A HISTORY OF
MODERN JEWRY
1780–1815

A HISTORY OF MODERN JEWRY

1780–1815

Raphael Mahler

SCHOCKEN BOOKS—NEW YORK

First published in Great Britain
by Valentine, Mitchell & Co. Ltd. 1971

Published in U.S.A. in 1971
by Schocken Books Inc.
67 Park Avenue, New York, N.Y. 10016

Printed and bound in Great Britain

CONTENTS

C. REVOLUTIONARY DECLINE AND THE RULE OF NAPOLEON

CHAPTER FOUR: HOLLAND

CHAPTER FIVE: ITALY

CHAPTER SIX: SWITZERLAND

CHAPTER SEVEN: GERMANY

A. SECOND HALF OF THE EIGHTEENTH CENTURY

B. THE FRENCH REVOLUTION AND THE NAPOLEONIC WARS

CONTENTS

vii

CONTENTS

CONTENTS

CONTENTS

PREFACE

For a number of reasons, there is an urgent need today for a new, comprehensive and synthesized reworking of the history of the Jewish people in modern times. Historical science has been enriched by an abundance of new knowledge since the appearance of the ten-volume *History of the Jewish People* by Simon Dubnow—the first scholar after the master of Jewish historiography, Graetz, to carry out a project on a similarly extensive scale. On the basis of this new knowledge, it is possible to revise and expand the factual outline Dubnow presented.

Even more urgent is the task of reassessing and amending value judgements *vis-à-vis* the theoretical approach prevalent in Jewish historiography, largely determined by social viewpoints. This approach may also have been directly influenced by political programmes concerning the present, though these are now generally considered obsolete.

Notwithstanding the good intentions of the adherents of the school described by its originator, S. Dubnow, as "sociological-realistic," it must be said that they were unable to grasp the exuberant and colourful reality of Jewish life, its past and its present alike: they overlooked the principal factor in the development of the people—namely, its social dynamics. Social antagonisms, class struggle and social opposition within the community have never been accorded their appropriate place in the history of the Jews of any period, and they have been almost completely omitted from the portrayal of the events of modern times for fear of overstepping political bounds, and, sometimes, precisely because of obvious political intentions. Phenomena and institutions concerning the ruling classes among the Jewish people were presented as general, national matters, and the Jewish policy of the ruling nations with regard to each and every class of the people under their rule was not properly analysed. Thus, instead of a national history of the Jews, we have been presented by the dominant school in Jewish historiography with a history that is largely nationalistic.

Autonomy as a political programme and historical outlook caused its originator to devote scant attention to the problem of the attitude of the Jewish people in the Diaspora, and its class-groups in particular, towards the historic tendency of Return to Zion and Restoration in Zion. In the depiction of the history of recent times this problem was not given the slightest attention, apart from a chapter on modern Zionism. And thus

xi

the dynamics of the national history of the Jewish people have not fared better than its social dynamics: both were forced off the main road of Jewish history by its writers.

Nor was justice done to the economic aspect of life, the basis of the national and social development of the Jewish people, as of all other people in the world. The economic structure of the people, its economic activities and the functions it fulfilled in the economic life of the countries of its dispersion in each particular period, were given only sporadic mention rather than exhaustive treatment. Because of this disregard of economic problems, no explanation was given for the causal nexus with those aspects of the people's life which occupy pride of place in the portrayal of modern history—the legal and political status. There was no clarification either of the fundamentals of the spiritual trends which shaped the structure of Jewish culture in modern times. Their social roots were not laid bare, and no attempt was made to establish how those trends reflected the interests, aspirations and ideals of the social classes which originated them.

To sum up, the history of the Jewish people in modern times has been squeezed into a framework comprised principally of a description of the process of equalizing the rights of European Jewry, with the addition of an account of anti-semitic movements and trends. It is not surprising, therefore, that in this scheme, in which the Emancipation served to delineate historical development, no place was assigned to the great Jewish community of America, since the question of Jewish emancipation had been solved there (with the exception of a few States) as early as the War of Independence. In the same way, only a very modest section was devoted to the history of the new *Yishuv* and of settlement in the Land of Israel.

Moreover, even an explanation of the Emancipation itself, however detailed in its account, cannot be satisfactory unless it is based on an analysis of the economic and social processes in the Jewish community during the period under discussion. Nor can the history of Emancipation be complete without consideration of the active part of the Jewish communities in their rebellion against the obsolete feudal régime which prevailed in the Jewish autonomous organizations and institutions as well as in the State. The Jewish people not only benefited from the achievements of the political revolution, but were also drawn into the great ferment it aroused and began debating Jewry's particular problems and aims.

Simon Dubnow did not live to see the Restoration of Israel. He died a martyr's death, together with the millions of his brethren whose history he had made it his whole life's work to investigate. His memory will be engraved forever in the hearts of our people by virtue of his creative achievements. He will also be accorded his rightful place in the annals of Jewish historiography on an historical scale, when we consider that, both in his many achievements and in his fundamental shortcomings, he was but a child of his times, which saw the hegemony of capitalism in the world, and the civil emancipation of the Jewish people. In our day it is the task of Jewish historiography to keep step with the spirit of the great revolution of our age, the age of humanity's struggle for auto-emancipation, for the Restoration in Zion and the Ingathering of the Exiles.

Despite the abnormality of Jewish life during the long era of the Diaspora, our history does not depart from the general rules of social development. On the contrary, this abnormality itself can be explained only on the basis of these very rules. It is precisely at this stage, when our people, after the appalling Holocaust, has reached its rehabilitation and liberation, that the duty is laid upon us of unfolding the full socio-realistic picture of its historical development and of scrutinizing it closely in all its tragic wrestling. Objective scientific clarification of the past is an essential prerequisite to rectifying the distortion in our national life and fully solidifying the foundations of our existence.

Only by a consistent social approach to our past can we delve deeply into the historical problem of "Israel and the Nations" in all its vitality, and at the same time determine our people's place in the modern world. Finally, clear historical consciousness is an imperative fundamental in the culture of our people, now in the process of its renaissance. From this viewpoint, Jewish historiography has a national role to fulfil, an important national mission to carry out.

A History of Modern Jewry presented here for the reader is the first, self contained part of a projected multi-volume history. It begins in the middle of the eighteenth century and includes the period of enlightened absolutism, the French Revolution and the Napoleonic Wars, down to the Congress of Vienna, 1815. I considered it necessary to deal with this period in particular at some length because of its great importance as a transitional period to the modern age in which the principal problems that confront our own generation emerge. Because of this lengthy description I have been unable to deal here with the Jewish communities of the Balkan Peninsula, North Africa and the Middle East, with the exception of Israel. In the next volume, which will deal with the period of European reaction—1815-48—the chapters on these communities will be preceded by an account of the history of each community during the previous period, 1750-1815.

This work constitutes an abridgement of the four volumes of the Hebrew original which appeared in Tel-Aviv as a publication of the Sifriat Poalim between 1952 and 1956. In this translation, the revised text of the 1960 edition has been followed. The bibliography—with omission of the Hebrew and Yiddish publications—has been here brought up to date by the addition of a selected number of recently published works.

I recall with gratitude the memory of the late Yirmeyahu Haggai, of Kibbutz Ein Hashofet, who prepared the first draft of the translation.

The publication of this work in English would not have been possible without the generous aid of the following organizations: The World Jewish Congress, Cultural Department, London; the Americans for Progressive Israel; Hashomer Hatzair in New York, who took upon themselves the costs of translating; the Jewish Agency in Jerusalem, Department of Organization and Information; the National Foundation for Jewish Culture in New York and the Dr. Mahler Book Committee in New York, who granted subsidies towards the publication. I owe all of them my gratitude. Last, but not least, I am deeply thankful to my wife who spared no effort on behalf of this book.

Tel-Aviv University, Summer, 1969   RAPHAEL MAHLER

THE AGE OF ENLIGHTENED DESPOTISM, THE FRENCH REVOLUTION AND THE NAPOLEONIC WARS

State of the Jews on the Eve of Revolution

The outbreak of the French Revolution found the Jewish people divided and dispersed over four continents, from India and Persia in the east to the British North American colonies in the west; from Sweden in northern Europe to Dutch Guinea (Surinam) in South America. The vast majority, however—more than four-fifths of all the Jews in the world—was concentrated in Europe, for it was to Europe that the focal centre of the Diaspora had shifted as far back as the early Middle Ages. The history of the Jewish people at the beginning of modern times is largely the history of European Jewry.

The size and relative significance of the Jewish communities varied in accordance with the socio-economic, political and cultural development of the various regions of Jewish settlement. Although the Jews of Europe numbered more than 2 million, less than one-tenth lived in the highly developed countries of western Europe: England, Holland, France and Italy. In the central European lands of Germany, Bohemia, Moravia, Austria and Hungary, mid-way in their economic development between the foremost mercantile nations of the west and the backward feudal, agrarian countries of eastern Europe, the Jews numbered less than one-fourth of the European Jewish community. More than one and a quarter million Jews, some two-thirds of all the Jews on the continent, lived in the countries of eastern Europe: in the vast Kingdom of Poland, including Lithuania, White Russia, and the Ukraine, and in the Balkan Peninsula, still under Turkish rule.

Owing to the varying development of the various European countries, there was a wide range of differences in the legal status of the Jews. There was no nationality anywhere in the world whose economic existence had been so affected by its legal status as was that of the Jews. First, legislation had barred the Jews from such activities as agriculture in almost every country, and from a majority of the crafts in most of the countries in which they lived. Such legal restrictions, however, were themselves the product of specific economic conditions in any given country where, generally, the economic activities of the Jews now constituted an important factor. Thus, the important role of the Jews in the commercial life of a number of countries, and particularly in the whole-sale trade, not only breached the wall of legal prohibitions but led in fact to a partial revision of such laws, thereby securing legal sanction for Jewish commerce as a whole or for the trade in certain commodities. Eventually, entry into certain crafts, such as tailoring and its related trades, which had begun to spread among the Jews in several central and eastern European countries, was also countenanced.

Outside North America, where the small Jewish community had achieved equality of civil rights even before the Revolutionary War (though they were still denied political enfranchisement), the status of the Jews was comparatively favourable in the highly developed countries of western Europe. In England and Holland, where the first rifts in the political and feudal systems had appeared in the wake of mercantile capitalist development and the rise of manufactures, Jewish capitalists enjoyed privileges that allowed them to engage freely in the foreign and wholesale trades as well as in banking. The Jewish middle class also benefited from the removal of some disabilities. They were, for instance, permitted to reside in nearly all the cities and were taxed on an equal basis with other citizens. On the other hand, Jewish petty traders and Jewish craftsmen were still hemmed in by legal restraints.

In the countries of central Europe, Germany, Austria, Bohemia-Moravia, and Hungary, harsh restrictions and the brutal exploitation of the Jewish population through taxation and special levies constituted a veritable system. This situation also prevailed in the adjoining French provinces of Alsace-Lorraine and in Italy. In these countries, remote from the routes of world commerce after the great voyages of discovery, the urban lower middle classes during the period of feudal decline were suffering from an extremely harsh economic depression. The official policy of persecuting the Jews in these countries was not only intended to divert the attention of the masses into the channels of religious ortho-doxy and bigotry, but was also motivated by the express purpose of shield-ing the impoverished, lower middle class gentiles from Jewish competition in commerce and the crafts. In some of the countries of this region, Jewish residence was forbidden outright. In others, the number of Jews was limited by law from the very outset. Throughout Germany and Austria, Jews were forbidden to ply any of the guild crafts. Jewish petty trade was restricted to a fixed number of stores and the sale of cheap goods. In Alsace-Lorraine, Germany and a few Italian provinces, the Jewish population in general engaged in usury, petty trade, peddling, and in the grain and cattle business in the countryside. In Bohemia-Moravia and in Hungary, the Jews paid the nobles for the right to lease breweries and distilleries.

The political and social backwardness of eastern Europe, as well as the large population of its Jewish communities, which this very backwardness itself postulated, determined both the legal status as well as the economic structure of these communities. In Poland, the largest of these Jewish centres, one in fifteen of the total population was a Jew, but one out of every two inhabitants in the cities and towns was Jewish. As a corollary to this relative and absolute numerical preponderance, and a phenomenon unique in all Europe, a very large proportion of the Jewish population (in Poland, about one-third) was scattered throughout the rural areas. The presence of Jews in large numbers also accounted for the widespread activity of the Jews in such productive occupations as the various handicrafts and transport. Retarded economic development explains in the main the fact that eastern European Jews on the whole held incontestable rights of domicile in all but a few of the major cities and towns. Jews had a predominant share in foreign trade, in inter-provincial commerce and in urban-rural barter. The ruling nobility's favourable disposition towards Jewish commerce and handicrafts was dictated by the national economy and its own class interests. Both required a counter-balance to the economic and political status of the Christian middle class. Incomes derived principally from distilleries, breweries, ale houses, inns, road and bridge tolls, and similar sources of revenue, were almost exclusively a Jewish sources of livelihood. They were leased from the nobles in the towns and villages.

In this eastern part of Europe, deeply sunk in feudalism as late as the eighteenth century, the Jews held a position, economically and legally, that was in many respects similar to that formerly held by the Jews of western Europe at the onset of the Middle Ages. But whereas the earlier period had been one of economic and political prosperity, eastern European feudalism during the eighteenth century had begun to stagnate and decay. The political rule of the nobles was based on the frightful ignorance of the urban and rural masses, on their ruthless exploitation, and on the repression of any aspirations to social opposition. Amidst this backwardness, poverty, and serfdom, the bulk of the Jewish masses also languished in want and distress. The ban on the purchase of land by Jews, as a result of the nobility's desire to retain its exclusive status as a class of landed proprietors, closed the main avenue to Jewish productive activity. In the crown cities, in commerce as well as in the crafts, the Jews were compelled to fight bitterly in the struggle forced upon them by the bourgeoisie and to purchase the least of legal concessions with sizeable sums of money. Hence, though in terms of economic rights the position of the Jews in feudal eastern Europe was still superior to that of their fellow Jews in the neighbouring central European countries, the stifling atmosphere of clericalism and Jesuit dominance, and the subservience of the Jews to the nobility, were of a kind hitherto unknown anywhere else in Europe. The nobility's treatment of its Jews, the waves of terror accompanying the ritual blood accusations, all seemed to reproduce the medieval Inquisition at the very beginning of the new era.

Simultaneously with the aggravation of the socio-economic crisis of the Jewish masses, an acute crisis was manifest in their existence as a nationality, and in their organizational patterns and culture. With the decline of feudalism, the autonomous functions of the Jewish community organization, the *Kehillah*, were greatly reduced. In the countries under the rule of enlightened despotism, they shrank to a minimum, while in eastern Europe the Kehillah became an agency within the state apparatus, its chief function being to ensure the prompt collection of taxes from the Jewish population. The traditional culture, the Talmudic-rabbinical literature, wilted, shrank, and lost any semblance whatsoever of originality and creativeness. Apart from such dying flashes as the Vilno Gaon* in eastern Europe, there were no longer any creations of lasting value in the field of *Halakhah* (the accumulated commentaries and pronouncements, theoretical and applied, on problems of Jewish religious practice). On the other hand, the first indications of a general awakening from the paralysis of feudalism were accompanied among the Jewish masses by the first signs of an awakening from the torpor of religious dogmatism. In eastern Europe, the tide of Hassidism, calling for a deepening of religious values, swet the Jewish masses to revolt against the outmoded, repressive Kehillah régime and the primacy of the rabbis. It also revived a profound yearning for social emancipation and national renaissance. The Jewish Enlightenment (*Haskalah*) of central Europe was expressive of the ascendant modern Jewish middle class and voiced the latter's demands for a fundamental revision of Jewish way of life by means of higher education, opportunity for a more productive economic existence and increased cultural and social rapprochement with the peoples amongst whom they lived.

The French Revolution and Jewish Enfranchisement in Western Europe

The French Revolution set itself the task of altering the structure of society and the state in accordance with the requirements of capitalism and its ruling class, the bourgeoisie. After a bitter struggle the Revolution accomplished this task. This presupposed the abolition of the special privileges enjoyed by the clergy and aristocracy and the enfranchisement of all citizens before the law, without distinction as to origin or religion. It presupposed the liberation of the peasantry from the bonds of serfdom and empowered the peasantry to own land. It required the overthrow of absolutism and entrusted the bourgeoisie with governmental power. It presupposed the abolition of separate, autonomous provinces within the state, the liquidation of the system of guilds and corporations and the

* See p. 540.

establishment of one unified state with a centralized administrative machinery and a single, uniform legal code.

In its very essence and character, the French Revolution postulated Jewish emancipation within the general corpus of its achievements. The true cause of all this—the urgent need of the capitalist system to integrate into the national economy all elements able to contribute labour and, more especially, resources and initiative—is perhaps best exemplified in the enfranchisement of the wealthy Sephardi Jews in France, bourgeois *par excellence*. This was proclaimed by the National Assembly barely six months after the outbreak of the Revolution, whereas the mass of the Jewish lower middle classes in the eastern provinces of Alsace-Lorraine had to wait another two years for enfranchisement. Eventually, however, the Revolution extended equal rights to the Jewish community of France as a whole, by virtue of its inherent capitalist economic tendencies.

The *ideological* manifestation of these tendencies also exerted a powerful influence. The consistency of the slogans proclaimed by the Revolution and by the political system it established was likewise influential. Precisely this ideological factor serves to explain why it was that the Commune of Paris provided the Jews with some of the most ardent champions of their rights. The population of Paris, organized in its Municipal Commune, fully comprehended that this was no casual matter involving some few hundreds of people in Paris or some ten thousand on the state's eastern frontier. They saw it as a matter of principle, a measure of the Revolution's very capacity to endure.

The enfranchisement of the Jews by the French Revolution served in time as a model for the enfranchisement which the Jews subsequently achieved, though not simultaneously, in all the capitalist countries (together with the superficiality and deficiencies of the French precedent). Although the Jews were proclaimed equal before the law with other citizens, the state did not feel obliged to take such measures as were necessary to ensure that this equality, fully implemented in practice, would prevent anti-Jewish discrimination in elections to municipal or central representative bodies, or in securing appointments to government posts. Likewise, the state did nothing whatsoever to establish the Jews in industry or agriculture with the object of putting them on a footing of economic equality with the general population.

As the Revolution marched triumphantly through Europe, so did the enfranchisement of the Jews on the French pattern spread from France to its neighbours. After the French conquest of the Low Countries and of northern and southern Italy, a new political system arose in which the Jews achieved equal rights between 1796 and 1798. Only in the Helvetian Republic, set up by France on Swiss soil, did the backwardness and bigotry of the ruling petty bourgeoisie force the Jewish community to remain totally disfranchised, even under the new régime which, on the whole, succumbed rapidly enough to the growing tide of reaction.

Under Napoleon, the Jewish communities in the greater part of western Germany also became enfranchised. In all the areas of Germany that had been annexed outright to France, e.g. the districts west of the Rhone and the city of Hamburg, and in the vassal states of Westphalia, Brunswick, Hanover and Frankfurt-on-Main, the legal equality of the Jews was promulgated in the wake of the new constitution. However, by contrast with the initial phase of Jewish enfranchisement during the wars of the Revolution, which had been accompanied by spontaneous popular outbursts of sympathy (e.g. the razing of the ghetto walls in the cities of Italy), the liberation of the Jews under Napoleon in the regions of Germany mentioned above was hardly more than a prosaic act of legislation. In all the other German states, the legal status of the Jewish population failed to undergo any substantial change for the better, save for the abolition of the humiliating poll tax. The sole exception was Prussia, which, following its crushing defeat in the war against Napoleon, was compelled to reform its system drastically in order to encourage the growth of a capitalist economy. In the wake of these reforms, Prussia also granted its Jewish inhabitants full civil rights, which were even accompanied by a number of political rights. The Kingdom of Denmark emancipated its Jews in like fashion.

Enfranchisement of the Jews, like the French Revolution itself, came to a halt at the eastern borders of Prussia. In the eastern part of central Europe, as in eastern Europe, the Jews gained nothing more than slight improvements in their existing condition.

During the last few decades before the French Revolution, enlightened despotism in the Hapsburg empire, Austria, Bohemia-Moravia, and Hungary inaugurated a number of changes in the legal status of the Jewish inhabitants. But what these actually amounted to was some extension of those exclusive rights already enjoyed by the more affluent Jewish merchants, bankers, and manufacturers. By contrast, there was hardly any change in the plight of the Jewish masses. After the death of Joseph II, when the counter-revolution gathered pace, no further reforms were undertaken on behalf of the Jews; there was a general cessation of all reforming activity on the part of enlightened despotism. The Jewish plutocracy did indeed continue to benefit from the privileges granted by Joseph II. It even extended the range of its economic activities quite considerably. As against this, however, new laws whittled down what few rights had been granted to the general Jewish population during the earlier period.

The third and final partition of Poland, that large and backward feudal kingdom of eastern Europe, took place in 1795, just a few years after the outbreak of the French Revolution. Austria, Russia and Prussia, which both dismembered and inherited Poland, displayed a number of common tendencies in their policy towards the Jews, which had their roots in the absolutist régime common to all three powers. Together with the systematic regulation of Jewish economic activity, which was most rigorously enforced in the part of Poland occupied by Prussia, these three partitioning powers drafted plans to enable the Jewish population to lead a more productive economic existence, e.g. by opening to it handicrafts and agriculture. But in fact their plans brought no significant results, except for a number of farming settlements in the south of Russia. On the other hand, despite the system of discrimination which was most keenly felt in the form of special taxes—these were never abolished and were in fact made considerably more burdensome—there was a marked improvement in the legal and political status of the Jews in the conquered Polish territories.

Schools were opened to them; they were granted rights of domicile in many cities in which, under Polish rule, they had had no foothold; and in the area under Russian administration the Jews were declared city burghers with the right to serve on the municipal councils. Nevertheless, the broad masses of the Jewish population derived no practical benefits from these concessions, owing to the heavy tax burden and the oppressive discrimination that undermined their existing sources of livelihood even before they were given the opportunity to transfer to those approved by the authorities—industry, the handicrafts, and agriculture. By contrast, this new legal and political situation opened fields of enterprise in large-scale commerce and industry to the Jewish propertied classes. In underdeveloped eastern Europe, the foundation was laid for the growth of the modern Jewish bourgeoisie.

In general, it is necessary to differentiate amongst the diverse results the Revolution had for the various classes of the Jewish population. This applies even to the first period of western European Jewish emancipation, which followed hard on the heels of the French Revolution. It was mainly in terms of legal status that the circumstances of a majority of the Jewish population improved. In their economic situation, on the other hand, there was no perceptible change: the economic benefits accruing from enfranchisement were reaped by the Jewish plutocracy.

The French Revolution anticipated all the subsequent bourgeois revolutions in that the total liquidation of the Jews as a nationality was made an explicit or implicit term of their enfranchisement. The spokesmen of the new régime not only demanded the termination of Jewish autonomy but even assumed, and therefore anticipated, that the Jews would, to all intents and purposes, become Frenchmen in language and culture. The continued existence of the Jewish faith was the sole exception. During the Revolutionary period, the concept of *nationality* was still synonymous with that of the *state*. It was thus beyond the capacity of that generation to conceive of more than one people existing within one and the same sovereign entity. This concept was particularly baffling with regard to the Jews. Their extra-territoriality was in itself obvious, but not the tragedy inherent in this condition of extra-territoriality. Hence, there was no endeavour to seek out the only practical solution; full civil equality without the stipulated or even concomitant demand for the renunciation of Jewish language and culture, history and national tradition, and, in particular, the ancient aspiration for a rebirth of Jewish national life in Palestine.

The degree in which the Jews responded to this demand for extreme assimilation varied from one country to another, and from one class to another. The most decadent in form was the assimilationist movement of the Jewish bourgeoisie in Germany and especially in Prussia. It was there that the upper middle class, the Jewish salon-bourgeoisie, in its passion to assimilate, went to the extreme of utter dissolution, to conversion, severing the remaining bonds of unity with its own people. This was, of course, the outcome of unique conditions. There was no other country where the gap between traditional Jewish culture and the culture of its environment was as wide as in renascent Germany. It was also in Germany that the most glaring contradiction existed between the outstanding importance of the new Jewish bourgeoisie to the country's economic, cultural and social life, and the wretched economic, legal, and political status of the broad Jewish masses.

In its attitude to the Jewish people and their culture Italian Jewry at this time, alone amongst the Jewish communities of western Europe, took a diametrically opposed and praiseworthy position. Assimilation by choice did not extend to Italy. The sole exception was a group of financiers who were close to the ruling circles. In contradistinction to their brethren in Germany, the Jews of Italy had been firmly embedded in the Italian population for many generations. They were linked to it by language, culture, and social relationships. The culture of Italian Jewry was always suffused with secular elements. In the light of Jewish historical development, enfranchisement in Italy in no way necessitated a violent clash between the ancient mode of life and a new one. What it signified was the removal of obstacles to a line of development long since marked out. The attitude of Italian Jewry to the historic aspiration of the Jewish people to return to Zion is especially noteworthy. Their spokesmen and, above all, the intellectuals amongst them, were not caught up in the torrent that persuaded the Jewish bourgeoisie in most of the countries of western Europe to repudiate the idea of their people's redemption. On the contrary, at that time as throughout the nineteenth century, the Jews of Italy gave fine expression to their national allegiance in Hebrew poetry and in other literary media in Hebrew and Italian.

The small and remote settlement of Jews in America, which achieved enfranchisement earlier than the Jews of western Europe, was also undisturbed in its loyalty to the Jewish people's historic goal while in the Diaspora. More, the triumph of the national revolution imbued the hearts of American Jews with a sense of Jewish national pride and stirred anew their longing for the return to Zion.

In eastern Europe not even the thin crust of a modern Jewish middle class had yet formed; only here and there did slight indications suggest that capitalist groups on the western European lines were in the process of formation. Hence the trend towards total assimilation never reached the Jewish masses in this part of the continent. Even the enlightenment movement was only in its initial stages. The great struggle on the Jewish scene in eastern Europe was, as hitherto, fought out mainly between the Mitnagdim, speaking for the class of well-to-do conservatives, and the Hassidim, who expressed the motivations and attitudes prevalent among the mass of lower middle class Jews.

The French Revolution, and the revolutions of 1848, brought national stability to the peoples and inspired a vast upsurge in the development of national cultures. It was the bitter historical lot of the Jews, precisely because they were an extra-territorial people, separated from their own country, that these revolutions, which for the world as a whole spelled progress, did not bring a Jewish rebirth but on the contrary heralded a period of national disintegration and assimilation. The opposition to assimilationism, in which the Jewish masses had persisted for many decades, acquired the form and content of religious ultra-conservatism. The result was a rift in European Jewry that became progressively deeper. Until the end of the eighteenth century the Jews of Europe had been united by a common way of life, and for the most part, by a common Jewish language and popular culture. Now, however, a new type of Jew emerged in western Europe. His estrangement from the Jewish masses of eastern Europe, from their distress and their struggle for national existence, grew *pari passu* with his own socio-economic integration into the surrounding bourgeoisie and his linguistic-cultural absorption into the general environment.

In the final count, however, the advancing power of the revolution did not withhold its vitalizing influence from the national existence and development of the Jewish people. Gradually, the revolutionary ideas penetrated into the numerous and large Jewish communities of eastern Europe and awakened them to struggle not only for enfranchisement but also for auto-emancipation, for national activity and self-liberation, for the consummation of the Jewish people's historical yearning to return and reconstitute itself a nation in its own country. These watchwords of Jewish national rebirth were gradually to evoke a response even in the Jewish communities of western Europe that were partly or almost entirely assimilated.

CHAPTER ONE

NORTH AMERICA

The Colonial Period

In 1775, at the time when the thirteen North American colonies were in revolt against England, the American Jewish community was amongst the smallest in the world. All estimates indicate that the Jews in North America in the latter part of the eighteenth century numbered some 2,000 or 2,500 souls out of a total population of approximately 4 million (according to the census of 1790). But as in the case of the newly independent United States as a nation a measure of historical importance far transcending its actual size may be attributed to this diminutive American Jewish community. The 2,000 Jews who laid the foundation of what was to become the largest Jewish community in history had already attained a level of social and legal equality unprecedented in the history of the Diaspora.

Before the Revolutionary War, most of North America's Jewish population was concentrated in five Kehillot: Newport, Rhode Island; New York, New York; Philadelphia, Pennsylvania; Charleston, South Carolina; and Savannah, Georgia. Smaller communities or groups of Jews existed in other places in these colonies as well as at Lancaster and Reading, Pennsylvania; Boston, Massachusetts; New Haven, Connecticut; and at various centres in New Jersey. The oldest and also the largest of these Jewish communities was in New York, where the first group of Jews to reach the North American mainland had settled in 1654. In 1759, the *Shearith Israel* Congregation of New York numbered more than sixty families, or 350-400 souls (2 per cent of the city's total population at that time). The second community, in seniority and size, was at Newport, with thirty families in 1740. At this period Philadelphia and Charleston had little more than twelve families. Charleston, however, though it was a younger community, continued to grow until by the end of the eighteenth century it had overtaken all the others in size. The community at Savannah was then in process of reconstruction, after its evacuation to South Carolina, together with most of the city's other inhabitants, in 1740-41.

The modest but uninterrupted growth of the Jewish community in the New World was the result of a small, slow, but continuous flow of Jewish immigration. Although Sephardi Jews, great grandchildren of the Marranos, still held the leading positions in the Kehillot their forefathers had established, this immigration made them a minority. The majority of the new Jewish inhabitants were Ashkenazim from Holland, Germany, and England; there was also a not inconsiderable number from Poland.

The location of the five important communities in seaport towns is indicative of the role played by trade in the economic life of this young Jewish settlement. The Jewish share in commerce with the West Indies—a vital sector in the economy of the American colonies—was particularly prominent. The Jews of Newport took an outstanding position in this trade. Their contacts with the local Jewish Kehillot, in some instances members of their own families, was a great advantage to Jewish merchants in West Indian ports of call such as Barbados, Jamaica, Surinam, and Curaçao. Jewish businessmen in most of the important seaport towns played a conspicuous role in the commerce, finance and industry of the prospering colonies. Two New York Jews, Benjamin Seixas and Ephraim Hart, were among the founders of the New York Stock Exchange. New York and Philadelphia Jewish merchants were distinguished particularly in the Indian trade, which dealt in furs. Moses Lindo, an important Charleston merchant from London, organized the export of indigo so skilfully that the authorities appointed him general supervisor of the indigo industry.

Thus the role that Jewish businessmen played in economic affairs was a factor in their extensive participation in the commercial boycott directed against England which prepared the ground for the Revolution.

A few Jews, in Georgia, New York, and Pennsylvania, owned landed property in addition to business establishments. The former included mainly granaries, dairy farms, and other agricultural installations—tangible proof that they engaged also in agriculture. Jewish artisans followed many trades at this time. There were Jewish tailors, tanners, saddlers, carpenters, glaziers, engravers, chandlers, distillers, tobacconists, bakers, butchers, goldsmiths, silversmiths, coppersmiths, watchmakers and barbers.

Yet however highly we estimate the importance of the Jews and their pioneering role in certain branches of trade and industry in the American colonies at the outbreak of the revolt against England, the American Jewish community was not unique in this respect. Jews had discharged the same functions with the rise of mercantile capitalism on the other side of the Atlantic, in Holland, the south of France, England, and Italy (at Leghorn). In the perspective of Jewish historical development in the Diaspora, the innovation here was the broad scope of the rights which the Jews of America enjoyed even before the Revolution and, even more, the degree of their social integration.

The marked importance of the Jews in economic affairs and the achievement of social and economic equality with the indigenous bourgeoisie characterized all the countries in which capitalism was in the ascendant. But additional and unique factors operated in America. The white inhabitants were all either immigrants or recent descendants of immigrants; to flaunt family lineage or length of residence would have been ludicrous. Even though English language and culture predominated throughout the colonies by that time, the population comprised a motley of nationalities. Its religious composition in particular was so varied that no single sect or denomination could claim an absolute majority. When it is remembered that most of the Christian denominations then flourishing in North America had been persecuted in England and the other European countries whence the colonists had come, it is not surprising that interdenominational tolerance marked their mutual relations and that this eventually came also to apply to members of the Jewish faith.

In the five colonies containing most of the Jewish population up to the War of Independence, the Jews had already not only acquired complete freedom of worship, but even economic equality, notably the right to own stores and to engage in crafts. The Plantation Act (1740) permitted Jews in the British colonies to apply to a colonial court for citizenship after seven years' residence. They were thus specifically released from the need to take a Christian oath. Jews in the North American colonies and the West Indies now enjoyed the rights of British subjects—a vastly different state of affairs to conditions in Britain, where a law enabling Jews to become citizens had been both adopted and repealed in 1753. Most of the American Jewish families did submit applications for citizenship. These were approved by the courts without difficulty (the sole exception being Rhode Island). In 1774, when the Revolution broke out, Francis Salvador, a young Jewish planter who had only been in the country for a year, was elected to the First and Second South Carolina Provincial Congress. In Savannah, Georgia, too, Jews were appointed to public positions on the eve of the War. Daniel and Moses Nunez were appointed Port Inspectors by a resolution of the Provincial Assembly.

The chief factor in this closer association of Jew and non-Jew was economic development, especially in the fields of commerce, industry, and banking. Apart from business partnerships, there were cases of Christians serving as clerks in Jewish businesses in New York, e.g. John Jacob Astor, founder of the Astor millions, and in Reading, Pennsylvania. Jews could be found serving not only as salesmen but as office clerks in large commercial houses, e.g. Newport. They exerted a very great influence in the Masonic movement, and some authorities even assume that they were among the founders of the first Masonic lodges in America.

The Revolution and Equal Rights

It is hardly surprising, given these economic, legal, and social circumstances, that the few Jews then in the country participated in the American Revolution of 1775 on a scale out of all proportion to their numbers in the general population. The Jewish community as a whole espoused the revolutionary aims that inspired the masses in the cities—the mechanics, labourers, farmers, and the enlightened section of the American public. They rose against British rule to seek, in independence, liberation from a fiscal burden that was only of benefit to England and to acquire a safeguard for the uninterrupted development of commerce and industry and the free development of the vast expanses to the west.

As we have already stated, Jewish merchants actively participated in organizing the boycott of English merchandise even before the War of Independence. Most of the Jews of New York displayed their solidarity with the Revolution in 1776 when they decided, under the leadership of the Reverend Gresham Mendes Seixas, to move to Philadelphia rather than swear allegiance to the British, who were besieging the city. At the end of the same year, the Jews of Newport likewise dispersed to other localities. The aid proffered by Jewish merchants—especially in Philadelphia—to the Continental Congress as suppliers to the armed forces and purchasers of Federal Bonds (though their motives presumably involved profits as well as patriotism) is further proof of their belief in the Revolution. Until the Battle of Yorktown in 1781, the outcome of the war hung in the balance; and in Philadelphia indeed some highly respected citizens were hostile to anyone known to support the Revolution. Given this situation, the unquestionably valuable activity of the Polish Jew, Hayim Salomon, merits appreciation (though later generations have attributed exaggerated importance to it). The records show that following his escape from British captivity in New York, Salomon was employed in Philadelphia to sell Continental Congress Treasury Bonds at a broker's fee. Jews also took part in another form of enterprise—privateering on the high seas. This likewise combined private with public interest.

The Jews who fought in the Continental Army hailed from every Kehilla in the country. The handful of Jewish combatants known to us by name comprised equal numbers of officers and privates, possibly because the sons of merchants could be commissioned as a matter of course due to their propertied status and educational level. One of these officers, Colonel David Salisbury Franks, served on United States diplomatic missions to Europe and Morocco after the War. Apart from the regular army, Jews also served in the local militia.

A small minority of Jews remained loyal to the British during the Revolutionary War. These were mainly large merchants who had previously had close business relations with English firms and also dealt with the British army. While such "loyalists" were common among the wealthier classes of the general public, they included only a few Jews amongst their ranks. The patriotism shown by the Jewish community as a whole during the struggle was indisputable—so much so, that immediately after the victorious peace the Jews could refer to their patriotism in official declarations.

As a result of the Revolution the Jews of America eventually obtained the equality of rights they had yearned for, total enfranchisement under the Constitution, even though it was not implemented all at once. The Constitution of the United States of America was adopted in 1787. Article VI concludes with the following clause:

> ... but no religious Test shall ever be required as a qualification to any Office or public Trust under the United States.

In 1791, the first ten Amendments, constituting the Bill of Rights, were adopted. Article I reads as follows:

> Congress shall make no law respecting an establishment of religion, or prohibiting the free exercise thereof; or abridging the freedom of speech, or of the press; or the right of the people peaceably to assemble, and to petition the Government for a redress of grievances.

The United States of America thus became the first modern state to grant full equality of rights to its Jewish population.

On the other hand, within the individual states of the Union the situation relating to equality of religious rights in general varied according to their respective constitutions. Whereas the New York State Constitution of 1777 had abolished all religious discrimination, laws in certain other states still discriminated against Christian minorities as well as against Jews. In Pennsylvania the discriminatory clause only disappeared when the new constitution was adopted in 1790. In Maryland, a law according Jews political rights was not passed until 1824.

However, in some states, limitation for the most part only existed on paper and was never enforced. Only a small minority of the Jews in North America were therefore actually involved. Where the great majority of American Jews were concentrated, and certainly in all the major Jewish centres, complete equality of rights prevailed under both Federal and State constitutions.

The exchange of letters between the Jewish communities and General George Washington also emphasized equality for all citizens without distinction as to national origin or religion as an achievement of the American Revolution. The Newport letter, sent in the name of "The Children of the Stock of Abraham," hailed the equality introduced by the new government as not only religious equality but also as equality of peoples. In his reply to the Jews of Newport, Washington wrote:

> May the Children of the Stock of Abraham, who dwell in this land, continue to merit and enjoy the good will of the other inhabitants, while every one shall sit in safety under his own vine and fig tree and there shall be none to make them afraid.

Replying to the Jews of Savannah, Washington declared that America might indeed pride itself on having presented humanity with an example of liberty of conscience and immunity of citizenship possessed by all Americans alike. He rejoiced in the fact that

> ...a spirit of liberality and philanthropy is much more prevalent than it formerly was among the enlightened nations of the earth and that your brethren will benefit thereby in proportion as it shall become still more extensive....

Despite official declarations, the population of the time did not display a consistently benign attitude towards the Jews. Indications of animosity towards them appeared simultaneously with anti-democratic tendencies which emerged in the course of a controversy between the two rival parties, the plutocratic Federalists and the agrarian Democratic Republicans, led respectively by Alexander Hamilton and Thomas Jefferson. The ultra-conservative Federalists detested democracy, urged war on France, and were hostile to Negroes. They were dismayed by the fact that Jews were active in the country's democratic movement, particularly in New York and Philadelphia. The leader of the Jewish community of New York, Solomon Simson, was elected vice-president and later president of the Democratic Club founded in New York in 1794. The printer and publisher, Naphtali Juda, was an active member of the Democratic Club. He was also, in the company of other Jews, a prominent member of the Tammany Association, parent organization to Tammany Hall of New York. Active members of the Democratic Club in Philadelphia included Benjamin Nones, for many years the president of the Kehillah. The religious leader of the New York Kehillah, the Reverend Gershom Seixas, also acted with boldness and brilliance. On May 9, 1798, which had been proclaimed a Day of National Fasting by the President of the United States, Seixas delivered a sermon advocating peace and unity—in contrast with most of the speakers that day, who used their pulpits to agitate for war against France.

These facts gave some Federalist journalists an excuse to launch an attack on the Jews. In his introduction to the American edition of a British novel antagonistic to the French Revolution, James Rivington, the editor of a New York Federalist paper, denounced the Democratic Clubs as French agencies and described the New York Democratic Club as "an itinerant gang . . . easily known by their physiognomy. They seem to be like their vice-president, of the tribe of Shylock."

A particularly abusive attack on Benjamin Nones was published in the Philadelphia organ of the Federalist Party in 1800. "I am accused of being a *Jew*, of being a *Republican* and of being *poor*" was Nones' brilliant and proud rejoinder.

> I am a Jew. I glory in belonging to that persuasion which even its opponents, whether Christian, or Mahomedan, allow to be of

6

divine origin, of that persuasion on which Christianity itself was originally founded and must ultimately rest, which has preserved its faith secure and undefiled, for near three thousand years—whose votaries have never murdered each other in religious wars.

... How then can a Jew but be a Republican. In America particularly. Unfeeling and ungrateful would he be, if he were callous to the glorious and benevolent cause of the difference between his situation in this land of freedom, and among the proud and privileged law givers of Europe.

... But I am *poor*. I know that to purse-proud aristocracy poverty is a crime, but it may sometimes be accompanied with honesty even in a Jew.

In general, however, manifestations of antisemitism in the United States at the end of the eighteenth century, though typical concomitants of reaction, never gained the proportions of a movement, not even in Federalist circles. Still less did they leave any imprint on contemporary American society.

The War of 1812 and the Spread of the Jewish Community

The British-American War of 1812 on the whole aroused far less patriotic fervour throughout the country than had the War of Independence nearly forty years before. The New England states in particular were actively opposed to the war because of its detrimental effects upon their maritime trade. Against this background, the Jewish participation in the War of 1812 is conspicuous, judging by the number of Jewish officers and men who served. It was no less than in the War of Independence. The remarkable number of Jewish officers in particular is a measure of their advanced social and political status. During the Revolutionary War, only one Jewish officer holding the rank of captain in South Carolina can be definitely identified. In the War of 1812, we find six Jewish Army officers from that state alone, apart from two in the state militia. By that time also there was a Jew holding a commission who had completed his studies at West Point Academy. Already several Jews were serving in the Navy, including Captain Uriah Levi, who eventually reached the rank of commodore.

During the thirty-seven years between the two wars, from 1775 to 1812, the Jewish population of the United States had increased to between 3,000 and 3,500 people. At the time of the Revolutionary War, a number of Jews had come to America from Germany with the Hessians (German mercenaries in the British service) as army suppliers and traffickers. After the Revolution, small groups immigrated from England, Germany, France, Holland, Poland, and the West Indies. The Jewish community at Charleston, South Carolina, benefited most from this immigration. By 1812, it numbered between six and seven hundred people and at the end of the first quarter of the nineteenth century it was the largest Jewish community in America. The Philadelphia Jewish community also grew; by 1812 it had increased to some thirty families (150-200 people). The city of Richmond (Virginia), now boasted its own Kehillah also with thirty families. Jews also entered states where no Jew had resided before the Revolution. These included Maryland (Baltimore) and Massachusetts (Boston). On the other hand, the community at Savannah, Georgia, had shrunk as a result of migration to South Carolina. Similarly, the formerly prosperous community of Newport had ceased to exist by the end of the eighteenth century, following the economic collapse caused by the abolition of the slave-trade in the North, the deterioration of colonial trade and the barter trade in raw materials and British products. The great colonial traders of the past gave way to traders with the new areas of the Middle West. Jewish fur-traders from Pennsylvania, notably the Gratz family, penetrated into Ohio, Kentucky, Indiana, Michigan, Illinois, and Mississippi. They set up trading posts and were active in companies formed to set up new settlements in these territories. These traders were also involved in land transactions in the older areas of the United States: the town of Aaronsburg, Pennsylvania, was founded in 1780 by the Jewish trader, Aaron Levi. At the end of this period, the first itinerant Jewish pedlars made their appearance, supplying farmers with dry goods and other wares.

Kehillah Organization, Language, Education, and Culture

All the Jewish Kehillot in America during the Colonial period and the years immediately following the War of Independence were organized by Sephardi Jews. Their organizational pattern and religious ritual remained Sephardi even after the Ashkenazim had become an overwhelming majority. The Ashkenazim in fact already outnumbered their Sephardi co-religionists before the Revolution broke out; their predominance was greatly increased by the continued influx of Jewish immigrants from the warring countries of western Europe at the beginning of the nineteenth century. However, it was not until several years later that the first independent Ashkenazi congregations were founded. Until then, the Sephardi synagogues ministered to the religious needs of both elements. In the Kehillah organization the Sephardi Jews, because of their advantages in education, wealth and social status, generally, though not exclusively, filled the important posts. At the head of the Kehillah was the *Parnass*, with two *Vice-Parnassim*—the *Hatan-B'reshit* and *Hatan-Torah*—and three or five additional officers (*Ajuntos*). The wealthiest men in the community were elected to the office of Parnass, such as Aaron Lopez and his brother Moses at Newport, Barnard Gratz in

Philadelphia, and Hyman Levy in New York. Eventually, the Newport Kehillah introduced the custom of electing Sephardi and Ashkenazi Parnassim in alternate years. In 1784, the New York Kehillah was registered under the Religious Societies Ordinance. In compliance with this law, it ruled that all persons paying for a "place" in the synagogue were entitled to vote in the elections to the Kehillah's governing body and to its offices. Despite this provision, however, persons who were entirely destitute or in arrears with their Kehillah taxes were not allowed to vote.

The American Kehillah was responsible for the maintenance of the synagogue, the cemetery and the Kehillah officials—a cantor (*Hazan*), sexton, ritual slaughterer, and teacher. Its activities, like its European counterpart, also included aid to the poor. During the eighteenth century, the Kehillot usually maintained separate charitable organizations.

Jewish education during that period was at a low ebb partly because the Kehillot were few in number and widely separated, but principally because of the small number of Jews in each Kehillah. None had a rabbi; for the most part they had to be content with a cantor for spiritual leadership. He was usually imported from London, Amsterdam, or the West Indies. This was equally true of *Talmud-Torah* teachers (in those centres where the cantor had not assumed such duties) and *Shokhtim* (ritual slaughterers). When important religious issues arose, the American Kehillot turned to the Sephardi *Bet-Din* (Religious Court) in London, and orders for their religious appurtenances had also to be sent to London, Amsterdam or Hamburg. In view of these difficulties the perseverance shown by these Kehillot in their efforts to impart a Jewish education to their children was quite extraordinary. The opening of a Talmud-Torah was considered a primary obligation by each new Kehillah. Originally, the Talmud-Torah curriculum only comprised religious studies; in the middle of the eighteenth century, however, the New York Talmud-Torah introduced the study of English and, occasionally, Spanish. Arithmetic was also taught. Secular studies were an absolute necessity. Jewish children attended no other school apart from the Talmud-Torah, as practically all the elementary schools in existence were under the jurisdiction of the various Christian denominations. At the end of the eighteenth century, all the children in the Kehillot attended Talmud-Torah. Poor pupils were excused from paying for their tuition. Girls, though in limited numbers, also attended Talmud-Torah by the end of the eighteenth century.

A knowledge of Hebrew was not widespread during the period preceding the Revolution. When the wealthy Isaac Hart of Newport received a Hebrew letter from Hebron in 1771 he had to ask the Christian scholar, Ezra Stiles, President of Yale University, to translate it for him. In 1761, an English translation of the *Makhzor* (prayer book for the Holy Days)

9

was published for the first time. In his introduction, the translator, Isaac Pinto, explained that "a veneration for the language sacred by being that in which it pleased Almighty God to reveal Himself to our ancestors and a desire to preserve it, in firm persuasion that it will again be re-established in Israel, are probably leading reasons for our performing divine service in Hebrew." However, he continues, the translation was urgently needed, Hebrew "being imperfectly understood by many, by some, not at all." On the whole, however, Hebrew still served as the language of prayer and featured in religious documents, such as marriage contracts, divorces, and gravestone inscriptions (accompanied by English translations). It was during the second half of the eighteenth century and in the English minutes of the New York Kehillah's proceedings, that frequent use began to be made of Hebrew sentences or Hebrew words written in Hebrew characters. This strengthening of the Hebrew foundation, indicating some revival in the knowledge of the language, undoubtedly resulted from two concurrent factors: the immigration of Ashkenazi Jews and improved Talmud-Torah education. It is most relevant in this context to note that an American-born Jew, Gershom Mendes Seixas, cantor to the New York Kehillah in 1768, was able to prescribe ritual procedure according to the *Shulkhan Arukh* and also to compose a Hebrew speech which he wrote out without an error.

A marked change occurred in Jewish education during the Revolutionary period. The children of the well-to-do now received their secular education in private schools and the Talmud-Torah was confined to imparting Jewish knowledge. The Jews of America were making a great advance in the acquisition of a general education, parallel to the general rise in the country's cultural level. Before the Revolution, only one Jewish student is known to have graduated from Columbia University in New York (of which, at a later date, Gershom Seixas was a trustee and incorporator), and a few more from the University of Pennsylvania. By the end of the eighteenth century there was a striking increase in Jewish student enrolment in universities, especially in the law schools. Equality of rights had opened the legal profession to the Jews. Jewish attorneys-at-law now appeared in every state which had a Jewish population. They constituted the first Jewish professional group in the United States.

Changes also occurred in the religious way of life, as a result of the expansion of education in the American population as a whole, and also because of the peculiar circumstances surrounding the smaller, distant, and unorganized Jewish settlements. In the Colonial Period, the Sabbath laws, holidays, and dietary customs were commonly observed, not only in the organized Kehillot, but also in the remotest localities. As early as 1757, however, mention is made of Jewish villagers in the colony of New York trading on Saturday and failing to observe *Kashrut*. The New York Kehillah Board therefore decided to withdraw their membership rights, including the right to participate in all duties performed within the synagogue, and also "not to inter them after the custom of our brethren." In future years the New York Kehillah was to display more leniency towards religious transgressors and even towards mixed marriage—this, apparently, was not only because of a general decline in religious sentiment, but also because of the difficulty in contracting marriages, as a result of the scarcity of female immigrants.

During the eighteenth century linguistic assimilation amongst American Jews accelerated, and the transition was made from languages such as Spanish, Portuguese, Dutch, and Yiddish to English. The rate of assimilation was more rapid among the earlier Sephardi immigrants. By the end of the eighteenth century, American Jews of Spanish or Portuguese origin depended exclusively on English in all their secular, and a large proportion of their religious, activities. In this context it is to be noted that there has been no significant Sephardi Jewish immigration to the United States since the beginning of the nineteenth century.

Yiddish exerted a more powerful influence on Ashkenazi Jews than Spanish or Ladino on the Sephardim. Yiddish was the principal medium of spoken and written intercourse amongst Ashkenazim. The constant trickle of immigration from Europe, even before the great immigration movements towards the end of the nineteenth century, kept it alive and ensured that it left its imprint—even after the older generations of immigrants and their progeny increasingly resorted to English. In fact, Yiddish exerted such a dynamic influence on the Jewish community as a whole that outstanding Sephardi Jewish leaders (Gershom Seixas, for example) can be found interspersing Yiddish expressions and Hebrew words and phrases *in Yiddish pronunciation* in their English correspondence. As in Europe at that time, Yiddish usage abounded in Hebrew phrases and words that have since been dropped from the language. On the other hand, letters written in Yiddish two centuries ago contained innumerable words that are peculiar to American Yiddish to this day (*gleichen*—to like, *store*—a store, *spring*—the vernal season of the year, *tryen*—to try, *chair*—a chair, etc.). It may well be that later generations of Jewish immigrants from Europe did not have to renew the process of absorbing English words into their vernacular; instead, they received a ready-made vocabulary from their Yiddish-speaking predecessors. Nevertheless, the negative aspects of linguistic assimilation, from a Jewish national point of view, already constituted a potent force on the eve of the nineteenth century. This is borne out by the Gratz family of Philadelphia, to whom we owe most of the Yiddish letters preserved from colonial times. As far back as 1776, Jonas Phillips wrote from Philadelphia on business matters in good Yiddish but apologized for the fact that "*Ich kennt mein meinung bezir shreibn in English als Yiddish.*" ("I can write down my thoughts better in English than in Yiddish.")

American Jews and Palestine

The small Jewish community of North America kept its bonds with Palestine intact despite increased linguistic and cultural assimilation and the inadequate scope of Jewish education. It continued to maintain its hope for national liberation—expressed at that time in the belief in Messianic redemption. In fact, unlike a number of Jewish communities in western Europe, it was outstanding in the extent of its national cohesion and pride. Several factors explain this, all of them related to the peculiar situation of the few, widely separated Kehillot on the new continent. The Jews of America, separated from the Jewish population centres of Europe by vast expanses of ocean, thought of themselves as the captives, "the exiled ones of Israel," who, according to the predictions of the prophets, would be gathered in from the four corners of the earth. Their natural longing for a normal Jewish way of life, for reunion with the body of the Jewish people, drew sustenance from an intensified hope for Messianic redemption. These spiritual trends were reinforced by the presence of a considerable number of erstwhile Marranos, particularly in the Newport and Charleston Kehillot. Such Jews as Aaron Lopez and his brother, who had returned to Judaism from Christianity in a spirit of exemplary devotion, general amongst the Marranos, had deep-rooted faith in the imminent and palpable advent of the Messiah. This faith was supported by the belief, widespread amongst the Christian sects in early America, that the Messianic redemption of the People of Israel was a precondition for the establishment of the Kingdom of Heaven on Earth, and was similarly linked to the Second Coming of Christ.

The principal reason why the Jews of America, even after they had become politically enfranchised, did not renounce their national ties or foreswear their national aspirations arose from the country's social and political conditions. The North American states, unlike western Europe during the Revolutionary and the Napoleonic era, were not faced with the task of consolidating a centralized state authority through the abolition of feudal particularism. On the contrary, their problem was to mark out the scope of self-government within the general framework of the Federal Union. The Federal Constitution made this possible by granting specific prerogatives to the central government and accompanying these with a detailed statement of the private citizen's rights in all the states. Rights, prerogatives and functions not specified in the Constitution were left to the respective state governments, *provided that they did not conflict with the basic law of the land: the Federal Constitution*. The Federal Constitution guaranteed freedom of speech, of press, and of worship in accordance with the individual's religious creed. The question of abolishing the autonomy of the Jewish Kehillah therefore never became an issue, primarily because autonomy, on the feudal pattern, had never been granted to the Jews in the thirteen colonies. Consequently, the American

Revolution never made any express demand for the linguistic, cultural, and national unification of this country of immigrants, nor did it consider of crucial importance the fact that national minorities might cling to their own languages and culture (for example, the "Dutch" in Pennsylvania, the French Creoles in Louisiana, or the Indian tribes). Not only did the Jews regard themselves as a nationality, but proclamations by official figures (such as Washington in his replies to the congratulations sent by Jewish communities) described them as both a religious sect and a nationality. The political emancipation of the Jews in America did not, therefore, in itself engender any crisis in respect of their acknowledgement of their affiliation with the Jewish people or their conception of the Land of Israel as the homeland to which the people would return at the proper time. On the contrary, there are indications that the victorious struggle for independence by the American people served, at least for a part of the American Jewish community, as an ideal of national liberation and intensified their own longing for Messianic deliverance.

The contributions made to the Palestine Jewish community were a powerful link between the American Kehillot and Palestine. Special collectors were usually appointed for this purpose. From the middle of the eighteenth century onwards representatives of the communities in the sacred cities of the Holy Land (Jerusalem, Hebron, Safed, Tiberias) frequently visited North America. One of the most distinguished of these was the Talmudic scholar from Hebron, Rabbi Isaac Carrigal. The fact that the sermon he delivered on the Feast of Tabernacles at Newport in 1773 was translated by Aaron Lopez from Spanish into English and published as a booklet testifies to the degree of honour enjoyed by this illustrious sage. Rabbi Carrigal was received by Stiles, the president of Yale University, and engaged in lengthy conversations with him on the subject of Israel's redemption by the Messiah, a matter of great mystic concern to this devout and pious Christian scholar.

However, the Messianic belief amongst American Jews was quite distinct from the Messianic searchings in Christian circles. It had become deeply embedded in their consciousness in its political aspects of rebuilding the Jewish state in Palestine. An obvious demonstration of the deep roots of this belief is to be found in a prayer composed by Rabbi Hendla Jochanan van Oettingen. It was publicly read by his assistant, Cantor Jacob Cohen, at the New York Synagogue in 1784 on the termination of hostilities in the War of Independence. In his prayer, the supplication, on behalf of Governor Clinton of New York and of General Washington, ended:

> As Thou hast granted to these thirteen states of America ever-lasting freedom, so mayst Thou bring us forth once again from bondage into freedom, and mayst Thou sound the great horn for our freedom as it is said: And it shall be on that day, the great horn shall be blown and the wanderers in the land of Assyria and the

dispersed in the land of Egypt shall come and bow down to the Lord on the Holy mount in Jerusalem ... May he send us the priest of righteousness who will lead us upright to our Land.

Amongst those who ardently spread the belief in the Restoration of Zion as an event of the near future, particular note must be taken of Reverend Seixas, at that time the spiritual leader of the New York Kehillah. Of the many sermons in which he reiterated his belief in the Jewish people's eventual return to the Land of Israel, his *A Religious Discourse*, delivered in honour of Thanksgiving Day, November 26, 1789, emphasized the idea that equality of civil rights, for all its great importance, did not signify the end of the Exile or, as he termed it, the Captivity. Later events, especially the conquest of Palestine by Napoleon, the Assembly of Jewish Notables and the convocation of the Sanhedrin at Paris, fortified Seixas' hope that deliverance and redemption were close at hand. In the sermons he preached between 1799 and 1807 his appeal to his fellow-Jews to return to acts of piety was based on the argument that they would thereby fulfil a condition for redemption, the happy omens of which could already be seen in the events of the day.

In another Thanksgiving Day sermon, delivered apparently in 1804, he declared that the Lord "will gather us again from all corners of the earth wherein we shall be scattered and reinstate us in our former possessions, in our own Land and under our own Government."

This outlook, this yearning for the Land of Israel, left its impress on the life of American Jewry for many more decades. Even the new generation, born after the outbreak of the Revolutionary War, produced a number of outstanding men who took a special interest in Palestine. They included Judah Touro, who fought in the War in 1812 and later became a magnate and philanthropist of renown, and the attorney Sampson Simson, who launched his career with an address in Hebrew when he received his university degree. These two endeavoured to establish a Palestine Fund and both bequeathed a large share of their estates to the fostering of handicrafts and agriculture among the Jews of Palestine. Mordechai Emmanuel Noah, one of the pioneers of American journalism, belonged to the same generation. He conceived the original idea of establishing a Jewish territory in America in preparation for the renewal of Jewish statehood in the Land of Israel.

Only in the latter half of the nineteenth century did ideologically motivated assimilationist trends begin to infiltrate the American Jewish community, as they had already permeated the Jewish bourgeoisie of western Europe. Indeed, many, if not most, of these assimilationist concepts were transferred to the New World when their advocates had to flee the reaction that engulfed many areas of western, and especially central, Europe in the aftermath of the revolutions of 1848.

CHAPTER TWO

ENGLAND

English Jewry at the End of the Eighteenth and the Beginning of the Nineteenth Century

The legal status of the Jews in England, the greatest empire and commercial power in the world, was the most favourable in Europe on the eve of the French Revolution. Immediately after their resettlement in the middle of the seventeenth century, Anglo-Jewry began to take advantage of the opportunities offered by the import and export trade with the colonies, and by banking. By the middle of the eighteenth century, the Jewish merchant class in this, the most highly developed capitalist country of the period, had become the wealthiest Jewish community in Europe. The Jewish population grew steadily from a few score families in 1660 to 6,000-8,000 people a hundred years later. By the end of the eighteenth century, the Jewish community in England numbered some 20,000-25,000 people.

This increase was mainly the result of the immigration of Ashkenazi Jews; the Sephardic community at the time was numerically almost static. Nevertheless, in terms of social status, the Sephardi community was still prominent amongst the Jews of England at the beginning of the nineteenth century. They were the most affluent merchants, engaged in the colonial trade with the Americas, India, and the Near East. The *Parnass* of the *Sha'ar Ha'Shamayim* Congregation, Joseph Salvador (Yeshurun Rodriguez), was elected Director of the East India Company in the middle of the eighteenth century. During the same period wealthy Sephardi Jews arranged loans for the Government. They participated in the development of the textile industry and formed half of London's sixteen large-scale exporters of coral. Twelve out of the total of 124 Royal Stock Exchange brokers were drawn from their ranks. Companies organized by Sephardi Jews acted as army suppliers. The Ashkenazi Jews, although they constituted by far the majority of the community, were in an altogether different—and inferior—position. With the exception of a small group of well-to-do wholesalers, stockbrokers and jewellers, and a somewhat larger lower-middle-class group, mainly shopkeepers, goldsmiths and watchmakers, the Ashkenazim comprised an abject mass of people whose poverty had become proverbial. For the most part, they earned their living in ways which had become associated with the penurious Jews of western and central Europe during the eighteenth century—rag dealing, street peddling, and itinerant barter in the villages and countryside. At frequent intervals they fell victim to assault and degradation of the worst possible kind. Yet by patience and perseverance some of these pedlars succeeded in establishing themselves in various English towns and in organizing local Kehillot. By the end of the eighteenth century some five or six thousand Jews were already living in places other than London—Portsmouth, Bristol, Plymouth, Liverpool, Manchester, Birmingham and fifteen other towns.

The only actual limitation on Jewish economic rights was a prohibition on opening retail stores in the City of London. However, apart from individual Jews who obtained the rights of freemen, other merchants circumvented this restriction by defining their shops as "wholesale businesses," or established them in the evergrowing suburbs, where freemen's privileges did not apply.

The question of Jewish *political* rights alone remained unresolved until the age of Parliamentary reform at the beginning of the 1840's. In practice Jews had been permitted to take part in Parliamentary elections by the end of the eighteenth century. Socially, the Jewish plutocracy of London had achieved equality with the bourgeoisie to such an extent that its members held high office in Masonic lodges at the beginning of the eighteenth century, and Jewish dignitaries were included in official delegations received in audience by the King.

However, British authority in the early days of the industrial revolution fell heavily on the mass of itinerant pedlars and the incessant stream of huddled, ragged immigrants from Europe. In this they received wholehearted support from representatives of the established Jewish bourgeoisie who even showed some appalling initiative of their own. In 1771, the Home Secretary directed the Postmaster-General not to allow passage on English mail packets sailing from the port of Hellevoetsluis in Holland to Jews who did not pay the full price for their tickets and held no passport from the British Ambassador. This order was issued by the British minister in response to a memorandum submitted by representatives of the Ashkenazi Great Synagogue of London. At the same time, the police launched an extensive roundup of Jewish pedlars throughout England; those arrested were deported from the country. A delegation from the Great Synagogue called on the Minister, Lord Suffolk, to offer thanks for this service.

While all manner of decrees were being directed against the Jewish immigrants, marked social progress and economic consolidation was taking place within an important segment of the Jewish population. As a result of the industrial revolution and the favourable conjunction of events during the war years in France, former rag dealers and pedlars in London were rapidly transformed into merchants, craftsmen, industrialists, and exporters; and a number of Jews became shipping agents in some seaport towns. An upper middle class gradually emerged from these circles. They began to displace the old Sephardi plutocracy, which had never recovered from the crisis in the West Indies trade following the French Revolution and the decline of the East India Company. In the middle of the eighteenth century, Sephardi families, such as the Gideon Salvadors, were bankers to the government; in the Napoleonic wars the Goldsmid brothers took a prominent part in floating Government loans; by the end of our period the house of Nathan Meyer Rothschild had moved to the fore.

The Jewish population was organized into two separate Kehillot, Sephardi and Ashkenazi. In 1760, representatives of the Sephardim agreed to consult with the representatives of the Ashkenazi synagogues whenever the necessity arose for concerted political action concerning the "two peoples." The foundation was thus laid for the Jewish Board of Deputies, representing all British Jewry. Apart from the educational and charitable activities of the Kehillot, special associations existed for the maintenance of rabbinical colleges, for the study of Maimonides, the Talmud, and similar works. Despite the stern attitude of the Kehillah leaders, Sephardim and Ashkenazim alike, towards the immigrant poor, they were not completely impervious to requests for monetary aid or political intercession from Jewish communities throughout the world. On many occasions (e.g. the temporary expulsion of the Jews from Bohemia in the middle of the eighteenth century) the Sephardi and Ashkenazi Kehillot of London conducted joint campaigns for funds on their behalf.

The cultural life of the wealthy English Jews during the eighteenth and at the beginning of the nineteenth century was characterized by outward assimilation and formal conservatism in religious matters. The Sephardi Jews grew no beards, used English in their daily intercourse and correspondence, and in general hardly differed from Englishmen of the same class. There was still a large group among the Ashkenazim, consisting mainly of new immigrants from Poland, who did grow beards and clung to the traditional long gaberdines. But the leaders of the Ashkenazi Kehillah were less conservative than the Sephardim. By 1815 they had introduced English sermons into their synagogues. The immigrant character of the Ashkenazi community and the strict conservatism of the Sephardim impeded any cultural development amongst English Jews. Against this background, a wave of conversions and extreme assimilation affected large numbers of the Jewish plutocracy. It was especially pronounced in the Sephardi community (defections from Judaism involved such prominent families as the Gideons, D'Israelis, Barnells and Ricardos). On the other hand, the Jewish poor and even the middle class were unaffected by the tendency towards deliberate assimilation. On the contrary, they remained loyal to the ideal of the restoration to Zion. During the first half of the nineteenth century they gave realistic and modern expression to the historic aspirations of the Jewish people in the form of plans for the colonization of Palestine. This spiritual climate inspired the pioneering activities of Sir Moses Montefiore for improving the condition of the *Old Yishuv* in Palestine.*

* The *Old Yishuv*—"the old settlement"—the term used to describe the religious Jewish communities of Palestine who depended on charitable contributions from the Diaspora for their material existence.

CHAPTER THREE

FRANCE

A. *THE PERIOD OF FEUDALISM AND ABSOLUTISM*

The Economic and Legal Situation

At the outbreak of the Revolution that was to change the very foundations of Jewish life in western Europe, the Jewish community in France numbered no more than 40,000 people out of a total population of 25 million. There were barely 1.5 Jews per 1,000 inhabitants. The Jews were concentrated in three widely separated areas: Alsace-Lorraine in the east; the district of Avignon in the south-east; and the ancient province of Guienne in the vicinity of Bordeaux in the south-west.

The Sephardim in the south-west enjoyed a certain prestige as the descendants of wealthy Portuguese Marranos. They were engaged in the wholesale trade as late as the eighteenth century and played a distinguished role in the economic affairs of the localities where they lived. The great seaport town of Bordeaux was the home of the wealthiest and most important Sephardi Kehillah, comprising 2,000 people. Second in size was the Sephardi Kehillah at Bayonne: domiciled in the suburb of Saint Esprit, its members made up a third of the local population. Smaller Sephardi communities lived in the nearby cities of Biarritz and Peyrehorade. There were also groups of Sephardi Jews in the seaport towns of Nantes, Marseilles, and other southern towns.

Because of their wealth and commercial activity the Sephardi Jews had received *lettres patentes* from Henry II of France, as early as the sixteenth century. These granted them rights of domicile in whichever province they settled, the right to trade without hindrance, and the right to own real estate. Louis XVI supplemented the rights of the Jews of Bordeaux in 1776 by allowing them to settle and conduct their commercial activities anywhere within the borders of France. The Jews of Bordeaux included great bankers, exporters and importers, silk and other cloth merchants, and suppliers to the Royal Navy. All that they lacked was political enfranchisement, particularly the right to become members of the Municipal Council and Chamber of Commerce.

But not all Sephardi Jews were in such favourable circumstances. The Jews of Bayonne occupied a lower position in the social and economic hierarchy than those of Bordeaux. They were forbidden by municipal law to reside within the city precincts (which is why they lived in the suburb of Saint Esprit), to engage in retail trade, or to own real estate. However, like the Jews of Bordeaux, they were granted various rights and even allowed to participate in the elections to the Estates General in 1789.

Religious orthodoxy began to wane among many Sephardi Jews of France, especially the Jewish plutocrats of Bordeaux, in the face of the attractions of the Enlightenment of the eighteenth century. Their community leaders included Voltaireans who considered all religion a superstition and acknowledged rationalist deism as their only creed. The enlightened Jews of Bordeaux were so attached to the French culture and language that the first Jewish writers in the French language emerged from their ranks. They included Isaac Pinto, author of several essays on banking and also of a French pamphlet which, as early as 1762, refuted Voltaire's invectives against the Jews, and Jacques Roderiguez Pereyra.

The Jews in the Avignon region were subject to the temporal authority of the Pope and lived in the ghettos (carrière) of *The Four Kehillot*, the name by which the four cities of Avignon, Carpentras, Cavaillon, and Ile-sur-Sorgue were known. There were about 2,500 Jews in the entire area, of whom 1,500 lived inside the ghetto of Carpentras. Congested buildings ten storeys high lined the one long and narrow street of this ghetto, for the small frontage available had caused structure to be piled upon structure.

The Jews of the Four Kehillot were forbidden by Papal edicts to pursue any calling other than moneylending, street peddling, and junk dealing. They were forbidden to rent rooms outside the ghetto, for even one night's lodging. But the needs of the economy helped them to overcome many restrictions. In the eighteenth century the Jews in the Papal States extended their trade to include horses and mules, grains, wines and oils, woven cloth and silk, ornaments, and fancy goods. They attended the fairs in all the important towns of southern France and their activities spread to Toulouse, Montpellier, Bordeaux, and Nîmes. Handicrafts, particularly tailoring, took an important position in the economic life of the Jews of Avignon, and there were also Jewish silk spinners. There were several Jewish commercial magnates at Carpentras, assessed at 100,000 *livres* or more.

Even the Papal administration had finally to reckon with the demands of economic development and in 1781 it consented to certain relaxations in the anti-Jewish segregation measures. Thus, Jews were now permitted to rent cow-barns and haylofts from Christians outside the ghetto. However, despite these legal exemptions and illegal permits, the Jews of Avignon, like the great majority of French Jews, were totally deprived of rights. Throughout the year, except on days when they travelled to fairs, the Jews of the Four Kehillot were compelled to live in the narrow, choking alleys of the ghetto. In addition to the regular taxes paid by all inhabitants, they had to pay special taxes and levies, and to make "gifts" to officials and the clergy. Not surprisingly in view of these heavy expenses, the Kehillot staggered under a heavy burden of indebtedness, all the more so as a sizeable proportion of the ghetto population was dependent on charity.

Humiliating Church decrees exacerbated the position: for example, all Jews were ordered to wear yellow hats; they were forced to listen to missionary preaching by clergymen (and each Kehillah had to pay the priest a regular fee for this); and they were forbidden to keep any volumes of the Talmud or *Kabbalah* in their homes. Despite this latter injunction, the Jews of Avignon applied themselves to the study of the *Gemara*. Not only this, but in the eighteenth century a visitor from Palestine reported that they even included some brilliant scholars. A Hebrew pronunciation and a prayer ritual peculiar to themselves persisted among the Jews of Avignon. Furthermore, their spoken vernacular consisted of a Jewish idiom based on Provençal which had also developed amongst themselves.

Over four-fifths of all French Jews were Ashkenazim, concentrated in the north-eastern provinces of Alsace-Lorraine, with its mixed Franco-German population. The number of Jews "suffered" to reside in the province of Alsace by a Royal edict of 1784 reached the figure of 20,000 However, a not unjustified theory suggests that an additional number of unregistered Jews also lived there. In any event, in 1789, an official memorandum from the *Shtadlan* (intercessor), Cerf-Berr, referred to 5,000 Jewish families in Alsace. Jews thus represented 3 per cent of the 700,000-800,000 inhabitants of the province. Practically all the Jews lived in the smaller towns and villages, especially in the southern region of Sundgau. Jews were completely banned from residence in the larger cities—the capital, Strasbourg, Colmar, and Mulhouse. Cerf-Berr, a wealthy grain dealer, only obtained royal permission in 1771 to settle with his family at Strasbourg and even to buy houses there, despite the vigorous opposition of the municipal council and the citizens of the town.

Refused access to the larger cities, which were forearmed with privileges from the king, the Jews of Alsace were dispersed among the small towns and villages where they could enjoy seignorial protection, though at a high price. Throughout Alsace, Jews were not allowed to engage in agriculture, or to belong to the craft guilds. Hence, they could practise no craft except that of the goldsmith. Nor could they buy real property except at their place of domicile for personal use. Similarly, in most of the province, Jews were excluded from all commercial pursuits except rag dealing. Within their towns and villages, they were limited to petty trade, peddling—which they mostly carried out surreptitiously—and usury.

The practice of usury by the Jews of Alsace was a grave matter, from the outbreak of the Revolution and until the Napoleonic period and after. Usury was undoubtedly a social blight, but it was a blight, after all, that was caused by the social and economic crisis of the régime. It is clear from the cahiers presented by the inhabitants of Alsace to the Estates General in 1789, that Jews were not the only ones in Alsace to deal in credit; and this was even more true of Lorraine. The large banking houses definitely belonged to non-Jews. Jewish usury was mostly confined to loans to peasants—loans which the borrower could in no circumstances have obtained from a bank. It was not the actual existence of the Jewish usurer that enslaved the peasant to the rate of interest. On the contrary, it was the peasant's condition, his utter inability to sustain the heavy burden of taxation exacted by the landed proprietors, which compelled him to turn to the Jew in his search for credit. The Jewish moneylenders were mostly not even well-off. Christian writers of the period reported that nearly the entire Jewish population of Alsace lived in abject poverty. The Jewish petty usurer had not infrequently to borrow money from bankers himself—even Christian bankers—thus incurring heavy debts.

In any event, the ruling classes in Alsace did not fail to exploit the fact that Jewish usurers were discharging the unsavoury functions of predatory capital in order to shift responsibility for the dire predicament of the peasants on to the Jewish population. A few years before the Revolution, *lettres patentes* did grant slight concessions to the Jews, but only very small groups benefited. On the one hand, the declining absolutist régime in France strove to keep the Jews as a whole in a totally under-privileged condition or even to aggravate their situation. On the other hand, it sought some improvement in the position of Jewish groups which might contribute towards the economic development of the state. Thus, Jews were permitted to engage in manufacture, banking, and commerce, on condition that their accounts were kept not in Hebrew but in French, and in Latin script. Similarly, some Jews were allowed to engage in agriculture where they had obtained domiciliary rights, but only as leaseholders and not as owners, and on condition that they cultivated the soil themselves and did not employ Christian ploughmen. The *lettres patentes* imposed stringent administrative restrictions on Jewish credit. Moreover, they included new provisions, entirely depriving them of all security of existence: Jews who could not produce proof of a permanent place of residence or of having paid patronage fees to King, noble or city, and of having discharged their Kehillah taxes, were required to quit Alsace within three months or suffer the penalties meted out to vagabonds.

Permission to engage in agriculture was, as a matter of fact, a mere illusion, since no Jew could take advantage of the right to lease farmlands without the help of experienced Christian farmers. The new decrees concerning the expulsion of Jews who did not possess domiciliary rights, as well as the prohibition of marriages without royal sanction, were on the other hand grim reality.

The number of Jews in Lorraine was small compared with Alsace. They numbered about 8,000 out of a total population of more than 1 million (by 1806, nearly 1,400,000). The largest Jewish community in the area—in all of Alsace-Lorraine, in fact—was in the city of Metz, which, together with the cities of Verdun and Toul, comprised a separate province known as "The Three Bishoprics." *Lettres patentes* issued between 1718 and 1777 permitted 480 Jewish families to reside in Metz. The limitations on Jewish rights in Lorraine were just as oppressive and, in some respects, even worse, than in Alsace. Until shortly before the outbreak of the Revolution, no Jew had the right to change his residence. In some cities, the right of domicile was limited to one stipulated quarter. The Jewish community in Metz was confined to a ghetto, notorious for its narrow streets and buildings of five and six storeys.

The great majority of Lorraine Jews did not practise usury, even as an auxiliary occupation. Instead, they worked as travelling merchants and pedlars. This provided a very precarious income, all the more so because of oppressive taxes as well as "gifts" that had to be presented to various officials—King, noble patrons, Church, monks, and all the clerks of the provincial administration. Nevertheless, it is true that a group of well-to-do middle-class Jews and an even thinner crust of very wealthy wholesale merchants and bankers, existed amidst the general poverty, particularly at Metz, and to a smaller extent at Nancy.

A few of the wealthy Jews of Alsace-Lorraine such as Cerf-Berr, purveyor and contractor to the King, Cerf-Worms, and other individual Jews at Avignon, received *Lettres de Naturalisation* which gave them freedom to live and trade anywhere in France and even to purchase real estate. However, in 1787 the number of such privileged Jews in the whole of France, excluding Bordeaux, hardly exceeded ten.

Cultural Life and the Kehillah

The character of the cultural life of the Jews of Alsace-Lorraine was fundamentally the same as in neighbouring Germany. Their mode of life followed the traditional-religious pattern, taken to the extreme, and the rabbis scrupulously guarded against any inroads that new customs might make in the established order. Gemara was taught at the *Yeshivot*. The largest, in Metz, had at its head during the eighteenth century such illustrious scholars as Rabbi Jonathan Eibeschuetz, and—until just before the Revolution—Rabbi Aryeh Leib Ben-Asher, author of *Sheagat-Aryeh* (Responsa on the *Shulkhan Arukh*). The spoken vernacular was a peculiar Alsatian variety of Yiddish.

Nevertheless, shortly before the outbreak of the Revolution, currents of the Enlightenment also reached the Jewish community of Alsace-Lorraine: there, as everywhere else, the protagonists of Enlightenment arose from the Jewish bourgeois class, then in the process of formation, and the small group of intellectuals associated with it, economically and ideologically. The views held by the latter were more moderate and conservative than those of Moses Mendelssohn's disciples at Berlin. Even though they advocated the dissemination of secular education and productive labour (in the textile factory founded by Cerf-Berr's relatives Jewish workers also were employed) they themselves still observed the traditional mode of life. The presidents of the Kehillah and the men who led the fight for the enfranchisement of the Jews of Alsace-Lorraine came from amongst their ranks.

The Jewish communities of Alsace-Lorraine enjoyed wide powers of autonomy, although under state supervision. The Kehillah was empowered to settle all problems of religious life and its law courts were authorized to give a first hearing to civil lawsuits between Jews concerning inheritances, custodianships, contracts, and similar matters. Because of the widespread poverty, one of the most important fields of Kehillah activity was the distribution of charity. The Kehillot also regularly allocated a definite sum from their annual budgets for the emissaries from Palestine.

As in all countries where a feudal régime persisted, the wealthier class dominated the Kehillah. At Bordeaux, the management of the Kehillah was in the hands of a few of the richest families, e.g. the families of Gradis, Fernandez, Silva, Lameira, D'Acosta, Pereyra, Peixotto and others. At Avignon and Carpentras, an individual whose property was assessed at less than 5,000 livres—actually about half the Kehillah membership—did not have a vote. In Alsace-Lorraine, the office of Kehillah president was held by a few families of bankers, big merchants, and purveyors. Where the wealthiest Jew of the city did not himself serve as Kehillah leader, he forced the community to elect a man of his own choice. The bye-laws of the Jews of Alsace for 1777, made wealth a qualification for eligibility to the office of Kehillah president.

Apart from the communities in southern France and in Alsace-Lorraine, a small Jewish community also existed in Paris before the Revolution. On the eve of the Revolution, there were 500 Jewish families, about 800 people, registered as officially resident in the capital. This community was composed of representatives of all three sectors of French Jewry: Sephardim, *Avignonnais* and Ashkenazim: the Ashkenazim, who were in the majority, came mainly from Alsace-Lorraine; the remainder were from Holland, Germany, and even Poland. The wealthy Jews of Paris hailed from Bordeaux and they included bankers, merchants, and suppliers, whereas the Ashkenazim for the most part scraped a livelihood by itinerant peddling, rag-dealing, and money-changing. The presence of the Ashkenazim in the city was only semi-legal: the police (who had a special division for "supervising Jews and thieves") carried out night searches every week or so and arrested any Jew whose passport had expired. The Jews of Paris had also to battle against constant attempts by the merchant guilds to hamper their trading activity.

In such circumstances, the Jewish population of the capital was isolated from the buoyant cultural life of its gentile environment. For most of the Jews of Paris, Yiddish was their everyday language, but even

23

before the Revolution a number of them were already highly educated. This was true of the Sephardi syndic, Jacob Rodriguez Pereyra, founder of the first school for deaf mutes; Moses Ansheim, of Metz, mathematician and author of Hebrew poems; and Zalkind Hourwitz, an ex-rabbinical student from Poland, who became the leading advocate of extreme assimilation (when the Revolution broke out he was working as librarian in the oriental division of the Royal Library).

So far as their internal organization was concerned, even in Paris, where the three regional groups of French Jewry were in contact, no ability to coalesce into one organized unit was evident. The gap was particularly marked between the proud Sephardim from Bordeaux and the Ashkenazim. The Sephardim of France displayed a tendency towards selfish separatism, both at the time of the Revolution and in their earlier efforts at improving Jewish conditions. The instructions issued by the leaders of the Portuguese community at Bordeaux to their representatives in Paris in May, 1788 were characteristic. In presenting their demands to the government mediator the representatives were ordered, on the one hand, not to create the impression that any articles of faith were in dispute between them and the "other" Jews. On the other hand, they were to explain that those Jews clung to ridiculous and superstitious orthodox rituals, so that the Sephardim could never intermarry with them. "Should it be absolutely necessary," the Sephardi representatives were authorized to emphasise that they were the descendants of members of the tribe of Judah who, having been exiled by Nebuchadnezzar even before the Babylonian captivity (with King Jehoiachin), had at once departed for Spain.

The Jewish Problem in Political Literature

The economic interests of the rising bourgeoisie postulated the abolition of the legal restrictions to which Jewish capital was subjected. This was in accordance with one of the chief slogans of the new class: an unimpeded, clear path for the economic forces of capitalism, which had already made inroads into the old system. The ideas of human equality and of the natural rights of every human being were rightfully applicable to the Jewish problem and the status of the Jews. Small wonder, then, that the Jewish problem was brought up in the writings of several of the thinkers who appeared on the public scene prior to the Revolution with new political programmes and ideas. It was to be expected that educated Jews would participate in this literature, either directly or by giving information and guidance to non-Jewish writers. At times they even took the initiative in publishing brochures.

In 1782, a French translation of Christian Dohm's famous essay, *On the Improvement of the Civil Status of the Jews*, was published on the initiative of Cerf-Berr. In the same year, Anacharsis Cloots, who became famous as a Jacobin during the Revolution, published his essay, *Letters on the Jews*. In 1787, a booklet was published by the Jewish intellectual Isaiah Berr-Bing in reply to a defamatory anti-Jewish paper that had gained some circulation in Metz. Also in 1787, Mirabeau published his monograph, *The Political Reform of the Jews*, which dealt with Moses Mendelssohn and other related topics.

In 1785, the Royal Academy at Metz announced a competition on the subject: *Is it Possible to Make the Jews of France More Useful and Happy?* Nine replies were received, seven in the affirmative. These contestants, who included three clergymen and a jurist from Lorraine, a barrister, Thierry of Nancy, almost with one voice argued that the shortcomings of the Jews were the result of their disenfranchisement and that, given full economic opportunity, they would become useful, contented citizens. Two years later, the Metz Academy published the results of this competition and three of the participants received wide publicity. They were Thierry, Abbé Grégoire, a famous liberal and friend of the Jews, and the self-styled "Polish Jew," Zalkind Hourwitz. Thierry took a positive stand on the question of autonomy and in any case thought that it would be a good thing to allow the Jews to maintain their Kehillot and Kehillah leaders for some time to come. Abbé Grégoire and Zalkind Hourwitz on the other hand expressed the opinion—in the spirit of Moses Mendelssohn—that in no circumstances should rabbis be allowed authority in anything but religious matters and in no case should they possess any civil jurisdiction. Hourwitz even went as far as to state at the conclusion of his essay: "It would even be desirable to forbid them to maintain rabbis, whose upkeep is most costly and who are absolutely useless."

At the same time, the government decided to convene an assembly of Jewish notables to discuss improvement in the situation of the Jews in France. Eight Jewish leaders were invited to appear before a committee under the chairmanship of the minister, Malesherbes. But before he had decided to set the committee in operation, the decaying structure of absolute monarchy collapsed under the thunderous impact of the Revolution which now broke out in all France.

B. *THE FRENCH REVOLUTION AND THE ENFRANCHISEMENT OF THE JEWS IN FRANCE*

Jewish Efforts in 1789 to Acquire Equality of Rights

In the spring of 1789, Louis XVI found it imperative to convene the Estates General in order to avoid bankruptcy. This body, representing the three classes in the realm, had not met for 175 years. It never occurred to the King that his action would give the signal for the outbreak of revolution. With its life drawing to a close, its every foundation rocking, the *Ancien Régime* once more perpetrated an enormous injustice against the Jewish population: the vast majority of its members were excluded from participation in the elections to the States General. Only the Sephardi Jews were permitted to attend election meetings. Even so, because there were so few of them at Bordeaux and because of the discriminatory electoral system at Bayonne, they did not send a single representative to the Assembly.

The Jewish representatives in Alsace-Lorraine did not dare demand the right to participate in the general elections. However, they took advantage of the occasion to present a series of demands for improvements in their condition. Organized anti-Jewish activities in Alsace during the elections proved that there was no time to be lost. At the beginning of April, 1789, Cerf-Berr, apparently at the instigation of Abbé Grégoire, submitted a memorandum to the Director General of Finances, M. Necker. He claimed that the Jews, as tax payers, had the same right to submit their requests in the *Cahiers de Doléance* as the rest of the population, and also to designate one or more of the Christian deputies already elected to represent them at the Assembly of the Estates General.

On May 15, after the Estates General had already convened, the Minister notified Cerf-Berr that the Jews of Alsace-Lorraine might elect six delegates, two from each of the three provinces, at special assemblies. The delegates would meet in Paris under the chairmanship of Cerf-Berr (now officially named State Intermediary) to draw up their own *Cahier* based on the resolutions of their electors. The assemblies duly took place and duly elected six delegates, all Jewish leaders of their respective provinces. The six included Berr Isaac Berr and three members of Cerf-Berr's family: they did not complete their task until August, when the Revolution was at boiling point.

The Revolution erupted and rolled onwards when the Estates General at Versailles yielded to popular pressure on June 17, 1789, and resolved in a historic declaration to form itself into a National Assembly. The capture of the Bastille by the Paris masses on July 14, 1789, was the signal for the people throughout the country to take the reins of revolution into their own hands. The wave of popular wrath wrought such panic amongst the ruling classes that they agreed to conduct a debate in the National Assembly on the abolition of serfdom. A resolution abolishing all feudal privileges was adopted at the session which took place on the evening of August 4. But the way in which this resolution was to be implemented *in practice* was the subject of prolonged debate. In the meantime, the National Assembly met to formulate *The Declaration of the Rights of Man and the Citizen* as the basis of the new political régime. It was on this occasion that the problem of Jewish rights was first raised at the National Assembly. In a fiery speech, Mirabeau denounced the principle of a dominant religion and the concept of mere toleration for other creeds. This actually contravened genuine freedom of belief, he argued. The Protestant Minister, St. Etienne, openly supported the Jews: "It is not even toleration that I demand, it is liberty . . . for the Protestants of France, for all the non-Catholics of the kingdom, I demand what you demand for yourselves; liberty and equal rights. I demand them also for that people, uprooted from the soil of Asia, wandering, ostracized and persecuted for almost eighteen hundred years, who would undoubtedly adopt our ways and customs, if only our law permitted them to be incorporated in us. Let us not censure this people for their morality, for this is but the fruit of our own barbarism, of that humiliation to which we have unjustly condemned them."

Etienne's speech set the pattern for all subsequent debates at the National Assembly in support of the Jews. However, the Jewish problem was not at this time included in the agenda. Article X of the *Declaration of the Rights of Man* was only passed in the face of powerful opposition. Later it provided the principle behind the claim to equality of rights for the Jews. The Article stated that "no person shall be molested for his opinions even such as are religious, provided that the manifestation of their opinions does not disturb the public order as established by the law."

The Jews, and particularly the Jews of Paris, were caught up in the stormy events of the first months of the Revolution. "Many Jews too, inhabitants of Paris," states a Yiddish pamphlet, *Beshreibung fun der Revolusion*, dated August 5, "entered the National Civil Guard. They were received with honour. One of them has been commissioned as a captain and another, as a sergeant-major. The citizens did not distinguish [between the Jews] and the Catholics." In Bordeaux, Jews enlisted in the National Guard and there, too, were commissioned. The Jews of Alsace-Lorraine received information directly from the author of the pamphlet quoted above. He was Abraham Ben-Getschlik Speier-Shamesh, a resident of Metz, and printer by trade. He was staying in Paris at the time and "with his own eyes had beheld the great Revolution."

The six Jewish delegates elected by the Kehillot of Alsace-Lorraine, met at the beginning of August after lengthy consultations. At Paris, under Cerf-Berr's leadership, they prepared their *Cahiers de Doléance*. The joint *Cahier* submitted to the Government for all three provinces, demanded equal taxes for Jews as "for all other citizens," the right to engage in crafts and agriculture, permission to settle in all the provinces of the state including, first and foremost, any district in any city. The *Cahier* ended by demanding freedom to practise the Jewish faith and, incidentally, the retention of the rabbis, Parnassim, and Kehillot. Particular demands from each of three provinces were attached to the joint demands. The Jews of Alsace specifically petitioned for the right to employ Christian labour in agriculture and demanded that the decree forbidding marriages between Jews without special permits be revoked. They also demanded a prohibition on the use of insulting terms in official documents to describe Jews. The demands from the Jews of Metz called, amongst other things, for the abolition of the extortionate patronage fees amounting to twenty thousand livres per annum and declared that the Kehillah itself had issued regulations against moneylending abuses. In view of the great indebtedness of the Kehillah, the Jews of Metz also demanded that nobody be allowed to leave the Kehillah without paying his share towards the liquidation of the Kehillah's debt. The Jews of Lorraine demanded permission to build a synagogue "without outside adornments," and also asked for the admission of Jewish students to colleges and universities. They outlined in detail the authority of the Rabbinical Court and requested that right of entry into Lorraine be withheld from Jews lacking a definite minimum of funds.

It would seem from this that the chief spokesmen for the Jewish community were not as yet imbued with the spirit of the Revolution. Instead of insisting on the principle of full enfranchisement, they were only demanding certain economic rights, and even then only in timorous, inconclusively formulated phrases. The Jewish leaders from each of the three provinces found it imperative to come forward with local grievances, even with demands (as in the case of the Lorraine delegation) intended only to protect their own, narrow, parochial interests at the expense of the Jews in the adjoining provinces.

The address that the same delegates from Alsace-Lorraine brought before the National Assembly on August 31 was somewhat bolder both in tone and contents. Now, under the influence of the *Declaration of the Rights of Man*, they expressly demanded that the "title and rights of citizens" be granted the Jews—although they still repeated individual demands concerning rights of domicile and equal taxation.

Moreover, the Jewish delegates still stressed, and at great length, the demand "to leave at their posts our rabbis and Parnassim as was the custom till this day." Autonomy meant so much to them, that in their representations they solemnly adjured the National Assembly: "Certainly you do not propose on the one hand to elevate us and on the other to degrade us." The Kehillah, they explained, was instrumental in maintaining the Jewish religion and in any case strengthened the loyalty of the Jews to the King and to the French people. They concluded with the most telling argument of all: liquidation of the Kehillot might "suddenly be followed by widespread panic amidst many creditors, mostly *Catholics*." (Emphasis in the original.) However, a group of Lorraine Jews, from the neighbouring Kehillot of Lunéville and Sarreguemines, flouted the discipline of the elected authorised leaders and presented their own demands for complete enfranchisement. Local circumstances explain their awareness of the right of the Jews to full emancipation: they wished to be freed from the supervision exercised over them by the leaders of the chief Kehillah at Nancy. After the Jewish delegates from Alsace-Lorraine had sent their memorandum of August 31 to the National Assembly, the Jews of Lunéville and Sarreguemines delivered a written protest. In their opinion, these delegates had no authority to speak in the name of their own two Kehillot. They protested in particular against the delegation's request that Jewish autonomy be retained as hitherto. They did not wish to be subject to the authority of the Kehillah at Nancy, which, they alleged, imposed a disproportionate amount of the Kehillah taxes upon them without their consent. They also did not wish to submit to the rabbi of that Kehillah, since he exacted many fees from them—for wedding rites, wills, and similar matters. They considered themselves citizens of their own cities; they were therefore entitled to choose their rabbis and Parnassim from amongst themselves.

An anonymous comment (apparently by Zalkind Hourwitz) in the margin of one of their memoranda subtly illuminates the contradiction inherent in the respective attitudes of the two Lorraine communities. "If they are becoming citizens and no longer have to pay special taxes to the government," it asks in surprise, "why then must they have their own community heads, why cannot they be subject to the local authorities?" The author of the comment, moreover, is of the opinion that the institution of Parnassim, like that of the rabbis, ran counter to the "regeneration" and "the cultural advancement of this people."

The petition that the Jews of Paris submitted to the National Assembly on August 26 avoided such contradictory demands as those made by the Kehillot of Lunéville and Sarreguemines. On this occasion, for the first time, the three Jewish groups in the capital, the Sephardim, the community of Avignon, and the Ashkenazim, combined to elect a committee of six. In their memorandum, the Jews of Paris cited the *Declaration of the Rights of Man*, adopted just a few days previously, and demanded that a special order be issued confirming the rights of the Jews as citizens. Such an order, they suggested, would arouse the admiration of the whole world and France would become a model for all countries to emulate. So far as autonomy was concerned, they declared "we therefore renounce, for the general cause and our own advantage, which is ever subordinate to the general interest, that privilege which had entitled us to have our own leaders, drawn from our members and appointed by the Government." While expressly foregoing Kehillah autonomy, the Jews of Paris nevertheless felt duty bound to dwell at length on their spiritual attachment to "our religion, which differs from that which is dominant in France." In their opinion this was to the advantage of the state; and they emphasized that their loyalty to the Jewish religion served as a guarantee that in the future too they would remain as steadfast in their civic loyalty as in the past, since no greater evil was conceivable than indifference to religious matters.

Only the Sephardi Jews took no separate action in the question of Jewish rights. The representatives of the Bordeaux Sephardim at Paris expounded their point of view in a communication of August 14, 1789, to Abbé Grégoire, which was later printed and published: in their opinion, the fundamental principles of the new constitution, expressed in the *Declaration of the Rights of Man*, rendered any special law concerning the Jews superfluous. At the same time, they made the following declarations: "Should the conduct or, rather, the ill fortune of some Jews in Alsace and the Three Bishoprics move the National Assembly to issue decrees applying equally to all the Jews in the country, then the Jews of Bordeaux and likewise their fellow-citizens, will have to complain about it as a needless and most cruel injustice." Thus the propertied Sephardic Jews sought, from the very outset, assurances that they would not be considered part of the general body of Jewry should any special legislation be enacted concerning the Jews of Alsace-Lorraine. This was not the final betrayal of the cause of Jewish unity by men secure and proud in their wealth.

By the end of August the National Assembly therefore had before it three different memoranda concerning the Jews. They were read on September 3 and passed on to the Committee. The National Assembly, at that time, was occupied with a matter that had aroused a storm of passion throughout the country: the struggle over the King's power of veto. However, in view of the exposed position of the Jews in Alsace-Lorraine, the National Assembly placed the Jewish problem on its agenda shortly afterwards, at least so far as the security of the Jews was concerned.

An anti-Jewish movement had already appeared in Alsace and spread into parts of Lorraine by the end of July, 1789, although this was quite a while after the outbreak of the peasant uprising against the nobility. Peasants attacked Jewish homes and plundered everything within sight. But first and foremost they destroyed the account books in which their debts were entered. At the beginning of August, nineteen towns and villages in the vicinity of Sundgau were affected. Hundreds of Jews fled destitute, with only the clothes on their backs, to nearby Switzerland where the city of Basle gave them refuge. A number of them also found asylum in the Alsatian city of Mulhouse, where the inhabitants treated them exceptionally kindly. On August 3, Abbé Grégoire appeared before the National Assembly and demanded the adoption of security measures for Jewish life and property. Three days later, the Provincial Committee of Lorraine sent an urgent report to the National Assembly on the pillage of the Jews.

All the signs indicate that the anti-Jewish disorders in Alsace-Lorraine were not spontaneous outbreaks of "popular indignation"—the explanation offered by reactionary enemies of the Jews at the time. They were rather the result of premeditated and organized activity to divert attention from the Revolution. It is very significant that the onslaughts on Jewish homes were not the work of the serfs who had attacked their masters' *châteaux*. There were two separate movements at work.

Under the impact of the anti-Jewish disorders, the Jewish leaders of Alsace-Lorraine petitioned the National Assembly to accelerate its deliberations on Jewish enfranchisement. As the practice of receiving delegations was common by this time, the Jewish leaders asked that their delegation also be received by the Assembly. They argued persuasively that a rejection of their request for a hearing might be construed as disparagement and would thus increase antagonism towards the Jews. On October 14, 1789, the delegation, evidently composed of the six leaders headed by Berr Isaac Berr of Nancy, appeared before the National Assembly. At the suggestion of Abbé Grégoire it was decided, despite opposition from a few of the deputies, to invite the Jews into the Assembly chamber.

According to the custom of the time, they took up their position outside the partition separating the general public from members of the Chamber of Deputies. Berr Isaac Berr's address in the name of the delegation was brief, as a written memorandum was submitted at the same time. But the fervour of his delivery impressed the deputies, although neither address nor memorandum explicitly demanded complete equality of rights. They were both formulated in the traditional spirit of *Shtadlanut* (private intercession) and so evinced a lack of comprehension of the Revolution already shaking the very foundations of the world.

Amidst shouts of acclaim in the chamber, the presiding officer promised that the National Assembly would devote its attention to the matter and "would be glad to restore your brethren to a position of tranquillity and happiness." Agreeing to a demand by Abbé Grégoire (though a murmur of disapproval was heard from the clergy) the Assembly resolved to honour the delegation by inviting it to pass the partition and remain present during the session as its guests.

The National Assembly's Debates on Jewish Enfranchisement

Meanwhile, under pressure from the people of Paris, the King and then the National Assembly were moved to Paris. Henceforth its proceedings were conducted under the surveillance of a population in the throes of revolutionary excitement.

The resolution of November 2 whereby the Assembly confiscated all Church properties on behalf of the State was passed amidst protest from the clergy and the reactionary aristocracy. The latter then attempted to interpret the confiscation as a Jewish plot aimed at the destruction of France. In such an atmosphere the National Assembly could not broach the question of Jewish enfranchisement. Only Abbé Grégoire persisted in his efforts. It was at this time that he published his pamphlet, *Motion en Faveur des Juifs*, in which he called upon the deputies to liberate "fifty thousand Frenchmen" still in bondage.

The question of Jewish enfranchisement came before the National Assembly in its widest scope at the end of December 1789, when active civil rights for Protestants were under discussion. A liberal deputy to the National Assembly had introduced a bill on December 21, explicitly conferring active civil rights on the Protestants, i.e. the right to elect and to be elected to all public offices. During the debate, Count Stanislaus de Clermont-Tonnerre proposed that no active citizen who complied with all other requirements should be barred from any public office because of his calling or religion. The anti-Jewish bloc at once perceived that his objective was to enfranchise the Jews. There was a great commotion. The Alsatian Deputy, Reubell, took the floor and declared, "I view the Jews as the Jews view themselves. They do not consider themselves citizens. It is in this opinion that I accept Clermont-Tonnerre's amendment since in employing the term 'active citizen' it follows that he excludes them." At this, Clermont-Tonnerre declared that it was precisely his intention to include the Jews. This rejoinder aroused a tumult that forced the speaker to adjourn the session.

The discussion on Jewish enfranchisement was resumed on December 23. Clermont-Tonnerre again took the floor. He began by arguing that it followed inexorably from the *Declaration of the Rights of Man* that no person was to be barred from any public office because of his calling. He then discussed the Jewish question: "I wish now to pass on to the matter of religion. . . . You have already pronounced on this matter by saying in the *Declaration of the Rights of Man* that no person is to be molested, even for his religious views . . . is it not in essence to molest citizens if one wishes to deprive them of the most cherished right because of their opinions . . . leave consciences free therefore; let not feelings or thoughts, however directed to heaven, become crimes that society punishes by the loss of social rights; or else create a national religion, arm it with a sword and tear up your *Declaration of Rights*. . . .

"Each religion has only one proof to show, that of morality. If there is one which demands theft and incendiariasm, not only must eligibility be refused to those who profess it but they must be proscribed. This observation cannot apply to the Jews. The reproaches made against them are numerous. The most serious are unjust, the others are only misdemeanours. Usury, it is said, is permitted to them. This assertion is only founded on an erroneous interpretation of a principle of benevolence and fraternity which forbids them to lend on interest amongst themselves . . . .

"Everything must be refused to the Jews as a nation; everything must be granted to them as individuals. They must be citizens. It is claimed that they do not wish to be citizens. Let them say so and let them be banished; there cannot be a nation within a nation . . . the Roman

Emperors had admitted Jews to all honours, to all duties. They have exercised in France the most important of all public functions ... the Jews are presumed to be citizens so long as it has not been proved they are not, so long as they have not refused to be citizens. In their petition they demand to be considered such. The law must acknowledge a title that prejudice alone refuses them."

The notorious Abbé Maury, representative of the *Black Bloc*, took the floor. "The word 'Jew'," he said, "is not that of a sect but of a nation with laws it has maintained at all times and proposes also to maintain in the future. To call the Jews citizens, is as though one were to say that Englishmen or Danes could become Frenchmen without certificates of naturalization and without ceasing to be Englishmen and Danes." The remainder of Maury's speech abounded in stereotyped demagogic vituperations about Jewish "laziness," the Jews' passion for money and usury, and their exploitation of gullible gentiles. Warning of the dangers of popular violence, he professed to be in favour of protecting their individual rights as "human beings, as our brethren, but not as Frenchmen, for they are incapable of becoming citizens."

Robespierre spoke next. No champion of Jewish rights before or after him formulated the theoretical issue so incisively and lucidly, or indicated so unreservedly the responsibility that oppression bore for the abject plight of the Jews. "They have told you tales about the Jews which are gross exaggerations, and many of them are the direct opposite of the historical truth. Jewish vices are rooted in the lowly status to which you have reduced them. They will become decent people if they will see any advantage in becoming decent ... How can one hold against the Jews the persecutions of which they have been the victims amongst the various nations? On the contrary, it is our misdeeds as a nation which we must atone for by restoring to them those inalienable human rights of which no human power may deprive them ... Let us restore them to happiness, to a fatherland, to propriety, by restoring to them the dignity of human beings and of citizens." In his conclusion, Robespierre appealed both to the sense of justice and to the self-interest of his audience: "Pray, let us take note of this, that it can never be politic, say what you will, to condemn to humiliation and oppression an entire body of people living in our midst. How can the interests of society rest upon the violation of those eternal principles of justice and reason which are the very foundations of every human society?"

A discordant note was sounded when de La Fare, a member of the same party as Abbé Maury, replied to this speech, though as the Bishop of Nancy he tried to sweeten his venomous remarks with high-flown humanitarian platitudes. He even lavished compliments on the Jews. "The Jews," he said, "beyond any doubt have wrongs that call for redress. We must abolish the laws which were passed oblivious of the fact that Jews are human beings and unfortunate human beings. They must be afforded protection, security, liberty. Is it, though, proper to adopt into the family an alien tribe which will ever direct its gaze to its own Homeland, whose driving urge is to quit its land of domicile?"

The reply to the Bishop was made by Adrien Duport, one of the foremost leaders of the left wing in the National Assembly, a champion of general suffrage and sponsor of bills ensuring trial by jury and abolishing capital punishment. As an erudite and experienced lawyer, he formulated the problem from a purely legalistic point of view, without polished phrases. His approach was more realistic than that of Clermont-Tonnerre, both in respect of the zealous adherence of the Jews (whom he termed a nation and not a religion) to the tenets of their faith and of the prospect for an imminent change in the attitude of the general population towards the Jews: "Were some nation to come to assimilate in our midst, were it to request the right of French citizenship for the individuals of which it is composed, could you reject such a request? This is virtually the position of the Jewish nationality. We are by no means under obligation to investigate whether or not the Jews observe their own laws. It will suffice us if they carry out the duties we shall entrust to them and share with them. It has already been stated here that it does not lie within the power of the law to impose an opinion, since the law itself is but the outcome of opinions. One must distinguish between the law, which is the substance of justice, and between customs, which are the consequence of things actually countenanced under the law. The law will pronounce the Jews eligible for election as public servants; custom may thwart their being elected. Ultimately, however, custom is reconciled with the law. Come what may, you have not the right to refuse to ratify this exalted principle if it be brought before you."

Duport introduced a new, more comprehensive bill which omitted any reference to calling or religion (Protestant or Jewish). "Both with regard to active citizenship," it stipulated, "and with regard to the right to hold public office, no Frenchmen shall be barred for any reason not specified in ordinances of the National Assembly. All laws and directives to the contrary are hereby pronounced null and void." Put to the vote, Duport's motion was defeated by a small majority (408 to 403) and the session was immediately adjourned.

Prince de Broglie, a royalist from Colmar in Alsace, introduced a revised version of Duport's bill on December 24, and, at the same time, proposed a postponement of the debate on the Jewish issue. Clermont-Tonnerre immediately supported the motion. The National Assembly finally adopted the ordinance concerning the active civil rights of non-Catholics with the following reservation: "It is to be understood, that no innovation will be made concerning the Jews, on the status of whom the National Assembly reserves its opinion." This formula was repeated on several occasions in the following two years until the Jews of France at last obtained their decree of enfranchisement.

Equality of Rights for the Sephardi Group

The vote of December 24, 1789, in the National Assembly was a bitter disappointment to all Jews of France, but particularly to the Sephardi Jews of Bordeaux. Until then, they had trusted in the commonly declared principles of the rights of man and in their own distinguished status and privileged position. Now they had been put in the same category as the poor Ashkenazim of the eastern provinces and, together with them, excluded from the enjoyment of civil rights. On January 22, 1790, they sent a petition to the National Assembly which they printed, published and circulated throughout the country. The petition expressed their amazement at the Jews of the east, who, "if one may judge by published writings . . . seek to live in France under special régime, to have exclusive laws of their own and to constitute a class of citizens separate from all others." They, the Jews of Bordeaux, were inclined to see the root of all the efforts (of the Alsace-Lorraine Jews) "only in a religious zeal improperly understood." For them, the Sephardim, by contrast, "the issue, more than it relates to the acquisition (of rights), bears on the maintenance (of already existing rights)." They referred to their *Lettres Patentes* granted by the Kings of France and cited their participation in the elections to the Estates General and their share in the patriotic regiments in which some of them had attained the rank of captain, lieutenant and other positions of command. In conclusion, they expressed the hope "that they, the sons of Judah, would not be confused with Jews descended from other nations." The Portuguese and the Spanish Jews, "had never assimilated or intermixed with the mass of the other sons of Jacob . . . ."

The petition was tantamount to a vindication of the opposition of the French reaction to the extension of civil rights to the Jews of Alsace-Lorraine, in that it specifically branded them as benighted religious zealots and obstinate separatists. The Jewish notables of Bordeaux also showed no grain of solidarity with the other members of their own fold, the lower status Sephardi community of Bayonne, "their racial brethren, sons of Judah" by their own confession. They did not invite them to participate in their efforts, and the Bayonne Kehillah was forced to send a separate petition to the National Assembly.

A delegation brought the petition of the Bordeaux Jews, signed by their Parnassim and 215 heads of families, before the Legislative Committee of the National Assembly. The Committee invited the Bishop of Autun, (better known as Talleyrand when he later achieved distinction as a diplomat), to prepare a report for the plenary session. On January 28, 1790, in the name of the Committee, Talleyrand advised the National Assembly "to comply with the just request of the Jews of Bordeaux and to pronounce them active citizens under the conditions applicable to all the other citizens." He argued that "the Revolution, which has restored to all Frenchmen their rights, cannot lead to the loss of rights by certain citizens." Talleyrand based his statement on the claim of the Bordeaux Jews that their rights were inherent in their royal privileges, and he extolled their achievements in support of his thesis.

The division in the National Assembly during the discussions on the Bordeaux Jews was of an entirely different character from that of the previous month, when the Jewish community as a whole was the subject of debate. The upper middle class and the liberal aristocracy felt obliged to prove their class solidarity with the wealthy and semi-assimilated bourgeois élite of French Jewry. Talleyrand's proposal was not only supported by the deputy from Bordeaux, de Sèze, who in the name of justice and righteousness enumerated the great achievements of his Jewish fellow-townsmen; and not only by the deputies of the left, such as Abbé Grégoire and Le Chapelier, who found it necessary to emphasize that the Jews of Bordeaux bore no resemblance to the Jews of Alsace. Support also came from self-professed liberal aristocrats such as Vicomte Noailles and Vicomte de Beauharnais, whose loyalty to the Revolution was later found to be somewhat dubious. In these circumstances, Abbé Maury did not venture to make a frontal attack on the bill as a whole. He attempted rather to emasculate it as much as possible, by proposing that the Jews of Bordeaux continue "provisionally" in possession of their local rights on the basis of the Royal *Lettres Patentes*. Only Abbé Grégoire remembered, even on this occasion, the wronged communities of Alsace-Lorraine. After suggesting that the terms of the proposed ordinance be extended to embrace all the Jews of southern France, known as Portuguese, Spanish and Avignonnais, he demanded that a precise date be set for a debate on the enfranchisement of the Ashkenazi Jews.

From the start, the proposal had every prospect of success and for this reason the clergy and the aristocracy created more difficulties than during the December discussions on the Jewish community as a whole. Twice the Speaker tried to obtain a vote by asking those supporting the motion to rise—twice he failed because the opposition deliberately milled around on the floor of the chamber. A vote by roll-call was attempted *twenty times* and repeatedly interrupted by commotion from the Black Bloc. The speaker then announced that voting would take place whatever the circumstances, though many deputies had left the chamber. With only two-thirds of the House voting (374:224) the bill was finally passed:

> All those Jews who in France are known as Portuguese, Spanish and Avignonnais, will retain those rights which they have enjoyed hitherto and had confirmed in *Lettres Patentes*, and in consequence thereof they will enjoy active civil rights if in addition thereto they will fulfil the conditions required by the decrees of this Assembly.

To clarify the situation beyond all shadow of doubt, the Deputy from

Alsace, Schwendt, demanded the following day, January 29, that a statement be attached to the order guaranteeing that it only concerned equality of rights for the Sephardim and did not in any way apply to the Jews of Alsace-Lorraine. Though Schwendt, like his colleague, Reubell, insisted that the only purpose behind his amendment was to ensure public order in Alsace and the security of the local Jews, the Assembly disregarded his motion and proceeded with the order of the day. However, this only made it obvious that there had been no change in the legal status of the Jews apart from that of the small Sephardi minority.

The Intervention of the Paris Commune

On January 28, 1790, before the decision about the Sephardim had been made, the leaders of the Jews of Alsace-Lorraine and representatives of the Ashkenazi Jews in Paris sent a petition to the National Assembly. It was very different in spirit from previous solicitations. Now they demanded complete equality of rights for all Jews and asked that their request be considered with that of the Jews of Bordeaux, with which it was "completely identical." They declared that "it would be both unjust and dangerous" if equality of rights were to be conferred by stages and not "with the utmost celerity." As long as the Jews continued to be disenfranchised, the people would continue to believe that the *Declaration of the Rights of Man* did not apply to them. They utterly rejected the concept of mere toleration and cited the United States "to whom politics owes a debt of gratitude for so many helpful examples," and who have "removed this word from their statute books."

In all matters not pertaining to religion, declared the representatives of the Ashkenazi community, it was just that the Jews be subject to the laws of the land. The new attitude to Kehillah autonomy, as revealed in this petition, was most characteristic. Not only was the demand for autonomy no longer mentioned, but all manner of "special provisions" for the Jews (apart from internal regulations "concerning the observance of religious laws") were now described as "frontier barriers" that had hitherto divided Christian and Jew. It was their wish that "in all matters Jews mingle, be linked, and united with Frenchmen."

The order by the National Assembly concerning the rights of the Sephardim underlined the failure of the joint petition presented by the Ashkenazi Jews. But on the same day, January 28, 1790, the Jews of Paris embarked on a course of action of great importance for the campaign for Jewish enfranchisement. They decided to enlist the most positive of the revolutionary forces, the Commune of Paris, in the fight for Jewish rights. A delegation of fifty Jews, members of the *Garde Nationale,* including Zalkind Hourwitz, appeared at the Hotel de Ville during a meeting of the Commune. The delegation was presented to the Commune by the attorney Godard, who was a member of the Commune himself. As adviser to the Alsace-Lorraine Jews, he had also drawn up their petition to the National Assembly. He began his address to the Commune by announcing that he was the authorized representative of "the majority of this country's Jews" at the National Assembly and also of the Jews of Paris. He expressed gratitude on behalf of the local Jews to the city of Paris for beginning to treat them as brothers, even before they had been recognized as citizens. He eagerly described the enthusiasm of the Jewish population of Paris and mentioned the large number of members of the National Guard amongst the Jews present. Out of 500 Jews in the city* 100 had joined the National Guard.

He cited the Jewish scholar, Zalkind Hourwitz, who was present at the time, as an example of the warm support that the Jews accorded to the Revolution. Hourwitz had covenanted for life a quarter of his modest income as a librarian to the welfare of his country—though the customary contribution was for one year only. Speaking in the name of these patriotic Jews, Godard requested the Commune to testify in public to their noble qualities and their patriotism. The Commune would thus not only render a service to the Jews of Paris but would "create happiness" for 50,000 Jews† throughout France. In reply to Godard's speech, the Chairman of the Commune Assembly, Abbé Mulot, promised the Jewish delegation that the Assembly's decision would be in accordance "with the laws of reason and humanity." He would be the "first to applaud what was decided in favour of your people." Finally, he invited the delegation to remain in the chamber, as "the first testimony to our feelings of fraternity."

The following day, January 29, 1790, a plenary session was held of the Carmelite Section, which contained the largest Jewish population of the sixty districts of the capital. The Section decided to ask the General Assembly of the Commune to do its utmost to persuade the National Assembly to proclaim equality of rights for the Jews. The following day, a delegation representing this Section was received by the General Assembly of the Commune. De Gerville, on behalf of the delegation, urged the Commune to support at the National Assembly the claim to the civil rights of these "new brethren." He emphasized that it should not be difficult for the Assembly to grant the Jews of Paris those rights that the Sephardi Jews had already achieved, "for by what right are the latter preferred? Do not all the Jews have one doctrine? Is not our political attitude similar towards these as towards the others? If the forefathers of these Jews—whose cause we espouse—were subjected to even more

---

* The number of Jews in Paris at the time was, in fact, greater and totalled about 800.

† Abbé Grégoire also gave this figure, though the number of French Jews at the time is thought not to have exceeded 40,000.

persecution and the frenzies of arbitrary power than the Portuguese Jews, then it is but fitting that this prolonged, brutal oppression should serve as an additional title to national justice . . ."

Some opposition emerged in the subsequent debate in the Commune Assembly. It was countered in a detailed speech by Abbé Bertolio, a clergyman and lawyer, deputy to the elected assembly and later ambassador of Revolutionary France at Rome. Referring to the *Declaration of the Rights of Man*, and to the equality of rights granted to the Protestants, he declared: "We have at last reached the point of rectifying an erroneous opinion that has raised so many barriers of separation between human beings who should more appropriately form one family . . . These principles have but recently won their victory over another prejudice, even more deeply rooted than that under which the Protestants were groaning." So far as state policy was concerned, Bertolio concluded, the granting of civil rights to the Jews would be a great achievement: the neglected economy of the country would acquire "the toiling hands and capital of the Jews" of France. Furthermore, he contended, "You will yet behold them gathering together and coming hither from all corners of the earth on hearing that the sun of liberty is to shine forth in France upon all those who have been born or have settled there. And the state will acquire new subjects, reaping the benefits of their diligence, brains, money and skill . . ." On the subject of the Jewish religion, he argued that the state had no right to interfere in religious matters and should only concern itself with matters of morality. Christian morality, he asserted, was only a development of Jewish morality, since both were based on the commandment *"Thou shalt love thy neighbour as thyself."*

The speaker dealt extremely sharply with contentions of the opposition. Refuting the argument that "Heaven was opposed to the Jewish proposals," that the fate of the Jews represented divine vengeance, Bertolio cried out as if inspired, "What, Messieurs, will one never cease to slander the Lord God? . . . God is not a god of vengeance . . . With this kind of sophistry we may well justify all the grave crimes against humanity . . . the abominable enslavement of the negroes." He described the development of Jewish citizenship in England, despite the repeal of the abortive enfranchisement act of 1753, as a veritable vindication of Jewish enfranchisement. It proved that advanced public opinion in England shared his views and also those of enlightened France on the Jewish question.

Bertolio's formulation of the Jewish problem in the light of the most progressive views of rising capitalism, combined with his firm adherence to the loftiest concepts of the Revolution, captured the sympathy of the Commune Assembly. It was decided at once to make public its position on granting equality of rights to the Jews, and also to testify to the patriotism and other virtues of the Jews of Paris. However, the resolution would not be presented to the National Assembly until all sections of the city had had the opportunity to give their views at meetings to be convened forthwith.

Replies from fifty-three section meetings were received at the Commune within the next three weeks, expressing agreement with the resolution of the General Assembly. In most cases they were accompanied by such remarks as "adopted unanimously," "absolutely concur," or "total agreement." Some credit for this could be claimed by the Jews of Paris, who conducted a lively publicity campaign in the sections. Only one section (Mathurins) made its agreement conditional on a referendum among the entire population of France. Six sections failed to submit replies, which they did not make public even at any later date.

On the strength of the replies from its sections, the General Assembly of the Paris Commune adopted on February 24 a new, more detailed resolution on enfranchisement for the Jews and intercession at the National Assembly. The resolution repeated the main principles of Bertolio's speech, with particular reference to the manifold benefits that would accrue to France from the grant of equal rights to the Jews, since it would encourage Jews from other countries to immigrate to France. The resolution further stated that such immigration would compensate for the harmful consequences of the Edict of Nantes which had expelled the Huguenots from France and caused damage from which the country had hitherto been unable to recover. The resolution also dealt with the renunciation of Kehillah autonomy: "Taking into consideration that even though certain principles of the Jewish religion would appear to contradict the laws of the French state, it is impossible to bar the Jews from the field of their own conscience since, agreeing as they do to be judged by our courts and not by their own separate laws and having renounced all their peculiar privileges, they will no longer be separated from other citizens in all matters appertaining to external law . . ."

It must be noted that the Commune's memorandum to the National Assembly gave an additional reason for its resolution—lest "a manner of aristocracy" (of the Sephardim) be created amongst the Jews. This would seem to indicate that the enthusiastic espousal of the Ashkenazi Jewish cause by the Commune was prompted, apart from the reasons already mentioned, by their direct political interest, as democrats, in ensuring democratic rule amongst the Jews of France, at any rate insofar as it affected the legal status of the various groups.

A delegation of the most prominent members of the Commune of Paris, including the speaker of the Assembly, Abbé Mulot, Godard, and Abbé Bertolio, appeared before the National Assembly on the day after the Assembly of the Commune, February 25. Mulot presented the Commune's resolution in a fiery speech which concluded with the statement: "We regard them (the Jews) as brethren; most impatiently do we look forward to calling them brother citizens."

The Chairman of the National Assembly, Talleyrand, promised the delegation that the problem would be dealt with in accordance with the accepted principles of the Rights of Man and the recognized laws concerning active rights of citizenship. Consideration would then be given to the reasons "so touchingly expressed" by the delegation. This was purely a diplomatic gesture of no more practical value than the invitation extended to the Commune's delegation to remain present at the session. The next day, the Duc de la Rochefoucauld de Liancourt demanded that the National Assembly fix a date for the discussion of the legal status of the Jews. The next speaker (a deputy whose name was not given in the minutes) declared that despite "the unquestionably great importance of the Jewish question" it only involved a small group of people, whereas the agenda included many questions of greater importance to the country as a whole. The most urgent of these were the organization of the courts and of the army, and a statute involving the currency. As these questions would take up all the time available, the deputy moved that discussion of the Jewish question be deferred. His motion was carried. The democratic Commune of Paris might proclaim that it was impatiently awaiting the grant of equal rights to the Jews, whom it had adopted as its brethren. The liberal bourgeoisie and aristocracy temporized with the opposition of the Black Clergy and royalist aristocracy. But the National Assembly as a whole remained unmoved by the insecurity and disfranchisement that the Jews would have to endure for many months to come.

The Anti-Jewish Campaign and the Rejection of Jewish Enfranchisement

At the end of February 1790, the reactionary clergy and aristocracy intensified their anti-Jewish campaign with redoubled fervour both in Paris and in the provinces, in an attempt to counteract the strong intervention of the Paris Commune in support of Jewish rights. The immediate object was, of course, to prevent a Jewish bill for equality of rights becoming law. But the campaign was also directed towards a much greater political issue: it was planned to divert public attention away from the Revolution by involving it in a movement against the alleged foes of the Catholic faith. This is confirmed by the fact that clerical propaganda throughout France was at this precise moment also directed against the Calvinists and other Protestant groups. It accused them of being in league with the Jews and frequently referred to both groups in the same context.

No lie, no act of demagogy was too extravagant for the yellow clerical press so long as it incited antagonism to the Jews. Two days after the intervention by the Paris Commune, a clericalist journal reported that "the sons of Aaron, Moses, Elijah, and all the Palestinian patriarchs, are going to seize one by one the tranquil, smiling retreats of the disciples of St. Bruno, of St. Benedict, of that angel of the Lord, St. Francis, where you now see uncircumcised monks, you will see an unending stream of circumcised usurers." It was claimed that all the liberal deputies, particularly those who spoke in favour of Jewish rights, had taken bribes. Even the sums they were supposed to have received from the Jews and also from the Protestants were specified. A special attempt was made to compromise Abbé Grégoire: the rumour was circulated that he prayed every Saturday at the National Assembly, which had been converted into a Synagogue! The reactionary representatives from Alsace in the National Assembly also organized from Paris systematic anti-Jewish activities in the province. At the beginning of 1790, a pamphlet by Bishop de La Fare of Nancy was circulated (to which replies were published by Berr Isaac Berr and Jacob Berr), and some new writers of Alsace also published anti-Jewish diatribes in French and German accusing the Jews of usury and incidentally attacking the Jewish religion. This literature depicted Jewish enfranchisement as an imminent danger that might plunge the entire population into ruin and disaster. Provincial government officials and local intellectual groups (such as those later known as the Jacobins) did not support this movement and counselled a liberal attitude towards the Jews in the name of the new régime and the *Declaration of the Rights of Man*. But the local authorities in the areas concerned stood solidly behind the reactionaries. The Strasbourg Commune, as if to caricature the Paris Commune's referendum on the Jewish question, also convened meetings of all sections of the city and then convened a general assembly of all "active citizens." The Strasbourg upper classes not only tried to arouse the worst sort of religious antagonism by organizing the affair exactly a week before Easter; they even intimidated anybody who evinced a desire to speak in favour of the Jews at the section meetings (ten such daring votes were recorded in the proceedings). The movement was led by the clergy and wealthy merchants. Their motives included fear of competition from the Jews, should they receive equal rights, and this was specifically stated in some of the section resolutions together with other "reasons": for example, that the Jews were maligning the name of Jesus. These resolutions were the direct opposite of those formed by the Paris sections. They went so far as to predict that equal rights for French Jews might lead to so great an incursion of "dangerous German and Polish Jews" that the citizens of Strasbourg would eventually be forced to emigrate. After this "referendum," on April 8, 1790, the General Assembly of the "active citizens" of Strasbourg had no difficulty in adopting a resolution opposing both the Jewish petition of January 28 and the memorandum of the Strasbourg *Association of Friends of the Constitution* (precursors of the Jacobins). The resolution was printed, circulated within the city, and sent to the National Assembly. Similar movements were promptly organized in other cities. The citizens of Colmar (which had no Jewish inhabitants) and three other towns were quick to follow Strasbourg's example.

The untiring activity of the Black Bloc in Alsace was co-ordinated to perfection with its manoeuvres in the National Assembly to forestall any resolution on Jewish enfranchisement. Whenever the liberals sought to introduce the Jewish question, the Blacks, through the Alsatians, demanded that it be entirely removed from the agenda in order to prevent the outbreak of "popular indignation." By a decree promulgated in the National Assembly on April 30, all foreigners who had resided in France for at least five years were eligible under certain conditions (ownership of real property, independent business establishments, or marriage with a French woman) to receive the franchise. This decree was mainly intended to regularize the legal status of the population in the border provinces and the seaport towns, but the injustice and, once again, the evasion of the question of Jewish enfranchisement was blatantly paradoxical. Even though they were regarded as aliens, Jews had been living in France not for five years but since Roman times! The right wing leaders of Alsace gave appropriate attention to this matter. While the minutes were being read on the following day, Reubell proposed what had become a routine amendment: "It is to be understood that nothing is resolved herewith as to the legal status of the Jews, concerning which the decision is deferred." The amendment was adopted.

On April 14, Comte Mirabeau, in his *Courier de Provence,* explicitly informed the Jews that their enfranchisement depended on themselves and on their agreeing to renounce all autonomy. Whether of his own accord or under the inspiration of a group of liberals, he wrote, "Two or three articles of faith must decide this issue! Gentlemen! Are our laws your laws? Are our courts of justice yours too? Are you legally our fellow-citizens, our brethren? Will you be able to take the civic oath in your hearts as well as by word of mouth? If such be the case, excellent! Then you are good Frenchmen, then you will be active citizens. If not, then remain passive citizens and wait until your city, Jerusalem, is rebuilt, and there you can be active or passive, as you choose."

By April, 1790, the abolition of Kehillah autonomy as a condition of enfranchisement had clearly become nothing but an excuse, though the entire plebeian bloc thought that the equality of rights and autonomy were incompatible. The Jews of Alsace-Lorraine had already completely waived all claim to Kehillah autonomy in their joint representations with the Ashkenazi Jews of Paris at the end of January. It was not the issue of Jewish autonomy that inhibited the National Assembly from placing the question of Jewish enfranchisement on its agenda but the lack of principles and tendency to compromise within the disunited liberal bloc. Meanwhile the Commune of Paris persevered in its efforts on behalf of Jewish rights with the utmost sincerity and good faith.

Further Intercessions by the Paris Commune: the Promulgation of Jewish Enfranchisement

The Jews could not remain silent in face of the decree of April 30, 1790, which enfranchised foreigners and discriminated against them. Nor could they ignore the parallel anti-Jewish activity in the form of memoranda which a number of municipal administrations in Alsace, led by Strasbourg, were sending to the National Assembly. In these circumstances the Jews of Paris, who had assumed leadership in the struggle for Jewish rights in January, 1790, decided to launch a new drive in the National Assembly and once again to enlist the active assistance of the Paris Commune. The formal motive behind this new move was provided by the reorganization of the city administration. This also involved the right to vote in municipal elections, a matter with which the National Assembly was then concerned.

After they had reached agreement with a number of leaders of the Commune, the Jews of Paris sent a petition to the National Assembly at the beginning of May, 1790, signed by Mordecai Eli, demanding recognition of their active civil rights. The document was read out at the session of May 10. At the same time, the representative of the Paris Commune at the National Assembly, De Bourges, sent a memorandum to the Constitutional Committee giving detailed reasons for conceding complete equality of rights to the Jews. The memorandum, which was also published as a pamphlet, contained some particularly valuable passages explaining realistically that the promulgation of complete enfranchisement for the Jews would in any event only mean gradual progress towards equality between the Jews and the Christian population, "for the prejudices of the Christians will not be eradicated at once. Granting political rights to the Jews merely means not to eliminate them from a lottery the results of which for many days to come will be unpropitious for them." De Bourges also firmly dismissed the charges made against the moral deficiencies of the Jews. In his opinion, the Constitution existed for the purpose of improving mankind, and this the Christians required as much as did the Jews.

De Bourges also sent his memorandum to the Commune of Paris with the request that it officially adopt the memorandum as its own manifesto. The Commune Assembly appointed a Committee of Three to report on the memorandum. On May 29, Brissot de Warville read the report on behalf of the Committee. It included large sections of the memorandum, which was enthusiastically commended. It was decided to bring de Warville's report and De Bourges' memorandum before the Constitutional Committee of the National Assembly and to advise that more attention be given the matter.

This second intercession by the Commune of Paris was also fruitless. The National Assembly took no notice of a petition of June 13, 1790, presented by the Jews of Alsace, in which they expressed their sorrow that the Jewish question was still pending in the Constitutional Committee. On every occasion that a National Assembly resolution called for a decree confirming complete enfranchisement for non-Catholics—for example, in the case of provincial town representation or the election of judges—no opportunity was lost of amending it by a reservation stipulating that in the case of Jews, the matter would be dealt with separately. Only one extraordinary instance of disfranchisement came to an end without any procrastination pending a decision in principle. A resolution, proposed by Deputy Vismes, was carried in the National Assembly on July 20, 1790 abolishing the enormous patronage tax paid by the Jews of Metz to the baronial house of Brancas. All the other special taxes levied on Jews throughout the country were likewise abolished.

On May 7, 1791, in the face of bitter opposition from the clergy, the National Assembly confirmed a decree of the Paris District concerning the Catholic faith. The important churches of the Catholic dioceses were placed under secular administration. All other houses of worship were put up for sale for the benefit of the State and their purchasers had the right to use them in any way they might wish. The implication of this decree was to implement religious freedom. It encouraged the Jews of Paris to send a new petition to the National Assembly two days later on May 9. This time they concentrated on the contradiction inherent in the fact that notwithstanding their long residence in Paris, their proven patriotism and their ardent devotion to liberty, not only were they not considered citizens, but they did not even have the right to become citizens as did foreigners of five years' residence. The National Assembly resolved at its session of May 16 to refer this petition, too, to Committee. But now they not only sent it to the Constitutional Committee, but also to the Committee on Reports. The Jews of Paris had no confidence in the justice of even the Constitutional Committee. They again asked for help from the Paris City Council, which had replaced the Commune. Their petition, drawn up by Godard, cited the Law on Religious Liberties which had recently been ratified. They declared their intention to buy or lease a building in Paris in which to establish a synagogue. Their position would be even more paradoxical than before: "Could they be citizens only in their synagogues, and outside aliens, or slaves? ... There can be no half-liberty today, just as there is no half-justice ..." The City Council, at its session of May 26, 1791, decided to approach the National Assembly again, with the request that it consider both the Jewish petition and the City Council's own plea, exhorting it to apply the conclusions derived from those fine principles in regard to religious freedom that it had just confirmed to the Jews of Paris.

The National Assembly was once again unable to spare time to discuss the petition of the Paris City Council on the enfranchisement of Paris Jewry. On the night of June 20, 1791, Louis XVI fled from the Palace of the Tuileries and was apprehended at Varennes, near the frontier. Once again, the country was immersed in conflict, on this occasion precipitated by a plot between opponents of the Revolution and foreign powers. The right wing was undermined by the resignation of numerous royalist deputies and the emigration or arrest of others. This bloc no longer dared obstruct legislative activity as it had previously done. The views of the revolutionary faction on the Jewish problem, so magnificently expressed in the intercessions of the Paris Commune, could no longer be ignored. The new Constitution, adopted on September 14, 1791 and signed by the King, was itself the result of the changed balance of forces in the National Assembly and the country as a whole. This Constitution provided a formal basis for Jewish enfranchisement. In the final reckoning, both Jewish enfranchisement and the new Constitution were the consequence of the termination of the first phase of the Revolution.

On September 27, 1791, two weeks after the adoption of the Constitution and three days before the National Assembly was dispersed, Deputy Adrien Duport proposed a decree investing all the Jews of France with active civil rights. He based his argument on the recently adopted Constitution, which incorporated the *Declaration of the Rights of Man*, with its guarantee of religious liberty (Article VI). He declared that religious liberty also meant that there could be no differentiation between one citizen and another in respect of the franchise on the grounds of religious faith. Since members of various religions and sects, such as Turks and Moslems, had already received full political rights, it certainly followed that an exception could no longer be made in the case of the Jews alone, or the matter of their enfranchisement be deferred, as had hitherto been done. The Assembly decided almost unanimously to discuss Duport's motion. The motion was carried, though in a temporary form.

The following day, September 28, the leaders of the reactionary wing had no alternative but to amend the law with addenda and reservations; and in this, they succeeded. Duke de Broglie of Alsace declared that the decree might aggravate public feeling in Alsace. To avoid the misrepresentation of the law, he proposed that the Jews be required to take an oath of citizenship (an oath of loyalty to the laws) "which would be considered a formal renunciation of such civil and political laws as the Jews consider to be binding exclusively upon themselves." The proposal was adopted with an amendment introduced by Deputy Prugnon to the effect that the oath taken by the Jews "would be considered a renunciation of their special privileges." Prugnon argued that "the civil laws of the Jew are held to be identical with their religious laws, and it is not our intention to demand that they abjure their religion."

That the Jews should renounce their autonomy in local administration and law courts as a form of special privilege deriving from feudal particularism was no new proposition. During the two and a half years of struggle for the enfranchisement of the Jews, from the outbreak of the

Revolution onwards, the demand was repeatedly heard—even the Paris Commune had introduced it—that the Jews be subject to the same laws and authorities as all other citizens. The concession made to the reactionaries lay in the explicit mention of this demand in the Decree of Enfranchisement. An even greater compromise with the right wing was the resolution that the Jews formally confirm the renunciation of their "special privileges" by an oath of citizenship. At the same session, the National Assembly made another concession to the anti-Jewish bloc; on a motion by Reubell, a special law was passed against Jewish usurers. The law thus complemented the Decree of Enfranchisement of September 27, and both were signed by the King on November 13.

The circumstances in which the Enfranchisement Decree of September 27, 1791 was adopted by the National Assembly do not detract from the great historic importance of the emancipation of French Jewry. For France, the Revolution, the *Declaration of the Rights of Man* and the new Constitution ended a thousand years of serfdom, feudalism, and absolutism and opened up the era of the modern, bourgeois state. Likewise, for the Jews of France, the Enfranchisement Decree signified the end of their oppressed, medieval status and the beginning of a new era, in which they were equal by law with every other citizen. The French Revolution was not confined to one country; as it spread it undermined everywhere the foundations of the ancient régime in Europe. In the same way, the emancipation of the Jews proclaimed by the Revolution opened the way to the gradual liberation of Jews throughout the old world from a medieval state of bondage.

Under Jacobin Rule

The Enfranchisement Decree not only altered the legal status of French Jews; it also enabled them, for the first time in European history, to take an active part in the political struggle in France, rather than remain passive onlookers. However, there were too few modern intellectuals among French Jewry to take as significant a part in the French Revolution as they were to take in the revolutions of the nineteenth century. Only in Paris and in the south, at Bordeaux and Bayonne, did sizeable groups of Jews enthusiastically engage in the agitated political events of the period. At the beginning of the Revolution, Jews in Paris had joined the political societies of the various factions and taken part in the activities of the sections of the Commune. This Jewish participation increased as the Revolution gathered force.

The second period of the Revolution began, in fact, with street fighting in Paris at the beginning of August, 1792; officially, however, it began with the proclamation of the Republic on September 21. During this period Jews held office in the Revolutionary Committees of the Sections and some were elected to the law courts. In 1793, one Jew, a cantor by profession, was appointed secretary of the Jacobin *Comité de Surveillance Générale*. But the smallness of the Jewish intellectual class at this time and its lack of experience, even in Paris, were shown in the fact that not a single Jew was to be found amongst the foremost leaders of the Revolution and, even more so, in the insignificant number of Jewish journalists A few Jews occasionally sent letters to the editor of a liberal paper, mostly in connection with Jewish rights and religious liberty, but Zalkind Hourwitz, a gifted writer with a flair for polemics, was the only Jewish free-lance writer to contribute to the liberal Parisian press.

Zalkind Hourwitz used his barbed style primarily in order to parry reactionary assaults on the Jews. But he felt deeply involved in the political life of the country and frequently declared his position on vital current affairs in the press—for example, when the death sentence was passed on the King (Hourwitz, a Girondist, was in favour of a verdict of guilty but opposed the decision to execute Louis XVI). He also published proposals on the Garde Nationale (in which he had enlisted), military affairs, issues of foreign policy, and—in 1810—an interesting plan for cheap soup-kitchens for the people. Characteristically, after 1790, Hourwitz no longer signed his articles *Juif Polonais* (Polish Jew) but merely *Polonais* (Pole). Presumably, he did this in order to demonstrate both his conception of religion as the private affair of the citizen and his sympathy for Poland, to which he remained loyal all his life.

The Revolution entered a new phase at the end of December, 1792. The Legislative Assembly, which had replaced the National Assembly after the elections of 1791, was dispersed. In the ensuing elections to the Convention, the Jacobins finally displaced the bourgeois Girondists and officially became the sole leaders of the Revolution. They assumed their role amidst the most formidable circumstances. Abroad, they had to wage war on all fronts against a coalition of the leading feudal powers of Europe. At home, they were faced with an economic crisis caused by the exigencies of war and revolution and aggravated by the unscrupulous profiteering of merchants and bankers, the rising cost of goods and the decreasing value of paper currency.

The open and avowed enemies of the Revolution conspired and plotted throughout the entire country. Nobles and clergy, but particularly Girondists—more powerful and dangerous than the other two factions—reviled and threatened the democratic political régime, its laws for the protection of the common man, maximum prices for commodities, and taxation of the wealthy for the benefit of the state. The radical Jacobin lower middle class had to employ the most stringent form of dictatorship against hostile classes and parties to rescue and strengthen the Revolution.

The principle of equality of rights for the Jews, together with all the other principles of the Revolution remained in full force under Jacobin rule, which was rule by the Convention in 1793-94. However, because of their formalist principles, the Jacobins had arrived at an abstract outlook which made them reluctant to view the Jewish problem in its practical context. They attempted to solve it through the application of formulas. Not only did they regard any discrimination against the Jews as a crime against the Revolution, but they also refused to acknowledge the presence of Jews in the country as a separate community. When it was absolutely necessary in any official document to mention that the matter under consideration concerned a Jew, they employed a set phrase, "formerly a Jew." But practice did not always coincide with theory. There were serious deviations, especially in Alsace-Lorraine. Here, on the one hand, the old economic structure of the Jewish community had hardly been affected by the changes in the outside world, and in some places had become even more extreme. On the other hand, the economic resentment and cultural backwardness of the surrounding lower middle class even breached the iron ramparts of Jacobin principle.

Jewish bankers, merchants, and market pedlars were amongst profiteers arrested in Paris during 1793 and the "Jewish Café" was raided more than once. In nearly every case, however, the arrested Jews proved their innocence and were released.

At Bordeaux, the Jacobins were from the start suspicious of the great Jewish magnates, both because of the extent of their property, which even increased during the war, and because the city, at the heart of the Gironde, was a stronghold of the Girondist underground movement. The banker Abraham Furtado, an active Girondist, fled in time to save his life, but his property was confiscated. All the wealthy Jews accused of profiteering and of opposition to the régime, were heavily fined by the state. At Nîmes and Lyons, two Jewish merchants were sentenced to death, one of them for defrauding the state in supply transactions.

The condition of the Jews in Alsace-Lorraine under the Jacobins was an entirely different story. The stormy years of war and revolution were not especially propitious for the Jews to utilize their emancipation for organized economic change. As it was, Jewish money-lenders had entered into deals with those peasants who were buying parcels of land, carved out of the nationalized estates, even though the Jews themselves had, for the most part, to borrow the money from wealthy burghers and the nobility. Because of the decline in normal trade, some Jewish businessmen and pedlars began to trade in the furniture of noble refugees, and a few even dealt in capital and merchandise. These things seemed to the onlooker to be on a larger scale than they were in reality. The embittered lower middle class, impoverished by the high cost of living, scarcely shuffled off its deep-rooted hatred of the Jews during the years of revolution and, as before, saw its salvation in the liquidation of Jewish competition or, as it was now called, "Jewish profiteering." In 1793, when a disagreement arose between Baruch-Cerf-Berr and General Custine, the Department of Colmar demanded of the Departmental

Council, that the Jews, "those most dangerous of internal enemies," be barred from permanent residence in the cities. In the autumn of 1793, the Jacobin Clubs of Strasbourg, Nancy, Toul, and the Department of Meurthe, to which the two Lorraine cities belonged, decided to petition for the expulsion of the Jews from the country. The resolution of the Nancy Jacobin Club, sent to both the Jacobin Club of Paris and to the Convention, labelled the Jews "eternal speculators, eternal swindlers, eternally separating themselves from the rest of the Republic's population." Even after a resolution of the central bodies of the Party and state at Paris had condemned this in principle, the governing agencies of the Department did not desist from their acrimonious attacks on "those who were formerly called Jews."

The Cult of Reason, introduced by the Convention at the instance of Hébert in 1793 and maintained until May, 1794, was expressly aimed at the Catholic Church and its counter-revolutionary force. But inevitably the struggle spread and encompassed other religions, including the Jewish. Though there was no direct official interference with the Jews, synagogues were included amongst the houses of worship forcibly or voluntarily converted into "Temples of Reason."

Many Jews, particularly in Paris, were swept along with the current. In Paris, their cultural and linguistic assimilation had already made considerable progress by this stage and a not inconsiderable number of Jews were showing indifference to their religion. It is recorded that a delegation of Sephardi Jews from the suburb of St. Germain (though the Ashkenazim, too, participated in these "rites") appeared before the Convention to hand over sacramental appurtenances from their synagogue with the declaration: "Our forefathers bequeathed unto us laws that were promulgated from a mountain top (Sinai), even so the laws which you bequeath to France are handed down from a Mountain which is no less revered by us . . ." (This was an obvious allusion to the ruling Jacobins, known as *La Montagne*.) In a number of cities in southern France, such as Nimes, Avignon and Saint Esprit, Jewish congregations contributed to the Cult golden and silver crowns that had formed the decoration of Torah scrolls. At a public ceremony in Nîmes, the cantor of the congregation even renounced his office and religion. On the other hand, it is recorded that six Jews at Carpentras signed a declaration stating that "we are too interested in supporting the Republican order not to conform to the common good and the national will. God, who—so we are convinced— even the Heavens cannot contain, can be worshipped throughout all the land. We shall all gather together in the Temple of Reason, wherein all men are brethren . . ." The tone of this declaration gives legitimate grounds to suppose that it was presented by a group of Jews who had not in their hearts completely forsaken their faith but had yielded to pressure or to open compulsion in order to prove their loyalty. Even in Paris, the vast majority of the Jewish community remained loyal to its ancestral faith. This is substantiated by the fact that in the spring of 1794, Moses Pimentel, of the Marat Section, requested permission from the Commune to import flour with which to bake Passover *Matzot* for 220 families. The Commune rejected the request on the grounds that a uniform bread decree was in force.

Apart from isolated instances elsewhere (the Four Kehillot of the Avignon area) reports of compulsion and anti-religious measures came from the provinces of Alsace and Lorraine. Even so, the local Jacobin Committee which ordered the closing down of two synagogues in Saint Esprit, near Bayonne (the leaders of a third handed it over voluntarily, "to strike at the foundations of fanaticism"), was composed almost entirely of Jews. Its chairman later became the Chief Rabbi of Bordeaux. The same Jacobin Committee forbade the observation of the Jewish Sabbath, on pain of a money fine. The situation was different in Alsace-Lorraine; there it was the municipal councils that closed down Jewish prayer houses, converted them into clubs or storehouses, and even destroyed cemeteries. At Strasbourg, Torah scrolls were confiscated and publicly burned; at Metz they were saved when the city decided to use them for drumheads. Observation of the Jewish Sabbath was forbidden throughout Alsace-Lorraine. The Catholic faith was similarly persecuted. Equipment was also destroyed and silver and golden vessels confiscated from the Christian churches of Alsace-Lorraine. At Hagenau and Nancy, Rabbis were compelled to make a public renunciation of their faith and to burn their rabbinical letters of authorization at ceremonies during which scores of Catholic clergymen were present.

These measures were ostensibly directed against the Jewish *religion*. But events in Alsace would seem to suggest that antagonism towards the Jews as Jews had become widespread amongst the local petty bourgeoisie. In November 1793, the Procurator General of the Strasbourg area approached the Departmental Committee, with regard to issuing decrees against the Jewish religion. He demanded the prohibition of circumcision as an inhuman practice, "as though nature were not perfect," and of the use of Hebrew as "a tongue which they themselves do not understand." The Jews, he said, grew their beards long, "for reasons of vanity and to ape the patriarchs, whose virtues they have failed to inherit." It was imperative to have an *auto-da-fé* for all Hebrew books, especially the Talmud, whose author was enough of a swindler to allow them to lend money to the members of other faiths at usurious rates. Once again, the vast difference was manifest between the provincial Jacobins of Alsace and the Jacobin centre in Paris. The Convention disregarded these demands and issued no decree against circumcision (the journal of the *Sans-Culottes* in Paris had made the same demand), Sabbath observance, the growing of beards, or Hebrew books.

Devout Frenchmen saw this coercive Jacobin anti-clerical radicalism—itself only the result of the need to defend the Revolution—as a suppression of the religious conscience of the individual. But to orthodox Jews it was a personal and national tragedy. At a time when new forms of Judaism had not yet taken shape, to abjure in its entirety traditional religious Judaism was tantamount to the severance of all bonds with the Jewish people throughout the world, the Jewish past, and its historical aspiration for national deliverance. The anti-religious decrees, especially in Alsace-Lorraine, were expressly designed to destroy every form of Jewish community life at its core. The war against Jewish "schismaticism" was carried so far that a member of the General Council of the Commune at Nancy demanded that any Jew who failed to marry a Catholic should be treated with suspicion, *a priori*.

It is not surprising therefore that the Jews of Hagenau, Metz, and even Nice began to meet in secret, wearing their workday clothes, for congregational prayer services on Sabbaths or on the Day of Atonement. A profoundly moving incident records how a Jewish woman, Hademard of Metz, came to the pro-consul of the city to request permission to hold a Passover *Seder* and eat *Matzot*. When the official exclaimed, "What, you still cling to this nonsense with the sun of Reason shining on the horizon?", she replied, "The *Matzot* have already been baked. It is a much cherished tradition of ours, a commemoration of liberty." The official gave his permission with a good-natured folk-proverb, "Oh well, since the wine is drawn, let it be drunk!" At that moment, he may have realized that some connection did exist between *Z'man Herutenu* ("The Season of Our Liberation")—an integral phrase in the Passover ritual and service—and the liberation at which the French Revolution aimed.

The active participation of a class of enlightened Jews in political life during the Revolution inevitably meant that a number of Jews was included amongst those guillotined in the final months of Robespierre's dictatorship, when the Jacobin terror against the enemies of the Revolution and the régime reached its peak.

The Colmar brothers, scions of a Dutch Jewish banking family, are known to have died in this way. The elder brother, Isaac, who had been Chairman of the Revolutionary Committee at Clichy, was condemned for profiteering, abuse of official prerogatives and despotism; the younger, Louis-Benjamin, was executed as a Royalist. Junius and Emmanuel Frey, sons of a converted commissionary from Moravia, were sentenced for espionage, together with the Dantonist, Chabot, to whom they had married off their sixteen-year-old sister—with a dowry of a quarter of a million *livres*—for reasons which will not bear too close an inspection. Most interesting, however, is the case of Jacob Pereyra, both for his colourful, adventurous and highly contradictory personality, and because he was a prominent member of the Jacobin Party. Originally from Bayonne, he came to Paris when Revolution broke out and opened a tobacco factory. At first, he belonged to the Royalist Feuillants, but he later joined the Jacobin camp. The Jacobins appointed him a court judiciary, Vice-Chairman of one of the Paris Clubs and head of one of the Municipal Sections, and entrusted him with an important political role as government liaison officer with the army. He was also one of the delegates to the Central Committee which carried out the Jacobin uprising and was later reorganized as the Comité de Salut Public. He was a friend of Anacharsis Cloots and participated in the scheme whereby the Catholic Bishop of Paris, Goebel, was persuaded to appear before the Convention and proclaim his withdrawal from the Catholic faith. Pereyra fell victim to Robespierre's new policy directed against the Hébertists and their religion of reason. The court charged him, *inter alia*, with having had relations with Beaumarchais, then an *émigré* in London. Pereyra apologized, and explained that it had only been in jest. He was convicted of counter-revolutionary conspiracy to restore tyranny (i.e. monarchy) and died at the guillotine on the 4th Germinal (March), 1794, in company with his friends Hébert and Cloots.

On July 27, 1794, Robespierre was himself arrested and guillotined the following day, the 9th Thermidor. The Revolution began to decline.

C. *REVOLUTIONARY DECLINE AND THE RULE OF NAPOLEON*

From the 9th Thermidor to the Proclamation of the Empire

When Robespierre's dictatorship fell in the upheavals at the end of July, 1794, an illusory hope still remained with the régime which lingered on under the Convention. In reality however, the 9th Thermidor marked the end of the revolutionary dominance of the Jacobins. The upper middle class now seized power and gradually destroyed what the Revolution had accomplished, according to a political régime conceived solely in the interests of its own class. In 1795, the Convention was dispersed and power passed to the Directory. At the end of December, 1799 (18th Brumaire), Napoleon Bonaparte proclaimed himself First Consul in the Triumvirate and virtually became sole ruler of France. On May 20, 1804, he crowned himself "Emperor of all the French," officially bringing the Republic to an end, though actually it had long since ceased to exist. Democracy, won at the expense of so much French blood, was completely effaced. The only revolutionary achievements to be retained were those that the bourgeoisie required for its class rule and capitalist development: unification under a centralized administrative power; the abolition of the privileges of feudalism and serfdom (though preferential status was restored to the nobility in government and in the army); and formal equality under the law for all citizens. But under the monarchical régime, they were known, as before, as *subjects*.

Equality of all inhabitants by law signified, of course, equality without

distinction as to religion. Equality of the Jews was therefore an acknowledged principle and no régime, not even the Revolution at its lowest
point, had dared question it—or, until Napoleon, even concieved of
attacking it. All the same, the Jews were affected by the perceptible and
unimpeded retreat of the Revolution.

Immediately after the 9th Thermidor, propaganda against the remnants of Robespierre's mutilated party took on an antisemitic bias in some
journals. Robespierre's supporters were dubbed "Maximilian's Israelites," or "Robespierre's Israelites," and anyone who let slip a word in
praise of the previous government was immediately labelled "Jew." This
propaganda in governing circles ceased when the new régime under the
Directory was firmly ensconced, and towards the end of 1797 a member
of the Council of Five Hundred (the Assembly of Deputies) was officially
reprimanded for an anti-Jewish speech and particularly for "still obstinately regarding the Jews only as Jews, whereas they are to be regarded
exclusively as Frenchmen." But the days of revolutionary drive and
vigour did not return.

In Alsace, where the ancient hatred of the Jews even smouldered
under the Jacobins, the political change betokened a redoubled attack on
all fronts. It took the form of repression and the imposition of heavy fines
on the Jews. In some towns, Jews were not allowed to participate in the
sale or purchase of public assets; in others, Jews recently settled were
expelled. Strasbourg even tried to renew the edicts expelling foreign
Jews from the city. One of the final actions of the Convention before its
dissolution was made in response to a complaint by the Jews. At the
beginning of November, 1794, its Constitutional Committee ordered the
local authorities of Alsace to put an end to all violations of the principle
of equal rights.

The legal enfranchisement of the Jews in France had an important
effect on the distribution of Jews within the country. Towards the end of
the Napoleonic era, in 1811, when France had annexed Switzerland,
north and central Italy, Belgium, Holland, and parts of Germany, official
statistics put the number of Jews in the Empire as a whole at over
141,000, including more than 47,000 in France itself. In the same year,
there were 37,000 Jews in Alsace-Lorraine, constituting four-fifths of the
entire Jewish community of the country. Changes in distribution had
nevertheless taken place. The Jewish population of Paris had grown
threefold since 1789 and numbered 3,000, though this was still only 0.5
per cent of the half-million inhabitants of the capital. An almost entirely
new Jewish community of 200 people had grown up at Lyons. Similarly,
large Jewish communities had come into being at Marseilles, Toulouse,
Dijon and Lille, in the extreme north. Before the Revolution, Jews had
only lived in ten of the seventy-two departments (under the new
division). Under the Empire, forty-four departments had Jewish populations—though in some cases these were small.

Even within the provinces of Alsace-Lorraine, Jews had settled in several new localities. In Alsace, there were twenty-six new urban Kehillot, (the total number of urban Kehillot had risen to 203 from 177). In Lorraine, where more severe restrictions had previously been in force, the number of cities and towns with Jewish populations rose from 51 to 168. In Strasbourg itself, the Jewish community in 1808 numbered approximately 1,500 as opposed to the handful of Jews related to the Cerf-Berr family who had formerly lived there.

Most of the Jews living between the borders of Alsace and Bordeaux and Avignon, continued to find their chief source of income in trading and peddling, but some changes for the better had taken place. In the two largest communities of the south, at Bordeaux and Bayonne, the means whereby Jews made a living had hardly altered, since nothing had happened to force the wealthy élite there to abandon its large-scale commerce and banking or the remainder to retire from petty trade and peddling in favour of more lucrative occupations. In Provence, however, where the Jewish population had grown, some of them did take advantage of new opportunities: a group of Jewish capitalists established textile factories, while their poorer brethren turned to tailoring or became goldsmiths, potters and other kinds of craftsmen.

In Paris, according to the Jewish Consistory's census of 1809, nearly a third of the community was also composed of artisans—mainly tailors, goldsmiths or cobblers. Approximately one half of the community still earned a living in retail trade, and there were 365 registered pedlars, who comprised over two-fifths of the heads of families. In Alsace and Lorraine, where the need for a transfer to productive occupations was greatest, it had become correspondingly more difficult than elsewhere to enter the skilled trades or agriculture. Even Departmental Prefects acknowledged in their reports to their Ministry that Christian artisans as a rule refused to accept Jewish apprentices. The deep-rooted antagonism of the peasants made it difficult for Jews to settle on the land in a gentile environment where there were no guarantees for the security of their life or property. Nevertheless, some progress was made in these eastern provinces. Butchers, like the cattle dealers before them, were fairly common, but an increasing number of Jewish householders and, even more, of young people became tailors, cobblers, bakers, tanners and goldsmiths. Jewish working men also began to appear in the factories, particularly in the spinning mills recently built by Jews and non-Jews. About one hundred Jewish boys were employed in the government arms factory in the town of Mutzig, with permission to work on Sundays instead of on Saturdays. Jewish land-owners and, even more significantly, Jewish husbandmen, for the first time appeared in the two provinces. According to the report of the Central Jewish Consistory of June, 1810, there were 1,232 Jews engaged in agriculture in all France. The same report puts the number of Jewish manufacturers in the country as a whole at 250.

From the period of the Revolution onwards, internal social conflict amongst the Jews of France became even more pronounced than amongst the general population of the country. Despite the widening scope of productive employment already mentioned, there was little if any alleviation of the chronic distress amongst the Jewish masses. If anything, it became more acute. The retreat of the Revolution after 1794 offered the opportunity for Jewish capitalists, and, for that matter, for all capitalists, to increase their profit margins without interference. The same period saw increasing poverty amongst the Jewish population as a whole, still mainly composed of pedlars and traders. Similarly, the non-Jewish lower middle class were impoverished by the depreciation in the value of the currency. However, they found some support in the wealthy peasantry and had some security in the houses and land they owned. The existence of the Jewish pedlar and petty trader was rootless and unstable.

Under Napoleon, these penurious urban Jews of Alsace-Lorraine were faced with vociferous charges of usury and exploitation. Jewish money-lending in Alsace-Lorraine had become the principal issue in all controversies and legal debates concerning the Jews at this time. It was largely in this connection that the Assembly of Jewish Notables and the Great Sanhedrin of Paris were convened.

Usury was a national disgrace in the Napoleonic period, the product of incessant, costly wars, profiteering and crises. The situation was most acute in Alsace. Here, more than anywhere else in France, the peasants lacked land and were therefore most heavily in debt. They had bought parcels of nationalized land—mostly through middlemen, who were wealthy Christian land speculators—at correspondingly high prices. To meet the cost, they borrowed money at interest. In these cases, the Jewish moneylender fulfilled the function of supplying loan capital. The lender either charged a high rate of interest or else took a low rate and a mortgage. Only a small number of Jews in Alsace, and even fewer in Lorraine, took part in these loan transactions. Many Jewish moneylenders lost the little capital they possessed in the process of making loans to peasants who paid their debts in depreciated bank notes. The peasants, on the other hand, acquired great wealth by selling their products for cash at high prices. Obviously, moneylending in Alsace-Lorraine involved a reprehensible exploitation of the poorer peasant, by the forces of capitalism, and, as such, had to be exterminated. But opprobrium was vociferously directed against Jewish moneylending rather than against the extortionate interest on loans as such. The Christian moneylenders, as Abbé Grégoire rightly indicated, tried to employ this stratagem to free themselves from Jewish competition and thus to acquire a monopoly in their specific field. Christian speculators had bought up most of the more desirable nationalized properties. The peasants were therefore faced with the choice of buying the miserable land which remained, or, alternatively, of purchasing better properties from the speculators at any price they might care to name. This new landed aristocracy tried to place the onus of responsibility on the Jews for the dearth of land and the shortage of capital of the peasant poor. In actual fact, the bourgeoisie of Alsace-Lorraine endeavoured to be free of Jewish competition by agitating against the Jews because of the growth in number of Jewish petty traders and pedlars following the impoverishment of the moneylenders. Above all, France during the growing political reaction of the Napoleonic period needed a scapegoat, particularly during the economic crisis of 1805-6. Resorting to the formula that had withstood the test of generations, it found its most convenient victim in the Jews and its easiest diversion in the Jewish problem.

One form that this social and political diversion assumed—though negligible in scope and importance—was propaganda concerning alleged Jewish evasion of military service, and this, in turn, led to specific anti-Jewish legislation. Recorded facts prove this accusation false. Statistics for the country as a whole are not available but the statistics of the particular departments are evidence enough. In 1808, the Prefect of Paris stated that 150 of the city's Jews were serving in the Army either as volunteers or as conscripts; some of them were even acting as substitutes for Christians! There was a large contingent of Jewish soldiers from various cities in the south of France. Even in Lorraine, where the traditional form of life, still widely observed, might have restrained Jews from enlisting, the Prefects noted with satisfaction the increased number of Jews in military service in 1801-10. In 1801, the Prefect of the Department of Moselle (Metz area) concluded that "by virtue of their heroism they were worthy of being called Frenchmen." In Alsace, which contained over half the Jews of France, the proportion of Jews in the army was certainly somewhat lower because of local factors: apart from the fact that religious orthodoxy was more prevalent here than amongst the Jews in other areas of France, prejudice against Jews was no less rife in the army than amongst the civilian Christian population of the department. Because of this, the recruiting officers rejected Jews for service, particularly during the Napoleonic period. Official reports verify this, not only for Alsace but also for the departments of Lorraine. In Alsace, the official report of the chief departmental statistician records that most of the young Jews were exempt from service because of skin disease and general physical disability. Yet young French Jews shed their blood on all the battlefields of Europe, sharing with their comrades-in-arms the conviction that their bayonets were bringing liberty and equality to enslaved peoples.

Greater than their economic progress after enfranchisement was the cultural progress made by the French Jews. This was mainly evident in the field of secular education. Here again, the Paris area was in the forefront. A large number of Jewish children attended elementary public schools; two hundred received training in crafts, and a number of young Jews attended lycées and polytechnic institutes. The same situation prevailed at Bordeaux. By 1808, in some southern departments and even in central France, all Jewish children of school age were attending public school.

As usual, Alsace-Lorraine presented a different picture. Jewish pupils could be found in the secondary schools, lycées, polytechnic institutes, and colleges there, but only in insignificant numbers. The number of Jewish pupils in the elementary public schools was also relatively small; in some departments of Lorraine it amounted to no more than a fifth or even less. In Alsace, in 1810, only one in every ten Jewish children of school age attended public school. This was primarily because of the old, traditional mode of life and the religious orthodoxy of the Jews in Alsace and, to a considerable extent, also in Lorraine.

The lack of support that the Jews of Alsace-Lorraine gave to public school education was reinforced by rabbinical prohibitions. This, in turn, was influenced by fear, which was not entirely unfounded, of assimilation and conversion. After Napoleon had signed the Concordat with the Vatican in 1801, public school education was placed under the supervision of the Catholic clergy. As a result the number of Jewish (and also Protestant) pupils attending school in several departments of Lorraine actually decreased. Added to this, the Jewish pupils were the victims of assaults and humiliations at the hands of their Christian companions. Finally, public school principals were unwilling to accept Jewish children! In such circumstances, wealthy Jewish parents in northern and eastern France customarily engaged private tutors for French language and other secular studies.

The linguistic and cultural assimilation of the Jews in the east and north of France proceeded so slowly that even in the state of Luxembourg, only one Jewish petty trader out of the seventy-five who applied for a trader's licence after the decree of 1808 could sign his name in Latin characters. In Paris, too Yiddish was still the everyday language of the Jewish petty trader and pedlar. Chief Rabbi Seligmann of Paris, whose appointment was confirmed by the Consistory, could only understand Yiddish. In the whole of France, linguistic assimilation primarily affected the new Jewish middle class: merchants, contractors, bankers, and manufacturers—a class that had already taken shape after the Revolution. Assimilation here, apart from language, mainly took the form of indifference to religion, and imitation of the French bourgeoisie in its luxury-loving way of life. Most profoundly affected by cultural assimilation were those Jews in the professions and skilled crafts, who had considerably increased in number in Paris. During the Napoleonic era, there were already several Jewish mathematicians (Orly Terquem was the most prominent), naturalists, master-engravers, artistic metal workers, musicians and doctors. However, there were very few Jewish writers in French, apart from Zalkind Hourwitz and Berr Isaac Berr, and they earned no reputation except for their Jewish *apologiae*. The rapid assimilation of the Jewish bourgeoisie and intellectuals in France left no room for a distinct *Haskalah* movement, save for a few casual authors of poems in praise of Napoleon in Hebrew, including the gifted Eli Halévy, father of the composer.

When Napoleon brutally raised the Jewish question, it was the totally or partially assimilated Jewish plutocrats who arrogated to themselves the right to act as spokesmen for the Jews of France and even for the Jewish people as a whole.

Napoleon and the First Discriminatory Law against the Jews

Napoleon disliked and despised the Jews and he gave vent to his prejudice on more than one occasion in letters and speeches. The aversion he felt as a soldier for bankers and merchants (who nonetheless profited from his dictatorial régime) was directed against the Jewish bourgeoisie. As a parvenu to greatness, his acute awareness of poverty and destitution was transformed into contempt for the ragged and tattered, bewildered and panic-stricken Jewish traders and pedlars he encountered on his campaigns through Europe, especially in the poor Jewish towns of Poland far more than France itself. Napoleon reinstated Catholicism as a bulwark against the defeated Revolution and believed the Jewish religion inferior to the "civilization" of the Gospel. Like all despots, he was a determined "unifier" and could not reconcile himself to the fact that the Jews conducted themselves as a separate people, with language, religion, customs and internal organization of their own. He considered them insolent and ungrateful for the "favour" of enfranchisement. With the penetration of a statesman, he realised that Jewish separatism was not merely a problem of religion but rather the expression of the impregnable will of a great and historic people. (During his military expedition to Palestine in 1799, he issued a proclamation based on this glorious history calling upon the Jews of the world to return and re-establish the Jewish State.) And as this realization grew, so too did his dictatorial, chauvinistic ambition to destroy the national unity of the Jews and forcibly to transform them into Frenchmen.

However, as in all political questions relating to the Jews, the personal attitude of the Emperor or his advisers could only influence the planning of *tactical detail*. The *strategy* was determined by the system, by the political order which had entrusted Napoleon with dictatorial power. The

Jewish policies followed during the Napoleonic era were a true reflection of the political level to which the bourgeoisie had reduced the achievements of the popular Revolution. "Napoleon," the Jewish historian Graetz wrote, "murdered the Revolution, which mothered him, and, one might say, exhaled its dying breath... He retained but one of the Revolution's achievements, equality..." For the sake of accuracy, this should be modified to read: the equality of all citizens *by law*. The essentially two-faced character of Napoleon's régime is revealed in his policy and legislation on Jewish matters. The régime was already so reactionary, both in its aims and achievements, that it could assail the Jews with accusations, abuse and restrictions which reduced the ideals of the frustrated Revolution to absurdity. Yet the formal basis of civil equality by law still remained as a sole surviving element of the revolutionary heritage and, despite all the restrictions that hampered the Jews, their civil enfranchisement, in theory at least, was not abolished.

In 1806, Napoleon finally reached a decision on his anti-Jewish policy. As early as spring, 1805, the Minister of Justice, at the Emperor's request, submitted a report on Jewish moneylending activities, recommending that usury in general be limited by law. The Council of State rejected this proposal on the grounds that it was contrary to the Civil Code. At the end of January, 1806, on his return from victory at Austerlitz, Napoleon broke march for one day at Strasbourg. The confirmed Jew-haters there had not yet grown accustomed to the fact that, since enfranchisement, a sizeable Jewish community had grown up in a city that had formerly been *Judenrein*. Then hastily organized a demonstration of "popular indignation" against the Jews. The Prefect and the delegation of honour submitted a lengthy series of complaints condemning Jewish usury to the Emperor, while a large mob surrounded him shouting angrily against the Jews. When he arrived in Paris, Napoleon showed the effect this had had on him and proposed to the Council of State a series of severe regulations against the Jews, based on a new plan drawn up by the Minister of Justice. The plan was to forbid the Jews, for ten years, to issue mortgage loans; to nullify mortgages previously issued to and held by Jews, if drawn up at usurious rates; and even revoke the citizenship rights of Jews who owned no real estate whatsoever. This was aimed primarily at Jews who had emigrated to France from Germany or Poland within the past ten years.

The State Council, which discussed these proposals, included a number of liberals who had not yet entirely discarded their revolutionary ideals, especially where opposition to the clergy was involved. At appropriate moments they even attempted to convince the dictator that this body, actually Napoleon's privy council, was occasionally entitled to speak its own mind. Their attempts to alleviate the harshness of the decrees and to defend the Jews did not succeed. On May 30, 1806, the

"Moratorium Decree" was promulgated. The Preamble explained its purpose:

> In several northern departments, certain Jews who engage in no calling other than usury, have, through the accumulation of a very high rate of interest, brought many husbandmen to a position of great loss. We have therefore considered it our duty to extend our help to those of our subjects whom an unscrupulous greed for profit has forced to these sorrowful extremes. Likewise, these circumstances have shown us how urgent it is that we essay once more to arouse in the hearts of those who adhere to the Jewish religion that sense of civic morality which, to our regret, seems to have expired and vanished because of the lowly state in which they languished for so long, a state which it is our intention neither to maintain nor to renew. To achieve this aim, we have decided to convene an assembly of Jewish leaders, to inform them of our intentions through Commissioners whom we shall appoint to that end and through whom we shall hear their wishes as to the appropriate measures which, in their opinion, should be employed to re-establish amongst their brethren the pursuit of useful crafts and professions so that honest industry may take the place of the shameful livelihoods whereby so many of them have been supporting themselves from generation to generation for hundreds of years past.

The Decree suspended in eight specified departments, including all of Alsace and parts of Lorraine and the Rhineland, the execution of court orders and contractual provisions relating to debts owed by agriculturalists to Jews. An assembly of Jewish representatives was summoned for July 15, 1806; and the precise number of delegates to be appointed by the Prefect of each department was specified. Thus the first discriminatory measure against the Jews came into effect. It is interesting to note that, whereas two additional departments asked to be included by the Ministry in those provisions of the Decree that declared a moratorium on debts owed to *Jewish* lenders, a number of departments demanded that a law be passed against *usury in general*. They stated that Christian usurers were no better than their Jewish colleagues (the city of Beziers and the Prefect of Meurthe), or that in their departments there were only Christian moneylenders the Prefects of six different departments).

One such department, the Eastern Pyrenees, launched a campaign against local moneylenders, who were all Christians and whose crimes were so serious that the police had preferred charges against them. Private individuals in various departments, including two Deputies to the "Legislative Body," sent memoranda to the Ministry, or letters to Regnaul, stressing how grave was the abuse of usury throughout the country as a whole and stating that Christians, including high officials, participated in usury as much as the Jews.

The memoranda setting out the true state of affairs regarding usurious interest rates brought a response from the other side. As though to affirm that the guilt lay entirely on Jewish shoulders, Napoleon's intimate friend, Molé, on the Emperor's instruction, published an article in the official publication *Moniteur*. It appeared virtually on the eve of the opening of the assembly of Jewish representatives and denounced the Jews as the eternal foes of Christianity and usurers from the time of Moses. It held up Saint Louis (Louis XI), as a model ruler, who had perceived that the Jews should certainly not be expelled from the countries in which they lived, but should be compelled to mend their ways. This was a clear hint to the forthcoming Jewish assembly.

The Assembly of Jewish Notables at Paris (1806)

By the decree of May 30, 1806, the Prefects were to appoint delegates to the Paris assembly "from amongst the Rabbis, landowners, and other Jews who were outstanding among their communal brethren for their integrity and enlightenment." Both the Prefects and the Kehillah representatives, whom they consulted, tried to follow the spirit of the decree, and ensure, as far as they could, that the Assembly be composed of the enlightened and the wealthy. In the Department of the Seine (district of Paris), the barrister, Michael Berr, described the list of personages which the banker, Olry Hayim Worms, submitted to the Prefect "as permeated with prejudice against all source of authority amongst the Jews save that of money." Conditions attached to the decree provided that the southern departments, where the wealthiest and most enlightened French Jews lived, might nominate twice as many delegates as the northern, in proportion to their Jewish population. In some departments, the Prefects appointed no delegates at all, even though the decree stated that the Jews were entitled to one delegate if there was a minimum of a hundred residents. There were, at first, ninety-five delegates from France, including the German Rhine Provinces. At the end of July, the Kehillot of the Kingdom of Italy (the north) were also ordered to send delegates. By the beginning of August, the Assembly numbered 111 delegates in all. Apart from fifteen rabbis, nearly all of them gave their profession as commerce, banking, industry or property. The merchants, particularly from the eastern areas, which sent relatively the largest delegations, included some exceptionally wealthy individuals.

The lack of enthusiasm that the Jewish "Parliament" generated amongst the Jewish population is illustrated by the fact that the Kehillot, especially in Alsace, failed to remit the sums designated to cover the delegates' expenses—despite intervention by the Ministry and the Prefects. Many delegates, therefore, had to depend on loans from the banker, Worms, who was officially appointed treasurer to the Assembly. Its

President, Furtado, even stipulated a figure above the fixed minimum for the subsistence allowance of delegates whose "personal situation" was difficult, or who had displayed "perseverance in the discharge of their mission." Some of the delegates could not stay in Paris—because of business affairs, or because of the expense—for the nine consecutive months of the Assembly's duration, and either travelled home for varying periods, or disappeared entirely. As a result, the Assembly was never fully attended by all its 111 delegates; and in these circumstances, the Furtado group of plutocrats and extreme assimilationists was able to stamp its imprint on the proceedings and resolutions of this Assembly of Jewish Notables.

Apart from a few rabbis, the most prominent speakers at the Assembly were Abraham Furtado, Olry Hayim Worms, Berr Isaac Berr and his son, Michel Berr, the three sons of Cerf-Berr, the younger Isaac Roderiguez, and Jacob Lazard, all very wealthy bankers. Abraham Furtado and Berr Isaac Berr fought for supremacy and were also men of very different views. Whereas Berr Isaac Berr was an enlightened man, of a conservative outlook in Jewish religious matters, Furtado was a devout Voltairean, who regarded all religion as so much prejudice and superstition.

The outstanding figure amongst the rabbis was Cerf-Berr's brother-in-law, David Sinzheim of Strasbourg, famous for his knowledge of the Talmud. Skilled in the art of compromise, he played an important role in drafting replies and resolutions at the sessions of the Committee of Twelve. The main representatives of those enlightened rabbis inclined to conscious assimilation, came from Italy—Abraham Vita di Cologna. the Rabbi of Mantua, and Joshua Segre of Vercelli. Nearly all the conservative rabbis were delegates from the German provinces and from Avignon. An Italian delegate, Rabbi Graciadio (Hananel) Nepi, Kabalah scholar and doctor of medicine, was also opposed to any reform of the Jewish religion. Jacob Israele Carmi from Reggio likewise supported a traditionalist point of view. Opposition from this group of conservative rabbis was energetically organized at all times by the Rabbi of Coblenz, Emmanuel Deutz. Some rabbis, such as Mordecia Crémieux of Aix (near Marseilles) foresaw the character of the Assembly of Notables and on grounds of religious principle expressly refused to be included amongst the delegates.

At the informal session held before it opened, the Assembly already made it clear to Napoleon that it had no intentions of opposing him, even on matters relating to the Jewish religion. The opening session was scheduled for July 26, a Saturday—certainly not by accident. The Minister informed the delegates that the choice of postponing the opening to another day lay with them. Despite the opposition of the rabbis and, apparently, also of a group led by Berr Isaac Berr, they decided, after consultation, to convene the opening session on the

Sabbath. They met in the assembly hall, near the Hôtel de Ville. At the entrance, a military guard presented arms to the accompaniment of rolling drums in honour of the notables. Abraham Furtado was elected chairman by a two-thirds majority vote over the candidacy of Berr Isaac Berr. When his opening speech made mention of the greatness of the hero of the nation, Napoleon, all present burst into loud cheers of "Long live the Emperor! Long live the House of the Emperor!" This was adopted as part of the routine of future sessions. The three Commissioners, appointed by Napoleon as representatives of the Government, did not attend until the second session, on July 29. They were Count Molé, young Portalis, and Pasquier. Molé described the Emperor's purpose in convening the Assembly: to help the Government eradicate an evil, whose spread the Emperor had already arrested. He was referring, of course, to usury. In his speech Molé repeatedly mentioned the threat of withdrawal of enfranchisement that hung over the Jews: "It is His Majesty's wish that you become Frenchmen, and it is for you to decide whether you accept this title or to reflect that you renounce it if you do not make yourselves worthy of it." Similarly, he warned the delegates that failure to reply sincerely to all questions would be contrary to the interests of the Jews. Molé followed up these introductory remarks with twelve questions, divided into three groups: questions of Jewish marriage laws; of the attitude of Jews to Frenchmen; and questions of usury in Jewish law. The delegates rose to their feet with shouts of acclaim in honour of the Emperor when the Commissioners entered. They remained standing until the twelve questions had been read. When Molé came to the sixth question: "Do the Jews who were born in France and who are treated as French citizens regard France as their fatherland? Do they consider it their duty to defend it?"—the delegates cried out: "Yes! To our dying breath."

The Assembly entrusted a committee of twelve with the task of formulating a reply to the twelve questions. This committee consisted of nine wealthy men who were active in communal affairs, and three rabbis, including David Sinzheim. On August 4, it put forward provisional answers to the first three questions to the Assembly. The answer proposed to the first question, whether Jews were permitted to have more than one wife, cited the ban of Rabbenu Gershom (forbidding polygamy in any form) and also the influence of European customs on the Jews. The second question asked whether a divorce decree not issued in a court of justice was legal in Jewish religious law. The proposed reply proved, by quoting the *Shulhan Arukh*, that no divorce was binding, if any impediments were involved, and argued that as "The Law of the Land is the Law" (according to the Talmud), no divorce could be binding unless executed in accordance with the laws of the state, that is, by a court of justice. Both these proposed replies received unanimous approval. The third question, on the other hand, whether mixed marriages between

Jews and Christians were permitted by Jewish law, aroused a stormy debate in the plenary session. The majority, which included the enlightened rabbis from the south of France and Rabbi Segre from Italy, accepted unreservedly the answer formulated by the committee. Opposition came from the German rabbis and the other Italian rabbis, who argued that this was a question of religious conscience, not to be resolved by majority vote, and they proposed a reply of their own. After a recess, a reply which compromised between the committee's formulation and the point of view of the rabbis was adopted: according to the letter of the Jewish law, Jews were forbidden to marry idol worshippers, and the modern peoples of Europe were not idol worshippers. Nevertheless, the rabbis opposed intermarriage as they were forbidden to perform the religious ceremony in such cases, in the same way as Catholic priests could not bestow their blessings in similar circumstances. However, the rabbis were also of the opinion that a Jew who married a Christian woman did not cease to be a Jew any more than did a Jew who married a Jewess under the civil code alone, without the religious ceremony of *Hupah ve-Kiddushin*.

At that session also, a declaration was adopted "in the name of those Frenchmen who believe in the Mosaic religion" which formed a sort of preamble to all twelve replies. It expressed gratitude, devotion, awe and admiration for his Imperial Majesty's sacred presence: "That they might be worthy of all the benefits which his Imperial Majesty proposes to bestow upon them, they are prepared to accept the authority of his paternal will. . . . Their religion commands them, in all civil and political questions, to regard the law of the land as the law of Israel." Hence, the mandatory nature of the religious laws or their interpretation was null and void insofar as they were not in accord with the French law in civil and political matters.

This declaration, by establishing the concept of "Frenchmen of the Mosaic persuasion" and basing Judaism solely on religious premises, prepared the way for the fundamentally assimilationist replies to the other questions, which were discussed at two sessions. The replies to the three questions concerning the Jewish attitude to Frenchmen in France contained a declaration of love for humanity, "a pious deed ordained by the Torah and the Talmud." The general tone can be gauged from the following: "Yes, France is our fatherland. . . . Today, when the Jews no longer constitute a nation and have finally been privileged to be included in this great nation—a thing which they view as an act of political deliverance—it cannot be that a Jew should not behave towards a Frenchman who is not of his religious persuasion as he does towards his co-religionist. . . . The Prophet Jeremiah persuaded the Jews to look upon Babylon as upon their own fatherland, even though they were not destined to sojourn there more than seventy years. . . . And so far did they heed his counsel that when Cyrus permitted them to return to Jerusalem to erect the Second Temple there, only 42,000, all proletarians, left that country, while all the wealthy remained.* Love of country is so vital and consistent with their religious faith, that a French Jew in Great Britain regards himself, even in the midst of other Jews, as a stranger, and even so an English Jew in France. This emotion is so powerful, that in the last war French Jews were to be seen fighting to the death against the Jews of those countries against whom France was warring . . . ."

The Jewish notables of France, self-appointed and approved by Napoleon's prefects, had indeed come to the point of undisguised betrayal of the unity, dreams, and historic efforts of the Jewish people. This could not fail to have repercussions. Even their declarations of loyalty to France were greeted with unconcealed scepticism by many of Napoleon's supporters and openly challenged in the press. The Jews read them with mixed emotions. Outside of France, F. D. Kirwan, in his introduction to the English edition of the Assembly's proceedings, interpreted the reply to the sixth question, "Wherein the Jews acknowledged France unreservedly as their fatherland," as a reprehensible denial of the tenets of the Mosaic faith. If the Jews did this, he argued, they were abandoning their hope in the Messiah and eternal heritage of the promised land, part of the holy covenant between the Lord of all creation and His chosen people.

The reply to the seventh, eighth, and ninth questions claimed that the rabbis possessed no authority except in religion and that their law courts had been abolished since the Revolution. The Assembly gave a detailed reply to the three remaining questions concerning usury, supported by quotations from the Torah, the Talmud, and the Codifiers: the Torah made no mention of usury but only of interest on loans; the Torah sought to protect the property rights of an agricultural population and therefore forbade the taking of interest from Jews or even from non-Jews living in the country: it was only permitted to take interest from foreigners. During the Talmudic period, when commerce was quite developed, the taking of interest from Jews was permitted, a sort of partnership thus being created. But even the Talmud regarded it as a great virtue to grant loans without interest, even to idol worshippers. Only Maimonides interpreted the passage *Unto a foreigner thou mayest lend upon interest* in such a way that he might be thought to have implied that taking interest from non-Jews was an act of piety. Actually he had in mind the

---

* This quotation from the Book of Jeremiah, used at the Paris meeting, gained currency among the assimilationists. It was, of course, a fabrication. In Chapter 29, Jeremiah adjured the captives taken to Babylon with their King, Jeconiah: "Build ye houses and dwell in them; and plant gardens and eat the fruit of them; take ye wives and beget sons and daughters . . . and seek the peace of the city whether I have caused you to be carried away. . . ." He told them all this and gave them the hope that, after seventy years of exile, they would return to Jerusalem (see verse 10). The example of Jeremiah, therefore, was used only to stand the evidence on its head: even when he was urging loyalty to Babylon, Jeremiah held fast to the hope of a return to Zion.

Canaanites, a people accursed of God. It must be added moreover, that all the other prominent sages, such as Nachmanides, the Rashba,* and Abrabanel, had ruled contrary to Maimonides. It would therefore be as unjust to indict the entire Jewish religion because of one interpretation of the Law, as to consider the entire New Testament responsible for judgments by individual Catholic theologians. Similarly, it was a myth that "the inclination to usury is innate in the Hebrews. True, there are amongst them, albeit fewer in number than is believed, those who pursue this nefarious vocation, forbidden though it is by their religion.... Is it not a misdeed (even so) to censure all Christians for the sins of individuals amongst them, who allow themselves to be thus occupied?"

Napoleon's birthday, on August 15, provided the Assembly of Notables with the opportunity to carry to the utmost limits their submissiveness to Napoleon. The delegates marched in formation to the synagogue, where they processioned round with the Torah Scrolls in their arms while a choir sang Napoleon's praises in Hebrew and French. Speeches were delivered in French, Italian and German. Rabbi Segre called Napoleon "The King Solomon of our Day"; Rabbi Sinzheim compared him to Cyrus.

Napoleon regarded the Assembly of Notables merely as a springboard from which to launch his plans for the Jews. These never excluded the use of compulsion or the discriminatory laws he had presented to the Council of State in the spring, several months previously. It was his intention that the resolutions of the Assembly of Notables constitute a framework for his future actions to "reform" the Jews. But these appeared to lack the necessary authority in the eyes of the Jews themselves. Napoleon therefore resolved to convene a *Grand Sanhedrin*, in Paris (such as had functioned in the time of the Second Temple) in order to ratify the resolutions of the Assembly of Notables and invest them with the power of religious laws "which would be established side by side with the Talmud." Napoleon thought of the *Sanhedrin* purely in terms of the internal affairs of his own country, both in its programme and its composition. However, in the initial stages, he ordered a public announcement to be made with full ceremony, "to all the synagogues of Europe." In this way, he hoped, on the one hand, to appear in a sympathetic light to European Jewry as a whole. On the other, he wanted to give the Jews of France the impression that the *Sanhedrin* would be a religious body with the power and authority to speak in the name of all Jews. But the reality—that the *Sanhedrin* would be no more than a religious façade for the Assembly of Notables—was confirmed when Napoleon stipulated that the majority of the *Sanhedrin's* members should be the rabbis and other delegates participating in the Assembly.

In the session of the Assembly on September 18, the Emperor's

* *Rabbi Sh'lomo ibn Adret*, Talmudic scholar and writer of *responsa* of the fourteenth century.

commissioners initiated the second act in the tragi-comedy of Napoleon's Jewish policy: the convocation of the *Sanhedrin*. The speech of the commissioner, Count Molé, did not lack flattery and high-flown phraseology. "The Emperor is satisfied with the Twelve Replies and he is greatly moved by the spirit that has actuated them, for how then shall one not be amazed on beholding this assemblage of enlightened personages, the chosen sons of the most ancient of this world's peoples?" In the Emperor's name he promised freedom of worship for the Jewish religion and all political rights—except that the Emperor "requires a religious pledge that the principles embodied in your replies shall be strictly adhered to." For that purpose a *Sanhedrin* was to be convoked whose decisions would "enjoy the utmost authority in the eyes of Jews in all countries." It was the task of the *Sanhedrin* to interpret the Torah truthfully and to reject all false interpretations. Similarly, the *Sanhedrin* would teach the Jewish people "to love and to defend the country they inherit; it will convince them that the land, where, for the first time since their dispersion, they have been able to raise their voice, is entitled to all those sentiments which rendered their ancient country so dear to them."

On September 24, the Assembly of Notables issued a manifesto "To the Synagogues of Europe" concerning their participation in the *Sanhedrin*. The *Sanhedrin* was scheduled to meet on October 20 but the date was later postponed to the beginning of February, 1807. The Assembly spent the intervening four months preparing for the *Sanhedrin*, and also planning the organization of the Jewish Consistory of the French Empire. After a ceremonial session of February 5, 1807, the Assembly of Notables adjourned for a month in deference to the convocation of the *Sanhedrin*. A lengthy speech by one of its secretaries, delegate Samuel Avigdor of Nice, at this ceremonial session, surpassed all the obsequiousness in which the Assembly had so lamentably excelled. It ended with the following resolution:

"The Hebrew Deputies of the French Empire and of the Kingdom of Italy to the Jewish assembly convened by the decree of May 30, deeply impressed with gratitude for the manifold favours conferred on the Israelites, in former centuries, by the Christian clergy in various parts of Europe; no less grateful for the kind reception given by several pontiffs and many other clergymen at various epochs to the Israelites of all countries, when barbarism, ignorance and prejudice, leagued together, chased the Jews from the bosom of society: *Resolve* that the expression of these sentiments shall be registered in the minutes of the proceedings of this day, to remain for ever a lasting monument of the gratitude of the Israelites who compose this assembly, for the favours received by the generations which preceded them from clergymen of various parts of Europe.

Resolve also that a copy of these minutes shall be sent to His Excellency the Minister of Public Worship."

The Assembly adopted Avigdor's resolution by acclamation. After kneeling idolatrously before the Emperor, the delegates prostrated themselves to kiss the feet of that Church which had trampled upon the Jewish people for 1,500 years.

The Grand Sanhedrin of Paris and the Final Discussions of the Assembly of Notables

The Manifesto issued by the Assembly of Notables at the end of September, 1806, "To the Synagogues of Europe" was printed in four languages: Hebrew, French, German and Italian. It described the convocation of the *Sanhedrin* by Napoleon as a "great event" which would initiate "a period of enthusiasm" and serve "the remnants of the scattered children of Abraham as the beginning of a new age of redemption and joy." The Jews of Europe were invited to send delegates to the *Sanhedrin* to contribute "their judicious and enlightened opinion and to endow its resolutions with greater significance" and "to establish in our midst that uniformity of doctrine appropriate in larger measure to the civil rights and the policies of those kingdoms which you have adopted as your fatherlands." The actual results of the Manifesto were minimal. Its message failed to reach the mass of the Jewish people, sunk in poverty and hardship, while the orthodox leaders could see from the very formulation of the Manifesto that the aim of the *Sanhedrin* was to effect reforms in the Jewish religion, and this was precisely what they regarded as a mortal danger to Judaism.

It was only individuals unacquainted with the precise nature of the programme for the *Sanhedrin* who thought that Napoleon had not yet abandoned his plan to help the Jews establish a state in Palestine. Their hopes of imminent redemption revived. The *Maskilim* of central and eastern Europe evinced considerable sympathy for the *Sanhedrin*. They turned to France for help in their struggle against religious bigotry and backwardness amongst the Jews, and some sort of alleviation of the disenfranchised status of the Jews in their countries. But it was in the very countries under Austrian and Russian rule that the governments employed the most forceful police measures (they even opened the mails and raided private homes), so that no-one dared make the illicit journey to Paris or even post a written message of support.

From Europe as a whole, delegations to the *Sanhedrin* came only from a circle of *Maskilim* at Frankfurt-on-Main and from the small, progressive *Adat-Yeshurun* Kehillah of Amsterdam. In both instances, the rulers of the areas concerned were vassals of Napoleon. The motive behind the deliberately equivocal style of the Manifesto, and the demagogy behind its attempt to summon the Jews of all Europe, immediately became apparent. The Frankfurt and Amsterdam delegations were not allowed to participate in the *Sanhedrin* as delegates and were only permitted to take the floor in order to welcome the convocation. The *Sanhedrin* scrupulously observed the framework that Napoleon had laid down: that of an internal state conclave of dumb lawyers, enjoined to sign the resolutions of the Assembly of Notables.

As the government had directed, the *Sanhedrin* included all seventeen rabbis and twenty-five of the laymen who had participated in the Assembly of Notables. This lay delegation had been elected by the Notables and consisted of the plutocratic bloc already mentioned, headed by Abraham Furtado. Nor were the remaining twenty-nine members of the *Sanhedrin*—the rabbis—elected by the Jewish population. The Minister of the Interior had circulated among the Prefects a list of candidates submitted to him by the Assembly of Notables, through the Imperial Commissioners. The Prefects also had the right to appoint people other than those named in the list. It eventually came to light that most of the twenty-nine appointed delegates had never served as rabbis. The official membership of the *Sanhedrin* was seventy-one, the traditional number of members of the ancient *Sanhedrin* at Jerusalem (forty-six rabbis, twenty-five laymen).

The *Sanhedrin's* Presidium, as proposed by the Commissioners, consisted of David Sinzheim, *Nassi* (President); Joshua Segre, *Av Bet-Din* (President of the Rabbinical Court); and Abraham di Cologna, *Hakham* (Counsellor). All titles were taken from the ancient *Sanhedrin*. The Commissioners said of Sinzheim, that he "is venerable, respected, helped draw up the Twelve Replies," and, as a German, could be expected to command influence over the Jews of the north. The Commissioners attributed to Segre and Cologna the advantages of higher education, though Sinzheim once described Segre (in a letter to Baruch Jeiteles) as an ordinary schoolmaster who had never been a rabbi and was not even a scholar. On the whole, the Presidium was of no importance. Furtado controlled the *Sanhedrin*.

The eight sessions of the *Sanhedrin*, covering a period of one month, were mostly filled with tedious speeches by Furtado and his associates. There were no debates, as all the resolutions had been drawn up by a Committee of Nine, members of the Assembly of Notables, in whose name Furtado or Cracovia, the rabbi of Venice, spoke. The *Sanhedrin* unanimously adopted all the resolutions. Fundamentally, they ratified the twelve replies of the Assembly of Notables in broader terms. Napoleon's express demand, that intermarriage should not be punished by excommunication, was accepted. On the other hand, his demand that the *Sanhedrin* recommend mixed marriages, "since they were for the good of the nation," was not conceded. But this was the sole occasion when the *Sanhedrin* dared reject a demand of Napoleon presented to it by Furtado. On the question of military service, the *Sanhedrin* resolved that service was not only an act of religious piety but also absolved all Jewish soldiers from observing such religious laws as were incompatible with military service. The *Sanhedrin* also adopted resolutions urging Jews to turn to agriculture, the crafts, and trades. It prohibited usury on loans to Jews and non-Jews alike, since "this is an abomination in the eyes of the Lord."

On March 9, 1807, the *Sanhedrin* came to an official end, and on March 25, the Assembly of Notables resumed its sessions. The Assembly, had since December, 1806, been engaged in planning the organization of Jewish consistories by order of the Ministry of the Interior. The request that the Jewish Kehillah leaders presented to the Government immediately after the signature of the Concordat between the Vatican and Napoleon in 1801, coincided with the Emperor's intentions. Since the Catholic Church had been placed under Government supervision, the clergy had been obliged to preach about military service and the duties owed to the imperial crown. It was not surprising therefore, that in January, 1807, Napoleon ordered the establishment of Jewish consistories "which would have the duty to maintain rigid supervision over the rabbis." The only difference was that the Catholic clergy drew the salaries and enjoyed the privileges of government officials, whereas the Jewish Kehillot were required to act as state police without corresponding recompense. The great majority of the Assembly of Notables submissively agreed to burden the Kehillot with the task of acting as informers for the authorities; the Catholic Church had been spared this task.

One of the first reforms passed by the Assembly of Notables in accordance with the Government's plan, was to change the "Jews" into "Israelites." The motive behind this step was obvious: "the epithet Jew recalls a nation rather than a religion," apart from which there were "unhappy prejudices" associated with the epithet. The Assembly of Notables also accepted the Consistory plan proposed and prepared in its minutest detail by the Government. Not unexpectedly, in view of its social composition, the Assembly raised no opposition to the proposal that the consistories be elected by twenty-five notables selected by each Prefect from amongst the highest taxpayers. However, the docile acceptance by the Notables of the programme for consistories and of their onerous police duties was not enough for Napoleon. His instructions to the Minister of the Interior, Champagny, at the end of January, 1807, demanded that the Assembly include in its resolutions all the decrees concerning the Jews that he had been trying for some years past to promulgate. By these tactics, he hoped to remain "the great benefactor" in Jewish eyes and be free of the need to bring his anti-Jewish writs before the Council of State. Apart from anything else, he no longer had complete confidence in the Council after his experience in the spring of 1806.

The decrees presented to the Jews for acceptance, in accordance with Napoleon's wishes, prohibited any Jew from engaging in commerce without special permission from the authorities in every case. Jews who owned no real estate were not to be permitted to issue mortgage loans. The consistories were not to allow more than two-thirds of all marriages to be between co-religionists; one-third must be mixed, between Jew and Christian. If this proved difficult to implement, then "persuasion, training, encouragement and command" must be employed "in any matter conducive to that end." Jews would be required to perform military service in person and not by proxy, in proportion to their numbers in the population.

All the declarations made by the Assembly of Notables and the *Grand Sanhedrin*, had not apparently convinced Napoleon that the Jews were a religious sect rather than a distinct nationality and, moreover, a nationality of evil character bent on exploiting the Frenchman. He was determined to compel the Jews to become French by decrees that would force them to change their occupations, to assimilate by intermarriage, and to endure large-scale disproportionate conscription for army service.* Even before the Paris *Sanhedrin*, Napoleon was preparing to mock those "representatives of the Jews" whom he would compel to flagellate the Jewish people with their own hands.

The resolutions of the Assembly of Notables virtually broke the ground for the discriminatory laws, which already hung over the heads of French Jewry. Yet even this did not prevent Furtado from eulogizing the Emperor and his Commissioners at the final session of the Assembly on April 6, 1807. He rapturously announced that "the day of justice is come at last. . . . The Israelites have been incorporated into the community of their fellow citizens."

The "Infamous Decree" and the Organization of the Jewish Consistories

On March 17, 1808, Napoleon signed two decrees concerning the Jews, one dealing with the discriminatory laws, the other with the organization of consistories for the Jewish religion. The simultaneous publication of the two orders was a deliberate attempt to demonstrate Napoleon's justice: with one hand he attacked, with the other he lavished paternal benevolence. In actual fact, the main effect of the ordinance on consistories was to force the Jews into a system of police surveillance. It complemented the discriminatory provisions of the other ordinance, known as *Le Decret Infâme*—the Infamous Decree.

The first section of the Decree dealt with special procedures governing the credit activities of the Jews. The moratorium of May 30, 1806 on all debts due to Jewish moneylenders was originally only to have remained

---

* Disproportionate, because the Jews had been deprived of the right to send proxies to serve in their stead, although the rest of the population still retained this right.

in force for one year. In practice it had been extended indefinitely by the Arch-Chancellor. It was now announced that it had expired. Instead, new restrictions were introduced: for example, all promissory notes held by Jews from minors without their parents' consent, from wives without their husbands' consent, or from military personnel, officers and men, without the consent of their commanding officers, were declared null and void. A Jew could not demand payment of a note or any other written obligation, signed by a merchant, if he were unable to adduce proof that the sum mentioned had been loaned in full and "without deception." In the case of loans, where the principal had increased through the accretion of interest above 5 per cent, courts of justice were authorised to make appropriate reductions in any past or future debt. Should the interest rate exceed 10 per cent, the debt would be regarded as an usurious transaction and, as such, cancelled.

The second section of the ordinance was mainly devoted to restrictions on Jewish trade: from July 1, 1808, no Jew could engage in any form of trade without a prefectorial licence. This would not be issued unless two documents were presented, one from the city council confirming that the applicant was not engaged in usury or any other illegal business, the other a certificate of character and good behaviour from the Kehillah. The licence had to be renewed annually and could be revoked by the court if information were received that the applicant had practised usury or engaged in deceptive practices. Any Jewish business transacted without a licence and any mortgage received by an unlicensed Jew in the form of a note or in a commercial transaction, was declared null and void. The court was empowered to reduce, at its own discretion, any debt owed to an unlicensed Jew or to cancel it entirely if the debtor could prove that the debt originated in usury or unfair business practice.

Section three forbade Jews to settle in two departments of Alsace and they were not allowed to settle elsewhere in France unless they purchased land and engaged solely in agriculture. Exceptions to this rule would require special Imperial consent. Jews were not allowed to discharge their military service by proxy; every Jewish conscript had to serve in person. Finally, the ordinance provided that the restrictions should remain in force for ten years and expressed the hope that within that time "there will no longer exist any difference between them (the Jews) and the other citizens of our Empire." Should this not be so, the ordinance would continue in force for as long as the Emperor saw fit. From its inception, the ordinance did not apply to the Jews of Bordeaux and the two southern departments of Gironde and Landes (including the municipal area of Bayonne-St. Esprit) "since they have caused no complaints and engage in no forbidden practices."

On the pretext that it was reforming Jewish characteristics, Napoleon's régime employed these discriminatory decrees to abolish equality of rights for the Jews for the ensuing decade and possibly longer. The

73

Infamous Decree stunned the plutocratic spokesmen of French Jewry. But instead of a unified concerted protest by French Jews as a whole, their reaction took the form of a mad race by Jewish community leaders, each seeking to prove that the Jews of his respective department or city deserved exemption from the decree. Napoleon could certainly boast in having caused dissension rather than unity amongst the Jews. Even now they could think of him in terms of "Merciful King" or "Just King." Wealthy Jews from various departments, provinces, or countries even submitted petitions imploring that they and they alone be exempt because of their individual virtues.

On the whole, the Departmental Prefects showed a large measure of liberalism and understanding for the plight of the Jewish population. They not only replied to the questionnaire from the Ministry of the Interior on the proportion of Jews in agriculture, handicraft, and industry, the actual extent of Jewish usury, the proportion of Jews in the Army and, particularly, public school attendance by Jewish children. For the most part, they also honestly supported Jewish requests for exemption from the ordinance and sometimes even submitted memoranda to that effect on their own initiative. Some emphasized the economic harm inherent in the ordinance, pointed to the spread of Christian usury (in Lorraine), and expressed fear lest the ordinance interrupt the process of education and assimilation amongst the Jews. The fact that these officials could take up such a position was a reflection of the progress that had taken place amongst the enlightened section of the French population in its attitude towards the Jews since the Revolution's proclamation of Jewish enfranchisement.

On the basis of these reports and in response to the suggestion of his Minister of the Interior, Napoleon consented to exempt the Jews in a number of departments from the provisions of the decree; he was not in favour of exempting individuals or even single cities. By April 20, 1808, the Jews of Paris and the Department of the Seine were released from the decree. A few months later the Jews of Leghorn and the Pyrenees were treated likewise. On April 11, 1810, fifteen more departments, mostly in Italy and southern France, were exempted. In 1810, the Central Consistory informed the Minister of the Interior of the results of a poll which indicated the great advance made by the Jews in turning to productive employment, education, and military service. It humbly suggested that Jewish rehabilitation would be more successful if the decree of 1808 were rescinded. However, the Government was even unwilling to continue to make exemptions. By the end of Napoleon's rule, only twenty of the sixty-eight departments into which France and Italy were at that time divided (excluding Holland and the northern occupied territories) had been exempted from the terms of the decree. The situation can be seen more clearly in the context of a total of at least

79,000 Jews, of whom only 14,000, or one-sixth, had been exempted from the terms of the Infamous Decree.

The great majority of French Jewry was hard hit by the anti-Jewish laws. But the worst effects were felt by the Jews of Alsace-Lorraine. Many debtors completely ceased to make repayment of their debts to the Jewish moneylenders, on the basis of the decree. In the last resort, however, the main benefit from the provisions against Jewish usury was gained by Christian usurers, who could now press home their advantage. In some areas, they completely eliminated their Jewish competitors; in some cases they formed partnerships with Jews under the cover of a legal "firm." The licence provision in the decree mainly hit the Jewish poor, the petty traders and pedlars who now depended upon the approval of the municipal councils. In some towns of Alsace, beating drums called the population together to announce that anyone with a complaint against a Jew might present it to the municipal council. A municipal council could refuse a Jewish applicant the certificate needed to obtain his licence to trade on grounds of slander alone. In some towns in Alsace, Jewish tradesmen came to the city council with children and aged parents to plead for mercy, begging for the grant of a certificate. In most instances the municipal councils of the large cities responded favourably (at Strasbourg and Nancy approximately 90 per cent were granted), but the smaller towns indulged in harsher tactics either from competitive motives or from sheer hatred. Once again, the prefects' sense of decency was in evidence and in several cases they compelled the local authorities to issue the certificates, or even issued licences without the certificate of the municipal council.

The new Jewish bourgeoisie in metropolitan France and the Italian and German provinces of the Empire not only accepted Napoleon's decrees against the Jewish masses. They even threw themselves energetically into establishing the consistories which would place these masses under complete government surveillance. To feel that they had some share in the machinery of government was a source of some satisfaction; but voluntary surveillance over the Jewish population in the service of the police also gave the wealthy Jews the opportunity to achieve, through the machinery of government, a dominant influence over the Kehillot, so that they could mould them to their own class interests and draw them along in the advance towards assimilation. The Government appointed the three rabbis who had been members of the Presidium of the *Grand Sanhedrin* to the Central Consistory: Sinzheim, Segre, and Cologna, and also Baruch Cerf-Berr and Jacob Lazard. The local consistories, each of which included three laymen and one rabbi (though the law called for two rabbis), were elected by dignitaries appointed by the prefects but subject to the approval of the Central Consistory in agreement with the Minister for Religions. When any unpropertied Jew obtained a place amongst the consistory electorate, the Central Consistory nullified the appointment. Therefore, it was obviously impossible for a member of what the Central Consistory designated "the most inferior classes" to be elected to the provincial consistories.

Actually, the Central Consistory never issued a directive to the Kehillot without first consulting the Ministry, nor did the departmental consistories make a decision without the agreement of the prefects. The satisfaction of the Central Consistory was only marred by the Government's refusal to allow the Imperial eagle to be stamped on its official documents (it had to be content with the heading *Religion—Fatherland*). Moreover, Napoleon treated it with contempt and did not invite it to participate in public celebrations.

Seven consistories were organized in France itself, six in the German provinces of the Empire, five in Italy, and four in Holland. The consistories appointed "supervisory Commissioners" in every Kehillah within their departmental jurisdiction. Initially, the consistories did not carry on any educational or welfare activity at all, both because of the shortage of funds and because the governmental authorities were unwilling to increase the monetary burden of the Kehillot, which maintained the consistory apparatus. Only in 1812 did the Minister of the Interior agree to allow the consistories to establish elementary schools for Jewish children at Kehillah expense. Even though Christian schools were maintained by the State, the Central Consistory was overwhelmed with gratitude to the Minister for "his paternal solicitude."

The educational activity of the consistories began after 1815. During the Napoleonic period, their only positive actions comprised occasional protests made by the Central Consistory to the authorities, condemning anti-Jewish propaganda in the press and on the stage. Unsuccessful objections were also made to the administering of oaths *More Judaico* in several departments, particularly Alsace-Lorraine, the German Rhineland cities, and Italy, where law courts had reverted to pre-revolutionary medieval practice in litigation involving Jews. The Jew was not given the same oath as other citizens. Instead, an oath was sworn in the synagogue by a special ritual, with a repetition of all the curses and vilifications incurred by a false oath. Even in this matter, the Central Consistory hardly dared invoke the principle of civil equality in its protest to the Government. Instead, it cited religious reasons for its protest and called upon the rabbis to refuse to conduct the ritual of administering the oath in such circumstances, since it desecrated the Jewish religion.

Apart from occasional intervention against affronts to Jews, the energies of the consistories were taken up in the main with changing the Jews into loyal citizens of the state and into Frenchmen of the Mosaic persuasion. The Central Consistory published regular instructions about the recruitment of young men for military service, the observance of the anti-British boycott, participation in patriotic celebrations, and so on. The consistories zealously pursued the task of *closing down* synagogues, houses for religious studies, and prayer houses; and in this they were supported by the authorities. The object of this exercise was to secure the financial status of the modern, recently opened temples of worship and to do away with the old religious way of life that tended to arrest assimilation. The Central Consistory even gave the local consistories express authority to summon police assistance "to disperse the clandestine communal prayer assemblies."

The consistories mark an unhappy episode in the chronicles of French Jewry, with their campaign against the Jewish poor which delivered them into the hands of the authorities. The Central Consistory even issued a circular letter, dated November 14, 1808, offering Jews a last chance to repudiate "this wretched solidarity which has lain upon us like a heavy burden for so many centuries." Several consistories attempted to rid themselves of itinerant beggars by prohibiting *pletn* (lodging coupons) for Jews possessing no passports (at Krefeld, Metz); elsewhere, at Wintzenheim for example, the use of *pletn* was prohibited and in general, taking in lodgers overnight. But the Paris Consistory went even further: it proposed to the Prefect that he issue an order forbidding any Jew to stay in the capital without a Consistory permit. The Prefect willingly agreed to this request and in 1812 the Consistory submitted a list of thirty Jews "of no discernible sources of livelihood, who must be expelled from the country . . ." Thus, the consistories most adequately supplemented both Napoleon's policy of forced assimilation for the Jews and his methods of policing the Jewish masses.

CHAPTER FOUR

HOLLAND

On the Eve of the Revolution, 1795

The tiny state of Holland was the richest country in the world in the second half of the eighteenth century. The Dutch Jewish community formed a larger proportion of the general population than anywhere else in western Europe. This community was also distinguished for its vital and colourful culture and communal life. The unceasing flow of Jews from central and eastern Europe had prevented Dutch Jewry from congealing into the pattern of time-hallowed orthodoxy, as had happened with the Jewish community of Alsace-Lorraine. Furthermore, unlike English Jewry with its predominantly immigrant element, Dutch Jewry was firmly rooted in Holland and concentrated in number, and was thus able to develop its own creative culture. Living in close contact with the highly developed culture of western Europe, the Sephardi Jews of Holland found, as did the Italian Jews too, conditions which were propitious for the existence and development of their rich cultural heritage of medieval Spanish origin. Here too, among the German and Polish-Lithuanian Jews, a new secular culture and a previously unknown way of life grew up.

Towards the end of the eighteenth century, Jews in Holland, according to official estimates, numbered about 50,000, representing over 2 per cent of the country's total population. Nearly half, about 24,000, lived in the metropolis of Amsterdam, where they formed over one-tenth of the city's population. No sizeable Jewish communities existed outside Amsterdam with the exception of Rotterdam (over 3,000 in 1810) and The Hague (over 2,600 in 1810). The Sephardi, or Portuguese, Jews, who pioneered the Jewish community in Holland at the beginning of the seventeenth century, still represented one-tenth of all Jews in Amsterdam and The Hague at the end of the eighteenth century. In the provincial towns, there were only a few scattered groups of Sephardim.

The economic activity of the Jews in Holland, as in all Europe at that time, was directly conditioned by the country's economic development and their own legal status, in itself a consequence of the social and political régime. Despite increasing indications of decline, Holland in the closing years of the eighteenth century, was still the world's richest country in proportion to its population. Its national capital in 1795 had risen to 3,000 million guilders for a population of 2 million. Amsterdam still conducted a large-scale sea-borne trade, twice that of London, and supplied all Europe with aromatics, spices, tea, coffee, and other colonial products. Through its commerce, Holland maintained lines of communication between eastern and western, northern and southern Europe. Amsterdam, with its commodities and stock markets, was the broker for world trade; the local finance market was the European credit centre for both private banks and government bond issues.

Jewish capital took a prominent part in Dutch banking and commerce at that time. The Sephardi Jews showed particular skill in overseas trade and stock manipulations. During the eighteenth century, approximately a quarter of all shareholders in the Dutch East India Company were Jews, though their invested capital was on the average considerably smaller than that of the other shareholders. Jews were similarly quite well represented in the Dutch West Indies Company, as the Sephardi Jews could call on their connections in Jamaica, Barbados, Surinam and Brazil. As a result of these traditional business links, the Sephardi Jews of Amsterdam also dominated a large portion of the trade with southern European countries, France, Portugal, Italy, and Turkey and with North Africa and the Near East (the Levant trade). In industry, on the other hand, especially the production of silk, tobacco, and sugar—industries in which the Sephardi Jews had played a pioneering role in the seventeenth century—their share in the eighteenth was much reduced. This came about because of the general decline in industrial development in contrast to the rise of banking and commerce, and also because of restrictions imposed by the guilds (in the silk industry). As opposed to this the Jewish share in the tobacco trade outside Amsterdam (at Amersfoort) had considerably increased and hundreds of Jewish families were also engaged in the diamond trade. A large number of Jews was employed in diamond polishing, despite a temporary ban by the city authorities.

The wealthy Sephardi Jews, descendants of the Jewish merchants who had left Portugal, mainly engaged in commerce and stockbroking, whereas the wealthy Ashkenazim of Amsterdam—with their tradition of credit dealings—dealt for the most part in finance and promissory notes.

But the great bankers, stock-market speculators, and official stock-exchange brokers only formed the thin upper crust of Dutch Jewry. It was this plutocratic élite which enjoyed complete economic liberty and had achieved social prominence. The legal restrictions imposed on the great majority of the Jewish population were so severe up to the Revolution, that there were few sources of livelihood left open to them. It is true that the legal status of the Jews in Holland was incomparably better than in other European countries. They were not burdened with special Jewish tax levies, nor forced to live in ghettos. However, they were severely limited in the economic field. They did not even possess the right to settle unreservedly in all parts of the country. There were cities where Jews were not permitted to live, and others where their right of domicile was confined to certain quarters. In many cities, the right of domicile was only granted to a few Jewish families by special dispensation of the municipal council and for a given fee payable by all new citizens. Jews were not eligible for public office and not permitted to practise law. Even Jewish surgeons were periodically forbidden to treat Christian patients. Jews were not accepted at any schools apart from the medical faculties of the universities.

The Jewish population was most affected by the restrictions in commerce and in the crafts. In the provincial towns, where the Jews enjoyed "secondary" rights of citizenship (with limitations), all the guilds were closed to them except the shop-keepers' guild. This guild allowed them to keep their stores open to all customers, but prohibited them from selling certain commodities (e.g. wine and other beverages).

The limitations on Jewish economic activity in Amsterdam were more severe than in the provincial towns. As early as 1632, the Burgomaster of Amsterdam published an order prohibiting the pursuit of "civil callings" even by those Jews who had acquired upon payment of a fee the status of burghers (*poorters*). The municipal laws permitted Jews to engage in addition to wholesale trade in any occupation related to religion or *Kashrut* (the preparation of ritually edible foodstuffs). They had the right to print and sell sacred writings, to slaughter cattle and poultry, to sell meat, and to keep spice shops. Jews in Amsterdam were also allowed to keep pharmacies and to peddle old clothes on the streets. A maximum of fifty stockbrokers' licences could be issued to Amsterdam Jews, according to a law enacted in 1760; at Rotterdam, Jews were totally barred from this profession.

The patricians of Amsterdam and other cities complied with the demands that the craft guilds made at the expense of the Jews. Similarly, they established monopolies for the merchants and middle-class store-keepers of the dominant Calvinist faith. The fact that the Jews of Holland were legally royal subjects and enjoyed undisputed religious liberty only brought the lowly economic status of the Jewish masses into sharper relief. The legal and social status of the Jewish capitalists in this highly developed capitalist country was in marked contrast to the restricted economic activity allowed to the poverty-stricken.

In actual fact, and despite the ban, by the end of the eighteenth century there were numerous Jewish craftsmen in Amsterdam. Jewish tailors worked on the pretext that they were repairing old clothes for resale; cobblers, saddlers, watchmakers, and even blacksmiths unobtrusively pursued their crafts. The great majority of the ordinary Jews of Amsterdam, however, depended on all kinds of insecure occupations and earned less than a pittance. Their most common source of livelihood was peddling and street barter. In fact, their position was so desperate that the Jews of Amsterdam were prepared to enter a profession entirely foreign to Jewish economic tradition and way of life: in 1782, during the war with Britain, the Dutch East Indies Company consented to employ

Jews as seamen. By a special agreement between representatives of the Ashkenazi Kehillot and the Company, the Jewish sailors were promised every opportunity to observe their religious and dietary laws, to keep the Sabbath and the Holy days, and to pray (for half an hour after sunset and before sunrise). The agreement even went into detail: they were forbidden to shave with a barber's razor. Married seamen were also required formally to divorce their wives, lest disasters at sea or in foreign ports reduced the latter to the status of deserted wives.

During the economic and political crises of the last third of the eighteenth century Holland's economic position continued to deteriorate. The crisis of 1772-73, which came immediately after the collapse of the English East India Company, upset the Dutch currency market for a long time: a large amount, some 40 million guilders, of Dutch capital, was invested in the British company. Furthermore, the war against England between 1780 (before the American War of Independence had ended) and 1784, affected Holland's position in the West Indies trade. Because of its particular economic structure, the Jewish population was more severely affected by these disturbances than the general population. Some Jews who lost their capital emigrated to London, others to North America and to Surinam (Dutch Guiana). Jews in a less favourable position did not even have this alternative, for the West Indies Company would not issue them passports. Local municipal councils even obstructed the exodus of some Amsterdam Jews to the provinces. The poverty of the Jewish masses in Amsterdam increased so greatly that it moved public and Dutch Government agencies to make gestures of generosity. When an unusually cold spell during the winter of 1773-74 added to the difficulties of the severe economic crisis, Christian individuals and a Christian philanthropic society allotted several thousand guilders to the Jewish poor. The municipal council allotted a total of 8,500 guilders for the same purpose with express instructions that part of the sum be used to purchase clothing for Jews who were roaming the streets clad in rags. The crisis of 1784 also impoverished the Sephardi Kehillah of Amsterdam and the Stathouder contributed 18,000 guilders—the equivalent of his salary as Director of the Dutch East Indies Company—to the Kehillah poor. According to an estimate derived from documents of 1799 the percentage of poor in proportion to membership in the large Ashkenazi Kehillah of Amsterdam was one and one-half times greater than in the Sephardi Kehillah.

The great majority of Dutch Jews, who hardly earned a living wage, had no representation whatsoever in the Kehillot. The administrative system of the Kehillot was based on the same plutocratic and oligarchical principles as the city administrations of Holland at the dawn of capitalism. Seven *Parnassim* stood at the head of the Amsterdam Ashkenazi Kehillah, each holding office for two years, so that only three or four were elected annually. The *Parnassim* were elected by seven arbitrators from a list of candidates submitted by the outgoing *Parnassim*. The arbitrators were chosen by lot at an assembly of those Kehillah members who donated at least 2.10 guilders annually for philanthropic purposes. A candidate for the office of *Parnass* was required to have paid an annual charity tax of at least twenty-five guilders. The treasurer of the charitable funds and the treasurers of all other committees came under the authority of the *Parnass*. The Kehillah bye-laws were passed at a meeting of past and present *Parnassim*. This system, introduced in 1639, placed all power in the hands of a group of the wealthiest Jewish families of the city. In almost every particular, this situation paralleled the administrative organization of the city of Amsterdam. The provincial Kehillot were organized on the same undemocratic model.

In both Amsterdam and the provincial towns, the Kehillot were entirely under the supervision of the municipal councils. No bye-laws were valid without the confirmation of the municipal authorities, even those of societies that fell under the strict supervision of the Kehillah. The municipal authorities reciprocated by supporting Kehillah leaders against internal opposition, and endorsed the congregational tax system even when it was based on undisguised exploitation of the unpropertied masses. Common or similar class interests promoted harmonious co-operation between Kehillah and *Poorter* (Burgher) Councils in Amsterdam and all the provincial towns.

This identity of interests of the municipal authorities and the leaders of the Kehillah régime accounted for the loyalty that the latter showed to the Stathouder and the Orange Party of the nobility. When the Patriots' Rebellion broke out in 1787, the *Parnassim* preached Jewish neutrality in all synagogues. Actually, however, the Jewish plutocracy was entirely in sympathy with the reigning dynasty and its régime. Community of economic interests grew stronger in face of external political events in the civil war. Prussia and England, where Dutch-Jewish bankers had invested heavily, supported the house of Orange. The marginal elements of the Dutch population, even some working-men, dockworkers, and unskilled labourers in town and country, had been won over by the philanthropic gestures of the Prince of Orange and unhesitatingly rallied to his side (they were known as *Bjeltjes*, or "The Fishing Rods"). In the same way, the Orange Party was solidly established amongst the Jewish poor of Amsterdam. In one instance, Jewish working-men intervened actively: they repelled an assault by the Patriots on the building of the deputy mayor. This incident enraged the Patriots, and lower middle class elements from amongst their ranks voiced open antagonism towards the Jews. The *Parnassim* of both Kehillot actually posted guards around the Jewish quarters, but no attacks were made. However, one of the most important Patriot journals reproached the Jews for their policy and described it as both contradictory to Jewish tradition (the wrath of the Lord against Saul, first King of Israel!) and as unwarranted ingratitude towards the revolutionaries, in view of the bondage suffered by Jews under monarchies. It is equally true, that this same journal warned its readers against the exaggeration that "not more than ten per cent of all the Jews are preaching the Patriots' cause." It noted that Jews in the Orange Party comprised the rich Ashkenazim and Sephardim, allies of the nobility, on the one hand, and, on the other, many poor Jews, swayed by a malicious rumour of the Orange party that the Patriots intended to expel the Jews from the city. Nevertheless, bitterness against Jews in general remained alive amongst the Patriots; one of them wrote to France (as early as 1794) of his party's "burning desire" to avenge itself.

After the Patriots' Rebellion had been quelled by Prussian forces in the autumn of 1787, the *Parnassim* of both Kehillot paid visits to Prince William V, now restored to authority. At the City Hall, they took the same oath of allegiance to the old constitution as the city leaders.

Dutch Jewry made a unique contribution to Jewish culture in the period of transition before the turn of the century. With the decline in Holland's economic and political position its once flourishing culture also began to wilt. Similarly, the day had long since passed when the pioneers of the Dutch-Jewish community had won universal renown with works of philosophy and critical thought and enriched Jewish poetry and drama with original creations and translations in Hebrew, Spanish, Portuguese, and Dutch. The increasing linguistic assimilation of the wealthy and enlightened classes of the Sephardi community to a large extent inhibited creative activity. By 1791-93, a complete translation of the prayer book according to the Sephardi ritual had appeared in Dutch. But some remnants of the golden age still remained. In the Sephardi rabbinical colleges and elementary religious schools, the old method of instruction was still employed; Sephardi rabbis were still publishing theoretical discourses on the religious law; and the poet, David Franco Mendes, wrote *Responsa* for the *Etz Hayim* Rabbinical College. The Portuguese Jews in Holland still maintained a Spanish theatre during the second half of the eighteenth century and also held frequent musical soirées in private houses. The deep-seated tradition of writing poems in Hebrew remained alive among the Sephardim, to such an extent that rabbis even set their *Haskamot* (approbations) to authoritative rabbinical works in metre. There was no need here for the *Haskalah* movement to encourage the revival of the Hebrew language. Its function was to disseminate its ideas more widely and to seek adherents from the new, enlightened stratum of art patrons, readers, and writers that had grown up amongst the Ashkenazim. An organized circle of Hebrew writers was formed around David Franco Mendes, author of a play, *Gemul Atalyah*, which was a free arrangement of a work by Racine. The group called itself *Mikra Kodesh*—The Holy Convocation. Another central figure in *Haskalah* circles was Solomon Dubno, Moses Mendelssohn's assistant, who had settled in Amsterdam after Mendelssohn's death. A woman also gained a reputation as a composer of Hebrew poems: Dinah, wife of the Ashkenazi rabbi of the Hague, Saul Halevi. In philosophy, Naphtali Hirsch Ullmann, author of the work *Hokhmat Ha-shorashim* (The Science of Radicals), was noted for his application of the system of the German philosopher Wolff. His work was published at the Hague, where the writings on problems of hygiene and mathematics by the Russian *Maskil*, Baruch of Shklov, were also printed. However, Dutch Jewry's most original field of creative activity during that period was not Hebrew literature. For all its wide diffusion, the movement in Holland never attained the stature of the *Haskalah* centre in Germany. It was remarkable rather for its folk-literature and theatrical art in Yiddish.

Amsterdam was then the largest Jewish community in Europe and, indeed, in the world. It also housed the largest urban community of Yiddish-speaking Jews. The German Jews provided the dominant dialect in Dutch Yiddish and, though corrupted by "Dutchisms," it had lost none of its succulence, elasticity, and homeliness, and retained a vast number of Hebrew words and expressions. Jewish Amsterdam was a miniature forerunner of the Jewish community which was to grow up in New York at the beginning of the twentieth century: a concentration of Yiddish-speaking people following a Jewish way of life in the turbulent metropolitan environment of a commercial centre.

The Jewish population of Amsterdam lived and toiled in the crowded, congested Jewish quarter of the city. Its thirst for knowledge appeared primarily in its curiosity about the important events in the Kehillah in the country as a whole, and in the world outside. This interest was met by the publication of pamphlets, leaflets and songs, giving serious accounts of even the more sensational events, often accompanied by a moral. It supplied information on dramatic occurrences in local Jewish life with epigrams, humour and satire. The chronicles which covered longer periods of time were more enduring and historically quite important, e.g. the writings of Zalman ben Moshe Printz, a barrel hooper by trade. The events that followed the outbreak of revolution in Holland brought a marked increase in popular interest in current affairs, drew the masses into political activity and involved them in the party struggle within the Kehillah and throughout the country. Apart from political pamphlets and songs, the Jewish liberal group published a weekly journal, the *Discours*, which was more than a mere revival of the first Yiddish-language periodical, the seventeenth-century *Kurant*. The *Discours*, published during 1797–98, heralded serious political journalism in Yiddish.

The folk literature in Yiddish which reflected the natural quest of the people for gaiety, entertainment, and light-hearted inspiration was richer than the news sheets and political publications. The *Purim Kurant* was a typical example. They were printed under such headings as *Kuntres* (pamphlets), *Almanach*, and *Purim Lied* (Purim Song), circulated at Purim and sung or even dramatized. They reached a wide audience of the ordinary people with their good-humoured satire of the lives of the poorest of the poor. Their popular appeal was so strong that they were still read by the working-men of the fish-market at the beginning of the nineteenth century, when linguistic assimilation was already putting an end to the popular, carnival-like Purim celebrations. Hayim Joseph David Azulai, the emissary from Palestine, visited Amsterdam in 1778, and reported that these celebrations lasted a whole week and captivated the entire city with street-dancing, Purim plays, and general merry-making. Injunctions were regularly issued by orthodox *Parnassim* against play-houses, dance-halls, and comedians, but the young people still spent their Saturday nights merrily dancing to the calls of the master of ceremonies or the tunes of an orchestra and listening to the rhymesters (*Badhanim*). Auditions for posts of cantors and bass singers held in the synagogues, especially the Great Synagogue (*Beit Ha-Knesset Ha-Gadol*), were an important event which constituted a major celebration for the Jewish population.

In the 1780's, the original Purim plays developed into a permanent Yiddish theatre, directed by Jacob Dessauer, with a large company and orchestra. The group continued to perform until the 1830's, but the assimilationist programme of the Jewish consistories under Napoleon had deprived it of its original character and aims long before. In 1808, German replaced Yiddish as the language employed and ten years later all performances were given in Dutch. With enfranchisement, the lively and creative cultural life of the Jews in Holland was slowly stifled by the deliberate action of the representatives of the Jewish bourgeoisie. Their goal was the linguistic and cultural assimilation of what had been a magnificent Jewish community.

The Batavian Republic and the Struggle for Enfranchisement

On January 18, 1795, the Revolution, engineered by the Patriots with the help of the French Army, broke out in Holland. On January 29, the Prince escaped to England and the Batavian Republic was proclaimed. The same month, the "Provisional Representatives of the People of Holland" published *The Rights of Man and the Citizen*, which, like the French *Declaration of the Rights of Man*, promised equality and freedom of religion to all inhabitants. On February 6, a group of Jewish intellectuals organized the *Felix Libertate* Society, on the pattern of Patriot Clubs which had been founded in Amsterdam and throughout the country, to disseminate the ideals of "liberty and equality." The founders of the Society set themselves the special task of propagating revolutionary ideals and encouraging the pursuit of enlightenment amongst the Jews. But the establishment of a *separate* club of this type must certainly have been occasioned by the fact that the atmosphere in the Patriot Clubs of

Amsterdam was still unfriendly towards the Jews. The leaders of the Society were the merchant Moses Solomon Asser, his son Karl, later to become a lawyer, Hertz (Hermann) Bromet, Dr. Hartog de Lemon and Jacob Saportas, a banker and one of the few Sephardi Jews in the Society. An important role was also played by the mathematician Judah Littwack, and the Hebrew-German writer David Friedrichsfeld. The Society very soon formed links with the other Patriot clubs in the city, the Revolutionary Committee, the municipality and the French military authorities. On March 11, it participated in a patriotic demonstration when the Liberty Tree was planted in front of the City Hall in the presence of government representatives and all the Patriot Societies of Amsterdam. On this occasion, Judah Littwack delivered a speech in Hebrew and in Dutch. The celebration marked the first act of fraternization between the Jews of Holland and the Dutch people.

The small but active *Felix Libertate* group met immediate and obdurate opposition from the Kehillah leaders as soon as it started to propagate revolutionary ideas among the Jewish masses in Holland. The attitude of the Kehillah leaders towards the Revolution and the struggle for Jewish rights was the result of the unique position of the Jewish bourgeoisie in Holland. In France and in other countries where most of the Jewish bourgeoisie had possessed no rights under the old régime, their representatives hastened to secure their own interests by embarking on a campaign for general Jewish enfranchisement as soon as Revolution broke out. In Holland, under the house of Orange, in contrast, the Jewish plutocracy and the upper ranks of the Jewish middle class had enjoyed a wide range of economic privileges. These classes not only saw no need to ally themselves with the Revolution; they actually hoped for its failure— as in the Patriot Rebellion of 1787. The triumph of the Revolution would make the new republic dependent on France and also entail war with England; and the Jewish bankers and trading magnates had numerous economic connections with England. They also quite rightly anticipated that defeat in the war against England would signify the end of Dutch colonial rule, in which they also had a large share. Hence the aristocratic Sephardim were entirely opposed to the Revolution. For the same reasons, the *Parnassim*, Kehillah treasurers, and rabbis of the Ashkenazi community, the representatives of its plutocracy, and the bulk of the Jewish middle class were far from sympathetic to the Revolution. They were not interested in the fact that the mass of Jews in Holland lacked all rights and suffered from the severe restrictions on small trade and craft. On the contrary, the élite were fighting for their very existence against a new order which would abolish the Kehillah régime and thus put an end to their oligarchy and their dominant position within the Jewish community. What they were defending, in the name of religious conservatism and concern for the continued existence of traditional Judaism, was the feudal plutocratic régime in general, and in particular their own preferential status amongst their fellow Jews and the control they exercised over Jewish life.

The numerically small but enterprising membership of *Felix Libertate* represented diametrically opposed interests and therefore adopted an opposite political position. They were the Jewish avant-garde of the Patriot movement, which was turning its attention to the development of modern industrial capitalism at the expense of Holland's moribund mercantilism. The Jews who belonged to *Felix Libertate* represented the economic interests of wider Jewish bourgeois circles and these interests were identical with those of the modern bourgeoisie. This may also explain why the Jewish middle class in the provincial towns (whose incomes came mainly from domestic rather than colonial trade or banking and the stock-exchange) displayed more sympathy for the activities of the Jewish club than members of the same class in Amsterdam. However, the Jewish Patriots were mainly concerned with the importance of the Revolution in regard to the legal and political status of the Jewish middle class and the Jewish population as a whole. The Revolution in Holland destroyed what remained of the nobility's supremacy over the peasants together with government by the urban aristocracy. It also aimed to abolish the craft guilds; this was finally achieved in 1798. The members of *Felix Libertate* hoped that, as in France, the new régime would bring enfranchisement to the Jewish population as a corollary of the principle that all citizens were equal. This equality of rights was as vital a necessity for the Jewish masses as for the middle class and the intellectuals who comprised the membership of the Jewish club. However, the backward condition of the Jewish populace made it difficult for the club to recruit adherents from amongst the masses. It gradually began to move openly towards a programme of assimilation identical with that of the enfranchised Jewish bourgeoisie in France. In so doing, it drew even further away from the mass of the people who clung instinctively to their language, culture and tradition.

The activities of *Felix Libertate* within the Jewish community met spirited opposition from the Kehillah leaders, despite the fact that the Jewish revolutionaries used Yiddish in their propaganda and swore that as good Jews it was far from their intention to destroy the faith and customs they believed in. The Society's energies were therefore devoted even more to the external task of achieving Jewish civil emancipation. In Amsterdam, more than anywhere else in Holland, the Dutch lower middle class, which made up the bulk of the triumphant Patriot movement, stubbornly resisted any step leading to Jewish enfranchisement. They were so afraid of competition in trades and crafts that they compounded a strange collection of arguments ranging from extreme republican, democratic slogans to demands for the retention of craft guild monopolies. Unlike the Hague, Groningen, Leiden, and Amersfoort, where Jews were accepted in the National Guard and even commissioned as officers, the municipality of Amsterdam, under pressure from the Quarters, rejected a *Felix Libertate* petition that Jews be allowed to serve in the National Guard companies of the city. Similar lack of success characterized attempts by *Felix Libertate* to obtain Jewish participation in the Amsterdam Quarter Assemblies, which had been organized on the pattern of the Paris Sections at the time of the French Revolution. A speech by Saportas in one of the Quarters for a time aroused great enthusiasm but his proposal was still rejected by a large majority. Other Quarter assemblies adopted resolutions expressly opposed to pedlars and the curtailment of craft guild privileges. Here again, the provincial towns proved more liberal than Amsterdam; the Jews there took part in Quarter assemblies without restrictions.

While the debates at Club meetings and the quarter assemblies continued, a stormy discussion had developed in the Dutch press and current political literature over the issue of Jewish enfranchisement. Not even the opposition denied that in principle the Jews deserved to enjoy *human* rights. The controversy concerned the question of *civil* rights: the equality of *political* rights. Professor W. H. van Swinden led the anti-Jewish school. His pamphlet, *Advice to the People's Representatives*, concentrated mainly on the claim that the Jews in the country were aliens because of their origin, character, and history; they even regarded themselves as such, as was seen in their continued belief in the coming of the Messiah and the Return to Zion. The most impressive literary efforts on behalf of Jewish enfranchisement included pamphlets by W. A. van Bloomendaal on *The Right of the Jews to Vote*, and J. Krap—*The Jews are our Brother Citizens*.

In no other country where the question of Jewish enfranchisement came to the fore was the argument drawn from their belief in the coming of the Messiah so frequently, so systematically and so persistently hurled at the Jews as in Holland. On the other hand, here, as elsewhere, it was merely a rationalization to cloak political conservatism and the lower middle class fear of competition. The exceptional persistence with which the argument was produced probably arose from the fact that the Jews of Holland at the time of the Revolution were distinguished more than any other western European Jewish community by their marked national culture and their particularly Jewish way of life. The sectarian orthodoxy of the Dutch people, more pronounced than in neighbouring countries, was undoubtedly a contributory factor. The thesis that Jewish Messianism was directly opposed to the belief in Christ as the Messiah had therefore more meaning for the petty bourgeois masses here than in other countries. *Felix Libertate*, in its enlightenment activities both amongst Jews and abroad through articles and pamphlets by Jewish and non-Jewish members, could not remain silent, still less ignore, its opponents' arguments on this issue. An active member, the Maskil David Friedrichsfeld, published a pamphlet, *The Jewish Messiah, or Republican Senti-*

ments Toward Him. In answer to the claim that Jews were not Dutch-men, he wrote: "Every right thinking man knows that the Jews of our day are a religious sect and not a people." The belief in the Messiah was one of the articles of faith that had no connection with practical existence. In their attitude towards the belief in the Messiah, Jews were divided into three classes: the heterodox, who believed only in a rationalistic, deistic religion; those whose creed was intermediate between heterodoxy and orthodoxy, interpreting the Bible poetically and explaining the prophecies concerning the Messiah as the gospel of statesmen on general reforms in divine worship of which Zion and Jerusalem were but poetic symbols; the orthodox, from whose patriotism not even their belief in the Messiah detracted. Friedrichsfeld illustrated his argument with a parable. "If my house catches fire in the middle of April," he asked, "shall I then not quench the flames because on the first of May I repair to another?" The main point, he contended, was that the Messianic ideal, as described in the book of Isaiah and the Talmud, did not conflict with republicanism, in the same way as it did not inhibit Isaac Abrabanel, "one of the greatest of democrats," in his opposition to princes and the very institution of princedom. The Messianic ideal, wrote Friedrichsfeld, meant popular rule based on liberty, equality, and fraternity. He also drew a parallel between the majority of the Jews, who had not returned to Palestine at the time of the Biblical Restoration of Zion, but had remained in Spain and Portugal whither they had emigrated from Tyre (according to Joseph Flavius), and the French Protestants abroad, who did not return to France after the revocation of the Edict of Nantes in 1685.

Thus, ten years before the Assembly of Jewish Notables in Paris, an eminent and enlightened member of Dutch Jewry not only repudiated the religious dogma that was attached to the concept of Messianic redemption but was proclaiming beliefs which entirely abandoned the historic aspirations of the Jewish people to return to their ancient homeland. And he was openly declaring that the Jews had ceased to be a nation and were merely a religious sect. Future years proved conclusively that this was in fact the attitude of the forerunners of the modern Jewish middle class in Holland, organized in *Felix Libertate*. Shortly afterwards they vociferously demanded complete assimilation with the Dutch people—religious faith alone excepted.

The fundamental tragedy of the Jewish masses in Holland, as in all the other countries where Jews were enfranchised, was that they had to choose between loyalty to the *Parnassim* and the rabbis on the one hand, and to the representative of the new Jewish middle class on the other. The *Parnassim* and rabbis did defend the traditional Jewish creed and Jewish national individuality but they also defended feudal reaction in Jewish life and in society in general. The representatives of the modern bourgeoisie fought for progressive reforms in Jewish life but at the same time persistently voiced their desire for assimilation. A typical example of this attitude was a poem *To the Free Jews* signed "Judaeus Batavus." Its closing stanza proclaimed:

> *Thus she [the goddess of Liberty] to us doth call,*
> *Hearken ye then to her voice!*
> *Amsterdam, be thou Jerusalem!*
> *Her law, be thy Messiah!*
> *Justice and Honour, be ye twain the Temple!*
> *Truth, be Thou the Holy Torah!*

Only the verse form of these sentiments was original. Some three years earlier on April 3, 1792, a contemporary, Samuel Halevi (who dubbed himself "Exilarch, Leader-in-Chief of all the Synagogues of East and West") had published an open letter to the same effect in the *Chronique de Paris* and dedicated it to the renowned revolutionary, Anacharsis Clautus (Cloots). It referred to: "France, who first wiped out the disgrace of Judah and broke the shackles of all the captives, she is our Land of Israel; her mountains—our Zion; her rivers—our Jordan . . ." Universal features can therefore be found not only in the intellectual formula for assimilation but even in its extreme manifestations.

Debate in the National Assembly and Jewish Enfranchisement

Elections to the National Assembly of the Batavian Republic were held at the beginning of 1796. Though Jews in all localities were entitled to participate in these elections, not one Jewish candidate was elected, even in Amsterdam. Only very few Jews took part because of inadequate electioneering arrangements; altogether thirteen Jewish arbitrators were chosen, whereas thirty were required to elect one deputy. Since the clubs did not have the right to submit petitions, six members of *Felix Libertate* sent a memorandum on Jewish enfranchisement to the National Assembly. It asserted that the Jews had already been recognized *de facto* as citizens of the Republic, since they had voted in the elections; they were now requesting the opportunity fully to enjoy their rights without impediment. The men responsible for this petition had no authorization from the Kehillot, but the Jews of Amsterdam possessed sufficient political wisdom not to interfere. An attempt by a small group of *Parnassim* to collect signatures for a counter-petition, and to intercede with some of the deputies to the National Assembly yielded no results.

On March 29, 1796, the memorandum was read at a session of the National Assembly. Some claims were made that the matter should not be discussed. One deputy, van Hoof, took the opportunity to declare that the Jews were a separate nationality living temporarily in Holland and that their real homeland was Palestine. Nevertheless, a majority vote decided to elect a Committee of Eight to prepare a report. This report was read at the plenary session on August 1. The Committee proposed full enfranchisement, equal rights and equal duties for "those who are called Netherland Jews," on the grounds that they were part of the Dutch people and by virtue of the principle that Batavian civil rights did not depend upon religion. On August 5, the National Assembly decided on the separation of Church and State, thus removing all obstacles to a discussion of the Committee's Report on the Jewish question. However, the debate on the report went on for eight consecutive days, August 22 to August 30; 34 out of a total of 126 deputies took part.

The atmosphere during the Dutch National Assembly's debate on Jewish enfranchisement was more favourable towards the Jews than it had been seven years earlier in the National Assembly of Revolutionary France. No echo of vindictiveness or hate appeared in the speeches. On the contrary, they were moderate and, on the whole, composed both in tenor and content. And this was not only because the opponents of enfranchisement could not exploit the argument of Jewish usury to stir up discord. Even before the debate, the Jews of Holland had been treated with religious tolerance and formally recognized as subjects and, to some extent, as burghers. They had acquired additional rights after the outbreak of the Revolution and had participated in the elections. Enfranchisement was therefore in essence only a formal acknowledgement of existing facts. Furthermore, French pressure and French demands for the establishment of a political régime based on civil equality before the law could not be ignored. Not even the opponents of Jewish enfranchisement dared deny the principle of Jewish rights. For the most part, they resorted to delaying tactics: proposals that the issue be returned to the Constitutional Committee, or that the scope of enfranchisement be reduced to the minimum. With that in view, some deputies proposed that the franchise be extended only to those individual Jews who regarded themselves as part of the Dutch people and repudiated the separate Jewish laws, which they identified with the Kehillah and Kehillah legal autonomy. In one respect, they faced an easier task than the opponents of Jewish enfranchisement in France. They could and repeatedly did employ the argument that the Jews themselves were by no means eager for enfranchisement—except for a small group unauthorized to speak on behalf of the entire people. Some deputies did discuss the negative qualities of the Jews, such as their pride and their antagonism towards gentiles. One of them, van Hoorn, even criticized their greed for money (in the face of their widespread destitution and poverty!) But the main argument was the separatism and the alien character of the Jews, based on their individuality as a national group and their hopes of a return to the Land of Israel in the days of the Messiah.

The protagonists of Jewish enfranchisement were led by Deputy Jacob Hahn, a leader of the Patriot movement. They concentrated mainly on convincing the opposition that the Jews did not constitute a separate people but were a religious sect. Some deputies accused the *Parnassim* and the "theologians" of using their own laws to force separatism upon the Jews in order to slake their own thirst for power—an argument already used by the municipalities of the old régime. Deputy Vonck asked how it was that Frenchmen and Italians who had lived in the country for a year could become Batavian citizens, whereas the Jews, "who have lived in our midst these two hundred years, who helped introduce great sums of capital and commercial traffic to our country ... they who achieved greatness with its success and sustained losses when it failed ... shall these people be considered aliens?" Supporters of the Jews did not deny that the Jews believed in the Messiah, but they attempted to prove that the belief need not prevent their enfranchisement. They based their claim on principles such as Christian charity and especially religious liberalism, and, occasionally, on some understanding of Jewish historical aspirations. Deputy Kantelaar, in fact, did not try to demonstrate that the Jews were not a people. Instead, he presented weighty arguments to prove that even as a nationality the Jews were entitled to equal rights. "Is it right," he asked, "that one people say to others that co-exist with it in one state, 'you are strangers'? Even when two peoples, or one people and part of another live in the same state without uniting into one?"

The eight day debate resulted in a compromise resolution, carried by a large majority. It incorporated the argument voiced by Deputy R. J. Schimmelpenninck that the law only recognized individuals, since "society is composed only of individuals." The Jews therefore could only be enfranchised as individuals, "by individual process, and not collectively, as a nationality." The Jewish Enfranchisement Bill was finally passed with this as its rationale, on September 2, 1796. The law read as follows:

> No Jew shall be excluded from exercising any rights or advantages which are attached to Batavian citizen rights and which he might wish to enjoy, provided that he meets the requirements and fulfils all conditions demanded by the general constitution.

Holland, as a result of the French Revolution, was thus the second European country to grant the Jews equal rights by law.

The actual process of emancipation was tortuous in almost every field. Just as the craft guilds continued to exist after their abolition by the law of 1798, so did discrimination against the Jews linger on. At times, the municipal authorities were forced to intervene to ensure the return of confiscated merchandise to Jewish merchants. Jews now began to settle in cities hitherto closed to them, but a whole province, Friesland, still imposed on its Jewish inhabitants all the old restrictions, not excluding the patronage fee. As far as representation was concerned, the Jews of Holland scored some success. In 1797, two Jewish deputies from Amsterdam, Bromet and Dr. de Lemon, were elected to the Second National

Assembly. A Jewish deputy, Isaac da Costa Athias, was also elected to the Third National Assembly in 1798. In the same year, the Jews had two representatives on the board of the Amsterdam municipality. However, it was a very rare phenomenon for a Jew to hold government office anywhere in the country.

In 1798, a Federalist revolution broke out. Furthermore, the decline of the French Revolution, leading to the proclamation of the Empire, likewise limited the scope of the Revolution in Holland. These political circumstances were naturally not propitious to substantial *concrete* advances in the process of Jewish enfranchisement. However, the Constitution adopted on April 23, 1798, did include an article on the equality of all citizens, regardless of religious creed.

Adat Yeshurun against the Old Kehillah

Despite the National Assembly resolution, scarcely any change occurred in the administrative prerogatives and the system employed by the Kehillot, especially at Amsterdam—except that the law separating church and state made compulsory affiliation with the Kehillah no longer possible. *Felix Libertate* took advantage of this new legal position. On March 20, 1797, after the Amsterdam Kehillah had rejected its proposals for financial reform and reorganization and even threatened to impose heavy fines (according to seventeenth century bye-laws) for the open violation of Kehillah discipline, twenty-one members publicly announced that they were withdrawing from the Kehillah. A new Kehillah was immediately founded, called *Adat Yeshurun* (Community of Israel), with its own synagogue, ritual bath, cemetery, and rabbi (the proselyte Isaac ben Abraham Gruenbaum). The dedication ceremony of the new synagogue took place in June. The president of the new Kehillah was Dr. Hartog Lemon; its membership eventually rose to one hundred families. Thus the largest urban Jewish community in Europe was the scene of the first Kehillah schism, based on the status of enfranchisement.

The new Kehillah made only moderate religious reforms confined to details such as abolishing the prayer *Ve'la'malshinim Alt'hi Tikvah* (Let there be no hope for Informers), which could be interpreted as an affront to Christian honour, or instituting new burial customs (e.g. interment in a casket and not necessarily on the day of decease). However, it was not only the religious reforms of *Adat Yeshurun*—themselves of minor importance—that infuriated the conservative *Parnassim* of the old Ashkenazi Kehillah (though they did consider them a danger to traditional Judaism). The immediate source of conflict lay in the threat of the new Kehillah to the very foundations of the existence of the old Kehillah. By opening its own butcher's shop, it was breaking the monopoly held by the *Parnassim* of the sale of slaughtered meat, which was the Kehillah's principal source of revenue. The *Parnassim* retaliated against the schism with a proclamation virtually excommunicating the members of the new Kehillah: they forbade inter-marriage with them, in effect declared the offspring of such marriages illegitimate and proclaimed their ritual bath (*Mikveh*) unfit. It was, of course, forbidden to eat the meat sold at the new butcher's shop as being unkosher.

For obvious financial reasons, the Amsterdam municipal authorities supported the *Parnassim* in this controversy. As the economic crisis became more severe, the number of poor in the city increased and they had to be supported from public funds. It suited the municipality to be relieved of responsibility for the Jewish poor and preferable that the Kehillah's revenues from the meat tax provide the necessary finance. *Adat Yeshurun* could not have opposed this powerful alliance without the political support it received from the French protecting authorities, and particularly the unconcealed sympathy of the French Ambassador, Noel. To begin with, the new Kehillah tried to win over the Jewish masses, whose social, economic and political interests it was assiduously and courageously defending by disseminating information and propaganda. The conflict inside the Amsterdam Jewish community became a social and political issue, conducted, for the first time in the history of European Jewry, by a party acquainted with all the methods of modern propaganda and furnished with the slogans of a socio-political programme.

As late as 1807, a memorandum from the Burgomaster of Amsterdam, J. W. Van de Poll, to Louis Bonaparte, compared *Adat Yeshurun* to the old Kehillah in the following derogatory terms: he called it a band of "individuals who were almost entirely destitute and therefore having little or nothing to lose." Even without this highly exaggerated testimony on the social position of the intellectuals and merchants at the head of *Adat Yeshurun*, it is known that this Kehillah continued the policy of the *Felix Libertate* society, and took up the defence of the subjugated Jewish masses against the old, feudalistic Kehillah and that it did so on the basis of its own political programme for the rehabilitation of Jewish life. Despite its ultimate plan for the linguistic and cultural assimilation of Dutch Jewry, its propaganda was firmly based on Yiddish as the vernacular of the people, making occasional references to "our Yiddish tongue." *Felix Libertate* had published manifestos and simple dialogues in Yiddish though it had at the same time distributed propaganda literature in Dutch. The *Adat Yeshurun* Kehillah published its bye-laws in Yiddish. Authors of literature directed against the old Kehillah had always to consider the need to prevent their subject matter compromising the Jews in the eyes of the general population. But the chief obstacle to the use of Dutch was the sheer fact that the Jewish public, generally, was unable to read *Galokhes*—that is, Dutch in Latin characters. The number of people who could read Hebrew was also decidedly smaller than the Yiddish-reading circle. *Felix Libertate* propagandists and some of its writers did publish some poems in Hebrew (*A Song on Liberty*, by Lipmann Bronfeld), documents (*The Declaration of the Rights of Man*, translated by Friedrichsfeld), and even larger works such as Zvi Hirsch Ilfeld's *Divrei Neggidim* (Words of the Rulers, a record of the National Assembly's debates on Jewish enfranchisement). All the same, the language mainly employed for propaganda and polemical literature was Yiddish. At first the *Adat Yeshurun* group was scornful of the language of the *Tze'enah-Re'enah* (Bible stories and commentaries for women) and the *Teitsch-Chumesh* (the accepted vernacular translation of the Pentateuch still used by the old Kehillah), and attempted to write "High German" in Hebrew characters. In view of the need to attract the masses, however, it wrote increasingly in the spoken Yiddish vernacular with its wealth of Dutch idioms and Hebrew words. The earliest *political* literature in Yiddish, like the earliest modern Yiddish literature in general, came into being not because its authors cherished the language of the people but because they wanted their information and propaganda to reach the broadest possible section of the masses.

Apart from a weekly, *Der Discours*, which appeared more or less regularly from the early autumn of 1797 until the spring of 1798, *Adat Yeshurun* published a series of popular dialogues, political pamphlets, and songs. These abused the *Parnassim* of the old Kehillah as ignoramuses, blind fanatics, puffed up nonentities and hypocrites. Even more stinging attacks were made against social oppression and reactionary politics of the old Kehillah leaders. "There is no king as sovereign as the Kehillah," they fulminated. Besides official and legal exploitation, the *Parnassim* and charity fund collectors were accused of theft, wastage of Kehillah funds and fraud. Citing all kinds of data the propagandists tried to convince the public that the *Parnassim*'s opposition to the new order was based on the fact that their authority depended on the old régime, which had itself depended on the "aristocracy," and on the disenfranchisement of the Jewish masses. Under this régime the Kehillah member was oppressed both by the state and the *Parnassim*. Enthusiastic exponents of capitalist democracy, the leaders of *Adat Yeshurun* explained that their aim was not social equality between poor and rich but the equality of legal democracy. However, this propaganda was permeated with the spirit of social protest and was in fact directed towards winning over the socially oppressed and embittered. As in the period of the French Revolution generally, the campaign against the "aristocrats" was carried on under the slogan of abolishing the prerogatives and social domination of the rich and elevating the "common man," the man of the people. In all sincerity they assured the masses that they wanted to arouse their fortitude and self-respect. "No! Fear not! It is tranquillity I wish to lavish upon you!" an *Adat Yeshurun* pamphlet proclaimed. Two satirical ditties about the old Kehillah published in *Discours*, were typical of the propaganda that used the slogans of the French Revolution: one was to the tune of the Marseillaise, the other to the tune of the Carmagnole. These songs expressed the short-lived triumph of *Adat Yeshurun* in the spring of 1798, when the government ousted the old *Parnassim*.

Faced with this vigorous and systematic propaganda by *Adat Yeshurun*, religious excommunication or even a boycott of the printing press where the booklets were published could not satisfy the old Kehillah. It launched a counter-offensive. Its *Discours* series, a complete visual imitation of the new Kehillah's weekly, charged the reformers with Sabbath violation, not using phylacteries (*T'filin*) and also with speaking Dutch in their synagogue: "They are learning strange tongues and have quite forgotten our mother tongue." It accused them of changing their names (Kalman, for example, had become Carolus) and concluded from this that "they are ashamed unto themselves for being Jews." They "even deny that the Messiah will come." It would appear from this that the old Kehillah's propaganda not only appealed to religious sentiments but also to the national traditions of the masses. "Because we are Jews," a dialogue between partisans of the old Kehillah declared, "we should talk Yiddish with one another."

Characteristically, the arguments put forward by the new Kehillah evaded the question of language and the essential attributes of the Jews as a nationality. But they firmly countered the claim that, as the Jews were inexile, they could hope for no advantage from the struggle for equality of rights: "We paupers are in exile," they said. "Had they really so desired, all Jews would have been released from this captivity of hunger and starvation." *Adat Yeshurun* mainly justified itself by the assertion that it was the true custodian of "our Holy Faith" whereas the heads of the old Kehillah were hypocrites who exploited religious motives in order to rule the masses irresponsibly.

In the long run, the counter-propaganda of the old Kehillah demonstrated its true strength. Its charity system, despite its abuses and many defects, retained its hold on the poor of the community, who were afraid to forfeit the allowance it doled out. *Adat Yeshurun* claimed that only "the Polish sycophants and mendicants" clung to the *Parnassim*, yet the new Kehillah remained a small group consisting of no more than two per cent of Amsterdam's total Jewish population.

The events of March 18, 1798, did not greatly alter this situation. On that day the *Parnassim* of the old Kehillah were removed from power by the Directory of the Republic for "aristocratic tyranny" following the radical revolution of January 22 (modelled on the French upheaval of the 18th of Fructidor—September 4, 1797). The *Parnassim* were replaced by five more liberally inclined Kehillah heads. *Adat Yeshurun*, doubtful of its own strength, went so far as to approach the ousted *Parnassim* with a view to reorganizing the Kehillah and restoring its unity. However, a few months later, on June 12, 1798, a right wing coup swept the country (again, according to the French precedent of the 22nd of Floreal—May

11, 1798) and the old *Parnassim* were restored to office by the municipal council. No elections were held for the next ten years, until the establishment of the consistory.

A group of intellectuals at The Hague, under the leadership of the *Maskil*, Moses Belinfante, were stimulated by the example of *Felix Libertate* and the *Adat Yeshurun* Kehillah to found a society in 1797 (*Through Industry and Unity*). Their fifty members, including several non-Jews, wanted to bring influence to bear to have Dutch taught in the Jewish schools and to secure the admission of Jewish children to the municipal schools. They also tried to encourage the spread of crafts amongst young Jewish people and the Jewish unemployed. The society was disbanded in 1799 because of the war. A similar society *For Work and Industriousness* was founded in Amsterdam in 1798 to increase productive labour amongst the Jews. By 1807 it had about 450 members. All their efforts, however, failed to produce any response except in limited circles of the Jewish population until the end of the Batavian Republic. The situation changed during the reign of Louis Bonaparte, when the new trend was supported by the State, particularly because of its assimilationist aims.

The Reign of Louis Bonaparte and the Jewish Consistorial Régime

In 1806, after the Batavian Republic had passed through all the phases of its decline, Holland, by the will of Napoleon, was proclaimed a Kingdom under the rule of his brother Louis. The country's economic depression, chronic ever since the final decades of the eighteenth century, had now become acute because of the blockade that England imposed in 1805. Even earlier, England had deprived Holland of its monopoly of the colonial trade. Holland was particularly affected by the crisis in the city of Amsterdam. Both trade and banking activities there were greatly reduced. The number of Jewish poor in the city (which became the capital in 1807) far exceeded the poor amongst the general population. Official reports confirmed this fact: Burgomaster Van de Poll reported in 1807 that 18,000 out of a total of 30,000 members of the Ashkenazi Kehillah—nearly two-thirds—required public support. Similarly, 1,420 of the 2,518 members of the Sephardi Kehillah could not exist without public support, in 1812. With the decline of the Revolution, the Dutch middle classes as a whole discarded the old slogans, which had coincided with the interests of the people, and frankly proclaimed their own selfish class programme. The enlightened vanguard of the new Jewish middle classes in Holland followed suit during the Napoleonic period. They rapidly forgot the golden age of the Revolution, when they had used every persuasive device to draw the masses into the struggle for the new order. Now they were aware of the new trends in Paris, at the Assembly of Notables and the *Grand Sanhedrin*; in wonder and envy they noted the close connections with the régime that the Jewish middle class enjoyed in France and Italy, which enabled it to institute reforms favouring the interests and prestige of its own class. In this way, reforms had been made in the Jewish religion and religious organization, compulsory linguistic and cultural assimilation had been instituted, and laws against mendicants, paupers, and propertyless immigrants had been enacted. In Holland, where the Jewish masses were more concentrated and more firmly rooted in their own language and national cultural environment, the reformers took more persistent and more offensive measures to enforce assimilation than in France. But their fanatical assimilationist policy met with no success in face of the instinctive disapproval of the masses—even the progressive measures of the programme which were given greater emphasis than in France. These measures were also in the interests of assimilation, as can be seen by the propaganda calling for the establishment of modern schools to give secular education and vocational training. The reformers wanted in this way to remedy the widespread destitution of the Jewish masses, which contradicted their own economic interests and imperilled their own enfranchisement and class prestige.

King Louis, his position in Holland none too secure, could not discount the political support of his Jewish subjects. He therefore exercised great caution in carrying out those reforms which his brother Napoleon had forcibly imposed on his own Jewish subjects. When the Sephardi and Ashkenazi Kehillot of Holland declined the invitation of the Assembly of Notables to send delegates to the Paris Sanhedrin, he granted the request of the *Adat Yeshurun* Kehillah for permission to send a delegation of its own, on the express condition that it would only be representing itself. The report that the delegation made to the King on its return to Holland called attention to the "regeneration" of the Jews which had taken place in France and Italy and which would spread even further following the resolutions of the Sanhedrin. The report particularly stressed that "many of our brethren have been awarded the Cross of the Legion of Honour and others are serving in the most eminent positions in the magistracy." The delegates reached the general conclusion that something should be done in Holland towards the education of the Jewish youth and that mendicancy and idleness should be forbidden.

A month later, at the end of June, 1807, *Adat Yeshurun* sent a memorandum to the King containing their plan for "bringing happiness to 60,000 of His subjects." It advised the King to award decorations and positions of rank to a number of Jews, as his brother Napoleon had proved that this was the best way to eradicate prejudices against the Jewish population. It openly requested the King to bear in mind, when making these awards, their "new Kehillah," which "by furthering the desires of the immortal Napoleon, has not ceased to profess liberal prin-

ciples and inculcate in its co-religionists the practice of social virtues."
At the same period, in 1806-08, a lawyer, Karl Asser, and a wealthy,
highly reputed jurist, Jonas Daniel Meyer, submitted a number of
memoranda to the King exposing discrimination against Jews in government and public institutions in Holland, and disclosing the unusual
extent of poverty, accompanied by mendicancy, amongst the Jews of
Amsterdam. They proposed that Jews be employed as government
officials and appointed municipal council members. They also suggested
reorganizing the Kehillot, which had been declining steadily under the
administration of the old *Parnassim*, and opening schools and institutions
for the poor.

The Asser-Meyer memorandum of 1806 formed the basis for an edict
published by the King at the end of January, 1807, ordering the
provincial authorities to see that "there be no distinctions practised
between Jews and the other inhabitants but that they (the Jews) must be
treated on the same footing." Having enunciated this general principle
(which only confirmed the provisions of the constitution), the government was content in practice to abolish several of the more glaring
examples of discrimination. At Amsterdam, a number of Jews was
accepted into the Civil Guard, and in 1808 the municipal welfare fund
was ordered to pay out 12,000 guilders over a period of five months
towards the support of the poor in the Ashkenazi Kehillah. In the
province of Friesland, a royal command totally abolished the special
Jewish taxes together with the anti-Jewish laws. A special edict
demanded that fairs scheduled for Saturdays be postponed, "insofar as
possible," to a weekday. With its commercial interests in mind Holland
interceded to secure exemption for Dutch Jewry from special Jewish
taxes at the Leipzig and Nuremberg fairs.

The government did not go much beyond these edicts, which in fact
only removed impediments to Jewish commerce, and were, in any case,
contrary to the law. The masses of the Jewish poor remained excluded
from access to the crafts because not only individual artisans but
government and municipal workshops would not accept young Jews as
apprentices. The Christian character of the public schools meant that
only a few Jewish children studied at them, and even fewer attended the
"Latin Schools" (high schools). In some cities, such as Rotterdam,
Jewish pupils were not accepted at all. Jews were totally excluded from
philanthropic and scientific institutions.

In 1808, the King agreed to a request by his enlightened Jewish
advisers to establish a Jewish Consistory in Holland modelled on the one
in France. Explaining this action, the King expressed sorrow at "the dire
poverty afflicting the Ashkenazi Israelites in our country, especially in
Amsterdam," and emphasized the urgent need for the Jews to enjoy equal
rights in practice. A Committee of nine was appointed, consisting of three
Parnassim of the old Amsterdam Kehillah, three *Parnassim* from *Adat*

Yeshurun, and Jonas D. Meyer, I. Littwack and B. Lemans. Despite orthodox objections to the committee, the recommendations that it presented to the King were accepted unanimously—a reflection of the rapprochement in ideas between these two Kehillot, which had engaged in bitter conflict for over a decade. In the first place, it was decided that the name of the Hoog-Duitsche, or Ashkenazi Jews, be changed to Netherland Jews. The reasons given for this move were the need to demonstrate to the younger generation that "this is their fatherland," and also to prove that they were repudiating the "corrupted Hoog-Duitsch,"—in other words, Yiddish. The "Netherland Jews" would be organized into a consistory of thirteen members, including a representative appointed by *Adat Yeshurun,* which would cease to exist as a separate Kehillah. The duties of the consistory would include attending to the needs of the poor and founding orphanages. It would appear that the old source of income was still considered in this context: it was expressly decided to retain the butcher shops intact and only to limit the requirement to purchase meat there to a definite quota. This marked the end of *Adat Yeshurun's* ancient battle to lift the burden of the meat tax from the people.

The Committee's decision not to permit Jews from abroad to settle in Holland without the local consistory's approval was equally characteristic of the social attitude of the two Jewish bourgeois factions that had now reached a compromise. This approval would require a guarantee by two local residents that the immigrant owned property to the value of three hundred guilders. The government itself had some doubt as to whether such a decree was constitutional and withheld its confirmation until the State Council ruled that the Constitution only applied to Netherland subjects. Even then, the decree was only to be in force for five years although the Committee recommended that it remain in operation for ten. The middle-class descendants of the refugees from Poland and Germany did not show the same compassion towards their brethren as the Dutch people had shown to their persecuted forebears for two hundred years. On September 12, 1808, in accordance with the committee's resolutions, the King issued an edict establishing the Consistory. Karl Asser was appointed a director in the Ministry of Religions, and thus assumed the task of supervising co-operation between the Consistory and the Government.

The sentimental King had indicated aid to the Jewish poor as one of the chief aims of the new organization. However, the Consistory considered that one of its principal missions was to raise the cultural level of the Jewish population. It was, in the first place, anxious to put the Jewish propertied classes on an equal footing with the Dutch middle classes and feared that the existing cultural image might compromise its efforts. The idea that the cultural level of the Jewish masses was responsible for their position was expressed by the former president of *Adat Yeshurun,* Dr. H.

Lemon. His communication to the Supreme Consistory stated: "One may hate a Jew for his belief in another religion, but he is held in contempt for his contemptible behaviour." The Supreme Consistory considered linguistic assimilation the best way to raise the cultural level of the Jewish masses and devoted most of its energies to attacking the Yiddish language. On its advice, the King published an edict in February, 1809, forbidding the use of Yiddish in legal documents.

The leaders of the Consistory realized that the proven and best method to inculcate the use of Dutch and to dislodge Yiddish from amongst the Jewish population was to instruct the younger generation in the language of the state. On August 20, 1808, at the initiative of Moses Cohen Belinfante, the Association for *Training The Child in the Way he should go* (Proverbs 22, 5) was founded. The objects of the Association were to publish textbooks in Hebrew and Dutch, establish new schools, train teachers, translate the prayers of the Ashkenazi ritual into Dutch, and, above all, to publish a Dutch translation of the Bible. At the request of the Supreme Consistory, the King issued an edict on July 10, 1809, ordering that the Bible be taught in Dutch for the purpose of "spreading civilization amongst our Israelite subjects," and "to abolish that tongue which is called Jewish." Teachers who gave Biblical instruction in Yiddish were liable to have their licences revoked for six months and if the offence were repeated, *in perpetuum*. Rabbis and preachers were instructed to recommend the new translation of the Bible in their synagogue and to propagate it as the only authorized translation. No Jew could, in future, be granted a teacher's licence if he failed to pass a proficiency examination in the Dutch language before a Government School Committee; Jewish teachers of religion could not teach without the approval of the Supreme Consistory.

The enforced use of the Dutch translation of the Bible considerably restricted education in Yiddish in general, and the Jewish population offered widespread and stubborn resistance to the decree. Even an assimilationist Dutch historian of this period, M. Wolff, wrote in 1920 that "a language in which the ordinary folk had been brought up, in which for generations it had thought, sung its songs and also wept, in which alone, so it thought, it could achieve intimate communion, a language which in this people's consciousness was superior to all others for depth, powers of expression and warmth—such a language was not to be abolished by the stroke of a pen."*

Jewish teachers ignored the rule to give Biblical instruction in Dutch and continued the centuries' old tradition of teaching the Pentateuch by reading each verse in Hebrew and then translating it into Yiddish. The Consistory attempted to enforce compulsory measures by ordering the *Parnassim* to dismiss all teachers who would not sign an undertaking to

---

* M. Wolff, *De Beteekenis der Regeering van Lodewijk Napoleon voor de Joden van Nederland,* 'S Gravenhagen, 1920, p. 79.

teach the Bible in Dutch—even before the translation had been completed. However, at Amsterdam, only thirty-eight teachers acknowledged the communication at all, and of these, fourteen refused to sign the commitment.

Publication of the translation was suspended with the work half completed, because of shortage of funds—a direct consequence of the general laxity of the Kehillot in remitting tax fees to the Consistory.

King Louis chose different measures from those of his brother Napoleon in order to attract the Jews of Holland into military service. He took account of the religious orthodoxy of the Jewish population and on July 10, 1809, published an edict establishing a Jewish corps. The Supreme Consistory showed considerable initiative throughout this episode and sent an enthusiastic letter of thanks to the King, praising the edict as one of the most exemplary in history. A ritual slaughterer (*Shochet*) was appointed to ensure *Kashrut* for officers and men, but the single battalion provisionally established never reached full strength and by the beginning of 1810 did not number more than four hundred men.

The edict on the Jewish corps was really directed solely against the Jewish poor. The King indirectly confirmed this. When a number of Hanoverian Jews wanted to serve in the corps, the King replied that the corps was not intended simply to create a Jewish army but to provide honest means of sustenance for the Jewish poor. In practice, the Consistory removed from the welfare rolls poor Jewish families whose sons refused to enlist. In desperation, the Consistory even resorted to the forced enlistment of sixteen-year-olds, who were rounded up from orphanages by military squads in the dead of night. The population reacted spontaneously and unanimously to prevent the victimization of the poverty-stricken in face of the brutal, socially repressive character that this operation assumed. In these circumstances, the Consistory informed the King that it preferred not to continue with coercive measures against needy families "because of the cruelty involved . . ." But it was extremely anxious to see a Jewish corps established. In the first place, the evasion of military service by Jews might provide an argument against Jewish enfranchisement. Second, the Consistory regarded military service as an excellent medium for the assimilation of the Jewish masses. When the King was on the point of disbanding the corps at the beginning of November, 1809, the Supreme Consistory persuaded him to postpone the date for three months, on the grounds that the poor individuals eligible for conscription were the sole means of support for their families. However, lack of funds formed the basis of the King's actions in disbanding the corps. The attempt to establish a Jewish military unit in Europe was thus brought to a close and with it ended an agonizing ordeal in the history of the poorest sections of Dutch Jewry.

Following Louis Bonaparte's rupture with his brother and forced abdication on July 1, 1810, Holland was annexed to Napoleon's French Empire. This political change signified for the Jewish population, as much as for the Dutch population in general, the stern rule of French imperialism. The French occupation authorities relentlessly enforced the Napoleonic decrees against the Jews of Holland. The Sephardi and Ashkenazi Jews were forced to unite into one organization consisting of four consistories, subject to the Central Consistory at Paris. The French governor emphasized the implementation of the resolutions passed by the Paris Sanhedrin as the main objective of the new consistorial régime, particularly the requirement that the rabbis advocate military service from the pulpit. The members of the consistory had to swear allegiance and obedience to the Emperor in the presence of the prefect and also to pledge themselves to inform the authorities of everything made known to them "that was contrary to the interests of the Sovereign or the State." The head of the Dutch consistory was Jonas Daniel Meyer, who co-operated closely with Paris.

In 1813, after Napoleon's downfall, the House of Orange was restored in Holland. Jonas Daniel Meyer held a leading position in the provisional government which was set up after the uprising against the French. The chief spokesmen of the Jewish middle class, in common with the Dutch middle class as a whole, quickly adapted itself to the change in régime.

CHAPTER FIVE

ITALY

The Ghetto Period

Italy, at the end of the eighteenth century was, as Metternich later described it, a geographical, not a political concept. The country was divided into a dozen independent states. The largest of these were the Kingdom of Naples in the south, the Papal States and the Grand Duchy of Tuscany in central Italy, and the Republic of Venice, the Duchy of Milan and the Duchy of Piedmont (Kingdom of Sardinia) in the north. Smaller states, in the area between Tuscany and Piedmont, were Modena, Mantua, Lucca, Parma, Piacenza and Genoa (Liguria). The country had begun to decline economically when world commercial sea routes shifted during the age of discovery. It reached its lowest point in the middle of the eighteenth century. The Italian provinces fell from a position high in the ranks of world economic powers to the level of third-rate states, with a limited commercial range, even within the Mediterranean area. What survived of Italian culture now sheltered in the shadow of past riches, still visible in the humbled "queens of the sea," Venice and Genoa. A pale ghost of the old splendour still shimmered in Italian music and theatre; original works also appeared in the social and natural sciences.

Italian Jewry during this period was, for the most part, exceptionally impoverished, confined to ghettos and oppressed by severe decrees. However, it too still displayed some of the marks of the splendid cultural tradition which had distinguished it during the age of Humanism and the Renaissance. It is true that not one name of major significance emerged in Hebrew poetry, philosophy or science in the second half of the eighteenth century from Italian Jewry. But a valuable tradition of awareness of all branches of secular culture survived from the past. Italy was the one country in Europe where secular science and art were considered an inseparable part of Jewish education.

After the expulsions of the post-medieval era, Jews no longer lived in the Neapolitan state in the south, including Sicily, the island of Sardinia, the Duchy of Milan in central Lombardy, or the Republic of Genoa. There were approximately 30,000 Jews in the other half of the country, in central and northern Italy, at the end of the ghetto period: about 0.2 per cent of the total population of 16 million. In the areas open to Jewish domicile, the Jews did not constitute more than 0.5 per cent of the total population. Between the end of the sixteenth century and the end of the eighteenth century, the Jewish population increased by a maximum of 5,000 to 8,000 persons, that is to say, by no more than a third, or more accurately, a fifth. This low natural increase was the direct result of economic depression, severe restrictions and unhygienic conditions in the ghettos. These circumstances even caused Kehillah members to emigrate, though not to any considerable extent. A thin, but continuous flow of Italian Jews left for Holland and England, while compulsory or semi-compulsory conversion, especially in the Papal States, reduced the number of Jews by scores every year.

Approximately two-thirds of the Jewish population were concentrated in ten urban Kehillot, each with over a thousand members. The largest Kehillot were at Leghorn—over 4,000 Jews (4,327 in 1784)—and Rome, which had nearly the same number. However, while the Leghorn Kehillah constantly expanded, the number of Jews in Rome consistently decreased. An official census of 1810 showed only 3,038 members. A similar decline occurred in the Venice Kehillah, which only contained 1,517 Jews (about 1 per cent of the 136,803 inhabitants of the city) in 1790. Kehillot with over 1,000 or nearly 1,000 members also existed in the cities of Mantua (1,962 Jews in 1793), Trieste, under Austrian rule (about 1,500 Jews), Modena (1,260 Jews in 1795), Ancona and Ferrara, both in the Papal States, Turin in Piedmont, Verona in the Venetian republic (822 Jews in 1795), and Florence (939 Jews in 1784). The remaining third of Italian Jewry was dispersed in over sixty Kehillot, nearly all of them numbering less than 500 souls, and half of them small groups of barely a hundred members.

During the Middle Ages, Italy showed greater tolerance towards the Jews than anywhere else in Europe. From the time of the Catholic Counter-Reformation in the middle of the sixteenth century, it set the classic example of Jewish ghettos and became increasingly strict as the country's economic state deteriorated. The largest ghetto and the one that lasted longer than any other in Europe (until 1870) was in Rome. It occupied a whole district of the city on the Tiber, and was crossed by two streets and six lanes. Stone walls separated it from the surrounding city. Jews were only permitted to leave the ghetto by one of its five gates during daytime; at sunset, the gates were locked. In Venice, the section of the city in which the Jews lived, gave the actual word *ghetto* to all segregated Jewish quarters throughout the world. The segregation of the Jews in the ghetto was completed by the "badge of the Jew," called *Sciamano* (from the Hebrew *Siman*, badge, or mark) by the Italian Jews. Men were required to wear a hat and women a kerchief, of a specified colour. In the Papal States, it was yellow, in Venice and Florence, red. In the Duchy of Modena, a red band round the hat was sufficient, while in Piedmont, Jews had to sew a yellow patch on their right shoulders. For the most part, Jews were only permitted to appear without this badge of shame when travelling, but individual dignitaries, such as doctors, people with state connections, or Jewish students at the University of Padua, were entirely exempt from wearing the badge. At times, the Popes found a useful source of revenue in exempting Jews from wearing the badge— for a fee. The advantage in this case fell to the Jewish rich. The impoverished masses continued to wear the badges.

A decree compelling Jews to attend the sermons of missionaries was still enforced in some of the Italian states, especially the Papal States, during the eighteenth century.

The most infamous oppression of the period however, related to forced conversion. The Jews were practically compelled to fill the *Case dei Catecumeni* which had existed in various parts of Italy since the middle of the sixteenth century. In the Papal States they were maintained—as were the missionaries—at the expense of the Kehillot. Voluntary conversion was not a common occurrence; the Church therefore resorted to false conversions. A Christian would deliberately sprinkle water over a Jew's head and simultaneously pronounce the baptismal formula. This was sufficient pretext to have the Jew taken to a house for catechumens. Similarly, the children of such "catechumens" (in reality, converts by coercion) were taken from their mother's arms and brought up as Christians.

The staunchness of the adult Jews, who were forcibly and on all kinds of pretexts brought to these hostels, is amazing. After a few weeks, a large proportion were released because they refused to yield and remained unconverted. It is not surprising that during this period the Jews made use of a magic charm against conversion. Hayim Y.D. Azoulai attributed this charm to the Kabbalist and scholar, Menahem Azariah da Fano, who lived at the end of the sixteenth and beginning of the seventeenth century. It consisted of swallowing a calfskin talisman with an inscription of the *Sh'ma*,* soaked in the milk of a mother and her daughter, and in lemon juice. This was in addition to the customary fast and bath of purification.

Besides the social segregation and degradation that it entailed, the ghetto system was designed to curtail the economic activity of the Jews and to confine them to a limited number of economic functions least likely to conflict with the interests of the Christian population. Purchase of land by Jews was forbidden everywhere and this naturally barred them from agriculture. Retail trade in public shops was a monopoly of Christian tradesmen, as in nearly all western Europe, while even Jewish wholesale trade, particularly in textile products, was obstructed by the guilds. The only occupation Jewish merchants might engage in with comparative freedom was the import-export trade. Jews were completely forbidden to belong to the craft guilds, and therefore could not legally work at the most important crafts. That was even true in provinces such

---

* *Sh'ma*—hear! First word in the verse which became declaration of faith: *Hear oh Israel! The Lord thy God, the Lord is One!* (Deut. 6, 4.)

as Piedmont and Modena, where it was not expressly prohibited by the state. Industry was also mostly organized within the craft guilds, even in sectors that had been established by Jewish initiative, and Jewish industrialists often met serious obstructions which they could not always surmount. Furthermore in some states, notably Venice and the Papal States, the employment of Christian workers by Jews was prohibited.

Despite these repressive conditions, large and medium scale Jewish capitalists found it possible to make very profitable investments and played a quite significant role in the country's economy. Jews controlled a substantial amount of trade through the two seaports of Leghorn and Trieste. These ports had expanded and developed at the expense of the established Italian mercantile cities and were now of primary importance in Mediterranean seaborne commerce. At Leghorn, in the early days, Sephardi Jews of Portuguese origin handled a large volume of the city's commerce in grain and oil, and particularly imports of spices. They were joined in the course of time by Jews who had migrated from other Italian districts, mostly the Papal States. The Jews of Leghorn also practically dominated manufactures in the city as well as trade in coral beads which they sold throughout Europe and to the remotest Asian countries. At Trieste, where the Jewish Kehillah had grown larger than the one in Venice by the end of the eighteenth century, Jewish merchants imported tobacco, coffee, and sugar, and Jews such as Marco Levi, and Joseph Eleazar Morpurgo, the poet, founded the *Assecurazione Generali* insurance company, which later became famous. In Venice, leading Christian merchant families had become an aristocracy and now considered all economic activity debasing. Levant and North African trade during the eighteenth century was therefore largely in the hands of Jews, especially Sephardim. This trade was generally conducted by merchants who had immigrated from abroad. Jews also played the leading role in trade with Turkey in the Papal sea ports of Pesaro and Ancona. In Rome, the Jews traded with the Near East, exported spices to western Europe, kept public stores for woven goods (permitted in 1740) and iron products, and Jews from Germany and Holland traded in foreign merchandise. Benedetto Frizzi, a Jewish physician and economist, reported in 1784, that the wheat trade was a Jewish monopoly throughout Italy. Jews transported wheat from provinces which produced a surplus to deficit areas, which had to import supplies from abroad during drought periods.

Jewish banking activities were very limited compared with earlier centuries. In Rome, following the Papal decree of 1682, Jewish short-term loan credits had contracted to such an extent that the remaining Jewish moneylenders often had to pawn the collateral they held at the Christian people's bank, *Monte di Pietà*.

In the face of innumerable obstacles the Jews played a large part in the development of the country's industry, especially the textile industry, which also exported its products abroad. In the Venetian Republic, Jews owned large wool and silk spinning mills in Venice itself and in certain provincial towns such as Padua, Rovigo and Verona. The Jews owned an even greater share of the weaving industry, where they purchased on credit goods manufactured to order by workers in their homes. In this way, seven Jews of Padua employed five thousand workers, mostly women, in the silk industry (which, incidentally, had been founded in the fifteenth century by a Jew). In Venice, a textile magnate, Gentili, employed about one thousand workers, both in his mill and as home workers. In Rome, the work of the Christian silk spinners was largely organized and administered by Jewish merchants. In the middle of the eighteenth century, a group of Christian industrialists operating in this sphere tried to organize a guild in order to eliminate the Jews. The Kehillah thereupon dispatched a lengthy memorandum to the Papal Vicar describing the abundant experience of the Jews in the manufacture of silk and the benefit the state derived from their activity. In Piedmont, the Jews were active in the twine and silk industry, especially as manufacturers. In addition to a number of Jewish firms in the capital city of Turin, there were large spinning mills in six other Piedmontese cities. The four Jewish industrialists and two contractors at Turin were worth several millions. In 1797, they asked for government permission to purchase a building outside the ghetto, hinting that if their request was refused, they would emigrate, taking their capital with them. In Tuscany, the Jews of Siena owned a large share of the local textile industry.

However, despite their prominent position in the country's economy, the Jewish merchants, bankers and manufacturers, even including the brokers, who were particularly numerous at Venice, only comprised a small stratum of Italian Jewry. The major part of the Jewish population suffered under the burden of brutal decrees imposed by Church and State. Disenfranchised, only two occupations were open to the ordinary Italian Jew: street barter and peddling in second-hand articles and tailoring. Rome, Venice, and all the cities and towns of northern and central Italy resounded with the call of *"Strazi!"* ("Rags!") or *"Robi Vecchi!"* ("Old clothes!") or *"Heb!"* (apparently a shortening of *Hebraio*, a Jew). In Venice, *Strazzaria*, rag-dealing, was the only legal occupation of the Jewish population—apart from the foreign trade of the wealthy. The authorities, by agreement with the Kehillah, renewed the licence every ten years.

As a result, very few Jews in Venice were engaged in productive activity. A census taken after the 1797 Revolution showed the following occupational distribution of the 473 families of the Venice Kehillah: fifty-five merchants; seventy-five rag-dealers; thirty-four brokers; twenty-three retail grocers; seven small general traders; forty-one clerks in commercial establishments; eighteen pawnbrokers; twenty-nine workmen and day labourers (including three letter-carriers); sixteen artisans; forty-five in the free professions (religious instructors, religious officials, physicians, etc.); eighty-four servants; twenty-nine paupers; and seventeen sundry other occupations. Artisans and workers together therefore did not even comprise one-tenth of the heads of families of the Venice Kehillah.

This occupational distribution was not typical of eighteenth century Italian Jewry as a whole. Trade in old rags developed into a peculiarly Jewish occupation: the repair, beating out and cleaning of old mattresses. Particularly after funerals, Christians would call in a Jew to renovate the mattress of the deceased. A more respectable trade at which Jews became adept was supplying furniture for dwellings, which developed from the purchase of old furniture and other second-hand articles. In Rome, the Kehillah was not only the sole supplier of beds and bedding, with coverlets and sheets included, to the Papal troops, but Jews generally were engaged as experts to install palace furniture in honour of guests or in preparation for new tenants. This business was also a prime function of the Venetian Jews. The fact that the Jews had become experts in this line provided a pretext for additional extortions by Church and State. At Rome, during conclaves for the election of a new Pope, the Jewish Kehillah was ordered to decorate the Cardinals chambers with tapestries at its own expense. At Venice, several times a year, for all great celebrations, the Kehillah was required to decorate a number of the city's cathedrals with tapestries—and this was in addition to its obligation to supply the army with bedding during manoeuvres. The Kehillot in the Venetian province and in Verona had similar obligations towards the municipality; they had, for example, to furnish and decorate palaces for official guests.

Tailoring had been an important Jewish trade as far back as the Middle Ages, especially at Rome and Venice. But it was trade in old clothes which made tailoring, in Italy more than anywhere else in Europe, the most common occupation of Jewish men and women. By the seventeenth century, the Jews of Italy had become remarkably proficient in repairing old garments for resale. At Venice and Rome, the ability to mend a tear so that the repair was invisible became synonymous with Jewish tailoring. Cardinals at Rome would have their pontifical robes mended by Jewish tailors. Many Jewish women and young girls worked at this trade throughout Italy. In Piedmont, small-scale trade was the main occupation of the men, while the women worked as seamstresses, garment-makers and spinners. The women sat in the doorways of their homes in the alleys of the Roman ghetto from sunrise to sunset, working with needle or bobbin. In the dark alleys of Venice, the women worked at their windows by daylight and well into the night by candle-light. Jewish women everywhere had a high reputation as expert button-makers.

As a consequence of their trade in used articles, the Jews of Italy specialized in crafts such as carpentry, leather-work, metal work and painting. Jewish engravers and jewellers existed throughout Italy. In

Rome, in direct contrast with Venice, repression of the Jews assumed a religious rather than an economic character, and during the eighteenth century there were large numbers of Jewish carpenters, tanners, saddlers and harness-makers. However, in Italy as a whole, tailoring and upholstery were the leading crafts among the Jews. These vocations affected the health of the Jewish population. At the turn of the eighteenth century, skin and lung diseases, resulting from constant contact with dusty old clothes, filthy rags and worn-out mattresses, were common ailments among the Jews of Italy, not to speak of eye diseases and chronic headaches caused by incessant needlework.

Though they mostly worked hard and productively, greater poverty existed amongst these Jews than among any other Jewish community in western Europe, with the possible exception of Amsterdam. Rag-pickers and patch-workers had to share the heavy tax burden that the Italian states imposed on the ghettos. This taxation was heaviest at Rome, where the cost of maintaining the *Case dei Catecumeni* hostels, at the rate of 1,400 *scudi** a year, was a significant item in the Kehillah's tax expenditure, only equalled by the interest on deferred loans. In 1755, the Kehillah at Rome was declared bankrupt. None the less, it was still required to pay the Pope interest due on loans at a rate of more than 15,500 *scudi* annually, albeit with assistance from the Christian people's banks. Between 1725 and 1795, the number of declared Jewish property owners at Rome increased from 139 to 143 and the assessed value of taxable Jewish property declined from 117,975 to 38,525 *scudi*—a decrease in wealth of two-thirds within a period of seventy years.

The large number of philanthropic organizations in all the Italian Kehillot, and their varied activities, were an indication of the widespread poverty among the Jewish masses as well as of the generosity of the well-to-do and the spirit of mutual aid and solidarity amongst the poor and labourers in the Kehillah. The Rome Kehillah in particular possessed twenty-five or so charity organizations covering a range of highly diversified functions. *Orah Hayim* and *Nevei Ha-Shalom*, for example, supplied pillows and cushions to the poor in the Kehillah, and seven different organizations distributed clothing to widows, orphans and paupers and even presented dowries to impoverished brides.

Life in the Kehillah; Culture and Education

In Italy, as in the other Jewish communities of Europe, Kehillah administration was monopolized by the heads of the wealthy families. Only the largest taxpayers in each locality participated in the elections, so that in fact only a very few Kehillah members had the right to vote. The

---

* Officially, the *scudo* was equivalent to a Venetian ducat. Its actual value was half a ducat, or six gold livres.

election assembly chose the *Parnassim*, variously known as *Masari* or *Fattori*, and also a limited committee. At Venice this committee was known as the *Vaad Katon* (Small Committee); at Rome it consisted of sixty members. At Leghorn, this plutocratic system actually developed into formal rule by an aristocracy in which the various offices in the limited assembly of sixty were no longer elected but hereditary. It received ducal approval in 1715. In 1769, however, the Duke of Tuscany limited the hereditary rights of these sixty "Rulers of the Hebrew Nation" to the third generation, but added a proviso excluding retail merchants, brokers and clerks *a priori* from Kehillah administration.

A large part of the Kehillah's revenue, in a régime such as this, must obviously have been derived from indirect taxation. At Rome, the Kehillah budget for 1744 showed that the direct property tax accounted for one-half of the Kehillah's income, 9,168 *scudi*, while the other half consisted of meat, bread, dwelling and similar taxes. Direct tax revenues in the Kehillah's slender budget fell absolutely and proportionately as the middle class became progressively poorer, but indirect taxes were scarcely reduced or not at all.

During the second half of the eighteenth century, the Jews of Italy no longer possessed Talmudic scholars with international reputations such as Isaac Lampronti, author of the great Talmudic encyclopaedia *Pahad Yitzhak*, or poets of the stature of Moses Hayim Luzzatto. But a thorough knowledge of *Halakhah* was still common throughout Italy and Hayim Joseph David Azoulai still met great Talmudic scholars on his second journey there in 1776-77, with whom he was able to hold learned discussions. Rabbinical Colleges existed in nearly every large Kehillah—with the exception of the Papal States, where the Talmud was officially banned—and there were also *Batei Midrash* (houses of learning), known as *Esger*.* During the 1770's, there were two *Batei Midrash* at Leghorn, each accommodating ten scholars, and maintained by bequests specifically for this purpose. One was devoted to the study of the Talmud, the other to the *Zohar*. The Kehillot at Ancona and Leghorn conferred on prominent scholars the title of *Maskil*. In Italy, as in most countries of Europe at that time, knowledge of the Talmud was highly esteemed and of great practical value to the Kehillah leaders. Rabbis and distinguished merchants sat on the same tribunals in the Kehillah law courts, which were autonomous in litigation between Jews.

A widespread knowledge of Hebrew and the Bible, and consequently the existence of a large number of Hebrew poets, was characteristic of Italian Jewry. Hebrew poets could be found through the length and breadth of Italy, from Gorizia in the north to Leghorn and the Papal States in the south. In several cities, such as Gorizia, Padua, Venice, Reggio, Ancona and Leghorn, a number of poets was active at the same period. Their position in their Kehillot was equal to that of the foremost

* From the Hebrew word *hesger*, a closed place, an enclosure.

scholars; the Kehillah of Leghorn actually conferred the title of *Paytan**
on one of its poets.

Their poems were mainly composed for special occasions, the wedding
of a friend, an elegy or a description of an event. But there was also
genuine creative verse; a leading example of this is the work of the
brothers Ephraim and Isaac Luzzatto. Jewish poets also wrote in Italian
during this period. The Court Poet of the Duke of Tuscany was a Jew.
The Jews of Italy generally had a perfect command of the language of the
country, though amongst themselves they conversed in a Judeo-Italian
dialect, generously interspersed with Hebrew words.

The architecture and the tasteful decor of the synagogues and the
artistic quality of the sacramental objects—illuminated Scrolls of the
Book of Esther and *Kethubot*† and the like—are evidence of the high
standard of artistry among the Jews of Italy. The fact that fifteen
musicians are known in the Kehillah of Mantua up to the end of the
eighteenth century is a gauge of the widespread popularity of music. The
night before a circumcision ceremony was spent in song and dance. At
Purim, the ghetto celebrated its own carnival, with masked balls, dances
and Purim plays. Purim songs were included in the *Heder* curriculum for
beginners. Theatrical performances were given at Passover and during
the Feast of Tabernacles (in the city of Siena).

The Jews of Italy were able to maintain their cultural level in the
ghettos because of their excellent educational system. The wealthy
municipality of Leghorn only maintained one public elementary school
before 1785, with only two classes. But the Jews maintained a *Talmud-
Torah* in the smallest of their Kehillot. Private *Hadarim* and home tutors
were employed, but for the most part, the sons of the wealthy also
attended the Kehillah *Talmud-Torah*, though exceptions could be found
in extremely wealthy Kehillot, such as Leghorn and Trieste. In the
beginners' classes, girls and boys were taught together, mostly by women.
Women also taught at the *Talmud-Torah* for girls founded at Rome in
1745. A reform introduced at Ferrara in 1776 ruled that parents should
pay tuition fees to the Kehillah treasurer instead of directly to the
teacher—probably to prevent preferential treatment for the sons of the
rich. Poor pupils received a suit of clothes and other forms of maintenance at *Hannukah* (Maccabean Feast of Lights). In 1751, the bye-laws of
the Ferrara Kehillah forbade pupils to leave the *Talmud-Torah* before
the age of sixteen without the Kehillah treasurer's consent or a Heder
before the age of thirteen. In 1767, the same Kehillah decided in favour
of compulsory education, as far as possible, until the age of eighteen.
Another bye-law adopted in 1767 was typical of the general trend:
grown-up pupils unsuited to abstract studies were to be sent for several

---

* The *Paytanim* of the early Middle Ages were the authors of religious verse,
much of which has been incorporated in the Jewish Prayer Books.

† *Kethubah*—religious marriage contract, read at the wedding ceremony.

hours daily to the local printer to learn typesetting. In this instance, the authorities were more concerned with preserving the tradition of Hebrew printing (which had originated in Italy and reached a high level of development there) than with directing Jewish man-power into productive trades. The curriculum in all *Talmud-Torahs* included arithmetic, Hebrew grammar, Italian grammar, Hebrew writing, Italian writing in Latin characters, and translations from one language to the other, as well as the traditional study of the Bible and Talmud. For a time, the *Talmud-Torah* at Rome even employed a Christian to teach Latin. In the sphere of private education, it was characteristic that boys and girls as well as adult men and women learned dancing together under a Jewish instructor. The study of music was also common.

Generally speaking, there was never any conflict in Italy between the champions of enlightenment and the orthodox as opposed to the situation which arose in western European Jewry as a whole. Similarly, at a later date no controversy broke out between reform and orthodox Judaism. The atmosphere was not conducive to such dissension. Conservatives and radicals in Italy certainly differed on matters of culture and religion, but their secular culture was traditional—an integral and basic part of Italian Jewish life. Differences of opinion that did appear later, under the impact of the French Revolution, centred on the proper balance to be struck between secular and religious studies rather than on the elimination of either. Because of this, Italian Jewry was spared the vast expenditure of energy—more constructively required for the modernization of Jewish life—and the process of political emancipation of Italian Jewry lacked many of the odious manifestations that characterized other Jewish communities in western Europe.

The ghetto system and geographical proximity to the Middle East (with which there was regular overseas communication) caused Italian Jewry to entertain strong hopes of the Messianic redemption and made it particularly conscious of the Jewish community in Palestine. All the larger Italian Kehillot supported a society of *Shomrim Laboker*—Morning Watchers; its members prayed daily at sunrise for speedy redemption. From the beginning of the seventeenth century in Italy, on the initiative of the Venice Kehillah, the members of the Kehillot were required to contribute a fixed annual sum (in the nature of a half-shekel) towards the settlement of Palestine. Several other countries followed suit. These societies for the support of the Holy Land were known as *Yerushalayim* (Jerusalem).

A Messianic attitude began to spread through Italy in about 1770. It was expressed in the *Responsa* correspondence and in rabbinical *Haskamot* (approbations on books published). During the same period, the Jews of Leghorn devised a concrete plan to exploit the political anarchy current in Palestine in order to seize the country from the Turkish Empire for the Jewish people. In 1771, a Russian fleet, which had taken part in the war with the Turks, put in at Leghorn, from which the *M'kubal* (religious mystic) Hayim ibn Atar had sailed in 1751 with a group of Italian Jews to settle in Palestine. A number of German officers in the fleet approached the Jews of Leghorn, proposing that they, the Jews, raise a sum of money to redeem Palestine from Ali Bey, leader of a military band then in power in the country. Some thought was given to Russian support during the negotiations. The Jews of Leghorn were also in touch with the Kehillot of England and Holland regarding the necessary sum. But the entire matter was dropped on the death of Ali Bey. The rise of Napoleon, his prosecution of the Palestine campaign, and the general revolution in world politics gave the Italian Jews new hopes for the imminent redemption of the Jewish people.

Despite its many repressive measures, the Church in Italy never succeeded in implanting hatred of the Jews amongst the Italian population. On the contrary, in Italy, the land of ghettos, mutual relations between Jews and native gentiles were more friendly than in any other country in Europe. The mere fact that the Church found it necessary to prohibit Christians from indulging in social recreations, (e.g. dancing with Jews) on several occasions during the seventeenth and eighteenth centuries, affords ample proof that the decrees were simply not obeyed. The high level of the ordinary Italian's cultural tradition, his *joie de vivre*, affable temperament, and the fact that he had intermingled with Jews for hundreds of years on the same soil, proved more powerful than any sort of artificial barrier. Even in Rome, Church supervision was powerless to prevent Christians from visiting the homes of their Jewish friends, or to dissuade them from taking an oath in the Jewish manner, *Badonai* (a contraction of the Hebrew *B'Adonai*—By my Lord!), or even from asking Jewish women to interpret their dreams. Similarly, the ordinary Jew in Rome adopted many customs of the Italian people and not only used Italian oaths, such as *Corpo di Dio*, often corrupting it to *Corpo di Leo*, but often, during a brawl, even flourished a dagger. The Jews of Rome and Trieste often spent their leisure hours in coffee houses, and they took part in the noisy revelry of the carnivals. Conversely, Christian intellectuals frequently attended the synagogue to hear the rabbi's sermon.

On the Eve of Revolution

The legal position of the Jews in most of the Italian states worsened in the last quarter of the eighteenth century as a result of new oppressive decrees or the revival of those that had lapsed. As the domestic and foreign markets in commerce, industry and the crafts continued to shrink, the governments yielded increasingly to pressure from the Christian lower middle class, which hoped to gain by eliminating competition from Jews and unorganized pedlars and artisans. An obvious political motive lay behind these anti-Jewish measures: in the stormy political atmosphere of approaching revolution, the ruling classes—the clergy, the aristocracy and the urban rich—attempted to divert the masses from the new anti-clerical and anti-feudal trends, by imbuing them with religious fanaticism and anti-Jewish hatred. The Church led this movement. The centre of its activity was at Rome, the capital of Catholicism and the Papal States.

The Jews of the Papal States found the policy of Pius VI particularly offensive, because his predecessor, Clement XIV, had modified several restrictions, especially those affecting Jewish commerce. Clement XIV, as Bishop Ganganelli, had drawn up the Papal Bull of 1760, directed against the horrible ritual blood accusations in Poland. During his period as Pope, the Inquisition's direct jurisdiction over the Kehillah in Rome had been abolished. The direction of the Church's new campaign against the Jews was clearly demonstrated by a pamphlet on the ritual blood accusation at Trent in 1475, which appeared on the streets of Rome immediately after Pius VI became Pope. Several months later, more inflammatory anti-Jewish sheets were published. Dissemination of this literature only ceased after great efforts by the Kehillah and the payment of vast sums of money to the Pope's courtiers. Even so, an edict issued by Pius VI on April 5, 1775, was expressly motivated, according to the preamble, by the necessity of "removing from the faithful the danger of revolution which too much fraternization with the Jews may bring upon them."

The *Editto sopra gli Ebrei* assembled in forty-four articles every Papal decree hostile to the Jews since the Middle Ages and the Catholic Counter-Reformation. It forbade Jews, native or foreign, to spend the night outside the ghetto walls, on pain of "being drawn three times on the rack." Jews were not permitted to keep a store, workshop, or warehouse outside the ghetto except by special permission, and even then only in the close vicinity of the ghetto. They were not permitted to remain outside Rome for more than one day, "not even under the pretext that they require a change of air." A Jew who wished to travel to a fair had to obtain a permit from a Bishop or an Inquisitor and then report to the Church authorities at his destination. In Rome, Jews were forbidden to ride in a coach or a chaise. They had to wear a distinctive badge inside or outside the ghetto, except during their journeys. In the case of men, this consisted of a yellow badge on their hats; of women, a yellow kerchief. Jews were not allowed to employ Christian women as maids, nurses, midwives, washerwomen, or even as fire-lighters on the Jewish sabbath. Other equally harsh prohibitions were imposed on a wide range of Jewish religious practices, and the rabbis were held responsible for the attendance of three hundred Jewish men and two hundred Jewish women at weekly missionary sermons on Saturday afternoons.

In the Venetian Republic, anti-Jewish decrees were inspired by the clerical reactionaries, supported by Rome, and also by a growing tendency to curtail the privileges of artisans, industrialists and merchants, especially if they were aliens, who did not belong to a guild. Jews were forbidden to engage in any kind of manufacture, to employ Christian workers or to carry on trade in grain and other food-stuffs. Jews could not accept commercial agencies, government agencies, government monopolies, or take on lease any branch of government finances. Similarly, they were not allowed to function as licensed brokers. The restrictions, in fact, left no occupation open to the Jews of Venice except the large scale import and export business in the hands of the upper stratum of wealthy merchants and the rag and second-hand goods trade for the common people. The Jews of the Papal States were also hardest hit by the renewed wave of economic reaction. In Venice, the economic anti-Jewish measures were considerably modified in 1788, but in Rome a vicious system was enforced and restrictions on commerce heavily affected the wealthiest Jewish establishments, halving their assets. However, the worst consequence of Pius VI's new edict was to intensify the terror accompanying forced baptism. A particularly shocking incident occurred in 1784 when a Jewish apostate claimed that two orphans in the ghetto were his blood relations. The Kehillah refused to hand over the children for conversion and the Papal authorities threw a large number of Jewish boys into prison as hostages, seized the two victims, and carried them to the baptismal font.

In the few areas of Italy not economically or culturally affected by the country's general decline, no such decrees restricted the Jews and the scope of their rights was even extended. The ghetto was abolished in the prosperous port of Trieste in 1784, and Jews were allowed to enter the governing body of the stock exchange. The Edict on Toleration of Joseph II was in force throughout all Austrian Italy. This made it possible for Jews to become craftsmen and to enter the free professions, to acquire real estate, and to send their sons to school. The advance in the legal and social status of the Jews in the Grand Duchy of Tuscany— also under Austrian influence—was even more noticeable. At Florence, Jews were granted the right to enrol in the local literary academy, while at Leghorn, the salons of the Jewish intellectuals were centres of the city's cultural life by the first half of the eighteenth century. At Leghorn too, an order promulgated in 1780 granted the "Hebrew Nation" the right to return one representative to the municipal council and to the municipal administration. This was just one of the many reforms instituted to promote free trade and industry and break down the guild monopolies. In other states of northern Italy such as Mantua, Parma, Piacenza and Modena, the legal status of the Jews improved during this period, especially in respect of their right to engage in the crafts, own real estate and study medicine. However, this progress only demonstrated the extent to which the old régime of Jewish disenfranchisement conflicted with the contemporary requirements of capitalist economy and society. Even the general reforms of enlightened capitalism failed to avert the Revolution; they only accelerated its inevitable eruption.

The French Revolution

The triumphant advance of the French Revolution brought panic to feudal and clerical circles in Italy. The reactionaries did their utmost to denounce it as a Jewish plot against the Church and to turn the people's bitterness against the Jews. On May 30, 1790, rioting broke out in Leghorn under the slogan of limiting the unrestricted import of wheat, of defending the Church against the reforms of enlightened despotism instituted by the Austrian Emperor, and against the danger purportedly threatening it from the Jews. A mob of dock workers and porters broke into the Jewish quarter and attacked the synagogue. It was dispersed by the military, and the Kehillah donated a sum of money to the Church for distribution among the city's poor. At Florence, the ghetto was saved by the intervention of the local archbishop, during political and social disorders there.

At Rome, the clergy systematically organized a counter-revolutionary movement, inciting the mob to take up arms against the French and the Jews. Christian merchants joined this movement in order to spread propaganda against the Jews. It was alleged that the Jews were sabotaging Christian commerce and had arrogated to themselves a degree of commercial freedom in excess of the Papal edicts. A revolutionary demonstration organized on January 13, 1793, by the French representative, Basseville, provided the pretext for an assault on the Jews. Basseville was murdered and the mob stormed on to pillage French business establishments. It was repulsed by the French and turned towards the ghetto gates. Wooden poles were stacked in front of the gates, and only pouring rain prevented the attackers from sending the ghetto up in flames. The siege of the ghetto lasted for eight days, with a contingent of Papal guards stationed outside to protect it. "In order to maintain proper order," the Pope renewed the harsh edict of 1775 in Rome and the other cities under his temporal rule. In fact, the decrees against Jewish commerce were intended to arouse the sympathy of the reactionary mob, but the reason given by the Grand Inquisitor for the severe ban on Christians entering the ghetto both in Rome and at Ancona was that it was a defensive measure against a revolutionary plot.

This was by no means the final measure by the Papal government to incite feeling against the Jews. A rumour was circulated that thousands of revolutionary tricolour badges had been found in the possession of a Jewish trader and the leaders and notables of the Kehillah were thrown into jail with the demand that large sums of money be paid for their release. The accusation that the *Parnassim* of the Rome Kehillah were in league with the Revolution was certainly false. A chronicle of the events of 1793, written by a member of the Kehillah Committee, specifically describes their fear of the Revolution. Their political aspirations went no further than the submission of pleas for mercy and large gifts of money to the Pope, that he might temper the implementation of his decrees. However, the cringing attitude of the leaders of the Rome Kehillah, who were loyal to the Pope as their temporal ruler, did not reflect the political inclinations of the Jewish population of Italy. This was proved by their enthusiastic participation in revolutionary events a few years later, culminating in the liberation of the country by French arms. Individual Jews, at great personal risk, even took part in preparing the ground for the revolution in Italy, despite the terrorism of the moribund régime. At Padua, in 1791, Dr. Michael Salom was reprimanded by the government of Venice for taking part in the student revolutionary movement, and in 1793 he was led in chains to a Venice prison. In 1797, a number of Jews were arrested at Ancona and charged with supplying arms to the approaching French army. The manuscript of a book containing the date 1793 in ornate characters with drawing of the Liberty Tree and the Phrygian cap of the Revolution reveals the sympathy that the Jews of Piedmont felt for the French Revolution.

In the spring of 1796, French forces, led by Bonaparte, invaded Italy through Piedmont. During the next two years, until the beginning of 1798, they conquered the northern and central parts of the country, including the Papal States. More powerful than Napoleon's military genius was the revolutionary impetus of the masses, which threw open the portals of ducal and ecclesiastical palaces to the French soldiers bringing the new order. *Liberty, Equality, Fraternity!* was still the clarion call of the Revolution, which was already showing marked signs of decline in the land of its birth. The score of duchies and aristocratic republics of Italy crashed in ruins, and the rule of the Holy Fathers of the Eternal City collapsed like a house of cards. Northern Italy was annexed by stages to the Cisalpine Republic, while the Papal "Heritage of Saint Peter" was proclaimed the Roman Republic. For Italian Jewry it signalled the advent of a political rebirth after centuries of Catholic reaction.

One of the first acts of the commanders of the victorious French army on arriving anywhere was to proclaim the equality of the Jews with all other citizens. In no other country did Jewish emancipation so *literally* mean destruction of the ghetto walls or arouse such spontaneous demonstrations of sympathy by gentiles, as in Italy. In several cities, the Christian population surged forward of its own accord with hatchets and axes to raze the ghetto walls. The most impressive demonstrations of fraternity with the Jews were held in the Venetian Republic. In the towns of the province of Venice, the *Terra Firma*, the revolutionary movement, was more powerful than anywhere else in Italy, even before the French invasion, because of its exploitation by the government of Venice. In Venice itself the aristocratic régime aroused violent discontent. The French army received an enthusiastic welcome everywhere there. In 1796, the population of Verona pulled up the ghetto gates and ceremonially burned them in an adjacent square. At Padua, after its liberation in April, 1797, large numbers of young Jews enlisted in the National Guard despite propaganda against the acceptance of Jews, foreigners and clergymen. The Jewish revolutionary hero, Dr. Michael Salom, was elected to the City Council, and the recently founded *Patriotic Society for the Education of the People* incorporated Jewish enfranchisement in its *Declaration of Principles*. At the end of August, 1797, "the barbaric and senseless name of the ghetto" was altered by government edict to *Via Libera*—Freedom Road. Two weeks later an order was issued to raze the ghetto walls to their foundations, so that "every vestige of segregation, which contradicts the rights of the free man, be wiped out." At Venice, by order of the new City Council, the Kehillah was reorganized on a democratic basis of general suffrage—with the exception, as in the municipal elections, of servants and mendicants.

The greater part of the Papal States was also conquered at this period. Immediately after Ferrara was taken, the French General Robert ordered the Jews, via the Kehillah delegation, to stop wearing the yellow badge and to leave the ghetto gates open day and night. At Lugo and Cento, Jews tore the badge of shame from their clothes at a public ceremony, to the accompaniment of shouts of joy from their neighbours. At Cento, also a National Guard Company spontaneously pulled up the three gates of the ghetto, carried them to the public square, and burned them amidst cries of "Hurrah for Liberty!" At Ancona, the French soldiers entered the city just as a mob was laying siege to the ghetto gates. The troops tore the yellow badges off the hats of Jewish passers-by. Here, a Jew was elected to the delegation sent to Napoleon to obtain his confirmation of the republican constitution. As elsewhere, the Jews in Ancona were elected deputies to the Constituent Assembly of the Cispadane Republic, and Jewish officers and men served in the National Guard.

The Jews of Italy, after hundred of years of unparalleled subjection and virtual servitude at the hands of the Papal Inquisition, awoke to the awareness and pride of equal citizenship at the first sign of civil liberty.

At the beginning of 1798, the Jews of Rome in their turn saw the beginning of freedom. On February 15, immediately after the proclamation of the Roman Republic, and five days after the entry of the French forces, the Jews removed the yellow badge. In the evening of February 17, the entire ghetto was illuminated and the Jews celebrated the planting of the Tree of Liberty in front of the synagogue to the accompaniment of music and games. Unfortunately their neighbours from across the Tiber were not yet free of their clerical prejudices. A few days later, they pinned miniature crosses on their coloured cap-badges, and at a city assembly in March, protested against the enlistment of Jews in the National Guard. The authorities retaliated by conferring a commission (the rank of major) on a Jew, Bar Raphael, in the National Guard and by organizing a special battalion composed mainly of Jews with Jewish commanding officers. On July 9, 1798 (21st of Messidor, Year VI, according to the calendar of the Revolution), the French commander proclaimed complete enfranchisement for the Jews on an equal basis with all other citizens of the Roman Republic. A week later, Ezekiel Morpurgo was appointed a member of the Senate. To avoid misunderstanding, on November 18 (28th of Brumaire, Year VII), the military authorities ordered that Jews be released from the payment of all *special* taxes "in view of the fact that such taxes have had their origin in religious tyranny."

French troops had been stationed at Leghorn, the largest Jewish community in Italy, since 1796, but the Grand Duchy of Tuscany was not totally conquered by France and proclaimed a republic until the end of March, 1799. The Jews of Florence and Siena had suffered greatly during the transition years because of anti-French and anti-Jewish agitation. They joyfully welcomed their enfranchisement and also commemorated it by planting a Liberty Tree. The aristocratic leaders of the Leghorn Kehillah displayed a different attitude towards the new régime, though the Jews there had also faced danger on the eve of the French occupation. Leghorn's commerce, like that of Amsterdam, had been gravely compromised by the French war against England, and, like the Jewish plutocracy of Holland, the Sephardi aristocrats were not anxious to renounce their domination of the Kehillah. But the new attitude to Jewish enfranchisement was also in evidence here. An Italian wrote a song in honour of the planting of the Liberty Tree in the Jewish quarter of Leghorn, dedicated to "those of our citizens who are members of the Hebrew Nation." Two Jews were elected to the new city council. Two others served as captains in the local National Guard, which also included two Jewish companies, each of one hundred men.

The Napoleonic period

The temporary withdrawal of the French from Italy when Napoleon embarked on his Egyptian campaign enabled the clerical and feudal forces of the counter-revolution to annul the achievements of the short-lived democratic régime. They instituted a reign of terror against the Jews, depriving them of their newly won liberties, reimposing the special taxes and war indemnities and in some places, such as Senigalia and Siena, they claimed a heavy toll of Jewish life. Elsewhere, pillaging and arson occurred, and Jews who had participated in the establishment of the democratic order were thrown into jail. A wave of anti-Jewish feeling swept across literature, the press and the stage.

In 1800, Napoleon, now First Consul of the Republic, again crossed the Alps into Italy and, following his victories, French hegemony and the French political system were reinstated. Piedmont and Parma were summarily annexed to France, followed by Tuscany (the Kingdom of Etruria) in 1807, and the Papal States, including Rome, in 1809. The north-eastern part of the country and Venice were formed into the Kingdom of Italy, with Napoleon as King. Thus all of northern and central Italy was actually—and part of it, officially—under French rule. Jewish enfranchisement was an acknowledged principle of the régime in Italy, as throughout the Empire. However, whereas the emancipation of Italy's Jews in 1796-97 had had the character of a revolutionary upheaval borne along by fervent popular enthusiasm, the renewed enfranchisement under the rule of Napoleon was now an official action authorized from above, in which the people had no share whatsoever. The governing authorities in Italy, as in France, did not give much thought to implementing the enfranchisement and the abolition of various forms of discrimination. Rome was typical of the way in which enfranchisement was put into effect. Although the ghetto gates were now open day and night, in 1810 many Jews raised objections to the removal of the gateposts because they feared attacks. The Mayor of Rome submitted their case to the prefect, with an additional reason of his own: the demolition work might damage buildings in the neighbouring quarter.

The thin crust of wealthy merchants, industrialists and large land-owners drew the main benefit from the Napoleonic régime. Prominent and wealthy Jews were appointed municipal councillors, judges in the civil courts, members of chambers of commerce, etc., in most of the provinces of Italy. But the Government paid remarkably close attention to reaction-ary, anti-Jewish tendencies, even in its relations with this élite. The Prefect of the Province of Po in Piedmont expressly explained in his report to the government that there were so few Jewish officials because of the population's prejudice against the Jews.

The leading spokesmen of the Jewish upper middle class were mainly concerned with securing aristocratic titles and other honours for them-selves, although the social and economic conditions of the mass of the Jewish population had not improved substantially, except in a few provinces. Slight changes had occurred in the occupational structure of the Jewish communities of Piedmont, even if the prefects' official reports to the government concerning the abolition of the Infamous Decree of 1808 contained some exaggerations. Their efforts to emphasize the new government's achievements led them to claim the credit for the fact that Jews were working at trades which they had actually already pursued under the old régime. Be that as it may, the reports showed that nearly one-third of all the Jews in the province were engaged in crafts, mainly as tailors, but also as goldsmiths, smiths, mechanics, cobblers, saddlers, carpenters and the like. About a quarter of the Jewish population, as a result of their new legal status, was able to work in agriculture, nearly two-fifths earned a living in commerce and the textile industry and a negligible percentage were functionaries.

The picture of the general economic structure of Jewish life in other Italian provinces was less cheerful. A bare $2\frac{1}{2}$ per cent of the 1,180 Jews of Florence were engaged in industry and the crafts in 1810, and about the same number in moneylending. The remainder were mainly pedlars or junk—and rag—dealers. In the same year, the Rome Kehillah possessed 3,038 members comprising 683 wage earners. Of these, only 12 per cent were registered as artisans, mainly tailors, hat-makers, mattress-makers and similar tradesmen. However, many tailors were listed among the 164 old clothes dealers who represented a quarter of all bread-winners. Shopkeepers and dealers in cloth and ready-made garments accounted for 162, and pedlars and hucksters for 128 families—nearly one-fifth of the Kehillah.

The poverty among the Jews of Rome was "unusual" and "horrible," according to the official evidence of the Consistory, the Prefect and the Governor-General. Many Kehillah members lived on a dole. Jews in the provinces of Parma and Tuscany (Department of Taro) were described as very poor, in reports by the Consistory and the Prefect. Even in the relatively affluent Kehillah of Florence, statistics on housing conditions in 1810 classified 55 per cent as poor, and another 14 per cent as welfare cases. The Prefect of the Piedmontese Department of Duara could only describe forty Jewish families (ninety-eight people) as wealthy industria-lists—cotton mill owners who employed many Christian workers.

Despite the favourable attitude of Italian Jewry towards secular education, only very few Jewish children attended public schools because of the clericalism of the Napoleonic era. Only ninety Jewish children in the whole province of Piedmont took advantage of their opportunity; in Rome, there was not a single Jewish child in any public school.

The thin upper stratum of the Jewish plutocracy represented the Jewish population to the state authorities and played a major role in the Assembly of Notables at Paris and in the *Grand Sanhedrin*. This plutocracy welcomed the Consistory Edict, which strengthened its rule over the Kehillot in every region annexed to the French Empire. A section of the enlightened Jewish middle class in Italy now became anxious for an official reform of the Jewish religion. They were led by Moses Formigini, a man close to government circles, who addressed a memoran-dum to the Ministry. It concerned the introduction of a modern ritual, the institution of a catechism in accordance with the *Sanhedrin's* resolu-tions, reform in education, and similar reforms. However, most of the Jews in Italy found these suggestions displeasing. In 1814 the Kehillah of Leghorn even burned all copies of an essay in Italian by a local Jew,

Aaron Fernando, advocating a basic reform of the Jewish law. The trend in Italy was in complete contrast with this striving for assimilation. At this period, against a background of world upheaval caused by the Napoleonic Wars, Italian Jews, like the *Hasidim* in Poland, were inspired by hope of the imminent coming of the Messiah and the redemption of Israel. The degree of patience and endurance evinced by the Jewish masses in the face of growing anti-Jewish reaction and conformist Kehillah leadership varied from place to place. In the Jewish quarter of Rome, a self-defence unit was organized against bands of Christian clerical reactionaries, who were not yet resigned to the equality of Jewish commercial rights. The French commandant, at the request of the *Parnassim*, ordered the arrest of the two leaders of the Jewish rebel organization, Abraham Citoni and Jacob Amati. This caused a tremendous uproar in the ghetto, with the French guard siding with the insurgents. Additional arrests were useless and the fury only subsided when the victims were released.

CHAPTER SIX

SWITZERLAND

The Eve of Revolution and the Helvetian Republic

The civil enfranchisement of the Jews which spread over western Europe with the victorious advance of the French armies eventually reached Switzerland. After the expulsions of the Middle Ages no Jewish inhabitants had remained in any part of this small, sparsely populated country, except in the two villages of Endingen and Lengnau in the county of Baden. In 1774, there was a total of 108 Jewish families in these two neighbouring communities. Subsequently, despite all legal restrictions, there was an influx of Jewish immigrants from Germany, Alsace, and even from Poland. During the Napoleonic period, the number of Jews in the two villages rose to between 1,500 and 2,000.

The legal status of the small Jewish community in Switzerland was governed by the aristocratic political régime of the Federation. A hereditary aristocracy of burghers ruled the country and had given birth to a hereditary élite, which controlled the cities. In the villages, the communities of burghers, which had all rights, were closed to foreigners, however long their residence. *Ansässe* (residents) either had no right whatsoever to buy or lease land, or were severely restricted in so doing; nor could they engage independently in crafts or commerce. The Jews in the two Baden villages were only tolerated because they paid a regular fee to the county and to each of its many representatives when their writs of protection were renewed, and also and most important, an annual tax to the *Landvogt*. The writs of protection had to be renewed once every sixteen years, when the rotating office of *Landvogt* came round to each canton. Deprived of the right to own land and excluded from the craft guilds, the only occupation permitted to the Jews was commerce, more specifically, peddling and collateral loaning, but not mortgage loaning. Jews also had permission to slaughter and sell meat. Under Napoleon, seven-eighths of the Jews in the two villages were still pedlars, fair traders or cattle merchants. Quite frequently, they combined their ordinary business with moneylending as they made their rounds of the villages. They would make loans to the peasants, taking a cow or several measures of wheat as surety. The most important estate agents in the entire county of Baden were also drawn from this small Jewish community.

The eighteenth-century writs of protection forbade the Jews to buy houses, but it became customary for a purchase to be valid if, after three public auctions, no Christian buyer made a suitable bid. Jews attending fairs anywhere in the country, but particularly at Zurzach in Canton Aargau, had to pay, apart from a poll tax, double or triple the excise paid by Christians on merchandise, and even more on horses. In order to limit the number of Jews, the writ of protection for 1776 forbade unpropertied Jews to marry, while a bride from abroad could not enter the country unless she brought a dowry of at least 500 *gulden*.

The social and economic composition, economic functions and legal status of the small Jewish community of Switzerland resembled the Jewish communities of Germany and Alsace-Lorraine. Its Kehillah life was also conducted along the same lines as in the neighbouring countries. Each of the two villages had its own synagogue; the one at Lengnau was built in 1750, that at Endingen in 1764. They had a common cemetery and one rabbi ministered to the spiritual needs of both. The Kehillah income was derived from property- and profit-taxes, marriage taxes and meat and wine taxes. Until the end of the eighteenth century, their language was Yiddish, but Jewish folklore persisted beyond this date, with native lullabies, Sabbath and *Havdalah* songs, Purim jingles, as well as characteristic satires on the modern way of life which penetrated these two Kehillot in the eighteenth century. Evidence of the cultural level of this tiny community is supported by an original prayer for peace composed in 1794 by the Kehillah's rabbi, Raphael Ben-Abraham Riess. Jewish folk-art flourished here even during the nineteenth century, in the form of lace *Matzot* napkins, traditional female clothing of original design, tombstone engravings, and illustrated religious calendars.

Even before the outbreak of the Revolution, enlightened Swiss statesmen had included demands for improved legal status for the few Jews in the country in their programme of political reform. In March, 1798, the Swiss revolution broke out and, with help from France, transformed the feudal federation into a unified "Helvetian Republic." The new state was organized on the French pattern, with a governing Directory, and a Grand Council and Senate comprising the two legislative chambers. The abolition of serfdom and the acceptance in principle of the enfranchisement of all citizens by law would logically seem to imply the recognition of equal rights for the Jews.

However, despite the negligible number of Jews, the reactionaries offered stubborn opposition whenever the Jewish question was placed on the agenda. The reactionaries were more powerful in Switzerland than in any other of the new republics because of the lower middle class agrarian composition of the population. The discussion of Jewish enfranchisement was continually deferred until a reversion to federalism restored all power to the cantons and thus removed even the formal possibility of dealing with a question that concerned the country as a whole. Though the debates in the legislative chambers in 1799 produced no concrete results, the alignment of political forces that they created was most instructive.

The government, representing the new political régime and the radical senators and deputies, particularly those from the French cantons, supported the extention of equal rights to the Jews. The opponents of enfranchisement resorted to the usual reactionary political and clerical arguments, but they also voiced the undisguised apprehension of the backward lower middle class faced with an expanding capitalist economy and economic competition from the Jews.

The debate on the subject was resumed from time to time and involved a dreary repetition by the right-wing deputies of all the worst arguments against granting the Jews equal rights of citizenship, such as had been heard in the French National Assembly. The moral stature of the Jews was questioned; their allegedly nefarious economic pursuits were castigated and their loyalty to Switzerland was challenged on the grounds of their religion and their belief in the return to Zion with the coming of the Messiah. When the radical wing put on the pressure, the reactionaries turned to devious legislative stratagems to reduce the number of Jews who would, in practice, be eligible for enfranchisement. Deputy Elmlinger emotionally exploited the fact that Napoleon had at that time just led his expedition to the Holy Land and had addressed a proclamation to the Jews of the world on the re-establishment of a Jewish state in Palestine. Elmlinger concluded his diatribe against the Jews by pointing to a group of Jews in the visitors' gallery and exclaiming: "Let them go, let them go and beg Napoleon to lead them to Jerusalem . . ." An outcry ensued and the Speaker refused to allow Elmlinger to continue his speech. But most of the deputies stood firm in their opposition and their statements were no less drastic than Elmlinger's.

A majority vote in the two legislative chambers of the Republic rejected the motion to alter the legal status of the handful of Swiss Jews. The Directory then exercised its governmental authority and decided to enforce at least one reform. The Grand Council had passed a resolution classifying the Jews as foreigners. The appointed governor of the Canton of Baden was therefore ordered to allow the Jews in the Canton to live outside the two Kehillot and also to buy and own land on the same basis as other foreigners.

The decline of the French Revolution encouraged the Swiss reactionaries, who had long been looking for an opportunity to overthrow the new régime. In the summer of 1802, when the French military forces left the country, counter-revolutionary rebellions broke out in many places. The reactionaries also began to stir up the peasants against the two Jewish communities. Mounted couriers were dispatched to regions around Endingen and Lengnau to provoke a crusade against the Jews. They were successful. On September 21, hundreds of peasants marched on the two villages. They smashed the windows, and broke in the doors of Jewish homes, pillaging as they went. In memory of this pogrom, the Jews of Switzerland declared a fast on the first day of *S'lihot* (penitential prayers offered during the week before the New Year). This custom continued to be observed for many decades during the nineteenth century.

The counter-revolutionary ferment in Switzerland abated at the beginning of 1803, following Napoleon's Act of Mediation. By agreement with France, the old, loose federal system was restored, with each canton free to decide on its own internal policies. This implied the end of hopes for Jewish enfranchisement. In 1803, the Jews submitted a petition to the Federal Council requesting equal rights in trade and taxation. They specifically waived their claim to political rights. The French ambassador, General Ney, supported this request, but the Council decided to postpone discussion on the question for one year. At the end of this period, in 1804, the representative of Canton Aargau (to which the Canton of Baden had been annexed) served notice that under the existing régime only the cantonal authorities were empowered to deal with such matters. The Federal Council agreed, and the question of Jewish rights henceforth remained under the jurisdiction of the cantonal authorities, government and council. In 1805, the Aargau cantonal government drafted a law conferring civil rights—with the exception of political rights which the Jews themselves had eliminated from their petition—on all Jews who had resided in the canton for the twenty years before 1798. The cantonal Grand Council rejected the proposal, and only in 1809 did it ratify a "Law Concerning the Jews Resident in the Canton." Instead of civil rights, the Jews of the two Kehillot had "the rights of protection," that they had possessed before the Revolution, with only one difference: they were now subject to all the canton's orders and police injunctions. The right to reside outside the two Kehillot was made conditional on the possession of a diploma or a master craftsman's certificate. These conditions could never be entirely fulfilled because of government policy. No instance of a Jew utilising this right was recorded until the middle of the nineteenth century.

A number of Jews from abroad, particularly from France, succeeded in settling in other cantons, in the cities of Basle, Zurich, Berne, Neuchâtel and in the neighbourhood of Geneva, by virtue of the rights granted to citizens of foreign countries. In Canton Aargau, the permission to engage in the crafts and in agriculture which the government conceded to the Jews, was of no practical value, as the ban on land purchases continued to apply and Christian craftsmen would not accept Jewish boys as apprentices. Jewish marriages also required permission from the cantonal government, which depended on the ages of bride and groom, the state of their possessions, and the groom's profession. On the other hand, the government was almost paternal in its "concern" for the German education of Jewish youths, and in 1813 ordered the two Kehillot to establish schools under the supervision of the cantonal education authorities. The Jews were not over-enthusiastic about this compulsory education order and until the beginning of the 1820's less than one-third of all Jewish school-age boys attended as pupils. Girls did not go to school at all.

It was certainly no coincidence that the reactionary Jewish law which oppressed the Jews of Switzerland for many decades was enacted in the Canton of Aargau a year after Napoleon's Infamous Degree on the Jews of France. The growing anti-Jewish reaction which continued in France under Napoleon's government had many fervent admirers in Switzerland, where the achievements of the French Revolution were stifled at birth.

CHAPTER SEVEN

GERMANY

A. *SECOND HALF OF THE EIGHTEENTH CENTURY*

The Jewish Diaspora in Germany; the Legal Position

German Jewry occupied a unique position in the history of the Jews. Its situation in the heart of Europe offered it the task of mediating between western culture and the great centre of the Jewish people in eastern Europe. During the Middle Ages, it was from the rabbinical academies of *Ashkenaz*—Germany—that learning had reached the Jews of Austria, Bohemia and Poland. The *Haskalah* Movement, which revived and reinvigorated Jewish culture in Bohemia, Moravia, Poland and Russia, originated with German Jewry at the end of the eighteenth century. The Jews of Germany retained their spiritual hegemony during the nineteenth century in the field of modern Jewish studies, in which they led all the communities of the Diaspora.

The intellectual emergence of the upper classes of German Jewry took place in the second half of the eighteenth century, when the legal and social condition of the majority of the community was the most squalid and abject in all Europe. This was the result of the retarded economic and political development of the country. Germany was cut off from the main channels of world commerce (which had moved to the shores of the Atlantic in the great Age of Discoveries) and this caused an economic decline which lasted until the second half of the nineteenth century. Germany was no smaller than France in area or population (over 24 million at the beginning of the nineteenth century), but Germany was several decades behind in development. Approximately two-thirds of its population still subsisted on agriculture, while about three-quarters of the total lived in rural areas. Economic conditions determined the pattern of social relationships in Germany: the peculiar direction they followed was determined by the absence of a middle class on the western European pattern. In 1800, less than 1,000 people in all Germany—apart from the nobility—possessed an annual income of 10,000 marks. The feudal nobles, who were the legal rulers, also dominated economic and social life. The shopkeepers and artisans were not socially or culturally superior to the peasants. The only class which possessed political views and an educational level free of the limitations of narrow provincialism was made up of senior officials—abundant in this land of many states. Germany's political disintegration had resulted in the creation of over three hundred sovereign entities. These included large countries such as Bavaria, Saxony, and above all, Prussia, and diminutive duchies and principalities, "free cities," and baronial states, some only consisting of a few, or perhaps only one village.

Pettiness, lower middle-class envy, and guild parochialism were all active in forming administrative policy and determining the German population's attitude to its small and widely scattered Jewish community. Almost all the German states built up a minutely planned system for the restriction of Jewish rights, unequalled elsewhere.

The total number of Jews in Germany at the end of the eighteenth century, did not exceed 175,000 souls* and constituted less than 1 per cent of the entire German population. The Jewish communities were distributed in a semi-circle stretching from the banks of the Rhine in the west, through the duchies of the south, to the eastern areas. The largest German state, Prussia, also possessed the most Jews. In 1803, it was estimated that 43,000 Jews lived on Prussian territory (not counting the areas annexed after the partition of Poland). There was only a small number of Jews in the north German states of Hanover and Mecklenburg; Saxony, the largest central German state, had no Jewish settlements except at Dresden and Leipzig.

The great port of Hamburg held the largest Kehillah in the country: including the Jews of nearby Altona, it had a membership of 9,000 at the end of the eighteenth century. Two other Kehillot in all Germany could claim over 3,000 members: those at Berlin and Frankfurt-on-Main. Only a few other Kehillot had over 1,000 members. The vast majority of German Jews were scattered in medium- and small-sized Kehillot. Cities in some states, such as Baden, only granted the right of domicile to one Jewish family. The Jewish communities were most dispersed in the south of Germany, where considerable numbers existed in small towns and villages. Some of these contained several score of Jewish families; in others, individual Jews were sheltered by the local baron, in some instances, actually living in his castle.

Every German state had special laws relating to the Jews and elaborate limitations on their rights of domicile and occupation. In common, however, they all defined in advance the number of Jews legally permitted to reside in their territory, either by a fixed quota of protected Jewish families or by exacting an exorbitant fee for a special protection permit, which only few Jews could afford. In all of them, manual trades and cultivation of the soil were forbidden to Jews. They were only allowed to trade within the bounds of a variety of restrictions and limitations.

---

* This figure does not include the Polish Jews who came under Prussian rule in 1793 and 1795; they alone numbered over 170,000. It does include the Jews of the River Netze area, some 13,000, who became Prussian subjects after the first partition of Poland in 1772.

Throughout the country, heavy taxation levied specifically on the Jews consumed their resources. The purpose of this pressure was not purely financial; the authorities also intended it to prevent as far as possible competition between Jewish and Christian retail traders, shopkeepers and artisans, and also to allay the bitterness of the increasingly impoverished lower middle class by a display of concern for its monopoly rights. In pursuit of this policy Jews were forbidden to conduct trade in open stores in most of the German states. In the remainder, detailed legislation kept their commercial activities within narrow limits. For the most part, they were only permitted to engage in petty trade and peddling. Even then, the merchant and storekeepers' guilds ceaselessly denounced this pitiable Jewish trade as an encroachment on sacred Christian privilege. Yet the function that these Jews discharged in developing the country's trade was so important that even the authorities protected them against their adversaries on most occasions—though always scrupulously ensuring that their numbers never exceeded the quota.

A strain of fabulously wealthy individual Jews emerged, scarcely affected by the repressive measures which burdened the main body of the Jewish population. The big wholesalers and export merchants in particular, the money brokers, government suppliers, army commissionaries and, above all, the factory owners enjoyed a wide range of privileges in their domiciliary rights and economic activities.

Prussia led the other German states in meticulously contriving restrictions and special taxes. The Revised General Privilege and Regulation for the Jewry of the Kingdom of Prussia,* was promulgated by Frederick II—the "Philosopher on the Throne"—in 1750 and remained in force until enfranchisement during the Napoleonic era. It limited the number of Jewish families possessing the right of domicile, fixing it *a priori* for every district throughout the state, from the banks of the Rhine to Silesia, and for each of the large cities, such as Berlin, Halberstadt and Breslau. First in rank were the "protected and generally privileged Jews" (*General-privilegierte Schutzjuden*), of whom there were barely a few score in all (some twenty in Berlin, forty in Breslau). They were entitled to settle in any city they chose, to engage in all branches of wholesale trade and industry, and to bequeath their rights of domicile to their sons. Most of the Jews legally entitled to reside in the state were classified as "ordinary protected Jews" (*Ordentliche Schutzjuden*). They were granted the right of domicile in one specified city and could only bequeath it to their eldest son. In 1763, on payment of the vast sum of 70,000 thaler, the king agreed to grant hereditary rights of domicile to second-born sons. More limited rights were conceded to "extraordinary protected Jews" (*Ausserordentliche Schutzjuden*); their number was fixed at sixty-three families in Berlin, as compared with 203 "ordinary"

---

* *Revidiertes General-Privilegium und Reglement fuer die Judenschaft im Koenigreiche Preussen.*

Jews. At Breslau, they exceeded those in the "ordinary" category. The heads of these "extraordinary" families were, for the most part, widows of ordinary protected Jews or the husbands of such widows by remarriage. As a matter of principle, they were not allowed to bequeath their rights of domicile unless their son obtained special permission—and one condition for this was possession of a minimum sum of 1,000 thaler. This category also included members of the liberal professions and public servants (*Publique Bediente*). Their numbers were *not* rigidly restricted (fifty-five in Berlin) but they were subject to a high fee which the Kehillah undertook to pay for the right to employ them. This category of Jew and also sons who had not inherited the right of domicile from their fathers, were not allowed to marry amongst themselves. Domestic servants, employees, private tutors, and similar individuals were included in the category of tolerated Jews (*Geduldete Juden*), to whom marriage was generally prohibited on pain of expulsion.

Innumerable repressive measures also limited the sources of livelihood open to ordinary protected Jews. They were categorically forbidden to work in any occupation represented by a craft guild; they were allowed to work at a few specified light trades such as polishing precious stones and optical lenses, gold and silver cording, seal engraving and the sewing of undergarments. Detailed qualifications even restricted trade, which the *Privilegium* defined, together with usury, as the Jew's main source of livelihood. The right to trade in items such as livestock, wines and other beverages, perfumes and spices, wool and untanned hides, was denied to Jews. Prussian absolutism thus established a detailed classification of Jews according to their social position, from "generally privileged" Jewish capitalists enjoying wide rights to pedlars and *Betteljuden* (mendicants) who were subject to merciless expulsion.

The special taxes levied on the Jews of Prussia increased as their rights contracted. Even worse, in 1768, the Jews of Prussia were required to purchase the products of the Government's Templin Factory (stockings, caps) and also to comply with the "porcelain" decree. This made a marriage licence for a first or second son and permission to buy a house, or transfer the ownership of a building, conditional upon the purchase of 300 thalers' worth of porcelain from the government factory which must be sold abroad. The gap between the official and the market price of porcelain was so great that the Jews lost hundreds of thousands of thaler in this forced barter between 1779 and 1787.

The few Jews in other north German lands, including some two thousand in Mecklenburg-Schwerin, and several hundred in Hanover, were in a legal position similar to that of the Jews in Prussia.

The Imperial Free City of Frankfurt-on-Main, one of the great commercial centres of Germany, operated a unique system of oppression of the Jews. Jews here were still confined to a ghetto, as in the Middle Ages. On Sundays and Christian holidays, they were not allowed to appear on the city streets even in daylight, or to journey out of town, which might mean that they passed through the city. Five hundred Jewish families were permitted in the ghetto; twelve marriages were allowed annually. The Jews of Frankfurt were absolutely forbidden to work at any handicraft, and their freedom to trade was also carefully restricted. A decree, for example, allowed for the maintenance of no more than six shops within the ghetto precincts.

Similar decrees to those in Frankfurt were in force against the Jews in the Imperial Free City of Hamburg, but they were not enforced with such unyielding severity in all matters. The pioneers of the Hamburg Jewish community had been Sephardi Jews (the "Portuguese"), who, as at Amsterdam in Holland, had become a small minority as compared with the constantly increasing number of Ashkenazi Jews by the eighteenth century. Special contracts drawn up with the small Sephardi community and the large Ashkenazi community determined the privileges that the Jews should enjoy and the sums they paid to the city. At first, the Jewish residential quarter was limited to a few streets without being actually confined to a ghetto. It expanded during the eighteenth century to include a few adjacent streets and by the end of the century there were over 150 house-owners amongst the Ashkenazim, despite the fact that they were forbidden to acquire houses. The municipality consistently enforced the ban on Jewish artisanship, but the city council vacillated between the aim of preventing Jewish competition with the burghers and the need to acknowledge the efficacy of the role the Jews actually played in the import and domestic trade. A statute that forbade Jews to keep stores was increasingly honoured in the breach.

In the middle of the eighteenth century, the requirements of commercial development were such that a Jewish community was even established in the capital city of Saxony, previously closed to Jewish settlement. Dresden granted legal domicile to privileged individuals in 1746, and again at later dates. Despite enactments against poor Jews,* the Jewish population of the city had grown to 1,000 by the end of the century. Jews were not allowed to enter the large commercial centre of Leipzig, except when fairs were being held, and until the end of the eighteenth century only some forty or fifty had been able to settle there. The severity of the anti-Jewish measures in Saxony was definitely aimed at mollifying the general population, embittered by exploitation under the absolutist régime.

Only a very few Jews were allowed to reside inside Bavaria proper. They were mostly court Jews, army commissionaries, money brokers, and their servants; by the end of the eighteenth century there were 220 of these Jews in Munich, the capital. There were many Kehillot scattered in the towns and villages of the adjoining areas of Upper Palatinate

---

* An expulsion decree against hundreds of indigents in 1777 was never carried out because of intercession by Moses Mendelssohn.

(Oberpfalz), Upper, Middle and Lower Franconia. Jews were not permitted to settle permanently in the large cities of Würzburg and Nuremberg, and large Kehillot therefore grew up in their vicinity, at Heidingsfeld and Fürth. Despite the variety of protection taxes and "gifts" that were collected from these Jews by princes, barons, government officials and clergy, the trade permitted to these Jews was severely restricted.

Some 500 Jews lived in a number of annexed towns west of Bavaria, in the Duchy of Württemberg. Only at the end of the eighteenth century were a few families allowed to reside in the capital, Stuttgart, and in the city of Ludwigsburg.

A similar legal situation to that existing in the duchies that ringed Bavaria, applied to the Jews in the duchies of southwest Germany, Oberhessen (capital, Giessen), Hesse-Kassel, Baden, and the Electoral Palatinate (Kurpfalz). There, too, they were obliged to pay a protection fee, an annual protection payment and various taxes, as well as to make compulsory "gifts." Furthermore, a poll-tax was levied whenever they crossed provincial or municipal boundary lines. A peculiar Jewish tax charged in some German states was the "Horse Tax," paid in lieu of the compulsory purchase of defective horses from ducal stables at fixed prices. For the first half of the nineteenth century the Jews of Baden still had to pay twenty-five different taxes and fees. The tax burden increased to such an extent during the eighteenth century that wide classes of Jews found their resources depleted, and were reduced to the level of pedlars.

Wealthy Jews in several large and developing west German cities prospered during this period in contrast with the situation in the small towns. At Karlsruhe, in the Duchy of Baden-Durlach, Jews had their own homes in every street in the city and conducted their shops undisturbed. At Mannheim, the Electors Palatinate granted them such extensive trading rights that a pamphlet published in 1738 referred to the city as "The New Jerusalem." The privileges, of course, were of use only to wealthy Jews, who were able to meet the demand for ever-growing protection taxes.

Thus the Jews of Germany might generally be described as victims of the administrative machinery of hundreds of sovereign entities, bound by decrees that limited their residential and occupational rights, and reduced them to a wretched trade in order to earn a bare livelihood and meet the protection and tax payments exacted from them. Their every right depended on these remissions. If they were unable to make them, they and their families were doomed to endless wandering from state to state and from city to city. Even the right to set foot in a city or state for a day, or even a few hours, could only be procured on payment of a special fee. Everywhere in Germany, a Jew had to pay the *Leibzoll* (body toll) on entering or leaving a state or on moving from one province to another within the same state. On entering cities such as Nuremberg or Augsburg, he had to pay a *Geleitzoll* (escort toll) to compensate for the services of the guard (usually a woman) who dogged his every step.

The wretched condition of the Jews in Germany inevitably left its mark on their character. Oppression of every possible type accompanied by incessant scorn and contempt over a period of centuries reduced them to a state of spiritual depression. Their self-confidence was broken and their sense of human dignity impoverished. Their troubles made cowardice and self-abasement before the most menial gentile second nature. Peddling, the occupation which most of the Jews in Germany followed through lack of choice, invariably fostered a sense of absolute dependence on the "mercy" of the customer and a fear of all officials, even the lowest ranking policeman. This attitude of subservience and self-abasement before the ruling classes lay behind the growing assimilationist movement amongst the German Jews which, through the absence of human and national pride, was unequalled anywhere else.

The Economic and Social Situation

The repressive measures in force made the occupational structure of the German Jews the most one-sided and unproductive in all Europe. Tailoring, the most common craft in the Jewish communities of other countries, was only legally permitted to one Jew even in such large Kehillot as Berlin or Mannheim. Even then, the lone tailor, usually known as a *Koscher-Schneider*, was tolerated only in order to ensure the avoidance of *Sha'atnez*.*

The few crafts not subject to guild restrictions offered a poor livelihood to a very small minority of the Jewish population. There were only a few artisans in the large Kehillot: diamond polishers, painters, glaziers (in the Duchy of Cleve), gold braiders and goldsmiths and silversmiths. (In Prussia not even this was permitted to the Jews. They were only permitted to remove "metal leprosy," or oxidization flakes). Seal engravers were more common. Some of them—for example, Jacob and Abraham Abrahamssohn of Berlin, medallion strikers and minters of the royal coinage—earned international reputations as master-craftsmen. A seal engraver, Aaron Itzigs, author of a highly interesting book of memoirs, became the pioneer of the Jewish community in Sweden in 1774, by virtue of his craftsmanship. During the second half of the eighteenth century, the number of Jews manufacturing buttons and other small items, which they peddled from town to town and sold at fairs, increased. It was common practice throughout the country for Jewish women to sew undergarments and make lace. In the east German states

* The prohibition on wearing materials woven of animal stuff and plant fibres, e.g. flax and wool.

of Mecklenburg and Prussia, and especially in eastern Prussia, Jews often manufactured intoxicating liquors at the manorial distilleries.

The butcher's trade, licensed as a matter of religious tolerance, was the only craft which supported a considerable number of Jewish wage-earners. In Prussia, the licence was issued only to cover the slaughtered meat requirements of the Jewish population. In the south of Germany, however, and even more in the west, Jewish butchers also supplied Christian customers. In the Kehillot in Cleve, under Prussian rule, and in the cities of Mannheim and Karlsruhe, butchers accounted for one-tenth of the heads of local Jewish families. At Hamburg, the largest Kehillah in the country, 10 per cent of wage-earners were artisans and workmen and this group also possessed the most diversified occupational distribution. Despite the city's stern injunctions against Jewish participation in crafts, the 1764 census reported that seventy-five were engaged in craft and industry out of 785 Jews with a specified occupation.

The inordinately large number of Kehillah employees and members of the liberal professions serving the public reflected the anomalous occupational structure and shortage of occupations among German Jews. In Prussia, however, many of them were only registered in this category to procure a residence permit from the authorities.

These two categories, artisans and members of the liberal professions (mainly Kehillah employees), together accounted for about one-fifth of the Jewish population, while over three-quarters were engaged in various forms of commerce and credit finance.

As a consequence of their legal status, the part played by the German Jews in commerce was largest at the two extremes, the wholesale trade and peddling. Within the wholesale trade, Jews concentrated on special areas, determined by the law, by the economic structure of the state, and also by their relative strength in face of the guilds. Jews throughout the country participated to a marked extent in the trade in silk, linen and other textiles, hides, wool, and various other raw materials. They were a determining factor in the clothing business, particularly in old clothes. The trade in silver, gold, and polished stones was also primarily in Jewish hands. In Berlin, at the end of the eighteenth century, Jewish wholesalers dealt chiefly in clothing, hides, and luxury articles, while silk and wool-cloth traders also owned stores. By 1773, there were seven Jewish brokers on the stock exchange and five Christian. In 1805, the Berlin Merchants Guild agreed to grant Jewish merchants equal rights of representation by accepting two members into the management.

In Frankfurt-on-Main, large groups of Jewish merchants dealt in linen, woollen and other cloths, and in new clothing. A sizable number of hide, raw wool, stocking and jewellery merchants were also in business there. Trade with Hamburg and Holland and the traffic in grains was also in Jewish hands. At Hamburg, tobacco and sugar imports in particular, but also wine, spices, oil and fruit imports were largely conducted by

Sephardi Jews. At the beginning of the nineteenth century, Jewish ship owners appeared upon the scene. Commerce in gold, silver, precious stones and fancy goods was considered a Jewish monopoly. Merchandise from the East Indies reached customers through Jewish wholesalers and dealers.

The range of Jewish trading activity in country towns and villages was very different from that in the large centres. In the eighteenth century, the Jews of Mecklenburg developed the wool export business and helped foster the growth of sheep-raising in the state. They were also very active in trade in raw hides. Throughout northern Germany, in Brandenburg, Mecklenburg, and Hanover-Brunswick, horse-trading was as common among the Jews as trade in old clothes and other commodities. In southern Germany, horse-trading was also frequently found, e.g., in the principality of Ansbach, and especially in the Rhineland provinces (at Kurmainz, in Baden), but cattle trading was most characteristic of the Jews in these areas. At the beginning of the eighteenth century, it was an acknowledged fact that cattle shows in the city of Giessen and elsewhere could not take place without the Jews of Oberhessen.

Large numbers of moneychangers were to be found, particularly in the large Kehillot. Moneychanging bridged the gap between commerce and credit. Credit dealing was still a source of income for a considerable number of German Jews, but during the eighteenth century its share in the Jewish economy declined in favour of a growing interest in trade.

Jewish banking was a familiar feature of all German commercial centres. At Hamburg, banking was the prerogative of the wealthy members of the Kehillah. The 1764 census only showed six Jewish bankers, but some of the registered merchants or moneychangers also dealt in credit. At Frankfurt-on-Main, Jewish bankers combined large credit transactions with purveyorships to the emperor and some of the German princes, and with ventures into international trade. The wealthy Kahn and Drach families were associated in loan activities with Jewish banking houses in Holland. During the Napoleonic period, the banking house of Rothschild gained ascendancy. At Berlin, during the reign of Frederick II, the banking houses of Veitl Ephraim, Daniel Itzig, Gumpertz, Wulf and Moses Isaac, amassed vast fortunes by taking over the mint on lease during the Seven Years' War. They were later joined, by the end of the Napoleonic era, by the banking houses of the Bendix, Levin and Mendheim families. At Breslau, the banking house of Daniel Kuh gained distinction during the eighteenth century. At Mannheim, Jewish bankers, including the Levi and Meier families, financed government manufacture of tobacco during the first half of the eighteenth century; in the latter half they were engaged in providing supplies for the army. These banking magnates however, only formed the upper stratum of the Jews dealing in credit. The remainder were petty bill brokers and moneylenders, sometimes only thus engaged to supplement their incomes from the crafts or other forms of employment.

The accumulation of capital from banking and commerce by the Jewish money magnates provided one of the foundations for the manufacturing industry which flourished in the second half of the eighteenth century. At Hamburg, Jews owned tobacco, cotton and silk factories. In the city of Breisach in southern Baden (under Austrian rule), Gideon Jakob Oppenheimer founded a linen spinning mill in 1785 and also employed over 300 home workers in the neighbouring villages. However, Jewish financiers played their greatest role in the development of manufacturing in Prussia, and of the silk cloth industry in particular. By the 1760's, Jewish-owned factories contained 380 out of a total of 598 looms and already accounted for two-thirds of the Prussian silk industry. Their owners also took the initiative in founding new branches of production with improved working methods, and in marketing their products at home and abroad. The largest silk manufacturing establishment in the country belonged to the partners, Israel Marcus and Halle, and distributed its products in Poland, Russia and even the East Indies. When it came to marketing their products, Jewish producers were able to utilise their business connections with Jewish merchants in the provincial towns, such as Breslau, Frankfurt-on-the-Oder, and Königsberg, who in turn were in direct contact with Jews coming to the fairs from Poland. These advantages also enabled Jews to operate factories in their capacity as receivers to bankrupt Christian owners.

The Prussian government certainly preferred to grant privileges to Christian industrialists, but did not deny the Jews the broad rights necessary to the development of industry—the prime factor in economic policy under the mercantile system. Jewish manufacturers received government development loans for their plants, monopoly rights in marketing their products, the right to maintain warehouses even in cities otherwise closed to Jews (Stettin, Magdeburg), and the right to import workers from abroad.

The function fulfilled by petty trade, which supported the broad mass of the Jews, was as important in the development of capitalism in Germany, as the large-scale activities of the great bankers, industrialists and wholesalers. Most of the petty traders did not concentrate on any particular line of goods but combined all kinds of commodities: old clothes and fancy goods; undergarments and old clothes; cattle or horses and general articles, hides, or stockings; watches and fancy goods; hair and garments; garments and silver. As a result, census reports and other official papers show a large number of traders in "casual" goods. The largest group of Jews within the country engaged in trade consisted of petty tradesmen and pedlars. Official census reports describe them as very numerous even in the large cities, although fear of the restrictive decrees caused many either to evade registration altogether, or else to register under other professions. The country and small town pedlars were more important in the development of the country's economy than those in the large cities. They brought industrial products to customers in the remotest parts of the country, and in turn, bought their raw materials and crops to supply the urban market.

The types of trade followed by German Jews shed light on their social condition and social stratification—which was complex, despite the generally lop-sided occupational structure. Social contrasts were greatest in the large Kehillot. At Hamburg, the wealthy class formed less than half the large Ashkenazi Kehillah; the majority of members struggled to earn a penurious living as middlemen, pedlars, craftsmen, Kehillah servants, or clerks in commercial establishments. At Berlin, capital of the German-Jewish financial magnates, the half-dozen actual millionaires had built palatial residences; but at the end of the eighteenth century, David Friedlaender reported that about half the Kehillah membership was dependent on dole. Moses Hirschel, a contemporary of Friedlaender, examined the approximate total of 600 Jewish families in Berlin in more detail. They included 50 fabulously wealthy bankers; about 150 well-to-do merchants; 150 rich industrialists and free professionals; and about 100 middlemen-pedlars, "court Jews," and petty "house Jews" (*Hausjuden*); the remaining 150 families lived on charity. At Frankfurt-on-Main, the Kehillah registered one-third of its membership as well-to-do in 1722, and classified a quarter as poor and living on the dole.

The small Kehillot in the towns showed little marked social differentiation, as few of their members achieved any degree of wealth. The pedlars who sold their wares in the cities and villages, carrying them literally on their backs (hence, *Packenträger*), were largely dependent for their livelihood on the rich merchants of the Kehillot. At times, the merchants also bought goods from pedlars from other towns. The reverse process was, however, more usual: the pedlar received goods on credit or *aufgesetzt* (on a commission basis) from the merchants, and settled their accounts at the end of each week or when he sold out the entire allotment of the merchandise.

But the pedlars were not the poorest German Jews. Really wretched were the thousands of beggars, the so-called *Betteljuden*. Gaunt and emaciated, they trudged with their wives and children from city to city, from state to state, ragged and destitute. There was nowhere they could find shelter. The extent of this social evil in Germany was unparalleled. No law or *Privilegium* relating to Jews, even in the smallest principality, omitted provisions against the admittance of these "undesirables"; and no Kehillah failed to draw up regulations with detailed clauses providing for such "guests."

The social boundary between the pedlar class soliciting trade from door to door in town and village and the vast number of mendicant Jews driven from place to place was by no means fixed. Petty artisans and pedlars, who failed and lost their meagre "capital" or were unable to meet the demands of the exorbitant protection tax and therefore forfeited their *Kiyum*, or residence permits, were frequently reduced to the level of beggars and joined their ranks. Surprisingly enough, when this stage was reached, they did not invariably despair completely of working for their living and were unflagging in their efforts to support themselves without begging for alms. Official documents often mention vendors of ribbons and other kinds of fancy goods in connection with the *Betteljuden*. There were examples of whole columns of *Betteljuden* with the mendicant and pedlar elements intermingled and with the craftsmen amongst them endeavouring to sell their own handiwork. These vagrants did not lack for cantors, religious teachers, and other religious officials, who did not possess rights of domicile in any Kehillah and were therefore forced to join the wanderers. This vagrant *Lumpenproletariat* very commonly included the *Kle'zmer* and *Badchanim*,* travelling to weddings from town to town, and also clowns and acrobats, who performed at the fairs.

The upper level of the Jewish mendicant class was thus open to frequent reinforcements from pauperized artisans, pedlars and members of the "free professions." Its lower levels were a transit route to the underworld of crooks and thieves. It is true that few Jewish brigands were hanged for murder, but gangs of Jewish thieves were common throughout Germany; their connections with their Christian colleagues left their stamp upon German underworld jargon.

The impoverishment of the broad mass of German Jews was the result of the pressure applied to the Jews under the absolutist régime. By forcing them into a few limited fields of trade and simultaneously weighing them down with a massive burden of special taxes, it had pushed the rapidly increasing fringe population of the Jewish masses into destitution. The internal social life of the German Jews presented an equally gloomy picture. The wealthy class, who dominated the Kehillot and the central organs of Jewish autonomy, made no effort to alleviate the distress of the poor masses. It even added to their burden by its method of apportioning state and Kehillah taxes. Furthermore, it collaborated with the authorities in implementing all the repressive decrees aimed at these unfortunates.

The Kehillah Régime

During the period of absolutist rule, the autonomous rights of the Kehillah as an institution were still acknowledged by the authorities. Some states, of course, already showed a tendency to curtail Kehillah prerogatives, especially in respect of law courts. The Prussian *General-*

---

* *Kle'zmer*—a musician, contracted from the Hebrew *Klei-Zemer*, musical instruments; *Badchan*— a rhymester, literally an impromptu jokester (Hebrew).

Reglement of 1750 stipulated that a court formed of a rabbi and the heads of the Kehillah could only hear disputes involving religious matters, wills, and marital relationships. Civil litigation between Jews and criminal lawsuits were subject to state jurisdiction.

The Kehillah's principal function was to apportion taxes and to collect them on behalf of the state exchequer. But it also continued to supervise economic affairs (with the aim of preventing undue competition), religious matters, education and charity. As far as education was concerned, it was usually content to superintend a *Talmud-Torah* for the children of the poor and a rabbinical *Yeshivah* (in the large Kehillot), both maintained by obligatory donations from individuals. The Kehillah's direct activity in the sphere of charity was also fairly limited (an almshouse for the poor) and in the main it merely ensured that households welcomed poor "guests" on Sabbaths and Holy Days or paid for their hostel accommodation. At Frankfurt-on-Main, the Kehillah was also responsible for various ghetto services, such as sanitation. It was the function of the Kehillot and the inter-Kehillah councils of the German states, as in the neighbouring countries, to administer contributions for "The Poor of Jerusalem." Funds were transmitted by a special Palestine treasurer of the largest Kehillah within any given area—for example, Fürth in Bavaria—and by the general treasurer who resided at Frankfurt-on-Main.

The pattern of Kehillah leadership was similar to the one followed throughout central and eastern Europe, based on traditional regulations dating from as early as the seventeenth or even the sixteenth century. At the head of the Kehillah were the *Parnassim*, usually three in number, occasionally four, five (at Berlin), or twelve (the *Baumeister* of Frankfurt-on-Main), and their *Tovim* (deputies). The *Parnassim* held the office of president of the executive in turn for monthly or quarterly periods. Tax collection was in the hands of collectors; Kehillah ledgers were supervised by accountants; and the assessment of Kehillah members for taxation purposes was carried out by assessors (*shamaim*). In addition to these officials, there were charity, almshouse, *Talmud-Torah*, and Palestine stewards elected annually or appointed by the Kehillah leaders. At Berlin and some other Kehillot, these functionaries, and even the Kehillah leaders, were elected or appointed every three years. The "State" board of management, chosen by the Inter-Kehillah Council at its triennial meetings, resembled the Kehillah board of management in composition.

In Prussia, two State *Parnassim* (*Oberlandesälteste*) were responsible for taxes. They were chosen by the *Parnassim* of Berlin—invariably from amongst the notables of the Kehillah—and then officially appointed by the King. The authorities were so interested in having the State Councils assemble to apportion taxes that in some states all heads of families were obliged to attend Council meetings, or render themselves liable to heavy fines.

The regulations governing the procedure for electing the Kehillah leaders were designed to protect the wealthy and to strengthen their control over the Kehillot. Property qualifications were everywhere a condition of the right to vote and, from the outset, at election time the only names in the ballot box (from which the official electors, or *borerim*, were drawn) were of Kehillah members who paid a specified property tax. In small Kehillot, such as at Warburg or Hildesheim, the minimum property qualification was 300 to 400 reichsthaler.* Similar conditions applied in elections held by the councils for leaders of the State Council and for Chief Rabbis in each state. Only recognized scholars (*Talmidei-Hakhamim*), with the title of *Haver* (fellow) were eligible for a reduction in the minimum obligatory assessment. In the large Kehillot, the property qualification for eligibility to participate in the balloting was higher. The Kehillah of Hamburg, which granted the right to vote to anybody whose property was assessed at 300 reichsthaler, was reasonably moderate. (For men over forty years of age, an assessment of 200 reichsthaler ensured eligibility.) At Fürth, a minimum property qualification of 600 gulden was in force, while at Frankfurt-on-Main, the sum was 1,000 gulden which, according to official data, deprived two-fifths of the Kehillah's families of the right to vote. Even within the wealthy class itself, the electoral system ensured that the small minority of financial magnates had the casting vote. People of means were divided into categories, each of equal electoral weight, however small the number of individuals it comprised.

Property qualifications also applied in the election of the State *Parnassim*, State Rabbis, and the other executive officers of the central autonomous institutions—but the minimum property requirement was higher than in the medium-sized Kehillot. The few families of money magnates therefore had to all intents and purposes a monopoly of control of the Kehillot and of the Provincial Councils. In Berlin, at the end of the eighteenth century, the offices of *Parnassim* were jealously guarded by a small group of "silk Jews," "mint Jews," and "Court bankers." These included individuals such as Veitl Ephraim, Daniel Itzig, Jakob Moses, David Friedlaender, and the Wulf, Riess and Gumpertz families. At Frankfurt, the tycoon Drach and Kahn families, and at a later date, Kahn and Kulp, competed for control of the Kehillah. A few Kehillot and Provincial Councils went one stage further. There, power did not rest even with cliques of this sort but the sole rulers were powerful individuals, Court Jews (*Hofjuden*), who were close to government circles. Instances occurred of these officials, especially if appointed by the government, punishing anyone who defied them with imprisonment, arbitrarily adding to the Kehillah tax burden, and not infrequently embezzling community

* One reichsthaler in the eighteenth century was the equivalent of 1.50 gulden.

funds. During the second half of the eighteenth century, the Kehillah population rebelled against these despots and often obtained their dismissal either at the hands of the authorities or by the decision of the Kehillot and the Provincial Councils. But even when the Kehillot did adopt new regulations in such cases, they only served to strengthen the oligarchy and the plutocracy in its domination of the Kehillah.

The ruling wealthy class in the Kehillot also determined the rules for apportioning taxes. In this, their policy was to shift the burden as much as possible on to the less prosperous families or those who were actually impecunious. For the most part, they employed the method of collecting part of the state taxes and Kehillah levies on an equal basis from all heads of families, and the remainder from each taxpayer according to the assessed value of his property. The proportions in which they combined these two systems of tax apportionment varied according to the size of the Kehillah. A typical example of a small Kehillah was Wied-Runkel in the first half of the eighteenth century. Here, in the case of regular taxes, such as the protection tax, all heads of families paid one-third on an equal basis and two-thirds according to their individual property rating; when extraordinary tax levies were involved, every family paid half on an equal basis and half on the basis of property rating. The tax system in operation in large Kehillot, such as Hamburg or Fürth, discriminated more strongly against the underpropertied. The Berlin Kehillah's taxation system was a triumph of social injustice. The protection tax and recruits tax (in lieu of military service, from which Jews were still barred) together amounted to twenty-five reichsthaler annually for each head of family. Everyone, whether or not he owned property, had to pay this sum to the Kehillah. Widows were the only exception; they were allowed a reduction, not exceeding 50 per cent on the protection tax. In contrast to this tax, which affected all Kehillah members, the additional tax collected from property owners was of relatively small value. The man who owned property "valued" at 1,000 reichsthaler (for taxation purposes, property was only assessed at part of its actual value; from 1794, at only a quarter) paid a maximum of 18 reichsthaler—in addition, of course, to the general taxes (protection and recruits).

To supplement the direct Kehillah tax, some German Kehillot also levied an indirect tax on the consumption of ritually slaughtered meat. The Berlin Kehillah used this meat excise as a means of ensuring that Kehillah members paid their direct taxes on time. The poorer members of the Kehillah bore the brunt of this indirect taxation; the rich were fully compensated as the amount collected by the excise was deducted from both the general tax and the property tax. The same system of indirect taxes, with a different method of collection, was employed at Fürth: everybody had to pay the meat excise and no deductions were made from the Kehillah tax; but the rate of the excise was so high that it covered half the Kehillah's expenditures, which were mainly borne by the poorer sections.

The taxation system at Breslau was openly extortionate. All Kehillah revenue and part of the state taxes into the bargain were financed by the excise tax on meat. The tax was fixed at first at a rate of two pfennigs per pound of meat. It was raised so many times during the ensuing decades that by the end of the 1780's, it had reached one groschen. The authorities finally realized that this exploitation of the poor Jewish population could be harmful to the royal treasury. An ordinance issued by the Prussian King in 1790 established a new Reglement for the Jews of Breslau, halved the excise on meat (to six pfennigs), and ordered the Kehillah to cover the remaining half of its expenditure by a direct tax based on property value and income. This royal ordinance specifically denounced the old meat excise, "which had especially afflicted the poor, the large sized families, and those who scrupulously observe the Jewish law" (the allusion is to *Kashrut*). Affairs had thus come to a fine pass when even the Prussian government, itself squeezing the Jews to the utmost, felt the need to advise the Kehillah on a fair apportionment of taxes.

Although the Kehillot of Germany were engaged in continual defensive action against the municipalities and guilds for rights of domicile and trade, the members of the Kehillot who were protected by domiciliary privileges looked askance upon those of their fellow-Jews who were not. The Kehillah leaders also jealously guarded their class privileges against competition from outside Jews. Numerous Kehillah and Provincial Council regulations were designed to prohibit within their Kehillot all trade by Jews from outside. Frequent cases occurred when Kehillah heads informed on Jewish pedlars and petty traders who lacked certificates of protection and demanded their expulsion by the authorities. They were ruthless in their treatment of the completely destitute vagabonds, expelling them or handing them over to the authorities. As their poverty throughout the country increased, a constantly rising number of Jews without rights of domicile wandered aimlessly from town to town, from state to state. In earlier times, the poor were maintained by charity and were thus mainly the internal concern of each Kehillah. During the eighteenth century, charity centred almost exclusively on the problem of vagrant mendicants. The Kehillah leaders, especially in the large cities, no longer saw any possibility of continuing the traditional method of lodging such "guests" in the homes of Kehillah members, the so-called *pletn* (lodging cards) system. For the most part, the beggars were now put up for a day or two in almshouses and then sent on their way with a small pittance. The main problem in this connection was not lodging the "guests" but sending them away. The erection of almshouses for the poor outside the Kehillah precincts, near the city gates, was an indication of the new trend. The Kehillot posted special guards near the gates to keep a strict watch against incursions by paupers. The famous Palestinian emissary, Rabbi Haim Joseph David Azoulai, gained first-hand experiences of these almshouses when he travelled through Germany in 1754. The keepers at the gates of Hanau (east of Frankfurt), Düsseldorf, and Cleve, refused him entry, and even in a town like Arnstein "the (officer) did not permit Israel to cross his boundary . . ."

Several of the Kehillot did not even refrain from employing police forces against infiltrating mendicants. The Kehillah of Ansbach made frequent complaints to the government about the "appalling penetration" of paupers into the city. The chiefs of the fire brigades at the Frankfurt-on-Main Kehillah, who were also responsible for the supervision of strangers and the prevention of dissolute behaviour, performed their duties very conscientiously, especially in the case of Jewish beggars from Poland, whom they delivered to the municipal police for expulsion. By the end of the eighteenth century, their zeal was subsiding and thenceforth they left it to the police to handle expulsions.

The spread of the evil of *Betteljuden* throughout Germany certainly resulted largely from the repressiveness of the régime. Still it is an unfortunate truth that the suffering endured by these enforced vagrants was also caused to no small degree by the Kehillah leadership, which entertained no feelings of solidarity whatsoever with their unfortunate brethren.

At Hamburg, the Kehillah leaders were also party to the Marriage Decree which struck a heavy blow at the indigent masses. The various governments already prevented poor Jews from marrying by making ownership of large property holdings and the payment of a high protection tax prerequisites for obtaining a licence. The Kehillah in the Duchy of Cleve, with a population of 491 in 1787, included fifty-two unmarried men and women between the ages of twenty and thirty and twenty-three over thirty. Now the leaders of the great Kehillah of Hamburg, in the face of protest from Rabbi Jacob Emden, added a repressive measure of their own: marriage licences were only to be issued when the parties concerned had met all their obligations to the Kehillah. Transgressors were punished by excommunication and by forfeiting their right of domicile within the Kehillah. Furthermore, a Kehillah regulation of 1726 prohibited the marriage of any couple if the bride's dowry was below 250 reichsthaler. The poor who defied this prohibition and succeeded in marrying outside the city were deprived of their right to reside within its boundaries. As a consequence of these measures, large numbers of children were born out of wedlock.

In some places, the Jewish "élite" of Germany integrated so successfully into the absolutist feudal régime and its system of restraints, that it collected the *Leibzoll*, or poll tax itself, either as individuals or as Kehillot. The revenue from this tax remained in the hands of the Kehillah of Hamburg until the French administration abolished the

Leibzoll in general. Though subject to ordinary inter-Kehillah rivalry and competition between factions within the separate Kehillot, the wealthy displayed absolute class solidarity when confronting the working classes, particularly their business employees and servants. Regulations at some Kehillot (Hamburg, Bamberg, Düsseldorf) ruled that one property owner might not engage a servant discharged by another "save with the consent of the master with whom he had previously been." At others, they stipulated that no servant who had been in service in one place might be employed until he had stayed for two years elsewhere. The employers thus ensured that servants would be bound to their masters and in no hurry to improve their working conditions. They also safeguarded themselves against the possibility that their servants might try to become independent and compete with their former employers.

Some examples of arbitrariness, bullying and exploitation by the *Parnassim* and their rabbis were so glaring, even against this background of prevailing Kehillah government, based on all the social abuses inherent in the current systems of government, that they evoked protest from many of the great rabbis. Rabbi Jonathan Eybeschütz, then Rabbi at Metz, delivered a sermon in 1746 castigating itinerant preachers for their indulgence towards the Kehillah *Parnassim*, whom he accused of nepotism, of currying favour with the gentile masters, and of ignoring the troubles of the people or worse still of exploiting them for personal advantage. The memoirs of Rabbi Jacob Emden give a sombre description of the situation in three Kehillot in the Hamburg area—Altona, Hamburg and Wandsbeck—when Rabbi Ezekiel Katzenelbogen (Eybeschütz's predecessor and, like him, Emden's opponent) was in office:

> In those days—Emden wrote—the *Parnassim* and the leaders held sway over that aged elder of the Rabbinical Court. For all that his hand was strong upon the poor and the malcontent, he being empowered and authorized by His Majesty the King to pass judgment and to order fines and mete out punishment from which there was no appeal, and assuredly he did possess authority over the *Parnassim* and the leaders; howbeit he did yield to them; for in this wise did they each recompense the other.*

Yet in the middle of the eighteenth century, when dissident rabbis were only protesting at the unjust leadership of the *Parnassim* and rabbis, without actually touching on the hierarchical system of control itself, criticism of the existing order could already be heard. This heralded the rise of the *Haskalah* Movement. A Yiddish homiletical manuscript entitled *Liebes Briev* (*Letter of Endearment*) and written by Isaac Wetzlar of Zell, spoke out on behalf of "the common man" in the face of the increasingly powerful *Parnassim*, and especially the rabbis and scholars who misled the people and kept them in darkness.

* *Megillat Sefer* (*Scroll of the Book*) Warsaw, 1897, p. 133.

Culture and Education

During the second half of the eighteenth century, the great majority of German Jews continued to lead a drab and static existence and were deeply embedded in their traditionalist religious atmosphere. In every Kehillah, community life and cultural activity were centred around the synagogues and the *Batei-midrash* (the *Klaus*), which devoted fixed periods to the study of the religious law. The precepts of the *Shulhan Arukh* were meticulously observed, as well as a great variety of local customs, mainly communal fast days that commemorated the martyrdom of individual Kehillot during the Middle Ages. All social ambition was gratified within the Kehillah. The reading of the Torah on the Sabbath, holding the Torah Scroll at the *Simhat-Torah Hakafot* (processions round the Almemor) and other honours peculiar to the synagogue were subjects of envy and frequent recrimination which eventually necessitated the inclusion of several long and detailed articles in Kehillah or Provincial Council constitutions.

Holiday and family celebrations, *Bar-Mitzvah* and circumcision ceremonies and weddings gave the Jew some compensation for the persecution and abuse of the working week. Wedding celebrations became occasions for such public extravagance that the authorities found it necessary at times to intervene. In Baden, for example, the custom of riding out to meet the groom was prohibited. The Kehillot also issued detailed ordinances curtailing luxuries: the *Klez'mer* was limited to four instruments; the groom's gift of shoes should be made only to the bride, instead of to all her female relatives. The German Jews also preserved the traditional atmosphere in the clothes they wore. They wore black thoughout the week and also came to synagogue on the Sabbath and on holidays dressed in black, broad-sleeved caftans and their own peculiar headgear—a black cap at Frankfurt; a black, broad-rimmed hat at Hamburg. The Kehillah leaders stressed the distinctions in the social hierarchy by appearing at the synagogue in their special traditional garb on weekdays as well as Sabbaths and Holy days (at Hamburg). Scholars who bore the title of *Haver* wore a special type of hat (the *Rabbihaub*) which could still be seen during the first half of the nineteenth century in some places in Bavaria.

Yiddish, the spoken language of the Jews in Germany, differed from German through its large admixture of Hebrew words, its pronunciation of German words, and in its sentence structure. It was unintelligible to the German speaking gentile. The Jews were scarcely more able to understand German. Even the *Maskilim*, the advocates of enlightenment among the Jews, with their programme of establishing "pure German" and uprooting Yiddish (which they despised as a "jargon,") did not for the most part possess a thorough command of the German language. Even Moses Mendelssohn did not feel completely at home in German. His struggle with the complexities of expressing himself in German (he corresponded with his friends in rich Yiddish vernacular) was a major factor in the personal tragedy of his life.

The educational system of the German Jews of the eighteenth century followed the same lines as in Poland. The system of instruction practised in Poland had come to be widely accepted in Germany as most of the teachers were of Polish origin. Most of the rabbis in the large Kehillot were also natives of Poland and some had held rabbinical posts there before accepting appointments in Germany. All the defects in teaching methods, vainly criticised by the authors of homilectical discourses from the sixteenth century onwards (Maharal of Prague, Rabbi Ephraim Luntschitz, and others), were still practised in Germany in the eighteenth century. The homilectical writers and the *Maskilim* were as one in their sharp criticism of this system—though the former saw no need for general enlightenment. The pioneer of the *Haskalah* movement in Germany, Naphtali Hertz Wesel,* launched his campaign for modernized education in a famous Hebrew pamphlet, *Words of Peace and Truth*. Part II (*An Abundance of Good for the House of Israel*) declared:

> I recall that I never did study the Bible and the *Mishnah* at school, but when I was five years old and could read Hebrew words, they sent me to school, and a rabbi began to teach me the *Halakhah* from the middle of the *Gemara* Tractate (*Kiddushin*.) Matters continued thus until I was nine years old, when I could read *Gemara* by myself. But I swear that I never did know what was written in the Torah, which from Genesis to Deuteronomy was for me a concealed treasure.

Isaac Wetzlar had given a virtually identical description of the education handed out to Jewish children at this age in the *Liebes Briev*, written some thirty years before Wesel's work. Wetzlar also complained bitterly about the system of instruction in the *Yeshivot* and *Batei-Midrash*, based on casuistic reasoning (*pilpul*) and exposition.

None the less, within the framework of Kehillah autonomy and the traditionalist religious environment, Talmudic education gave its scholars the requisite professional knowledge to enter several of the liberal professions. They were qualified for employment as teachers (*melamed*), ritual slaughterers (*shochet*), scribes (*sofer*), and judges (*dayyan*), as well as for the honourable and highly lucrative post of rabbi, often held by merchants, bankers or influential court Jews.† The practice of law also provided a remunerative source of income. In the large Kehillot, at Frankfurt-on-Main and Hamburg, the parties to a dispute customarily argued their case before the rabbinical court through *murshim* (attorneys), versed in the theory and practice of the law. At some litigations, there

---

* Also known by his Germanized name, Hartwig Wessely.
† Ostensibly vindicated by the traditional aphorism, "Torah and eminence in one."

were as many as four *murshim* in attendance. The 1726 Regulations of the Hamburg-Altona Kehillah required that an attorney bear the title of *Haver*. In many German states, *Parnassim* were also empowered to judge between litigants of their own Kehillah in lawsuits involving financial matters. This made it necessary for them too, to have a knowledge of the Talmud and its codifiers. However, despite the professional prospects it offered, Talmudic education in German Jewry, as in all contemporary European Jewish communities, was chiefly a matter of social status. The title of *Haver*, and even more, of *Morenu* ("our Teacher"), conferred all the honours of the synagogue and Kehillah. In some cases, possession of the title was a statutory condition of passive or active voting right to Kehillah offices. The financial and intellectual élite were not only complementary, somewhat similar to the nobility and clergy under the feudal system; they were also to a large degree actually linked as one class in two contiguous fields; in particular, learning and the titles that went with it were indispensable to the wealthy and well-to-do merchants for the maintenance of their social prestige within the Kehillah. The lack of social contact between the scholars and the common people deepened the social cleavage amongst the Jews of Germany. The author of *Liebes Briev* vehemently reproved the *Parnassim*, the Provincial Council members, and the wealthy for ignoring their obligation to spread learning among the masses (*Die gemeine Leit*), whose educational level was extremely low.

While the Talmud and the Codifiers were primarily studied by reasoning (*pilpul*), the books of commentary and exegesis were full of far-fetched explanations or rehashed arguments, completely devoid of creative thought. *Maskilim* and orthodox homileticists were again in agreement in their acid criticism of this late rabbinical literature. A form of book censorship did exist in some German Kehillot. The Hamburg Kehillah's regulations for 1726 made reference to the fact that authors were canvassing the Kehillah and bothering it with their books. Henceforth, the *Parnassim* were only to recommend books which had the approval of the Rabbi of Frankfurt-on-Main, his *Bet-Din*, or the *Bet-Din* of the Rabbi of Hamburg-Altona. However, this censorship was obviously not aimed at casuistic and exegetical works. Its effect was rather to limit books of ethical protest, criticising casuistic and exegetical works or, of course, criticising the behaviour of the *Parnassim* and rabbis (e.g. *Liebes Briev*). They remained in manuscript form unwanted and unpublished.

By the beginning of the eighteenth century, against this background of spiritual stagnation, the first glimmerings of general enlightenment had appeared amongst the Jews of Germany. The new trend, characterized by its ambitions for affinity with the gentiles in culture and manners, began to spread. The opulent merchants and bankers were especially susceptible; not content with giving their sons the traditional education, they thought that they should also possess a general knowledge, particularly of

European languages. The fact that some Kehillah laws prohibited attendance at the opera (Hamburg 1715), or a *"Komedie* or *Spiel"* (Fürth, 1747), reflects the extent to which these new customs had become fashionable in the large cities.

An important factor in the dissemination of serious general learning was the appearance at this time of a progressive intellectual class of German Jewry. The foundations of this class were laid by Jewish physicians, who had increased in number as the universities opened their gates to Jewish students. They had been allowed to attend that of Frankfurt-on-Oder at the end of the seventeenth century, and Giessen, Halle, Göttingen, Heidelberg, Duisburg, Königsberg, Marburg, Mainz, Bonn and others followed suit during the following century. These Jewish physicians, with their broad education in the natural sciences and philosophy, were among the first authors of scientific books in Hebrew. Dr. Asher Anschel Worms, a practitioner at Frankfurt, published a *Key to the New Algebra* in Hebrew as early as 1721. The well-known Dr. Mordecai Gumpbel Schnaber (Marcus Levisohn) anticipated the *Me'asef* series* by many years with his *Essay on Learning and Wisdom* (*Maamar Ha-Torah Ve-ha-Hokhmah*, London, 1771). The essay expounded the fundamentals of mathematics, physics, and astronomy and also reproached the Jews for having "forsaken our sacred tongue." It is no coincidence that two doctors were among the preceptors of Moses Mendelssohn. They were Dr. Abraham Kisch of Prague, and particularly, Dr. Aaron Gumpertz, whose work, *An Essay on Science*, published in 1765, had already exhorted the people to turn their attention to the secular sciences, despite the religious zealotry of "the ignorant among the people." The spread of general education for the sons of the rich resulted in an increase in the number of private tutors. Outstanding *Maskilim* such as Naphtali Hertz Wesel, Isaac Euchel, Aaron Wolfssohn and Hertz Homberg were employed as tutors in Berlin, Königsberg and Breslau.

The spreading popularity of Enlightenment amongst the wealthy at the top of the social scale was matched by an increasing penetration of "the modern way of life" into the traditional environment at the bottom, especially in the large cities. The severest injunctions that the Kehillot could impose and all the sermons against dissoluteness were of no avail. The Hamburg-Altona enactments for 1726 contained the following prohibition: "Boys and girls, and most emphatically servant boys and servant girls (were) forbidden to learn dancing with dancing masters" on pain of heavy fines and the threat of excommunication. In their concern for virtue, the Kehillah leaders even eyed the pleasure of taking a stroll in the city streets with suspicion; in 1731, Jewish and Christian night watchmen were ordered to keep a vigilant eye on transgressors. Servant girls who violated the injunction against Sabbath strolls were threatened

* See p. 169.

with loss of their right to work for Kehillah members. The Frankfurt-on-Main Kehillah also scrupulously enforced a ban on Sabbath strolls by young girls in the city streets outside the ghetto.

The autonomy of the Kehillot and the Provincial Councils had been whittled down by the absolutist authorities. Now it was progressively undermined internally by the slackening discipline of the Kehillah population. Kehillah members in various German states, such as the Palatinate, Mainz or Mecklenburg, began to be lax or actually to default on their payment of the remittance necessary to maintain the office of the Provincial Chief Rabbi. Increasingly frequently too, Jews applied to civil law courts instead of submitting their litigation to rabbinical tribunals.

At the same time, the first signs of a reversal of German public opinion towards the Jews became discernible. Books on the science of government (Johann Albrecht Phillipi in 1795; Johann Heinrich Justi in 1760) proposed directing the Jews into useful occupations in industry, handicrafts and farming. In 1754, the official gazette of the state of Bamberg expressed the view that the only difference between Jew and Christian was one of religion, and that the Jews deserved all the kindness ordered by humanity. The broad mass of the German people of course still regarded the Jews with deep-rooted distrust and contempt, implanted by long centuries of incitement and religious bigotry. In 1781, Christian W. Dohm complained that "in the eyes of the broad masses not even such splendid qualities as nobility of soul and heart can ever atone for the Jew's major fault of being a Jew."* Nevertheless, members of the German population increasingly expressed a humane attitude towards their Jewish neighbours, and the press was always quick to report, as worthy of emulation, any instances of care for Jewish orphans or of help given to Jewish victims of fire or flood.

Social relations between the Jews and their neighbours made their appearance in the main amongst the wealthy circles of both parties, encouraged by economic developments at the beginning of industrial capitalism. In the course of their economic activities, the Jewish industrialists, wholesalers, and financiers from Berlin, Königsberg, and Breslau, came into social contact with the French colony in Prussia (at Berlin), and with German importers, nobles, and high government officials. In Hamburg, at the end of the eighteenth century, a stage had been reached in intercourse between the Jewish and German upper middle class such that senators and burgomasters visited Jewish homes, and there was reciprocal attendance at celebrations, funerals, and the like. Inevitably, this change in relationship among the upper classes was, in some measure, reflected among the broad mass of Germans. The Enlightenment was also directly instrumental in changing public opinion towards the Jews.

* See below p. 172.

During the eighteenth century, intellectual influences from England and France, two western European countries with a highly advanced culture, penetrated backward Germany. The backwardness, which had resulted in the absence of a firmly established, politically alert middle class in Germany, was still palpably present—even in spheres affected by the intellectual renaissance. Enlightened circles had not advanced beyond benevolent despotism in their political outlook, and they could not accept Rousseau's republican and democratic concepts. They took similar exception to the materialism of the French philosophers. Thus, with the exception of a handful of disciples of Spinoza, they were satisfied with the moderate "heresy" of deism. Yet, for all its moderation and reserve, this rebirth of philosophy and literature created a new intellectual climate amongst the German people. As the new outlook continued to spread, it necessarily caused a change in the views prevalent in enlightened circles concerning the Jews and the Jewish question. The concept of deism, with its negation of the divine revelation and its foundation of all applied religion on "natural morality," required the abandonment of religious fanaticism at which the dominant Christian religions, Catholicism and Protestantism, excelled. Locke's political theory, based on the separation of church and state, demanded the abolition of all discrimination against any religious sect within the state. Similarly, his psycho-philosophical teaching that man, at birth, was a *tabula rasa*, would confute every existing prejudice about the evil qualities allegedly inherent in the Jews or any other people. The French rationalists' ideas on the equality of the human race were reinforced with regard to the Jews by the Physiocrats' theory of the free play of economic forces. The individualism which taught that a man's worth depended solely on his personal qualities formed the very foundation of the outlook of the Enlightenment and was also conducive to an objective evaluation of the Jews. Lessing had already broached this idea in his play, *Die Juden*, in 1749: the first practical attempt to realize it in the educational field was made by the *Philantropin* Institute, opened at Dessau in 1774.

Beginning of the Haskalah Movement; Moses Mendelssohn

The birth of a modern German culture and the advance in science, the arts and *belles lettres* to the level of the rest of western Europe, roused the subjugated Jewish population from the torpor of petrified, tradition-laden rabbinical culture and fertilized its intellectual development. This was the more so since the new culture officially championed the ideals of humanitarianism, the unity of man, the removal of sectarian barriers, and the eradication of religious bigotry, prejudice and superstition—and, into the bargain, enthroned reason as the final arbiter of the political and social system and of relations between man and man.

This was not, of course, the first time in the long history of the Diaspora that the Jewish people had lived in close proximity to a rich and highly developed culture. However, in medieval Spain and Provence, in Italy during the age of Humanism, and in Holland in the seventeenth century, the Jews, in a spirit of imitative rivalry, had been partners in the culture concerned, during the various stages of its development. In these cases, the rise of a secular Jewish culture had been the growth of a new branch on an old tree. This was not so during the *Haskalah* period in Germany. The traditional Jewish culture, which had taken shape over the centuries and was now petrified and impervious to external influences, came into sudden conflict with an alien culture clamouring for "universal citizenship," and the breakdown of the barriers of religion. The result was a crisis, unprecedented in the history of Jewish culture in Europe.

Wide circles of German Jewry—the middle and lower middle classes—continued in their traditional forms of existence for a long time. The new Jewish middle class bore the brunt of the intellectual crisis. A knowledge of the German language and culture had become not only a matter of social prestige for this class, but also an economic necessity. The industrialists, bankers, and commercial magnates needed the German language, general schooling and the ability to conform to the manners of the country, both in their business affairs and in their frequent dealings with the authorities and rulers. But the decisive motive was the ambition to break free from the restrictions of their peculiar legal status and achieve equal civil rights. "Spiritual emancipation," not only in the sense of cultural progress, but also imitation of the speech, behaviour and culture of the German ruling classes, was considered a *sine qua non* for legal enfranchisement—even by the German exponents of the Enlightenment. The new Jewish middle class, therefore, was unflagging in its efforts to prove that it already deserved equality in this respect. To the same end, the enlightened Jewish middle class produced a programme to reform the Jewish way of life, with particular regard to religion, Kehillah autonomy and education.

The severity of religious laws and prohibitions conflicted not only with the *Weltanschauung* of the enlightened Jewish middle class and its deist inclinations, but also with its economic activities. This class also found Kehillah autonomy a serious handicap. In the first place, it involved subjection to rabbinical authority. Secondly, it entailed shared responsibility for the payment of taxes by all Kehillah members—or, for that matter, by all Jews in the state. The reform programme also supported modern education for the children of the ordinary people, particularly the study of German. This would not only enable them to move from peddling, speculation, and moneylending to more productive activities such as handicraft and agriculture. It was also vital for the prestige and prosperity of the middle class; as long as the Jewish masses were culturally isolated and their trading methods evoked unfavourable comment, the Jewish middle class feared that public opinion in Germany might identify "enlightened" Jews with this "contemptible" nation.

In this way, the new Jewish middle class became the active force in the *Haskalah* movement. It laid down the programme of the movement and supported its literature (including its writers) and its educational institutions. The headquarters of the *Haskalah* were in Berlin, the capital of Prussia. Prussia led all the states of Germany in industrial and cultural development, and the most important branches of the *Haskalah* movement (apart from Hamburg), were located in the two largest Prussian provincial cities—Königsberg and Breslau. Nearly half of the 190 subscribers to the *Me'asef* at the beginning of 1785 lived in Berlin or Königsberg.

From the beginning, the German middle-class Jews who joined the *Haskalah* movement could be divided into three categories. The first consisted of a small number of Jews, lacking both the ambition and the creative power to find a synthesis between the rich and developing general culture and the historical legacy of their own. They seized upon German culture without effecting the slightest change in their practice of the Jewish religion, which they identified with the essence of Jewishness. The second group in its initial stage was the most characteristic of the German-Jewish Enlightenment movement, the enlightenment that gave birth to the *Haskalah* movement amongst the Jews of Galicia and Russia. Its members preached the revival of the Hebrew language and literature and the people's renaissance in terms of a synthesis between the Jewish and the European culture. The extremist wing of the movement was represented by enlightened assimilationists who saw no possibility or need to maintain a distinct Jewish culture. They eroded the tenets of Judaism until they only retained those elements of the ancestral faith which were compatible with deism. Representatives of these three factions were still united within the same fold when the *Haskalah* movement mounted its first offensive, and the demarcations between them were blurred. The extremist wing of deliberate assimilationists, in particular, had not yet acquired a clearly defined outline. But the future trend of the Jewish Enlightenment movement in Germany was already established by the fact that even in its early, formative stages, the destructive tendency was the strongest and engulfed the entire movement in a flood of assimilation.

"From Moses to Moses, there was none like Moses." In these terms, the German *Maskilim* lauded Moses Mendelssohn during his lifetime. The words had originally been applied to Moses Maimonides, the greatest Jewish thinker of the Middle Ages. The disciples of the *Maskilim* in eastern Europe faithfully followed them in their veneration of Mendelssohn. If the truth be told, however, Moses Mendelssohn was only one of the foremost exponents of the moderate *Haskalah* movement in intellectual power, ability and outlook, even judged by the criteria of his own generation. He was not even the main power behind the *Mas-*

kilim—precisely because he embodied the middle stream of German Enlightenment, with all its backwardness, added to the unique backwardness which characterized the Jewish Enlightenment movement of his time. Mendelssohn was, in fact, typically representative of the ultra-conservative right wing of the *Haskalah* movement, which demonstrated how thoroughly powerless it was to solve the crucial problem confronting the Jewish world: how to rejuvenate Jewish culture by combining it with the best in universal culture. Instead of a synthesis, Mendelssohn merely produced a delineation of Judaism and humanity as two apparently separate provinces. This strange distinction was also exemplified in his personal life and literary activity. The sense of pride and achievement with which Mendelssohn inspired his contemporaries in the *Haskalah* movement came principally from the eminence which he achieved in non-Jewish Enlightenment circles—an eminence that was evanescent and short lived.

Moses Mendelssohn was born in 1729, the son of a Jewish scroll writer at Dessau—he was known to the people as Moshe Dessauer, even in the early twentieth century. In 1743, when he was fourteen, he knocked on the *Rosenthalthor* in Berlin and convinced the strict Jewish gatekeeper that he was worthy to enter the city. He had come to study at the rabbinical school of his mentor and fellow-townsman, Rabbi David Fraenkel, recently appointed Rabbi of the Berlin Kehillah. After years of poverty as a *Yeshivah Bachur* (rabbinical student), obtaining his meals by "eating days,"* Mendelssohn was employed in 1750 as a tutor in the home of Isaac Bernhard. Later Bernhard appointed him accountant at his silk factory and he eventually became a partner. While still a young man, Mendelssohn had acquired a broad general education from his teachers, who were among the first *Maskilim* of Berlin. Rabbi Israel Zamosc (1700-72) taught him mathematics and also tutored him in the understanding of Maimonides' *Guide to the Perplexed* and other medieval works of philosophical inquiry. In 1741, Rabbi Zamosc had published *Eternity of Israel* (*Netzach Yisrael*), including Talmudic mathematics and astronomy, and had been forced to leave Poland because of his preoccupation with such "heretical" matters. Dr. Abraham Kisch, a physician, taught Mendelssohn Latin, and Dr. Aaron Gumpertz, German literature and, in particular, the German philosophy of Leibnitz and Wolff. Through Gumpertz, Mendelssohn met the German writer and dramatist, Gotthold Ephraim Lessing, and a close friendship developed. This also marked the beginning of the fame that Mendelssohn later achieved in the field of German literature.

In 1755, Lessing published Mendelssohn's first work in German, *Philosophical Discourses*, which tried to prove an essentially incongruous thesis: the common aspects in the philosophies of Spinoza and Leibnitz.

---

* In Yiddish, *essn teg*. Needy students took their meals with a different family, by arrangement, each day of the week.

In the same year, Mendelssohn published his first inquiry into aesthetics, which displayed more original thought than all his popular philosophical writings and influenced to some extent the German literature of his generation. Mendelssohn's success in the field of philosophy lay principally in his light and lucid style, which presented the systems of Leibnitz and Wolff to a wide circle of readers. Ironically, in 1763, Moses Mendelssohn was awarded the prize of the Berlin Academy of Science for his inquiry into *The Application of Mathematical Proofs to Metaphysics* in a competition in which Kant was only awarded honourable mention. In that work, Mendelssohn's definitive distinction between mathematical, empirical, and metaphysical truth only contained a glimmer of one of the ideas basic to the philosophy of Kant. Mendelssohn reached the height of his fame both in Germany and abroad with his book *Phaedon, or the Immortality of the Soul*, published in 1767. It rapidly passed through several successive editions in German, was translated into nearly all European languages, and earned its author the epithet of "The Jewish Plato." Any man of letters visiting Berlin felt duty-bound to pay his respects to the "Socrates of Berlin." The Dukes of Brunswick and Schaumburg-Lippe sought his company and cultivated his friendship. Ecclesiastics and Christian theologians corresponded with him and even sought his advice in solving religious problems which had proved beyond their own capacity. In 1771, the Academy of Science proposed to Frederick II that Mendelssohn be appointed a member of the Academy. But the King, who hated Jews—although in 1763, at the request of Marquis D'Argens, he had condescended to grant Mendelssohn the status of *Schutzjude* (protected Jew)—struck his name off the list.

Mendelssohn's *Phaedon* became a favourite with Enlightenment circles, and especially with the semi-enlightened in Germany, as it reinforced the tenets of faith which the spread of rationalism was undermining. It was a collection and arrangement of extracts from Plato's *Phaedon*, augmented by the theological opinions of Leibnitz and Wolff, and written in a pleasantly attractive style. The author based his view of immortality on the premise of God's existence, as proved by the scholastic method of the Middle Ages (the common ontological proof deriving from a definition of the concept of God), and on the theories of the soul advanced by his teachers, Leibnitz and Wolff, which negated both materialism and Lockian sensualism. A year before his death, in 1785, Mendelssohn published *Morgenstunden* (*Morning Hours*), in which he again sought to prove the existence of God by the scholastic ontological method, only in a revised formulation. The book was written with the intention of controverting the Spinozist system. At the time the subject was of increasing interest amongst leading German writers. The German author, Jacobi, revealed that even Lessing had become addicted to the philosophy of Spinoza and this revelation embittered Mendelssohn's last days and apparently hastened his end. This revival of interest in the hitherto neglected Spinoza during the declining years of "The Jewish Plato," who had spent his life in vain efforts to resurrect an antiquated theology and theodicy, may contain some intimation of the verdict of history.

Mendelssohn was a kind and sensitive man, not easily angered, and generally well-liked by his fellows. His friends and acquaintances included the representative German writers of the day. His kindheartedness, however, also had its negative aspects. Although he was revered as their leader by a generation of enlightened Jews, he was neither a fighter by nature nor a revolutionary in his opinions. It is greatly to his credit that on several crucial occasions he overcame his innate love of peace and took action against the adversaries of his people. As early as 1754, he published an open letter defending the Jews against criticism by the theologian, Johann Michaelis, of Lessing's play, *Die Juden*. This was followed by a long period when Mendelssohn published nothing concerning the Jews. In 1770, however, he was forced to clarify his attitude to the Jewish question in order to vindicate his own honour. A Christian clergyman at Zürich, and an admirer of Mendelssohn, Lavater, published the German translation of a booklet by Professor Bonnet of Geneva entitled *Untersuchung der Beweise für das Christentum gegen Ungläubige*. He prefaced this with an open letter to the author of *Phaedon* challenging him to confute the *Beweise* or draw the logical conclusions—in other words, convert to Christianity. Mendelssohn ignored the advice of the leaders of the Berlin Kehillah, that he hold his peace, and published an open letter in reply. "I cannot conceive," he wrote, in a reply which scrupulously avoided any offence to the Christian faith, "what could bind me to a religion ostensibly so harsh and so universally held in contempt were I not convinced in the depths of my heart of its Truth . . . I hereby testify before the Creator who gives sustenance to my life and to yours . . . that I shall stand upon my principle so long as my soul remains essentially unchanged." The friendship with Lavater continued even after this incident. In 1775, Mendelssohn requested him to intercede on behalf of the Jewish poor of Switzerland when their expulsion was ordered. Mendelssohn himself interceded effectively for the withdrawal of a similar expulsion decree against several hundred indigent Jews in Dresden in 1777. In the same year, he defended the Königsberg Kehillah against slanderous reports by the Government Supervisor of Synagogues, including criticism of the prayer '*Aleinu Le'shabeach (We Should Give Praise)*'.

Mendelssohn unwittingly played an important part in the emancipation of the Jews in Germany and beyond its borders. To them, and to their enlightened supporters, he was a shining example and a living proof that it was not beyond their capacity to achieve eminence in the field of general learning and to make an important contribution to the culture of the country. However, in the final years of his life, Mendelssohn also engaged in literary activity which was invaluable in rousing European public opinion on behalf of the civil liberation of the Jews. He was forced into this by a new development in the controversy on the Jewish question. In 1780, the Jews of Alsace, attacked by the venomous propaganda of a certain Hell, approached Mendelssohn with the request that he write a memorandum to the French government on their abject condition. Mendelssohn delegated this task to his friend, the Prussian government official and statesman, Christian W. Dohm. Dohm elaborated on the subject and his work, *Uber die bügerliche Verbesserung der Juden* (*On the Civil Betterment of the Jews*) 1781, made a great impression everywhere. Dohm's opinions found a certain number of opponents, including Professor Michaelis in Germany; Dohm included Mendelssohn's reply to the Professor's indictment in the second volume of the work. To silence the critics, Mendelssohn encouraged his learned friend, Dr. Marcus Hertz, to publish a German translation of Menasseh ben-Israel's Latin *Vindiciae Judaeorum* (*A Defence of the Jews*). Mendelssohn wrote a trenchant introduction to this book, with pointed references to matters of current interest. The medieval hatred of the Jews, he argued, had only changed its outward form. The public were no longer convinced by ritual blood accusations, charges of well-poisoning and similar travesties. New accusations were therefore being heaped upon the Jews to justify the curtailment of their rights. They were libelled as immoral and ill-mannered, incapable of pursuing useful occupations or of engaging in science or the crafts. "They bind our hands," he wrote, "then condemn us for not using them."

In this introduction, Mendelssohn also expressed disagreement with Dohm's opinion that it was desirable to leave Kehillah autonomy *in statu quo*, particularly in respect of the judiciary authority of the rabbis and *Parnassim* to excommunicate and banish. Mendelssohn had personal experience of the zealotry of the rabbis—they had banned his commentary on the Pentateuch—and he advised the rabbis and Kehillah leaders not to learn from the religious animosity of other nations, but to refrain from all coercion in religious matters. This introduction revived the controversy, and Mendelssohn decided to investigate in depth the questions of the interrelation of state and religion. In 1785, he published *Jerusalem, oder über religiöse Macht und Judentum* (*Jerusalem, or Religious Authority and Judaism*). This work brought together and affirmed all the views on the state, religion, and Judaism which he had voiced in previous polemics, beginning with the Lavater incident.

In the general section of the book, Mendelssohn discussed the functions of state and religion and their inter-relationship. The state and religion had one common objective: to sustain human society and individual happiness, which included immortality. Mendelssohn, like Spinoza in his *Theological-Political Treatise*, submitted that the state only controlled the overt acts of men, irrespective of their intent. On the other hand, religion and the church were concerned with human intent and thought. Religion, therefore, had no coercive authority, for matters of the spirit and the mind were not subject to fiats. As the state had no right to intervene in religious matters, it had no legal grounds for infringing the rights of its citizens on account of their religious creed, so long as they obeyed its laws. Thus, the principle of liberty of religious conscience in a state postulated total equality of rights for the Jews.

Mendelssohn reinforced the case for Jewish civil enfranchisement by discoursing on the essence of the Jewish religion, juxtaposing the methods of Maimonides, Spinoza in his *Treatise*, and the deists in their doctrine of natural religion. The Jewish religion did not try to impose tenets and views by decree, since God had implanted these in man's native intelligence. Mendelssohn was convinced that everything in the Jewish religion concerning faith and the outlook on life and the universe could be rationally demonstrated. Hence the Jewish religion, in contrast with Christianity, did not depend on divine revelation in matters of faith but on practical laws enacted by God Himself. Mendelssohn, like Maimonides, thought that the laws and precepts were handed down by God in order to instruct man in an ethical way of life, to educate him in a lucid conception of the Divinity, and thus to draw him away from idolatry and false beliefs. However, Mendelssohn also followed Spinoza's view on the specific natural circumstances of the Jewish religion. While the Jewish people inhabited their own land, they did not differentiate between religion and the state. The religious laws were also the laws of the body politic; anyone who broke them was punished as though he had violated a law of the state. This religion had been given to the Children of Israel alone; the historical connection between God and the people was sealed in the covenant that He made with the Patriarchs and through the miracles recounted in the Torah. The Oral Law was given when God revealed Himself and it was equal in sacredness to the Written Law. The Torah was not given in writing alone, in order to prevent the people becoming enslaved to the graven letter, since that would smack of idolatry. The political nature of the Jewish religion ceased to exist with the destruction of the temple and the Jewish state. Since then the Jews had been obliged to obey the laws of the state in the countries of their dispersion and the coercive political power of the Jewish religion had lapsed. Nevertheless, in every detail and particular—apart from those obligations depending on residence in the Land of Israel—the Jewish religion postulated that "it lies not with man to grant that which God has forbidden."

Mendelssohn concluded with an appeal to his "brother men" among the nations of the world not to withhold their civil rights from the Jews, merely because they were loyal to their religion. This religion, he proclaimed, was binding upon the Jewish people and was dearer to them than anything else in the world, even than equality of rights, should that be conditional on conversion. He also addressed a stirring appeal to his

159

people, to the "House of Jacob," which, in a sense, was a testament for coming generations: "Integrate yourself into the customs and the order of the state in whose midst you have been placed, but also cling steadfastly to the religion of your fathers. Carry both these burdens to the best of your ability."

There are obvious conceptual defects and contradictions in *Jerusalem*; and even Mendelssohn's contemporaries were aware of them. The author had sought to prove that the Jewish religion was based entirely on reason and on natural religion, but he did not explain satisfactorily why the practical duties of this religion should have been ordained for the Children of Israel alone and not for all the peoples of the world. The idea of a chosen people which lay behind his method was entirely opposed to the rationalist pan-humanist religion that Mendelssohn, together with the enlightened men of his generation, upheld; its exponent, Lessing, was his intimate friend. His utter lack of any historical approach—essential to understand the national particularity of the Jewish religion—involved Mendelssohn in a contradiction between the political nature of the Torah's laws and precepts and the view that all its requirements were binding, even after the loss of Jewish statehood. Spinoza, from whom Mendelssohn derived his concept of the connection between the Torah and the ancient state of Israel, was similarly limited in historical perception. But as a consistent rationalist, he solved the contradiction with the proposal that the obligations ordained by the Torah were devoid of meaning, from the destruction of the temple until the Jewish State were reconstituted as of old. Solomon Maimon also sensed the contradiction in Mendelssohn's statement that the Kehillah did not have the right of coercion through excommunication and similar methods "at a time when he himself had decided that the statehood of the Jewish religion is everlasting and will neither be altered nor disestablished for all eternity."

Mendelssohn's book did not reach the level of Spinoza's *Treatise*, not only because of inconsistencies in its actual conception, but also because of the inconsistent radicalism of his views on the freedom of conscience. Spinoza and Locke had granted the state no authority to interfere in matters of religion. Mendelssohn evinced theoretical moderation and political conservatism on this issue. His opinions on the principle of freedom of conscience, as expressed in *Jerusalem*, did not extend beyond the limits set by the accepted religions. He thought that the state had the right and was qualified, when faced with epicureanism and the atheistic rejection of God, to adopt measures "from a distance," for assuredly the well-being of mankind, for whom society was created, was inconceivable without the existence of God, Divine Providence, and the immortality of the soul. A contention by the Calvinist-born critic and fore-runner of rationalism, Pierre Bayle, that atheism should be tolerated within the state as, unlike superstition, it did not undermine its foundations, was rejected, with consternation, by Mendelssohn. "Which is preferable, cancer or typhoid fever?" he asked.

However, *Jerusalem*, with all its manifold contradictions and regressive tendencies, played the same positive role as so many of Mendelssohn's other works: in the retarded atmosphere of Germany, even these moderate ideas could exert a progressive influence. Not surprisingly, therefore, it was attacked by German conservatives, for daring to oppose the authority of the Church and for preaching the existence of a natural religion. At the same time, it won abundant praise from the genuinely enlightened, such as Herder, Kant, and even Mirabeau.

Mendelssohn's counsel of patience to his fellow Jews in bearing their "dual burden" of Jewish religious law and the laws of the land, actually represented his own formulation of the problem confronting Judaism and humanity. In his view, the quintessence of Jewry was its religion, whereas culture was a matter concerning all humanity. The solution Moses Mendelssohn offered the Jewish people to the problem of their enlightenment was a strange combination—on the one hand, rigid conservatism regarding the religious heritage, and, on the other, hope of cultural attainment to the rank of "world citizenship."

It was only in his early youth that Mendelssohn engaged in any literary activity in Hebrew that revealed a hope of recasting the culture of his people in an essentially national sense. In 1750, with a friend, Tobias Bock, he published a Hebrew weekly *Kohelet Musar (Preacher of Ethics)*, which expressed the view and aspirations of the whole moderate wing of the *Haskalah* Movement. It called for a revival of Hebrew, was written in an ornate style, exclusively in Biblical idiom, propounded the love of beauty and of nature, and stressed the social import of ethical relations among men. It ceased publication, apparently under orthodox pressure, after two issues. For the next twenty years, Mendelssohn published nothing in Hebrew. Then, in 1770, his *Commentary* on Ecclesiastes appeared. Eight years later, he published his specimen *Commentary* on the Pentateuch, which, with the German translation of the Pentateuch, launched a new era in the history of the Jewish Enlightenment.

Mendelssohn hoped that his *Commentary* and translation would raise the level of learning among the Jewish people, the *Commentary* by inculcating a sense of the beauty of biblical style, the translation by teaching the German language and thereby opening the door to European literature and culture. However, in disseminating a knowledge of German, Mendelssohn also had a definite negative purpose: to uproot and displace Yiddish as the people's vernacular. Mendelssohn described the language of the Yiddish translations of the Pentateuch as "a tongue of buffoons, very inadequate and corrupt; a reader capable of elegant speech must recoil from it in disgust." A letter that Mendelssohn wrote to a Prussian state official, Professor Ernst Klein, in 1782, emphatically demanded that the Jewish oath be couched in "pure German" and not "in a Judeo-German mixture."

Mendelssohn's contempt for the spoken language of the people expressed the view of the new Jewish middle class, its hope of resembling the country's ruling classes in all things, of rising above the lower middle class and the poor, who were looked down upon by the dominant nation. The motive of social prestige was all the more emphasized by the fact that, like many other of his enlightened contemporaries, Mendelssohn continued to conduct his personal correspondence with intimate friends and family in Yiddish. Neither he nor all the *Maskilim* who followed him realized that by jettisoning Yiddish they were destroying one of the chief foundations of a distinct Jewish culture and thereby endangering the basis for the existence of Hebrew. But Mendelssohn was genuinely concerned for the survival of the ancient language (even though for purely religious reasons and possibly, at a sub-conscious level, in response to an urge for national survival).

Mendelssohn translated the Pentateuch and three books of Hagiographa—Ecclesiastes, Psalms, and the Song of Songs—entirely on his own. The *Commentary*, on the other hand, incorporated the work of a number of other *Maskilim*; Mendelssohn himself wrote the *Commentary* to the Book of Exodus. The *Commentary* to Genesis was mainly written by Rabbi Solomon Dubno, an outstanding grammarian from Poland; to Leviticus by Naphtali Hertz Wesel (Wessely); to Numbers, by Rabbi Aaron of Jaroslaw; and to Deuteronomy by Hertz Homberg. Mendelssohn nevertheless had a share in all the Commentaries and his outlook was indelibly stamped on each composition. He was very restrained in his methods of interpreting the Torah and was no advocate of Bible criticism then developing in the *Haskalah* generation. Even with his preference for *prima facie* explanations of the Bible, he carried his caution to the point of stating that, where the *D'rush* (homiletical interpretation) of the Sages contradicted the obvious meaning, "we are beholden to follow in the path of the *D'rush*."

Mendelssohn's moderation was of no avail against the attacks of the orthodox extremists. They realized that any tendency towards a direct "explanation" of the Biblical text, however cautious, was an innovation which could conceal a movement to divert the attention of the young people from the Talmud to the Old Testament. These conservative circles directed a furious campaign against Mendelssohn's German translation. Rabbi Raphael Hacohen, Chief Rabbi of Hamburg, excommunicated anyone who read the book; he only refrained from excommunicating the author because the King of Denmark was among the subscribers.

The fear in orthodox circles of the consequences of the *Beur*, as Mendelssohn's *Commentary* was known in Hebrew, was justified. It was not so much a knowledge of the Torah that it diffused, but rather of the German language. This provided a stepping stone for generations of

Maskilim to the acquisition of European learning, "a first step to culture," as Mendelssohn had hoped.

Naphtali Hertz Wessely and the Manifesto of the Haskalah

Mendelssohn's influence on Jewish Enlightenment was mostly indirect. The new movement found an ardent champion in his contemporary, the Hebrew grammarian and poet, Naphtali Hertz Wesel (Hartwig Wessely, 1725-1805). He was born in Hamburg of a family that had fled from Poland during the Chmielnicki outrages of 1648. He spent his childhood and youth in Copenhagen, his middle years in Amsterdam, and his old age in Berlin. He engaged in commerce as an agent for the wealthy Ephraim family, and later earned a living by teaching and literary activity. His interest in Hebrew grammar and the Bible was aroused at the age of ten by his teacher, Solomon Zalman Hanau, a grammarian, persecuted by the orthodox camp on account of an essay he had written. He had acquired a general education largely through his own efforts, though in geography he was advised by his father, a wealthy merchant; and he read widely amongst the commentators and Hebrew scientific works of the Middle Ages and Renaissance, including works by the seventeenth century physician and thinker, Joseph Solomon Delmedigo of Candia (Yosef Sh'lomo Rofei).

Wessely's development towards Enlightenment was but another symptom of the historical continuity represented by the *Haskalah* movement, despite its distance in time from previous periods of rationalism in the history of Jewish culture. Every individual amongst the *Maskilim* with any claim to literary repute had gained his initial knowledge of science and philosophy from the books of the Jewish thinkers of the Middle Ages. Maimonides was particularly important in this respect as the link connecting the golden age of Hebrew literature in medieval times with the Hebrew renaissance of the modern period. One of Moses Mendelssohn's favourite jokes was that the many hours of his early youth passed bent in assiduous study of Maimonides' *Guide to the Perplexed*, had made him a hunchback.

Wessely's first books were a valuable factor in the revival of the Hebrew language, though as yet they contained nothing to stir up orthodox opposition. In 1765-66, two parts of his *Lebanon, The Closed Garden*, a book of synonyms, appeared. In 1775 he published *The Wine of Lebanon*, a commentary on the Mishnaic Tractate *Avot* (Patriarchs) which even gained the approval of the orthodox rabbis who later became his chief adversaries. In 1778, he published a Hebrew translation of *The Wisdom of Solomon*, one of the Apocrypha, with a commentary, (*Ruah Hen, The Spirit of Grace*). But his importance in the history of the *Haskalah* Movement was really the result of his *Songs of Grandeur*

(*Shirei Tif'eret*), the first part of which was published in 1789. This work may of course be described as the literary child of his old age, since even Klopstock's *The Messiah*, which Wessely used as a model, had aged in its author's life-time. (It was written and published over a span of more than twenty years in a progressively deteriorating style, pseudo-classic at its early best and monotonously bombastic towards the end.) Lessing, in a frequently quoted *bon mot*, said: "Everybody praises Klopstock and nobody reads him." Wessely's epic, apart from a very few cantos, lacked even Klopstock's lyricism and flights of imagination. It overflowed with unnecessary phraseology, digressions and moralizing. Yet *Songs of Grandeur* met enthusiastic acclaim not only from Wessely's own contemporaries (current issues of the *Me'asef* were full of praise). Later generations of *Haskalah* poets, including J. L. Gordon, wrote poems modelled on its pattern.

Wessely became the father of *Haskalah* as a *social* movement by virtue of a booklet he wrote and published in 1782 entitled *Words of Peace and Truth* (*Divrei Shalom ve'Emet*). In 1781, Joseph II issued his *Edict of Toleration* granting economic concessions to the Jews of his realm, and allowing them to establish schools for general education. The orthodox Jewish population greeted this as a repressive decree that jeopardized the structure of traditional Judaism and threatened to erase the hope of Messianic redemption and the restoration of Zion from amongst the people. Mendelssohn, as a moderate, was also highly suspicious of Joseph's reform and justly charged him not only with intent to increase taxation, but also with hypocrisy and plotting to convert the Jews. "Of what use are ordinary schools to us if we are neither permitted to engage in manual vocations nor to serve in public office?" he wrote to his friend Hertz Homberg. "Many thanks for all this toleration, if, incidentally, efforts still are made, as before, to unite all the religions . . ." Wessely, on the other hand, though even more orthodox than Mendelssohn, agreed with the majority of the *Maskilim* that the decree opened a new era of enlightenment and happiness in the history of the Jewish people.

Wessely prefaced his proposals for reform in Jewish education with a historical survey of the development of Jewish culture in *Words of Peace and of Truth.** This survey established the premises for the educational programme and general outlook of the *Haskalah* movement. Total culture, he wrote, comprehended the law of God and the law of man, the latter embracing all the sciences and technical developments. While the Jewish people occupied its own land, it had recourse to the law of man like all the other peoples of the world, for without this law, the Jewish state could not have existed. In the Diaspora, the Jewish people neglected the law of man as a whole and therefore was left solely with the law of

---

* For Wessely's views, as summarized here, we have also drawn upon their later expansion in three further epistles on the subject, and especially on the second of these, *An Abundance of Good for the House of Israel* (*Rav Tuv le'Beth Israel*) cf. p. 167.

God. This was the result of repression and affliction. Decadence became especially marked amongst the Jews "dwelling in Ashkenaz (Germany) and Poland" for geographical reasons and because of the generally backward economic, political and cultural development of these countries. The persecution of the Jews during this sad period was only one symptom of the atmosphere of religious animosity, when there still prevailed "that division of faiths and opinions in unfeeling hearts" which had led to bloody religious conflicts. Wessely mentioned all the monarchs of Europe with generous praise for their gracious acts on behalf of the Jews. In particular, he named as "the Jewish people's great benefactor" the Emperor, "who has done so much for the cause of toleration," in other words, Joseph II. He "has loosened the bonds from their existence" and "has perceived, in his concern, that but few of them speak the German language properly and do not therefore understand its books . . . Nor can they converse correctly with the inhabitants of the country and its rulers." "To converse correctly"—this took top priority in an open letter that Wessely addressed to "the Congregation of the flock of Israel who dwell in the lands under the rule of the great Emperor." The Jews of Germany and Poland did not know German and spoke Yiddish, a "mutilated and confused," "desolate and arid" tongue, purely as a result of their bitter exile. And because they did not possess this command of "correct speech" the people were remote from all the wisdom and virtues which comprised the law of man. Wessely appealed to "my brethren, the Children of Israel," to make use of the benevolence the Emperor had evinced and to reform their educational methods. Enlightenment and, in particular, "good German," apart from their importance *per se*, were also essential to earn a living, especially "for the great merchants" who "have access to the courts of rulers." These accomplishments would efface the disgrace that his people bore in the eyes of the world; and a knowledge of the arts, history, geography, and the natural sciences, would also be of great help in understanding the Torah and the Talmud.

Wessely proposed a course of studies for the schools, based on these principles, to include both the "law of man" and the "law of God." The Bible would only be taught in conjunction with a German translation, in the manner of Mendelssohn's *Commentary*, so that the pupils would acquire both a grammatical knowledge of Hebrew and a knowledge of German, which in turn would introduce them to the arts. *Mishnah* would be taught in the third grade to pupils who had already studied the Bible. Talmud would only be introduced after the pupils had "previously become fully conversant in good manners and the arts" and only to those "who showed an aptitude" for it, "since not all of us have been destined to become Talmudists." Wessely gave preference to the handicrafts amongst occupations "because the land cannot contain so many mer-chants. May knowledge multiply and God's flock not consist entirely of traders. . ." He concluded with a word of encouragement to the Jews of Austria:

> All beginnings are difficult, and especially in this matter. Do not weaken, for your deeds will be recompensed; for that which you now do is but a revival of those proper customs which we practised in ancient times.

The entire programme of the *Haskalah* was contained in this manifesto by Wessely. The distinction between "the law of God" and "the law of man," followed by Mendelssohn in *Jerusalem*, was also an early formulation of J. L. Gordon's aphorism, "Be a Jew at home and a man abroad." The emphasis on knowledge of a "pure language" as the basis for general erudition; the complete opposition to Yiddish; the faith that an era was beginning when reason and human fraternity would prevail in all religious communities; the fervent expectations engendered by the enlightened "benevolent kings" and the Jewish notables who "attend upon monarchs;" the appeal for loyalty to the ruler and obedience to the laws of the land; the exhortation to become productive by learning manual trades—these were the basic slogans of the *Haskalah* school of thought for a long period.

Wessely's work aroused even greater anger in orthodox circles than Mendelssohn's *Commentary*. It precipitated a conflict between *Haskalah* and ultra-orthodoxy that raged throughout the nineteenth century. The same ultra-orthodox rabbis who had protested against the *Commentary* were prominent here. Ezekiel Landau of Prague, Pinchas Horowitz of Frankfurt-on-Main and David Tebele (Harif) of Lissa acrimoniously attacked Wessely. They were joined by the Chief Rabbi of Berlin, Hirschel Levin, who had been one of the few rabbis to approve of Mendelssohn's *Commentary*. Their bitter antagonism to Wessely's book came from their instinctive realization that it contained the germ of the approaching revolution in educational methods and cultural condition of European Jewry. Wessely, despite his moderation and orthodox devotion to his religion, had set out to disturb not only the traditional order of studies but also the whole system based on study of the *Gemara* and built on a hierarchy of Talmudic scholars. The ultra-orthodox certainly exaggerated when they accused Wessely of trying to render "the principal (religious studies) secondary and the secondary (general knowledge) principal." But they were not unjustified when they claimed that he had made a frontal assault on their view that "the German language and other branches of knowledge" be permitted only as "minor accessories of wisdom." They also regarded the emphasis that his book placed on the study of the Bible and ethics and its suggestion to leave the study of the Talmud to those who have a talent for it as a negation of the whole concept of religion. What particularly infuriated the rabbis, however, was the reflection on their honour contained in Wessely's interpretation of the

Midrashic epigram: "If a Talmudic scholar be without knowledge, then is a lifeless carcass superior to him."

The Jews of Italy found nothing revolutionary in Wessely's assertions. They had been steeped in general enlightenment since the Humanist period, and had adopted an identical policy in educational matters. It was they who rallied to Wessely's side. A few months after the first epistle, Wessely, in order to confute his opponents, published a second, entitled *Rav Tuv le'Beth Israel* (*An Abundance of Good for the House of Israel*), addressed to the Kehillah at Trieste. In 1784, he published his third Open Letter, *The Well of Judgement*.* Here he cited the views of the rabbis of Trieste, Ferrara, Venice, Ancona and Gorizia, as well as poems written in his honour by Italian Hebrew poets. The fourth Open Letter, *Rehovoth* (Wide Vistas), published in 1784, summarized Wessely's views on education and Enlightenment, but it concluded with an expression of disappointment at the way in which Joseph II's *Edict* concerning elementary schools was being implemented. The pupils were not receiving their general elementary education and their Hebrew education (to be based on Mendelssohn's *Commentary* and Pentateuch translation) at the same school. Instead, they still received instruction in the *Heder*, as before, "in that mutilated, confused tongue." The text books on ethics, too, were written by gentile scholars, in German, and not by Jewish authors, in Hebrew.

The Maskilim Organize; First Issues of the Me'asef

Words of Peace and of Truth became the declaration of the *Haskalah* movement's principles for the Jews of Germany. Once the controversy became open, all the *Maskilim* of Berlin rallied to Wessely's side against attack from all directions. The four epistles were printed at the press of the *Jüdische Freischule* under the direction of David Friedlaender—who also translated the first pamphlet into German. In support of Wessely, a satire, *Ke'tav Yosher* (*Writ of Justice*) was published. It was one of the finest creations in the Hebrew literature of that generation. Its author, who withheld his name at the time of publication, was Rabbi Saul Berlin, one of the most tragic fighters in the *Haskalah* movement.

Saul Berlin was the son of Rabbi Hirschel Levin of Berlin, and was himself ordained for the rabbinate at the age of eighteen. He drew close to *Haskalah* circles at Berlin and Breslau, where he had family connections, and became convinced that the ignorance of his people and their vicissitudes were the result of rabbinical domination. His position—he was employed as Rabbi at Frankfurt-on-Oder, and lacked the courage to resign—limited his activities in the campaign for Enlightenment to

* The Hebrew title, *Ein Mishpat*, contains a subtle play on words; it can also mean the *Eye of Judgment*.

underground methods. *Writ of Justice*, completed in 1784 and published by the *Maskilim* after his death was his first work in this direction. In 1789, with the help of *Haskalah* friends, and under a pseudonym, he published *The Watch-Tower of Yekutiel*. The book ridiculed a new exegetical work on the *Halakhah*, known as *Torat Yekutiel*, by the Chief Rabbi of Hamburg, Raphael Hacohen, who was also the foremost opponent of Mendelssohn's *Commentary*. So strong was the ridicule that it provoked violent reaction in orthodox ranks and Berlin's work was condemned to be publicly burned at Hamburg. The author continued undeterred, and published a new pamphlet, under his own name, defending the fictitious writer of *The Watch-Tower of Yekutiel*. In 1793, before orthodox anger at this escapade had abated, Berlin published a collection of Responsa, *Be'samim Rosh (Chief of Spices)*, again at the Berlin *Haskalah* press. The introduction stated that he had discovered the book in manuscript form and alleged that it was the authentic work of the Rosh—Rabenu Asher, the famous fourteenth-century codifier.* The fraud was immediately recognized and evoked the wrath of the entire rabbinate. Its author had to resign his rabbinical post and emigrated to London in 1794, where he died shortly afterwards, deserted and forlorn. His will requested that he be buried in his clothes—"in one of the woodlands—far from the burial grounds of his people." Even when he died at the age of fifty-four, he had still found no solution to the formidable contradictions between his own *Weltanschauung* and a hostile, rigidly conservative environment.

Saul Berlin's *Writ of Justice* was written in the form of a dialogue between the author, a Polish *Melamed*, and a rabbi. It was a keen and wonderfully humorous satire on the fanatics who opposed Wessely. The *Melamed*, speaking on behalf of his colleagues, cursed Wessely for "embittering their lives with the threat of robbing them of their livelihood and killing them by starvation, for which alone he is worthy of being uprooted from this world." The *Melamed*, as portrayed by Berlin, typified the ignorance and cultural depths to which the old-fashioned educational methods employed in *Heder* and *Yeshivot* had led. However, Berlin had advanced far beyond the moderate Wessely in rationalist outlook. He was not content to defend the propositions expounded in *Words of Peace and of Truth*; his barbed satire attacked the very essence of the traditional culture, based on Talmud and Kabbalah. The dialogue openly poked fun at casuistic arguments (*pilpul*), homiletics, and the multifarious commandments (*mitzvot*). Indirectly, it also struck at several Talmudic dicta, derided all superstitions, and *en passant* made a laughing stock of the Kabbalah. Berlin bitterly criticized both the Talmud and Talmudical casuistry and proved the existence of a causal

---

* The Hebrew title was, in fact, a deliberate pun on the accepted mnemonic for the name of the codifier to whom Berlin attributed authorship. The word *rosh* in Hebrew means "head" or chief."

relationhip between the poverty of the poeple and their ignorance. "For all that we desire, all the salvation we wish," he went on to explain, "is but that poverty multiply; for so long as the people are impoverished and crushed amongst the grits with the pestle, they will endure oppression to sharpen this learning in ever greater abundance. As our teachers of blessed memory said, 'Poverty is becoming to Israel.'" His stinging humour did not even spare ideas hallowed by religious tradition, such as the *Oneg Shabbat* (Joy of the Sabbath), the distinctiveness of the Chosen People, or *Kiddush Ha-sham* (death by martyrdom for the sanctification of God's name). If *Writ of Justice* had been published during the lifetime of its author, a Jewish Voltaire seated on a rabbinical throne, it would have caused a far greater storm amongst the ultra-orthodox than the entire controversy aroused by *Words of Peace and of Truth*.

Mendelssohn's *Commentary* and Wessely's pamphlet on education opened a new chapter in the history of the German *Haskalah* movement by encouraging the scattered and unorganized *Maskilim* to undertake concerted action. At about this time, groups of *Maskilim* were already forming to implement their educational programme and to spread knowledge among the people. In 1778, David Friedlaender and his brother-in-law, Isaac Itzig, founded the first German school for Jewish youth. In German, it was called the *Jüdische Freischule* (Jewish Free School) because poor pupils were not required to pay for their tuition; in Hebrew, it was known simply as *Hinukh Ne'arim* (Education for the Young). Apart from general courses in German, French, geography, and commerce, the curriculum included Hebrew and the Old Testament. In 1780, the *Maskilim* of Breslau formed the *Hevrat Achim* (Society of Brethren).

Under the impetus of Mendelssohn's *Commentary* and Wessely's *Words of Peace and of Truth*, the *Maskilim* grew bolder and initiated regular publications of their own. The idea originated with the circle of *Maskilim* at Königsberg, where the geographical situation had created both a commercial and a cultural centre of communication between the Jews of Germany and Poland. In 1783, at the suggestion of Isaac Euchel, a university student studying under Kant, the Königsberg *Maskilim* formed the Society for the Promotion of Hebrew (*Hevrat Dor'shei Leshon Ever*) with the aim of publishing a Hebrew periodical modelled on the widely read *Berliner Monatsschrift*. The first issue of the monthly *Me'asef* (Collector) appeared at Königsberg in autumn 1783. It was the symbol and standard bearer of the *Haskalah* movement for many decades.

The founders of the *Me'asef* were committed to the cosmopolitan outlook of eighteenth century rationalism, but the movement to revive Hebrew was associated with the newly awakened sense of national pride. "Our aim is wholly to restore to grandeur the language of Judah which now dwells in the dust of oblivion and the dunghill of contempt," the editors declared in their comment on Mordecai Gumpel Schnaber's article in praise of the "Holy Tongue" towards the end of 1783. Of course, their motive here was peculiarly tinged with questions of class prestige, which exerted an important influence on the *Haskalah* programme as a whole. The *Maskilim* felt that the revival of the Hebrew language and literature would serve the same purpose as the dissemination of general enlightenment among the Jewish masses: it would improve the standing of the enlightened wealthy class amongst the ruling classes and the rulers of their respective countries. The editors of *Me'asef* were also aware of the practical value of Hebrew for spreading general enlightenment under contemporary conditions, when only very few people could read a non-Jewish language. *The Brook of Besor*,* the first announcement of the *Me'asef's* programme, expressly justified the need for a news section:

> ... So that every reader *who knows not how to read the languages of the nations* be informed about the condition of God's people in his day, of the events transpiring amongst them, and of what God inspires the hearts of monarchs to do on their behalf ...

This attitude exposed the linguistic dualism which obstructed the further development of Hebrew and its literature during the modern era until it was rectified in the course of rebuilding the Land of Israel. The root of the dualism was deeply embedded in the conditions of life in the Diaspora. Hebrew had lacked the environment essential to the normal development of a living tongue throughout the history of the people in the Diaspora. A further limitation closely connected with the very nature of the Enlightenment movement among the Jews hampered Hebrew literature during the age of the first *Me'asfim*. Although the development of Jewish Enlightenment occurred at a time when rationalism was flowering among the civilized nations, the movement was marked by many characteristics of the humanist outlook which were anachronisms in eighteenth-century Europe. Hebrew culture appeared to find difficulties in negotiating the historical leap from feudalism to rationalism, without pausing at the intermediate phase of humanism. The linguistic dualism prevalent amongst a dispersed people was intensified by the linguistic dualism associated with Humanism. The humanists had regarded Latin as the classical tongue for poetry and works of historical philology, while concomitantly, they retained the popular vernacular, raising it to the level of a cultural medium for polite literature and the sciences. Hebrew replaced Latin as a classical language for the *Haskalah* writers, but they allowed all subject matter outside the limits of classicism to come within the scope of the non-Jewish vernacular of the country. This strange cultural and linguistic dualism was undoubtedly to some extent responsible for the short life of the Hebrew Enlightenment in Germany. The younger

* The title is derived from I Samuel, 30, 9. *Besor* also means a "heralding" or "a tiding."

generation of German Jews quickly found complete satisfaction in German culture. They had been dependent on it even earlier because of the limited scope of Hebrew culture.

Be that as it may, Humanist classicism left its mark on the revived Hebrew of the *Maskilim* and also affected their literary and scientific interests. They proclaimed that Hebrew must be revived in its ancient form, that the weeds in the corrupt language of the rabbinical works must be uprooted, that there must be a return to the pristine freshness of the original tongue. However, the *Maskilim* derived their language exclusively from the Bible. They claimed that the language of the *Mishnah* and its grammatical forms was "a defective tongue" of homiletics and casuistry. This reversion to the Bible expressed the negative attitude of the *Maskilim* towards the old mode of life, to the prevalence of fanaticism and orthodoxy in the cultural existence of the dispersed Jews, to the entire historical development which they thought gave rise to the evil. They revered the Bible as both symbol and prototype of all that was normal and healthy in Judaism—in much the same way as the Reformers had found the wholesome source of religion in the Gospels, or as the ideologists of the French Revolution drew their inspiration from the republican institutions of ancient Rome.

The literary creations and the socio-political aims of the Jewish Enlightenment movement revealed how the latter lagged behind contemporary European literature and culture. The *Me'asef* was characterized by extreme moderation during its first three years of publication at Königsberg. Its editors adhered so closely to the advice of the conservative Wessely, that they did not publish poems which contained references to the Greek gods, they would not include love songs among "sacred gems," and they took care that no satirical attack, however light-hearted, was directed against the orthodox rabbis. Their tastes ran so much to the pseudo-classical style that the excerpts of translated German poetry, printed in every issue, were chosen exclusively from the *Idylls* of Gessner, Haller, and similar poets. Ignoring the current *Sturm und Drang* movement in German literature, these early issues of the *Me'asef* did not mention Schiller or Goethe, or even writers such as Lessing and Herder.

Similarly in their social and political attitudes the *Maskilim* of the *Me'asef* did not rise above the concept of enlightened despotism, which they saw as the peak of human political development. Every issue contained a paean in praise of some living or dead ruler, even Frederick II, a notorious enemy of the Jews. Wessely himself wrote poems extolling reigning monarchs and also flattering such magnates as David Friedlaender, Daniel Itzig and Cerf-Berr. The "celestial" *Haskalah* movement was closely bound up with the interests of the new middle class in its rise to eminence under the protection of the enlightened despots whom it served and whose attitudes and aims it expressed.

Nevertheless, despite their moderation and the narrowness of their class and political horizons, the first issues of the *Me'asef* discharged an important historic function in the stagnant environment of contemporary German Jewry. Here was a Hebrew periodical devoted to secular matters —literature, articles, historical accounts of great figures in the Jewish past, and current affairs. The successive issues aroused interest in the Bible as a literary creation, spread a knowledge of Hebrew grammar, brought the question of educational reform to the attention of the reader, and first bridged the gap between the isolated Jewish culture and European culture.

When publication recommenced at Berlin in 1787, the *Me'asef*, and with it the German *Haskalah* movement, entered upon a new phase of development. The upheaval of the French Revolution in Europe aroused the new Jewish middle class in Germany to demand its rights, and also broadened the scope of its spiritual movement, the *Haskalah*.

Enlightened Opinion on the Jewish Question and Proposals for Reform

During the decade before the French Revolution, while the *Haskalah* movement was taking shape, the Jewish question was also brought to the fore by the spokesmen of the German Enlightenment. In 1779, Lessing published his play, *Nathan der Weise*, which gave powerful expression to the idea of religious toleration. It was based on the well-known medieval parable of the three rings, symbolizing the three great monotheistic religions of the world. Lessing voiced his belief in deism and cosmopolitanism through the medium of a Knight Templar:

> What doth a people signify? Is then a Christian or a Jew a Christian first, or Jew? And not a man? . . .

Christian Wilhelm Dohm also applied the concepts of religious toleration and the equality of man when, in *On the Civil Betterment of the Jews* (1781), he demanded the enfranchisement of the Jews. But, as a statesman, he based his programme on the benefits that could accrue to the state.

Dohm, an enlightened Prussian official, proved logically and incisively that current policy towards the Jews in most European countries, and especially in Germany, could not survive criticism, as it conflicted with every principle to which an enlightened government adhered.

> What are the reasons—he asked—that have impelled the governments of the kingdoms of Europe to be almost uniformly severe in the decrees levelled against the Jewish people? Why have they, even the wisest among them, found it necessary to exclude them alone from the general body of enlightened legislation? Is this multitude of

good and diligent citizens less beneficial to the state solely because they are of Asian origin, because they grow beards, practise the rite of circumcision, and worship that Supreme Being in their own way, a heritage from their ancient forbears?

The tenets of Judaism, he argued, in no way precluded the highest civic virtues. And even if there were some fanatical Jews amongst the masses who evinced hatred for members of other religions, they were no worse in that respect than the bigots of other religions. Dohm contended that the shortcomings of the Jews were merely the shortcomings of a trading class, and were common to a people which had been entirely channelled into trade—and, furthermore, not of its own free will, but by repressive decrees. On the other hand, the Jews excelled in qualities such as solidarity, the purity of their family life and loyalty to the tradition of their fathers. If they received civil rights, he said, their own vices would disappear, for man's nature depended on the circumstances of his life. The state of repression in which the Jews were kept was nothing but a vestige of "principles which contradict alike humanity and politics and clearly bear the impress of the dark centuries in which they originated (and) are unworthy of the enlightenment of our own day." Dohm concluded with the proposal to grant the Jews equality of rights with all the other subjects of the kingdom for the benefit of the state and the human happiness of the Jews. In particular, he claimed unqualified rights for the Jews to settle anywhere in the country, to engage in manual trades, agriculture and the liberal professions, and to pay equal taxes with all other citizens. Dohm suggested not only that all schools be opened to Jewish youth, but that it be made compulsory for the Jews to have their children educated. On the other hand, he also demanded reforms in the education of Christian youth to eradicate anti-Jewish prejudice. He would even have obliged every clergyman to restate the principles of human fraternity as applied to the Jews in his church. In return for equal rights, Dohm stated, the Jews would have to assume all civil duties towards the state, including the performance of military service. They would have to keep their business ledgers in the language of the state, with a view both to intercourse with Christian merchants and to appearing before government law courts. Actually, Dohm would have left Kehillah autonomy, like municipal autonomy, intact in juridical matters. Even appeals before government courts could best be conducted in conformity with Jewish law. Rabbinical powers of excommunication would continue in religious affairs only, subject to suspension when they threatened human and civil rights. Only the right to work in public on Sundays would be denied to Jews—and this prohibition would not apply to work done inside their own homes. They did not deserve to endure two days of forced idleness a week.

Dohm, the physiocrat, was so intent on directing the Jews into productive manual or agricultural occupations that he was prepared to contemplate temporary restrictions on their enfranchisement to achieve this end. He thought that the government was also entitled to apply coercive measures against the Jews—for example, to force the head of a family to teach one of his sons a craft, to impose a special tax on Jewish traders to prevent their becoming too numerous in any one place, and even to define the scope of Jewish trade in each city. On the other hand, he proposed that special privileges be granted to Jewish craftsmen, such as exemption from tax payments for a number of years, or special emoluments. He did not want to compel the guilds to receive Jews as members. Instead, he would have given Jewish tradesmen equal rights with all unaffiliated Christian tradesmen. As his main objective was to move the Jews into productive activities, Dohm was not in favour of appointing Jewish officials except in cases of outstanding ability. He added that there was no lack of gifted officials in most states. His suggestions included encouraging the Jews to move into agriculture, especially as husbandmen, and, to the same purpose, restricting the right to purchase or lease large farming estates to men who would undertake to employ a fixed quota of Jewish labourers.

Dohm, in fact, began with high principles of equality for the Jews. He ended, as befitted a German physiocrat and Prussian official, by providing protection for the Christian merchant class against Jewish competition, and defending the firmly entrenched position of Christian officialdom, and the nobility's monopoly of landed property. Nevertheless, within the political limits of enlightened despotism, Dohm's essay vigorously expressed a progressive middle class outlook on the Jewish question. Theoretically and practically, his proposals were superior to the reforms of Joseph II for Austrian Jews, published in the same year. Dohm's manifesto also evoked a great response in Enlightenment circles outside Germany. A French edition prepared by Mirabeau served as a guide for advocates of Jewish enfranchisement during the French Revolution. In Poland, liberal spokesmen referred to Dohm when they proposed reforms in the condition of the Jews. In Germany itself, his work made such a deep impression that Dohm was flooded with letters from all parts of the country, and discussion of the Jewish problem was continued in special articles and pamphlets.

The opposition to Dohm was led by Professor Michaelis of Göttingen, a reactionary theologian. The real reasons behind his antagonism emerged in a seemingly casual expression of fear lest Jews eliminate Germans from the manual vocations, commerce, and landed property. Michaelis went to some lengths to disguise these material considerations, presenting "psychological" and historical arguments on the great natural increase of the Jews, their ineptitude for military service and, above all, their national and religious distinctiveness. "The Jews," he said, "will always regard the state as a temporary abode which they will be very happy to leave one day to return to Palestine, quite like their forefathers, who were suspect in the eyes of the Egyptians. . . ." The same argument was used by other opponents of Dohm who had some conception of the importance of humanitarian principles to the Jews. They included Pastor Schwager and the writers, Hartmann and Lange.

Both Christian Dohm and his friend, Moses Mendelssohn, tried with slight variations to refute Michaelis' contention that Jewish hopes for the restoration of Zion precluded their acquiring German citizenship. Mendelssohn argued that "the hoped-for return to Palestine . . . exerts no influence whatsoever on our civil deportment—experience has always taught everywhere where Jews have enjoyed tolerance—and it is in accordance with human nature that if a man is not actually a visionary, he loves the soil on which he prospers; and if his religious views be opposed thereto, he reserves them for the house of worship and for prayers and thinks of the matter no longer. . . ." He reinforced this by quotations from the Talmudic sages who had warned the people "not to mount the ramparts and not to hasten the end." Dohm was less cautious, openly stating that the Messianic ideal was the result of the tribulations and repressions to which the Jews had been subjected. A change in their status would bind them to the state and eventually cause them to forget the prophetic promises of deliverance. In this expectation Dohm was the spiritual father of subsequent generations who espoused the cause of civil rights for the Jews. Michaelis, on the other hand, was a source of inspiration to a host of reactionaries and opponents who exploited Jewish hopes of redemption and return to the homeland, as an excuse to deny them civil liberation. Michaelis foreshadowed the policy of a later generation of antisemites in the fundamental solution he offered to the Jewish problem: deportation of the Jews to island sugar plantations unfit for colonization by Europeans because of the noxious climate. He would not contemplate any project to settle the Jews within Germany in separate farming villages of their own, lest they revolt and join forces with the enemies of the state.

However, the enlightened German public agreed with Dohm, and not with Michaelis and his faction, on the need to improve the position of the Jews, both in principle and for the good of the state. It is significant that the spokesmen for the Dohm school of thought advocating equal rights for the Jews were, by and large, government officials. Germany's retarded development and its lack (as distinct from France) of a stable and class-conscious middle class meant that the principal exponents of the Enlightenment were drawn mainly from among high-ranking officials who considered the welfare of the state from the viewpoint of enlightened despotism. In Prussia, and the states of Mainz and Baden, reforms in the condition of the Jews were propounded by senior officials such as Goethe's brother-in-law, Schlosser, who was especially concerned with the attendance of Jewish children at general schools.

Despite these suggestions, no significant change—apart from a few slim concessions—occurred in the legal status of German Jewry until the period of the French Revolution. When Frederick William II ascended the Prussian throne, the Jewish *Leibzoll* was abolished (1787). The following year, after paying the King 40,000 thalers in compensation, the Jews were also freed from payment of the rebate on porcelain. In 1783, when freedom of movement was permitted to the peasants, the Jews of Baden were also allowed to transfer their domicile from one province to another. In Mainz, in 1784, under the influence of the reforms of Joseph II, the government allowed the Jews to engage in industry and trades which were not organized into guilds, and also to buy buildings and land—on condition that they cultivated it themselves. With the outbreak of the French Revolution, the German-Jewish question entered a new phase. The Jews themselves became more politically conscious and expressed the demand for civil enfranchisement.

B. *THE FRENCH REVOLUTION AND THE NAPOLEONIC WARS*

The Foundations of the new Policy

The retarded state of Germany's economy, society, and politics was manifest during the period of the French Revolution. At a time when the foundations of the old system in France and its western neighbours were collapsing under a mighty revolt by the masses against their oppressors, fragmented Germany remained in a state of sluggish apathy. Without a consolidated Third Estate to make a stand against the feudal oppressors, the German peasants, living in a state of virtual slavery, lacked the force to mobilize and organize themselves to cast off their yoke. The parochial middle classes were bewildered and frightened by events which they were incapable of understanding, and impoverished by the economic crisis that gripped the continent. They buried themselves even more deeply in their own affairs and guarded their ancient privileges in the municipalities and guilds with redoubled vigilance against all competitors and intruders, tainted in any way with the spirit of modern capitalism. The German followers of the Enlightenment, who had worshipped at the shrine of Montesquieu, Voltaire and Rousseau had never at any time been very numerous. Now they were shocked to see the gigantic conflagration that the theories of these philosophers had helped to ignite, and clung more closely than ever before to royal power. They completely disavowed the French Revolution as soon as it violated the sacred institution of monarchy and thrust ahead under the republican rule of the Jacobins.

In these circumstances, no change whatsoever took place in the legal status of the Jews in Germany during the period of the French Revolution, just as nothing changed in the foundations of the ancient political régime. Only the Jews in German territory on the west bank of the Rhine, which had been annexed to France after its conquest by the revolutionary armies, achieved civil enfranchisement under the new constitution in force throughout the Republic. The system of repression continued unchanged in all the other German states, whether they joined the coalition against revolutionary France or supported her, until the establishment of Napoleon's empire.

The position of the Jews of Germany was certainly not helped by the fact that during this vital period, they had achieved no ideological, political or organizational cohesion. The schism between the conservatives and the disciples of the Enlightenment increased under the impact of the crucial political problems. The conservatives, who dominated the Kehillot, were, in fact, so afraid of any political change in case it upset their position, that their opposition to secular enlightenment also embraced the entire programme for reforms in the economic and legal status of the Jewish population. Even the advocates of enlightenment failed to show any sense of solidarity with the masses of their people or any responsibility for their destiny when suitable occasions arose. In several instances they pursued their own, narrow class interests, contrary to the welfare of the Jewish people.

The first attempt to arouse German public opinion (and the conscience of the world) to the problem of German Jewry was made in 1797-98 during the peace congress between France and the German princes at Rastadt. The Jews of Holland made representations to the Congress on behalf of their fellow Jews in Germany, but with negligible results. In 1802, at Regensburg, the German *Reichstag* convened and elected a deputation to determine the new boundaries between the states. A memorandum was submitted to this deputation in the name of the Jews of Germany, drawn up by Christian Grund, the attorney-at-law who had interceded at Rastadt. It would seem that the memorandum was written at the initiative of the Jews of Frankfurt-on-Main, since it drew mainly upon conditions in that Kehillah for its examples of the oppression to which the German Jews were subjected. The repercussions that the document aroused in official circles also chiefly involved the Frankfurt Kehillah. The Kehillah sent three representatives to Regensburg, including one of its *Parnassim*, the banker, Jacob Baruch, father of the writer Ludwig Boerne. Their complaints made a profound impression on the delegates of the countries represented at Regensburg, especially on the French representatives. The French press devoted articles to the Jews of Frankfurt, condemning the brutal ghetto decree. None the less, the policy towards the Jews remained unchanged amongst the German deputies at Regensburg and the memorandum submitted on behalf of all the Jews in Germany was a lone voice in the wilderness.

It was only indirectly and under the influence of victorious France that the German Jews benefited from the *Reichstag* meeting at Regensburg. In accordance with a resolution of the deputation and prompted by France, over a hundred German states, most of them minute entities, ceased to exist. They included "free cities," (all but six), and ecclesiastical states, which were annexed to the large principalities. The fragmentation of the German-Jewish community was correspondingly reduced and the domiciliary rights of the Jewish inhabitants increased. Similarly, the number of frontiers at which Jews had to pay the *Leibzoll* diminished. Pressure from the representatives of revolutionary France on the German princes was also responsible for the first inroads into the *Leibzoll* decree. Jews were freed from payment of the toll in Brunswick in 1803, as a result of intercession by the court Jew, Israel Jacobson. It was also abolished in all the principalities on the banks of the Rhine and Main rivers, notably Frankfurt, and in the state of Bavaria, following efforts by another court Jew, Wolff Breidenbach. Yet even this "gracious gesture" had to be paid for by sizable cash gifts to the rulers.

With Napoleon victorious and in control of most of the German principalities after the liquidation of the Holy Roman Empire in 1806, a period of reforms in the political system ensued. They brought in their wake changes in the legal position of the Jews. They received complete civil enfranchisement only in those German states which, by order of Napoleon, had instituted the French system. These included two territories indirectly under his rule: the Kingdom of Westphalia, which had placed Napoleon's brother on the throne; and the Grand Duchy of Frankfurt, which was promised to Napoleon on the death of the Duke. Also involved were the states ceded to the Empire at a later date, such as Hamburg and the other Hanseatic towns. The reforms effected in the legal status of the Jews in the states under Napoleon's patronage and ruled by his allies were as inadequate or defective as the partial reforms in the political régime as a whole, introduced under government auspices. Even in the most progressive of these states, such as Baden, the new régime was scarcely more than a superficial and distorted version of the system prevailing in France. Baden only granted limited rights to the class of wealthy Jews, whose financial resources were required for the promotion of its capitalist development. Some of Napoleon's allies, such as Saxony, did not even feel the need to change the existing feudal régime at all—apart from some insignificant reforming for the sake of appearances. Saxony did not relax its anti-Jewish laws, which were amongst the severest in all Germany. In fact, the improvements in the Jewish situation were not determined by alliance with Napoleon, but by the rate of progress towards capitalism. In Prussia, overwhelming military defeat—it had led the coalition against Napoleon—was followed by drastic reforms in the old régime. In the wake of these reforms, that state was compelled to extend equal economic rights and a modicum of political rights to its Jewish inhabitants.

It is significant that when civil rights were finally conferred on their Jewish subjects a number of German princes proved more concerned with monetary gain than with any consistent political or ethical principles, as had already been evident when the Jews were released from payment of the *Leibzoll*. The Duke of Frankfurt did not consent to grant his Jewish inhabitants civil rights until they had agreed to pay an enormous sum in compensation. The Duke of Mecklenburg reproduced precisely the Prussian reforms, including the extension of economic rights to the Jews. But the paragraph abolishing all special Jewish taxes included an exception to the new rule: a protection tax had to be paid to him annually by each Jewish family. If the enlightened princes who proclaimed their religious tolerance behaved in this way, it was not surprising that other German princes, who had never acknowledged the principle of Jewish equality, continued to burden the Jews with special taxes.

The complete enfranchisement which the Jews had acquired in a few German states during the age of Napoleon from rulers under his command, quickly disappeared with the triumph of reaction after his downfall.

The Jewish Question in Prussia during the French Revolution; Romantic Reaction and Libellous Polemics

The question of reforming the legal position of the Jews in Prussia was placed on the agenda two years before the outbreak of the French Revolution. The Prussian Government began to discuss measures to relieve the condition of "this oppressed people" at the beginning of 1787 by command of Frederick William II, who came to the throne in 1786 on the death of his father Frederick II ("The Great"). From the outset, it was evident that the sole aim of the King and his Cabinet was to increase the revenue from the special Jewish taxes without making the slightest alleviation of the oppressive decrees against the Jews. Fruitless discussions continued over the ensuing fifteen years between a hypocritical, reactionary government and the Jewish representatives, who failed to take up any steadfast militant position. Only the crushing military defeat of Prussia compelled it to introduce meaningful reforms both in the rights of the population as a whole and in the legal status of the Jews.

Authorized representatives of the Kehillot of the Kingdom of Prussia met in Berlin, with government permission. In May, 1787, they submitted a detailed memorandum to the Government Committee on Reforms in the Condition of the Jews. The representative, David Friedlaender, participated in formulating their modest demands. These included freedom of trade, permission to engage in certain crafts which were not within the scope of the guild monopolies, and the right to purchase land and to engage in agriculture. The memorandum particularly emphasized a request for a reform in the system of Jewish taxes and asked that the collective responsibility of all the Kehillot for payment of the Jewish taxes be terminated. It argued that the progressive impoverishment of the majority of the Jewish population meant that the remainder (i.e., the wealthy Jews!) had to remit tax payments on behalf of their indigent brethren.

The *General-Direktorium* (the Prussian Cabinet), based its reply on the proposals of the Special Committee of July, 1788. It was published at the beginning of 1790 and did nothing more than strengthen the old decrees by the addition of new ones, in the guise of false promises. The Kehillah representatives, heartened by events in France, totally rejected the government's offers. David Friedlaender expressed their position in February, 1790: "We do not request that the chains which now weigh upon us be placed upon us afresh but that they be removed entirely. . . . And if it be the intent of an all-just Providence which we may not question, to cause us disappointment in this hope, we must perforce express our wish that His Majesty deign to leave us under our old order . . ." Yet even this declaration specified that the chains which shackled them were—apart from the vocational and domiciliary disabilities—mainly "the bonds of mutual liability imposed upon us." Four of the chief spokesmen of the representatives, including Friedlaender, were not fully satisfied with this standpoint. They submitted an obsequious memorandum of their own to the King, demanding general abolition of the Kehillah as such and its replacement by the establishment of a purely religious organization.

The new programme of reforms that the government proposed at the beginning of 1792 did not differ essentially from the first and was also rejected by the *Parnassim* of Berlin and the Prussian state. This time the *General-Direktorium* expressly acknowledged in its report to the King that its motive in refusing to better the condition of the Jews to any significant extent was fear that it might engender antagonism amongst his Christian subjects which it would be wise to avoid "on the eve of war." The government was prepared to revoke the joint Kehillah liability for all payments of taxes on condition that agreement be reached on a new apportionment. The majority of the authorized Kehillah representatives refused to assist the government in working out a new tax apportionment until the legal position of the Jews was improved. The delegates from Königsberg caused the first rift in the unity of the body of representatives.

In January, 1793, thirty-four family heads from amongst the financial magnates of the Königsberg Kehillah sent a memorandum to the King. They declared that if he ignored their plea, conversions would multiply among "the wealthy, good, and noble section of the people" with harmful consequences for the King's exchequer, for "the poor, orthodox, uncultured, and ignorant section" would be unable to sustain the burden of the taxes. They asked the King to distinguish between themselves and the Kehillah as a whole, by conferring on them certain rights which would not harm the rights of his other subjects, before making any decision on reforms for the general body of Jews. They also requested him to refrain from describing them as Jews in official documents, "for this appellation to our sorrow is associated with the idea of degradation," and, above all, to revoke joint Kehillah liability, both in the matter of royal taxes and in respect of their dependence on the *Parnassim* and the Kehillah heads. When the representatives met again at Berlin the following autumn these signatories submitted a new memorandum to the King, signifying their desire to co-operate with the government in the plan for a fixed tax apportionment. In December, a similar memorandum was submitted by twenty family heads of the Berlin Kehillah. The position held by the majority of the representatives prevailed and the government had to withdraw its demand for a fixed tax apportionment—if only to avoid concessions concerning Jewish rights. It was not until 1800, after a series of negative replies, that the Prussian government finally agreed to the request made by the State and Berlin *Parnassim* in 1795 to abolish Kehillah liability for the delinquency of individual Jews in such matters as robbery or bankruptcy.

While these fruitless discussions in Prussian government circles were in progress, a sharp debate on the Jewish question erupted in the political literature of Germany, and in particular, of Prussia. Every stage in the enfranchisement of the Jews in France had been reported in detail in the German press, and this had caused the German reactionaries to fear that the liberation of the Jews in Germany might be imminent. Violent opposition greeted any suggestion of relaxation, however slight, in the legal position of the Jews, such as permission to work for the Army, or engage in a manual trade, as proposed by the *Berliner Monatsschrift*, the organ of the Enlightenment. The reactionaries revealed their motives in their views on general economic and cultural policy. Together with the Jews, they also attacked the Enlightenment as a manifestation of moral depravity undermining the foundations of the Christian religion and the monarchy. But they also openly admitted that their main concern was to arrest competition from the Jews who were taking trade away from Christian merchants. Their opposition to Jewish entry into the manual trades merely echoed the guild spirit with its harsh system of qualifying regulations. An incident at Breslau revealed their attitude: a Jew there dared to work as a day labourer; several other impecunious Jews had learned the cobbler's trade and opened their own shops. The working man was beaten up and expelled by his Christian "colleagues"; and the guild confiscated all the equipment of the Jewish shoemakers. But the open support given to the reactionary régime and the feudal privileges enjoyed by the merchant and craft guilds was not enough for these antisemites. They adopted all the tactics of social demagogy and fore-shadowed all the anti-Jewish movements of modern times. Jews were accused of exploiting the working classes, both urban and rural. They were charged with teaching honest Christian tradesmen the arts of deceit and usury, with corrupting officials and even princes by bribery, and with vitiating Christian morality by licentiousness, prostitution and other vices. Berlin journalists who displayed some sympathy with the Jews were reviled as "Protectors of Zion." The Jewish religion also came in for attack, again heralding modern antisemitic tactics: the "jealous, venge-ful" God of Israel was described as a despot, who made all the oriental potentates seem by contrast "virtual angels." Proposals for solving the Jewish problem included "dispatching all of them back to Canaan," or putting them to work at paving roads, reclaiming waste lands, and dry swamps "with mortar and bricks," and other types of hard labour "as in the times of Egypt."

The Breslau *Haskalah* extremist, Moses Hirschel, published a reply *In Defence of the Rights of Man* (Zürich, 1793), to a denunciatory diatribe of *Cosmopolite* consisting of a summary of several contemporary anti-Jewish pamphlets. Hirschel's work evoked a response in only one Prus-sian publication, the *Berliner Monatsschrift*, which commented on it favourably. The *Monatsschrift* and the Berlin *Vossische Zeitung* also published documents concerning the emancipation of the French Jews, translated into German by David Friedlaender and Lazarus Ben-David. Articles in support of the Jews also appeared in the *Schlesische Provinz-blätter* at the turn of the century.

The military successes of revolutionary France, the Congress of Rastadt and the efforts by the German Jews to secure their rights, drove the reactionary clergy of Prussia and their supporters to renew the literary attack on the Jews. This time it was based on an open letter which David Friedlaender sent anonymously in 1799 to Pastor Teller. The letter proposed that "a few 'housefathers' of the Jewish faith" be accepted into Christianity on condition that certain concessions were made regarding the tenets of faith. The political and economic aims of the antisemites clearly emerged from the torrent of abuse directed against the Jewish religion and the national character of the Jews, the two attributes which, so they argued, were the cause of their disabilities. A Prussian official, Paalzow, openly voiced anxiety lest the Jews possessing equal civil rights should eliminate Christians from all trade and handicraft and gain monopolistic control of the country's economy. A clergyman and profes-sor at Göttingen reproached the Jews for their philosophic rationalism and their devout adherence to the revolutionary slogan of the rights of man. Only one of the seven authors who participated in this debate was in favour of enfranchising the Jews, and even he did not conceal the hope that in return they would convert.

Meanwhile, the reaction which had begun to spread in Prussia following the death of Frederick the Great in 1786 became more powerful with the decline of the French Revolution. The ideals of clericalist and religious romanticism, propounded by Schleiermacher and Schlegel, and nationalistic Germanism on the lines of the philosopher Fichte, gained ground in German enlightenment circles. The government of Prussia ceased even to pretend to devote attention to proposed reforms for the Jews; rather, it plotted new strategems against them. The East Prussian authorities reinterpreted the domicile decree for the Königsberg Jews to signify that the second-born son of a protected Jew might not bequeath his privilege to his progeny. The Prussian minister, Schroetter, observed that the government had a duty to protect the Königsberg burghers in commerce against the Jews, who were turning the city into a "New Jerusalem."

On the other hand, the public and official attitude towards the Jews was changing in many German states: the Regensburg Council of Princes consented to deal with Jewish grievances, and several German rulers agreed to abolish the *Leibzoll*. This incited the Prussian anti-semites to further action. In 1803-04, they embarked upon a campaign which surpassed all previous stages of the controversy in its bitterness. Paalzow, an implacable enemy of the French Revolution, led off with a Latin dissertation, *De Civitate Judaeorum* (*Concerning the Citizenship of the Jews*), published in 1803. Writing as an exponent of the wide-spread romanticist ideal of the "Christian State" and basing his arguments on allegedly scientific views on the evil qualities of the Jews, which had their origin in the Talmud, he denied the validity of their claim to enjoy the rights of citizenship. Another Prussian official, Karl Wilhelm Fried-rich Grattenauer, took the first step in inciting public opinion at large. Grattenauer moved freely in romantic circles, was an intimate friend of Gentz and the Schlegel brothers, and publicly styled himself The New Haman. His essay, *Against the Jews*, recapitulated all the calumnies written against the Jews from the Middle Ages to Eisenmenger* and contemporary Jew-baiters in order to prove that the Jewish people had possessed evil impulses from its earliest days and that its endeavours were directed solely towards plundering the Christians. Grattenauer drew his principal arguments from the writings of Fichte, who ten years earlier had already accused the Jews of separatist behaviour and a contemptuous attitude towards Christians and had suggested that "their promised land be conquered for them and that they all be sent thither." Fichte, however, had felt duty-bound to denounce all persecution of the Jews and had stated that they were not to be deprived of human rights even though they were unworthy of civil rights. Grattenauer, in contrast, copiously and unrestrainedly abused the Jewish people. He expressed sorrow that in "this age of Enlightenment" one might not murder a Jew with

* Johann Andreas Eisenmenger (1654-1704), German anti-Jewish author of *Entdecktes Judentum* (Judaism Revealed).

impunity, compared the Jewish people to a varied assortment of prosti-
tutes, and thought it unnecessary to reintroduce the compulsory wearing
of the badge of shame because their foul odour was an adequate mark of
identity. He repeatedly reiterated that the Jews were "a separate race of
men," "a foreign nation of Asian origin," and therefore "even Jews who
have been converted to Christianity remain Jews." His defamatory
writings included a warning against "the world government" which the
Jews were plotting to set up by intrigue through their international
connections. His political views were contained in the assertion that the
ideals of human equality were a Jacobin, *sans-culotte* sacrilege "which
dare not even be mouthed." His reactionary and feudal inclinations were
combined with a warning of the threat which "the pecuniary power of the
Jews constituted to the system founded on the sacrosanct rights of the
nobility whose rank is theirs by birth."

Grattenauer's pamphlet went through three editions; 13,000 copies
were in circulation. Two supplements to the pamphlet appeared within a
year, and several similar compositions were published by authors who
rivalled Grattenauer in antagonism towards the Jews. One of these
pamphlets, which went into two editions, contained a new proposal for
solving the Jewish problem in addition to re-establishing the ghetto and
restoring the medieval badge of shame: castration of all Jewish male
offspring, except the first-born. An essay by a Christian tradesman
proposing that the Jews be segregated in a separate colony in order to
prevent them from competing in commerce was already more restrained.
A spokesman of the German nationalist faction, Friedrich Buchholz,
advised "educating" all Jews by compulsory military service.

An equal number of German writers rose indeed to the defence of the
Jews in this discussion but their argument lacked a basis of consistent
principles and they were incapable of influencing public opinion. Characteristically, those periodicals which had remained loyal to the ideals of
the Enlightenment published articles vindicating the Jews, whereas
Zeitung, edited by Spazier and close to the romantic movement, did not
conceal its sympathy with Grattenauer. Pastor Johann Hermes, a writer
who espoused the spirit of eighteenth-century Enlightenment, was an
open and logical defender of the Jews as "the people who have dwelt in
our midst and, in any event, no less than we ourselves carry the burden of
state taxes."

Two excellent satires on Grattenauer were written by Jews, one a
doctor from Königsberg, and the other a Hamburg Jew who signed his
name Lefrank and entitled his work *Bellerophon*. Lefrank was convinced
that the antisemitic literature was nothing but the final death spasm of a
system of "persecution, fanaticism, and superstition." Three outstanding
Hebrew authors of the *Haskalah* school, all living in Silesia, also
published German pamphlets against Grattenauer: Joseph Ha-Efratti
Troplowitz, author of a play *M'lukhat Sh'aul* (*The Kingdom of Saul*);

Solomon Pappenheim; and Aaron Wolfssohn, editor oɪ the *Me'asef* and author of a comedy *Leichtsinn und Frömmelei* (*Levity and Self-Righteousness*). The enlightened leaders of the Berlin Kehillah thought their personal participation in the debate was unnecessary and preferred to intercede with the state authorities. The government of Prussia took action against Grattenauer, only, and his activities were discontinued by order of the authorities.

The debate on the Jewish problem was also carried on in Hamburg at the same period—the beginning of the nineteenth century—but in a more restrained fashion than in Prussia. The supporters of Jewish rights showered praise on the Jews of the city, precisely because of the important part they played in its commerce, banking and discounting of bills of exchange. The memory of a revolt by apprentices and craftsmen when a number of Kehillah members had volunteered for and been rejected by the city militia and when other Jews had donated funds for the same purpose also reflected favourably on the Jews. In fact, the first indication of a rapprochement between the German and Jewish middle classes on the basis of joint economic and social interests appeared in Hamburg.

Emancipation in the French Fashion in the West German States

When in the autumn of 1792, the armies of revolutionary France stormed the German territories west of the Rhine in their first victorious advance, the Paris press published a Jewish appeal to General Custine begging him to observe their affliction and put an end to their bondage.

> "Great hero," the appeal read "bestow your mercy on the impoverished, oppressed Jews for whom our hearts cry out! Behold the posts at every crossroads with signs proclaiming, "Jüdisches *Leibzoll!*""

The general replied with a public announcement on November 1, 1792 from his military headquarters at Mainz:

> "For long the Children of Israel have been oppressed in vile servitude. Be patient for but a short while, and soon, wherever the sacred banners of freedom wave, none will have reason to weep any longer but slaves and tyrants."

In fact, several years passed before the Jews of the Rhineland were completely enfranchised. The delay was partially the result of the temporary status of the régime, which also made the Kehillah leaders hesitate to take the oath of allegiance to the Republic. Their conservatism and orthodoxy were not conducive to sympathy with the Revolution and they tended rather to look forward to the restoration of the dethroned

German princes. There were few enlightened members of these Kehillot, and even fewer were active in the republican movements in their cities.

The uncertain political situation in the Rhine territory came to an end in 1797. In the spring of that year, the French authorities launched a propaganda campaign to establish an independent western Rhineland Republic, and in the autumn the government of the Directory at Paris decided to annex the entire territory to France. Meanwhile, the Jewish population became increasingly aware of the superiority of the new régime, founded on the principle of civil equality. In 1797, Jews from many Kehillot participated in the formal planting of the Liberty Trees and appended their signatures to the declarations in favour of the Rhine Republic issued by their cities. In 1798, the signatories of petitions to the Paris government from the Rhineland asking to be annexed to France included Jews, many of whom signed in Hebrew letters. About a quarter of the Jewish heads of families actually signed—the same proportion as between all the signatories and the general population.

The ghetto gates in the cities of Mainz and Bonn were smashed as a symbol of civil emancipation and Jewish youth there participated in the tumultuous celebrations of the liberty of the citizenry. The return of the Jews to the cities of Cologne and Speyer, where they had been forbidden to set foot since the expulsions of the Middle Ages, was also symptomatic of the spirit of the times. Over twenty thousand Jews lived in this area of Germany annexed to France.

After his decisive victories over Austria and Prussia in 1805-06, Napoleon founded the Kingdom of Westphalia, comprising the territories of Hesse-Kassel, Brunswick, several adjoining areas, part of Hanover (including the city of Halberstadt), and all the Prussian provinces west of the river Elbe. In 1810, the Duchy of Hanover was also annexed to this kingdom. In the Kingdom of Westphalia, where Napoleon enthroned his brother Jerome as King, the new system completely imitated the French imperial régime. Article X of its constitution, promulgated in November, 1807, provided that "all citizens will be equal under the Law and all the various religions will enjoy freedom of worship." In January, 1808, King Jerome issued a special ordinance on the equality of rights for the Jews in accordance with the constitution, with express reference thereto, and by agreement with his government and the Royal Council. Westphalia thus became the first German state (apart from the Rhineland territories annexed to France) where the fifteen thousand or so Jews achieved absolute legal equality under the aegis of the French Revolution.

A Jewish Consistory was organized in Westphalia as in France, to supervise the Kehillot of the Kingdom. This organization, like all the other government reforms concerning the Jews, was initiated by Israel Jacobson, agent to the Duke of Brunswick and subsequently appointed Court Banker to the Kingdom of Westphalia. His speech before the King at the head of the Kehillah delegates (convened for consultation on the central organization), compared Jerome to Cyrus and described emancipation as the total salvation of the Jewish people. "The songs of Zion," he declared ecstatically, "will be heard on high in the hills of Westphalia." At the end of March, 1808, a royal command establishing the Consistory was published. However, its aims were formulated somewhat differently from Napoleon's decree concerning the Consistory in France. In addition to the supervisory function of ensuring "that the Jewish religion shall not conflict in practice with the laws of the state and public morality," the Consistory was also committed to strive so "that the Jews shall not continue to constitute a separate public body within the State but that they shall be obliged, like all the rest of Our subjects, to merge within the nation of which they are part." The preface to the Consistory Ordinance also stressed that the requirement to assimilate did not exempt the Jews from meeting expenditure on their religious needs or from remitting their Kehillah debts, old and new. Westphalia, therefore, Napoleon's empire in miniature, guaranteed both the preservation of religion amongst the Jewish population and the remittance of Kehillah debts which had originated in the repression of the feudal age.

Jacobson was appointed president of the Consistory. He ruled it arbitrarily, and selected three rabbis, two advisors, and a secretary (a Christian!) after the government had confirmed his suggested appointments. Provincial rabbis were also appointed on his advice. The Westphalian Consistory was, to a large extent, occupied with educational affairs. Apart from supervising the new schools opened on its initiative in provincial towns, it maintained a school in the capital, Kassel, at its own expense. It intervened in religious affairs and synagogal organization rather more than the French Consistory and passed reforms affecting the observance of religious laws and the form of worship which caused dismay in orthodox circles because of their assimilationist tendency. The Westphalian Consistory also aroused popular resentment because of the heavy taxation it imposed.

The Jews of Frankfurt-on-Main had to struggle much longer for their rights, in the face of the hostile attitude of the government of the "Free City" which would not countenance any concessions. It feared Jewish competition with the city's merchants and also hoped that its severe restrictions on the ghetto inhabitants would placate the lower middle classes, embittered by the rule of the conservative orthodox patricians. The compromising, deferential attitude of the Kehillah leaders was certainly not calculated to improve conditions for the oppressed Jewish population. In October, 1792, when the armies of revolutionary France penetrated into Frankfurt, a number of Jews were discovered mocking a Liberty Tree which had been planted in one of the suburbs. The Prussian forces, who drove the French from the city, were welcomed by the Jews with cries of joy, "as though the Messiah had come." However, the second temporary occupation of Frankfurt by the French armies in

1796 produced an abrupt change in the history of the local Jews. Most of the buildings of the ghetto had been burned during the fighting, and the municipal council had no alternative but to agree to allow large numbers of Jews to shelter in the homes of burghers. For the first time, social relations were established between the Jews and their Christian neighbours.

The French Revolution was indirectly instrumental, as in the case of the *Leibzoll*, in removing one of the most distressing discriminations in force at Frankfurt. Vigorous demands by the Mainz commandant to exempt Mainz Jews, as French citizens, from the prohibition on entering or leaving Frankfurt on Sundays were successful. The decree enforcing the prohibition was suspended in relation to the ghetto Jews as well, though only for a period of ten years and on payment of compensation. The Kehillah fathers felt duty-bound to shower abundant praise on the city council for this "generosity." On the other hand, they abhorred the Revolution and suspected the supporters of enlightenment in the Kehillah of sympathizing with its ideals. In 1794, a group of Jews was excommunicated by authority of the Kehillah, for preparing to establish a school of secular studies. When the city council ordered them to revoke the writ of excommunication, the Kehillah leaders appealed to the Council and to the Imperial Court in Chancery (*Kammergericht*). They denounced the initiators of the school project as "frivolous Jews, a species of that band which wishes to tear asunder sacred bonds of human society, morality, and religion under the notorious cloak of enlightenment and betterment. Those who plan to introduce a new system of teaching into the Kehillah in order to clear a path for pestilential revolution also belong to this class." The writ of excommunication was not restored. This was not the sole occasion when the reactionary municipal and court authorities proved more liberal than the Kehillah leaders, who, given their way, would have preserved the ignorance of their people. At least one other instance is recorded involving the degrading way of burial of a Frankfurt Jew who had violated the Sabbath in his lifetime.

Shortly afterwards, the conservative leaders were compelled to demand the rights of the most repressed Kehillah in Germany. The inhabitants of the city were no longer unanimously opposed to an extension of Jewish rights. Many Christians living in streets near the Jewish quarter were influenced by events in German territory west of the Rhine. They approached the city council with the demand to tear down the ghetto walls, as had occurred in Bonn. The inhabitants of other streets demanded that Jews be allowed to keep stores in their buildings so that, as landlords, they might collect the rents. Opinions favourable to the Jews and against the (Christian) Union of Stock Exchange dealers, were also voiced by senior municipal officials. The Kehillah acted by publishing a new memorandum (an earlier one had been rejected by Francis II of Austria in 1803). This time the Emperor did not have the chance to reject it. In August, 1806, he was forced by Napoleon to abdicate his German throne. Napoleon's new disposition made the city of Frankfurt-on-Main part of the principality of Prince Bishop Dalberg of Mainz.

Meanwhile, the numbers and importance of the enlightened progressives in the Kehillah had increased and they gained new hope under the new government of the principality. The *Société d'Israélites*, founded in autumn 1806, sent its congratulations to the Assembly of Notables at Paris. Another letter was sent in the name of 250 Kehillah members. This letter heaped flattery on Napoleon, and expressed the hope that "the glorious example of France would spread beyond the boundaries of her Empire." Frankfurt sent two delegates to the *Grand Sanhedrin* which was convoked at Paris in the spring of 1807, but, as foreign citizens, they could only attend the sessions as guests.

The hopes which the Jews of Frankfurt had attached to Prince Dalberg were soon proved groundless. All of the Prince's enlightenment—he had corresponded with German writers and Jewish communal leaders and scholars—failed to meet the test of practical statecraft. His greed for money prevented him from renouncing the revenues derived from the special Jewish taxes. He was too dilatory to oppose firmly the municipal senate when it refused to grant the Jews any extension of rights.

Dalberg paid no attention to the pleading and flattery of the "enlightened" self-appointed Kehillah spokesmen—even though one of the reasons they gave for their requests was the accretion of economic benefit to a capitalist economy. They referred to Adam Smith's theory of supply and demand, and argued that Jewish competition could only lower prices and thus advance commercial prosperity. This was proved by the fact that the spice trade, which was forbidden to Jews, was declining in Frankfurt. Similarly, trade in general was at a low ebb in German cities such as Erfurt, Würzburg, Cologne and Schweinfürth, where Jews were forbidden entry, in contrast with Frankfurt, Leipzig and Mainz, where Jews had a considerable share of trade in general. The Prince, despite his alleged progressiveness, seized on the common excuse of all opponents of Jewish rights: that the entire matter depended on the Jews alone, on their reforming their ways. He did, however, make one "original" theoretical contribution: it was not religion as much as "the national element in the environment and customs of the Jews as an oriental people." He was undoubtedly strengthened in his refusal by Napoleon's current policy towards the Jews of France as reflected in the Infamous Decree.

At the beginning of 1808, the new *Stetigkeit** for the Jews of Frankfurt was made public. It left their state of subjugation unchanged except for some slight relaxations, such as the enlargement of the ghetto and permission to learn manual trades. The number of Jewish families

* Ordinance on the Permanent Status. The original *Stetigkeit*, that remained in force until the promulgation of the new one, went back to 1616!

was again limited to five hundred, while the special Jewish taxes were raised to 22,000 gulden annually under the title of "licence fees." The distress of the Frankfurt Jews aroused public opinion. The President of the Westphalian Jewish Consistory, Israel Jacobson, who had earlier attempted to have the Jewish *Leibzoll* abolished in the German principalities, published a Humble Petition to Prince Dalberg. The petition criticised all the repressive decrees against the Jews of Frankfurt on the grounds of justice and common sense, and justifiably argued that the new *Stetigkeit* jeopardized "his co-religionists throughout Europe." The controversy stirred up by Jacobson's pamphlet produced a notable work by an anonymous author who contended that the Jews, as an alien people, had no choice but to acquiesce gratefully in all the conditions dictated to them or else to return to their homeland. A young Frankfurt Jew, who later changed his religion and achieved fame as a German writer under the name of Ludwig Boerne, replied in detail to all the arguments of the anonymous author—but his father restrained him from publishing it.

Goethe, himself a native of Frankfurt-on-Main, showed great interest in the debate on the new *Stetigkeit* for the Jews of his city, but was not in sympathy with their cause. A letter he wrote in February, 1808, made scornful comment on the Jews of Frankfurt: "I would like to see how the modern Israelites conduct themselves regarding the new *Stetigkeit* wherein they are treated as real Jews and as former servants of the imperial treasury." A subsequent letter, dated April 3, revealed the reasons behind his attitude: his contempt for Israel Jacobson and his opinion that the Jews were in need of a political education. "That Jew Messiah from Brunswick," he wrote of Jacobson, "It pleases him indeed to contemplate his people as it should be and become, but one should not look askance on the Prince Primate (Dalberg) who deals with this tribe as it is (now) and will remain for some time to come." Goethe regarded the Jews of his time with aristocratic disdain, for all his admiration of the poetry of the Old Testament and his faith in the eternity of Israel and its historic mission. Similarly, notwithstanding his pantheistic and universalistic *Weltanschauung*, he considered Judaism merely a religion which had not reached the zenith of that human culture, the roots of which were purportedly embedded in Christianity. For these reasons Jews were excluded from the commonalty of citizens of the model state in his *Wilhelm Meister*. Goethe, despite his stature as poet and philosopher, was caught up in Germany's political regressiveness, as far as his opinion of the Jews and the French Revolution were concerned.

Legal emancipation of the Jews of Frankfurt was eventually realized during the final stage of Napoleon's victories. After the defeat of Austria in 1809, Prince Dalberg was raised to the rank of Grand Duke and his Duchy expanded to include the Principality of Hanau and the Prince-Bishopric of Fulda. A totally French-type of régime was now introduced into the Grand Duchy of Frankfurt, based on the Constitution of 1810, which proclaimed the equality of all the inhabitants of the state and the abolition of serfdom. On the advice of his officials, the Duke finally agreed to the complete enfranchisement of the Jews of Frankfurt on condition that they paid 440,000 gulden in compensation, or the equivalent of "licence fees" over a twenty-year period. Similarly, compensation was demanded as a condition for the civil emancipation of Christian "protected individuals" and serfs. The Kehillah could not pay the whole sum in cash and paid mainly in promissory notes, discounted by the banker Anschel Meyer Rothschild, who had moved into prominence during the age of Napoleon. Not until 1811 was the entire sum finally remitted to the Duke. Then, and only then, was an order published in the *Official Gazette* legally establishing the civil equality of the Jews.

In the interim, the new Kehillah leaders demonstrated that they were no less narrow in their class interests than the conservative *Parnassim* who had ruled the Kehillah during the ghetto period. In 1810, the Kehillah leaders had already decided to expel from the city "alien Jews, their wives and children, and, whenever necessary, to enlist the assistance of the police administration." The Kehillah administration even refused to grant domicile rights to well-to-do Jews whose property was valued at less than 6,000 gulden, and in 1813 it asked the government to legalize this practice.

Thus, even the Jewish middle class did not free itself over-hastily from the feudal guild and oligarchical frame of mind, though its civil equality depended on the continued existence of the new system. It is not surprising, therefore, that the Frankfurt burghers did not wholeheartedly surrender their former advantages over the Jews. While the Duke still ruled by Napoleon's consent, they attempted to prevent the appointment of a Jewish city councillor. After Napoleon's defeat, they set out determinedly to destroy the principle of Jewish citizenship itself.

The nine thousand Jews in the three Kehillot of Altona, Hamburg and Wandsbeck obtained emancipation after Hamburg was captured by the French armies and annexed to the Empire in 1810, in order to tighten up the anti-British blockade (the "continental system"). In 1811, the Jews in these three communities became citizens in accordance with the French Constitution, and enjoyed completely equal rights with all other citizens. The same law also applied to the other two Hanseatic ports, Bremen and Lübeck, after they had been declared part of France— although previously Jews had not even had the right of domicile there. However, the blockade affected trade in these ports so seriously that the Jews of Hamburg welcomed the news of Napoleon's defeat in 1813, and many young people also volunteered to fight for Germany in her war of liberation against France. They did not realize that Napoleon's defeat would engulf Germany in reaction and return them, together with the Jews of Westphalia and Frankfurt, to servitude.

The System of Reforms in States Allied to France—Bavaria and Other South German States

Outside of Westphalia, Frankfurt, and the seaport towns (either directly under French rule or under rulers appointed by Napoleon), the Jews of Germany only acquired equal rights in two or three tiny states where they were very few in number.

The rights that the Jews acquired in the Grand Duchy of Berg, where Jewish communities in the province of Nassau, the city of Düsseldorf, and the neighbourhood of Cologne and Mainz contained slightly over three thousand members were more extensive than in any other states of this type. A government edict in 1808 abolished the special Jewish taxes, on the grounds that Jews had to pay state taxes and also perform military service. At the same time, the Duke announced that he was desirous of "gradually equalizing the Jews in their rights and liberties with the rest of the Grand Duchy's inhabitants."

There were about 12,000 Jews in the Grand Duchy of Baden which, like Berg, had a population of 900,000 after the Electoral Palatinate was annexed to it with the city of Mannheim and the adjacent districts. The Palatinate government had already appointed a special committee to consider reforms in the condition of the Jews in 1799-1801. The municipal authorities notified this committee of their views—for example, the city of Wiesloch demanded that no Jew be allowed to marry unless he had served in the Army for a number of years. The Jews, they explained, had not demonstrated any fortitude as fighters except in America, Holland, and France, "in all the wars against the princes and the existing order." The princes were advised to be wary "of what they might expect from them (the Jews) in these revolutionary times." However, the chief argument that the municipalities employed was that the Talmudic wall segregated the Jews from the rest of the inhabitants, therefore enfranchisement was only conceivable by degrees, to the extent that they were educated in general schools. The summary of the report to the committee repeated this view. The dominant upper segment of the Jewish community also followed this line of thought, so much so that they betrayed a saddening sense of inferiority. In 1803, the leaders of the Provincial Council of Kehillot sent a memorandum to the Prince requesting that civil rights be granted to all Jews at present capable of enjoying them. It added an argument borrowed from Christian Dohm's essay: "their attachment to their religion would decline as they became more attached to the state in their civil devotion."

The government of the Grand Duchy of Baden was guided in its new legislation by the differentiation between rich and poor, as well as by the aim of uprooting the Talmud and educating the Jews as followers of the Mosaic persuasion. The state constitution, promulgated in seven ducal edicts between 1807-09, was a patchwork of legislation. It provided for two classes of burghers. "local citizens" and "protected citizens." The Jewish population was similarly divided into categories according to their rights, except that the discriminations against the Jews were incomparably greater than against any class of Christian inhabitant. Jewish citizens were classified as "protected citizens" who, unlike "local citizens," did not have the right to elect or be elected to the local communal authorities. Only exceptional individuals could acquire local citizenship by special ducal dispensation. The right to serve in government positions had already been reserved exclusively to Christians by the previous constitution of 1807. The special Jewish taxes remained in force and the double *Leibzoll*, known as the "Pocket Escort Fee" (*Taschengeleit*) and the "Trade Escort Fee" (*Handelsgeleit*), was retained for transient foreign Jews. Jews were still obliged to pay protection taxes to the landed nobility and the local communities, even after the state protection tax was abolished in 1816. Even so, as "protected citizens," the Jews still had to discharge their duties to the state, including military service.

An edict relating to the Jews was promulgated on the first anniversary of the new constitution, at the beginning of 1809. It outlined in forty-seven lengthy articles the system that was to govern them. They were allowed to attend school at all levels and to engage in agriculture and the manual trades. The police were required to ensure that the guilds did not place any obstacles in their way. However, Jewish tradesmen were not to enjoy the rights of protected citizens unless they were merchants and owned some property. Pedlars, second-hand dealers, brokers, and petty moneylenders were allowed to trade only as a last resort (and then only if they possessed an earlier writ of protection) and on condition that they were aged twenty-one or more. The Jews who were engaged in these "poverty trades" (*Nothandel*) were barred like their Christian colleagues from giving evidence and were forbidden to marry under the age of thirty. The Baden Kehillot were reorganized, on the pattern set by the Consistory, as local and regional religious communities under the leadership of a supreme council at the governmental centre of Karlsruhe. Its members consisted of three rabbis and seven supreme councillors, who were appointed by the Duke. In 1812, a government commissioner was appointed to supervise the supreme council with a deciding vote on all its resolutions. This religious organization also had to ensure that religious instructors only educated their young pupils in the tenets of Moses and the Prophets and in a spirit of subservience to the state authorities.

The supreme council of the Jews of Baden was particularly successful in popularizing manual and agricultural training amongst the Kehillah population both by stipends for apprentices and farmers and by propaganda on the virtues of useful labour. Yet even in 1814, only some 350 Jews in the Grand Duchy of Baden were registered as living by occupations other than trade. All the expenses incurred during the transition to productive occupations were to be defrayed by the Kehillot. The Supreme Council, which included some of the wealthiest merchants, imposed such heavy taxes on the Kehillot for this purpose that they were unable to meet their obligations. Official reports from all the districts of the Grand Duchy emphasized the extreme poverty of the Jewish population. Some 80 or even 90 per cent of the total number of wage-earners continued to engage in the "poverty trades" as before. They evaded the government decrees, helped by the landed proprietors in return for protection fees. The law was more effective in the matter of compulsory school attendance, despite the hostility that the Jewish children encountered. The Jewish trading magnates, bankers, and industrialists derived most benefit from the new law. The banking house of Seligmann obtained a franchise of the salt monopoly for an annual payment of 250,000 gulden, and also employed 400 workers in its firearms and spinning machinery factory. Such members of the élite were granted "local citizenship" without delay.

However, the Jews in most other German states lived in such abject conditions that they actually envied the "Jews' Law" of the Grand Duchy of Baden as though it were virtually an act of emancipation. These states included the Kingdom of Bavaria which had a larger number of Jewish inhabitants during Napoleon's times than Prussia, even though it withheld the right of domicile from all but a negligible few. It had nearly 50,000 Jewish subjects, about one and a half per cent of the Kingdom's total population*, when the neighbouring lands, including Franconia, the Palatinate and Swabia, had been annexed to it between 1801 and 1805. Backward and clericalist, the political reforms actually decreed during the age of Napoleon were mediocre and most were never enforced. Complete enfranchisement of the Bavarian Jews was therefore entirely out of the question; any improvements in their conditions which were actually approved came later than in any other German state, and even then failed to strike at the roots of their servitude.

In 1803, the Jews of Franconia addressed a humble petition to the Prince. They asked for equality with the rest of his subjects in taxation, trade, and other rights "insofar as this can be implemented and does not conflict with other calculations and circumstances of the state." Even while making these minimal demands, the Kehillah representatives were still concerned with their own class interests and urged the Prince to take measures against "the large number and wretched condition" of the Jews who lived under the protection of the country squires and to abolish the "mendicant Jew (das Betteljudentum)." They also asked for the establishment of a home for the aged, a factory for the employment of the

* In 1818, the population of Bavaria was 3,660,452, including 53,208 Jews. In Prussia, the 1811 census returns indicated no more than 32,617 Jews in that state; following the Peace of Tilsit in 1807 not only the Polish areas but all its territories west of the Elbe had been severed from Prussia. In 1816, the number of Jews in Prussia rose to 72,000, not counting the state of Posen, which had a Jewish population of 52,000.

able-bodied poor, and a children's educational institution. This petition was fruitless, although non-Catholics were granted religious freedom by royal command in the same year.

The Bavarian government first took measures to improve the condition of the Jews of Munich before it finally decided to effect reforms in the whole Kingdom. The Jewish community in Munich had grown at the end of the eighteenth and especially at the beginning of the nineteenth century without achieving any clearly defined legal status. From ten families in the middle of the eighteenth century, the Jews of Munich had increased tenfold to a hundred families, over 400 individuals, by 1804. Eighty per cent of them were engaged in trade or moneychanging, with a group of factory-owners (potash, hides, spinning mills) prominent at the upper level. Jewish contractors achieved particular importance by supplying the quarter-master's branch of the Bavarian Army during the Napoleonic Wars. However, most influential were the Jewish bankers, and over 80 per cent of all state loans between 1801 and 1808 were floated under their auspices. The largest banker, Aaron Elijah Seligmann, who was also Commissionary-in-Chief to the Bavarian Army during 1799-1802, arranged a 3 million gulden loan for the state. Men such as these were spokesmen and official legates for the Munich Jewish community when its official status was established in 1805. They also held the offices of *Parnassim* in the religious Kehillah founded in 1815. The great role the Jews of Munich played in the economy of the state resulted in the promulgation of a government ordinance in 1805, the Munich Regulation for Jews (*Münchener Judenregulativ*), determining their legal status. It gave them permission to pray in a *minyan*; to buy houses and reside in any street in the city; to establish factories and engage in certain branches of commerce, on condition that their ledgers were kept in German. Peddling was specifically prohibited, and police licence to marry depended on the ownership of property valued at a minimum of 1,000 reichsthaler. The *Münchener Judenregulativ* also contained a provision whereby the *Matrikel*, the protection privilege held by the head of a Jewish family, could be inherited by only one son. This provision served as the prototype for the 1813 law applying to all Bavarian Jews.

The leaders of the Jewish community at Munich were no more generous or broadminded than their colleagues in the other large Kehillot of Germany. They were also unfavourably disposed towards those Jews, mostly of the poorer classes, who ventured into the capital and sheltered under cover of their own privileges. On at least two occasions, in 1801 and 1813, they addressed memoranda to the authorities dissociating themselves from these "alien Jews."

Amongst provincial towns, Fürth was a large commercial centre as a result of the activity of the Jews there (they controlled the trade in household textiles, spices, gems, and moneychanging). The mirror factories, producing for export, employed a large number of Jewish and

Christian workers. The Fürth Kehillah drew attention to its economic importance in memoranda to the government in 1809 and 1813. The Kehillah leaders specifically asked that they should not be deprived of the *Privilegium* of 1719, which empowered the *Parnassim* to accept new inhabitants into the Kehillah, with due regard to the candidates' favourable qualities and the property they owned.

The advance in emancipation in Germany encouraged the Jews of Bavaria to renew their efforts to acquire civil rights. On June 10, 1813, a "regulatory ordinance for the members of the Jewish religion" was finally issued and described by the King "as proof of his concern for the welfare of all his subjects . . . wherefore the Jews residing in the realm should be beholden to him." As in the Grand Duchy of Baden, Jews were permitted to engage in industry, in all manual occupations, in the wholesale and retail trades, and in farming. On the other hand, peddling, referred to as "poverty trading," here also was not allowed, except in the last resort, as in Baden, and those practising it were forbidden to marry. The protection tax and all the other special Jewish taxes and fees had in theory been abrogated earlier but continued to be collected in some districts for many years to come. The Kehillah courts were abolished together with the autonomous status of the Kehillah as an institution; it was replaced by a merely religious Kehillah. The general schools were opened to Jews and they were also permitted to establish schools of their own. However, side by side with these reforms, the most repressive laws of the old régime were retained in full and even made more severe: e.g., decrees requiring domicile permits and curbing natural increase. Jews from abroad were totally forbidden to take up permanent residence and "any increase in the number of Jewish families in the localities where they now exist is, in general, forbidden. On the contrary, if too large, it should be gradually reduced." For the same purpose it was decreed that a father might bequeath his right of domicile—now newly described as a *Matrikel* rather than a Writ of Protection—to one son only. The remaining children were allowed to live with their parents as long as they did not marry; when they did, they had to leave not merely the city but also the country. The King reserved to himself the right to issue a new *Matrikel* for a Jew settling in a place where a Jewish community already existed, or even in a new locality, on condition that he established a factory or large trading establishment, or was engaged as mastercraftsman or cultivator.

The hypocrisy of this law, published in the name of freedom of conscience, annoyed enlightened circles in the country and was later condemned by the Bavarian historian Von Lerchenfeld. But it was merely a further reflection of the backwardness of a state faced with the conflicting aims of furthering capitalist development and protecting the shopkeepers and craftsmen against growing competition from the "alien" people.

An incidental result of this legislation was that the *Matrikel*, being transferable, became a saleable merchandise; its price was sometimes as high as 1,000 gulden. The category of "tolerated" Jews, as opposed to the holders of the *Matrikel*, was also revived. The "tolerated" Jews included army supply contractors from abroad, religious teachers, hospital watchmen, or aged relatives of *Matrikel* holders. They were only allowed to stay for a few years, at times only for one year, unless permission was specifically given by the King, when it covered longer periods. Temporary residence in the country was also granted to apprentices, servants and to Jews passing through Bavaria *en route*. Here again, therefore, in the age of the Declaration of the Rights of Man, the Jews were divided into various categories with their right to live and work measured out in limited quantities.

The neighbouring state of Württemberg had instituted somewhat earlier a system similar to the Bavarian. There were nearly 6,000 Jews in Württemberg, following its territorial expansion between 1802 and 1805. Its ruler had been crowned king and the new absolutist régime extended its system of reforms to include the Jews. However, the Supreme Court rejected the King's proposal for a comprehensive programme of reform legislation on the grounds that it was deeply concerned "for the livelihood of the other inhabitants." Instead, individual reforms were passed. The Jews were required to perform military service, though, as in Bavaria, they were given the alternative of paying an exemption charge. They were permitted to engage in handicrafts, join the guilds, and buy houses and land for farming; but, again as in Bavaria, they were forbidden to engage in the buying and selling of property. The Kehillot even improved their status, though only as religious communities: their *Parnassim* were now elected by the Kehillah members and not, as formerly, appointed by the sovereign, and they were no longer held collectively responsible for payment of individual protection taxes. The Jews now paid the ordinary civil taxes instead of the other special taxes. Protection taxes and the prohibition on Jewish residence remained in force in all places where Jews had not previously resided. Some wealthy individuals, with property valued at 30,000 gulden or over, rose above the category of "protected Jews" and acquired the title and rights of subjects. At the other end of the social scale, severe laws were directed against *Betteljuden* (mendicant Jews) coming from other states.

A number of the small states in 1810 granted the Jews broad rights which brought them closer to full enfranchisement. These included Saxe-Weimar, the Principality of Lippe-Detmold, and the Principality of Anhalt-Bernburg. Although the Duchy of Anhalt-Dessau was ruled by an enlightened duke, no fundamental change occurred in the legal status of the Jews (except for the abolition of the *Leibzoll*, as was universal throughout Germany). In 1810, however, they were allowed to learn manual trades and crafts.

In western Germany, on the banks of the Rhine, only one moderate-sized state in the Confederation of the Rhine possessed a relatively large Jewish population (because of the segmentation of German Jewry): the ecclesiastical state of Hesse-Darmstadt.* Its ruler had assumed the title of Grand Duke in 1806. The Jewish population had only been granted a few meagre rights during the revolutionary period but apart from the revocation of the *Leibzoll* and permission to acquire real estate, their servitude had not diminished. The Jews in the Kingdom of Saxony, where no change whatsoever had taken place, were in an even worse legal position. They were forbidden to reside anywhere in the kingdom unless they held residence permits in the capital city of Dresden. The thousands of Jews who gathered in the city of Leipzig for the fairs were not allowed to erect a synagogue. Even the *Leibzoll* was not abolished in Saxony until 1813—by the Russian armies of occupation. The régime instituted for the Jews in France was only imitated in so far as the anti-Jewish measures modelled on Napoleon's Infamous Decree of 1808 were concerned. In 1811, an order curbed the extension by Jews of interest-bearing loans. There was nothing surprising in this as, despite strong ties with Napoleon against neighbouring Prussia, the political system of Saxony had not been even ostensibly reformed. The nobility preserved its privileges and the King dared not override the representatives of the feudal estates even on the issue of compulsory military service, though it was practised in all the neighbouring German states.

Enfranchisement: Inside Prussia and in the Prussian Fashion (Mecklenburg, Denmark)

Prussia's crushing defeat by Napoleon after the battle of Jena, and the loss of the greater portion of her territories at the Peace of Tilsit in 1807†, brought on an economic crisis. This was so severe that the government was forced to reform the out-dated absolutist and feudal régime. The period that now ensued was spent in overhauling the state with the object of promoting capitalist development.

The first indication that the organized Prussian middle class had become aware of its common interests with the Jewish middle class had already appeared on the eve of political reform. In 1805, the two separate Christian and Jewish mercantile, banking, and industrial guilds of Berlin addressed a memorandum to the government requesting approval for a new charter for the stock exchange. Jews had not previously been admitted to the exchange. Now, with royal approval, a new exchange

---

* In 1822, the Grand Duchy of Hesse, which had expanded territorially after the Congress of Vienna, had a Jewish population of just under 20,000.

† All the areas west of the Elbe as well as all the sections of Poland occupied by Prussia following the second and third Partitions.

management was set up, consisting of two Christians and two Jews—one banker and one wholesaler on each side. Another indication of the growing social rapprochement was the participation of Jewish volunteers in the Berlin Civil Guard, organized in 1809.

Members of the Prussian government, although not greatly in sympathy with the Jews, also realized the need to improve their condition. This need became still more urgent after the civil enfranchisement of the Jews of Westphalia; a highly placed official admitted to some anxiety lest "the educated and wealthy Jews" emigrated from Prussia. Even Schroetter, a Cabinet member nicknamed "Haman the Jew-baiter" in government circles, submitted a proposal to Frederick William III in November, 1808 concerning equal rights for the Jews. His proposal arose from the conviction that it was necessary "to undermine the nationality of the Jews ... so that they shall not continue to be a state within a state." He therefore suggested granting them civil rights in return for the civil duties that they would assume, but with stringent qualifications to achieve his ultimate aim: their assimilation. Jews would have to wear German clothes and shave their beards; they would have heavier military service obligations than other citizens. Schroetter particularly hoped that permission for mixed marriages between Jew and Christian without requiring either party to change religion would result in the assimilation of the Jews. In this way Christian society would receive an influx of some of the Jewish capital accumulated in commerce, "which, in accordance with all their spiritual endowments, is their principal inclination."

The *General-Direktorium* was dissolved in December, 1808, and a council of five royal ministers set up. Schroetter's programme was considered by several ministries and brought to light conflicting opinions, particularly between the War Ministry and the Ministry of Religions, on the one hand, and the Ministry of Justice, on the other. The former demanded complete equality of rights for the Jews; the latter wished to retain certain restrictions. The chief spokesman for the Ministry of Religions was the statesman-scholar, Wilhelm von Humboldt. His views on the Jews were influenced by social contact and were free of all popular prejudices, but he still held to the prime axiom of the German Enlightenment movement: the superiority of Christianity to Judaism.* Like Napoleon, he was amazed at "their (the Jews') wondrous capacity for passive resistance" and the stubbornness with which they preserved their religion. But, again like Napoleon, he felt that the state must endeavour to subjugate this force, to destroy their segregation to the point of total absorption. He completely rejected any suggestion to grant rights to the Jews by gradual rather than by immediate enfranchisement. The state, he maintained, was not an educational but a legal institution.

The other officials of the Ministry of Religions also recommended that

* In his youth, Wilhelm, together with his brother, the naturalist Alexander von Humboldt, had been close disciples of Mendelssohn.

the Jews receive complete enfranchisement, although they were not as optimistic as Humboldt that total assimilation would eventually ensue. Only one, Süvern, concluded that the Jews would eventually be assimilated both as a people and as a religious community as a consequence of civil equality. "It may be," he declared, "that the Jews will forget Palestine when they are allowed to become fully naturalized in Europe, and it is possible that they will even believe that Jesus is the Messiah when they are no longer compelled to await another Messiah . . ."

Reforms in the Prussian régime reached their final stage when Karl August von Hardenberg was appointed Chancellor in 1810. All serfs were fully liberated and received the ownership of their land (the landowners were compensated to one-third of the value of their holdings). Complete freedom of occupation was established; and merchants and craftsmen were no longer compelled to affiliate with the guilds. Not surprisingly, Hardenberg wholeheartedly supported the proposals for enfranchising the Jews. He prepared his emancipation programme in close contact with David Friedlaender, at that time a *Parnass* of the Berlin Kehillah. (Particularly significant was a letter that Friedlaender sent to Hardenberg at the beginning of January, 1811. It complained of the spread of religious conversion among the wealthy Jews of Berlin, Breslau, and Königsberg, which might lead to the complete deterioration of the Kehillot.) Hardenberg also suggested that the Jews be allowed to hold public office, though with the proviso that for the first fifteen years they would require special royal consent. However, Frederick William preferred the negative attitude of the Justice Ministry, though he rejected its other proposals for additional restrictions.

On March 11, 1812, *An Edict Concerning the Civil Status of the Jews in the State of Prussia* was published. All Jews and their families who held the *General-Privilegium*, letters of protection, and domiciliary concessions, were declared *Einländer* (natives) and citizens of the state of Prussia. All anti-Jewish residential restrictions in cities and villages, all special taxes and all limitations on economic activity were abolished. In peddling too, they were henceforth subject to the same laws as all the other citizens. They were expressly allowed to hold municipal office and to work as teachers in schools with academic status. The King promised to promulgate a special law determining their right to hold government office at a later date. The adoption of a permanent surname was made a condition for receiving citizenship papers. They were required to keep their business ledgers and all other records and contracts in black letters, or Latin characters, and in German or any other living language—except Hebrew. Jews had to assume all civic duties towards the state, including military service. The special Jewish *Batei-Din* were abolished with the temporary exception of Berlin. Foreign Jews were permitted to live in Königsberg, Breslau, and Frankfurt-on-Oder while fairs were in progress. Matters relating to religious communities and education would be dealt with by special ordinance in the future. In this way the Jews achieved absolute civil rights and some political rights together with a promise of complete political enfranchisement in a Prussia where their subjection had formerly been so complete.

The partial emancipation of the Jews of Prussia served as an example to the adjoining state of Mecklenburg-Schwerin. It undoubtedly stimulated the local ruler to expedite the promulgation of a similar law in order to forestall the possible emigration of his wealthy Jews. On February 22, 1813, "The Sovereign's Law, establishing an appropriate régime for the members of the Jewish religion in the states of the Duchy of Mecklenburg-Schwerin" was published. It was little more than an imitation of the Prussian law of 1812. It mainly differed in that it retained the annual reception fee for Jews, though they were released from all other special taxes.

The neighbouring country of Denmark also prepared a law concerning the Jews, modelled on the Prussian enactment. About 400 Jewish families, 2,400 individuals, lived in Copenhagen and several other cities at that time. The rich members of this community owned silk and cloth factories—thirty-four in 1816—or engaged in wholesale trade. A third of all heads of family were craftsmen. Copenhagen had become an important centre of the *Haskalah* movement, and the young people attended both Jewish and general schools (a Jewish school for girls was opened in 1809). A sharp discussion flared up in Denmark in 1813 on the issue of Jewish enfranchisement. Its opponents admitted that their main fear was of Jewish competition. The supporters of Jewish rights included the well-known Danish poet, Jans Baggasen, as well as a number of bishops, pastors, and privy councillors. Several educated Jews, such as Euchel, Nathan, and David Werfel, also took part in the debate. On March 29, 1814, Frederick VI issued a command establishing civil equality for "the members of the Mosaic Faith," including permission to engage in any occupation, but, as in Prussia, excluding political rights.

The Danish equal rights law did not apply to Jews in the province of Schleswig-Holstein, which was under Danish administration. Here a number of severe restrictions remained in force.

Zenith and Decline of the Haskalah Movement in Germany

The *Haskalah* movement in Germany matured, became more intense, and reached the peak of its development during the period of the French Revolution. The organ of the movement was the Hebrew monthly, the *Me'asef*, which resumed publication in 1787 in Berlin, after a lapse of a year. Its new editors were Aaron Wolfssohn and Joel Brill, with frequent assistance from Isaac Euchel and Mendel Breslau, the former editors, and from David Friedlaender and other writers, who mainly lived in Prussia and Silesia. The main strength of the *Me'asef* did not lie in the field of political thought and the struggle for a new régime. In the retarded state of Germany, revolutionary activity of any sort concentrated on intellectual issues, literature and speculative thought. How much more unlikely, therefore, that the *Maskilim* should propose a militant political programme calling for a change in the régime as a pre-condition for the civil enfranchisement of the Jews. The new middle class in the German Jewish community based all its hopes for the acquisition of civil rights—its highest aspiration—on the dissemination of enlightenment, raising the cultural level of the masses and destroying the barriers of ancient tradition, superstition and way of life which separated them from the German people. The *Maskilim* did not venture outside the framework of enlightened despotism in their political thought or go beyond the concepts of Voltairian deism and the rationalism of the Encyclopedists which reflected the absolutist régime in their broad philosophical outlook, however great an impression the Revolution in France and the civil equality achieved in its wake by the Jews of France and Holland may have made upon them.

Nevertheless, the revived *Me'asef* at Berlin rose to far greater heights than during its earlier, Königsberg phase, both in its scientific and literary content and in the radicalism of its general outlook, despite the moderation and narrowness of its political horizons. Natural science, described by one author, Mendel Breslau, as "a ladder set up on the earth, and the top of it reaching the heaven," replaced "Commentaries on the Holy Scriptures" or interpretations of difficult passages in the Bible in the most prominent position in the monthly. In the field of history, publications included *The Chronicles of the Great Men of Israel,* a *Contemporary Chronicle* and a *Record of the Times* for ancient history. The editors devoted the utmost seriousness and enthusiasm to their project of spreading real knowledge among the people. Several of the poems which appeared side by side with empty and grandiloquent verse also introduced a new trend. The advice that the conservative, Naphtali Hertz Wessely, had given to the founders of the *Me'asef*—"Do not pour into your vessels songs of passion, words of lust and love"—was laid aside. The two new editors wrote paeans to wine and love. Joel Brill voiced the spirit of the Renaissance poets of Spain and Italy in a poem overflowing with the joy of living:

> *Without love and wine*
> *What destiny is mine?*

The editors also neglected Wessely's moderate advice not to provoke the orthodox and refrain from "speaking in a satirical manner." The only consideration the new editors gave to the orthodox circles, to conserve the peace, was to publish a number of eulogies on the deaths of famous rabbis. The living rabbis and the traditional religion were made the subject of satirical attacks. The first of these was published anonymously in 1789 and entitled *The Letters of Meshulam Ben Uriah the Eshtamoite*. It was written by Isaac Euchel on the lines of Montesquieu's *Lettres Persanes*. However, it was the second of these satires, *A Dialogue in the Land of the Living*, published by Wolfssohn in the last volume of the *Me'asef* (1794-97), which caused real anger in orthodox circles. The *Dialogue* took place in "The True World" (i.e., the Hereafter) between Maimonides, Moses Mendelssohn and *Ish Ploni* ("a certain man"), an orthodox Ashkenazic rabbi. Wolfssohn used it as a vehicle to give open expression to his views on religion and enlightenment. He poured scathing contempt and ridicule on "leaders to err" and "the rebels against the light," particularly on the grounds of their opposition to Mendelssohn's translation and commentary, and made sport of the Kabbalah and its theory of reincarnation. He angrily derided the *Zohar*, making Maimonides (in Paradise) state: "I have heard nothing of this." He recommended that prayers be offered "in the language of this country" and suggested that it might also be as well if the Pentateuch were read in German. He differentiated between rational commandments which depended neither on time nor on place and practical commandments which "are rational, but depend both on the time and the place and possibly, without that time and place, were not given at all; these are indeed profound matters." The *Me'asef* went too far with the *Dialogue* in the eyes of moderate *Maskilim* who had formerly supported it. The split amongst the *Maskilim*, stirred up by the controversy over religious radicalism, hastened the end of the *Me'asef*. Its final issues were only produced with great difficulty and monthly publication ceased in 1790. It was resumed in 1794 but only four more issues appeared up to 1797, when the number of subscribers had dwindled to 120 in all, and "The *Gatherer* (i.e., *Collector*) was gathered (unto its fathers)."*

Both the interruption in publication and the contracting readership of the Hebrew periodical were only indications of a profound crisis in the German *Haskalah* movement. But the movement had, nevertheless, given a new appearance to Hebrew literature and to the culture of the Jewish people at the beginning of a new era. The Jewish writers of Germany during the generation of the *Me'asfim* bequeathed a great and invaluable heritage to the people. Hebrew poetry flowed afresh after centuries of stagnation in central and eastern Europe. Besides the empty, loud-sounding songs and panegyrics in honour of rulers and wealthy men, there were also Wessely's *Shirei Tif'eret* (*Songs of Grandeur*) which, despite their defects, exerted a tremendous influence on the Hebrew poets of the following generation. Other poetic creations included an original play in

---

* *Me'asef* in Hebrew also means Gleaner, or Gatherer. The Biblical euphemism for death is "to be gathered unto one's father." This play on words was used by Ben Ze'ev in the introduction to his *Thesaurus of Radicals* (*Otzar Ha-shorashim*), Vienna, 1807, under the heading *A Proposal*.

1794, *The Reign of King Saul*, by Joseph Ha-Efratti of Troplowitz, Silesia, and in 1790 Solomon Pappenheim broke new ground with the poetical quality of his prose in an elegy, *The Legend of the Four Cups*. In narrative prose, *A Journey to Araby*, describing Morocco and the life of the Jews there, was published at Berlin in 1792 by the roving poet, Samuel Romanelli of Mantua. Isaac Euchel and Saul Berlin, author of the *Writ of Justice*, showed outstanding talent in satire, the favourite weapon of the *Maskilim* in their war against fanaticism and ignorance. The scholarly literature produced by that generation was not inferior in quality or quantity to the *belles lettres* of the *Haskalah* movement. Mendelssohn's *Commentary* on the Pentateuch was followed by translations of and commentaries on Job, Proverbs, and Psalms, the *Five Scrolls*, and several chapters from other books of the Old Testament by his disciples, Isaac Euchel, Aaron Wolfssohn, and Joel Brill. Research into the Hebrew language was enriched by lexicographic works and books on synonyms such as *The Curtains of Solomon*, by Solomon Pappenheim and Benjamin Ze'ev Heidenheim, on lines already followed by Wessely. Apart from articles in the *Me'asef*, Barukh Lindau's book on *Reishit Limmudim* (Elementary Studies) (Part 1, 1789) was of great value in diffusing natural science. Educational problems were also treated by Ze'ev Wolff of Dessau and other teachers in the spirit of the new methods of instruction. Another great historical project by these *me'asfim*—or anthologizers—was to publish works of inquiry and collections of poetry of the golden age of Hebrew literature and scholarship during the Middle Ages and the Renaissance. Maimonides' *Guide to the Perplexed* was published with the commentary by Moses Narboni and with a new commentary in the spirit of modern philosophy, *Giv'at Ha'moreh* (*The Mount of the Guide*) by Solomon Maimon. Similarly, Judah Ha-Levi's *Al-Khuzari*, Saadya Gaon's *Beliefs and Opinions*, the *Compositions* (*Machbarot*) of Emmanuel Ha-Romi, and the *Be'chinat Olam* (*Examination of the World*) of Jedaiah Ha-P'nini, were brought out in new editions by Judah Ben-Ze'ev at Vienna. Most of these books were published as a result of the efforts of Isaac Satanow.

This very varied literary activity of the *Me'asef* collaborators came to an end almost at the same time as the magazine ceased publication at the end of the eighteenth century. The new Jewish middle class of Germany, which had been the mainstay of the Berlin *Haskalah*, now turned its back on the movement and all its aims, particularly the revival of the Hebrew language and literature. The *Haskalah* movement was followed by a strange extremist assimilation movement hitherto unknown in the history of the Jewish people. The *Haskalah* movement, flourishing only during the last quarter of the eighteenth century, seemed almost to have served the Jewish middle class of Germany merely as a springboard from the petrified traditional culture to the "spacious" atmosphere of assimilation.

The reasons for its rapid decline could be discerned in the character of the Berlin *Haskalah* itself. The exponents of the cultural renaissance had not only failed to provide a protective barrier between the people and assimilation; but their programme itself shook the foundations of national existence and destroyed the walls that had shielded the people from national extinction. In the cosmopolitan atmosphere of the Age of Reason, the sole distinction they could discover between the Jews and other "citizens of the world" was that of religion. And religion to them did not mean traditional popular beliefs imbued with a national spirit and deeply rooted in the nation's historical continuity. It meant a deistic creed of "rational commandments" tenuously attached to an Old Testament which could be rationally interpreted. In other nations, those settled in their own countries, the conflict between reason and religious tradition did not shake the foundations of national life in any way. On the contrary, it liberated them from bondage to the church and cleared the way for a budding national culture in the atmosphere of capitalist society. But for the Jewish people, dislodged from their own soil and dispersed, the vacuum created by the collapse of traditional religion could only be filled by a deeper awareness of the historic connection with their homeland, and the strengthening of their hope of achieving a renaissance and renewed existence in Zion. Not even the most extreme *Haskalah* writers ever contemplated attacking or rejecting the concept of the Restoration of Zion (*Shivat Zion*), which the people held sacred above all else. Their attitude, however, can be gathered from their omissions: they did their utmost to eradicate this idea, in their ceaseless advocacy of loyalty to the ruling "gracious monarchs," and devotion to "the land of their birth," its language and culture. Furthermore, they expressly taught that the concept of the Diaspora only accorded with a state of bondage and repression, and they welcomed every law that proclaimed equality of rights as a "redemption and deliverance" for the people of Israel. Inevitably, the dissemination of this viewpoint as one of the principles of the new outlook erased all the ideals and feelings of attachment to Zion from the hearts of *Haskalah* followers, though this attachment had given Jewish national life in the Diaspora the stability and historical perspective necessary for survival.

Similarly, the Berlin school of *Haskalah* directly—though not deliberately—undermined the existence of the Hebrew language by its attitude to the spoken vernacular and culture—even though it gave prime place in its programme to fostering Hebrew. The *Maskilim's* war against Yiddish continued from the days of Mendelssohn and Wessely throughout the *Me'asef* period. It never occurred to them that the danger to Hebrew did not lie in Yiddish but in the very "correct" native language they championed. Similarly, they did not realize that destroying the foundations of the spoken Jewish vernacular—interspersed with almost 25 per cent of Hebrew vocabulary—would lead to the collapse and disappearance of the popular cultural background which was also the *sine qua non* for the existence and growth of Hebrew as a cultural medium. From the beginning, the *Maskilim* of Berlin deliberately specified such narrow spheres for the use of Hebrew in literature and education that it was hardly left an adequate basis on which to exist and compete with the non-Jewish rival. Most of the *Maskilim*, even the moderates, were not in favour of the view of Wolfssohn and Friedlaender that Hebrew be eliminated from the liturgy. But they did agree with the idea of linguistic dualism in culture whereby the alien language would be incontestably dominant, although this eventually was to bring about the elimination of Hebrew entirely. The small circle of *Me'asef* readers invariably followed to its logical conclusions this acknowledgement that Hebrew was irrevocably limited as a scholarly language. They set about acquiring scientific and general information from German books as far as their knowledge of the language permitted. They began to read German *belles lettres* in the original; all the more so as the *Me'asef* generally lagged behind the times in its choice of translations and arrangements from German originals. It entertained its readers with the sentimental idylls of Gessner at a time when Schiller and Goethe were at the height of their powers. The small number of original literary works in Hebrew prevented them competing with literature in contemporary European languages. It was characteristic of this contradictory dualism and the complete inability of the Berlin *Haskalah* to solve the problem of the dynamic of Hebrew cultural existence that the last two editors of the *Me'asef*, Aaron Wolfssohn and Joel Brill, were at the head of the Breslau *Wilhelmschule*. The basic aim of the *Wilhelmschule* was to imbue Jewish youth with the German language and culture—together with a smattering of knowledge of the Bible and Hebrew grammar. Even its editors thought that the *Me'asef* was only designed for "a certain class": those who still depended on Hebrew to acquire general enlightenment.

Deliberate Assimilationism and its Exponents; Solomon Maimon

After its migration and dissemination through eastern Europe, the *Haskalah* movement was long-lived, highly productive, and influential during the nineteenth century. This in itself proved that its rapid collapse in Germany was not caused by anything fundamental in the movement, but rather by its particular objective, a product of the time and place. It was affected by the demographic circumstances of the Jewish middle class in Germany—and in Prussia particularly—which made it easy for current cosmopolitan ideals to be transformed into deliberate assimilation. Germany's small Kehillot were dispersed throughout the country and composed of a thin layer of well-to-do middle-class Jews and an unstable mass of pedlars and petty traders. They could not be relied on to present any great defence against assimilation. The subjugation of the

Jewish masses stimulated the middle class to make every effort to assimilate in order to achieve civil equality. The contrast between the legal status of the Jewish masses, who had no rights at all, and the position that the Jewish bourgeoisie occupied in the economy of the state and its social and cultural life was more striking in Prussia than anywhere else. As the gap widened, the bourgeoisie endeavoured to withdraw further and further away from their miserable and despised lower middle class co-religionists and to strengthen their foothold in the culture and way of life of the German ruling classes. In Germany also the gap between the traditional Jewish culture, the old Jewish pattern of life, and the universal human culture now opening up to the Jews was deeper than in any other country. There was on the one hand the ancient and unyielding rabbinical culture, completely lacking the freshness of original, rejuvenating thought and totally closed to any external influence. On the other hand, there was the new, revolutionary bourgeois culture of the *Weltbürger* (citizen of the world), out to destroy every prejudice and every barrier between men in the name of pure reason, the force which was giving birth to prolific creativity in literature and science. The clash of these two cultural extremes gave the assimilationist drive amongst German Jews (though actually rooted in the political background) its peculiarly unwholesome quality and whipped it up to the proportions of a mania.

Not all the Jewish middle class succumbed to complete cultural assimilation. The most common form of deviation from the extreme trend was the outward, superficial "enlightenment" of the younger generation of the middle class. In possession of a general education, they were content to be able to converse in "correct" German, to own a slight knowledge of French, and to devote their time to dissolute, luxurious living, in imitation of the "gilded youth" of the nobility. This behaviour pattern became so widespread amongst the sons of the wealthy Prussian Jews, and particularly their daughters—who were enchanted by any association with army officers and noblemen's sons—that it was criticised by both Isaac Euchel and Aaron Wolfssohn, in their respective satirical comedies *Reb Hennich* and *Leichtsinn und Frömmelei* (*Levity and Self-Righteousness*), together with ignorance and fanaticism.

David Friedlaender (1750-1834), the political leader of the enlightened assimilationist Prussian Jewish middle class was a typical example. He was born into a wealthy Jewish Königsberg family and was the son-in-law of Daniel Itzig, one of the great Jewish bankers of Berlin. Friedlaender himself was a prosperous merchant and factory owner, and wielded a powerful influence in the Berlin Kehillah, where he was a *Parnass* for many years, and over Prussian Jewry as a whole, negotiating with the government in their name. He was a disciple and admirer of Mendelssohn and was amongst the leading founders of all the institutions of the Enlightenment in Berlin, for example, the school and printing press, *Hinukh Ne'arim* (Youth Education), *Hevrat Scocharei ha-Tov ve-ha-Tushiah* (Society for Promotion of the Good and the Useful), and the *Hevrat Re'im* (Society of Friends), founded in 1792 mainly to introduce burial of the dead on the third day after decease and modern burial customs. His generous payment to *Haskalah* writers and his literary activity on the German *Berliner Monatsschrift* and the Hebrew *Me'asef* gave the editors of the *Me'asef* the pretext to proclaim him Mendelssohn's heir and to honour him by the publication of innumerable eulogies in somewhat poor taste. More applicable was the description of Friedlaender, coined by the historian, Heinrich Graetz, as "petty of mind, the ape of Mendelssohn." He differed markedly from his mentor in his mediocre ability, superficial knowledge, general attitude and conception of Judaism, and in his personal character, which was that of a slave, cringing before the dominant race and religion both on his own behalf and that of his people. Voltaire's deism and the reign of reason were the basic principles behind his struggle against the whole Jewish cultural heritage and every manifestation of Jewish national life, which he saw as the chief obstacles to enfranchisement. He regarded the Talmud, the rabbinical religion, merely as "mysticism" in conflict with "common sense." From the vast body of Judaism he only selected a distilled Mosaic creed expressed according to the tenets of a naturalistic, deistic religion. Needless to say, he opposed the use of Yiddish, as "distorted and unintelligible outside our own circles," and demanded that it be replaced by "the German language, the parent tongue." He frequently voiced his love for Hebrew and yet, as early as 1786, published a German translation of the liturgy with the *a priori* intention of eliminating the Hebrew. However, Friedlaender's letter to Pastor Teller in 1799 really revealed his innermost feelings about Judaism and his main intentions—and that of the members of his class—to undermine the foundations of the national existence of the Jewish people. The letter, on behalf of "a number of 'house fathers' of the Jewish faith," expressed their willingness "to assume the ritual duties (*Zeremonien*) of the Protestant faith, on condition, however, that this be understood as an acknowledgement of eternal truths and not as belief in the tenets of the Church."

This was in 1799. The Prussian-Jewish bourgeoisie had been disappointed in all its expectations of acquiring civil rights, after the government had even moved away from effecting reforms in their existing status. As a reaction to this, a group of enlightened Berlin Jews, under the leadership of a Kehillah notable, a generous patron of the *Haskalah* movement, declared that they were prepared to what amounted to "be Christianized somewhat," on the sole condition that they be permitted to remain deists at heart.

The men who drafted this declaration decided to address it to Pastor Teller, as he was known to be an enlightened man and the author of several essays on Christianity in a spirit akin to deism. However, the enlightened Pastor held more tenaciously to the principles of his religion than Friedlaender and his group to the principles of theirs. The Pastor declined to accept anybody who did not believe in the rite of baptism, in the Host, and in Jesus of Nazareth, into the Christian fold. "Why should you not be content for the present with refining the pure gold of your original Israelitic tenets of faith from all the impurities that have accrued to it with time?" he asked the would-be Christians in mock amazement, in full awareness of the answer. He added that the question of civil rights was not under Church but under state jurisdiction. Several years elapsed before David Friedlaender admitted publicly that he had been the author of this letter but it had been an open secret in all Berlin circles. The theologian and exponent of religious romanticism, Friedrich Schleiermacher commented ironically on the letter in an anonymous pamphlet: "How deeply the feelings of that excellent man, Friedlaender, must have been hurt! I wonder whether he will raise his voice against this betrayal of a treasured asset." He like Teller, reproached the sponsors of the letter on grounds of social morality and maintained that they should work amongst and for their people rather than abandon them.

The theories on Judaism illogically jumbled together in Friedlaender's letter of apostasy had previously been expressed in condensed and systematic form by Lazarus Ben-David, a man of superior character. Like most people of his class and generation, Ben-David (1762-1832) had received in his youth a basic education in the Bible and Talmud. Despite his philosophical learning (he was a pupil of Kant), he did not remain as a lecturer at the University of Vienna, where he had expected to find a more liberal atmosphere than in Prussia. Instead, he became the principal of the *Jüdische Freischule* of Berlin. He expounded his views on Judaism in a pamphlet, *On the Characteristics of the Jews*, published in 1793. According to Ben-David, the pure unadulterated Jewish religion, the religion of Moses, had been distorted by fanaticism and the multifarious mandatory observances which came into common use after the destruction of the Second Temple. The Jewish people saw no way of propitiating the Lord except by increasing the precepts and prohibitions and by rendering the Torah immune through an intricate system of protective laws. The subjugation caused by Diaspora existence and the economic links between people who were only allowed to earn a living by trade had intensified Jewish segregation from the nations of the world and universal human culture. Now, the darkness of the Middle Ages had lifted and the Age of Enlightenment had begun. A brighter future was open to the Jews too and they had only to mend their ways to partake of the benefits available to all citizens of the state. The essential reform required was that the Jews discard the outer case, the ceremonial laws, which were pernicious both to themselves and to the state. They should then return to the core—the religion of Moses—which was the natural and rational religion and the religion of pure morality.

The identification of Judaism with naturalist religion, that is to say, with deism, was also the central theme of a German pamphlet *Leviathan, or Religion in Relation to Judaism*, published in 1792 by Dr. Saul Ascher (1767-1822). Ascher was another German assimilationist Jewish intellectual. However, whereas Ben-David stressed the moral teachings of Judaism, Ascher demanded that the essentials of the Jewish faith be formulated in such a way as to provide a basis for adherence to Judaism by enlightened elements who could not intellectually tolerate the ceremonial laws (*mitzvot*). By the emphasis he placed on the element of faith in the Jewish religion, Ascher was in fact expressing a positive development in the attitude to religion that had occurred in contemporary German "Enlightenment" circles. His standpoint was also the first indication of the religious reform movement that spread through German Jewry during the first half of the nineteenth century.

Moses Mendelssohn's exposition of Judaism, as interpreted by his disciples, had thus reached an *impasse* where its very *raison d'être* hung in the balance. Mendelssohn, both an assimilationist and a conservative, had tried to mediate between the traditional Jewish religion and the ideas of deism and religious rationalism. His disciples, seeking an ideological basis for the rapid assimilation of the Jewish middle class in the following generation, had only to eliminate their master's final conclusions from his teachings in order to nullify their obvious dualism. As reason was also the final arbiter in religious matters, there was no sense in the mandatory observances. Apart from compromising the Jews in the eyes of the gentiles and thus delaying their political and cultural "emancipation," these observances were not dictated by reason, and some of them actually conflicted with it. The essence of Judaism, they concluded, was only rational religion; and this was also the foundation of Christianity.

None the less, these enlightened men recoiled from religious conversion through a personal sense of honour, family ties, and above all, because of their economic connections with their own people and a sense of national solidarity which, unconsciously perhaps, they still possessed.

Solomon Maimon, who towered head and shoulders above the enlightened Jews of his generation, both in talent and integrity, was also aware of these contradictions. The tragedy of his life and personality prevented him from becoming a guide to his people in this spiritual crisis. Maimon was born in about 1753 in a remote village in the neighbourhood of Nieswiezh, Lithuania, the son of an impecunious lessee. He was an outstanding Talmudic scholar. At the age of eleven, Maimon was so well versed in the Talmud and the Codifiers that he was considered competent to become a teacher. At the age of twelve he was married off and forced to become a village *melamed* in order to maintain a home. He had already learned the fundamentals of general and Jewish history from the sixteenth century chronicle entitled *Tzemach David* (*The Flower of David*), by David Gans, and made his first acquaintance with mathematics and astronomy from another book, also by Gans, found on his father's bookshelf. When he was still a child, he had satisfied his taste for philosophical enquiry with Maimonides' *Guide to the Perplexed*, and, as a youth, made a copious study of Kabbalah, where he was particularly attracted by the method of Rabbi Moses Cordovero. His quest for the truth also led him towards Hasidism and he only became disillusioned with it after he had visited the *Magid* Dov Ber of Mezericz. His overpowering thirst for knowledge and his vast creative urge could not be satisfied in his native environment, where there were not even foreign language books available. Maimon mastered the Latin alphabet by applying a peculiar invention of his own; he learnt to correlate the letters that spelled out the number of sheets in Hebrew books. Even when he could read German, the only books he could find were several physics text-books, and he had to travel to a distant city to obtain them. Maimon was about twenty-five years old when he left his family and country of his birth in order to go to Germany and study at a university. His ragged clothes, tangled beard, queer gestures, and succulent Lithuanian Yiddish, aroused laughter and derision from the refined and enlightened men of Königsberg and Berlin. After many vicissitudes he reached Stettin from Königsberg and proceeded to Berlin on foot. When he innocently told the *Parnassim* who interrogated him that it was his ambition to publish a commentary to the *Guide to the Perplexed* and to specialize in the sciences, he was mercilessly driven from the city gates. In the company of a beggar, he trudged to Posen, where he finally found asylum with its Rabbi Zvi Hirsch of Janow, who cared for him like a father. However, all the honours that the Kehillah dignitaries accorded to the brilliant young scholar rapidly ceased when it became known that he was openly flouting accepted superstitions. Maimon set out for Berlin a second time, but on this occasion a recommendation from Moses Mendelssohn stood him in good stead. The support of wealthy patrons provided his livelihood and also enabled him to study pharmacy. Until then, all his philosophical knowledge had been derived from the works of Maimonides. Now the new world of philosophy, the systems of Descartes, Spinoza, Locke, Leibnitz and Wolff, were open to him. His brilliant mind enabled him to master the essence of Wolff's metaphysics even before he had learned German, and he wrote a devastating critique of it in Hebrew. Three years later, his sponsor, Mendelssohn, withdrew his favour. Conservative and cautious in his thinking and lower middle class in his attitude, Mendelssohn found many aspects of Maimon's conduct unforgivable: that all his efforts were devoted to perfecting his intellectual faculties and not to acquiring a skill which would equip him to earn a respectable living; that in his search for absolute truth, he had dared to express views contrary to the dogmas of religion at a friendly gathering; and finally, oblivious of the fact that he had obviously received no schooling in manners and deportment, that he should spend his nights at taverns in the company of frivolous companions. A new chapter of peregrinations fraught with unending tribulation began in Maimon's life.

In Holland, he provoked anger in orthodox circles by his free-thinking conduct. At the age of thirty he arrived in Hamburg and, despite his age, spent two years as a student at a *Gymnasium*, learning German and Latin. After innumerable wanderings between Berlin, Dessau, and Breslau, he again succeeded in settling in Berlin for a number of years. His views on Kant's *Critique of Pure Reason* earned him a letter of praise from the philosopher (though Kant later changed his mind about it). It also gave him entrée to the serious German periodicals, and his books on philosophy easily found publishers. His autobiography (published in German in 1792) brought him nation-wide repute and even the admiration of Goethe and Schiller. Yet, though now famous, his material condition remained wretched. The same Berlin Kehillah élite who had forced him to leave the city after he had lost Mendelssohn's favour, still ignored him because of his behaviour and even more because of his personal characteristics. They were embarrassed by his neglected appearance, disgusted by his speech, interspersed with Yiddish, and appalled by his Talmudic casuistry. They could not forgive his lack of deference and felt insulted by his derogatory opinion of them. Maimon spent his last years in the palace of one of his admirers, the enlightened Silesian nobleman, Count Kalkreuth zu Nieder-Siegersdorf, who provided all he required. But continual wandering and hardship had broken his health. He died of tuberculosis in 1800 at the age of forty-six. Ruffians stoned his coffin and he was given an anonymous burial in the potter's field outside the enclosure of the Kehillah cemetery at Glogau.

Solomon Maimon has come to be known in the history of philosophy as a transitional link between the systems of Kant and Fichte. The freshness and originality of his thought, however, was also evident in his approach to the problems of the Jewish people in his own and former times. He saw, in the developments which occurred in Jewish religion after the destruction of the Second Temple, a consistent tendency to buttress the Jewish nation's existence. In this he anticipated the theories propounded by Zhitlowsky, Ahad-Ha'am (Asher Ginsburg) and Simon Dubnow over a century later, including their fundamental errors. Maimon showed a real historical sense in his exposition of the Talmudic system, defending the Talmud against both denunciatory Christian writings and against "Jews who profess to be enlightened." The laws enacted by the members of the *K'nesset Ha-gedolah* (Men of the Great Assembly) and the Sages of the Talmud answered the "needs of the times." They did not ordain a multitude of commandments and proscriptions in order to expound the Torah; on the contrary, they interpreted passages in the Pentateuch with the express purpose of revealing any coincidental authorization for the new laws they introduced. Maimon proudly extolled the morality of the Talmud, which he defined as an outstanding example of stoicism based on love of humanity. He stood alone in his generation in his positive historical appraisal of the Jewish cultural past, with which the development of the Talmud was associated. He was not ashamed of his own origins in Polish Jewry—the object of derision to the "enlightened" Jews of Berlin. In fact, he cited the Jews of Poland as exemplifying the transition from theory to practice of the moral values of the Talmud. The Jews of Poland had not been forced to engage solely in usury and peddling, as in other countries. They earned their living by honest and useful toil. They excelled in pious and charitable actions, in the purity of their family life and their modest behaviour. Such praise of the virtues of Polish Jewry, coupled with biting satire of the hypocritical middle class manners of western European society, was not heard again in German-Jewish literature until Heinrich Heine.

In his apologia for the Talmud, Maimon did not overlook the negative social aspects of the historic development of the Jewish people. He thought that Talmudic domination over the life of the people had caused the elevation of the class of Talmudic scholars over the people and the establishment of a régime of spiritual aristocracy. He regarded early Christianity, the Kabbalah, the Messianic movements (e.g., Sabbatai Zvi), and Hassidism, as links in one historic chain of opposition to this régime. The common denominator of all these movements was their attempt to elevate moral precepts above the multiple system of mandatory observances. Maimon's evaluation of Polish Jewry and his own profound personal affection for it did not blind him to its cultural state. He sadly described the low level of general education amongst the Jews of Poland and, as befitted the age of reason, saw the diffusion of scientific knowledge as a panacea for the political ills of his people.

The numerous works Maimon wrote in Hebrew—including original philosophical inquiries, comprehensive books on mathematics and physics, and a translation of the history of the Jews by Basnage—were evidence of the broad scope of his programme and the earnestness of his endeavours to spread learning and enlightenment amongst his people. But apart from their comprehensiveness and intrinsic worth, they bear eloquent witness to his love of the Jewish national language.

The method he employed should have earned Maimon the merit of fostering profound and creative learning among his people. Most of his Hebrew books on philosophy, and several on the natural sciences, were written in the form of commentaries on works of medieval inquirers. But of all these, only a single instalment in the *Me'asef*, and the first part of *Givat Ha-Moreh*, his commentary on the *Guide to the Perplexed* of Maimonides, was ever published. This confirmed the tragic truth which Maimon himself voiced in his autobiography, when he dwelt on the difficulty of disseminating in Hebrew scholarly works and works of research. "The unenlightened," he wrote, "the preponderant majority of the people, severely prohibit all reading of secular books; the few enlightened ones will certainly not trouble themselves to study the sciences in Hebrew. . . ." His personal tragedy was that of his people, torn between fanatical religious ignorance on the one hand and enlightened assimilationism, on the other.

The Salons and the Conversion Mania; the Beginning of Religious Reform

Maimon's death took place at the same time as the monthly *Me'asef* expired. The coincidence was historically symbolic. The age of Berlin *Haskalah* had come to an end, and the process of assimilation and total absorption which engulfed the Jewish middle class of Prussia reached its climax. The cultural life of the enlightened Jewish finance magnates, who held a *General-Privilegium* conferred by the rulers, was now character-ized by the grand *salons* of Berlin, Königsberg and Breslau, which also became meeting places for the cream of the German Enlightenment. The social and political backwardness of Germany, as compared with western Europe, which was the prime cause of the unique phenomenon of assimilation within the Jewish capitalist class, was also the reason why this class discharged such an important function in the diffusion of bourgeois culture in Germany.

Moneyed Jews filled the vacuum caused by the absence of a German middle class in the chief cities of Prussia. This new Jewish middle class was not only distinguished by its wealth but also by the high level of its general erudition and its sensitivity to every new cultural development. The Jewish merchants and bankers were now turning the thirst for learning inherited from their fathers to the study of literature, philosophy and the sciences. Their mental acumen, sharpened by Talmudic disputa-tions, stood them in good stead in the debates on issues of contemporary interest in German culture that took place at gatherings of scholars and enlightened intellectuals. The enlightened Jewish middle class also had the advantage of being free from the prejudices and out of date traditions which oppressed the German middle class. As a result of their commer-cial links with all the European countries, the homes of the Jewish middle class could offer the additional attraction of frequent visitors from abroad. The salons of the Jewish upper middle class of Berlin thus became a focal point of social life for enlightened Germans. As early as 1772, the Danish scholar-statesman, August Hennings, found the principal centres of social life in Berlin at the homes of Moses Mendelssohn and the wealthy Itzig family. In 1798, the theologian, Schleiermacher, explained the reason for this in a letter to his sister written from Berlin.

> It is but natural that young scholars and dandies here regularly visit the large homes of the Jews, for these are the wealthiest urban families here and almost the only ones who keep open house . . . and also because the Jewish women . . . are highly educated . . . .

However, the *salons* of the Berlin Jewish financial magnates were not used solely as clubrooms for literary circles. As the members of the German ruling circles met together there, they also became centres of all the libertinism and moral laxity which pervaded that class at the time. The more Germany withdrew in essence from the political revolution of the middle class, the more enthusiastically did its capitalist class embrace the individualistic principles of French Revolutionary theory as a mode of middle class life. This new trend towards a reversal in morals did not supply an outlet for revolutionary fervour but rather diverted it into the libidinous channels of sensuous and emotional stimulation. The women who dominated these Jewish *salons* were ideally suited to play the role that this process of breaking free of convention required of them. In the first place they were well versed in the new *belles lettres*; in the second, they were remote from any traditional or historical background. They had received no schooling whatsoever in the traditions of the Jewish people— beyond for some of them, a routine religious education—and had not as yet struck roots in German tradition.

While the *salons* of the Berlin Jewish financiers were frequented by officers and scions of the nobility, the *salon* of the Herz family became the most famous in Berlin as a centre for intellectuals after Mendelssohn's death. Dr. Marcus (Mordecai) Herz (1747-1803) was both a distinguished physician and an accomplished student of philosophy, especially of Kant. He did a great deal to make known the Kantian system. His lectures on the teachings of Kant, and on experimental physics, brought the best of the enlightened elements in the city to his home. However, his knowledgeable, pretty and vivacious wife, Henriette, was the greatest attraction of the *salon*. As time passed, German authors and intimate friends, such as Lessing and Mendelssohn, were replaced by representatives of the Romantic school, Gentz, Friedrich von Schlegel and Schleiermacher. They were joined by the Humboldt brothers—the future statesman, Wilhelm, and Alexander, who made a name for himself in the natural sciences—and the German men-about-town of Berlin. Under the rule of Henriette Herz and her pretty, intelligent companions, this parlour became the centre for a group which implemented the principles of the Romantic movement. Friendships and liaisons were formed in defiance of all conventional decorum and morality—between Henriette Herz and Wilhelm von Humboldt; later between Henriette Herz and Pastor Schleiermacher; between Dorothea Mendelssohn, the elder daughter of Moses Mendelssohn, and Friedrich von Schlegel (she became his mistress and eventually married him).

Rachel Levin (1771-1833) was by far the most profound of this group of Jewish women. She was a jeweller's daughter whose attic apartment became a meeting place for the most distinguished intellectual leaders of Germany. Her lively and sensitive personality emerges from her letters. The historian Leopold von Ranke commented: "She writes her letters the way I write my books." Towards the end, her preoccupation with mysticism turned towards St. Simonism and her pacifist ideals led her to launch a programme calling upon the women of Europe to abolish war.

All three *salon* heroines consummated their careers or concluded the romance of their lives by religious conversion. Dorothea Mendelssohn-Veit became a Christian when she married Friedrich Schlegel. Rachel Levin was converted on her marriage to a senior Prussian official, the writer Varnhagen von Ense. Only Henriette Herz postponed this step for several years after her husband's death until her mother also had died. Conversion also engulfed most of the families associated with the Berlin *salons*: the Ephraims and Solomons, the Itzigs and Friedlaenders. All the sons and daughters of Moses Mendelssohn were affected and only his eldest, Joseph, died a Jew. As far as the Jewish women were concerned, the ease with which they were converted to Christianity was in no small measure due to their complete lack of Jewish education, which might have implanted some feeling for their people and a pride in its past. Even Rachel Levin first read the Old Testament when she was over forty, and was moved by the German mystic Angelus Silesius through sheer ignorance of the mysteries of the Kabbalah and Hasidism. A few days before her death, she was overtaken by remorse and expressed deep emotion at having been born a daughter of the ancient Jewish people.

Reactionary romanticism, especially dominant in contemporary Germany, gave the act of baptism in the name of Jesus the Nazarene an aura of mystery, accompanied by the nobility of devotion to humanity and the sensation of holding all creation in one's loving embrace. These Jewish matrons had experienced every excess of romantic love in their youth. In their old age they did not neglect the latest fashion for Christian self-righteousness then prevalent amongst aesthetes and fashionable gentlemen. These ladies were not even particularly disturbed when exponents of romanticism, in extolling Christianity, voiced contempt for the Jewish religion, and sometimes even preached perpetual hatred of the Jewish people (Schleiermacher, Friedrich Schlegel, Gentz). Dorothea von Schlegel *née* Mendelssohn descended to the lowest depths of hatred for her people, possibly engendered by a sad sense of inferiority. In 1802, she wrote to Schleiermacher:

> I have been reading the Old and New Testaments attentively, and my heart tells me that Protestant Christianity, in any event, is purer and superior to Catholicism: the latter appears to me to be too similar to that old Judaism which I greatly condemn.

This female apostate later changed her mind with regard to Catholicism. A few years later she and her husband entered the Catholic Church and both her sons were raised strictly according to its tenets.

The women wrapped their flight into the dominant religion in a veil of romanticism. The men tried to justify their own and their sons' baptisms by deistic arguments still surviving from Mendelssohn's time. In 1810, Simon Veit, the first husband of Dorothea Schleiermacher *née* Mendelssohn, wrote in a tone of forgiveness to his son Philipp, who, with his brother, had undergone conversion to the Christian faith, "I shall not cease to love you both . . . So long as we differ only in religion but share one opinion on the fundamentals of morality, there will never be any division between us." In 1820, before his own conversion, Abraham Mendelssohn, Moses Mendelssohn's younger son and the father of Felix, the composer, wrote to his daughter Fanny, "with congratulations from the depths of a father's heart" on the occasion of her formal adoption of the Christian religion.

This wave of conversions was essentially a social phenomenon, the final stage in a process of elective assimilation which had infected the Jewish finance magnates and intellectuals of Prussia, and especially Berlin, from the second half of the eighteenth century. They had become impervious to their own people, long before they decided to be baptized. As the number of conversions within the class multiplied, many who had hesitated at first were also drawn into the movement, either because they believed that the old class solidarity could no longer be maintained or because of a new sense of family and class solidarity with those already outside the Jewish fold. At the beginning of 1811, David Friedlaender submitted a memorandum to Chancellor Hardenberg, containing the names of fifty Berlin Jews (thirty-two heads of families and eighteen individuals) who "had left the faith of their fathers" during the preceding five or eight years. The memorandum stated that the Berlin Jewish community had consisted of 405 families in 1806, which would indicate that a tenth of the Kehillah had adopted Christianity within a few years. According to Friedlaender, the proportion of conversions in the Kehillot of Königsberg and Breslau had been on the same scale. Friedlaender's memorandum hinted at the material damages this had caused to the Jewish community and indirectly to the state, and this undoubtedly hastened the promulgation of the Prussian government's Jewish emancipation ordinance at the beginning of the following year. The ordinance was followed by a sharp decrease in the number of religious conversions, indisputable evidence of the extent to which the ambition of the Jewish middle class to achieve civil equality had been the decisive factor in the movement. The same ambition gave the conversionist movement renewed momentum when political reaction set in under the Holy Alliance. This was particularly the case amongst Jewish intellectuals, whose careers were once again blocked.

The general Prussian-Jewish population, the bulk of whom lived outside the provincial capitals, continued to preserve their traditional culture and religion, even during the period of mass conversion in the upper layers of the new Jewish middle class. The open defection of the small minority only strengthened the conservative orthodoxy and the resistance to assimilation of the majority. However, this did not precisely apply to the middle class as a whole. Within its ranks the assimilationist, as distinct from the conversionist, trend, became more powerful in the Napoleonic age, even outside Prussia, in German states where the Jewish communities were as yet remote from the influence of the Berlin *Haskalah*. A division took place within the new Jewish middle class throughout all of Germany during the Napoleonic Wars. This class consisted not only of large merchants, army and government contractors (some of whom had been in Spain and Russia with Napoleon's armies) but also groups of bankers and industrialists. Under the stimulus of the political reforms in most of the German states, this class increased its efforts to assimilate, in the hope of thus achieving civil and political enfranchisement. The *Me'asef* had been the organ of the *Haskalah* during the preceding period of Berlin enlightenment. Now a monthly, *Sulamith*, began to appear in German in July, 1806 as the mouthpiece of the new Jewish middle class in Germany during the age of Napoleon. The fact that *Sulamith* was published in the German language showed the transformation that had taken place in German-Jewish life since the last years of the eighteenth century and also heralded the new assimilationist programme.

The editors of *Sulamith*, David Fraenkel and, for the first year of publication, Joseph Wolff, both taught at the German school for Jewish children in Dessau. They kept up close connections with the Jewish Consistory of Westphalia, to which Fraenkel belonged, but carefully avoided propaganda in favour of the French constitutional régime and specifically opposed any "interference in political affairs."

Sulamith's dual programme of enlightenment embodied its new aim. In their statement of intent, the editors were most emphatic in their advocacy of religion and published such articles as "On the Essence, Nature, and Necessity of Religion." The religious tendency lay at the very basis of the cultural programme of this organ of the assimilating Jewish middle class of Germany: its efforts towards assimilation inevitably caused it to focus on religion as the only cogent aspect of Jewishness, once all national elements had been removed. The affirmation of religion also reflected the current attitude under Napoleon; the middle class, now secure in its domination, had long since renounced the atheism and rationalism of the Encyclopedists, and the theories of the reign of reason which had prevailed during the French Revolution.

Sulamith's affirmative attitude towards the Talmud and Midrash was also symptomatic of the *volte face* in regard to religion, while articles on Jewish history by *Maskilim* such as Judah Jeiteles of Prague, Shalom Cohen of Berlin, Peter Beer, and the German writer A. W. Spieker, showed a positive approach to the historical continuity of the Jewish people. But in encouraging religion and religious education, the editors of *Sulamith* and their contributors never lost sight of their prime objective:

linguistic and cultural assimilation. The obviously national characteristics of traditional Jewish religion lay behind their continual emphasis of the necessity to "refine" the religion and purge it of all national tradition— termed "superstitions," or "strange customs." The spokesmen for the assimilationist programme were well aware of the fact that it would be impossible to re-model German Jewry as a community of Germans of the Mosaic persuasion as long as they remained loyal to the historical striving towards Zion. Not surprisingly therefore, the enlightened men grouped around *Sulamith* attempted to eradicate the belief in the coming of the Messiah and the ingathering of the exiles from the minds of their readers. In their pursuit of assimilation, they had no compunction in distorting the implications of passages in the Talmud and the works of Maimonides, which they cited as authority for their statements. For example, David Fraenkel twisted the simile derived from Talmudic and Midrashic legend, comparing Israel's deliverance to the dawn of a new day which breaks "bit by bit," to mean that the civil emancipation of the Jews would come about by degrees rather than instantaneously. The well-known aphorism of the Sage of the Gemara Samuel Yarchinai: *Between this world and the days of the Messiah there is naught but the enslavement to the ruling monarchies* was frequently quoted. Moses Abraham Fraenkel, an associate of the editor, interpreted this to imply that "the correct and true meaning of the Messiah is but this, that the time will come when the Jews will be liberated from pressure and burdens, that is, that they will enjoy the Rights of Man like all others . . ." He reinforced this distorted interpretation by citing Maimonides' *Mishneh Torah*, Chapter XII, Section *Laws of Monarchs*: "Let it not be thought that in the days of the Messiah anything in the ways of this world will be abolished or that aught will be created anew as in the act of Genesis; the world will continue in its wonted manner." But Maimonides had made his views clear in the subsequent sentence which Fraenkel saw fit to omit from his quotation: "In the days of Messiah the King, when his Kingdom will be established and all (the people of) Israel will be gathered unto him."

Maimonides was even more unequivocally outspoken in the preceding chapter:

> And think not that Messiah the King must perform signs and tokens.* This is not so, for Rabbi Akiva was a great sage among the sages of the Mishnah, yet did he attend upon Ben Koziva (Bar-Kokhba) the King and of him he did say that he was Messiah the King.

There might, at first glance, appear to be some excuse for this rejection by the spokesmen of the new Jewish middle class of the ideal of Zion restored. They were, after all, born of a generation of Voltairean

* Biblical term for miracles.

intellectuals, enlightened men, disciples of rationalist philosophy, who could not tolerate any belief in miracles or supernatural phenomena. And it could be argued that the Jewish people's expectation of Messianic redemption was only founded on the belief in a great miracle to take place at the end of days. However, *Sulamith* adequately proved this excuse to be entirely erroneous. It was not on philosophical grounds that the Jewish middle class of Germany in the age of emancipation discarded the creed of redemption in the Land of Israel, sanctified by a thousand-year-old tradition. It was motivated more by the atrophy of its national consciousness, its adjustment to the ruling class with the sole aim of achieving equality of rights or retaining those rights they had already acquired. The fact that they discarded the Jewish hope of redemption as so much superstition, and yet emphasized their belief in the immortality of the soul—in accordance with the spiritual climate of the times, but in contradiction of all natural law—demonstrated just how "rational" their philosophy was.

Actually, in contrast to the concept of immortality, the belief in Messianic deliverance was capable of rational interpretation in no way contradicting the naturalistic outlook. Maimonides, the leading exponent of Jewish thought during the Middle Ages, had brought a rationalistic and realistic approach to bear on the Messianic belief, based on the principle that nature functions according to a logical pattern of inter-related laws. However, the "enlightened" Jews of the emancipation period in Germany did not favour this interpretation, although they unceasingly depicted Maimonides as a paragon worthy of emulation for his work in separating Judaism from its gross superstitions. Some of the enlightened writers carefully concealed Maimonides' views on the Messianic belief from their readers. Others actually tried to find confirmation for their diametrically opposed conceptions in his work. Not rationalist thought, therefore, but sheer blindness to their national affiliations, lay at the roots of the irreconcilably negative attitude that the western European Jewish middle class assumed, towards the ideal of restoration. And the new Jewish middle class of Germany were leading exponents of this attitude. They had never entirely lost the sense of inferiority of the despised and "tolerated" pedlars who had risen to the eminence of "Court Jews." From a Jewish national point of view, they sank to even lower depths than the emancipated members of their own class in other countries.

The "Consistory of Israelites in the Kingdom of Westphalia" attempted to carry out the programme of reforms in religion and customs that *Sulamith* had advocated in 1806. This Consistory was the only institution in Germany which gave to the modern Jewish middle class the opportunity to adapt Kehillah, religious and educational affairs to its own inclinations. Not surprisingly therefore, all the leaders of the Jewish Enlightenment movement in Germany and Austria felt the need to advise the Consistory President, Jacobson, on his reform plans. These advisers included David Friedlaender and Aaron Wolfssohn of Berlin, Eleazar Riesser (father of the statesman Gabriel Riesser) of Hamburg, Hertz Homberg and Peter Beer of Prague, and Ben-Ze'ev of Vienna. Their numbers were augmented by Christian dignitaries, whose advice was sought by Jacobson.

Israel Jacobson tried to implement a large part of his project in the city of Seesen, near Göttingen, in Brunswick-Hanover, after its union with Westphalia in 1810. Next door to a school he himself had endowed, he erected a temple of worship. He installed an organ, introduced choral music in Hebrew and German as a required part of the communal prayer service, ordained that the Pentateuchal portions be read in the original Hebrew and in German translation, added a number of new prayers in German, and made a sermon in the German language compulsory.

His reforms of the Kehillot of the Kingdom of Westphalia, made through the Consistory, pursued the same aims: to tie the Jews more firmly to the German "fatherland"; to encourage their assimilation; and to modify the service in the synagogue so that it might resemble the Christian service as far as possible. In view of the strong opposition of the great majority of the Jewish population, he employed caution and moderation. His initial object was to do away with as many as possible of the customs popularly practised at synagogal services and religious festivities. Under the pretext of the need to establish more "decorum and concentration" during prayer, the Consistory published a detailed ordinance at the end of September, 1810, containing over forty items. It prohibited convocation of a *minyan* outside official synagogue hours (the Central Consistory of France had also instituted this prohibition); it forbade the rabbis to teach Talmud and Kabbalah within the synagogues and only allowed them to deliver sermons; it decreed the elimination of certain passages in the prayers sung by cantor and congregation, as well as the recitation of *piyuttim* (medieval religious poetry), except on the High Holy Days; and it abolished marriage customs such as stamping on the wine-glass by the groom, the showering of bride and groom with seeds of grain, and the bride's circuit of the marriage canopy.

Jakobson and the Consistory only ventured to eliminate a few prayers from the accepted orthodox prayer service. They included Merciful Father (*Av Ha-Rachamim*), the Memorial Prayer for the deceased, and the *Akdamut* (recited before the reading of the Law at Pentecost). Also deleted was a prayer, recited at the morning service every Monday and Thursday.

> Look from heaven and see how we have become a scorn and a derision among the nations; we are accounted as sheep brought to the slaughter, to be slain and destroyed, or to be smitten and reproached .... Strangers say, There is no hope or expectancy. Be gracious unto a people that trust in Thy name. Pure One, hasten our Rescue ....

This deletion was typical of the reformers; they could not tolerate any appeal for mercy or for the early deliverance of the persecuted people. Jakobson undoubtedly struck this prayer from the service on the advice of David Friedlaender, who also influenced him in other matters. Friedlaender had already termed this prayer an anachronism, in a letter of March 30, 1799, to the Glogau merchant, Meyer Eger.

The Consistory only made a few exploratory attempts to introduce German into the prayer service, but it did substitute a prayer in the German language for the conventional Hebrew prayer of supplication for the welfare of the ruling power: *He who giveth salvation unto kings* ... On the other hand, rabbis were obliged to deliver their addresses both in the synagogues and at weddings in German. In imitation of Christian procedure, the Consistory introduced an obligatory confirmation ceremony for Jewish boys and girls on reaching the age of religious responsibility.

The Westphalian Consistory's decrees for Cassel provoked stubborn and persistent resistance from the Kehillot there. Only three Kehillot outside the capital city of Cassel—Seesen, Wolfenbüttel and Brunswick—introduced the new confirmation ceremony. In the State of Hanover, the Kehillot, armed with a recommendation from the Chancellor, Hardenberg, obtained permission to conduct the traditional prayer service. The remaining Kehillot tried to avoid the revised service by worshipping outside the synagogues, and sent innumerable applications to the government for special permits to conduct such *minyanim*.

Some rabbis refused to comply with the Consistorial decrees and actually expressed their position in statements reflecting deep concern for their religion and for the unity and national existence of the people. In a letter to Jacobson, Rabbi Zavel Eger of Halberstadt disagreed with the exclusion of certain prayers and stressed the dangers of ignorance which could result from the relegation of Hebrew to an inferior position. He powerfully proclaimed that "all Israel are brethren and comrades wheresoever they sojourn by virtue of one language ... And now, if we here shall pray in German, and the Jews who dwell in France in French, and in Italy in Italian, the bundle assuredly will fall apart ..."

While Jacobson and his associates were gradually truncating religious and traditional customs to adapt their class to the society of the dominant middle class, the first programme of extensive reforms in the Jewish religion was drawn up at Berlin, with the aim of achieving total assimilation. David Friedlaender was not satisfied with the moderation of Jacobson's plan. In October, 1812, he published an anonymous pamphlet entitled *On Reforms in Worship, in Schools, and in Education, Which Have Become Indispensable in View of the New Organization of the Jews in the Prussian States*. He submitted this pamphlet to the King, to Hardenberg, and to the General-Director of the government Department of Education. He demanded the deletion of all prayers of mourning and lamentation at the loss of Jewish national independence and of supplication for national revival and Messianic deliverance. These were, he argued, justifiable while the Jews were the victims of oppression and filled with longing to return to Palestine, which they regarded as their motherland. "Now that their political liberation has been consummated," he declared, "we acknowledge but one fatherland, Prussia, and only for its well-being is it our duty to pray." He also thought it necessary to further Prussian patriotism by the introduction of worship in German—"our mother tongue"—instead of in Hebrew, especially as Hebrew could no longer serve as a sacred or inspiring language. Finally, he stressed the importance of installing organs in synagogues as music had the power to arouse dormant faith.

Friedlaender's religious reforms were only intended for enlightened people who felt that they were needed, and he was prepared to allow orthodox Jews to conduct their religious affairs as they wished. His educational programme, however, was designed to embrace Jewish youth as a whole. The basis of reforms in religious education was the total removal of Hebrew from the curriculum of the Jewish schools. He also proposed that a catechism be drawn up, as an adjunct to the study of Jewish religion, which would comprehend in a "scientific system" all the principles of faith based solely on the "Old Testament."

Most of Friedlaender's colleagues on the Berlin Kehillah Board voiced their support of his reform programme in memoranda to the government, and he also gained adherents from amongst the extreme assimilationists in Berlin and the Breslau Kehillah. However, the vast majority of Prussian Jews violently opposed the proposed reforms in religion and education. Even the spokesmen of Enlightenment circles treated them with extreme caution: they were unhappy about the suggestions to eliminate Hebrew from the prayer service and to eradicate the ideal of Messianic redemption. Enlightened circles in the Silesian area were particularly vociferous in their reservations. Their arguments in favour of retaining Hebrew for at least some time ranged from expedience to a positive respect for the sacred status of the language of the Scriptures and prayer service.

The Chanceller, Hardenberg, wholeheartedly supported Friedlaender's programme both in his replies to its critics and his suggestions to the King. To ascertain the Jewish population's opinion of the reforms, the government ordered the Kehillot of Berlin, Potsdam, Breslau, and Königsberg to elect by general ballot two deputies from each Kehillah who would communicate with the Department of Education. The results of the elections in the Berlin Kehillah at the beginning of 1813 proved that the extreme reformists were in an absolute minority even in the capital city—they obtained approximately one-third of all votes. In the event, the conclave of Kehillah deputies never took place; the war against Napoleon broke out a few days later. However, the main obstacle to the implementation of the programme was the refusal of the King. He notified his Minister that "as long as the Jews want to be Jews," he would sanction no changes except those which did not contradict the basic elements of Jewish faith. His true motives became apparent some years later when he opposed the erection of a reformed temple at Berlin: the Prussian King was afraid that a reformed religion would not be sufficient to stem the spread of freethinking amongst the Jews and that this might have an unfavourable influence upon their Christian neighbours.

The New Education; Last of the Me'asfim

While religious reform was still only a dream cherished by Friedlaender and his group and the initial experiment in Westphalia had barely been launched, the spokesmen for the German-Jewish assimilationists were wholeheartedly engaged in establishing German schools for Jewish youth. At the end of the eighteenth century, there were only three such institutions in all Germany: the *Hinukh Nearim* (*Freischule*) at Berlin, founded in 1778, the *Wilhelmschule* at Breslau (1791) and the *Jüdische Freischule* at Dessau (1799). At the beginning of the nineteenth century, several additional schools were founded by individual Jewish magnates or by societies of wealthy donors. In 1801, Israel Jacobson established a school at Seesen, in the State of Brunswick; in 1804, the *Maskilim* finally realised their ambition and founded the *Philantropin* School at Frankfurt-on-Main; and in 1807, a *Freischule* was erected at Wolfenbüttel in Brunswick in memory of the philanthropist Isaac Hertz Samson, Jacobson's brother-in-law. After the Westphalian Consistory had been established, it opened schools in the capital city of Cassel (in 1809), in the cities of Brunswick, Halberstadt, Hildesheim, Peine, Hanover and Paderborn, and in a few cities in the Department of Fulda. Schools were even founded in backward Bavaria, in 1810: in Munich, Bamberg, and in the village of Altenkunstadt. In Hamburg, the Kehillah introduced the teaching of handwriting and arithmetic into the Talmud-Torah, and, while under French administration, it undertook to pay for the tuition of a number of needy children. The first schools in Europe for Jewish girls were opened in Breslau and Dessau in 1804. Altogether, by the end of the Napoleonic era, there were over twenty Jewish schools in Germany, more than half of them located within the Kingdom of Westphalia and under the supervision of the Westphalian Jewish Consistory.

The general curriculum in these schools varied with local conditions and the number of pupils and classes. In the advanced schools, such as those at Berlin, Breslau, Dessau, Frankfurt, Seesen, Wolfenbüttel and Cassel, the curriculum was quite comprehensive. Apart from German and elementary arithmetic, it also included French, history, geography, the natural sciences and drawing. The Berlin schools also taught geometry and book-keeping. The study of Latin was initially introduced at Seesen, and of Polish at Breslau (because of its importance in trade with Poland). The teaching methods employed at the best of these schools incorporated the most progressive in educational theory of the time. The Dessau school, in particular, was strongly influenced by the fathers of the new education: Basedow, Campe and Pestalozzi.

In conjunction with the new educational institutions, steps were also taken to teach Jewish youth useful occupations. Only the Berlin *Freischule* proposed to train clerks and merchants. The Westphalian Consistory, instead, drew up a curriculum that also gave instruction in handicrafts. The curriculum was never carried out in full, but the school at Seesen did assign a plot of land to each pupil for agricultural training.

The programmes of Jewish studies in the German Jewish Schools included varying degrees of Hebrew and the Bible. At the Berlin School, the only Jewish subject at first taught was Hebrew, and the pupils had to supplement their Jewish education by private tuition or at a *Heder*. The Pentateuch was later added—though more additions had in fact been contemplated. At Breslau, Wolfenbüttel, and the Consistory school at Cassel, Hebrew grammar and the whole Old Testament were taught. At Cassel, twenty-four hours a week were devoted to Jewish studies in the upper classes. At Wolfenbüttel a small group of pupils were taught Mishnah and Talmud. Talmud and the *Mishneth-Torah* of Maimonides were compulsory subjects at the Teachers' Seminary that the Consistory opened at Cassel in 1810. In Breslau, instruction in Talmud was the subject of a controversy between the orthodox Kehillah leaders and the enlightened school board. The Kehillah leaders, who were responsible for the conduct of the *Hadarim*, thought religious education would be jeopardized if entrusted to unbelievers.

The open assimilationism of the new schools and their rejection of traditional religion antagonized the orthodox mass of the Jewish population. Because of orthodox opposition, the school at Munich in Bavaria only lasted three years. The *Hadarim* continued to exist in Westphalia despite a request from the Consistory to the Departmental Prefects that "clandestine schools" be prohibited wherever qualified teachers were available. The decree banning the *Heder* was only effectively enforced in Mendelssohn's native town of Dessau, where instruction by private teachers was prohibited.

In addition to religious opposition, most of these schools also ran into grave financial difficulties. They were mainly intended for the children of the poor. The wealthier classes, apart from a group of philanthropists, hired private tutors to teach their sons and were indifferent to the schools. The poorer members of the Kehillot were neither willing nor able to maintain the schools by supplementary Kehillah taxes. They were able to exist in these circumstances on funds provided by individual donors, or on annual contributions by patrons. Some of the leading schools, at Dessau, Hildesheim, Frankfurt, and Bamberg, for example, received sizable annual government subsidies as well as donations from generous nobles (as at Hildesheim). However, the only school that prospered in Westphalia was in the capital, Cassel, where it was directly maintained by the Consistory. The schools in the provincial towns, which depended on Kehillah support, struggled along in great straits. By 1815, the first year of post-Napoleonic reaction, only three Consistorial schools in the now defunct kingdom of Westphalia survived: at Paderborn, Brunswick and Hildesheim. Even the school at Cassel had completely closed down. In the course of time, under the impetus of the growing reaction, the Kehillot themselves felt the need to establish special schools for Jewish children. Yet the schools of the Napoleonic period, though none survived for long, succeeded in intensifying that process of linguistic and cultural assimilation amongst the Jewish youth of Germany for which they had been intended.

The *Me'asef* resumed publication in Berlin, as a quarterly, in autumn 1809, reflecting the last glow of the Hebrew *Haskalah* movement of Germany. Its list of subscribers and the origins of its contributors showed the effects of the spread of linguistic assimilation and the corresponding decline in the number of people conversant with Hebrew. The centre of the *Haskalah* movement had begun to move to the eastern fringes of central Europe, with branches stretching into eastern Europe. Even the new editor of the *Me'asef* was a Polish Jew from Mezheritch, (a district of Posen), Shalom Hacohen, and its regular contributors were mostly *Maskilim* from Bohemia, Hungary, and the provincial towns of Silesia and Poland, particularly the Posen area.

The main object of the earlier issues of the *Me'asef* had been to disseminate Enlightenment. But the editor of the revived periodical deliberately set out to rally the few *Maskilim* scattered throughout Germany for the purpose of fostering the now neglected Hebrew language and literature. The emphasis was not laid on the *Haskalah* movement *per se* but on Hebrew as the language of *Haskalah*. The principal aim of the *Me'asef* quarterly was therefore to provide a means of expression for all who cherished the Hebrew language, and Shalom Hacohen took care not to offend the orthodox circles whom he hoped to add to his reading public. The time was long past when the Hebrew *Haskalah* movement of Germany had, in the name of rationalism, attacked any manifestation of religious fanaticism, superstitious credulity, or anything that seemed outdated in religious tradition. However, this change in attitude towards religion was dictated not only by the desire to widen the ranks of the "Lovers of Hebrew." The spirit of "religiosity" that pervaded the Jewish middle class during the period of Napoleonic rule was expressed in the new *Me'asef*—in Hebrew—and had in fact already appeared in the monthly German-language *Sulamith*. In the German introduction to a collection of his Hebrew poems, *Oriental Plants on Northern Soil* (1807), Shalom Hacohen deplored the fact that enlightened Jews thought that a cultural "rapprochement" with other peoples could only be reached by casting off traditional customs.

The revived *Me'asef* totally lacked the militant tone which had characterized the previous series, especially under the editorship of Isaac Euchel and his colleagues, and had given it the freshness of a regeneration of Jewish life. Its contents were not enough to fill the void. As before, every issue contained poems, commentaries on biblical passages, "explanations of Hebrew words," popularly written chapters on general history and on outstanding figures in Jewish history, articles on natural science, and a review of current Jewish events. But the translations from Gessner in the old *Me'asfim* had already been a sign of literary stagnation at the end of the preceding century. Now, in the Hebrew quarterly published at the climax of the Napoleonic age, they were certain proof of cultural decay. Only a few of the poems published in the *Me'asef*, showed a modicum of poetic inspiration—for example, the dramatic poem *Moses and Zipporah* by Gabriel Berger of Prague, or romance in verse, *There, in the Land of Galilee* by Dov Ber Ginzburg of Brody. Shalom Hacohen, himself a teacher at the Berlin *Freischule*, published in addition to his *Oriental Plants* an allegorical tale, *Amal and Tirzah*, in 1812, after the quarterly *Me'asef* had ceased publication. Naphtali Hertz Wessely regarded Hacohen as heir to his poetic mission, "destined to be the saviour of the Hebrew tongue," and he did in fact make a positive contribution to Hebrew poetry. He was much influenced by Rousseau in his glorification of the natural life and the happiness of the tiller of the soil, while his romantic idyll also expressed the concept of "productive labour" which had been one of the main tenets of the *Haskalah* movement. The spirit of Rousseau's social theory and the social radicalism of the French Revolution was also reflected in the protest of the oppressed against the rule of tyrants and social evils in his *A Tale of Naboth the Jezreelite* and *Amal and Tirzah*. But in his role as editor of the *Me'asef* Shalom Hacohen did not convey the slightest intimation of this revolt. He converted the Hebrew periodical, on the lines of the German *Sulamith*, into an auxiliary of the Westphalian and Dutch Consistories and the assimilated Jewish middle class who controlled them.

It would appear that Shalom Hacohen agreed with the charitable plutocrats who supported his magazine on the programme for assimilation as far as the spoken vernacular was concerned, and made wholehearted efforts to promote it. In the summer of 1809 he published an *Epistle to the Sages of Israel in Poland*, urging them to follow the example of the Jews of Holland, extirpate Yiddish, "that vile and ridiculous language of Ashkenaz," and replace it by Polish. The Epistle followed an announcement by the *Train a Child Society* (*Hanokh La-Na'ar*) of Amsterdam concerning the translation of the Pentateuch into Dutch by Moses Belinfante. Hacohen, a representative of the surviving remnants of the German *Maskilim*, used all the arguments in *Haskalah* literature to prove the need as well as the advantages that would result if the Jews of Poland, like those of Holland, France, and Germany, could speak with one another and with "the people of their fatherlands and birthplaces" in an unblemished tongue, the "language of the country of their birth." Polish, he contended, was necessary for them "when holding converse with the country's great men and its leaders, or when granted audience by kings." In this way, "the people of God" would cease to be the object of "scorn and defamation" in the eyes of the country's inhabitants, "their brethren." He also used the argument already employed by his mentor, Wessely, at an earlier date: a proper understanding of the Old Testament, "the niceties of expression in Hebrew," and "some of the sayings of our sages" was impossible without a knowledge of "the tongue of our native land."

The same factors which had precipitated the end of the earlier *Me'asfim* were also responsible for the failure of the revived quarterly version. At the beginning of 1812, after only three years' existence, it too ceased publication. The progressive Jewish middle class in Germany no longer needed the *Haskalah* movement—all the more as its own spokesmen cordially supported the programme of linguistic assimilation and did not even openly condemn cultural assimilation. A common front was now shared by the Hebrew poet, Shalom Hacohen, the associates of Israel Jacobson, founder of the "temple," and the Hebrew writers, Solomon Pappenheim and Peter Beer, the authorized "Germanizer" of Bohemian and Moravian Jewry. The result of this was to strengthen the position of the members of the group who felt no remorse at the fate of the Hebrew language—the one surviving glory of the *Haskalah* movement in Germany, which in its decline lacked all social content and objective. Within German Jewry, only the orthodox conservatives persevered in their loyalty to the Hebrew tongue and still associated with its revival their hope for their people's redemption in their own country.

CHAPTER EIGHT

THE HABSBURG EMPIRE

Policy under Joseph II and during the Period of Reaction

Approximately 400,000 Jews lived in the countries under Austrian domination during the reign of the enlightened despot, Joseph II, though the census of 1785 only showed 356,962. Of the official total, 212,000 lived in Galicia, a Polish-Ukrainian province beyond the Carpathians, which was severed from Poland by the First Partition (1772). There were two other large Jewish communities: one in Hungary, with 75,089 people; the other in Bohemia-Moravia, numbering 68,794. There were very few Jews in the German-Austrian lands. A total of 652 Jews was recorded in all Upper and Lower Austria, most of them in Vienna. No Jews at all were registered in Tyrol, Styria, or Carinthia. The Kehillah in Trieste, with approximately 1,500 people was not included in the census returns.

Joseph II's policy was to promote the economic development of the countries of his realm. He was particularly concerned with commerce and industry, where he favoured a system of mercantilism. To facilitate the expansion of manual trades and crafts, he released all occupations which did not require particular specialization—for example, weaving or knitting—from guild authority. His social policy was linked to his economic system. On the one hand, he curtailed the prerogatives of the nobles and placed them under the jurisdiction of the governmental authorities, laws and courts. On the other, he improved the legal status of the peasants. With the total concentration of governing power in the hands of the absolutist régime, the autonomy of the estates was curbed or reduced to a minimum, and what survived was subject to strict administrative supervision. The Catholic Church was also made subject to imperial control, though the Emperor generously supported it. He was anxious to spread learning amongst his subjects; he introduced compulsory school education and raised the rank of the teaching profession in the hierarchy of state service.

In 1781, in accordance with his general policy, in economic matters, administration, education and national and religious questions, the Emperor set about revising the legal position of the Jews in his Empire. On March 13, 1781, he sent an imperial writ to the court chancelleries in Austria and Hungary outlining reforms for the Jews to be instituted in all the lands under his rule. In the same year, imperial edicts affecting the Jews of Bohemia, Silesia and Austrian Italy (Trieste and its surrounding areas) were issued. At the beginning of 1782, a *Toleranzpatent* was promulgated for the Jews of Lower Austria (Vienna) and Moravia. Others followed for the Jews of Hungary, in 1783, and Galicia, in 1789. The enlightened circles of Europe were greatly impressed by the first intimations of Joseph's enactments on behalf of the Jews in 1781. And the grandiloquent phraseology of the conventional preamble to his *Toleranzpatent* for the Jews certainly gave the impression that the Emperor honestly hoped to offer the Jews the same privileges as all his other subjects. In reality however, the Emperor's actions were governed by the prospect of benefit to his own domains, rather than of civil equality for the Jews or their welfare: "... In order to make the members of the Jewish nation, who are so numerous in the lands of my inheritance, more useful to the State than they hitherto could be with their sources of livelihood so limited that in consequence they have deemed the pathways of learning superfluous ..." Despite this declaration, only a few new branches of employment were opened to the Jews, and even these grudgingly, with petty obstacles and innumerable limitations inherent in a Christian police state. Thus, Jews were now allowed to till the soil, but under conditions that nullified the permission: they were still forbidden to buy estates or peasant holdings, and were allowed to rent estates (excluding peasant holdings) only in places where they held domiciliary rights and on condition that they cultivated the soil themselves and not with the assistance of hired Christians (whom they were only permitted to employ during the first years of tenure). In much the same way, Jews were allowed to practise all crafts and "free trades" that were not organized. As to guild crafts, Jews could learn these skills from Christian craftsmen, but it was specifically stated that the latter were not obliged to accept Jewish apprentices, or assistants. As a result, few Jews, on the strength of the new edict of toleration, could enter occupations previously closed to them. Concessions granted to the Jews in commerce were more substantial. The wholesale trade, petty trading and peddling were now specifically opened to Jews. When fairs were held, Jews could lodge in cities where rights of permanent domicile were denied them—in contrast with previous prohibitions. Trade was also facilitated by the abolition of the special Jewish *Leibmaut* (the Austrian *Leibzoll*, or poll tax) and double court fees. All these reforms naturally increased Jewish self-respect. On the other hand, the severest restraints on Jewish retail trade remained in force: stores could not be opened outside the Jewish quarter, and the ban on storekeeping in general, and on "the burgher trades," continued to be effective in most of these countries.

On the whole, therefore, Joseph's economic concessions were not far different from those granted to the Jews in any other country under a benevolent despot. From the outset, the principal object of the reforms was to clear the way for large-scale Jewish capital, which was of greater significance in terms of mercantilist policy, and which would not encroach on the monopolistic rights of the Christian middle class. The mass of the Jewish population only gained the benefit of some relaxation of a few restrictions on trade and the manual occupations, while they were still oppressed by the cruel institution of family quotas and the prohibition of natural increase (this proscription did not apply to the Jews of Galicia and Hungary). Similarly, the Emperor's *Toleranzpatent* fully confirmed the exclusion of Jews from residence in the cities and villages outside their permanent habitat. The special Jewish taxes were increased and most of them were converted into indirect taxes (for example, the Kosher meat tax) under the fiscal system of the absolutist régime so that the burden fell even more on the poor and the lower classes.

The Emperor's reasons for retaining these, the harshest of the anti-Jewish decrees, were intrinsically linked with his economic and ecclesiastical policy. His desire to improve trade and industry conflicted with his publicly avowed aim of protecting the established position of the Christian burghers. In any case, Joseph II was not fond of the Jews and agreed with his high-ranking officials, that "their morals are exceedingly depraved."

He never entirely abandoned an idea of his mother's, the Empress Maria Theresa, to convert her Jewish subjects. But he was not unaware of the difficulties involved in such a drastic programme. As far as the Jews of his own and the following generation were concerned, he confined his efforts to educational measures designed to change them into "useful" citizens of the state. An important feature of this programme to reform Jewish education and thereby bring Jew closer to Christian was compulsory school attendance. The Jews were ordered to found special German schools. If they were unable to establish a school of their own, they were required to send their children to a Christian school. Secondary schools and universities were also thrown open to Jewish youth without proviso or restriction—except that occasionally the permission was deliberately phrased so that it only applied to the sons of well-to-do-parents (as in the *Letters Patent* to the Jews of Moravia). Jewish secondary school pupils were allowed to go to school after morning prayers and allowed to leave before the closing service. Furthermore, Jewish pupils were permitted to sit in class with covered heads if they so wished. In 1786, an Imperial Court decree ruled that any Jew in the Austrian Empire who wished to obtain a marriage licence must possess a certificate of elementary school education. As a result of the consistent implementation of this policy, a larger proportion of Jewish young people attended school in the Austrian Empire before the French Revolution than in all the countries of western Europe during the initial period of enfranchisement following the outbreak of the Revolution!

From the inception of his reform, the Emperor's attempts to raise the educational level of the Jews were inseparably connected with his desire to bring about their linguistic and national assimilation. His announcement to the Court Chancellery of his intention to grant the Jews *Toleranzpatent* gave priority in the list of effective ways of reforming the Jews to "the abolition of their national speech." The Letters Patent subsequently published specifically mentioned abolishing "the tongue called Jewish, which is a mixture of Hebrew and German," and the Hebrew language. Any document written in Hebrew, Yiddish, or even in Hebrew script was invalid for legal or other official purposes. The *Patent* of 1787 concerning Jewish names represented a further step towards eradicating Hebrew and Yiddish. It required Jews to adopt German names and even surnames (excluding Yiddish surnames), and obliged rabbis—on pain of severe penalties—to keep records of births, circumcisions, marriages, and deaths in the German language. Between 1783 and 1785 Jewish jurisdiction in litigation between Jews had already been terminated and placed under the imperial law courts.

Thus, after the reforms of Joseph II, the Jews of the Austrian Empire lived under the centralized régime of a modern state subject to its uniform administration and laws and, like other subjects, obliged to fulfil all the duties of citizenship. But they did not possess the corresponding rights. The large Jewish population of the Habsburg Empire—with the exception of Galicia—enjoyed a mere caricature of emancipation.

A period of political reaction followed Joseph's death in 1790 and continued unabated until the revolution of 1848. During the two years of his reign (1790-92), Joseph's brother, Leopold II, succeeded in restoring some of their special privileges to the nobility and the Church, but there was no adverse change in policy towards the Jews—apart from the first of the decrees against their entry into the capital. Leopold's desire to strengthen religion even led to some relaxation in those regulations, introduced by Joseph, that had interfered with the observance of Jewish laws.

The full weight of reaction in the Austrian Empire fell on the Jews during the reign of Francis II (1792-1835) who was crowned Emperor Francis I of Austria when Napoleon liquidated the Holy Roman Empire in 1806. Narrow-minded and of limited vision, he led all the coalitions of the feudal kingdoms of Europe against revolutionary France and later against Napoleon. He also enforced a policy of absolutism, national repression, clericalism and unremitting police surveillance. He only retained those of Joseph II's reforms for the Jews which were directed towards their "Germanization" and the abolition of communal autonomy—and he strengthened these with fresh decrees. He abolished all the Kehillot in Bohemia except that at Prague; he left the Kehillot intact in the other countries of the Empire mainly to ensure the efficient collection of imperial taxes. The Kehillot were ordered to elect *Parnassim* who could write and speak German (in Moravia and at Prague), while the rabbis in Bohemia were not only required to know the language of the state but also to complete a course of university studies. The government openly acknowledged its intention of "distilling" the Jewish religion by "purging" the Talmud and rabbinical literature of "obnoxious ideas". Joseph II had hoped to achieve assimilation of the Jews mainly by new methods of education. Francis feared the spread of Enlightenment amongst the Jews and was content with "Germanization" decrees. During his reign the special German schools for Jews in Galicia and Hungary were closed and Jewish youth there left with no secular education whatsoever.

Together with the increase in "Germanization" decrees, frequent restrictions reduced the rights of domicile and the economic rights of the Jews. The Jewish trading magnates and industrialists alone continued to partake of the special concessions and privileges they had enjoyed under Joseph II, so that the Jewish factories in Bohemia, Moravia and Austria, actually prospered during Francis's reign. The mass of the Jewish population in Bohemia was oppressed by new decrees published in the *Patent* of 1797, by strict limitations on their right of entry into Vienna, and by prohibitions on their pursuit of certain branches of trade (grains, salt, gunpowder, and other commodities). The Jews now had to bear a particularly heavy burden of special taxes: rates were doubled and trebled under Francis and new taxes, such as the candle tax in Galicia, were added. During the reign of Joseph II, Jews had fulfilled their military service obligations in the transport corps; this was no longer considered sufficient and henceforth they had to risk their lives on European battle-fields on behalf of a sovereign who despised the Jews and fought the Revolution.

According to the official census, 451,161 Jews lived under this reactionary régime within the boundaries of the Austrian Empire in 1803. This also included Jews in a province recently severed from Poland: by the Third Partition in 1795, Austria acquired the eastern, Lublin, part of central Poland (with the cities of Lublin, Siedlce and Radom), which was included in the Empire as "Western Galicia." The 1803 census recorded 95,586 Jews in this province. Austria lost it again in 1809 in the war against Napoleon and it was ceded to the Duchy of Warsaw. However, even without "Western Galicia," the authorities in Lower Austria had (with some exaggeration) estimated that a total of over 600,000 Jews lived in Austria in 1791.

A. THE CAPITAL, VIENNA

From Maria Theresa to the Reaction

The history of the Jews in Vienna during the period of transition from feudalism to capitalism reflected two major factors. In the first place, it was governed by the changes in the Jewish policies of the Austrian rulers, which always depended on the aims of the current régime. In the second, it was influenced by the increasingly important role the Jewish population played in the Empire's economy—which enabled them to overcome imperial edicts and harsh police repression.

At the beginning of the age of enlightened despotism, in 1781, there were only thirty-three "tolerated" Jewish families in the capital city of Austria. With their households and servants, they consisted of 550 people. Even these "tolerated" few were not allowed to organize themselves into a Kehillah or build a synagogue. This was one of the oldest Jewish communities in Europe, but its historical continuity had been twice interrupted by expulsions: 214 Jewish men and women were burned at the stake, charged under the *Vienna Decree* of 1421 with desecrating the Sacramental Host. All the remaining Jews in the city and throughout the country were stripped of all their belongings and expelled. Again, in 1670, the Jews of Vienna (who had grown into a sizable Kehillah of three or four thousand during the seventeenth century) were expelled from the city by command of Leopold I. Their ghetto was renamed Leopoldstadt (today the IInd District of Vienna).

In actual fact, the religious zeal of the devout Catholic rulers was not the most important factor in the elimination of the Jews from Vienna and from the state as a whole. Of decisive significance was their desire to protect the urban Christians against competition from Jewish merchants, petty tradesmen and pedlars. However, the Austrian rulers never denied permission to enter the capital to individual Jews possessing large sums of capital. The early eighteenth century was a golden age for the Court Jews. Groups of Jews, who dealt with the rulers, were allowed to settle in a number of German capitals such as Munich and Stuttgart. The limited number of Jewish families of finance magnates, bankers, suppliers, monopoly lessees (salt, tobacco), and contractors to the Imperial Mint, who rose to eminence at Vienna, included Samuel Oppenheimer, Samson Wertheimer and Diego d'Aguilar.

During the second half of the eighteeenth century, the golden age of the Court Jews came to an end in Vienna and indeed throughout all Germany. The lack of stability in the economic position of the Jews meant that the capital inherited from wealthy magnates did not survive. However, the constant growth of the city as a commercial centre continued to palliate the repressive decrees directed against Jewish trade and the increase in the Jewish population. In 1764, Maria Theresa allowed Viennese Jews to trade in the products of Austrian factories. She even encouraged them to establish their own factories—on condition, of course, they only employed Christian workmen. Although servants were forbidden to engage in any type of commerce, as were the families of these "tolerated" Jews, many Jews actually lived permanently in Vienna where they conducted their affairs under the cover of service with the holders of domiciliary rights. An incomparably greater number of Jews arrived in the capital on business from all the countries of the Empire: Bohemia, Moravia, Hungary,

Trieste, Gorizia, and also—after 1772—from Galicia. Under the statute of 1764, these people had to pay a poll tax of one gulden when they entered the city on ordinary days and two gulden when a fair was being held. This tax was farmed out to Jewish partnerships for an annual sum of 6,000 gulden. The number of Jews entering and leaving Vienna in the course of one year reached several thousand, and included two exceptionally wealthy merchants, partners from the ancient city of Buda in Hungary, who annually purchased goods to the value of 100,000 gulden at the Vienna fairs.

Despite the increasingly important role that the Jews played in the city's trade, Maria Theresa refused to make the slightest concession in any of the decrees that burdened them. All Jewish traders from out of town, except those from Trieste and Turkey, were compelled to crowd together in two prescribed inns. The "tolerated" Jewish residents of Vienna were forbidden to live in buildings that housed Christian tenants. In 1772, all Jews who did not live in special houses were forced to evacuate their homes and move into a special building. To increase the distinction between Jew and Christian, the Statute of 1764 ordered Jewish males to grow beards!

The new Emperor abolished many of his mother's worst decrees and at the beginning of 1782 issued his *Toleranzpatent* for the Jews of Lower Austria and Vienna. Despite the numerous stern prohibitions which remained, Joseph's modifications benefited the Jews of Vienna immeasurably more than the Jews of any other part of his Empire, because of the marked contrast with their previous state of subjection.

The Vienna *Letters Patent* like the *Letters Patent* for Jews throughout the Empire, granted them permission to learn a trade under Christian craftsmen, to work for them as assistants, and to engage in any trade or calling. It added a proviso preventing them acquiring the status of *Stradtbürger* (freeman, or burgher), or the title of *Meister* (master craftsman); Christian craftsmen were not obliged to accept Jews as apprentices or assistants. Jews were allowed to pursue *Grosshandel* (wholesale trade) on the same conditions as Christian traders. This also applied to all "non-burgher trade," with the exception of storekeeping, which was a monopoly of the Christian townsmen. The right of Jews to open factories was not only confirmed but actually encouraged. Jews who established factories anywhere within Austria outside of the capital were allowed to take up residence there—although this was generally forbidden otherwise. They were permitted to grant mortgage loans on condition Jews in Vienna were allowed to employ Christian and Jewish servants as hitherto, Jews were not allowed to acquire immovable assets). "Tolerated" Jews in Vienna were allowed to employ Christian and Jewish servants as required, but with the stipulation that the Jewish servants must not engage in commerce independently. As before, married Jewish servants were forbidden to live in Vienna with their families unless their wives (or husbands in the case of maid-servants) and children who had reached their majority were similarly employed as servants. All restrictions on the dwelling rights of "tolerated" Jews were revoked and they were free to live wherever they pleased amongst Christians in the city and its suburbs. As in the Empire generally, the Jews of Vienna were freed from the requirement to pay a double fee in the courts of justice. Laws imposing special marks of identification such as beards, segregating Jew from Christian, were rescinded. Jews were no longer forbidden to appear on the streets on Sundays or on Christian holidays before noon, or to frequent gaming houses. Prosperous Jewish merchants and *Honoratiores** were permitted to wear swords as a mark of honour. All institutions of learning, from elementary schools to colleges, were opened to Jewish youth, and the Viennese Jews were also instructed to open a special school of their own. Jews from out of town were allowed to stay in the city on business for a specified period of time on condition that they registered with the authorities and did not prolong their stay beyond the time limit indicated on their permits. They were relieved of payment of the poll tax and permitted to take lodgings and rent warehouses in any part of the city.

Yet, despite all these concessions, the age-old attitude towards the Jews of Vienna, maintained throughout the city's history, was expressly reaffirmed: their presence there was merely tolerated. "Tolerated status" permits were granted at the government's discretion, contingent on the extent of the applicant's property, the nature of his affairs, and the amount of protection tax he undertook to pay.

During Joseph II's brief reign, his *Toleranzpatent* achieved precisely the results he had envisaged. Despite permission to engage in manual trades, not a single Jewish artisan emerged from Vienna's Jewish population during the decade. On the other hand, Jewish wholesale trade in Vienna prospered and reached extensive proportions, primarily as a result of the activity of out-of-town Jews who had easier access to the city after the removal of the severest restrictions. The number of Jews allowed to reside permanently in Vienna had more than doubled, but still comprised less than a hundred families and thus virtually fulfilled the Emperor's wish not to see the capital's Jewish population increased. These Jews however, included a class of enormously wealthy merchants and powerful financiers.

The importance of Jews in Vienna's commerce during this period may best be gauged by the constant rise in the numbers of temporary business visitors from all corners of the Empire. Official statistics recorded that 10,546 Jews entered Vienna in 1789, although only 3,240 had registered on entry as required by law. Several of these "guests" visited the city at frequent, sometimes monthly, intervals. Many merchants from nearby Moravia actually lived in the city for all practical purposes for years on end, by regularly renewing their entry permits. Traders and pedlars dealing in old clothes and fancy goods also made their way into town in

---

* An official title, with attendant privileges, conferred on distinguished burghers.

the wake of the merchants. The Catholic merchants were only waiting for an appropriate occasion to protest against "the Jewish invasion" of the capital. Their opportunity came with the death of the reforming Emperor, when a wave of reaction engulfed the realm of the Habsburgs.

New decrees governing the entry of Jews into Vienna signalled the growing strength of reaction during the first year of Francis's reign. In 1792 a law was promulgated establishing a *Judenamt*, a special office to supervise the entry and departure of Jews to and from the city. Every Jew who arrived had, without exception, to obtain permission from this office. It was only granted for fourteen days and was renewable for an additional fourteen days at the discretion of the officials. The permit entailed the payment of a fee of half a gulden, known as a *Billet* (ticket). This was raised to one gulden in 1807, and to two gulden for foreign Jews. Jewish pedlars, grocers, and artisans such as engravers, musicians, and paper-dyers, were expressly barred from receiving permits. All Jews in Vienna who did not possess a "ticket" were expelled from the city. The "tolerated" Jews of the capital considered this measure a blow to their pride and they realized the danger it represented to the *Toleranzpatent*. They interceded with the government and even offered to pay an annual compensation fee in return for the abolition of the *Billet*. Their request was rejected. Both the *Judenamt* and the payment of the *Billet* remained in effect until the revolution of 1848!

The government now issued a series of new decrees aimed at preventing an increase in Vienna's Jewish population, especially the settlement of people without substantial assets. In 1794, they decided not to issue any further toleration permits except for limited periods; a ruling stated that in future the Emperor himself would issue "toleration" permits. Two years later, the widows of deceased "tolerated" Jews were required to apply for "toleration" permits in their own names, six weeks after the death of their husbands. In 1807, a new edict provided that "toleration" permits would only be granted in exceptional cases—such as wholesalers who possessed a capital of at least 60,000 gulden. The "toleration" fee was continuously increased as a result of a decision by the Emperor that people who were "tolerated" for an unlimited period or for the duration of their lives must report on the state of their assets every three years. Those "tolerated" for specified periods had to give a report whenever they applied for an extension.

As a result of these rigid enactments the Jewish population officially allowed to live in Vienna did not increase during the first decades of the nineteenth century. But its importance in the economy of the city and the Empire as a whole certainly did. The 130 "tolerated" Jewish families, some 1,300 individuals, altogether constituted less than one-half per cent of Vienna's total population of 300,000. Records for 1804 show that a quarter of the number of Jewish families was occupied in catering for the needs of the small Jewish community (kosher wine bottlers, butchers, restaurant keepers) which could not possibly bring them wealth. However, there was also a significant group of financial magnates. In 1789 five *Grosshändler* were registered; in 1804 fifteen of these big merchants were mentioned by name. Socially, this group also included ten bankers, suppliers and monopoly leaseholders, as well as the banking house of Nathan Arnstein and his partner, Bernhard Eskeles, which earned a wide reputation. The great economic role that these financiers filled was confirmed by the fact that by 1804 nine of them were already listed as *noblemen*, and that this title had, for the most part, been conferred after the accession of that zealous Catholic, Emperor Francis.

Merchants with lesser capital assets also occupied an important position in the commerce of the capital. Some of the wholesalers dealt in grains and raw materials such as wool and hides, while others exported the finished products of the textile, silk and dry-goods factories in and around Vienna to all the imperial territories, benefiting from the fact that Vienna was at the crossroads of the vast empire's trade routes. The Viennese Jews were able to maintain these commercial connections through their contacts with the Jews who flocked to the capital in their thousands from all parts of the Kingdom: Bohemia and Moravia, Hungary and Galicia. Despite the frequently renewed bans on entry, over ten thousand Jewish imperial subjects entered Vienna every year. They employed every conceivable stratagem to prolong their stay in the city beyond the legal period: some claimed the need for extended medical care by Viennese doctors, others submitted applications to the authorities and then awaited the replies; others contrived to land in jail under arrest—whence they sallied forth daily to attend to their business affairs. Only very few succeeded in obtaining official permits to remain in the city for one or two years as the agents of provincial trading firms. In actual fact, Jewish merchants from provincial towns also played a great role in the city's commerce. Up to the end of the eighteenth century, the only occasions for the purchase of the products of the Styrian steel industry and the textile goods of Bohemia and Moravia had been the fairs at Vienna, Linz, Graz, and especially Brünn. The development of the textile and fancy goods industry at Vienna produced the need for round-the-year supplies instead of the customary market days. Their quickness and experience in provincial trade made the Jewish merchants most suited to the task of commercial reorganization. These men bought the products of the factories in the Vienna suburbs and sold them in their home towns. Similarly, they purchased the handiwork of the Bohemian and Moravian weavers who brought it to Vienna. Persecuted by a reactionary government, the Jews none the less pioneered modern methods in Austrian trade and promoted the development of industry in the capital—where they were strictly forbidden to live.

Vienna was thus important as a political metropolis and economic centre for the Jews of the Austrian Empire. In contrast, it had not yet acquired any significance as a centre of Jewish culture and enlightenment. Unlike Berlin, it lacked organized Jewish community life and a hinterland of Jews in the provincial towns with communal links with the capital.

The ban on an organized Kehillah in Vienna remained in effect. However, an unofficial body, apart from the Old and the New Burial Societies, had existed since 1784 to discharge the Kehillah functions of supervising ritual slaughtering, butchers, and charity organizations, particularly the paupers' hostel erected in 1792. In 1792, the Jews of Vienna were allowed to select representatives to superintend the affairs of the "tolerated" Jews, to transmit government orders, and to give their opinion to the Government Committee on Jewish Affairs (as the *Judenamt* was renamed between 1793 and 1797) if required when the domiciliary rights of any family came under discussion. Actually, because of pressure by the authorities and indifference on the part of the Jewish community, these positions (five representatives and four deputies) remained in the hands of a few families of financiers and years passed before new elections were held.

The condition in which these few "tolerated" Jews of Vienna lived, helped to accelerate the process of assimilation which gripped the Jewish middle class in all the large cities of Germany at that time. The changes that took place in the New Burial Society of the Vienna Jews were characteristic of the early stages of this process. The bye-laws of the society, founded in 1763, were signed by members of forty-seven of the city's notable Jewish families—some destined to occupy leading positions in the Jewish plutocracy several decades later, and to be closely associated with government circles. The Society not only fulfilled charitable functions such as making anonymous donations, marrying off brides, clothing the destitute, visiting the sick, ransoming prisoners, and supporting the poor in Palestine. It also undertook to recite the *Kaddish* for the dead, to study *Mishnayot* (paragraphs from the *Mishnah*) in honour of the departed, "to designate periods for Torah study, to welcome and accommodate rabbis and teachers, to listen to Talmudic debates and interpretations, and to hear excerpts from Talmudic legend." By 1782, an amendment had released members from the duty of listening to a "lesson" by the rabbi of the Society "since for diverse reasons this is impossible." The rabbi was only obliged to deliver a Sabbath sermon. The final minutes of the Society were written in fluent German (though still in the Hebrew alphabet) and not in a Hebrew/Yiddish mixture as before.

The upper-class plutocracy of Viennese Jewry were the first to assimilate, together with favoured individuals who had been raised to the nobility by Imperial grace, and others, close to the Imperial Court, who were connected both with government circles and with the Christian aristocracy, through their banking, commissionary, or activities in the wholesale trade. The big Jewish banking firms, such as Arnstein-Eskeles, or Hertz-Leidesdorf, were interested in Austria's military success against Napoleon because of their capital investments: they had loaned the principal resources to finance these wars. The firm of Arnstein-Eskeles also organized the financing of the Tyrolean revolt in 1809 against Bavaria and the French régime, under the leadership of Andreas Hofer. This in no way deterred the victorious rebels, who carried the banner of the Catholic Church, from looting the homes and shops of the few Jews of Innsbrück. (The Jews of Hohenems in the Vorarlberg—some ninety families—saved themselves from violence by paying the rebels a huge tribute.)

These favoured families enjoyed a social position befitting their economic importance. The appearance of the Jewish *salons* of Berlin was repeated here, on an even grander and more lavish scale. The tradition of the Berlin Jewish middle class was also conveyed to Vienna by family ties: leading Viennesse Jewish bankers, Nathan, Baron von Arnstein, and Ritter Bernhard von Eskeles (son of State Rabbi Berush Eskeles of Moravia) married the daughters of the Berlin banker, Daniel Itzig. Fanny von Arnstein had already impressed Joseph II with her beauty* and she was later described as "the Viennesse Madame Récamier." Her salon was "the largest and, to some extent, the only meeting place for all those visiting here from abroad," according to the reactionary romantic writer, Friedrich Gentz, in a letter in 1802. The Arnstein *salon* reached the height of its splendour at the time of the Congress of Vienna, when it was visited by practically all the innumerable princes and ministers at the Congress. However, the apathy that these powerful magnates showed towards Jewish communal affairs and their detachment from their own people grew as they rose in the social scale. During the 1780's they could still be approached and did, in fact, agree to subscribe to newly published Hebrew books and to the *Me'asef*. (Reb Nathan Arnstein and his wife, then still known as Fegliche, subscribed to Mendelssohn's *Commentary* and translation.) The conspicuous absence of Viennese names from the subscription list when the *Me'asef* renewed publication in 1809 was not a coincidence. The only things from which they did not dissociate themselves were charitable concerns.

Assimilationist ambitions also grew stronger amongst the well-to-do Jews of Vienna. In 1812, a school was founded with government permission, for the sole purpose of teaching Jewish religion, as it was not taught at the public schools. A house in Seitenstettengasse accommodated the school, the synagogue, the home for the aged, and the ritual bath, and thenceforth became the centre of religious and communal life for the "tolerated" Jews of Vienna. In 1814, the government and the Jewish representatives collaborated to draw up a curriculum for the school. It included the study of religion on lines laid down in the official German text-books prepared by Hertz Homberg (*B'nei Zion* and *Imrei Shefer*) and his intellectual colleague, Peter Beer (*A History of the Jewish People*

* The Emperor's comment: "The *belle* is queen wherever she appears."

240

in Biblical Times); the Bible; Hebrew ("That they may understand the meaning of the words in the benedictions and prayers"), and the writing of German, in Hebrew letters, in order to communicate with Jews abroad. The teaching of Yiddish was expressly forbidden.

The constant stream of Bohemian, Moravian, Hungarian and Galician Jews visiting the capital on business exercised a unique restraining influence on the process of assimilation among the Jews of Vienna. On the other hand, outstanding *Haskalah* writers in Vienna at the beginning of the nineteenth century were already far more influential in the diffusion of Enlightenment amongst Jews in the provinces, especially Galicia, than in the cultural life of the diminutive and disrupted Jewish colony in Vienna. These writers had obtained temporary rights of domicile in the city, a few as private tutors in the homes of the rich, some as proof-readers of Hebrew books in Christian printing establishments, including the outstanding firm of Anton Schmidt. The most impressive intellectual figure in the group was the grammarian Judah Leib Ben-Ze'ev. Not many years later, in the early 1820's, Vienna became the centre of the *Haskalah* movement for the countries of the Habsburg Empire, particularly Galicia.

B. BOHEMIA-MORAVIA

On the Eve of the Reforms of Enlightened Despotism
(The Economic and Legal Situation)

The economy, legal position and cultural life of the Jewish community in the two Czech lands under Austrian rule, Bohemia and Moravia (together with Silesia), at the end of the eighteenth century, represented a transitional link between German Jewry in the west and the great centre of the Polish Jews to the east. Their economy was the same as in eastern Europe: a manorial system based on the forced labour of serfs. The nobility consisted entirely of men of Germanic stock or of Germanized Czechs and they controlled the cities, which were largely their own property. Unlike Poland, however, mercantile capitalism had made continual progress in Bohemia and Moravia, although slowed down by external and internal wars during the seventeenth century and again in the eighteenth (the Seven Years' War). Nevertheless, export trade showed a constant growth, especially in raw materials and agricultural produce, and the crafts were also partly organized on a credit basis for foreign marketing purposes. The absolutist régime was able to utilize these elements of early capitalism as a basis for its mercantilist economic policies and the consolidation of governing power along western lines. This intermediate stage of development also determined the policy towards the

Jews of the country: it represented a middle way between meticulous German repression and the system of Jewish rights as permitted under an aristocratic feudal régime.

The edicts of Charles VI fixed the countries' Jewish population in 1725-26 at 8,541 "tolerated" families for Bohemia and 5,106 for Moravia, and these figures did not, in fact, show much increase during the eighteenth century. In 1792, the Jews of Bohemia constituted 1½ per cent of a total population of approximately 3 million.

Jewish residence in the imperial cities of Bohemia and Moravia was prohibited. However, a large Kehillah existed in the capital of Bohemia, Prague, and over 8,000 Jews lived in the *Judenstadt* (as the ghetto was called) in 1791. On the other hand, only a number of tax farmers and monopoly leaseholders and their families was allowed to live in Brünn, the capital of Moravia at that date. Nevertheless, the Jewish population of Bohemia outside the city of Prague was more dispersed than in Moravia. The census of 1724 showed that nearly half the Bohemian Jews outside Prague were scattered over the rural areas and only a third of all the Jews in provincial towns and villages lived in Kehillot of over a hundred people. A considerable proportion of them remained in the smaller towns and villages, even during the eighteenth century, when the Jews of Bohemia tended to concentrate increasingly in the large cities which were mostly subservient to the nobles. The rural Jewish population of Moravia was appreciably smaller than in Bohemia. Although they were spread over more than fifty Kehillot, about a third of the total number of Moravian Jews were gathered in the four great Kehillot of Nikolsburg (620 "tolerated" families), Prossnitz, Boskowitz and Holleschau.

The occupational distribution and economic activities of the Bohemian-Moravian Jews were also the direct outcome of the social and economic structure of the country and the legal status it ordained. The 1724 census reported that 52 per cent of Bohemian Jews (not including those in Prague) lived on trade, twenty per cent were artisans, while the remainder were equally divided between lessees, religious functionaries, members of the free professions, and various other occupations (15 per cent). The 1729 census showed a different occupational distribution within the great Kehillah of Prague. Of a total of 2,335 Jewish families, 2,306 wage-earners were registered, comprising seventy-four money-changers (3 per cent); 1,030 merchants, storekeepers, itinerant traders, and pedlars (nearly half or 45 per cent of the total); and 742 (or about a third) miscellaneous craftsmen. The remainder earned a living as porters (2 per cent), Kehillah clerks, members of the free professions, and similar occupations. Of the 1,418 Jews who returned to Prague in 1748-49 (following the expulsion in 1745) over 5,000, or 35 per cent, were artisans—a considerable increase over previous figures. On the whole, however, the changes in the distribution of the Jewish population as a result of its increasing concentration in urban centres produced no significant change in the main branches of its occupational structure. In any event, statistics from a number of Moravian Kehillot definitely proved that craftsmen there did not form less than 20 per cent of the total and in some towns as much as 25, 30, or even, as at Budschwitz, over 40 per cent. In Bohemia, manual occupations for Jews were no more severely restricted than in Moravia and therefore it can be assumed that the percentage of craftsmen amongst the Jews was no lower than in Moravia. In fact, no Jewish community in western Europe could claim so high a percentage of productive elements. The Jewish community of Bohemia-Moravia bore a greater resemblance, in terms of occupational structure, to the community in the east, in Poland and beyond, except that the percentage engaged in trade was somewhat higher and the percentage of lessees proportionately lower.

Jews engaged in all branches of trade in both countries, both as far as the goods they handled and the level at which they traded were concerned. On the whole, however, Jewish tradesmen were concentrated at the two extremes of the trading process: in the wholesale trade, including imports and exports, and in peddling. Shop-owning by Jews was very limited, except in the small towns, by the repressive measures of the Christian merchant guilds, which had state approval and were designed to prevent Jewish competition. On the other hand, trade in wool, linen, leather and raw hides, furs, feathers, and potash was almost entirely in Jewish hands. The fact that large numbers of Jews dealt in the raw materials trade was a result of their legal status in the small towns and villages. The landed proprietors compelled their Jewish subjects to purchase their products, often at arbitrarily fixed prices. At times they even ordered their serfs to sell their wool, feathers, and other goods only to the local Jews. This monopolistic régime changed slightly at the end of the eighteenth century by an Imperial Decree of 1774 that forbade forced sales by serfs.

Trade in woven materials developed as a natural consequence of the wool trade. The traders who sold the wool to the carders, in turn bought their processed goods and sold them at home and abroad. In 1772, there were 459 Jewish linen, woollen and dry goods merchants in Prague, as compared with only thirty-nine Christians dealing in the same commodities. Cases were also reported of estate owners forcing their Jewish subjects to supply all the commodities they required—in much the same way as they forced them to purchase all their agricultural produce. Trade in clothing, especially old clothes, alcoholic beverages, (as a result of the leasing of distilleries), and gold and silver (connected with the jewellery and ornamental crafts which were widespread amongst them) was in Jewish hands. Not surprisingly, therefore, the Jews played a very large part at the fairs held in Bohemia and Moravia; by government order, market days were fixed so as not to coincide with the Jewish holidays. In the Bohemian town of Neuern, the national feather trade was concentrated in Jewish hands. Jewish merchants from Bohemia and Moravia also attended fairs in neighbouring countries, at Leipzig, Dresden, Linz and Laibach, selling raw materials and industrial products, especially textiles. During the second half of the eighteenth century, their acquisition of leases of the government tobacco monopoly opened a wide field of activity to Jewish capitalists and merchants.

The Jewish merchant class formed a broad social hierarchy, headed by the great wholesalers, the import and export merchants, who were frequently also army suppliers. In second place came the wholesalers in agricultural and industrial products. They were followed by the retailers in the small towns and villages. The largest trading class consisted of the pedlars who travelled, pack on back, between the small towns and, especially, the villages. In Bohemia, some of these pedlars also lived in the villages, but in Moravia their domicile was confined exclusively to the towns and cities, and they only travelled to the villages to ply their trade. A memorandum prepared in 1781 by the Moravian authorities stated that about a third of all Jewish family men in Moravia were pedlars. They faced harsh municipal regulations against trading in the cities and even in the villages they had to obtain permits from the local landowners. These pedlars were traders in every sense of the word: they sold linen and woollen fabrics, fancy goods and other commodities to their customers, most of whom were peasants; in return, they bought their old clothes, scrap iron and other metals, hides, wool, feathers, tallow, flax and other raw materials. They either obtained their stock-in-trade on credit, on a contract basis from Jewish wholesalers, or else borrowed to finance their purchases from the villages. Most of them lived in abject poverty. However, the poorest of the traders were the "brokers," or middlemen, who collected meagre commissions for serving as intermediaries to the more "prosperous" purveyors.

The Jewish lessees in Bohemia and Moravia were connected with commerce, industry, and even, to some extent, with agriculture. Most of them leased liquor distilleries from the village and town squires and were known as *Randarn*, a variant of the term *Arendarn* employed in Poland.* However, the large number of Jews who operated tanneries and potash kilns was the most characteristic feature of economic life in Bohemia-Moravia. Most of the distilleries and potash kilns were located in the villages, whereas tanneries were more common in the towns. The distillery lessees often leased the village or town ale-house as well, but as a rule they were content with their monopoly rights. The publicans in the manorial taverns, some of them Jews, were required to purchase their liquor exclusively from the lessees. Some Moravian towns possessed a Jewish lessee and also two or three Jewish publicans, jointly classified as *Bestand-juden* (enterprise lessees). The lessees were usually well-to-do, some even extremely wealthy, but a rural lessee might find his income so unstable as to force him to collect his remuneration from the proprietor in the form of

---

* The medieval Latin word *arrendare*, "to rent."

produce or else to take supplementary work as a butcher, perhaps, or tradesman. On the other hand, a fair number of the lessees in the Moravian cities were registered as both tannery and distillery lessees. In most cases, it would appear that the Jewish tavern-keepers never achieved any degree of prosperity.

At the beginning of the modern period in the main, but to some extent also during the eighteenth century, numerous oppressive measures were introduced against Jewish crafts in Bohemia, and, even more, in Moravia. The government's main intention was to prevent Jewish artisans from competing with Christians. Jews were therefore forbidden to engage in most of the crafts where the Christian masters were organized into guilds. Even in those that they were allowed to practice, they might not employ Christian apprentices, assistants, or workmen. In 1753, a regulation concerning the manual trades in Moravia provided that even Jewish craftsmen who were legally engaged in their callings could only work for Jewish clients. Nevertheless, Jewish artisanship throughout Bohemia and Moravia was marked by its variety, particularly in the capital city of Prague, which was unique amongst European Jewish communities of the period for its diversity of crafts. The 1729 census reported 742 Jewish craftsmen at Prague practising over sixty different crafts (as well as forty-five porters in the cartage business), and the picture was, to a large extent, the same during the latter half of the eighteenth century. The Jewish craftsmen in the large Prague Kehillah were specifically allowed, by an Imperial command during the seventeenth century, to work without let or hindrance "amongst themselves"—that is to say, to carry out orders for Jewish customers. The largest group consisted of 179 tailors (including eighteen women) in addition to thirty-nine seamstresses. There were also 116 shoemakers (including five women) and over forty in each group of butchers, cord makers, cap makers and furriers. The Jewish craft groups of Prague each had their own display of banners and emblems, like the Christian guilds. Jewish craft organizations also existed in the larger Kehillot in the provincial cities. An etching of the processions in Prague to celebrate the birth of the Crown Prince (subsequently Emperor Joseph II) in 1741, showed the Jewish craft banners, including the butchers': an embroidered Bohemian lion grasping a butcher's cleaver above the Hebrew inscription "Kasher."

Many of the Jewish artisans of Bohemia lived in the villages, where their customers were peasants. In Moravia, Jewish residence in rural areas was prohibited, but government and guild restrictions were circumvented by the sale of finished products at markets and fairs. The Jewish craftsmen, especially those in the clothing industry, like some of their Christian colleagues, accepted orders on credit from Jewish merchants or wealthier Jewish craftsmen; most of the independent Jewish artisans, except the butchers and tanners, were also poor men.

In the large Kehillot a considerable number of men also earned their living in transport as porters (Jews were legally barred from being carters). Most members of the free occupations and Kehillah employees belonged to the poorer classes. Jewish medical orderlies and bath attendants also worked for Christians, and Jewish orchestras and musicians were often hired to perform at Christian festivities. Official census returns showed a large percentage of the Jewish population either as having no source of income or as actual paupers. But, in many cases, paupers possessed no rights of domicile and evaded the census officials.

The great majority of the Jews of Bohemia and Moravia had been able to overcome all the legal obstacles created by the antiquated feudal system. They played an important part in the country's economy because of their initiative, energy and quickness. Their landless condition, economic tradition, and above all their legal status, had caused them to concentrate in special areas of the general economy. They discharged an important function pioneering the capitalist system in this region of central Europe by introducing new types of organization into commerce and the manual trades (the *Verlags* system in the clothing industry), and also by their agricultural activities as lessees of industrial installations in the rural areas. Against this background of early, mercantile capitalism, industrial capitalism here made its first beginnings. To facilitate its development, enlightened despotism, in accordance with its economic policy, made concessions to the thin upper layer of Jewish capitalists in Bohemia and Moravia, as it had in all the other countries under its rule.

The imposition of family quotas was the cruellest measure that the absolutist régime took against the Jews of Bohemia and Moravia. To prevent increase in Jewish families, only the firstborn son was allowed to marry; the remaining sons had to postpone marriage until a vacancy arose through the death of a *Familiant* without male issue. This decree weighed most heavily on the poorer classes. The Jewish Statutes of Moravia in 1754 did not even permit the firstborn son of a Jewish family to take a wife unless he could prove his ability to pay a tax quota imposed by the Kehillah for the three consecutive years following the wedding. The tax burden sustained by the Jewish population was indeed intolerable. In spite of all the severe restrictions on occupations and rights of domicile in the cities and villages of her kingdom, Maria Theresa decreed a threefold increase in taxes for the Jews of Bohemia in 1748—from 72,000 florins to 216,000—over and above the provisions tax of 17,000 florins collected from the Jews of Prague. On a *per capita* basis, the taxes paid by the Jewish population of Bohemia to the government were three times as high as those paid by the rest of the population. This did not exempt the Jews from compulsory payment of various general taxes, such as the consumers' tax, the capital tax, protection tax, and trade tax, to mention but a few. In Moravia, Jews visiting fairs at Brünn and other imperial towns were required to pay a toll (*Judenleibmaut*), which the government usually farmed out to wealthy Jews—at a later date to the Dobruschka family, who also held the tobacco monopoly on lease.

Most of the Bohemian and Moravian Jews lived in towns and villages which were the ancestral property of members of the nobility. In Moravia, even Jews who lived in municipally incorporated cities were under the jurisdiction of the neighbouring manorial proprietors. The right of domicile under noble patronage entailed high taxes for the Jews, in addition to the government taxes. The protection tax alone sometimes amounted to half the tax money owed to the central government. There was also an annual cemetery tax, sometimes a Kehillah bath-house tax (at Nikolsburg), a butcher's tax, and various merchandise taxes, especially on hides and wine. An excise duty was sometimes even levied on baking permits for the Sabbath loaf. As in most European countries at that time, "gifts" to public officials and clerics also formed part of the expenses of the Kehillah. The budget of the Central Council of Moravian Jews in the middle of the eighteenth century included 500 florins in gifts to officials and deputies of the country's estates.

Kehillot and Cultural Life

The apportionment and collection of taxes was the principal function of the Kehillot and the autonomous central bodies of Bohemian and Moravian Jewry at that time. The communal organization was headed by the Kehillah leaders, assisted by the community "Optimates" (*Tovim*). The large Kehillot of Bohemia, such as Kolin, elected one *Parnass* (*Primator*), four Kehillah leaders, and four "Optimates." The office of *"Parnass* of the Month," which involved presiding over sessions, rotated on a monthly basis between the Kehillah leaders and the *Parnass*. At Prague, the Kehillah was led by a *Parnass*, known as the *Primus* (or *Primator*), five leaders and four "Optimates." When important matters, such as the adoption of new regulations, had to be decided, they formed themselves into the Grand Council, by the addition of the rabbi, the religious court (*Bet Din Gadol*) and fifteen "Elite" (*yehidei s'gulah*) drawn from amongst the highest taxpayers in the Kehillah. The Bohemian Kehillot were organized into a Council including representatives from all twelve provinces of the country and also from the Kehillah of Prague. This Council, known as the *Landesjudenschaft*, including delegates from every district, twelve in all, met representatives of the Prague Kehillah every three years at the town of Smichov near Prague. When agreement had been reached on the share of the total tax quota to be allotted to the Prague Kehillah, they apportioned the remaining sum amongst all the districts and then determined each Kehillah's allocation in the district's total. The Kehillot of the provincial cities elected a State *Parnass* (*Landesprimator*) and Intercessor (*Shtadlan*), who lived permanently in

Prague, and also a recorder and trustee. Besides apportioning taxes, this Council also passed occasional regulations concerning religious matters, Kehillah organization, and economic affairs. In Moravia, Kehillah representatives convened (latterly at Brünn) once every three years to elect three "Heads of the Land," or "Heads of the District," six "Deputies and Tax Collectors," and six Tax Assessors, two from each of the three districts (in 1757 six districts were set up). The "Heads of the Land" elected a head rabbi for lifetime tenure to live in Nikolsburg. The main function of the Moravian Council also was to apportion taxes to the districts and Kehillot and to ensure their collection. However, this Council enjoyed a greater degree of autonomy than its Bohemian counterpart, and the regulations of the "Moravian Land Council" embraced all areas of Kehillah life, amongst which charity and educational affairs were of considerable importance. In 1754, most of the Council's regulations— mainly drawn up as long ago as 1650 ("The 311 Regulations")—were ratified by the government and acquired legal status as the *General-Polizei-Prozess und Kommerzial-Ordnung* (General Administration, Procedure and Trade Ordinance).

The Moravian Kehillot also commanded greater autonomous prerogatives than in Bohemia. In Bohemia, outside the city of Prague, Kehillah leaders were officially recognized only as heads of synagogues. Although they were officially known as *Judenrichter* (Jewish judges), the provincial city Kehillot, except in Kolin and Jung-Bunzlau, had no juridical authority, even in financial litigation. In Moravia, in contrast, the Kehillah Court had legal authority to preside over financial litigation, the Land *Parnassim* were empowered to sit as a court of first appeal, and the Land Rabbi was authorized to hear a second appeal. As a result of their concentration within ghettos, the Moravian Kehillot were generally organized very much as autonomous townships; at times they even had their own police, fire-fighters, and nightwatchmen. However, in both Bohemia and Moravia, these autonomous institutions were used as instruments to serve the purposes of the government authorities.

As the functions of the Kehillah management were reduced to the level of auxiliary government agencies for tax apportionment and collection purposes a corresponding contraction in the scope of their activities took place. In Bohemia, the task of supervising synagogues and charitable activities was in the hands of "Local Overseers" who had no voice in Kehillah administration. *Talmud-Torah* institutions (Charity schools) in Bohemia were also supported by contributions and administered by their own treasurers. The indigent Jewish population had no part in electing Kehillah officials and the state authorities ensured that the plutocratic Kehillah régime was kept intact.

From the very beginning, and in accordance with the old regulations, Kehillah organization in Moravia had been based on the principle of "superiority in wealth or in *Torah*." Those holding the title of *Morenu*

(Our teacher) or *Haver* (Fellow) possessed extraordinary privileges both in elections to the Kehillah administration and in taxation. However, except in the case of judges, heads of rabbinical academies and similar officials whose professions were their assets, acquisition of these appellations did not depend on learning alone. The candidate might devote a specified portion of his time to the *Torah* (to receive the title of *Haver*) or display his knowledge of the Talmud and the Codifiers (to receive the title of *Morenu*). But the title of *Haver* could be purchased for the sum of fifteen florins (Austrian guldens), that of *Morenu* for between forty and sixty florins. The title was even on occasion granted solely on account of the candidate's respected social status. People who worked for their living or might even in the past have soiled their hands by labour, or engaged in disreputable occupations, were specifically ineligible for these titles. With the passage of time, however, it would seem that this regulation was less scrupulously observed—if the candidate were a man of substance.

"The Chiefs and Rulers, Heads of the Land" took constant care to ensure that Kehillah and Council administration did not pass out of the hands of their own wealthy mercantile class. In the eighteenth century they continued to invoke the regulations passed in the previous century whereby "at least four" of the five Kehillah leaders (one Kehillah leader and four Optimates) in the large Kehillot, were to be appointed from among the wealthy and only one from the intermediate classes. Similarly, they renewed an old ruling "that no 'Head of the Land' was to be elected save from amongst the foremost five of the Kehillah's membership." Men engaged in "contemptible occupations," such as meat trading or tanning, were, under the regulations, ineligible to serve as Kehillah representatives on the Council ("unless he shall have borne the title of *Haver* for ten years...and is also one of the Heads and the Optimates in that Kehillah").

The Moravian Kehillot employed a system based primarily on assessments for the collection of imperial taxes. Other payments such as debt remission costs and Kehillah needs derived mostly—unlike the earlier period—from the indirect *pardon* tax on merchandise and incomes, and the excise duty on meat, wine and other beverages. The tax apportionment and collection system was the cause of frequent controversy and conflict. In Moravia, there were cases of Kehillah members rebelling against the tax apportionment by the assessors, who placed the main load on the lower income groups and spared the rich. In 1765 at Prague, and in 1768 at Kolin, clandestine protest meetings were dispersed by Kehillah officials, helped by the municipal police. In Bohemia and Moravia, there were numerous complaints by the smaller Kehillot against the Kehillot in the provincial capitals, on the grounds of discriminatory and arbitrary tax apportionment and Council expenditure. In the middle of the eighteenth century, the Moravian Council's expenditures, including the salaries of the Council *Parnassim* and the Land Rabbi, amounted to 12,500 florins, or one-seventh of the "Toleration Tax" (82,200 florins) levied on the Jews of the country. The post of the Land Rabbi in Moravia was another cause of dissatisfaction to the Kehillot. His multifarious income included his fees for conferring the title of *Haver* or *Morenu*—his prerogative for all the Kehillot of the country.*

The family quotas decree also gave the Kehillah authorities wide scope for arbitrary practice and the exploitation of the poor. The poor were not only refused marriage licences, under the repressive statutes of Moravia and the decrees of the Bohemian authorities, but the records of the Kremsier and Ungarisch-Brod Kehillot of Moravia proved that bargaining over marriage licences was a common occurrence. People from outside the town could frequently purchase a *Familiennummer* (family number) at an exorbitant price when one fell vacant within the legal quota, while the natives of the community who could not afford bribery were barred from legitimate marriage and even forced to forfeit their rights of domicile in the country.

The social abuses that the leaders of the Bohemian-Moravian Kehillah practiced was also reflected in the homiletical literature of the late eighteenth century. The well-known Prague judge and *darshan* (homileticist), Eleazar Fleckeles, in the introduction to his collection of sermons published in 1785, related how he was forced to leave Prague in his youth, because of the intolerable pressure of taxation. He described the poverty and utter destitution of his home, inveighed against the unhappy position of Talmudic scholars and protested against the pressure to which the poor were subjected. "With this transgression," he writes, "whereby we drive the poor from one affliction to another, from house to house, from shelter to shelter, we are also driving out the Divine Presence Itself."

However, the plutocratic régime and the frequency of arbitrary abuse never reached the degree of license then prevalent in the large Kehillot of Poland and Lithuania. In contrast with the degenerate Polish feudal régime, civil administration in Bohemia-Moravia was under the restraining influence of absolutism, which also kept a check on Kehillah affairs. However, the collapse of the Kehillah and the organs of central autonomy with the exhaustion of their function in organizing the affairs of the people characterized the state of affairs in both regions.

The Jewish way of life and culture in Bohemia and Moravia was not at that time essentially different from that of Polish Jewry. Religious tradition was minutely observed. The men wore beards and the women a colourful head-dress. The dietary laws were so scrupulously followed that pedlars on the road carried provisions for a week with them. These provisions usually consisted of a jar of dough-crumbs wrapped in linen and a packet of ground coffee. The pedlar stored them in a locked chest at

* In the Moravian town of Pohrlitz, which had one hundred "tolerated" Jewish families in 1788, nineteen men possessed the title of *Rav* (*Haver*) and one the title of *Rav-Rabi* (*Morenu*) in 1740.

the home of a peasant with whom he regularly lodged. Yiddish was the spoken vernacular of the entire Jewish population, as well as the language of instruction in *Hadarim* and *Yeshivot*. Kehillah and Land Council regulations were sometimes drawn up in Hebrew, sometimes in Yiddish interspersed with Hebrew words and phrases. Kehillah administration and court notices were written in a form of Yiddish filled with Hebrew expressions. The close ties between the Kehillot were reflected in the geographical appellations found in local Jewish folklore: the Jews of Nikolsburg were called "The Proud Ones" because the Land Rabbi lived in their Kehillah; the people of Prossnitz were *Shebsen** because the Shabbetai Zvi and Frankist apostasies had found adherents there; Holleschau achieved notoriety as the Khelm† of Moravia in the expression *Holleschauer Narronim.‡* The Kehillah régime was intimately bound up with traditional folk customs. In the small towns, it was customary for the candidate for the office of Kehillah treasurer to distribute *Havdalah* candles to all the wealthy members and wax candles to the children at *Simchat Torah* to decorate their flags. The successful candidate tossed apples and pears into the crowd of young people who gathered in front of his house. The expression *Sharblech Geld* (shard money) meaning wedding gifts, perpetuated a custom unique to the Moravian Jews: the shards of the earthenware pot broken for luck at the celebration of the marriage contract served as invitation cards for the wedding ceremony.

The Jews of Bohemia and Moravia, like their co-religionists throughout the Diaspora, firmly maintained the hope of redemption. They were deeply and personally involved with the Land of Israel and all their views on the future of their people centred around it. Even the smallest Bohemian Kehillot (see Rules and Regulations at Kuttenplan for 1768) required all members aged twenty or over, including "servants and even 'bonded' pedlars" (who obtained their goods on bond from merchants) to donate half a *shekel* annually for "the poor of Jerusalem." Some Kehillot, such as Kremsier in Moravia, supported a *Jerusalem Society* similar to the one founded in Hamburg in 1659. Moravian Land Council bye-laws dating from 1750 stated, under the heading *If I Forget Thee O Jerusalem, May My Right Hand Forget Its Cunning*, that the Jews of Moravia undertook to contribute fifty thaler annually to the poor of Jerusalem, they "and their posterity and the posterity of their posterity unto all generations till the coming of the Deliverer."

The Prossnitz Kehillah issued a public announcement in 1772 forbidding extravagance in male and female dress, on grounds not only of the sin of pride and the threat of "Gentile jealousy" but also "because it is in addition meet and just that we grieve and lament over the destruction of

---

* Literally meaning sheep. It represented a play on words involving the Yiddish pronunciation of the Hebrew name Shabbetai, *Shabbseh*, and the Yiddish word *Shebs*, a sheep.

† In eastern European Yiddish folklore the equivalent of Gotham.

‡ Hebraized plural of the Judaeo-German *Narr*, a simpleton, or fool.

Jerusalem in appropriate garments, as it has been explained . . . that the adornments of grooms and of brides have been forbidden from the day of the Destruction and but with difficulty have coloured raiments been permitted to womenfolk."

The education available to the Jews of Bohemia and Moravia was much the same as in the east of Europe. Talmud was taught to very young boys even before they had completely mastered the Pentateuch, though the extreme form of *pilpul* in the teaching of the Talmud and the Codifiers had been moderated, mainly through the influence of Ezekiel Landau, the well-known Rabbi of Prague. The centre of Talmudic instruction in Bohemia was the *Yeshivah* of Prague, to which students flocked from Germany, Hungary, and Galicia. *Yeshivot* did exist in all the large Kehillot of Moravia, Nikolsburg, Kremsier, Holleschau, Prossnitz, Ungarish-Brod and Leipnik, but, with the exception of the school at Nikolsburg, they were all in a state of decline. The teaching of the Talmud and the Codifiers was extremely one-sided. The scholars were not even in favour of the study of the body of Talmudic legends traditionally known as the *Agadah*, which had become popular with the common people through the activities of the *darshanim* (preachers). In addition to this class motive on the part of the spiritual aristocracy, the rabbis also feared that concentration on the *Agadah*, which involved neglect of the *Halakhah* would tend to draw the people closer to the rapidly expanding Hasidic movement of the neighbouring countries to the east. They were even afraid that it might actually lead to Frankist apostasy, traces of which could be found in Bohemia-Moravia.

The rabbis of that generation were utterly opposed to secular studies. Rabbi Ezekiel Landau was among the first of his contemporaries to do battle against the *Haskalah* movement of Wessely and Mendelssohn. Only Hebrew grammar was spared from the attack of the rabbinical leaders. "The Renowned One of Judah"—as Rabbi Landau was known after his book of *responsa*—even expressed pleasure that a textbook of grammar offered the opportunity "to teach the sons of Judah a language of instruction, whereby the youth might be instructed from its earliest years, trained in a lucid and precise style of the Holy Tongue . . . and thus a proper knowledge of the Holy Tongue would spread to young and old." But though study of this subject was sanctioned, it was nevertheless regarded as an intellectual trifle, and Rabbi Landau gave a specific warning against spending "more than one half-hour or an hour daily at most" on the study of grammar.

Despite the efforts of the most distinguished rabbis, secular enlightenment was already gaining adherents amongst the Jewish population. The process was greatly facilitated by the fact that the Jews in this area generally knew the German language. A small group of professional intellectuals began to take shape. At Prague, it consisted of Jewish surgical orderlies, who had learned their profession at the university in the city, and a number of Jewish doctors with medical degrees from universities abroad (for example, Halle). Furthermore, the political and cultural atmosphere engendered by the absolutist régime was more conducive to an incipient rapprochement between the Jews and their Christian neighbours than the rigid feudal atmosphere of eastern Europe. Christian as well as Jewish views vindicating the Jews were expressed in the polemical literature on the Jewish question published in Bohemia during 1781-82. It is significant that government censors erased some of the more venomous passages from the diatribes of the anti-Jewish pamphleteers. At the same time, the rabbis of Bohemia and Moravia maintained and even strengthened their entrée into government circles—through whose protection they obtained their posts (for example, the Land Rabbis of Moravia). Ezekiel Landau corresponded regularly with the censor; one of his letters mentioned that he was calling upon his Jewish brethren to honour those nations "in whose countries and states we are sheltered." The custom of printing an *Apologia* in this vein on the reverse side of the title page of all books published had originated in 1767 as a result of provocation by the Prague censor. The declaration expressed gratitude to those nations "who are generous with us and enable us to maintain ourselves and abide in this country." In addition, it contained a theme which was typical of the constantly increasing spirit of religious toleration even among the orthodox: "And how much the more so to those nations of our times who believe in the cardinal principles of religion, who believe in the creation of the world and in the Prophets and their Prophecy, in all the miracles and wondrous things of which it has been written in the Torah and in the books of the Prophets . . ." Not surprisingly, therefore, Joseph II's reforms, and the establishment of German-language schools for the Jews in Bohemia and Moravia did not encounter the lively opposition that it aroused amongst the orthodox elements of Galicia.

Joseph II's Reforms and their Consequences

On October 18, 1781, Joseph II's decree on reforms for the Jews of Bohemia was published. It was followed on February 13, 1782, by another decree, slightly differently formulated, for the Jews of Moravia. They made some concessions in respect of the occupations permitted to the Jews. Jews were allowed to engage in wholesale and retail trade and to peddle. They were permitted to learn manual crafts from Christian artisans, but the right to practise these crafts depended on "existing laws," which meant that, as before, it was limited by guild privileges. All crafts, such as weaving, which were not under guild supervision, were now open to Jews. They were allowed to build factories, "especially those in which expensive machinery is required," and also to be employed in factories as workmen. The ban on Jewish carters was removed. Jews were permitted to lease parcels of land, especially virgin soil, but not the land of serfs, and only in places where they held rights of residence. Lessees would only be allowed to own land if they were baptized.

The Jews of Bohemia and Moravia were ordered to establish elementary schools in every Kehillah; in places which failed to maintain a school of this type, the Jews were enjoined to send their children to local Christian schools. Jewish youths were allowed to study at secondary schools and universities. The ordinance for the Jews of Moravia specifically indicated that this permission was only granted to the sons of the wealthy.

Special imperial writs abolished the "Jewish body toll" and the double fee paid by Jews in the law courts. In general, however, taxes levied exclusively on the Jews continued at their former rate, though some of the less significant were abolished—for example, the tax on capital and the excise on consumption. But the actual method of taxation was changed: instead of a uniform Jewish tax, a graduated family tax based on property classification, and property and grocery taxes, were imposed in Bohemia. Jews still had to pay taxes and fees to estate owners. This new system of government taxation placed the burden of these taxes, most of them indirect, even more heavily on the impoverished Jewish population.

The Kehillah continued to be responsible for these taxes. In Moravia, however, collection was handed over to lessees and the central autonomous body was thus rendered superfluous, as its main function, as far as the government was concerned, had been to apportion the taxes amongst the Kehillot. In 1788, it was abolished. In Bohemia, the Land Council continued to exist as a government-sanctioned institution since it undertook to accept tax collections from Jews on lease on the terms offered by private lessees. These terms included the provisions tax as an obligatory condition laid down by the tax farmer, Sheindel Dobrushka of Moravia. Ordinances of 1783 and 1785 abolished the Kehillah courts in Bohemia and Moravia. Thereafter Jews had to submit their lawsuits to state courts of justice.

In practice, therefore, the "reforms" of Joseph II were confined to concessions which only affected the Jewish capitalists, and they thenceforth took advantage of the opportunity to engage in wholesale trade and industry without interference. Even after the reforms had been promulgated, Jewish storekeepers and pedlars were still faced with all the decrees that limited their rights and were designed to protect the Christian middle class. Only a few of them could make use of the right to learn a trade from a Christian master, as Jewish apprentices were rarely accepted by Christian craftsmen. Needless to say, the right to lease land was rendered void of all practical meaning by innumerable restrictive clauses; for example, a Jewish home was forbidden to lodge the hired Christian hand necessary to teach the Jew farming. The Imperial Edict of 1786 declared that the Emperor's intention was not to increase the number of Jews, but only to reform their way of life so that they might be of greater service to the state. Its negative aspects were fully implemented. The domiciliary rights decrees remained in full force; only Jews who possessed assets valued at 10,000 florins or more and furthermore agreed to invest them in the establishment of factories were permitted to settle in the country by special imperial court licence. The family quota decree was not relaxed either for the state as a whole or for the individual Kehillot.

The Emperor issued two more edicts during the remaining years of his reign aimed at eradicating the national character of the Jews. Both made far-reaching changes in the traditional way of life of the Jews in his realm. The Imperial Edict "Concerning Jewish Names" was published in 1787. Article Four of this Edict decreed that all birth, marriage and death records be kept in German. On New Year's day, 1788, the Recruiting Act was promulgated, making Austria the first European state to impose compulsory military service on the Jews. The fact that military service at that time was only compulsory for serfs and the inhabitants of manorial towns, indisputably proved that the Emperor's sole purpose in adding the Jews to these categories was to accelerate their assimilation. Christian clergy, aristocracy and bureaucracy were exempt from the terms of this decree, as well as the freemen of the imperial cities and the yeomanry. At first, the Jewish soldiers were only detailed for service as carters, but in March, 1789, they were given the option of "rifle service." Whereas the upper class of wealthy merchants profited to the full from their extended rights, the broad masses of the Jewish population not only lacked elementary human rights, but were burdened with this additional duty—a duty which the Imperial Council in 1793 admitted to be the harshest of all duties toward the state: it was customary at that time not to discharge a soldier till the day he died.

The economic and legal status of the wealthy upper class Jews showed considerable change following the Emperor's reform measures. The freedom they acquired in the wholesale trade together with the increased facilities for visiting fairs in the imperial cities (where Jewish merchants were also permitted to take lodgings for the night) resulted in a thriving Jewish trade in raw materials and finished products. The Jewish merchants of Moravia, especially the textile and clothing merchants of Prossnitz, came to the imperial cities on market days and attended the fairs at Brünn, Olmütz, Troppau and other cities. The Bohemian-Jewish wool trade which supplied the local weavers with raw material was centred in the city of Reichenberg; the feather trade entered a new phase of development. Jewish merchant associations were founded, both local (as in the second-hand clothes trade at Prossnitz) and national (as in the feather trade). At Prague, wealthy Jewish merchants took advantage of their right to lease dwellings and to establish warehouses outside the ghetto. By 1811, seventy Jewish families, including fifteen commercial magnates and eighteen manufacturers were recorded in the Christian section of the city. Individual instances were also reported of permission being received to own buildings outside the Jewish quarters of Prague and the provincial cities. The group of Jewish factory owners was a new phenomenon. Jewish merchants had gained influence in some of the principal branches of industry by means of the commercial credit system. The Jews of Bohemia and Moravia built textile mills for the manufacture of woollens, cotton goods and silk cloth in Prague, Brünn and the provincial cities. Some of them settled in Vienna and established a widely diversified industry in the neighbourhood. The textile industry flourished, particularly during the French Revolution and the Napoleonic Wars, on the copious supplies consumed by the Army and the blockade which cut off imports from abroad. By 1807 the total of fifty-eight linen and cotton textile manufacturers in Bohemia already included fifteen Jews. The largest of these enterprises employed some 300 workers; in Prague alone, about 1,000 workers were employed by Jewish textile manufacturers.

The deterioration in the condition of the general Jewish population of the country contrasted dismally with the quick rise of the upper classes. During discussions of Jewish taxes in the middle of the 1790's, the gubernatorial advisor of Bohemia, J. A. Rieger, calculated that over half the Jews of Bohemia (4,600 out of 8,600 "tolerated" families) and a third of the Jews of Moravia (1,800 out of 5,400) were excluded by their poverty from estimates relating to the fowl consumption tax. The inability of the masses to pay the exorbitant Jewish taxes caused an annual increase in Kehillah indebtedness to the central government. By 1797, the Jews of Bohemia were estimated to be 500,000 florins in arrears with their tax payments.

Unlike his economic reforms, the Emperor's measures to disseminate the German language and culture amongst the Jewish masses had an immediate and tangible effect on their daily lives. The imperial decree was very powerful. The German-Jewish school at Prague was opened on May 2, 1782, with an official ceremony attended by the Chief Rabbi, Ezekiel Landau, who even wrote a Hebrew poem in honour of the event. The Kehillot were required to establish these schools with their own funds, but the government assisted them by allocating a share of the special fees (marriage and *minyan* payments) for this purpose. By 1787, twenty-five of these schools, with an enrolment of 559 pupils, existed in Bohemia. In the same year, 278 Jewish children were attending Christian schools in fifty-six cities and towns. By 1784, schools had been established in forty-two Moravian Kehillot. Unlike Bohemia, however, it was rare to find Jewish children in the Christian schools, undoubtedly because of the high concentration of the Moravian Jews in ghettos and the fact that their religious devoutness and traditionalism were stronger than those of their brethren in Bohemia. Study only lasted for four hours a day in these schools, as the pupils also attended *Heder* or *Talmud-Torah*. Yet, despite government pressure and Kehillah efforts to carry out their commitments, only a negligible minority of school-age children, recruited mainly from amongst the poor, attended the schools. The sons of the wealthy learned to read and write German from private tutors, while the majority of the Jewish population regarded the schools as dens of heresy and continued with an exclusively traditional education as before. The German-Jewish school did not become a widespread institution throughout all the Kehillot of Bohemia and Moravia until the first half of the nineteenth century and even then it was still, for the most part, supplemented by religious instruction at *Heder* or *Talmud-Torah*.

The spokesmen for the Jews of Bohemia realized the dangers of assimilation inherent in the imperial command concerning cognomens, and resisted it much more strongly. The people were deeply conscious of the Talmudical legend which tells how the children of Israel were delivered from Egypt because they had not changed their names. The Emperor's order only permitted the Jews to adopt German names, but the authorities also confirmed a number of Czech names which remained as historical evidence of friendly relations between Jewish pedlars and Czech peasants during the eighteenth century. The peasants had been accustomed to call the pedlars visiting their villages by the surnames of the hosts with whom they lodged—for example, Kafka, Kraupa, Mostny, Marudi, Studnitzka—and not by their Hebrew names, which they found difficult to pronounce. These appellations had become so firmly established, that not even the authorities ventured to change them.

The orthodox Jews of Bohemia and Moravia generally found Joseph II's order imposing compulsory military service the most oppressive of the imperial decrees. The Jews of Moravia sent a delegation to the Emperor to intercede for the annulment of the decree, and the Jews of Nikolsburg set up prayer groups to recite psalms in the synagogue throughout the night for the success of this mission. When all intercession failed, the Kehillah leaders were compelled not only to enforce the order, but also (as with the opening of the schools) to hold public celebrations in honour of the first conscripts (who were to serve as carters). An address to the recruits, delivered by the Chief Rabbi, Ezekiel Landau, at a celebration of this type at Prague in 1789, exposed his fear of the authorities and his anxiety over the dangers confronting the traditional religion. On the one hand, he urged the conscripts to obey their superior officers in all things and expressed the hope that devotion to duty would eliminate other discrimination against their brethren throughout the country. On the other hand, he tearfully bade them obey the dietary laws and, as circumstances permitted, the Sabbath laws as well. He presented each of them with a prayer shawl, phylacteries, and a prayer book. The recruits, when they left, kissed the hand of "the Renowned One of Judah" and embraced his knees in accordance with the homage customarily given a rabbi in that country. Barely a year later, the question of military service became the paramount issue in a controversy between the orthodox and enlightened factions in the Kehillah of the capital city of Bohemia.

Beginning of Reaction (1790-1815); First Signs of Haskalah; the Frankists

No significant changes occurred in the legal status of the Jews of Bohemia-Moravia in particular or of the Empire as a whole during Leopold's two-year reign from February, 1790, to March, 1792.

During the last years of his reign, Joseph II had expressed a wish to include the Jews of Bohemia and Moravia in some of the reforms he had already made for the Jews of Galicia. This raised the hopes of the enlightened Jews of Bohemia. At the beginning of May, 1790, Joachim Popper, *Landesprimator* for the Jews of Bohemia, sent a petition to the new Emperor asking that Joseph II's *Letter Patent* for the Jews of Galicia be extended to include the Jews of Bohemia. The orthodox circles were immediately spurred on to take action on their own account. A meeting was convened at the home of Rabbi Landau in Prague and a delegation was chosen. It submitted a memorandum to the Emperor "in the name of the entire Kehillah" of Prague asking for the restoration of the ancient privileges of the Jews of Bohemia. The memorandum was entirely devoted to religious matters, apart from a request for greater leniency in government issue of marriage licences.

The enlightened circles submitted their memorandum to the Emperor very shortly afterwards. The signatories of the orthodox memorandum had included some of the wealthy men of the Kehillah; but it was characteristic of the social rank of the enlightened faction that the eleven signatories who stated their occupations (out of the seventy men who signed the memorandum) consisted of five factory owners, three wholesalers (in the wool trade), and three members of the liberal professions. This memorandum protested against the orthodox memorandum and claimed that its sponsors had no authority to speak on behalf of the Kehillah as a whole. Its enlightened signatories stated before the Bohemian *Gubernium* Committee that the Jewish faith was not being persecuted by the government; on the contrary, it enjoyed the protection of its laws. In an additional memorandum, submitted in November, 1790, they also repudiated the orthodox demand for the reinstatement of the Jewish religious law in questions of marital relationships and inheritances. They considered that civil law did in fact avert conflicts and family squabbles in these matters. The supplementary memorandum dealt at length with the question of Jewish military service. It attempted, on the basis of quotations from the Talmud, the Codifiers, and international law, to prove that religion could not interfere with the discharge of civic obligations, especially "since the rulers of the state do not go forth to do battle unless the cause is just."

The narrow class egoism and obsequious attitude towards the government in the memorandum of the Jewish plutocracy of Bohemia closely resembled the behaviour of the French-Jewish plutocracy during the early revolutionary period and the rule of Napoleon Bonaparte. Just as the Sephardi money magnates at Bordeaux had tried to convince the National Assembly that they were superior to their co-religionists of Alsace-Lorraine, so the great Jewish merchants and industrialists of Bohemia apologetically submitted to the government that they deserved more indulgent laws than those enacted for the Jews of Galicia. The Jewish plutocrats of Bohemia actually anticipated the Paris Assembly of Notables by a decade and a half in their protestations of undying "love for the fatherland." The only difference was that the spokesmen of French Jewry acted as they did because of the complete equality of rights that they already possessed, whereas the pioneers of the Jewish middle class of Bohemia (like the members of their class in Prussia) abased themselves before the imperial authority because of the slightly improved legal status gained by their class alone. It is equally true, however, that the conservative orthodox circles had no qualms about demanding that the old, essentially feudal, régime be restored, in spite of all its oppression of the Jewish population.

Enlightened and orthodox alike were disappointed in their hopes of Leopold. The Emperor only replied to one of the demands submitted by the orthodox: their request for alleviation ... facilitating the observation of the Sabbath and the dietary laws by imprisoned Jews. Compulsory military service remained in full force for the Jews of Bohemia, in sharp contrast with Galicia, where the Emperor had entirely replaced it by exemption which could be purchased at thirty florins per head. However, the full weight of reaction did not fall upon the Jews of Bohemia until the reign of the Emperor Francis. In an Edict of 1794, the Emperor instructed the *Gubernium* of Bohemia, even in places where the number of Jewish families was below the established quota, not to issue marriage licences or residence permits unless there was a decline in the Jewish population in places where it exceeded the quota. New decrees also made compulsory military service more onerous. At the end of 1792, the fee for the purchase of exemption was raised from thirty to 140 florins and the Jews of the entire province were made responsible for remission. In practice, the municipal authorities collected a fifth of the general conscript quota from amongst the Jews, ten times more than the ratio of their numbers to the general population. The payment of exemption money weighed heavily on the Kehillot which were already greatly in debt because of their inability to pay government taxes on time. Yet the government even claimed that this system was merciful and just. In 1796, when the Austrian campaign against revolutionary France was intensified, a new imperial decree compelled Jewish conscripts to discharge their military service in person, without the privilege of purchasing exemption. This was justified by the argument that it would lighten the heavy burden of military service which lay upon the Christian population.

At the beginning of Francis's reign, the *Gubernium* and the Imperial Council considered a new reform project for the Jews of Bohemia. In 1792, in connection with these discussions, the *Landesprimator*, Joachim Popper, submitted a memorandum to the government in the name of the Jews of the provincial cities of Bohemia, requesting an improvement in their condition. The authorities acknowledged the fact that the Jews were paying taxes above their means, and higher than the rest of the population, but they did not suggest even the slightest concession. Some even declared that at a time when the state so badly needed funds, "one does not hearken unto the voice of humanity." In contrast, the authorities promptly accepted those of the *Landesprimator's* recommendations which suited their own policy, such as his proposal not to issue a wedding permit unless the applicant could prove his capacity to pay at least ten florins yearly in taxes for three consecutive years. They also failed to react to any of the proposals in a memorandum submitted by the spokesman for the extreme assimilationists, Hertz Homberg—though he had written it at the request of the Ministry and received a gold medal from the Emperor for his efforts.

Hertz Homberg (1749-1841) represented the extremist branch of the *Haskalah* movement which was prepared to countenance the most brutal acts against the Jews in its anxiety to merge with the dominant nation and win the favour of the ruling power. Voicing a superficial rationalist doctrine that had its origins in a vulgarized Voltaireanism, Homberg regarded traditional Judaism as nothing but a collection of prejudices and superstitions that had gathered around the pure Biblical faith. He conceived this faith as identical with deism and akin to the distilled Christianity of the enlightened rulers. However, all Homberg's actions, though ostensibly motivated by philosophical principles, were actually impelled by the desire to enhance his own reputation and gain material reward. This trait of his character, coupled with his contempt for his own people, increased the dangers inherent in his official affiliation with the Jewish religious community. In the eyes of his own contemporaries in Galicia and Bohemia, he became the epitome of the slave of the régime and the enemy of the Jewish people.

Homberg was born in Lieben, near Prague, and educated at the *Yeshivot* of Prague and Pressburg. Caught up in the current of the Berlin *Haskalah* movement, he travelled to Germany to study philosophy and education. At Berlin he met Moses Mendelssohn, who took him into his home as a tutor for his children and also engaged him to participate in the German translation of the Pentateuch. When Joseph II's Jewish reform regulations were announced, Homberg returned to Bohemia and in 1784 was appointed Superintendent-in-Chief of all the German-Jewish schools in Galicia. When the discussions on reforms for the Jews of Bohemia were in progress, the government invited him to Vienna to draft a programme for a new law.

Homberg's memorandum to the government in 1794 explained that there were two main reasons for the unfortunate condition of the Jews: their own orthodoxy and their lack of permanent fixed rights under the law. Orthodoxy, he asserted, was the result of rabbinical greed for power and their consequent education of the people on the basis of the Talmud, which was "an unbounded ocean of casuistic, futile, disputations." Worst of all, he declared, were the emissaries from the Land of Israel, "Talmudic idlers from Palestine, who grew fat on the sweated brows of European Jews, who misled their brethren ... and return with their booty to the Promised Land ..." He also thought that the peculiar legal situation of the Jews had caused their economy to resemble an inverted pyramid, in that the majority were traders rather than agriculturalists. Homberg's proposals for promoting the enlightenment of the Jews were extreme: a strict censorship to purge the Talmud and all Hebrew writings of the warped ideas and redundant accretions of several thousand years, "in order to restore Judaism to its pristine source"; dissolution of the Kehillot, even in the form retained by law in Galicia; synagogue societies alone might continue to exist, but by choice and not by coercion; and the abolition of all rabbinical posts except in Prague, where no more than one rabbinical position could be permitted. The teachers at the Jewish schools would replace the rabbis as the spiritual leaders of the people and Jewish youth would be required to listen to their sermons (chapters from their textbooks) every Saturday. The government would, of course, have to play its part. It should extend civil rights to those Jews who earned them by observing all the following conditions for ten years: shaving their beards and in no way differing from Christians externally; not violating any of the laws of the state or engaging in moneylending; engaging in useful occupations such as legally sanctioned commerce, manual crafts, or cultivation of the land; holding certificates of graduation from a school; and possessing affidavits confirming that they were not in arrears with their taxes. Jews serving in the army would immediately obtain citizenship rights. Homberg followed these assimilationist proposals (divided by a hair's breadth from total apostasy) by the naive question: "If there be such Jews who, from the state's point of view, have ceased to be Jews, is it not meet that the State finally desist from treating them as though they were Jews?"

The government accepted Homberg's proposals to accelerate the assimilation of the Jews, in principle, though not in all their details. In 1797, an Imperial *Letters Patent* for the Jews of Bohemia merely confirmed the existing decrees with greater severity and added several more. The decree concerning religious affairs laid down that popular preachers (*darshanim*) and cantors travelling from city to city were to be classed as vagabonds and expelled from the country. The maintenance of rabbis at community expense became optional and not compulsory. Only men holding degrees from the philosophy faculty of the State University could be appointed to rabbinical posts. The Jews were forbidden to employ special teachers or *Yeshivah* Heads to give instruction in the Talmud. This task was to fall to the rabbi alone. Any youth who failed to present a certificate from the principal of a Christian school testifying to his complete knowledge of spoken and written German could not be taught Talmud. The same certificate was a prerequisite for obtaining a marriage licence. Three years from the date of promulgation of the decree no religious books were to be in use, in a home or a synagogue, that were not printed within the country. Only the Prague Kehillah was left unscathed and even then its *Parnassim* were to be elected solely by the property owners and subject to confirmation by the municipality and the *Gubernium*. To convince the Jewish population that it was equally concerned with the cause of justice, the government, in the same law, prohibited all acts of oppression and exploitation by the *Parnassim* on pain of flogging and expulsion from the country.

The clauses of the law governing Jewish rights of domicile and occupation were even more stringent than the assimilation provisions. A further condition was added to the fixed family quota and the obligation to learn German, on which permission to marry depended. It stipulated that the groom earn his living in a legally sanctioned occupation and that he possess assets of at least 300 florins in a village, or 500 florins in a city. Emigration was only allowed on the payment of 10 per cent of the individual's property if he were moving to another part of the Empire, or 20 per cent if leaving the Empire. The branches of trade permitted to the Jews specifically included the wholesale trade, trade in special commodities such as potash, hides and wool, and peddling (but only old clothes and second-hand articles inside Prague!). To engage in crafts, the Jew had to pass an examination by the heads of the Christian craft guilds. Jews were forbidden to lease public houses and mills. Jews engaging in commerce had to obtain permits from the authorities specifying the class of merchandise authorised. The government probably thought that it was being most considerate in allowing Jews to work as day labourers, shop assistants, and porters (this latter only in Prague and within a quota determined by the authorities). Jews who volunteered for the army, worked on the land, or worked as artisans in the guild crafts were to receive preferential treatment: they would be allowed to marry outside the regular family quota and would be taxed on the same basis as Christians. On the other hand, any Jew who failed, within one year, to prove that he was engaged in a legal occupation was subject to deportation from the country, "as befits a non-useful, harmful subject."

The *Patent* left the Jews of Bohemia no trace of the fractional rights that the régime of enlightened despotism had bequeathed, which might have offset the demand for complete assimilation. In fact, they aggravated the situation by the imposition of renewed police injunctions in economic matters and on their rights of natural increase. Even Homberg in his memorandum was forced to define these measures as "a regrettable necessity" or "an unnatural thing." And yet the Emperor prefaced his *Patent* with the customary cant reaffirming his love of humanity and describing the reforms as the outcome of his attempts totally to abolish discrimination between his Christian and Jewish subjects under the law.

Towards the end of 1798, the representatives of the Jews of Prague presented their grievances against the *Letters Patent* to the Emperor. The government replied at the beginning of 1801, refusing any modification whatsoever of any decree. The repressive *Letters Patent* therefore remained in force for the Jews of Bohemia until the revolution in 1848. The rich found ways to circumvent the restrictions, particularly those aimed at curbing natural increase. They bribed government officials, paid "ransom money" to Kehillah heads for possession of a *Familiant* when one fell vacant, and occasionally obtained testimonials from the local authorities that their sons were employed as agricultural workers in the fields of the estate proprietors. The sons of the poor were forced to resort to secret marriage ceremonies and go into hiding because of their illegal status or else emigrate to neighbouring Hungary.

Jewish young men, like the Christian peasants, fled from the recruiting edict and wandered from Kehillah to Kehillah. None the less, thousands of Bohemian and Moravian Jews worked in the military camps of the Austrian Army and died in battle in the war against the French Revolution and Napoleon Bonaparte. Under the guidance of the *Parnassim* and rabbis, the Kehillot felt obliged to contribute their share towards the war, which the Emperor had been "forced" to wage. In 1810, the Kehillot complied with an imperial command to surrender to the mint all silver objects in the synagogues and those held by the various societies. They did not spare even ancient works of Jewish art. Orthodox circles were in fact in sympathy with the Austrian cause, not only because of their traditional loyalty to the ruling power, but also because of their antagonism to the French Revolution. Even the spokesman of the moderate *Maskilim*, Abraham Trebitsch, in his news summary, *A Chronicle of the Times*, published in Hebrew at Brünn in 1801, expressed his anger at the "errant scourge." He was particularly vehement on the subject of the "Jacobins, who hate all monarchs, acknowledge no king or master, and rule with a government of iniquity," and quoted a passage from the Scriptures in this context: "For three things the earth doth quake, and for four it cannot endure: for a servant when he reigneth . . . and a handmaid that is heir to her mistress." (Proverbs, 30, 21-23). The restoration of the monarchy by Napoleon was instrumental in modifying the attitude of Jewish conservatives towards France.

Despite the official, though naive, "patriotism" that they displayed towards the Austrian crown, Francis I was still afraid that his oppressed Jews might sympathize with progressive France. When, in the autumn of 1806, news first reached Austria of the manifesto of the Paris Assembly of Notables inviting all the Kehillot of Europe to participate in the *Grand Sanhedrin*, Francis instructed his authorities to keep a special watch on teachers in German-Jewish schools and on any Jews whose views tended towards deism. The authorities at Prague, Bidschov and Trebitsch reported that the young Jewish intellectual class was enthusiastic about Napoleon and had high hopes of him, both because of the enfranchisement achieved by the Jews in the lands under his rule and because of the reforms he was enacting in the Jewish religion—which they would dearly like to see in Bohemia and Moravia. On the other side, orthodox aversion to any religious reform made conservative Jewish circles generally suspicious of the *Sanhedrin*, though some members felt sympathy for the supposed plans of the French Emperor. According to a report by the Nikolsburg police, the Jews of Moravia were still under the delusion that Napoleon intended to rebuild Jerusalem and establish the state of Israel "and would settle there the dignitaries, the wealthy, and the diligent of the world's Jews in order to promote the colonial trade." The same ideas were also cherished by the remnants of the Shabbetai Zvi movement, the repercussions of which had not yet died out in Moravia, while Frankist groups in Bohemia sought to revive it.

During the Napoleonic Wars, it was already obvious that the Austrian government's promise that the Jews would achieve equal rights after "they had mended their ways," and especially learned to speak German, contained no substance. In 1811, the Jews of Bohemia submitted a new memorandum on the amelioration of their legal status. In 1813, the *Gubernium* administration—now under the control of officials educated in the spirit of Joseph II's reforms—supported the Jewish request and suggested improving their position by gradual enfranchisement. The *Gubernium* reported that according to information submitted by the local authorities, the Jews had complied with all the conditions stipulated in the *Letters Patent* of 1797. "In respect of dwelling, customs, attire, and speech they now differ but little from the Christian population; they aspire to an even greater degree of equality with the Christians by being trained in science, commercial matters and industry; they have ceased to engage in moneylending and their patriotism, too, is constantly growing." This description by the enlightened officials was, in the main, a true picture of the life and aspirations of the Jewish plutocracy of Bohemia, which was desperately anxious to imitate the Christian middle class. Nevertheless, the government was unwilling to grant any concessions, even to Jews who had earned this official testimony to their "good behaviour." The Austrian régime was based on a system of national and religious oppression, inseparable from the rigid feudal order.

Despite government measures to accelerate their assimilation, most of the Jews of Bohemia and the great majority in Moravia were devoted, even during that period, to their traditional religious way of life, the Yiddish language and their cultural heritage. Studies at the *Yeshivot* of Prague and the Moravian cities continued as before, and exegetical books on the Talmud and the Codifiers were still published—to the dismay of the censors. These books included publications which were acclaimed by Jews throughout the Diaspora, for example, Rabbi Landau's *Responsa* and his exegeses on *Tractates of the Talmud, Tziyun Le'nefesh Chayyah* (*Commemoration for a Living Soul*). During the same period, *Machatzit Ha'shekel* (*A Half Shekel*) was published. It was written by Samuel Halevi of Kolin, head of the *Yeshivah* at Boskowitz, and was a supplementary commentary to the *Magen Avraham* (Shield of Abraham), which in turn had been written by Abraham of Gombin as a Commentary to the first part of Joseph Caro's *Shulhan Arukh*.

None the less, the scope of orthodox control decreased in the face of the *Haskalah* movement which was now spreading to the provincial cities. This was apparent from the defensive attitude that the conservative camp assumed. Travelling *darshanim* visiting the Kehillot frequently preached against Jews engaging in secular studies or reading books such as Mendelssohn's *Commentary*—for the *Haskalah* movement already numbered individual rabbis in the provincial towns of Bohemia among its new devotees.

The capital, Prague, was the centre of the movement in Bohemia. Its supporters and benefactors belonged to the thin, newly-formed layer of the Jewish middle class: the industrialists and trading magnates who had close ties with the government had benefited from its "generosity" and even, in some instances, been officially decorated. Titles of nobility had actually been granted to Joachim Popper, *Landesprimator* for the Jews of Bohemia, and the Hoenigsberg family. The subscription list to the Berlin *Me'asef* showed an increasing number of wealthy families. In 1785, there were twelve subscribers in Prague. When publication was renewed in 1809, there were fifty-three in Prague alone. The principal exponents of the *Haskalah* movement were the teachers in the German-Jewish schools, including authors of German language text-books, Hebrew grammar books in the German language, and Hebrew-German dictionaries. A group of extreme assimilationists amongst these teachers tended strongly towards the views of Hertz Homberg. Like Homberg, they sent memoranda to the authorities on effective methods for spreading "the pure German language" amongst the Jews and for establishing German as the language of religious instruction. With the exception of the government-inspired Germanizers however, extreme assimilationism had so far made no headway even within the new Jewish middle class and cases of religious conversion were extremely rare.

The old printing houses of Prague (though by the beginning of the nineteenth century only one remained) and a new one at Brünn, played an important part in disseminating *Haskalah* ideas in Bohemia-Moravia. These establishments printed several works by the outstanding *Maskilim* of Germany as well as the essays of the first eastern European *Maskilim*, such as Baruch of Shklov. Some members of the group of young Hebrew writers, born and educated in Bohemia, were already rising to prominence at that time. They included the philologist and grammarian, Judah Jeiteles, and the poet-grammarian, Solomon Loewisohn (actually born in Hungary, but educated at the *Yeshivah* and University of Prague). The views of the moderate *Maskilim* were expressed by Baruch Jeiteles, brother of Judah, and Abraham Trebitsch of Nikolsburg. Trebitsch, though an admirer of Mendelssohn and Wessely, wrote his *Chronicle of the Times* deliberately to prove the force of Divine Providence in the history of the Jewish people and to discredit the "fallacious opinions" of those who, "like primitive aborigines, attribute all things to nature."

The orthodox faction retained the upper hand in the first clash between conservatism and the rising *Haskalah* movement. Even at Prague, their authority over the Kehillah was still so great that young Jews went outside the city to read the works of classical German writers; even in their own homes, they only dared to read secular books furtively, by night.

The Frankist episode in Bohemia was also linked with the unique cultural situation of the Jews there. At the beginning of the nineteenth century, the *Haskalah* movement in Bohemia had barely begun and religious orthodoxy was still all-powerful. The ground was therefore ripe for the strange emergence of Frankism. On the one hand, it actively revolted against the type of congealed orthodoxy which even found fault with Hasidism; on the other, it counter-balanced the early *Maskilim*'s disregard for the historic ideal of Jewish regeneration in the ancient homeland. The stormy political atmosphere of the period following the French Revolution, and particularly Napoleon's 1799 campaign for the conquest of Palestine, inspired a few brave souls with hope and prompted them to band together to achieve their mystic aims.

Frank's sojourn in Moravia left some remnants of his sect in that country and in Bohemia, even after he himself moved to Offenbach in 1786. He died there five years later. Rabbi Ezekiel Landau had investigated Frankist customs in Podolia while he was still Rabbi at Yampol. He took measures against them in Prague and actually called a meeting of people suspected of sympathizing with the sect. The Frankists renewed their activity in Bohemia after his death, in 1793. At the end of the eighteenth century, they numbered fifty in all, mostly in Prague, and included members of the prominent and wealthy Wehle, Porges, and Bondy families. The remainder lived in the provincial cities of Jitschin and Kolin, and the area around Teplitz. Unlike the Polish Frankists, they did not break completely with the Jewish religion, and in public they behaved like any other Jews. Two very different anonymous accounts (one by an informer against them to the Prague authorities in 1799, the other a written defence by a *Maskil* in 1800) describe the tenet of their faith as their firm conviction of the imminence of Messianic redemption. Their isolation increased after some of them had made a pilgrimage to the centre of the movement at Offenbach and been disillusioned to discover that the band, led by Eva Frank (the founder's daughter), was motivated entirely by material gain.

The leaders of the Prague group met violent attack from Landau's disciple, the rabbinical judge, Eleazar Fleckeles. In 1799, in a sermon at the New Synagogue, he accused them of all the evils—which, in actual fact, had only been practised by Frank's individual followers. At the beginning of 1800 the Frankist chiefs at Offenbach embarked on a lively propaganda campaign. They issued a proclamation in Hebrew (written in red ink and thus reminiscent of *Edom*, a common designation for Christians) to "Our Loved Ones of the Houses of Israel" and sent it to scores of Kehillot in Poland and the Ukraine as well as Bohemia and Moravia. The proclamation announced that according to a vision, "this year of 5560 After the Creation will be a time of troubles for the Jews." On the basis of Frank's *Sacred Epistles*, written during his incarceration in the fortress of Czestochowa, they summoned them "to go unto the holy faith of Edom," whereby "you shall speedily enjoy all the consolations promised us by his servants, the prophets ..." Fleckeles no longer felt that mere sermons were sufficient in the face of this propaganda, openly urging conversion to Christianity. In company with his two associates in the rabbinical judiciary, he issued a court order against the Frankists. The proclamation of 5486 (1725) against Shabbetai Zvi was read out before the *Kol Nidrei* service in the year 5561 (autumn, 1800) in all the synagogues of Prague, and nailed on the doors of all houses of prayer, together with a new proclamation against the Frankists. Thenceforth, the Frankists were fair game for every kind of insult and humiliation at the hands of an excited crowd in the streets. Their persecution only ceased after intervention by the authorities and intercession by a number of *Maskilim*. The movement expired after it had been proscribed by the government.

The sympathy that some Bohemian *Maskilim* felt for these sectarians arose from the need for a common defence against orthodox aggression. A memorandum that the *Maskil*, Loew Hanokh Hoenig von Hoenigsberg, submitted to the police in 1800, showed that the predicament of the *Maskilim* in the Prague Kehillah was not much better than that of the outcast Frankists. They were subjected to insolence in the synagogues and on the streets. Private teachers suspected of being *Haskalah* adherents found that their jobs were jeopardized.

The first indications that the orthodox were succumbing to the contemporary atmosphere appeared while the crusade against the Frankists was at its height. In 1800, Rabbi Elazar Fleckeles published a booklet of sermons against this sect under the title *Love of David*. He quoted from a letter by Wessely "to one of the residents of the city of Prague" to corroborate his view that prying into Kabbalah was dangerous for someone not thoroughly cognizant of the Talmud and the Codifiers. He prefaced his quotation with fulsome praise of "this writer of beautiful poems." Scarcely twenty years later, Rabbi Samuel Landau, son of "The Renowned One In Judah," then Chief Rabbinical Judge at Prague, recommended in a sermon Mendelssohn's translation "in its precise and lucid German," thus in a sense resurrecting Wessely's educational programme of *Words of Peace and of Truth*. Whereas his late father had regarded that same book of Wessely as "a root begetting bitter fruits," the younger Landau could now concede that not all Jews were born to be Talmudic scholars and that secular studies might therefore be useful in preparing young Jews for life.

C. HUNGARY

Economic and Legal Status; The Kehillah Régime

Hungary, with its retarded economic and social development, was inseparably a part of feudal eastern Europe. As late as 1840, its urban population only formed a twentieth of the total, and even then a considerable proportion of the townspeople also engaged in agriculture. As in neighbouring Poland, the Jews of Hungary had the advantage of the protection of the estate-owning magnates and nobility. Their patronage and the favours they granted enabled the Jews to earn their living as middlemen between squire and peasant, circumventing the burghers' measures to restrain their trade. Assistance from the aristocracy, which jealously guarded its privileges against the ruling Austrian foreigners, was again instrumental in helping the Jews of Hungary to avoid the full impact of the severe repression that the absolutist Habsburg régime enforced in neighbouring Austria, Bohemia and Moravia. However, in contrast with Poland, where the cities only possessed limited rights, Hungary's Crown cities, mostly populated by Germans, enjoyed a wide measure of autonomy. Hence the Hungarian Jews, who were mostly concentrated in the economically more developed west central region, had to engage, in a prolonged struggle for domiciliary and trading rights against the burghers—who insisted on their privileges and rights of seniority in the country as a whole, as well as in its cities.

The Hungarian Jewish community already included a large number of immigrants during the first half of the eighteenth century. As had been the case with late medieval fifteenth- and sixteenth-century Poland, eighteenth-century Hungary provided a refuge for Jews from the west. After 1725, the pressures to which the Jews of Germany were subjected, and especially the imposition of family quotas in Bohemia and Moravia, brought new waves of Jewish immigrants to Hungary every year. Polish Jews were prominent among the new settlers, especially from the Galician districts beyond the Carpathians, where the situation had deteriorated progressively as a result of economic decline and irresponsible rule by the nobility. Census returns for 1735 and 1737 showed that the majority of Jews in the major Kehillah of Pressburg (Bratislava), and at Buda, were not born in Hungary. Instead, they came from Germany, Poland, Moravia and Bohemia. During the second half of the eighteenth century, the immigration to Hungary of Moravian Jews in particular took on vast proportions and continued unabated; at the beginning of the nineteenth century, it rose to even greater heights. In addition there was a stream of immigrants from Galicia, most of whom settled in the northern counties (comitatus) of the country. In 1787, nearly 81,000 Jews were registered in Hungary; by 1805 their number had increased to 127,816.

The Jewish community was unevenly distributed over the country. In 1729, a royal decree expelled the Jews from Dalmatia, Croatia, and Slavonia, where they had been living illegally. In 1803, only 2,108 Jews were registered in Transylvania. As already stated, most of the country's Jews lived in the west central areas, on both sides of the Danube. The largest Kehillah in the country was situated there, in the city of Pressburg; this was also the region of the ancient "Seven Kehillot" of Eisenstadt, Marchegg, Mattersdorf, and four lesser communities in the small area of the county of Oedenburg (Burgenland) on the Austrian frontier. A handful of Jews lived in towns and villages in the west-Slovakian area of mountainous northern "Upper Hungary," and in Carpatho-Russia. The principal occupation of the Jews in the cities of the developed western area was trade. Import and export merchants formed the upper stratum of these traders. They brought woollens and linen, as well as various fancy goods from neighbouring Moravia, and shipped raw wool and hides to Bohemia and Moravia, in particular. The Jewish merchants of Hungary, especially those from Pressburg, also held partnerships in Moravian-Jewish trading firms which imported woven fabrics. The wine trade became widespread amongst the Jews of Hungary despite the prohibition that the *Landtag* (The Estates General, or Diet) imposed and renewed in 1741, and which affected Greek and Armenian traders as well. The Pressburg Jews traded in wine as far afield as the cities of Poland, using the credit system in their dealing: they extended interest-bearing loans to the owners of the vineyards on account of the coming grape harvest. So much of the country's copper exports were concentrated in Jewish hands that the government did not consider it feasible to close this field of commerce to them. The wealthy Jewish merchant class also included the liquor distillery lessees, found in all the Kehillot, army suppliers, and customs duty farmers, maintained by the authorities in various places contrary to the law.

The middle-class Jewish merchants owned linen and woollen stores. Beneath them in the social scale and more numerous were the dealers in fancy goods, tobacco, old clothes, scrap iron, and junk. As in neighbouring Moravia, the largest trading group consisted of pedlars. They obtained their wares—linen, woollens and trinkets—on credit from Jewish merchants, and occasionally from Christian storekeepers in town. Some of them peddled from house to house in the cities, visiting the courtyards of noblemen and innkeepers particularly assiduously, while a few travelled through the countryside, trading with peasants on credit or by barter. The servants and traders' assistants ranked as the proletariat and at times comprised a third (in Pressburg, actually a half) of all the family heads in any Kehillah. The numbers of Jewish women servants (cooks) suggested the wealth commanded by the Jewish merchant class of western Hungary at that time.

The *Litterae Privilegiorum* (Letters of Rights) granted by the lords of the cities and their suburbs (as at Pressburg) specifically allowed Jews to practise manual trades. However, they usually added the qualification that a craft could only be practised to fill mutual requirements by fellow-Jews (as at Eisenstadt). The quota of Jewish artisans allowed was sometimes determined separately for each craft (e.g., Mattersdorf). In actual fact, the number of Jewish artisans was not large, not merely because of these provisos (in Poland the Jews had found ways to circumvent more stringent regulations concerning manual trades), but because of economic conditions in the country and in the cities where the Jews resided. The Jews were attracted more powerfully to trade than to handicraft and, despite all the decrees promulgated by the municipalities, a wide field of activity was open to them in western Hungary. The western origins of the Hungarian Jews would have represented an additional factor in their commercial success. Census returns for 1735-37 showed that the Jewish artisans in the old city of Buda scarcely comprised 25 per cent of all the family heads in the Kehillah. In the city of Eisenstadt they were hardly a fifth; while in Pressburg, only a few individuals were registered as artisans. Apart from butchers, who were the most numerous, those registered included tailors, cobblers, belt-makers, jewellers, glaziers, tanners and bookbinders. Needlework, for the most part, was the occupation of impoverished widows.

Most of the Jews in Upper Hungary lived in villages. The Jews were generally not permitted to live in the royal free cities. The private cities, on the other hand, which were the property of the magnates, were not essentially different from the villages and most of their inhabitants were peasants as far as economic and legal status were concerned. In one of these cities, Munkacz, Jews did not form a religious prayer quorum until the middle of the eighteenth century, and their numbers were not sufficient to warrant the erection of a synagogue until the end of that century. Only a few Jews engaged in trade as their main source of income, either making their own transport arrangements to send raw wool, potash, and wine to Poland, or using Polish Jews as middlemen for these exports. Artisans were even rarer, with the sole exception of butchers. The main Jewish source of income was obtained by acting as lessees and publicans. The lessees obtained the right to distil liquor and to operate inns and taverns from the estate owners and were usually also granted leases on flour mills, on the sale of meat, and toll collections from transients. Even those Jews engaged in petty trade often resorted to leaseholding. On some estates, payments for lease rights were also associated with the raw wool and wine trades, as well as with the sale of candles and soap in taverns.

The village innkeepers and publicans were only the paid employees of the lessees. Their difficult economic position is indicated by the fact that not one of them was ever registered as the owner of a single horse or cow—at a time when lessees owned numerous horses, cows and beehives. Documents specifically listed the servant and tenant families in the houses of lessees as abjectly poor (*miserabiles*) and this category also included ritual slaughterers, religious teachers, and musicians (*kle'zmer*). In some places, *miserabiles* comprised a quarter of all Jewish families on a proprietor's estate. Apart from the actual lessees, Jewish *compossessores* (co-occupants) who leased part of the noble's estate to raise herds of cattle were also widespread in Upper Hungary. In some villages in the Carpatho-Russian district Jewish peasants cultivated plots of land.

The legal status of the Jews on the estates and in the private towns of the nobles and magnates was secure. The Jews of the Crown cities, conversely, had to struggle persistently and obstinately for rights of domicile and trade. The burghers explained that their campaign against the Jews was to defend local trade against foreigners in general. Their memoranda to the *Landtag* and to the King* often included the Jews in the same category as Armenians, Turks, Wallachians (Rumanians), and Greeks. The Jews were obviously not the burghers' only competitors, therefore, when the capitalist trend towards free trade conflicted with the antiquated feudal monopoly of the burghers' merchant guilds, with their extraordinary privileges of immunity. They were only the most serious and the most skilful. However, the King's interest in the development of trade prevailed over all racial and religious prejudice. As a result also of the protection of the magnates, who collected substantial revenues from their subjects, the Jews succeeded in establishing a foothold in several royal cities and trading in most of them despite bitter opposition from the municipalities and merchant guilds. In 1746, it is true, an order by Maria Theresa expelled the ancient Kehillah of Buda where Jews had lived since the second century. But during the same period, Jewish merchants attended fairs in nearly all the royal cities and in some of them succeeded in extending both their trading rights and the area where they could stay. In the provincial capital of Pressburg, Jews had lived under ducal

* The Habsburg Emperor of Austria was officially the King of Hungary.

patronage at the foot of the Schlossberg and the surrounding neighbourhood since the end of the sixteenth century, separated from the rest of the
city by an iron gate. The Kehillah there continued to grow until it became
the largest in the country during the eighteenth century.

The state authorities and the aristocracy were both very anxious to
preserve the broad autonomous powers vested in the Kehillot—though
under government supervision. Kehillah regulations were ineffective
unless ratified by the city proprietor. In some instances, his permission
was required to hold the annual election to the office of Kehillah leader.
As in neighbouring Moravia, the Kehillah was governed by seven Optimates consisting of the Kehillah leader (*Judenrichter*), four Associates
(*Beisitzer*), and two Charity Stewards (*Gabba'ei-Tz'dakah*), who handled
charity affairs and supervised the synagogues. In most cases an additional
trustee was elected, two or three members were appointed to take charge
of sanitation and weights and measures, and others to serve as tax-
assessors—a collector each for *Talmud-Torah*, the local poor, and for
Palestine. The large Kehillot, such as Pressburg, also elected law enforcement officials (*Polizeimacher*) as well as special appraisers (triennially) to
estimate the number of *Pletn* (lodging tickets) to be issued to feed and
shelter mendicant "guests" from out of town. In 1740, the Kehillah of
Pressburg, in wholehearted co-operation with the estate proprietor, passed
a regulation disenfranchising people who had not paid their Kehillah taxes
or patronage fees on time The latter were not even allowed to give their
children in marriage; the same injunction was also adopted by the
Eisenstadt Kehillah. At Pressburg, a regular hierarchical system prevailed
in the election of Kehillah officers. No one could be elected to the position
of Optimate unless he had previously served as a trustee, charity steward,
or law enforcement official; he could not be elected Kehillah leader unless
he had held office as an Optimate.

The Kehillah leader and the Optimates adjudicated in matters of
financial litigation, though the contestants also had the right to appeal to
the rabbinical court and even to the "Kehillah Assembly," which included
"distinguished individuals" as well as the Kehillah leaders. The *Letters of
Privilege* for the Kehillot of western Hungary required any Christian
bringing a charge against a Jew to appear before a Jewish judge. Only in a
few places were suits of this type heard by an official representing the
proprietor of the city, in the presence of the Jewish judge (as in Moravia).
Kehillah revenues were derived from taxes on liquor, beer and salt, but
particularly on meat and wine; as in Moravia, they were known as *Brievel
Geld*. Again on the Moravian pattern, a *Pardon*, or excise was levied on
commodities, artisan's fees and wages.

The Kehillah regulations were designed to guard the prerogatives
of the merchants and to prevent unfair competition. To protect the
interests of property owners, it was illegal to employ a male or female
servant without the consent of their previous employers. The Kehillah

leaders jealously defended, with the same narrow economic parochialism as the Christian merchant guilds, their own commercial interests against Jewish traders from out of town. Not only were they determined to protect themselves against competition, but the Kehillot were also jealous of their control of the acceptance of new Jewish residents from outside because of their responsibility for tax remissions by the local Jewish inhabitants. Hungarian Kehillah organization on a basis of central and regional autonomy had been established by government initiative to ensure greater efficiency in the collection of taxes from the Jews. The Pressburg Council was convened to apportion toleration tax quotas amongst the Jews of the various counties (the tax was humorously termed *Queen Money*, after Queen Maria Theresa). The Jewish county leaders in their turn apportioned it amongst the various Kehillot.

The traditional method of apportioning the tax within the Kehillah and amongst the various Kehillot, was based on the opinions of the early codifiers of Talmudic Law, and represented a "compromise" between a fixed per capita levy and an income-property tax. Controversies usually revolved around the proportions in which the two principles were to be combined, and in the course of time, the less prosperous ventured to demand that the per capita basis be abolished entirely. In practice, the *Queen Money* was, for the most part, collected from the Kehillot in proportion to family assets. There were ceaseless complaints about the Kehillah assessors by Kehillot which felt ill-treated in the tax-apportionment by the County Councils. These grievances were frequently submitted to the County authorities and occasionally to government tribunals for judgement.

Culturally, immigration had made Hungarian Jewry during that period a branch of the Jewish community of Moravia and Bohemia, from which it had been built up. The Kehillah régime was a replica of the system prevalent in Moravia. In addition to the small *Yeshivot* in cities such as Eisenstadt and Mattersdorf, the *Yeshivah* at Pressburg became a centre of Talmudic study for the entire country when (like the Mattersdorf *Yeshivah*) it was re-opened at the beginning of the nineteenth century by Rabbi Moses Sofer, already distinguished for his achievements in the neighbouring countries.

The Hungarian Jews preserved the old atmosphere and customs with all their colourful folk-characteristics during that period (the "Seven Kehillot" did it even throughout the nineteenth century). The synagogue beadle (*shamash*) went from door to door knocking three times—only twice in token of mourning for funerals and on the Ninth of Av—to call the occupants to prayer or to a meeting at the synagogue. On Sabbath eve he called out, "*Gebreit zum Shabbes!*" ("Prepare for the Sabbath!") and on the morning of the day before Passover his cry was "*Chometz is osser zu essen!*"* Every day at noon, during the three weeks preceding the fast

* Literally, "It is forbidden to eat leavened!"

of the Ninth of Av, commemorating the destruction of the First and Second Temples at Jerusalem, the beadle would summon the members of the congregation to midnight services. On the eve of the Ninth of Av, it was the custom to drink lentil soup as a sign of mourning. "Pious men and men of accomplishment" remained in the synagogue throughout the night, studying legends associated with the destruction, and recited the midnight prayers (*Tikun Chatzot*) for the redemption of Israel. It was a widespread custom on the Ninth of Av throughout central and eastern Europe for children to walk to the cemeteries with bows and arrows. Once there, they shot the arrows into the air, then laid them on the graves. In the "Seven Kehillot" an ancient democratic tradition survived: at Mattersdorf, for example, the procedure was similar to the "Interruption of the Reading" still the custom in many countries during the nineteenth century. Every Monday and Thursday, a pause was made between one reading of the Torah portion and the next for *koivel sein*—voicing grievances. Anyone with a complaint against Kehillah management or Kehillah members could state his charge when the beadle had announced, "That we may fulfil (the saying) 'Then ye shall be clear . . .' "* On the other hand, anyone who slandered the leaders or the Optimates, "the Leaders and Directors of the Flock of Israel," was not only fined and temporarily deprived of his right to participate in the Assembly and the privilege of membership, but was also required to beg forgiveness. Even as late as the beginning of the nineteenth century (at Eisenstadt, in 1803) all kinds of innovations in female clothing "which have not formerly been in our Congregation here" were very conscientiously ostracized.

The educational system of Hungarian Jewry was also not much different from the Moravian. A large number of their teachers came from Moravia, though there were others from Bohemia, Germany and Poland. Nevertheless, the Berlin *Haskalah* penetrated to the homes of some of the wealthy merchants and lessees through these teachers, enlightened young men from Bohemia and Moravia who even succeeded in circulating Mendelssohn's *Commentary* in the remotest villages. The *Haskalah* movement was particularly successful in the "Seven Kehillot" and in Pressburg—both closer to Austria than to Hungary, while the Mattersdorf Kehillah forged ahead of events by opening a German language school even before the promulgation of Joseph II's decree.

Joseph II's reforms for the Jews of Hungary, which were essentially included in the *Toleranzpatent* of 1783, were no different from those for the neighbouring countries except for slight adaptations to local conditions. In addition to the freedom acquired for wholesale trading and peddling, the ban on Jewish trade in gunpowder and salt was specifically removed. On the other hand, the injunction against Jewish residence in the free cities of the Crown was not in practice withdrawn, except for

* According to the book of Numbers, 32,22, "And then ye shall be clear before the Lord and before Israel . . ."

favoured individual large-scale merchants, who were expressly granted this right by the King or his Imperial Palatine. The absolute ban on Jewish residence in the mining towns or in their neighbourhood remained fully effective. The permission obtained for Jews to cultivate the land was of no practical significance, even though it covered the leasing of peasant farmsteads, which was not the case in Bohemia or Moravia. Fortunately for the Jews, the King's decrees against the leasing of liquor distilleries were ineffectual in practice. The estate proprietors adopted the stratagem of registering their Jewish lessees as employees operating public houses. When Jews were also forbidden to work in this capacity in 1786, the nobles continued to retain their lessees and publicans in defiance of the law.

The Emperor's measures for the education of the Jews of Hungary were drawn up in even greater detail than for the other countries of his realm. In the case of the Hungarian Jews, his object was not to Germanize them, but rather to eradicate Jewish nationality and particularly the "Jewish jargon" (Yiddish). Thus, the law required all business ledgers, contracts, and other documents to be written in one of three languages, Latin, German, or Hungarian. A two years' period of grace was allowed. The Jewish curriculum was brought into line with the Christian schools in the country, to include the study of Hungarian and Slovakian as well as German. A number of special provisions designed to defeat the "notorious obstinacy" and "cunning" of the Jews was inserted in the compulsory school education law. Children were not to be privately taught in places where schools had been opened, or, for that matter, anywhere else, after a period of four years had elapsed, except in the case of children who held school leaving certificates. All badges of shame were abolished and Jews were permitted to wear swords—this was, of course, one of the devices intended to expedite assimilation.

The year following the promulgation of this ordinance saw the opening of the first of the schools in the large Kehillot, with official ceremonies held in the presence of the authorities and the Kehillah leaders. The schools and their enrolment increased rapidly after an edict in 1786 made the issuing of marriage licences to Jews depend upon documentary proof of graduation from a school. Teachers and textbooks were imported from Germany and Bohemia. Generally, the Kehillah schools did not teach any of the languages of the country except German. However, even towards the end of Joseph II's reign, hardly more than thirty of these schools existed in all Hungary and the number of pupils enrolled was below 2,000. The number of Jewish children attending Christian schools was negligible. After the Emperor's death, the secular schools were either liquidated by the Kehillot or converted into traditional *Hadarim*.

During Joseph II's reign, the burghers' campaign against Jewish domiciliary rights and trade had subsided. It flared up again immediately after his death. Letters were exchanged by the merchant guilds in the cities of Kosice, Raab and Pressburg, with a view to taking action in the *Landtag* and sending a deputation to the Emperor in order to limit the expansion of Jewish rights. The Jews, for their part, were also moved to action by the prospect of the convocation of the *Landtag* at the beginning of Leopold's reign. They would seem to have been encouraged both by the French Revolution and by the information that the *Landtag* (similarly influenced by the spirit of the Revolution) was to consider increasing the rights of the Protestants. In 1790, the Jews of Hungary presented a nine article memorandum to the *Landtag*, with the following requests: freedom to settle in all parts of the country; the right to buy houses and fields; freedom to trade on market days and fair days; freedom to engage in peddling throughout the year; and the right to engage in manual trades and agriculture with the help of Christian employees. In 1792, a committee appointed by the *Landtag* drew up a programme for extending Jewish rights by allowing them to trade in every city, to buy houses on certain streets, and to engage in the handicrafts, for example. But the programme never even came to a debate at a plenary session of the *Landtag*. The only result of the discussions was a resolution of the *Landtag* in 1790 which was confirmed by a royal ordinance. This decreed that all the Jews in all the cities would retain the status they had possessed at the beginning of the year. Even this minute concession displeased the municipalities and guilds, but Leopold's successor, Francis, was nevertheless compelled to attach to the Ordinance of 1790 an official interpretation that corresponded to the arguments of the Jews. Similarly, in 1798, he did not grant the Pressburg merchant guild's demand that Jews be forbidden to engage in peddling. Thus, despite the narrow-minded attacks of the antagonistic municipalities, the Jews were able to establish themselves and to enlarge their precincts in several of the "free" cities. In Buda, which had replaced Pressburg as the state administrative centre, there were already sixty "tolerated" Jewish families by 1783. Only fourteen Jewish families had been registered as temporary residents (*commorantes*) in the neighbouring city of Pest in 1785; by the end of the eighteenth century, it numbered nearly 1,100 Jews with their own Kehillah.

However, as the Jewish community in the country continued to grow through the constant influx of immigrants, the limitations on rights of residence and occupation became correspondingly harder to endure. With the advance in Jewish enfranchisement in other European countries during the Napoleonic Wars, the Jews of Hungary became increasingly conscious that they, too, were entitled to civil rights. When the *Landtag* met in 1807, they submitted a memorandum modestly formulating their demands. They emphasized the benefits that the state derived from their activities through their export trade in its products. They requested confirmation of the proposals of the *Landtag* Committee of 1792, with the addition of several supplementary articles; equality of rights with other inhabitants (not of the aristocracy), especially in so far as they concerned freedom of trade; classification of the Jewish population into five categories: farmers, industrialists and artisans, traders, burghers, and pedlars; freedom of religion; and legal status for religious communities. On the whole, the *Landtag* Committee accepted the demands contained in the Jewish memorandum, but as a result of growing reaction in Francis's government, the proposals on Jewish rights were not even put to a vote.

All the loyalty that Hungarian Jewry felt towards the sovereign—and which it demonstrated with great ceremony in his presence in 1802 at the Pressburg synagogue—was of no avail against the increasingly severe system of extortion. As early as 1793, the "Toleration Tax" which weighed heavily on the poverty-stricken masses, had raised Kehillah tax indebtedness to the government to a total of over 370,000 florins. In 1807, the Jews suggested abolishing this purely Jewish tax in return for the payment of 1,600,000 florins over a period of five years. The *Landtag* Committee not only supported this proposal but entreated the Emperor "to pity, as a father would his sons, the lot of these people" and to accept this compensation in part, at least, if not wholly. The Emperor refused to make any concessions whatsoever. In 1811, the Jews repeated the request for the cancellation of the *Queen Money* in a memorandum to the Imperial Palatine, the Emperor's representative, and also asked him to intercede on their behalf on the issue of civil rights at the forthcoming *Landtag* session. The Emperor replied by doubling the "Toleration Tax" (to a total of 160,000 florins) in 1812. He had imposed compulsory military service on these "tolerated" people in 1807. Severe restrictions were imposed on the immigration of Jews into Hungary by Imperial decree, in 1806, and again in 1808. Jews who sheltered illegal immigrants were threatened with deportation. The triumph of reaction throughout Europe after 1815 added new restrictions to the legal discrimination against the Jews of Hungary.

The *Haskalah* movement made further headway amongst the Jews of Hungary during the Napoleonic era. In 1810, the leading merchants in the Kehillah of Pressburg, supported by a number of Hungarian magnates, initiated a movement to found a school to include a large proportion of secular studies as well as the study of Hebrew, the Bible, and portions of the *Mishnah* in its curriculum. An announcement, published in Hebrew and German, promised that study of the Talmud would be added when advanced classes were opened. The Chief Rabbi of the city, Moses Sofer (also known as *Hatam Sofer*), immediately responded with an attack on "these unbridled ones amongst our people" in a sermon in 1810. As early as 1802, he had delivered a sermon denouncing "the wicked, the heretics, and the unbelievers." Yet another sermon, this time in 1811, sounded a sharp warning against "newcomers who would estrange God's people from the Divine Torah," "who incite and foment" and wish to institute studies "in such fashion that most of their pupils will leave with a knowledge of

the Bible and of Latin and such like . . ." At this time too, the first
religious reformers, led by Rabbi Aaron Chorin of Arad, arose in
Hungary and started a conflict, that was to continue for several decades,
between the orthodox and enlightened Hungarian Jews, between religious
conservatism and national Jewish loyalty on the one hand, and assimilation on the other. Orthodoxy temporarily prevailed, and the project for
the school at Pressburg was dropped until 1822.

CHAPTER NINE

POLAND

A. ON THE EVE OF THE THREE PARTITIONS

Economic Life

In the sixteenth century the vast expanse of the Kingdom of Poland was constituted as a dual monarchy consisting of the Polish crown domains and the Grand Duchy of Lithuania. In the eighteenth century, in addition to the area inhabited by Poles, the Crown domains still included all the Ukrainian territories, except the areas east of the Dnieper which, with the city of Kiev, had passed to Russia in the seventeenth century. The Grand Duchy of Lithuania covered all of White Russia, in addition to the ethnically Lithuanian territories. It was united with Poland under one sovereign as far as foreign relations, the conduct of war, and the joint parliamentary body, the *Sejm*, were concerned.

In both parts of the Kingdom, the nobility, or *szlachta*, was the ruling class. The Jews in both areas were also united by virtue of their economic and legal position as well as by a common, centuries-old tradition reflected in their culture and way of life. The Jewish community of Poland and Lithuania accounted for approximately a half of all European Jewry. It stood out from amongst all the Diaspora settlements because of its closeness to the land it lived in, the wide degree of autonomy that its institutions enjoyed, and the unique attributes of its national culture.

A government census at the end of 1764 listed 430,009 Jews living in the Polish Crown domains and 157,649 in the Grand Duchy of Lithuania, a total of 587,658 people over a year old who were required to pay the poll tax. The actual number of Jews in the Kingdom of Poland that year, including infants under a year old, was closer to 750,000. Less than a third of the Kingdom's Jews lived in the Polish areas of western and Little Poland. Over two-fifths lived in the Ukrainian territories, and again less than a third in the Lithuanian-White Russian region. Nearly a third of the Jews of Poland (27 per cent in the crown domains) lived in villages, and a large proportion of the Jewish urban population was actually dispersed over the small towns, which, economically and physically, resembled rural rather than urban settlements. No other Jewish community in the world at that time contained such a high percentage of rural Jews, and this fact explained the unique character of the economic activities and pattern of living of Polish Jewry. According to the census, there were only forty-four cities in 1764 (but in terms of the true number of Jewish inhabitants—about sixty) where the Jewish population exceeded a thousand persons, and twenty-seven of these were in Ukrainian areas. Only twelve urban Kehillot possessed a membership of over two thousand: Brody (7,198); Lwow (6,159); Lissa (4,989); Krakow (3,458); Vilno (3,390); Brest (3,175 with the environs); Grodno (2,148 with the environs); Pinczow (2,164); Zaslaw (2,162); Dubno (2,117); Posen (2,060); and Zolkiew (2,017).

Even its size in relation to the population as a whole, and the urban population in particular, made the Jewish community in the Kingdom of Poland unique in world Jewry. In 1790, the total population of the Kingdom was 9 million. The Jewish population was 800,000 or 9 per cent of all the inhabitants. The number of urban Jews alone exceeded the number of urban Christians (only 500,000 that year). Furthermore, taking into account the fact that a large proportion of the Christian inhabitants of the small towns were, like the peasants, engaged in agriculture, it would appear that the Jews constituted the bulk of Poland's urban population in the eighteenth century. The large number of Polish Jews, and their special weight in the general population, were instrumental in determining their economic and legal status. The decisive factor, however, was the economic, social and political condition of the country in which they lived.

The deterioration in the economic situation in Poland during the eighteenth century was bound up with its social system. The absolute subjugation of the peasants and the unbridled rule of the *szlachta* over the townsmen and the Jews were the main causes of the sharp economic, political and cultural decline. The closed manorial economy prevailing in western Europe at the beginning of the Middle Ages was a characteristic feature of Polish feudalism in the eighteenth century. The inhabitants of the cities had also come increasingly under the direct domination of the grand *szlachta*. Large cities like Krotoszyn and Lissa in the west, and Bialystok, Siedlce, and Brody in the east, were the private property of manorial lords or magnates. In the small crown cities, royal administrators, *starostas*, governed without restraint, in the same way as the landed nobles ruled their private towns. In the large crown cities, such as Posen, Krakow, Warsaw, Lwow, or Vilno, only part of the metropolitan area possessed any autonomy; the sovereign *juridicae* of magnates, clergy, and monastic orders controlled the suburbs.

The social and economic structure of feudal society in Poland was reflected in an appropriate feudal political organization. The *szlachta* made free use of its privilege of *liberum veto* ("I forbid it") which effectively obstructed discussions and usually led to the dispersal, without decision, of the *Sejm*, occasionally also of the supreme royal tribunals, and even of the *Sejmiki* (regional councils of the nobility). In actual fact, the state was not ruled by the *szlachta* as a whole, but rather by a small group of magnates. The *szlachta* actually included a large number of nobles who scarcely possessed more land than the peasants or might even be totally landless (the "empty-handed *szlachta*"). The anarchic domination of the magnates was supported by the Catholic Church and especially by the Jesuits. This was a time of uninhibited incitement to violent fanaticism and intolerance against non-Catholics, both Protestant and Greek Orthodox (in the Ukraine and White Russia). Poland was a far cry from the economic development and political progress then current in western Europe, and equally sealed off from western culture. The average member of the *szlachta* derived his knowledge from almanacs which taught astrology, belief in spirits, devils, witchcraft, the evil eye and other superstitions. Witch-hunting trials, when the victim was accused of "consorting with a devil" were not unusual in contemporary Poland and scores of innocent peasants (men and women) were burned alive at the stake.

It was against this background of economic decline, prolonged wars, *szlachta* anarchy, Jesuit fanaticism, and the ignorance of the population as a whole, that the Jews of Poland carried on their daily struggle for existence. Their function in the stagnant feudal economy was that of economic intermediaries between the manorial lords, the peasants in the villages and the burghers in the small towns. The tenuous economic link between village and town, which consisted of the exchange of agricultural produce for urban commodities, had for the most part passed into Jewish hands. This economic role dominated the occupational structure of the Jewish community. Leaseholding, innkeeping, and the selling of liquor were almost the sole occupations of the village Jews and also formed the main source of income for a considerable section of the urban Jews, especially in the eastern districts. Most of the Jews in the cities and towns were engaged in trade, but they also included a high proportion of artisans—sometimes as many as a quarter, a third, or even more (in Vilno, 44 per cent!) of all the family heads in the Kehillah.

Only a small percentage of the rural Jews earned their living outside lesseeship or liquor selling. They were millers, storekeepers, brokers, dairymen, artisans and teachers. But about nine-tenths of the village Jews relied for their income on activities connected with the leasing of liquor distillery plant and the sale of liquor and beer. There was a wide range of social differentiation amongst them. The chief lessors were the wealthiest. They leased their distilleries and breweries directly from the estate owners, together with village inns and, quite often, mills and road and bridge toll collections as well. The innkeepers and publicans actually served as sublessees under the principal lessor, though they were often classified under the general heading of lessors (*arendars*). The publicans were solely concerned with selling alcoholic beverages, whereas the inns also served as hostels and stores. Below the publicans on the social scale of village Jews came the *winers*, who distilled and brewed spirits for the lessors.

Although the lessors were on the whole more prosperous than the innkeepers, most of the rural lessees never leased more than one inn and the position of this class was scarcely better than that of the innkeepers. The small lessees barely, if at all, made a living from their tenure. The estate proprietors continually raised rentals so that the lessees remained heavily in debt. Altogether, most of the village Jews were scarcely better off than the serfs who drank themselves into a stupor at the Jewish inns. "Although the peasant's drink was sold him by the Jew," the Polish historian Wladyslav Smolenski rightly observed, "the liquor in his glass belonged to the owner of the estate; it was in the latter's tavern that the lessee lived and filled the nobleman's coffers with coins of the realm."

The numerous hostelers among the vast number of Jewish publicans and innkeepers were of great value to the economy of the country. They are described in Polish literature, scurrying around purchasing hay and oats when a guest put in for the night. Their hostelries enabled trade connections between all parts of the country to be maintained; no journey would have been possible at that time, in prevailing transport conditions, without the food, rest, and lodgings that they provided for the traveller.

The Jewish share in Polish foreign trade was particularly large at the fairs in the German cities of Leipzig, Frankfurt-on-Oder, and Breslau. The most important commodities they brought from Poland to the fairs in Germany were agricultural products such as beeswax, potash, saltpetre and hides. They returned to Poland with "Glogau wares"—buttons, clasps, and French jewels—or "Nuremberg wares" such as needles, pins and pen-knives. They also brought back various delicate woven fabrics of spun or raw silk, flax or wool, lace work and similar articles. Commercial connections with seaports and other large towns in the north such as Torun, Danzig, Königsberg, Memel and Riga, were also largely maintained by Jews. The Council of the Four Lands* appointed judges (*dayyanim*) to be present at the Torun and Danzig fairs (as was the practice at Breslau); the large Kehillot of Great Poland, such as Posen or Lissa, sent court-beadles. It was mainly Jews from the border towns of eastern Galicia in the Carpathians who participated in the trade with Hungary. They sent liquors to Hungary and brought back Hungarian wines. Jewish merchants from Krakow maintained a very varied system of trade relations with Moravia. Despite all the difficulties which hampered their entry into Russia proper, Jewish traders from White Russia travelled to the fairs at Smolensk, Moscow, and—at a later period—St. Petersburg, mainly to buy furs, hides and linen (produced by the *muzhiks*), which they later sold at Leipzig.

The Jews relied on help from the *szlachta* also in their foreign trade activity. Very frequently they registered their merchandise in the name of their manorial overlords in order to avoid the high custom duties; and the

* In Hebrew, *Va'ad Arba Ha'aratzot*; the Central Council of Jewish Kehillot in the four Crown domains of Great Poland, Little Poland, Red Russia (Galicia) and Volhynia.

nobles often brought back foreign goods for the Jews, declaring them as their own property, again in order to evade payment of custom duties. The loans which Jewish merchants took from the estate owners at high interest rates—in the wine trade with Hungary, for example—again indicated the monetary dependence of the Jewish middle class on the *szlachta*. In Riga and Königsberg, Jews sometimes took merchandise on credit or paid for it with money borrowed from the gentile burghers of the city. The Jews at that time also played an important part in the *szlachta*'s export trade. They bought timber, grain and other products and transported them to the port cities; but they also refined potash, felled the trees on a contract basis on the forest lands of the nobility, and even of the clergy. Jewish traders and owners of barges and rafts undertook to ship consignments from the estate owners via the waterways.

Jews also played an important role in Poland's domestic trade during the eighteenth century. Within the Polish Crown domains, the cities of Jaroslaw, Belzyce, Ryczywol, and Pinczow, as well as Lublin, had developed into important centres for commercial fairs. The extent to which Jews attended these fairs could be gathered from the fact that the Council of the Four Lands usually held its conferences in one of these cities. The Lithuanian Kehillot were represented by their *dayyanim* at the Lublin and other fairs in cities in the Polish Crown Domain. The large Lithuanian Kehillot were also represented by *dayyanim* at Mir, Nieswiez, and other fairs held within the Grand Duchy itself. Thousands of Jews gathered at the Zelwa Fair, including visitors from far-off Great Poland.

Merchants, in the full sense of the word, only represented about a third of all the Jewish heads of families in Poland, who traded in the medium-size or even the larger cities. Most of these traders, both wholesalers and retailers, never possessed enough capital and regularly obtained their goods on credit or through loans. A large proportion were itinerant traders, who obtained their merchandise by "contract", i.e., on bond, and worked on a commission basis. Peddling was widespread amongst Polish Jews during the eighteenth century, partly because it could evade the supervision of the municipalities but mainly because intensive competition between Jewish storekeepers had led to their decline in the social scale. The rules and regulations of the large Kehillot contained detailed restrictions to prevent pedlars competing with the merchants.

In addition to the itinerant traders and storekeepers, agents, brokers, pedlars and market-women, those engaged in commerce also included assistants, or "servants," some of whom were married. This was especially true of the large and medium-sized Kehillot. In conjunction with trading activity, Jewish carters and porters abounded everywhere; in the small towns of White Russia they constituted about a tenth of all the local Jewish families.

The large Crown cities and the small towns showed different proportions of Jews and Christians engaged in trade. In the small towns, the important branches of trade were generally in Jewish hands; in the large cities of the Crown, the Jews were a minority among the large Christian merchants with their vast resources.

The Jewish artisans of Poland, unlike the merchants, were concentrated in only a few manual trades. Over half were engaged in clothing manufacture, particularly as tailors, furriers, and cap-makers. Some of the tailors made dresses to order, but others worked on *tandet*, that is to say, they produced cheap off-the-peg garments which they peddled in the streets or sold at fairs. The furriers and cap-makers were even more engaged in the manufacture of ready-to-wear articles for sale at the fairs. Cobblers were still rare amongst the Jews of Poland at that time, mainly because the Christian craft guilds held sway in this sphere. Two of the most common Jewish handicrafts in Poland were "edging" (silken buttonholes, fancy goods) and the manufacture of brocaded belts and other ornaments. Most Jews in the food trade were butchers; baking, for the most part, was still done at home. Gold refining and precious stone polishing, brass-ware, tobacco, soap and candle manufacture, tanning, glazing and bookbinding were amongst industries which employed large numbers of Jews.

The craft guild bye-laws would seem to indicate that there were far more assistants and apprentices than master craftsmen themselves. Jewish artisans actually predominated in certain occupations—tailors, furriers, cap-makers, glaziers and butchers—even in the large cities. They also held a commanding position in several crafts which were not elsewhere typically Jewish—in the small towns of the eastern districts, the Ukraine, Lithuania and White Russia, where the Christian inhabitants mostly lived by farming. In all the villages of the realm, practically all the tailors and butchers were Jews, and this also applied to the "court tailors," who worked only for their respective manorial lords.

Medicine was the only liberal profession open to Jews. The Jewish doctors, who held degrees from the Universities of Padua and Prague, as well as from the German universities (e.g., Frankfurt-on-Oder), were ranked amongst the outstanding specialists in their profession. Nearly all the kings of Poland retained Jewish court physicians, and their example was followed by princes and magnates. Every large Kehillah could claim several qualified Jewish doctors and they were not rare in the small towns. A large number of Jews worked as barbers, which included both hair-dressing and nursing.

A significant facet of the cultural life of Polish Jewry at that time was the presence of three or four musicians to a community, even in the smallest towns, with less than a hundred Jewish families. They were listed according to their individual speciality: fiddlers, bass viol players, and cymbalists. A fair proportion of the population were engaged in Kehillah duties, religion and education in both large (eight per cent at Brody) and medium-sized Kehillot. This category included rabbis, judges, ritual slaughterers, cantors, intercessors (officially designated by the Polish authorities as Syndics), trustees, beadles, and, especially, teachers. The Kehillot also employed various manual labourers, sanitary workers and watchmen.

Husbandry as a primary source of income was limited to Jewish dairymen, and there were many of these in the villages. Still, it was quite common for Jews in the villages and the small towns to practise agriculture as a supplementary source of income. The rural Jews who held taverns, mills, breweries or liquor distilleries on lease, often owned milch cows and operated dairy farms. Many also leased strips of land or gardens from the estate owners in addition to their principal lease. In Lithuania, it would appear that leases on undertakings where the agricultural factor was as important as the inn or distillery, were not uncommon. Animal husbandry as an auxiliary source of income was also widely practised by Jews in the small towns of Crown Poland. In some towns, such as Kolomyja, Jews mowed hay in the meadows, side by side with the Christian inhabitants.

Servants constituted a considerable proportion of the Jewish labour force. The census of 1764 showed Jewish servant girls registered as seven per cent or more of urban and rural Jews. There were fewer Jewish man-servants, working as *parobki*, or hired helps, for village lessees or innkeepers, and in the cities as traders' assistants or errand boys.

Statistics on married couples living with their parents emphasize the unsatisfactory social and economic structure of Jewish life in Poland during those years. In 1764, one-seventh of the total number of families were in this position in the District (*Wojewodztwo*) of Lublin. The custom of living at parents' expense did not, of course, gain much ground amongst the artisans and other toiling elements, such as carters and porters. The vast proportion of unemployed, dependent families accentuated the severe problems arising from the unstable sources of income and the insecure occupations in which so large a segment of the Polish Jewish population was engaged.

Struggle for Rights of Domicile, Trade and Craft; The Tax Burden

The legal status of the Jews in the Kingdom of Poland during this period continued on the general lines determined at an earlier date. The kings still vacillated between the Jews (confirming their general and special privileges) and the municipal and Christian guild administrations. Only Augustus III, in his aversion for the Jews, tended on the whole to concede the demands of the Christian inhabitants of any city. The country's general economic decline had exacerbated the burghers' resentment of Jewish competition, and it erupted more frequently than in previous years. However, as the governmental centre was in a state of disruption, the *szlachta* now enjoyed completely unrestrained supremacy, and the

Jews were able to retain their commercial positions and even enlarge their area of settlement and extend their economic operations, both as publicans and as artisans. The *juridicae* of the magnates in all the large royal cities had grown so much that the Jews could, through them, circumvent the enactments of the municipalities and the craft guilds. Similarly, the increased power of the *starostas*, the King's administrators, in the smaller royal cities now provided protection for Jewish trade and crafts. None the less, time and again, the Jews were forced to disburse vast sums of money to the King, committees and governors and to engage in costly litigation to win the right to live, trade and work.

The capital city of Warsaw was one of the centres of the grim and protracted struggle for rights of domicile, trade and artisanship. Jewish residence there had been prohibited since the expulsion decree of 1527. However, Jews were living inside the city in the eighteenth century, in the palaces and courtyards of the magnates. By the end of 1764, 1,274 were registered inhabitants. In 1768, the *Sejm* legalized an old custom which allowed Jews to enter Warsaw two weeks before the opening of the *Sejm* (which theoretically convened bi-annually) and to remain there for two weeks after the adjournment. The two dates were marked by a bugle call from the Crown Marshal's militia. In 1770, the Marshal also permitted Jews to come to Warsaw on market days—provided they purchased a "billet" valid for fourteen days at a price of three grosze. At approximately the same time, Sulkowski, a magnate, allowed Jews to settle on the outskirts of the city in an area called *Nowa Jerozolima* (New Jerusalem); later it was known as *Aleje Jerozolimskie* (Jerusalem Avenue). Following brutal expulsions ordered by the Crown Marshal in 1775 and 1784, Jewish merchants, artisans and brokers resettled in the capital; by 1787, their numbers had reached 3,342. In 1788, the Jews received permission to stay in Warsaw for the duration of the historic Quadrennial *Sejm*. This aroused vociferous protests from the Warsaw magistracy, who initiated a nation-wide action by the burghers to have the Jews expelled from all the crown cities. In May, 1790, rioting against the Jews ensued, followed by their temporary expulsion from the capital. Nevertheless, two years later, 6,750 Jews lived in Warsaw and became the largest Kehillah in Poland.

The burghers in most of the large Crown cities were not as precipitate as to demand the outright expulsion of the Jews. Instead, they requested that Jews be forbidden to buy new houses or move into streets and districts which they had not previously inhabited; that the sale of alcoholic beverages, brewing of beer, and distilling of liquor by Jews be prohibited; that Jewish trade be restricted to definite commodities; that the Jewish retail trade and particularly Jewish peddling be made illegal; that Jewish artisanship be either banned or limited to the utmost; and that the Jews be made liable to contribute to all city taxes and fees. This was actually the situation in the cities of Lwow and Vilno, except that in Vilno, after prolonged litigation, the Jews eventually obtained a favourable decision from a tribunal of the royal court. As a result, in 1783, they were permitted to buy houses and reside in all parts of the city (with the exception of two streets), to trade without restriction, to operate public houses and to engage in crafts. Although this decision reflected new economic trends in Poland during the age of reform, it still cost the Vilno Kehillah 27,000 zloty. At Krakow, the issue of expanding the Jewish quarter in the suburb of Kazimierz and allowing Jews to keep shops within the city was the cause of incessant strife. In all the cities, the Jews were able to alleviate the harshness of the decrees, but principally they circumvented them. They did this primarily through the patronage of the magnates and the ecclesiastics in the *juridicae*, but also with the assistance of the *woyewodas*, and, in part, of some burghers who profited from their presence.

The Christian merchants were supported in their campaign against the Jews by Christian artisans, who very often made even more extreme demands. Apart from their desire to be free from Jewish competition, they were interested—at times even more interested than the Christian merchants—in the imposition of a ban on Jewish trade in goods, production of which was considered a craft monopoly. These goods included furs, hats, clothing, fancy goods, pottery, tin vessels and iron products. The Jewish artisans therefore had to struggle even more desperately than the merchants, especially in the Crown cities. At times, the Jewish artisans' corporations were forced to reach agreements with the craft guilds on a quota, determining the number of Jews allowed to engage in any one craft (at Lublin, no more than twenty-four tailors were allowed until 1789, when the limit was raised to forty-four) and also the number of journeymen and apprentices. Furthermore, Jewish craftsmen were compelled, in practice, to make regular payments to the Christian guilds.

Apart from the direct and indirect taxes imposed on the urban population as a whole, the Jewish population also bore an additional burden of special taxes. In 1717, the *Sejm* raised the Jewish poll tax to 220,000 zloty in the Crown domains and to 60,000 zloty in Lithuania. In addition to the poll tax, the Jews were required to pay nearly 15,000 zloty annually to the Minister of Finance and his officials in wages, as well as "charitable gifts" to the bookkeepers for rendering accounts of tax apportionment, and to the commissioners who superintended the inter-Kehillah Council meetings. The cost of these regular "gifts" to government district officials, *woyewodas*, lieutenant-*woyewodas* and *starostas* reached such proportions that in some Kehillot it far exceeded the total assessment for the poll tax. On top of these expenses, the Kehillot had to pay the municipal housing tax and also to share in the cost of billeting army personnel, at a rate far above the ratio of the Jews to the general population. In connection with army expenditure, the Kehillot were also liable to permanent levies to pay for such items as the carcass of an animal to feed the dogs of a battalion commander or even of medical orderlies—

as at Vilno. In the manorial towns, the Jews did not have to make contributions to government officials, instead, they were forced to meet heavy taxes imposed by the estate owners. In both Crown and manorial cities the Jews were obliged to present "gifts" to the Catholic Church which virtually constituted a regular annual tax. These "gifts" for the most part included the so-called *Kozubalec** for Church beadles and Jesuit college students, as a means to prevent anti-Jewish riots by the students.

Very often, because of the political repression of the Jews in Poland, the sums extracted from the Jewish population by "extraordinary expenditures" for intercessions, averting persecution (ritual blood accusations!) or its alleviation, were higher than all their ordinary annual tax payments and fees. For example, the special budget of the Vilno Kehillah for 1773-74 was three times greater than its normal expenditure for the period. The Four Lands' Council budget for 1726 earmarked over 28,000 zloty, or approximately forty per cent of its total expenditure (besides the poll tax) for various kinds of intercession.

To meet this rising expenditure, the Kehillot and the district and central councils were forced to borrow funds from the clergy and the nobility. But as Kehillah needs grew, they were less and less able to cover their obligations and had to apply for additional loans—if only to underwrite their existing budgets and to pay the interest on their previous debts. By the end of 1764, the debt of the Council of the Four Lands and District Councils of the Polish Crown domains amounted to 2,500,000 zloty. Large individual Kehillot such as Lwow, or Lissa, had debts of 500,000 zloty at that period. The debts of the Posen Kehillah stood at nearly 1,000,000 zloty. The interest on debts and the special taxes and payments levied on the Jews were merely two aspects of the same phenomenon: the policy of extortion which the ruling classes, the clergy and the *szlachta*, applied to the Jewish population of old Poland.

The economic decline in Poland during the eighteenth century brought to a peak the clerical reaction which had engulfed it since the late sixteenth century. The *szlachta* had only been able to continue to exploit the population unrestrainedly because of the power of the clergy. The clergy used every available method to incite anti-Jewish feeling and the economic antagonism between burghers and Jews furthered their campaign. The impoverished shopkeepers and artisans, incited by the systematic propaganda of the priesthood and the Jesuits, regarded the Jews as the most important cause of their economic deterioration. The patricians, who had aggravated the economic ruin of the cities by their irresponsible orgies, did their utmost to intensify mass hatred of the Jews. The growth of religious fanaticism and intolerance in general also influenced the *szlachta*, particularly because of widening social differentiation in its

---

* From the word *kozub*, a box or receptacle made of bark. Jews passing a church or Jesuit College were expected to deposit their toll in this container. Failure to do so, or inadequate contributions, resulted in serious disorders on many occasions.

ranks. In 1768, peasant opposition to the Jewish stewards, lessors, and publicans of the landed proprietors finally erupted in the bloody riots of the Ukrainian *Haidamaks*. However, the economic benefit that the state as a whole and all the various sectors of the population derived from the Jews was sufficient to outweigh this ill-feeling and, even at this period, they were able to retain and, in certain fields, actually to extend their position. None the less, the political element in this reaction inaugurated for the Jews a cycle of suffering, servitude, bloody excesses, and degradation.

The memoirs of the priest, Kitowicz, relate that assaults on Jews by Jesuit students, the *Schiller Geloif* as they came to be known in Yiddish, or scholastic riots, were widespread in Poland. The clergy had never before interfered so arrogantly in the internal life of the Jews. Bishops issued decrees against the Kehillot to humiliate the Jews, keep them in constant fear of the Church and isolate them from all social contact with Christians. A further manifestation of the increasing power of the Church in Poland occurred in 1757 when Bishop Dembowski of Kamieniec-Podolsk was able to force *Parnassim* and rabbis to enter into public disputations with the Frankists and subsequently order the Talmud to be banned, stage *autos-da-fe*, and have the books burned in the market place. This was followed by the disputations with the Frankists at the cathedral of Lwow in 1759, a strange disputation that terrorized Jews throughout the country. Some bishops staged these disputations at regular intervals and also compelled the Jews to listen to Catholic sermons—as in the Middle Ages or in the Italian Papal States.

However, all other clerical persecution of the Jews was relatively insignificant by comparison with the systematically engineered ritual blood accusations, the charge of desecrating the Host (The Holy Water), and other unspeakable religious crimes that were imputed to the Jews. Under the Saxon Kings these became chronic occurrences. The clergy methodically incited public opinion by issuing inflammatory anti-Jewish books and pamphlets and ensured that every charge of ritual murder during the eighteenth century aroused bloody repercussions throughout Poland. In the preceding period, ritual blood accusations had been staged by the Jesuits and unworthy priests. In the eighteenth century, on the other hand, the highest church prelates, even bishops, directed this activity and employed every means to renew the trials and obtain a positive verdict even when the accused Jews had been acquitted by the courts. The ritual murder charge at Posen between 1736 and 1740 was jointly organized by the Church and the rulers of the city, and resulted in the King issuing new edicts against the local Jews. In 1747, a ritual murder trial at Zaslaw, Volhynia, was conducted by clergymen and the municipal court. In Szepetowka, in the same region, two Jews were sentenced to death in 1748 following a charge made by the Carmelite Brotherhood. Also in 1748, Bishop Dembowski initiated a ritual murder trial at Dunaygrod. The ritual murder trial at Zhitomir in 1753 claimed the largest number of innocent victims. It was organized in minute detail by the Bishop of Kiev, Kajetan Soltyk, and resulted in the execution of twelve Jews by torture including flaying alive. In 1756, Anton Wolowicz, Bishop of Lutzk, staged a ritual murder trial at Jampol and in 1759, six Jews, brought to trial by the Jesuits for a ritual blood murder in the village of Stupnica, were beheaded at Przemysl. The bloody wave of ritual murder trials swept all the provinces of the Polish state. In 1751, trials are recorded in the Carpathian towns of Biecz and Nowy Sacz, the verdicts of which have not reached us. Ten years later, another trial in Nowy Sacz was staged in which an entire family was involved. Three death sentences were passed and carried out. In 1760, five Jews from the Grodno area in the north, were accused of murdering a nobleman and a cleric, and were sentenced to death by torture. In 1761, the death sentence was carried out on several Jews of Woyslawice charged with ritual murder. Even as late as 1763, the last year of Augustus III's reign, there was a ritual blood accusation at Kalisz. Impalement, disembowelling, quartering, and other forms of torture were amongst the methods employed at these executions. All the trials were regularly accompanied by offers of absolution through baptism, preceded by the infliction of physical and mental torture to obtain "confessions."

The main purpose of the ritual blood accusations in Poland was to incite religious fanaticism amongst the masses. But, as with the Spanish Inquisition, they were also directed towards the gratification of the clergy's greed. In the course of 150 years, Jesuits, monks, and other members of the clerical class obtained vast sums in cash and promissory notes from terrorized Kehillot by this means. The Roman Cardinal Ganganelli, later Pope Clement XIV, specifically wrote of Bishop Soltyk, "from the words he utters gleams his accursed love of mammon." Cardinal Ganganelli also submitted a memorandum to Pope Clement XIII in response to intercession by Eliakim Ben Asher Selig of Jampol, specifically sent to Rome for that purpose by the Council of the Four Lands. The memorandum proved that the Polish ritual murder charges were on a par with the blood accusation the Romans had levelled against the early Christians. The Pope made a carefully formulated declaration to the clergy in Poland that there was no evidence of any kind to substantiate the prejudice. But of even greater service to the Polish Jews was the reign of Stanislas August Poniatowski when European Enlightenment began to penetrate the country. Henceforth, ritual murder charges were rare in Poland, witch trials finally ceased, and torture as an instrument of legal examination was abolished. In all other respects, few if any changes were made in the position of the Jews of Poland, even during the period of initial reforms.

During the age of reaction, the persecution of the Jews by the dominant *szlachta* had also grown to formidable proportions. The *szlachta's* deputies had certainly, on numerous occasions, in the *Sejm* and elsewhere, openly proclaimed their interest in the economic existence of the Jews. Apart from the sizable profits they made from the Jews, the *szlachta*, as the ruling class, could not fail to acknowledge their growing role in the country's trade and industry. Furthermore, the *szlachta* had invested large sums of money in loans to the Kehillot; in the *Sejm*, Deputy Miroslawski in 1740 unequivocally admitted their unwillingness to forfeit these. But this vital concern on the part of the *szlachta* was inhibited by religious fanaticism, and the lower, impoverished ranks, who had themselves turned to trade and lesseeship, began to regard the Jews as rivals. Generally, the interests of the magnates, the middle-rank *szlachta*, and above all, the economic and political interests of the nobility as a whole prevailed over these of the poorer, lower-class *szlachta*. Ironically, while the limited economic activity of the Jews was dependent on the patronage of the *szlachta*, they still made life miserable for the people they were theoretically protecting by continual repetition of innumerable excesses. Assaults on Jews by *szlachta* were made whenever the provincial diets, or *sejmiki* convened. Estate owners applied the severest pressure to collect debts from the Kehillot—even closing down the synagogues. Jews embarking on a journey were terrified lest they meet a noble. Jewish lessees were whipped by nobles on the road because the local village proprietor had failed to order a bridge to be repaired, or because fodder or a meal had not been prepared at the inn. The attitude of estate owners to their "own" lessees was, on many occasions, cruel. The episodes depicting the life of village Jews in *The Praise of the Besht** and Hasidic lore were not exaggerated. Recently published documents† prove that the occurrences described in the tales were quite commonplace at that time throughout Poland. The tragedy always followed the same pattern: a lessee who could not pay the high rental fee on time was locked in a pig-sty or thrown into a pit, while his wife and children were cruelly tortured and occasionally forcibly converted. In those days, every large Kehillah kept a special reserve fund or budgeted for a special item of expenditure, the "redemption of captives," intended for these victims. The grievances of Jewish lessees tortured by their masters were also submitted to the Finance Committee of the Polish Crown domain. The Jews of feudal Poland purchased manorial protection, not only with large sums of money, but also with their abasement as human beings.

The Kehillah and Central Autonomy

During the period of uncontrolled *szlachta* domination in Poland, the Kehillot also came under the administrative machinery of the ruling class.

* Contraction of Rabbi Israel *Ba'al SH*em *Tov*, founder of Hasidism, cf. belof, p. 455.
† E. Ringelblum, cf. bibliography.

The election of Kehillah leaders and, usually of society treasurers as well, required confirmation by the *Woyewoda* or, in private cities, by the manorial lords. A candidate for the position of rabbi had to pay out large sums to receive approval. Important enactments by the Kehillah and its auxiliary societies needed the sanction of the government supervisory administration or of the city-proprietors—who also supervised the Kehillah budget. The social, cultural and even the religious needs of the Jewish population were met almost entirely by charity societies and only to a slight extent by the Kehillah itself. To all intents and purposes, the Kehillah had become an administrative organ which the government, nobility and clergy exploited for the extortion of taxes, fees, "gifts," and interest on debts from the Jewish population. The budgets of the period reflected this trend. In return, Crown or manorial officials helped the Kehillah to suppress all opposition, and, at times, put military or municipal police assistance at its disposal for collecting the *korobka*—an indirect tax levied on foodstuffs and frequently on professional services as well.

The Kehillah interfered in every aspect of its members' lives. Without permission from the Kehillah and without the purchase of a licence, no Jew could pursue any occupation such as liquor selling, trade, or handicraft; he could not even rent a dwelling. It was also necessary to purchase a permit to settle in another Kehillah: the *Hezkat ha-Yishuv* (right of domicile), which only the rich could afford. The ordinary Jew was chained to his Kehillah like a serf to his master. Power in the Kehillah was vested in an oligarchy of wealthy men by specific provisions in the Kehillah and central council regulations, as in Lithuania. All the Kehillot of Poland and Lithuania applied the same criteria in granting active and passive membership rights: property and learning. As in the neighbouring countries of Germany, Bohemia, and Moravia, individuals with the official title of *morenu* or *haver* enjoyed special privileges. However, according to a regulation of the Lithuanian State Council of 1761, men who were not scholars but merely conversant with the book could also acquire these titles. The combination of the property and scholastic qualifications precluded any possibility that the broad masses of the Jewish population might influence Kehillah policy.

The electoral laws of the backward and conservative Lithuanian Kehillot were more oligarchical and exclusive than any of the others. Only men with the title of *morenu* or *haver* could participate in the Vilno election assembly, which was also the Kehillah council. With the increase in the number of artisans, some Lithuanian Kehillot adopted regulations specifically excluding artisans from the right to hold Kehillah office.

The taxation system of the Kehillot was based on unrestricted exploitation of the lower class masses, the shopkeepers, publicans, artisans, and the like. The system of basing tax assessments on property holdings had been almost universally replaced by the *korobka*. The *korobka* on food articles was particularly oppressive. The tax on kosher meat alone accounted for a third of the revenue in the smaller Kehillot; in larger Kehillot, such as Posen or Vilno, it provided two-fifths of the income.

The condition of the Jewish masses deteriorated further during the eighteenth century as a result of the excesses of the Kehillah oligarchs. In some Kehillot, the *Kahal* (the elected Board of the Community) even ceased to function as the organ of the wealthy class as a whole, but became an instrument of exploitation in the hands of Kehillah cliques. In all the large Kehillot, the highest posts became the hereditary property of a few select families. Throughout Poland, from Posen to Vilno and Minsk, it was an accepted custom for the *Kahal* to collect money in return for appointments to all salaried positions, from the rabbi to the beadle. At Vilno, even the right to elect or be elected ("passive" and "active" voting rights) to Kehillah institutions was converted into a saleable commodity. Conflict between the cliques often resulted in one of the oligarchs usurping dictatorial power. These Kehillah dictators were quite often the most notorious reprobates, thieves and felons (for example, at Krakow, Drohobycz, Warsaw) and, like the cliques, they resorted for support to government dignitaries, city owners, *starostas* and *woyewodas*. As each such dictatorial episode came to an end, the "normal" but no less brutal rule of entire cliques would resume.

The Kehillah rulers introduced new methods to break down the resistance of the masses to this régime of exploitation. In addition to the old system of excommunication, public disgrace and imprisonment, they employed new devices such as blacklisting opponents and forcing them to redeem promissory notes, signed on their behalf by the synagogue beadle. A body known as the "Anonymous Persecutor" was established in the Kehillot of Lithuania and White Russia with power relentlessly to persecute any recalcitrant until he yielded. When opposition to the ruling clique exploded into open warfare, the Kehillah leaders declared a state of emergency known as "The Sin Against the Kahal."

This hierarchical system of oligarchy also prevailed in the large societies, particularly the burial societies, the major charity societies, and the *Talmud-Torah* organizations for instructing the children of the poor. But despite their hierarchical constitution, these bodies also fulfilled important social functions. The Jewish craft organizations were similarly under the direct supervision of the Kehillah. One of their chief tasks was to defend the rights of Jewish artisans against the municipalities and the Christian craft guilds. However, the need to curb competition between artisans of the same trade was equally important to them—as it was to the Christian guilds. The Jewish craft organizations also protected the monopoly rights of their members against "outsiders" and incompetents, and watched over the employers' interests in face of demands from journeymen and apprentices. Like the members of a craft organization who enjoyed preferential rights over other artisans, so certain restricted groups within each organization possessed greater powers and privileges than ordinary members. Nevertheless, these organizations were also concerned with mutual aid and looked after fraternal relationships as well as the religious and cultural needs of their members. The inner differentiation notwithstanding, the Jewish artisan class was subjected to more repressions than any other section of the Jewish population. The Jewish artisan in old Poland laboured under oppressive laws and was burdened with payments that had to be made to government officials, municipalities and Christian craft guilds; he was also more heavily exploited than others by the Kehillah oligarchies. No wonder that the Jewish artisans were foremost in the struggle of the Jewish masses against the oppression of the Kehillah despots.

The organs of Jewish regional and central autonomy had by this time, to an even greater degree than the Kehillot, become nothing more than instruments of the government for the extortion of a constantly increasing poll tax and other levies from the Jewish population. The Council, both in its open actions and its official prerogatives, resembled an auxiliary of the Ministry of Finance rather than an autonomous Jewish institution. During the eighteenth century, Council meetings were mostly held in towns belonging to the Minister of Finance, including Tyszowce, Ryczywol, Konstantynow and Pilica. The system of cliques and strong-arm dictatorship that caused the decline of the Kehillot, also brought anarchy into the institution of central Jewish autonomy. This was scarcely surprising, as the Kehillah leaders who ruled their own communities so arbitrarily had also arrogated the privilege of making decisions for the Jews of the entire state.

The largest and wealthiest Kehillot made use of the power they exercised in their own districts. Hardly a year in the eighteenth century passed without some conflict breaking out between the leading Kehillah in any district and the lesser ones. Apart from this direct abuse of power, Council leaders frequently took advantage of the opportunities for embezzlement that regional fund administration offered—just as certain *Parnassim* availed themselves of Kehillah funds. The oppression of the lesser Kehillot by the central bodies in the various districts disrupted the organization of regional autonomy and it began to disintegrate. By the middle of the eighteenth century twenty local and regional Kehillah organizations were directly dependent on the Council of the Four Lands as compared with five in the sixteenth century.

The small Kehillot broke away from the central Kehillot and the regional organizations and put themselves under the protection of the ruling authority. Similarly, under the aegis of the landed nobility, the dependent outlying communities—termed *s'vivot*, or in Yiddish *svives*,* by the Jews and *przykahalki* by the Polish authorities—began to dispute the authority of the guardian Kehillot and found Kehillot of their own. Apart from unjust apportionment of taxes, the economic rights of the inhabitants

* *S'vivot* in Hebrew: environs.

of the *s'vivot* were curtailed: they were not even allowed to trade freely within the Kehillot, to which they paid taxes. The Jews in the suburbs rebelled against the Kehillot for the same reasons, and at times, with the connivance of their landlords, the *juridicae* holders, succeeded in founding separate Kehillot.

The struggle against the Kehillah leaders had begun as early as the seventeenth century; it was renewed in the eighteenth. This time, the first outbreak occurred in the western districts of Poland. (It was some years before it spread to Lithuania, where domination by Kehillah leaders was extremely powerful and the struggle of the masses, therefore, harder and more bitter.) In 1753, the Kehillah leaders at Posen were forced as a concession to the opposition to adopt a new regulation allowing a bloc of twenty-one men to be elected to the Kehillah board in addition to the seven "K'sherim." At Lissa (Leszno), the largest Kehillah in Great Poland, a permanent reform in the taxation system was not introduced until 1792, after a violent internal struggle lasting twenty-nine years. Thenceforth, the regulations required the Kehillah leaders to convoke the Assembly Members for discussion of all important matters. This Assembly was composed of ten elected trade groups, including merchants, publicans, shopkeepers, brokers, tailors, furriers, and cordmakers. The fact that Jewish artisans were most numerous in the western area of Poland and their influence therefore more decisive in relation to the other classes of the Jewish population might explain these partial reforms. Moreover, this was the most advanced region in the Kingdom of Poland as far as economic, political and cultural development was concerned. At Krakow, where the Kehillah consisted mainly of merchants, and artisans were in a minority, the leadership cliques remained firmly in power in the Kehillah until the end of the eighteenth century—though sharp outbreaks of opposition occurred even there from time to time.

The artisans of the Wolhynian Kehillah of Dubno openly rebelled against the Kehillah leaders, but they were defeated, as the leaders had the support of the manorial landlord of the city. In 1765, the societies of "Weavers" (probably the official title of the tailors), butchers, bakers and other manual workers were disbanded and forbidden to reorganize. However, the bitterness of the poor population remained and in the Regulations for 1766, 1781 and 1792, the Dubno Kehillah leaders were forced to make certain concessions. Three *regierers* (wardens) were designated to supervise Kehillah funds and reforms in the meat and Kehillah tax systems were instituted so "that the poor should no longer need to cry out" and "in order to lighten the load of the people."

In the backward regions of Lithuania and White Russia, a furious revolt against the Kehillah leaders broke out in the last quarter of the eighteenth century. It took the form of an open uprising against the Kehillah leaders. At Minsk, the artisans organized the urban Jewish population and selected representatives of "the common people," demanding that elections be held for a new management. The Kehillah leaders succeeded in obtaining the support of the government courts, leaving the insurgents no alternative but open conflict. In 1777, the artisans attacked the office of the Kehillah leaders and evicted the management. They broke into the Kehillah archives, confiscated the ledgers and documents and handed them over to the *Starosta*'s office. They organized a Kehillah tax boycott, seized the synagogue and prevented the *Parnassim* from entering. However, the Kehillah rulers restored "order" with the assistance of the local authorities, bitterly avenged themselves on the opposition, and carried on with their abusive practices. A memorandum that the elected representatives of the people of the Minsk Kehillah submitted to the Lithuanian Tribunal in 1782 was equally futile.

The struggle that broke out in the Kehillah of Vilno in 1781 was a classic example of the united front that the various classes of the Jewish population presented to the *Kahal* cliques. On the one hand, the party of Rabbi Samuel Ben Avigdor consisted essentially of reformers who wanted to establish the rule of the moneyed class over the Kehillah while preserving some semblance of democratic forms. On the other, the old *Kahal* clique was representative of the feudal exploitation system as a whole, as well as the economic exploitation of the Jewish masses. In its struggle against the *Kahal* leaders, the Rabbi's party appealed for the support of the broad masses of the "common people," and therefore included amongst its grievances the oppression of "the mass" by the *Kahal* leaders. When these leaders imposed a new tax on the Kehillah population for the "Great Charity" funds the Rabbi proclaimed, "These ruffians are impoverishing the public!" Joseph Ben Elijah, the wealthiest merchant in Vilno and one of the leaders of the Rabbi's party, wrote in a memorandum to the Vice-Chancellor: "The poor masses have to pay heavy taxes. Nobody with a human heart can contemplate this pressure without weeping." The representative body of the common people, which called itself the *Plenipotentiaries of the Commonalty* and consisted mostly of members elected by the artisans, only entered the scene in Vilno, as at Minsk, Lissa, and other Kehillot, when the phase of open warfare against the Kehillah rulers began in 1785. The controversy at Vilno lasted for the next five years, because both factions—the Kehillah leaders and the opposition—were supported by a representative of an important third party. In the case of the Kehillah leaders, this was the *Wojewoda*, Prince Radziwill; where the Rabbi's party and the "representatives of the common people" were concerned, it was the *Wojewoda's* rival, Bishop Ignacy Massalski. The dispute between the two parties passed through several law courts and eventually reached the Royal Court in Chancery. Both sides published polemical pamphlets in Polish and also expounded their case in a local Polish paper. One of the main arguments raised by the Kehillah leaders was that the opposition was trying to destroy the Jewish religion. They dealt the opposition many severe blows, but the greatest ordeal was inflicted on the leader of the "Tribune of the Common People" (*Trybun Ludu*), Simon Ben-Wolff, who was subjected to hard labour in Prince Radziwill's prison at Nieswiez. The civil war in the Vilno Kehillah, the greatest rebellion of the "Mass" against the oppressors, the Kehillah leaders, ended in a compromise. Both parties were represented on the new Kehillah management elected in 1790. Not one of the reforms the working people had so loyally fought for—reduction of the Kehillah tax, abolition of the meat sales *korobka*, appointment of a special supervisory committee for *Kahal* loans—was put into effect.

The rebellion that broke out in the Lithuanian city of Szawle in 1790 against the Kehillah leaders differed from that at Vilno. Here, the Rabbi, who had been supporting the Kehillah rulers with decrees of excommunication, also came under attack. The rebels petitioned the authorities to abolish both the Kehillah organization and the office of rabbi. However, as at Vilno, a compromise between the contending factions of the wealthy class brought the people's uprising in the Szawle Kehillah to an end.

At Witebsk, an unconcealed plot by artisans against the Kehillah leaders in 1782-83 ended in defeat. The municipal administration supported the Kehillah leaders and sentenced a number of artisans to the lash. All the artisans in the city were forced to sign a declaration "that they would no longer form any plots or engage in oppositionist activities . . ."

These bitter campaigns on the part of the "common mass," and especially the artisans, against oppression by the Kehillah leaders were confined to the individual Kehillah, with no interconnection of any kind. However, as in the preceding period, contemporary ethical literature and books by homileticists and forerunners of the *Haskalah* movement criticized the oppression of the people. Some individuals rose from the ranks of rabbis and scholars who shared responsibility for the misdeeds of the wealthy oligarchy. These men of stature and integrity felt an affinity with the popular masses and participated in their anguish. They were usually to be found among the homileticists who were employed in the shopkeepers' and artisans' associations. The pioneers of the *Haskalah* movement amongst the rabbis also came to realize that no cultural reforms could be introduced amongst the people as long as they were kept in a state of servility by the Kehillah leaders. Berachiah Ben Eliakim Getzel of Krakow, an itinerant preacher and homileticist, rebuked the rabbis and Kehillah leaders in the introduction to *Zera Berakh Shlishi*, his commentary on the *Mishnah* tractate, *B'rakhot* (Benedictions), published in 1730. In this instance, the crime named was accepting gifts before trials, in addition to the court fee, on a scale large enough to keep those judges for lengthy periods. In a book entitled *Pillars of the House of Judah* (1766), Judah Hurwitz, a Vilno physician, expressed his bitterness at the wealthy who built luxurious three-storey homes for themselves and drove poor, and even "respectable itinerants," from their doors. However, Rabbi Judah Leib Margaliot, a young contemporary of Hurwitz, exposed the dissoluteness of "some leaders in Israel" with greater clarity than all the ethical writers. Like Hurwitz, he was a precursor of the *Haskalah* movement, and had also wandered from one Kehillah to another over the length and breadth of Poland. His book, *Beth Midoth A House of Virtues* gave a complete and vivid description of the current evils in Kehillah life. He also attacked the rabbis who abetted the Kehillah rulers in all their crimes and themselves drank "of the blood of humble men." He proved that the rabbis' attitude towards the wealthy members of the Kehillah was a manifestation of class solidarity:

> And since he also comports himself like the governors of the country and its nobility in his food and drink, in his fine ointments and elaborate garments, while like them he is avid for money, if even he does at times reproach the wicked man for his fault, yet is this fault his own. Will his hue and cry be hearkened unto by one who may well say to himself, Tomorrow will he do even as I have this day and be upbraided ...

This sense of social morality was shared by a later forerunner of the *Haskalah* movement in Poland, Pinhas Elijah Hurwitz of Vilno. He was the author of a popular scientific work, the Book of the Covenant (*Sefer Ha'B'rit*), published in 1797, and he carried his social outlook to even greater lengths than his predecessors. His targets included the Kehillah leaders "and the mighty tax officials who themselves give nothing and, sparing one another, it is the poor man they afflict." He also directed his attack against those self-satisfied scholars who, "though with their own eyes they behold the impoverished who fall in the streets overcome by the pangs of hunger and the lack of clothing on a frosty day, yet they will not budge from their own shelter to perform acts of charity." But he also berated those Jews who lived by fraud and usury and exploited their neighbours of other faiths.

This social protest by individual moralists and rabbis expressed the anger and despair of the Jewish masses. The Frankist movement drew its adherents in Poland from these rebellious elements amongst the Jewish poor—though under misguided leadership, it ultimately became an arrant enemy of the Jewish people. Similarly, when the hardship of the people reached a certain limit, the Hasidic movement emerged. It was the first time in the long history of the Diaspora that a general democratic movement had arisen to dispute the rule of the social élite and the scholars, proclaiming the rights of the common people as one of its ideological principles.*

* See Chapter Twelve.

B. *THE AGE OF REFORMS AND PARTITION*

The Social and Legal Situation

The last thirty years of the old Kingdom of Poland, from 1764 to 1795, were the most tempestuous in its history, both in domestic politics and foreign relations. It was actually a period of economic, political and social progress for Poland, when the question of reforming the régime was never absent from public debate. But, ironically, it was also the time of the three partitions which brought about the end of the independent existence of the Kingdom. The contradiction is explained by the fact that the cultural and political reforms were superficial only and had not fundamentally touched the corrupt feudal system of the state. The selfish policies pursued by the class of feudal *szlachta* made it impossible for Poland to withstand the expansionist imperialism of its three powerful neighbours, the absolute monarchies of Prussia, Russia and Austria.

The internal wars and disorders that ravaged Poland during the period up to the first partition in 1772 destroyed whole Jewish communities and even exterminated the Jewish population in entire regions. The *Haidamak* massacres of 1768 in the Ukraine not only claimed tens of thousands of Jewish lives but left an even greater number of Jews in a state of utter privation as a result of pillage and arson. The robbery, extortion and forced contributions which accompanied the Bar Confederacy Rebellion, waged for four years by conservative *szlachta* in many parts of Poland against curtailment of its privileges, wrought economic havoc in innumerable Jewish settlements. The Russian army formed another burden for the Jewish population, which was charged with providing food, billets and money for the Tzar's troops.

Increases in the taxation levied on the Jews constantly worsened their already poor financial state. The *Sejm* of 1764, which carried out the first of the Kingdom's fiscal reforms also passed and eventually implemented a demand which the *szlachta* had made unceasingly over the previous hundred years: it abolished central and regional Jewish autonomy, leaving only the local autonomy of the Kehillot in force. This greatly increased the tax burden borne by the Jews. They were now required to pay a poll tax of two zloty annually for every person of a year or over which increased tax payments from the 220,000 zloty, which the Jews of the Crown Domains had been paying since 1717, to nearly 860,000 zloty. Further increases in the Jewish poll tax occurred in 1775—to three zloty per capita—and in 1789—by 50 per cent. A decision by the 1789 *Sejm* to liquidate the debts of the central and regional bodies as well as those of the Kehillot, imposed new and heavy obligations on the Jewish population. Instead of paying the usual rates to the landed proprietors and the clergy, the Kehillot had thenceforth to remit a considerable portion of their debt every year so that the debtors might be completely remunerated by a fixed date. Meanwhile, in 1775, a new special tax consisting of a stamp-tax on Jewish books had been levied.

In addition to the new tax burden and the monetary obligations it had imposed on the Jews, the *szlachta* also adopted repressive resolutions depriving a large proportion of them of all source of income. In the *Sejm* of 1768, the *szlachta* was not satisfied merely with refusing to grant the burgher estate political concessions, but went even further and strengthened *starosta* control of the cities both in fiscal and legal matters. To compensate the burghers for this most recent curtailment of municipal autonomy, it penalized the Jews. It enacted a law prohibiting all Jewish trade, liquor sales, or handicrafts except within limits permitted by agreement with the municipalities "since Jewry is guilty of intolerable wrongs against the cities and burghers." Where no such agreement had ever existed, it must immediately be made, in conformity with the precedent set by cities where such agreements had already been in existence before the enactment of the law. This law formed the basis for a new attack on Jewish trade and artisanship, the confiscation of Jewish merchandise, and the closing of Jewish stores by the municipal governments of large cities such as Krakow, Posen, Lwow, and Vilno. The smaller cities proceeded to expel Jews on the pretext that they had no agreement with them. Approximately a fifth of the cities of Poland expelled their Jewish inhabitants in the years immediately following the adoption of the law, on the basis of the paragraph relating to these agreements.

Jewish life in the villages was further disrupted by oppressive measures against Jewish innkeepers and publicans. To shift responsibility for the plight of the peasantry from its own shoulders, the *szlachta* openly and incessantly incited hostility towards Jewish lessees and innkeepers, "who suck Christian blood like leeches." In actual fact, the *szlachta* was unwilling and legally unable to prohibit Jewish liquor selling throughout the state. Generally, it genuinely needed its Jewish lessees and innkeepers, particularly as there was no abundance of Christian lessees to replace them. At the session of the *Sejm* in 1775, the Marshal of the Confederacy opposed the proposal to ban Jewish lessees, on the grounds that "this prohibition would reduce revenue from these leases." In several regional *sejmiki* however, the *szlachta* succeeded in carrying resolutions depriving Jews of the right to hold leases and to sell liquor. In some areas of Poland, the gentry did not wait for *Sejm* resolutions, but drove the Jewish lessees, innkeepers and publicans from their villages on their own initiative. Many of these squires took over the management of the breweries, distilleries, mills and inns as part of the process of reorganizing the administration of their estates. The increasingly destitute lower ranks of the *szlachta*, who had by now been reduced to the level of a landless *lumpenproletariat*, seized upon the lesseeships as the only remaining occupation offering some claim to gentility. This new situation with regard to lesseeships contributed greatly to the spread of large-scale persecution of Jewish lessees. Manorial lords who could now manage without the Jews—because they no longer required lessees at all, or because they wanted to establish "their own" Christian people in the lesseeships—took the opportunity to torment "their" Jews before evicting them. In Great Poland, where the number of Jewish lessees had, in any case, been comparatively small, the *szlachta* began to expel them from the villages. These expulsions assumed vast proportions in Little Poland, and especially in the administrative district (*wojewodstwo*) of Sandomierz and in Ruthenia. The largest number of expulsions was recorded in the Ukraine. In 1765, one per cent of the Ukrainian villages contained no Jews; thirteen years later, in 1778, seven per cent had been "purged" of Jews. In the following six years, up to 1784, the number of Christian lessees doubled. As a rule, the Jews were expelled by those wealthy estate owners who had reorganized their holdings on a rental basis to replace serf labour.

The number of Jewish poor without visible means of support and of door-to-door beggars was greatly increased by the recent law requiring agreements with the municipal governments, the expulsion of the Jews from the smaller Crown cities, and particularly by the expulsion of many Jewish liquor purveyors from the villages. After the first partition of Poland, thousands more joined their ranks following the deportation of the *Betteljuden* from Galicia and Prussia. Some 40,000 paupers entered Poland in this way in 1788 from the areas of "enlightened" despotic rule in Austrian-occupied Galicia and in Prussia. Figures compiled by a contemporary Polish statesman, Tadeusz Czacki, indicated that 72,000 Jews in Poland were unemployed at that time, while 9,000 were complete paupers. Czacki calculated that the Jewish population of Poland was then 900,000, which would imply that nine per cent of the total was on the brink of the most abject poverty.

Hosts of destitute Jews, with their wives and children, were thus wandering from city to city, from Kehillah to Kehillah. Not surprisingly in these circumstances, the number of criminals—thieves and robbers— amongst the Polish Jews increased. Apart from gangs of Jewish robbers, there were also gangs of bandits composed of Jews, gipsies, dispossessed members of the *szlachta*, burghers, and peasants, all uprooted from their native environments. Fear of these constantly increasing bands moved the government authorities to issue directives concerning Jewish mendicants. However, their practical results were negligible, as the Kehillot were unable "to employ them gainfully for the common good" and the municipalities were unwilling to permit their presence.

The problem created by the vast numbers of unemployed and mendicant Jews only emphasized the wider, over-all question inherent in the abnormal economic structure of Polish Jewry: the need to transfer the Jewish masses to productive occupations. But Poland's decaying feudal system, which had created these depths of Jewish poverty, was hardly competent to solve the problem.

As far as predisposition was concerned, circumstances had never before in the history of Polish Jewry been so favourable to large-scale agricultural settlement as during this period, when approximately a third of the country's Jewish population consisted of rural inhabitants associated to a greater or lesser degree with agricultural activity. But outside factors frustrated all serious attempts at colonization. The *Sejm* of 1775, which raised the Jewish poll tax to three zloty, also heard a lengthy debate on the Jewish question. It decided that Jews who settled on the soil and cultivated it themselves would be exempt from paying the poll tax for the rest of their lives. However, this resolution was entirely theoretical. Apart from the fact that Jews were only allowed to settle as tenants on wastelands, which demanded inhuman effort and vast sums of capital for improvement and cultivation, the law ignored the need to provide the settlers with building materials, livestock and tools. However, the greatest obstacle to the conversion of Jews into agriculturists was the general social predicament of the Polish peasants. Jews who settled on government, manorial, or Church lands were faced with unending serfdom. Although they were to be registered as tenant farmers under the law, they would ultimately have been "written into the soil," like all the other peasants. The prospect of permanent bondage for themselves, their children and the generations to come was not inviting, however great their distress. Not surprisingly, the law of 1775, like the ensuing propaganda for the settlement of Jews on the soil, brought no results. Scarcely a hundred Jewish families in the whole of Poland chose to settle on the soil during that period.

The alternative productive activity offered by industry was equally ineffective, because of the country's backward feudal economy. The number of Jews who worked in manufacturing enterprises belonging to magnates is known in several localities. At Korzec, Wolhynia, a total of sixty Jews worked at two of the ten looms in Prince Jozef Czartoryski's mill. The 300 workers at a Nemirow textile factory founded by the magnate Wincenty Potocki, included a limited number of Jewish women. A Lithuanian magnate, Tyzenhaus, Assistant Minister of Finance, is known to have employed Jewish women in their homes to process threads for his Grodno textile plant. In fact, as the factory system was then in its infancy, a large number of Jewish workers, mostly female lace workers, was engaged under the domestic system which had begun to flourish at that time in certain areas, especially in Great (western) Poland. Veitel Heine, a contractor, employed 800 women in this way, 520 of them at Lissa. A limited number of Jews was also accepted on public work projects, such as dredging the Niemen river. Jews were also known to work in the newly developing Polish mining industry.

All in all, however, this early movement into industry only accounted for negligible percentage of the country's Jewish—or, for that matter, its general—population. The abnormal social and economic Jewish structure, and in fact, the retarded economy of the state were in no way altered. Increases in productive capacity and the programme for moving the Jews into productive occupations never advanced beyond the planning stage. Yet some of the men who had outlined these plans regarded even these insignificant initial efforts to divert the Jews into agriculture and industry as proof of the tremendous potential which generations of repressive decrees, violence and persecution had restricted.

Plans to Reform Jewish Life in Poland

The Jewish problem obviously took a prominent position in the reform programme for the Kingdom, if only because the Jews comprised about a tenth of the country's total population. No reform programme that aimed to improve the country's economic position could ignore a section of the population which had fulfilled such an important function in its commerce and even more in the little industry that it possessed. Furthermore, apart from political and economic considerations, the Jewish problem in Poland was inextricably linked with improvements in the condition of the cities and the peasants. The problems of municipal self-government, for example, could not be solved without taking into account the question of the rights of Jews to reside in the cities and to engage in trade, to sell liquor, and to practise handicrafts. In any case, the problem of municipal self-government brought to the fore the question of the functions and powers of the Kehillah, as well as its juridical relationship with the municipality. The peasant reform programme brought up the subject of Jewish innkeepers and lessees with full force. The issue of transferring the displaced village Jews to new occupations was automatically raised, in conjunction with the plan to prohibit Jewish innkeeping, and inevitably led to the more comprehensive question of moving the Jewish population into productive occupations. Governing circles considered the question of maintaining or abolishing Jewish national autonomy to be of the utmost urgency, and of equal importance to economic and political reforms.

The legislation that the neighbouring absolute monarchies had enacted for their Jews—particularly Joseph II's *Toleranzpatent* for the Jews of Galicia, published in 1789—greatly influenced the manner in which these issues were propounded. They served the authors of the Polish programme as models for their own "reforms." These reforms included a ban on Jewish residence and liquor selling in the villages; the adoption of the principle of transferring the Jews to the cultivation of the soil; the subordination of the Jews to the municipal governments; the abolition of Kehillah autonomy and the restriction of the Kehillot to purely religious matters; the granting of privileges to Jewish merchants and contractors and the strict repression of shopkeepers, pedlars, brokers and people engaged in unstable occupations (*Luftmenschen*); and the cultural and linguistic assimilation of the Jews by law through admittance to the public schools.

The conservative wing of the *szlachta* did not deal at great length with reforms for the Jews because in general it was opposed to any reform in any field. The *szlachta* only regarded the rehabilitation of Jews as farmers as a means of preventing them from increasing too rapidly. An anonymous pamphleteer from this faction demanded that all Jews who were transferred to farming should be declared the chattels of the *szlachta*. "Let them know what the yoke of serfdom is!" The former Chancellor Andrzej Zamoyski also produced a programme which was deliberately antagonistic to the Jews. In 1778, he drafted a legislative code in the spirit of the conservative *szlachta*, but it included certain minimal concessions to the peasants and the burghers. Other projects suggested by *szlachta* conservatives were equally hostile to the Jews.

Representatives of the *szlachta's* progressive party published the most detailed, as well as the most liberal, reform plans for the Jews. A booklet entitled *Jews, or the Urgent Necessity of a Reform Amongst the Jews in the Lands of the Republic* appeared in 1782, signed by *Bezimienny* (i.e., anonymous). The most significant section of this work levelled sharp and accurate criticism at the legal status of the Jews of Poland:

> The Jews have been ejected from all of the country's classes; they have been hedged off by special laws, eliminated from civil posts, ordered to pay double in the law courts. Their religion has been made the butt of scorn and vilification ... And after all this, the Jew has been expected to wear his chains respectfully and to kiss the hand that shackles him. We have wanted him to be useful to the State, though the State has been no motherland to him; we have wanted him to be persevering, yet we have not been willing to guarantee him the fruits of his labour; to be friendly and devoted to those who have ceaselessly tormented him ...

Anonymous proposed that Jews be allowed to engage in commerce and the crafts. He suggested that they be permitted to sell liquor in the cities but not in the countryside, and to settle on the soil as tenant farmers but with the right to change from one landowner to another; that they be released from payment of a special poll tax; and that they be accepted for military service. On the other hand, he insisted that they abandon their "separatism," discard their characteristic Jewish attire, cease to employ Yiddish and Hebrew, and translate their religious books into Polish. The Kehillah should only deal with religious matters; administratively, the Jews should be under the jurisdiction of the city government like the rest of the inhabitants. Judgement in litigation between Jews would either be given by the municipal law court or by Jewish judges in the presence of assessors appointed by the municipal authority. Reforms should also be introduced into the Jewish religion with a view to relaxing the dietary laws and reducing the number of holidays.

This programme, in company with other proposals put forward by the liberal *szlachta** would have allowed the Jews to engage in trade, handicraft and industry while renouncing the sale of liquor, especially in rural areas. All the reformers considered the idea of settling the Jews on the soil, but only Tadeusz Czacki went so far as to indicate some of the methods to achieve it.

All the liberal proposals stipulated that the Jews would be required to forfeit their autonomy and be subject to municipal jurisdiction in return for the freedom to trade and engage in handicraft. Furthermore, total assimilation in speech and culture was also demanded. They were not even promised participation in the administration of the cities to compensate for this sacrifice, or, needless to add, political rights in the state, such as participating at the *Sejm* or holding positions in the civil service, as had been promised to the burghers. In their limited liberalism, the progressive members of the *szlachta* thought that their proposals to grant the Jews legal opportunities to engage in urban professions were quite generous.

Some of the reforming gentry even thought that this programme was too liberal. They suggested that Jews be forbidden to engage in brokerage, peddling, and street hawking. They also proposed to restrict the right of Jewish merchants to live in the cities to those possessing a required minimum of capital or owning building property in the town.

The leading spokesmen of the burgher class were definitely not disposed to acquiesce in the programme of reforms for the Jews proposed by the *szlachta* liberals. Their one policy towards the Jews was to rid themselves of Jewish competition. The burgher representatives of the Warsaw *woyewodztwo* demanded the expulsion of the Jews from all the cities in their district. During this revolutionary period, when the middle class in western Europe was demanding equality for the Jews in the name of equality for all citizens, their Polish counterpart made its first appearance in the political arena to launch a total attack on the Jews. Ironically, the *szlachta*, which had protected the Jews from the burghers throughout the feudal period in Poland, once again fulfilled this function during the age of "great reforms." This was inevitable in a country where social development was so retarded that its revolutionary debt was discharged by superficial and outmoded measures.

The reform programme that the Jews propounded were for the most part the intellectual product of the first pioneers of the Enlightenment movement in Poland. These men were influenced by the spirit of European Enlightenment and regarded the Jewish question in terms of

---

* e.g., Butrymowicz, a Deputy from the Department of Pinsk, in his pamphlet, *A Reform for the Jews*; the statesman Tadeusz Czacki; and the ecclesiastic, Hugo Kollontay.

education, enlightenment, and the movement into productive employment. They showed no signs of any depth in their social and political conceptions. Thus, they remained silent on the subject of the deprivation of Jewish rights, or else only touched casually upon the question. They were enchanted by the generosity of the liberal Polish reformers and gave their programme almost unreserved support.

In 1786, a year after the appearance of a second edition of the booklet on the Jews by *Anonymous*, it was published in German by a Warsaw Jewish physician, Elias Accord, who added his own comments. In 1792, an eminent *Maskil*, Mendel Lefin of Satanow, who was supported by the enlightened Prince Adam Czartoryski, published anonymously a French booklet, *Essay on a Programme of Reform with the Aim of Enlightening the Israelitic People in Poland and Mending its Ways*. Even the title indicated that the author saw the Jewish problem fundamentally as consisting of the spread of Enlightenment and refinement. He suggested setting up Jewish schools in Warsaw and other cities with Polish as the language of instruction. The graduates of these schools would disseminate Enlightenment and wisdom amongst the Jewish masses. The government would need to combat Hasidism, which was, he claimed, spreading fanaticism and superstition and constituted the main obstacle to the advance of Enlightenment amongst the Jews. In order to transfer the Jews gradually to productive occupations, he proposed the establishment of trade schools where Jewish youths could learn handicrafts and agriculture. The rabbis could accustom the Jews to work in the fields in the early stages by compelling them to raise wheat for the Passover *matzot . . .* Mendicants and idlers would be forced to work in workshops to be established by the Kehillot. The Jewish people would have to be trained to obey the laws of the state; the state, on the other hand, would have to abolish all special Jewish taxes.

Mendel Lefin had been preceded by the Königsberg physician, Dr. Moses Markuse, who had settled in Poland in 1773. In 1789, he published a *Book on Curatives (Sefer R'fuot)* in Yiddish. Like Lefin of Satanow, Dr. Markuse also had a powerful patron, in this case an enlightened magnate, the Court Chamberlain Michael Bobrowski, who defrayed the costs of his small book. But while Lefin based his solution to the Jewish problem primarily on Enlightenment, Dr. Markuse emphasized the movement of the Jews into productive activities. His plan was realistic and adapted to the means available. He proposed an evolutionary transition to productive occupations, assisted by auxiliary activities. He told elderly women that "instead of furtive whisperings about the evil eye, it were better that they should comb flax, spin, and pluck feathers." He told the preachers that "instead of distorting the *Torah* and twisting its obvious meaning" they should go into the forests and "make rakes, winnowing shovels, and brooms . . ." He informed the Jewish innkeepers that they could obtain their own vegetables and fresh air into the bargain—if they converted the refuse-covered parcels around their taverns into gardens and flower beds.

A royal broker, Abraham Hirszowicz, was also concerned with the question of the movement into productive activity. He submitted a plan to the King, requesting that the Jews be permitted to engage in all manual trades. He, like Dr. Markuse, saw the need to spread agricultural activity, such as vegetable and flower growing and bee-keeping, amongst the Jews in the smaller towns. But he also proposed that the government allot lands in Podolia and the Ukraine for concentrated Jewish settlement. Jewish beggars would be employed in paving roads, digging canals, and draining swamps—and would in return receive a fair wage.

The popular Jewish leader of Vilno, Szimel Wolfowicz (Simon Ben-Wolff), while in prison in 1789* also published a Jewish reform programme, influenced by the pamphlets by *Anonymous* and Butrymowicz. The booklet carried the striking title: *The Prisoner at Nieswiez to the Estates in the Sejm on the Necessity of a Jewish Reform*. Wolfowicz was principally concerned with the question of abolishing Kehillah autonomy, which he considered an instrument of repression and a superfluous institution. He felt that the Jewish courts should be abolished together with the Kehillot, and only religious tribunals for religious matters be retained. These would consist of one rabbi and two arbitrators approved by the two parties to a dispute. Jewish religious expenses should not be defrayed by Kehillah taxes but by voluntary contributions.

Another Vilno Jew, Dr. Solomon Polonus, a physician to the royal court, drew up a Jewish reform plan in 1792 which included some of Szimel Wolfowicz's proposals, but in a more moderate version. Polonus advanced this plan to supplement an address by the pro-Jewish French liberal, Abbé Grégoire, which he translated into Polish. Polonus also thought that the Kehillah should only be concerned with religious affairs. In all non-religious matters, the Jews should be tried by government courts, with two Jewish assessors participating. The Jews should be called *Hebrews* or *Old Believers*. They should be granted complete freedom to trade, take up manual occupations, engage in industry, and live wherever they chose. Jewish craftsmen should belong to the general craft guilds. Jews who were not traders, artisans, or servants, should be transferred to work on the land. Dr. Polonus supported Butrymowicz' suggestion that Jews should dress like Poles. Kehillah correspondence and ledgers should be conducted in Polish. A principal task of the Kehillah would be to educate the children in the Polish language. No marriage licences would be issued to people not conversant with the Polish language. Jews would acquire citizenship rights after five years of military service or twelve years of observing the "reform." Enlightened Jews would acquire the rights of citizenship immediately.

The idea that citizenship should be granted in the first instance to a

* See above, p. 297.

select group of enlightened persons was not unusual. In 1790, a number of wholesale merchants, led by the "enlightened" David Königsberger, submitted a memorandum to the *Sejm* requesting rights of citizenship in Warsaw for the 250 families of local wholesalers and bankers. They were apparently not particularly concerned about the fate of the several thousand other Jewish families in Warsaw, faced with the threat of impending expulsion.

The highly assimilationist programme of these Jewish authors was the direct result of the ambition of Polish Jewry's newly developed middle-class to assimilate with and merge into the Polish burgher class and to enjoy all its rights. Ironically—or, from the point of view of the Polish-Jewish intellectuals and plutocrats, tragically—the Polish middle class remained unmoved by their protestations of affection. The Polish burghers —or *mieszczanie*—obstinately retained their own programme of bringing the Jews to utter ruin.

The Jewish masses in Poland were still too remote from European Enlightenment and culture to make their views heard in the political debates on reforms. The conservative section of the Polish-Jewish middle-class gave the sole reply to the plans published by Butrymowicz and his enlightened Jewish disciples. The Rabbi of Chelm, Herschel Jozefowicz, published a Polish pamphlet criticizing the reform proposals. He attempted to prove that the planned reforms threatened to destroy the Jewish religion. Everything, therefore, should remain as before: the Jews must be different in their clothing; Kehillah autonomy and Jewish law courts must remain unrestrained; and Jewish education must continue along traditional lines.

The opposition of the Rabbi of Chelm expressed the attitude of the official Kehillah leaders. The conservative group exercised a firm hege-mony over the Jews, very similar to the power wielded by the conservative *szlachta* over the realm as a whole. And the leaders of the latter camp employed every means during the Great *Sejm* to ensure that the reform programme for the Jews did not pass into law.

The Jewish problem at the Quadrennial Sejm;
The Kosciuszko Revolt

The Jewish problem and the peasant question shared a like fate at the *Quadrennial Sejm* which lasted from 1788 to 1792. None of the reform programmes for the Polish peasants ever went beyond the verbal stage and the *Sejm* passed no law whatsoever to improve their condition. The same applied to the Jewish question. However, the Jewish problem and the peasant question were also closely linked at another level. The problem of reviving Jewish economic life was essentially concerned with settling large sections of the Jewish population on the soil. But this was impossible as long as no change was made in the legal status of the peasants, at least to the extent of emancipating them from their serfdom. The Jews were unwilling to become serfs, and there was no conceivable way of forcing them to do so. On the other hand, the *szlachta* could not transgress its own limits by establishing Jewish agricultural colonists at a higher legal level than that of the peasants.

The *szlachta* rejected peasant reform because of its greed as a feudal estate and it had only been prepared to enact a "reform" for the Jews insofar as it would not conflict with the demands of the burghers. But even the slightest improvement in the legal position of the Jews in the cities necessarily conflicted with the plans of the *mieszczanie*. The burghers wanted to exploit these reforms purely in order to eliminate their Jewish competitors in commerce and trade. The committee appointed to handle the problem was composed of three senators and six deputies. The advocates of reform were represented on the committee by Senator Jezierski and Deputy Butrymowicz. The *szlachta's* contradictory attitude to the Jewish question, and differences of opinion amongst the committee members, prevented the committee making any progress until the end of 1791.

Meanwhile, in April, 1791, the *Sejm* enacted the Royal Cities Law which became an integral part of the constitution of May 3, 1791. The Law made no mention whatsoever of the rights of the Jews and discharged its obligations to the peasants with a non-committal reference to their protection by law. More important, however, the provisions governing the cities were explicitly formulated so that the Jews forfeited the few rights they possessed as well as the opportunity to acquire citizenship rights in the future. One section stipulated that the inhabitants of a city could only conduct retail trading enterprises (dealing in goods measured by weight or volume) when they had obtained the status of citizenship in that city. Another section decreed that the cities could not withhold citizenship rights from Christians, whether local residents or strangers.

The consequences of these laws appeared immediately. The ensuing persecution and expulsion of Jewish traders, brokers and artisans was not confined to Warsaw. The municipal governments of several cities in Poland, Lithuania and the Ukraine promulgated new decrees against their Jewish business men and artisans.

In the latter half of 1791, the Jews took organized action on the reform issue. The Kehillah leaders resolved to employ all means to mitigate the forced assimilation in language and dress and to obtain the withdrawal of the proposed legislative programme to reduce Kehillah authority—to them, an equally formidable decree. At the Zelwa fair in August, 1791, delegates from the Lithuanian Kehillot decided to levy a tax on all the Jews, "that there might not, Providence forbid, be new reforms." A month later, the Lublin regional Rabbi, Hirsh Ben-Saul, submitted a proposal to the King in the name of all the rabbis of Poland: the Jews would undertake to pay several hundred thousand zloty annually to the King for his own exclusive disposition, on condition that the reform projected did not conflict with Jewish law. In autumn, 1791, deputies from the Kehillot of Poland and Lithuania convened at Warsaw. Court brokers and royal bankers obtained an audience with the royal scribe, Father Scipione Piattoli. Pessah Haimowicz, a former intercessor (sh'tadlan) for the Jews of Warsaw, presented Piattoli with a memorandum in the name of the Kehillah deputies, requesting him to prevent the abuse of Jewish religious customs, and to assert Jewish rights against the opposition of the mieszczanie, with law courts of their own, the right to buy houses, and civil rights in the cities.

The King was heavily in debt and was mainly interested in receiving as much money from the Jews as possible. At a royal audience granted to the Jewish delegates at the end of 1791, he compelled them to sign a commitment for 2,000,000 zloty, partly to be put at the disposal of the government, and partly to cover the King's debts. In addition, the delegates deposited 15,000 red zloty (170,000 ordinary Polish zloty) in cash at the sovereign's feet. A few month's later, when the Jews of Warsaw were faced with a new threat of expulsion, they donated a further 40,000 zloty to the King with promises of more to come.

These money gifts and commitments enabled Piattoli to introduce certain revisions into the Jewish reform programme that he submitted to the Sejm in the name of the King. This programme contained some important provisions. The Jews were to discard their special dress and to be educated at Polish schools which the Kehillot were required to open. No Jew could marry without a certificate from one of these schools. The Jews would be permitted to live in the villages and in the manorial cities if they possessed a permit granted by the gentry. In the cities of the Crown Jews would be permitted to live only with the consent of the municipal governments. Liquor selling by Jews would require the consent of the departments concerned. Jews would be subject to municipal law courts for civil affairs and punishable offences, but with a Jewish assessor present at the litigation or trial. They could purchase for cash exemption from compulsory military service. The Jewish poll tax was to be abolished and replaced by a tax on kosher meat and a Jewish stamp tax. The income to be derived from these Jewish taxes was fixed at 5,000,000 zloty annually, including 1,500,000 zloty to be earmarked for covering the King's debts.

The Sejm Committee on Jewish Affairs found even this programme too liberal. At the beginning of 1792, the Committee was reorganized under the chairmanship of Father Kollontay and a number of urban representatives were co-opted on to it. The section on Jewish economic rights in the cities naturally aroused most opposition. The burgher representatives were particularly adamant in their demand that Jews be prohibited from selling liquor so that Christians would face no competition in this field. The only innovation that the Sejm made in connection with the Jewish problem was a resolution to introduce special courts for the liquidation of Kehillah debts. A few months later, war broke out with Russia and led to the second partition of Poland.

The debates on the Jewish question in the Great *Sejm* had not produced a single legal enactment. This complete inability to solve the Jewish problem was another example of the social and political bankruptcy of the feudal republic of the *szlachta*.

In March, 1794, under Tadeusz Kosciuszko, revolt broke out. From the start, the leaders of the uprising appealed to the patriotism of all the inhabitants of the country and did not hesitate to include the Jews in this appeal. In his speech proclaiming the revolt in the market place of Krakow on March 24, Kosciuszko declared: "Worthy gentlemen! In the defence of our country, all are equal in my eyes, and I therefore hold in equal esteem the Jew, the peasant, the nobleman, the priest and the freeman." Kosciuszko is also purported to have made a speech in the Krakow synagogue stating that "in his ambition to bring happiness to his fellow-countrymen he also meant the Jews."*

The leaders of the revolt regarded the Jews in much the same way as the peasants: it declared them all equal in defence, but failed to grant them equality.

These leaders imposed the same heavy duties on the Jews as on the population as a whole, except for personal military service. Until October, 1794, Jews everywhere in Poland could purchase exemption from service in the armed forces. In October, a proclamation by the Supreme National Council announced that the Jews would have to supply foot and cavalry recruits on the same basis as the rest of the country's inhabitants. As the revolt was then nearing its end, this could hardly have secured the enlistment of very many Jews. On the other hand, large numbers of Jews had served in municipal militias and popular mobilizations throughout the revolt, especially in the large cities of Warsaw, Vilno, and Grodno. In Warsaw alone, several hundred Jews served in the militia. Jews also provided auxiliary services for the army as carters, as well as by digging trenches, erecting embattlements, and in fighting fires to the same extent as the rest of the city's population. Jewish artisans, tailors, cap-makers, tent-makers, furriers and bakers worked for the army and were thus important to the success of the revolt. The Jews participated in national loans both by collective money contributions through the Kehillot and in private loans in cash and supplies.

In fact, the leaders of the revolt considered the Jews a factor so important to its success that they forbade any excesses against them and issued an order of the day to all personnel on "keeping order and treating all citizens justly, regardless of class or religion." Even so, they did nothing to redress the legal status of the Jews, though they found it expedient to make some slight concessions to the peasants. In addition to

* As told by the Chief Rabbi of Krakow, H. D. Lewi.

the Jewish poll tax, the Jews of Warsaw were still forced to pay for the day ticket (*billet*) to spend fourteen days in the capital and this had been raised from three groszy to five or more for one person. The Warsaw Jews asked in vain for the abolition of this ticket. Kosciuszko demonstrated his own liberalism in a letter to the Supreme National Council dated September 18:

> The old government (i.e., prior to the revolt) compelled the Jews to endure this (the ticket) along with other discriminations. Now, however, when our country is as a mother to all of us, when our country must prove its justice for all, it is neither meet nor just that this class of people (the Jews), which has been so helpful together with all the rest and is desirous of contributing, with the rest, to the common defence, should not enjoy the government's generosity.

Kosciuszko did not go beyond making these recommendations. He was unwilling to quarrel with the leaders of the revolt by insisting on his own point of view.

The revolt failed to arouse any enthusiasm which might have led to action amongst the Jewish masses. The deeply-rooted, traditional mode of life of the body of Polish Jewry contained no basis for any feelings of patriotic affinity with the surrounding urban population. The antagonism that the Polish burghers had felt towards the Jews for generations made such a rapprochement even more difficult. However, the domestic policy of the revolutionary government was the prime reason for the lack of enthusiasm that the Jewish masses in Poland evinced towards the revolt. The Jews did not observe any practical manifestations by the revolutionary authorities in confirmation of their announcements of the fraternization of the whole population.

However, even though the Jews showed no inclination to participate in the conflict with wholehearted dedication, they felt great sympathy for the revolt. They appreciated the new, friendly attitude of the leaders of the revolt, and especially of Kosciuszko's pronouncements, when, in the past, the Polish governments had never had a good word to say for them. Some elements in the poor Jewish population, especially in the larger cities, even participated actively in the revolt. They were artisans, servants, working men and the socially uprooted, less obsessed with religious zeal than the Jewish lower middle class. They did not have much to lose and hoped they might gain something by participating in the war. They also tried to obtain the protection of the revolutionary government against the rich. A petition that "The Organized Jewish Poor of Warsaw" addressed to the President of the Warsaw Municipality accused the wealthy Jews of "planning to collect their property and ship it abroad."

These "poor Jews" of Warsaw distinguished themselves in the battles of April 17 and 18, when the Warsaw populace drove the Russians from the capital. Their bravery was made known throughout the country and was even held up as an example for the Poles to emulate. In September, Berek Joselowicz, a Jew who had participated in the Warsaw fighting in April, organized a Jewish cavalry troop. It was partly composed of volunteers and partly of "idlers" and unemployed, forcibly conscripted for army service, like the Christian *Lumpenproletariat*. All in all, it numbered 500 men, under Jewish officers. When, on November 4, the Russian General Suvorov began to shell Praga, the historic Warsaw suburb, Berek Joselowicz' Jewish cavalry troop was heroic in its defence of the capital. Only a handful of his men survived. Suvorov's cossacks took a bloody revenge on the inhabitants of Praga and mercilessly slaughtered the entire Jewish population. In the annihilation of old Poland, that ensued, their bloodshed was the basis for an incipient fraternity between the Jewish and Polish peoples. The "Anonymous" Polish writer first had described them as "two nations inhabiting one fatherland." Kosciuszko later wrote in the *Government Gazette*, "... They proved to the world that wherever Humanity has hopes to prevail, they gladly offer their lives."

CHAPTER TEN

POLAND AFTER THE PARTITION

A. *GALICIA*

The Population and the Economic Situation

The area taken from Poland by Austria in the first partition in 1772 was renamed Galicia, after the town of Halicz. It remained under Austrian domination for the following 146 years, until the Habsburg Empire disintegrated in 1918, at the end of the First World War. Their geographical position and political circumstances enabled the Jews of Galicia to occupy a unique position in the history of modern Jewish culture. They were the only large eastern European Jewish community to be incorporated into the immediate sphere of influence of a central European cultural centre. The Jews of Germany only formed an intermediate link between the traditional culture of eastern European Jewry and the culture of the west. The Galician Jews, on the other hand, were the first Jewish community to bring about an organic fusion of these two cultures. However, this only occurred after a first, transitional period. Anything that the Jews of Galicia gained as a result of the superiority of the absolutist régime over the antiquated feudal order—especially in its reactionary phase—was, as in the case of the Jews of western Poland who had come under Prussian rule, offset by harsh fiscal exploitation and discriminatory decrees. The mass of the Jewish population lived in poverty. Only the rising Jewish middle class, laboriously working its way to the fore as the capitalist system slowly advanced, benefited from the new régime in Galicia—as it did in Prussia and Tzarist Russia. However, when the force of political reaction in the Austrian Empire disappeared, at a later stage of capitalist development, the Jewish masses in retarded Galicia also obtained civil rights, which was not the case with their fellow Jews throughout eastern Europe.

The new Austrian province included the southern portion of the woyewodships of Krakow and Sandomierz, Red Ruthenia, a strip of Podolia and, until 1809, the district of Zamosc. Between 1772 and 1776, the Krakow suburb of Kazimierz, which contained Krakow's Jewish quarter, was also under Austrian administration. After the third partition of Poland in 1795, the entire city of Krakow, as well as the Lublin district, named "Western Galicia," was ceded to Austria.* A census held in

* The Lublin district only remained under Austrian rule until 1809.

Galicia in 1772 for military purposes and known to be inaccurate put the number of Jews in the area at 171,851, or 6.5 per cent of the total population of 2,656,152. In reality, there were about 200,000 Jews in Galicia that year, over 7 per cent of the total population. The censuses of the period, however faulty, clearly indicated the uneven spread of the Jewish population between the eastern and western regions of Galicia. In the western half, the general population was actually Polish and the percentage of Jews (according to the 1776 census) was only 3.1; whereas in the eastern half, inhabited chiefly by Ukrainians (known there as Ruthenians or Russinians), the Jews constituted 8.7 per cent of the total. The contrast between the proportion of Jews amongst the urban population in the eastern and western areas was even greater. In eastern Galicia in the 1830's, Jews accounted for a third of the population in cities such as Lwow (Lemberg), Drohobycz, Stryj, Kalusz, Tysmienica, Jaroslaw and Przemysl. They formed an absolute majority in the cities of Tarnopol, Kolomyja, Skole, Turka, Starasol, Stary Sambor, Zolkiew, and also in the central Galician city of Rzeszow. In a number of cities, for example, Brody, Rohatyn, Przemyslany, Delatyn, Sokal and Belz, practically all the inhabitants were Jewish. On the other hand, only a small proportion of Jews lived in the cities of western Galicia, with the exception of Krakow, Wisnicz, Tarnow and a few towns in the Tarnow district. In some cities in this area, such as Bochnia and Wieliczka (two salt mining centres), Jewish domicile was totally forbidden on the basis of ancient municipal privileges "not to tolerate Jews."

Galicia, which held the largest Jewish community, was also the poorest and most retarded province in all Austria. In common with all the other areas of Poland and most of eastern Europe, its development had been hampered by a decadent feudal system. The serfdom of the peasants and the poor plots of land that the landowners left them had reduced their standard of living to an inordinately low level. This was further aggravated in Galicia by the fact that the breaking up of peasant holdings into minute plots through inheritance, was greater there than in most other regions of Poland. The peasant lived on coarse and inadequate food and dressed only in a shirt over rough denim trousers. His living quarters were equally wretched. In the mountain villages in the eastern area, he did not even have a hut but occupied a clay hovel without a chimney, which served as a house and a cow-shed combined.

Drunkenness was the main vice of the Galician—and in fact of all eastern European—peasantry. The misery of the peasant's life, as a number of provincial administrators testified, drew him to alcohol, both as a means of enlivening his coarse diet and of finding some consolation for his drab existence. The feudal régime deliberately acted as the primary agent in spreading alcoholism. Income returns that the Galician nobles submitted to the Exchequer in 1774 showed that liquor sales in many cases contributed a third and even a half of all the profits from their estates. Here, as in most parts of Poland, the peasant was forced to purchase a fixed quota of liquor at the nobleman's tavern; in addition, he was frequently remunerated with manorial credit slips redeemable in kind by the liquor lessee in place of cash payments.

The reform-conscious Austrian government during Joseph's reign took a number of steps to improve the welfare of the peasantry in order to ensure the flow of tax revenues (the peasants formed the largest class in the population) and also to expand the domestic market for trade, handicrafts and industry. By the end of Maria Theresa's reign, estate owners had been forbidden to add to the peasant's quota of labour for taxes and court revenues over and above the long established practice. Joseph II issued several *Letters Patent* on the Galician peasant question, culminating in the *Patent* of 1786, the most comprehensive of all. Peasant servitude was thenceforth defined as "limited subjection" and not as "serfdom." Trials involving peasants were entrusted to officials appointed by the manorial lords, but appeal against their verdicts could be made to the district authorities, to the *Gubernium* (Central Provincial Government), or even to the Imperial Court. Peasants who had purchased and owned their own landholdings were granted freedom of movement. A peasant no longer required his lord's permission to marry or engage in handicraft. A number of limitations was imposed on the service quota that the peasant owed his lord, particularly the establishment of a three day maximum of labour in the lord's fields. Ordinances were also issued to stop the spread of drunkenness. The peasants' obligation to purchase fixed quantities of liquor at the manorial taverns had already been abolished during Maria Theresa's reign and a prohibition was placed on serving liquor on credit to a value exceeding three Polish zloty at the same time. The monopoly that many estate owners held, compelling the peasants to sell their crop surpluses to the lords or their lessees and to purchase in return commodities such as salt, herring, or agricultural implements, was also abolished.

All these reforms were inadequate because of the superficiality and contradiction inherent in enlightened absolutism and even more so in the absolute régime that soon succeeded it. The absolutist system tried to improve the condition of the peasants without impairing the feudal basis of the régime and the privileges of the dominant nobility. As a result, no substantial changes were effected in the circumstances of rural life. The estate owners were able to evade the legal injunctions against intoxication by various devices, especially as the government had entrusted them with the lease for collecting the liquor excise—the rate of which was predetermined by reference to large-scale consumption. That section of the law which permitted peasants to be punished with the lash, as before, provided a high-ranking official of the lord of the manor was present, was symbolic of the spirit behind these reforms.

Descriptions by early nineteenth-century travellers proved conclusively how little the condition of the Galician peasants changed, even after the reforms of Joseph II. Josef August Schultes, Professor of Chemistry and Botany at the University of Krakow, in an account of his travels in Galicia published in 1806, made the following comment on the Galician peasant:

> Culture here is at an extremely low level. Only the liquor known as *aqua vitae*, which is actually Poland's *aqua mortis*, is the chief reason for the paralysis of the Polish peasant and his apathy towards anything human. It is as though the sun shines in Galicia only to light the peasant's way to the tavern.

The Galician towns were also bound to the feudal régime. In 1776, 311 cities and towns were registered in Galicia, but not more than a dozen actually resembled urban communities. Economically, most of the towns were more like villages than cities. Some of the townsfolk were occupied as liquor purveyors or artisans, but the majority earned their living chiefly from the land. The peasant only came to town on market day or, particularly, fair days, when he sold his surplus crops (if he were not already committed to selling them to the village innkeeper) and purchased his few supplies, mainly fancy goods and trinkets. This was another opportunity to get drunk, as in many towns practically every building housed a tavern. Drunkenness was even more prevalent amongst the Christian townsmen than amongst the peasants, and the former were, by all official accounts, far less diligent or skilful than the latter.

The poverty of the Christian townsmen made the economic role of the Jews in Galicia even greater in some respects than in the other countries of eastern Europe. The village Jews, who comprised about a third of the total Jewish population, held leases, sold liquor and kept inns, like the Jews of Poland as a whole. Their social differentiation was also much the same as in neighbouring lands. The big lessee obtained a leasehold on the manorial distillery and taverns, on the mill, dairy farm, fish ponds, fruit orchards, road and bridge tolls, and usually also on a plot of land which included serf labour. By contrast, the minor lessees or sub-lessees, the innkeepers and publicans, who were also classified as lessors, only earned a precarious living. Even the district administrators, despite their unconcealed hostility towards the Jews, had to admit that these rural Jews were poor, destitute and, for all their exploitation of the peasants, themselves exploited by the owners of the *latifundia*. The small-scale Jewish publicans and lessees in the numerous privately-owned towns of the province were in an even worse position. Their numbers exceeded the towns, capacity to contain them and they had to compete with many Christian townsmen, especially artisans, who also engaged in the sale of liquors, either as their principal or as a secondary source of income.

Nearly half of the Jewish population of Galicia were lessors and publicans in towns and villages. Their function as middlemen between the landed proprietors and peasantry on the one hand, and the cities and villages on the other, was symptomatic of the dual economic system. They supported the feudal economy in two of its principal activities: the production and the sale of liquors. They were the chief factor in the accumulation of capital by the estate owners, a process which undermined the foundations of feudalism and eventually cleared the way for the emergence of a capitalist system. But they were also of great direct importance in developing the foundations of the capitalist system in Galicia. In the first place, to a large extent, they still discharged the capitalist function of supplying loans in that they sold liquor on credit and granted cash loans to the peasants. Secondly, and more important, the urban Jews were the leading promoters of mercantile capitalism. Jewish lessees, innkeepers and publicans in villages and towns, together with Jewish pedlars and small-traders, were practically the only promoters of trade in the area they inhabited.

The Jewish lessee very often also marketed the estate owner's grain, flax and sometimes even his timber. The Jewish innkeeper in the village and the Jewish publican in the town bought the peasant's produce both for consumption by the Jewish population in the town (the Christian inhabitants were agriculturists themselves) and for sale to urban whole-salers. The role of the village innkeeper in this trade was doubly useful: he relieved the peasants of the need to go to market in the town, and thus also averted the bouts of drunkenness that invariably followed such visits.

The sale of liquor only came third in the list of occupations of towns and city Jews. Their two principal sources of income were trade and handi-craft. Both the Galician authorities and travellers to the country concurred that trade there was predominantly in Jewish hands. Large entrepreneurs were the most prominent of the Christian merchants and some of them owned business establishments with branch stores in several of the large cities. But Christian trade in Galicia was insignificant, both in volume and complexity, by comparison with that of the Jews. The Jews controlled both wholesale and retail trade. "Were it not for the Jews," stated a memorandum from the District Administrator of Sambor to the govern-ment, in which he described the Jews as a necessary evil, "it would be impossible to procure even a strand of cotton or silken thread in the cities for the price of a few pennies; were it not for them, the estate owners would not sell their grain and linen, the peasants would be unable to buy on credit and thus obtain their most vital commodities. In this land, which is so lacking in diligence, they are the ones who are infusing its economy with a breath of life and serving all classes of the population."

Imports by Jewish traders were closely linked with the export trade, which was also for the most part, in Jewish hands. They shipped timber and potash, flax and linen, salt, beeswax, honey and also some grain via the Vistula to Danzig and imported mainly herrings, spices and coffee by the same route. They transported potash, hides, flax, honey, wax, liquor and cattle by the overland route to Breslau, Leipzig and Frankfurt-on-the-

Oder, and in return bought woven fabrics and various other dry goods. Jews from the Carpathian mountains in eastern Galicia imported wine from northern Hungary (now Slovakia) and distributed it throughout Poland. In exchange, they exported honey, linen and grain. The grain trade between the various regions of Galicia was also conducted entirely by Jews. But more important even than the import and export trade was the transit trade that Galician Jews carried on between Russia and Turkey in the east and Germany in the west. The city of Brody, the largest commercial centre in Galicia and almost entirely Jewish, had become the great centre for this traffic while it was still under the Polish régime. A significant anecdote that circulated through Galicia at that time, related that when Francis I visited Brody, he commented derisively, "It is now clear to me why I bear the title 'King of Jerusalem.' " Between 1778 and 1799, the population of Brody grew from 10,997 to 16,359 including 14,105 Jews or 86 per cent of the total. By 1820, Jews represented 88 per cent of the city's inhabitants (16,392 out of 18,471). There were only a handful of Christian merchants in the city, though certainly they were the most opulent. The big merchants were the most important of the hundreds of Jewish family heads in Brody who were engaged in trade. According to the official report of 1784, several of them held assets valued at between 10,000 and 20,000 florins, and about ten possessed capital assets of between 25,000 and 60,000 florins. It should be noted that the wealthiest Christian merchant in the city was worth 105,000 florins. Needless to say, in all of the cities, and even more in the towns, there were far more retail dealers, storekeepers, small traders and pedlars than wholesale merchants. Official statistics for 1806 showed that even such an international centre as Brody had 281 retailers, as compared with 244 wholesale dealers. In addition, there must have been several thousand storekeepers and hucksters, as 5,000 families in that city earned their living by trade, according to an estimate by the District Administrator for 1797. The official census of 1772 for two communities, each with less than 1,000 Jewish inhabitants, illustrated the stratification of the Jews engaged in trade in the towns. Two silk merchants and ten shopkeepers were registered at Jazlowiec. One merchant was reported at Zaleszczyki and twenty-five shopkeepers. Many of the family heads who failed to indicate their occupations would appear also to have been engaged in trade and brokerage as pedlars, small traders, agents and the like.

Travellers' accounts indicated that brokerage was not as widespread amongst the Jews of Galicia as in neighbouring Poland and the Ukraine. Nevertheless, there were social and economic variations between the brokers, ranging from the nobility's "factors," and the official commercial brokers (at Brody and Lwow), to poverty-stricken wretches who offered their services to all newcomers to the city. In large commercial centres groups of Jews also made a living by moneylending. However, usury as a primary occupation was rare amongst the Galician Jews, though it provided a secondary source of income for Jews in the towns and villages. On the other hand, even German writers, such as Franz Kratter (in 1786) and Professor Belthasar Hacquet (in 1789) who did not like the Jews, one way or another, complained of the Armenians, nearly all of whom engaged in usury and extorted "from 25 to 100 per cent." Kratter denounced the German usurers who had recently settled in Galicia even more vehemently: they were more harmful than all the others because of their widespread activities and the assistance they received from the authorities. As well as the village inns, the Jews maintained lodging houses in the cities and towns. Linked to their trading activities, carters were common amongst the Galician Jews, as in all other areas of Poland, and Jewish porters were also frequently found. An anti-Jewish author, Rohrer, reluctantly confirms the honesty of these men who carried on their backs the furniture of tenants moving house.

Direct participation by Jews in home industry was limited to a few places. In the town of Skalat in eastern Galicia, Jews manufactured cheap ornaments—rings, metal blouse-buttons, and similar articles—for the peasants. Jewish manufacture in the city of Rzeszow, with 4,604 inhabitants was more important. Pastor Samuel Bredetzky described it in his travel book as worthy of the title of the Jerusalem of Galicia. Jewish engravers there made some of the finest seals; a native of the city, Ze'ev Isaiah Finkelsteiner, was employed at the court of the King of Sweden. Rohrer cited the products of Rzeszow's engravers as an example of the developed artistic sense of the Jews. Jewellery was the chief product of the Jews of Rzeszow and it acquired an international reputation as "Rzeszow gold." Gold alloy work by these craftsmen won them the markets of Prussia, Hungary and Russia and occasionally reached as far afield as Leghorn or even Alexandria. Rohrer described this gold handiwork as no less delicate in form than the golden ornaments of Prague, despite its cheap price.

The Jewish share in the home production of Christian workers thriving at that time throughout Galicia was immeasurably greater. All contemporary descriptions of Galicia showed that the Jews not only marketed these products at home and abroad in their capacity as traders, but at times actually controlled production through the credit system.

The majority of artisans in the towns were also Jews, although in this field they did not achieve the same superiority as in trade. Cobbling, in conjunction with tanning, was the chief occupation of the Christian artisans in the towns; the Jews dominated the crafts of tailors, furriers, cap-makers, braiders, goldsmiths, coppersmiths, glazier, meat dealers and bakers. The Christian craftsmen were to the fore in the larger cities but Jewish artisans nevertheless penetrated into many occupations in addition to tailoring which was, as in the smaller towns, their chief occupation.

At this period, Jewish handicraft was very diversified in the Kehillah of Brody. An official report for the year 1806 reported 41 independent Jewish artisans, comprising, with their families, 14 per cent of the Jewish population—approximately 2,000 out of 14,000 people. As the Jews were in a majority amongst the inhabitants of the city (86 per cent of the total), it was not surprising to find that there were more Jewish than Christian artisans, though less than 100 per cent more—418 Jews as against 228 Christians. Here again, the vocational distribution was different amongst Jews and Christians—so much so that in effect a mutual division of trade occurred. Even so, the Jewish craftsmen included four lathe-workers, seven coppersmiths, thirteen saddlers, two tinkers, four painters, one gold embroiderer and four boiler-makers, though none of these trades was represented amongst the Christian population of the city. Jewish artisans also followed crafts on the same lines as the list of Christian occupations: two house-painters, five watchmakers, nine carpenters, twenty wood-workers and four tinsmiths.

Contradictory contemporary opinions on the Jewish share in the manual trades in Galicia are to be explained by the different relative proportions of Jewish and Christian artisans in the cities, on the one hand, and in the towns, on the other, and by the differences in their respective occupational distribution. Reports by district administrators uniformly stated that handicraft was mainly a Christian occupation. By contrast, the authors of travel books, whether in favour of the Jews or not, invariably recorded that they had seized all or the most important manual trades. Undoubtedly, the administrators were only interested in relationships in the basic manual trades and the domestic industries in the cities and villages. The authors, on the other hand, were mainly looking at the small towns, where the Jews were generally preponderant in the artisan trades. They also based their conclusions on the observation of typically Jewish occupations in the cities.

However, despite the great importance of the Jewish population to the Galician economy, and the significant proportion of productive elements it contained, the Jewish problem in Galicia—as in all the areas of what had once been Poland—was exceedingly grave and inevitably demanded a solution. That vast numbers of Jews depended for their livelihood on the manufacture and sale of spirits was only one of the more obvious symptoms of the feudal decay which was consuming the population as a whole and debilitating the increasingly impoverished Jewish community. "Brokerage," was a further evil prevalent amongst the Jewish masses; most of those engaged in it came from a *Lumpenproletariat* unequalled in extent amongst other peoples.

When Austria annexed Galicia from Poland, it also inherited the acute problem of its Jewish inhabitants. The first attempts that Austrian absolutism made to solve this problem took the form of a series of harsh decrees directed against Galician Jewry.

Beginning of the Absolutist Régime: Maria Theresa's Reign and the early Government of Joseph II

During Maria Theresa's rule over Galicia (1772-80), her son and the heir to her throne, Joseph, participated officially and actively in the government as "Emperor Co-Regent." As a result, basic Austrian policy did not change with the death of the Empress but continued for some years to come. During this period, Joseph's centralization of the country's administration had not yet been fully completed and the implementation of the peasant reform programme was still in its initial stages. On the other hand, the full force of the police system of the absolutist state and its exorbitant fiscal policies were brought to bear on the Jews of Galicia immediately after the establishment of the new régime.

The new German administrative machinery of Galicia, from the governors and the *Gubernium* advisers at Lwow (Lemberg) down to the district administrators and lowest clerks, was permeated with hatred of the Jews. Reports by some of them acknowledged the tremendous task that the Jews discharged in the country's economy and described them as a vitalizing factor in all branches of economic endeavour. But, in the words of the Talmud, they "began with a pitcher and finished with a barrel;" they concluded by depicting the Jews as a "necessary evil," "the destroyers and despoilers of the land" and "leeches sucking the blood of the country's inhabitants." For the most part, these denigrations were intended to vindicate the nobility, exonerating it from all guilt for the pitiable condition of the peasants. This hatred of the Jews by the Austro-German officials was sometimes coupled with a contempt for the defeated nation generally, which embraced all classes of Poles—nobles, burghers and peasants alike. These "exponents of German culture" were recruited, especially during the first decade, from the lowest grades of imperial bureaucracy, and the coarseness of their methods was exceeded only by their moral corruption. This situation remained unchanged as far as lower-ranking officials were concerned for many years to come. Bureaucrats of this type were entrusted with the implementation of the new anti-Jewish decrees that the Austrian police state issued at frequent intervals. The only advantage for the well-to-do was that these representatives of the monarchy were not usually averse to accepting bribes.

The first ordinances relating to the Jews of Galicia demonstrated that the government had decided to impose on the Jews of this province the same severe restrictions that had been long since imposed upon the Jews of Bohemia and Moravia. It even augmented them with decrees modelled on Frederick II's policy towards the Jews of the area of Poland he had acquired. Barriers were erected against their natural increase, deportation of all "non-useful" indigents was instituted, and the tolerated Jews were exploited to provide a special source of revenue for the exchequer. The Austrian government was quite unimpressed by the fact that the Jews of

Galicia—like those in the Polish regions conquered by Prussia and Russia—had joyfully welcomed "the new kingdom." Kehillah representatives, together with the other inhabitants, had publicly taken an oath of allegiance and a popular celebration had been held at the Brody synagogue with all pomp and dignity. Disappointment quickly followed. In March 1773, a royal warrant was issued embodying two decrees: one relating to marriages, the other ordering the deportation of "beggars."

The law of 1773 forbade Jews, "on pain of confiscation of all their property and of physical punishment, according to their capacity," to marry without the special permission of the *Gubernium* (the Galician Provincial Administration) at Lwow. Such permission was to be issued on payment of a marriage tax. This measure remained in effect until 1789 but the severity with which it was enforced varied. During the first years, many cases of informing occurred and the property of the parents of the transgressors was often confiscated and part of it passed on to the informers as recompense. However, the law was evaded in most cases by the performance of clandestine ceremonies—even though the government threatened rabbis who sanctified marriages without permission with grave penalties. In any event, the law kept the Jewish population of Galicia in a state of depression and constant fear for many years.

The second law, which decreed the expulsion of all *Betteljuden* was a further trial for the Jewish poor of Galicia. As well as actual vagrants, it also affected all Jewish inhabitants of Galicia who had failed to pay on time the Jewish poll tax for themselves and their families for three consecutive years, and all Jews who had entered Galicia at the Polish frontier. An exception was made in the case of owners of property valued at 5,000 gulden who had paid the naturalization tax of 10 per cent on the assessed value of their property. The Kehillot, ordered to prepare lists of deportable mendicants for the government, defended the victims to the best of their ability with every kind of stratagem. They entered fictitious names or the names of individuals who had died or already left the country. However, despite the solidarity that the Jewish population maintained, expulsions repeatedly took place under Maria Theresa and became even more frequent during Joseph's rule. The visiting German author, Kratter, describes incidents when entire families of the poor were driven out of Lwow in the winter and deposited on the Polish frontier. The Polish authorities finally posted guards along the Galician border with orders to fire at these unwanted guests. The deportees were simply shunted back and forth across the line. According to official reports, dispatched to the Emperor, 1,192 "beggar-Jews" were deported between September, 1781 and the end of 1782. A further 659 deportations took place in 1784.

Following the marriage tax decree, the Jewish poll tax was doubled in 1774 from two Polish zloty to one gulden per person.* In 1776, this tax

* One Austrian gulden was equivalent to four Polish zloty.

was characteristically renamed the *Toleranzsteuer* (Toleration Levy) or *Schutzsteuer* (Protection Levy), and the collection rate was altered to four gulden per family. In addition, a business and property tax was imposed on all Jews, with an average total assessment of four gulden per family. In practice, each family's payment was apportioned in accordance with its financial position. The indirect Kehillah taxes, the excise on meat and other foods, long known as the *krupka* (in Russian, korobka; cf. Chapter IX), were left in Kehillah hands as previously, except that they were now earmarked in the main for paying off Kehillah debts but partly for the government Exchequer. A special fee had to be paid to the Exchequer when the title of *Haver* or *Morenu* was conferred and when new burial grounds were consecrated or old ones expanded. Apart from all this, the Galician Jews were not exempt from payment of the village properties tax (the rustic tax) and the military personnel billetting tax, and no reductions were made in their taxes to estate owners and city proprietors.

To ensure efficient tax collections, the government did not interfere with Kehillah autonomy throughout this period—and this autonomy was also maintained in the other Austrian dominions. Furthermore, and again to guarantee the Exchequer's revenues, Maria Theresa established a new agency for the central autonomy of the Galician Jews. By the Jews' Law of 1776, the Kehillot elected a district elder from each of the six districts of the province. These six district elders, together with six provincial elders met under the chairmanship of the provincial Chief Rabbi, and constituted the *General-Direktion der Judenschaft* (General Directory of the Jews) with headquarters at Lwow. The chief function of the General Directory was to apportion the total income and property tax amongst the Kehillot. The Kehillot in turn divided the sums apportioned to them amongst the families within the individual Kehillah. The provincial Chief Rabbi was empowered to supervise all religious and educational matters within the Kehillot, to confirm the appointment of rabbis, cantors and ritual slaughterers (for a fee), to confer the titles of *Haver* and *Morenu* (similarly, for a fee), to hear appeals against rabbinical verdicts, and to judge litigation between individuals and Kehillot or between one Kehillah and another. Although any rabbi could effect "minor excommunications" or ostracisms with the agreement of the Kehillah leaders, the major excommunications required the permission of the General Directory and the *Gubernium*.

Contrary to appearances, the new Kehillah organization lacked the autonomy that Kehillot and Councils enjoyed under the Polish régime. For all practical purposes, the Kehillah leaders, district and provincial elders, and even the provincial Chief Rabbi were merely officials appointed by the authorities. Furthermore, the domination of the wealthy class over the Kehillot was secured by the ruling that only the highest taxpayers, paying a minimum of 80 guldens annually in the towns, and 200 guldens in the large cities, might be elected to the office of *Parnass*.

The poverty of the Jewish population prevented the government from accomplishing a great deal even with the establishment of this tax collection machinery. The calculations by the authorities showed that the General Directory was responsible for an annual tax remission ten times higher than the total poll tax for which the Galician Jews had been liable under the Polish régime (300,000 compared with 28,824 gulden). But Kehillah indebtedness for unpaid taxes grew yearly. By 1781 it amounted to 363,372 gulden, or more than the total annual obligation. The General Directory added to the tax burden of the Kehillah population by its inequitable system of apportionment. In this respect, it repeated the abuses condoned by the central Jewish autonomy in Poland during its declining years. The large Kehillot, and especially the Kehillah of Lwow, whose representatives had a decisive voice in the General Directory, shifted the tax burden on to the small and impoverished Kehillot so far as they were able. The number of complaints against the General Directory that the victimized Kehillot made to the *Gubernium* and also to the government at Vienna steadily increased. They were particularly bitter towards the provincial Chief Rabbi, Aryeh Leib Bernstein, and he was the target of organized opposition in his native city of Brody, as well as at Lwow. The Jewish "autonomy" which the Austrian régime had instituted for its own benefit—much like the "autonomy" re-introduced several decades later in the Grand Duchy of Warsaw—was a strange marriage of convenience between an absolutist fiscal system and a decadent feudal institution.

The inefficacy of the General-Directory and the resulting Kehillah resentment accelerated the Emperor's decision to abolish this autonomous representation. In any event, it conflicted with the system of centralized administration that his government was perfecting in Galicia. Tax apportionment by a central body of Kehillah representatives had already in fact been made redundant by 1784, as a result of a basic change in the tax system: the *Toleranzsteuer* was retained at a higher rate of five gulden per family, but the business and property tax was replaced by a kosher meat tax. Beef was now taxed at 1.75 kreutzers per pound, and poultry at an even higher rate. Collection of the tax was farmed out to Jews and non-Jews alike. This measure was symbolic of absolutist justice. The direct tax on property and income was replaced by an indirect tax on consumption which affected the masses, most of whom already lived in dire poverty. Joseph II had introduced a similar system in the form of a grocery tax for the Jews of Bohemia and Moravia.

An imperial edict liquidated the General Directory of Galician Jewry and with it the office of provincial Chief Rabbi, officially in 1785, but actually towards the end of 1786. Simultaneously, the Emperor abolished the autonomy of the individual Kehillot with the goal of centralization in mind, made possible by the new tax system. The law now restricted their activites exclusively to religious and charitable affairs. The details of the new Kehillah régime were established in their final form in the Imperial *Letters Patent* of 1789 for the Jews of Galicia.

The abolition of Jewish autonomy was only one of the reforms that the Emperor instituted during that period in order to reorganize Jewish affairs to accord with his general programme for the rehabilitation of Galicia. In the implementation of this programme two issues directly affected his policy towards the Jews: the settlement of Germans in this province, and the improvement of the conditions of the peasants.

The results of Joseph II's peasant reforms rocked the foundations of Galician Jewry's economic existence during this period. The legislative policy that linked the question of Jewish lessees and liquor purveyors to enactments on behalf of the peasantry had already been adopted during the reign of Maria Theresa. However, the proposal to forbid Jews to engage in all types of leaseholding or liquor sales actually originated from amongst representatives of the nobility.

The movement to evict the Jews from their leaseholds facilitated the tactical exploitation by representatives of the nobility of the comprehensive proposal for legislation against the Jewish lessees during the discussions on peasant reforms. Absolutist Austria had made no changes in the special privileges of the aristocracy, which included its exclusive right to political representation. The Galician *Sejm* was only composed of deputies from two estates: the magnates and the knights, with an additional two deputies from the city of Lwow. This *Sejm* was now faced with the news that the government, not content with the law of 1781 restricting the labour obligations of the peasants, was in process of preparing new legislation circumscribing all the obligations that the serfs owed to their masters. The *Collegium* of the Galician *Sejm* considered this an opportune moment to submit to the government a legislative proposal prohibiting the Jews from engaging in the liquor business and in lesseeship. The proposal served a dual purpose as far as the representatives of the nobility were concerned: it demonstrated their "concern" for the peasants and it was an attempt to forestall the extension of reforms which threatened to curb their exploitation of the serfs.

The government considered the *Sejm Collegium*'s proposal in 1783 in conjunction with the general legislative programme for the regulation of Galician affairs. In the same year, the Lord Privy Councillor and High Commissioner for Galician Affairs, Johann Margelik, was sent to the province. The High Commissioner consulted the district administrators on various matters, including the *Sejm Collegium*'s proposal. Only eight of the eighteen district administrators supported the proposed decree against the Jewish lessees without reservations. Five were opposed to the decree, mainly because they feared it might be harmful to the Imperial Exchequer. The remaining five requested that it be deferred or else implemented by stages, in order to avert the complete ruination of its Jewish victims. All the district administrators expressed anxiety about the adverse effects of the scheme on the revenue of the estate owners, as the existing social and political system was based on the domination of the aristocracy. Nevertheless, in some instances, their differences of opinion on the anti-Jewish decree depended on their views regarding the extent to which reform of peasant conditions was necessary. Four of the five who opposed the decree unequivocally advocated the economic development of the province. They were the most enlightened district administrators in all Galicia. The most outstanding personality amongst them, Josef von Baum, administrator of the district of Bochnia, was considered a typical left-wing Galician official. Baum's extremist programme for the germanization of Galicia was coupled with a sharply critical attitude towards the despotism that the nobles exercised over the peasants. The opinion he submitted to the government emissary denounced the nobles not only for fraudulent practice in the payment of government taxes and their evasion of the laws of the state, but it also exposed their irresponsibility and profligacy in the management of their estates. Some of them spiced their liquor with herbs so that the peasants were more easily intoxicated and more easily cheated by the lessees. They deliberately brewed low quality beer to prevent the peasants overcoming the liquor habit. Their servants were whipped and always hungry. The wives and daughters of the peasants were completely at the mercy of the estate officials. The village priests were ignorant men who exploited the peasants and their morals were no better than those of the stewards of the nobility. It is not surprising therefore, that Baum would not consent to sacrifice the Jews as scapegoats for the exploitation of the peasants by their masters, nor that he suggested that the government abolish the deportation decree against the Jewish "mendicants."

The government emissary, Margelik, although he himself was antagonistic to the Jews, informed Vienna of the results of his inquiry amongst the district administrators. Nevertheless, the government did not act in accordance with the opinions of Baum and his supporters. It did not even relent so far as to postpone the date when the decree became effective. In 1784, a *Gubernium* order was issued forbidding Jews in cities and towns to lease public houses, inns, distilleries, breweries or wineries from landed proprietors. Jews in the small towns were only allowed to sell liquor in their own homes, at their own expense, and not as lessees—and then only if they were already so engaged. Barely two months later, at the beginning of 1785, an Imperial *Letters Patent* for the Jews of Galicia prohibited Jews from holding any lesseeships, including the leasing of estates, operating mills and collecting tolls and similar revenues. It would appear that the Emperor did not intend this decree to arrest the spread of drunkenness, as the estate owners' rights of *propination* (the sale of alcoholic beverages) was not in any way affected. In fact, the government was so anxious to maintain the nobility's revenue from this source, that it published an additional order in 1786 requiring the Jews in the towns who were still allowed to sell spirits to purchase their stock from the manorial lords and not from Jewish distilleries. The government profited from the peasants' drunkenness no less than the nobility. It increased the excise on alcoholic beverages at three yearly intervals so that government revenue from this tax in Galicia accounted for 330,000 gulden in the 1785 budget, or over half the principal *Dominikal-Steuer* (Manorial Tax) collected from the estate owners according to data for 1792. In the following years, the excise on liquors actually exceeded the whole *Dominikal-Steuer*. It can only be surmised that the government was trying to gain the sympathy of the peasants at the expense of the weaker, more oppressed people, the Jews. It also hoped to obtain some immediate advantages for its German peasant and artisan settlement programme by the expulsion of the Jews from the villages. Jews were expressly forbidden to rent dwellings in the villages intended for the settlement of German immigrants.

If every detail of this decree had been implemented, some 100,000 people, about half the Jewish population of Galicia, would have been rendered unemployed and also homeless, as the Jewish lessees and liquor purveyors lived at their inns and taverns in the towns and villages. Fortunately, the authorities did not hurry scrupulously to implement the decree. The Austrian government bureaucracy in Galicia was not only amenable to bribes, but was also not noted for its alacrity. Furthermore, it lacked the courage to enforce the law in full against the ruling class of the nobility. Most important, administration in the villages and manorial towns was actually in the hands of the landowners who were unable to do without the services of the Jews and generally found ways to evade the law and the financial consequences with which it threatened them. Their actions passed uncensured by the inspection authorities. These authorities were only compelled to enforce the law during the short reign of Joseph II in a number of instances when violation was too obvious. In these cases, several estate owners, including Count Potocki, caught in the act of granting lesseeships to Jews, were heavily fined and their punishment publicized "so that all might hear and behold." However, many landlords also took advantage of the government decrees to evict their Jewish lessees and publicans or arbitrarily to raise rentals under the threat of enforcing the law.

The consequences of the liquor decree promulgated under Joseph II—however transient—were sufficient to aggravate the impoverishment of the Jewish population, which had, in any event, become increasingly severe during the first twenty years of Austrian rule. Thousands of Jews had been forced to leave the villages they lived in and migrate to the cities. They were joined by Jews from the small towns who had been deprived of their source of income. It took many years for the people thus expelled from the rural areas to become adapted to the new urban conditions and to reinforce the Jewish merchant and artisan classes. In the interim, their poverty reached proportions which at times led to acts of desperation.

The urgent need to compensate the thousands of Jews who had lost their means of support as a result of the liquor decree, moved the Emperor to accelerate the Jewish agricultural settlement programme. He had already announced this in the Galician *Gubernium* in 1781. In July, 1785, he issued an order to proceed immediately with the establishment of a Jewish farm colony. Less than a year later, in the spring of 1786, the first Jewish farming settlement in Galicia—indeed, in all Europe—was founded in the village of Dabrowka, near the city of Nowy Sacz. It was called New Jerusalem and comprised twenty families. In the following three years, up to 1789, a few more colonies were established on the same pattern, including New Babylon, near the city of Bolechov, with twelve families.

The Jews of Galicia were familiar with agricultural matters and were also anxious for agrarian settlement. This was, therefore, a unique opportunity in the history of Galician Jewry to execute a programme which could completely alter the economic basis of thousands and possibly tens of thousands of families. In the course of their lesseeships and liquor dealings, the village and also some of the urban Jews of Galicia had been engaged in truck farming and pasturage and some had also kept bees. They were thus in a position to adopt farming as their chief occupation. News of the government's farm settlement project for the Jews aroused great interest in Kehillot throughout all Galicia.

Nonetheless, colonization was a failure because of government dilatoriness and lack of enthusiasm. Most of the settlers waited a year or more for their land allotments, and, when they had exhausted their savings, eventually received low-grade land which could be used as arable only with the greatest difficulty. For example, the settlers from Zaleszczyki were granted a plot of land in Bukovina, which had already been deserted by its previous Transylvanian German settlers, because of the poor quality of the soil. The settlers of New Babylon were deliberately allotted land which the Galician *Gubernium* admitted "had been unsuitable for colonization by the Germans precisely because of its extremely poor quality." The people from Lezajsk were given rocky land in a remote hill area which was of no use for grain crops; the settlers had to buy the cereals they needed for their own consumption. The areas assigned and the size of the subsidy given to each family showed great discrimination between the German and Jewish settlers. Land awarded to each family of Jewish settlers was two-thirds the size of that received by a German family. One Jewish family cost the government 100 gulden in the form of a four-year loan; the government spent 556 gulden on settling a German family, without stipulating repayment. Finally, implementation of the settlement law was entrusted to the Galician *Gubernium*, which was hostile to the Jews. It evaded all action for settling them, on the excuse that, first, it was preoccupied with the current German colonization programme and, second, that the Jewish candidates for colonization were only interested from the point of view of speculation in liquor selling under cover of farming.

Not surprisingly, in view of the attitude of the government, and especially of the Galician authorities, the whole Jewish colonization experiment was a failure. Jewish colonization activities were suspended on the intercession of anti-Jewish officials during the last year of Joseph II's reign. Within a year, the settlements founded on government land were either deserted or resettled by Germans. In 1800, Rohrer recorded that there were only a few score agricultural Jewish families in all Galicia. Inevitably, the few settlements of Jewish cultivators that some noblemen had established on their estates did not last long either. They were not settled on more favourable terms than the peasants who paid a tax in lieu of serf labour. In 1789, a *Letters Patent* by Joseph placed the responsibility for colonization activities on the Kehillot, at their own expense, and fixed a compulsory quota of 1,410 families. The Kehillot, however, were reluctant to undertake such a large expenditure and in most cases only apparently carried out the registration of settlers. Meanwhile, a large number of the potential settlers took advantage of the opportunity offered by the fact that they were rural inhabitants to engage in liquor sales. The plan prepared by the enlightened despotic régime for transferring Jews to agriculture came to nothing, in the same way as all its other programmes for improving conditions in Galicia lapsed when reaction set in throughout the Austrian Empire.

The 1789 Toleranzpatent for the Galician Jews

The results of the scheme to settle Germans in the cities to promote commercial and industrial prosperity in Galicia and to germanize the population as a whole were disappointing. Lacking an alternative, Joseph II turned to the Jews to replace the settlers in these capacities. The Imperial *Letters Patent* for the Jews of Galicia which appeared in 1789 was the most liberal of the Emperor's Decrees of Toleration for the Jews in any country of his empire.

This *Toleranzpatent* had been preceded by a number of laws attempting to germanize the Galician Jews and to make them subject to the same legal code as all other citizens. In 1786, the Jews of Galicia were placed under the general law governing marriages. In 1787, they were ordered to select surnames by the end of the year; in practice, state officials assigned the names and practically all of them were German. In the same year, an ordinance was promulgated on founding German schools for Jewish youth. In 1788, all distinctive Jewish clothing was banned as from 1791. In 1788 too, the Jews of Galicia and all other countries of the Empire became liable for military service. These laws, together with the previous prohibitions on lesseeship and liquor sales and the abolition of Kehillah autonomy were included in the sixty-four paragraphs of the *Patent* of May 7, 1789, outlining in detail the rights and duties of the Jews of Galicia.

In accordance with the principle of "equality," all limitations on the growth or number of the Jewish population were abolished. The expulsion decree against the *Betteljuden*, and the marriage quota decree, including the special marriage licence fee, therefore lapsed. Furthermore, the principle was established that "all vocations and all branches of livelihood are open to them as to all other inhabitants of the province, and all restrictions hitherto in effect and applicable to Jews only are hereby revoked." A special paragraph allowed peddling, which had been proscribed for some years past. Trade was permitted in all commodities and all industries (Jews engaged in industry were exempt from paying the Toleration Tax) and handicrafts were now legally opened to Jews, even for trade with Christian customers. Jewish artisans were allowed to belong to the craft guilds and paid the same dues to these associations as other artisans. In 1784, all restrictions on Jewish physicians and medical attendants were removed. Jews were also permitted to engage in farming in the rural areas and to lease or purchase whole estates from their owners; they were, however, forbidden to lease the peasant's plots. The ban on Jewish purchase of houses in the cities from Christian owners was rescinded. Jewish civil rights were specifically acknowledged in respect of the municipalities. Following the abolition of the Kehillot as autonomous communities, the Jews were declared members of the communities in which they lived (cities, towns) with the right to vote and to be elected to municipal councils.

In return for these rights, the Jews now had to assume the same obligations as all other citizens, from which they were previously exempt, such as compulsory labour at public works, road repairs, and—above all—military service. At first they were only conscripted as carters, but from 1789 were given the choice of "serving under arms."

The Jews may have obtained equality as far as obligations were concerned, but the *Patent*, despite its grandiloquent preamble, left most of the discriminations and decrees specifically applicable to them, in force. It was no coincidence that the *Patent* omitted all mention of the civil right to hold government office. The Emperor's proposal on this score had encountered lively opposition from the Imperial Council. As a result, the only appointments open to Jews were as district medical officers, and these had already been opened to them by the Ordinance of 1784 because of the shortage of physicians in Galicia. The *Patent* specifically confirmed the severest discrimination, the decree forbidding Jews to hold leases or sell liquors, and even expanded it to bar Jews from residence in rural areas except to work on the land or as artisans. The hypocrisy of the *Patent*, which concealed discrimination behind lofty professions of equality, was particularly apparent in the fifteen paragraphs dealing with special Jewish taxes. The toleration tax and the kosher meat tax were retained, without modification—in fact, the publication of the *Patent* was the occasion for a 50 per cent rise in the poultry tax. Apart from the concessions granted to men of property, such as permission to buy houses in the cities as well as entire estates, the principal innovation that the *Patent* contained lay in the provisions subjecting the Jews to the absolutist centralized régime and those aiming at their germanization.

The Kehillot were deprived of all their authority as autonomous institutions and confined to their functions as religious communities and to their charitable activities. As Jews had become subject to the government law courts, all the special Jewish Kehillah courts were abolished. The number of Kehillot was fixed at 143, including two in Bukovina, which was then only one of the nineteen districts in Galicia. Three Kehillah leaders were placed over each Kehillah, with the exception of Lwow and Brody, each of which had seven leaders. Only district centres were permitted to engage rabbis; the remaining Kehillot had to be content with religious advisers (*Religionsweiser*) or cantors (*Schulsinger*). Kehillah leaders and rabbis were elected for three year terms, and only Kehillah members who owned their own homes were allowed to vote. Rabbis were elected by all the Jews of the district. After a six year transition period, only people with a command of the German language would be eligible for election as Kehillah leaders. In addition to their religious duties, the rabbis, like Christian clergymen, were obliged to keep birth, marriage, and death registers—in German. All Kehillah members had to share its expenses and were divided into three categories of wealth for that purpose. Kehillah leaders were permitted to draw a salary for their services.

The Emperor still regarded the Kehillot as instruments of government policy, even though they were limited to matters of religion and charity. The number of candidates for election to the offices of Kehillah leaders and rabbis was double the number of posts vacant; from amongst them, the district authorities appointed those they judged desirable. The Kehillot also continued to function as an auxiliary apparatus for the collection of taxes. In 1785, in contradiction to the principle abolishing the administrative functions of the Kehillot, the Emperor decreed that they were still responsible for collecting government taxes from the Jews. The *Toleranzpatent* of 1789 neither mentioned nor rescinded this order.

In the main Joseph II delegated the task of germanization to the German schools for Jewish youth. The Emperor did not offer the Jews of Galicia the alternative, available in Bohemia and Moravia, of sending their children to Christian schools—even though Jewish children had been allowed to attend such schools in the last year of Maria Theresa's reign. Instead, each Kehillah was required to found a German school of its own.

The law for compulsory school attendance was reinforced by a provision forbidding parents and religious teachers, on pain of imprisonment, to give instruction in the Talmud to anybody who had not completed the course of studies at the school. Similarly, the issue of a marriage licence required a certificate of school attendance. The Kehillah had to meet the cost of school buildings and their maintenance as well as teachers' rents, but their salaries were paid out of a fifth of the Jewish toleration tax (the fifth florin out of the five paid by each family). The annual payment of fifty gulden for each *"minyan* with a Torah Scroll" was also set aside for school expenditure, particularly for the clothing of poor pupils. By 1788, forty-eight schools had been founded, two in the city of Lwow. By 1792, Galicia boasted of a hundred German Jewish schools.

Joseph II died barely a year after the *Patent* for the Jews of Galicia had been issued. His death marked the end of enlightened absolutism in Austria. The political reaction which replaced it reduced the few advantages that Galician Jewry had acquired through the *Toleranzpatent*.

Under the Rod of Austrian Officialdom and Jewish Tax Farmers; Beginning of Reaction, 1790–1815

The abolition of the Galician Peasant Reform Act by Leopold II was an indication of the reaction that set in after the death of his predecessor. Still, no new decrees affected the Jews of Galicia during the two years of Leopold's rule. In fact, Leopold, in his role as patron of religion, acceded to several requests made by a delegation from Galician Jewry.* By the concessions granted to the Jewish religion throughout the Empire, the Jews of Galicia were allowed to have marriages performed between relatives (involving kinships forbidden to Roman Catholics) and they were promised that observation of the dietary laws, the Sabbath, and the Holy Days would be facilitated for Jewish prisoners. In 1790, compulsory military service for Galician Jews was replaced by exemption through purchase—though this was withheld from the Jews of Bohemia for a further two years. In the same year, the paragraph in Joseph II's *Patent* prohibiting the traditional Jewish apparel was also abolished, though the motives behind this move were economic: thousands of silk weavers and velvet makers in Bohemia and Vienna supported the Jewish request in a memorandum to the Emperor in which they pointed out that the law decreeing a change of dress might deprive them of their living. The petition by Galician Jewry, particularly by the Brody Kehillah, to restore the authority of the rabbinical courts, was rejected, but the Jews were granted permission to maintain courts of arbitration under conditions specified by law.

The reign of Francis II was a period of increasingly harsh repression

* *cf. supra*, Chapter Eight, p. 259.

333

for the Jews of Galicia, as for the Jews of the whole Empire. Hardly one of the concessions that Joseph II had made to the Jews remained untouched—except for the right to engage in commerce and handicraft—either by restriction or by complete abolition. Even the legal status which the Jews of Austria had possessed since the times of Maria Theresa was progressively impaired.

From 1792, Joseph II's enactment whereby Jews could be elected to the municipalities was interpreted to require the Emperor's special permission on every occasion that it was evoked. In 1806, the government ruled by order of the imperial court that "the Jews are not citizens of the municipalities but only tolerated inhabitants." Two years later, the Jews were deprived of all rights to acquire a lease on the liquor monopoly in the cities. In 1813, they were forbidden to lease any municipal source of revenue whatsoever, including municipally owned lands. In 1791, Emperor Leopold had confirmed the right of Jews to buy houses in the cities from Christian owners. In 1805, they were not only forbidden to buy Christian-owned buildings but even former Jewish buildings, once they had been sold to Christians. Cities where Jewish residence had been prohibited under the Polish régime retained this privilege, and in 1798 Jews were banned from the mining towns even when fairs were being held. In some cities, similar decrees, dating from Polish times, which confined Jews to a special quarter, street or suburb, were never abolished. Government enforcement of these decrees was particularly assiduous in the Galician metropolis of Lwow. By special orders, repeated periodically between 1793 and 1811, Jewish residence in the city was prohibited outside the two suburbs and the streets they had occupied under Polish rule, and a few adjoining streets. Exceptions were made to this rule in the case of Jewish merchant magnates with capital valued at a minimum of 30,000 gulden—if their assets fell below that level they were to be expelled to the Jewish area. In 1804, to curb the increase in the number of Jews in Lwow, Jews from elsewhere were forbidden to settle there. Jews at Krakow were forbidden to renew residence, even in the suburb of Kazimierz. In 1799, an imperial order required Jews who owned stores or warehouses in the city of Krakow proper (ninety-two tradesmen and artisans) or even in Kazimierz (outside the Jewish quarter) to quit their premises within six months.

The right of Jews to lease or purchase estates was rescinded in 1793 to eliminate the possibility that they might percolate into the class of landed proprietors, and in 1794 their employment in any clerical capacity by estate owners was declared illegal. In 1805, Jews were forbidden to lease special farming enterprises and they were not even allowed to lease plots of land unless they cultivated them themselves. The old Polish ban on the employment of Jewish apprentices or journeymen by Christian craftsmen was revived to reduce competition between Jews and Christian artisans. Fear of Jewish religious influence on the Christians with whom they came in contact led to the reinstatement of the former prohibition on the employment by Jews of Christian male and female servants, including wet nurses. A medieval decree restored with the deliberate intention of humiliating the Jews, was the strict injunction against appearing on the street or even peering through a window with covered head "to the dismay of Christians" during a holy procession or when a priest was passing with the Host or Extreme Unction for the dying. Offenders were punished with the lash. Antagonism towards the Jews and desire for revenue caused this régime to resurrect the Jewish *Leibzoll* which had almost been forgotten throughout nearly all of Europe. Any Polish Jew crossing the Galician frontier on business (except for transit trade) had to pay a five gulden escort duty (*Geleitzoll*) in addition to a reduced fee for his wife and children. Jewish vagrants, or *Betteljuden*, arriving from beyond the frontier were summarily deported.

The reactionary régime did not even show to the Jews that small measure of political justice with which the absolutist régime of the eighteenth century had treated them. They had then been regarded as tolerated non-citizens and the obligations exacted from other subjects had not been imposed on them. This was not the case with the newer version of Austrian reaction. In 1804, Jews were required to fulfil their military service obligations in person and they forfeited the right, open to all other sections of the population, to send proxies. Even earlier, in 1803, an estimated 15,000 Jews had been in the Austrian army. Taking into account the proportion of Galician to the total number of Jews in the Empire, about half of these were Galician Jews. Jews were thus forced to shed blood on all the battle-fields of Europe on behalf of the monarchy that led every anti-Napoleonic coalition.

The special tax burden weighed more heavily than all the discriminations and restrictions on the Jewish masses of Galicia. It became even harder to endure as reactions grew stronger. Not content with one indirect tax on kosher meat (in place of the business and property tax), the government in 1795 also substituted an indirect tax on ritual candles for the Jewish toleration tax (the protection tax). This duty, like the kosher meat tax, was easier for the state to collect than a direct tax, and it also represented a tremendous increase in total revenue from Jewish taxes. Every Jewish family head, including young couples and widows dependent on parents or children, was obliged to pay the minimum sum for two Sabbath and holiday candles at the rate of two kreutzers a candle. A higher duty was levied on *Jahrzeit* (death anniversary) candles and *Hannukah* candles were taxed at half a kreutzer a candle. Candles for the Day of Atonement, whether lit at home or in the synagogue, required the payment of ten kreutzers a candle, and wedding candles one gulden each. Lighting a ritual candle without first paying the tax was punishable by an extortionate fine—one gulden for each Sabbath candle. Anyone unable to pay the fine was sentenced to forced labour and later also to imprisonment.

This tax, together with the kosher meat tax, more than doubled within a decade. To compensate the Imperial Exchequer for annual budgetary deficits in total revenue from these two indirect taxes, the Kehillot were required to pay a "supplementary tax." Nonetheless, the Jews were still required to pay the government war tax, charged at a uniform rate for all Jewish families ($7\frac{1}{2}$ gulden in 1806) rather than on the property assessment applied to the rest of the population. They were also not exempt from the income tax collected, as from 1813, by a fresh increase in the candle tax. The average annual taxes paid by one Jewish family rose from eight gulden in 1784 to thirty-eight gulden by 1810.

The system of taxation employed placed the burden most heavily on the impoverished masses. The kosher meat tax had raised the price of kosher meat to double that of unkosher meat and the poor were forced to abstain from such "luxuries" even on the Sabbath. The very poorest had to pay the candle tax, even if it meant leaving their home on the Sabbath eve to beg for alms to meet this expense. People who could not afford to buy meat could certainly not pay the candle tax, as the five kreutzer tax on a single candle (it had risen to seven kreutzers a few years later) was equal to the cost of one pound of meat (without the tax on *Kashrut*).

This systematic exploitation of the Jewish population through indirect taxation provoked an unprecedented degree of lawlessness and corruption in Galician Kehillah affairs, unequalled even during the period of feudal decadence. Both kosher meat tax and candle tax collection were farmed out to Jewish contractors who occasionally accepted Christian partners into the business. The candle tax had even originated at the initiative of a Jew, Solomon Kofler, a liquor tax farmer in Stanislawow. He, together with partners, was rewarded with the lease for the collection of this tax throughout all Galicia. The government had approved his proposal after consulting Hertz Homberg, then serving as government superintendent of the German Jewish schools that he had organized in Galicia. Homberg, the servile assimilationist, expressed the opinion that the candle tax did not constitute an offence against the Jewish religion. Court proceedings subsequently proved that he had been promised two per cent of the leasehold profits by Kofler in return for this statement. Kofler was the prototype of the usurers, embezzlers of public funds, informers and thieves from those ranks the candle tax and most of the kosher meat tax farmers, as well as their sub-lessees, agents and collectors were recruited. They exploited the Galician Jews to the maximum and beyond for their personal financial benefit and also in order to provide funds for the Imperial Treasury. The *Lichtpächter* (candle tax farmers) did not stop short of taking in pawn the shirts the poor were wearing in payment of tax or even extinguishing unpaid Sabbath candles. These collectors were so greatly hated by the people that in 1808 at Lwow they requested permission to live in the centre of the city as their lives were in danger in the Jewish quarter.

The lessees, especially those collecting the candle tax, acquired control of the Galician Kehillot through their function as tax farmers. The government established their authority in its ordinances regulating the Kehillah régime. Voting rights were only granted to those paying tax for three Sabbath candles in the small Kehillot, eight in the medium, and ten in the large. As a result, Kehillah offices were restricted to money lords alone, and even then, those chosen were the ones who were on friendly terms with the tax farmers. Thus, only a limited few were entitled to participate in the elections—in a Kehillah as large as Krakow, there were only twenty-eight electors—and legal supervision of the elections was entrusted to the candle tax farmers. In several Kehillot, especially large ones such as Lwow and Krakow, the tax lessors themselves held the offices of Kehillah leaders. At Krakow, a candle tax farmer, Berl Luxemburg (who also held a lease on liquor tax collections and was the leader of the city's Hasidim), was approved by the authorities as leader of the Kehillah whenever he submitted his own candidacy, even though he was elected by only one voter. All the grievances that Kehillah members lodged with the authorities against the election abuses of the tax farmers and their corrupt administration of Kehillah affairs were of no avail.

The law authorized the lessees to dominate the Jewish population even if they did not themselves participate in Kehillah management. As from 1800, a certificate from the candle tax farmer became one of the prerequisites for obtaining a marriage licence. The *Letters Patent* of 1810 stated that no Jew might transfer his abode within Galicia without permission from the district administrator's office. This could only be procured with the consent of the candle tax farmer, accompanied by a statement of tax remissions "so that the leaseholder in the district to which the family was moving would know the date from which he was to begin collecting the tax." The government restored to the Kehillot the right of excommunication, abolished under Joseph II, as a means of avoiding a deficit in tax revenues. District Chief Rabbis were required to announce the excommunication in the synagogue of men who had defaulted on their payments of the kosher meat tax (four times a year), and the candle tax (twice a year), in the presence of representatives of the authorities. Under the Holy Alliance, political offenders and supporters of the revolutionary *Carbonari* were also excommunicated. The text of these excommunications had to remain posted on the "Black Notice Board" throughout the year, by government order.

Although Joseph II's *Letters Patent* theoretically remained in force, Kehillah authority was extended to encompass both administration and tax collection. Until 1806, the Kehillah executive was responsible for the delivery of Jewish conscripts to the army; in 1806 this function was transferred to the local authorities, but the Kehillah leaders continued to play a part in it. Merchants with official trading rights, master craftsmen and tax farmers and their collectors were legally exempt from military service. This arrangement automatically made it easier for the Kehillah leaders to conscript the sons of poor families only. All direct government taxes, such as the supplementary tax and the war tax, were apportioned by the Kehillah executive. In some communities, Kehillah taxes were collected indirectly, through excises, on milk, butter, honey and other food-stuffs for example, and usually by the tax farmers. In Krakow, direct tax payments between 1801 and 1805 never accounted for more than a sixth or a fifth of the Kehillah's budgetary income; the remainder was derived from excise on a number of food-stuffs. The house owners in the "Jewish city" of Kazimierz, a suburb of Krakow, provided another example of selfish concern for their own class interests to the detriment of the general welfare. In 1806, the district administration granted Jewish merchants permission to lease stores in the adjoining Christian streets and also to erect buildings on an additional area, because of the great congestion in the Jewish quarter. The house owners submitted a "supplication" asking the throne to forbid departure from the crowded ghetto, "since it has already been your supreme desire to have all the Jews concentrated in one locality."

The restoration of their principal prerogatives to the Kehillot in order to increase the Imperial Exchequer's revenue did not prevent the reactionary government from continuing with its germanization decrees. The German Jewish schools spread to nearly a hundred towns and cities, and their number throughout the province increased to 104, with a staff of 150 teachers. At Lwow and Brody, girls' schools were also opened. The authorities strictly enforced Joseph II's law requiring bride and groom to present certificates of graduation in the study of the German language in order to obtain a marriage licence. The Jewish population of Galicia, deeply absorbed in religious orthodoxy, which had grown even more powerful with the spread of Hasidism, regarded the German schools mainly as a danger to their religion, though unconsciously they also feared for the existence of their national culture.

The dubious quality of the teachers aroused even more antagonism than the schools' curricula. Most of the teachers were imported from Bohemia and Germany, and almost equalled their leader, Hertz Homberg, government superintendent of the German Jewish schools, in their extreme assimilationism, and in their coarseness towards the religious sensibilities of the people, as well as in their activities as informers, intriguers and bribe-takers. Legends of Homberg's provocative and public flouting of Jewish religious customs have not unjustifiably persisted amongst Jews of Galician origin. Galician Jews adopted innumerable schemes to evade the decrees of "dictated enlightenment" and to counteract the influence of its despised agents on Jewish youth. Its eagerness to enforce the imperial order for compulsory attendance at these schools even led the executive of the Lwow Kehillah to employ coercive measures such as quartering the military personnel—placed at its disposal for tax-collection—in the homes of defaulting parents. Despite all this, only a minority of the Jewish school-age children of Galicia actually attended these schools.

An imperial edict of 1806 liquidated the German Jewish schools of Galicia. This decisive step was one of the results of growing reaction in the Austrian Empire. More than anything, the Emperor feared that the teachers might spread indifference towards religion. Furthermore, the existence of separate schools for the Jews conflicted with the government's new educational policy. In 1805, shortly before the edict, the Emperor had drawn up a Concordat with the Pope whereby all the schools in the Empire reverted to the Catholic priesthood. The Jewish youth of Galicia remained without any institutions of general education for many decades to come.

The reactionary absolutist system was not notable for its logical consistency. Even after it had abolished all general educational institutions for the Jews, the government still retained its programme of compulsory germanization. Jewish merchants were still required to keep their books in German (or, alternatively, in French or Italian), and Kehillah leaders and rabbis were required to know German as a condition of their confirmation in office by the authorities. In 1810, the certificate of completion of studies in a German school as a pre-requisite for the issue of a marriage licence was replaced by proof of a knowledge of the catechism of morality and the Jewish religion—in the German language. Hertz Homberg's book in German, *B'nei Zion*, was the obligatory textbook for the acquisition of this knowledge. The Austrian government was well aware of the fact that Homberg was "not beloved of his people" because of "his immoral deeds, which conflict utterly with righteousness," and therefore resolved to publish this work anonymously. The government favoured this book because its exposition of the Jewish faith omitted all "exaggerated hopes and fantasies" (a hint at the ideal of Messianic redemption) and because it based religion on subservience to the monarchy. Engaged couples throughout Galicia, and in fact, in all Austria, were required to purchase a copy of this book and to obtain their religious instruction from it. They were subsequently examined on their knowledge of its contents at the district administrator's office in the presence of a municipal or manorial representative and the Kehillah rabbi. These compulsory, tragi-comic examinations were one of the causes of the widespread custom of "clandestine marriages" amongst the Jews of Galicia.

This was an unhappy period in the history of Galician Jewry, oppressed by district administrators, meat and candle tax farmers, and the unpropitious atmosphere embodied in the antisemitic Emperor and his employee, Hertz Homberg. The impoverishment of the Jews grew steadily worse and only a few of them found relief through emigration to neighbouring Hungary and Bukovina.

Nonetheless, during this period of reaction, the decrees against the

Jewish liquor purveyors and lessees lapsed in practice, if not officially. Enforcement of the laws to improve the condition of the peasant, as well as of the decree to check the spread of drunkenness, was relaxed, with the restoration of the nobility to its former eminence. The authorities, who condoned the unrestrained control of the landlords over their peasants, would hardly dare, even outwardly, to implement a decree that affected the nobles financially. Galicia was the only one of the former Polish territories (the area under Prussian rule, the Congress Kingdom of Poland) where lesseeship and liquor sales remained a principal source of income for the multitudinous rural Jews as well as for a large part of the Jewish population in the cities and towns.

The same feudal atmosphere overcame all the Imperial *Letters Patent* abolishing Kehillah autonomy and demanding germanization. The Jews of Galicia were subject to the authority of the Kehillah leaders and rabbinical jurisdiction during the feudal period under Austrian absolutist domination as they had been in feudal Poland. The German schools founded by Homberg also turned out to be a transitory phase which left no lasting residue in the culture of Galician Jewry. Development in the cultural sphere came eventually from another internal source: the emergence of a modern Jewish middle class, linked with the development of commerce, even amidst a retarded feudal environment. This class became the vehicle of the *Haskalah* movement which revived and resurrected Jewish culture throughout eastern Europe.

In 1774, during the war against Turkey, Austria conquered the territory of northern Moldavia, known as Bukovina, and this area, like neighbouring Galicia, thenceforth became a province of the Austrian Empire. This tiny province, tucked away in the Carpathians, had a total population of 17,000 families at the time of its conquest according to the official census, and contained a maximum of 526 Jewish families. However, this minute community already possessed the marked individual characteristics which made it conspicuous amongst the other Jewish communities of eastern Europe during the nineteenth and twentieth centuries. In the first place, the Jews of Bukovina combined a decisive role in the commerce and handicraft of the province, with deep roots in the soil, equalled only by the Jews of neighbouring Carpatho-Russia. Secondly, they played an increasingly important part in the cultural life of the country, because of their comparative weight amidst the general polyglot population of Moldavians, Ukrainians, Armenians, Greeks, Poles, Szeklers (from Transylvania), Hungarians, gypsies and Germans.

Expulsion decrees against new Jewish inhabitants of Bukovina were first issued at the beginning of Joseph II's reign and repeated every few years until the end of the first half of the nineteenth century. These expulsions, however, only interrupted a growing stream of Jewish immigration into the province, especially from Galicia. In 1782, when the authorities estimated that the number of Jews in Bukovina exceeded 1,000 families, the War Council in Vienna ordered the expulsion of all Jews who had settled in the area after 1769 (following the outbreak of hostilities between Russia and Turkey) and of all *Betteljuden*. The decree was implemented with the utmost severity and official figures for 1785 only recorded a maximum of 175 Jewish families left in the province. Those expelled settled mainly in Moldavia, but a few emigrated to Bessarabia.

The *Patent* for the Jews of Galicia was applied to Bukovina in 1785 and circumstances became easier for the Jews there. The entire province was incorporated into Galicia, six months later, as one of its nineteen districts. (In 1850, Bukovina again became a separate province within the Austrian Empire.) The economic opportunities that the constant development of the area provided led to a steady influx of Jews from Galicia. By the end of 1816 the official statistics showed 1,031 Jewish families living in Bukovina, of whom a third lacked the status of long-term residents.

B. *WESTERN AND CENTRAL POLAND UNDER PRUSSIAN RULE*

Oppressive "Reglement" and Extension of Rights

A number of Polish Jews came under Prussian rule as a result of the first partition of Poland in 1772. There were 10,000 Jews in the Netze District of Greater Poland which was annexed to the coastal province as West Prussia. The transition from the centuries-old feudal system to the absolutist régime of the conquerors was not easy for the Polish Jews, either in the territory occupied by Austria (Galicia) or by Russia (White Russia). But the peculiar character of Prussian absolutism made its first encounter with its new Jewish subjects brutal and repressive.

The antisemitic King, Frederick II, aimed to establish the same "system" in the conquered Polish territory as was in effect for Jews in the Prussian states: domiciliary rights exclusively for the wealthy, who were engaged in industry and the wholesale trade and who enriched the treasury by the payment of huge protection taxes. In 1772, following the conquest, the King's Chamber issued a warrant for the expulsion of all Jews of Netze with assets of less than 1,000 thaler. During the following decade, about 4,000 *Betteljuden* were deported to the Polish frontier. In most cases, the Kehillah leaders withheld support from these victims, in the hope of gaining the King's favour. Some Kehillot, Lobsen for example, collaborated with the government to the extent of preparing lists of Jews to be protected and of others who could be deported. In contrast, the Kehillah of Inowroclaw defended its poor families against expulsion, although the cost was enormous.

In the second partition, of 1793, Prussia annexed Greater Poland with the city of Posen and re-named the area Southern Prussia. In 1795, its rule was extended to Masovia (with the city of Warsaw) and Podlasie (with the city of Bialystok) and the area as a whole designated New East Prussia. There were over 170,000 Jews in the two provinces.

The Polish Jews who came under Prussia's rule were completely different from the few "protected Jews" of Prussia in their geographical concentration, occupational distribution and their function in the country's economy. Jews constituted a fifth of the inhabitants in the cities of the Posen area, a third in the cities of New East Prussia. Forty per cent of the merchants in the two provinces were Jews. A report submitted in 1793 by a Prussian official, Zimmermann, contained the following description of Jewish trade in Southern Prussia (the Posen area), recently annexed to the Kingdom of Prussia:

> The Jewish wholesale merchants bring woollen fabrics, linen, caps, "Nuremberg goods," and colonial goods from Breslau, Reichenbach and the Sudeten Mountains, or from the fairs at Frankfurt-on-the-Oder and Leipzig. They distribute these wares to pedlars, who canvass the towns and villages with them, selling them for cash or bartering them for such products as flax, raw wool, hemp, honey, wax, hides and feathers. The pedlars return with all these goods to their merchants and the latter market them at Königsberg, Berlin, Frankfurt-on-the-Oder, Danzig and especially at Breslau. There are also Jewish wholesalers who export commodities purchased at Breslau, Frankfurt and Leipzig, to the Ukraine, Russia and Turkey; and they bring the goods imported from those countries, especially from Russia (furs), to the markets of these German cities.

Jews had a large share in the crafts, especially in several varieties which they controlled by virtue of a centuries'-old tradition. The Prussian officials regarded this as quite miraculous. Immediately after the first partition, in 1773, the Financial Adviser, Roden, described this novelty to the Chancellor in great astonishment:

> Here (in the Netze District) I am involved with so many Jews that I am totally bewildered. If I want a doctor, a Jew calls; a carpenter— a Jew turns up. The butcher, the baker, they are Jews. All the artisans in the world are Jews.

This exaggeration originated in the fact that the Jews there were actually concentrated in a definite number of crafts. Lacework was a common occupation amongst Jewish women and girls and several hundred were thus engaged in the city of Leszno (Lissa) alone. A merchant, Ephraim Veitel Heine, employed 1,500 women throughout Greater Poland manufacturing lacework for him on credit. Because Jews were reputed to be expert carters, the Prussian authorities considered a proposal to draft them into the army as cavalrymen.

Despite the prominent position that the productive elements of the

Jewish population held, its occupational structure was, on the whole, unsatisfactory and was reflected in poor social conditions. Jewish artisans were concentrated in a few branches of activity, particularly the needle trade, and most of them therefore made only a poor living. Two-thirds of the Jewish population was chiefly engaged in trade and brokerage, most of them small shopkeepers and pedlars, and here too, great poverty prevailed. Jewish liquor sellers and innkeepers were comparatively few in the Posen area, more numerous in the Kalisz district, while in New East Prussia, in the districts of Warsaw and Bialystok, rural Jews were almost as numerous as urban Jews. In proportion to their dispersal throughout the eastern areas, the poverty of those subsisting on the manufacture and sale of beer, liquor, and other beverages increased. The newly arrived Prussian officials emphasized the straitened circumstances of the Jewish inhabitants in the conquered areas, as compared with the wealthy Jews of Prussia, at the same time as they expressed surprise at their unusual productive activity.

The Jews, together with all the inhabitants of the Polish territories seized by Prussia in 1793 and 1796, welcomed the new régime with joyful demonstrations. A demonstration in honour of the Prussian régime in the town of Oberzicko illustrated the prevailing mood amongst the Jews in the small towns in the transition period. As the black eagle symbolizing the Prussian state was nailed to the post in the market square in the presence of all the inhabitants of the town summoned to swear allegiance to the conquerors, a Jew by the name of Herschel rose and delivered an impassioned speech in fluent Polish. He began by quoting the traditional passage, *We were slaves to Pharoah in Egypt*, to recall Jewish servitude under the old régime. He concluded amidst general acclaim with a paean in honour of the new rulers of the land.

The expectations aroused amongst the Jews by the new order were only realized in the case of propertied and wealthy classes. The poor Jewish population only gained a few additional rights, while their tax burden became heavier, and their economic activities were hampered by a strict supervisory system.

Immediately after the conquest of the western region of Poland, in 1793, the Prussian authorities realized that it would be impossible to employ the routine system in operation for the Jews of Prussia in relation to the Jews of the occupied territory. The decisive role that the Jews took in commerce and their large share in the manual trades made quick action by the Prussian government with its reform plans essential. On April 17, 1797, after an additional acquisition of Polish territory by the third partition, the Prussian government issued regulations for the Jews of South and New East Prussia entitled, *General Juden—Reglement für Süd und Neu Ost Preussen*. On one hand, the government, as the government of a Christian state, wanted to check the increase in the Jewish population and to restrict its competition with Christian trade and handicraft. On the other hand, it could not relinquish the economic activities of the Jews, and, in keeping with absolutist economic policy, actually extended in large measure their domiciliary rights as well as their rights to engage in trade, industry and the manual vocations. The Prussian government, again like all the absolutist governments, and particularly Emperor Joseph II in his reforms, announced the aims of transferring the Jews in South and New East Prussia to useful occupations, especially cultivation of the soil and handicraft, and above all, of ejecting rural Jews from their positions as lessees and publicans in the villages. In actuality, the project to move Jews into productive activities was never carried out in the slightest degree because of government reluctance to allot funds for the purpose. A government plan to convert the Kehillot into exclusively religious institutions and a programme for germanization by the establishment of schools was also never fully implemented for similar financial reasons. On the other hand, the law levied far higher taxes on the Jews than had been customary under the independent Polish state.

A provision making a specific permit from the government Exchequer necessary before a Jew could pursue any occupation, transfer his residence from place to another, or even change quarters within the same place marked the climax of *Reglementiererei*—regulation mania. The ancient Polish poll tax for Jews was retained in open contradiction to the principle of Jewish equality in taxation with all other citizens, and raised from three zloty to ten for every individual between the ages of fourteen and sixty. The title of this tax was changed to *Rekruten- und Schutzgeld* (Recruit and Protection Fee) and it was imposed as a form of compensation to the state for exempting the Jews from military service "and also since this entire matter of Jewry entails the expenditure of much effort and resources by the state . . ." The Jews of South and New East Prussia were also required to pay a *Geleitzoll* (Escort Duty) when they crossed the country's frontiers in either direction. No pretext was offered for this.

The *Reglement* limiting Jewish economic activity by stringent controls and tying Jewish trade and manual occupations to the securing of special licences was the most difficult to bear of all the numerous enactments of the 1797 statute. However, the Kehillah leaders, who not only feared the loss of their own control over Jewish communal affairs as a result of the abolition of the Kehillah's autonomous prerogatives, also realized the danger to the Jewish population of being subjected to the jurisdiction of the municipal courts. On August 30, 1797, the Kehillah leaders of South and New East Prussia, mostly from the Posen district, met at Kleczew in the vicinity of Posen for consultations on the new juridical situation. The council elected a delegation to intercede with the government at Berlin for the revocation of new restrictions.

As a result of this intercession, on November 20, the Ministry for Silesia (with jurisdiction over the conquered areas of Poland till 1799) issued a warrant appreciably relaxing most of the harsher economic restrictions. It established that the licence permitting Jews to engage in trade and craft would not in every instance be conditional on the assets of the applicant or the number of merchants in the locality. Jews were also allowed to engage in peddling by government licence in the rural areas. Jewish artisans were to be included amongst the examiners of Jewish candidates for the craft. At the beginning of 1798, the Minister for Silesia, Von Hoym, also agreed to modify the marriage restrictions; the requirement that the groom be at least twenty-five years old was specifically withdrawn.

In practice, the Jews had not been affected by the fact that the right of residence depended on a warrant of protection, except that they had to pay for the certificate. The government only refused the request of the Kehillah emissaries for the abolition of Kehillah courts, despite the convincing argument that there were very few Jews who knew German well enough to present their claims orally or in writing before a municipal court.

On the other hand, as already stated, basic constructive reforms such as settlement on the land were never instituted. When land was available, the government openly admitted that there was no shortage of German Christians to settle on it. The Prussian régime not only surpassed the Austrian and Russian governments in unconcealed discrimination against the Jews, but also in its unwillingness to make any expenditures on behalf of the Jews' reform. This hard-fisted niggardliness hindered the Prussian government in the implementation of its programme for the germanization and assimilation of the Jewish population. With each accretion of Polish territory following the three partitions, the Prussian officials reiterated their surprise at the high cultural level of the Jews as compared with the remainder of the population. In the Netze district, they found twenty Jewish *Me'lamdim* in the villages and not one Christian teacher. After the seizure of the province of Posen, the Minister, Von Voss, wrote to the King, "The Jews of South Prussia are generally more cultured than the burghers in the towns and the peasants in the country." Because of their geographical proximity and close commercial ties with Germany, the Jews in the western areas of Poland were not as fanatically antagonistic towards general enlightenment and secular education as the Jews of Galicia under Austrian rule, or the Jews of Lithuania, White Russia, and the Ukraine under Russia. In the 1797 memorandum to the government, the Posen Kehillah stated that 200 children were learning to write and studying a foreign language under private Jewish and Christian tutors. A report by the provincial official mentioned that there were also Jewish young people learning Polish and German in the Kehillah of Lissa. Similar instances of wealthy Jews taking advantage of all available opportunities for secular studies and sending their sons to Lutheran church cantors to study German were recorded in the smaller towns. It was also quite common for the Jews to be almost the only people in a small town possessing a general education! The German writer, Von

Kloeden, described in his Memoirs how in his youth in the city of Friedland, he had learned geography and arithmetic from a Jew who had once been a business official in Berlin, and French and piano from the town physician, a Jew, Dr. Phoebus. The Kehillot of the western district therefore did not oppose the erection of schools when the law of 1797 was enacted; they only requested that the government provide the monetary support the law promised. But the government was unwilling to allocate any funds whatsoever. Despite the *Reglement*, not a single school for Jews was established in any of the Polish territories under Prussian control.

And yet, the Prussian régime fulfilled a positive function for Jewry in western Poland despite the contradiction between its grandiose declarations and actual discriminatory practice and the *Reglementiererei* embodied in its repressive tax system. The trend inherent in the absolutist régime of fostering capitalism impelled the Prussian government to abolish several oppressive restrictions that had hampered the Jews under the feudal system of independent Poland, alike as it inexorably led to the improvement of the legal status of the peasantry. Frederick William III's Royal Warrant of 1802 considerably modified the laws curtailing Jewish rights to engage in the manual trades. It ruled that the craft guilds could not withhold the right of membership from Jewish artisans and even less the right to engage in any craft. It also confirmed the *Reglement* of 1797 curbing the prerogative of the municipalities "not to tolerate Jews"; to reinforce this, it stated that only government authorities had the right to decide on matters of this nature. In fact, under Prussian rule the Jews gained access to scores of cities and towns in the Posen province which they had been forbidden to enter under the Poles or where a maximum of two per city had previously lived. The city of Bydgoszcz (Bromberg) was an outstanding example of the new legal situation. In 1772, before the Prussian occupation, only four Jewish families had lived there; in 1815, it numbered 233 Jewish inhabitants. Throughout the province of Posen, up to the interruption of Prussian rule in 1806, there were only three secular cities and a few ecclesiastical towns in which there were no Jews at all. In 1825, in the entire Grand Duchy of Posen, there were only six towns without Jewish inhabitants. The number of wealthy Jews who acquired homes of their own increased despite qualifications attached to the new law, such as Christian priority in the purchase of houses and plots. Similarly, discrimination by the authorities against Jewish trade failed to arrest their economic activities.

The legal position of the Jews in the large cities of Warsaw and Posen improved appreciably as a result of the new order. In Posen the Jews had lived within the Jewish quarter during the Polish period. Now the government urgently demanded that the municipal administration set aside a new area for a Jewish quarter in consideration of the congestion in the old one and the consequent unhygienic conditions which this had caused. The municipality refused but the government insisted on the execution of its order. It also demanded that Jews who had settled in streets outside the Jewish quarter be granted domiciliary rights in the city, even though it encountered determined opposition from a strange combination of the magistracy and the Kehillah leaders in this matter. The Kehillah leaders contended that the Jews in question had arrived from outside the city, possessed no Kehillah authorization to reside there, and were harming the business interests of legitimate Kehillah inhabitants! A conflagration destroyed the Jewish quarter of Posen in 1803 and accelerated the abolition of the ancient law decreeing a pale of Jewish settlement within the city—in much the same way as the ghetto in Frankfurt-on-Main had been liquidated in 1796 following a fire. After the fire at Posen, the Jews were allowed to live unimpeded in any street in the city, with the proviso that they should not possess more houses than they had owned inside the quarter. However, the Jews of Posen preferred to erect their new homes in the area of their old quarter and its immediate vicinity so as to concentrate their trading activities and communal affairs. At Leszno (Lissa), too, the fire of 1790 served as a pretext for permitting settlement outside the ghetto pale up to the disruption of Prussian rule. At Kalisz and Krotoszyn, even without this pretext, the authorities raised no objections to Jews taking up residence in city streets outside the Jewish quarter.

An even more fundamental change occurred in the condition of the Jews of Warsaw. Although nearly 7,000 Jews lived in the city in 1796 when it was annexed to Prussia, Polish law only granted them rights of temporary residence and they lived continually under the threat of expulsion. Under Prussian rule, the Warsaw Jews who had lived in the city before 1796 were specifically granted the right to live there. Only Jews who had arrived after that date were required, as formerly, to pay a "sojourn" tax known as the "ticket" (*Billet*). In conjunction with this permission to reside in the city, an organized Kehillah was founded in Warsaw with the approval of the authorities for the first time since the expulsion of the Middle Ages. In 1806, the first Jewish cemetery inside the Warsaw city limits was consecrated. This was the Ulica Gesia cemetery, which exists at the present time. The Jews of Warsaw had previously buried their dead on the other side of the River Vistula, in the suburb of Praga. In the decade ending in 1805, the number of Jews in Warsaw grew to 12,000 people—over a sixth of its total population.

C. THE GRAND DUCHY OF WARSAW

The Napoleonic Code in a Feudal State; the "Infamous Decree"

On October 27, 1806, two weeks after Prussia's defeat at Jena, Napoleon's armies entered Berlin. A month later, Warsaw was in their hands. A peace treaty between Napoleon on the one hand and the King of Prussia and his ally, the Czar, on the other, was signed at Tilsit at the end of spring, 1807. Prussia forfeited nearly all the Polish territories it had acquired by the second and third partitions. With the exception of the district of Bialystok, which went to Russia, they were formed into an independent state: the Grand Duchy of Warsaw.

In 1809, following Napoleon's victory over Austria at Wagram, a peace treaty was signed at Vienna. Austria was forced to cede all the Polish territory she had gained from the third partition ("Western Galicia") as well as the district of Zamosc and Krakow and its environs to the Grand Duchy of Warsaw. This annexation increased the population of the Grand Duchy to 4,334,280, according to the census of 1810.

The economic structure of the Grand Duchy still showed the main characteristics of a feudal system. Eighty-four per cent of the Christian population was rural in 1808 and only 16.3 per cent lived in cities. Even many of the inhabitants of the cities and towns still engaged in agriculture, like the peasants. The leading "industry" of the Duchy was the manufacture of beverages, liquors and beer; far behind, in second place came the flour milling industry.

The new political régime of this backward state was also merely the result of a compromise between rigid feudalism and the desire to promote capitalist development. Napoleon appointed Frederick Augustus, King of Saxony, his loyal ally and heir to the throne of Poland under the defunct constitution of May 3, 1791, as ruler of the Grand Duchy. The Grand Duchy's new constitution, drawn up by Napoleon and ratified by his signature, was proclaimed on July 22, 1807. This constitution instituted the French civil code, the *Code Napoléon*, in the Duchy and established an apparently parliamentary but actually absolutist régime. Freedom of all religions was guaranteed (sec. I, para. 2), although the Catholic religion was declared the state religion. Its chief innovation was contained in a few brief words in Paragraph 4 of Section I of the Constitution:

Serfdom is abolished. All citizens are equal before the law. Personal status (i.e., personal freedom) has the protection of the courts of law.

On the basis of this paragraph, the peasants were freed from serfdom for the first time in Polish history, and the Jews, who had existed in servitude for hundreds of years, were also granted rights on a basis of complete equality with all other citizens. However, the Constitution contradicted the principle of civil equality that it had proclaimed, above all by extending extraordinary privileges to the Church and the nobility.

Furthermore, even within the framework of this compromise, the constitution was never fully implemented. The peasants and the Jews who shared a common fate in Poland, as in all eastern Europe throughout the new age, were both deprived of their rights to such an extent as to render the guarantees in the new Constitution absurd. As far as the peasants were concerned, a ducal warrant of December 21, 1807, construed the constitutional paragraph abolishing serfdom to mean that the peasant was free to leave his master and his village at will; but the landlord was equally free to evict the peasant from his home and plot and to expel him from the village. Thus, in practice, despite their new freedom of movement, the condition of the peasants deteriorated considerably, even by comparison with the feudal system.

The census of 1808 gave the population of the Grand Duchy of Warsaw as 2,048,653, including 205,000 Jews, over a tenth of the total and nearly 28 per cent of the town dwellers. Nearly two-thirds of the Jews of the Grand Duchy—63.65 per cent—lived in cities and towns, while over a third—36.35 per cent—were in the villages. According to the census of 1810, 112,000 Jews lived in the territory of "Western Galicia," annexed to the Duchy in 1809. There were over 360,000 Jews in the Duchy as a whole in 1810, comprising approximately 9 per cent of the general population.

The proportion of Jews amongst the urban population reflected their importance to the economy of the Grand Duchy. In 1810, there were over 14,000 Jews in Warsaw, or 18 per cent of its total of 77,727 inhabitants. Posen had 3,729 Jews, 21 per cent of the total there. At Leszno (Lissa), 3,381 Jews formed 34 per cent of the total. At Kalisz, 38 per cent of the population—2,535 people—were Jewish. Piotrkov had 1,817 (46 per cent), Krakow 5,014 (21 per cent) and Lublin 2,973 (42 per cent of the total). The census of 1808 showed that Jews outnumbered Christians amongst the population of many small towns and several medium-sized cities. In view of the fact that even in cities and towns where Jews were in the minority, most of the Christian inhabitants still lived on agriculture, the evidence produced by contemporary Polish economists illustrating the large role that the Jews took in trade and the large share they possessed of the country's artisanship can be understood.

The statesman and economist, W. Surowiecki, evaluated the economic activity of the Jews in his book, *On the Decline of Industry in the Cities of Poland* (1810) in the following terms:

> If we rule out several of the larger cities, in which the magnates were wont occasionally to disburse their income, then in nearly all localities Poland has salvaged her trade and industry thanks to the Jews. . . . Through their assistance, the Polish husbandman is more assured that his yield will be marketed. In their frequent journeyings about the country, they collect and purchase for cash even products which, because of their worthlessness, would either be wasted or else would impoverish the poor agriculturist, with their price not even defraying transport costs. . . . Up to now, the Jews, more than all others, have maintained Poland's commerce, and without them this trade, requiring such diligence, would either have reached the

vanishing point, or would long since have reduced the population to poverty. None are more agile in seeking out needed crops and commodities than they are; none so well acquainted with these items; nobody transports them with greater economy; and none is so content with so little profits as this people. . . .

The role of the Jews in the manual trades was certainly less important than in trade, but "poverty, ridicule, and a prejudiced attitude towards their workmanship, together with the desire to obtain cheap articles, are the principal reasons for the poor state of their handicraft," according to Surowiecki. "Nobody can justly deny his (the Jew's) talent for manual vocations. When he does not lack the necessary funds, and when his market is assured, he demonstrates the same good taste and perfection that others do."

Jews took a particularly large share of the foreign trade of the Grand Duchy at the Leipzig fairs. Grain, on the other hand, which was Poland's main export, was apparently handled by the nobles. Between 1807 and 1813, 97 per cent of all the traders who went to the fairs at Leipzig from the Grand Duchy of Warsaw were Jews. In 1811, for example, only twenty-one out of 1,143 merchants from Poland attending the Leipzig fair were gentiles. The remaining 1,122 were Jews.

When Napoleon visited Warsaw in December, 1806, a large Kehillah delegation came to welcome him and presented him with a Song of Praise in Hebrew, accompanied by a French translation printed in his honour. It expressed their joy at the rebirth of Sarmatia (a poetic appelation for Poland) and also expressed the conviction that by the Emperor's grace "Israel would burgeon and bloom, Jacob strike root. . . ."

It would seem that Napoleon was gratified by the attitude of the Polish Jews towards himself and his forces. Tradition records a joke of the Emperor when he saw so many Jews helping his forces in Poland as middlemen, suppliers, and spies: *"Voilà pourtant à quoi me sert le grand Sanhédrin."*

Nevertheless, when the Jewish question appeared on the agenda for discussion by the government of the Grand Duchy, neither the Jews' manifold services to Napoleon and his armies, nor their tremendous role in the country's economy, were of any help. The ruling class of this absolutist feudal state, consisting of nobles and proprietors who retained their own peasants in bondage, could not countenance the idea of an enslaved people enjoying equal rights with the dominant nation. Its sovereign, the King of Saxony—a state which even in Germany was renowned for its brutal repression of the Jewish community—was certainly not inclined to protect the Jews against the curtailment of their rights. It should be noted, however, that he reformulated several of the decrees the government of the Duchy presented to him, in order to eliminate any offence that the original text might give to the Jews; on some occasions he actually modified their content. Nonetheless, the reactionary government had no difficulty in securing the assent of Napoleon, the supreme ruler of the state, to its anti-Jewish activities. Napoleon had already demonstrated his cautious policy towards the Polish nobles by his ambiguous paragraph in the Constitution respecting the emancipation of the serfs. He did not propose to quarrel with the ruling class in the Grand Duchy of Warsaw over the Jewish question. He had, after all, himself encouraged reactionary anti-Jewish tendencies throughout Europe and provided them with a model in the *Infamous Decree* of March, 1808, against the Jews of his Empire.

The conventional argument of Jewish national distinctiveness and self-segregation served as a convenient excuse for the government of the Grand Duchy, which from the outset sought every means to circumvent the constitution on the issue of Jewish citizenship. Napoleon's *Infamous Decree* curtailing the civil rights of most French Jews for ten years was promulgated on March 17, 1808. To the government of the Grand Duchy of Warsaw this decree was of unbelievable assistance. It did not neglect the opportunity. On April 4, 1808, the Minister of Justice, Lubienski, proposed to the Grand Duke Frederick Augustus that he act on the authority of Napoleon's warrant to reject the enfranchisement of the Jews in the Duchy. This suggestion that the Council of State (the Cabinet) submitted to the King on May 30, 1808, was supported by the argument of the self-segregation of the Jews as well as by new grievances regarding their noxious economic effects. It was claimed that they rejected agriculture and were barely concerned with industry: "They impair their commerce and even their artisanship with their excessive haggling; and on the other hand they are involved in brokerage." They were also accused of engaging in usury and occasionally of smuggling contraband goods. To sum up: "They live a life of idleness and instead of augmenting national assets destroy them while enjoying the fruits of other men's labours." This condemnation of Jewish trading activities hardly concealed the motive behind the government's projected repeal of Jewish rights: to employ political means to arrest Jewish competition with the Polish merchant class, always from its wretched beginnings a protégé of the mercantile system of the semi-independent state. The repeated emphasis in the government proposal of the claim that "the Jewish people are present here in too large a number," unlike the neighbouring countries, "in which sensible laws prevent the undue multiplying of the Jewish people," was conclusive proof of this aim.

However, Frederick Augustus dared not take a decision in this matter, with its constitutional implications, without the consent of his master, as Napoleon had confirmed the constitution with his signature. In spring, 1808, negotiations on the debt payments which France was demanding from the Grand Duchy took place between the emissaries of the government of the Grand Duchy of Warsaw and the Saxon Minister Plenipotentiary, on the one hand, and Napoleon and the French Minister for the Interior, Champagny, on the other. During these negotiations, concluded at Bayonne on May 10, Frederick Augustus authorized his Minister to raise the question of revoking the political rights of the Jews in Poland for a period of ten years "taking as an example Napoleon's legislation." However, the Emperor only gave verbal approval to the anti-Jewish decree in the Grand Duchy of Warsaw—possibly because he anticipated a new war (which, in fact, broke out in 1809) and was therefore reluctant to antagonize entirely the Jews of Poland by officially agreeing to the abrogation of their rights.

The government of the Grand Duchy had secretly suspended implementation of the Jewish enfranchisement ordained by the constitution in a Warrant surreptitiously signed by the King on September 7, 1808, pending a final decision on their active civil rights. Nonetheless, the King did not sign the following decree until October 17:

> We hereby suspend for ten years the political rights eventually to be enjoyed by those inhabitants of Our Grand Duchy of Warsaw who profess the Mosaic faith, in the hope that within this period they will eradicate those traits which so divide them from all others. This Ordinance, of course, will not prevent Us from permitting individual members of this faith to enjoy political rights prior to the aforementioned time, provided they shall merit Our Exalted Grace by fulfilling conditions We shall ordain in a special Enactment for those professing the Mosaic faith.

Characteristically, this decree was not published in the Duchy's legal gazette—probably because of the open contradiction between the decree and the Grand Duchy's constitution; possibly also because it had not been confirmed in writing by Napoleon, the final arbiter of the Duchy's affairs.

The revocation of civil and political rights was the prelude to severe repressive measures against the Jewish economy and Jewish domiciliary rights in the cities, as well as to the imposition of special taxes that drained the people's resources. The policy that the government of the Grand Duchy pursued towards the Jews was lacking even in the small measure of consistency that enlightened absolutism had possessed. Absolutism, while imposing new restrictions, had at least granted the Jews certain rights and had attempted to carry out programmes for their enlightenment and movement into productive activities—even if they were only intended to encourage their assimilation. Under the absolutist régime of the Grand Duchy of Warsaw, the only measures adopted in regard to the Jews, with the exception of a limited few men of finance, were those of harsh repression. The fine phrases about the need to raise the level of their civilization served as a pretext for acts of oppression. Enlightened absolutism had regarded the Jews in the light of the capitalist progress it favoured. The Jewish policy of the Polish state, re-established by Napoleon, mainly revealed the dual reactionary tendencies which hampered it, despite its incipient capitalist development: feudal regression, on the one hand, and the increasingly powerful counter-revolutionary policy of the Napoleonic régime on the other.

On November 19, 1808, barely a month after the ducal warrant curtailing their political rights, an order was issued forbidding Jews to acquire landed estates from the nobility pending the publication of a new order. The decree reinforced the monopoly of acquisition of landed property held by the Polish nobles, whose economic position had been weakened by the abolition of serfdom and the grain export slump (access to the sea had been cut off when Danzig was declared a free city). The government was also concerned about the exclusive privileges of the Polish middle class and proposed to renew the Jewish ghetto decree to assist it to compete with Jewish trade and handicraft. It was particularly reluctant to accept the fact that the Jews of the capital had been living at will without interference in any street in the city since the Prussian occupation. On March 16, 1809, a royal warrant forbade the Warsaw Jews to reside in the Old City and in any of the main thoroughfares of the city specified by name. Jews with dwellings on prohibited streets were required to move within six months. "In order that the Jewish people may understand that it is not the Government's intention to make any exception of them amongst the other inhabitants," exemption from the decree was granted to "those individuals who will endeavour to be worthy thereof." It was referring to Jews whose assets totalled 60,000 zloty, wholesale merchants, founders of manufacturing enterprises employing Jewish labour, doctors and other members of the liberal professions, and people who had built new homes, provided they could write Polish, French or German, sent their children to general schools, and did not dress differently from other inhabitants.

The purpose of the warrant was contained in its preamble:

> We have considered the fact that the excessive congestion caused by the people of the Old Testament exposes the other inhabitants of the capital to all kinds of dangers, such as fires and the loss of health, and We have noted that uncleanliness, disorder, and lawlessness are the natural result of excessive crowding into a small area.

This rationalism would appear to lack conviction: to avoid congestion, the Jews were ordered to vacate the entire central area of the city and to crowd into a few specified streets. It was, in fact, generally known in Warsaw that owners of buildings far away from the centre of the town who hoped to rent homes to the evicted Jews had exerted considerable influence on the issue of this decree. The same concern for the property owners was also evident in some of the legal details laid down. Residence in the streets near the centre of the city where Jews were still permitted to reside, was restricted to a maximum of one family to every two rooms and of five families to any building. On the other hand, no limitation was placed on the number of Jewish tenants "in vacant houses in the outlying suburbs. . . ." The Council of State, in its reply to the Jewish protest, openly admitted that the resettlement of the Jews on the more distant streets besides "being of great benefit to the Jews . . . would afford the Christian owners considerable income. . . ." However, it was the economic motive of curbing Jewish competition in trade that predominated in the expulsion of the Jews from the centre of the capital. An order dated September 7, 1809, forbade Jews to open stores on streets where Jewish residence was prohibited. "It is the jealousy of a number of Christian merchants that has hounded us," the Jews of Warsaw complained in their request of August 24 to Frederick Augustus to rescind the expulsion decree.

Once again, this ghetto decree, like the prohibition of the acquisition of landed property and the abolition of Jewish political rights, was not published in the Grand Duchy's legal gazette. It would appear that the government was reluctant to disclose to all Europe its attitude towards Napoleon's constitution that was apparently still valid.

The sole achievement of the expulsion decree was to help to fill the empty houses on the Warsaw streets allotted for Jewish residence. It also led to the construction of new buildings there by Jews and Poles. However no change occurred in the nature and scope of Jewish trade in the capital. The inhabitants of the city, as well as customers from outside who had previously patronized the Jewish stores, continued to travel out to them to purchase their wares even after they had been segregated in a district of their own.

The Warsaw decree was only a beginning. Only the short life of the Grand Duchy prevented the programme being implemented in its entirety. In 1810, at the request of the burghers of Wschowa (Fraustadt), the government ordered the Jews to be expelled from the Old City to the new suburb where they had lived before the fire. In 1811, a warrant was issued, establishing a Jewish quarter in Plock. On January 29, 1813, orders were signed setting up special Jewish quarters in Makow and Przasznysz, at the request of the burghers there. As in Warsaw and Plock exemptions were granted to Jews with capital.

The government of the Grand Duchy did not require new legislation in what had been Western Galicia, but in actual practice confirmed the existing decrees dating back to the period of Polish independence, which the Austrian government had not revoked. At Lublin, the Old City continued closed to Jewish settlement. At Krakow, the ban on Jewish residence and business establishments in the city proper remained in force. Jews could not even rent additional stores in the Christian quarter of the suburb of Kazimierz, into which they were crowded and could only retain the ones already rented for a maximum of six years, by which time they should have built homes in the "Jewish City." Cities such as Kielce and the smaller towns around it which had retained their medieval privilege not to tolerate the Jews under Austrian rule, were absolutely closed to Jewish settlement under the Grand Duchy of Warsaw. The special Jewish *Revirs* (quarters) subsequently introduced into scores of cities and towns in Congress Poland were only a continuation and full implementation of the policy laid down by the Grand Duchy of Warsaw. The Provisional Government which ruled the Grand Duchy after Napoleon's defeat immediately established *Revirs* in additional cities, such as Radom, in 1814.

The Kosher Meat Tax and "Autonomy" by Patronage

While it abolished all the concessions relating to the rights of domicile granted to the Jews under Prussian rule, the government of the Grand Duchy retained all the restrictions embodied in the Prussian *Reglement* of 1797. Thus, a special permit from the authorities was still required for every purchase of a building by a Jew. The government also retained the Prussian enactment requiring payment of the *Geleitzoll,* or escort fee, by all foreign Jews crossing the Duchy's frontiers. Despite the proof that this decree was harmful to the country's trade, the government refused to revoke it, except in the case of Jews in transit with their merchandise (1810). The only one of the former régime's repressive measures definitely abolished was the *Billet* (*biletowe* in Polish, *tugtzettl* in Yiddish) which Jews from outside had to pay on arriving in Warsaw and which dated from the period of Polish independence. Even then, this concession was only granted in 1811, after intervention by the King and to the dismay of the Minister of the Interior, the Prefect, and the municipal authorities of the city of Warsaw.

The innumerable special taxes weighed more heavily on the Jewish population than all the other measures of discrimination. They had been introduced under Prussian rule and were not abolished by the government of the Grand Duchy despite the civil equality promised by the Constitution. In 1809, the *Sejm* decided to replace all these taxes with one uniform tax, the kosher meat tax, but the law, passed on March 25, 1809, specified that this special tax did not exempt the Jews from the general taxes applying to the population as a whole. Thus the Jews had to pay the general taxes (which the *Sejm* more than doubled) and, in addition, a further tax which was fixed at considerably more than the sum total of the previous special taxes. Based on an estimated average consumption of one pound of meat per family weekly, a tax of six grosz was placed on each pound; the current price of one pound of non-kosher meat did not exceed six or eight grosz. Thus the tax was fixed at 2,400,000 zloty a year, which later increased to 3,300,000 zloty.

The system of collection made the kosher meat tax a direct rather than indirect tax. To ensure effective collection, Kehillah executives were authorized to impose on "those rebellious or delinquent in their payments all the religious punishments meted out by their faith," in fact, even excommunication. In such instances, the authorities were obliged to support the Kehillot. The government did not even shrink from restricting Jewish freedom of movement in order to prevent tax evasion. A law of March 25, 1809, required departmental, district and municipal authorities to ensure "that no family of those who adhere to the Old Testament" moved its residence from one place to another without permission to settle in the new locality if it did not possess a receipt for payment of all due kosher meat tax instalments. The personal liberty of the Jewish, and for that matter, of the peasant "citizens" became a travesty of justice under the absolutist and feudal Grand Duchy of Warsaw, behind the façade of the *Code Napoléon*.

The system of special Jewish taxes also revived the central organs of Jewish autonomy, although with narrower prerogatives than under the ancient Polish régime. Already, under Prussian rule Kehillah representatives were meeting for consultation on communal matters, especially the revocation of repressive measures. These meetings became an urgent necessity under the Grand Duchy of Warsaw. Furthermore, the law explicitly provided for meetings of Kehillah representatives within the districts for purposes of consultation with the vice-prefects on the apportionment of kosher meat tax quotas. In several districts, Kehillah representatives took advantage of these occasions to hold discussions amongst themselves on taxation matters in general and the question of intercession with the authorities.

The arguments that the Kehillah representatives of the Warsaw district produced indicated a high level of political intelligence, undoubtedly influenced to a considerable extent by the *Haskalah* spirit, and a familiarity with the detail of the law. They also reflected the interests of the ruling classes in the Kehillot. They claimed that the kosher meat tax constituted a double burden; as it was not indirect, the rich had to pay it even on behalf of Jews who could not afford to buy meat. The representative of the Kehillah leaders also complained that as the kosher meat tax had to be paid into the State Exchequer, the Kehillot were unable to continue with their own system of indirect taxes (the so-called *krupka*), because they could not possibly impose a double meat tax on the people of the Kehillot. The class aims already involved at this stage of the intercession by the Kehillot produced a conflict between the interests of the large and the small Kehillot. The large Kehillot tried—as had been their custom in pre-partition Poland—to shift the heavy tax burden on to the smaller Kehillot of their respective departments or districts by all available means. Inter-Kehillah conflict and, especially the desire of the Warsaw Kehillah to achieve hegemony over the others, frustrated an attempt by the Kehillot of Posen and Leszno to convene a central council of all the Kehillot of the Grand Duchy at Slezyn in autumn 1809.

However, the great increase in poverty amongst the Jewish population and its inability to meet the demands of the tax eventually moved the Kehillot to take joint consultation on united action. In the interim, the condition of the Jewish population had deteriorated so much that not even half of the kosher meat tax quota for the entire Grand Duchy had been collected. In these circumstances, the Minister of the Exchequer himself agreed to convene a conference of invited individuals from the six original departments of the Grand Duchy in March, 1811. Despite the proposal of the conference spokesmen that the tax be reduced to a quarter (on the basis of estimated meat consumption), the Minister issued an order reducing it only by a third of the total sum. The members of the Conference reacted by co-opting representatives from the remaining four departments annexed to the Duchy in 1809. This broadened conference thenceforth spoke on behalf of all the Jews in the Grand Duchy. It submitted a memorandum to the Council of State relating the issue of the kosher meat tax to the exemption of Jews from military service. Discussion on the question of military service, Kehillah autonomy and central representation for the Jews entered a new phase.

According to the existing law (royal warrants of May 9 and November 10, 1808), Jews were liable for military service like all other inhabitants of the Grand Duchy. In practice, very few Jews served in the Grand Duchy's forces. Most of those liable to conscription avoided it, either by virtue of being married or by paying a service fee to a proxy. A dozen or so Jews distinguished themselves by their valiant service in the Grand Duchy's army, but the widest popularity in Poland and throughout Europe was achieved by Berek Joselewicz, the Jewish battalion commander at the time of the Kosciuszko rebellion. He was an officer in the Polish Legions of General Jozef Dombrowski, fought in the Italian campaigns, entered Poland with Napoleon's armies, and as a colonel of cavalry was killed in action near the city of Klock in the war against Austria in 1809. The Polish press eulogized him; Prince Poniatowski mentioned his death in dispatches to Napoleon, and a Polish folk song praised his heroic death. Some of the Jewish officers, army doctors and soldiers who became renowned for their acts of courage were proud to be Jews and never forgot their Jewish heritage. However, observance of the Sabbath and of the dietary laws were out of the question in military service, so that Polish Jewry, the most orthodox in Europe, naturally regarded compulsory service in the army as the worst oppression. The French resident in Warsaw at the time, E. Bignon, stated that the Polish soldiers were also opposed to serving together with Jews. But even without these religious grounds and the hostile atmosphere in the army, Jewish enthusiasm could hardly be great for service in the military forces of a state which was doing its utmost to oppress them by ever new discriminating decrees. Even former volunteers for military service were not exempt from the special Jewish taxes and could not enter the city of Warsaw unless they paid the

Billet fee. The memorandum on the abolition of military service for the Jews which the Committee of Jewish Deputies submitted to the Council of State in April, 1811, primarily expressed trenchant political conviction rather than religious orthodoxy. Was it just, they asked, that inhabitants already burdened with special taxes and denied all civil rights should still be required to perform all civic duties.*

This time, however, the attempts by the Kehillah representatives to have the military service annulled encountered a receptive attitude in government circles. At the beginning of December, 1811, by order of the Minister of the Exchequer, a national meeting of Jewish deputies took place at Warsaw. The subject of the discussions which ensued between the Conference of Jewish Deputies and exchequer officials was the rate of the recruits' tax to be collected in lieu of military service. An agreement was finally signed whereby the conference deputies, acting on behalf of the Jewish population, undertook to pay punctually an annual recruits' tax totalling 700,000 zloty. The ducal warrant of January 29, 1812, was framed in the light of that agreement.

In 1812, the special taxes imposed on the Jews reached their highest level. In the same year, the government issued a new edict of unprecedented harshness. The royal warrant of October, 1812 decreed that as from July 1, 1814, Jews in cities and rural areas were forbidden to trade in alcoholic beverages, serve them, engage in their manufacture, or even live in taverns, inns, breweries or distilleries. This measure, which would have deprived practically half the Jewish population of its income, was unique in the history of the modern period. Even the severe repressive measure enacted by Joseph II against the Jews of Galicia had only applied to rural Jews. Explanations accompanying the warrant mentioned the detrimental effect of the Jewish liquor business on the Duchy's inhabitants, especially the peasants, and also a "desire, this time, to transfer those Jewish families engaged in these callings to occupations more useful for the country's population as a whole." However, despite this promise the government of the Grand Duchy did not even attempt to compensate the Jewish liquor purveyors as had been done in Galicia and Russia. There, the governments—if only for the sake of appearances—had announced government-aided colonization of the Jews simultaneously with the enactments against the publicans. The Warsaw government's sole object was to eliminate the Jews from an area of economic activity that was of great importance in the backward state. The Jews were to be replaced by estate-owners or their friends in the rural areas, and in the cities and towns by the Polish burghers, who became increasingly involved in the liquor trade under the Grand Duchy of Warsaw. In the western areas of the Duchy, Jews had been driven out of liquor selling and innkeeping under the old Polish

* A divergent attitude was adopted by the leaders of the Inowroclaw Kehillah. They accompanied their approval of military service for Jews with the demand for release from payment of special taxes.

régime. It was no coincidence that this decree was issued at a time when Napoleon's forces had occupied areas of Lithuania and White Russia in the Russian campaign. The Minister of Police of the Grand Duchy specifically cited Poland's hope of annexing this land as a decisive reason for expediting implementation of the decree. A memorandum which the Jewish representatives submitted to the Tsar in 1814 stated that 200,000 Jews had been affected by the 1812 decree. Strong intercession by the Jewish Council and the delegates from the Warsaw Kehillah persuaded the Provisional Government in 1815 to defer implementation of the decree for an additional year. It was gradually implemented under the Congress Kingdom of Poland.

The harsh governmental decrees in the Grand Duchy all struck at the poverty-stricken Jewish masses. They bore the heavy load of general and special taxes; were crowded into ghettos at Warsaw, Plock, Krakow, Lublin, and other cities; restricted in their retail trading activities and hampered by the craft guilds by decrees barring them from manual occupations. Indubitable proof of the extent of their increasing poverty was provided by the fact that, despite the heavy punishments imposed on Kehillot and individual Jews who defaulted in their kosher meat tax payments, the total actually collected constantly decreased. During the fiscal year 1812-13, total revenue from the kosher meat tax amounted to 942,000 zloty—only 29 per cent of the budgetary figure of 3,263,040 zloty! At the same time, however, there was a progressive increase in capital held by the Jewish propertied class and especially the leading magnates whose businesses expanded and prospered in conditions of unceasing warfare. This sector of Jewish society included a few bankers, some of them German Jews who had settled in Warsaw under the Prussian régime, wholesale merchants, suppliers, purveyors and kosher meat tax farmers. Most of them lived in Warsaw. Although there were no more than forty families of this type in the capital, their function in the country's economy, especially as army contractors, was very great.

Even the well-to-do formed only a tiny minority of the Jewish population. The Krakow Kehillah was a typical example of income distribution, though most of its members did, in fact, engage in trade, and artisans only constituted a quarter of Kehillah membership. When the Departmental Prefect ruled that only those paying a direct annual Kehillah tax of at least forty zloty could exercise the right to vote in elections to the Kehillah executive, it appeared that only twelve individuals out of approximately 1,000 family heads (5,000 people) qualified. When the Prefect reduced the required annual minimum to twenty zloty in the light of this situation, there were still only seventy-five qualified voters. This thin layer of wealthy people, headed by the powerful magnates, exercised control over all the Kehillot. Towards the end of the period of the Grand Duchy, the six leaders of the Warsaw Kehillah (three *Parnassim*, three administrators) included three major suppliers (Berek Szmulewicz, Moses Aaron Fuerstenberg, Jakob Epstein), and one banker (Samuel Kronenberg).

With this social composition, the Kehillah executive obviously gave fullest support to the wealthy class that had entrusted it with power. A letter of protest to the Krakow Kehillah leaders in 1812 indicated the degree of resentment which their policy had evoked amongst the Kehillah poor:

> To the Kehillah Heads,
>   We warn you to stop collecting taxes from the poor; we do not even have enough bread to eat, and know this, that if you will not cease to inflict these taxes on us, we shall be forced to set fire to the entire Jewish quarter and you will not be able to prevent this. We are twenty who have banded together because we have nothing to eat . . . We would be prepared to become servants except that, first, that would be humiliating, and, second, nobody will employ us.*

At Inowroclaw in 1809, the Kehillah leaders reported to the Prefect that eighty family heads were preparing to offer "concerted resistance by force" if an attempt were made to collect their tax according to the assessors' apportionment.

The line of demarcation between the various classes in the Jewish population clearly appeared in the intercessions made by the Jewish representatives for the abolition of the various decrees. The representatives of Kehillot in provincial towns, who had closer links with the broad Jewish population, repeatedly submitted memoranda to the government protesting against the heavy taxes. When these failed, they still endeavoured to secure all possible concessions in the size of the tax. The Warsaw Kehillah leaders, on the other hand, represented the rising class of great Jewish capitalists in the capital and devoted their efforts to the removal of restrictions affecting the Jewish financiers and to the achievement of complete civil equality, promised under the Constitution, for a small group within their own class. It was characteristic that, in 1809, when the government consulted the Warsaw Kehillah leaders about replacing the various special taxes with one uniform tax, the leaders proposed a kosher meat tax. On November 30, 1808, shortly after the royal warrant suspending Jewish political rights and their right to purchase land, a petition was submitted to the King in the name of the Kehillah of Warsaw and in the name of the signatories—five wealthy Jews, suppliers and merchants. They complained that they had not been granted permission to purchase plots of land and houses in the city of Warsaw and to build factories. They also voiced their grievance at the ban on marriages between the daughters of Warsaw Jews and men from outside the city.

* This letter has been preserved in a Polish translation prepared by the Kehillah secretary in 1812. It is quoted in M. Balaban's *Historja Zydow w Krakowie i na Kazimierzu*, Vol. 11, p. 594, Krakow, 1936.

Finally, they requested that the Jewish people not be regarded as distinct from the nation of which it was a part, and that the Jews be granted all the civil and political rights enjoyed by the rest of the population on the basis of the Constitution "the creation of Napoleon the Great."

The King not only rejected this complaint and indicated that Jewish reforms were in preparation (he was referring to the Government Committee, which never completed its work). He also issued the warrant already mentioned for the expulsion of the Jews from Warsaw's main thoroughfares. On March 17, 1809, the day after the promulgation of this measure, a request was submitted to the Senate in the name of the Warsaw Kehillah, bearing the signatures of the same five wealthy men. Basing their arguments on the concept of human equality and "the wisdom of Napoleon's legislation," the laws "of God and nature," they enumerated the worst evils afflicting Poles "who adhere to the Old Testament." These included the burden of special taxes and the ban on "purchasing estates and building homes, establishing farms, factories, or carrying on unrestricted trade." Furthermore, the announcement of their exclusion from the main streets of Warsaw now added to their problems. And, naturally, they did not omit complaint about the denial of the right to vote. While maintaining this attitude of solidarity with the common body of Jews, they could not abstain from an allusion to themselves and their class as most worthy of the government's good graces. They answered the argument that Jews were not in favour of cleanliness by explaining that this was the result of poverty and was common to members of all religions. As part of their arguments they asked, "Are the many to be penalized for the wrongdoing of the few?" and answered, with the obvious intention of strengthening their own case, "To us, especially, no man can prove that we have transgressed, that we have done evil through usury, or other offences. . . ." They even declared, without mentioning that they did so on their own responsibility, that the Jews would be willing to change their traditional dress should the supreme authorities issue an order to that effect.

This request was also rejected. The Warsaw Kehillah representatives ceased to intercede for the rights of the Jewish community as a whole and the class that they themselves represented.

Even earlier, however, the Jewish *nouveau bourgeois* group of Warsaw had taken positive action to secure for its own class the rights withheld from the Jews in general. On January 5, 1809, the Minister of Justice was presented with a petition, signed by seventeen merchants, bankers and contractors.* It referred to the promise in paragraph 2 of the Royal Warrant of political rights to individuals who deserved them and declared:

* Including the banker, Samuel Kronenberg, and the supplier, Jacob Epstein, who were members of the Warsaw Kehillah executive during the Grand Duchy's final years, if not actually at the time the petition was signed.

... The undersigned have for a long time now endeavoured to draw closer to the rest of the inhabitants in their moral comportment and similarity of attire, and they are now certain that they have ceased to be unworthy of civil rights. They are also certain of this because they ardently desire to be of help to the country in which they were born or reside and loyally to discharge all the duties the government and the state will impose on them.

It ended with the hope that should the Minister respond to their request, many "members of the Mosaic persuasion" would make an effort to follow their example and win the grace of the Grand Duchy's Constitution by the acquisition of learning.

Several men who signed this petition were too impatient to wait for a reply from the Minister of Justice. Despite "the utmost certitude" expressed in their memorandum, they determined to make doubly certain of success. Four days later, on January 9, 1809, a petition was submitted to Frederick Augustus of Saxony, Grand Duke of Warsaw, in the name of thirteen of the signatories and "in the name of other German (Jewish) families that had been born or had settled in this city (Warsaw)." They included three bankers, two foreign exchange dealers, three wholesale merchants, one supplier, one book dealer and publisher, and one engraver. This memorandum was largely a copy of the one that had been submitted to the Minister of Justice a few days earlier, except that it carried obsequiousness even further.

However, neither their social "polish" nor their empty "enlightenment" was of any help to the financial magnates. Similar failure was encountered by various private individuals who pleaded for Royal exemption solely for themselves. A wealthy Warsaw merchant, Michael Ettinger Rawski (originally Reb Mikheleh Raver), addressed a personal entreaty to the King on March 21, 1809, hardly four days after signing a joint partition to the Senate with four other representatives of the Warsaw Kehillah. Rawski, according to his petition, was willing to be the sole recipient of civil rights. "In every society," he contended, "there are good people and there are boors." The characteristics distinguishing the Jews from the remainder of the population, and which had caused their exclusion by Royal Warrant from the enjoyment of civil rights, were, "their unethical demeanour, their lack of utility to the country, and their attitude of indifference towards its best interests." He himself excelled in all these things. "Hence," he wrote, "it is clear that an individual differing from the other members of his persuasion should be excepted from the general body of people to whom this severe legislation applies."

Michael Rawski was not unique amongst the Jews. The reaction to the royal decree of the first representatives of the modern Jewish capitalist group, which was beginning to break away from the old Jewish community of Poland, was no different from that of the *nouveau bourgeois* Jews of

France to Napoleon's *Infamous Decree*. In both cases, the decrees aroused a panic of abasement before the authorities and an abandonment of the masses of their own people in order to secure their own privileges.*

The indefatigable efforts of the Jewish financial magnates to obtain political rights for their class as a whole or for themselves as individuals were not directed towards the title of citizenship *per se*. Their principal aim was to gain the right to acquire immovable property and especially landholdings through unqualified citizenship. If the Jewish bankers and commissionaries had been allowed to acquire estates from the nobles, they could also have appropriated the debts that the landed proprietors owed to them and invested their capital in profitable enterprises. At this time, the estates of the nobility were selling at public auctions at extremely low prices, often at a quarter of their value. The fact that enfranchisement would have involved this economic right explained the obstinacy of the government at Warsaw on the issue.

Still, the new Jewish middle class in the Grand Duchy, especially in the capital, did record some successes. A few score of the "enlightened" families (their "enlightenment" consisted of the possession of vast riches, of having shaved their beards, donned modern clothing and learned how to sign their names in a non-Jewish language) received permission to live wherever they chose in Warsaw at a time when their unpropertied, "unenlightened" fellow Jews had been ordered to crowd into a special quarter. The government programme to promote capitalist development also caused it to retract its ruling on Jewish purchases of buildings and lots in the cities, in contrast with its attitude on the acquisition of rural estates. In Warsaw, the same group of Jewish capitalists that had gained the right to live anywhere in the city, now enjoyed this right as well. In the larger provincial cities, and in a number of small towns, several score of buildings in each place passed into the hands of Jewish purchasers. This process, which associated the slow but constant progress of capitalist relationships in production prompted the government of Congress Poland several years later to hasten promulgation of the decree establishing special Jewish *Revirs* in most cities in the country.

Predawn of Haskalah and the beginning of Assimilation;
Expectations of Redemption

The changes that took place in the cultural life of the Jews of Poland at the beginning of the nineteenth century, during the twenty years of Prussian rule and under the Grand Duchy of Warsaw, only affected the summit of the middle class, just emerging from the general community which was congealed in its hereditary way of life. The Warsaw salons of some members of this topmost social stratum of contractors and bankers

* *cf. supra*, Chapter Three, C.p. 74

had even become meeting places for senior French officers. Isolated instances of conversion within plutocratic Jewish families were already reported at that time, resembling on a miniature scale the conversion mania that had seized the Jewish financial magnates and *salon* hosts of Berlin. A case in point was that of the two daughters, together with their own families, of Samuel Zbytkower, a prominent commissionary and communal leader during the reign of Stanislaus Augustus. These converts had begun to take an active part in the cultural life of the capital together with the Frankist colony, which had not hitherto intermarried. The *Haskalah* movement, which at that time was moving from Germany to the eastern part of central Europe, Bohemia, Moravia and Silesia, and had even penetrated into the Posen district and Galicia, seemed to have halted at the frontiers of central Poland. There was only one subscriber to the *Me'asef* in all central Poland—a resident of Warsaw. Not one organized group of central Polish *Maskilim* was recorded in that period, and there were only two *Haskalah* writers in the whole country, Abraham Stern, a physicist from Hrubieszow, who first came to the fore during the time of Congress Poland (i.e., under Russian rule), and the grammarian, Tobias Feder.

In the absence of any broad, general *Haskalah* movement, the thin layer of Jewish *nouveaux riches* in Warsaw was attracted towards a superficial form of assimilation. The initiative here came from German Jews who had settled in Warsaw under Prussian rule. At the opening of the nineteenth century, a group of German Jews had founded their own synagogue in Warsaw which came to be known popularly as the German Synagogue (*Die Daitshe Shul*) because the members of its congregation differed from the other Jews in their German language and "German" dress. Several enlightened and semi-enlightened people close to this small circle also made a number of attempts to found a secular school for Jewish children in Warsaw.

However, the Jewish masses in Poland remained remote from all *Haskalah* influence, and it was just at this time that Hasidism, which had already swept the Ukraine, Galicia, and several areas of Lithuania and White Russia, now spread to this territory.

The atmosphere at the end of the eighteenth and beginning of the nineteenth centuries was particularly propitious to the spread of this popular religious movement amongst the vast number of Polish Jews. The ever-increasing oppression that had begun under Prussian and Austrian rule and continued under the Grand Duchy of Warsaw, the heavy tax burden and deepening poverty, forced them to seek support and refuge in religious ecstasy. As exile and servitude became continually harder to endure, they put increasing hope in divine salvation. They turned to their leaders, the *Tzaddikim* to whom they attributed the power to nullify repressive decrees and hasten the coming of deliverance. Furthermore, this era which was giving birth to a new world when revolution and incessant war was shaking the foundations of powerful kingdoms, could only strengthen the faith that the ordeals they were suffering were merely Messianic travails heralding imminent redemption. Even Poland had experienced several decisive changes of régime within less than twenty years. The Kings of Prussia and Austria had inherited the ancient Kingdom of Poland; Napoleon's armies had established the Grand Duchy of Warsaw; and Napoleon's defeat had brought the Czar to power. They calculated the date of the approaching climax on the basis of the numerical value of scriptural passages, attempting appropriate interpretations of Biblical prophecies, and meanwhile expected deliverance from one year to the next. Even in the Posen district, where Hasidism never gained a serious foothold, the rabbis summoned the people to repentance, so that they could partake of the coming redemption, for example, Rabbi Joel Asch of Schoenlanke. Popular opinion credited the year 1810 with intimations of redemption, on the evidence of the prayer opening with the words *Blow the Great Horn for our Freedom*.* The rabbis, therefore, warned their congregations to stay awake during the night of the Eve of Passover (traditionally termed "The Night of Vigil") lest they miss the arrival of the Prophet Elijah. When these expectations were not fulfilled, fresh hopes arose in 1812 in connection with the defeat of Napoleon. In this case, homiletical interpretations were made of the prophecy concerning *The End of the Days* made by Balaam: *But ships shall come from the coast of Kittim, and they shall afflict Asshur, and shall afflict Eber, and he shall also come to destruction* (Numbers, 24, 24). Again, 1814, by Hebrew reckoning the year 574 of the sixth millennium, was construed as forecasting the Messiah's clarion.† Unceasing efforts to calculate when the End would arrive continued until the end of the sixth century of the sixth millennium.‡

The hearts of all the Hasidim overflowed with the anticipation of Deliverance. So strongly did their leaders in Poland and neighbouring Galicia believe that the Days of Deliverance were at hand that, the three leading figures of the generation—the *Tzaddikim* of Lublin, Kozienice and Rymanow—are reported to have met to arouse the quality of Divine Mercy by joint prayer and thus bring about the coming of the Messiah. At this meeting, after deliberation, they resolved in accordance with the prophecy of Zachariah that the Ninth of Av would become a day of rejoicing after the coming of the Messiah. This meeting was traditionally said to have been arranged after Napoleon's final defeat was assured. Previously, under the Grand Duchy, the *Tzaddikim* had differed on Napoleon's function in the pattern of Israel's Redemption. A number of Hasidic legends showed that this divergence of opinion had not yet

---

* The Hebrew year, stated in centuries of the sixth millenium from the Creation, was 570: and the letters expressing this number (*Tav* (400) + *qof* (100) + *'Ain* (70)), as a word read *Te'qa*, which is the imperative of the verb "blow".

† The letter Daleth read as the conventional abbreviation for the name of God.

‡ 5600, or 1839–40 C.E.

appeared in 1809 when Napoleon and the Grand Duchy of Warsaw were at war with Austria. The Hasidim hated Austria so passionately, particularly because of the heavy taxes and the assimilation decrees, that even *Tzaddikim* who were not particularly sympathetic either to Napoleon or to Poland prayed for its defeat, comparing it to the Amalek of biblical times. Disagreements on the attitude towards Napoleon and the Grand Duchy of Warsaw were especially prominent in 1812, when Napoleon marched on Russia.

An unqualified supporter of Napoleon was Rabbi Mendel of Frysztak in Galicia, known as Rymanower since he had transferred his seat to the town of Rymanow. Rabbi Mendel regarded Napoleon as both the warrior for justice and the commander-in-chief in the war of Gog and Magog which was to precede the Deliverance. He knew that Deliverance must be purchased with bloodshed and endless suffering, and was reported as saying: "It is well that the blood of Israel should be spilled and that from Frysztak to Rymanow people should walk up to their knees in blood, that our Deliverance may come." That year, Passover was not only celebrated as a commemoration of the Deliverance from Egyptian bondage but also as the spring season holiday heralding the springtime of Redemption. Legend, not always reliable in the matter of correct historical sequence, also associated Rabbi Mendel's prayers with Napoleon's victory over the Russians on Passover 1812, although that particular war was only imminent at the time; it did not break out until June 23. The same legend depicted Rabbi Mendel on Passover Eve, "on which day there was a great and mighty battle, standing holding the *Matzot* out towards the oven, repeating 'another 500 Russians will fall,' and thus it happened in the war." Hasidic legend gave the following account of Rabbi Mendel's reasons for supporting Napoleon: when Rabbi Mendel ordered all those visiting him to pray for Napoleon's victory, Rabbi Naphtali of Ropczyce asked him in amazement, "Are they to pray then for the spread of apostasy?" Rabbi Mendel answered him, "They are all apostates, they all want *Shkolles* (schools). Now, *his* patron angel is an angel of justice! Let Napoleon triumph and let all behold and realize. (As Hillel the Elder has said in *The Ethics of the Fathers*), *Because thou drownedst others, they have drowned thee.* . . . Nations that have conquered . . . now shall they be conquered nations. Let all men know that there is a law and a judge!"

Many contradictory legends surrounded the standpoint that the two leaders of Hasidism in central Poland, Rabbi Jacob Isaac of Lublin and Rabbi Israel the *Maggid* of Kozienice took up. However, the historical truth they concealed indicates that the *Maggid* of Kozienice was a close friend of Prince Adam Czartoryski and was also greatly respected by the provincial authorities. It would seem that this *Tzaddik* was also expressing the political views of the Prince in his attitude towards Napoleon. At first, his position towards Napoleon was purely negative, but under the Grand Duchy of Warsaw, he prayed for his victory; after his first defeat, he turned away from him and predicted his downfall. The "seer" of Lublin, who was more moderate than his colleagues, adopted a neutral stand of no confidence in either belligerent and was content to wait and hope for the Messiah's coming after both sides had been vanquished.

The great majority of the Jewish population of the Grand Duchy would seem to have adhered to this neutrality during the war of 1812. There were, of course, individual young Jews then, as in the war of 1809, who were swept away by the current of patriotism that gripped the country and volunteered for the crusade to expand and glorify Poland. The small number of "enlightened" Jews, the suppliers and bankers, who had profited greatly from the war, were in absolute and unqualified sympathy with the Grand Duchy and Napoleon. The great mass of Jews, however, could say in the words of a gentile poet—with whom many of them only later became familiar, as the *Haskalah* movement gained momentum—*A Plague on both your houses!* The anti-Jewish measures of the government of the Grand Duchy and particularly the prohibition on their engaging in the liquor trade, made known at the beginning of that year, in no way encouraged the oppressed Jews to hope that their situation would improve should the Duchy be victorious and the Polish Kingdom reconstituted with its former broad boundaries. On the other hand, they could hardly pray for the victory of Russian arms, knowing, as they undoubtedly did, of the régime's decrees against Jewish occupations, including their expulsion from the villages, and vividly remembering Cossack excesses at Praga scarcely eighteen years before. Not surprisingly, therefore, some Hasidic legends consistently described the war of 1812 as the War of the Angel of Esau (Poland) against the Angel of Yavan (Greece, i.e., Russia).

This attitude did not prevent Kehillot throughout the Grand Duchy feeling an obligation to refrain from open dissidence and also to demonstrate their patriotism in public manifestos, by participation in war loans, and by contributing to the needs of the war.

The religious leaders of the Jewish people in Poland, the rabbis and Hasidic *Tzaddikim*, received the news of Napoleon's defeat in Russia with mixed emotions. The well-known *Halakhah* scholar, Rabbi Akiva Eiger, then Chief Rabbi in the city of Markisch-Friedland in Prussian Pomerania, applied to the vanquished leader the passage from Psalms, 92, 8: *When the wicked spring up as the grass, and when all the workers of iniquity do flourish, it is that they may be destroyed forever.* This attitude concealed the hatred the conservative felt for the symbol of revolution and the threat to religion that he represented. But it also expressed the hope that the restoration of Prussian rule to western Poland would lead to an improvement in the position of the Jews. The *Tzaddikim*, who dominated the Jewish mood in central Poland, regarded Napoleon's defeat as a new portent of the approaching Days of the Messiah. Confidence was widespread amongst the Hasidim that the *Tzaddikim* had actually predicted the end of Napoleon from intimations in the Bible, for example, the phonetic similarity to Napoleon's name in passages such as *Thou shalt surely fall* in the Book of Esther, 6, 13. By the beginning of 1813, the forces of Alexander I had entered Warsaw and the Jews of Poland were plunged in hopelessness. Existing discriminatory laws were coupled in autonomous Congress Poland with new rigid enactments which the government of the Grand Duchy had already planned, but had been unable to carry through. The triumph of reaction throughout Europe also affected the life of the Jews of Poland, smarting in their state of oppression and yearning for deliverance.

CHAPTER ELEVEN

RUSSIA

(RUSSIA, WHITE RUSSIA, LITHUANIA AND THE UKRAINE)

First Jewish Settlements in the Eighteenth Century (up to the first partition of Poland)

By the end of the eighteenth century, Russia—the largest state in Europe—held the greatest Jewish centre in the Diaspora. Until about the beginning of the century, it was still almost totally without Jews. From the Middle Ages, when the Russian capital was transferred from Kiev to Moscow, Jews were no longer allowed to enter its territories, except for temporary visits by Polish and Lithuanian Jews for purposes of trade—and even they encountered great difficulties. The jealousy that Russian merchants evinced towards any foreign competition assumed in the case of the Jews the form of religious animosity as well as fear of the influence of the Jewish faith. The rulers of Russia, influenced by economic considerations and religious bigotry, had inserted clauses "except for Jews" in the peace treaties with Poland in 1678 and 1686, which allowed trade between the countries to flow unimpeded. This qualifying phrase henceforth became a permanent feature of all Russian legislation until the revolution of 1917 overthrew the Czarist régime. The anti-Jewish prejudice, the result of continuous incitement by the dominant Greek Orthodox Church over the centuries, was so deeply rooted in the Russian population that even the radical reformer, Peter the Great, did not find it possible to relax any of the existing decrees during his consolidation of Russian absolutism.

Nevertheless, despite repeated prohibitions, a small number of Jews did succeed in penetrating three frontier provinces, which had been annexed to Russia during the wars with Poland, as early as the second half of the seventeenth century and, especially, during Peter's reign at the beginning of the eighteenth century. In all three provinces concerned, the Ukraine beyond the Dnieper, the province of Smolensk, and Livonia (the Latvian city of Riga), Jews from beyond the frontier traded whenever fairs were held, and also throughout the year; some had even settled permanently with their families. However, temporary business visits as well as permanent residence inside the borders of the state were subject to frequent interruptions by expulsion decrees during this period.

The Czarina Elizabeth, in the throes of religious fanaticism, determined to bring all the Christian inhabitants of her realm into the Greek Orthodox Church. Her harsh measures against apostates incidentally served to distract the clergy from her plans to appropriate Church properties for the state. During her reign, many dissident sectarians (*Raskolniki*) were forced to flee to neighbouring provinces in the Kingdom of Poland. Persecution was also directed against the Moslem Tartars and idol-worshippers in the eastern areas of her lands (Kirghizians, Kalmuks) whom she attempted forcibly to christianize even after they had adopted Islam from their Tartar neighbours. In 1742, she expelled the Jews from all her territories and threatened drastic reprisals against all officials who delayed implementing this order. The decree also applied to the temporary entry of Jews concerned with trade. A Senate request that Jewish traders be allowed into the Ukraine to prevent injury to the country's commerce was refused. Its proposal that temporary entry be permitted to Jewish traders provoked the Empress to reply, "From the enemies of Christ I desire neither benefits nor profits." Nonetheless, the Empress stipulated in her expulsion decree that Jews driven out of the Ukraine were to surrender all the silver and gold coins in their possession to the authorities and to receive only copper coins in exchange.

The Jews of White Russia under the Russian Empire

In the second half of the eighteenth century, as a result of the partition of Poland, the Jews of White Russia, Lithuania, and the Ukrainian districts came under the rule of the Russian Empire. The Russian state was now confronted with the problem of hundreds of thousands of Jews inside its boundaries together with all its other newly acquired subjects, instead of facing only questions of temporary entry permits for individual Jews or the expulsion of a few hundred who had crept into the frontier areas. However, the revision in the Russian government's policy towards the Jews was also necessitated by changes taking place at the same time in the economy, the social and political régime, and the cultural situation.

This vast empire, stretching across the Eurasian land-mass to the Pacific Ocean in the Far East, had already acquired an outlet on the Baltic Sea with the conquests of Peter the Great. It reached the shores of the Black Sea in the south following Catherine II's wars against Turkey. Its increasing productive capacity affected all branches of the economy and was followed by marked progress in Russian culture and learning. In the second half of the eighteenth-century, during Catherine's reign (1762-96), Russia entered the stage of enlightened absolutism in its economic, political, and cultural development. The "enlightened" sovereign herself espoused the ideas of Montesquieu, Voltaire and Beccaria, corresponded with the French Encyclopedists, and composed essays in the spirit of the European Enlightenment.

The new dynamic economic forces were not sufficient to alter the foundations of the political and social system and Russia continued to be a feudal monarchy with a powerful nobility. Nevertheless, economic development exerted a strong influence on the policies of this monarchy, despite its firm feudal basis. At the same time as it conferred practically absolute feudal privilege upon the dominant nobility over their serfs, the government was compelled to promote the country's economic development by fostering industry and trade—if only to entrench its position at home and abroad.

This dual trend also determined the Russian government's attitude towards the Jews who had come under its rule after the partition of Poland. Its new Jewish subjects benefited from the Russian monarchy's interest in the development of trade and industry, which founded its ideological expression in the Enlightenment concepts of the importance of the burghers and of human equality regardless of racial origins or religious principles. They were granted legal status, economic rights and even some political rights. This represented appreciable progress in relation to their position under feudal Poland. On the other hand, the essentially feudal character of the Russian régime, which had firm ties with the dominant Christian Church, required that Jewish economic rights be limited in order to preserve intact the privileges of the nobles and prevent competition with the Russian merchant class. Furthermore, measures were taken to ensure that the Jews should not achieve total equality with burghers of the Christian faith, even in terms of political rights.

In 1772, the first partition of Poland took place and the greater part of White Russia was annexed to Russia. In September, 1772, the provincial General-Gubernator, Count Chernyshev, published a proclamation (*Plakat*) to the population in the name of the Empress promising the new subjects, "without exceptions," all rights enjoyed by the other subjects of the realm. The Jews were specifically mentioned:

> By virtue of the aforementioned solemn commitment concerning freedom of religious worship and the inviolability of each individual's property, it is self-evident that all these liberties of religion and property which they now enjoy, will be maintained and preserved for the Hebrew communities residing in the cities and territories that have been added to the Russian Empire: for her Imperial Majesty's love of her fellow men does not allow her to exclude them from those favours bestowed upon all under her blessed reign so long as they, for their part, will abide by the obedience befitting loyal subjects and will persevere in their callings, the various contemporary branches of trade and the crafts.

The Jews were accordingly designated *Yevreii* (Hebrews) in the imperial proclamation and in all future official documents, instead of *Zhidi* as before, which had an approbrious connotation in the Russian language.

(Only documents drawn up by local authorities continued to employ the old appelation during the first few years after the inauguration of this policy.)

A census taken in 1772, during the year following the annexation, showed 25,018 males, or a total of 50,000 Jews, in the province of White Russia, or Byelorussia. However, as the object of the census was to assess the Poll Tax, a considerable number of "vanished" individuals should be added. A more accurate estimate would therefore be between 60,000 and 65,000 Jews. Sixty per cent of those counted lived in cities and towns, the remainder in villages.

The Jews constituted 29 per cent or less than a third of all the inhabitants in the cities and towns of the province. However, the proportion was distinctly greater in specifically urban economies, especially in the private cities and towns, where they were the decisive factor in commerce. Even in the gubernatorial district of Polotzk (renamed the district of Vitebsk in 1802), where Christian traders prevailed, there were cities where the Jewish inhabitants were almost the only people engaged in commerce. Shklov, a private city belonging to a nobleman, had a wider range of trade than all the others, and practically all its merchants were Jews. Shklov became the centre of trade between White Russia and the interior from the beginning of Russian rule. Traders from Moscow, Kursk, Orlov, Kiev and other cities of the Empire came to the Shklov fairs, though they were primarily a meeting place for merchants from the entire province. The merchants of Shklov also exported Moscow merchandise to the Leipzig fairs (especially furs, which Jewish artisans dressed and dyed).

In contrast with their role in trade, the Jews only formed a small minority in most branches of handicraft as compared with Christians. Because of the economic and social backwardness of the area, most of the White Russian Jews—all the rural Jews and many of those in the towns—were engaged in some way in the leasing of liquor distilleries, taverns and inns. Nearly all the village inns and most of the inns and taverns in the towns were held on lease by Jews. For the most part, they also held leases on the flour mills as well as on road and bridge tolls. Occasionally, the lease contracts even specifically stipulated that the peasants purchase their small supplies, usually consisting of salt, herrings, sickles, tar and similar consumer goods from the Jewish innkeeper. Similarly they were required to sell him their surplus agricultural products: grain, poultry, flax, hemp, honey and so on. It was also quite a common occurrence for the peasants to repay the principal and interest of their debts to the innkeeper for liquor with produce to the value of the money due. The rural Jews thus complemented the very valuable function that the urban Jews fulfilled in Russian trade: apart from the fact that their inns were indispensable to the transport system of the country, they supplied goods to the peasants and sent peasant produce to the market. It was only through the medium of the Jewish lessees, innkeepers and liquor sellers that the White Russian peasant's flax, hemp and honey reached Riga and Königsberg and from there the most distant markets of Europe. In White Russia, as in most of the eastern European countries, the Jews were the decisive factor in the development of a mercantile economy.

The government faced a complicated problem when determining the organizational pattern for the Jews and their position within the class system of the state. Under the current system in Russia, every subject belonged to a corporate body and was attached to it in all fiscal, legal and administrative matters. The peasants were attached to their masters and, in the imperial estates, to their village communes; the townsmen were liable to the local authorities. Rural and urban communities were responsible for tax payments by their respective members. In the light of this general situation, the government at first attached all Jews to the existing Kehillot. In 1772, an order was issued, in connection with the poll tax, also levied on burghers and peasants, "to have the Jews registered in their Kehillot and also to found new Kehillot, if necessary, as the governors saw fit."

This situation, where the Jews constituted a distinct class in the hierarchy of the general population and where their Kehillah institutions enjoyed a wide range of autonomy, was drastically revised in 1778, when the law of 1775 on the organization of the gubernatorial departments became operative in White Russia. This law subdivided the urban population into merchants, with assets assessed at 500 rubles or more, and burghers, whose property was valued at less than this sum. It also made the Jews subject to the general law courts instead of the Kehillah tribunals. Urban Jews were required to submit their litigation to the magistrates and rural Jews to the district courts, which tried the cases of free peasants. The Jews could, like the free peasants who sat as assessors in the district courts, also have the assistance of a representative of the district Kehillah in their litigation. However, this new scheme basically altered the status of the Jews as a distinctive class even more than it curtailed the autonomy of the individual Kehillot.

By 1779, wealthy Jewish merchants were applying to the Chief Governor of the two gubernias of White Russia for permission to be included in the merchant class. At the beginning of 1780, Catherine granted these requests and specifically observed that Jewish merchants were under no obligations to pay a larger capital tax than other members of the merchant class. This decision logically resulted in a government directive of 1783 to include all White Russian Jews, with lower assets, in the burgher class.

In addition to total fiscal equality, their new status as burghers and merchants endowed the Jews with the political rights of electing and being elected to municipal administration bodies and law courts. The Czarina actually replied in 1785 to objections from representatives of the burghers to these equal rights, with an explicit order not to hinder the Jews from serving in any offices to which they might be elected. The Charter of Rights and Privileges for the Towns, also issued in 1785, granted the towns a new system of self-government, though under stringent government supervision, in the form of a Council, or *Duma*, elected every three years by inhabitants of the city who belonged to any of the six established categories. A Senate resolution confirmed Jewish electoral rights to these municipal *dumas*. To all appearances then, the Jews of White Russia enjoyed equal rights with all the other inhabitants of the cities and were only inferior to their neighbours as far as the rights to hold government positions and to acquire immovables were concerned (in 1776 this had been made conditional on religious conversion). No other country in Europe prior to the French Revolution could compare with Russia in respect of the legal status of the Jews and certainly in all matters pertaining to their rights of participation in municipal government.

It is not surprising, therefore, that the spokesmen of the enlightened Jewish middle class of Germany were entranced with the "favours" that the Russian monarchy showered upon the Jews. During the Napoleonic age, they still envied their co-religionists in the east, and the German-language periodical *Sulamith* cited Russia, together with France, as a model for all European states. Needless to say, the White Russian Kehillot themselves were generous in their praise of the Empress.

In fact, only the wealthy Jewish traders benefited from inclusion in the merchant or burgher class, whereas the danger to the majority of the Jewish population inherent in the new legal position soon became obvious. Even the right to vote in municipal elections encountered obstacles in practice and at times its actual benefits were offset by disadvantages. Through the inclusion of Jewish village inhabitants amongst the burghers, the Jews had become a majority in the burgher and merchant class of White Russia. The census of 1783 already showed that they constituted three-fifths, or 59 per cent, of the burgher class. Their proportions within the merchant class were even higher (63 per cent in 1783, 66 per cent in 1785), though within the Jewish population only one in every fourteen Jews was registered as a merchant. Christian merchants outnumbered the Jews only in the small gubernia of Polotzk, by 646 to 467. If the Jews had been allowed to employ their voting rights in proportion to their numbers within these two classes, they would certainly have gained control of municipal and judicial offices in most of the cities. However, when actually enforcing this law, the government was not prepared to renounce the principles of the feudal system and found it necessary to secure a majority for its Christian subjects in the municipal institutions.

The instruction of the White Russian authorities only permitted half the number of qualified electors to be placed by Jews on the voting lists in cities where they formed a majority of the population; in other cities they had the right to participate in election meetings with the general body of merchants and townsmen. As a result, in 1784, twenty-five Jews were elected to municipal posts in ten cities of the Moghilev gubernia: seven mayors, nine councillors, eight judges and one city elder. But in both the cities of Moghilev and Orsha, where the Jewish merchants far outnumbered their Christian colleagues, only one Jewish judge was chosen. The population of the Polotzk gubernia evinced even greater opposition to the Jews: a total of four Jews in two cities out of eleven in the gubernia as a whole were elected to office. Jewish representatives complained, in a letter to the Empress in 1784, that a Jewish defendant could expect all kinds of abuses at his trial in the absence of Jewish judges from the municipal courts, as a result of the electoral system in force: "The Jew, who has none to defend him in the courtroom, cannot be sure, what with his fear and his ignorance of the Russian language, that no evil will befall him even though not guilty. . . ." Furthermore, this memorandum openly charged the Christian municipal authorities with discrimination against the Jews.

The partial emancipation that Russian absolutism had granted to the Jews thus created certain problems: they had forfeited the protection that the former régime of administrative and judicial Kehillah autonomy had provided without receiving in exchange the full protection of the new order. However, the "enlightened" régime, with its egalitarian façade and feudal substance, then proceeded to deal an immeasurably more severe blow aimed directly at the economic existence of the majority of the Jewish population.

The classification of the Jews as burghers could be interpreted as a legal basis for expelling them from the villages. The Russian government had long since adopted a policy of tying the burghers to their cities like the peasants to their villages. This was an obvious outcome of the feudal system which demanded clear-cut demarcations between the classes of society. The interests of the Imperial Exchequer were an even more compelling reason for such a policy. Freedom of movement for the population might have disturbed the regular flow of revenue from the communities and enabled vagrant elements to evade tax payments. In 1782, an Imperial Warrant required all merchants and burghers living in villages throughout Russia to transfer their residence immediately to the cities. Few of the Christian burghers could feel seriously threatened by this measure—and they were not in fact dealt with too severely—but to the Jews the new law could spell severe repression. Though all of them had recently been classified as burghers and merchants, most of the White Russian Jews actually lived in the small towns and villages.

A new measure at the beginning of 1783 aggravated the situation of the Jews, though to all appearances it was not directed specifically against them. The right to brew or distil and sell liquor in White Russia was withdrawn from the burghers and restricted to the municipal magistracies, to the government in the imperial estates, and to the landed proprietors in the villages and towns. The Kehillah leaders dispatched a delegation to the Empress in 1784 with detailed representations of all the wrongs done to the Jewish population. Their cause was assisted by the fact that the government still felt committed to the principle of equality that it had proclaimed for the Jewish population and therefore did not support the repressive acts of the White Russian authorities. The Czarina's directive to the Senate stated:

> Her Majesty has ordered that attention be given to the fact that since these members of the Hebrew faith have already, through Her Majesty's Warrants, acquired equal status with others, the rule laid down by Her Majesty must be observed in every instance, namely, that every individual shall enjoy the concessions and rights adhering to his occupation and class without distinction of religion or nationality.

On the authority of this directive, the Senate issued an order in 1786 replying to the Jewish representations in detail.

The Senate ruled in favour of the Jews in the two principal items in the Jewish deposition and against the ordinances of the White Russian authorities threatening their sources of income. The estate-owners were specifically permitted to lease town and village liquor distilleries and inns to whomsoever they chose, including Jews, and village proprietors were ordered to ensure that the peasants did not succumb to drunkenness. As the Jews were now allowed to hold leases in villages and towns, their expulsion from villages and towns was obviously annulled. Explaining this decision, the Senate stated that the law did not forbid townsmen to quit the cities provided only that they paid their taxes in full; it added that it was pointless to drive the Jews into the cities while they did not own land there to build homes on and while they did not have assured means of support.

On the issue of discrimination against Jewish rights in elections to municipal bodies, the Senate ruled that the Jews were entitled to vote and hold office in the municipal institutions "in equal measure, according to the numerical strength of each class." When, even after this pronouncement, the municipal council of the city of Vitebsk reduced Jewish participation in the elections, even employing violence to achieve it, the Jews appealed to the Empress. Catherine, during the summer of the same year, "most sternly" ordered the Chief Governor of White Russia to fulfil the Senate's decision "at once and with no delays."

The Senate confirmed the jurisdiction in all religious matters of the Kehillah courts in county and gubernia centres. As the Senate also did not refuse Jews the right to settle civil disputes amongst themselves by arbitration, the Kehillah courts to all intents and purposes continued to exist as before with official sanction, and their jurisdiction remained available to any Jew who preferred not to seek a fair trial in the "Gentile courts of law." By implication rather than by an explicit ruling, the Senate empowered the Kehillah leaders to issue passports to Jews as travel permits. It also entrusted the Kehillah authorities with apportioning and collecting taxes, except from those registered as members of the merchant class, who paid a percentage of their individual capital. The government's object in all this was obviously to strengthen the Kehillah régime in the services of the Exchequer.

Considerable changes in this legal situation occurred a few years later. The political reaction already setting in in Russia during that period sharply reduced the rights that the Russian legislation had bestowed upon the Jews at the height of Catherine's reign, during her liberal phase. The dual character of the legal status of the Jews did not end, but dual rights were replaced by double discrimination: Jewish activity in the villages was greatly curtailed and the rights of Jews as members of the burgher class were reduced to the point of open national oppression.

Beginning of Reaction and Oppression; the Jews of Lithuania and the Ukraine under Russian rule

The French Revolution evoked a deep response amongst the enlightened Russian nobility, middle class, and, particularly, intellectual circles. It spread fear and trepidation amongst the rulers of the absolutist Empire. The "enlightened" Empress discarded all her programme for reform and instituted a régime of open terrorism designed to crush all ideas of freedom and progress. At this period the last two partitions of Poland were made by Russia, Prussia and Austria, alleging the need "to halt the spread of the Jacobin plague." By far the largest portion of the liquidated Polish Kingdom fell to Russia. In the prevalent atmosphere of reaction, the government policy towards the Jews obviously changed for the worse. The oppressive decrees which were now enacted affected not only the tens of thousands of Jews in White Russia but also hundreds of thousands of Jews in Lithuania and the Ukraine who had become Russian subjects as a result of the partition of Poland at the height of the reaction.

The first step taken by the Russian government in the direction of the new policy was to legalize the existing restrictions of the Jews, which were to last as long as the Czarist régime itself. The main points of this policy were the confinement of the Jews to the gubernatorial districts in which they lived and a ban on Jewish settlement elsewhere in the vast realm. A number of Jews from White Russia had taken advantage of their official status as merchants to get their names included in the merchant registries of Smolensk and Moscow. The merchants of Moscow had more than once protested at the competition from Russian petty traders trading in the city without licence. Early in 1790, they submitted a series of memoranda to the government complaining of the cunning and deceit of the Jews who were underselling them, demanding the expulsion of all Jews in Moscow, and calling for an investigation of those illegally registered as merchants.

The Imperial Council took up this grievance together with a memorandum from the Jews complaining of the refusal to include them in the merchant registries of Smolensk and Moscow. The Council agreed that Jews should not be permitted "to be registered in the commercial and port cities of Russia . . . since . . . no benefit is to be seen in such permission." Jews could enjoy the rights of citizenship in White Russia only, but "there might also be some advantage in granting them such permission in Yekaterinoslav and in the Tavrida areas." On December 23, 1791, the Empress issued a warrant in precisely the same formulation, fully agreeing with the Council's decision.

The establishment of a pale of settlement for the Jews in Russia was thus given specific legal sanction. It was not a coincidence that the government promulgated the decree establishing the pale of settlement during the period of reaction. At a time when political repression was increasing and when the Empress was already considering the second partition of Poland, egalitarian principles would obviously not prevent her from restricting Jewish rights in an open act of persecution. However, Catherine's preparations for another partition of Poland were more directly connected with the edict on the Jewish pale of settlement. By accelerating the act, the Empress was preparing in advance for the enlargement of her country by vast areas of the Polish Kingdom. It was meant to block the movement of White Russian Jews, but, more important, it was intended to arrest the settlement in the Russian interior of large numbers of Polish Jews who were soon to become Russian subjects.

Despite the formulation of the law of 1791, it contained nothing expressly indicating any expansion of the pale of settlement, for it actually only permitted Jews to settle in districts where Jewish communities already existed by sanction of previous laws. Apart from the two White Russian districts, Jews at that time already lived in several cities of "New Russia," now called the Vice-Royalty of Yekaterinoslav, by permission granted in 1764. There had also already been several thousand Rabbinate Jews and Karaites in the Crimean Peninsula, which had been renamed the Tavrida Area, when it was captured from the Turks. In the Crimean cities alone, 469 Jewish households had been counted in 1783. The 1792 census also recorded 966 Jews in the three large gubernatorial districts of Kiev, Chernikhov and Novgorod-Seversk in the Ukraine, scattered through the cities, towns and villages. Half of these had come from beyond the Polish frontier, the other half from White Russia. As the Ukraine was not mentioned in the law of 1791, the local authorities asked the government at St. Petersburg whether it would not be proper to expel the Jews. The government decided in favour of the Jews, and later resolved to include them in the pale of permitted settlement together with the Jews in the areas annexed after the latest partition of Poland.

In the spring of 1792, Russian forces invaded the Ukrainian territory west of the Dnieper and Lithuania. By the beginning of 1793, a treaty dividing Poland was signed between the three powers. Russia absorbed the rest of White Russia (the Minsk and Novogrudok areas), the eastern portions of Polesia and Volhynia, the Podolia area, and all of the Ukraine west of the Dnieper (the Kiev and Bratzlav areas). The third partition of Poland took place in January, 1795, after the suppression of the Kosciuszko revolt. Russia obtained Courland, Lithuania and the rest of Polesia and Volhynia. The western borders of the Empire now extended to the rivers Niemen, Bug, and Zbrucz. All the Jews in the Ukrainian territories (excepting Eastern Galicia, which remained under Austrian rule), the White Russian territory, Lithuania, and the other Baltic lands, were now united under the domination of the Russian Empire. The census of 1800 (in Lithuania in 1797), recorded 152,346 taxable Jewish males, 300,000 people in all these territories. Actually a minimum of 750,000 was closer to the truth.* As had occurred earlier with the White Russian Jews, all Jews were now officially listed as merchants and burghers. Even on the basis of the 1800 census returns, they were almost equal in number to the Christians in this category (178,000 taxable males).

The laws already in force for the Jews of the two White Russian gubernatorial districts were also applied to those in the territories acquired by the last two partitions of Poland. By the decree of June 23, 1794, Jews, as merchants and burghers, were permitted to inhabit the three gubernias of the Ukraine east of the Dnieper, in addition to the gubernias listed in 1791. This explicit inclusion of the eastern Ukraine in the pale of settlement is a conclusive proof that in fixing the limits of the settlement the Empress was guided by ethnographic policy rather than by the principle of the status quo: Jews were permitted to dwell in all territories in the west inhabited by non-Russians, but no further to the east, lest they compete with Russian merchants.

The prevailing reaction also produced other anti-Jewish decrees. The warrant of 1794 defining the pale of settlement decreed that Jews "must pay double the tax owed by burghers and merchants of the various Christian communities," as a condition for receiving domiciliary and economic rights. "Those who will not wish to remain shall be permitted, under the law governing the cities and after having paid (double) taxes covering three years, to leave Our Empire."

With the end of Catherine's liberal phase, the full extent of the decadence of the absolutist régime was disclosed. Like Austria and

* Inefficiency in the collection, tabulation and interpretation of data, together with the fact that large numbers of individuals "disappeared" during the census, accounted for marked discrepancies between the results of this census and later estimates prepared for the Government Committee on Jewish Reform set up in 1809. The consensus of these later estimates placed the total number of Jews in the Russian Empire for the period under discussion at between 750,000 and 800,000.

Prussia, it now only tolerated its Jews on account of the special revenue they paid into the Imperial Treasury.

The doubling of the taxes to be paid by the Jews applied to all government taxation: merchant tax, burghers' poll tax, postal tax and so on. In addition, Jews had to pay a military tax of 500 roubles per recruit in lieu of army service. Amongst the Christians who lived in the cities only the merchant class had to pay this tax; the Christian burghers had to do combatant duty in the army, like the peasants. Apart from the double government taxes, the Jews were also required to pay all municipal taxes, and in the private towns they paid heavy "subject" taxes to their noble masters. In actual fact, the Jews also paid dual municipal taxes, as even under the imperial law they were not exempt from the taxes imposed by their own religious community, the Kehillah. The burden of all these taxes became intolerably heavy and resulted in Kehillot indebtedness and increasing poverty amongst the Jewish masses.

The reactionary trend was equally injurious to the electoral rights in municipal administrations which the Jews had secured. Catherine's edict of 1795 had ruled that Jews in the newly-annexed territory were also entitled to participate in municipal elections "without distinction of race or religion." But the Empress did not intervene when the Governor-General of the gubernias of Minsk, Volhynia and Podolia reduced Jewish representation to one third of council membership. In the cities of Lithuania, the municipalities continued to bar all Jewish participation in elections as they had under Polish rule, generally without any protest by the authorities against this infringement of the law.

The administrative decrees expelling the Jews from the villages, which had been nullified by the Senate's edict of 1786, were revived during the final years of Catherine's reign, though their implementation was deferred. Meanwhile a new Czar, Paul, had come to the throne. He inherited his mother's general reactionary policy, together with her aim of "reforming" the Jews by repression.

Paul mobilized vast armies against revolutionary France and subdued his subjects by a "reign of terror." He, even more than his predecessors, based the monarchy on the entrenchment of the position of the noble class. Paul gave particular support to the nobility in the western provinces annexed from Poland. He granted the Polish nobles unlimited authority over their serfs, wide powers of self-government and local administration. He restored the *Statute*, the legal code of the sixteenth century, in the former Lithuanian territories. The Jesuits especially benefited from his rule; their confiscated properties were returned to them and all educational institutions in the annexed territories placed under their control.

The Polish estate owners now accumulated wealth to an extent unknown under Polish rule. Unrestricted exaction of hard labour from their serfs enabled them to increase the production of crops from their own estates and from the plots of their peasants and export them through the port of Riga in the north and Odessa on the Black Sea in the south. A commodity which had acquired a wide export market was whisky, and this impelled many estate owners to repossess the liquor distilleries from the lessees and operate them themselves.

The new trend in Russian domestic policy also determined the legal status of Russian Jewry during Paul's reign. Even this reactionary government was concerned for the Royal Exchequer's revenues and willing to recognize the rights of domicile, trade and craftsmanship that the Jews enjoyed by law or in practice—as long as they had no adverse effect on the privileges and advantages of the nobles. Thus, Jews who had migrated from White Russia to the district of Novgorod-Seversk, in the Ukraine, were allowed to remain there (1795). Similarly, despite the fact that the ancient privileges that the Crown cities of the west held from the Polish Kings had been reconfirmed, the Czar did not grant a request by these municipalities that the Jews be expelled on the basis of their privilege *de non tolerandis Judaeis* (i.e., the right not to tolerate Jews). A warrant in 1797 expressly confirmed the right of the Jews in the city of Kamenetz-Podolsk to live "as they choose, just like in other cities." An order issued in 1798 allowed them to live in the city of Kovno despite the municipality's objections and to engage freely in handicraft and trade. In Kiev, the capital of the Ukraine, the Jewish population increased constantly, to the dismay of the municipal government. By 1801, the number of Jews in this city had risen to 656 officially registered burghers and eleven merchants. The municipality then requested the government to expel the Jews from the city on the basis of a *Letter of Privileges* dating from 1619. The government, however, preferred to follow the Gubernator's report, which proved that expert master craftsmen were only to be found amongst the Jews of Kiev and that only Jewish merchants stocked their stores with all the commodities the local population required. On these grounds, the Czar ordered that "the Jews should not be transferred to any other place but are to be left in their residences at Kiev."

In regard to the Jews of Courland also, government policy was directed towards the assiduous promotion of trade and the imperial revenues. Russia had annexed Courland in 1795 during the third partition of Poland. The official census of taxable males made in 1797 recorded 4,581 Jews. Official descriptions of the Jews of Courland state that for the most part, they were destitute paupers "who only with the greatest difficulty keep body and soul together." In an ordinance confirmed by the Czar in 1800, the Senate agreed to allow Jews to live in Courland under the same conditions as in all other parts of the Russian pale of settlement, except that more stringent regulations were enforced in respect of delinquent taxpayers.

In contrast to the Jewish city dwellers, whose rights were confirmed by the government, the legal position of the Jews under the domination of the nobility in private cities, towns and villages deteriorated throughout this period. In White Russia and the Ukraine, there were daily instances of Jews being expelled from their villages by nobles on the pretext that they were legally registered as city dwellers (in fact, it was usually because the nobles had ceased to require their services). Very many of those not threatened with outright expulsion were harassed by steady increases in leasehold rates and other payments.

The increasing number of Jews evicted from the villages and their ever more ruthless exploitation at the hands of the nobles only reflected the general growth of social oppression on the manorial estates. During Paul's reign, peasant impoverishment resulting from intensified serfdom reached such proportions that the government was obliged to take action. The discussions on social conditions in the rural areas revealed the reactionary features of the political régime in the Russian state. To conceal the real source of the problem—the system of serfdom—principal responsibility was attributed to the Jewish lessees, innkeepers and publicans, who were actually only the instruments of the nobility and mostly lived in poverty and want themselves. Now that the prime motive was no longer the official inclusion of the Jews in the burgher class but rather the diversion of public opinion from a social abuse, the threat of expulsion from the villages (which had hung over the Jews even since they came under Russian rule) took substantial and practicable shape. As on other occasions, the government was not unconscious of the incidental advantages such a measure offered: the reduction of liquor production and sales in the western districts would lessen competition with the liquor monopoly that existed in the Russian interior.

In spring, 1797, the government received reports that starvation was rife amongst the peasants of the gubernatorial district of Minsk. The Gubernator of the district was ordered to ascertain the reasons for this deterioration in conditions, after obtaining the opinion of the nobles, and to suggest means to remedy the situation. Barely two months later he submitted to the Czar the resolutions adopted by the nobles at regional meetings and confirmed by the marshals of the district nobility at an assembly in Minsk. The nobles believed that the local peasants could not achieve any degree of affluence because they lacked elementary knowledge of agriculture, because of their illiteracy, and because they were utterly deficient in any capacity for financial calculation. Furthermore, they suffered from such afflictions as revolutions, wars, droughts and cattle plagues, while the underdeveloped state of trade and the shortage of roads in good repair represented additional problems. It was further stated that:

> Amongst these many deficiencies, the most formidable by far is caused by the Jews, who are employed as lessees and publicans by the estate owners contrary to the Government Ordinance defining them as city dwellers ... (They) live in the villages with their

numerous families, secure their livelihoods without physical toil, and wrest from the peasant his remaining resources by means in which they are well tried. That is to say, they give the peasants liquor on credit and reduce them to intoxication. They beset them with lies and all kinds of false accusations and thus cause them to waste their resources and lose their capacities for self-support ... Furthermore—the nobles explained—there are occasions when clergymen of all denominations collect too high a fee for baptisms, marriages and funerals, thus thrusting the peasants into poverty.

To prevent drunkenness amongst the peasants, they demanded that publicans should not be allowed to serve any spirits except the landlords' and that "the Jews, publicans and other lessees," should be forbidden to manufacture alcoholic beverages. A similar measure proposed that publicans should not derive profits but should draw a salary by contract with the estate owners. The nobles also urged that the sale of liquor on credit be limited to those publicans who were granted this right in their contracts with the estate owners. Finally, they stated that the peasants deserved permission to sell crops, such as hemp, as they chose, without the service of a lessee. They did not mention their own monopoly on the sale to the peasants of vital commodities, such as salt.

The Senate dealt with all the principal proposals of the nobles of the Minsk gubernia in an imperial command dated July 28, 1797. It accepted in full the proposals concerning the clergy, terms of tenure of manorial leasehold (fixed at a minimum of three years), forest protection, and peasants' rights to sell their own produce. The Senate considered the Czar's warrant on "The Limitation of the Rights of Jews Who are Destroying the Peasant Class" in extreme detail. As "it had been proved" that the main reason for the poverty of the peasantry was the leasing of taverns to Jews by the estate owners, a strict injunction against the manufacture of liquors by "Jews and others" was passed. In this connection, the Senate cited Catherine II's edict of 1795 on the need "to endeavour to transfer the Jews to the district towns."

When the order to the Governor of the Minsk District was issued, the governors of Volhynia, Podolia and Lithuania were instructed to make similar inquiries of all the leading nobles within their jurisdiction and to enclose their own opinions with their reports. The leading nobles of Podolia met at Kamenetz-Podolsk in June, 1798, and on the whole approved of all the proposals made by the Minsk nobility. However, they appended a number of proposals related to their own specific circumstances and interests. As evidence that "the condition of the peasants has ever been the chief concern of their noble patrons," they pointed out that most of the nobles in the Podolian gubernia had established a monopoly of liquor manufacture and sales "in order to protect the people from the robbery of the Jews." It was essential that this monopoly became an inviolable law throughout the gubernia. Contrary to the Minsk nobles, therefore, they requested that not only the manufacture of liquor but also the rights of leasing in villages and towns should be an exclusive privilege of the nobility. Jews and gentiles who were not members of the nobility would not be allowed to engage in the sale of liquor except as publicans. The request by the Podolian nobles for an absolute monopoly in the leasing of liquor enterprises is not surprising in the light of their further claim for the right to export liquor.

The Podolian nobles, who were expanding their economic activities at that time, were fully aware that they could not gain control of foreign trade without the mediation of the Jews, even with legal protection. Hence, they requested that "this people by whose skill and agility for the most part trade is carried on and through whom alone the country's produce is exported," should be permitted to continue to engage in the export of liquor, honey, wax, tallow, "and everything now exportable from the country." They also thought it desirable that the Jews in the towns and villages should retain their positions as liquor purveyors and even replace the peasant purveyors, "so that the latter should not forsake the tilling of the soil. . . ." The remaining Jews should be forced to turn to the cultivation of the soil and manual trades on noble and royal estates, "and thus the multitudinous Jews who live in this gubernia would be removed from the opportunity to cheat the masses of the people and would also increase their occupation with manual vocations, trade and agriculture."

The harshest and most repressive anti-Jewish programme was proposed by the nobles of Lithuania. This was not fortuitous. The nobles there were the most reactionary of all the nobles of the former Polish state. They reposed such confidence in the legal system that the Czar had specifically confirmed in their behalf that they refused to agree to the negligible reforms suggested by the nobles of the other gubernias even with regard to the peasant conditions under consideration by the Senate. Furthermore, the spokesmen for Lithuania's nobility went as far as to demand "counter-reforms" in peasant status. For the purpose of "eliminating inequality among the peasant class" and in order to prevent "idleness and indolence," they requested that the rent-paying class of peasants, who had enjoyed the right to change employers for generations, should be bound to their masters like all other serfs and be required to perform serf labour.

This Lithuanian nobility claimed to be protecting the peasants against the Jews "who pauperize them through their deceitfulness." Only three of the nineteen delegates at the assembly of Lithuanian nobles were prepared to leave the Jews in their previous state. They gave as their reasons that "this people has already formed close ties with the Christians through all kinds of money dealings and various obligations" (thus hinting at their fear of forfeiting the debts that the Jews owed to the nobles) and also that the peasants could only obtain the money to pay their taxes through the

Jews, who facilitated the sale of their crop surpluses. The rest of the delegates demanded that the Jews not only be forbidden to manufacture liquor independently or as lessees but even to sell liquor, even as publicans—"in order to uproot the evil." However, the Polish magnates in Lithuania were still so dependent on Jewish help in administering their estates that they proposed that the Jews be allowed to lease estates and hold them on mortgage.

First Reform Programmes for the Jews

Several of the proposals made by the Lithuanian nobility were nothing more than an identical copy of the programme propounded by the Governor-General of Lithuania, Ivan Friesel, a typical example of the superficially liberal noblemen. He was influenced by the ideas of enlightened absolutism, mainly of the Prussian and Austrian variety, and hoped to reform the condition of the peasants and the Jews without touching the foundations of the feudal régime. He, like all the disciples of Frederick II's version of Enlightenment, regarded the reform of society primarily as a matter of eradicating religious fanaticism and superstition, restricting the authority of the clergy of every religion, and disseminating knowledge. This strange combination of radicalism in religious affairs and conservative or reactionary views on vital social issues is characteristic of the opinion he forwarded to the Senate together with the resolutions of the Lithuanian nobles.

Apart from the dilemma of a conservative noble who had espoused the theory of "Enlightenment," Friesel's opinion also revealed an overriding contempt for "this people (the Jews) which has brought to every country it has reached in the course of its wanderings the indolence of Asia coupled with repulsive uncleanliness, characteristics which it preserves to this very day." His long introduction reviewed the history of the Jews in Poland—how they had multiplied, extended their activities and dominated trade, credit, brokerage, light handicrafts, liquor lesseeships and any other trade which did not entail hard work. A reform of the Jews was an urgent necessity both to improve their own situation and for the welfare of the state. He agreed with the opinion of the marshals of the Lithuanian nobility that the Jews should be forbidden to engage in any form of liquor trade after a transitional period of two years. All Jews should be divided into three estates: merchants, artisans and peasants. Jewish merchants and artisans should be granted the same privileges as the other members of their estates, including guild membership and passive and active electoral rights in the municipalities. All other Jews should be directed into cultivation of the soil "since there is no land shortage in the vast expanses of the Russian Empire." To avoid the oppression of the Jewish cultivators by the landed proprietors, royal lands should be set aside for them and they should be exempt from tax payments for a period of ten years. Those who chose to settle in villages owned by the nobility should be supplied with timber to build houses and they should be free to move to other localities after each census (in connection with tax assessments). Marriage should only be permitted at the age of twenty or more and on condition that the couple were able to support a family.

"The education of the Jewish people towards Enlightenment should commence with religion, the prime factor on which all others depend," Friesel declared, and, in the spirit of Frederick's deism, added, "for all religions have but one aim." It was therefore necessary to determine the tenets of the Jewish faith, free it from all the laws added by Jewish leaders for their own advantage, and, primarily, "to root out all the sects, all the superstitions, with the utmost severity to prohibit the introduction of new ones with which charlatans dupe the masses and plunge them into still greater ignorance, extort from them their remaining possessions, whether acquired by toil or themselves the fruits of deceitfulness." Hasidism, which he described in sinister terms (at one point, he referred to the Hasidic *Tzaddikim* as "sorcerers"), should be eradicated. The General-Gubernator also demanded the total liquidation of the Kehillah, both because it constituted a government in itself and violated all the laws of the state and because of its oppression of the Jewish poor. The Kehillah leaders were burdening the people with taxes and fees for their own benefit, increasing its problems with laws of tenure and clientage, and subjugating it by the threat of excommunication. The Kehillah leaders were deliberately keeping the Jewish masses in abysmal ignorance for their own purposes; the very few erudite men "lead an ascetic life, exist on alms, and depart this life without having been of any service to the community."* Each gubernia should possess only one rabbinical court dealing exclusively with religious matters, and in the Polish language, rather than in "that depraved Jewish speech" which "veils them from the authorities." To raise their educational standards and moral level, their sons should be sent to public schools and Jewish education confined solely to matters of religion. It would also be necessary for the Jews to resemble the rest of the inhabitants in their dress, to save money, because "the garb at present affected by the Jews of Lithuania is definitely unsuited to any kind of work," and, principally, "because it keeps them dirty and untidy, a thing that intensifies the contempt in which all persons hold this people."

This opinion by the Governor of the district of Lithuania contained the first programme for educating the Jews and for moving them into productive activities to be proposed by a government official under the Russian monarchy. However, before the Senate had the opportunity to consider the opinions that leading nobles and the gubernators had

---

* This faithful description of the sufferings of the *Maskilim* suggests that Friesel obtained his information on the Hasidim as well as his programme for the dissemination of Enlightenment from the few *Haskalah* circles in Lithuania at that time.

submitted, the Jewish question again appeared on the agenda in conjunction with new information on the condition of the peasants in White Russia. In March, 1800, the Senate learned that an epidemic of intumescence was raging amongst the peasants there, resulting from a deficiency of salt, which they could not afford to buy. Again, on this occasion the only remedy that occurred to the Senate was a fresh decree against the Jews in the villages. The Polish Senator, Ilinski, in his report, blamed the Jews, alleging that they were impoverishing the peasants by intoxicating and defrauding them. However, when the Senate asked Governor Severin of White Russia why the Jews in his gubernia had not yet been expelled from the villages, he sent a detailed report proving that such a decree could not be implemented, and would not, in any case, improve the situation. Most of the Jews, he pointed out, were poor and did not possess the means to build homes in the cities, where, moreover, there was a shortage of land for construction purposes. Furthermore, a mass migration of Jews to the cities was liable to raise prices of food, houses and land. The General-Gubernator of White Russia, in company with a minority of leading Lithuanian nobles, observed that the eviction of the Jews from the villages would not only fail to solve the peasant problem but would aggravate it further. The Jewish innkeepers helped to save the peasants' time: the peasants sold their produce to the innkeepers or to Jews in neighbouring villages and thus were spared the trouble of long trading journeys. The Jewish innkeepers also discharged a useful function by supplying travellers with provisions. The Governor of White Russia also repeated the views of his Volhynian and Podolian colleagues regarding the detrimental effect on the Royal Exchequer if large numbers of Jews were to lose their income and be unable to pay the double tax levied on them. However, the governor mainly enumerated the losses to the estate-owners if the Jews were expelled from the villages. If hostelry and flour mill leases were given to the peasants, the landlords would not earn half the revenues produced by the Jewish lessees, and would, therefore, neither be able to pay their personal debts nor make their tax payments to the state. Landlords who refused to expel their Jews depended on the authority of Paul's warrant of 1796 reaffirming the rights and privileges formerly enjoyed by White Russian nobles under Polish rule.

Despite this candid official acknowledgement of the role the Jews played in enriching the nobles at the expense of the exploited peasantry, the Senate decided to proceed with its inquiry into the situation in White Russia, with regard not only to the nobles (the prime cause of oppression), but also to the Jews (whose existence depended on the nobles' good will). In June, 1800, Senator Derzhavin was sent to look into the situation. Derzhavin was a well-known Russian poet, who had already carried out a government mission the previous year investigating Jewish grievances against Zoritch, the proprietor of the city of Shklov. Imperial command empowered this senior emissary with close government connections to act with the utmost severity against "those of the landed proprietors who for inordinate love of profit neglect their peasants and fail to support them with food supplies." Derzhavin was authorized to "relieve them of their estates and to appoint custodians who would allot grains to the peasants from their masters' granaries." However, the Chief Procurator to the Senate, Obolianinov, hastily amended this order with instructions issued in the Czar's name:

> ... Since it has become known that the Jews constitute a significant factor in the impoverishment of the peasants in White Russia, with their trafficking, depriving them of their assets, it is His Supreme demand that Your Honour shall devote special thought and attention to this calling of theirs and submit your opinion as to how to do away with the evil they are inflicting upon the public.

Derzhavin, far more conservative and reactionary in political affairs than in his poetry, was hostile to peasant reform. When he first arrived in White Russia, he did initiate a few energetic measures against the nobles and the Jews, by virtue of the wide powers he wielded. Here, however, the Senator's practical activities came to an end and he then proceeded to collect material for his report on the Jews of White Russia. He obtained his information mainly from the Polish nobles, practically all of whom placed the responsibility for the condition of the peasants upon the Jews, contrary to the opinion they had expressed to the government. He gathered further facts from the burghers, who were antagonistic to their Jewish competitors, and also from the fanatical instructors in the Jesuit college. On the other hand, he took care not to enter into discussion with those most directly concerned in the situation—the oppressed peasants themselves—and he certainly paid no attention to the Kehillot's claim that the blame for peasant starvation lay with the nobles, who not only subjugated their peasants but increased the quota of serf labour obligations and raised their rentals.

Derzhavin's report was not confined to the Jewish question in White Russia. On his own initiative he widened the scope of his reform proposals to include all the Jews in Russia. To that end, he added all the material the Senate already held, the opinions of the leading nobles and governors, especially that submitted by the Lithuanian Gubernator, Friesel, to the information he himself had collected in White Russia. The Senator also made considerable use in his programme of the legislation in operation for Jews in the enlightened absolutist régimes of Austria and Prussia. He even referred specifically to anti-Jewish decrees promulgated by the Byzantine Emperors at the beginning of the Dark Ages. On the other hand, he was prepared to listen to the advice of two Jewish *Maskilim* who presented him with their reform proposals. The wealthy St. Petersburg merchant, Nathan Nota of Shklov, drew up a detailed plan for moving the Russian Jews into productive occupations by establishing textile mills and colonies of Jewish farmers, vinegrowers, silkworm cultivators and sheep farmers. Dr. Elijah Frank of Kreslavka (near Dinaburg), was convinced that the reforms of the Jews consisted mainly in separating the essence of the Jewish religion from the "Talmudic nonsense" and in educating the youth at modern schools. The programme that Derzhavin submitted to the government for the solution of the Jewish problem was permeated with a spirit of religious and political reaction and imbued with the absolutist aim of improving "the Czar's subjects" by decrees from the bureaucracy and the secret police. Derzhavin, it should be added, had come into contact with Jewish communities for the first time only a year before he presented his report.

The title of Derzhavin's report to the government in December, 1800, reflected his conclusions: *Opinion of Senator Derzhavin on the Prevention of Grain Shortages in White Russia by Restricting Avaricious Jewish Callings, on Reforming the Jews, etc*. He thought, with Governor Friesel, that the Jews were congenitally averse to physical labour. However, he explained it by a religious theory of his own: they had acquired this characteristic from the Talmudic teaching that it was the mission of the Children of Israel to subjugate all the nations. The rabbis, he alleged, strengthened this belief amongst the Jews by instructing the youth in the Talmud and spreading superstition, prejudice and hatred of the gentiles. "They have no concept of the love of man, of the abhorrence of material gain, or of any other virtues," and "a sense of honour is utterly worthless to the Jew. ... All they wish is but to accumulate capital and treasures with the object of rebuilding Solomon's Temple or for their own pleasures of the flesh." Jewish leasing, innkeeping, brokerage, and trade were all only "cunning devices for appropriating the resources of their neighbours under the pretence of profits and services." Their trade was of no value whatsoever either to the state or to the Treasury. Their purchases of the country's produce only raised the price of foodstuffs. The Jewish brokers, "stewards in the domestic establishments of the estate owners, who have their hands in everything," were draining the peasants' resources. The Jewish innkeepers bore the heaviest responsibility for making the peasants' life miserable by causing their total impoverishment through the sale of liquor on credit and at high interest rates. "A peasant, once indebted to them," had no possibility of extricating himself from his debt. An urgent need therefore existed "to reform the Jews politically and morally, that they might become like the enlightened nations."

Derzhavin's reform for the Jews filled eighty-eight paragraphs. A special Christian "protector" was to be appointed over the Jews to supervise the reforms. A special committee would be set up in White Russia for liquidating mutual debts between Jews and Christians in collaboration with the Jews. Only when that had been accomplished would it be possible to begin to execute the reforms, which would entail a new census of the Jews and their compulsory adoption of surnames. All Jews would be divided into four categories: merchants; burghers (only half of whom in any city would be permitted to engage in trade; the remaining half would have to turn to manual occupations); villagers (who would work in industry and handicrafts); and peasants. In White Russia, the proportion of Jews was fixed at one merchant and four burghers to every hundred Christian inhabitants; the remainder would have to transfer to agriculture if they wished to stay in the same place, or else resettle in Jewish towns and villages in the gubernias of New Russia and Astrakhan. The most talented Jewish youth would be sent to St. Petersburg, Moscow, and Riga to study bookkeeping, languages, handicraft and agriculture. The Kehillot would be abolished, leaving only the "synagogues" for religious affairs and these would be under the authority of a *Sendarin** and Patriarch (Chief Rabbi) at St. Petersburg. To disseminate Enlightenment, Derzhavin suggested prohibiting peculiarly Jewish styles of dress, requiring all documents to be written in Russian, Polish or German, compulsory attendance of all children from the age of twelve at general schools (until then, they would have been taught at the religious schools), the creation of a censorship organization to destroy all superstitious books, and the publication of Hebrew books in Russian translation with "philosophical commentaries."

Derzhavin's programme basically resembled Friesel's, but it also contained several new restrictions illustrating the difference in general outlook between the reactionary clericalist on the one hand and his predecessor on the other, who superimposed his reactionary proposals on a pattern of Enlightenment. Derzhavin proposed a prohibition on the employment of Christian men and women by Jews, on threat of punishment for insulting the Christian religion. Jews would have to live on special streets, segregated from the Christians. They would not participate in municipalities or municipal departments, so that they would not boast that Messianic times had arrived. They would only serve in the army as carters and musicians, "since they are cowards by nature" and because they observed the Sabbath. "Thus," concluded Derzhavin, "the Jews, that stubborn and fanatical people, enemies of the Christians, although by Divine Decree they shall remain in exile unchanged so long as that is the will of God on high, yet in this sorry condition of theirs they will get some sort of a good constitution."

The Jews of White Russia could not accept these insults in silence, and they sent a complaint about Derzhavin to the Czar. However, very shortly afterwards, in March, 1801, Paul was assassinated as the result of a plot in which his son and heir, Alexander, participated. Derzhavin's report became the main foundation for the "Jewish statute" enacted under the new Czar.

* Derzhavin's corruption of *Sanhedrin,* a word he had learned from hearsay.

The Jews in Russia at the Beginning of the Nineteenth Century: their Economic and Social Condition

At the beginning of the nineteenth century, the foundations of capitalism were developing in Russia, though the process was slow because of the obstructive nature of the absolutist régime. In 1812, the urban population represented 4.4 per cent of the total population. The number of factories in operation and the proportion of wage earners they employed constantly increased, though they were still fewer than the serfs employed in factories. The textile industry was particularly prosperous because of the state's need for army uniforms. The expansion of domestic and foreign trade stimulated the landed proprietors to further exploitation of their serfs both by means of compulsory labour quotas and farm rents.

Alexander I's reign only differed from those of his predecessors on the surface. The principal aim of the government remained the strengthening of the absolutist régime and the dominant noble estate. Napoleon had described Alexander I as "a virtual Byzantine." His outstanding psychological characteristics appeared to be insincerity, deceit and a love of the theatrical. He created a public image of a liberal and humanitarian sovereign for the benefit of his subjects and even more so of western European opinion. But in practice, even during the early years of his reign, which were apparently marked by liberalism, his reforms did not rise above organizational changes in government institutions intended to ensure greater efficiency and yield some concessions to the merchant and industrialist classes.

After his defeat in the war against Napoleon, culminating in the Peace of Tilsit (1807), Alexander decided that new reforms were necessary to stabilize his unsettled position. He entrusted the task of drawing up the reforms to Michael Speranski, who had prepared broad proposals for a nationwide reform as early as 1803. In 1810, the Council of State was founded, with Speranski as secretary. Speranski, a man of wide and profound erudition, held genuinely liberal views and possessed great political and administrative ability. But his official programme only contained a proposal for a constitutional régime with a *Duma* (parliament) to represent the noble and middle estates. At the beginning of 1812, the Czar, fearful of antagonizing the dominant class when he was feverishly preparing for war against Napoleon, decided to placate the nobility. Speranski was sent far away from the capital. The Russian Empire was rapidly proceeding in the direction of the political reaction which broke out in full force in 1815, when feudal-clerical reaction engulfed all of Europe.

The fate of the largest single body of world Jewry depended on the policies of this régime. Russia now contained most of the Jews formerly under Poland's rule inside her borders. The official census counts did not, of course, yield even an approximation of the actual number of Jews in the

Empire. Under the bureaucratic census system then in use in Russia, data collected in earlier counts were repeated for decades. Thus, only 153,653 taxable male Jews were registered for the entire Empire (apart from the Bialystok area) in the census of 1812, though the census of 1800 had recorded nearly the same total (152,346). However, the number of these Jews who "disappeared" was not much larger than the number actually counted, so that the total of Jews in the Russian Empire at the beginning of the nineteenth century, together with women and children, would be approximately three-quarters of a million.*

The economic condition of the Jews in Russia at the beginning of Alexander's reign changed at the same slow rate as capitalist progress in the feudal state. Congestion within the pale of settlement was only slightly relieved by internal migration to south eastern districts. There was constant movement from the populous Kehillot of White Russia, Volhynia, and Podolia to the east bank of the Dnieper in the gubernias of Chernikhov and Poltava. The Kehillah in Kiev grew to 1,500 people by 1815. The rate of Jewish settlement on the plains of "New Russia" in the Yekaterinoslav and Kherson districts was even higher. In addition to government-sponsored agricultural resettlement, Jews from the western gubernias were attracted to the seaport towns of Odessa, Nikolaiev, and Kherson on the Black Sea, where new Kehillot were prospering. However, this resettlement could not materially alter the general economic situation of the vast Jewish population still crowded into the western districts of the Empire.

A strong indication that the defective economic pattern of Russian Jewish life continued was the proportion engaged in the manufacture and sale of liquor. At the beginning of the nineteenth century, about two-fifths of the Jewish population still lived in the villages. Most of these village Jews were publicans and innkeepers who lived in the inns and taverns owned by the nobles and also engaged in retail trade to supplement their income from selling liquor. Despite their role as middlemen in the nobility's exploitation of the peasantry, most of them barely eked out a livelihood. Even their staunchest adversaries, such as Derzhavin and Friesel, confirmed the poverty of the Jews. Their need was obvious during the years of expulsion from the villages, when they wandered destitute from city to city.

Lesseeship, innkeeping and liquor purveying also provided an income for many Jews in the cities and especially the towns. But the actual proportion so engaged varied according to the economic structure of each district within the pale. The economy of a Jewish town was largely linked to the method of feudal exploitation prevalent in the adjacent villages. Apart from visitors to towns on market and fair days, the publican's customers also consisted of local gentile artisans to whom it was customary to sell liquor on credit—which caused them to accumulate debts,

* cf. *supra*, p. 379 text and footnote.

like the village peasants. However, the condition of the Jewish publicans in the towns did not differ either in poverty or subjugation to the estate-owning nobles from that in the villages. This was, in the first place, because the distilleries and breweries belonged to the *Pritzim** who also monopolized the sale of liquor and merely leased the right of sale to the Jews. Second, most of the profits of the liquor salesmen were indirectly claimed by the town proprietors in the form of rentals and other payments. Even Friesel, though he had denounced the widespread sale of liquor by the Jews, could not ignore the evidence of the worsening material circumstances of the publicans. He reported that it was common to find the women alone in the town taverns and also in the village inns. "Their men," he observed, "are busy at secondary occupations, since very frequently the sale of liquor does not suffice to provide those so engaged with a livelihood. . . ."

By contrast, the position of the lessees in the towns was even better than in the villages. These lessees took over from the estate owners the operation of the distilleries and breweries, the sales monopoly of beverages and commodities such as candles and glass, the flour mills and the exclusive right of milling, the collection of excise duties on all commercial transactions in the town, market fees, road and bridge tolls and other sources of revenue. Exceptionally large incomes were earned by men who held government contracts for the sale of beverages in the Crown cities. They first appeared on the scene at the beginning of the nineteenth century and their numbers steadily rose during the first half of the century.

The principal Jewish economic activity in the villages and towns of Russia was trade in beverages. The city Jews, however, were mainly spread over all categories of business. In the gubernias open to Jewish domicile in the western districts of Russia, they generally took a decisive share in trade, even though they were in a minority amongst the members of registered merchant guilds. Only 2,309 Jewish members were registered in 1800 in the three guilds of the merchant estate in all of the western districts (except the two Lithuanian gubernias, for which no data are available), as compared with 11,637 Christians. However, these official figures of guild membership did not, of course, reflect the true situation, as many Jewish merchants refrained from enrolment in the merchant estate to avoid the high tax payments—especially while Jews were subject to a double assessment (Jewish merchants, until 1807). The role the Jews played in the trade of the western areas could be more accurately assessed from the figures for the burgher estate. The census of 1800 reported 166,713 registered Christian burghers and 148,968 Jews in all of the western gubernias (including the two in Lithuania). Taking into account the fact that the total for the gentiles in the towns primarily consisted of agriculturists and that they included a larger number of artisans than the Jews, it would inevitably follow that Jews were predominant in trade. This

* Plural of the Hebrew *Paritz* (in Yiddish, *Poretz*), a landed proprietor of the nobility.

is even more evident from figures for all the western gubernias excluding the gubernia of Courland (where there had been a firmly established German merchant class for a long time), the two eastern Ukrainian gubernias of Chernikhov and Poltava (which had not been officially opened to Jewish settlement until 1794—4,234 adult Jewish males in 1800), and the "New Russian" districts (where Jews had only begun to settle recently—1,306 adult Jewish males in 1800). All the other western gubernias had already possessed a large Jewish population in Polish times. The 1800 census showed 140,333 Jewish burghers as against 104,188 Christians; in other words, the Jews were in a 34 per cent majority. There were, of course, in reality over twice as many Jewish as Gentile burghers. The number of Jews that had "escaped" the census was almost equal to those included.

One consequence of the prosperous Jewish wholesale trade was the founding of a new Jewish community in the Imperial capital, St. Petersburg. According to a letter that Catherine wrote to Diderot, at the beginning of her reign in 1762, there were three or four Jews in St. Petersburg. By 1803, during the early years of the reign of Alexander, there were over ten Jewish families in the capital. It was no mere coincidence that the pioneers of this community came mostly from the city of Shklov, the great centre of Jewish trade in White Russia. At the beginning of 1802, the St. Petersburg Jews, who called themselves "sojourners" in the capital as they had no rights of permanent domicile there, established a cemetery on a plot of land purchased from the Evangelical Church.

Foreign trade in the western districts was largely in Jewish hands, even though they were far more important as importers than as exporters. Imports from the west were handled almost entirely by Jews. Jewish merchants imported colonial products and iron goods, fancy goods, silver and gold jewellery, and, in particular, a range of linen, woollen, cotton and silk fabrics from Riga, Königsburg, Frankfurt-on-the-Oder, Leipzig and Breslau. Jews were especially active at the Leipzig fairs. They travelled to Leipzig to purchase goods not only from the big cities such as Shklov and Berditchev, which held their own fairs, but also from medium-sized cities such as Uman in the Ukraine, and even from towns such as Glubok in Lithuania and Dokshitzy in White Russia. At the beginning of the nineteenth century it became a widespread practice for middle grade Jewish merchants to attend the Leipzig fairs, not only to purchase goods for themselves, but also for other traders who contributed towards their travelling expenses. The number of Jews attending the Leipzig fairs from the gubernias of western Russia was several times higher than the total number of Christian traders from all Russia.

Jewish trading activities maintained commercial connections between the western districts of Russia and other European countries. Similarly, they were the chief factor in the exchange of goods between the various areas of the pale of settlement. Attendance at the fairs at Shklov in White

Russia and at Berditchev and Dubno in Volhynia was absolutely essential for traders from all the western territories. They also attracted merchants from the Russian interior and from Brody, in Galicia. Large numbers of Jews were also present at the fairs at the provincial capitals and the smaller towns. A Russian author, Prince I. M. Dolgorukov, describing his trip through the Ukraine in 1810, told of his arrival in the city of Boguslav on the day of the fair—according to the calendar, "but since it was on Saturday, the Jews were not trading and the fair, therefore, was actually without a single visitor." He visited the city of Uman on market day and reported that "the city is full of Jews; and there are also many *Khokhols* . . ."* "We were in Uman on market day," he wrote, "when multitudes of people congregated. There was much trading and one could obtain whatever one fancied. The merchandise had been brought directly from abroad . . ." On the road to Zvenigorodka he found "crowds everywhere. The Jews were trading in every place and swarming like bees in a hive." In the town of Zlatopol, in the heart of the southern steppe, he saw to his amazement that "there are booths set up here in which, to judge by their external appearance, one would not expect to find a thing. Inside them Jews deal in every conceivable item. There one finds lovely fabrics, cashmere cloth and velvet, women's adornments, ancient and elegant courtiers' attire." Jewish trade also spread in the villages: "In many communities, in the vicinity of Kaniev, market days are held every week . . . The Jews bring their wares to every spot, selling, bartering, and cheating; you will find them everywhere, like the pedlars in our own Russia, canvassing the villages in their carts and offering all kinds of goods for sale."

The social condition of the Jewish trading class in no way reflected the importance of their function in the country's economy. Even many middle grade merchants had to conduct their business with borrowed money. Prince Dolgorukov allowed a note of contempt to steal into his description of the extensive trade carried on by the Jews on market day in the city of Uman: "The *Zhids* in their stalls swarm about the passers-by like flies. You will not escape from them unless you buy something. I experienced this personally. One grabbed me by one of my coat-tails and a second by the other, each in his deceitfulness seeking to lead me off to his own store . . ."

The mass of Jews engaged in trade also included the brokers, who embodied all the squalor and uncertainty of a rootless economic existence. Prince Dolgorukov's account of his stay in Uman gives a vivid description of the feverish activities of these *Luftmenschen*† which disclosed their extreme poverty:

* *Khokhol*, a derogatory epithet applied by Russians to Ukrainians.

† *Luftmensch*, a designation applied by eastern European Jews to describe those amongst them who tried to make a living by uncertain, insubstantial occupations—no more solid than the empty air. The literal meaning of the word is precisely that—a man of air.

Amongst them (the Jews) there are individuals offering special services and known as "factors." My advice is to beware of them: in plain Russian, they are what is known as—intermediaries. Such a person will procure for you anything you need or do not need. Whatever occurs to you, one word to the factor is sufficient—and you have it. He will drag along to you any quantity of bread, wine or meat; he will bring you on the run a reserve team or a column of horses for chaise or coach. He will deliver your letters, run errands, drive in a storekeeper with merchandise, change your money. In brief, there is nothing beyond the range of a broker's possibilities. But weep not when the time for settling accounts arrives . . . It is not enough that he will collect a double price for everything and add to this his brokerage fee; he will also collect a supplementary price for every rouble note to equalize it with the value of a copper rouble. More, after he has settled accounts with you, he will also collect a wage from the person from whom he obtained your food or wares, merely for having secured the things from him rather than from somebody else. Hah! Factors! People with a peculiar sense of honour and kindheartedness. Yet withal, naked and barefooted. If you see a ragged Jew, don't ask his name. It is Factor! . . .

It is not by chance that this excerpt specifically mentioned the provision of horses for travellers amongst the typical services rendered by the brokers. Together with trade and the maintenance of inns and hostelries, transport and carting enterprises were widespread amongst the Jews in the Russian pale of settlement, as they had been in Poland. Contemporary accounts by foreign tourists of their travels through Lithuania, White Russia and the Ukraine assign an important place to their haggling with Jews over horse rentals and the cost of coachmen. In many places, according to official census returns (as in the Minsk gubernia), tourist travel accounts (Dolgorukov), and the memoirs of officers in Napoleon's armies, government mail was also in the hands of Jewish innkeepers. The Senate's suspension of the decree expelling the Jews from the villages in 1812 specifically mentioned that "the most orderly postal depots are the ones in Jewish hands."

The artisans were the productive element in the Jewish population of the cities and towns. According to the census of 1812, artisans constituted 14 per cent of the Jewish population. The Kehillah members were anxious to conceal the presence of the members of this class (and also that of the middlemen and other indigents) from the census, because of their poverty, as the Kehillah was responsible for tax payments to the state on behalf of all Jewish family heads. Nevertheless, all other sources, and especially the proceedings of the authorities on the Jewish question, would seem to indicate that far fewer men were engaged in handicraft than in trade and brokerage, even in the urban Jewish population alone. The artisan class, according to the official census, represented only a quarter of the total number of Jews living in the cities and towns, who constituted some three-fifths of the entire Jewish population.

The proportion of Jewish artisans was higher in the large cities. In Minsk, according to census returns for 1808 and 1811, craftsmen represented 30 per cent of the Jewish population. In Riga, in 1811, the proportion was 36 per cent. In the Vilno Kehillah, they had reached this level by the middle of the eighteenth century. Novogrudok with 22 per cent, Slutzk with 21 per cent, and Pinsk with 19 per cent were typical of medium sized Kehillot where the proportion of artisans hardly exceeded 20 per cent.

The occupational structure of the Jewish artisan class in the Russian pale at the beginning of the nineteenth century was absolutely one-sided. According to government records for 1807 in the Minsk, Kiev, and Yekaterinoslav gubernias, the clothing industry accounted for nearly 70 per cent of all the Jewish artisans in the three districts. Within the industry, tailors were in an overwhelming majority; they actually constituted 47 per cent of the total of Jewish artisans in the area. However, there are indications of an incipient broadening out process with Jewish craftsmen penetrating into new occupational fields. By contrast with the eighteenth century, these records already revealed an appreciable number of Jewish cobblers, especially in the Ukraine; in the three gubernias there were 388 out of 3,735, or a tenth of all Jewish artisans. Similarly, in 1807, there were already 193 Jewish coppersmiths and boilermakers, and several score of tinsmiths, carpenters, engravers, watchmakers and painters. In a number of Kehillot, these new occupations were organized into separate craft organizations, proving that their numbers were much higher than the official statistics. In Vilno, there were Jewish craft guilds for tailors, furriers, butchers, glaziers, cobblers, brass-workers, goldsmiths, cord-makers, musicians, tinsmiths and woodworkers.* The Pinsk Kehillah's books for that period mentioned craft guilds of tailors, jewellery makers, barbers, and cordmakers and a joint association of engravers, glaziers and comb-makers, founded in 1803.

Comparison with gentile artisans emphasizes even more the one-sided occupational structure of the Jewish artisan class. According to the records of 1802, there were 248 Jewish artisans in the city of Minsk out of a total of 507, or 49 per cent. However, whereas 160 of the 164 tailors were Jews, all eighteen cordmakers, sixteen of the twenty-one furriers, and ten of the twelve barbers, the ratios were reversed in other occupations: two Jews among 137 cobblers, thirty Christian building construction workers and no Jews, one Jewish woodworker out of twenty-six, two Jewish carpenters out of twelve, fifteen gentile tanners and no Jews, three Jewish metal workers out of fifteen, and twelve Christian and no Jewish

---

* This is the order in which a letter from the municipality of Vilno to the Kehillah leaders in 1810 listed the Jewish guilds. The tinsmiths and woodworkers were only mentioned in the Kehillah's register for 1809.

saddlers. According to Governor-General Friesel of Lithuania, this was the situation throughout the entire pale of settlement.

Nonetheless, Friesel's statement that the Jews preferred light, clean occupations was exaggerated. As already stated, the carters were mainly Jews and this occupation demanded great physical exertion. Similarly, the barges floated down the River Dvina to Riga were chiefly manned by Jewish crews. The marked difference between the occupational composition of the Jewish artisan class in the north of the pale of settlement and in the Ukraine proved how strongly local conditions, especially competition, affected the introduction of new manual trades amongst the Jews. In Lithuania and White Russia, where Christian cobblers had worked for generations, the number of Jewish cobblers was negligible. On the other hand, the number of Jewish cobblers in the Kiev gubernia was three times as high as in that of Minsk—279 as compared with 94. Competition amongst the shoemakers of the Ukraine was merely not as keen, the peasants were better off than in White Russia and the demand for footwear was greater. The different market conditions in the two areas also accounted for the existence of over twice as many coppersmiths in the Kiev as in the Minsk gubernia, 136 against 57.

The Jews were master craftsmen in the occupations they dominated—contrary to Friesel's generalization. Jewish tailors sewed the most expensive garments and drew their customers from all social classes. In eighteenth-century Poland, records show that Jewish "court tailors" had worked for magnates. The Jewish craft guild books contained numerous regulations aimed mainly at preventing competition for the custom of the *P'ritzim*, or nobles. Prince Dolgorukov expressed surprise at the agility of the Uman Jewish tailor who delivered his dress suit "complete and perfect" on the evening of the day he took his measurements. The Jewish furriers, cordmakers and goldsmiths produced work of an equally high standard.

Friesel's contention that Jewish craftsmen did not learn their trade thoroughly, was frequently heard at a later period, and was, of course, not entirely unfounded. There were in fact, more unskilled workers in the trades dominated by the Jews than in those where Christians prevailed. Jews had successfully penetrated into some branches of handicraft, despite obstruction from the Christian guilds, merely because their cheaper products found a market amongst the masses.* Jewish tailors in Poland had pioneered the manufacture of ready-to-wear garments which they sold at fairs during earlier centuries. The proportion of inferior products produced by Jews was determined by their peculiar economic situation, which only offered them a limited number of occupations. Because Jews had established themselves in certain manual trades, especially the clothing trade, these occupations were steadily filled beyond their absorptive

* For comments by Polish economists on the similar situation in the Duchy of Warsaw, cf. *supra*, pp. 349–50.

capacity and many people attracted to them did not have the chance of an adequate training. It was not early marriage, as Friesel claimed, that was responsible for the lack of expertise of so many Jewish artisans, but the limitations placed upon the Jewish economy, the basic cause of Jewish poverty and destitution in general.

The overcrowding in the Jewish trades was the cause of the poor condition of the Jewish artisans. They employed the same methods as the shopkeepers in their attempts to obtain customers. Prince Dolgorukov recounted with gusto how five Jewish tailors grabbed hold of him as he was leaving a textile emporium and set to work with their tape measures. This was a common daily occurrence. The bye-laws of the artisan associations (for example, the Protocols of the Keidany Association for 1810) were often mainly concerned with measures to be taken against groups of tailors, furriers, and cordmakers who accosted a *Paritz* when he arrived in a town, on the street, in a shop, or at his inn. These bye-laws set out in detail the regulations against "cutting in" on craftsmen who had obtained the nobleman's custom legitimately. The fact that the Jewish artisans as a group were classed amongst the poor masses is reflected in all the literature of the period and is corroborated by data on their housing conditions included in late eighteenth century census returns. Large numbers in communities such as the Podolian town of Yampol all lived in clay huts, in contrast with the stone or wooden buildings occupied by the more prosperous.

The social and economic structure of the Russian Jewish population, resulting from centuries of oppression under the feudal system, was basically unsound. Agriculturalists constituted the overwhelming majority of the surrounding population and were almost non-existent amongst Russian Jews. Over half of them depended on liquor selling, in which they acted as intermediaries in the nobility's exploitation of the peasantry and the populations of the small towns. The Jewish population, lacking economic roots, mostly lived in a state of utter poverty. A fundamental reorganization of the Jewish economy was essential to right the wrongs of an oppressed people. But it was also indispensable to the capitalist system in Russia, which was making constant progress in the face of unceasing conflict with the dominant feudal régime. Instead, the policy that Alexander and his government chose to pursue bore no relationship to their liberal phrases, but frustrated all attempts at a basic improvement in the system. They discharged their obligation to the Jews by drawing up programmes without actually implementing a single reform.

First Government Committee for Jewish Reform and the Statute of 1804

All the reform proposals raised at the beginning of Alexander's reign came up against the question of peasant serfdom, and to interfere with serfdom was to interfere with the basic principle of the régime. However, the wretched situation of the Jews could not be remedied without a basic solution to the peasant problem. Instead of attempting to solve both interrelated problems, the government, anxious to make recompense for its unwillingness to improve the lot of the peasants, introduced pseudo-reforms for the Jews, which, even when partially implemented, brought upon them economic ruin and endless hardship.

Alexander set up some ten different committees to attend to the special problems facing the state, e.g. those relating to certain cities, the ports, the Imperial Navy and the Tartar lands. Following an imperial directive to the Senate dated November 9, 1802, a Committee on the Jewish Question was added. The primary task of this Committee was to review Derzhavin's report on the problem of the Jews and Jewish reforms in White Russia. However, it was also required "to extend these reforms to the Jews in all the gubernias annexed from Poland and the southern gubernias as well," or, in other words, for all the Jews in the entire pale of settlement. The Committee included the Minister of the Interior, V. P. Kotchubey; the Minister of Justice, Derzhavin; General Count V. A. Zubov and two Poles, on close terms with the Czar; Senator Seweryn Potocki; and the Assistant Minister for Foreign Affairs, Prince Adam Czartoryski.

The news of the St. Petersburg Committee alarmed the Jews in the pale of settlement, and especially those in White Russia, who had heard of Derzhavin and his proposals. By December, 1802, the heads of the Minsk Kehillah and its leading members had met and decided to send delegates to St. Petersburg "to petition His Majesty the Czar that his Ministers should not make any new reforms for us." Three days of fasting were decreed and the entire Kehillah was ordered to attend prayer services in the large synagogue of the city. In January, 1803, to calm the agitated Jews, the Minister of the Interior, Count Kotchubey, ordered all western Governors to notify the Kehillot that it was not the government's intention to restrict Jewish rights but, on the contrary, "to promote their improvement and prosperity." Immediately afterwards, the authorities notified the Kehillot that the Committee on the Jewish Question had decided to invite representatives of the chief Kehillot in the gubernias' capitals for consultations on reforms. However, not all the Kehillot could afford the expense involved in sending delegates, and even by the summer of 1803 only the representatives of Kehillot in the four gubernias of Minsk, Moghilev, Podolia and Kiev had gathered at St. Petersburg.

The enlightened St. Petersburg Jews advocated economic and educational reforms within the Jewish population, while the delegates from the provincial Kehillot, though they were also mostly wholesale merchants and members of leading guilds, were conservative in their views. When the Committee on the Jewish Question asked them to state their opinion on the projected reforms, they replied that they were not authorized to do so without first consulting their constituencies. They requested a period of six months for this purpose. The Committee did not agree to this postponement and circulated a summary of its proposals to the Kehillot through the governors "so that they would forward their replies on the matter of implementing the reforms without altering any of its sections." The Kehillot only made two requests: that all the reforms be deferred for a period of fifteen or twenty years and that, in any event, Jewish rights to engage in lesseeships and liquor selling should not be affected. In these circumstances, the government Committee decided to proceed with its discussions regardless of the opinion of the Kehillot. Thus the welfare of three-quarters of a million Jews was arbitrarily decided.

The composition of the Committee was enough to determine the direction of its programme for the Jews. Its members were Russian and Polish magnates, the owners of vast estates worked by serfs. In their views on Jewish reforms they were guided purely by the interests of their own class, the nobility, and of the Exchequer of the Empire which they ruled. Even the few concessions to the Jews included in the reforms for the promotion of trade and industry showed care on the part of the Committee not to infringe the special privileges of the dominant nationality and religion of the state.

The Committee based its discussions on the Jewish problem on the declared principles of human liberty, the encouragement of individual initiative, and the avoidance of all acts of coercion. However, the contradiction between its declaration propounding reform of the Jews through their own activities and the harsh decrees it proposed against the village Jews was so blatantly obvious that the Committee even introduced a note of apology into its programme. It explained that the contradiction was only superficial:

> As long as this occupation (alcoholic beverages) is permitted the Jews ... it will be impossible to divert them into other vocations and there will be no cessation of the general population's enmity towards them ... Furthermore can this be termed a repressive decree, if at the same time many new sources of livelihood are thrown open to the Jews—agriculture, factories and handicrafts? ...

On December 9, 1804, the Czar published his *Jewish Statute,* incorporating all the Committee's proposals, and accompanied them by an explanation of his action. The preamble stated that the Committee on the Jewish Question had been formed "owing to the numerous complaints about abuse and irregularities harmful to the agricultural and other vocations of the inhabitants of the districts in which the Jews are domiciled." The Czar considered the principles on which the Committee had based its statute "very just," as were also "all those sections of the Statute moderate and solicitous of the genuine welfare of the Jews on the one hand, and on the other hand founded on the best interests of the inhabitants rooted in those districts in which these people have been permitted to dwell." In this way, and almost incidentally, the Czar ratified the decree establishing a pale of settlement for the Jews; even within the pale, he distinguished between Jews and "the native inhabitants." This detailed act of legislation consisted of six sections and fifty-four articles. It was the result of the efforts of the first government Committee on the Jewish Question in Russia. It was also Russia's first law regulating Jewish life economically, communally, educationally and in terms of general enlightenment.

The principal innovation of the Statute was the ban it placed on all lesseeships and dealings in beverages in the villages. Under Section 34 no Jew might "acquire on lease any enterprise, ale-house or inn in any village or settlement, neither in his own name nor in the name of any other party, nor may he purvey liquors in them or dwell in them. . . ." This was to come into effect on January 1, 1807, in the gubernias of Astrakhan, the Caucasus,* Little Russia (the Ukraine) and White Russia; on January 1, 1808 in all other gubernias. The Jews were divided according to the type of employment permitted them into four estates: agriculturists; factory owners and artisans; merchants; and burghers. Every Jew was required to register in one of these estates within the following two years on threat of punishment for vagrancy. Jews in all four estates were permitted to buy unsettled land in all districts of the pale of settlement as well as in the two gubernias of south eastern Russia—Astrakhan and the Caucasus—and to employ wage earning cultivators. Jews were also allowed to lease plots of land from the landed proprietors for agricultural settlement. The government promised to place certain areas of the Crown lands in the western gubernias (except those in White Russia and the Ukraine) and in the two gubernias of Astrakhan and the Caucasus at the disposal of Jews who wished to transfer to agriculture. Groups of Jews who settled on manorial lands would be exempt from the payment of all taxes for a period of five years, and on Crown lands for ten years. Neither type of settler would be required to pay the double tax like other Jews even after his tax-exemption had expired.

The law encouraged manufacturing and handicraft as well as agriculture amongst the Jews. They were permitted to establish factories in all the western districts and also to acquire leases on factories built by the landed proprietors. Factory owners were promised state treasury loans and were immediately exempted from double taxation. Artisans were also exempt from this special taxation. They were allowed to engage in all crafts (but only within the pale of settlement) and also to be enrolled in the craft guilds, on condition that this did not conflict with the privileges enjoyed by the cities they lived in. The law promised that the Ministry of the Interior would arrange for Jewish artisans who could not make a living in their present districts to have an opportunity to transfer (like the agricultural settlers) to sparsely-populated gubernias in New Russia

* The two *gubernias* open to settlement by Jewish agriculturalists and artisans.

(Yekaterinoslav and Kherson gubernias), in the gubernia of Tavrida (Crimea), and in the two gubernias of Astrakhan and the Caucasus. Factory owners, artisans and merchants were permitted to enter the Russian interior "and even the capital city" with their families for temporary residence, on condition that they obtained passports from the district governors and wore "German" dress.

By contrast with the drastic economic reforms, the paragraphs of the law concerning "the civil government of the Jews" (Article IV) essentially confirmed the *status quo*. In deference to its declared principles regarding the rights of the Jews as citizens of the state, the Statute prohibited any offence to their religion or "their civil life" in speech or action. Contracts between the manorial proprietors of the towns and the Jews had to be observed equally by both parties, and the estate owners had no judicial rights over the Jews. Nevertheless, the law scrupulously maintained the privileges of the nobility: no Jew was free to transfer his residence from one city to another without a certificate from the estate-owner stating that he had "in the latter's opinion" discharged all his obligations towards him. Jews without passports would be arrested by the police and deported to the southern steppes. The P'ritzim's authority over the Jews was also guaranteed as far as Kehillah supervision was concerned. The Kehillah leaders in the private towns were required to submit an account of Kehillah finances to their respective proprietors in the same way as the Kehillah leaders in the county centres were obliged to render their accounts to the municipal authorities. In both cases they were forbidden to impose new taxes on Kehillah members without permission from the respective authorities—proprietor or municipality. The authority of the Kehillah boards as autonomous institutions was specifically confirmed by the requirement that they "ensure that government taxes were paid on the due date and in full." Abolition of Kehillah court jurisdiction was repeated and the permissive clause officially empowering them to sit as courts of arbitration was retained. Kehillah leaders and rabbis were to be elected every three years, subject to confirmation in office by the gubernias. Proprietors in the private cities had no right to interfere with these elections or to collect payment on the election of a rabbi. The rabbis were to supervise the observance of religious affairs and to give judgement in religious matters, but they were forbidden to punish wrong-doers by depriving them of kosher meat or Passover *matzot*, and certainly not by excommunication. Rabbis were not allowed to collect any fees beyond their own salaries.

The government believed that these regulations restricting rabbinical authority fulfilled its obligations to the demands of the *Maskilim* for a basic reform of the Kehillah régime. The enactments concerning general enlightenment among the Jews contained in Article 1 of the Statute were no more substantial. All public schools, secondary schools and universities were declared open to Jewish pupils without discrimination, and it was specifically forbidden to entice them away from the Jewish religion or to teach them anything contrary to its precepts. Pupils would be allowed to appear in Jewish dress only in the elementary schools; in the *gymnasia* (secondary schools) and universities they were required to wear German or Polish style clothes "for uniform and pleasing appearance." If the Jews were unwilling to enrol their children in the general public schools despite this encouragement, special schools would have to be founded at their expense and a special tax levied on them for that purpose. The study of one of three languages—Russian, Polish or German—would be required at these schools. At the end of six years, Jewish business ledgers and documents would have to be kept in one of these languages if they were to be legally valid in the law courts. The ability to read and write in one of these languages was also made obligatory for Jewish members of municipalities in 1808, and for Kehillah leaders and rabbis in 1812. Furthermore, Jewish members of municipalities were required to dress in the German, Polish or Russian fashion.

For all the high-flown phraseology of the Committee's declarations, the Statute for the Jews of Russia was fundamentally only an imitation of the paternalist system that enlightened absolutism in the neighbouring countries had introduced for its Jewish subjects some years earlier (cf. Joseph II's reforms and the Prussian *Reglement* of 1797). Its only improvement lay in its broad programme for Jewish agricultural settlement (more theoretical than practical) and this was the result of circumstances peculiar to this vast country. The need for a labour force to develop the steppes of New Russia (southern Ukraine) made the religion or nationality of the settlers irrelevant. This project, however, like all the Jewish reform measures decreed by law, was hampered by the inefficiency of the unwieldy absolutist state and its government through police *dicta*.

The government of the absolutist régime attempted to eliminate the problem of Jewish lesseeship and liquor selling at one blow. However, the estate owners saw no possibility of finding efficient replacements for the Jewish lessees and liquor purveyors in their private cities and towns— in contrast to the villages. The Jews were after all best suited to the task in the towns where they lived amongst their own kind and were experienced in its affairs. When it came to a question of their own incomes, the nobles were indifferent to the fact that the liquor business in the towns and in the villages exploited the peasants in exactly the same way. The very law on the expulsion of the Jews from the villages in fact expressly allowed lesseeship and liquor sales by Jews in the cities and towns, with the sole qualification that no liquor was to be sold on credit.

The Statute of 1804 for the Jews in Russia not only protected the estate owners' profits; it also strengthened their authority over the small-town Jews under their jurisdiction. It also left in force the discrimination between Jewish and Christian burghers. The slight expansion of the pale of settlement, by the permission granted to Jewish agriculturists and artisans to settle in Astrakhan and the Caucasus, had no practical value. Agricultural settlement in the area did not take place and settlement permits for artisans were not issued on individual request but depended mainly on special arrangements by the Minister for the Interior. Even the formulation of this item in the law was more suggestive of a deportation measure. The double tax decree was not rescinded by the 1804 Statute, except in so far as it affected factory owners, artisans and cultivators. The taxes paid by Jewish merchants, members of one of the three guilds, were brought into line with those paid by all other merchants (a 1 per cent capital tax) in 1807. The remaining Jews, who were classifiel as burghers, were only freed from the double tax during the wars with Napoleon, when taxes for the population as a whole were raised to such a height that there was no prospect of collecting double the amount from the Jews.

All limitations on Jewish rights not specifically mentioned in the Statute of 1804 remained automatically in force. A number of cities still retained the ancient privilege of "not tolerating Jews," while others only permitted Jewish residence in certain streets (Kovno for example), or else forbade Jews to live in certain streets (Vilno). The question of Jewish rights of participation in the municipalities and other urban institutions was not fortuitously omitted from the law. This right had been greatly curtailed at the beginning of Alexander's reign, initially in the gubernias of Volhynia and Podolia. In 1802, the Military Governor of Podolia ordered that the Jews there only be allowed to elect one-third of the members of a municipal administration. Furthermore, they were no longer permitted to participate in the election of Christian members of municipal administrations. The Senate confirmed the Governor's order and even extended these restrictions to cover both gubernias of Lithuania, the two gubernias of White Russia and the Kiev gubernia. The inclusion of the Lithuanian districts in the Senate's ordinance provoked an outcry amongst the Polish burghers in that area who considered even these restricted Jewish civil rights to be too liberal. At the instigation of the Minister of the Interior, and with Alexander's consent, the Senate, in 1804, repealed its ordinance on the voting rights of Jews in the cities of Lithuania. Actually the Jews were deprived of the right to participate in the municipal administration not only in Lithuania, but in several other localities as well. The omission of municipal electoral rights from the 1804 Statute provided the city of Kiev and the cities of the Tavrida gubernia (Crimea) with a basis for denying their Jewish inhabitants these rights.

Reaction was thus constantly spreading with regard to the Jews as well as to the country as a whole. In contrast with the period of enlightened absolutism, when Catherine II firmly insisted on active Jewish enfranchisement in the municipalities, the Jews were deprived of all their political rights as burghers in part of the pale of settlement under the "liberal" Alexander I. In the remaining districts of the pale, their representation was confined to a fixed minority. However, the decree expelling the Jews from the villages, the essential point of the Jewish Statute of 1804, was immeasurably more oppressive than this discrimination.

The Decree of Expulsion from the Villages; Delays in Implementation

Evidence of the insuperable economic and social difficulties involved in implementing the decree expelling the Jews from the villages appeared almost immediately after it was announced. While many landowners could not even wait for the expulsion decree to become legally operative but began at once to evict the Jews from their villages, most of the village proprietors had so great a need of their lessees and innkeepers that they drew up lease contracts with them for the coming years despite the law. However, political events forced the government to act with moderation in implementing the decree rather more than did these circumstances or the unhappy situation of the first victims of the expulsion. The news that the Assembly of Jewish Notables had met in Paris by order of Napoleon came as a warning to Russian government circles, and on August 24, 1806, Alexander directed his Committee on the Jewish Question to renew its activities and take into consideration the current trends in Russian Jewry. The report of the convening of the *Grand Sanhedrin* in France came towards the end of the year, when Russia entered the Prussian war against Napoleon. The government, despite its anti-French propaganda campaign conducted through the Orthodox Church and the reactionary press and its criticism of Napoleon as "the saviour of the Jews", still attempted to gain the favour of the Jews.

On February 10, 1807, the Minister of the Interior, Kotchubey, proposed to Alexander that the expulsion of the Jews from the villages be deferred. He gave as his reasons the need "to put this people in a cautious frame of mind towards the French government's intentions" and also the shortage of means to transfer the expelled Jews to work in factories or agriculture. The Czar did not agree to the actual proposal but decided nevertheless to proceed with caution, in view of the political situation.

In July, 1807, the Franco-Russian War came to an end with the Peace of Tilsit, and the Paris *Sanhedrin* was dispersed. The Russian government now did not hesitate to start the implementation of the expulsion decree. On October 19, 1807, an Imperial Warrant was issued to the governors of the western gubernias "for the transfer of the Jews from the villages to the cities." The preface to the Warrant did mention the petition that the Kehillah delegates had submitted to the governors for postponement of the expulsion "for several years" in view of "the extreme poverty of the majority," the double taxes, and the high cost of living—all factors preventing them from building factories and purchasing land. But Alexander only agreed to one concession: that the expulsion be carried out over a three-year period, a third each in 1808, 1809 and 1810. To compensate to some extent for this measure, the authorities in all gubernias of the pale of settlement were ordered to establish committees of the nobility for the rehabilitation of the victims of the expulsion. These committees were instructed to suggest to the Kehillot that they raise funds to assist the settlers, to urge the estate-owners to settle Jews on their land and to establish factories, and to draw up plans for the colonization of Jews in New Russia, Astrakhan and the Caucasus. Nonetheless, the order still gave specific assurance to the estate-owners that their privileges were guaranteed. "It is self-evident," it stated, "that proprietors and villages are free to establish other lessees in the inns and also to open new inns, provided that Jews are excluded from the leasings."

All the provisions that the Warrant made for the transfer of the village Jews to land settlements were completely insubstantial. The noblemen's committees were set up in accordance with the law but took no action of any kind. The estate-owners did not even contemplate settling Jews on their lands, partly out of fear that free peasant colonies were liable to inspire rebellion amongst their serfs. From the outset, it became obvious that colonization in the southern Ukraine would be limited to very few Jewish settlers. The government itself later admitted the reasons for this in an order postponing the expulsions which was published at the end of that year: the Kehillot, in their reduced circumstances, could not afford to support the settlers, and the government refused, or—in its own words—was "unable" to allot the necessary sums of money. However, in spite of this, the authorities began to carry out the expulsion that year according to plan. Hundreds of evicted families wandered along roads or thronged city streets, without a roof over their heads, in search of food.

Meanwhile Senator Alexeiev had submitted another report. On the basis of the opinion of the authorities in the western gubernias, he warned that implementation of the expulsion might be disastrous to the Jews. Alexander, at the suggestion of a new Minister for the Interior, Kurakin, who recapitulated the reasons advanced by his predecessor, Kotchubey, to prove that "transferring them (the village Jews) gradually to settlement on government lands would take many decades owing to their very great numbers," finally consented on December 29, 1808 to defer the expulsion until further notice. On January 5, 1809, a new Committee was formed to suggest new ways of carrying out the expulsion as well as to deal with petitions submitted to the gubernial authorities by representatives of the Kehillot on that question, and on other changes made in the Statute of 1804. This Committee was headed by Senator V. S. Popov.

The State Secretary, Speranski, appointed in 1810, reached the peak of his influence at this time and a spirit of liberation also pervaded the Committee on the Jewish Question. In March, 1812, after three years of discussion, Senator Alexeiev submitted a report to the Czar on behalf of the Committee. The report was prepared after hearing views from local authorities, estate-owners and Jewish representatives. The Committee, for the first time since the question of Jewish liquor selling had been placed on the agenda, considered the problem in its report comprehensively and in depth. The essential points made were that:

> ... neither Jewish obstinacy nor the helplessness of the authorities but the material and political situation in the districts of the Jewish Pale of Settlement were the reasons why Section 34 (expelling the Jews from the villages) of the Jewish Statute has been impossible to implement. The Jews seized the liquor business as an occupation because there was a dearth of other sources of livelihoods, while the nobles found this beneficial to themselves. The Jewish innkeepers have never amassed fortunes but have earned barely enough to support themselves. Expulsion of the Jews from the villages would not necessarily reduce drunkenness amongst the peasants, for the Jews would be replaced in the inns by other peasants who would behave as they have in order to reap greater profits for the proprietors. Replacement of the Jews might harm the economy by removing 60,000 peasants from agriculture. The Jewish innkeepers have also possessed many advantages: because of the trading activities they conduct as a supplementary occupation, the peasants are spared the waste of time consumed in travelling to town to sell their grains and buy salt, iron implements and other items. When in need, the peasants have obtained loans from the Jewish innkeepers. The Jewish inns have been of benefit to travellers and their keepers have also maintained postal traffic. The reduced circumstances of the White Russian peasants cannot be attributed to the Jews; for there are also Jews in the villages of the southwest gubernias, yet peasant conditions there are far more favourable than in the north. The origin of drunkenness amongst the White Russian peasants lies in the economic system of the landed proprietors, which has facilitated the spread of this evil. There are no Jews at all in the Districts of St. Petersburg, Livland, and Estonia; nevertheless, drunkenness there is very widespread. The prohibition of Jewish liquor purveying would be a signal to the estate-owners to expel the Jews from the villages and would thus foment persecutions of the Jews, the like of which has already been forgotten, thanks to our Imperial Master's love of his fellow creatures. The best interests of the State Exchequer also demand nullification of the expulsion decree in view of the tax revenues deriving from 60,000 Jewish family heads in the villages as well as tax payments by the peasants who also depend on Jewish help.

The Committee used similarly logical arguments to prove that, in present circumstances, no other source of income was available to the village Jews. Demand was not large enough for trade and the manual occupations to provide an income for tens of thousands of additional families. If, despite this, the village Jews were forced into these branches of the economy, it would only cause the complete impoverishment of those Jews who had long been established in these occupations. There were no factories, and the Jews did not have the capital to build them. Even if the government decided to spend several million rubles on the construction of factories, it could not solve the problem, as industry depended primarily on the marketing of its products. The Jews could not, in all justice, be forced to work in factories, as they were not serfs. On the question of the implementation of the agricultural settlement programme, the Chairman of the Committee, Popov, pointed out that this had been hampered by lack of funds and Jewish inexperience in the cultivation of the soil. The Committee summed up in conclusion that the Jews were too destitute to be able to improve their condition by themselves and the government did not command the necessary funds.

Needless to say, the Government Committee on the Jewish Question never for a moment considered any proposal to put an end to the feudal system, which would inevitably have involved the emancipation of the serfs. However, its liberal views and political and economic sanity were reflected in its demand that the financial destruction of the Jews be prevented, especially as this anyhow would not improve the condition of the peasants. In its conclusions, the Committee recommended that Section 34 of the Statute for the Jews be revoked, both for the reasons already mentioned (on which it was in total agreement with the representatives of the Kehillot) "and also considering that in present political circumstances it is in general appropriate not to deal severely with the Jewish people, which even so is oppressed to the utmost."

The allusion to Russia's political situation signified the preparation for war against Napoleon, and it was this argument that now carried weight with the government, as it had in 1806. It became even more convincing several months later, when the war broke out and Napoleon invaded Russia. Nevertheless, although the paragraph in the law concerning the expulsion was not put into effect, the government was unwilling to repeal it completely and it remained as a threat suspended over the rural Jews. When a new wave of reaction set in towards the end of Alexander's reign, it descended in full force upon the Jews of White Russia.

Attempts to Move the Jews into Productive Activities: Agricultural Colonies

The Statute of 1804 offered the Jews two means of reorienting their unbalanced economy: establishing factories and settling on the land. Individual officials had proposed the fostering of industry amongst the Jews in reform programmes they submitted to the government at that time. Detailed plans for spreading useful occupations amongst the Jews were also drawn up by the Jewish merchant and supplier, Nathan Nota (now Notkin) of Shklov, who lived in St. Petersburg.

The government disregarded Notkin's arguments for abolishing the double tax imposed on the Jews and revoking the village expulsion decree. It did, however, pay some attention to his plan for spreading industry amongst the Jews. The establishment of textile factories to supply woollens and linens to the army had become an urgent necessity with the intensification of the anti-British blockade which was seriously interfering with Russian imports of textiles. The Statute of 1804 allowed Jews in the pale of settlement to operate factories under the regulations governing all other Russian subjects. Factory owners, like artisans and cultivators, were exempt from double tax payments. Jews establishing important factories, especially in the "woollen linen and leather" trades, were promised Treasury loans and building sites. But all these incentives were impotent in face of the lack of funds amongst the Jews. In 1806, there was a total of twenty-six textile mills with ninety-eight looms in all the western gubernias. Eight mills with no more than twenty-five looms belonged to Jews. Even the few factories owned by Jews hardly employed any Jewish workers. They were definitely present only in the textile industries of a few cities like Moghilev, Dubrowne (where prayer shawls were manufactured!) and in the government factory at Poltava, where in 1810, Prince Dolgorukov reported that "Jewish idlers were employed."*

The Russian government was so anxious to develop the textile industry to supply the army and the navy that in 1809 it built a factory at Kremenchug in the Ukrainian district of Poltava especially to teach Jews the textile trade. By the beginning of 1810, it already employed forty Jewish families, 232 individuals. Its craftsmen and instructors included Jewish experts, brought there from distant Grodno. Its initial results were satisfactory and workers who mastered their trade within a year were rewarded with cash prizes. As time passed, however, conditions in the factory became intolerable: punishments such as lashings by the police were introduced and the small payments made for food supplies discontinued. The factory was closed in 1817.

The cruelty of the police methods, inseparably associated with the absolutist régime, was also partially responsible for the failure of the Jewish agricultural resettlement programme, even though the government's activity in this field was on a much broader scale than in the industrial venture. The Statute of 1804 mentioned Jewish agricultural colonization both on manorial lands in all districts of the pale of settlement and on government lands in nine gubernias of the pale. White Russia, Kiev and the Ukraine were not mentioned. Before long, however,

* In 1815, the Jewish owner of the textile plant at Vilno, Moses Leib Klaczko, applied to the authorities for permission to employ child labourers, the sons of poor Jews, in addition to his sixteen workmen.

it became obvious that permission to settle on the manorial lands had no practical significance, while the possibilities of settlement on government lands were limited, in practice, to one definite area. From the beginning, the government had actually only seriously considered the steppes of "New Russia," the southern Ukraine, for its Jewish resettlement programme. While it wanted to reduce the large Jewish population of the western districts, it also was very anxious to populate the desolate areas in the southern part of the country.

Energetic action to colonize the steppes of New Russia had already begun during the reign of Catherine II and was continued during the first half of the nineteenth century. Numerous colonists were brought from abroad without distinction as to nationality or religion. When the enactment of the Jewish Statute of 1804 had made it clear that there was no possibility of agricultural settlement in their own districts, many Jewish families, especially those recently expelled from the villages, agreed to migrate to the remote areas of New Russia to try their hand at farming.

These families, anxious for the "grace of His Exalted Majesty, the Czar, His Ministers and Advisers," had not anticipated that their colonization would be hampered by the slow-moving Russian bureaucratic machine. Nor had they expected that, even when they had overcome this obstacle, they would have to endure new difficulties and incalculable weariness. In 1806, Nahum Finkelstein applied to the Governor of the Moghilev District on behalf of thirty-six families of the Tcherikov locality who were prepared to settle in New Russia. However, it appeared that the government had not drawn up any plan of action for such eventualities. After prolonged negotiations between the Governor of Moghilev and the Minister of the Interior, Kotchubey, a plot of nearly 60,000 acres of arid steppe in the Kherson Gubernia, on the banks of the river Inguletz, was allotted for settlement by these Jews. It was agreed between Kotchubey and Duke Richelieu, Governor of the Kherson District, that they were to be settled in separate colonies, "both for their own good as regards their religion, and in order to facilitate supervision by the authorities . . ." After Finkelstein had made innumerable journeys between the district offices and Kotchubey's Ministry at St. Petersburg, he was finally sent to New Russia to select the land for his group. This group was followed by another of fifty-two families from Mstislav, and the colonization movement immediately spread to other districts of the pale, such as the gubernias of Vitebsk, Chernikhov, Podolia and Kherson. By the end of 1806, according to official data, 1,479 families had applied for colonization in New Russia.

The monetary support supplied by the gubernial authorities for travelling expenses was so meagre (five kopeks a day for food) that the Kehillot were obliged to help the migrants. At the suggestion of the Moghilev District Governor, representatives of the Kehillot in the district met and agreed to allot 6,000 rubles from money accumulated over a fifteen-year period from hiring out ritual citrus fruits* for travelling expenses for the settlers. In addition, an entry in the Mstislav Kehillah records for the year 1808, indicated that the journeys were also financed by the treasuries of the Kehillot which the settlers were leaving, the burial society and other communal organizations, and by a fund-raising campaign amongst property owners in the Kehillah. The Mstislav Kehillah "also equipped them with seven rubles' worth of pharmaceutical supplies which they took with them on the journey . . ." The Vilno Kehillah leaders responded by issuing a regulation in 1809 requiring that gold and silver ornaments on women's dresses and silver collars on the "kittels" be donated "for the needs of the poor that they may exist by tilling the soil."

The Kehillah leaders did not neglect to provide for the religious and ceremonial requirements and cultural needs of the settlers. They were not ignorant peasants moving to new lands but *yode'ei sefer*—people versed in the Books—to whom a lesson in the *Mishnah* and *Ein-Ya'akov*† was of vital importance. The scribe of the Mstislav Kehillah reported:

> With the permission of the Kehillah dignitaries I also gave them two Scrolls of the Law from the Synagogue collection; six tomes of the *Mishnah*, Dyhernfurth Edition; one Bible, Dyhernf. Ed.; one old *Midrash*; one large *Ein-Ya'akov*, Amsterdam Ed., with all the Commentaries; one *Shevet Musar*‡ one complete *Shulhan Arukh*; the *Tze'enah Re'anah*§ and *Nachalat Zevi*.¶

However, even the assistance given by the Kehillot was not sufficient to cover the expenses of a journey which, at that time, took several months. Most of the settlers used up their funds en route and arrived in the Kherson District in a wretched condition. The office for the welfare of the settlers in the southern Ukraine was totally unprepared to receive such a large number of families, and the Governor-General requested Kotchubey to restrict colonization to between 200 and 300 families a year. Nevertheless, migration continued and actually increased in volume during 1808, when the authorities began to expel Jews from the villages. By the end of 1809, 1,691 Jewish families, or a total of 9,757 people, had reached New Russia, a third of them at their own expense, without any government support. Over half of those who arrived in 1808 had to wait for a further two years before they were settled. Hundreds of families

---

* The *Etrog*, used for religious purposes on the Feast of Tabernacles—*Sukkot*.

† A collection of legends, ethical teachings and virtues gleaned from the Talmud and first published at Salonica in 1516 by Rabbi Jacob ben Habib. A constant companion of the religious masses for generations.

‡ Literally, *The Lash of Morality*, by Elijah Ben Solomon Abraham of Smyrna, seventeenth century, a collection of ethical discourses and admonitions promising brimstone and hellfire to the sinful, widely circulated amongst orthodox Jews throughout Europe during the eighteenth century.

§ Biblical homilies in Yiddish.

¶ i.e., *The Legacy of Zevi*, a collection of legends from the Zohar, in Yiddish.

wandered about the steppe without shelter, and some of them dispersed to distant villages and cities.

The families who were received by the settlers' office did not fare better. Until their homes were built, they suffered from the scorching summer winds of the steppe, and froze in the winter for lack of fuel. A shortage of drinking water in most places and a scarcity of bread gave rise to contagious diseases that spread disaster amongst the colonists: in the colony of Se'deh-Menuchah* alone, 200 people died within three years. Those strong enough to survive suffered for many years at the hands of a bureaucratic régime. Government loans for oxen, ploughs and other implements were not even sufficient to obtain half their actual requirements. Seed-grain was delivered months after the season. Above all, the corrupt practices of the "superintending" officials made considerable inroads into the loans intended for the settlers. In these conditions, the farm colonies of the Jews in the southern Ukraine were built. In 1807, the colonies of Bobrovy Kut (with settlers from Moghilev), Izrailevka (from Chernikhov), Se'deh-Menuchah and Ya'azor* (Dobroye) were founded. Four more were added in 1809: Inguletz, Kamianka, Nahar-Tov* and Ye'feh-Nahar* (corrupted in Russian to Yefengar). The number of inhabitants in these settlements, as registered by the Ministry of the Interior, totalled 646 families or 3,618 people.

On April 6, 1810, an imperial warrant discontinued the colonization of Jews in New Russia. This was basically because of the government's reluctance to allocate funds for the support of Jewish settlement on the land. It was not the result of a shortage of candidates, for even after that date, groups of Jews who had not heard of the warrant still submitted applications for settlement to the authorities. Neither was it caused by the difficulties the Jewish colonists were experiencing in adjustment (of which the Kherson Governor had complained to the Czar when he proposed that settlement be restricted); contagious diseases had also broken out amongst the German colonists, accustomed for generations to agricultural work (and the German settlers had been allotted larger plots of land than the Jews).

The *ukase* issued by the government had begun the transfer of the Jewish population to agriculture and industry within a rigid feudal régime. Another *ukase* terminated the few attempts to move them into productive activity. If they had continued under a changed system, they might have met with success.

The Kehillah Régime

The economic, social and political system within the Jewish pale of settlement in Russia was essentially the same feudal régime that had

* Hebrew names: *Se'deh-Menuchah*—Field of Repose; *Ya'azor*—He Will Succour; *Nahar-Tov*—A Good River; *Ye'feh-Nahar*—Beautiful River.

prevailed in the Kingdom of Poland. The Kehillah also retained its status as the institution of feudal autonomy for the Jewish population. None of the severe laws that the Russian absolute monarchy enacted to reduce the Kehillah's functions exclusively to religious affairs were effective, particularly as all of them, including the Statute of 1804, within their own context, pronounced the Kehillah responsible for collecting government taxes from the Jews. Although the Russians, unlike Poland in the past, did regard the Jews as burghers both in judicial and electoral matters, at first granting them equal and later restricted rights, the Kehillah constituted a municipality within a municipality. Its activities continued to embrace all spheres of life of the members and it imposed its authority with the utmost severity. Government and municipal taxes were not paid directly by the individual but through the Kehillah Board and by a system which the Kehillah determined. Jewish representatives to municipal bodies and in the law courts were appointed by the Kehillah Board or at elections held under its authority. Although the law had only left the Kehillah court powers of arbitration, it continued to judge civil and criminal lawsuits; for a Jew to file a suit with "gentile tribunals" was considered an act of betrayal, punishable under Kehillah law by excommunication.

The character of the Kehillah as an autonomous community with the authority of a feudal corporation was most clearly apparent in its supervision of the economic affairs of its members. As before, even the right to live in a city depended on permission from the Kehillah administration. When population censuses were conducted by the government, the Kehillah Board drew up the register of the Jews in the city. Before the returns were submitted, the Kehillah leaders ordered non-indigenous poor, especially servants, to leave the city in an attempt to escape the responsibility for paying government taxes on behalf of the poor families. For the same reason, no new inhabitant was granted permission to live in a city unless he had received permission from the Kehillah Board, and this depended on payment of a special fee (at Minsk, fifteen rubles) and a pledge on the part of the prospective member to pay all taxes. Occasionally, the Kehillah also demanded a written guarantee from a local resident. If the new member was an artisan, the consent of the artisans' association, which involved payment of a registration fee, was also required. A permit from the Kehillah authorities was needed if a member wished to travel out of town; the Statute of 1804 specifically authorized the Kehillot to issue these permits. Sometimes they would not issue them without the traveller's assurance that he "would not cause any evil to any person in the world." In a few Kehillot, a house outside the quarter or the "Jews' Street" could still not be bought without a special licence from the Kehillah Board. The law of *Hazakah* (tenure licence) applied in all the Kehillot to buildings, flats and stores, especially if they were rented or bought from Christian proprietors. The right of tenure was granted by the Kehillah Board against the payment of a sum fixed at intervals. To preclude violation of prerogatives and economic competition (an integral facet of government by corporation) the Jewish artisan associations scrupulously enforced the individual clientage rights of each member in relation to the *Paritz* who patronized him. The Kehillah authorities also interfered in the affairs of the professional class which depended on the wealthy members for their income: musicians, rhymesters, cantors, beadles, midwives. Members of these and similar professions had to obtain a licence to engage in their professions by paying a fee into the Kehillah treasury (rabbis had to pay vast sums for their appointments). They were subject to various restrictions and sometimes even had to take colleagues specifically designated by name into partnership. The Kehillah Boards, like the autonomous municipalities under the old régime, established maximum prices for food commodities, especially meat and fish, and forbade speculation in grain, flour and similar commodities. Amongst their economic functions, the Kehillah Boards also represented the interests of the liquor purveyors in negotiations with the beverage monopoly lease-holders (at Minsk), the nobles, and the city proprietors (at Dubno). They determined the number of liquor sellers in a city (at Pruzhany), and, in some cases, all arrangements with the nobleman concerning lesseeships in a town had to have the approval of the Kehillah leaders. The custom whereby the Kehillah attended to Jewish affairs by interceding with the authorities did not change during that period, except that the municipality was now an important factor amongst these authorities. The frequent gifts to public officials, and especially to city authorities (the magistrates) on Christian holidays, entailed such heavy expenditure that the Kehillah leaders often had to make a special levy on their members for this purpose.

The Kehillot continued rigidly to supervise the organizations within its aegis, whether artisan associations or charitable and religious societies. No new society could be founded without permission from the Kehillah Board. Their laws and bye-laws had to be approved by the Kehillah Board; in some cases it even drew up their regulations for them. Disciplinary offences against society officials were punished by the Kehillah heads. Charitable expenditure was financed by fund raising on behalf of the societies, but the Kehillah executive decided on all their activities and determined the procedure for supporting the poor. In times of drought or severe economic crisis, the Kehillah Boards also imposed a special tax on family heads on behalf of the poor. The Kehillot tried to curb expenditure on luxuries by detailed regulations governing celebrations at circumcisions and weddings. The Kehillah leaders closely supervised the practice of religion and religious ethics. In the great Kehillah of Minsk, special inspectors were appointed to ensure that the flour sold in the stores did not contain worms. Special regulations were passed to secure proper observance of the Sabbath; for example, liquor purveyors were required to sell their taverns to a gentile woman against a "bill of sale" every Sabbath Eve. Serious offences such as prostitution were heavily punished. At times of repressive government legislation or other hardships, all Kehillah members were ordered to observe public fasts. In 1803, during one such fast, the Minsk Kehillah appointed three officials to supervise its observance and issued a proclamation in all the synagogues of the city declaring that "anybody who knows of anything that merely suggests the possibility of a transgression committed by man or woman must, on pain of excommunication, notify the three officials."

The organization within the Kehillot had continued the traditional system of Polish times, with its plutocratic, oligarchic characteristics. The historical roots of the Polish Kehillah lay in the Kehillot structure of Germany and, especially, Bohemia and Moravia, as it had crystallized during the seventeenth and the beginning of the eighteenth century. The Russian Kehillot during the first half of the nineteenth century still resembled those central European Kehillot of two centuries or more earlier.

The right to participate in Kehillah assemblies was only granted, in practice, to wealthy men and those with titles of erudition. In some instances, Kehillah bye-laws specifically denied to low ratepayers or artisans the right of election to Kehillah office (the Kehillah of Petrovitchi in the Moghilev gubernia in 1777; the Kehillah of Sukhari in the same gubernia in 1781). However, even without these regulations, the practice of selling the right to be elected at all levels effectively excluded the unpropertied from any participation in the Kehillah executive. The only restriction imposed by the Minsk Kehillah Regulations of 1808 forbade the electors to accept money from candidates for appointment to positions in the Kehillah or any society.

The wealthy class that ruled the Kehillot determined the collection system for all taxes: Kehillah rates, government taxes, municipal taxes in the crown cities and taxes for the proprietors in the private cities. The indirect tax system, collectively known as the *korobka*, was employed on an even wider scale under Russian rule than in the past under Poland. In some of the small Kehillot, it was still the practice to collect part of the taxes directly, but in the large cities the *korobka* was the chief source of Kehillah revenue. As before, the meat excise, the *taxa*, which varied from one Kehillah to another was the principal source of the *korobka*. In addition to the *korobka* on beef, mutton and poultry, some Kehillot also introduced an occasional *korobka* on other foods, such as fish, butter or bread, to raise funds for the poor. When the *korobka* was not enough to cover government taxation and particularly when an urgent debt had to be paid, merchants and artisans were taxed in proportion to the value of their property and capital. Jewish merchants from outside a city had to pay a special tax representing a fixed percentage of the various commodities they handled. The *korobka* system of taxation weighed heavily on the large poverty-stricken population and also involved the employment of inspectors by the Kehillot—usually chosen from amongst the family and friends of the leaders.

The class interests of the Kehillah executive, representing the merchants and the wealthy lessees, continued, as in the preceding period, to conflict sharply with those of the artisans, who had no share in Kehillah administration. In some instances, Kehillah leaders refused the artisans permission to found a society of their own, unless a definite agreement were reached that the society would accept their authority. The Kehillah Board at Minsk hampered efforts by the Jewish musicians to organize a professional society for many decades until their ban was finally confirmed by an unequivocal resolution in 1803. Artisan status was inferior in the Kehillah hierarchy. Only one tailor figures amongst the scores of entries in the Minsk Kehillah register at the end of the eighteenth and beginning of the nineteenth centuries recording recipients of the title of *Morenu* by Kehillah resolution—and he paid a larger fee than was customary for the honour. Artisans, because of their lowly status, were even denied the privilege of wearing the same garments as respected *balebatim*.* In the spring of 1815, in the city of Keidany, the Jewish tailors had the audacity to appear in synagogue on the Grand Sabbath (the Sabbath preceding Passover) with *yarmulkes* (skull caps) and *shtreimlakh* (fur-brimmed headgear) on their heads. The "insolent ones" were handed over by decision of the Kehillah Board to the city proprietor, who had them whipped for insubordination "that they might tell of it unto the last generation and never again transgress." The artisans won their case on appealing to a government court.

Kehillah leaders were also suspicious of the separate prayer congregations (*minyanim*) that the artisans established to avoid depending on others for honours such as being called up to the Reading of the Law on the Sabbath.

The position of the poor in the Kehillot of Lithuania, White Russia and the Ukraine was no better than that of their co-religionists in most European Kehillot at the time. The Kehillah's task here was to supervise the charity societies, to direct their activities, and to levy regular taxes on their members for charitable purposes, quite apart from the fund-raising drives it organized at times when poverty assumed unusual proportions. On the other hand, the Kehillah authorities considered it their duty to issue decrees to ensure that charity would not become a burden on the wealthy and, particularly, that the number of local poor would not increase by an influx from outside their communities. Some Kehillot forbade their *balebatim* to give alms to the poor, "not even a half kopek,"

---

* Yiddish corruption of the Hebrew *ba'alei-batim*—house-owners, hence men of wealth and social position.

without the authority contained in a slip from the leader of the congregation or the Kehillah Board. Infringement was punishable by ostracism. For the most part, the Kehillah poor were only allowed to beg for alms from door to door on two days a week. Mendicants from out of town could not even be sheltered in the homes of residents for one night, and no one, in any circumstances, was allowed to rent a room in a dwelling without the Kehillah Board's permission. The only lodgings permitted mendicants from outside were in the *hekdesh* (almshouse), which also served as an infirmary for the poor—and they could only stay there for two or three days. The caretaker of the *hekdesh* was required to keep a horse in preparation for sending them away when their time was up. A poor man who returned to a city was forbidden access to the almshouse.

In order to implement their decisions and execute their sentences, the Kehillah leaders continued to employ all the forms of punishment that had been practised during the period of Kehillah autonomy under Polish rule. Offenders were punished by losing the title of *Morenu* or the right to participate in Kehillah assemblies, by being removed from office in their society, or by paying a fine into the Kehillah treasury. A severe penalty, imposed for insulting a Kehillah leader, was to expel the miscreant from all societies. In the case of an artisan, this meant that he was deprived of his source of income as it was forbidden to engage in any trade without the approval of the trade association. Records of the period mention the pillory (*kuneh*) as a punishment for adultery. Abusive criticism of the Kehillah executive or of a *Parnass* was sometimes punished by depriving the offender of the right to lease enterprises, but occasionally the Kehillah authorities were satisfied if the culprit publicly begged forgiveness instead of being expelled from his society. At Minsk, "police," (*dyesyatniki*) supervised enforcement of Kehillah decisions, especially concerning taxes. These functionaries formed a professional association in 1805. Burial societies also exercised authority over all Kehillah members so that anybody sinning against religion or offending its functionaries was liable to be punished on his dying day (by a dishonourable funeral).

However, despite all the coercion employed, the authority of the Kehillah as an institution was not as complete as under the Polish kingdom. Increasing social differentiation on the one hand, and absolutism on the other, were steadily undermining the foundations of an institution which had bound the Jewish population with all the chains of the outmoded feudal system. The modern Jewish middle class, which was beginning to take shape in Russia too, disapproved of the existing Kehillah régime. The oligarchy of family cliques mainly relied on the big merchants, but it also required the support of the moderately wealthy classes and even, to a slight extent, of the unpropertied elements, who depended on the Kehillah leaders for their jobs as Kehillah functionaries or for their trades. The financial magnates, on the other hand, wanted to establish exclusive domination of the Kehillot by the merchants. Although the tax system enforced by the Kehillot was based on exploitation of the poor masses, it also placed a heavy burden on the merchant class, and occasionally under popular pressure the Kehillah leaders were forced to abandon obvious injustices in the apportionment of government levies. However, the avant-garde of the modern capitalist class within the Russian-Jewish community was primarily incensed by the systematic waste of Kehillah funds for non-productive purposes, including the numerous fund-raising drives for charity. The number of occasions when Jews turned to the "Gentile courts" to settle private litigation or even conflicts with Kehillah authorities steadily increased, despite all the prohibitions and ostracisms with which the Kehillah tribunals surrounded this practice. The wealthy merchant class, the guild members, depended less and less on Kehillah institutions, as they paid the capital tax (which they paid in place of the poll tax) directly to the local authorities and not through the Kehillot. In the crown cities, Kehillah autonomy was restricted by the supervision of the authorities, whose official consent was required for the introduction of *korobkas* and other Kehillah rates.

The poor masses, and especially the artisans, were even more opposed to the Kehillah system than was the thin layer of large state privileged merchants. In the cities of Lithuania, the relationships of the various sectors within the Kehillot was altered by the rise of the Hassidic movement, which became a rallying point for opposition to the Kehillah leaders. For a long time, the sharp controversy between Hassidim and Mitnagdim* in the Lithuanian Kehillot at the end of the eighteenth and the beginning of the nineteenth centuries pushed the economic and social conflict between the merchant and artisan class into the background, although it could not prevent occasional outbursts.

Social pressure, fear of intervention by the government and municipal authorities and the popular unrest following on the spread of Hassidism, combined to force the Kehillah authorities to make some concessions to the principle of popular representation. The new representative institutions that appeared in the Minsk Kehillah at this time were characteristic of the tendency. In 1798, the Kehillah convened representatives of three classes, wealthy, intermediate and poor in order to apportion its debt to the Government Exchequer. In 1803, a committee of seven members of the Kehillah Assembly was elected and two representatives of the artisans were co-opted to determine the conditions for farming out the *korobka* on meat.

Some remnants of Jewish regional autonomy continued to exist under Russian rule, despite the fact that it had been abolished for the Jews of Lithuania, White Russia, the Ukrainian areas, and all of the Kingdom of Poland as early as 1764. As before, Jews in the villages and the small towns were under the jurisdiction of a Chief Kehillah. Delegates from all the Kehillot within one gubernia, and at times from the Kehillot of

* *cf.* Chapter Twelve, p. 477.

neighbouring gubernias, met in council whenever joint affairs required a decision. Special inter-Kehillah councils met in Lithuania and White Russia to devise means to contain the spread of Hassidism (at Moghilev in 1784 and at the Zelva Fair in 1797). Nonetheless, the inter-Kehillah councils never extended beyond one gubernia or several neighbouring gubernias, even in emergencies, when it was necessary to secure the revocation of decrees threatening all the Jews in the Empire, possibly because of anxiety that the authorities might regard the joint organization of all the Jews in the country unfavourably. This was the case in 1784, 1798, 1802, 1804 and 1807, in connection with the village expulsion act and similar measures.

The comments by Kehillah deputies on specific sections of the Statute of 1804 "Concerning the Jews" showed a wide knowledge of economic and social problems and constant concern for the rights of the Jewish population. On the other hand, they also reflected the rigid social and religious conservatism of the Kehillah leaders and their fear of any innovation in the existing economic, social, and cultural situation. They openly expressed anxiety for the preservation of traditional Jewish customs and requested that Jewish members of municipalities and Jews travelling into the Russian interior on business should wear Russian clothes (long gaberdines) instead of having to assume German attire. With the beards prescribed by their religion, they argued, they would be the objects of ridicule in shortened garments. The Kehillah leaders had a deep psychological understanding of the rulers of the absolutist feudal state. Their request that the rabbis be invested with authority to judge and pass sentence on offenders was based on the contention that

> . . . the abolition of this prerogative of the rabbis, besides loosening the bonds of conscience amongst the Jews, might rapidly lead them to extreme dissoluteness . . .

This argument did, in fact, evoke a response from the Government Committee on the Jewish Question. Its recommendation to the Czar that the rabbis be empowered to inflict all punishments except excommunication, advised the government not to concern itself with their religion, as "any incautious act against it might shake the foundations of morality, upon which rest their loyalty to the Imperial Master and their obedience to the government."

The Kehillah representatives considered even the provisions of the 1804 Statute for the dissemination of general enlightenment amongst Jewish youth to be a severe trial. The law offered the Jews the alternative of setting up special schools at their own expense with a curriculum including general studies if they were unwilling to send their sons to the general schools, but the Kehillot usually avoided this on grounds of lack of funds.

Jewish education in Lithuania, White Russia and the Ukraine followed the traditional lines of previous generations. The greatest ethical expositors of the sixteenth and seventeenth centuries had criticized their own generations for the lack of balance, order, and method in their instruction. Yet it persisted unchanged in eastern Europe during the period of Enlightenment and the Revolution, when modern forms of education were spreading amongst the Jews of western and central Europe. Study was centred mainly on the Talmud, the Codifiers, their commentators and the super-commentators. The sons of the spiritual leader of the Mitnagdim, Rabbi Elijah, the *Gaon* of Vilno related how he advised his contemporaries "to be well versed in all 'Twenty-Four Books' (i.e., the Old Testament), with their vowel punctuation and accents," to study grammar and the six tractates of the Mishnah.* To no avail—the accepted method was described by the forerunner of eastern European *Haskalah*, Naphtali Hertz Bar-Abraham of Bykhov, in the introduction to a book published at Shklov in 1797:

> And as soon as the boy has mastered the letters and some of the syllables, they teach him the Prayer Book; when they announce that he is able to pray, he has to start learning the Pentateuch ... And what he learns is but the first chapter of each portion, and of that only the first passages ... When he already knows some passages here and some there, he is told that the time has come to study Gemara. Before long they will accustom him to the *Tosaphot;*† and the Commentaries of Rabbi Samuel Edels;‡ and the boy is left wanting in all respects: he has neither knowledge nor manners. To train the boys in the virtues and in upright behaviour is a thing lacking in this country save for those few whom the Almighty calleth.

Judah Leib Margaliot, another outstanding forerunner of eastern European *Haskalah*, a former rabbi in Polish and Lithuanian Kehillot and finally at Frankfurt-on-the-Oder, also appealed to his contemporaries to train their children in "the virtues." Margaliot constituted a link between the literature of ethical exhortations§ and the moderate *Haskalah* trend.

In his book, *The Trees of Eden*, published in 1802, Rabbi Margaliot called upon the elementary teachers:

> ... to teach the sons of the Children of Israel ... all the noble virtues which the Sages taught in the *Mishnayot* of the *Tractate of the Fathers*. "To be truthful men, to condemn evil, to love their fellow-men, to rejoice in the well-being of their comrades and their honour, to be humble in spirit and forgiving, rejecting spurious honours and wealth unjustly acquired ..." And should the teachers

---

* *cf.* Chapter Thirteen, p. 541–2.

† *Tosaphot*, super commentary to the Talmud.

‡ Polish rabbi, born Posen 1555, died Ostiog (Volhynia) 1631. Author of celebrated commentaries on the *Tosaphot*.

§ *cf.* Chapter Nine (excerpt from *A House of Virtues*).

not instruct their pupils in these things, then we and our progeny shall be more deficient in these qualities than all other peoples. For other peoples observe these customs for fear of the rulers and judges who are over them. And we, we have no rulers and judges in our day with any power or authority to chastise the evildoers.

The criticism by the pioneers of *Haskalah* that education neglected virtues, did of course mainly refer to education in correct social comportment. Virtue in the religious-ethical sense was preached at that time by the Hassidic movement, which was gaining strength in the southern areas of the Russian pale of Jewish settlement and also spreading to Lithuania, the stronghold of the Mitnagdim. The ethical literature of the Kabbalists and the Hassidim replaced the study of Talmud, even in Lithuania, to such an extent that Rabbi Haim of Volozhin mainly attributed the neglect of Talmudic studies to the new religious movement when he arose to found the *Yeshivah* in his city in 1803. In fact, Rabbi Haim's activities eventually contributed greatly to the rehabilitation of Talmudic studies throughout Lithuania and White Russia. *Yeshivot* on the model of his Talmudic school, which became the central institution for these areas, were established in other cities such as Vilno and Minsk and declining *Yeshivot* experienced a revival.

The revival of the *Yeshivot* had resulted from the desire to arrest the advance of Hassidism on the one hand and to prevent the spread of the rising *Haskalah* movement, on the other. The same motive impelled the Kehillah leaders in Lithuania and White Russia to take their own measures by establishing *Talmud-Torah* institutions for the children of the poor and by rehabilitating existing institutions which had deteriorated. At the beginning of the nineteenth century, the Kehillot of Minsk and Vilno passed new regulations requiring their constituents to contribute to the *Talmud-Torah* and also introduced new procedures for the instruction of the children of the poor. Fund-raising drives were held for clothing the pupils and a supplementary tax was imposed on Kehillah members. Arrangements for feeding the children consisted either of assigning them fixed "days" to be fed at the homes of congregation officials, as at Minsk, or by installing soup kitchens at the *Heder*.

Several notable attempts at general education occurred amongst the Jews of the Russian pale, despite the atmosphere of stagnation and ultra-orthodoxy. The first efforts were actually made by the Jews themselves. Even before the Statute of 1804 opened general schools to Jews, individual Jewish pupils or entire groups enrolled in general elementary schools in the cities and towns of Lithuania and White Russia. Several Kehillot, as in the city of Vielizh for example, reacted conscientiously to the study of a non-Jewish language required by the 1804 Statute and designated special Jewish teachers to study Russian. Another White Russian Kehillah, Moghilev, announced similar arrangements for the study of Russian in 1808, when a questionnaire was received from the government inspector of schools.

The education authorities inside the pale of settlement who had been placed under the Polish nobles, were even more anxious to instil general enlightenment in the Jews than the central Russian government. The enlightened Polish nobles were particularly interested in giving the Jews a Polish education in order to draw them away from the influence of Russian language and culture. In 1808, a special Polish school for Jews was founded under the auspices of the University of Vilno, with the outlook that its graduates should become teachers in future schools for the Jews. As pupils were accepted between the ages of ten and forty, the school could have functioned as a combined elementary school and teachers' seminary. However, although enrolment reached a hundred, this institution was closed in the same year. The government had not found it possible to allocate the necessary funds and the Vilno Kehillah leaders had not approved of the idea from its inception. The University of Vilno exercised a more enduring influence on the initial propagation of Enlightenment amongst the Jews of Lithuania. Its students included a certain number of Jews, especially in the medical faculty; some of them subsidised by enlightened Polish magnates.

The War of 1812: First Indications of Class Solidarity Between Jews and Peasants

On June 24, 1812, Napoleon Bonaparte led his *Grande Armée* across the River Niemen. The war thus launched by France and her allies against Czarist Russia decided the fate of Europe. Russian Jewry, despite the exemption from military service it acquired by payment of the Recruit Tax, was an important factor in this war because of its vast role in commerce and trade and because of the proportions of its urban population in the western districts where the battle raged. A number of factors decided the Russian Jews to adopt a position generally favourable to Russia and opposed to Napoleon. There was, in the first place, a natural feeling of solidarity with the native population of the country in face of the invaders—especially as the Jews suffered as much as anyone else from French military requisitioning and plundering by the wild marauders. Jewish hostility towards the French became even more apparent during the second phase of the war, when the whole population, and particularly the White Russian peasants, joined forces to harass the straggling rear of Napoleon's broken army in its panic-stricken, disorderly retreat. Jewish patriotism represented the loyalty to the "reigning sovereign" cultivated by a persecuted people seeking protection in the law and constituted authority from becoming a victim of the class conflicts of the country's inhabitants. It was encouraged and reassured by the fact that the ruling class in White Russia, the Polish nobles, fearing peasant reforms, were also not in sympathy with Napoleon, while the clergy, especially the Jesuits, stood solidly in support of Alexander and the Russian Empire. The principal grievances the Jews had harboured against the state disappeared on the eve of the war, with the revocation, for all practical purposes, of the decree evicting the liquor sellers from the villages. In taxation too, Jews had been placed on an equal footing with the other burghers and merchants. The Jewish population did not, as yet, regard segregation inside the pale of settlement as serious discrimination. On the contrary, the Jewish traders appreciated Russian generosity in permitting them to make temporary and unmolested visits in connection with their business to all parts of the Empire.

In the second place, Jewish political attitudes were influenced by distrust of the régime that a Napoleonic victory would inaugurate in the provinces of Lithuania and White Russia. They remembered their "humiliating position"—as they termed it—under Polish rule, and were not ignorant of the repression and discrimination inflicted on their fellow-Jews in the reduced Polish Kingdom that Napoleon had established as the Grand Duchy of Warsaw. Moreover, the Jews of Lithuania and White Russia had already experienced the Jewish policy of the provisional Polish Government in Lithuania—an indication of their future if the country were ceded to the Grand Duchy of Warsaw. They had been subjected to double tax levies, had to pay a double war tax on all commodities (one tax by virtue of their status as burghers, another as Kehillah constituents) and "the heavy burden of the forced labour quota weighed down threefold on the Children of Israel," according to the grievances the Vilno Kehillah leaders submitted to the authorities. The Government which treated the Jews in this manner was sponsored by Napoleon who, despite his declarations on the need to abolish serfdom, took no action whatsoever on the issue of peasant enslavement except to promise favourable treatment in the future.

Finally, the Jewish population, and particularly the Kehillah leaders, tended to support Russia for orthodox religious reasons. Napoleon's reputation had preceded him among eastern European Jews. He had, it was true, legally enfranchised the Jews in the west. But he had also forced them to accept obligatory public school education and other reforms that undermined the traditional religious Jewish way of life. The Russian government, on the other hand, had practically demonstrated that, despite the reform programme contained in the Statute of 1804, it was anxious to preserve the Kehillot with all their broad powers, and rabbinical domination as a safeguard against the spread of apostasy. It had, therefore, done nothing to implement the public school "gezerah."* The Hassidim were especially grateful to the Sovereign for Section 53 of the Statute of 1804 which granted specific permission for the existence of "religious sects"

---

* Hebrew term for Draconic, oppressive decree.

with their own rabbis and synagogues. The leader of the Hassidic movement in Lithuania and White Russia, Rabbi Shneur Zalman of Lady, expressed the attitude of the Hassidim and of orthodox Jews in general in a letter to a friend:

> On the first of the New Year, before the *Musaf* prayer, it was revealed to me (from on High) that if Bonaparte triumphs, then will wealth multiply in Israel and its horn will be raised, but the hearts of Israel will break away and grow distant from their Heavenly Father. And should our Master, Alexander, triumph, poverty will multiply in Israel and its horn will be lowered, but the hearts of Israel will be joined together and unite and become an offering for their Heavenly father ...

The small circle of *Maskilim*, on the other hand, was convinced that it was under Russian rule that "wealth was going to multiply"—for the Jewish wholesale trade was already thriving as a result of access to the broad markets of the vast Empire—and also that "the horn of Israel had been raised," as Jewish members of the first guild had been granted a wide range of privileges. The Russian-Jewish *Maskilim* at that time were also optimistic about the government's programme for the propagation of Enlightenment, even though its implementation was slow.

The Russian government, the General Staff and the military commanders promptly exploited the prevalent attitude amongst the Jews and employed all the propaganda at their disposal to strengthen their loyalty. A proclamation was circulated amongst the Jews, with the knowledge of General Headquarters, and possibly at its initiative. It contained a warning by Rabbi Shneur Zalman against believing the spurious promises of Napoleon and advised them rather to support Russia, "the Cherished Motherland." Even if the Czar had generously exempted them from military service, it continued, they should aid the army by intelligence work. In fact, dispatches from military and guerilla commanders as well as from the governors of the north-western districts invariably praised Jewish help to the Russian forces.

A few Jews did, of course, side with the provisional Polish Government in Lithuania in the war of 1812 and also assisted Napoleon's armies with risky espionage activities. The character of Yankiel the Innkeeper, an accomplished Jewish musician, with access to the nobility and a Polish patriot in their confidence during the revolt against Russia in the epic poem, *Pan Tadeusz* by Adam Mickiewicz, was not altogether a figment of the poet's imagination. Several of the same factors that impelled the Jews of White Russia to give practical demonstrations of their loyalty to Russia also caused the Jews of Lithuania to hold divided opinions on the war, and some of them actually helped Napoleon's army. The traditional loyalty and "reverence for the ruling power" common to orthodox Jews led some Lithuanian Jews to favour the new "power," the provisional

Government of Lithuania. Inevitably therefore, they did not refuse assistance to Napoleon's armies when the authorities demanded it. In November, 1812, when Napoleon's forces were already in flight, three prominent leaders of the Vilno Kehillah still agreed to a plan by the French agent to establish an espionage network with the help of the Kehillot in the provincial cities. The efforts of the Polish nobles in Lithuania to spread Enlightenment amongst the Jews there would also appear to have engendered an enduring sympathy for Poland amongst the Jewish *Haskalah* groups in Vilno, which survived even when the moment of decision between Poles and Russians came. Napoleon's reputation as a ruler who had abolished Jewish servitude might similarly have attracted the support of some rabbis and spiritual leaders in the Lithuanian province in the same way as it had drawn some of the Hassidic leaders in Poland and Galicia. However, the cases of active assistance by Jews to French forces, confirmed in a document dated as late as August, 1813, were also in some way connected with the condition of the innkeepers. The innkeepers, dependent on their aristocratic masters for their incomes, also tended to adhere to their political view. They sometimes performed intelligence services at the nobles' request, either willingly or by coercion, and always at the risk of their lives. Many Polish nobles in Lithuania, and especially the magnates, unlike their counterparts in White Russia, sided with Napoleon.

The isolated incidents of active solidarity between the village Jews and insurgent peasants against the oppression of their masters were notable features of the tumultuous years. This class solidarity which bridged the gap of alien nationalities and ancient religious prejudices, first appeared in Lithuania in 1794, at the time of the Kosciuszko revolt. Instances were recorded not only of Jewish sympathy and assistance for the national revolt but of Jews actually inciting the peasants to insurrection. This did not only occur in Lithuania. A command from Alexander to the Military Governor of the Kherson district dated July 14, 1803 mentioned the name of a Jew who organized peasants to rise against their masters in one of the provinces of the southern Ukraine. The command confirmed a dispatch by the Governor to the Ministry of the Interior concerning the peasant uprising in the province of Tiraspol (on the Bessarabian border) which had been provoked by "the agitation of the Jew Berko (Dov Ber) Yankielewicz (Ben-Ya'akov), who for some time past had been sowing the seeds of insolence and disobedience to legal authority." As it was rumoured that Berko had already left those regions and was then in White Russia, an order was issued to the Military Governor there to deliver him to St. Petersburg, thence to extradite him to the Military Governor of the Kherson district. The Czar ordered that the rebellious peasants should be persuaded verbally to submit to their masters and obey them in all things. If this proved useless, the Military Governor was permitted to employ military force "to check the insurgents and restore them to orderly behaviour. . . ."

Peasant uprisings against the landed proprietors broke out in Lithuania and White Russia during the war of 1812, on rumours that Napoleon intended to abolish serfdom. The attitude of the rebellious peasants towards the French forces varied according to the local situation and the specific phase that the war had reached. Instances occurred of peasants accompanying French troops on marauding expeditions to loot the property of the magnates and set fire to their holdings. On numerous occasions also, the peasants both revolted against their masters and decimated the French "marauders" as a revenge for pillaging. Amidst this chaos, some individual Jews also joined the movement against the manorial lords.

The leader of the peasants in the town of Wilki (Rassieny District, Vilno Gubernia), Abraham Marcus, deserves honourable mention for his courage and devotion to the peasant cause. The inhabitants of Wilki had enjoyed burgher autonomy (the "Magdeburg Law") but under Russian rule they had been degraded to the status of serfs. In 1812, the peasants of Wilki, like the village peasants in the neighbourhood of the town, revolted. A resident of the town, commissionary to the Army, Abraham Leib Ben-Mordecai (whom the peasants called Mord'khelevitch, and who signed all his documents Abraham Marcus) espoused their cause. His actions were based on his belief in the ideals of the French revolution, but he nevertheless considered it his duty to help the Russian army against the invaders. The Military Commander officially acknowledged his gratitude for Marcus' "great service" as an espionage agent. After 1813, when the peasants commissioned him in writing to lead their cause, he untiringly interceded with the authorities to obtain justice and also spent many years in St. Petersburg for that purpose. He wrote letters to his principals, to "The Republic of the City of Wilki," encouraging them "not to obey the Court and not to labour for the lord, and, whatever might be done by the Court, not to yield but to fight" for their existence. The peasants gave proof of their loyalty and affection for their protagonist. In 1814, when the Czar's brother, the Grand Duke Constantin Pavlovitch Romanov, ordered Marcus and his son to be arrested, the peasants of Wilki attacked the police with heavy clubs, rescued the prisoners and hid them. However, "the inciter of the peasants, the Jew Marcus," was apprehended in the same year and imprisoned with his family and several leaders of the peasant revolt. In 1826 Marcus and his wife and son were exiled to Siberia for life, after sentence by a military court. But even in 1833, Abraham Leib Marcus sent a memorandum (in Yiddish!) from his exile to the Third Section* enumerating the evils and abuses that the peasants of his town endured at the hands of their manorial lord. He did not know that in the

---

* Established by Nicholas I as the Third Section of the Imperial Chancellery for uncovering and eliminating administrative abuses, this agency became the extra-legal instrument of terror employed by the Russian secret police.

interim these peasants had become reconciled to their serfdom and apologized in writing to their master for having succumbed in the past to the persuasion of "people who had incited them to demand liberty . . ." These isolated pioneers of the struggle for liberty and justice on a basis of international solidarity—as exemplified by Mord'khelevitch—hardly envisaged that their isolated efforts within Russian Jewry would be vindicated by the widespread revolutionary Jewish socialist movement of later decades.

The Jews of Russia endured formidable hardships during the War of 1812. The Jewish population was in the first place impoverished by the paralysis of trade and handicraft as well as by requisitioning by both belligerent parties. Jewish towns were sacked or burned. Finally, the Jews were the victims of excesses perpetrated with the extraordinary license by Russian and some French forces (the Saxons). Jewish towns were sometimes plundered successively by both armies, first the Cossacks, then the French. Amongst the French it was mainly the "marauder" troops that engaged in pillage; amongst the Russians, the regular army equally participated.

At the end of the war, the Russian Jews hoped that the government would take their material exhaustion into account and reward them for the loyalty they had displayed to the state during its ordeal. In 1812–13, two Jews at Imperial Headquarters, Zundel Sonnenberg of Grodno and Eliezer Dillon of Nieswiez, who had served in the quartermaster section of the army, acted in liaison with the country's Kehillot as "Deputies of the Jewish People" or "Kehillah Deputies." In 1813, Sonnenberg, together with the representatives of other Kehillot, submitted a memorandum to the Czar on improving the condition of the Jews in Russia. The Kehillah deputies were not aware that the government had ignored their memorandum and sent a further request for an audience with the Czar when he came to Bruchsal, in Baden. This time the Czar "made known to the Kehillot of the Jews that he is favourably inclined towards them" and agreed that delegates elected by the Kehillot should come to St. Petersburg to submit their wishes and to hear the Czar's views. However, the authorized representatives of the Kehillot did not appear before the Czar until 1817. By then, following the Congress of Vienna, the Autocrat of All the Russias had adopted an avowedly reactionary policy towards the Jews.

The only positive results to accrue to the Jews of Russia from the war of 1812 were in the cultural field. For the first time, Jews in the remote townlets of Lithuania and White Russia encountered western European culture in the form of Napoleon's cosmopolitan armies. It also represented their first contact with their enfranchised and educated fellow-Jews in the west. The Jewish suppliers, doctors and soldiers in the French forces were as surprised as the Frenchmen and Germans at the firmly-rooted national way of life of the Russian Jews, their vast role in the economy of the pale as merchants, lessees and artisans, by the considerable proportion of productive elements amongst them and by the positive differences in their character from the Jews of the west, deriving from the different circumstances of their life. German army officers later recorded in their memoirs that Russian Jews were generally excellent horseback riders and that in their physical appearance both men and women were more robust than the German Jews. The officers were enchanted by the beauty of the Jewish girls and they also emphasized the strength and sense of inner security shown by the Jews of Poland and Lithuania in contrast with the impulsiveness, restlessness and timidity of the German Jews. They realized that this difference was the result of the confidence the Russian Jews had acquired by living amongst large numbers of their own people, in stable and generally firmly established occupations, frequently also in association with land cultivation and pasturage. Their comments also included a certain amount of criticism—of the insanitary state of the Jewish towns, for example. The honesty of the Russian Jews in their business dealings was unanimously confirmed both by western Jewish writers in their memoirs and by a few non-Jews. Western Jews praised their hospitality and the spirit of fraternity that stood them in good stead in the troubled period during the retreat of Napoleon's armies. Many Jewish captives were saved from death by dressing up as local Jews and being concealed by their fellow Jews in private homes, hospitals and prayer houses. Their encounter with western Europe in the war of 1812, though transient, awakened the Jews of Poland and Russia from the intellectual stagnation of centuries. It encouraged the growth of Enlightenment which had sporadically shown itself since the closing years of the eighteenth century.

CHAPTER TWELVE

THE RISE OF HASSIDISM
AND ITS FLOWERING

A. *SOCIAL AND NATIONAL BACKGROUND OF THE HASSIDIC MOVEMENT*

National Oppression and the Kehillah Régime

The abundant creative force accumulated by the teeming and seething masses of eastern European Jewry erupted for the first time in its full splendour with the Hassidic movement. For centuries, the literature of the Polish Jews had only differed from that of the neighbouring central European countries in the quantity of its creative output. Poland had been a major centre of orthodox Jewry from the sixteenth century and its influence had extended beyond the communities of Moravia, Bohemia and Germany into Alsace-Lorraine and Holland. However, its creative activity was confined to exegeses and commentaries on the Talmud and the Codifiers. The literature of ethics was also on the same pattern in Poland as in all other Ashkenazi Jewish settlements. The appearance of Hassidism revealed for the first time the uniqueness and originality of a culture deeply rooted in a colourful folk life, fashioned by a community of people which had been living in Poland and the countries around for many centuries. This body of Polish Jewry had moreover covered the cities, towns and villages of the country with a tight network of Kehillot. A mass religious movement such as this, which overwhelmed and inspired with enthusiasm vast numbers of Jews in Poland, Lithuania, White Russia and the Ukraine, was altogether inconceivable in central or western Europe: even in geographic terms, the tiny, scattered Jewish communities there, shut away in their ghettos and their separate streets, were not conducive to such a development. However, the differences in economic, social and political condition and cultural level between eastern and western European Jewry were more decisive with regard to Hassidism than the demographic and geographic factors. The spiritual exhaustion of religious orthodoxy and the decadence of the Kehillah and other organs of Jewish communal autonomy had become evident throughout the European Diaspora—East and West—by the second half of the eighteenth century. In western Europe, however, this period of enlightened absolutism saw the rise of capitalism so that western Jews found an outlet for their aspirations to transform public and cultural life in *Haskalah* and the movement for civil enfranchisement. By contrast, the social, economic and political backwardness of eastern Europe, with its intractable feudal system, caused the Jews there to express their hopes for social, national and cultural regeneration in a religious movement—Hassidism. Nonetheless, although Hassidism was confined to eastern Europe, it exerted the most pervasive influence of all Jewish religious movements during the centuries of exile. It was also the last such movement in the Jewish people's history. It represented the crowning achievement of religious Jewry and passed on to the modern, secular culture of the Jewish people what was best in the ancient culture which had for a long period (longer by far than in the case of other European nations) been exclusively dominated by religion.

Like all the religious movements amongst the Jewish people in the Diaspora, particularly the various mystical systems, Hassidism possessed all the characteristics of a redemption movement. Like them too, it developed and extended because of the yearning of a people living in captivity amongst gentiles for deliverance from exile and for restoration in Zion and Jerusalem. At every crisis in the diaspora history of the Jewish people—every increase in economic distress or national oppression, repressive legislation or persecution—the longing of the masses for deliverance became more acute. The expulsion of the Jews from Spain, Sicily, southern Italy, Provence and the cities of Germany at the end of the fifteenth century gave rise to the Kabbalah movement founded by Isaac Luria (HaARI) and his disciples at Safed. After the massacres of 1648 and 1649 in the Ukraine, Lithuania and White Russia, and the Czarniecki pogroms in Greater Poland, the Sabbetai Zvi messianic movement arose and caused such an upheaval in the Jewish world that its consequences were in evidence until the end of the eighteenth century. Hassidism was born during the "Saxon" period, when Polish Jewry was all but overwhelmed by persecution and oppression. At this time Poland was in the state of chaos that preceded its fall. The noblemen, who dominated the private cities, the towns and villages, indulged in atrocity towards the Jews, who were totally thrown at their mercy. During this period, the Catholic clergy too, had reached the height of its power in the state. Religious fanaticism against non-Catholics, and especially against the Protestants, was given free rein. Bloody assaults by students and apprentices under inflammatory Jesuit incitement were a daily occurrence for Jews inhabiting the Crown cities. The clergy re-introduced the system of public disputations—as if to revive the horrors of the Middle Ages. The most terrifying of the compulsory debates, those held with the Frankists at Kamenietz-Podolsk and Lwow, spread terror amongst all the Jews of Poland. Innocent Jews were publicly executed on ritual murder charges in all the provinces of the state on an almost Inquisitional pattern. Finally, the Jews of the Ukraine were struck by the Haidamak peasant revolt. "The Terrible Tale of Uman," a massacre of Jews in the fortress of that city in 1768, seemed almost a repetition of episodes during the massacres of 1648. In 1768, too, the retrograde, fanatical and chauvinistic Polish nobility founded a union "For the Defence of the Faith and the Fatherland," the Bar Confederation. Its forces roamed through most of the districts of Poland for several years, regularly extorting war levies from the impoverished Jewish Kehillot.

During the closing decades of the eighteenth century when Hassidism experienced its greatest growth and expansion, the condition of Polish Jewry actually changed for the better in several respects. The government under the last king of Poland, Stanislaw August Poniatowski, reduced the power of the clergy, and ritual murder accusations and anti-Jewish riots occurred less frequently. But at the same time the legal position of the Jews in Poland deteriorated. The poll tax was raised several times after the liquidation of the Council of the Four Lands and the abolition of regional Jewish autonomy. Furthermore, the law of 1768 expelled the Jews from a number of cities; in the remaining Crown cities they had to wage a difficult struggle for the right to engage in trade and the crafts. As a result of the various repressions, the poverty of the Jewish population became even more desperate. Over a tenth of all Jewish family heads were totally without income and columns of beggars wandered from city to city, from Kehillah to Kehillah, begging for alms to keep themselves alive. The position of the village Jews, the lessees, innkeepers and liquor purveyors was undermined to an even greater extent than that of the urban Jews. Following changes in the management of manorial estates, tens of thousands of petty lessees were deprived of their leaseholds and left without employment. The same trend caused an arbitrary increase in rentals by the landed proprietors; lessees and their families who could not meet their contractual obligations were subject to incarceration and other forms of abuse by their masters.* It is no coincidence that summary increases in lease rentals, the threat of expulsion from the villages, and the attendant "ransoming of captives" (the liberation of lessees held prisoner by estate owners) are recurrent themes in Hassidic legends about the miracle-working *Tzaddikim*.

The only improvement that took place at the beginning of the nineteenth century, under the absolutist régime of the three powers that had partitioned the Kingdom of Poland, was in the condition of the wholesale merchant class, the contractors and army suppliers. The burden of special taxes was even heavier than under independent Polish rule and weighed desperately heavily on the Jewish masses in the cities and villages. The double tax in Russia, the kosher meat tax in Galicia and the Grand Duchy of Warsaw, and the candle tax in Galicia sapped the vitality of the oppressed Jewish poor. The brunt of the repression fell on the rural Jews, as the partitioning powers paid special attention to implementing the enactments which Poland, on the verge of collapse, had not found the opportunity to enforce. Decrees expelling the Jews from the villages were

* *cf.* the details in the preceding chapter (Chapter Eleven).

issued in Russia, Austria and the Grand Duchy of Warsaw, and some were actually put into effect in Galicia and White Russia. The national oppression of the eastern European Jewish masses at the end of the Napoleonic period was as effective as in the days of Rabbi Israel Ba'al Shem Tov, during the reign of Poland's Saxon kings. Only the outward form was different.

It was not surprising, therefore, that Hassidic teaching interpreted "this bitter exile" as a total metaphysical, spiritual, ethical and even an economic antagonism between the Jewish people and the gentiles. Israel's position amongst the nations was compared with "a lamb amongst wolves." In their daily lives, the Jews encountered "the nations of the world" in the form of the arrogant, brutal and lustful *Paritz* or nobleman, the priests, with their hatred of the Jewish religion and their incitement of the mob against its adherents, the domineering, pompous officials whose goodwill could only be obtained by bribes, and the crude peasants who drank them-selves into oblivion to escape from squalor and wretchedness. All the pent-up suffering and humiliation accumulated over the generations achieved a catharsis in the Hassidic doctrine of the Cosmic Axis, with its poles represented by Tyre and Jerusalem, Esau and Jacob, idolatry and the worship of God, defilement and purity, Satan's domain and the domain of Holiness. "Tyre was built up only through the Destruction of Jeru-salem.... When the one falls, the other arises"—this was the key to the mystic interaction of supreme forces, which also affected livelihood and maintenance. Prayer, the study of the Law and the observance of the divine commandments functioned in such a way that ultimate affluence did not flow entirely towards the gentiles but was also allotted to the children of Israel. Their share of the bounty of the world increased to the extent that they proved themselves worthy. In this way too, the people of Israel were able to "assuage the sternness," to mitigate unfavourable decisions and decrees that the gentiles contrived against them and sometimes even to abolish those decrees completely.

The virtue of love for Israel was one of the cardinal tenets of Hassidism related to its consistent teaching of the identity between the people of Israel and the good positive and noble substance of the Universe. All the natural emotions of love for humanity and all the scriptural talmudic precepts, and those of ethical literature on the love of fellow-men were construed as references to the Jewish people—and not only as the chosen people but also as mankind personified. Love of Israel meant love of the people as a whole and of every living individual Jewish soul. It was as though the suffering of the Jewish people and its mission of reforming the world atoned for the sins of the entire community of Israel and of every Jew. When a people was troubled and in captivity and still served the one true God, its actions were not subject to minute scrutiny. Hassidic literature abounded in glorification of the people of Israel. One of the highest qualities that Hassidic lore attributed to all its *Tzaddikim* (the leaders of the movement beginning with Ba'al Shem Tov) was the vindication of Israel. Some of them were even crowned with the epithet *Ohev Yisrael*—a lover of Israel—(Moses Leib of Sasow, Davidl of Lelow, Levi Isaac of Berditchev, Abraham Joshua Heshel of Opator).

The "assuagement of sternness" and the bringing down of affluence represented only a modicum of salvation to a people exiled from its country—together with the *She'khinah* (the divine presence)—and delivered into the lands of the profane gentiles. Only complete deliverance would constitute total triumph in the contest between Israel and the nations of the world. In messianic times, the *She'khinah* would be redeemed from its exile to become a perfect entity with the Holy One Blessed Be He, the people of Israel would be restored to its own land, and the world would achieve its perfection (*Tikkun*) in the kingdom of the Almighty. The yearnings for deliverance, which had filled the hearts of the people throughout the generations of its long exile, became an overwhelmingly powerful and continuous longing amongst the masses who supported the Hassidic movement. Hassidism was, in fact, heir to all the religious folk movements in the history of the people, but it did not possess the attributes of a straightforward messianic movement in the accepted sense. On the contrary, from its inception its aim was a total negation of the Sabbetai Zvi movement and its offshoots, despite the fact that it adopted some of its mystic elements and even some of the customs from its mode of life.

Hassidism followed the pattern of the essentially evolutionary redemption movement and not that of the messianic movements, which had the character of national religious revolutions in the history of the exiled people. In that respect, Hassidism might rather be compared with the Karaite movement of some 1,000 years earlier. The emphasis that the Karaite movement placed on the striving for deliverance and the restoration of Zion was so great that it formed the basis for the principal divergence of opinion between it and rabbinical teaching on most of the religious laws and customs. Even so, Karaism did not fundamentally arise as a messianic movement but rather in opposition to the messianic movements that had preceded it, such as Abu Isa in Persia and Serene in Syria. The failure of these movements had strengthened Karaite belief that the end could not be hastened by acts of desperation, but that redemption lay in a wholehearted return to the God of Israel and literal observance of the Torah without the distortions of the talmudic sages and the rabbis. Analogically, Hassidism sought an answer and solution for the despondence and impotence which attacked large numbers of people after the defeat of the Sabbetai Zvi movement, sealed by Frankist treachery precisely when the new movement was beginning to grow. The founders of Hassidism counteracted the bitter disappointment that followed these attempts to hasten the end, by teaching that deliverance was a mystical-historical process in which each and every person in Israel was destined to play an active and decisive role. Every improvement in the soul of the individual through loving and worshipful adhesion (*De'vekut*) to God contributed to the attainment of perfection in the highest realms and thus accelerated the deliverance of the people and the *She'khinah* from exile. Prayer with intention (*Kavvanah*), the study of the Law for its own sake (*Torah Le'she'mah*), ardent observance of all precepts (*Mitzvot*) and the performance of acts of piety and charity would lead to individual wholeness and to communal redemption. As Hassidism revealed this truth concerning behaviour in the service of the Creator, its adherents were convinced that their movement was the messenger of deliverance—much in the same way as the publication of the *Zohar* had prompted the view amongst the Kabbalists that the age of deliverance had dawned with the revelation of Kabbalah. Proof that expectations of imminent deliverance existed and gained in strength as Hassidism grew was demonstrated by the Hassidic *aliyot* (ascents, i.e. migrations) to the Land of Israel led by the disciples of Ba'al Shem Tov and their pupils.

At the turn of the eighteenth and nineteenth centuries, the people gained new hope of the Messiah's advent from the cataclysmic events inaugurated by the French Revolution and the Napoleonic wars. But even amidst the spiritual tension of the time, Hassidism did not abandon its principles relating to the conditions for deliverance. It did not succumb to a spirit of adventurousness engendered by despair, but called for penitence as the only means of achieving the desired end.

Another common characteristic linking Hassidism to the other religious folk-movements in the history of the Jews was the fact that the forces motivating its aspiration for national redemption were inextricably connected with the dynamic factors of social development, and the aspiration on the part of the destitute and oppressed classes for social advancement, and with their struggle for liberation. As social pressures grew, the classes discriminated against by the Kehillah régime yearned for deliverance even in the widest sense: deliverance from bondage amongst the nations, from poverty, and from oppression by their own ruling classes. The yearning for national redemption, for an improvement in social conditions and for a reform of the régime were fused into one movement for total redemption, which called for a revival of the faith from its decadence and a purge of all its abuses. This social aspect of the redemption movement gave rise to violent hatred and ruthless persecution by the defenders of the existing régime and by the guardians of the traditional version of the Jewish religion.

In fact, the Kehillah régime in Poland had deteriorated to the lowest level of decadence during the period of the rise of Hassidism. The decay of the antiquated feudal order in the Kingdom had eroded the organs of Jewish autonomy, which were interlocked with its framework. The Kehillah had long ago ceased to discharge its functions of organizing the Jewish population to defend its rights and of ministering to its communal and cultural needs. It had become a tool of the monarchy and the noblemen who owned the towns. The rural Jews, including the wealthy lessees and suburban inhabitants, were denied electoral rights in the Kehillot and thus the right to hold Kehillah office, though they were required to pay all Kehillah rates and observe all its regulations. The authority of the Kehillot weighed heavily on towns in their immediate vicinity and their inhabitants were the victims of discrimination in the apportionment of government taxes. In the cities, not only the destitute but even Jews who were not actually prosperous were deprived of electoral rights.

Even wealth did not assure its owners of the official right to participate in Kehillah administration, as this had come under the control of cliques. The office of *Parnass* in the Kehillot had become a kind of concession (*arenda*), which, like other lesseeship transactions, depended on access to nobles and government officials. These leaders, with the support of the authorities, ruled the Kehillot like private estates. Their position sometimes provided a lucrative source of personal income for themselves, their relations and friends. The taxation system in the Kehillot was almost entirely based on various indirect levies generically designated as the *korobka* and the full weight was borne by the working classes—artisans, storekeepers, the pedlars and the publicans. Charitable activities had been removed from the scope of Kehillah functions and long since entrusted to societies, the largest of which were in turn organized on the same hierarchical pattern as the Kehillah executive.

Generally, the rabbis not only failed to protect the people against oppression but actually lent their approval to the activities of the Kehillah leaders, established their own control over the people and prospered from their office. A rabbinical post could only be obtained in return for huge sums paid into the Kehillah treasury and its organs, and appointments were awarded to the candidate who paid most. Therefore, the office of rabbi was usually in the hands of the sons and sons-in-law of the wealthy who also controlled the position of *Parnass*. The rabbis lived on a similarly luxurious scale as their relations, and they recouped many times over in fees and obligatory gifts from their congregation the sums they had paid for their appointments. Nor were the Kehillah judges innocent of partiality during court proceedings or of accepting gifts from litigants, according to the critics of the time, the popular preachers (*darshanim*). The judges, like all Kehillah officials, received their appointment in return for a sum paid into the Kehillah treasury. The highest strata of the scholar class were tightly linked to the wealthy class which ruled the Kehillot. Even scholars who did not actually hold office were mostly related to the wealthy, either by social origin or by social position. The children of artisans and the poor usually had no opportunity to matriculate in the study of religious law and scholars were not common amongst the rural Jews, who were remote from rabbinical seminaries and religious schools. The rank of scholar not only conferred many rights in Kehillah institutions and societies—such as electoral rights or qualification to serve in public office—but also many honours within the synagogue (such as to be called to attend the reading of the Law) at ritual celebrations and similar occasions. As a result, the social position of the *am-Ha'aretz** was of the lowest grade and they were even humiliated in their status as human beings. According to prevalent concepts an *am-Ha'aretz* could read the Scriptures but knew no *Gemara*. Even those who regularly studied Talmudic legends (the *Ein-Ya'akov Societies*) were classed amongst the lower orders. These caste distinctions isolated the lofty scholar from the broad masses.

The detachment and seclusion of the scholar class was also a symptom of the spiritual crisis that had developed amongst the Jews of Poland and orthodox Jewry as a whole. The fact that *pilpul* (casuistry) had become the predominant method in the study of the Talmud and the Codifiers proved that the Torah had ceased to be a rule for living and therefore correspondingly less of a guide to the masses of the Jewish people in Europe. It had become "a spade wherewith to dig" the means to a social career and distinction in the hierarchy of Jewish community life. This mode of *Halakhah* instruction had not given birth to any fruitful or enlightening concept and no innovations whatsoever had been made in the negative and positive laws, let alone in the religious way of life. All the precepts and prohibitions had been formulated and sanctified over the past two hundred years in the *Shulhan Arukh* and fortified for a hundred years by detailed commentaries. Any working man of Polish Jewry in the eighteenth century could justifiably have asked like Benjamin Assia, cited in the Talmud (*Sanhedrin, 99*) as a typical heretic "Of what use have our rabbis been to us? They have never permitted us to eat raven flesh nor forbidden us to eat dove..." Contemporary ethical literature had become permeated with the belief in demons, spirits and the transmigration of the soul under the influence of theurgic, or practical Kabbalah, and was equally incapable of supplying the spiritual mainstay of the people. Instead of encouraging them, raising their spirits, consoling them in their troubles and moral depression, and giving them renewed hope, the moralists urged them to forswear the vanities of this world, praised the virtue of asceticism and provided all the tortures of hell for the slightest transgression or suggestion of transgression.

During the final decades of the Polish Kingdom, when the spread of Hassidism had already made considerable headway, mass revolt broke out in the large Kehillot of Lithuania, White Russia and Volhynia (at Dubno), especially amongst the artisans, who organized themselves against the *Parnassim* and demanded a democratic Kehillah régime.† The Hassidic movement was in sympathy with this mass uprising, though it never integrated with its organization and was not identified with its ideals. In

---

* *am-Ha'aretz*, literally, the people of the land (*cf.* etymological connotation of the word *peasant*), hence a common or ignorant person, a boor.

† *cf.* Chapter Nine, 295–6.

some places, however, the Hassidim supported the rebellious masses in their demands for Kehillah reforms, and voiced complaints on their own behalf against abuses in Kehillah affairs (at Vilno and Minsk). Conversely, many of the oppressed who were in revolt against Kehillah despotism, were attracted by the democratic nature of the doctrines of Hassidism.

The theoretical basis of Hassidic doctrine rested on the Kabbalah, in all its phases of development, from the old *Sefer Ha'yetzirah* (*Book of Creation*) down to the concepts of the last Polish Kabbalists before the Ba'al Shem Tov. However, the Kabbalah system which influenced Hassidism most was that of Isaac Luria, as formulated by his disciple, Haim Vital. Until the rise of Hassidism, Kabbalah had only been a school of the occult in the mainstream of Judaism. Its sanctity was so widely recognized that none of the acknowledged sages dared challenge it, but its study was limited exclusively to individuals and circles concerned with the occult. Hassidism elevated Kabbalah to the rank of a superior doctrine, which endowed the revealed Law with meaning and purpose. Hassidism explained the mystic doctrine in such facile and simple terms that its secrets became a commonplace, an occult teaching which had, as it were, become a second version of revealed Law. The elements of Kabbalah assimilated by Hassidism became the property of the masses. The Hassidic movement ensured the publication of new editions of the principal Kabbalist books and also caused ancient manuscripts of the doctrine (*Sefer Ha'pe'lia—The Book of Miracles*, and *Sefer Ha'Kanah*, composed in the fourteenth century) to be printed for the first time. As a result, knowledge of Kabbalah and its original methods became widespread amongst the Jewish masses. The entire religious life of the Hassidim was permeated with Kabbalah doctrine after they had generally adopted the custom of conforming to Isaac Luria's method of preceding every prayer and every act of piety with a formula interpreting its mystic connotation. Furthermore, Hassidim were instructed by their masters never to depart from Kabbalah doctrine for a moment in their daily lives. In everything they did, they were conscious of the precept of adhesion to God and effecting perfection in the upper worlds. The influx of Kabbalist concepts into broad sections of the common people together with the spread of the Hassidic movement was reflected in the numerous Kabbalist terms which became an integral part of Yiddish vocabulary: *

> *Nitzotz Ke'dushah* (a spark of holiness of divine sanctity), *Sitra-Achra* (Aramaic: the "other side," i.e., the devil's domain); *Koah-Ha'tum'ah* (the force of defilement); *Ke'lipah* (the impure, or material shell); *Tikkun* (literally, a perfecting, or reforming; *cf*.

---

* All Hebrew, or Aramaic, words listed here as Yiddish vocabulary have been transliterated according to the accent commonly employed in modern Israel. In Yiddish they have actually undergone changes in phonetics and accent.

supra); *metakken zein* (Yiddishized Hebrew, to effect *Tikkunim*); *madregah* (level, stage); *be'chinah* (category, criterion); *Olamot Elyonim* (the upper worlds); *Galut Ha'She'khinah* (exile of the abode of the divine presence).

Likewise, the vernacular of eastern European Jewry absorbed expressions such as the following directly from Hassidic teachings: *Hitbodedut* (solitary communion; literally, being solitary); *de'vekut* (literally, adhesion, clinging; hence, devotion); *hitlahavut* (enthusiasm, fervour); *atzvut* (sadness, grief); *kavvanah* (literally, purpose; by implication in Hassidic contexts and by derivation in all acts involving application, concentration of purpose); *aliyat ha'ne'shamah* (ascent of the soul); *hitpa'alut* (ecstasy); *nitgaleh vern* (Yiddishized Hebrew phonetically: *nisgaleh vern*—to be revealed); *hitgalut* (becoming revealed, revelation).

The authority given to Kabbalah by Hassidism, as well as its spread and popularization by this movement, brought about a religious revolution—directly, through the propagation of a mystical outlook amongst the people and indirectly, by reducing the hegemony of Talmudic doctrine. However, Hassidism did not adopt Kabbalah unaltered. It discovered new facets of it and created a new system of mystics by its mode of presentation, its emphasis and its development of those ideas which were appropriate to the movement's aims. The central theme of Hassidic Kabbalah was not contained in the speculation on divinity and the nature of the upper worlds, or in the search for the "Story of the Divine Chariot" or "the Acts of Genesis." Its dominant interest was man, his conduct in reverence and his way of worshipping God.

Main Tenets of the New Doctrine

Despite its diverse ramifications and numerous schools during its growth and development, Hassidism, as a universal attitude and way of life, was based on a number of consistently interconnected principles reflecting one invariable tendency. God was omnipresent throughout the cosmos, in the inanimate, the growing plant, the animated and the articulate creature, in all man's actions, thoughts, emotions and desires. His glory filled the universe and the universe was full of His glory: everything was part of divinity, for divinity was everything, the substance of being. The world was tainted at its creation, by Adam's sin, by the "Breaking of the Vessels," when the sparks of holiness were scattered and fallen into the captivity of defilement. The exile of the sparks was the exile of the She'khinah, which was the exile of the people of Israel amongst the Gentiles. The ultimate purpose to the earthly life of a Jew was to rectify the imperfections of the world and thus to contribute towards the deliverance of the *She'khinah* from its exile and the deliverance of the people of Israel from its bondage amongst the Gentiles. Every rectification accomplished by an individual added to his own perfection and thus rectified the imperfection of the universe. All perfections would thus merge into a complete perfection in the days of the Messiah, when all the sparks of holiness would be purged of their defilement and defilement itself thus rendered a nullity. The *She'khinah* would become one with the Holy One Blessed Be He in complete and eternally enduring oneness, and the Universe would become entirely of the spirit, entirely good, and the people of Israel would dwell securely in its land, on the holy soil. A person achieved *Tikkunim* while redeeming the sparks of holiness within himself, in his soul, and all about him in his fellow men, in the entire cosmos; and by restoring these sparks to their source in the upper worlds.

Hassidism had adopted this pantheistic attitude to life, in conjunction with the doctrine of evolutionary redemption from the Kabbalah system of Isaac Luria. However, here again, Hassidism superimposed its own idealistic trend by stressing pantheism in respect of man's intellectual capacities, both rational and emotional. Its doctrine related to the manner whereby a man might restore the sparks of holiness to the upper world and achieve *Yihud* (unification) with God for himself and this world was an innovation of its own. The fundamental principle was categorical belief in God, independent of rational or logical inductions or inquiry. It was a faith in the Torah of heavenly origin, in the choice of Israel as the treasured nation and in the coming of redemption. This unconditional, unreserved faith postulated the virtue of uttermost trust in God, who was goodness and did good to all, who watched over every man individually, hearkened to his prayer, and did not desert those who called upon Him. Sterling faith and certain trust led man to the love of God with his whole being. This love did not depend on any physical or material cause. In the face of it, all his lust and ambitions disappeared, for it was God who infused the cosmos with life, and there was no goodness, truth or beauty other than God. Man achieved the level of adhesion, which was the acme and ultimate purpose of the worship of God, through profound faith and ardent love of God. True adhesion was only consummated in the "voiding of one's own existence," could only be achieved when a man had totally negated himself before God, removed every barrier of materialism within himself together with every vestige of cognizance of self as a distinct personality. Only then was the complete *Yihud* of man with his Creator possible.

The assumption that worship of God was based on faith and love, inevitably led Hassidism to see wholehearted purposefulness as the essence of prayer, the study of the Law, and the observance of the Precepts. Prayer without concentrated purpose was of no value, for if the heart was far removed from God, then the prayer was only "service of the lips," while the observance of a precept without concentrated purpose was only "a commandment of men learned by rote" (Isaiah, 29:13). This also applied to any study of the Torah which was not for its own sake and lacked concentration of purpose, for such study had nothing whatsoever in common with the worship of God. It was not an abundance of prayer, meticulous observance of the precepts or copious study of the Law that decided in a man's favour but the degree of ecstasy he attained in the worship of God. Hence, the scholar enjoyed no advantage over the man who worshipped God in love. In fact, the opposite was true; a man who had not had opportunity to study could attain the highest level by worshipping God with all his heart, while one who studied the Law, but not for its own sake, was a sinner. The worship of God did not end with prayer, the study of the Law or the performance of preceptual acts of piety. The commandment was explicit: *I have set the Lord always before me* (Psalms, 16:8). In fact, it was not the act of worship which was the measure of adhesion but the quality of concentration of purpose (*kavvanah*). Therefore man could and was actually obliged to worship God in all his activities—in eating and drinking, in his business dealings, and even in conversation with others. By worshipping God in his daily profane acts, he redeemed the sparks of holiness present in material substance, and elevated the material life which surrounded him to the level of spirituality. But man himself was composed of matter and form, in which materialism and spirituality were firmly interwoven. Divinity, the vital essence of the universe, penetrated all his thoughts, emotions and appetites. Therefore, he was advised not to be depressed by sinful reflections and earthly appetites—such as desire for a woman—even when such thoughts intruded in time of prayer ("alien thoughts"), but had to restore them to their divine roots and thus refine from them the sparks of holiness.

Belief in God, Whose glory filled the universe, absolute trust, whole-hearted love of God and the acknowledgement of man's noble task in the reintegration (*Yihud*) of the Holy One Blessed Be He with the *She'k-hinah* (as though actually a partner in the acts of creation daily wrought anew), necessarily brought the believer unbounded and unceasing joy. Therefore, worship of the creator could not be dissociated from joy in the Lord, in the same way as the worship of God was inconceivable without love. Sadness was an evil quality widening the distance between man and God; even transient moments of sadness were ominous, betraying "pettiness of mind" resulting from a descent in the level of adhesion to God. The love of God had to accompany man at every step in his life and similarly he had to persevere in his love of his fellow-men, and even of animals.

This was even more the case where his love of the children of Israel, collectively and severally, was concerned. The virtues of truth, humility and faith in social intercourse were amongst the chief precepts and all those who observed them thereby secured rectification of the blemished world, and naturally, hastened deliverance. A man's virtue was particularly highly estimated in acts of charity, for the more mercy, generosity and charity he displayed, the more he aroused the quality of generosity in the world of divine emanations (se'phirot) and secured affluence for the world and for all of the people of Israel. A Tzaddik was one who had attained the highest level in the worship of God and in adhesion to Him. Men should therefore associate themselves with the Tzaddik, both to learn his ways and to be aided by his prayers and intercessions on behalf of Israel.

Its explicitly national character was one of the most salient features of Hassidism and made it unique amongst the popular religious reform movements in history. Yet although the concept of national redemption was integrated into Hassidism to the degree of complete fusion, the character of the movement and its doctrines can be comprehended only by analyzing its universal humanitarian elements, which were also inherent in other world religious movements of a similar social trend. For distinctly mundane, social and essentially democratic tendencies were discernible behind the Hassidic mystique of the perfection of the Godhead, the universe and the soul of man.

Hassidism, by representing faith as the cardinal virtue in the worship of God, voiced the aspiration of the mass of the people to rise from their lowly status in religious and Kehillah life. The severe ethical protest that the first Hassidim made against the arrogant scholars, who towered above the people, was imbued with the aim of improving the status of the common people and recognizing their social and religious value. Hassidic legend, even more than Hassidic doctrine, took up the defence of the masses, by encouraging the wholehearted believer—even if he were only a Psalm-reciting or totally illiterate Jew (e.g., the village lad in The Praises of Ba'al Shem Tov who prayed by whistling)—to a level equal if not higher than the brilliant scholars. In any event, praise of the virtue of faith also fulfilled a democratizing and regenerative function in the cultural sphere. Rejection of the absolute hegemony of the scholars made possible a challenge to the hegemony of the Talmud and the Codifiers as alone worthy of spiritual consumption. The study of Kabbalah was entitled to equal honours with the Gemara, and the study of the Midrash and the ethical books became more important and widespread. In the course of time, the movement created its own literature and reading the tales and legends of the Tzaddikim came to be considered as much an act of piety as the study of books on Hassidic doctrine and even the study of the Torah. Hassidism therefore was responsible for the fact that Hebrew literature finally extricated itself from the Talmudical exclusiveness and stagnation of generations.

Like all other socio-religious movements amongst the Jews and other peoples, Hassidism set out to strengthen the supremacy of religion and to strengthen the people's faith. All such movements had been convinced that this was the way to end affliction and suffering and to achieve salvation. However, the Hassidic doctrine of heartfelt purpose, the principle underlying the observance of precepts and the study of the Law, possessed characteristics peculiar to reformation movements and expressed a new attitude opposed to that of the Middle Ages. The concept of religion as the fulfilment of detailed commandments was associated with formalism and a stereotyped outlook. But the assertion that the law within man's heart was the quintessence of religion revealed a deepening of philosophy accompanied by a more percipient understanding of the soul of man as the motivating force of his actions. This new approach to the human being was a concomitant expression of the individualist trend in the conception of man's place in society. The rejection of "a commandment of men learned by rote" in religious matters, for matters that lay within the heart defied formulation, necessarily relaxed the bonds of communal tradition which pressed on the individual. In this incipient awareness of individualism, every religious reformation has contained a message of humanism, however thoroughly it might be enveloped in doctrines of resurgent faith. But the trend towards individualism was only one of the reformation characteristics inherent in the Hassidic movement. The entire outlook and ethos of Hassidism presaged a new humanitarian doctrine in the spirit of pre-humanism, similarly an attribute of religious reformation.

The medieval outlook had essentially been based on an irreducible dualism in the concept of man and the universe and in ethical doctrine. God and the cosmos, heaven and earth, spirituality and materialism, purity and defilement, the next world and this, paradise and hell, soul and body, the sanctity of religion and the profanity of daily life, good and evil impulses, commandments and sins, reward and punishment, were opposites in a dual series. No link or bridge between them was conceivable, despite the principle of faith which asserted that everything had been created out of nothing by the word of God. The vast chasm between noble spirituality on the one hand and coarse matter on the other was only a reflection of the *social* division in feudal society between the ruling class of "spiritual men" and the toiling masses whom they subjugated. Kabbalah, like Christian mystic doctrine, made the first inroads into this dualist base by its efforts towards a uniform, monistic outlook. This monism was, of course, still directed entirely towards idealism and the first bridges over the gulf of dualism were all of a spiritual nature. The middle class, which was just beginning to emerge from feudal society, was composed of a small number of patricians who did not venture to reject the feudal hierarchy in its entirety but demanded for themselves a share with the ruling class in the existing system. The doctrine of mysticism, including Kabbalah, did not eliminate the dichotomy between the two elements of universal dualism but tried to draw the opposites closer together and reduce the distance between them.

The elements of a monistic trend present in the Hassidic outlook were based on Kabbalah. The Hassidic doctrines of God's omnipresence, of sparks of spirituality, the sparks of holiness that permeated the world of fauna, flora and inanimate objects and constituted the vital element within them showed an obvious tendency towards monistic idealism. This Hassidic Kabbalah doctrine represented a spiritual effort to surmount the doctrine of dualism sanctified by religious tradition, not withstanding the thorough idealism inherent in the pantheistic theory which was diametrically opposed to the Spinozist system and to monistic materialism in general. God and the universe, the spheres of divine emanation and the earth, the spirit and matter—all these opposites were one entity, one reality, one essence, manifestations of divinity, besides which nothing else existed. The imperfection in unitary existence was only a function of perfection—the function of man's life on earth. By worshipping God in love, in study of the Law, and in acts of piety, the individual would restore the sparks of holiness to their divine source, convert defilement into sanctity, sensuality into spirituality, matter (*chomer*) into form (*tzurah*). He would thus bring about unification (*yihud*) in the higher *Sephirot*, unification of The Holy One Blessed Be He with the *She'khinah*, unification of the *Sephirah* of mercy with the *Sephirah* of might (i.e., justice), and thus strengthen the precedence of mercy over stern justice in the rule of the universe. The same definite trend towards a unitary conception of the universe also affirmed the significance of this world and of earthy substantiality despite all idealistic reservations. This explained why the idea of the world to come did not occupy a prominent position in Hassidic doctrine and was only mentioned casually. Man could actually elevate himself to the highest level of spirituality and perfection in this world, by communion with God, through self-negation, "voiding his own self," and thus achieve a state of ultimate beatitude.

This conception of man and his mission in the rectification of the world already showed a glimmering of the humanistic tendencies that were emerging from the medieval outlook. Man born of woman was not "a vessel filled with shame and disgrace." On the contrary, he resembled "a ladder planted on earth with its head reaching up towards Heaven." He was superior to the ministering angels, for the latter were incapable of perfecting themselves, just because they were of the essence of spirituality. However, the doctrine of humanity that Hassidism revived was also permeated with a tendency towards monism in the sphere of morality. Hassidism did, of course, repeatedly remind the individual of his duty to avoid even a semblance of any sinful behaviour—in contradistinction to the moral dissoluteness of the Frankists. Nevertheless, it did not subscribe to the principle that absolute evil was fundamental to man's animal nature, exactly as it denied the presence of absolute evil in the universe as a whole. Instead of considering the human *psyche* as the sphere of conflict between the good and evil impulses, Hassidism regarded man as an integral creature progressively perfecting himself on a spiritual level. "The contemplation of sin was much worse than sin itself," but a sin which spontaneously entered a man's thoughts could incite him to strengthen his adhesion to God. Thus it was also the function of material desire to arouse man to greater ecstasy in the love of the Creator. Hassidism vindicated man's natural tendency to enjoy eating, drinking, and sexual passion, the joy of living which was part of his pristine nature, on an idealistic-religious ground, based on the doctrine that man's life on the "material" level could and should be elevated to the rank of sanctity. An affirmation of "the needs of the material substance" as a "chariot" or a "throne" for spirituality replaced the moral dualism which preached the duty of self-mortification as an ideal for human life. The same tendency towards monism embraced all man's economic activities. Commercial intercourse was not a totally secular activity, unavoidably involving a corresponding loss in the study of the Law and the observance of the precepts on the part of its participants. Instead, it was elevated to the level of a holy service when accompanied by adhesion to God. The changes which appeared in the attitude of Hassidim towards the world of nature are explicable both in the light of its withdrawal from asceticism and in its inclination towards some affirmation of the "material world." Even if the frequent adjurations in Hassidic lore (Ba'al Shem Tov, Moses Leib of Sasow, Davidl of Lelow) to commiserate with dumb animals followed from the doctrine of mercifulness, the same legends also stated that Ba'al Shem Tov was fond of horses and was accustomed to indulge in solitary prayer in forests and meadows as did his great-grandson, Rabbi Nahman of Bratzlav, in later years.

Unlike its new attitude to the universe, Hassidism left the theurgic religion as had been handed down by tradition entirely untouched. On the contrary, under the Hassidic system, the study of the Torah and the observance of all the precepts still constituted the main basis for worshipping the Creator and the foundation for the perfection of the universe. The only "transgressions" the Mitnagdim could point out, even in their severest anti-Hassidic polemics, were that the Hassidim had altered the recognized Ashkenazi form of prayer and substituted the "Sephardic rite" for certain prayers, that they conducted prayers later in the day because of hygienic preparations and were consequently late in their recitation of the She'ma, and that they insisted on ground and not whetted knives for ritual slaughtering. Nevertheless, the warning of the Mitnagdim that the Hassidim were fresh "sectarians," who threatened to undermine the foundations of the dominant religion was not misplaced. It was the Hassidic ideas, the expression of a new trend in the attitude to life and the social order, that aroused indignation among the zealots of the old orthodoxy. The criticism by the Mitnagdim that the Hassidim above all else, slighted the dignity of scholars, neglected the study of the Talmud, removed sadness from life and indulged in extravagant merriment and levity were not unjustified. These were clear manifestations of the democratic aspirations of the new movement, its rejection of the hegemony of the scholars

445

in the Kehillot, and its advocacy of a natural joy in living. Its denial of the absolute dualism of spirituality and materialism in the metaphysical and moral sense, and its tendency to link them by idealistic monism merely reflected Hassidism's aim of raising the status of the masses, the "material" element in society, and of bridging the gulf between them and the "people of the Form," the scholars, by special rapprochement and co-operation.

Social Character of the Movement

An analysis of the social theme in Hassidic doctrine and legend reveals which social groups led the advance of the new religious movement. Social unrest as well as an intensified yearning for deliverance had gripped wide circles of the Jewish masses at the period when Hassidism was born. But the social stratum which actually led the movement and determined its social complexion from the very outset was the underprivileged middle-class group in the Kehillot. It included the inhabitants of the suburbs and the small towns who were oppressed by the major Kehillot and also the villagers, the middle and petty lessees.

The continually deteriorating economic position of these lessees drove them to seek refuge and security in the idea of heavenly salvation and the righting of the balance of abundance forecast in the teachings of Hassidism. These middle classes in the villages, suburbs and towns were united in their opposition to the system of Kehillah exploitation which affected most of the population, including themselves. They also shared a mutual desire to be free of the humiliation of a status inferior to that of the scholars, who enjoyed pre-eminence in Kehillah society. This middle-class opposition found a broad social basis for its reform programme and religious policy amongst the lower middle class and the poor in the city and country. These masses, especially those who lived in the suburbs and towns, lent Hassidism its clearly democratic character and marked it with the popular quality of their religion, environment and customs. The Kehillah members in the cities and towns attracted to the new movement were the small shopkeepers, publicans, pedlars, hawkers, middlemen and all the unemployed who had no place whatsoever in economic life. The village Jews—the innkeepers, liquor-sellers and the middle and small lessees—for the most part also adopted Hassidism and firmly supported the movement at all stages of its development. In Lithuanian territories, where Hassidism only caught on in a few areas, it gained more adherents in White Russia, with its large rural Jewish population, than in Lithuania proper.

The rural and urban adherents of the Hassidic movement were not only brought close to each other by social conditions and by similar aspirations for greater equality in the Kehillah order and a more dignified status in the socio-religious sphere. The absence of deep economic roots affected both groups to the extent of rendering their livelihoods extremely precarious. The shopkeepers, publicans and particularly the hawkers, pedlars and middlemen earned a subsistence almost literally by "miracles" in the form of occasional customers. When their luck failed, they starved. Similarly, the village innkeepers and publicans depended for their income on the mercy of estate-owning noblemen; and "the nobleman's mercy," according to an apposite Polish proverb, "rides a striped horse." The sense of complete security that Hassidic doctrine provided, reflected the innate optimism of the people and encouraged them and gave them strength to face the future amidst their daily troubles.

Whereas lessees and publicans constituted the most frequent characters encountered in Hassidic legend, artisans were fairly rare. Even the earliest legends, compiled in *The Praises of Ba'al Shem Tov*, only mentioned a few. Despite the lowly status of the majority of artisans, their economic basis was far more stable than that of the Jewish small traders, middlemen and liquor-sellers. Their lack of privileges in the Kehillah régime was notorious, but they did not elect to remain passive or to put their faith in moral preachings. Instead, they organized active resistance against the Kehillah leaders wherever they were able, and especially in the large Kehillot of Lithuania and White Russia. In a number of Kehillot, the rebellious artisans at times found allies in the Hassidim, but for the most part they went their separate ways, as Hassidic teaching never at any time advocated actual class warfare as a means of changing the Kehillah régime. Furthermore, a distinct cultural and social demarcation divided the artisans from the lower middle class hawkers and liquor-sellers. The shopkeepers and the liquor purveyors customarily had their sons instructed in Gemara, while the sons of artisans usually completed their education at the age of confirmation—*barmitzvah*—and entered workshops as apprentices, even before they had acquired a knowledge of the Pentateuch. Unlike the shopkeepers and liquor sellers, whose wives could take their place in the store and the ale-house, the artisans could not observe the Hassidic customs of ritual personal hygiene which entailed frequent visits to the *mikveh* (ritual baths) and delayed prayer service. Often even the dress of a "master" (*ba'al-bayyit*, or *balle-buss*), though he might be nothing more than a hawker or a lowly liquor seller, differed from that of the artisan, who was considered an *am-ha'aretz*—an ignorant boor. In fact, the artisans were not amongst the devotees of Hassidism, despite its mass character, and although it would appear logical that they should have acknowledged its democratic aims in its quarrel with the Mitnagdim.

The men who moulded the ideas of the movement, the thinkers who expressed Hassidic ideology, came from the lower stratum of professional religious intellectuals. They were preachers and moralists, ritual slaughterers, cantors and teachers who were in closer touch with wide circles of the masses, both because of their profession and because of their own poverty. The active campaign that these underprivileged scholars led against the arrogant scholar class and the stern rejection of the Kehillah leaders who were robbing the common people expressed and reflected their own bitterness at their wretched status, as well as the popular opposition in the Kehillot as a whole. It was not surprising that the founder of Hassidism, Israel Ba'al Shem Tov had worked as an assistant to a village teacher, as a teacher and as a slaughterer, as well as in such undistinguished capacities as servant, watchman at a synagogue-school, clay-digger and bartender. It was even more typical that most of his disciples were preachers, moralists, teachers and slaughterers.* The group only included two or three ordained rabbis.

However, despite all its emphatic democratic tendencies, Hassidism never arrived at a lucid, outspoken programme of reforms in the Kehillah régime and social relationships. Hassidism, unlike non-Jewish socio-religious movements, lacked a solid social class (e.g. peasants, urban poor or proletariat) capable of undertaking the struggle from a clearly defined social and political platform. This was mainly because of the abnormal social and economic structure of the Jewish population, resulting from the absence of a territorial basis of its own, and the consequent absence of a national political life. Furthermore, national oppression affected all classes of Jews, even though it weighed most heavily on the weak and impoverished groups. The affliction of exile, even within an oppositionist religious movement, was sufficient to relegate the social problem to a secondary position and to cause it to be absorbed into a general national aspiration for redemption—Messianic deliverance, envisaged only in the form of heavenly salvation.

The changes that Hassidism actually and successfully introduced were primarily in the sphere of rendering *social* life more democratic. Hassidism elevated the sense of human dignity and communal significance not only of the middle class, who ranked inferior to the scholars in learning, but also of the ordinary people, who had been denied both the distinction of wealth and the virtue of learning.

Hassidism was able to influence Kehillah affairs and public activities through its internal organization, a network which extended over numerous districts and, indeed, entire countries, far more than by direct action. In fact strong bonds of solidarity existed between supporters of the movement causing it, in some respects, to resemble a parallel organization to the Kehillah. This surprised its opponents and was mentioned in the reports of government officials. The principal task of the *Tzaddik* was to

* Professor B. Z. Dinur (Dinaburg) has stressed the significance of the social composition of Ba'al Shem Tov's group of disciples, and emphasized the place held by the "intellectual proletariat" in the ascendant Hassidic movement, a phenomenon previously suggested by such historians as H. Graetz and S. Dubnov, *cf.* B. Z. Dinaburg, *The Beginnings of Hassidism, Its Social and Messianic Foundations* (in Hebrew), *Zion* Quarterly, Vols. 8-10, particularly Chapter 8, Vol. 9, pp. 89-108.

offer guidance in the worship of God and the way of righteousness. But he was also a congregational leader, on a par with the Kehillah Rabbi, and, furthermore, exercised absolute and unchallengeable authority over his flock. In this capacity, he attended to the affairs of the Jews in towns and villages, pronounced decisions in disputes between his followers, prevented infringement of rights of tenure by lessees and liquor sellers and usually defended the poor against extortion and exploitation. Their integral organization and exceptional unity made it possible for the Hassidim not only to influence decisions on the appointment of cantors, ritual slaughterers (by forbidding all slaughtering except with ground knives), preachers and even rabbis—even in Kehillot where they did not command a majority. At times they were even able to force their will on the Kehillah leaders in the regulation of Kehillah affairs.

The reforms instituted by Hassidism did *not* transcend the framework of the existing social order. The mass character of Hassidism was expressed in a powerful demand for justice and honesty on the basis of what it regarded as an unalterable system, in its attempts to soften the existing sharp social antagonism, and in charity and mutual aid to the poor. A principal feature of all Hassidic instruction on comportment in revering God demanded that business dealings be conducted honestly and faithfully, without "robbery" and deceit, and expressly included a prohibition on deceiving gentiles. The social pathos which animated the warnings against "robbery" and deprivation of the abjectly poor given by the preachers among Ba'al Shem Tov's disciples represented a continuation of the best in the ethical literature of the Middle Ages and modern times. The principle stressed in the new social morality of Hassidism was the unity of Israel, which could only be maintained through justice, as well as love of Israel, which required the practice of grace between men, before brotherhood and companionship amongst the people could be established.

Charity, as a means of redressing social wrongs, acquired a unique organization under the Hassidic system, in addition to the existing charitable societies. This was linked to the fact that congregational life centred on the *Tzaddik's* "court." It was the custom for the *Tzaddik's* friends, who constituted a sort of entourage, to share his meals. Even the term used to describe them, *yosh'vim* (sitters), proved the extent to which the Hassidic order was grounded in the feudal system of the state—precisely the same expression (in Latin, *residentes*) was customarily attached to impoverished nobles in Poland who resided in the palaces of their magnate relatives and patrons, literally living at their expense. The meals served to the Hassidic congregation in the *Tzaddik's* court on the Sabbath and on holidays, gave the local poor, who could not afford such feasts in their own homes, the opportunity to eat their fill. Charitable activities were concentrated in the hands of the *Tzaddik*, mainly because of the custom of paying a *pidyon* (redemption) to the *Tzaddik*, observed by Hassidim who came to pay homage and obtain help through his prayers. During the period of Hassidic ascendancy, these *pidyonot* served as a large welfare chest enabling the *Tzaddik* to distribute generous alms to the very poor. At that time, the *Tzaddikim* also organized special charitable activities in times of need. The legends in *The Praises of Ba'al Shem Tov* described his attempts on behalf of the *Redemption of Captives*—the release of lessees imprisoned by their masters for failure to pay their rentals punctually. During the second and third generation of Ba'al Shem Tov's disciples, *Tzaddikim* travelled about the country to raise funds for the impoverished ones. Hassidic legend also praised *Tzaddikim* who married off orphans of both sexes with their own funds (thereby fulfilling the commandment on the giving of the bride in marriage). The *Tzaddik* thus became the "bestower of abundance" not only in his mystical role as mediator between the people of Israel and the world of divine emanations, but also in a practical sense.

The *Tzaddik* undertook a similar double task in matters concerning bodily health and practical help in times of trouble. He not only aided the sick, the barren, and the afflicted, by the cogency of his prayer and adhesion to God, but he was also the practical consultant in times of distress and confusion and provided remedies and cures when required. Theosophic and theurgic Kabbalah had always been linked in mystical doctrine. They had already been united in the teaching and practice of the founder of Hassidism and his disciples and their pupils usually followed his example. The folk character of Hassidism also appeared in this field. The *Tzaddikim*, in their capacity as "the healers of the sick ones amongst His people of Israel" did not rely exclusively on the secrets of Kabbalah but occasionally also drew on popular experience in their diagnosis of illness and the application of simple remedies. Remedy lists, like that of Rabbi Pinehas of Koretz, were a combination of secret cures with actual medicines, tried and tested by popular quacks over generations. In fact, Hassidism marked a singular fusion between the profound study by generations of the dialectics of the law and theology and the naïve, superstitious beliefs current amongst the simple people. On the one hand, it expressed a consistent philosophical and mystical ideal, in an effort to comprehend the universe in a unified concept of idealistic monism, a subtlety of thought that rejected miracles in the crudest sense because they conflicted with the natural course of events. On the other hand, it clung to the simple and primitive beliefs of the people. This dual character impregnated the social composition of the movement, which united democratic scholars with the common people in the cities and towns.

As a popular movement, Hassidism adopted the characteristics peculiar to the people—their optimism, *joie de vivre*, fertile imagination, depth of feeling, gift of observation of the external scene and their wisdom born of experience. The theoretical works by Hassidic thinkers displayed amazing skill in their attempts to expound complex problems in occult science with the aid of the subtle dialectics of *pilpul*. But these thinkers were able to recount their parables with the narrative skill intrinsic to folk tales, and express them in the keenly humorous idiom of Jewish folklore. These qualities, together with the aim of national redemption, constituted the principal difference between Hassidism and gentile religious sects. Not one of the Christian folk sects ever became a popular religion, mainly because the dominant church, whether Catholic or Protestant, persecuted them relentlessly and forced them to exist illegally. Hassidism, on the other hand, never bore any trace of sectarianism. Its nature, aims and the scope of its activities marked it from the beginning as a movement fated to win over an entire people to its ideas.

The folk element in the movement's doctrine acquired singular importance in the lives of the Hassidic masses. They received the Hassidic system as a religion which was accessible to all men, which had brought the Torah down from heaven to earth and even brought God infinitely closer to the individual through His apostle and prophet, the *Tzaddik*. Hassidism gave the lower classes confidence in their difficult struggle to earn a living and strengthened their hope of attaining salvation together with the whole nation. But it also elevated them by mystic visions from the depression and inanities of daily life to the heights of the upper spheres, to a world that was all spirituality and divine radiance. Hopes of redemption and of the triumph of the oppressed people over the depraved nations grew with the increased pressure of the bondage in exile. As the life of the small trader and liquor seller became more wretched and melancholy, his yearning for flight and refuge in a higher source of beauty, splendour and majesty grew more powerful. Above all, however, Hassidism inspired the lives of the people with a spirit of joyfulness, of the warmth and good cheer of communal life, the buoyance of nature, and the pleasure a man could derive from his actions—all of which were licensed and approved in Israel's rejoicing in the Creator. The process was reciprocal: Hassidism was nourished by the spirit and emotions of the people, their innermost hopes, desires, and visions; in its turn, it wielded a tremendous influence on the people by bolstering their inclinations and ambitions, shackled for many generations by the dominant religion of the *Shulchan Arukh*. Hassidism roused the people from the religious frigidity of legalistic minutiae to the freshness of a religion exuberant with life and creativity. It released their creative ability, held in check for many centuries. The forces of their emotions and imagination were released and a wealth of art and wisdom burst forth. In the art of the people ecstasy to the point of "voiding one's existence" in Hassidic dances and an emotional outpouring that attained the "divestment of materiality" in music expressed Hassidic doctrine: a tumultuous joy in living tempered by gnawing economic problems and the sadness of bondage in exile, an overwhelming desire for redemption in Zion and for a beautiful, happy existence, an everlasting life amidst a liberated people.

Hassidism did not escape the unfavourable development that had in the long run overtaken all the religious movements of the world. Its development followed similar lines to the Gentile religious movements that had attained power. However, its initial lack of a crystallized social pattern made the process of transformation in Hassidism far easier and more rapid. As the movement began to acquire adherents among the well-to-do and wealthy, its doctrine was increasingly adapted to fit their specific social outlook. And the more drastically the doctrine was changed in order to subdue social opposition and the more prominence and emphasis were given to the principles of the system which were acceptable to the ruling Kehillah class, the more members of that class eagerly joined the spreading movement.

Some of the principles which the Hassidic movement proclaimed could, by altering their original significance, not only avoid antagonizing its opponents but actually serve them as arguments for strengthening the existing social order and its religion. Hassidism's aim of strengthening religious faith accorded with the aspirations of the ruling class more than all its other principles. The condemnatory attitude of the conservative *Mitnagdim* increasingly changed to approval as *Haskalah* "apostasy" began to gain adherents and spread through Poland. More than that, Hassidism not only provided a mainstay for religious faith, but also for community life on a religious basis. As the Kehillah was continually weakened by inner schisms and underminings from within as well as by the absolutist monarchy's restrictions on its institutional activities and authority, the conservative *Mitnagdim* perceived the efficiency of the new organizational pattern of the Hassidic congregation in the maintenance of religious institutions and the re-establishment of their authority within the Kehillah. As a result, Hassidism not only spread geographically at the end of the eighteenth and beginning of the nineteenth centuries, but also across class boundaries. It steadily pervaded the very wealthy circles and ruling Kehillah groups which had been determined to destroy it in its early days as a new religious movement.

In keeping with the change in its social composition, the doctrines of the Hassidic movement began to gloss over the ideals of democracy and social opposition which had reflected the aspirations of the lower middle class and the poor masses which constituted its social basis. Open criticism of the scholars as an aloof and haughty class became far less frequent in the Hassidic literature of the third generation, even though it was still repeatedly advised that Torah be studied for its own sake. With this decreased antagonism towards the scholar class, a change also took place in the attitude of Hassidism towards the study of the Law.

The change in the essential nature and characteristics of Hassidism was not only produced by relegating several of its cardinal principles to the background until they were forgotten or repudiated, but also by amplifying other ideas already present in the teachings of the fathers of Hassidism and presenting them in a new light. The role of the *Tzaddik* had already been fundamental to the doctrine in Ba'al Shem Tov's system. The *Tzaddik*, as Ba'al Shem Tov conceived him, was not only a counsellor to the people in the worship of God. He also possessed special mystical attributes: he transmitted the prayers of his congregation and sent up its sparks of holiness even when he only communed with it in his thoughts: and he was also the vehicle of supreme abundance. Ba'al Shem Tov, however, still believed that communion with the *She'khinah* and the "assuagement of sternness" was the duty of every individual Jew. He actually served frequent warnings to the effect that a Jew should not depend on the agent of the congregation but should pray in his own individual act of adhesion. Ba'al Shem Tov's disciple, Jacob Joseph, still did not differentiate between a *Tzaddik* and a scholar (*Talmid-Chakham*) who was attached to the mass of the people, and he employed both terms interchangeably. A generation later, the doctrine of *Tzaddikism* was definitely perfected in the system of Rabbi Elimelekh of Lezajsk. The *Tzaddik* was "omnipotent," and he lavished an abundance of wealth not only on the world as a whole but on every individual by praying for him, even merely by conversing with him. He also healed the afflicted through his prayer; the precondition for this function of the *Tzaddik* was that the person who came for help should have faith in him. The role of the *Tzaddik* had thus been transposed to that of an agent of divinity and a miracle-worker. He procured a livelihood, healed the sick and dispelled barrenness. What had begun as a prehumanist regeneration of religion in the form of a democratic folk religion, developed towards a mass religion permeated with magic, superstition, and idolatrous adulation of the all-powerful *Tzaddik*, the "Eye of God" on earth. *Tzaddikism* as a theoretical system reached its acme in the doctrine of Ba'al Shem Tov's great-grandson, Rabbi Nahman of Bratzlav, who regarded the *Tzaddik* as only slightly inferior to the Almighty. Hassidism had begun with aims directed towards a popular religious reformation. At the very height of its development it deteriorated to quasi-Catholic *Tzaddikism*. Opposition to the scholars on the grounds that they held themselves above the people, was succeeded by worship of the *Tzaddikim*, who exercised unlimited power over their congregations to an extent never attained by even the most brilliant learned men. The doctrine that the rabbi's office was a sacred rank to be bequeathed from father to son, caused the number of *Tzaddik* dynasties to multiply and branch out as fathers passed both their glory and their material assets on to their sons. A new aristocracy of "grandsons" thus gained ascendancy over the people, the sons of *Tzaddik* families, who for the most part even married only amongst themselves. The material wealth and way of life of this spiritual aristocracy in no way fell below the most opulent of the rabbis during their period of greatest prosperity.

The change in its social trend and tenor eventually caused Hassidism to follow a jealously conservative policy which obstructed the spiritual and cultural progress of the people. Its unalterably hostile attitude towards all secular science and enlightenment in its decline was far in excess of Talmudic orthodoxy.

It must be noted, however, that because of the very gradual geographic diffusion of Hassidism, there was no strict parallel between the stages of its development and decline in various localities. The process of decline first began in the Ukrainian districts where it had been conceived. In Lithuania and White Russia, where it had only caught on amongst a minority of communities, it never descended to the belief in miracles and the *Tzaddik* cult, such as it had reached in other eastern European countries. In central Poland, where the movement was late in spreading, it preserved much of the pristine freshness with which it had infused religious life as late as the beginning of the nineteenth century. Even in the middle of the nineteenth century some remains of its early dynamic intellectual power were still in evidence there. Similarly, wherever the movement still held sway during that period, there remained individual *Tzaddikim* who continued to propagate in their teaching and behaviour the finest elements of the popular Hassidism represented by Ba'al Shem Tov and Rabbi Moses Leib of Sassow. However, these variations in development and even the thin rivulets of original Hassidism in the mainstream of the movement were of no decisive historical significance. When the process finally came to an end, the entire movement had been imbued with unyielding conservatism and social and cultural reaction.

The *Haskalah* movement in eastern Europe furnished the progressive cultural trend destined to regenerate all spheres of the people's life. It was fostered by the modern Jewish middle class and gained ascendancy during the period of Hassidism's intellectual and social decline. Furthermore, the *Haskalah* movement in eastern Europe had no prospect of propagating its message except by a persistent struggle against the steadily deteriorating Hassidic movement. The superiority of the *Haskalah* movement in this struggle was the advantage enjoyed by capitalist progress over antiquated feudalism. It was only after the triumph of the *Haskalah* movement that historical reappraisal vindicated Hassidism. The Jewish people were only able to assess the movement's position in its cultural development and to evaluate the legacy of national and humanitarian values bequeathed by early Hassidism when it was no longer an active cause but a historical phenomenon. It was remembered as a religious movement that had wrestled with God for the deliverance of the people, and with man for equality and justice amongst the people, and had not prevailed.

B. *THE AGE OF GROWTH AND OF CONTROVERSY*

Rabbi Israel Ba'al Shem Tov—The Teacher and his Doctrine

The image of the founder of Hassidism, like several of the founders of world religions, is heavily shrouded in legend. The legends circulating amongst Hassidim about their first master and teacher—collectively known as the *Praises of the BeShT*—were only published in 1815, over fifty years after his death.* These legends contain several grains of historical truth regarding his personality, and in substance present an outline of the story of his life.

Rabbi Israel Ben-Eliezer Ba'al Shem Tov was born in about 1700 at Okup, apparently a suburb of Kolomyja, in the foothills of the Carpathians in Red Ruthenia (subsequently eastern Galicia). Both his parents died in his early childhood and he was educated by a *me'lamed* at Kehillah expense. He was accustomed to play truant from the *Heder* and to run off alone to the forest, "and the lad grew not up in the custom of the land." Before he had reached confirmation age, he was employed as an assistant teacher to small boys and devoted himself to this profession with love. Later, he became a school-synagogue (*Bet-Midrash*) watchman. Meanwhile, he had married, but his wife died when he was twenty, and he then settled in a Kehillah near the city of Brody where he was employed as a teacher. Shortly afterwards, he married again, this time the divorced sister of Abraham Gershon Kutyver, named after the town of Kuty, south of Kolomyja. His brother-in-law was one of the Brody *Kloiz* Sages† and served in the same synagogue as prayer leader (*ba'al-te'fillah*). Kutyver, an accomplished Talmudist, was embarrassed by his brother-in-law, who posed as a crude village Jew. He therefore bought him a horse and cart and sent him away. Rabbi Israel returned with his wife to his native countryside and settled in a Carpathian village between the towns of Kuty and Kosow. He dug clay to earn a living, loaded it on his cart, and his wife hauled it to town. Amidst these high mountains, the years of solitude began for Israel Ben Eliezer. It was there that his pantheistic doctrine, the fundamentals of which he had drawn from the literature of Kabbalah, came to fruition. Amidst the murmurings of the primeval forests, the roaring River Prut and its tributaries, and the expanses of meadows, he heard creation sing its praises of the Almighty. The sight of the gigantic boulders and timeless mountains, snow-capped throughout most of the year, instilled him with a sacred passion to glorify the majesty of nature in

---

* *BeShT* are the Hebrew initials of Ba'al Shem Tov. The full name is employed hereafter in this translation.—Tr.

† The *Kloiz* was a kind of *Bet-Midrash,* or school, at which religious students, in seclusion from the outside world, devoted themselves to the study of Talmud. The Brody *Kloiz* Sages had already become known as *Hassidim* (pious men) even before Ba'al Shem Tov's movement acquired momentum, but they were inclined to asceticism, which the *BeShT* rejected.

its vesture of infinity. Even when he moved to another village, near Kuty, Rabbi Israel continued his solitary prayer and study of Kabbalah in a hut he built himself in the forest. At first he worked as a bartender at a tavern in the service of the village lessee, with the additional job of watering the lessee's cattle. But in later years he worked at many occupations; he was, amongst other things, a village teacher and itinerant slaughterer, until he settled in the town of Tluste as a *Me'lamed*. There too, he suffered extreme poverty. "His dress consisted of one coarse homespun garment, and his toes protruded from the holes in his boots."

When he was thirty-six years old, Rabbi Israel decided to reveal himself as a *ba'al shem*. Thenceforth, he was engaged in healing the sick and demented, aiding barren women, and proffering advice and remedies in times of trouble. In his healing activities, he made use of plants and herbs, blood-letting, and other remedies he had apparently learned from village quacks; but for the most part he became known as a writer of amulets, as prescribed by the Kabbalah. Within a few years, he had acquired a reputation as a miracle worker throughout Red Ruthenia and Podolia, Volhynia and the Ukraine. Estate-owners, *P'ritzim*, who required his cures, as well as village Jews, lessees and innkeepers, not only came to his house at Tluste from remote parts but also invited him to visit them. The people quickly distinguished between Rabbi Israel, the famous "son of a midwife," and ordinary *ba'alei-shemot*, who were common everywhere. They expressed their love and veneration by bestowing on him the title *Ba'al Shem Tov*, The Master of the Good Name.

He gained their confidence more by his personality and behaviour than by his remedies and miracles. The fervour with which Ba'al Shem Tov prayed, achieving extreme ecstasy, powerfully impressed those who beheld him. When he worshipped, he began to tremble, his face "would burn like a torch and his eyes would bulge, standing motionless like—Heaven forbid!—those of a dying man." His votaries described how the water in a vessel in the synagogue "actually whirled about," as he trembled during prayer. Once, while he was praying in a house with full grain bins ranged along the walls, "one saw the grains shaking." People attributed his power to work miracles, to heal the sick and to nullify the effects of decrees issued against the Jews to this devotion whilst praying. His great confidence in the efficacy of devout prayer was equalled by his profound belief that the Torah reflected the universe and its contents, and that intimations of all events throughout all of time should be sought in the Torah. The *Praises of Ba'al Shem Tov* recalled instances when Ba'al Shem Tov divined mysteries or predicted the future after opening and glancing briefly at the *Zohar*.

Ba'al Shem Tov had originated amongst the poor, grown up with the ordinary people, and spent all his life in intimate contact with them. He therefore taught them his doctrine "in the language of mortals." Like Socrates, the Athenian searcher for truth, also the son of a midwife, who struck up conversations with people in order to acquaint them with philosophical concepts, the midwife's son from a Carpathian mountain village was accustomed on his numerous travels to stand in market places and expound Hassidic doctrine to groups of ordinary people. But Ba'al Shem Tov held his audience with simple words, with the warmth of his speech, his pointed, lucid epigrams, his graphic parables, created by his fertile imagination, and with fables he had heard from the people and interpreted symbolically. He also considered it his personal duty to care for the observance of religion amongst the people, and especially amongst the village Jews who were left to their own devices.

Some of the legends praised Ba'al Shem Tov for his championship of the persecuted and the injured against their oppressors, for his advocacy of justice, his tribute to labourers living by the sweat of their brow and for his emphasis on the virtue of charity. He rebuked the lessors who deprived others of their incomes and increased rentals, and he defended the poor option-holding lessees against them. He and his disciples embarked on the "redemption of captives"—lessees arrested by estate owners for failing to pay arrears on their rents—though he himself was deeply in debt as a result of borrowing heavily from nobles to get these victims released. He was able to recognize any money which had been acquired by usury in any form, and on one occasion threw away a ring he had seen at a jeweller's because he had sensed its defiled origin when he picked it up. Another story concerned a stocking-maker who worked for a jobber, performed his work diligently, recited all the Psalms that he remembered by heart and prayed at the synagogue in a religious quorum. Ba'al Shem Tov used to say of him: "He will be the foundation of the synagogue till the Redeemer comes." He was also scrupulous about honesty in business dealings with gentiles. Nevertheless, he felt compassion for anyone who stole because of adversity. In practice, Ba'al Shem Tov thought that the precept of charity was of greater importance than quoting from the Torah, and his friends testified that "he never clung to any money; whenever he returned from a journey, he would pay his debts and on the same day disburse the remainder in alms."

His mercy was unlimited. His love for all his fellow-Jews and his compassion for every living creature made Ba'al Shem Tov the archetype of all those *Tzaddikim* who were venerated by the people for their conduct. In accordance with his teachings that the sparks of holiness were scattered in every impurity amongst the gentiles, Ba'al Shem Tov saw elements of sublimity in the Ukrainian folk songs, which he had heard since early youth in his mountainous birthplace. According to his grandson, Rabbi Ephraim, he would say, "When the Gentiles sing their songs, there is in all of them Reverence and Love that spread out and descend from on High to all the Lowest Levels."

However, despite his manifest humanitarian attitude to all human beings, the ultimate fullness of Ba'al Shem Tov's love was lavished upon the Jewish people, the nation of God, enduring all the agonies of exile and persevering in its faithfulness to the Torah and the Precepts. A traditional tale related in the *Praises of Ba'al Shem Tov* told how a preacher once "calumnied" the Jewish people in his sermon. Ba'al Shem Tov was so angry when he heard this that he sprang up from his seat with tears gushing from his eyes and remonstrated with the preacher:

> You would speak evil of Israel! Know then that day in and day out a son of Israel goes forth to market and with the fall of evening, when he is weary, he trembles, saying "Woe is me, that I should be late for the afternoon prayer!" And he repairs to a home and there he offers the afternoon prayer scarcely knowing what he says; yet have seraphim and angels been shaken thereby!

In fact, Ba'al Shem Tov also prepared the way for Hassidism by his vindication of the Jews, even to the extent of discounting the charge of the social abuses in their midst.

The man who created the Hassidic system, with the joyous worship of God and the rejection of sadness and asceticism as one of its principles, was himself, both temperamentally and in his intercourse with the common people, overflowing with the joy of life and he did not deny himself its pleasures. He was both a man of vision and a popular teacher who puffed continually at a meerschaum as he mingled and conversed with people on current events. He was accustomed to drop in at a tavern on his journeys, to pass the time of day with friends, and he enjoyed a good meal. Furthermore, he was enough of a gourmet to discriminate between good and poor wine. An ex-carter, he was a passionate lover of horses and affectionately patted and stroked every handsome beast he encountered on the road. Not even the fear of breaking the Commandment *Thou shalt not covet* could deter him when he wanted to buy a horse. He possessed a brilliant sense of humour, which pervaded his speech, and was willing to enjoy a subtle joke even if told by a thief.

At the beginning of the 1740's, Rabbi Israel Ba'al Shem Tov settled in the city of Mezhibozh in Podolia. This marked a turning point in his activities and in the history of the movement he had inaugurated. True, even during this period, Ba'al Shem Tov continued to heal the sick and prescribe remedies and charms as before, and he travelled about the country for that purpose. The *Praises of Ba'al Shem Tov* did not conceal the fact that because of this activity local Hassidim at first disparaged him. Before many years had elapsed, however, many disciples flocked to him at Mezhibozh, including brilliant Talmudic scholars. His brother-in-law, Rabbi Gershon of Kuty, was reconciled with him and became one of his ardent admirers. The miracle-working *Ba'al Shem* now became the spiritual leader and teacher of Hassidic doctrine to thousands of enthusiasts and led the new religious movement that was rapidly spreading. Ba'al Shem Tov was no different from the founders of other religious movements in that he himself did not hand down his teachings in writing. Nothing has been preserved of his doctrine except what his disciples, especially Rabbi Jacob Joseph, and their pupils, included in their books.

Ba'al Shem Tov once explained the arch-principle of his system, according to which God "fills all the universe with His glory, no place is vacant thereof," and "all movement and thought, all derive from Him," in the following parable:

> There was a great and wise king who erected illusory walls, towers, and gates, and he commanded that all coming to him should pass through the gates and the towers, and he commanded that the King's treasures should be dispensed at each gate. And some went to one gate taking money, and some to another gate and back; until his beloved son was very desirous of going to his father the king. And then he perceived that no barrier intervened between him and his father, for it was all but an illusion.

The moral: he who knows that "The Holy One Blessed Be He takes cover behind sundry raiments and partitions ... no partition divides such a one from Him, May He Be Blessed." The man who reached this stage of gnosis was also enabled to examine the ultimate root of everything in the universe, its "vitality and spirituality," without dwelling on its material covering:

> If a man suddenly beholds a comely woman, he may well ponder whence came she by this comeliness. Dead, she would no longer possess this countenance, consummate ugliness would be hers ... Therefore, it is hers by virtue of the Divinity which is diffused in her. It is that which bestows upon her the power of her beauty, the rosiness and comeliness of her features. It follows that the source of beauty is the Divine Force. Why then should I be drawn after the part? Better for me to cling to the Root and Principle of the entire Universe, where lie all manifestations of beauty.

Except for the absolute condition of unanticipated observation (the premeditated contemplation of a woman for the enjoyment of her beauty was a manifest transgression according to Ba'al Shem Tov also), this exposition might have been a recapitulation, though an unwitting one, of Socrates' discourse on beauty in Plato's Symposium. The essential Platonic doctrine of ideas was thus handed down in a winding chain of historical development over a period of two thousand years, via the channels of neo-Platonism in Hellenistic Egypt, the mystic doctrine of Provence and Spain, to the Kabbalah in Safed, whence it reached the Ukrainian steppes and was revived in the speculations of Hassidic thinkers who worshipped God with joy.

The rule for manifestations of beauty applied to all man's thoughts, emotions and yearnings. "In all of a person's thoughts, there is His

Blessed Presence," except that they had become encased in profane shells. Man was therefore obliged to restore them to their source. For this restoration, it was necessary to aspire to that particular upper world whence the *Idea* descended. And thus, "if one be seized by his lusts, then is he fallen from the World of Love; if by evil belief—from the World of Reverence; by pride—from the World of Splendour." On the same lines anger derived from the world of divine might (Justice). "And if, in the Blessed Name of God he bind them to the Love of the Creator and Reverence for the Creator, then has he restored them to their Source." Evil was only the throne of goodness, both in the sense of its oppositeness and as forming a lower stage of goodness, for the nether world and the upper worlds were bound together "as the flame is united with the burning coal, each to the other, up to on High."

Ba'al Shem Tov's ethical doctrine which aimed to span the gulf between the duality of the impulses for good and evil ran strictly parallel to this explicit tendency to integrate man's material world and mental forces within an idealist monistic outlook. Man's worship of the Creator was not directed towards a struggle against the impulse for evil, but instead to elevate and convert it into an impulse for good. Here again, a parable of an all-powerful king was offered:

> And he sent one of his servants to sound out the domains as though he were a servant rebelling against his master. And some of the domains made war upon him and overpowered him, and some of the states made their peace with him; and in one domain there were wise men who sensed that he was but doing the bidding of his king. And the moral is clear, for there be men who war upon the impulse to evil as though it were presuming to be like a servant rebelling against his master and enticing men not to do the Will of the Blessed Creator Who is King of the Universe, and they resist this until they have prevailed over their impulse in the mightiness of their struggle and through tremendous self-affliction. And there be men who have sensed that it is the Creator's Will that he is doing and that His Holy Name is clothed therein.

Ba'al Shem Tov offered yet another parable to illustrate this, while expounding the saying of the Sages that *A valiant man is he who subdueth his desire*:

> It is as in worldly affairs, when one who keeps guard over merchandise stored in a room hears the thief approaching stealthily he cries out, thus causing the thief to flee. But there is also one who prepares chains, and when the thief enters the room he fetters him in iron bonds. And thus it is that amongst saintly persons there be those who permit no idle thought to draw near ... But there is one who takes the covetousness or the lust or the evil belief on behalf of the

Worship of God, that they may be for the Love and Reverence of Him, Blessed Be He. And of such a one it is said that he is the more valiant, for it is he who subdues his desire and his qualities and his covetousness for the Worship of the Blessed Name.

In abolishing the irreconcilable contradiction inherent in moral duality, Ba'al Shem Tov was not satisfied with teaching a means of deceiving the impulse to evil but expressly established that material desires were the source of awakening of all spiritual powers, including the desire for goodness and the aspiration to holiness. Under Ba'al Shem Tov's system this idea, an intimation of modern psychological theory which had already been hinted at in the Talmud as well as in medieval theological works and Kabbalah, became one of the cardinal principles in the worship of God. In the name of Rabbi Sa'adyah Gaon, Ba'al Shem Tov taught that "it behooves a man to desire all material things and thence to come to desire the Law and the worship of God ..." Again he strengthened his argument with a parable:

There was a king who had a son, and he wished to teach him several wisdoms which were necessary, and he employed a number of scholars to teach him, but the son failed to acquire any of these wisdoms until his teachers despaired of him and there was but one scholar left. And once the king's son espied a virgin and he lusted for her charms, and the scholar complained to the king against his son concerning this, and the king replied, *"Even so, since he has lusted, albeit for things of the flesh, thence will he attain to all the wisdoms."** And he commanded the virgin to be brought unto the royal court, and he commanded her that when his son should lust for her she should not hearken save he did acquire one wisdom. And she did so. And then she said to him that he must learn yet another wisdom, and thus did he acquire all the wisdoms. And when he had become a scholar, he spurned this virgin, for then he took to wife a royal princess like himself. ...

By negating asceticism man also avoided sadness, which was the origin of all the shells of impurity which kept him apart from God. Also, "prayer in great joyousness is certainly more important than prayer amidst sadness and weeping ... And even though a man shall have erred in sin, let him not be profusely sad ... Let him but be sad for the sin he has committed and be abashed before the Blessed One, and let him weep and plead that his evil be done away with, and he shall again be happy in the Blessed One ..." Joyousness derived from the individual's knowledge, from his belief that God filled the Universe, and therefore "let him ever be joyous, let him think and believe wholeheartedly that the *She'khinah* is with him, that it watches over him, that he is gazing at the Blessed Creator and

* The Italics are the author's.

461

the Blessed Creator is gazing at him." This joyousness which arose from faith, naturally filled the individual with an abundance of confidence:

> For I am assured in Him that from the Void He hath created and doth sustain the Worlds through His Words, and that all is as nothing unto Him, and that He keepeth watch over them and doth bestow upon them their abundance and their life.

The primary rule in the worship of God was loving adhesion to Him. One of the pathways of adhesion was prayer, in which a man should divest himself of materiality, remove the curtain that separated him from God, and achieve breathless ecstasy. Prayer was union with the *She'khinah* and a man's emotions while praying showed the awakening of love.

The prime object in the study of the Torah was also concentration of purpose and adhesion. "A man who reads the Torah and beholds the clarity of the letters in the Torah, though he understand not properly the reasons, yet since he reads it with great love and fervour, the Blessed One will not be strict with him . . . For he is as an infant whose father loves him greatly and when he asks anything of his father, though he stammer and say it not properly, yet is his father greatly pleased." According to Hassidic legend, Ba'al Shem Tov sharply ridiculed scholars who quibbled over niceties of law with no practical purpose except to flaunt their skill. The *Praises of Ba'al Shem Tov* related how the *Parnass* of the Council of the Four Lands summoned Ba'al Shem Tov to appear before the Council Assembly. To humiliate him publicly by exposing his supposed ignorance, the rabbi asked Ba'al Shem Tov what should be the ruling for a man who had forgotten to recite *Let him rise up and come* at the beginning of the new month (i.e., whether or not he should repeat the prayer of the *She'moneh-Esrei*, the *Eighteen Benedictions*). Ba'al Shem Tov's reply was: "This ruling is necessary neither for Your Reverence nor for me. For Your Reverence even if you repeat the prayer, will forget it again, while I certainly shall not forget!" The cardinal purpose in studying the Torah was to know the precepts, to revere heaven, and to improve one's virtues; anybody who only studied Gemara had no purpose other than to boast of it:

> For certainly the impulse to evil does not entice a man to forswear all learning, for it knows that none will heed such a man; for if he learn not at all, he will not be meritorious in the eyes of men and will not be called a scholar. Therefore, the impulse to evil entices him not to learn that which will inspire him with the Awe of Heaven, like books of ethics or the *Shulchan Arukh*, whereby he may know the laws thoroughly, but it entices him at all times to engage only in Gemara with all of its commentators.

Concentration of purpose was as important in the observation of the precepts as in prayer and the study of the Torah.

And when he commences to worship God, let him not be overstrict in all that he does, for such indeed is the purpose of the impulse to evil, to make a man fear that he has not fulfilled his duty in this. . . . Even when he observes one precept with purpose and love, it is as though he had observed them all, for he deserves to know the secret of the Blessed One's Unity, for wheresoever I grasp and hold the edge and part of that Unity I have grasped it in its entirety.

The religious liberalism of Ba'al Shem Tov's system was most clearly evident in his affirmation of the individual's material life, whether his bodily needs, his business affairs or his table talk were concerned. Several reasons lay behind this permissive attitude in Ba'al Shem Tov's system. On the psycho-physiological plane, it was stated that fervent study of the Torah and devotion to God required rest and relaxation for their replenishment. Ba'al Shem Tov also explained the need for pauses in Divine Worship through "eating and drinking, and business intercourse and sundry matters," with what was virtually a psychological reason. "As an unceasing pleasure becomes natural and is no longer a pleasure, so one must rise and descend in the Worship of the Blessed One, in order to derive that pleasure which is the essential thing in the Worship of God." But all these reasons were only secondary as compared with the arch-principle in Ba'al Shem Tov's system, which was based on the unitary view intrinsic to his conception of the universe and man. Divinity permeated all of reality; the sparks of holiness were present in all facets of the material and spiritual universe. Therefore, the worship of God, which consisted of restoring the sparks to their source, the reintegration of the *She'khinah* with The Holy One Blessed Be He, necessarily encompassed all of life, not least secular existence. Ba'al Shem Tov's favourite maxim when formulating the doctrine for the worship of God and the means to accomplish it was a saying from Proverbs 3:6, *In all thy ways acknowledge Him.* From this it followed that the holiness of the worship of God also extended to man's economic activity, to his "dealings." Conversation amongst mortals was a way of worshipping the creator, if the subject under discussion was of an ethical nature or concerned love and reverence for the Lord. But "men of understanding" knew "how to derive communion even from the recounting of events with their comrades." In such narratives, speech was also exalted to its source. Ba'al Shem Tov thus removed the categorical contradiction between secular existence and the worship of God by destining man to exalt his secular life to the level of holiness.

Any individual could achieve the level of perfection and holiness, but he did require to bind himself to the sainted ones of his generation, the *Tzaddikim* for this purpose. It was the *Tzaddik* who guided the people in the ways of worshipping God and who moralized the members of his generation "not, Heaven forbid, to elevate themselves thereby to the enjoyment of wealth and such things" but for the sake of heaven. A *Tzaddik*, in expostulating with a man, also included himself. To make the people penitent, the *Tzaddik* needed to develop greater affinity for the people and descend to their level:

> Like the king who sent his son and companion on a distant journey, that later he might have more enjoyment. With the passage of time, the king's son forgot all of his father's pleasures. The king sent for him and he was loath to return to his father. However numerous the illustrious ministers whom the king sent for him, they availed him nought. Until there was one minister who assumed the attire and speech of the son and drew him close to him, at the son's own image, and he brought him back to his father.

The *Tzaddik*, who was linked with God in his devotion, was also the mediator between God and the world. The *Tzaddikim* were "the heads of the generation," "the eyes of the congregation." They raised up the sparks of holiness of the entire congregation in their prayer and from them the *She'khinah's* inspiration emanated to all other men of their generation. The *Tzaddik* also caused the abundant flow of God's light to the world, "assuaged sternness," transmuted the quality of justice into the quality of mercy and abolished evil decrees. In the same way as the *Tzaddik* clung to the people, so every individual had to cling to the *Tzaddik*, to learn ethics and the awe of heaven from him, and be linked with him in thought. Nevertheless, Ba'al Shem Tov warned that man must not depend on the *Tzaddik* in prayer: "Let every one endeavour to pray for himself."

Ba'al Shem Tov's teachings on the unity of the upper and nether worlds, the spiritual and material world, stated that man was predestined to pursue the exalted task of connecting the worlds and influencing the movement of the upper forces:

> In the extremes of humility, one draws distant from the worship of the Blessed One, not believing that man in his baseness may through his prayer and his study of the Law cause an abundance on all the worlds; yet even the angels are nurtured by his study of the Law and his prayer. For were he to believe in this, with what joyousness and reverence for all would he worship God and take care to utter with fitting accuracy every letter, syllable, word ... For the Holy One Blessed Be He carefully watches man's lips and kisses them when they have uttered Torah and Prayer in reverence and awe ... Thus it is meet that man pay heed, and say that he is a ladder planted on the earth while his head reaches up to Heaven and all his movements and affairs and speech leave an impression on high in all the worlds.

However, for all his greatness in the constellation of the worlds, man had to regard himself as a friend to all human beings and to every living creature on earth, down to the tiniest worm:

Let him not say in his heart that he is greater than his comrade, that he worships with greater devotion, for he is as all other creatures, that have been created that they may Worship Him, May He Be Blessed. And (let him not think) that the Blessed One has not granted his comrade intelligence while to him he has ... Let him think that he and the worm and other tiny creatures and living things are accounted in this world as companions, that all of them have been created of the Blessed One and they are not capable of more than the Blessed Creator has graced them with. And let this be evermore in his thoughts.

Ba'al Shem Tov consciously conceived of his new doctrine of life and ethics mainly as one of messianic deliverance. He thought that the course he prescribed for the worship of the Lord was destined to educate the people in holiness so that they might be rewarded with the coming of the messiah. The leaders of all the redemption movements, even those like the Karaites and the Kabbalists, who had propounded an evolutionary conception of the messianic ideal, had considered it essential to proceed to the Land of Israel in order to bring redemption closer. It is therefore not surprising that a longing to "go up to the Land of Israel" also appeared in Ba'al Shem Tov's group. Ba'al Shem Tov himself, on the evidence of his disciple, Rabbi Jacob Joseph, set out on a journey to Palestine, but never reached it and returned home. In 1747, his brother-in-law, Abraham Gershon of Kuty, went to Palestine and settled in the city of Hebron. Two of Abraham Gershon's letters and one of Ba'al Shem Tov's have been preserved from the correspondence between the two brothers-in-law, close friends for a long time now. In a letter from Hebron written about a year after his arrival, Gershon described the events of his life in Palestine and expressed dismay at the fact that Ba'al Shem Tov was not preparing to join him.

Ba'al Shem Tov's reply, written after 1750, sheds light on the closing stage of his intellectual development, his belief in his prophetic mission and his perfected doctrine on the course of redemption. He wrote:

> ... I ascended level after level until I entered the abode of the Messiah ... And I asked the Messiah, When wilt thou come, Master? And he replied, By this shalt thou know, when thy teaching will become known and revealed to the world and thy springs disperse abroad with what I have taught thee and which thou hast grasped, and when they too shall be able to Unify and to make ascensions even as thou hast done, then shall all the shells of impurity fall away and it will be a time of grace and salvation. And at all this I marvelled and great were the pangs of my regret for the long span of time ere this would be possible...

The intricacies of Ba'al Shem Tov's vision clearly contained the suggestion that the ascent to the highest level of holiness was a long process, to be continued until "all the shells of impurity fall away." It was a process of "worshipping God" through prayer, Torah, and acts of piety, in fact, the same procedure that the founder of Hassidism had prescribed in his own new doctrine.

But the years when Ba'al Shem Tov saw his visions of redemption were a time of bitter bondage, affliction, and calamities for the Jews of the Ukraine. On the one hand, the Haidamaks poured over the Ukraine perpetrating outrages on the Jews. On the other hand, horrifying ritual murder accusations spread panic and consternation amongst the Jews in Poland.

The latter years of Ba'al Shem Tov's life were embittered by the events which attended the growing strength of the Frankist sectarians, their abominations and the ensuing furore amongst the Jews of Poland. Yet Hassidic legends of the miracles Ba'al Shem Tov performed for his people at that time, when they suffered the most fearful trials, proved the great difference between his attitude towards the renegades and that of the dominant orthodox leaders. Despite his profound anxiety for the existence of Judaism, which the Frankists were bent on destroying, Ba'al Shem Tov unhesitatingly placed the responsibility for the catastrophe on the distorted teachings of the leaders of the people.

According to legend, Ba'al Shem Tov had a premonition of the public debates in 1757 between the rabbis and the Frankists at Kamienetz Podolsk, held by order of Bishop Dembowski, even before they were decreed. As a result of these debates, books of the Talmud were burned at the stake:

> Once on Yom Kippur Eve, Ba'al Shem Tov foresaw that a great doom was approaching the people of Israel, namely, that the Oral Law would be taken away from them. All day long Ba'al Shem Tov was agitated and full of sadness, and that evening in the synagogue, before the Holy Ark of the Scrolls, he prostrated himself and cried out, Woe! Because they sought to take the Law from us; and how shall we exist amongst the nations even half a day? And he was most indignant with the rabbis and he declared that it was because of them, because they fabricated falsehoods in their hearts, in their lying discourses. And he declared that they were to be judged by the Tannaim and the Amoraim.

Reliable historical sources completely disprove the traditional belief that Ba'al Shem Tov participated in the debate against the Frankists at Lwow in 1759. However, the words that legend imputed to Ba'al Shem Tov when he was apprised of the fact that Frank and his sect had been baptized were in complete harmony with his doctrine on the duty to seek extenuation for the wicked:

> The *She'khinah* wails and protests that so long as the limb is a

member, there is hope that some cure may be found, but when the limb is severed, there is no remedy for it. For every one in Israel is a member of the *She'khinah*.

The "mighty exertion" in his fight against the Sabbetai Zvi sect (i.e. the Frankists), namely his spiritual efforts at prayer and ascension of the soul (visions), as well as his deep distress at the dangers threatening Judaism hastened Ba'al Shem Tov's death, according to Hassidic tradition. Like Socrates, who ordered a rooster to be offered up as a sacrifice to Aesculapius before his death in gratitude for his recovery, legend states that Ba'al Shem Tov too, before his death comforted his close friends with the following words:

I do not worry for myself, because I assuredly know that no sooner shall I depart through this passage than I shall enter another.

And after he had listened devoutly to the Prayer *Let the Graciousness of the Lord*...he had himself covered with a sheet and thereupon began to tremble and to quiver as in reciting the *Eighteen Benedictions* and then he rested a while, and they observed that the little clock had stopped.

He had taught the doctrine of adhesion to God during his life. He died in the same supreme degree of ecstasy whereby he had attained in his lifetime to the level of the ascension of the soul.

Ba'al Shem Tov's Disciples and the Formulation of Hassidic Doctrine

Ba'al Shem Tov's doctrine was propagated by scores of disciples and companions. Many of his friends had been protagonists of ascetic Hassidism before they adhered to the new form of Hassidism. The Palestine migration movement, which had emerged in Ba'al Shem Tov's circle while he was still alive, grew stronger after his death. Apart from individuals, a group of Hassidim led by Rabbi Nahman of Horodenka and Rabbi Mendel of Premyslany left for the Land of Israel in 1764.

Rabbi Jacob Joseph Ben-Zvi Ha'cohen was the greatest of Ba'al Shem Tov's disciples and companions. He assembled his master's teachings and also compiled a systematic formulation of Hassidism. He was an accomplished scholar and in his youth had written exegeses employing the method of *pilpul*, as well as *responsa*. But he was also a brilliant master of Kabbalah and had made a deep study of the ethical literature and works of philosophic inquiry such as Bahya Ben-Joseph ibn-Pakuda's *Duties of the Heart*, Maimonides' *Guide to the Perplexed*, Joseph Albo's *Book of Roots*, and *The Offering of Isaac*, by Asaac Aramal (a well-known philosophical commentary on the Pentateuch). He was at first a great opponent of the new Hassidic doctrine, but he later drew close to Ba'al

Shem Tov and admired him wholeheartedly. His book referred to him alone by the title *Mori*—My Teacher. He was deposed from his position as Rabbi at Szarygrod, Podolia, for having joined the Hassidic "sect" and even expelled from the city. After serving for a number of years in the rabbinate of the town of Raszkow, he was accepted as Rabbi at Niemirow, the Podolian city noted for the bloodshed there in the violence of 1648. He remained at Niemirow for nearly twenty years. However, his name was better known to subsequent generations in association with the Volhynian city of Polonne (which also achieved notoriety in the sanguinary events of 1648) where he officiated as Rabbi and preacher from 1770 to his death in 1782.

In 1780, under the title of *The Chronicles of Jacob Joseph*, he first collected and published the teachings he had been expounding, as a commentary on the weekly portion during the "Third Repast" on Sabbaths, as was the custom of the Hassidic leaders. This book was received by both Hassidim and Mitnagdim as the manifesto of the new movement. During the remaining two years of his life, he published two more books, also commentaries on the Torah by Hassidic methods.

Rabbi Jacob Joseph's sermons all established the basis for and expounded the doctrine of Ba'al Shem Tov, which was thus presented for the first time in the works of his disciple. What Plato was to Socrates in ancient times, Rabbi Jacob Joseph was to Ba'al Shem Tov: he spread and made known his master's teachings and perfected them according to his own method until he unwittingly obscured the demarcation between the original doctrine and the accretions and alterations that had taken place in the course of its development. However, one tenet of Ba'al Shem Tov's teachings occupied a central position in the studies of Rabbi Jacob Joseph and he dealt with it exhaustively in all his works: the status of Talmudic intellectuals and their function amongst the people. The Rabbi of Polonne waged an unprecedented and unequalled struggle against the scholars and their provocatively haughty attitude towards the people. *The Chronicles of Jacob Joseph* expressed all the bitter opposition to the hegemony of the scholar class, which had united poor and underprivileged scholars with the masses in Hassidism. He used every unfavourable epithet to voice his anger at the conceited *Talmidei-Chakhamim*, who studied the Law "not for its own sake": "The rabbis standing on the pathway of money" were the little foxes damaging the vineyards; "scholars coarse in spirit" were vindictive and vengeful, "like snakes, for any negligible slighting of their dignity, of whom it was said, *And the Lord sent fiery serpents amongst the people, and they bit the people*..." (Numbers, 21:6); "They that learn not for the sake of Heaven, who are called asses ... are more amazing in their wickedness" than the ass, and they "in their studies are like the prophets of Ba'al, because of whom the Temple was destroyed." The most common phrase found in his invectives against this scholar class was drawn from the *Zohar*, "Jewish demons."

The more they learned, he explained, the more remote they became from "the object of all the Torah and the precepts, which is the Adoration of God." But the evil lay chiefly in the fact that these rabbis and scholars were evading their duty as the people's teachers and guides in Torah, the worship of God, and ethical behaviour. He included in this category the hypocritical sermonizers who flattered their listeners instead of reproaching them for neglecting the Torah and directing them towards penitence.

Rabbi Jacob Joseph's sermons also complained bitterly of the persecution of the "legitimate" scholars, the *Tzaddikim*, leaders of the Hassidim, by the "scholars," abetted by the Kehillah leaders. He repeatedly stated that there were three kinds of bondage, each worse than the other. consecutively: Israel's exile amongst the Gentiles; the captivity of the scholar amongst the ignorant masses; and the bondage of "rightful, sin-fearing" scholars amongst "those scholars who are Jewish demons."

However, the leader of a movement of religious regeneration, Rabbi Jacob Joseph could not find satisfaction solely in the prospect of solace in the future. "The coarse spirit" of the Talmudic scholars and their arrogance towards the people was not only the most heavy of the three classes of exile; it was also the cause of exile in all its forms, the source of Jewish enslavement amongst the Gentiles, and the factor which delayed their deliverance. Accordingly, the focal point of Rabbi Jacob Joseph's Hassidic doctrine was the wholesome structure of society as represented by a reciprocal relationship between scholars and the masses. He did, in a sense, confirm the veracity of the historical method which posits an absolute parallel between the *Weltanschauung* of each generation and its outlook on the social system, by repeatedly declaring that the social fabric was a reflection of the human fabric. "Man," he asserted, "was created of Matter and Form ... but ... Man was created to the end that he shall convert Matter into Form and thus become one Unity ... And just as that has been the objective for the individual man, even so has it been for the Jewish people as a whole." Within the people, the material substance was "the masses of ordinary folk, since their affairs are mainly concerned with the earthy aspects of matter." The form consisted of "the *Tzaddikim* who engage in Torah and the worship of God ... Their primary function is to convert matter into form" by disseminating the Torah amongst the people, but above all by guiding the people in reverence for God and in ethical behaviour. The man of the form was "a ladder planted on the earth with his head reaching up to heaven," since he joined his mundane, material activities with his thoughts, raising them to a heavenly level by concentrated purpose. The same pattern applied to the people as a whole: the masses of the people were the feet of the ladder, hence an integral part of the ladder planted on the earth, while the scholars were the top of the ladder reaching up to heaven.

The joining of "the masses of the people" with the scholars was an association of two social classes each of which undertook different social functions, not unlike the tribes of Issachar and Zebulun: of Zebulun were "the rich, who engage in business" and support the scholars, "providing them with the pleasure of their possessions"; and of Issachar were the scholars who taught Torah in abundance to the rich and led them to repentance. Thanks to Zebulun, who engaged in trade, "Issachar is free to engage in matters of the intellect." This social philosophy was so similar to the premises of the social doctrine contained in Maimonides' teaching that Rabbi Jacob Joseph specifically cited Maimonides to support his arguments. Nevertheless, fundamental differences did exist between the doctrine of a spiritual aristocracy, propounded by the spokesman of medieval rationalism, and the occult doctrine of Ba'al Shem Tov's disciple.

Rabbi Jacob Joseph's new message was that of union. The "spiritual" class and the "material" class should draw together in loving devotion and the worship of God. The duty of affinity devolved equally on both classes, "the masses of the people," and "the rich" and the scholars. In fact, the system was disrupted by the haughty scholars and therefore they were the class whom he castigated most severely.

Occasionally, in order to guide the people in ethics and heavenly reverence, and in order to approach them with affection, even those not engaged in the Torah but in "the life of the moment," it was necessary for the scholar to dispense with his studies, "that he may not thereby grow accustomed to be ever immersed in his learning but shall also mix with people." Rabbi Jacob Joseph gave psychological expression to Ba'al Shem Tov's maxim, *In all thy ways acknowledge Him*: a scholar who was "tough as a cedar" and applied himself exclusively to "Torah and prayer, fasting, sackcloth and lamentations," when "eventually he does go forth into the world and beholds people not comporting themselves as he does, evokes Divine Justice upon them." A descent from his own level by "colloquies with his friend" could also be instructive, for "a wise man is he who learns from all men."

The ultimate object of Rabbi Jacob Joseph's doctrine like that of his master, the founder of Hassidism, was to solve the problem that agitated the people, the problem of deliverance. He considered the crude-minded Talmudic scholars a disaster for the people and the cause of its exile. "The disruption of the hearts," the disruption amongst the people between the men of the spirit and those who dealt in material things was preventing the people from doing penance and winning redemption. But when "the masses of the people" joined with "the men of knowledge" to constitute one Unity, all three exiles would be ended and "a general deliverance of the matter from bondage and exile amongst the Gentiles" would ensue. Unity in the nether world was the foundation for integration in the upper world, for the deliverance of the *She'khinah* from its exile and the coming of the Messiah.

The unwavering, dynamic struggle that the Rabbi of Polonne waged against the class of "learners" still possessed all the audacity and resolution that characterized the Hassidic movement at the beginning of its forward movement. But Rabbi Jacob Joseph's doctrine lacked Ba'al Shem Tov's hearty, bracing popular spirit which permeates his epigrams and statements and lends charm to his personality. A factor even more significant than the contrast in the personalities of the itinerant master who "possessed the name" (*ba'al-shem*) and the disciple, safe in his rabbinical post, lay behind this difference. It inaugurated a new phase in the social development of Hassidism. Rabbi Jacob Joseph's use of the terms "masses of the people" and "the rich" as synonymous was no coincidence. The teaching and tendencies propounded by Ba'al Shem Tov had to a large measure expressed the mood of the actual masses, who represented the social basis of Hassidism. The doctrine of the Polonne Rabbi, on the contrary, definitely reflected the social force behind the new religious movement, the "rich" sector in the Jewish middle class which had not attained the distinction of the scholarly class. Simultaneous with this development, the first indications of a new conception of the *Tzaddik's* role appeared in Rabbi Jacob Joseph's expositions and heralded a development on the lines of a *Tzaddik* cult, or *Tzaddikism*. Ba'al Shem Tov's exemplary disciple had not, of course, reached the point of extolling the *Tzaddik's* virtues to the extent of negating the value that the "masses of the people" might have in influencing the upper worlds. But he did explicitly teach, amending what he had heard from his master, that the *Tzaddik* not only cleared a path and vehicle for delivering continued abundance to the world but that "he is himself called such a path and vehicle, for the abundance passes through his hands. . . ."

Rabbi Jacob Joseph was the leading theoretician of Hassidism and according to Hassidic legend, Ba'al Shem Tov had regarded him as the greatest of his disciples. He did not, however, receive the reward of inheriting his master's position as leader of the movement. This might have been because of his personal character as a "dweller in his tent," or because of his polemic with the Talmudic scholars, which none of Ba'al Shem Tov's other disciples pursued as bitterly or as angrily. After Ba'al Shem Tov's death, the *Maggid* Rabbi Dov Ber Ben Abraham of Mezhirich, Volhynia, known by the Hassidim as Rabbi Reb Ber, stood at the head of the Hassidic movement.

Apparently the *Maggid* did not regard himself as a disciple of Ba'al Shem Tov but rather as a teacher of Hassidism equal to him in rank. However, apart from the manner in which they were formulated, his teachings indicated complete dependence on the doctrine of the founder of the new movement. Ba'al Shem Tov tended to reduce his doctrine to laconic aphorisms and to expound it through parables; this was in keeping with his personal qualities and the popular character of his audiences. The *Maggid* of Mezhirich, and also the Rabbi of Polonne, did not dispense with parables in propounding their doctrine, but preferred to employ the device of homiletic dissertations on scriptural passages in conjunction with commentaries from the Sages and passages from the *Zohar*. They bequeathed this form of sermon to all subsequent leaders of Hassidism.

The teachings of Rabbi Ber were assembled by one of his pupils and first published in 1784 under the title *He Who Speaks His Word to Jacob—A Collection of Utterances.** Rabbi Ber had pored over Kabbalah since his youth and was particularly attached to the system of Isaac Luria. He gave a singularly methodical exposition of the pantheistic idea in Hassidism: "Every active force is immanent in the object acted upon and they all together constitute a single Unity; only the bodies are separate." And since "Torah and God are One . . . divisions are inapplicable to the Torah as well as to the Precepts." Characteristically, the *Maggid* elevated the fear of the Lord attendant upon love in the worship of God to a position of paramount importance and his pupils followed him in this.

In the main, however, the new phase in Hassidic doctrine was distinguished by its exaltation of the *Tzaddik's* superiority. "The world rests on one pillar, and that is the *Tzaddik*," and if the world were created, according to the Midrashic saying, "on behalf of Israel, who was the first to be summoned," then "the *Tzaddikim* are Israel . . . Like the father who has a small son. The small son wants a stick to ride like a horse . . . The father helps him and gives him the stick, thus gratifying the child's desire. Even so are the *Tzaddikim* desirous of leading the world, and The Holy One Blessed Be He created the worlds that they might take pleasure in leading them." In the same way as a father derived joy from his son, so God derived joy from the *Tzaddik*. Thus it was only natural that the *Tzaddik* should transform the quality of sternness into the quality of mercy, and "as the *Tzaddik* wishes, so wishes the Holy One Blessed Be He." In contrast with Rabbi Jacob Joseph of Polonne, who still employed the terms "rightful Talmudic scholar" and *Tzaddik* interchangeably, Rabbi Ber of Mezhirich only spoke of the *Tzaddikim* as God's elect. This marked the beginning of a process in which the centre of gravity in the leadership of the Hassidic movement was constantly shifting. It moved away from the opposition, composed of the stratum of poor scholars—preachers who travelled about to earn their living—towards the *Tzaddikim*, who were firmly established in their "courts."

The strength of the Mezhirich *Maggid's* power did not lie in his exegeses of Hassidic doctrine but rather in his personality as a spiritual leader and in his talent for organization. Unlike Ba'al Shem Tov, who travelled to towns and villages to propagate his creed, Rabbi Ber made his home town of Mezhirich the centre of Hassidism. But he was not satisfied with his influence in the city and vicinity and determined to conquer all of Polish and Lithuanian Jewry for Hassidism. The geographical position of the town in Volhynia, on the borders of the Ukraine and Lithuania, was most auspicious for the dissemination of Hassidism amongst the Jews of

* In Hebrew, *Maggid De'varav Le'Ya'akov—Likkutei Amarim.*

472

Lithuania and White Russia. According to Solomon Maimon, a Lithuanian and also according to Hassidic tradition, "the heads of the sect" sent emissaries throughout the country to propagate the new doctrine and enlist new adherents. This propaganda was quite productive and "many made pilgrimages to Karolin (the residence of Rabbi Aaron Karliner, a pupil of Rabbi Ber), to Mezhirich, and to other holy places, to the cities in which the heads of the sect, the *Tzaddikim*, resided. Young men left their parents, their wives and children, and proceeded in large parties to set eyes upon their exalted leaders and to hear of the new doctrine from their mouths." The *Maggid* even possessed the ability to attract "rabbis and Talmudic geniuses towards him" and the rabbis and *maggidim* who became leaders of the Hassidic movement after his death had in fact all been his pupils and admirers. The strength of his personal charm over even the most brilliant of these pupils was confirmed by a statement attributed to Rabbi Leib Sarahs, one of the venerated *Tzaddikim* of Hassidism. He used to say that he did not travel to Rabbi Ber the *Maggid* in order to hear Torah from his lips but to learn his ways in holiness, even the secular daily routine, "to see him remove his slippers, or lace them up." This form of adulation by the Hassidim for their rabbis was thenceforth a law in the Hassidic movement until its last years. The slightest unusual movement by the rabbi while praying—for that matter, every detail of his comportment whilst eating or strolling—was interpreted as a mystery of sacred portent, and the Hassidim felt in duty bound to imitate him.

Solomon Maimon had travelled to Mezhirich in his youth under the influence of a Lithuanian Hassid. He gave in his memoirs the following description of the *Maggid's* appearance at a Sabbath repast and the impression it made on him and on all present:

> So, on the Sabbath I came to a grand repast and there I met many notable men who had gathered from many localities. At last the great man appeared, an awe-inspiring figure, dressed in white satin clothes. Even his shoes and snuff box were white (white is a colour of grace amongst the Kabbalists). He extended his greetings to each one of the visitors. We were seated at the table and during the repast a holy silence prevailed. When the eating was done, the exalted leader raised his voice in a melody majestic in its sacredness and inspiring, and after he had held his hand for some time before his forehead, he began to call out, "Z. from the town of H.! S.M. from the town of N."* And thus he addressed all the visitors by name and mentioned the towns they lived in, and we were all greatly amazed by this. Every one of us had to quote some passage from the Bible. Every one

---

* i.e., Solomon Maimon of Niesviezh. Needless to say, the Lithuanian-born German Jewish philosopher (*cf.* Chapter Eight) committed an inaccuracy by including the surname of Maimon, which, as a matter of fact, he only adopted many years later, when he was living in Germany.

quoted his passage. And the exalted leader delivered a sermon on these passages in such a way that even though they had been selected at random from the various Books of the Bible, he so related them to one another as to make them appear as one complete section. And what is more amazing, every one of the visitors was convinced that in that part of the sermon referring to his own passage he had found something of import to his own inner disposition. It was but natural that under the circumstances we should regard this as little short of miraculous.

Solomon Maimon's enthusiasm declined within a short time and he found a natural explanation for what had previously seemed almost miraculous. He surmised that these rabbis received information about their guests from "spies" or in letters from their confederates and furthermore were able to sum up each new visitor themselves by skilful indirect questioning and a knowledge of the art of physiognomy. However, even the details of the *Maggid's* teaching, as cited by Maimon in the name of his pupils proved indisputably that the famous Hassidic leader himself believed that he possessed the divine spirit. Thus the passage in Kings II (3:15), *And it came to pass, when the minstrel played, that the hand of the Lord came upon him,* was interpreted to mean that the spirit of holiness did not dwell in a man unless he only considered himself a vessel for receiving the influence.

The great *Maggid*, Rabbi Ber, died at the end of 1772. A few months before his death, the first controversy between Mitnagdim and Hassidim openly erupted, and the first of the *Charamim* (singular, *Cherem*, i.e. excommunication) which ravaged the Kehillot of Poland and Lithuania was pronounced.

Another of Ba'al Shem Tov's disciples and friends, Rabbi Pinehas Shapira of Koretz (died *c.* 1790) lived in Volhynia, which had become the centre of Hassidism due to the influence of the great *Maggid* of Mezhirich. He was born in White Russia and was named after the city where he became known as a Hassidic leader. Rabbi Pinehas appeared more inclined to acknowledge Rabbi Jacob Joseph of Polonne as the heir to Ba'al Shem Tov's doctrine rather than the great *Maggid*. The teachings of Rabbi Pinehas, recorded in several of his sayings in their original Yiddish, retained much of Ba'al Shem Tov's simplicity as well as his strong opposition to the scholars. A characteristic of his teaching was his emphasis on the virtues, especially humility and truth. Like his master, Ba'al Shem Tov, he healed illnesses with popular medicaments, though he was actually employed as a *me'lamed*. His pupil, Rabbi Raphael of the Podolian town of Bershad, who founded the Bershad Hassidim group, followed in his footsteps and even surpassed him in the simplicity of his behaviour. In his humility, he accepted all offences without taking offence. At first he dressed like the ordinary people and lived in a poor dwelling with the roughest furniture. He included criminals, enemies and "even heathens" in his observance of the Precept *Love thy neighbour as thyself*. However, examples of the preservation of the folk-like simplicity of original Hassidism such as those of the *Tzaddik* of Bershad, were only isolated instances in the powerful general trend of Hassidism which extended from Mezhirich to cover Poland and Lithuania.

The Hassidim-Mitnagdim Controversy and Persecution of the Sect

As Hassidism spread through the Ukraine and penetrated into Lithuania and White Russia, a Hassidic way of life took shape which distinguished the members of the new sect from other Kehillah members. Hassidim assembled for prayer in *minyanim* (religious quorums) of their own. From the time of the Mezhirich *Maggid* it was an inviolable rule that they pray according to the ritual prescribed by Isaac Luria. Apart from the addition of a number of prayers in keeping with the Kabbalah, they also altered several of the prayers in the Ashkenazi ritual that had been employed in Poland for many generations. They were not punctual about time of prayers and were late in reading the *She'ma* because of the ritual immersions they performed and their preparations for devout prayer. In order to achieve a state of ecstasy in prayer, they occasionally held orgies of merriment beforehand. During his visit to Mezhirich, Solomon Maimon witnessed the following occurrence:

> When the *Maggid* Rabbi Ber heard that a daughter had been born to one of his Hassidim, he ordered his group to whip the man (for not having begotten a male offspring), and when in the course of executing this sentence the whippers reached a state of merry excitement, he urged them to commence to pray, saying, "And now, my brethren, Worship God in Joy!" Their prayer was noisy, with much swaying, clapping of hands, whirling about in circles, and weird motions of ecstasy, devotion, and also with determination to exorcise alien and confusing thoughts.

"The din and confusion of their prayer can split a city asunder," complained the *Epistle of Zeal* sent from Vilno to Brody in 1772. The Epistle also described the fact that its followers spent their days in unceasing merriment as a characteristic feature of Hassidic life. "They are loath to be sad, but are always laughing and gay ... They are forever raising a tumult with their laughing and jesting and the gaiety of their merry-making." The pronouncement of excommunication issued in the same year at Brody referred to another typical facet of this festive life: "All day long they do naught but give forth melodies." The Mitnagdim regarded the Hassidic habit of strolling in the streets pipe in mouth, as wanton and emanating from an idle existence and they were particularly indignant about their habit of smoking before praying. Numerous Hassidic groups sprang up in all parts of Lithuania and the Ukraine, and the extreme lengths to which they carried "worship through joy" gave rise to strange behaviour patterns. Some of them were accustomed to turn somersaults in the synagogue in front of the Ark of the Holy Scrolls as well as in the market places and on the streets. Besides expressing their religious zeal (*fun Gotts vegn un fun Rabbis vegn*, i.e., for the sake of God and the Rabbi), they justified this behaviour by stating that it subdued "conceit." However, the orgiastic behaviour of "some of them" described by Solomon Maimon must be regarded as truly exceptional:

> They offended the laws of good taste, ran about naked on the open street, relieved themselves in public, and such like.

Quite justifiably, Maimon dubbed such people "true cynics." There was indeed in this clowning something of a revolt against the outdated system, a revolt against the manners of the sedate men of property.

Other than the liturgical issue, even the sworn antagonists of the Hassidim could only discover one transgression against the traditional laws: the Hassidim had introduced ritual slaughter (*she'hitah*) with ground knives and declared that any meat not slaughtered in this way was unclean. The object of this innovation in the form of a reinterpretation of the slaughtering laws was an attempt by the Hassidim to justify the maintenance of special slaughterers for their own sect. Furthermore, as the ritual slaughterers, in common with all scholars of inferior rank, sympathized with the new movement, the Hassidim hoped that in the course of time, they could gain control of the official slaughterers' posts as a step towards taking over all the religious functions in the Kehillot.

However, the evaluation of the quality of joy in the worship of God, including secular life, represented a basic change of values in the religious sphere. The religion of joy practised by the Hassidim was precisely the opposite of the outlook which had been based on the nullification of this world and its "vanities" and had regarded asceticism as the acme of perfection in human behaviour. Similarly, another tenet of traditional religion was deeply undermined by Hassidism's assignment of a superior position to faith than to the Precept of studying the Torah. The Hassidim actually implemented this principle and in all their manifestos and polemics against them, the Mitnagdim charged them with "abolishing the study of Torah and divesting themselves of the burden of the Torah." In actual fact, the Hassidic custom of assembling in *minyanim* for communal feasts, singing, dancing, and conversation, left little time for studying the Torah, so that "the Torah was truly left in a corner," as the Mitnagdim complained. Adhesion to God in the individual's thoughts was immeasurably more important to the Hassidim than industrious study of the Torah. When Solomon Maimon saw that "members of the sect" walked about idly all day with their pipes in their mouths, he asked them what they

were thinking about. The reply was, "we are contemplating on God . . ."
Even the scholars amongst the Hassidim preferred to study Kabbalah
rather than Gemara and the Codifiers. Some, though not many, Hassidim
went to the extreme lengths of disparaging the study of religious law
(*Halakhah*) on principle. In some groups the bitter resentment that the
Hassidim felt for men who studied "not for its own sake," who engaged in
pointless casuistry, and used the Torah for their own glorification and
advancement, led to public disparagement of the scholars. There were
instances when the same Hassidic extremists who "clowned" in the
streets, "made sport of all the learners and hurled every manner of insult
against them." This contempt for the accepted courtesies of life and the
defamation of the Talmudic scholars were manifestations of one social
trend: the revolt against the Kehillah régime, which was controlled by
the men of wealth and the scholars attached to them. Indeed, in a number
of places, the first onslaught by the Hassidim was accompanied by active
efforts to reform the Kehillah régime. These reforms, several of which
were initiated by Rabbi Aaron of Karolin, did not only involve tax
revisions (they were especially aimed at the indirect *korobka* on food-
stuffs) but actual administrative changes as well, entitling the lowly placed
and poor to a voice in determining tax policies. In some places, such as
Leszniow (near Brody), in 1772, acts of actual violence were reported by
Hassidim against Kehillah leaders.

In view of the social trend of early Hassidism it is scarcely surprising
that it captured the hearts of the masses and spread as rapidly as it did
—especially in the eastern areas of Poland, the sphere of influence of the
Mezhirich *Maggid* and his pupils. Open warfare between the guardians of tradition and the "sect" began in Lithuania, the stronghold of
traditional rabbinic Judaism and the oligarchic Kehillah régime. Hassidic
centres had already been founded in Lithuania and White Russia by the
pupils of Rabbi Ber the *Maggid* during his lifetime. These Hassidim were
known in Lithuania as the Mezhirichers or the Karliners. They included a
group led by Rabbi Abraham of Kolyski which was marked by its
extremism, both in its contempt for scholars and its somersaulting
activities "feet over head in the market places and on the streets . . . and
with other diverse acts of clowning on the streets of Kolyski and Liozno."
Needless to say, Rabbi Abraham Kolysker's colleagues took exception to
these practices and his teacher, Rabbi Ber the *Maggid*, "also spoke
sternly to him of this matter." The Mitnagdim, however, were able to
exploit the eccentricities of groups such as these by accusing all Hassidim
of exceeding the bounds of propriety and profaning the dignity of learning. The struggle against the Hassidim was led by Rabbi Elijah of Vilno,
who was esteemed by Jews in Poland and abroad not only for his brilliant
erudition but also for his abstemious and ascetic way of life.

In the winter of 1771-72, a contagious children's disease broke out in
Vilno. The Kehillah élite took the opportunity "to examine deeds" and

discovered that the behaviour of the Hassidic group in the city had incurred the wrath of God. In accordance with a judgement passed by the *Parnassim* and *Dayyanim* of the Kehillah, "the *minyan* of 'Karliners'" in the city was disbanded and a severe penalty imposed on the leader of the Vilno Hassidim, the learned Rabbi Isser. On the Sabbath evening after Passover, he was lashed with a leather thong in the Kehillah chambers. The writings of the sect were burned near the pillory post. On the following day, the Sabbath, Rabbi Isser and his friends were led on to the pulpit platform at the synagogue and, in the presence of the congregation gathered for prayer service, required to listen while excommunication was pronounced against the Hassidic sect. The same judgement ordered letters to be sent to the chief Kehillot of Lithuania and White Russia demanding that they too excommunicate the Hassidim as at Vilno. The excommunication was proclaimed throughout Lithuania and White Russia, Hassidic *minyanim* were banned, and the movement in these two provinces was driven underground for a number of years.

The Vilno excommunication also caused repercussions in the southern Kehillot, in Volhynia and Podolia. The *Epistle of Zeal* from Vilno concerning events in the Lithuania capital, reached Brody, the largest Kehillah in the Kingdom of Poland, and prepared the *Parnassim* and rabbis there for action. On the twentieth day in the Hebrew month of Sivan (late spring), in 5532 (1772 C.E.), while the Great Fair was in progress, the rite of excommunication against the Hassidim there was carried out. However, as the differences between the Hassidim and the scholars were not as great in the districts of Volhynia and Podolia as in Lithuania, the Brody writ of excommunication only accused the Hassidim of the sin of separatism in organization and custom. In Lithuania, the Mitnagdim hoped to extirpate Hassidism completely. In the southern districts, instead, Hassidism had become so widespread that the authors of the excommunication writ felt constrained to limit themselves to decrees curtailing freedom of action by the Hassidim and obstructing the further spread of the movement. Prayer services in synagogues and private *minyanim* (an exception was made for the *minyan* of the Brody *Kloiz* Sages) based on the Isaac Luria ritual and alterations in the Ashkenazi versions were banned. It was forbidden to wear white clothes on Sabbaths and holidays—on pain of being stripped in the street (again, a concession was made to the *Kloiz* Hassidim). Meat slaughtered with ground knives was declared carrion and unclean. Any visitor to the city of Brody who practised the Hassidic custom in meat slaughtering and prayer was to be expelled. In fact, however, the political situation in Poland at the time favoured the Hassidic movement. The advocates of the acts of excommunication against the Hassidim did not command the same degree of authority or the same powers of implementation which had aided the leaders of Polish Jewry in their struggle against the Sabbetai Zvi movement and the Frankists. In 1764, six years prior to the Vilno and Brody

Kehillah manifestos against the Hassidim, a Sejm statute had liquidated the central and regional autonomous institutions of Polish and Lithuanian Jewry—the Council of the Four Lands, the Lithuanian National Council, and the Regional Councils—leaving only the local autonomy of each separate Kehillah intact. Shortly afterwards, the federative link between the Kehillot of Poland and Lithuania began to weaken. In the year when the first excommunications were pronounced against the Hassidim (1772), the first partition of Poland took place. Two government districts of White Russia passed into Russian hands, while Galicia, up to and including Brody, was annexed to the Austrian Empire. When the final dismemberment of Poland was completed by the partitions of 1793 and 1795, the Polish Jews found themselves divided by the boundaries of three powers—Russia, Austria and Prussia. These circumstances greatly hindered efficient combined action by the Polish and Lithuanian Kehillot against the new movement, even though all possibilities of co-ordination between them were not entirely eliminated.

In the same year as the excommunication at Brody, the "Kehillah Optimates" (*Yakirei Ha'Kehillah*) of the neighbouring town of Leszniow passed anti-Hassidic regulations. The rabbis and *Parnassim* of Vilno and Brody continued to co-operate against the Hassidim even after the rites of excommunication. By order of Elihah, the Vilno Gaon, and the metropolitan rabbis of Lithuania and Galicia, a pamphlet entitled *The Song of the Terrible Ones and Knives of Flint** was published, again in 1772, containing the texts of the writs of excommunication and the manifestos against the Hassidim, the letters from Vilno to Brody, and an appended *Beür*† written by the scribe of the Brody Kehillah.

The Hassidim did not remain passive in the face of this action. They bought up all available copies of the pamphlet *Song of the Terrible Ones and Knives of Flint*, tore them up, and burned them until only a few remained.

New *minyanim* of Hassidim were also founded in White Russia, in the districts of Vitebsk and Moghilev despite excommunication decrees from Vilno and the persecution that followed in their wake. This persecution became especially fierce in the city of Shklov and around the Lithuanian city of Grodno.

It was during these years of severe persecution in White Russia and Lithuania that the leaders of the movement determined to emigrate to Palestine. They were actuated in this, as the disciples of Ba'al Shem Tov twelve years earlier, by the ideal of deliverance, the basic motive of Hassidic doctrine. They hoped that by "ascending" to the Land of Israel

---

* *cf.* Isaiah, 25 : 5, and Joshua, 5 : 2.

† An untranslatable play on words in Hebrew, based on the Ashkenazi accent. Spelled one way, *beur* means "explanation." By substituting the letter "Ain" for "Aleph" after the initial "Bet" the word means "a burning" or "cleansing by extermination and removal." In the Brody scribe's *Beür*, the latter spelling was used and the intention was obvious.

and settling "on the Holy Soil" they would arouse "Supreme Grace" and thus hasten the consummation of redemption. The longing for "our cherished land" might also have gained strength as a result of the bitter ordeal of persecution by the Mitnagdim. Evidence shows that they hoped by coming to Palestine not only to establish a centre of Hassidism in the Land of Israel but also to increase the prestige of Hassidism, which had been damaged in the Diaspora, by the holiness of the country. In contrast with former Hassidic *Aliyot* (emigrations to Palestine), the migrants on this occasion formed a long procession. The numerous group of Hassidic *Olim* who travelled in 1777 was led by Rabbi Menahem Mendel of Vitebsk, Rabbi Abraham of Kolyski and Rabbi Israel of Polotzk, who, in his role of the great *Maggid's* emissary had done much to propagate Hassidism in Lithuania. The eminent Rabbi Shneur Zalman, foremost leader of Lithuanian Hassidism, also decided to go with them, but turned back on reaching the Wallachian frontier, apparently anxious lest the Hassidim of Lithuania and White Russia remain leaderless. They were joined by many people, not all Hassidim, on their way through Volhynia and Podolia, from the two regions as well as the Ukraine. Over 300 people reached the land and practically all of them settled in Safed* and struck deep roots in the country. However, the religious attack by the Mitnagdim did not abate and broke out with renewed strength and fury three years later to reach the shores of Palestine.

In 1780, the first book on Hassidic doctrine, *The Chronicles of Jacob Joseph*, by the Rabbi of Polonne, appeared in print, in the city of Koretz, near Mezhirich. The leaders of the Mitnagdim, consisting of the *Parnassim* and rabbis at Vilno and with the Vilno Gaon at their head, regarded this book on Hassidism as a call to arms and took new action against the "sect." On a Sabbath, the twentieth day in the Hebrew month of Av, 5441 (1781 C.E.), a writ of excommunication was once again issued against the Hassidim in the Grand Synagogue of Vilno and all the other Lithuanian synagogues. Not only Hassidic groups, but the Hassidim individually, were outlawed: "Whosoever performed their acts and customs ... was excommunicated, ostracized, cast out, and isolated from the entire Congregation of Israel." All contact or converse with them, even rental of dwelling places in Vilno and its surroundings was forbidden. Under the "Grand Excommunication," members of the "sect" were "required to terminate their residence in our Kehillah with their wives and children."

These new anti-Hassidic measures even applied in Galicia, except that on this occasion, they were confined exclusively to the large Kehillot there. At Brody, *The Chronicles of Jacob Joseph* were publicly burned by rabbinical court order. In the western area of Galicia, in Krakow, the Kehillah leaders pronounced excommunication on the Hassidim with the concurrence of the Rabbi in autumn of 1785, and this process was

* For an account of Hassidic settlement in Palestine, *cf*. Chapter Fourteen.

repeated in all the synagogues in the province. The Krakow Kehillah leaders, proud of the tradition associated with Rabbi Moses Isserles (RaMA), a native of the city, prohibited the establishment of any "*minyan* for the purpose of modifying the prayer service" or "the making of any kind of weird movements whilst praying, to the bewilderment of those who heard ... or to clap hands" while praying, or like gestures, under the terms of this excommunication writ. The Hassidim were accused of discarding the obligations of the Torah by erecting a "high place"* for themselves. However, this was one of the last acts of excommunication against Hassidism in Galicia. The movement was now constantly extending and within a short time had claimed most of the Kehillot in the province as in the neighbouring Ukraine. This was not the case in Lithuania and White Russia. Here the persecution of Hassidism was strengthened by the new writ of excommunication and continued intermittently until the beginning of the nineteenth century.

C. EFFLORESCENCE AND EXPANSION

a. HASSIDISM IN LITHUANIA AND WHITE RUSSIA

The Karliners in Lithuania; White Russian Hassidim Under the Leadership of Rabbi Mendel in Palestine; Rabbi Shneur Zalman of Lady and the HaBaD School

At the time when persecution was intensified, following the second Vilno excommunication, Hassidism in Lithuania and White Russia was in the process of dividing into two currents: the Karlinite Hassidism of Lithuania; and the *HaBaD* school of Hassidism founded by Rabbi Shneur Zalman in White Russia. They were separated not only by geographical spheres of influence, but also by their theoretical exposition and practical application of the new doctrine.

Karlinite Hassidism spread out from Polesia, the southern Lithuanian district bordering on Volhynia, and penetrated northwards into the adjoining districts of White Russia historically included in the designation, "Black Russia." A Hassidic "court" was established in the Grodno area by Rabbi Haim Haika of Amdur (Indura) forming a Karlinite Hassidic spearhead in the northwestern corner of Lithuania. Haim of Amdur retained the propaganda methods of the original school of Hassidism founded by his teacher, Rabbi Ber the *Maggid,* and the *Maggid's* friend, Rabbi Aaron Karliner. It was his practice "to send emissaries to all the cities with a Jewish population to incite and induce" people to accept Hassidism and to attract them to his court. He also joined in the recriminations against the scholars. The leader of the Amdur Hassidim

* *cf.* I Kings, 11:7.

was a typical folk *Tzaddik*, of the type then becoming prevalent, especially in the Ukraine. Even his adversaries conceded that poor Hassidim lodged for periods of six months and even for a whole year at Rabbi Haim's court, receiving sustenance from money the Rabbi had collected from the rich as *pidyonot*—redemption payments. The Jewish physician and *Maskil*, Jacob Calmanson of Warsaw, apparently had this custom in mind when he described the Hassidim as communists: in his pamphlet in French of 1796, *On the Present State of the Jews in Poland, and their Perfectibility*: *

> All their possessions are held in common and are almost always at the disposal of their leaders.†

A contributory factor in the existence and growth of the Hassidic groups in Lithuania and the closely-knit Hassidic community in White Russia was the social struggle against the Kehillah leaders and their methods of government. This struggle broke out in large communities such as Vilno, Minsk, Vitebsk, and Szawle at the time of the excommunication decree and continued for some twenty years. The leaders of the Kehillot involved in the conflict were forced to shelve the Hassidic problem and turn all their attention to suppressing the mass revolt, conducted mainly by artisans. The numerically few Hassidim in the towns were in sympathy with the rebels but apparently did not actively participate in the struggle. Nonetheless, there was a recurrence of anti-Hassidic measures during that period. Rabbi Shneur Zalman gave a moving account of the position of the persecuted Hassidim in his letter to the Kehillah leaders at Moghilev:

> ...For we have borne our shame amongst the Gentiles and disgrace has covered us amongst our brethren of Israel. Earth, cover not our blood! May there be no resting place for our outcry till God look down from the Heavens and behold. And he shall give us for mercy unto our merciful brethren, who are the descendants of merciful forefathers, to arouse much mercy for us and our infants and children, to let us live this day and grant us a name and a remnant on the face of the earth . . .

However, the Hassidim of White Russia were sustained in their troubles by the great solidarity that bound them to each other and also to their leaders. Rabbi Mendel of Vitebsk continued to serve as the spiritual leader of the White Russian Hassidim even after his departure for Palestine, while in the Diaspora, Rabbi Shneur Zalman and his friends were occupied with efforts at organization, which also included constant

---

* *Essai sur l'Etat actuel des Juifs de Pologne et leur Perfectibilité*, Warsaw, 1796.

† "Tous leurs biens sont en commun et presque toujours à la disposition de leurs chefs."

aid to the Hassidic community in Palestine. Rabbi Mendel and his group of Hassidim were forced to move to Tiberias as a result of the anti-Hassidic controversy that had erupted also in Safed after the Vilno excommunication decree of 1781. Only a small group remained in Safed, led by Rabbi Abraham Kolysker. In his person, Rabbi Mendel was the prototype and embodiment of all the unique characteristics by which Lithuanian Hassidic leaders came to be distinguished. He was far from considering himself a *Tzaddik* with power to bestow heavenly munificence in all things upon his Hassidim. Instead, he outlined the principles of Hassidism in a letter to his followers in White Russia and Volhynia in 1787 on questions of behaviour, strengthening their faith, and cheering them with words of comfort and affection. "You are my sons, as though I myself had begotten you . . . Therefore neither can heights nor expanses, nor horsemen nor chariots keep us apart." And they repaid his affection with love.

After the death of Rabbi Mendel at Tiberias in 1788, leadership of the White Russian Hassidim passed entirely into the hands of Rabbi Shneur Zalman, previously one of their counsellors. The outstanding personality of this man contained a more felicitous combination of the essential qualities required in a Hassidic leader than had ever before been found in the history of the movement. He was a thinker and a man of action; a brilliant Talmudist who was also deeply versed in the mysteries of Kabbalah. He possessed a sensitive poetic nature, despite a strong character. He sought solitude in his devotion and still commanded rare organizational energy. He was attached to his followers to the point of sacrifice but ruled them with the iron hand of a born leader.

Rabbi Shneur Zalman was born at Liozno, in the district of Orsha of the Vitebsk Gubernia in about 1748. Diligent and sharp-minded, he acquired a profound knowledge of the Talmud and the Codifiers in his early youth. By the time he was eighteen, he had gained a reputation as a brilliant Talmudist. At the age of twenty, after he had made a deep study of Kabbalah, he reached the "court" of the Mezhirich *Maggid* and at once became one of the most important members of his circle. At the *Maggid's* school, and on his advice, he embarked on the immense task of rewriting the *Shulchan Arukh* in a "lucid tongue," including the reasons behind the laws and their origins in the Talmud and the Codifiers. The pattern was in accordance with Hassidism's aim of facilitating the familiarity of the people with the laws without needing to depend on the dialectics of the official scholars. Rabbi Shneur completed part of this *Shulchan Arukh* by 1771, when he was twenty-three years old. After the *Maggid's* death, he returned to White Russia to assume the leadership, together with his friends, of the Hassidic movement there.

From 1788 to 1796, during the first years of Rabbi Shneur Zalman's authority over the White Russian Hassidic community, there was a relative lull in the Mitnagdim's campaign. Shneur Zalman at that time filled the office of Rabbi in his native city of Liozno (which caused the Hassidim simply to call him "The Rav"). He received large numbers of his followers, paid particular attention to his more recent adherents, "and interviewed them privately to offer them his counsel." For "the poor people, not so well-versed in the Law," he maintained, *"train up a child in the way he should go." (cf.* Proverbs, 22 : 6.) At the same time he was also engaged in writing and in 1796 his book on Hassidic doctrine, the *Selected Sayings,* also commonly known as the *Tanya,* was published.

Immediately following its publication, it was realized that the Hassidic doctrine expounded in the *Tanya* was a distinctive system of Hassidism, differing from conventional Hassidism in theory and application. The theoretical work of the founders of Hassidism and their disciples had concentrated mainly on the doctrine of the individual and his function in perfecting the upper worlds. Shneur Zalman, however, combined this doctrine with an inquiry into the nature of divinity which followed the lines of Isaac Luria's system of Kabbalah. On the basis of this theosophy—which was itself new to Hassidic method—the rabbi arrived at pantheistic views representing a compromise between original Hassidism and the Lurianic system.

In his theosophic doctrine on the progressive contraction of divinity, in accordance with the level of apperception, Rabbi Shneur Zalman expressed with systematic lucidity what the teachings of his master, the *Maggid,* had merely hinted at. In the system developed in the *Tanya,* this tenet was the uppermost layer in Rabbi Shneur's social doctrine of gradation in the virtues of souls:

> There are tens of thousands of divisions of levels amongst the souls, reaching higher and higher into infinity ... and in every generation there are thousands of heads of the Children of Israel whose souls are as a head and a brain to the souls of the mass and the illiterates.

The idea expressed in *The Chronicles of Jacob Joseph* received its theosophical reinforcement in Shneur Zalman's *Tanya.*

The principal exegesis that *Tanya* expounded was on the doctrine of man, which occupied the central position in the world of Hassidism. According to Rabbi Shneur Zalman, the ultimate goal in the creation of man was to raise up darkness into light, "that the Light of God, Blessed is His Name, may shine infinitely in place of darkness... that his soul may be elevated to its roots and origin." The individual fulfilled this objective in thought, speech and action, which were themselves only prayer, Torah, and observance of the Precepts. Of these three ways of worship, the *Tanya* laid the greatest stress on the virtue of studying the Torah, which "is balanced against all the Precepts" and which Rabbi Shneur considered superior even to prayer. The Torah to him contained both divine wisdom and divine will; the man who studied the Torah connected himself in speech and thought with "the speech and thought of The Holy One

Blessed Be He." However, the Rabbi repeatedly emphasized the inner-most essence of the laws, contrary to the ideas extant in the Hassidic movement concerning that Torah which was revealed as an externality and that Torah which was concealed in its own innermost essence. Every Law represented the effulgent vesture of divinity and the revelation of God's wisdom, not only the permissive and proscriptive laws—of clean-liness and defilement, exemption and obligation—but even such laws as "one who exchanges a cow for an ass." On the basis of this mysticism, Rabbi Shneur Zalman required his Hassidim to study Talmud and the Codifiers with the utmost diligence. He construed the passage in Psalms, 19:8, *The Law of the Lord is perfect, restoring the soul,* to mean that "this signifies the completion of the Talmud (studying) in most of the towns and *minyanim* of our people." His letters ordered "the entire Six Talmud to be studied every year in every city, to apportion the tractates by lot or by choice, and in those cities where they are many *minyanim*, each *minyan* will complete the studying...Nothing, Heaven forbid, is to be altered in this or disregarded." This kind of Hassidism could obviously only be practised by members of the middle class, the *Ba'lei-Batim* scholars, who had the opportunity to take time off from business to study the Torah daily.

The doctrine of the *Tanya* also differed from conventional Hassidism which was founded on the duties of the heart, on feeling. The *Tanya* did not reject worship from the heart, but it did demand the precedence of "mind over heart," of reason over emotion. All evil qualities had their origin in the "brute souls." The divine soul was reason. Rabbi Shneur distinguished between three criteria of reason: *Hokhmah*—Wisdom, *Binah*—Comprehension, and *Da'at*—Knowledge (hence the abridgement *HaBaD*, consisting of the initials of the three Hebrew words). According to Rabbi Shneur Zalman's definition, which was not quite identical in all the chapters of his teachings, wisdom was the source of reason, potential reason, as it were; comprehension was active reason, "the accurate and profound comprehension of an object;" and knowledge was an "associa-tion and conjunction for comprehending the grandeur of the Infinite One." Knowledge meant the profound contemplation of the deity and the planting of an individual's intelligence in the greatness of God, who filled the universe, for

> the essential thing is to accustom one's knowledge and thought of Him to dwell firmly in one's heart and mind at all times, so that whatsoever one's eyes behold in the Heavens and on earth and the abundance thereof, are all the outer raiments of The King, The Holy One Blessed Be He, and thus one will ever be mindful of their innermost essence and vitality.

The virtues which were the "purpose of the Torah and the Precepts," the reverence of God and the love of God stemmed from knowledge. This

HaBaD doctrine had nothing in common with philosophical or even theological rationalism, as the author of the *Tanya* was far from even suggesting a search into divinity, theology, or metaphysics, the subject matter of medieval Jewish philosophy. What rationalism was present in Zalman's system did not transcend theosophy, and its affirmation of reason was only the affirmation of the constant observation of God and the focusing of thought on God's unity. But even this type of theosophy conflicted with the system of Hassidism which based religion purely on faith.

Although Rabbi Shneur Zalman repudiated any rapture which did not originate in knowledge, he did promote ecstasy in the love of God to the highest levels of perfection. His own soul overflowed with this ecstasy and he passed it on as a living heritage in one of his melodies, which was permeated with devotion to such an extent that contemporary *HaBaD* Hassidim call it *The Rav's Devotion*, or simply, *The Rav's Melody* (in Yiddish, *Dem Rav's Nign*). The same ecstasy emanated from his teaching with the full impact of his poetic and religious sensibility. Observance of the Precepts was in the nature of a wife's love for her husband:

> ... For it has been written, *Thou Who has sanctified us with His Commandments*, which is to say, like a man who sanctifies a woman to be with him in total communion; and therefore Solomon, peace be upon him, in the *Song of Songs* likened this communion to the communion of groom and bride in their eager and willing devotion whilst embracing and kissing.

Man arrived at the state of "true happiness of the living soul" by observing the unity of the Lord, when he

> visualizes through his reason and comprehension the true oneness of the Blessed One, how He fills all the upper and nether worlds ... And behold, how great is the joy of the simplest and lowliest person in his propinquity to a king of blood and flesh when such a one lodges and lives with him in his home; how infinitely more so then in affinity and habitation with the King of all Kings, The Holy One Blessed Be He!

At first sight, these words suggest Spinoza's *amor Dei intellectualis*, but in actuality their only common feature was religious ecstasy. In Spinoza's system, the human being reached the height of ecstasy and love when he beheld the cosmic marvel of natural law revealed by degrees in the course of wearisome, exhausting inquiry. Rabbi Shneur, on the other hand, achieved ecstasy in the love of God by focusing his thought on "His Glory which fills the universe." There was, therefore, a vast difference between the Kabbalist and Hassidic system on one side and the Spinozist on the other, despite the deceptive similarity of their pantheistic monism. Spinoza reduced the concept of God to identity with nature, whereas the mystic doctrine attempted, by diverse sophistries about "the secret of contraction," to negate nature by reducing reality to a mere wan glimmer of God's hidden light. Not surprisingly, therefore, Rabbi Shneur scorned the sciences, "the wisdoms of this world," and his compilation of the *Shulchan Arukh* ruled that even "one who has already learned all the Torah may not study the wisdom of the Gentiles."

The *Rav* repeatedly taught his followers to love every individual Jew with the same passion with which he urged them to love God. It was as though he took the Kabbalist principle that "The Holy One Blessed Be He and the Congregation of Israel are One" as his standard. Indeed, by the logic of his system, the love of Israel was a corollary to the individual's duty to reject the pleasures of the flesh and to elevate the soul to its divine source. Hence, "All of Israel are virtually brethren in their divine origin and only their bodies are divided ... as Hillel the elder said concerning the observance of the Precept *Thou Shalt love thy neighbour as thyself*, 'That is all the Torah, the rest is commentary ...' "

Acknowledgement of the unity of Israel postulated first and foremost the quality of charity. Rabbi Shneur Zalman extolled charity more eloquently than any other leader of Hassidism. Few authors of Hassidic books, in fact, devoted the same amount of space to the clarification of social duties when expounding their doctrines. His letters to his associates dwelt upon this in detail:

> The *She'khinah* is essentially revealed neither in His Torah nor in prayer, but rather in charity ... As the lightning issues from the black clouds in which it lay concealed and with its flash illuminates the world, so the Light of God, dispersed and concealed in the penumbra of this world's materiality, shines forth in the act of charity.

A letter, probably written in 1807, following the expulsion of the White Russian Jews from the villages* made an impassioned appeal for aid to the poor. He described the situation in the following words: "... I am not unaware that these are trying times, when livelihoods have declined, and I know of cases amongst you in which all means of support have vanished and people literally have to borrow in order to eat ..."

He reproached those who "... as I have heard, to this day have clenched their hands tightly and refrained from giving generously and willingly for the essential requirements of the completely destitute who look to us. If we show no pity for them, which Heaven forbid, then who will take pity on them?"

Apparently Jews who had ceased to support the poor mainly excused themselves on the grounds that the community as a whole was in impoverished circumstances. Their leader replied in words which proved

* *cf.* Chapter Eleven, p. 406.

his detailed knowledge of the situation from the *Halakhic* point of view as well. Referring to Leviticus, 25 : 36, he stated:

> "It is written *And Thy brother shall live with thee*. On the other hand the Sages taught that *Thine own life cometh before that of thy companion* only in the event that *In the hands of one there is a jug of water etc*. If a poor man needs bread for his little ones, kindling wood and clothing against the cold, and such like, then all these things take precedence over resplendent clothes and family repasts of meat and fish and all delicacies wherein a man delights . . . This is entirely within the meaning of the Law. Yet in truth, even if one be poor . . . it is fitting that there should be no quibbling over the letter of the Law for one's own preservation; one should do one's utmost even beyond the letter of the Law . . ."*

Another letter to his friends on the subject of charity repeated his demand that they forfeit the profits derived from their business dealings and dedicate their incomes to reviving the unfortunate and to ministering to their needs, without reward.

The Hassidic thinkers, including Rabbi Shneur Zalman, related the precept of charity to the concept of deliverance in accordance with the tradition that had evolved from the Prophets and the Talmud. In many of his letters, Rabbi Shneur repeated the Talmudic principle that the people of "Israel may not be delivered save through charity, for it has been said, *Zion shall be redeemed with justice, and they that return of her with righteousness*." However, he also added an original reason for assigning singular importance to the quality of mercy. This was connected with the rise of his Messianic hopes as of most of his own generation, during those years of revolution and warfare. "The essential phase in the worship of God in these times, when the Messiah's footsteps draw nigh, is the act of charity," the *Rav* asserted. Like Rabbi Mendel of Vitebsk before him, Rabbi Shneur particularly praised the virtue of charity to solidify the Jewish community in the Land of Israel. He enthusiastically urged his Hassidim to multiply their contributions to those living there to the same extent, as the holiness of the land was not a constant but continually increased:

> Let us awake our old love and endearment for the Holy Land so that it burn with tongues of flame deep in the hearts of each one of us, as though only this day God had inspired us with generosity and

---

* Rabbi Shneur Zalman here expounded one of the most conscience-challenging issues facing Jewish ethics since Biblical times: the duty of self-preservation in adversity as and when confronted with responsibility for others. The Talmud, *Baba Metzia*, 62:71, poses the problem as follows: "Two were walking on the road and one held a jug of water. If both drank, both would die; if one drank, that one would reach a habitation. Ben Pe'turah opined, 'Better that both should drink and let not the one behold his companion die.' Then came Rabbi Akiva and taught, '*And thy brother shall live with thee*; now then, thine own life comes before that of thy companion.'"

the people do offer to fill their hands for God generously and in increasing abundance from year to year, like that supreme sanctity which shines upon the Holy Land and does ever increase, throughout all eternity.

The Renewal of Persecution and the Beginning of Compromise

The *HaBaD* Hassidism of White Russia and Lithuania differed considerably from the Hassidism then popular in the neighbouring countries to the south. The difference lay principally in the *HaBaD* insistence on the study of the Gemara, in its high opinion of scholars, and in its rejection of the *Tzaddik* cult. However, none of this served to exonerate it in the eyes of the Mitnagdim when the war against Hassidism broke out with renewed fury in Lithuania.

In fact, sporadic persecution of Hassidism in Lithuania had never ceased even at the beginning of the 1790's. The book entitled *Rabbi Israel Ba'al Shem Tov's Testament*, and containing the *Hanhagot Yesharot* (Upright Behaviour) by his disciple, the great *Maggid*, as well as Ba'al Shem Tov's doctrine, had been printed in 1793. When it reached Vilno, the Vilno Gaon decreed that it be burned publicly on one of the city's streets. The Hassidim themselves precipitated the new attack by the sharp tactics they employed in their defence. In order to shake the foundations of the anti-Hassidic crusade of the Mitnagdim they spread rumours that the Gaon, the aged Rabbi Elijah, had retracted his opinion and was now repentant. They dispatched special couriers with this news to the German Kehillot. The Gaon was extremely angry at this deceit, and in 1796, published an epistle, *To Those Who Tremble at God's Word*. In this he denied the lie and called for persecution of the Hassidim, "that scurvy affliction of Israel . . . wherever the hand of Israel reaches . . . to wipe their name off the earth." The Vilno Kehillah leaders sent the epistle to the Kehillot of Lithuania and White Russia, and two notables were entrusted with effecting mobilization for the new campaign against the sect. The Hassidim tried to repeat the same tactics by announcing that the epistle was a forgery, but the Gaon drew up a fresh communication to the Kehillot in the latter part of 1796 at the height of his anger. He vehemently denounced the Hassidic doctrine of pantheism and the "Lifting up of the Sparks of Holiness" and ordered that "no man have mercy on them nor spare them but set them apart for evil from all the tribes of Israel. And he who heeds them shall be pilloried. . . ."

Two messengers from the Kehillah of Vilno delivered the Gaon's new epistle at Minsk and it was read out in all the synagogues there. The Gubernia Kehillah Council, with the authority of the Governor-General, banned all Hassidic *minyanim* and their mode of slaughter throughout the gubernia. It also prohibited all travel outside the city precincts without a slip from an appointed official in order to prevent Hassidim from travelling to their *Rebbes*. It threatened excommunication if derogatory words were heard against "the great Gaon and true God-inspired Hassid," Rabbi Elijah of Vilno. The two Vilno couriers then proceeded on their mission to Shklov and the other large communities of White Russia.

The Hassidim, however, kept up secret *minyanim* at Vilno even when things were at their worst. The majority of the active group were members of the most notable and wealthy families in the city; they owned stone buildings and were rich merchants, distillery owners, liquor excise farmers or liquor lessees.

The aged Gaon died shortly afterwards, during the Feast of Tabernacles, 1797. On the day of his funeral, when the whole city was in deep mourning, the Hassidim celebrated the joyous festival and, according to Mitnaged testimony, even indulged in gaiety at a feast alleged to have been held to mark the death of their enemy. At his graveside, the Gaon's followers swore to avenge this affront to his memory, and a new chapter began in the struggle between Mitnagdim and Hassidim in Lithuania.

On the same day, an assembly of Kehillah dignitaries empowered a "Panel of Five" to conduct the war against the Hassidim, and a "secret persecutor" was appointed to implement their decisions. The Panel of Five began work immediately. The *minyan* where the *HaBaD* Hassidim met was closed down, and the tailor who provided the premises publicly whipped in the courtyard of the Grand Synagogue. One Hassid was heavily fined and the home of another raided and his property plundered. The purchase of liquor from Hassidim was prohibited in an effort to strike a blow at the leader of the city's *HaBaD* Hassidim, Meir Ben Raphael, a liquor merchant.

Persecution of the Hassidim spread through all Lithuania and White Russia. The victims were not particular about the means they employed in self-defence. Rabbi Israel Leibel, the *Maggid* of Slutzk, described scenes he personally witnessed while touring the Kehillot of White Russia to preach against the sect as authorized by the Vilno Kehillah emissaries. He wrote in his *Book of Debates*, published in 1798 at Warsaw:

> There were instances in which the Hassidim (apparently Karliners) set upon the rabbis and preachers with invective and abused and beat them up murderously.

As already stated, the Mitnagdim had obtained government permission to excommunicate the "sectarians" in pursuance of their anti-Hassidic action. Under pressure, the Hassidim in their turn now availed themselves of the "third party." When oppression had become intolerable, an audacious plan was drawn up in Vilno to overthrow the Mitnaged Kehillah administration with the assistance of the authorities and take over the management. The Gubernia published its decision on the grievance submitted by the Hassidim together with specific ordinances on

April 26, 1798. Hassidic *minyanim* were to be permitted in accordance with the government's municipal statute permitting freedom of religion; the Kehillah management was forbidden to administer corporal punishment or to impose fines for religious offences; the Kehillah and the rabbinical court were deprived of the right to preside over civil or criminal trials; the Kehillah management was warned not to levy excessive taxes and not to enforce its rights to issue tenure permits. The Vilno Hassidim took advantage of this first victory. They again informed against the Kehillah, this time in connection with a clandestine conference it had held with other Kehillot of the gubernia for the purpose of financing a delegation to St. Petersburg by a special tax levy to prevent the prohibition of Jewish liquor lesseeships in the villages.* As a result, the Vilno Kehillah leaders were summoned to an investigation by the local authorities.

The Mitnagdim, thus attacked within their own stronghold, embarked upon a counter-offensive to wipe out the Hassidic movement irrevocably. A letter denouncing the Hassidim, bearing a fictitious signature, was sent from Vilno to the Imperial Attorney-General at St. Petersburg. The leader of the Hassidim in Lithuania and White Russia, "Rabbi Zalman Borukhovitch (Ben Barukh), living in the Gubernia of White Russia in the town of Liozno," was accused of "acts detrimental to the state" and of sending money to Turkey every year. Rabbi Shneur Zalman and twenty-two other leaders of the "Karlinite" sect were brought to Vilno by Imperial Order, in October, 1798. After interrogation, all of them were released, save Rabbi Zalman, who was taken to St. Petersburg and incarcerated in the prison for political criminals. While under interrogation by the secret police, the *Rav* submitted a petition in Hebrew explaining the principles of the suspect "Karlinite" system, which was then sent to Vilno for translation into French. Communications between the *Rav* and his Hassidim were not disrupted even during his imprisonment, as a result of the assistance of one of his admirers living in St. Petersburg. Hassidic intercessions must have played a considerable part in expediting the release of their revered Rabbi. However, the issue was mainly decided by the fact that the investigators did not discover any evil in the Hassidic leader's doctrine. This was reinforced by documentary evidence submitted to the investigating body and containing definite proof of the complete loyalty of the accused: an invocation composed for the well-being of the Czar and *Re'mazim Ve'sodot* (Hints and Secrets) based on passages in the scriptural reading *Give Ear* (Deuteronomy, 32:1), concerning the downfall of "the leaders of the French rebels" and the destruction of "the man Bonaparte." It has been established that Rabbi Shneur believed that the danger to Judaism lay in the victory of "the rebellious ones" rather than of their enemies in the war that Paul was then waging against revolutionary France. At the end of November, 1798,

* *vide* Chapter Eleven, pp. 375–6.

Rabbi Shneur Zalman was released. An order issued by the Governor-General of White Russia, in accordance with Paul's decision, provided religious freedom for the "Karlinite" worshippers of the Liozna rabbi.

Rabbi Zalman's release and governmental sanction for Hassidism gave rise to great joy amongst the Hassidim of Lithuania and White Russia and also encouraged the Hassidic group at Vilno to take strong action to win control of the Kehillah. They addressed a new memorandum to the Gubernia Administration, complaining of Kehillah pressure and violation of government laws: during the latest census—in 1795—the Kehillah management had concealed a great many people in order to diminish the Poll Tax assessment; and money collected for the tax had been spent for other purposes. On the basis of this information, the Governor-General ordered that the Vilno Kehillah management be deposed and new elections held. Police officials, accompanied by gendarmes and Hassidim, arrived at the Grand Synagogue on Friday, February 4, 1799, interrupted the late afternoon service and announced the order. A number of Kehillah leaders who attempted to protest were beaten up by the gendarmes, with clubs as well as fists. The Kehillah ledgers were confiscated and a search conducted in the homes of the Kehillah leaders. The Hassidim, triumphant, attacked all Mitnagdim they met on the streets with clubs. Two days later, elections were held in the presence of the Chief of Police, with only Hassidim participating; eight Kehillah administrators, all of them Hassidim, were elected. Hassidic revenge on their opponents now descended to the level of petty extremes, not excluding the actual violation of religious sensibilities.

It is true that the actions by the victims of persecutions, who had in their turn become persecutors, met with the great disapproval of the leader of the *HaBaD* Hassidim and earned his vehement protests. But although the leaders at Vilno professed to act in accordance with his directions, they disregarded them in practice.

Although the Hassidim were now in control of the Kehillah, they introduced no positive tax reform. One of their complaints against the old administration had been that it unlawfully farmed out a quarter of the Kehillah *korobka*, earmarked for the remission of Kehillah indebtedness, to one Simon Ben-Wolff. Ben-Wolff was a "leader of the common people" at the time of the controversy between Rabbi Samuel Ben-Avigdor and the Vilno Kehillah management,* and had also leased collection of the Recruits', or Military Service Exemption Tax. Nevertheless, when the Hassidim came to power, they imposed a new Kosher Meat *Korobka* on the Kehillah population at the rate of one-fifth of the price (6 grosz out of every Polish zloty) despite their previous demands that the people's wrongs at the hands of the predatory Kehillah leaders be redressed.

The chairman of the Panel of Five, appointed by the former Vilno Kehillah management to subdue the sect after the death of the Gaon, now

---

* *cf.* Chapter Nine, p. 296.

led the Mitnagdim, who had been deposed from office. He petitioned Paul to ban the Hassidic sect and restore the old management to office. In reply, St. Petersburg confirmed the government's previous resolution granting the "Karlinites" religious freedom. However, at this time, the Mitnagdim acquired an ally who turned to new informing tactics in his bitter struggle against the Hassidim. He was Avigdor Ben-Haim, formerly Kehillah Rabbi at Pinsk and a typical member of the class of rabbis branded as "Jewish demons" in *The Chronicles of Jacob Joseph*, at the height of Hassidism. He had secured the office of Rabbi at Pinsk by his close connections with high ranking dignitaries and also by paying "full money" to the city's ruler. Furthermore, to obtain the Kehillah rabbinate, he had deposited the sum of 400 red zloty (over 4,400 ordinary zloty) in the form of a loan for the duration of his appointment. He had attempted to recoup this expenditure twofold or more by exacting heavy "taxes" and "grants" from the members of the Pinsk and provincial Kehillot, until finally the Hassidim succeeded in having him removed from his rabbinical post. The deposed rabbi was engaged in futile legal action against the Kehillah for six years, claiming the refund of the deposit he had made when he received his appointment. He then determined to resort to other methods to gain his end, and take his revenge on the hated sect. He arrived at St. Petersburg at the beginning of 1800 and petitioned the Imperial Throne. His memorandum, which was both denunciatory and obsequious, described the Hassidim as the reincarnation of the Sabbetai Zvi sect and claimed that they negated all the principles of the accepted religions. Several excerpts from *The Testament of Ba'al Shem Tov* were cited as proof that Hassidim rejected fear of sin as well as the individual's duty to subdue his carnal appetite and shun the vanities of this world. On the contrary, Avigdor alleged, they decreed a life of joy, pleasure and orgies. One of the tenets of their faith was to fear nothing, no man and not even a monarch of a country.

At first Avigdor's memorandum brought no results, as the Governor of the Minsk Gubernia had expressed a favourable opinion of the Hassidim: they differed from the rest of their Jewish brethren only in the fact that they worshipped the Lord joyously and not in sadness or fear; they were loyal to the government and paid their taxes promptly. However, when the Attorney-General received a memorandum from Senator Derzhavin containing condemnatory remarks about the Hassidim and their leader, Rabbi Shneur Zalman, the latter was once again arrested at the beginning of November, 1800, and taken to St. Petersburg. As before, he was interrogated by the secret police, but now the indictment was based on nineteen slanderous charges composed in Hebrew by Avigdor Ben-Haim. Even the "fact that on Holidays some one thousand Hassidim come to him" was treated as a felony on his part for "it is not proper for so many people to be together . . . and who knows of what they speak during their conclave?"—apart from the fact that such journeys involved "much expenditure." In his replies, which all expressed his respect and loyalty to the Czar, the accused *Rav* compared the charges that his enemies had brought against him to the ritual murder accusations which "the priests used to fabricate against the Jews in Polish times." Three weeks after his arrest, the *Rav* was released from prison, but ordered to remain in St. Petersburg for a further three months until his trial was held in the Senate. In March, 1801, Paul was assassinated, and his successor, Alexander I ordered that "the Jew, Zalman Borukhovitch," be permitted to return to his home.

The Jewish Statute of 1804 granted the Hassidim unreserved religious freedom by allowing any sect within the Kehillah to build its own synagogue and even to choose its own rabbi. It only demanded that there be no more than one, undivided Kehillah management in each city. The law also deprived rabbis of the right to pronounce excommunications or to impose any other kind of punishment on those guilty of religious transgressions. Persecution of the Hassidim by the Kehillot was henceforth impossible. The new régime of the absolutist monarchy thus helped the Hassidic movement in Lithuania and White Russia by restricting the autonomy of the Kehillot and bringing them all under its own supervision. But the ending of the controversy was equally facilitated by the social and intellectual development of Hassidism. It had changed from its earlier character as a movement opposed to the dominant Kehillah régime and to the hegemony of the scholars. The crystallization of the *HaBaD* system and the consolidation of the *HaBaD* Hassidic community in White Russia and a number of Hassidic centres in Lithuania, were only expressions of the movement towards compromise.

The process whereby the Kehillot of Lithuania and White Russia became reconciled to the existence of the Hassidic minority in their midst actually preceded the Statute of 1804 which granted the minority group religious tolerance. It was directly and considerably facilitated by Rabbi Shneur Zalman's active efforts to pacify the two sides. When he was liberated after his first imprisonment, he had appealed to his fellow Hassidim not to provoke the scholars or the *Mitnagdim* as a whole. Similarly, after his second release, he attempted to persuade his opponents that Hassidism contained nothing offensive to traditional Judaism. He worked tirelessly to achieve this, travelling to a number of rabbis in order to meet them personally. In fact, the *Rav*, who had moved from Liozna to Lady (with which his name was thenceforth associated) was highly respected by the rabbis and Kehillah leaders. The Kehillot now even gave explicit assent to ritual slaughter with ground knives as well as to Hassidic prayer services in separate *minyanim*. The resolution by the management of the Minsk Kehillah in 1803 to this effect was candidly explained on economic grounds connected with the numerical increase of Hassidim in town: the ban on ground knife *she'hitah* in Minsk had caused a deficit in Kehillah revenue from the meat *korobka*. The existence of the Hassidic prayer house was also officially acknowledged at the same time. The Vilno Kehillah administration, where Hassidim and Mitnagdim served together from 1802, allotted a house near the old *Bet-Midrash* to the Hassidim as permanent premises for their *minyan*.

Despite the toleration that now prevailed, the Hassidim remained a small minority in Lithuania as well as in the larger cities of White Russia. But in the provincial towns and villages of White Russia, the *HaBaD* school of Hassidism struck deep roots. In 1813, Rabbi Shneur Zalman, founder and leader of *HaBaD* Hassidism, died, in a village near Kursk, far from Lady, where he had wandered during the upheavals of war. For many years after that, the name most frequently found in many White Russian Kehillah registers for new-born baby boys was Shneur Zalman.

b. HASSIDISM IN THE UKRAINE AND GALICIA

Beginning of the Tzaddik Cult; Rabbi Elimelekh of Lezajsk and his Doctrine

The Hassidism of the Ukrainian regions of Eastern Galicia, Podolia, Volhynia and the Ukraine proper was entirely different from that of Lithuania and White Russia in extent, environment and doctrinal principles. In the Ukrainian regions, where it first developed, Hassidism spread rapidly especially among rural and small town Jews after the death of Ba'al Shem Tov's disciple, the *Maggid* of Mezhirich. By the end of the eighteenth century, it dominated most of the Jewish population in the small communities there.

Definite symptoms of a new stage in the development of the movement and its doctrine were already perceptible amongst the first generation of Rabbi Ber the *Maggid's* pupils. Certain principles of Ba'al Shem Tov's system still maintained a position of pre-eminence: the individual's influence on the upper worlds by strengthening the quality of mercy in relation to the quality of justice; the union of the *She'khinah* with The Holy One Blessed Be He; love of God and devotion to Him; ecstatic prayer; obedience to the Precepts; the study of Torah for its own sake; and above all the quality of absolute confidence and powerful faith. Also, as before, Hassidic ethical doctrine attached importance to the precept of loving Israel as the chosen people and to the concept of Israel's unity, together with its corollary of mutual aid and charity. Another basic Hassidic doctrine still prevailing at that period was the idea of accelerating Messianic deliverance by perfecting the living soul (*Tikkun Ha'nefesh*). On the other hand, certain principles were no longer assigned a major position in Hassidic doctrine: absolute pantheism (i.e., "No Place is Void of Him"); the elimination of sadness and the repudiation of asceticism; and the precept of joy in worship. The new trend was most characteristic in regard to the revolutionary principles of ethical monism enunciated by Ba'al Shem Tov. The theory that materiality was the "Throne" of "Spirituality," the elevation of "alien thoughts" (i.e., sinful thoughts) to their source in the upper world, affirmation of bodily desire by raising it to the level of sanctity—none of these tenets was any longer common to the doctrine taught by the first generation of the *Maggid's* pupils (i.e., the second generation after Ba'al Shem Tov). The following generation had practically consigned them to oblivion. Even the precept of worshipping God in secular acts—*In all thy ways, acknowledge Him*— had been preserved in its original context (as applying to every individual and not only to the *Tzaddik*) by the *Maggid's* pupils, mainly in the sermons of Hassidic *maggidim*. However, it too began to be forgotten in the course of time. The Hassidic *maggidim* were also responsible for preserving the tradition of social opposition and expressed it in their teachings. But even these *maggidim* were even more rare as the years passed and Hassidic doctrine became virtually monopolized by the *Tzaddikim*, who were increasing in number and spreading throughout the land.

One tenet figured more and more in this recasting and revaluation of Hassidic doctrine until it had relegated all the other principles to a totally subsidiary position: the superior virtue of the *Tzaddik*. Ba'al Shem Tov and his disciple, Rabbi Jacob Joseph, had taught that it was the individual's duty to associate closely with his *Tzaddik*. This was now transformed by the interpretations of several of Rabbi Ber the *Maggid's* pupils into a veritable cult of the *Tzaddik*. Blind faith in the *Tzaddik* and his mystic power was proclaimed the cornerstone of Hassidism and the true test of worshipping God. A complete transformation occurred in the character of the movement and its environment. The teacher and guide became a fortune-teller and miracle-worker. Hassidim streamed in their masses to the *Tzaddikim* not only to hear the Torah but primarily to ask for help in their troubles. The social exaltation of the *Tzaddikim* had not yet become a general phenomenon during the active lifetime of the *Maggid's* pupils. At that time the majority of the foremost Hassidic leaders were uninterested in the accumulation of wealth and distributed their "redemption money" to charity. Some of them actually canvassed their neighbourhoods to collect contributions to release prisoners and for other public requirements. However, in the following generation, and especially in the Ukraine, the *Tzaddik* who established a sumptuous "court" and lived luxuriously on "redemption money" received from his "holy flocks" became increasingly common. These *Tzaddikim* also bequeathed their "thrones" and "courts" together with their "Grades of Holiness" to their sons. The *Tzaddik* "dynasties" began to ramify exactly like feudal dynasties, ruling by "Divine Grace" over kingdoms divided up by legacies.

The new system giving the *Tzaddik* élite status was introduced into

Hassidic doctrine by the most highly reputed of Rabbi Ber the *Maggid's* pupils in Galicia, Rabbi Elimelekh of Lezajsk. His book, *No'am Elimelekh* (*Elimelekh's Graciousness*), was published two years after his death in 1786, and contained sermons on the Torah arranged in the sequence of the weekly portions, letters by the author and his son, and also instructions for "the conduct of men." In this *Guide*, Rabbi Elimelekh warned against evil characteristics: "Obsequiousness and falsehoods, levity and evilmongering, envy and hatred, rivalry, anger, pride and gazing upon women." (Though he proscribed it for his followers, Elimelekh himself was a strict ascetic during his lifetime.) The curriculum of study he ordained was indicative of the new spirit in Hassidism:

> At first, every one should study Gemara and the Commentary of Rashi, the Tosaphot (annotations to the Talmud) and Commentators, each according to his capacity, and the Codifiers.

He added that "the *Aggadah* (legend) in the Gemara also possess the merit of greatly refining one's soul," and he also recommended daily study of the ethical literature and—"occasionally"—the works of HaARI (Isaac Luria), for men who had previously "refined themselves and been cleansed of all sins ... and let them study it with awe and reverence and the fear of God." Rabbi Elimelekh's frequent admonitions to penitence for sins were even more typical of his way in Hassidism. A man should remember "his sins, iniquities and transgressions, small as the hills, large as the mountains" and especially "the offences of one's youth." He should weep in penitence "not once, nor twice, nor yet a hundred times ... but an untold number of times ... till Heaven have mercy ... And one should ever be mindful of the day of one's death." These words were far removed from *Ba'al Shem Tov's Testament*, which proclaimed that "even should one have defaulted by committing a sin, let him not multiply sadness; let him but feel sorrow for his transgression and then rejoice once more in his Creator!"

The body of *Elimelekh's Graciousness* dealt mainly with the doctrine of *Tzaddikism*. Even the creation of the world had taken place for the sake of the *Tzaddikim*, for "it is precisely the worship of the *Tzaddikim* that He of the Blessed Name desires, that they shall raise ... the sparks of holiness ... for it is written, *And God saw that it was good* (Genesis, 1:10)." The Scriptural injunction *He shall be brought unto the priest* (Leviticus, 13:9, 14:2) referred to the *Tzaddik*. The *She'khinah* dwelt within the *Tzaddik* while in exile instead of in the Temple, and it was a cardinal maxim that "whatsoever may come to pass at the time of deliverance, (May it come soon in our day!) should now be present in the person of the *Tzaddik*," for "in the *Tzaddik* the example of deliverance should rest." Therefore, the prophetic utterance *And the Lord shall be King over all the earth* (Zechariah, 14:9) was to be interpreted as meaning that "when The Holy One Blessed Be He confers rulership over the earth, it is upon the *Tzaddikim* (that he confers it), that the *Tzaddik* may be as a king ruling through the reverence of God." In the name of his teacher, the *Maggid*, Rabbi Elimelekh announced that *Tzaddikim* were called *Seraphim*, of whom it had been said that "they stand over Him." This meant that they ranked higher than the angels, who were called "The Standing Ones" for they proceeded from level to level. But the status of *Tzaddikim* was even more exalted than that of *Seraphim*, for "as The Holy One Blessed Be He is One and there is no one as he is One," so the *Tzaddik* "likewise is called One . . . and he is a part of God." Because the *Tzaddik*, in the strength of God, infused all the worlds with life, he was called Lord (*Elimelekh's Graciousness*, Portion Pinehas). Hence, it was only logical that "he who speaks against the *Tzaddikim* and opens his mouth upon them in imprecations and villifications . . . is blaspheming the Lord (Numbers, 15 : 30), for it is as though he were speaking of the Lord."

Not surprisingly, therefore, the *Tzaddik*, created with these attributes, was virtually omnipotent. The *Tzaddik* delivered abundance from on high, wealth, physical well-being and all the good things of life. The *Tzaddik* decreed, and The Holy One provided. The superior position of the *Tzaddik* rested essentially on the final purpose of creation. The world was only created for the *Tzaddikim*, for (according to the Talmud) "The Holy One Blessed Be He longs for the prayer of *Tzaddikim* to such a degree, that at times He, Blessed Is His Name, makes a decree that the *Tzaddik* may pray for its annulment." An additional justification for the function of the *Tzaddik* as mediator lay in the fact that "since the abundance of The Blessed Creator is manifold and it is impossible that each one should receive of His abundance without an intermediary, it is the *Tzaddik* who receives the abundance from On High and lavishes it upon all, even upon such as are not righteous or worthy of receiving thereof."

The *Tzaddik's* practice in order to secure continued abundance for the world and the revocation of nefarious decrees consisted of adhesion to God, prayer, charity and the study of the Torah. A *Tzaddik* who studied Torah for its own sake and formulated exegeses upon it was constructing a new heaven and a new universe. Merely by the process of thinking, the *Tzaddik* dwelt in the upper worlds "and there The Holy One Blessed Be He converses with him and causes His Spirit to rest upon him." The *Tzaddikim* also brought abundance to the world by eating in sanctity and purity. They "eat in privacy and solitude, for they are ashamed that they must eat, for their soul is ever desirous of adhesion to God."

In his activities in the upper worlds, the *Tzaddik* was reciprocally connected with *Tzaddikim* on a lower level than his own but also with the people as a whole. The *Tzaddik*, of course, "ennobled the thoughts of villainous men that stray about in this world," and in general "corrected what mortals spoiled," but nevertheless, it were preferable that "simple people . . . should endeavour to worship," as well, for then "the *Tzaddik* does not need a tremendous effort to reach the high grade." But the majority of the masses were unable to gather such strength in the worship of The Blessed One because of their crass materiality. They, therefore, were allotted another task: "He who bestows of his possessions on scholars and *Tzaddikim* will, through the ease so afforded them, sin the less readily." By granting charity to the *Tzaddik*, communion in the upper worlds was established: "Justice becomes Charity...and then the world is full and content with all good things, with abundance, blessing, mercy, life, food and peace, all without end or limitation, lavished by the *Tzaddik*, who has received the charity."

Rabbi Elimelekh's doctrine of deliverance also revolved around the concept of *Tzaddikism*. *Elimelekh's Graciousness* forcefully voiced the yearning of the Galician Jewish population, subjected to the harsh servitude of Austrian absolutism, for deliverance. The passage in Genesis, 32:5, *Thus shall ye say unto my lord Esau*, was interpreted to mean that "because we are in this bitter exile, we must be subservient to them and address them as lords." The passage taught, he claimed, "that it is sufficient for us to be subservient to him and to do him honours...forasmuch as he continue to harm you more than is fitting in taxes and levies, robbery will be in his hands, and thus God will have mercy on us." Yet although deliverance depended on the penitence of all of the people and its faith in the coming of the Messiah, the chief task, even here, devolved upon the *Tzaddik*. The *Tzaddik* "shall neither sleep nor slumber in this bitter exile which is called night...but will sorely trouble himself for the needs of Israel in their bitter exile with its taxes and levies, and all his ecstasy and devotion are as nothing to him because of his great anxiety for them." Rabbi Elimelekh was certain that deliverance would come through the *Tzaddik*, for "the initials represented by the name ADAM (i.e. a human being, a person, man) stand for *A*dam-*D*avid-*M*essiah, meaning that the *Tzaddik*, being all-powerful, can also act to cause the Coming of the Messiah."

However, although this doctrine elevated the *Tzaddik* to the level of Seraphim, if not even higher, the last vestiges of the *Tzaddik's* original task of teaching and guiding had not totally disappeared. *Elimelekh's Graciousness* gave occasional reminders that "the main thing for one was to learn the *Tzaddik's* deeds," for the *Tzaddik's* behaviour served as an example to his Hassidim, while the level the *Tzaddik* attained depended in turn on the behaviour of the children of Israel as a whole. However, all these warnings and reservations were of secondary importance compared with Rabbi Elimelekh's chief innovation which defined the sublime status of the *Tzaddikim* and their function as mediators between the individual and God, between "the base world" and the upper worlds, where they were completely at home. This new system not only provided the justification and theoretical foundation for the *Tzaddik* cult (which, incidentally, had already been current in the Ukraine for several decades) but actually accelerated the development of Hassidism on these erratic lines. The belief in the *Tzaddik* as God's factotum on earth, who provided a livelihood, cured the sick, visited the barren, rescued those in trouble, and performed all manner of miracles, was displacing all the other principles of Hassidism—at any rate amongst masses of ignorant believers —which in its early days had been based on a new individual and social morality and on a new world outlook.

The leadership of the Hassidic generation of Rabbi Elimelekh of Lezajsk still remained in the hands of a group of distinguished men of intellectual stature who evinced that vitality and creative drive in their teaching and philosophy, which had abounded at the height of Hassidism.

The evocative image of Rabbi Leib (Son of Sarah) emerges from a vast accumulation of remarkable legends. This wealth of legends the people built around their hero during his lifetime and for many generations after his death, concealed many fragments of historical truth. According to legend, Rabbi Leib Sarah was one of the invisible thirty-six sainted men (*Lamed-Vov Tzaddikim*) and he would suddenly appear whenever any Jew, but especially the Jewish people or any Jewish community, was being imperilled by ritual murder charges or other forms of oppression. He had the power to cover distances miraculously when he travelled and would arrive at the courts of princes, reproach them in person, and compel them to deal justly with Israel. He arrived in the same miraculous manner in the capital city of Vienna every Sabbath eve for many years, and employing his powers of invisibility, entered the palace of Joseph II and chastised him mercilessly to force him to withdraw his decrees against the Jews: expulsion of Jewish mendicants, compulsory attendance at German schools by Jews, the kosher meat tax and obligatory military service. He travelled to the great fairs in the Ukraine, to Berditchev, Yarmolinietz and other towns, and even to Lenczna in Poland, and set up stalls with barely any goods; hence, until recently, people called a poor, understocked shop, a *Reb Leib Sarah's* shop. He did not do this in order to trade but so that he could enter into conversation with the market people and collect contributions for ransoming prisoners and for anonymous *Tzaddikim*. He was also in the habit of entering the homes of rich lessees and the wealthy Jews of Lwow and Brody, where his appearance aroused such fear that they donated any sum he named. The "tabernacle" erected over his grave in the Podolian town of Yaltishkov was as simple as the charitable Hassidism of his life: a small wooden shed with a thatched roof. The date of his death is inscribed on his gravestone: the 4th day of Adar II, 5551 (1791). His legendary adversary, Joseph II, had died exactly a year before.

The Hassidic principles propagated in Galicia by the *Maggid* Rabbi Jehiel Michael of Zloczow differed from the innovations of his contemporary, Rabbi Elimelekh, who died in the same year, 1786. He was the son of a friend and disciple of Ba'al Shem Tov, Rabbi Isaac of Drohobycz, and in his youth had had the opportunity of visiting the founder of Hassidism at

Mezhibozh before he developed close links with the *Maggid* of Mezhirich. *Reb Mikhele,* as the people affectionately called him, served as *Maggid* in a *"minyan* of his own" in the city of Brody, in the Kehillah of neighbouring Zloczow, and towards the end of his life at Yampol in Podolia. Many Hassidic legends praised his special qualities. He despised money and refused to pander to the rich. He interpreted the passage in Deuteronomy, 5:5, *I Stood between the Lord and you* to mean that it was egoism which formed a barrier between the individual and God. The few fragments of his doctrine which were preserved in the books of his pupils emphasized the same theme of social morality. He castigated those who studied the Torah "for their own embellishment and not for its own sake" in the same severe terms as *The Chronicles of Jacob Joseph.* He applied the verse in Psalms, 107:26, *They mounted up to the heaven, they went down to the deeps* to them: "They think that by thus studying the Torah they will ascend to Heaven, but in truth, through much study they will plunge to the depths ..." "The essential thing in repentance," Reb Mikhele *Maggid* preached in the same sermon, in 1777, "is to do the virtual opposite of what one has done before, and also to restore the things one has stolen and obtained by cheating and not to plague oneself very much." His instructions for righteous behaviour which he formulated as a kind of testament in twenty or more articles, also included the following: "One must forbear from stealing even to the value of less than one copper coin, be the victim Jew or Gentile." His young contemporary, the Kabbalist Uri Feivel Ben-Aaron, quoted him as saying that "in our times all idol worship is but money."

The Grandsons of Ba'al Shem Tov

While Hassidism in Galicia was still facing obstacles created by both the Mitnagdim and the Austrian government with its plans for disseminating German culture amongst the Jews, the new movement was spreading in the neighbouring areas of the Ukraine with no interference from the Polish authorities or the Russian state—to which Volhynia, Podolia and the Ukraine had been annexed in 1793 and 1795. The proportion of *Tzaddikim* amongst the Jewish population of the Ukraine was also higher than in Galicia. The oldest member of this group of Hassidic leaders, former pupils of Rabbi Ber the *Maggid,* was the *Maggid* Rabbi Nahum of Tchernobyl (1730-98), who like Rabbi Michael of Zloczow, had learned from Ba'al Shem Tov himself. He unwittingly supplied evidence of the luxurious existence of contemporary *Tzaddikim.* To prove his thesis that a man's livelihood did not depend on "external causes," such as business and other dealings, but rather on the extent of his confidence and faith, he cited the circumstances of the *Tzaddikim:*

> For mostly *Tzaddikim* are not business men nor do they engage in earning a living in material ways, as is the custom in this world, yet they feed respectably without much trouble and there are those amongst them who feed and satisfy all their needs much more plentifully than those wealthy men who engage in earning a living . . .

His espousal of this strange economic theory was so naïve that he was entirely impervious to his own material circumstances. His position as *Maggid* in his own town and even his journeys to neighbouring cities and villages were barely sufficient to support him.

Nahum the *Maggid* was also loud in his praise of charity and his denunciation of the love of money: "In these generations . . . the principal cause of all the cupidity in the world." The phrase ascribed to him, "the stingy *per se* are rich," was evidently the result of his experience when appealing for funds to marry off poor brides and to purchase the release of Jewish prisoners. In his doctrine of deliverance, Rabbi Nahum gave prominence to the idea of a slow process: there was a part of the Messiah which belonged to the individual soul of every Jew and the worship of God meant essentially "to correct and complete that part of the Messiah that belongs to each individual . . . until the entire structure shall have been repaired and shall stand ready."

It was only natural that two of Ba'al Shem Tov's grandchildren, the sons of his daughter Odel, should occupy important positions amongst the leaders of Hassidism in the Ukraine. They were Rabbi Moses Haim Ephraim and Rabbi Barukh. The elder of the two, known as Rabbi Ephraim of Sudilkov, after the Volhynian town where he served as rabbi and *Maggid*, was brought up in the spirit of his grandfather and had even had the opportunity of being taught by him directly. Rabbi Jacob Joseph's work had instructed him in the essential elements of the doctrine which divided society into the people of the form (or image) and the people of matter (the raw substance)—scholars and *Tzaddikim*, the servants of God, on the one hand, and "the people of the mass," on the other—and their duty to be joined together. The people as a whole was an organism, like a complete human being:

> The Congregation has its heads, who possess the brains and the mind, and it has its eyes, those who supervise community affairs and their integrity, and it has its hands, those who implement its commandments and philanthropies, and it has its feet, the people of faith, who possess nothing but their faith . . . (Only) when they all follow the head and execute all things wisely as instructed by the Congregation and are bound to one another . . . are all the limbs sanctified . . . and they are like one complete man; and there the *She'khinah* resides.

A precept carried out by an individual elevated the entire congregation and similarly a transgression by each individual implied the "descent of all." This was in fact, a hierarchy, functionally divided like a feudal society, which was reformed by the obligation of mutual rapprochement between its leaders and the people.

Like all Hassidic thinkers of his generation, Ba'al Shem Tov's grandson, Ephraim, incessantly considered the concept of deliverance. In his outlook, that of a Kabbalist and Hassid, spiritual deliverance, the deliverance of the *She'khinah*, and the literal deliverance of the Jewish people, were inseparably merged. The following homiletical interpretation of a scriptural passage, which in the literal sense dealt only with sacrificial offerings, exemplifies the longing for deliverance which he shared with his contemporaries:

> The teaching concerning the burnt offering, the offering which is on the altar flames all during the night till the morning, means that the *She'khinah* is complaining and yearning for her Lover, for she is sick with a love that burns within her like the flames on the altar, for together with Israel she suffers all the sorrow and the anguish . . . the night long throughout all the bitter and precipitate exile. Therefore is she sick with love . . . recalling how long the exile must endure, till the morning, till Israel's morning come and shed its light.

But this mystic doctrine concealed a realistic, down-to-earth approach to the question of deliverance:

> There can be no deliverance other than through the reign of the House of David, and there is no other redemption besides this.

There were indications in Hassidic literature that the prevailing frame of mind amongst the Hassidim in Rabbi Ephraim's declining years, during the final partitions of Poland, the Revolution in France and the ensuing wars, was the expectancy of imminent deliverance. This could be adduced not only from the legend which placed the Messiah's crown, that of the son of Joseph, on the head of Rabbi Solomon Karliner, who was killed during the Russo-Polish war of 1792. The hope that the wars heralded deliverance was also expressed in the sermons of Rabbi Joseph Bloch, Rabbi at Olesko in Galicia and subsequently *Maggid* in the Podolian city of Satanow. He urged his congregation to do penance by unity, peace and love, in view of the impending deliverance, for "especially in such times as these, when kingdoms provoke one another, the Messiah's footsteps approach . . ."

The younger grandson of Ba'al Shem Tov, Rabbi Barukh (born a few years before Ba'al Shem Tov's death, died in 1811), represented a new social type of *Tzaddik*. He was called after the two cities of Podolia where he led Hassidic congregations, first at Tultchin, and later at Mezhibozh, formerly Ba'al Shem Tov's own seat. Even with the addition of the morsels preserved by his pupils, his vague doctrine hardly constitutes a collection of fragments (*A Brilliant Light*, first published in 1880), but it is sufficient to reveal his character and Hassidic thought. His capacity did not go beyond taking passages out of their context and interpreting them in an utterly irrelevant fashion, at times amounting to an absurd play on words. An example of this was supplied by the passage in Isaiah, 1:20, *For the mouth of the Lord hath spoken*, which he rendered in Yiddish as *My mouth speaks the Lord.** He raised this type of commentary to the level of a method, and "found" a premise for it in the Torah. Thus, he interpreted Genesis, 1:2, ... *and the spirit of God hovered over the face of the waters*, to mean that the *Tzaddikim* hovered over the Torah (according to a Talmudical dictum *there is no water but Torah*). The *Tzaddikim* only required the merest hint to predicate their words on the Torah. He was so conceited that he not only claimed that his knowledge of the *Zohar* was superior to that of any other mortal (for example, he addressed the following words to the legendary author of the *Zohar*, "Reb Simeon Bar-Yochai, I know you, and you know me ...") but he also boasted of his erudition in the entire Torah and its secrets. Moreover, he thought that no one in the world could equal him in humility. He disparaged all contemporary *Tzaddikim*, and hated some of them, the most illustrious, such as Rabbi Shneur Zalman of Lady, Rabbi Levi Isaac of Berditchev, and his nephew, Rabbi Nahman of Bratzlav.

Rabbi Barukh's facile doctrine propounded a lax and universally acceptable brand of Hassidism. He taught that the virtue of joy should not only be practised in the worship of the Creator but also in the individual's secular life, for "sadness greatly impairs a man's livelihood ..." Men should also indulge in meat and wine on secular occasions for two reasons. In the first place, an inordinate expansion of the menu from weekdays to the Sabbath might give rise to "changes of regularity on the Sabbath" and thus the joy of the Sabbath would not be perfect; secondly, on the Sabbath "one transfers (to the upper worlds) food consumed throughout the week, as is known." It would appear that these commandments of physical and spiritual hygiene were not on the whole intended for the poor. Love of money on the part of the *Tzaddik* was, according to Rabbi Barukh, considered a virtue:

> Now therefore God has implanted in the hearts of *Tzaddikim* the desire for the money which the world should afford them, since they attach themselves thereby to the Community of Israel as a whole and offer up their prayer.

Furthermore, the larger the *pidyonot* collected by the *Tzaddik*, the higher his level. *Tzaddikim* "who throw open the gates with their prayers" were like the guards of a royal court, for the nearer the guard to the king, the more money had to be paid to enter.

---

* The Hebrew *Pi* may mean either *the mouth of* or *my mouth*, depending on the context of the passage and the usages of Hebrew syntax.

Vast numbers of Hassidim flocked to Mezhibozh to prostrate themselves on Ba'al Shem Tov's grave and, particularly, to pay homage to his grandson who would pray for a supplicant's material security and physical welfare, on payment of a *pidyon*. His "court" at Mezhibozh was surrounded by splendour, with wardens and servants to obey his every command. Like a prince of the blood, he kept a court jester to amuse his guests and himself; this was the famous Hershele Ostropoler, the humorous rhymester, whose figure later acquired legendary proportions in the Jewish folklore and literature of eastern Europe. Rabbi Barukh rode in a stately carriage, very similar to those usual with the local nobility when he travelled from town to town in Podolia to collect donations from his Hassidim.

As Rabbi Barukh's accumulation of wealth increased, his anxiety lest other *Tzaddikim* trespass on his territory intensified correspondingly. Against this background, his hatred of Rabbi Shneur Zalman of Lady became open hostility. When Rabbi Shneur arrived in Podolia during a journey to raise funds for village Jews evicted from their homes in 1808 by the Czar's decree, Rabbi Barukh refused to forgive him for entering his domain. Rabbi Shneur Zalman relates his conversation with Rabbi Barukh when he visited him at Mezhibozh in a letter to his Hassidim:

> ... He then asked me, "What do you need all this for (i.e. collecting funds for the evicted)? The laws can be mitigated by passing the hand over the forehead and face..." And then he asked me, "And does it accord with your honour to wander about these distant towns? Why have you come to my country?" And I replied, "There are two answers to this. One, it is written, The earth is the Lord's and the fullness thereof (Psalms, 24 : 1). And two, I could no longer endure the sorrow and the agonies of these villagers exiled from their places to the towns and cast out into the streets bloated with starvation and dying of hunger." And he answered me, "What care you if they die? ..."

Rabbi Barukh's words quoted in this conversation revealed more eloquently than his doctrines or his actual behaviour the depths to which Hassidism had degenerated in various parts of the Ukraine by the beginning of the nineteenth century.

The Hassidic Maggidim; Rabbi Levi Isaac of Berditchev—Advocate of Israel

Large numbers of Hassidim came from far and wide to the courts of famous *Tzaddikim* to ask for help in their problems, destitution and distress. Only a few came to hear the teaching of their masters. Apart from these *Tzaddikim*, however, several of the Mezhirich *Maggid's* more retiring pupils actively disseminated Hassidic doctrine verbally and in writing in Galicia and the Ukraine in the closing years of the eighteenth century. Nearly all of these preachers served as *Maggidim* in their Kehillot, but they never occupied posts of "*Rebbes*" and therefore neither bequeathed their distinction to their progeny nor founded new *Tzaddik* dynasties. Their memory would have been expunged from the history of Hassidism if it were not for the collections of their sermons, mostly printed after their death. This group included Rabbi Jacob Joseph Ben Judah (died 1791), *Maggid* at Ostrog in Volhynia, who signed his book with his initials (*The Book of Rabbi YeYBY*, published in 1808), quite probably to avoid claiming the name of the famous author of *The Chronicles of Jacob Joseph*. Other Hassidic *Maggidim* were Rabbi Joseph Ben-Abraham Bloch, Rabbi at Olesko in eastern Galicia and later *Maggid* at Satanow in Podolia, "The Kabbalist Rabbi" Uri Feivel Ben-Aaron of Laszczow in the south Lublin district, Rabbi Eliezer Ben-Jacob Horowitz, Rabbi at Tarnogrod, and—the most prolific in literary activity—Rabbi Benjamin Ben-Aaron (died 1792), *Maggid* in the two eastern Galician towns of Zaleszczyki and Zalozice (after which he was called), as well as an itinerant *Maggid* in the neighbouring cities and the author of numerous books of sermons.

The sermons of all these Hassidic preachers shared several common features; the importance they attached to the precept of charity, their insistence on social morality, and the particular prominence they attached to the concept of deliverance. Their specifically social trend expressed the spirit of the masses of Hassidim, even though they did not go in their multitudes to the modest *Maggidim* but rather to the famous *Tzaddikim* to bask in their light.

Rabbi Ze'ev Wolf of Zhitomir should be classed with this group of *Maggidim*, both because of the social direction of his sermons and because he did not establish a dynasty. Unlike them, however, this prominent pupil of Rabbi Ber the *Maggid* was actually a famous *Tzaddik* in his day. His fame was confirmed by the inclusion of his name amongst the great *Tzaddikim* listed in the polemical works of the Mitnagdim. His book, *Or Ha'meir* (*A Shining Light*), published at about the time of his death in 1798, was written in more polished language than all the other Hassidic literature of his generation. The deep pathos of his social protest was equalled by his grief at the exile, "our being as one lamb amongst so many wolves, at the mercy of them who beat us." He regarded the severe decrees against the Jews of Galicia, adjoining his native Volhynia, and the harsh compulsory military service, as a divine visitation for the misdeeds of the assimilationists, who were abetting the government in promoting "the intermingling of Israel amongst the Gentiles to learn their ways" (*A Shining Light*, Portion Balak). He was distressed to note the spread of a superficial, banal and strident brand of Hassidism:

Our eyes have beheld many people, when the hour arrives to discourse upon the Torah and to pray, raising their voices to an ever greater distance, clapping their hands, and making alike motions with their limbs, dancing with their feet as is the custom in the world at large, and many of these are ignorant people who imagine that in this lies the essence of prayer. . . .

Similarly, he ridiculed the ignorance of Hassidim who believed that they had performed an act of piety by listening to their masters teach without understanding a word. However, his anger reached its peak on the subject of the numerous *Tzaddikim* who were unworthy of the power they enjoyed and professed to be the leaders of Hassidic congregations without possessing either Torah or reverence; some were consciously charlatans. These spurious *Tzaddikim* took it upon themselves "to pray for the sterile . . ., to open the wombs of barren women . . . They boast that their names are amongst those of the great in accomplishing *pidyonot* (redemption from sorrows) . . . and they are neither ashamed nor yet do they know abashment . . ." However, even *Tzaddikim* who were not frauds did not escape his stern judgement on the grounds of their insatiable greed for wealth: "Of such it has been said that 'they fly with two wings,* from town to town and from country to country . . .' He 'surrounds the whole land of Havilah where there is gold to be found't . . . everything for gold. . . ."

The travelling *Tzaddikim*, like the travelling rabbis, had nothing in view but their own gain. It would appear that decadence was deeply imbedded in the Hassidism of the Ukraine if the Hassidic *Maggid* from Zhitomir acknowledged that his generation was powerless to right the wrong. "We have not," he lamented, "that strength to redress this shameful quality, and we may only hope that at least the coming generation will do so . . ."

The court of Ba'al Shem Tov's younger grandson at Mezhibozh was typical of the process of decay of Ukrainian Hassidism. However, in the same country some of the original Hassidic principles which had not yet lost their vitality were embodied in the teachings and image of one of the greatest figures in Hassidism, Rabbi Levi Isaac of Berditchev, who was born in 1740 and died in 1809.

The essential Hassidic doctrine of the Berditchev Rabbi (during his lifetime he came to be known by the name of his book, *Ke'dushat Levi* (*The Sanctity of Levi*, published 1798) contained nothing new in comparison with the teachings of Ba'al Shem Tov and the Mezhirich *Maggid*, as expounded by other Hassidic leaders of his generation. The central theme of *The Sanctity of Levi* consisted of the ideas expressed by Hassidic literature as a whole in that period: the worship of the creator in the heart, the love and reverence of the creator, Israel as the chosen

* Isaiah, 6:2. † Genesis, 2:11.

people, the strengthening of the quality of mercy over that of justice, the provision of continued abundance upon earth through the mediation of the *Tzaddik*, and similar concepts. In particular, Rabbi Levi Isaac did not diverge from the other *Tzaddikim* in his grasp of the function of the *Tzaddik*. Like the other *Tzaddikim* of his time, Rabbi Levi Isaac was a practising *Tzaddik* and toured the villages within his orbit, dispensing nostrums, medicines and charms against illness and other afflictions.

The respect he received from his contemporaries was therefore not accorded for any original exegeses on Hassidic doctrine but for his brilliant personality, which also influenced his unique choice of essentials in the worship of God and ethical doctrine. The secret behind Levi Isaac Berditchiver's spiritual image lay in his genius for mercy, his compassion that flowed from unbounded love for his wretched and suffering people. This was the quality of mercy which, contained in the ethical doctrine of the persecuted people from Talmudic and Midrashic times onwards, had been made pre-eminent over all the precepts governing human relations. In the religious tradition it had shaped the image of God as a merciful God: "Forasmuch as He is merciful, thou too are merciful." But according to the Hassidic conception, Israel and its God were so closely connected in eternal love, that it was impossible to distinguish between Israel's love of God and God's love for His chosen people. As the *Tzaddik's* love for Israel was like the love of a father for his son, the love he felt for God was like that of a son for his father. The warmth of the intimacy was the strongest characteristic of the love of God in the doctrine and practice of Rabbi Levi Isaac. He taught that when an individual recited the *Eighteen Benedictions* he "should picture to himself that he is standing alone before The Blessed One, embracing Him and pleading with Him like a remorseful son with his father." According to Hassidic tradition Rabbi Levi Isaac was given the official surname of *Derbarmdiker* (Yiddish for The Merciful One), because he never for a moment omitted to mention God, referring to Him by this name.

Rabbi Levi Isaac poured his whole being into his prayer, very much like a son pleading with his father, not hesitating to introduce heartfelt words of his own in the Yiddish vernacular into his recitation of the *Eighteen Benedictions*. His love for God in the observance of the Precepts was so ardent that he attained a degree of ecstasy when he would passionately kiss ritual objects such as the *Etrog* (citrus) and *Lulav* (palm branch) used during benedictions on the Feast of Tabernacles. But his patriarchal attitude towards God was also permeated with a filial awe for his heavenly Father that was almost a pathological fear. This awe prevented him from staying in his place in front of the Ark of the Scrolls during prayers and he would run around inside the synagogue. On the eve of the Day of Atonement, he would crawl to synagogue on all fours, "with outstretched hands and feet." He stressed in his teachings ecstasy also in the observance of the Precepts. One who did not observe the Precepts "with a mighty desire" had not achieved sympathy with the quintessence of the precepts. It was like learning military tactics, "how to grasp the weapon and how to confront the enemy ... and when the fighting starts he seizes the weapon and does not fire." This was his interpretation of Numbers, 28:19, *But ye shall present an offering made by fire, a burnt-offering unto the Lord*. "That is to say," he explained, "the fire of ecstasy—a burnt-offering unto the Lord ..." Ecstasy in the worship of God was also essential in penitence for sins, as it says in Leviticus, 21:9, *And the daughter of any priest, if she profane herself by playing the harlot, she profaneth her father: she shall be burnt with fire*, meaning, in the fire of "ecstasy to which one later rises in the worship of the Creator."

Despite his emphasis on feeling in the worship of God, Rabbi Levi Isaac did not ignore the ethical doctrine of Hassidism in the matter of "obedience to the precepts and the performance of pious acts." The *Tzaddik's* task was not only to maintain his links with his congregation through devout thinking but also "to bring Israel closer through moral exhortation." Rabbi Levi Isaac's teaching preserved from the original Hassidic doctrine one of Ba'al Shem Tov's fundamental tenets: the worship of God in all secular actions:

> *In all thy ways acknowledge Him* applies not to the *Tzaddik* alone but to every individual. He who is careful in his business dealings not to transgress the prohibitions of the Torah, it is as though he has studied the Torah. And thus, he who is in the market-place where all is abandon and he may lie but does not lie, as though mindful of the passage *Neither shall ye deal falsely* (Leviticus, 19:11), it is as though he is then learning that passage. And so, when he arrives in his shop and somebody comes to buy from him and he serves him a correct measure, dealing out fairly liquids and solids and not burying his weights in salt, then is he mindful of the passage *A just ephah* * and *A just hin* * shall ye have (Leviticus, 19:36), so that when doing business in good faith, it is as though he were also learning.

All the individual's other secular activities should also be directed towards the service of the Lord; ploughing and harvesting for instance. "Let a man's intention be ... thereby to obtain food," Rabbi Levi Isaac taught, "so that he may be able to engage in Torah and in the worship of the Blessed One." This principle in his teaching was embodied in a well known story about Rabbi Levi Isaac:

> He was overjoyed on coming upon a carter who was rubbing pitch onto the hubs of his wheels and praying at the same time. *Ribbono shel Olam*—the Rabbi from Berditchev cried out—Oh Master of all the Universe, behold how great is a Jew's love for Thee: even when greasing his cartwheels he is not forgetful of Thee!

* *Ephah* and *hin*, respectively a solid and liquid measure (Biblical).

However, the most outstanding characteristic of Rabbi Levi Isaac, "the merciful one"—even more than his doctrinal principles or the virtues of his personal conduct—was his self-appointed role as the advocate of the people of Israel. It seemed as if all the immense love he bore humanity was focused on his own people, persecuted and suffering the ordeals of exile. This great love embraced every Jewish individual—child and adult, righteous and criminal. He regarded a nation that had remained steadfast in its faith, throughout the vicissitudes of long exile, without renouncing its covenant or forsaking its Law, to be wholly sacrosanct:

> How dear and lovely and sweet are to us all the anguish and blows to pass through fire and water, because through these blows His great Name is exalted and sanctified.

This persecuted people was superior in its spiritual capacities and virtues to all the nations of the world, who oppressed and abused it. "And even if we fail to do the will of The Blessed One, even then are we better than the other peoples." Of course, "We all have One God, and He is The Master and the Ruler ... and no evil can issue from Him," but the gentiles "have closed their hearts and do not comprehend what good things they enjoy." Israel was a chosen people:

> Every nation must have some virtue, and that is the essential of existence, but Israel possesses all the virtues ... The Creator, Blessed Be He, chose only Israel, therefore none may speak evil of Israel, he should speak only in vindication of Israel.

Even a *Tzaddik*, remonstrating with Israel, had to preach "with pleasant sayings, acceptable to the heart, that a sinner may depart from his evil ways."

One of the cardinal duties of a *Tzaddik* as the protagonist of his people, was to justify the people before the Lord. The Jews of eastern Europe created innumerable legends about Rabbi Levi Isaac's role as advocate, but they all drew one conclusion: the people of Israel worshipped God and only Him, and even the most uncouth scrupulously observed the precepts, such as washing their hands before taking food. A reliable legend told how the Berditchev Rabbi used to speak proudly of his people before prayer on Yom Kippur Eve:

> Behold Thy People Israel, all as one are now in the synagogue, not one absent, not one drunk and sleeping on his wine; nor is there one of them aslumber in his house for having eaten so much. All of them now stand barefoot before Thee.

Rabbi Levi Isaac reached the greatest heights of poetic expression in his *Converse With God*, preserved in its original language, half Hebrew, half Yiddish, and composed as an adjunct to the *Rosh Hashanah* canticle, *They That Dwell On High and They That Dwell Below*, and in a slightly revised version, as an introduction to the *Kaddish*. Here he exchanged his role of counsel for the defence to that of accuser and voiced the Job-like cry of all the generations of his people in its dispersion:

> (In Hebrew): What wouldst Thou of Israel? Speak! (In Yiddish): To whom, then, dost Thou speak? (In Hebrew): To the Children of Israel. Say! (In Yiddish): To whom dost Thou say? (In Hebrew): To the Children of Israel. Command! (In Yiddish): Whom dost Thou command? (In Hebrew): The Children of Israel! (In Yiddish): Now therefore do I ask Thee, (In Hebrew): What wouldst Thou of Israel? ...

The ardent longing for redemption permeates his work *The Sanctity of Levi*. "All the events that have befallen us while in exile," he asserted, "have been but a preparation for deliverance." The afflictions of exile were the travails of the Messiah, "for in truth, even now Zion grieves over her destruction, she is as a woman in her pains ... The Land of Israel is Israel's and will allow settlement only by Israel." Therefore, "when Israel was exiled from the Land, even though Gentiles live there, it has lain waste." Of course, redemption depended on the observance of "the precepts, the Torah, and acts of piety," but God is merciful and "in the fullness of His Mercy He shall deliver us soon though we be undeserving of deliverance." According to Hassidic legend,

> ... on the eve of the Ninth of Av, the Rabbi of Berditchev would gaze through the window, hoping that perchance the Messiah would come and this day of mourning would become a day of joy. When it was time to recite Lamentations, he would enter the synagogue and burst out crying, "Woe, the Messiah is not yet come! *How doth the city sit solitary!*"

Rabbi Levi Isaac's love for the Jewish people dynamically expressed the yearning for deliverance, one of the motive forces in the Hassidic movement. But the emphasis he placed upon this principle was also significant in another way: its rejection of the ideas of social opposition current amongst the Hassidic masses at the height of the movement's development. In fact, there is no information to indicate that any reforms were made in the plutocratic Kehillah régime during the period of his service as rabbi in the great Berditchev Kehillah. He did, however, protest at blatant social abuses. According to a Hassidic legend, the Berditchev Kehillah leaders at one point passed a regulation to prohibit beggars from soliciting alms from door to door, forcing them to content themselves with the support distributed from Kehillah funds. Rabbi Levi Isaac, only recently appointed to the office of rabbi in the city, scornfully denounced the new regulation as "an ancient custom," originating in Sodom.

The Attempt to revive declining Hassidism;
Rabbi Nahman of Bratzlav

The famous *Tzaddik* of Berditchev was incapable of confronting the increasing vulgarity and decadence of Ukrainian Hassidism, both because of his compulsive compassion and the essentials of his teaching, which were based on a vindication of the Jewish people. The attempt to restore the pristine glory of Hassidism in its native land and to re-create its original impetus as a movement of religious fervour was associated with the teaching and activities of Rabbi Nahman of Bratzlav during his short lifetime (1772-1810).

Nahman was a great-grandson of Ba'al Shem Tov on his mother's side, and of Rabbi Nahman of Horodenka, a friend of Ba'al Shem Tov, on his father's. He was born in Mezhibozh and spent his childhood in that town, which was steeped in the tradition of his great-grandfather, in mystical faith and miracle tales. This atmosphere inevitably strengthened the natural characteristics of a sensitive, imaginative child inclined to fantasy and solitude. When he was confirmed at the age of thirteen, he was married off to the daughter of a wealthy lessee and went to live at his father-in-law's home, in a village near the town of Medvedovka, district of Human (Uman), in the gubernia of Kiev. His great perseverance in the study of the Talmud, Kabbalah and the ethical literature did not prevent him from spending many days in woods and meadows. He used to ride great distances into the forest on horseback or row out on the river far away from the village in order to be alone and listen to "Creation's song to the Creator." "It is better," Rabbi Nahman later advised his Hassidim, "to be alone outside the city where the grass grows, for growing things cause the heart to awaken." He was particularly enchanted by the loveliness of nature in the springtime. "Winter is a time of conceiving, when all grasses and plants are lifeless—and then, as summer approaches, like giving birth, they all awaken and live." During that period, he was influenced by the Lurianic system of mysticism and resorted to a great deal of fasting and self-mortification in order "to shatter the lusts."

Rabbi Nahman was not more than twenty years old when he led a congregation of Hassidim in the town of Medvedovka, but he already saw that his mission was to restore Hassidism to its earlier glory. To obtain the inspiration for this task, he decided to travel to the land of Israel. "Whoever would be a Jew," he used to remark after his return from the Holy Land, "that is, to ascend from level to level, cannot do so save through the Land of Israel." To avoid any chance erroneous idea that he was speaking of the land of Israel in the heavenly sphere, he would add succinctly, "I really mean *this* land of Israel, with its homes and buildings."* On Jews who excused themselves from visiting Palestine because of the hardships of the journey, he commented derisively: "It

---

* In Yiddish: *Ikh mein takke dos Eretzisroel, mit di shtiber mit di haizer.*

often seems to them that they would like to go to the Land of Israel if they could travel thither in comfort but not in pain and hardship; but truly, this is not a total desire, for he who truly wishes to go to the Land of Israel must be content even with proceeding on foot, as it is written, *Go thee out of thy country* (Genesis, 12:1) in other words, even if you have to walk."

The grief of his family did not deter him from undertaking this journey. When his wife and daughters asked who would support them in his absence, he replied, very much in the same vein as Napoleon's grenadier in Heine's poem: "You will go to your father-in-law; somebody will take your older sister into his house to be a young servant girl, who is called a nursemaid; somebody will take your little sister into his house out of mercy, and your mother will be a maidservant, a cook, and all that is in my house I shall sell for travelling expenses." In spring 1798, Rabbi Nahman sailed from Odessa to Istanbul and travelled on from there, even though the members of the local Kehillah tried to restrain him because of the imminent danger to Turkish ships from Napoleon's forces, which were then approaching Palestine. On Rosh Hashanah eve he arrived at Haifa. After spending a few months in Tiberias, he moved on to Safed. However, on learning that the French were approaching Acre, he hastened to the port and escaped the danger in time. After many vicissitudes, Rabbi Nahman arrived home in summer, 1799.

The journey to Palestine proved to be the decisive event in Rabbi Nahman's life. Thenceforth, he considered himself bound to the land of Israel in all his thoughts and deeds. Every country, he stated, had its own melody, and the melody of the land of Israel was so overwhelming that it could entirely eliminate a man's desire for money. He himself had had the privilege of travelling to Palestine and now made great efforts on behalf of the poor of Palestine. He urged his Hassidim to associate with the country in the same two ways: "By making charitable contributions for the Land, one is absorbed into the atmosphere of the Land." Every individual "should entreat God that he may long and yearn for the Land of Israel until he succeeds in arriving there." The Hassidim of Bratzlav even composed a special prayer that they might overcome "all the hindrances and delays and confusions" and reach the Land of Israel.

From his early youth, Rabbi Nahman had believed that he was destined for great things. The conviction of his own genius grew stronger after his return from Palestine. All his numerous aphorisms in praise of himself are classic examples of pathological megalomania. "You," he announced to his Hassidim, "are lucky to have such a Rabbi. I envy you . . ." And on another occasion: "Not even breath escapes my mouth without some innovation." His pupil, Rabbi Nathan, said, "Once I heard his holy mouth utter these words, that through him one could understand something of the Blessed Lord's greatness, for if one perceived how great was his own comprehension . . . how much more so the greatness of the Blessed

Lord . . ." Like all megalomaniacs, he was embittered at the world for not appreciating his greatness. "If the world only knew how much it needs me," he once said when ill, "all would drop to their knees beseeching Almighty God that I recover my health." "You are very petty people and I have nobody to talk to," he complained to his Hassidim without fear of offending them.

The consciousness of his own superiority was not unjustified so far as his own generation of *Tzaddikim* in the Ukraine was concerned. He described them as "*Tzaddikim* of renown through deceit . . . who lyingly boast of their great and miraculous accomplishments." Rabbi Nahman considered the duty of a Hassidic leader to guide his congregation in the fear of heaven and the worship of God and not, like some *Tzaddikim*, to cure barren women, heal the sick and guarantee a livelihood.

The new attitude that Rabbi Nahman adopted, and especially his superior attitude towards the older *Tzaddikim*, aroused the anger of his rivals. About a year after his return from Palestine, he settled in the city of Zlatopol, near the town of Shpola, the seat of the famous *Tzaddik* Aryeh Leib. Leib, known as *Der Shpoler Zeideh* (*The Old Man of Shpola*), was *a guter Yid* (literally, a good Jew) of the type whom Rabbi Nahman ridiculed and condemned. He had been a *melamed* and beadle in a *Bet-Midrash* before he was "revealed" and travelled around the villages and towns attracting the simple people with his stories, curing the sick with herbs, nostrums and amulets, and bestowing his blessings for plenty. He also presented himself as an advocate for the people of Israel, much like Rabbi Levi Isaac of Berditchev, but he actually reached the stage of summoning the Lord to a rabbinical trial. Nonetheless, "Lover of Israel," as he was, caring for the young and a father to the poor (he regularly distributed the *pidyonot* he collected from his Hassidim), he was capable of violent hostility towards Rabbi Nahman, who was trespassing on his domain. The Hassidim of Shpola physically attacked Rabbi Nahman's Hassidim. Not even intervention by Rabbi Levi Isaac of Berditchev could halt the conflict. Rabbi Nahman was forced to leave Zlatopol and in 1802 moved to the city of Bratzlav, which gave him his name.

The years that Rabbi Nahman spent at Bratzlav were the most productive, both creatively and also in propagating his teachings amongst his followers. Almost as soon as he arrived at Bratzlav, he was fortunate enough to gain the close devotion of a young Hassid, Rabbi Nathan of Niemirov, the son of a family of Mitnagdim, who also excelled in Talmudic erudition and possessed outstanding literary ability. His regard for Rabbi Nahman was almost idolatrous and he enthusiastically and accurately recorded both his master's teachings and all his daily conversation. As a result of this collaboration, a book appeared in 1808, *Likutei MOHaRaN* (*The Gleanings of MOHaRaN*, an abbreviation of Rabbi Nahman's title and name), containing the essentials of Nahman of Bratzlav's Hassidic doctrine. In 1810, following a great conflagration that destroyed part of

Bratzlav, the Rabbi moved to the city of Human, where he died at the age of thirty-eight of tuberculosis.

Rabbi Nahman had set out to regenerate Hassidism. The principal aim of his doctrine was to strengthen faith. Faith, to him, was the quintessence of Judaism, the outstanding point of distinction between Israel and the gentiles. The wisdom of the gentiles consisted of "imputing all things to nature"; the wisdom of Israel lay in faith which nullified nature. There was no way of achieving redemption except by strengthening faith "for the exile is due mainly to the lack of faith . . . But it was impossible to acquire faith except by truth, and it was impossible to arrive at truth except by drawing continually closer to the *Tzaddikim*. . . ." The Bratzlav Rabbi thus developed the two Hassidic axioms he had linked together to their extreme limits: the axiom of absolute faith and the axiom of *Tzaddikism*. The *Tzaddik* to him resembled the Creator in that "he himself constantly sheds light, and the only obstruction is in the recipients thereof, . . . for ordinary mortals are preoccupied with this world and therefore are unable to receive the light of the *Tzaddik*." And in accordance with the *Tzaddik's* resemblance to God, who was unfathomable by creatures of the body, Rabbi Nahman taught "that the *Tzaddik* himself is unfathomable, for there is in him nothing fathomable, for he is above man's reason and only through those who are in intimate contact with the *Tzaddik* may one comprehend the *Tzaddik's* level." The *Tzaddik* possessed the power to decree life and death and good and evil, merely by the expression of his face:

> When The Blessed One displays smiling features, life and the goodness thereof are the earth's portion, and if—spare the mark!— the opposite, then the contrary is true. Even so, when the *Tzaddik* laughs, it is good, and so to the contrary.

Even the characteristics which Rabbi Elimelekh's principles accorded to the *Tzaddik* paled in comparison with this system of Ba'al Shem Tov's great-grandson. By elevating the *Tzaddik* to the loftiest position possible, Rabbi Nahman came to the ultimate conclusion that it was every individual's duty to affiliate to a *Tzaddik*. A system of closer association with the *Tzaddik*, peculiar to the Bratzlav Hassidim, was of confessing to the *Tzaddik*, "confessing on each occasion in speech to all that one has done." The resemblance of Hassidism to a kind of Jewish Catholicism is even more pronounced in the dogma of the *Tzaddik* of Bratzlav that non-belief in the *Tzaddik* was tantamount to a rejection of the axiom of faith itself.

Rabbi Nahman continually repeated the theory that the sciences and all types of philosophical speculation conflicted with faith, for "essentially Judaism means but to walk in innocence and simplicity without any subtleties . . . for in truth, it is the brain that should be eliminated . . . And this is the greatest wisdom of all, not to be a man of wisdom . . . for it is the heart that the Merciful One seeks." It is therefore not surprising that he rejected the slightest suggestion of rationalism and all secular studies as "alien thoughts." He was so afraid of the influence of *Haskalah*, "the evil study of sciences, languages and philosophy, which are now spreading, in the multitude of our sins," that he would not tolerate any compromise between blind faith and reason. He not only categorically forbade the "external wisdoms," including the traditional "Seven Pillars of Wisdom," but he even warned against "books of inquiry that great men amongst our fellow Jews have written.* From them, too, one must keep a great distance, for they are very damaging to faith." He asserted that it was possible to distinguish men who had studied Maimonides' *Guide to the Perplexed* by "the change for the worse in the cast of their countenance; the image of God in them has lost its aspect." Small wonder, therefore, that the item in the proposed Jewish Statute drawn up by the Russian government in 1804, which most deeply distressed him was "that Israel should, Heaven forbid, have to teach their sons sciences and languages ... And our master of blessed memory said—recalls his secretary—that for a decree such as this one must declare a day of fasting and cry out to the Blessed One more than against all other decrees." In conformity with the axiom of absolute faith which transcended nature, the Bratzlav *Tzaddik* dismissed all *doktorei* as valueless in the face of the power of prayer—somewhat like certain of the faith-healing sects in present day Christianity. Ba'al Shem Tov's great-grandson had wanted to regenerate Hassidism; in actuality, he reduced it to an ideology of utter cultural reaction, rejecting reason *a priori* as the negation of faith and completely discrediting all the achievements of human intelligence. However, despite his own personal inclination to asceticism, he did not deviate from the Hassidic trend and urged the virtue of joy in the worship of God. "It is a great act of piety always to be joyous, to surmount and repel sadness and melancholy with all one's might," he said. His numerous epigrams on the subject of song and dance not only bore witness to a finely-developed, innate poetical sense, but also revealed the joy of life appearing through his ascetic doctrine: "Every shepherd has his own peculiar melody, depending on the kind of grass and pasture lands he has, for every blade of grass has a song of its own, which is like an entire chapter of song ... And such is the power of melody, that through it one is united to the Blessed One." The virtue of dancing was no less significant than melody in the joy of obedience to the precepts: "When one is happy in the fulfilment of a precept, so much so that it affects one's feet, that is, one dances because of this happiness, that is what is meant when we read *That we may get us a heart of wisdom*" (Psalms, 90 : 12).

Dances were an antidote to anti-Jewish decrees, for "when, Heaven forbid, laws are passed against Israel, by dancing and clapping hands we may secure modification of the laws." Furthermore, the joy of dancing erased the memory of servitude in exile from man's heart and elevated

* i.e. works of philosophy and theology.

him to the atmosphere of the land of Israel. "One exhales the air of the Diaspora and inhales the air of the Land of Israel." He saw virtually the secret of inspiration by the divine spirit in the dizzying dances of *prisiudki*, or deep knee-bending movement, which the Jews of the Ukraine and White Russia adopted from their peasant neighbours. "The *prisiudki* in the dance mean, *I will go down with thee into Egypt*" (Genesis, 46:4).

Nevertheless, his teachings were pervaded by a sense of grief and sadness, very much like the *Weltschmerz* current in contemporary European literature. The tendency to asceticism, the exhortation to penance and confession, the negation of the material world and the struggle against the temptation to evil—all these elements in his doctrine had their foundation in a single aim: the repudiation of the world of action and the evasion of reality.

Undoubtedly, this outlook was, to a large extent, the result of the tuberculosis that was consuming and destroying his body. But in the main, it was based on the tragic contradiction between the aspirations of the visionary to a world of sheer beauty and loftiness and the turbid state of Jewish life in the Ukrainian villages at that time: the depressing bondage of exile, the demoralizing occupations pursued by the liquor purveyors, pedlars and middlemen on the one hand, and the feverish pursuit of money by the wealthy merchants and lessees on the other; the one immersed in degrading poverty, the other in the pettiness of commerce. It was from this aspect of "this world" that the sensitive soul of Rabbi Nahman—like the reactionary romantic poets of his generation—sought escape and refuge in blind faith, in a rejection of sciences, and in the higher spheres of fantasy. Two of his classic parables illustrate his attitude to the vanity and evil spirit that underlay the subjection to this world:

> The temptation to evil is like a person scurrying about amongst people with a clenched fist and none know what he holds therein; and he deceives the people, asking of each, What have I here? And each one imagines that he holds that which he desires, and therefore they all pursue him . . . And then he opens up his hand and behold, there is nothing in it.
>
> The appetites of this world also are like pillars of light that come into a house from the light of the sun, and one perceives with one's senses that they are like pillars because of the sun's radiance, but when one seeks to grasp those pillars of light, one grasps and grasps, but the hands remain empty.

Rabbi Nahman did not conform to the general pattern of Ukrainian *Tzaddikim* either in his Hassidic system or in his relationship with his followers. He also differed in another respect. In 1806, he began to express his ideas in a new literary form, and continued to do so during the last years of his life. He wrote stories, incorporating the full force of his rich imagination and narrative talent, inherited from his great-grandfather. But Ba'al Shem Tov's stories, as we know them, mostly take the form of short parables, only long enough to present his ideas. His great-grandson, on the other hand, told stories for his own and the reader's pleasure, giving free rein to his powers of imagery, concocting plots within plots, and describing experiences in the minutest detail. He endowed these literary creations, which had issued from amongst the people over generations, with an aura of mystic sanctity. In this way, he laid the foundations for the Yiddish and Hebrew *belles lettres* of a new age. The *Tzaddik* of Bratzlav was enchanted by an imaginary world, pleasing to look upon and arousing dormant yearnings. It was a world of kings and viziers, comely princesses, magnificent palaces and fortresses, merchants travelling to remote climes through forests infested with wild beasts and bandits, ships sailing to lands beyond the seas and Robinson Crusoe islands, great adventurers and ragged mendicants wandering from city to city. Nearly all of the thirteen stories, except one about a rabbi and his only son, were based on general themes, though some were placed against a Jewish background, as in the *Story of the Prayer-Leader*. "The Glory of God cries out to us even in the tales of the Gentiles," Rabbi Nahman taught, in conformity with Ba'al Shem Tov's theory. However, all of them, from their very inception, served the author as allegorical vehicles for his doctrinal concepts, in addition to the sheer pleasures he experienced in the product of his own imagination and in developing the tales current amongst the people. A western European contemporary, Goethe, regarded the world solely as the symbol of eternity—*Alles Vergängliche ist nur ein Gleichniss*. It was hardly surprising therefore, that the mystic leader of the Hassidic congregation in a Ukrainian town was confident "that all these things that take place throughout the world certainly are but intimations of higher things, that nothing exists solely in this world. In other words, all these things are but intimations of what is destined to be in the future."

His first story, *The Lost Princess*, was obviously an allusion to the *She'khinah* in exile, and not unexpectedly the author commented "that whoever heard it had thoughts of penitence . . ." The tale about *The Wise Man and the Innocent* was a biting satire on research and academic erudition, which were nothing in face of the innocence of faith. The *Story of the Prayer-Leader* was an obvious morality tale abounding in allegories, each with its own significance.

> The prayer-leader travelled from country to country, and each of these countries regarded as the objective of Man's existence its own particular lust or virtue, in accordance with which it chose its kings: wealth and the pursuit of money, the "profane sciences and heresies," eating and drinking, drunken merriment, distinction, the gift of speech, bodily health, love of athletics, the lust for women. To demonstrate the moral "that truly the only end is to worship God all

one's life ... in Torah, prayer, penitence, and pious deeds," the author presented a series of caricatures, excelling in wit, of the various countries, each pursuing its own imaginary end. He described the sect that saw its prime object in the assiduous consumption of fattening foods and drinks that would foster the growth of the limbs and therefore wanted as a king, "one who possessed mighty limbs and was careful to cultivate the growth of his limbs as described, for in having big limbs he also owned a larger portion of the world, for he occupied more space in the world. . . ."

The sect that craved distinction was only being consistent when it chose for its king an aged beggar, blind and bent, and chief of a gypsy tribe, who was always accompanied by hundreds of members of his clan who took turns in carrying him on their shoulders, "for he was a very irascible man and was very particular about his honour."

The votaries of the cult of speech, of the knowledge of languages and flowery expressions, crowned a king to suit their taste: "They went and found a crazy Frenchman who walked about talking to himself—and knew many languages ... And such a man," Rabbi Nahman explained with his satirical humour, "certainly achieved his end, since he was a linguist who commanded several languages and could talk a great deal, talking as he did mostly to himself. . . ."

Our Hassidic moralizer poured out all the bitterness of his satire on the lust for money, "which reeks offendingly, more than offal." In the plutocratic state of the worshippers of mammon, a utopian state turned upside down, "everything was determined by wealth ... The entire scale of rank was according to the money owned by each individual ... Whoever owned so many and so many thousands and tens of thousands, according to the sum determined by them, was king. And they also had banners, a banner for each measure of wealth to which those owning the appropriate sums belonged, and they enjoyed commensurate privileges. And it was established that if anybody possessed merely such and such a sum of money, he was merely a human, and if he had less than that, he was a beast, or a fowl, and so on. And they had many deities, that is, according to their money, and they arranged services and sacrifices, which they offered up, and they prayed to these gods. They also sacrificed human beings and themselves as well to these gods. . . ."

In the *Story of the Prayer-Leader*, the Rabbi of Bratzlav created one of the finest satires on the capitalist system in world literature, despite its folk-like simplicity and unpolished style.

The long story, *The Seven Mendicants*, is the best of the *Tales*, both in breadth of imagination and in depth of thought and sensibility. Rabbi Nahman, like Scheherazade, told it in instalments, recounting the story of each of the seven on successive nights—except for the last, of which he

said that he would never tell it. These tales of maimed beggars, symbolizing the imperfect state of the world, brought joy to a pair of orphans
throughout the seven days of their wedding. They were, in a way, the
swan-song of a moribund medieval outlook. The skilful story-teller
compressed the essence of Kabbalist and Hassidic mysticism into the tale
of the third mendicant, the stutterer, about "the heart of the world" which
"ever yearns and pines to reach the fountain, with a great longing in all its
soul, and the fountain, too, yearns for the heart. . . ."

Neither Rabbi Nahman's *Weltanschauung* nor his ethical doctrine
were consistent to the very end. In fact, they conflicted in almost every
essential. He was aware of some of these contradictions and tried to
reconcile them by means of his dialectic subtlety. In pursuit of this end,
he taught that the quality of humility, one of the fundamentals of
Hassidism, did not preclude "the individual's occasional deporting himself
with grandeur, as it is written, *And his heart was lifted up in the ways of
the Lord*" (Second Chronicles, 17:6). The precept of joyous worship and
avoidance of sadness was consistent with the instruction "in special
circumstances to have a 'broken heart.' " Innocence was a great virtue,
but "even in innocence one should not be stupid." His own psychological
conflicts were responsible for the chief contradiction in Rabbi Nahman's
doctrine. They were even more marked in the contradictions in his
Weltanschauung. His conflicting views on poverty and wealth were particularly obvious.

It was only natural that the author of a biting satire on the rule of
mammon should praise charity and cultivate the poor. "Why," he exclaimed, "when I see some poor fellow worshipping God in a torn cap,
ragged clothes, and worn-out shoes, I am greatly fond of him." But Rabbi
Nahman was also attracted to the world of the rich both by his personal
inclinations and his outlook on the realities of life. Although he incessantly
denounced the lust for worldly goods in his sermons, he himself was
scrupulously careful with his own money. He was an ascetic, denying all
the delights of this world, but he enjoyed agreeable furnishing and fine
clothes, explaining "that whenever a person dons a becoming new garment, a change takes place in him." Some of his aphorisms related to the
means of achieving wealth, including charity and the faith in *Tzaddikim*.
He even supplied a mystic explanation for the honoured status enjoyed
by the rich in the community as evinced in the Talmudic saying that
"Rabbi Judah HaNasi honours the rich." He said, "Money originates and
flows down from a higher sphere, which is also the source of the living
soul." He ridiculed those who converted to Hassidism "only such people
of lowly rank as the very poor, the ignorant, and such like . . ." and he
urged his associates to gain adherents amongst the scholars, the wealthy and
the élite.

The teachings of Rabbi Nahman thus closed the circle of Hassidic
social development which had begun when his great-grandfather Ba'al

Shem Tov set out to demand redress for the poor and oppressed. **Rabbi Nahman** had embarked upon a reform of the movement; he had proved unable to accomplish his task. Essentially, the glaring contradictions between the rejection of this world in theory and its acceptance in practice, and between ethical judgements on the unimportance and debasing influence of money and the enthusiasm for the advantages of wealth, reflected the deep-rooted contradictions in the social status of the lower middle class. This class still formed the social basis of Hassidism and most of the Bratzlav *Tzaddik's* admirers were drawn from its ranks. It was constantly torn between resentment of a social system which derived its strength from the exploitation and poverty of the Jewish population and its hope "to rise to greatness," to climb the social ladder and attain the rungs of the dominant men of wealth. Its conservatism and withdrawal to the safety of blind faith, which resulted in hostile opposition to all "speculations and sciences," originated in the fear of emergent capitalism. Nevertheless, a more progressive influence had also penetrated this backward environment and signs of it could be discerned in certain of Rabbi Nahman's doctrines and discourses. Although his theory and practice pledged allegiance to the outlook of medieval times, he also advanced startling, brilliantly new ideas, which were both timely and progressive in spirit.

He repeatedly taught that the individual's duty consisted of subservience and self-abnegation before the *Tzaddik* and renunciation of his own powers of reasoning. Nevertheless, he still proclaimed a concept of unadulterated individualism. "In every individual Jew," he stated, "there is a thing of value, a single point, not present in his comrade . . . and in that respect he possesses more than his comrade, influences, enlightens and arouses his comrade . . ." Rabbi Nahman's own personality was markedly dynamic and he was so incapable of conceiving perfection as a finite process that he propounded the daring idea that the individual's continuous improvement was an unceasing process even in the world to come. He expressed another original opinion in conjunction with this view. With incomparable imagery, he declared that in the future, too, even though the earth, in the words of Isaiah, shall be full of knowledge as the waters cover the sea, "in depth of wisdom, every individual will have his own level, just as the waters of the ocean, with the same surface level everywhere, reach bottom at greatly varying depths."

Thus Rabbi Nahman, the spokesman in his native Ukraine for the concept of perfection as attainable through the *Tzaddikim,* also arrived, through consistent ratiocination, at an acknowledgement of the concept of progress, proclaimed by rationalist contemporaries at the other end of Europe widely removed from him in world outlook. The Rabbi from Bratzlav—though he was deficient in all knowledge of "Gentile wisdom" and produced sheer puerile nonsense whenever he attempted to explain relevant scientific matters to his Hassidim—formulated those conclusions, based on the systems of Voltaire and Condorcet, on a broad study of world history and the natural sciences in charming, popular phrases. He said for example: "In fact the Almighty now administers His world much better than He did." Rabbi Hahman explained this progress in the following terms:

> The ways of The Holy One Blessed Be He are unlike those of blood and flesh ... for man dons a new garment which gradually wears out, whereas The Holy One Blessed Be He created the world which at first was defective, and then from time to time he improved it, and each time he valued it more ... Moses improved the world more than had the Patriarchs, Abraham, Isaac, and Jacob; and now there are always *Tzaddikim* who constantly add to this improvement, till eventually the Messiah will come, be it soon in our days, and then the improvement of the world will be complete.

Furthermore, in a similar way as Rabbi Nahman saw the mystical and ethical improvement of the world through the *Tzaddikim*, he also perceived and confirmed the need for substantial progress in the history of the human race. He was excited by the constant rise in the standard of living and conceded that humanity also progressed in religion and in thought:

> Many of the foolish things that misled and confused earlier generations, such as idolatry and the sacrifice of children to Moloch, and many similar acts of foolishness, have vanished.

He seemed almost to be referring directly to Voltaire's view on pacifism, when he protested against the strange contradiction between the advance of civilization and the wars then covering Europe with blood:

> Many of their errors have been done away with by now, yet this error and confusion of warfare has not been abolished. Monarchs war upon each other for some victory and spill much blood in vain.

In fact, he protested that all technical inventions were cleverly enlisted to multiply the carnage and destruction. His pupil recalled that

> ... he made sport of their wise men and jestingly said, "They are, indeed, exceedingly wise, and in their wisdom ponder and inquire how they may devise some wonderful weapon that will be able to kill thousands of living souls at once. And can there be anything more foolish than to destroy and kill many souls in vain?"

The life of Rabbi Nahman, dreamer and saint of Bratzlav, was replete with the sorrow and the tragedy of the contradictions in his own personality and between his dynamic, sublime aspirations and his stagnant, retarded environment. He had not only attempted to reform the Hassidic movement but had also considered the reform of the world as a whole. A romantic, whose life ended before it had reached its prime, he consummated in his own person what he demanded of others: "Life need not be long, but beautiful."

His hope that his preaching would check the decline of Ukrainian Hassidism and strike roots amongst the people, and "that his flame would flicker and flare till the Messiah came" was never realized. After his death, his Hassidim gave strong, faithful, and loving devotion to his memory and counsel until the end of their lives. He had been an elder brother and boon companion to them: it had been his custom to explain his teachings to them in friendly chats while seated "outside the synagogue wall on a block of wood," or strolling with them "on the hill-top outside the city." Just before his death, he repeated his promise that he would forget none of them, for "how could one forget? . . . Does not each and every one of you hold a place in my heart?"

The Bratzlav Hassidim did not choose a new rabbi after the death of their revered teacher. The affinity and solidarity they maintained amongst themselves as a virtually unique sect within the Hassidic movement continued in the face of later grim persecution. The formula of excommunication that the *Tzaddik* of Savran pronounced against the Bratzlav Hassidim was, with the irony of history, a repetition of that issued by the Vilno Gaon only a decade before against the entire Hassidic movement. The Bratzlavites were the exceptions to the Ukrainian Hassidic movement as a whole, which was in a state of progressive deterioration at the beginning of the nineteenth century. The extensive *Tzaddik* dynasties led by two houses, the descendants of either Rabbi Nahum of Tchernobyl or of the *Maggid* of Mezhirich, divided spiritual and temporal rule over the masses of Hassidim throughout the Ukraine between them.

A wide ramification of *Tzaddik* dynasties, mostly founded by the sons and pupils of the *Maggid* Rabbi Yehiel of Zloczow* also existed in eastern Galicia, the Ukrainian province beyond the frontier, which had been under Austrian rule since 1772. However, even during the second generation after Rabbi Ber, the *Maggid* of Mezhirich, Hassidism in Galicia was still markedly and favourably different from that of the neighbouring Ukraine. Not only was the study of the Talmud here more widespread even amongst the Hassidim, as compared with the uncouth ignorance of the Ukrainian Kehillot, but the type of behaviour current amongst the Ukrainian *Tzaddikim* had not yet been adopted in Galicia. In the Ukraine it had been inaugurated by Rabbi Barukh of Mezhibozh, Rabbi Mordecai (Mottl) of Tchernobyl and Rabbi Israel of Ruzhin (great-grandson of the *Maggid*), who revelled in luxurious living and grew rich on *pidyonot* received from lessees holding immense properties, quite frequent in the Ukraine at that time. On the contrary, the personalities most representative of the Hassidic leaders of Galicia still embodied the

* *cf.* above, p. 500.

finest traditions of early Hassidism, both in the simplicity of their bearing and in the social ethos they taught. Hassidic legend credited two East Galician *Tzaddikim*, Rabbi Wolf of Zbaraz and Rabbi Moses Leib of Sassow, with every virtue of ethical sanctity.

Rabbi Wolf of Zbaraz was one of the five sons of Rabbi Mikhel of Zloczow, compared by Hassidim to the five books of the Pentateuch. It was said that in the aura of sanctity surrounding him he symbolized the book of laws for the priests of Israel, i.e., Leviticus. His heart overflowed with love for humanity and he was devoted to all living creatures. "When he travelled in a coach, he protested against beating the horses because of his kindness to animals, and he even objected when they were yelled at." In his great love for his fellow-men, "he would call every individual a *Tzaddik*, even a carter or any ordinary person," and he showed astonishing delicacy in his consideration for the dignity of the individual. The naïveté with which he tried to vindicate all people was humorously described in legends:

> He would not suffer any condemnation of people who played cards into the night for days on end, explaining that by acquiring the habit of being awake nights the card players would reach the stage of nocturnal contemplation of the Torah and prayer ... His extreme naïveté did not prevent him from being aware of social evils and coming to defence of its victims. On being told that his wife was going to court to sue her maid for a sum of money, he dressed to accompany her and to plead the case for the orphan maid, in order to fulfil the words of Job, 31:13: *If I did despise the cause of my manservant, or of my maid-servant, when they contended with me—what then, shall I do when God riseth up? ... Did not He that made me in the womb make him?*

His contemporary, Rabbi Moses Leib of Sassow, possessed similar characteristics except that in his case, the love of his fellow-men was far more active and he was also successful in training in his views and practices pupils who became the greatest figures in Polish Hassidism. He identified himself with the sorrow of all Israel, "as though the trouble had come directly upon him," and engaged in the "redemption of captives ... to feed them and give them to drink and shoes to wear." He healed the sick "both with his money and body." He paid particular attention to orphans, supporting them and caring for them. He washed their hair with his own hands and applied poultices to their sores. He taught that this love for little children was a precept to be obeyed by all men, and, according to tradition, he used to say that "a man who is incapable of sucking the boils and sores of Jewish children has not yet attained to one half the measure of loving Israel." "If you are not a faithful lover of Israel, then you have not yet tasted truly of heavenly reverence," he taught in his rules of conduct *Likutei RaMaL (Gleanings from RaMaL,*

Item 32). Love of Israel was not only a thing of the heart but also involved the dispensing of charity, "that pillar on which the world rests." In fact, the legends concerning the charitable activities of the Rabbi of Sassow expressed the ultimate in the social ethics of Hassidism.

> Once, when he was late for *Kol Nidre* on the eve of the Day of Atonement, they found him in a certain house with a child whose mother had abandoned it in his arms. On the first night of *Se'lichot*, he was absent from the house of prayer because he had gone to light the stove for an ailing, solitary old woman.*

Moses Leib was so humble that he was always the first to greet all who came to the market place, "even Gentiles," like Rabbi Yohannan Ben-Zakkai in Talmudic legend. He obeyed the precept of "sparing beasts all anguish" literally, in a manner which was customary amongst the Hassidim who followed him as late as the twentieth century: he used to visit fairs and "water the calves hobbled in the sun in the market place."

However, the teachings of the Rabbi of Sassow, whose heart overflowed with love for mankind, placed the quality of mercy on a par with the call to social passivity and placidity, exactly as in early Christianity or amongst the Franciscans of the Middle Ages. In some paragraphs of his rules of conduct (Items 20-23), Rabbi Moses Leib repeatedly advised the individual to accept his lot in life and station in society, not to oppose those who are domineering him but rather to throw himself on God's mercy. The days of Hassidism's frontal attack, when the leaders of the movement had protested against social evils and even demanded reforms in the Kehillah régime, had long since passed. The only tradition of original Hassidism that Rabbi Moses Leib of Sassow emphasized, like some of his contemporaries such as Rabbi Levi Isaac and Rabbi Nahman of Bratzlav, was the doctrine that good faith in business transactions was one of the ways to worship the Lord, a manifestation of *In all thy ways acknowledge Him.*

C. THE BEGINNING OF HASSIDISM IN POLAND

The Age of "Miracles" and the "Holy Spirit"—The Maggid of Kozienice, "The Seer" of Lublin, and "The Jew" of Przyuscha

The final barrier to Hassidic expansion was central Poland. The growth of Hassidism in Poland began at the turn of the eighteenth and nineteenth centuries, when Ukrainian Hassidism was already showing definite signs of spiritual decline and deterioration. Before long Polish Hassidism was in full bloom. In Poland, as in Galicia, the movement drew its strength from

---

* *cf. The Rabbi of Niemirov,* from the tales of I. L. Peretz.

the wretched condition of the Jewish population, which was growing progressively poorer as a result of harsh oppression by the régime.

The movement very rapidly captured most of the Jewish population in the towns and villages and even won adherents in the large cities. It had entered Poland through two channels, from the two adjacent regions of Volhynia and Galicia. The two leaders of Polish Hassidism, Rabbi Jacob Isaac, "The Seer" of Lublin, and Rabbi Israel, the *Maggid* of Kozienice, had adopted the doctrine from the great *Maggid* of Volhynia, Rabbi Ber. After the Great *Maggid's* death his distinguished pupil, Rabbi Levi Isaac, recapitulated it for them during his term of office in the Polish town of Zelechow. However, his Galician contemporary, Rabbi Elimelekh of Lezajsk, exerted quite as much influence on the doctrine and conduct of the Polish *Tzaddik* as the Volhynian *Maggid*. According to a later legend, Rabbi Elimelekh is said to have blessed his four oldest pupils and bequeathed to each of them one of his spiritual qualities: to Rabbi Mendel of Rymanow he granted the spirit that was in his brain; to Rabbi Abraham Joshua Heschel of Apt (Opatow) his capacity for speech; to Rabbi Jacob Isaac, the light in his eyes; and to Rabbi Israel, the *Maggid* of Kozienice, he gave his heart.

Polish Hassidism during its development and efflorescence was no different from the Ukrainian movement (steadily deteriorating at that time) in that it maintained the cult of *Tzaddikim* who promised a livelihood and all prosperity, helped in time of trouble, healed the sick, cured the barren, and dispensed nostrums and amulets. Although the Polish Hassidic leaders had not yet succeeded in establishing dynasties of "the sons of holy men" the cult still enabled them to extend their rule throughout the land. But there were never more than two or three *Tzaddic* courts at any one time in all of Poland, as opposed to the fragmentation of the *Tzaddik* dynasties in the Ukraine and East Galicia. These formed the centres of the movement and Hassidim flocked to them from the remotest parts of the country, even from beyond its frontiers from Galicia. The two leaders divided their spheres of influence between them, one at Lublin and the other at Kozienice. At the time when Rabbi Jacob Joseph transferred his seat from Lantzut in Galicia to Lublin, the influence wielded by Rabbi Mendel of Rymanow did not extend beyond central Galicia. A feature peculiar to Polish Hassidism at this period was its combination of the powerful rule of the *Tzaddikim* and exaggerated "applied" *Tzaddikism* with a Hassidic doctrine centred on the concept of deliverance; for example, Rabbi Abraham Joshua Heschel of Apt concluded nearly all of his sermons with a prayer for deliverance, salvation and the coming of the Messiah.

The *Maggid* of Kozienice, Rabbi Israel Hofstein, was most respected by the vast numbers of Hassidim in Poland. A bookbinder's son, he was a brilliant scholar and Kabbalist, as well as the author of many books on *Halakhah*, Kabbalah, and Hassidism. However, he became famous more as a *Tzaddik* who mixed with the people and performed miracles. His reputation as a "holy man" who healed the sick and cured the barren even reached Christian Polish circles, both the nobles and highly placed personages such as Prince Adam Czartoryski, and the ordinary people. He acquired the doctrines of the *Tzaddik's* attributes from his masters, the *Maggid* of Mezhirich, Rabbi Elimelekh of Lezajsk, and Rabbi Levi Isaac. But he laid special stress on the *Tzaddik's* duty "to maintain intercourse with the people, to deal with and supervise their needs," even if they were "inferior to him . . . in order to raise them up and bind them to the Lord and His service." The *Maggid* of Kozienice still carried on the finest traditions of Ba'al Shem Tov and his disciples and spent the money he collected for *Pidyonot*, charms and nostrums on feeding the Hassidim who dined at his table, and supporting the poor, the orphaned and the widowed.

The Kozienice *Tzaddik* was so weak that a great part of his time was spent in bed, but his small, thin body burned with religious ardour. The erotic element in the Kabbalist system was more pronounced in the teaching of Rabbi Israel the *Maggid* than in any other Hassidic ideology.

> For this is the essential thing in the worship of the Blessed One—Rabbi Israel taught—that by a mighty love with flashes of fire from the Divine Flame we should cling to Him, with all those ways of love that we sense in the pleasures of this world, and even more so should the Love of God be in the hearts of His lovers, that they should ever dwell upon it as though sick with the sickness of love.

He taught that the erotic symbolism of the Kabbalist mysteries concerning the communion of the Holy One Blessed Be He with the *She'khinah* principally referred to the "passionate love" between the congregation of Israel and the God of Israel. The imagery and metaphors employed in his sermons invested them with the lyricism of a love song. His descriptions of love through the medium of parables impress us as prototypes for the love stories of I. L. Peretz, Shalom Asch and J. Opatoshu in modern Yiddish literature. They also expressed the peculiar quality of Jewish nuptial relationships between bride and groom, husband and wife, marked throughout the generations with the shyness and modesty instilled by ancestral traditions of marital purity.

His attitude towards God was the uninhibited intimacy of a small boy cuddling up to his father. In the same spirit of intimacy, Rabbi Israel interpreted a pertinent passage from the Tractate of the Fathers to mean "that the *Tzaddik* can nullify all severe decrees by saying to Him of the Blessed Name, 'Lord of the Universe, why must Thou contend with Thy sons that they should return unto Thee in hardship and perforce under evil decrees and afflictions? On the contrary, return them unto Thyself in love and endearment, that they may come back unto Thee in joy, as to a father whom it pleaseth to pardon his son.' "

His theory of deliverance reflected contemporary thought. It was inspired by an overwhelming longing for redemption, which became ever stronger during the world-shaking events of the period and the stream of new anti-Jewish legislation. "*For thou hast stumbled in thine iniquity* (Hosea, 14:2) portended the troubles and the time of the destruction of the Temple, when all of us are drunken and maddened by the heaviness of the destruction and the afflictions and persecutions from day to day . . .," he explained in a Sabbath sermon. At times, he was unable to contain his sorrow and protested to God, saying, "When *Tzaddikim*, though they be totally devoted to Him of the Blessed Name, see how humbled is the City of God and foxes leap in His Temple and all ask, Where is your God? then a mighty flame burns in their hearts and from the vastness of their grief they often begin to protest, saying, 'Why must our lot be less than that of the idol worshippers, for they are tranquil and undisturbed . . . and every one of their cities is built up on its hill, while Thy people of Israel are in exile?' "

Ostensibly all prayers that "The Holy One Blessed Be He may shed upon us in abundance all good things" were only granted because of the *Tzaddikim*, as it was the *Tzaddik* who ordained and The Holy One Blessed Be He who dispensed. But the *Maggid* of Kozienice claimed that this was only by virtue of the prayer for the *Restoration of Zion*, which, he asserted, was the prayer of the truly wretched, *A Prayer of the afflicted, when he fainteth* (Psalms, 102:1):

> For do not our eyes pine from day to day, because we have been in exile close to 1,800 years and there is no responding voice? Yet nevertheless it is only through this prayer of the wretched that all prayers meet with response, for they are all mantled in this one prayer, which is *A Prayer of the afflicted when he fainteth and poureth out his complaint before the Lord* . . . And that is the meaning of the passage in First Kings, 8:48, *And if they pray unto Thee toward their land* . . . it is only toward their land, for it lies in the strength of this prayer which we offer to bring us to our land when our Messiah comes, speedily and in our day, Amen! *

The people of Israel and the land of Israel were therefore inseparably bound together. According to a reliable Hassidic legend, the *Maggid* of Kozienice interpreted the phrase in Numbers, 34:2 as follows: . . . *When ye come into the land*: "You belong to the Land, you hold on to it and cling to it, like a lid attached to a vessel, of which the one without the other has no value." Thus, the people of Israel should cling to their Land and never release their hold on it, as the promise to Jacob in Genesis, 28:13, meant, *The land whereon thou liest, to thee will I give it, and to thy seed*. The *Maggid* explained, "The Land, in which thou hast thrust thy

---

* From this passage in *Kings* I, the Talmud (*Berachot*, 30b) has concluded that a Jew praying in the Diaspora "should face with his heart to the Land of Israel."

fingernails, like one who lieth on his place and moveth not therefrom, to thee will I give it and to thy seed . . ." In fact, Rabbi Israel Hofstein, the *Maggid* of Kozienice, was not content with eloquent sermons but urged the Hassidim of Poland actively to promote Hassidic settlement in Palestine.

The dominant figure in Polish Hassidism was the Kozienice *Maggid's* friend, Rabbi Jacob Isaac Horowitz, Rabbi of Lublin. He was surrounded by many pupils and even exercised his authority over *Tzaddikim* with their own congregations. Rabbi Jacob Isaac had transferred his seat from Lantzut to the Lublin suburb of Czechow (Wieniawa). Before long, however, he had gained so many adherents that he was able to establish a *Kloiz* in the centre of the city of Lublin, where the Chief Rabbi, Rabbi Azriel Horowitz, "the sharp-minded one" (or in Yiddish, "the iron-headed one") vigorously opposed Hassidism. Lublin had been famous for its *Yeshivot*, rabbis and Talmudic scholars since the sixteenth century; the leader of the Polish Hassidim also gained fame there as "the Seer of Lublin." His nickname of "seer" symbolized the secret of Rabbi Jacob Isaac's personality and his strong spiritual domination of tens of thousands of Hassidim. One of his distinguished pupils was the *Tzaddik* Rabbi Uriel of Strelisk in East Galicia, who came to be known as "The Seraph." Rabbi Uriel described the impression that the Lublin Hassidic centre made on the "pilgrims" who flocked there to pay homage to "the Seer":

> The city of Lublin is the Land of Israel: the courtyard of "The Seer's" *Bet-Midrash*—Jerusalem; the *Bet-Midrash* itself—the Mount of the Temple; "The Seer's" quarters—the Court, the Hall and the Hekal; "The Seer's" room—the Holy of Holies, and the *She'khinah* speaks from the throat of "The Seer."

Rabbi Jacob Isaac of Lublin did not attain the level of erudition achieved by the *Maggid* of Kozienice; even as a Hassidic ideologist he was markedly inferior to his friend, whose exegeses and lyrical profundity were great. But the Lublin *Tzaddik* did possess the indelible quality of religious leadership distinguishing the men who had led Jewish messianic movements. He himself was carried away by unbounded religious fervour and was able to inspire his followers with the joy of active faith. His intuition and his confidence that he himself was graced with the spirit of holiness enabled him to implant in the hearts of his Hassidim the belief that he was literally a prophet and a man of God, that he could see from one end of the world to the other and foresee the future to the end of all generations. Even some of his pupils who became great Hassidic rabbis themselves testified that he could detect what a person did, his nature, the origin of his soul, all of his past, and even his previous transmigrations by merely glancing at this man's scribbled note. In addition to his ability as a "seer," the Lublin Rabbi possessed the talent for attracting pupils and ennobling them with his spirit. Pupils from all parts of Poland and even abroad congregated at his court as if it were a school of prophecy. They included his colleagues of his age, hoping to achieve the grace of the holy spirit at this holy place, under the guidance of the holy man.

The atmosphere at the court of "The Seer" of Lublin was not only distinguished by a pervasive air of mysticism but also by a high degree of solemnity in expectation of the coming of the Messiah. The longing for deliverance that had beset the Jews of Poland and Hassidic circles with particular force during the Napoleonic age seemed to have its focal centre at the court of the Rabbi of Lublin. His sermons *Divvei Emet* (*Words of Truth*), repeated at nearly every weekly Portion the call to penitence, by grace of which deliverance would come. He continually emphasized the demand for unity and internal harmony amongst the Jews as the precondition for redemption. But nonetheless, the hope that deliverance was imminent still emerged from his doctrine, that "that time" was the time of "the Messiah's footsteps." This deliverance did not depend solely on penitence, but on "miracles and wondrous acts," and it was within the *Tzaddik's* power to bring about these miracles "at the time of the end" whereby the people would be spared the travails preceding the advent of the Messiah. According to the traditional conception of the advent of the Messiah, the Messiah born of Joseph was destined to be killed before the Messiah the son of David would come. "The Seer" optimistically believed that this calamitous event had taken place when the Kabbalist Rabbi Samson of Ostropol had died a martyr's death in the sanctification of the Name (*Kiddish Ha'Shem*) during the atrocities of 1648.

These homiletical sermons on deliverance would seem to indicate that a hard-core of historical truth was embedded in the vast complex of Hassidic legends: "The Seer" genuinely believed that redemption lay "just beyond the wall," and in his efforts to cause the Messiah to come he tried to unite the *Tzaddikim* of the time in prayer which intended unification.

Most characteristic of these legends was the following:

> Once, on Passover Eve, apparently in 1813, after Napoleon's defeat in Russia, the Lublin Rabbi was aroused to bring the Messiah and before that he actually handed over the secrets of unification to the great men of the generation who were his colleagues. But Rabbi Jacob Isaac was disappointed in his hope, because the other *Tzaddikim* failed to establish contact with him in their devotions.

The frustrated "Seer" felt that the Hassidic leaders were too preoccupied with the trivialities of family life or the *minutiae* of custom, and some were idyllically placid, at a time when a new world was being born and it lay within their power to bring about the redemption. After all, Hassidic doctrine had been founded essentially on the principle that "a

Tzaddik lives by his faith," and that his belief and devotion determined the victory of light over darkness in the forces arrayed in the upper worlds.

However, although the same tradition recorded that "The Seer" of Lublin not only reproached his fellow *Tzaddikim* for being unmindful of deliverance but also for their petty grasp of Hassidism, he himself in fact was also limited in his vision. He expressed the impatience of a persecuted people in its anticipation of deliverance most eloquently, but he never rose above the level of mass Hassidism and fostered it both in his teaching and his conduct. When the elect amongst his pupils were expecting to achieve "the Spirit of Holiness" at "The Seer's" court, their master would be attending to the mundane affairs of large numbers of Hassidim. To him, "sons, life, livelihood," were "the essence and the root of the world's existence" and "the *Tzaddik* was beholden to attract abundance to this world through his prayer and pious thoughts." He was not thinking of meagre incomes when he prayed for his Hassidim but of actual riches, "for one should enjoy the blessings and the grace, an ample share of food and income, and dignified attire, a pleasing dwelling in which all the chambers are good . . ." *A man's money sets him on his feet* recurred in the Lublin Rabbi's teaching. Not merely an income but wealth "is a necessity for heavenly worship," for "many precepts depend for their observance on a man's possession of wealth." Wealth was also appropriate to *Tzaddikim*, according to the Sages, for then it was possible to "worship Him, May He Be Blessed, in the expansiveness of one's heart." It would appear that "The Seer" of Lublin personally lived up to this point of view and thereby exposed himself as a primary target for polemical attack by Rabbi David of Makow, spokesman of the *Mitnagdim* in Poland. Rabbi David cited "Reb Itzig of Lantzut" on many occasions as an example of those *Tzaddikim* "whose obesity has caused him to make *Collops of fat on his loins* (Job, 15:27). They have become rich and risen on the money of others, on *Pidyon Nefesh* (redemption of the soul) payments they collect from the wretched poor . . ." This was not entirely accurate, as it did not take into account the share borne by the wealthy lessees in the Rabbi's "holy flock," and in the heat of debate overlooked the fact that he quite literally fed innumerable poor Hassidim.

Opposition amongst Hassidim to the kind of Hassidism that Lublin represented appeared within "the Seer's" lifetime. With slight alterations, the conflict that had begun in the Ukrainian movement with the activities of Rabbi Nahman of Bratzlav was repeated in Poland. But the Bratzlavite Hassidim remained an isolated sect without any discernible influence amongst the masses of Hassidim in its country. The doctrine that emanated from Przysucha on the other hand, struck root in Polish Hassidism and determined its pattern for future generations.

The other Rabbi Jacob Isaac, "The Jew" of Przysucha, was born about 1766. After studying at *Yeshivot*, he came to Apt (Opatow) and drew close to Hassidism under the influence of Rabbi Moses Leib of Sassow, at that time residing in that town. The tenet of "the Love of Israel" which distinguished the *Tzaddik* of Sassow, was stressed by "The Jew" when he came under the guidance of Rabbi Davidl of Lelow (a town in the vicinity of Czestochowa) who resembled the Galician type of "Lover of Israel" in his qualities and behaviour.

Rabbi Jacob Isaac served at Apt as dean of a *Yeshivah* and then moved to Przysucha, where he supported himself by teaching in the city and neighbouring villages. He soon joined a group of Hassidim to which Rabbi Davidl of Lelow also belonged. A number of trends had converged in this group. Like the first Hassidim in the days of Ba'al Shem Tov and his disciples, its members lived together, shared their slender funds in a common chest, had their meals together, and induced a state of religious ecstasy by alcoholic beverages, dancing and singing. Their mode of life involved the same rejection of convention and the same revolt against middle-class stolidity that had formerly characterized the Hassidic groups of Lithuania founded by Rabbi Abraham of Kolyski. However, the group at Przysucha was far removed from the clowning and provocative cynicism of the "somersaulters" and, above all, it differed from them in its attitude towards learning: its members were scholars who assembled for joint study and kept themselves aloof as a kind of élite in an environment of ignorant Hassidim. They travelled together to the Lublin Rabbi and separated themselves as a "holy band" at his court. Apart from "The Jew" and Rabbi Davidl of Lelow, the membership of this "band" also included a number of other distinguished scholars who later gained reputations as Hassidic leaders. The group was led by Rabbi Jacob Isaac of Przysucha and it was at the court of "The Seer," that he became known as "The Jew." The name was apparently given him mainly out of respect for the master, whose name was identical with his pupil's, though Hassidic tradition tried to embellish "The Jew's" memory further by explaining that he possessed a spark of Mordecai, the modest and humble Jew, for he was so humble that he would recite the Law merely as "another Jew"—*Stam a Yid*.

At first, "The Seer" was pleased with his learned pupil and even referred rabbis and scholars attending the court to him for guidance in Hassidism. Before long, however, "The Jew" began "to lay a table of his own" at the Lublin hostel where he lodged and relations between rabbi and pupil deteriorated until an open rupture took place. "The Jew" became an independent *Tzaddik* during "The Seer's" lifetime and conducted his congregation of Hassidim at his home in Przysucha. In fact, he became the founder of a new school of Hassidism which was more interested in raising Polish Hassidism out of its decline than in opposition to the enemies of Hassidism. "The Jew" espoused the cause of Hassidism as a means of achieving perfection in the worship of God as opposed to the malleable, shallow and stereotyped mass Hassidism issuing from the court of "The Seer." The Hassidim at "The Seer's" court used to extol their master by saying that "at Lublin miracles roll around under the table." In direct opposition to this miracle-Hassidism, "The Jew" asked "is there anything clever about being a miracle-worker? Even those on the meanest level can turn Heaven and Earth upside down. It's being a Jew that's difficult!" The Lublin Hassidim came to their rabbi "to be saved" by his counsel, his blessings, and especially by his miracles. The Hassid who came to Lublin discharged the obligation of "binding himself" to his *Tzaddik* mainly by paying his *pidyon* and placing implicit trust in the *Tzaddik*. "The Jew" interpreted the passage in Exodus, 23:5, *Thou shalt forbear to pass by him, thou shalt surely release it with him*, to mean that the Hassid must assist the *Tzaddik*, "for if he do nothing, only relying upon the *Tzaddik*, then, Heaven forbid, the *Tzaddik* will be unable to perform any action for him." Every individual, not only the *Tzaddik*, was an "ascender," rising from level to level. "The Jew," like Rabbi Nahman of Bratzlav, did not evade a pronouncement in favour of asceticism in his attempt to reform Hassidism. "The Seer" was conducting his court so extravagantly that Hassidim coming to Lublin regarded his household as "the Kingdom of David." "The Jew" maintained that the precept of charity stood above all the positive commandments. When an act of charity was to be performed in atonement for a sin, he disregarded all the legal maxima, even the assessed fifth part of one's property—but no more—as stipulated by the *Gemara*. He based this concept of charity on Job, 2:4, *Skin for skin, yea, all that a man hath will he give for his life*. He himself distributed all his money to the poor. According to legend, he was so careful not to retain a single coin in his home that if he chanced to receive a *pidyon* in the middle of the night, "he roused his household from their sleep to take the money to certain of the city's poor."

Despite the many aspirations for restoring the virtues of Hassidism that the *Tzaddik* of Bratzlav and "The Holy Jew" of Przysucha shared in common, the principal difference between their two systems was obvious. Rabbi Nahman of Bratzlav replaced the cult of mass *Tzaddikism* with a new doctrine of *Tzaddik*-worship that referred mainly to himself. "The Jew" of Przysucha instead maintained that the *Tzaddik's* function consisted in guiding his flock in piety and reverence. Though both the Bratzlav *Tzaddik's* faction and "The Jew's" Hassidism were élite congregations of virtuous men, "The Jew's" Przysucha Hassidim were unique in that they excelled in their capacity for learning. A slander against "The Jew" reported to "The Seer" by one of his followers, was not unjustified in stating that "The Jew" associated with scholars. His contemporaries had already begun to adopt the peculiar combination of "worshipping God in Torah and prayer alike," the chief innovation in the Przysucha school of Hassidism. "The Jew's" pupils, Rabbi Simha Bunim of Przysucha and Rabbi Mendel of Kotzk, also followed this trend and it was the view taken in the propagation of Hassidism in Poland during later generations. As in Poland, the type of Hassidism that prevailed in Galicia was that established by Rabbi Mendel of Rymanow and Rabbi Naphtali of Ropczyce, who were also remote from any similarity to the miracle-working type of *Tzaddik*.

The triumph of the Przysucha school of Hassidism was not fortuitous. The revival of Hassidism entailed a new advance and the need for adaptation to new social classes. The restraints that the school placed on miracle-working *Tzaddikism* and its frequent repetition of the obligation to study the Law attracted learned circles. As a result, the gulf which divided it from the Mitnagdim faction as a whole began to be bridged. Hassidism had been depleted of its original ideological content and could only achieve its aim of strengthening faith by intensifying the study of the Law. In this way, the Mitnagdim gained confidence in the value of the Hassidic doctrine of "the obligations of the heart" as a means of fortifying traditional religion—already being undermined by the forerunners of the *Haskalah* movement from within, in collusion with the government from without.

Not surprisingly, in view of this development, polemical literature by the Mitnagdim in Poland against the *Hassidim* almost completely lapsed when Przysucha Hassidism appeared. The struggle against Hassidism was eventually resumed by the *Maskilim*.

Przysucha Hassidism also marked a turning point in the attitude of the movement towards the concept of deliverance. "The Jew" of Przysucha was in fact overwhelmed by the atmosphere of imminent deliverance which prevailed in Polish Hassidism during the Napoleonic Wars. But he nevertheless expressed disapproval of "those *Tzaddikim* who already reveal the Messianic consummation, though it is truly a secret . . ." In this matter, "The Jew" again followed a course of his own in Hassidism, in contrast with "The Seer's" system. Just as he was opposed in principle to the Hassidism of "miracles" and "the Holy Spirit," he did not consider the means to redemption to lie in the magic of *Tzaddikim* but in the wholehearted penitence of the people as a whole: "Before the Messiah comes, there will be a great thirsting for worshipping God with all one's heart."

All three leaders of the Hassidim in Poland, as well as the leaders of the Galician Hassidim, died within the space of two years, as if history itself were signalling the end of an era in Hassidism. "The Jew" of Przysucha died during the Feast of Tabernacles in 1813; the *Maggid* of Kozienice on Tabernacles Eve, 1814; about six months later, he was followed by Rabbi Mendel of Rymanow; while on the Ninth of Av, 5575 (1815), "The Seer" of Lublin passed away. Hassidic legend regarded the death of the three *Tzaddikim* within a year as heavenly retribution for their desire to hasten the end. In fact, this legend reflected the subsequent development of Hassidism, when the tense anticipation of deliverance associated with the Napoleonic age had abated and disappeared. The Przysucha school with its policy of penitence and long enduring hope in the Messiah who would surely come "though he tarry," was triumphant.

At about the same time, the leaders of Ukrainian Hassidism also died: Rabbi Barukh of Mezhibozh and Rabbi Levi Isaac of Berditchev, the "old Man of Shpola" and Rabbi Nahman of Bratzlav. The leader of the White Russian Hassidim, Rabbi Shneur Zalman of Lady was also dead by then. The older *Tzaddikim*, who had had the privilege of hearing the teachings of the Great *Maggid*, Ba'al Shem Tov's disciple, made way for a new generation of Hassidic leaders throughout eastern Europe.

CHAPTER THIRTEEN

BEGINNING OF THE HASKALAH MOVEMENT IN EASTERN EUROPE

A. *ECONOMIC, SOCIAL AND POLITICAL BACKGROUND OF EAST EUROPEAN HASKALAH*

The Difference Between the Haskalah *in Eastern and Western Europe*

At the opening of the nineteenth century when Hassidism was in full flower, the *Haskalah* movement had made its first small beginnings amongst the Jews of eastern Europe. The economic, social and political feudalism that hampered the productive capacity of eastern Europe also impeded the cultural progress of the entire population, including the Jews. East European Jewish culture was stagnant and sealed off from all European cultural influence in an environment of oppressed and brutalized peasants, uncouth burghers, domineering nobles and fanatical priests. The complete absence of secular elements in its cultural life made this body of Jewry unique in Europe. The new religious movement of Hassidism had only added homiletical expositions, ethical books, Kabbalist works and Hassidic doctrine to the normal spiritual diet of the people, which had consisted exclusively of the Talmud, Codifiers, Commentaries and Super-commentaries. Secular science, physical or social, was non-existent among the east European Jews, and there was no trace of secular poetry or *belles lettres*. Even knowledge of the Old Testament had been limited mainly to the Pentateuch, which served as the basis of religious law. Only exceptional individuals were familiar with the grammar of the Hebrew language. The antiquated economic pattern which lay behind the petrified traditional environment was reinforced by religious ultra-conservatism. The Jewish population of Poland, Lithuania, White Russia and the Ukraine was thronged into those occupations which had become peculiarly its own—liquor purveying, trade, brokerage and a few handicrafts. This cul-de-sac in their economic activity was the primary cause of their increasing impoverishment. But this was not all. Legislation by the feudal government, municipalities and craft guilds blocked their entry to agriculture and various manual vocations. Their own ruling class, the *parnassim* and the rabbis, aligned themselves with the feudal régime and took fanatical care to preserve traditional economic relationships. The leaders of the popular religious movement, the Hassidic *Tzaddikim*, were equally conservative. To this stifled atmosphere the *Haskalah* movement brought a fresh current of cultural, educational and socio-economic reform. But against such a background, the first manifestations of *Haskalah* could not appear until the end of the eighteenth century, at a time when the slow rise of capitalism had made incursions into eastern Europe's feudal system.

Industrial capitalism made an appreciable advance in eastern Europe at the end of the eighteenth century, especially in the Russian Empire. Here, the merchants of the burgher class were active in this sphere, together with the nobility. In the backward Kingdom of Poland, too, the magnates had laid the foundations of "manufacture" (i.e., production in non-mechanized factories) on their estates.*

The slow development of industry and productive relations met parallel changes in the political régime. Poland's political reforms during its final decades of independence had been permeated with the spirit of enlightened absolutism. But they had been short-lived and eventually gave way to the absolutist régime of the three partitioning powers. A cultural advance also occurred in eastern Europe, in the wake of economic progress and the establishment of modern statehood. However, it was still mainly the preserve of enlightened aristocrats, from whose ranks the senior officials who supported reform were also recruited. Universities, such as those at Krakow and Vilno, were removed from the jurisdiction of the clergy and liberated from theological domination. State-sponsored academies were established and the courts of noblemen became meeting-places for writers. By the beginning of the nineteenth century, polite literature and several branches of science in Poland and Russia had already reached western European standards. The first schools founded by the state were providing an elementary education for the urban population, although educational institutions were still rare in the rural areas.

The progress of capitalism within the Jewish Pale in underdeveloped eastern Europe was immeasurably slower than amongst the Jews of central Europe. In Poland, Lithuania, White Russia and the Ukraine their participation in the industrial development initiated by the Polish magnates was still negligible. The emergent Jewish modern middle class in these countries was primarily developing its capital assets in the trade fostered by the economic advance. A special group within this class had business connections with the state exchequer. They were contractors and army suppliers, who were especially numerous during the Napoleonic period, and the revenue collectors, some of whom held leases on the liquor monopoly in Russia and the tobacco monopoly in Galicia. This group also included the Jewish tax farmers, who collected the kosher meat tax in the Grand Duchy of Warsaw and both meat and candle lighting tax in Galicia. A thin stratum of intellectual professionals, similarly a new phenomenon in the social structure of east European Jewry was attached to this new middle class in economic position and outlook. They included the

---

* *cf.* above, Chapter Nine, pp. 300, 302.

university-trained physicians, more common now than in the preceding period, as well as officials, agents and accountants employed by the wealthy group, and the tutors whom they engaged in their homes. In Austrian Galicia, scores of teachers in the government-sponsored schools for Jews added to their numbers.

Not surprisingly, the large cities of Warsaw, Vilno, Lwow, and, above all, the two great centres of Jewish foreign trade, Shklov in White Russia, and Brody in Galicia, formed the focal centres for the nascent *Haskalah* movement in eastern Europe. The number of subscriptions to the organ of the movement, the *Me'asef*, provides an infallible index of a positive attitude towards *Haskalah* ideas. This criterion proves conclusively that the *Haskalah* had only acquired a very few followers in eastern Europe at that time, and these mostly in Shklov, Brody and Vilno.

The east European *Haskalah* movement expanded as a result of changes in the political and national life of the countries in the area but it found a ready-made pattern to follow in the spiritual revolution that had taken place in German Jewry. The close commercial ties between the east European Jewish trader and Germany, which had for the most part been maintained by frequent attendance at the important German fairs, naturally played an important part in the diffusion of western *Haskalah* ideas amongst the Jewish populations in the east. All of the east European *Haskalah* writers had had direct contact with Berlin *Haskalah* circles. The forerunners of the *Haskalah* movement in Poland and Lithuania, Israel Zamosc and Solomon Dubno, and even moderates such as Judah Hurwitz and Judah Leib Margalioth, had spent some time in Berlin. They had made the acquaintance of Moses Mendelssohn, who was glorified by Jewish *Maskilim* in all countries as the leader of the movement. Outstanding Lithuanian and Polish *Haskalah* writers such as Barukh Shik of Shklov and Judah Ben-Ze'ev and Mendel Lefin of Satanow had established friendly relations with the Berlin *Maskilim* when they stayed in the city. The itinerant rhetorician, Tobias Feder, had also reached the cities of Germany in the course of his wanderings.

Personal contact with the German *Maskilim* gave an added stimulus to the pioneers of east European *Haskalah* in their endeavour to follow the Berlin example in their literary and social activity. In fact, the common denominator of the Enlightenment programme in both areas of Europe was based on the common aims of the emergent Jewish new middle class, which sustained this cultural trend. Demands, first heralded by Wessely and the *Me'asef* writers were now also expressed in eastern Europe: the reform of the educational system and the establishment of modern schools; the promotion of culture amongst the Jews by the propagation of the sciences; the fostering of "pure" Hebrew through a knowledge of grammar and more thorough Biblical studies; the spread of knowledge of modern languages, especially the dominant language in the country of residence; the desegregation of the Jews from the gentiles and the cultivation of affinity between all men "as human beings"; loyalty to the régime and, above all, to "the gracious monarchs of our day"; and a change in the defective economic structure of Jewish life by a movement into the productive activities of agriculture and "the useful arts."

Nonetheless, east European *Haskalah* displayed some unique features from the beginning and these became increasingly prominent during the century of its development. The rationalism of the Polish and Lithuanian *Maskilim* offered a far more moderate *Weltanschauung* than had the *Me'asef* at its zenith. It never reached the level of deism propounded by Euchel, Wolffsohn and Saul Berlin. The primary factor behind this moderation was the underdeveloped, almost exclusively commercial, Jewish middle class in these countries, compared with the industrial Jewish middle class of Prussia. The time factor was also very important in this context. In Germany, the *Haskalah* movement had reached its peak when rationalism dominated the European intellectual world and the ideas of Voltaire and the Encyclopedists dominated Enlightenment circles. When *Haskalah* first arrived in Poland and Lithuania, Enlightenment was already on the decline in Germany, and the Napoleonic Wars were in progress. During the ensuing period of reaction, religion was rehabilitated by the European middle class and patronized particularly by the reigning monarchies. Furthermore, for many decades, and until the age of liberal reform in Russia, the peculiar conditions of Jewish life in eastern Europe precluded the formation of an assimilationist wing which had been so influential in the German *Haskalah* movement. Programmes for assimilation which did appear in east European *Haskalah* were arbitrary, isolated and exceptional. They arose from temporary circumstances, such as the forced germanization decrees in Galicia or the formation of a privileged Jewish plutocratic group at St. Petersburg outside the Pale of Jewish settlement in Russia.

From its inception, *Haskalah* in Poland and Lithuania, unlike its German counterpart, was closely associated in its spiritual roots, literary creativeness and propaganda with the broad popular masses. This remained the case even when the masses continued unmoved by the new slogans. In contrast with the small, isolated German Kehillot, the Kehillot in eastern Europe were populous centres of a humming community life with a variegated pattern of national existence. No gulf gaped here between the two social extremes of *haute finance*, on the one hand, and a weak lower middle class living in poverty on a pedlar's earnings, on the other. Instead, a large and strong middle class bridged the social and cultural gap between the newly consolidating middle class and the masses of shopkeepers, artisans, liquor sellers and innkeepers. Thus, east European *Haskalah* was not entirely devoid of popular elements, despite the fact that it conflicted completely with the Hassidic folk movement. At times, its men-of-letters even undertook an affectionate "descent" to the mode of thought and robust vernacular of the simple people, in their public Enlightenment campaign.

The link between the prolific creation in the Hebrew language during the golden age of Spanish Jewry, the Jewish renaissance in Italy and the *Haskalah* movement of the eighteenth and nineteenth centuries, presents one of the most remarkable manifestations of historical continuity in Jewish cultural development. Like the *Maskilim* of Germany, who had been educated in the Jewish grammarians and the scholars and poets of the Middle Ages, those of Poland and Lithuania also drew copiously on this literature. It seemed almost to have been revealed anew to *Bet-Midrash* recluses weary of intensive study of the Talmud and the Codifiers. The stimulating influence of Maimonides was especially great in shaping the rationalist outlook of the *Haskalah* generations. However, medieval Jewish science and philosophy played a far larger part in east European *Haskalah* than in the German movement. In the first place, knowledge of Russian and Polish was not as widespread amongst the Jews of eastern Europe as German amongst German Jews. Secondly, the natural sciences, and especially philosophy, in these countries had not attained the German level. In fact, a Lithuanian *Haskalah* writer, Manasseh of Ilya, acquired his knowledge of the sciences and philosophy exclusively from Hebrew books. Consequently, the scope of *Haskalah* literature in eastern Europe was incomparably broader than in Germany. The division of labour between Hebrew and the gentile languages, envisaged in Naphtali Herz Wessely's programme, which assigned the "knowledge of Humanity" to the language of the state, found no place here.

From its first appearance in eastern Europe, the *Haskalah* movement was committed to the enormous task of disseminating knowledge amongst the Jews. Its greatest writers, imbued with pioneering endeavour, undertook to lead Jewry forward against the intractable conservatism of staunch orthodoxy.

B. *INCIPIENT CULTURAL REVIVAL AMONGST TRADITION-ALIST JEWS*

Elijah, the Gaon of Vilno, and the Dubno Maggid

The declining years of Talmudic Jewry were still brightened by the personality and work of Rabbi Elijah Ben She'lomo-Zalman, "The Gaon of Vilno." A genius in Talmudic doctrine, secluded day and night in his study, he seemed to personify all the generations of scholars who had ever emptied their hearts of "the vanities of this world" and mortified themselves in the Tabernacle of the Torah. His custom of studying the

Torah in prayer shawl and phylacteries symbolized, as it were, the link between the Torah and the Precepts, the two pillars of traditionalist Jewry in "The Service of the Creator." His extreme conservatism and exacting orthodox zealotry were unyielding on the minutest detail of preceptual observance and caused him to wage total war on Hassidism, which was making inroads into the dominant Kehillah régime and exalting religious emotion above both preceptual observance and Torah study. Nevertheless, his nobility of soul and sharp intellect enabled him to rise above the petrifying conventions which had pervaded Talmudic Judaism in the course of generations. In his attempt to solidify the study of Talmud and the Codes, he introduced method and criticism, based not only on his spiritual qualities and scholarship, but also on the spirit of the age of rationalism. However, Talmudism had declined too far for these measures to be effective. The fundamentals of the new method for the study of the ancient Torah introduced by the Vilno *Gaon* fulfilled a historical function quite contrary to his intentions: instead of reinforcing the traditional spiritual world of east European Jewry, they undermined its foundations and hastened its decline.

The *Gaon*'s opposition in principle to exaggerated casuistry (*pilpul*), the established method of teaching the Talmud and the Codifiers in *Yeshivot* and schools, was a startling innovation. As opposed to this casuistry, which had become an end in itself, he believed that the purpose of Torah study was to clarify the laws which were based on the Written and Oral Code. In order to secure a more profound and more comprehensive knowledge of *Halakhah*, he resolved to base it on its original sources. He regarded the Talmud as a sacred, unshakeable, undisputed source of authority by contrast with the *Shulhan Arukh* (which he had permitted himself to criticize wherever he believed that it deviated from Talmudic law). But even where the Talmud was concerned, he did not refrain from employing the same methodical criticism that was an innate part of his intellectual approach. The *Gaon* spent days and nights on end, throughout his life, amending versions and formulae in the Talmud and *Halakhic-Midrashim* which had become distorted through various recopyings. As the result of these amendments, he shed new light on many passages in Talmudic literature which had hitherto been obscure in meaning or else buried beneath an accumulation of baseless theories and irrelevant *pilpulist* subtleties. His method of studying the origins of the laws and their historical development led the *Gaon* Rabbi Elijah* to extend his inquiries back to the *Halakhah* literature parallel to the Babylonian Talmud and earlier. In this way, he reintroduced his own generation to the Jerusalem Talmud, the study of which had been completely neglected because of the hegemony of the Babylonian Talmud. Following his retrospective method, he turned back even further to contemplate the *Halakhic-Midrashim*,

* This full title has provided the mnemonic, or abbreviation HaGRA (*Ha'Gaon Rabbi Aeliyahu*) by which the Vilno *Gaon* is frequently referred to.

or expositions, compiled before the completion of the Mishnah: the *Me'khilta* on Exodus; the *Sifra*, on Leviticus; and *Sifre*, on Numbers and Deuteronomy. He also studied the *Tosefta* and the smaller Tractates to put the study of *Halakhah* on a comparative basis.

This original method of inquiry into the *Halakhah* necessarily led the Vilno *Gaon* on to a deeper study of the Old Testament as the foundation of the Oral law. As the Scriptures could not be properly understood without a basic knowledge of Hebrew grammar, he diligently pursued this task. He even wrote a Hebrew grammar himself, which was published posthumously (as were all his works) as *Elijah's Grammar*. The *Gaon* advocated systematic education in keeping with his own method of studying the Torah, proceeding from the simple to the complex, a system which his contemporaries entirely disregarded though the *Chapters of the Fathers* had explicitly advised it.

Reverently named the "Hasiol (Saint) of Vilno" by his contemporaries, the *Gaon* considered the only object in life for a Jew to be unceasing study of the Torah, day and night; for the Sages had declared, *In it there is everything, and in it thou shalt gaze, and thou shalt never move therefrom*. In his extreme fanaticism, he despised philosophy, even medieval theological inquiry, dubbing it "accursed." True, his own profundity, as well as the new trends of thought emanating from Germany and spreading through Lithuania, restrained him from a total negation of the "sciences." However, he approved of them only insofar as they were useful auxiliaries to the study of Talmud and the Torah. His basic method of study led him on from the Bible to the problems of the geography of Palestine. This resulted in a composition entitled *The Shape of the Land*, including a map which showed the division of the country amongst the tribes of Israel. Again, in order to explain Talmudic laws involving trigonometry, he especially wrote a book entitled the *Triangled Pilaster*. He encouraged his pupils and colleagues to translate scientific works into Hebrew, claiming that "all the sciences necessary for our Holy Torah are contained therein"; he even expressed a wish to see the work of Flavius Josephus translated. The *Maskil*, Barukh of Shklov, in the introduction to his own translation of *Euclid* (Amsterdam, 1780) reported a conversation in 1778 when the *Gaon* had encouraged him "to translate into our Holy Tongue whatever of the sciences it is possible," not only for their value to an understanding of the Torah but also out of a feeling of national pride.

The Vilno *Gaon* thus anticipated the *Maskilim* by indicating the need to study the "sciences." Similarly, he to some extent prepared the ground for the *Haskalah* movement by his programme of educational reforms and by emphasizing the advantage of studying the Bible and Hebrew grammar. Not surprisingly therefore, forerunners of moderate *Haskalah*, such as Barukh of Shklov, Solomon of Dubno and Manasseh of Ilya, courted his favour and were welcomed into his company. However, despite this apparent affinity, the *Haskalah* movement could not progress unless it freed itself from the medieval outlook which was the basis of the *Gaon's* Judaism. No lasting compromise between the old and the new world of ideas was possible. Not long after the death of the Vilno *Gaon*, the ultra-orthodox ranks adopted his name and teachings to lead the defence of old-style Judaism against the rise of *Haskalah*. Their wrath was experienced at close quarters by Manasseh of Ilya who was not even saved by the fact that he had been a favourite of the departed *Gaon*.

The Vilno Gaon had tried to revive *Halakhah* by new methods of study. Similarly, the *Maggid* of Dubno, another of his close associates, was something of a last manifestation of creative power in the realm of moral teaching which had generally atrophied with age. The Dubno *Maggid*, Rabbi Jacob Krantz (1740-1804), was a native of Zdzieciol near Vilno. He served as "a spokesman of justice and preacher of uprightness" at Mezhirich, Zolkiew, Dubno, Chelm and Zamosc, where he finally died. He was also an itinerant preacher and his travels led him to numerous Polish and Lithuanian Kehillot, and even to Germany. Known to the populace simply as the "*Maggid* of Dubno," after the Volhynian city where he lived continuously for eighteen years, he was to win the love and reverence of future generations. The unique qualities which endeared him to the common people more than any preacher before or after, were inherent both in the form of his sermons and the ideas they conveyed.

The Dubno *Maggid* was the spiritual heir to the leading masters of legend and homiletics. The tradition he followed had begun with the Mishnaic *Tannaim*, had continued with their successors, the *Amoraim*, and culminated in Rashi and Judah, the twelfth-century Hassid of Regensburg. A warm, folk-like charm invested his sermons and he expounded his doctrine in the language of the common people, in words which appealed to their hearts. He possessed the imagination of a poet and a powerful talent for observing events. Even the parables he composed followed the pattern set by the ancient masters of legend. However, the parables in Talmudic and Midrashic legend were mainly allegorical and therefore used words economically, confining themselves to the bare essentials required to eucidate a moral. The Dubno *Maggid*'s parables, on the other hand, were affably and expansively related. He captured the imagination and captivated the hearts of his audience with all the details of a plot, like a popular storyteller. The Hassidic masters of parable had, of course, preceded the Dubno *Maggid* in this respect. Some of them, like Ba'al Shem Tov and his great-grandson, Nahman of Bratzlav, had even surpassed him in the splendour of their creative imagination. The unique feature of the Dubno *Maggid*'s parables was the fact that most of them were drawn from the experiences of this world and the vicissitudes of daily life. Naturally stereotypes were not lacking and kings and royal princes, dignitaries, and villagers, frequently recurred. However the allegories were of small account compared with the abundance of parables derived from daily reality and experience. Thanks to this aspect, his sermons reflected Jewish life in Poland and Lithuania at the end of the eighteenth century.

The Dubno *Maggid* was a typical devout believer as far as his *Weltanschauung* was concerned, still adhering to the dualistic doctrine of the Middle Ages: man's purpose was to obey the precepts and study the Torah, to ensure that the inclination towards goodness prevailed over the inclination to evil in order to be rewarded with life in the world to come. True pleasure was spiritual, and a man's perfection lay in the perfection of his soul, which could be attained through sincere and loving worship of the creator. However, the most remarkable feature of his sermons was the emergence of an incipiently positive and realistic attitude towards the world of action—a message of regeneration—from out of the framework of an antiquated doctrine of man. In common with the Hassidim, the Dubno *Maggid* was far removed from medieval asceticism, and like them too, he unwittingly challenged the dualistic doctrine with its total negation of this world. But whereas the Hassidim tried to overcome duality by hallowing materiality and raising it to the level of spirituality, the Dubno *Maggid*'s system was based on concessions to these "ways of the flesh" which were necessary for the "civilization of the world" and indispensable to divine worship.

However, the sharpest contrast between the attitudes of this *Mitnaged* preacher and Hassidism with regard to the experiences of this world, on the one hand, and worship of the creator, on the other, was in the Dubno *Maggid*'s method of dealing with the quality of trust. The idealistic monism of the Hassidic outlook subordinated all human behaviour, in repose and in action, to the quality of trust. It emphasized the significance of this quality in matters concerning livelihood. The *Maggid* also made the quality of trust basic to his doctrine of heavenly reverence, but his tendency towards realism caused him to limit its function to areas not directly touching economic affairs. His doctrine in this matter was based on socio-psychological observation, perfected by the Talmudic and Maimonidean attitude towards those human actions "necessary for the settlement of the world" (i.e., civilization—a Talmudicism). Human labour had created civilization, thus complementing the act of Genesis. In fact, the impulse to work was only the inclination to evil, motivated by "foolishness" and lack of trust in the creator of the universe. But this inclination was reminiscent of Mephistoles in Goethe's *Faust*, who thirsted for evil and nevertheless performed good deeds. The *Maggid* thought that ". . . were trust implanted in the soul, man would naturally despise his labours and would not exert himself so heavily on realizing that the circumstances were powerless to supply his daily bread, without the consent of the Supremely Merciful One, May He Be Blessed."

As things were, man's role in the building of civilization increased with the growth of man's "foolishness, stupidity and folly," in the pursuit of pleasures, luxuries, and the other "vanities of this world." The *Maggid*'s psychological system was based on an aphorism of Maimonides (in his introduction to the Talmudic Tractate *Ze'ra'im*)—"Were it not for the mad, the world would remain waste." He taught that "as an article becomes more difficult to obtain and preserve, its value as appraised by human beings increases over that of available objects ... e.g., pearls and precious stones." This explained the fact that people were prepared, again in the words of Maimonides (ibid.) "to travel to distant lands, to go down to the sea in ships ... to imperil themselves in order to find and return with precious stones wherewith to trade ..." The desire for luxuries was also a necessary factor in economic development, as it provided employment for many workers. It would appear that the big wholesale merchants, whose activities formed the favourite subject of the *Maggid*'s parables, also inspired him with their spirit and outlook, that of mercantile capitalism.

In the same way as man's innate appetite led to continual progress in economy and civilization, so was he endowed with an insatiable desire to fathom the secrets of knowledge. With the strength of that desire "they (the Just) travel onward and upward to that perfection unceasingly and forever desired for the world by Him, May He Be Blessed." The *Maggid* did not reject secular disciplines as such. He was completely convinced that "whoever engages in Torah for its own sake ... will eventually be honoured by having revealed to him the Torah's secrets and those of all the 'external sciences.' " On the other hand, he applied the passage in Proverbs, 1 : 20, *Wisdom crieth aloud in the street* to him "who is empty of the wisdom of the Torah and occupies himself with the external sciences."

The flashes of realistic insight that marked the Dubno *Maggid*'s outlook were also evident in his conception of deliverance and the restoration of Zion. This idea emerged from most of his sermons. Undoubtedly, like most of the leaders of his generation, whether Mitnagdim or Hassidim, he was aroused by the historical events of the period to a more acute longing for deliverance. Several of his sermons were composed during the last years of his life, when the triumph of the Revolution in the west, and especially reports that Napoleon planned to revive the Jewish people's state in its own land, had given birth to new hopes of imminent deliverance amongst the people. Needless to say, the *Maggid* regarded deliverance as heavenly salvation which depended solely on repentance. He even glorified deliverance as spiritual redemption, as the end of the days, when "The Holy One Blessed Be He will renew His leadership on high over nature." But even while he voiced these tenets of the traditional faith, the Dubno *Maggid* revealed that he was essentially a popular leader at heart, grieving over the palpable afflictions of exile and dedicated to the economic and political improvement of his people in the land of its birth.

The *Maggid* of Dubno with his penetrating observation of the labour-based economy of society could not be oblivious to the unsound occupational structure of Diaspora Jewry. His longing for the restoration of Zion also concealed a deep yearning for the life of tilling the soil, ploughing, sowing, and harvesting. He constantly compared the life of the Jews "formerly, when we inhabited the land of the living, on the Holy Soil, each under his grapevine," with their questionable sources of income in exile. A sound situation consisted of

> each supporting himself by his toil, the body deriving sustenance from bodily cultivation of the land . . . But all this was so when we existed on our own soil . . . Now it is no longer so, when we have no known enterprise for maintaining our households, neither threshing-floors, nor wine-presses, neither the dew of the heavens nor the fat of the earth, nought save scheming from morn till night. And even at night there is no respite, but only thoughts concerning trade and how to procure one's bread from afar.

Not even holiday festivities were perfect in the Diaspora, "For now we have neither field nor vineyard in which to rejoice in gathering our fruits from the field." The *Maggid* continually reiterated the sad truth that in the Diaspora the Jews only subsisted on what the Gentiles left over, for "the dew of the heavens and the fat of the earth are no longer ours but theirs, for theirs is the land . . . They have a patrimony of field and vineyard." Furthermore, the Gentiles themselves "plunder and aggrandize one another, so what have we to hope for from them? . . ."

In exile, not even riches were assured their owners:

> . . . Even our lives hang in the balance and we are never sure of them for so much as an hour, let alone our money and property . . . It is like the man who erected a splendid building on a large river, so formidably frozen over in the wintertime that he thought it was solid ground . . . Then it became warm and the sun shone, the frost lifted, the ice melted and ran, and the entire building sank . . .

However, the occupations that the Jews of the Diaspora pursued were not only insubstantial but were "tainted bread . . . a crime of deceit, encroachment and such like." It was of this bread, "contaminated by encroachments and robbery, perjury and fraudulent scales," that the Prophet had foretold in the name of the Lord, *Even thus shall the children of Israel eat their bread unclean, among the nations whither I will drive them* (Ezekiel, 4 : 13).

A passage in the Talmud (*Be'rakhot*, 13) states: *Later troubles cause the earlier ones to be forgotten*. The Dubno *Maggid*, with profound psychological insight employed the passage to explain why the Jews in exile longed for deliverance mainly as a result of their troubles in the lands of their dispersion:

Each man's want is assessed according to his station and habits. Thus, should he who has ever been accustomed to meat and wine have to subsist on bread and water, it will be agony for him as against his former habit. Not so one who has lived on bread and water all his life; this he will not consider agonizing unless he starve and thirst ... Thus, too, it has been with the sequence of exile, from the lighter to the more severe, from one misfortune to the next. At first exile meant being in a land that was not ours, with a surfeit of humiliation and displeasure; but after we had grown accustomed to that, till it no longer aggrieved us, it was (as written) *and they shall afflict them*. But the truth of the matter lies in our having left our abodes and resided on alien soil.

The affliction of exile came about when the Lord "brought about separation between the devoted ones, that is, between Israel and that lovely land; for this had ever been a glorious coupling from the day God created earth and the heavens." According to a passage in the *Midrash*, and in the spirit of Judah Halevi's teaching, the *Maggid* construed the passage in Habakkuk, 3 : 6, *He standeth and measureth the earth*, to mean that

> ... the Holy One Blessed Be He measured all the countries and all the peoples, allotting a place of settlement to each nation, to each according to its heart's desire and temperament, for every state has its own unique merits and qualities ... And God weighed the merits and the temperament of the people of Israel and found it valuable because gifted only for worthy things, for the Commandments of God, the Commandments of Purity; and the most fitting place for this worthiness was only at the very head, at the cornerstone in Jerusalem and its precincts.

The Land of Israel was "the place of our physical existence, just as water is the medium of life for all that exists within it. On departing from it, there could be no greater punishment for us, for we were as fish caught in a net." Again, in the *Maggid's* parable, the Land of Israel was "veritably like a garment, individually made for one particular person according to his measurements, and it may not be worn by another without being spoiled through alterations in length and breadth."*

The *Maggid* also employed a touching parable to illustrate the people's longing for the restoration to Zion:

> It was like one who had lost his hen and gone in search of it, perchance he might find it at one of his neighbours. And when he came to a certain neighbour, he saw the hen tied by one of its legs to a bar. And he said to him, "Why, this is my hen." And the man disputed with him, saying, "Nay, it is mine, for did I not buy it of

---

* The parable is based on *Midrash Rabbah*, Numeri, 23.

such and such a one?" And his acquaintance said to him, "Lo, here is a sign that it is mine: do but unloosen the fetters from her legs and open but the door to her and your eyes will behold how she flies at once to my house, to her own roosting place . . ." Thus veritably does Israel dispute with the Lord . . . For our hands are manacled in the places of our dispersion, and this will be the sign: when the Blessed One but unties the bonds of them who have been banished, will we not run after him in happiness and with joy in our hearts to that place where our tents were pitched at the beginning, as has been said, *Who are these that fly as a cloud, and as the doves to their cotes?* (Isaiah, 60:8).

"In the perfecting of the common weal the good of the individual will be perfected," the Dubno *Maggid* declared. Only in the solidarity of the entire people could every individual Jew expect salvation:

> This is virtually like a flaming brand fallen between two houses. If each of the two masters will leave their immediate occupations and together help extinguish the flames, they will succeed and the fire will easily and rapidly die down . . . Not so if each separately busies himself with removing his effects from his own home.

Instead of every Jew praying for his own soul, for his own sustenance, he should plead for the deliverance of the people, "for the city ruined and waste, for the Holy of Holies, for the ingathering of the exiles, for the kingdom of the house of David."* He compared the people in exile to a sick person, and "the gravest symptom of his sickness, indicating the danger and the fatal affliction, is the patient's insensitivity to his pains."

The *Maggid* told the following parable to illustrate the insignificance of the people's efforts to achieve tranquillity in exile:

> There were some orphans with a grand heritage of many rooms on the first floor, the second floor and the third floor; and one who held it in mortgage lived there while they lived in the house of a stranger. After a long time, a fire broke out in the city, and they began to exert themselves to save the house in which they lived. Then a wise man said to them, "Why must you toil for the legacy of a stranger? How can you abandon your honour? How can you forget that you must toil to save your ancestral heritage, which is your own patrimony for all time?"

Another parable, aimed at arousing his people to a sense of national pride, went straight to their hearts:

---

* In this reproof, the *Maggid* of Dubno was definitely influenced by Judah Halevi, *cf. Kuzari*, Chapter II, 4: "Worship His holy hill—worship at His footstool—He who restoreth His glory to Zion (Psalms 99, 9:5) and other words, this is but as the chattering of the starling and the nightingale. We do not realize what we say by this sentence, nor others . . ."

There was a king who was wroth with his son and drove him from his palace and from the city. And the lad wandered about in search of bread until, perforce, he knocked at the door of a person of lowly station, perchance with him at least he might find lodgings. And that person rose and admitted him to his home . . . that he should serve him and perform his labours. Thus many years went by until he forgot his people and his father's house, and performed the rustic's tasks as though he were a slave in perpetuity, from birth. The years passed and the rustic died, and then he served the rustic's son, but the son was an evil, wicked man, and he forced him to toil with mortar and with bricks and at all difficult tasks, nor did he properly feed him the daily bread which was his due. And he was very bitter and wished that he might be dead. At that time the king became sad for his son, for he had not had word of him a long time . . . And, having taken counsel, he determined to search the land . . . And he travelled constantly, he and one of his companions . . . And where-soever he came, there he commanded that in all the market places and streets be it proclaimed that whosoever wished to ask aught of the king or to request judgement, a citizen against his comrade, or a slave against his master, let them all come before the king and he would take up their quarrel . . . And the king's son came also . . . to com-plain of his master . . . but he recognized not his father . . . And when the king beheld his beloved son . . . he fell upon his neck and kissed him and wept bitterly and he said to him, "My son, how could you forget your glory and your pride? How could you forget that the kingdom awaits you and when you were in my house, ministers and viceroys knelt before you in your path and grandeur? And now behold, how fallen you are! And all this you have forgotten. All that you sought was to find favour in this rustic's eyes, that he might lighten the burden of your labours and add a crust to your ration? . . .

His socio-psychological realism also enabled him to observe the nega-tive factors that stirred the people to recall their homeland and to long for deliverance in Zion. The *Maggid* gave his explanation of the ultimate purpose behind the Jewish people's ordeals:

If The Holy One Blessed Be He subjects us to the ordeal of a single punishment . . . his purpose therein . . . is to purge our sins . . . and thereby to save us from the doom of perdition. Not so if many troubles engulf us . . . If they have all been gathered together to come upon us as one, that is a sign and an omen that The Holy One Blessed Be He wishes to awaken our hearts to plead for mercy and to restore us to Jerusalem . . . to ingather our exiles from the four corners of the earth. It is truly like one who pursues his servant who has fled from him. Should he come upon him face to face and wish to seize him or delay him in his flight, will that suffice for the servant to return to his master's house? Is there not before him a plot of field into which he may swerve to the right or to the left? But if the master come and cut him off from three directions so that he can swerve neither left nor right, then the servant must necessarily return to his place. Thus The Holy One Blessed Be He, to compel us to return to our place, sends many troubles and evils upon us to surround us in all directions and from every corner... Then perforce *They shall inquire concerning Zion with their faces hitherward* (Jeremiah, 50: 5).

In yet another parable, the *Maggid* dealt with the need which led the Jewish people to yearn for the restoration of Zion:

There was a great minister whose son had sinned... Necessarily, the father banished the son to a distant land, but because the father's pity for his son was very great, be he what he might, he sent him gifts, open or clandestine, that he might not die of hunger... Many days passed and the minister walked about with angry mien, for he was aggrieved because of his son. He could not write him that he should return home, for it would compromise his honour, the son having sinned so shamefully, for the father to appease him. So he was sorely bitter and distracted. And one of his servants who waited upon him said to him, "Master, accept my counsel and the lad will return by himself. For I know that the boy's sustenance these days certainly comes only from you, else how would he exist? Withdraw your hand and from this day send nought for his support, and when he is helpless, he must necessarily suppress the wickedness in his heart and come to you to placate you that you may seat him again at your table."

The Dubno *Maggid* also regarded Messianic deliverance as complete deliverance, both nationally and socially, in keeping with the best traditions of the people, evolved from the prophetic visions concerning the end of days. "This entire establishment" (i.e., the division of the world into rich and poor), he said, "exists but in this world." In his promise for the future, he quoted the Prophet Isaiah (35: 10; also, 51: 11): *"And the ransomed of the Lord shall return and come with singing unto Zion, And everlasting joy shall be upon their heads; They shall obtain gladness and joy, And sorrow and sighing shall flee away."*

He gave an explanation through the use of simile:

When we observe the piece of land on which we stand, we find that it too is unequal, with elevations and descents, mountains and hills, valleys and lowlands, and logic dictates that what is lacking in one place is added in another; and as for the future, it has been said, *Every valley shall be lifted up, and every mountain and hill shall be made low* (Isaiah, 40: 4) and the world will be equal.

Absolute social equality, was therefore only possible in the future. Until the Messianic period, the world would pursue its customary course with the existing social division into rich and poor, according to the literal meaning of the written text, *For the poor shall never cease out of the land* (Deuteronomy, 15:2). The social problem, the reason for the presence of poverty in this world and society's obligation towards the poor, was one of the many axes around which the *Maggid*'s sermons revolved. He explained it as methodically as the Jewish people's deliverance in Zion. He had observed the way of life of two classes of society, the large merchants and the very poor, and they formed the principal theme of his parables. They also represented the two poles of his outlook on society. However, while his economic views presented a positive attitude in the spirit of capitalist enterprise and the middle-class individualism peculiar to the big merchants, his approach to the problem of poverty showed that he was still totally immersed in the organic feudalist concept of society and the traditional ethico-religious doctrine of charity. The Dubno *Maggid*'s teachings concerned a world order where God "supports the poor through the rich," and he demanded the utmost generosity in charity as a matter of duty and not of mercy. In this, he was in full agreement with the best Hassidic preachers of his generation. His originality, here again, lay in his unique expository talents and striking, heart-warming parables.

C. PRECURSORS OF HASKALAH IN EASTERN EUROPE

Pioneers of Science—Campaigners against Ignorance; Grammarians, Rhetoricians

The pioneers of the *Haskalah* and of secular creativeness in Poland and Lithuania arose from the ranks of the learned by virtue of their new ideas as early as the generation of the Vilno *Gaon* and the Dubno *Maggid*. They were guided in their rationalist thought by Maimonides' *Guide to the Perplexed,* and drew their initial knowledge of the natural sciences from works of Jewish scholars of Spain and Italy. This scientific literature had been forgotten in the course of centuries by a people shut away in the confines of the Mishnah, the Codifiers and their commentators. Now the few scholars in Poland and Lithuania who espoused Enlightenment in their communities, though themselves steeped in Talmudic Judaism, returned to them as a source of knowledge. The forerunners of the *Haskalah* in eastern Europe resurrected the hidden scientific treasures of Jewish origin, salvaged them from oblivion, and cleared the way for their people's advance towards contemporary European science and universal culture.

Some of them even preceded the *Haskalah*. With the courage of iconoclastic rebels against petrified tradition, they urged their people to abandon its narrow confines and raise its intellectual level. They fearlessly denounced the obscurantism, egoism and hypocrisy of the fanatical guardians of ignorance in whose mouth were the high praises of God. However, like the *Gaon* of Vilno, they still correlated study of the sciences with the need to understand the Talmud and elucidate the Laws (e.g., sanctification of the new moon and astronomy, dietary laws and medicine). The message of *Haskalah* was evident in their statements on Jewish national prestige, which had been compromised amongst the gentiles through neglect of the sciences extolled by scripture in the admonition: "For this is your wisdom and your understanding in the sight of the peoples" (Deuteronomy, 4:6).

One of the earliest precursors of *Haskalah* in Poland was Solomon Ben Moses Khelma. He was an outstanding Talmudist and had served as Rabbi in the city of Chelm (whence his name) and, later, in his native city of Zamosc. From 1771, he officiated in Lwow. He died at Salonica whilst returning from Palestine in 1781. His numerous writings include exegeses on the Six Tractates of the Mishnah and the *Shulhan Arukh, Responsa,* and—the greatest of his books—*Merkevet-Ha'mishneh (The Chariot of Mishneh)*, a *Halakhic* exegesis on Maimonides' *Mishneh-Torah*. Although he dealt with arithmetical and geometric propositions for interpreting certain passages in the Talmud, in the last chapter of *The Chariot of Mishneh* (first edition, 1751), his principal work, it was the introduction to the same book that established his position as a forerunner of east European *Haskalah*. It was an exposition of Khelma's views on the study of Torah and the sciences, composed in rhyming prose.

Khelma regarded the leaders of the new Hassidic sect as the most suspect figures, "a characteristic of our times." They were deficient in both the revealed and the hidden Torah, yet professed to know everything as though they saw it in "the mystic spectrum of light." He also unequivocally rejected the "pilpulist" trend, in a graphic description which contained one of the most trenchant satires on that devious and barren method of study. Rabbi Solomon Khelma identified himself with those "whose aim was, all in all, to understand the words of the Sages and their riddles," to understand what the Talmud and the Codifiers intended, so that he might prescribe correct *Halakhic* practice and "properly establish the precepts of our religion." This correct method of studying the Law also postulated the study of the "accessories of wisdom" which had absorbed the author during his youth: "the science of numbers, integers, and fractions; the science of geometry, algebra, engineering and astronomy." He confessed that he had "dabbled in the science of nature and what is beyond nature," that he had acquainted himself with the *Guide to the Perplexed* and with grammar and logic, and had "gleaned amongst the sheaves" (*cf.* Ruth, 2:15) of "meter and verse." In fact, he considered that "they speak nonsense who find the slightest fault with the study of the sciences." They spoke from envy and brought to mind the words of Ecclesiastes, 10:1: *Dead flies make the ointment of the perfumers fetid and putrid*. Of the sciences, Ecclesiastes 2:13 had said, ... *Wisdom excelleth folly as far as light excelleth darkness*. The sciences, besides being necessary to an understanding of the Talmud and the Laws, were valuable in their own right. "Practice in logic," he wrote, "makes perfect in thought ... The grammar of speech above all one must learn; its study to shirk is to fail, nought else will avail." A knowledge of grammar was indispensable to prayer and the reading of the Torah. In any case, "it is a learned commandment of the Lord to speak a lucid word." Algebra, arithmetic, surveying and astronomy strengthened "the power to depict through the intelligence acquired" and they "train the imagination." The student of astronomy climbed "the rungs of the ladder till his head reached the heavens and his heart was as an open chamber." Hence, it was not surprising that "all the great men of ancient times claimed a share in all the sciences." Neglect of the "sciences" in the course of time was a repudiation of the glorious tradition of the Jewish people and a lowering of its prestige amongst the Gentiles.

Israel Ben Moses Zamosc (1710-1772) was a contemporary and fellow-countryman of Rabbi Solomon Khelma and, like him, tried at first to enhance the position of both the Talmud and the sciences. However, the sciences were of prime importance for Israel Zamosc, both as far as his personal interest was concerned and his remarkable abilities. Thus this Polish Talmudist became the teacher of Germany's first *Maskilim* after his wanderings had brought him to that country. He was born at Bobrka (immortalized in Yiddish as Boiberik), in the neighbourhood of Lwow and served as "one of the *melamdim*," or instructors, at the Zamosc *Yeshivah*. In 1741, he published his book *Netzah Yisrael* (*The Eternity of Israel*) at Frankfurt-on-the-Oder. This work was a theoretical explanation of certain passages in the text of the Mishnah. It was also partly based on arithmetic, geometry and astronomy and an appendix to the text elucidated these scientific problems as they appeared in the Talmud. The manuscript of his work on mathematics and astronomy, entitled *Arubot Ha'shamayim* (*The Windows of Heaven*) had already been completed at that time, but his expectations of "obtaining funds to have it printed" were not fulfilled and the book was never published.

The rhymed prose and content of Israel Zamosc's introduction to *The Eternity of Israel* may be regarded as the prototype of Solomon Khelma's introduction to the *Chariot of Mishneh*. Israel Zamosc also protested against the idle pilpulistic method of Talmud study. He preceded Khelma in accusing those who employed this method of having no object except prestige, of "making a spade of their wisdom ... and thereby supporting themselves." Zamosc, however, went much further than Khelma in systematically expounding the actual purpose of studying the Talmud. He pursued Maimonides' line of thought in this: the study of the Talmud was unnecessary in any but a practical sense, to obtain a knowledge of the precepts and how they were to be obeyed.

The author of *The Eternity of Israel* made an even bolder evaluation of the sciences. A knowledge of astronomy was also infinitely more important than pilpulistic disputations on Talmudical matters, for practical reasons. The precept of sanctifying the new moon depended on this discipline, "and this aspect of study is forever and necessarily inseparable from the practice." There was also a category of learning "that existed in its own right" and did not depend on any practice (i.e., on familiarity with observance of the precepts). It included natural science, philosophy and metaphysics, although Zamosc, too, thought that "a cardinal thing, which brings us to the next world, is occupation with the Gemara." He described the fanatics as those "whose custom it is to condemn all science and all that is beyond their ken . . . who derogate the sciences as stupidity and folly . . . the authors of parables have said that when the cat finds the morsel of flesh suspended beyond its reach, it pretends to scorn it as putrescent." He was referring to the ignorant fanatics who angrily persecuted anybody engaged in the sciences.

Israel Zamosc complained of the unfortunate position of the science scholar and compared him to a lamb amongst the wolves. As a mathematician and admirer of Maimonides, he could not tolerate life within an environment of "oxen in the shape of men." He was violently persecuted after the publication of *The Eternity of Israel* and forced to leave Poland and settle in Berlin, where he was employed as a tutor in the home of the wealthy Daniel Itzig and subsequently as a teacher in the *Talmud-Torah* school founded by Veitel Ephraim. He himself was self-taught, and had obtained his knowledge of mathematics from Hebrew books such as those by Isaac Israeli and Joseph Solomon del Medigo of Candia, and his philosophical education from the *Guide to the Perplexed* and other medieval works of philosophy. Now he initiated a circle of young *Maskilim* in the fundamentals of mathematics and philosophy, and according to Solomon Maimon, greatly influenced the spiritual development of Moses Mendelssohn. Representative German authors such as Lessing and Friedrich Nicolai were overwhelmed by the profundity of his mathematical research. He spent his last years in Brody and undoubtedly inspired Enlightenment circles in that city—already coming to the fore as an east European *Haskalah* centre. During Israel Zamosc's lifetime, his only writing to be published, apart from *The Eternity of Israel*, was his commentary on the *Spirit of Grace*, a philosophical dictionary attributed to Jacob Anatoli. Shortly after his death, several of his works were published: *The Pottage of the Harvest*, ethical reflections in rhymed prose (Dührenfurt 1773); a commentary on Judah Halevi's *Kuzari* entitled *A Charming Treasure*; and a commentary on Bahya Ben Joseph ibn Pakuda's *Duties of the Hearts* entitled *The Goodness of Lebanon*. The commentary on the *Kuzari* gave Zamosc an opportunity to include detailed lectures on astronomy and questions of Hebrew grammar. However, the commentary also proved that in questions of philosophy and faith its author had become converted to Judah Halevi's conservatism, despite his grounding in the Maimonidean system.

Israel Zamosc revealed his traditionalist religious outlook in his ethical work *Nezed Ha'dema'* (*The Pottage of the Harvest*). He preached the virtue of abstention from pleasure and condemned the vanities of this world; but, typical forerunner of the *Haskalah* movement that he was, he denounced Hassidism in sharp and bitter satire which set a pattern for the anti-Hassidic literature of the following generation of *Haskalah*. His attitude towards Hassidism was marked by the contempt and aversion of the *Maskil* for the ignorant masses. He condemned Hassidism not only as a rationalist who loathed superstition and ignorance, but also as a champion of justice and defender of the wronged who could not endure the exploitation of people by the self-righteous. He maintained that while the Hassidic leaders spoke of lofty things, their eyes and hearts were actually only set upon material gain. The contradiction between the mystic phraseology of the *Tzaddikim* and their way of life, with its feasts and banquets, aroused him to the heights of sarcasm and indignation.

However, his satire did not only attack the Hassidim, but all manifestations of social abuse. Israel Zamosc exposed the reprehensible behaviour of the wealthy in a style worthy of the prophets: "they who hoard pillage and loot in their homes" spent their time in luxuries and delights and exploited the poor. He claimed that the sanctimonious rich, like the Hassidic leaders, imagined that their prayers, fasts and purported allegiance to the Torah atoned for their acts of oppression. "The essence of faith" was to "love thy neighbour as thyself," but they "have put to nought the precepts of behaviour between a man and his fellow men." "I could not constrain the spirit that was locked up within me, for it was stronger than I!" the author exclaimed in the introduction to his book of social chastisement. The spiritual characteristics of the scientist disseminating Enlightenment amongst his people and the ardent fighter for social justice were indistinguishably fused in Israel Zamosc's personality. But his social system still held traces of pre-capitalistic, traditional religious ethics. He regarded as evil all desire for luxury and the efforts of the unpropertied to attain the level of the wealthy in their way of life.

Self-educated intellectuals such as Solomon Khelma and Israel Zamosc had mastered mathematics and the natural sciences by their remarkable tenacity. Similarly, men with an outstanding knowledge of the Old Testament and the grammar of the Hebrew language, laboriously acquired in an ultra-orthodox environment that was hostile to anything outside the narrow limits of *Halakhah*, appeared in Poland and Lithuania during the second half of the eighteenth century. It was not a coincidence that both types of the precursors of *Haskalah* in eastern Europe came from Kehillot which were centres of Jewish foreign trade in Poland and

Lithuania. They included cities such as Zamosc, Lwow, Brody, Dubno, Jaroslaw, Shklov in White Russia, and even the Podolian city of Satanow. Trade with the neighbouring countries inevitably brought Polish Jews into contact with the culture of those countries, especially Germany, broadened their horizons and extended the scope of their intellectual interests. Frequently, Jewish wholesale merchants, conducting transactions with Polish magnates and clergymen, had to acquire a command of correct Polish speech, an ordinary appearance in public, and a knowledge of social protocol. A typical example of a contemporary Jewish merchant, with a fluent command of Polish and a broad education, was Ber of Bolechow (1723-1805). The town in East Galicia where he was born was only a small community, but its Jewish inhabitants maintained close commercial ties with neighbouring Hungary and they imported Hungarian wines for marketing throughout Poland. Ber of Bolechow already knew Polish and Latin when he was a youth. Later, he mastered German and studied widely amongst medieval books of inquiry, history and, especially, the history of religions. He recommended to his offspring the combined study of Torah, Gemara and the "sciences" which he practised himself. In this he referred to two sentences from Scripture and the Mishnah respectively, which were to serve the *Haskalah* as slogans: *For this is your wisdom and your understanding in the sight of the peoples* (Deuteronomy, 4:6) and *Torah is good with the way of the land*. His books, which remained unpublished until they were "discovered" in the twentieth century, consisted of *Memoirs*, containing a wealth of information on the life of eighteenth century Polish Jewry, and *Sage Sayings*, comments on the Frankist movement. The author had participated in the public debate with the Frankists at Lwow in 1759, both as an interpreter and as one of the formulators of the rabbinical rebuttals.

Two Hebrew grammarians who came to the fore in Poland during that period participated in writing Mendelssohn's *Commentary* on the Pentateuch. Aaron Friedenthal of Jaroslaw wrote the commentary to the Book of Numbers under Mendelssohn's editorship. After his return to Galicia, on Mendelssohn's recommendation, he was appointed principal of the Teachers' Seminary at Lwow, which trained the teachers for the Jewish German-language schools established by Joseph II. Solomon Dubno (1738-1813) played a much greater part in Mendelssohn's *Commentary*. He was a brilliant grammarian and stylist, but the few poems which he published lacked poetic elan. Solomon Ben Joel was born at Dubno and was taught Hebrew grammar and the Bible by Rabbi Solomon Khelma at Lwow. In 1766, he had a book by Khelma, *The Gateway to Melody*, printed, with a poem of his own in praise of music as introduction. After several years spent in research in the libraries of Amsterdam, he came to Berlin in 1772 and was employed as a tutor in Mendelssohn's home. When Solomon Dubno saw Mendelssohn's German translation of the Pentateuch, he accepted Mendelssohn's proposal to write the *Commen-*

tary as well as the glosses to the text of all five books of the Pentateuch. However, intellectual differences of opinion arose and Dubno abandoned his work on the *Commentary* and left Berlin. The differences arising from collaboration between a moderate advocate of Enlightenment, who was also a conservative, devoted to tradition and associated with the orthodox world, and representatives of the *Haskalah* movement, who had begun to make drastic revisions in the traditional faith, might have been predicted. The objections to Mendelssohn's *Commentary* voiced by the orthodox rabbis might have strengthened Solomon Dubno's resolve to sever relations with Berlin *Haskalah* circles, lest he lost favour with the rabbis. From Berlin, he proceeded to Vilno, where he was cordially welcomed and supported both by sympathizers with Berlin *Haskalah* and by the pupils and colleagues of the *Gaon*. He died at the end of a lifetime of wandering at Amsterdam, in 1813.

Solomon Dubno's principal aim in his lifetime of grammatical and Biblical research was the regeneration of the Hebrew language and its literature. Like all the precursors of *Haskalah* and the moderate *Maskilim*, he was filled with hope for deliverance in Zion and associated his plan for the regeneration of Hebrew in the Diaspora with the vision of its revival when the people returned to their homeland. His introduction to Moses Haim Luzzatto's *La'ye'sharim Te'hillah*, which he published in 1780, concluded with the following exhortation to his readers:

> Teach your sons to accustom themselves to this tongue, for God may pardon us and acquiesce, as of old, to restore us from captivity, to heal our tongue, so that speedily, in our day, stammerers may converse fluently.

A contemporary of Solomon Dubno, Ze'ev Wolf Ben David Buchner (d. *ca.* 1810) paved the way, in flowery prose, for the *Haskalah* movement in Galicia. He was born at Brody, the son of a noted rabbi and author of *Halakhic* works. He travelled a great deal between the cities of Poland, Lithuania, Bohemia, Moravia, Hungary and Germany on business and in connection with the publication of his own and his father's books. In the course of his travels, he became acquainted with the representative *Haskalah* writers of central Europe (Wessely, Barukh Jeiteles), and later corresponded with them. For some time, he served as secretary to the Kehillah in his native city of Brody. The poetry he wrote consisted mainly of prayers, but the collections of his letters which, like his poems, went through many editions, are of inestimable historical value. Buchner's florid, verbose and artificial style became the model for *Haskalah* writers, such as Samson Bloch and his successors. In reality, the difficulty which Buchner himself frequently pointed out in apology for his style of expressing all concepts in the Biblical vocabulary was only an excuse. The ornate rhetoric he affected and which was copied by those who adopted his pattern in writing, was chiefly a manifestation of the baroque phase that characterized the new Hebrew literature in its initial stages. Only baroque could have produced monstrosities such as "a-device-for-seeing-on-the-nose-being" (i.e., eyeglasses) or "a-large-weapon-rolled-on-wheels-when-marching" gun, cannon).

His collection of letters, *Tzahut Ha'me'litzah* (*Lucid Expression*), provides valuable historical source material for the study of economic, and particularly commercial, history, as well as the daily life and customs of Galician and Polish Jewry, at the beginning of the nineteenth century. With the curiosity of a natural journalist, Buchner collected every bit of information on politics and wars and also on sensational cases of theft, swindling, forgery and adultery in his own immediate area and in neighbouring countries. These letters also reported ordinary daily incidents in epic detail, reflecting the author's evident enjoyment in his own detailed accounts: the methods of production of various types of artisan; the quality and appearance of English and Prussian cloths; a bride's betrothal gifts and her wedding attire; the menu of a wealthy miser; military training in the Austrian army. He had the outlook of a conservative, well-to-do east European Jewish merchant who was still tied to the concepts of his own class, despite his education and familiarity with the ways of the world. He did not conceal his contempt for "the lowly, the vine-dressers and servants." He even regarded the imposition of compulsory military service on the Jews as an evil, not only because it applied to the common people, "the vinegrowers and grain farmers," but also because "the tempest rages about every man of stature, so that a priest is become as one of the people, a master as a slave, one may not distinguish between a magnate or a prince and the poor or inferior." Nor was he different from the other members of his Kehillah-dominating class, in his absolute loyalty to the Austrian régime and his hostile attitude to revolutionary France. When people consulted him on how to invest their capital, he advised them to lend their money on interest "as a prime business proposition" (except that "they should not defraud or collect usury"), since such an investment was safer than trade (Letter 45). However, this kind of practical advice did not prevent Buchner, as a precursor of *Haskalah* influenced by the economic theory of the physiocrats, from extolling the serene, tranquil life of the peasant, in redundant rhetoric. His role as a precursor of *Haskalah* also appeared in his pride in the Hebrew language.

D. ADVOCATES OF SCIENCE—THE ENEMIES OF SPECULATION

Judah Hurwitz and Judah Leib Margalioth

Judah Hurwitz, Judah Leib Margalioth and Pinhas Elijah Hurwitz, who wrote during the latter half of the eighteenth century, were in a class by themselves amongst the precursors of *Haskalah* in eastern Europe. They belonged, like the school of writers established by Israel Zamosc and Solomon Dubno, to the transitional generation between old orthodox Judaism and *Haskalah*. Their *Weltanschauung* too was firmly rooted in the traditional faith, but their work reflected the incipient formation of a secular Jewish culture. In fact, their cultural dualism was accentuated because they deliberately and systematically formulated it as a reform programme for the Jewish way of life. These orthodox believers launched a conscious attack on two fronts. They expressed support for such basic *Haskalah* premises as a change in attitude to the gentiles, allegiance to rulers and state, the movement into productive activity, and the study of secular branches of knowledge (some of them even wrote popular books on science to disseminate knowledge amongst the masses). At the same time, they evinced complete hostility to the "apostasy" that was infiltrating from Germany through *Haskalah* channels into the few Enlightenment circles of eastern Europe. They unanimously repudiated the rationalistic outlook and tirelessly demonstrated the danger that all philosophical works constituted to religion and faith. It was not a coincidence that these writers, all of them of Polish and Lithuanian origin, had spent long periods of their nomadic lives in western European countries, and especially in Germany. Their contact with western European culture and Jewish Enlightenment circles had deepened their erudition and also encouraged their hopes of raising the cultural level of their people in their native lands, especially by disseminating knowledge of the natural sciences. On the other hand, what they had personally seen of religious apathy in European metropolitan centres determined them to prevent this attitude from penetrating into the east European Kehillot—where the integrity of the traditional faith still prevailed.

These writers, like all the forerunners of *Haskalah*, still relied on the ethical and philosophical works of medieval Jewish authors, and even Aristotle, for their principal intellectual inspiration. The influence exerted by contemporary European science and literature was barely discernible in their ideas. The fact that their books contained frequent discussions on the insignificance of this world in comparison with the next was typical of their adherence to the medieval outlook. Furthermore, they did not depart from the social pattern of feudalism in their demands for the protection of the scholar caste in the Kehillot, or in their attitude towards a wife's obligations to her husband. In form and content, their books were only new editions of the traditional ethical literature. However, the clearly defined traditionalism in their approach to the social and national issue was a point in favour of this group of *Haskalah* precursors as compared with the literary spokesmen of the *Haskalah* movement proper. The *Maskilim* of eastern Europe, like their prototypes in Germany, usually ignored the problems of social antagonisms and social justice. In the spirit of eighteenth century Enlightenment, they regarded the diffusion of knowledge as the panacea for all ills. The precursors of *Haskalah* did not. They exposed the social abuses that were being perpetrated in the Kehillot and demanded relief for the poor and lowly from their oppressors and exploiters. The programme of the *Maskilim* rarely contained the idea of restoration and deliverance in the homeland. For one thing, they consciously strove to establish greater affinity between the Jews and their neighbours and to unite them in loyalty to the states in which they lived. Moreover, the idea of Palestine was not an immediate issue in the *Haskalah*'s practical schemes for reform through education and productive occupations. The *Maskilim* regarded Palestine merely as a fantasy, only serving to distract the people from the implementation of practicable tasks. By contrast, the precursors of the *Haskalah* felt duty bound to strengthen the people's hopes for redemption in Zion as a fundamental tenet of faith. In fact, one of them, the author of *The Book of the Covenant*,* brought to light new facets of the idea of the restoration of Zion, under the influence of the spirit of modern nationalism.

The first members of this group of *Haskalah* precursors, Judah Hurwitz, was also the most conservative and moderate in his views on society and education. He had studied medicine at Padua and served, first in his native city of Vilno as "physician to the Holy Kehillah of Vilno," later at Mitau in Courland, Latvia, and, towards the end of his life, in Grodno, where he died in 1797. In the course of innumerable journeys around western Europe, he became acquainted with the Berlin and Amsterdam *Maskilim*, but this contact tended to reinforce his vigorous opposition to the "apostasy" of rationalism. He had obtained his general knowledge of philosophy and the social sciences primarily from the works of inquiry of the Middle Ages, and his religious canticles were also influenced by the language and ideas of the poets of that period. The canticles were never published, but of his three papers on ethical and intellectual problems, all of them composed in rhymed verse, *Tzel-Ha'ma'alot* (*The Shadow of the Dial*) appeared in 1764; *Amudei-Bet-Ye'hudah* (*The Pillars of the House of Judah*), two years later, in 1766; and *Me'gillat-Se'darim* (*A Scroll of Systems*), in 1793. In his principal work, *The Pillars of the House of Judah*, Hurwitz expressed his views on social matters, on the Jews and the gentiles and on religion and philosophy, through three disputants.

* Pinhas Elijah Hurwitz, who will be discussed separately, see below, p. 564.

Judah Hurwitz, in something approaching a latter-day version of Plato's doctrine of the three classes of society corresponding to the three levels of the soul, taught that "this triple thread sustains the world." However, in his system, the second estate was not composed of warriors but of merchants, in keeping with the socio-economic position of the Jewish people. These three classes—agriculturalists and artisans, merchants and scholars (who dealt "in Torah and Wisdom")—corresponded to "the material spirit, the vital spirit, and the intelligent spirit." It was the duty of each of them to engage in their own occupation and not to violate their neighbour's precincts. Class equality was "impossible, alien to nature and to wisdom," for "if every person in Israel will be a physician and a seer . . . and if every cowherd engages in seven wisdoms . . . who will hew wood and draw water?" He also compared the estates of society to the limbs of the human body and stated that they were duty bound to live together in fraternity and amity. The duty of giving charity fell to the rich. At times, the author condemned the injustices that the rich committed against the poor and especially the scholars*—to such an extent that he seemed to echo the teachings of Rousseau in his advocacy of a return to nature.

His social theory never went beyond the feudal system of society; similarly, he expressed medieval religious bigotry towards all those peoples who lacked any monotheistic belief. Hurwitz's views were original in that they echoed, however faintly, the footsteps of approaching *Haskalah*. Despite his opposition to speculation and philosophy in principle, he made an exception in the case of the books of "pious philosophers" such as Moses Mendelssohn and he was able to add Mendelssohn's approval of his book to its rabbinical approvals. He also supported "Greek wisdom" and the natural sciences, with the proviso that these "external wisdoms" should not lead Jews to apostasy. Most expressive of the new spirit of the age, however, was his attitude to the monotheistic peoples of the world, the Christians and "Ishmaelities." Here, he demonstrated an absolutely tolerant view in glaring contrast to his hatred of the "heathen" nations.

> The peoples in whose midst we dwell—he wrote—are attracted by the true law of the people of Israel, believe in the cardinal tenets of the faith, in the existence of God, the creation *ex nihilo*, the divine origin of the Torah, reward and punishment, resurrection of the dead, *et cetera* . . . And they are not to be blamed if they agree not with us in all things . . . for our Torah is like "the mirror of the serving women" (Exodus, 38 : 8), and a mirror has the same property

---

* *cf*. Chapter Nine, p. 292; *cf*. also *The Shadow of the Dial*, p. 155: "The scholar acknowledges the prerogatives of wealth, yet the wealthy man does not acknowledge the prerogatives of wisdom and talent." Also: "For they who dwell in the shade of money are blessed, while the dwellers in the shade of learning sigh." (*ibid*. p. 101).

for all who gaze into it: the nations peered into the Torah and ceased from their abominations and abuses."

The gentiles were Israel's brethren, "for one God created us and we all have one Father ... Let us not hate them because they are opposed to us in some of their views, for if we are to hate our brothers because of conflicting opinions, then in our own midst, too, you will find varying and digressive views. ..."

Dr. Judah Hurwitz, like the other forerunners of *Haskalah*, was steadfast in his belief in the national rebirth of the Jewish people. His yearning for deliverance was so powerful that his grief burst out:

What are we to do with a world that restrains us, when to our exile there is no end? Our days have departed and are gone like a passing shadow, but we are without salvation. Have we not drunk enough of venom and of gall? Ye Heavens, have not the clouds of darkness and the pall dispersed? Must these days of terror persist?

Although the Jews longed for deliverance more than other peoples, when the Messiah finally came he would redeem humanity as a whole, the living and the dead, for "the Lord is most desirous that the human race should not be eternally disgraced and abhorred." But Judah Hurwitz still belonged to the age of reason and he also believed in the progress of civilization and technology. His broad imagination could envision the material abundance that awaited mankind in the future. Not only would "the desert become like the garden of the Lord" through re-settlement of the wasteland that constituted nine parts of the dry land, but "men, through their powers of choice and invention," would also convert the waters of the oceans into dry land, as the author had seen "in a number of countries" (an obvious allusion to the Netherlands). And then, "No man shall say, 'This place is too close for me ...' " Dr. Hurwitz's doctrine of messianic deliverance thus intermingled a technological Utopia, of the kind immortalized a century later by the school of writing inaugurated by Jules Verne, with intimations of immortality in conformity with the traditional faith. As always, in fact, he adhered to a religious and feudal tradition but had nevertheless succumbed to some of the progressive concepts current in contemporary Europe.

The writings of Rabbi Judah Leib Margalioth (1747-1811) showed appreciable progress in *Haskalah* thought as compared with the work of Dr. Judah Hurwitz. This precursor of *Haskalah* successively occupied the post of Rabbi in a number of Polish cities, ending up at Frankfurt-on-the-Oder in Germany. As an itinerant preacher, he gained the reputation of "a mouth producing pearls,"* while his Talmudical exegeses earned him a reputation in scholarly circles. Judah Leib Margalioth surpassed Dr.

---

* A tribute to the Rabbi's surname: the Hebrew word *margalit* (pl. *margaliyot*) means a gem, or pearl.—Tr.

Judah Hurwitz both in scientific erudition and in the breadth of his intellectual horizon. He too had read the works of Aristotle (in the Hebrew translation) and medieval works of inquiry, but he did not neglect *Haskalah* literature during his stay in Germany. As a rabbi and homilist, Margalioth was also firmly committed to traditional religion and tirelessly urged people to study the Law and to revere heaven. His attitude on the question of women's rights and the political régime expressed the unyielding conservatism of his views on society. He laid down the political axiom that monarchy was the organ for "improving the world," as stated in the Book of Proverbs, 24:21, *My son, fear thou the Lord and the king*. The Rabbi was still voicing these views in 1802, apparently with the idea of confuting republicanism which was constantly radiating from revolutionary France.

Rabbi Margalioth militantly opposed the study of philosophy in his concern for religion and faith. He contended that Maimonides and other men of inquiry of his time had dealt with philosophy in response to current requirements, that they might "reply to the heretics . . . But in our own generations we have but to spend our time in God's Torah . . . for it has not been said that He uttered His Words to Aristotle, His Laws and Judgments to Plato, but rather He uttered his Words to Jacob, His Laws and Judgments to Israel . . ."

His *'Atzei-'Eden* (*Trees of Eden*, Frankfurt-on-the-Oder, 1802) contained a graphic description of the spread of the rationalist apostasy which had resulted from the study of philosophy: people the author had known, "all of them charming young men, were persuaded by the study of philosophy to hate the Torah and those who learned it." Study of Voltaire (whose name Margalioth hated so much that he never mentioned it) was particularly liable to lead people astray.

Actually, however, Judah Leib Margalioth's uncompromising support of religious tradition was sustained by a strong sense of social morality that emphasized his leading position amongst the precursors of *Haskalah* in his generation. The courage and social pathos he displayed in exposing the victimization of his people by a "handful of the leaders of Israel"—the *Parnassim*, rabbis, and their supporters—are reminiscent of the fiery sixteenth century preacher, Ephraim Luntschitz. In fact, Margalioth cited him as an example for contemporary preachers. His criticism of the rabbis—like the *Parnassim*, they were "consumed with cupidity"—did not exclude the Hassidim (though he did not define them as the leaders of an independent sect). Several of his comments on the deceptions and hypocritical frauds perpetrated by some Hassidim were an almost word-for-word repetition of Israel Zamosc's sharp satire of the *Tzaddikim*.

Margalioth's loyalty to the tradition of his people and its religion extended to the ideals of deliverance and the restoration in Zion. Luxurious indulgence in finery and sumptuous repasts aroused his aversion, not only on the grounds of modesty but also because "even without that it is not fitting that we should adorn ourselves at a time when the People of Israel are exiled from their land, endure suffering and humiliation in the lands of their enemies, while the Sanctuary of God lies desolate because we have sinned, and His Great Name will be profaned among the Gentiles till He once again shall console and uplift His people."

Judah Leib Margalioth occupies an honourable position in the history of the precursors of *Haskalah* because of his unqualifiedly positive attitude towards the sciences, despite his vigorous opposition to the "apostasy" of philosophy. Even in his sharp polemic against "speculation" he always clarified his opinion: that the situation in respect of the sciences was altogether different. The sciences were not only permitted, but it was an act of piety to practise them. Rabbi Margalioth virtually anticipated the whole of the *Haskalah* doctrine in his reasons for encouraging the study of science. He even felt that congruence of theory and practice demanded that he disseminate the sciences amongst his fellow-Jews to the best of his ability. He wrote a popular book on "the wisdom of nature" principally devoted to chemistry. A first edition entitled *An Eternal Light*, was published in 1777. However, the need for a work of this kind was so great in his time that two more editions were published within the following six years.

In accordance with his view that morality was the foundation of human society, Judah Leib Margalioth also actively demanded the reform of traditional education, which he considered to have been neglected, especially as it affected "polite manners."

Pinhas Elijah Hurwitz, Author of The Book of the Covenant

The most influential of all the forerunners of *Haskalah* who attacked both heresy and ignorance, was Pinhas Elijah Hurwitz, author of *Sepher Ha'brit (The Book of the Covenant)*. It was first published at the Brünn press in 1797, and immediately began to circulate throughout the European Diaspora. It "reached the land of Uz, Damascus, Aram, Algeria, Barbary and Jerusalem, may it speedily be rebuilt in our day." It passed through several editions in its author's lifetime, and was still used as a sort of popular natural science encyclopedia by those east European Jews who still derived their knowledge from traditional sources as late as the twentieth century.

Pinhas Elijah Ben Meir Hurwitz of Vilno was born at Lwow in 1765 and died in Krakow in 1821. He wrote *The Book of the Covenant* during his travels through Poland, Hungary, Germany, Holland and England, and completed it in 1794. He obtained his knowledge of the natural sciences and philosophy laboriously, because of his ignorance of any European language. In his introduction to the book, he apologized for its

Hebrew style which was often awkward because he had originally written the work in Yiddish and had then translated it into Hebrew. The apology however, only expressed the author's humility. The light, flowing, agreeable style was what actually endeared the book to its many readers.

The wide circulation *The Book of the Covenant* enjoyed throughout the Jewish Diaspora was mainly due to its first part, which was an encyclopedia of all the natural sciences with a supplement of geographical information. It taught its readers about astronomy, physics, chemistry and zoology. They learned for the first time about "the globe of breath, the atmosphere," about "an air pressure gauge called *barometer*," and about "an air gauge called *thermometer*," about air pumps and balloons, whales, "burning mountains" (i.e., volcanos), "an iron bar called 'weather conductor' " (i.e., a lightning rod), and electricity. *The Book of the Covenant* played an enormous part in spreading elementary knowledge of the world and all it contained—despite its author's antiquated ideas on several fundamental scientific facts. Pinhas Elijah Hurwitz still retained the theory of the four basic elements (fire, water, air, earth), and he disputed the Copernican system, relying on the astronomer Tycho Brahe. In both instances, he was following the example of J. L. Margalioth, also the author of a popular book on the natural sciences. He formulated his reasons for propagating the sciences amongst his people almost exactly in the spirit of the *Haskalah* movement:

> It is most appropriate and right that every person in Israel should be conversant in all the sciences . . . that he may not remain as ignorant as a horse or mule in his understanding of nature and the world, that he should not be embarrassed on conversing with educated Gentiles in the city gate which is the sanctification of God,* so that the Gentiles will not say that the people of God are all simpletons and fools, none of them versed in any wisdom, a people without understanding.

A knowledge of nature was particularly important for heavenly reverence, "that the individual may be cognizant of the vastness of God's works in the secret recesses of the four elements."

Nevertheless, the propagation of nature study was only a subsidiary. The author's principal aim was to strengthen his readers in their traditional religious faith. He repeated the warning against the study of philosophy and preoccupation with any type of speculations, with even greater determination than Rabbi Margalioth. His familiarity with the new philosophy—he could quote the opinions of Leibnitz, Wolff, Spinoza, Kant and Solomon Maimon—only supplied him with polemical arguments to emphasize the insignificance of all metaphysical and other inquiries into the tenets of faith. What did appeal to him in the Kantian system was the opinion that faith was not subject to logical analysis, for

* A euphemistic circumlocution to avoid profanation of the Lord's name.

"that which may be ascertained by demonstration or through the senses is knowledge and not faith," and he blessed the Lord for creating that philosopher. He even differed from the medieval Jewish scholar Bahya ibn Pakuda, author of *Duties of the Hearts*, for having advocated such investigations. He contended that in the wake of "philosophical scholarship . . . heresy has multiplied in Israel in our times," and explained "though they be few in one country, they wax numerous in another" (the allusion was to Germany). He even found fault with polite literature in Hebrew because of the threat of apostasy. As for Hebrew poetry, the only poems he approved of were "songs of praise" in honour of God.

Rabbi Judah Leib Margalioth had merely spoken affirmatively of Kabbalah. Pinhas Elijah Hurwitz, on the other hand, wrote Kabbalist books himself. The theoretical section and the section devoted to ethical doctrine in *The Book of the Covenant* were both based on Kabbalah. The author actually stated in his introduction that the book as a whole, including its encyclopedia of natural science had been primarily conceived as a preface to Haim Vital's Kabbalist work, *The Gates of Holiness*. Hurwitz did not only deal with theosophical (theoretical) but also with theurgic (practical) Kabbalah. Although he had written a popular book on the natural sciences, he was not above disseminating ideas that were basically contradictory to any concept of natural law.

This dualism—reverence and orthodoxy on the one hand and intellectual enlightenment on the other—also characterized Pinhas Elijah Hurwitz's outlook on ethics and society. Charity and justice were balanced against all other acts of piety; for this was also the divine attitude as expressed by the prophets. In *The Book of the Covenant*, Hurwitz sternly reproached those who "robbed and abused" the needy, and especially "those mighty notables who are in charge of taxes . . . and harm the poor." Like Hurwitz the physician and Rabbi Margalioth, he protested against the wrong that was being done to scholars.

The moral and social doctrine contained in *The Book of the Covenant* rose above that of its predecessors by its emphasis on ideas which anticipated the essentials of the *Haskalah* reform programme for the Jews and their relationship with the Gentile world. Pinhas Elijah Hurwitz regarded the prime rule in "neighbourly love" to be "that a person should love all of the human race, of whatever nationality, because any other man is of the same image and shape and likewise inhabits this world." An orthodox, God-fearing man, attracted by the *Haskalah*, he repeatedly stressed the view of Maimonides that those nations which observed seven acts of piety were assured of a share in the next world. Kabbalist that he was, he also cited the words of Rabbi Haim Vital in *The Gates of Holiness* (Part I, Section 5), "And he shall love all men, yea, even the stranger." Love of mankind was the natural inclination of the individual human being, "for man was not created solely for himself . . . and the society of men generally is veritably like one person composed of many limbs . . .

Man is born lacking in all things . . . and in immediate need of another person besides himself." The Torah explicitly ordained the love of all peoples and not of the people of Israel alone, for it was written, *Thou shalt love thy neighbour as thyself*—thy neighbour "and not merely thy brother."

The precept of "loving the society of humankind" was no abstract matter in the doctrine of Pinhas Elijah Hurwitz. He gave an example of the observance of this precept by the gentiles themselves, in an incident involving a magnanimous ruler (Duke Leopold of Frankfurt-on-the-Oder) who risked his own life to rescue others from death during the flood of 1785. Another of his examples concerning scientists working all their lives on behalf of humanity was an even more typical anticipation of *Haskalah*. From the general principle of loving mankind, he also postulated the duty of allegiance to the ruler: "Each individual should cherish the king of the country in which he lives as he does his own soul, and especially in time of war." Of course, "it is fitting that the king should love every one of his countrymen," for the precept, *Thou shalt love thy neighbour as thyself* was also binding upon him. His exhortations to his fellow-Jews to love their rulers contained repeated prohibitions against defrauding the state of its custom revenues—which were all the more valid for being cited in the Talmud. In fact, he warned his readers against all fraudulent acts towards gentiles, "whatever their nationality," as a corollary to the rule of "neighbourly love" which was equally binding on every individual. Deceiving a gentile, apart from being strictly forbidden by the Torah, also disgraced the Jewish people, for as a consequence of such iniquitous actions, the gentiles denounced the Talmud for purportedly condoning them.

In the sphere of reform, Hurwitz was also concerned with the education of the young. In the best spirit of traditional ethical literature, he demanded that children be spoken to "not in the language of commands but in the language of counsel," so that "the staff of morality should not become the rod of sin." The social theory underlying his programme for educating the young to become useful members of society, displayed the originality and breadth of horizon of an innovator in the field. His proposal that young heirs should not inherit ample wealth but "just enough for their sustenance" came a hundred years before the ideas advanced by the social reform school of thought founded by Franz Oppenheimer. He hoped that an enactment of this nature would be of threefold benefit to society: the heirs would be encouraged to display alacrity and diligence; family strife over legacies would be avoided; and it would provide aid for the poor, as the bulk of all bequests would go to charity. He was, naturally, well aware that his plan was only "a wise man's counsel, for what would the poor man do?" His advice to the poor man on the education of his sons was "to teach all his children arts and crafts while yet young, that they might support themselves thereby."

Pinhas Elijah Hurwitz considered the question of handicraft training for the people to be "the cornerstone and foundation of all God's Commandments." He recapitulated all the reasons given in Bible and Talmud in praise of the handicrafts and added religious arguments of his own. However, he combined his traditionalist and religious reasons with a realistic one which bore the imprint of the current *Haskalah* attitude. He enthusiastically appealed to his fellow-Jews to abandon their questionable employments and take up useful trades in order to improve their own situation and enhance their prestige in the eyes of the gentiles. He complained bitterly of the derogatory attitude that his own generation displayed towards the crafts:

> . . . And I am troubled by the crudity of behaviour and custom manifested in this generation, when most of our people are unwilling to teach their children any crafts, saying in their pride and vanity that artisanship is disgraceful to us and only business dealings and the trade of hawkers and pedlars is honourable and enhancing.

Similarly, he protested against "the scholars who do not wish to teach their sons handicrafts, only the Torah . . . They take it for granted that their sons will be rabbis and judges," though in fact they ended up as *me'lamdim* "and barely earn half their sustenance . . . because there are more *me'lamdim* than pupils." Some of them worked as itinerant preachers, or wrote books and canvassed them from door to door, "and they are all needy and beg their daily bread."

> Whosoever—he wrote—transgresses against the words of our Sages of blessed memory in this matter and fails to teach his son a trade, will have to render an accounting before a heavenly court . . . especially in the Diaspora, where Jews do not own land nor slaves, nor fields; where they have no peasants, vineyards, or grain farmers; neither cattle nor sheep, and in some places not even homes, while even that most important trade in wholesale merchandises shipped from state to state by sea is forbidden to us. How then shall we exist amongst the Gentiles, we, our wives, and our children?

The exclusive preoccupation with trade and peddling led Jews to fraudulent practices, because, as the sages had already said, "poverty distracts a man from the knowledge of his Creator." Hurwitz added:

> By these nefarious acts . . . we profane God amongst the nations . . . for the Gentiles say of us, "This people resides among the nations, idle, lazy, and indolent; they will not perform physical labour and they avoid the manual callings. The only bread they enjoy is that of trade amongst the nations, yet are they a poor people, and when they trade in a country they defile the people about them through fraud, sleight of hand, forgery and quarrelling, and they derive their money from many nations by sucking their marrow . . ."

Like the *Haskalah* spokesmen, Hurwitz ignored the legal restrictions against Jews, although he himself had listed them amongst the reasons for their heavy concentration in trade. Instead, he accused them of ingratitude to the state, which had opened the crafts to them:

> . . . especially now, when most of the states favour the artisans, the craftsmen and smiths, and allow them to reside anywhere in their territory, lighten the tax load for Jewish artisans and add to that of the Jews who are not artisans.

Like all the precursors of the *Haskalah*, his programme of reforms for his people in the Diaspora did not prevent Pinhas Elijah Hurwitz from encouraging his readers with hopes of Messianic deliverance and the restoration of Zion. But his aspirations for deliverance were rather the fervent yearning of a Kabbalist awaiting ultimate salvation. It would appear that Hurwitz, like his friend, Eliakim Ben Abraham Hart of London, with whom he corresponded on the Copernican theory, believed that the great upheaval of the French Revolution and the Napoleonic wars portended imminent redemption. Like all Kabbalists, he believed that "the portals of light, the gateways of mercy have opened, for the End of the Days are approaching," as a result of the revelation of the Kabbalah in the sixth millenium since the creation. "Of course," he complained in a bitter mood in 1807, "because of our innumerable sins, 1,739 years have already elapsed since the destruction of the Second Temple and the Son of David is not yet come, and we have not yet returned to our land." He made a saintly man, mocked by a lout for lamenting the exile, utter the words of consolation: "Know then, that even were I to live in the last year of the Sixth Millennium, I would not cease to hope to God that I will yet offer Him thanks for His Anointed One's salvation . . ."

Even his description of the geography of India (Chapter XI, Article 9) in *The Book of the Covenant* gave Hurwitz an opportunity to introduce the issue of the return to Zion and to deal with it at length. He cited the *Bnei-Israel* of the Malabar Coast as an example of loyalty to the idea of deliverance:

> Why, they were already exiled in the days of Hoshea, the son of Elah, together with the ten tribes and they have more cause to protest against the duration of their exile than we, for they have spent there 816 years more, since we have been in exile only since the destruction of the Second Temple . . . Yet they endure the length of their exile, wholeheartedly see justification for the judgement meted out, always pray to God for deliverance, and daily await the coming of the righteous Messiah.

He criticized his contemporaries for their lack of Jewish patriotism in a long sermon couched in thoroughly modern nationalist terms:

Yet, if our Exile has been so long, it is we who are at fault. Our sojourn on alien soil has lasted so long a time that the Gentiles say we have given up hope . . . For how much longer shall we fail to do what we are able to? Other peoples fight each for its own state, for the land of its fathers (*Vaterland*) and sacrifice their lives for it, while we have been idle and helpless this long while. Why should not we too rise up to contend for our holy soil and the land of our fathers?

However, as an ardent Kabbalist, his religious reverence prevented him from drawing the ultimate conclusions from this striking comparison. On the contrary, he went on to prove that the strength of Jewish patriotism only lay in prayer and obedience to the precepts. Like Judah Halevi and his successors, Hurwitz assured his readers that he had "explored and inquired thoroughly and with all his heart into the reason for the long duration of this agonizing exile." He had discovered that even those who prayed and observed the precepts "have no intent in their actions save their own needs, their own benefits . . . be it for this world or the next or both . . . and they do not aspire to hasten the end and redeem the people and their God . . ."

Hurwitz turned a bitter and penetrating satire particularly on to the wealthy notables who had no ambition beyond the acquisition of wealth and property and the pursuit of glory in life and death—glory amidst a people subjected to contempt and depredation. All their praying for deliverance in Zion was only *a commandment of men learned by rote* (Isaiah, 29:13).

For all the salvation desired by such a Jew is but that he derive his livelihood with distinction and succeed in building himself a house of unpolished or polished stone, or bricks, after the custom of the state we know as *Kamienitza*, that it should endure for many years, to be inherited by his sons and his sons' sons who shall be born unto him in a Gentile land; and he should see his posterity and have long days in this exile and die at a hoary age; and then the rabbi of the town will, together with the other scholars of the Torah, eulogize him in front of the synagogue, and he will have a splendid funeral with the vast attendance of a reviled, despoiled people . . . Yea, the coming of the Messiah is ever on our tongues, but always *from the lips and outwards* . . . They say, *Next year in Jerusalem* . . . not *today*, nor *tomorrow*, and even that not wholeheartedly, for each is desirous of completing the structure he is putting up . . . and of carrying out the transaction he is negotiating for four or five years, having drawn up a written document in connection therewith with the nobleman or the state authorities, a so-called *Kontrakt*, and there is no calling for justice, no conforming to the truth.

These were the satirical diatribes of an embittered Kabbalist, helpless in the face of the ruling class of his people. It was a class indifferent to the yearnings of these people for Messianic deliverance.

While the programme the precursors of east European *Haskalah* drew up for improving the position of education and enlightenment amongst their fellow-Jews was a practical one, despite its shortcomings and limitations, they failed to rise above religious "activism," in regard to the ideal of Zion restored, despite their integral loyalty to that national aspiration. They only followed the practices of their forbears: the Torah, the precepts, and prayer. The same religious conservatism which narrowed their horizons in disseminating enlightenment and securing social-economic reforms also hindered them from becoming the guides of subsequent generations of east European *Maskilim* towards the goal of liberation in Zion.

E. *THE HASKALAH CENTRE IN RUSSIA*

Rabbi Barukh of Shklov, Advocate of Enlightenment

The *Haskalah* made its first appearance in the Jewish communities of Poland and Lithuania during the last quarter of the eighteenth century. Its earliest writers and propagators were no different from the precursors of *Haskalah* in their religious orthodoxy. They, too, adhered to the traditional religion in all essentials of outlook and ethical doctrine. They regarded their great activity in disseminating knowledge amongst the people merely as the fulfilment of the Talmudic proverb, *Torah is good with the custom of the land*. They did not act contrary to the Torah or the obligation to study it in any way whatsoever. Nevertheless, there was one main and significant difference between this generation of *Haskalah* pioneers and their predecessors, the precursors of spiritual regeneration. While the writings of the school of Solomon Khelma and Israel Zamosc exemplified the combined study of Torah and the "sciences," the literary creations of the first east European *Maskilim* were characterized by their essentially secular content. Furthermore, none of the first proper *Maskilim*, the moderates included, disparaged philosophy or advocated any limitation on the study of secular science for fear of heresy. It is true that the *Maskilim* of that generation were far removed from any idea of heresy, apart from individual, atypical exponents of the Enlightenment who were rather assimilationist by conviction than *Maskilim*. Still, they did not consider it either a duty or a necessity to propagate the strengthening of religion. The only task they set themselves was the eradication of ignorance through the dissemination of science and the new ideas.

Haskalah doctrine issued and spread through eastern Europe at that time from two centres, both large commercial cities: Shklov in White

Russia and Brody in Eastern Galicia.* The influence of these two centres reached individual *Maskilim* in neighbouring cities and also further removed areas. The first *Maskilim* in other White Russian cities and in Lithuania (e.g., Vilno, Slonim) maintained connections with the *Maskilim* of Shklov, while the *Maskilim* of Lwow, Tarnopol and the cities of Podolia cultivated personal contacts with the *Maskilim* in Brody.

Barukh Ben Jacob Shik, known, after his native city, as Barukh of Shklov, or Barukh Shklover, had been ordained as a rabbi in 1764 at the age of twenty-four. He later served as a *dayyan* (religious judge) in the city of Minsk. He conceived the idea of "transcribing into the language of the Hebrews books on every branch of learning and science to teach the sons of Judah, that they might not be embarrassed on conversing with the enemy at the gate" when he was still a youth studying Gemara, Rashi and the *Tosaphot* (Annotations) "day and night" under his father, a rabbi. His first work on science was destroyed, together with his collection of books, in a fire that swept the city. Later, poverty and "the burden of earning a livelihood" prevented him from realizing his plans. He set out in quest of knowledge, wandering "from house to house and from city to city" until he arrived in London. He completed a course of study in medicine and then once more roamed the cities of Europe, staying for some time in The Hague, Prague and Berlin (in 1777). In Berlin he made the acquaintance of the *Maskilim* there, including Moses Mendelssohn and Naphtali Hertz Wessely. Travelling via Vilno, he returned to Minsk (he maintained a "fixed residence" there until 1780) and settled for a while at Shklov. According to a family tradition, towards the end of his life he acted both as *dayyan* and court physician to prince Radziwill in the city of Slutzk. He died there some time after 1812.

The Shklov *dayyan* never ceased his efforts to carry out the life's work he had set himself in his youth: to disseminate science amongst the east European Jews, who totally lacked all secular education. The books he wrote incorporated the profound and extensive knowledge of the natural sciences he had acquired during his "years of study and travel" in western Europe. However like most of the *Haskalah* pioneers of his generation, he was forced to canvass the homes of "the generous" in order to get his writings published. In 1777 at Berlin, he published two books by Rabbi Isaac Israeli, a pupil of one of the first of the fourteenth century Codifiers, Rabbi Asher Ben-Yehiel: *The Art of Intercalation* on astronomy and *Foundation of the World* on the proclamation of the new moon. He had discovered the almost three centuries' old manuscript in the home of Rabbi Zvi Hirsch Levin. Barukh of Shklov had previously published a book on the fundamentals of geometry and trigonometry entitled '*Amudie-Ha'shamayim* (*The Pillars of Heaven*) explaining that "man, being a ladder planted on earth with his head reaching into the heavens,

---

* On the trade conducted by the Jews of Shklov, *cf.* Chapter Eleven, p. 372; for Jewish trade in the city of Brody, *cf.* Chapter Ten, p. 319.

must investigate and examine everything on earth, beginning with the human body and including the world as a whole, which he will place as a ladder to be climbed for inquiry into divine purpose . . ." He also offered this motive as his excuse for appending a popular book on anatomy and physiology entitled *Man's Beauty* to his book, *The Pillars of Heaven*. His Hebrew translation of Part I of *Euclid* (on Euclidean geometry) was ready for the press in the same year, but it was not published at Prague until 1780. In 1789, his book on hygiene, *Derekh Ye'sharah* (*A Righteous Path*), was published at The Hague; and in 1784 his book on trigonometry, *Ke'neh Midah* (*A Standard of Measurement*), came out in Prague. A second edition of this book was printed in 1791 at Shklov. However, several of his manuscripts, such as the translation of Part II of the *Euclid* which was ready for the press as early as 1780 and *The Book of Medicaments*, announced in *A Righteous Path* in 1779, never reached the publication stage. His hope that his "collection would be subscribed to by each and every one in Israel" (in a full-page announcement at the end of the *Euclid* volume) was not realized.

All his original works and translations appeared with an introduction, passionately encouraging his people to rouse themselves from the torpor of ignorance and stimulating them to study the natural sciences. Barukh, like the precursors of *Haskalah*, was convinced of the truth of the traditional outlook that "all wisdom and science have flowed from the fountain of Judah." The natural sciences and theologic-philosophical inquiry "have ever been our ancestral heritage," he declared. He also anticipated Wessely in his expression of the view that the primary reason for the popular neglect of science till "wisdom has been lost upon our sons" was the exile. However, he described in a more detailed manner the living conditions that had caused intellectual decline, persecution and poverty. In fact, his protest was not directed against those who had to worry about earning a living but against the wealthy who pursued "each his own profit." Even worse was the atmosphere of contempt and bitterness that surrounded "anybody who has been inspired to assume the burden of Torah and wisdom." He echoed the serious accusations that Israel Zamosc had previously levelled at the fanatics and exposed their sanctimonious self-righteousness. His scathing satire concluded with a bitter cry against this clique of fanatical, hypocritical religious leaders:

> Earth, oh earth! What will you do on the Day of Judgement, when your wickedness will be reckoned against you for not having opened your maws to swallow these sin-tainted men alive even as you swallowed Korah, for is not their evil greater than the evil of Korah?

The Kehillah *Parnassim* abetted the fanatical "protectors of the Faith" and instead of judging issues fairly, refused to listen to "the voices of understanding amongst the people." Because of these fanatical leaders, the people was sunk in the depths of ignorance:

It is through them the Children of Israel have betrayed the wisdoms and become stricken with blindness, disgraced and scorned in the eyes of the Gentiles, forsaken of their glory and their splendour.

National pride and the people's honour in respect of the gentiles formed one of the primary arguments in Barukh Shklover's dissertation postulating a rise in the educational level of the people. Gentile superiority to the Jews was reminiscent of the scriptural phrase, *A handmaid that is heir to her mistress* (Proverbs, 30:23). Thus this disparate situation over a period of generations had to be rectified, for wisdom "which was with us, unto us must return." The restoration of Jewish science to its original height postulated the revival of the Hebrew language, for it was in this language that the works of science intended for the people should be written. In the spirit of the *Haskalah* movement, Barukh of Shklov urged his fellow-Jews to repair the status of the Hebrew language by writing and speaking in "a precise, lucid tongue":

Go, go through the gates! Clear ye the way of the Holy Tongue! Lift up an ensign over the people! Let Israel proclaim—the right of the firstborn that is of the holy tongue! Why must the pillars thereof tremble, its buttresses and foundations be laid bare? Awake to strengthen the hand of our queen, to converse lucidly in pure tones, from the cedar which is in Lebanon and even unto the moss thereof, in a clear speech . . .

Significantly, the author concluded this manifesto by disclosing that he had not adopted *Haskalah* doctrine in all matters: he bestowed on the subscribers to his books the traditional blessing that all authors of religious works addressed to their readers:

May eternal happiness be yours, to behold with your own eyes the Lord's Restoration of Zion, and to be among those remembered, speedily in our day, Amen, so be His will.

The growth of Shklov as "a city full of wise men and scholars" took place at the end of the eighteenth century and the beginning of the nineteenth, when the importance of its Kehillah as the centre of White Russia's foreign trade was at its height. Like all *Haskalah* centres in that period, the literary creation of the Shklov *Maskilim* depended on the generosity of the wealthy patrons who supported them. Leading plutocrats in close contact with Russian government circles, who were accumulating capital as quartermasters and suppliers to the state, played a particularly large role in this activity—though only for a brief interval. The most prominent were Joshua Zeitlin, his son-in-law Abraham Peretz, and Nathan Nota (Notkin). Joshua Zeitlin ranked, both as a man of property and as a patron of enlightenment, with the enlightened Polish magnates whose courts were meeting-places for writers and scholars. He was a merchant, an outstanding Talmudic scholar and the author of *Halakhic* exegeses, but he was also an agent of Prince Potemkin and had co-operated with him in the settlement of the south Ukrainian (Kherson) steppes as a purveyor of supplies. His estate in the neighbourhood of Wielizh numbered over 900 serfs. When he retired from business, he settled on his estate at Ustie, near Shklov, and housed Talmudists and scholars in his palatial residence, erecting a special *Bet-Midrash* for them and establishing a large library for their use. The composition of this community reflected its patron's views: Zeitlin was a close friend of the Vilno *Gaon*, and saw no contradiction between Torah and "wisdom." The scholars who lived and wrote under one roof at the court of the "prince of Ustie" (as Joshua Zeitlin came to be known) included: Barukh of Shklov, who conducted experiments in a chemical laboratory; Rabbi Menaham Nahum, author of a commentary on the *Tosephta* entitled *Additional First Fruits*; the famous *Maskil*, Mendel Lefin of Satanow; and Rabbi Benjamin of Dribin (Benjamin Zalman Rivales), pupil of the Vilno *Gaon*, recluse and puritan, author of Mishnaic exegeses, and the owner of a collection of plants for the study of botany and pharmacy.

Several works by the group of scholars and *Maskilim* residing at the Zeitlin mansion were printed at the Hebrew press which had been established in Shklov at the end of the eighteenth century. An indication of renewed interest in Hebrew grammar amongst the Lithuanian and White Russian *Maskilim* was the new edition, printed at this press, of *A Great Remembrance*, a work on the roots of the language by Rabbi Benjamin Mussafia (first edition, Amsterdam, 1635). The publisher was Naphtali Herz Schulmann of Bychow, in White Russia, who became famous both as a grammarian and as a linguist. When he lived at Vilno, he founded a circle for the study of *The Guide to the Perplexed*. He included a booklet of his own on the rules of grammar as an appendix to the new edition of *A Great Remembrance* and also added an introduction which proved him to be a reformer influenced by several Berlin *Haskalah* concepts. His proposals for educational reforms (which he had already mentioned in a separate but unpublished essay) included the eradication of Yiddish, which he considered a "travesty of language," and the explanation of the Torah to children in "pure" German. At the end of the book, he published an announcement of the founding of a Hebrew weekly with a dual purpose: "To print the news and to spread Enlightenment." In the event, the number of subscriptions collected did not reach Schulmann's expectations, so that this first venture in publishing a Jewish periodical in eastern Europe was a failure.

Assimilationist Radicalism: "the Outcry of the Daughter of Judah"

Simultaneous with the beginnings of moderate *Haskalah* amongst the Jews of Lithuania and White Russia, individual supporters of the Berlin school of *Haskalah*, and particularly of its extremist wing, appeared in the same communities. The moderate *Maskilim* who were practically all Talmudists by profession, expressed the viewpoint of the progressive wing of wealthy merchants. They felt a need for some educational reform and progress which should be in harmony with the new framework of the absolutist state's economy and régime. Nevertheless, like their class as a whole, they were still attached to the traditional religion and the old Kehillah system, which had given them secure status for generations past. The radical *Maskilim* on the other hand, were drawn from amongst the enlightened merchants and professional *intelligentsia* (e.g., physicians) and represented the interests and outlook of a small segment of the Jewish middle class, more modern in origin in that it had emerged in the Russian Jewish community at the beginning of the nineteenth century. These merchant members of the First Guild—commissionaries, quartermaster agents and factory builders—enjoyed more privileges than any other Jews. They were assisted by those very reforms of the absolutist monarchy which were undermining the feudal régime and the Kehillah system, its corollary. Their connections with the autonomous Kehillah organizations became progressively more tenuous, particularly because of the law that required payment of government taxes through the municipal authorities. They were dependent on the government machinery for their widely ramified business affairs and maintained direct and frequent contact with it. Hence, their *Haskalah* programme represented the policy of the semi-enlightened absolute monarchy as well as an attempt to advance their own economic interests and class prestige by binding the Jewish population more firmly to this monarchy. They proposed to accomplish this by means of the new education and also by eradicating the traditional way of life—not least, its glaring manifestation in the conventional Jewish dress.

As early as 1783, during the reign of Catherine II, Jacob Hirsch, a *Maskil* and an admirer of Mendelssohn, had submitted to the Russian government a memorandum in German requesting the establishment of schools for Jewish youth. He was a Moghilev merchant, who was staying in St. Petersburg—apparently on business, for his memorandum expressed his gratitude to the Empress for her abundant generosity. Hirsch described his pride in the fact that all his life "his heart had been aflame with the desire to assist his unfortunate fellow-Jews in their ignorance and thereby also in their wretched and despised status." Courage to pursue this ambition had come from "the great enlightenment ... and magnanimity" of the Christians, and particularly from the state's toleration of all religions and the efforts of its sovereign, "great in her wisdom and a lover of humanity," to promote the cause of Enlightenment amongst the people. He proposed that all *Heder* and *Talmud-Torah* institutions in the Moghilev gubernia be converted into schools where ethics, science and the arts needed "by the useful members of society, each according to his status and mission," would be taught, in addition to religion. These schools would be divided into three categories: elementary schools in the towns; intermediate schools in the cities; and a main school in Moghilev. The author was convinced that well-to-do parents would willingly pay the tuition fees. The children of the poor would be free from payment, but there would be no difficulty in raising the sums needed to establish these schools from the *korobka* revenues, which were mostly squandered on the salaries of the parasitic collection overseers.* This memorandum was not only submitted in the name of its author. Jacob Hirsch assured the government Elementary School Commission that financial assistance for the project would be forthcoming from Jewish dignitaries in the Moghilev district, whom he had consulted.

Hirsch was an enlightened Moghilev merchant, who was convinced that the condition of the Jews could be improved mainly by founding schools which would include the crafts in their curriculum. Unlike him, Nathan Nota Notkin of Shklov, an active commissionary agent with close government connections, devoted his attention to the problem of the movement into productive activity through agricultural settlement and the establishment of factories.† However, Notkin did not ignore the question of educational reform through special schools to be founded by the Kehillot. His plans for moving the Jews into productive occupations were amongst the factors which influenced both Senator Derzhavin's *Opinion* of 1800 and the Jewish Statute of 1804. But his other Jewish adviser, Dr. Jacob Elijah Frank of Kreslavka, exercised an even greater influence on Derzhavin.‡

Frank, a physician, submitted a memorandum to Derzhavin, written in German, on the subject, *Can a Jew Become a Decent, Useful Citizen?* Some of Derzhavin's views on the "false beliefs" in the Jewish religion were borrowed verbatim from this document. Frank, like Jacob Hirsch had been converted by the Berlin *Haskalah*, but he absorbed the views of its extremist, Voltairean wing. In his opinion, the root of the evil lay in the distortion and deterioration of the wholesome Israelite religion of antiquity, based "on simple deism and the postulates of wholesome morality." The authors of the Talmud had come to the fore during the post-Biblical period, some of them "visionaries, deceivers who had themselves been deceived," but most of them were simply charlatans. These men perverted the Bible with their occult and devious interpretations. They distorted the truth and introduced meaningless, unfounded formulas.

---

* cf. Chapter Eleven, pp. 416–7. Hirsch's estimate, considerably exaggerated, placed actual Kehillah expenditure in the Moghilev district at a maximum of a third of the gross annual *korobka* revenues.

† cf. *ibid.* pp. 388–9, 410.

‡ cf. *ibid.* p. 389.

They blinded the people for their own advantage in order to dominate it, spread superstition, and segregated the Jews from other nations and religions by severe prohibitions and religious antagonism. What followed was only a consequence of this evil: because of the bitterness that the Jews felt towards them, the Christians would not tolerate Jews in their countries except on payment of disproportionate taxes; in order to meet these tax requirements, the Jews had been forced to engage in trade and usury; and these occupations had deprived them of all sense of dignity, morality and consciousnesss of noble actions and ethical perfection. This categorically demonstrated that the only way to reform the Jewish character was to restore the Jewish religion to its former, unsullied state. This project—to cleanse the Jewish religion of Talmudical impurities—was mainly to be achieved through a knowledge of pure Biblical Hebrew. In any event, a Jew who knew Hebrew and meditated on the Old Testament would not require the Talmud. Liberated from its seductions and nonsense, he could pursue the path of morality. This was Mendelssohn's way of education, which he had implemented in his translation of the Pentateuch into German—and thereby enabled the German Jews to raise themselves to the level of morality. The conclusion, therefore, was that Jewish reform lay in the founding of schools where Jewish youth would learn Russian, German and Hebrew. Frank did not ignore the driving ambition of the Jewish *intelligentsia* to carve careers in government service.

Hirsch Ber Hurwitz (1785-1857), who rose to fame in the 1820's as a *Maskil* of broad accomplishments shared Dr. Frank's views on the Talmud. Hurwitz had received a traditional as well as a modern education from his father, Haikel Hurwitz, a wealthy trader in the Ukrainian city of Uman, himself inclined to moderate *Haskalah*. In 1817, Haikel Hurwitz published *Zophnath Pa'aneah*,* his own Yiddish arrangement of a book by a well-known teacher, Joachim Heinrich Campe, on the discovery of America, in order to impart a knowledge of geography to his fellow-Jews. The younger Hurwitz spoke and wrote Russian, German and French. He had absorbed the ideas of the Berlin school of *Haskalah* on his trips to Prussia and to Leipzig on his father's business. The Russian Prince Dolgorukov† stayed at the Hurwitz home when he passed through Uman on his travels in 1810, and was so impressed by the profound erudition of the young man that he devoted several pages of his book to details of their conversation. When the Prince asked what the Jews needed in order to be happy, Hirsch replied: "What I wish first of all is that we should be forbidden to wear our clownish garments, for they stamp us with indignity and disgrace. He who is held in contempt loses his own self-respect . . . That is why our people is held in such contempt at present, why it is so

* Literally, "revealer of hidden things," the name given to Joseph by the Egyptians (Genesis, 40:45).
† *cf.* Chapter Eleven, p. 395.

ignorant and uneducated . . ." During this conversation, the young Hirsch expressed the opinion that the Talmud was full of superstition and trivial precepts, severe prohibitions, and limitations that misrepresented the original Mosaic Law, kept the people in ignorance, made its life a burden and held it up to ridicule. "It is time," he declared, "to burn our Talmud, which is only a book of vanities . . . Leave us nothing but the books of the teachings of Moses in their unblemished form, for their laws are best for us."

> Why—he continued—should not all this (Talmudic) foolishness be consigned to the flames? . . . The Jewish people would not dare to oppose this . . . All these absurdities are connected like the links in a chain. Sever the first link—I refer to the Talmud—and all these other nonsensical trivia would fall apart of themselves.

The young Hurwitz was convinced that "sooner or later we will have to be made happy against our will."

Prince Dolgorukov recalled that Hirsch Ber Hurwitz "loves his people, passionately, ardently defends its best interests, and appears to be prepared to offer his life if that could but further the happiness of his brethren." Hurwitz subsequently gave a practical demonstration of his concern for the education of his people. In 1822, he founded a modern school in his native city of Uman, one of the first schools in Russia for Jewish youth. Hurwitz was sure, in the tradition of the generation of the Enlightenment and in total accord with the views of the extremist German *Maskilim* as propounded by Wolffsohn, Euchel and Saul Berlin, that the prior condition for reforming his people was solely a revision of its ideology and faith, by eradicating superstition and fanaticism which, he believed, stemmed from the Talmud.*

A temporary centre for Russia's incipient *Haskalah* movement also grew up in St. Petersburg. The leaders and supporters of the movement in the Imperial capital were nearly all ex-Shklovites who had first established the small Jewish community in the city. The outstanding commissionaries and quartermaster agents of Shklov, Abraham Peretz and Nathan Nota Notkin, had transferred their residence to St. Petersburg at the end of the eighteenth century. They were joined from Shklov by the *Haskalah* writers Judah Leib Nevachovitch (1776-1831), a native of Latyczow, Podolia, who was Abraham Peretz' teacher and later his secretary, and Mendel Lefin of Satanow, who taught Peretz' son, Zvi Hirsch (Gregory) (later a leader of the Decembrist revolt). Their business dealings with the government brought Peretz and Notkin into close relations with ministers

---

* It should be added that Hirsch Ber Hurwitz later altered his opinion and expressed a positive attitude towards the Talmud. Forty years after his conversation with Prince Dolgorukov in 1810, he remarked *en passant* in a letter to the *Maskil* Jacob Goldenweiser, dated July 11, 1850 and written from the University of Cambridge, where he taught Hebrew, ". . . The Torah of Moses is my heritage here, the prophets and sages of the Talmud, my sustenance."

and high officials, and they also negotiated with them on reform plans for Russian Jewry. Notkin was a merchant, a business man and an intercessor (*shtadlan*). He identified himself completely with Jewish life in the Pale of Settlement, was particularly sensitive to Jewish economic distress and ceaselessly supplied the government with detailed programmes for moving the Jews into productive occupations. Peretz and his assistant, Judah Leib Nevachovitch, on the other hand, expressed the desires of the élite of the St. Petersburg Jewish colony, which comprised the fabulously wealthy and the intellectuals. They maintained direct connections with the Berlin *Haskalah* (in 1809, Abraham Peretz had secured six subscriptions to the *Me'asef*) but the main effect of its influence had been to stimulate their ambition to attain equality with the notables of the ruling nation in class prestige. In view of their own unqualified economic privileges, and their contact with the most exclusive aristocratic and official circles, the contemptuous attitude that Russia's ruling class as a whole displayed towards the oppressed Jews, with no exception made for wealthy and enlightened individuals, deeply offended their pride. In 1803, when the government set up its Jewish Reform Committee and summoned Jewish Kehillah deputies to St. Petersburg for consultation, the hopes of these "court Jews" were raised. Judah Leib Nevachovitch felt this to be an auspicious occasion to vent his bitterness and to speak in defence of his associates against those who slandered and humiliated them. He became the spokesman of this group. He published a Russian booklet, *The Outcry of the Daughter of Judah*, at St. Petersburg in 1804 and in the same year an abridged version in Hebrew, printed at Shklov. The author dedicated the Russian booklet to the Minister of the Interior, Count Kochubey, and the Hebrew translation to Nathan Nota Notkin and Abraham Peretz.

Nevachovitch's whole composition, the first ever published by a Jew in the Russian language, was an effusion of Russian patriotism and monarchist loyalty couched in an unrestrainedly obsequious style. Pride in "the land of his birth" was not enough for the newly-fledged Russian patriot, son of the "Daughter of Judah." He extolled it above all European countries and prophesied a great future for it. Russia was already, in his own generation, a guiding light for the nations in the love of humanity. Its monarchist régime was preferable to the new republics overcome by anarchy and fratricide. The blessed Lord had dealt generously with Israel in bringing it, after all the vicissitudes of its wandering, to this land, where it had found repose and happiness. The "wise Catherine" had already granted the Jews equal rights with all other citizens. Czar Alexander, "the good and beneficent," followed in her footsteps and "had not withheld his grace in consoling the mourners of Judah, that condemned of all the nations." He deigned to summon an assembly of Kehillah deputies at St. Petersburg. *The Outcry of the Daughter of Judah* called upon the Jews to thank the rulers of Russia for all the favours that the country had conferred upon them and to rejoice in their salvation, for "their King and

Saviour" was already come and, behold, he was seated on the royal throne!

The Outcry of the Daughter of Judah opened with the question "Why dost thou tarry, oh Daughter of Judah? What hindereth thee?" "The daughter of Judah's" reply did not complain of disenfranchisement, repression or impoverishment. The assimilationist author was secure in his own status of "court Jew" in the capital of the country. He therefore skilfully avoided mention of the ruling power's enactments against the Jews. On the contrary, he announced to them the joys of approaching salvation. What did grieve the "daughter of Judah" inconsolably was the fact that as yet "her brethren were denied a place in the hearts of their neighbours," in the hearts of their Russian "countrymen." Nevachovitch triumphantly proclaimed, in the spirit of the *Me'asef* and in unanimity with Wessely, the victory of reason over medieval ignorance. But even in that generation of reason and religious tolerance, the "daughter of Judah" was still despised in Russia merely because of the difference in religion. The designation *Jew* was enough to evoke scorn and hatred. *The Daughter of Judah* cited the words of "Moses Ben Menahem, that glorious writer of our people" (Mendelssohn) in *Jerusalem* to confirm the theory that religious conversion by the Jews without inner conviction would be of no benefit to the Christians. He abjectly begged for mercy for the Jews—that they should be respected as human beings: "Why shalt thou condemn a person like thyself created in the image of God?"

Nevachovitch's great desire was to be accepted as a brother by the Russian people. With extreme self-abasement and with tears in his eyes, he pleaded with the enlightened Russians in the name of "the daughter of Judah" that they at least suppress their prejudices and "show them (the Jews) merciful grace." His humility before the Russian ruling class, at the expense of all human and national pride, did not stop at a betrayal of national solidarity. He requested that he at least, and other "enlightened" individuals like himself, should not be condemned for the sins of the people as a whole and that they, in any event, should have the honour of being called brothers by the Russians.

This lachrymose appeal for mercy was without precedent, even in the servile pandering to the ruling nation by the representatives of the Prussian Jewish middle class, personified by David Friedländer. This is not surprising: the gulf between the oppressed Jewish people and the ruling class of the state was vastly deeper in Russia than in Prussia, because of the clericalist atmosphere then pervading the regressive Empire. Not long after the publication of *The Outcry of the Daughter of Judah*, its author, like his generous patron, Abraham Peretz, satisfied his offended sense of "honour" in the arms of the dominant Orthodox Church. Judah Leib Ben Noah became Lev Nikolaievitch.*

* With his conversion, Nevachovitch's career began as a Russian writer and high official. His daughter was the mother of the famous Russian biologist, Ilya Mietchnikov.

A Voice in the Wilderness: Manasseh of Ilya

While Jewish *haute finance* and intellectual circles in St. Petersburg indulged in unlimited humility before the high ranking nobles and officials, the Jewish community of Lithuania and White Russia steeped itself deeper in orthodoxy and shut itself off from all manifestations of enlightenment and secular culture. The religious reaction that seized the European ruling classes while Napoleon was still in power also affected the Russian Pale of Jewish settlement, while the spread of Hassidism undoubtedly strengthened religious fanaticism and isolationism. The defection represented by the Berlin *Haskalah* movement and the wave of assimilation amongst the Jewish middle class of Germany prompted the east European Kehillah leaders to redoubled efforts to strengthen religion and tradition in the face of the innovations and reform plans repeatedly launched by the *Maskilim*. These reform programmes appeared most dangerous since they coincided with the legislative aim of the Russian government to limit Kehillah autonomy and spread a modern form of education amongst the Jews. The Kehillah leaders, in contrast with the *Maskilim*, who based their hopes on high-sounding government declarations and the laws of the state, saw through the duplicity of the authorities' practice.

It became evident within a few years of the enactment of the Statute of 1804 that the government was not implementing too strictly those sections concerning the restriction of Kehillah and rabbinical prerogatives and the Kehillot's obligation to establish schools. Confident of the government's secret support, the well-to-do traders who dominated the Kehillot even discarded the moderate *Haskalah* programme with which many of them had still sympathized at the end of the eighteenth century. When reaction throughout the state became more powerful following Napoleon's defeat, orthodox domination of the Kehillot became even more securely entrenched. Manasseh of Ilya, an intrepid exponent of the *Haskalah* who came from the ranks of the religious scholars, was exposed to endless pain and suffering in this atmosphere. Manasseh of Ilya's outlook, way of life, and even the literary form of his writings, placed him in the category of the precursors of *Haskalah* rather than of the actual leaders of *Haskalah* itself. But he had the misfortune to appear too late upon the scene. In this tragedy lay his greatness. During the reaction that swept the Lithuanian Kehillot at the beginning of the nineteenth century, it took exemplary intellectual and physical courage to preach incessantly to the people the doctrine of moderate *Haskalah* which Israel Zamosc and Solomon Khelma had already taught in the middle of the eighteenth century.

Manasseh of Ilya (1767-1831) was born at Smorgon in the Vilno gubernia and was called after a nearby town, where he settled in his youth. He received a thorough education in the Talmud and Codifiers from his father, a *dayyan*, while his great memory already won him a reputation when he was a child. At the age of thirteen he was married off. Two years later he obtained a divorce and remarried. By then he was a famous prodigy and received offers of rabbinical posts in large Kehillot. However, he preferred to lead an austere and penurious existence as long as it enabled him to devote himself to studies. He drew his general education from medieval Hebrew books of philosophy and science, which he found in the library of a friend in a nearby town. It was only later that he obtained works of science in German and Polish, and, despite difficulties in understanding these languages, was able to grasp the rationalist ideas current in the eighteenth century. He gained his information on the events of the French Revolution from the Yiddish journal, *Zeitung*, published at Metz, and from *Words of the Rulers*, by the Dutch *Maskil* Zvi Ilfeld.* His attempts to travel abroad to study science were frustrated by the fanaticism of the environment. When he arrived in the city of Brody, he aroused the disfavour of Rabbi Jacob Landau (son of Rabbi Ezekiel Landau of Prague) by contradicting the Commentary of Rashi. He also had to give up a trip to Berlin because some ultra-orthodox traders he met at Königsberg informed on him to the authorities and hindered him from obtaining a passport, in order to prevent him from "going astray." In 1827, in his old age, he agreed to requests from his native city of Smorgon and accepted the post of local rabbi. He occupied the position only for a year and a half. On August 26, 1827, the royal decree for the military conscription of Jewish Recruits and Cantonists was promulgated,† and the rabbi could not stay silent and see his people suffer. His sermons castigated those who delivered helpless children into the hands of recruiting officers, as criminals entitled to no share in Israel, for their deeds proved "that their forefathers were not present at Mount Sinai." When his friends advised him to desist lest he jeopardize his own career, he resigned from the rabbinate.

Manasseh of Ilya possessed remarkable engineering and inventive talents. Once, after seeing a threshing machine on the estate of the Smorgon city proprietor, he invented a mechanical plough that increased efficiency tenfold. However, the nobles had no confidence in a Jewish mechanic and the Jews were certainly not interested in the mechanization of farming. For the same reasons a tobacco shredding machine he invented was not developed. His sense of national pride was hurt by the Russian government's allegations, at the debates of the St. Petersburg Jewish Reform Committee, that the Jews were uneducated. In order to correct this judgement, he wrote a book on mathematics and military engineering and arranged to have it translated into Russian so that he could submit it to the Senate. This book met the same fate as his inventions. The Kehillah leaders were so afraid that the book would

* *cf*. Chapters Three, Four.

† *Cantonists,* the term for minors (less than eighteen years old) conscripted for Russian military service.

furnish the government with another reason for forcing the Jews into productive labour, that they condemned the manuscript to be burned.

The tragedy of Manasseh's life, isolated in a hostile environment and spent in poverty and persecution, was infinitely deepened by the fate of his fertile literary creativity. His books never reached a circulation amongst the people and most of them remained in manuscript. Several of those that were published were almost entirely destroyed by orthodox fanatics as soon as they appeared from the press. His principal work, *Alphei-Me'nasheh (Manasseh's Thousands)*, was already set up and partly printed at a Volhynian press when the printer gave heed to a warning by a member of the orthodox faction, took fright, and burned the printed sheets together with the manuscript. The author rewrote the entire book from memory and had it printed at Vilno in 1822. This time the book was spared destruction only because its author gave in to the demands of the Vilno Rabbi, Saul Katzenelbogen, and expunged whatever the rabbi considered heretical. Furthermore, Manasseh agreed in principle to the rabbi's right to authorize a decision condemning his book if they should find that historical circumstances necessitated it. Manasseh of Ilya's last book, *The Holy Shekel*, urging his fellow Jews to abandon their idle existence and dubious occupations and to teach their youth the arts and crafts, was publicly burned in Vilno.

The works of Manasseh of Ilya were pervaded with his learning both in their form and in their contents. His method of presentation was characterized by a wealth of Talmudic interpretations, which makes understanding difficult for any reader not acquainted with the exegetical works on *Halakhah*. Manasseh, like his revered master, the Vilno *Gaon,* was entirely immersed in the world of the Talmud and, furthermore, did not question the sacredness of Kabbalah. He rejected the doctrine of deism as a fundamentally "distorted and erroneous view" and also considered the medieval Aristotelean outlook on the eternity of the world to be "perverted and unsound." Nonetheless, his great innovation lay in the fact that his theory of man and society, the Torah and ethics was founded on Maimonides' rationalist system. At the height of early nineteenth century reaction he taught on the basis of *The Guide to the Perplexed*, "that all the righteous conduct concerning the welfare of this transient world is a preparation for a state whereby truly wise men may be free to strive for the comprehension of Divinity." Reason was the final arbiter in matters of religion and therefore "it is necessary to devote attention to the Torah and the precepts, that they should accord with true reason . . . and not that Torah and the precepts should be opposed to common sense . . ."

Manasseh of Ilya repeatedly expounded to his generation Maimonides' doctrine of the rule of reason, for which he derived strength of conviction from eighteenth-century rationalism. Alas, his generation still considered the purpose of life to be in observance of the minutiae of the precepts and in futile casuistry, and was steeped in superstition and false beliefs. In the absence of reason, people could not perceive the purpose of society and the universe as a whole. This purpose was the common good, and Manasseh devoted his entire life to this ideal of the general welfare.

Manasseh did in fact explain in the spirit of capitalist individualism, that "essentially, the ultimate purpose is the welfare of the individual." However, he was not able to follow this doctrine to its extreme conclusion: that the general welfare would be advanced by each individual's pursuit of his own advantage. In this respect, he was influenced both by his own exceptionally socially-minded nature—he was attached to his people by the fervent love he bore them—and by his philosophical outlook on the inseparable bond beween the individual and the community, man and the universe. This outlook undoubtedly contained a spark of the system of Spinoza. The introduction to his book, *Deep Questioning*, which was never printed, explained the task he had set himself in investigating "what it is that has caused the evil and the defects in this world, to understand thereby general methods for improvement":

> For I said, what am I and of what worth, when confronted with the multitude of living, sentient, and articulate creatures in this world? And if conceivably the Sacred Creator had afforded me, my household, my cherished ones and relatives ever-lasting benefits, while yet abuses remained in this world, that is to say, to the disadvantage of any sentient, not to mention articulate creature, a thing from which I could not by choice derive pleasure—wherein then am I different from any other living creature, when we are both equally His handiwork?

In addition, however, the wretched condition of the Lithuanian Jewish community controverted the capitalist doctrine justifying the untrammelled initiative of every individual solely for his own gain. Its extreme poverty resulting from rootlessness was accentuated by social antagonism and the egoism of the wealthy. Manasseh of Ilya, in the introduction to another unpublished book, *A General Reform*, described the privation that his unfortunate brethren endured:

> My heart is sorely concerned with the excess of need and pain suffered in this world by living creatures ... Observe merely the injustice perpetrated in this world, with the stronger devouring his comrade alive ... But most of the evils in the world, and the main ones, are the result of unemployment, for most people are busy searching for a livelihood and do not find any. Only a negligible few out of every thousand have a dependable source of maintenance, while the majority consist of overburdened poor wanting a crust of bread, hungry, thirsty, unclothed, exposed in cold weather, without a house to live in. And in addition to all that, they are beset by natural afflictions and persistent, nagging illnesses ... My eyes are spent

with the daily contemplation of this and I am helpless... I cast about for schemes ... perchance with God's help I may contrive to remedy this, so that through me the world may be rewarded with some measure of relief. ...

Manasseh explained that the welfare of the individual depended on "the welfare and pleasure of every sentient being," and the nature of man was such "by the will of his Creator." He interpreted in this sense, the saying of the Sages, *All those who mourn for Jerusalem shall be rewarded by witnessing her joy.*

Manasseh of Ilya offered nightly prayers (*Tikkun Hatzot*) for the restoration of Israel, with heartfelt lamentations, which left an indelible impression on any chance listener. He tirelessly urged his fellow-Jews to make practical reforms "for the common good," and though he himself was predominantly a Talmudist, he also anticipated the best of the east European *Maskilim* by not disdaining to employ the popular vernacular, Yiddish, in propagating his views. In 1823, he published the first edition of his book, *Sammei de-Hayei*, simultaneously in Hebrew and in Yiddish "so that all should understand it, even simple folk."

Manasseh was concerned mainly with the natural sciences and mathematics in urging the dissemination of Enlightenment amongst the people. However, he was a realist and realized that reform could mainly be achieved by the movement into productive occupations. The title page of his book, *Pesher-Davar* (*The Meaning of Things*), already announced that he would voice "denunciation of that idleness which consumes and debases people to the lowest level, and (I shall) arouse the desire amongst all the impoverished classes of the people for work and manual vocations." He also objected, like an anonymous *Maskil* who had drawn up a memorandum on the subject in 1808, in his pamphlet, *The Sacred Shekel*, to the bad custom of child marriage. The young family heads, who lacked all vocational training, were forced to turn to trade and other insubstantial occupations, "most of which are sheer brigandage," and thus increased poverty amongst the Jews. With his historical perspicacity Manasseh understood that "there is nothing in the world absolutely good or bad; everything at the right time and in the proper place is good; at the wrong time and in the wrong place—bad." The general welfare also "changes with the passing generations ... according to the time and the place." Not all men were capable of understanding the common good; indeed, comprehension in this sphere belonged to those who possessed greatest knowledge and understanding of the foundations of society. Manasseh, true to the age of absolutism, placed his hopes in the monarchy. It is not surprising therefore, that he was moved to write *The Meaning of Things* when he learned of the discussion by the Russian Government Committee of the Jewish Statute. Similarly, he conceived the idea for his principal work, *Manasseh's Thousands*, when the government ordered the Kehillot to send delegates to meet a new Committee in 1818. Towards the end of his life, his ideas were vindicated in a programme systematically outlined in the works of the Russian *Haskalah* writers, especially Isaac Ber Levinson, the Mendelssohn of Russian Jewry.

F. *THE HASKALEH CENTRE IN GALICIA*

Mendel Lefin of Satanow, Father of the Haskalah in Galicia

Political conditions at the beginning of the *Haskalah* movement in Galicia were totally different from those in Russia. In Galicia, a period of forced enlightenment had preceded *Haskalah* as a social movement. German schools for Jewish children had been in existence in Galicia for about twenty years, until 1806, with the principal aim of spreading the German language amongst their pupils. The foundation of these schools had been accompanied by agitation and propaganda which, despite their official governmental character, had included a programme of reform of Jewish life in the spirit of the *Haskalah* movement. Hertz Homberg, government superintendent of the schools, displayed a large degree of skill and caution in concocting this propaganda. Instead of revealing himself in his true role as assimilatory extremist, he confined his propaganda to moderate *Haskalah* slogans based on the premise that "Torah is good with the way of the land." The Hebrew manifesto on educational reform that he published in 1788 was couched in entirely plausible terms which could have emanated from Naphtali Hertz Wessely.

Homberg also dealt with the question of the movement into productive occupations in his book on ethical instruction *Goodly Words*,* written in Hebrew and published simultaneously with a German translation in 1802. However, all the caution and moderation that Homberg employed to propagate enlightenment and useful occupations amongst the Jews of Galicia was in vain. Their rigid conservatism, coupled with religious fanaticism, was still so strong that the Kehillah leaders even considered a modest reform programme to introduce method and order into religious instruction as an innovation tainted with heresy. Their sentiments were of course, strengthened by the fact that Homberg was sponsored by the government and was known to be a lowly servant of the ruling power, and an extreme assimilationist, only one stage removed from conversion.† He also had a reputation for greed and susceptibility to bribery. He even went as far as to initiate repressive measures against his own people (e.g., the

---

* In Hebrew, *Imrei Shefer*; *cf.* Chapter Eight, p. 261.

† It is noteworthy that many years later, in 1833, when he petitioned the Emperor for permission to reside in Vienna, Homberg cited in his favour the fact that "four of his sons had already adopted Christianity."

Candle Tax). For decades after the liquidation of these German-Jewish schools, the memory of Hertz Homberg and the teachers who assisted him evoked the horror and curses of the Jews of Galicia. Thus, the project that Homberg and his faction launched, instead of advancing the process of Enlightenment in Galicia, actually impeded the spread of the movement. The advantage gained by the acquisition of an extremely elementary education by the pupils in these schools, who only numbered a few thousand throughout the country, was more than offset by the animosity towards anything savouring of secular education that was instilled in the great majority of the Galician Jewish population.

A *Haskalah* worthy of the name began to flower in Galicia at the beginning of the nineteenth century and after the decline of Shklov, the first *Haskalah* centre in Russia. There were three large Kehillot in Eastern Galicia: Lwow, Tarnopol and Brody. Brody occupied the leading position as a city of *Maskilim* and writers. Because of its geographical situation and its position as a centre of international trade, it quickly rose to eminence as the centre of *Haskalah* for the neighbouring regions of Volhynia, Podolia and the Ukraine. The central figure amongst the Brody *Maskilim* who advised and taught the leading Galician *Haskalah* writers was Mendel Lefin of Satanow. Mendel Lefin's prolific and extensive activity as a writer and propagator of *Haskalah* was actually associated with four countries: Germany, Poland, Russia and Galicia. He served personally as the intermediary between the movement's centre in Berlin and its focal points in the countries of eastern Europe as well as amongst the focal points themselves. Thus, to the father of the *Haskalah* in Galicia, also fell the historic role of fostering the movement in Poland and in Russia; he prepared the way for his pupil, Isaac Ber Levinson, who initiated the *Haskalah* in the two countries and brought it to maturity.

Mendel Lefin (1749-1826) was born in Satanow, a Podolian trading city near the Galician frontier, which had also been the home of his predecessor amongst *Haskalah* writers, Isaac of Satanow. After marriage, he moved to the nearby town of Mikolajow, which had belonged to Prince Adam Czartoryski. When he had learned his fill of Talmud and the Codifiers, he turned, like most contemporary *Maskilim*, to the *Elim** of the outstanding Jewish renaissance scholar, Joseph Solomon del Medigo (JaShaR) of Candia, for his initial knowledge of the natural sciences and mathematics. *The Guide to the Perplexed*, the guide for all *Haskalah* generations, introduced him also to philosophical inquiry. In 1780, he travelled to Berlin for eye treatment and spent four years there. While staying at the centre of the *Haskalah* movement, he was frequently in the company of Mendelssohn and his circle of friends, German and Hebrew writers. During the same period, he furthered his studies in the sciences and philosophy, and also began his literary work. When he returned home to Mikolajow, his fortune changed as a result of support from the town pro-

* *cf.* Numbers, 33:9.

prietor, Prince Czartoryski. Czartoryski, an enlightened nobleman, a brilliant statesman and leader of the Polish Patriot Party, remained Mendel Lefin's patron for the rest of his life. He contributed funds for the publication of his books, employed him as a tutor to his sons in mathematics and philosophy, and even supported him in his old age. The friendly relationship between Lefin and the Prince's family may be illustrated by the fact that his essay on philosophy, *The Legacy of a Strange Man of Abdera*, was dedicated to Princess Izabella Czartoryski on the occasion of her birthday. The essay was completed in 1794 and amended in 1823, but remained in manuscript form.

After a second trip to Berlin, at the end of the 1780's, Lefin only lived at Mikolajow sporadically and spent most of his time at the Czartoryski home in Sieniawa, Galicia, in Pulawy, near Lublin, and in Warsaw. He was in Warsaw for the convocation of the Quadrennial *Sejm*, which was in session from 1788 to 1792. In close co-operation with Prince Czartoryski, Lefin wrote a booklet in French on reforms for the Jews of Poland. In 1791, he submitted this to the special *Sejm* committee on the Jewish Problem and, on the Committee's recommendation, to the Government Commission on Education (*Komisya Edukacyjna*). It was printed anonymously the following year. At the end of the eighteenth century, Lefin lived on the estate of Joshua Zeitlin at Ustie as tutor to Zeitlin's grandson Hirsch (Gregory) Peretz. He continued in this capacity when his pupil moved to his father's home at St. Petersburg. Lefin's patron, Prince Czartoryski, was Deputy-Minister for Foreign Affairs in the St. Petersburg government during this period, and an active member of the Russian government's Committee on Jewish Reform. It might therefore be safely assumed that he maintained close contact with his Jewish friend while he was working out the Statute of 1804. By 1806, Lefin was back in his home town of Mikolajow, and in 1808 he settled in Galicia, living in Brody until 1817, and after that in Tarnopol, where he died in 1826. The last eighteen years of his life, spent in Galicia, were the most productive both in literary activity and in his personal educative influence on the younger generation of east European *Maskilim*. During these years, he completed and published his most important works, showing amazing perseverance in perfecting them. He did not even allow the ailments that attacked him in old age to interrupt his work. When his eyesight failed, he employed a reader and dictated his books to a copyist. In Galicia, Lefin also found a circle of *Maskilim* who regarded him as their mentor and guide. His disciples included all the prominent writers of the Galician *Haskalah* movement; amongst them, Samuel Jacob Byk, Joseph Perl, Nachman Krochmal and Solomon Judah Rappoport.

Lefin's historic importance lies in his unremitting efforts to raise the cultural level of his people and disseminate general enlightenment and scientific knowledge amongst them. This activity was particularly fruitful due to his exceptional linguistic and literary ability. His unusual and refreshing style, light and universally comprehensible, marked a new development in Hebrew literature and laid the foundations of modern Yiddish literature.

Lefin set out his programme for Jewish reform in the above-mentioned French pamphlet anonymously published in 1792.* He ascribed the wretched condition of Polish Jewry to the spread of ignorance, religious fanaticism and delusions. "Religion," according to the introduction to his essay, "is the most cogent, active motive force within the Jewish people." Thus, it was obviously necessary to examine the evolution of this religion in order to find the remedy. The Jewish religion, the essay stated, was based, first of all, on the Talmud, which was mainly a compilation of laws and precepts—in face of which any discussion on the details of preceptual observance was of no practical value. After the Talmud, a great Jewish leader, Maimonides, had arisen. His book, *A Guide to the Perplexed*, had established his outlook and religion on a scientific basis and had also attributed allegorical significance to the strange legends of the Talmud. However, Maimonides' disciples had placed greater importance on "the wisdom of the Greeks" than on the words of Israel's sages, had explained the entire Torah allegorically, discarded the burden of the precepts and ultimately arrived at a repudiation of religious principles. This apostasy had engendered a reaction in the form of vigorous opposition to every science, so that religious fanaticism now dominated the life of the people. *Pilpulistic* dialectics had become a widespread method of studying the Talmud and great credit rebounded on those who excelled at it. An even graver evil appeared with the spread of the occult doctrine based on the *Zohar*, ascribed to Rabbi Simeon Bar Yohai, and filled with miraculous interpretations and casual references—not to mention later annotations which were not part of the original text. The Kabbalah movement had produced the Hassidic sect of zealots and fervent believers, which originated in Podolia and spread over the entire Ukraine, Volhynia and also a large part of Lithuania. They believed in the miracle-working powers and prophetic inspiration of their leaders, the *Tzaddikim*, who had added innumerable new Kabbalistic customs to the minutely detailed traditional precepts. Even the rabbis had ceased to oppose the Hassidim for fear of their persecution. *Haskalah* had then triumphantly issued forth from Germany and special credit should be paid to the creator of the movement, Moses Mendelssohn, who had followed in Maimonides' footsteps. The first issues of the *Me'asef* had also proceeded along the right lines; however later ones had done great harm by declaring war on the rabbis, thereby antagonizing the people "while they themselves smugly affected an air of spiritual fastidiousness."

As opposed to the *Me'asef*, Lefin proposed attracting some of the rabbis to the *Haskalah* movement, a goal more easily to be accomplished

* *Essai d'un plan de Réforme ayant pour l'objet d'éclairer la Nation Juive en Pologne et de Redresser par là ses Moeurs.*

because of the low status to which the spread of Hassidism had reduced them. These rabbis would be urged to add their approval to *Haskalah* books and periodicals. Rabbis favourably disposed to *Haskalah* would be appointed district chief rabbis and granted exclusive rights to impose censorship and pronounce excommunications under the supervision of the government Commission on Education. The censors would be duty-bound to forbid occult books, *Kabbalah* and Hassidism, and to purge the *Zohar*. The categorical condition for the diffusion of Enlightenment was the eradication of Hassidism. All manifestations of fanaticism, superstition, "the nonsense of amulets," and "miracle healing" would be prohibited by the authority of the state. The rabbis would be encouraged to publish anti-Hassidic writings. However, this task would primarily be incumbent upon the *Maskilim* by writing books and publishing articles in current periodicals, attacking Hassidism and its *Tzaddikim* with devices such as irony and satire, and by exposing their inanities through quotations from Hassidic literature. A positive action would be simultaneously carried out by disseminating information and Enlightenment through the publication of *A Guide to the Perplexed* in easy Hebrew, comprehensible by all, and by popular works on natural and other sciences. It would be the duty of the rabbis to deliver sermons on ethics, castigating offences such as licentiousness, fraud and illegal trading. National chief rabbis with jurisdiction over district rabbis would have to be appointed. The chief rabbis would be empowered to decree, on pain of excommunication, that able-bodied mendicants find employment; those who refused would be forcibly sent to workhouses. Religious orthodoxy needed to be exploited to persuade Jews to transfer to agricultural occupations: the leaders of the religious extremists would be induced to urge their congregations to sow wheat for Passover *matzot*, and to grow flax in order to avoid the use of clothing manufactured with mixed fabrics. Men who propagated agricultural employment for reasons of piety would be rewarded with all the honours granted to the factory builders. However, Lefin remained convinced that the reform of Polish Jewry depended primarily on improved education. To that end, he proposed the establishment of "normal" schools, with Polish as the language of instruction, in Warsaw and all large cities (the tribunal cities). The schools would be open for boys aged fourteen years or over. In addition to the general curriculum, they would also study the Bible, in order to cultivate appreciation of the beauty in the poetry of their forefathers. Some parts of the Old Testament would also be taught in Polish translation to acquaint them with the Polish language. Only graduates of these schools would thenceforth be permitted to submit memoranda to the authorities on subjects of Jewish interest. Similarly, the district rabbis would only be allowed to engage secretaries from amongst these graduates. Thus a generation of Jews who would propagate Enlightenment would be raised.

Lefin's programme was typical of *Haskalah* ideas about improving the condition of the people. Lefin, as an advisor to Prince Czartoryski and the Government Commission on Education, was confident that Poland's enlightened government, now that it had begun to discuss state reforms, was concerned for the welfare of the Jews. He was also convinced that the improvement of their situation depended only on the Jews themselves. Close co-operation between *Maskilim* and the government (which he regarded as a just government) would gradually raise the level of the Jewish people so that fanaticism and ignorance would vanish and Enlightenment prevail. The Jews would become attached to "the land of their birth" and obey its beneficent legislation. The government, for its part, would give the Jews the advantages of its patronage.

Nevertheless, this programme also displayed Lefin's intellectual originality and versatility. He made satire his principal weapon in his war against the fanatics in the peculiar circumstances of Poland, with its widespread Hassidism. It had actually already been employed by extremist Berlin *Maskilim* such as Rabbi Saul Berlin, Isaac Euchel and Aaron Wolffsohn. In emulation of their master, Lefin, it became the method of propagating *Haskalah*, adopted by the *Maskilim* of Galicia, Poland and Russia. There was also a measure of innovation in Lefin's tactical scheme (which also provided the pattern for the *Haskalah* literature of eastern Europe) of creating a schism amongst the orthodox by persuading *Mitnaged* rabbis to enter an alliance with *Haskalah* and thus form one, united anti-Hassidic front.

To the one-sidedness of the reform programme formulated in the French pamphlet undoubtedly contributed the fact that it was intended for the Commission on Education, which, by its terms of reference, dealt only with educational and cultural matters. But it was not mere chance that Lefin saw fit to voice only the hope—and casually at that—that the special taxes be abolished. He made no mention, even indirectly, of the question of Jewish enfranchisement. Lefin's programme in this respect reflected the limited political horizons of the *Maskilim*, who in regarding the dissemination of knowledge as the panacea for all the ills of the people, in their turn reflected the narrow scope of the enlightened absolutist system. Still, even Lefin considered the movement into productive occupation as fundamental to the national reform of the Jews. He failed to enlarge on this subject in his French booklet only because its prime object was the enlightenment and education plan. A Hebrew booklet, found in manuscript amongst Lefin's papers, dealt with reforms for the Jews living on Prince Czartoryski's estates. He had worked out these reform projects in consultation with Moses Mendelssohn and they included a detailed programme for directing the Jews into productive activities. Lefin thought the root of Jewish poverty lay solely in petty trade, and that their condition could only be improved in manual professions. Lefin was aware of the Jews' tradition, as well as their means, capacity and training, for physical labour and proposed, in the first place, the choice of light handicrafts involving no physical effort or undue exertion; crafts not requiring large investment by the artisan or exceptional skill; crafts permanently assured of a profitable clientele and ensuring the artisan a secure and comfortable existence; and finally, simple crafts uncomplicated by the need for additional skills. In this plan Lefin also took into consideration the marketing opportunities for the products of the various crafts.

The schemes Mendel Lefin of Satanow propounded for restratification of the Jews by productive occupations, the reorganization of the Kehillot and the rabbinate, and the dissemination of Enlightenment with the help of the Polish government, came to nothing, like all the Jewish reform plans advanced in connection with the Quadrennial *Sejm*. "The Kingdom of Righteousness," on which he had pinned his hopes, could not muster the strength to implement any substantial reforms in the conditions of the oppressed urban and rural population. It expired with its final partition amongst the three neighbouring, absolutist, powers, a victim of its own feudal régime. Disappointment at this event made Mendel Lefin more than ever determined to devote all his talents and strength to his main task in life: "to compose writings" propagating Enlightenment and science amongst his people. His opinion that it was the duty of the scholar to enlighten the people with his learning and to consecrate his life to instilling this knowledge into his brethren was in the high tradition of the élite in Hebrew science during the Golden Age in Spain (for example, Abraham Bar Hiya Nasi) and the Renaissance period in Italy (Joseph Solomon del Medigo of Candia).

Mendel Lefin personally, and with distinction, practised what he demanded of others. He was indefatigable in his literary efforts. In 1789, his first book *Kinsman to Understanding* (*cf.* Proverbs, 7:4) was published at Berlin. It contained excerpts from two of his essays, *Iggarot Hokhmah* (*Epistles of Wisdom*) on the natural sciences, with a supplement on ethics, and *Re'fuat Ha'am* (*Popular Remedies*). His announcement to his readers on where to purchase his book proved that the distribution of *Haskalah* books at that time was advanced by the author's *Haskalah* colleagues and also by traders attending fairs (in large commercial centres such as Berlin, Frankfurt-on-the-Oder, Mezhirich, Satanow, and Miedzyboz), market days in Lenczna and the market at Berdichev.

In 1794, Lefin published a complete edition of *Popular Remedies*, the Hebrew translation of a popular book by a Swiss, Dr. Tissot. Moses Mendelssohn had encouraged him to translate this book, which had had a wide circulation throughout Europe, Prince Czartoryski advanced the money to print it, and a number of well-known rabbis honoured it with their approval. In contrast with the book on hygiene and anatomy by Barukh Shik, the Shklov *Maskil*, or even Dr. Moses Markuse's Yiddish *Book of Remedies*, Mendel Lefin's work was a marked success; 1,000 copies were sold within a short time and were "scattered through the length and breadth of Poland." Lefin, in a letter written in 1825, justifiably boasted that, as a result of the book, "from then until now many hundreds of Jewish souls have been kept alive." Some Kehillot accepted the advice Lefin offered in the introduction, bought the book in bulk and distributed copies to rabbis and hospital superintendents, so that they might learn how to tend their patients.

Lefin's book on morals, *Heshbon Ha'nefesh* (*The Soul's Reckoning*), published at Lwow at the end of 1808, also had a wide distribution. The late nineteenth century Hebrew writer, A. B. Gottlober, relates how young men's associations were founded in Galicia and Podolia with the aim of living according to the ethical precepts of that book. Some twelve rabbis gave their approval to the first edition; as late as 1844, Rabbi Israel Salanter Lipkin) had it republished for the enlightenment of the members of the movement he founded.

The Soul's Reckoning was partly an adaptation of Benjamin Franklin's autobiographical work, *Art of Virtue*. But Mendel Lefin added his own "Chapters on Morals" and "Selections" to Franklin's concepts of chastity and the art of cultivating the virtues. These incorporated a vast collection of psychological problems and new philosophical ideas (such as those of Locke and Kant), although he also occasionally employed ancient and medieval philosophical terminology (for example, Plato and Maimonides). He also propounded ideas of progress and the self-perfectibility of the human race as well as man's duty to dedicate himself to general welfare. The terms in which he formulated this latter concept contained intimations of democratic thought and also demonstrated surprisingly subtle psychological observation of personal and social human relationships.

Lefin's two popular books were also liked by the reading public because of their "light and easily comprehensible" language—to use the author's own definition of his style in translation. The flowery rhetoric commonly employed in *Haskalah* literature and consisting of fragmentary Biblical passages arbitrarily connected, was foreign to Mendel Lefin's taste. He avoided equally the other extreme: the stiff, difficult jargon of rabbinical literature, *Halakhic* exegeses, and *responsa*, which his contemporary, Manasseh of Ilya still employed. Lefin's style was a pleasing fusion of the language of the Bible, the Mishnah, and the Midrash, and it was in this that his felicitous linguistic innovations lay. He created this easy and attractive Hebrew medium out of deliberate democratic motives: not to adorn himself with rhetorical phrases but to write to "be understood by the mass of the people who do not thoroughly understand the Holy Tongue." Lefin's pupils and their pupils in turn quite explicably therefore inherited the democratic trend of *Haskalah* from him, as well as the folk medium. *Mendele Mokher Se'farim* (Shalom Jacob Abramowitz), "the grand old man" of modern Hebrew and Yiddish literature was taught at the Zhitomir Rabbinical Seminary by Mordecai Suchostaver and his colleague Eliezer Zvi Zweifel, both of whom had been Lefin's disciples.

Lefin published the *Sea Voyages* of the German writer and pedagogue, Joachim Heinrich Campe, in a popular, Talmudic Hebrew translation at the Zolkiew Press, in 1818, with the aim of spreading geographical knowledge amongst the Jews. Towards the end of his life, Mendel of Satanow completed the great undertaking he had begun in the 1780's: a new translation of Maimonides' *Guide to the Perplexed* "into a light, pure, Mishnaic tongue" based on Samuel ibn Tibbon's medieval Hebrew translation. His translation of Part I (up to Chapter LXXII), was only published in 1829-33, a number of years after Lefin's death, through the efforts of his pupil, Mordecai Suchostauer. The translation of the remaining two parts remained in manuscript and was never printed. Lefin had hoped that his translation of Maimonides' book would inculcate a rationalistic outlook based on the study of nature amongst the people and eradicate their belief in occult doctrine, Hassidism and Kabbalah. He made this dual purpose explicit in a separate introduction to the translation, published in the year of his death under the title *Alon-Moreh* (*The Oak of Moreh*, i.e., The Guide).

In this introduction, Lefin elucidated the classification of the branches of science and the principles of logical thought. He reiterated man's duty to gain familiarity with the world and to study it. The image of God, he asserted, was human intelligence, which enabled man to raise himself from his state of nonentity to the zenith of the heavens and to penetrate the secrets of nature. The Maimonidean system, therefore, only served Lefin as a frame of reference to propagate his own views; he omitted all mention of metaphysics—the "inquiry into divinity"—which Maimonides had regarded as the crowning glory of science.

Mendel Lefin again expounded his concept of progress, and particularly the unceasing progress of science, in this introduction—and even more lucidly than in *Soul's Reckoning*. He clearly stated that the increase in scientific knowledge constantly revealed new fields to be explored and claimed that scientific advance was the necessary result of the growing volume of information accumulated and correlated from generation to generation.

In addition to intelligence, the other attribute of the divine image, which God implanted in man, was, according to Lefin, ethical doctrine. "For Man is beholden to resemble Him and to cling to His ways; that is *And thou shalt love thy neighbour as thyself*, which is the Torah's intent and meaning." Mendel Lefin, like Israel Zamosc before him, inveighed wholeheartedly against the self-righteousness that based religion on "precepts concerning Man's relation with God" and placed little importance on "precepts concerning man's relations with his fellow men." He refused to reconcile rigid observance of ritual with dishonesty in business and was particularly incensed by the increase in vindictive religious fanaticism which accompanied the spread of Hassidism. He regarded the adherents of the Hassidic movement as simpletons, and its leaders as charlatans, who had become "false prophets in order to lead a pleasurable life on the toil of fools."

However, Lefin's attack on the occult doctrine in Hassidism, which, he argued, stultified the people with its meaningless superstitions, was even stronger than his rejection of it on ethical grounds. As a rationalist, a popular educator and a proponent of scientific inquiry, he compared Maimonides' pure reason with Kabbalah and Hassidism, pointing out the latter's inanity and insignificance.

Lefin had commented on the efficacy of satire as a means of exposing the religious fanatics in his French pamphlet and he himself wrote anti-Hassidic satires which were never published. By writing a Yiddish book against Hassidism, Lefin was merely following the same method he had adopted in the propagation of *Haskalah*. A letter found amongst his papers mentions an essay he had written in German on the importance of disseminating culture and Enlightenment amongst the Jews of Poland in Yiddish. His one aim in life was to raise the cultural standards of his people and implant knowledge in their midst. In pursuit of this goal, he had repudiated the Berlin school of *Haskalah*, which supported "pure" Biblical Hebrew, in order to regenerate the language of the Mishnah and the Midrash by his Hebrew writings. For the same reason, he did not hesitate to go against the prevalent trend amongst the *Maskilim* of his own generation and to write for the people in Yiddish—the language that the *Maskilim* despised. And it was into this popular spoken vernacular that Mendel Lefin of Satanow chose to translate some of the books of the Bible.

To spread the knowledge of the Bible was a fundamental point in the *Haskalah* programme throughout its existence. The Bible was considered the chief instrument for orientating the people from the Gemara atmosphere and the casuistry of rabbinical literature to new, improved patterns of living. It was felt that the study of the Bible would accustom them to read poetry and awaken their dormant sense of the beautiful. To Mendelssohn and his associates, in writing the *Commentary* and translating the Pentateuch, the educational aim had only been of secondary importance. Their main objective had been to spread the knowledge of German amongst the Jews as "a first step to culture." Mendel Lefin, on the contrary, regarded the dissemination of Biblical knowledge as the chief function of a *Maskil* educating his people. Despite Mendelssohn's hostility to the "jargon," Lefin was determined to translate the Holy Scriptures into Yiddish in the hope of making knowledge of the Bible the possession of the masses of the people.

Lefin therefore scrupulously translated the books of the Bible he selected into pure vernacular, "our Yiddish tongue, as it is spoken amongst us today." He quite deliberately avoided, as far as possible, the influence of German—which explains the large number of Slavic expressions in his translation, commonly found in colloquial Yiddish of the period—and liberally employed Hebrew words. It was these characteristics that gave his translations their peculiarly charming and moving popular quality. He did not consider it his function to translate verbatim but rather to render the idea of any given passage faithfully. As a result, he produced lively paraphrases instead of literal translations, colourful, supple, warm, with the succulence of the spoken word and often the humour of pithy folk expressions.

Lefin seems originally to have intended to translate Psalms, Proverbs and Job, as well as the Five Scrolls but he was only able to complete the translation of Psalms (with a few omissions), Proverbs, Job, Lamentations and Ecclesiastes. He chose to translate the books which were best adapted in content to the educational purpose he had set himself. He would appear to have selected Psalms and Lamentations as models of poetic creation, while Proverbs, Job and Ecclesiastes were intended to stimulate the reader's thoughts on universal matters and train him in philosophical meditation. Lefin wrote a Hebrew commentary to each of the books he translated, with a dual purpose in mind: to discredit laboured and distorted commentaries by providing a simple gloss of the written text; and, where expedient, as a vehicle for the insertion of *Haskalah* ideas. Even so, he adhered to the custom of traditional commentators by concluding his introductions (e.g., to Psalms and Ecclesiastes) with an expression of hope for deliverance.

Only one of the Biblical translations that Lefin completed was actually published in his lifetime: Proverbs (Tarnopol, 1813). His translation of Ecclesiastes was not published until 1873 and the rest remained in manuscript. But his Bible translations, like his other manuscripts, were passed from hand to hand in Podolia and the Ukraine, and, according to A. B. Gottlober, they induced many people to "seek enlightenment" and to teach their sons "the tongues and books of other nations."

The publication of Mendel Lefin's Yiddish translation of the Book of Proverbs provoked the first literary controversy in east European *Haskalah* on Yiddish, and on *Haskalah* ideology generally. The *Maskil* Tobias Feder recorded his unqualified opposition to the translation and to its author in a satirical work that precipitated a storm amongst the *Maskilim* of Eastern Galicia.

Tobias (Gutmann) Feder was born in 1760 in the city of Przedborz, near Piotrkow, in central Poland. He was an outstanding Hebrew grammarian and Biblical scholar and won acclaim with his critical book on Aaron Wolffsohn's commentary and on the Hebrew language research of Isaac of Satanow. He was a famous *Melitz* (rhetorician), still he spent his entire life wandering in search of employment, engaged in many occupations: correcting Torah scrolls, as a prayer leader on the High Holy Days, a synagogue preacher, and as private tutor in wealthy homes. Even with the support from rich *Haskalah* patrons, including Rabbi Joshua Heschel of Chelm, he lived in continual poverty until his death at

Tarnopol in 1817. His wanderings took him to Frankfurt-on-the-Oder and Berlin, and at one time or another he lived in Piotrkow, Chelm, Wolodarka in Volhynia, Berdichev, Brody and Tarnopol. His dependence on the generosity of benefactors was reflected in some grandiloquent verses, written in their honour. He also composed patriotic paeans celebrating the Russian triumph over Napoleon (1813-14) at the request of the Berdichev Kehillah leaders. Even his one poem redolent of social protest, describing the deprivation the poor endured at the hands of the Berdichev Kehillah leaders, was written in honour of someone described in high-flown rhetoric as the saviour of the Kehillah.

Feder's *Weltanschauung* was a conglomeration of *Haskalah* and ortho-doxy, like the strange combination of occupations he had followed. His radicalism was only expressed in his hostility to the Hassidim, who, in turn, persecuted him all his life. Even the one humorous work found amongst his papers, *A New Zohar for Purim*, written in a scholarly imitation of the language of the *Zohar*, was a deliberate satire on Hassidism. His ideological moderation did not prevent Feder from admiring Mendelssohn and the entire group of the Berlin *Haskalah* and re-garding them as the guiding spirits in everything concerning "purity of language," both Hebrew and German. Not surprisingly therefore, Feder, with his narrow horizons and a view of *Haskalah* confined exclusively to grammar and rhetoric, was incontrovertibly hostile to the trend developed in the *Haskalah* movement by Mendel Lefin. As a grammarian and rhetori-cian, he was appalled by the popular, light and flexible Hebrew that Lefin had so worthily regenerated. A hanger-on at the tables of the rich, he was contemptuous of the poor and inferior in station. He was therefore im-pervious to the utility of Lefin's project for publishing popular books on science for the education of the masses. The complete contrast between Feder, the backward humanist *Maskil*, servant of the patrician class, and Lefin, the rationalist *Maskil*, spokesman for the progressive, democratic faction, ambitious to raise the people as a whole to a modern cultural level, openly erupted in the controversy over the translation of the books of the Bible into Yiddish.

The appearance of the Yiddish version of the Book of Proverbs brought Feder's anger at the man who was revolutionizing *Haskalah* methods to boiling point. He gave vent to his wrath in a satirical diatribe against Lefin, entitled *Kol-Me'hatzetzim* (*The Voice of Archers*) published in the same year (1813). The satire attacked the abomination committed by translating a book from the Scriptures into Yiddish. It was a double infringement: neither the desecration of "Germany's fair language," nor the elevation of Yiddish, "that tongue of corruption," speech of the masses, to the rank of a literary medium, was forgivable.

The satire chiefly took the form of a "trial" of Lefin's translation, conducted as a *Discourse in the Land of the Living*. The participants were representative *Maskilim*, Moses Mendelssohn, Naphtali Hertz Wessely, Isaac Euchel, Joel Brill and Judah Leib Ben-Ze'ev, in addition to two representatives of earlier centuries, Moses Haim Luzzato and Manasseh Ben-Israel.

Mendel Lefin was so greatly respected by Galician *Maskilim* that even those who disagreed with his *Haskalah* methods rallied to demand satisfaction on his behalf for the abuse that Tobias Feder had hurled at him. A letter that the distinguished Brody *Maskil*, Jacob Samuel Byk (1772-1831), sent to Feder, expressed their unanimous opinion. The letter defended Lefin as a writer, but Byk also took the opportunity to expatiate as a matter of principle on the rights, historical value and philological nature of the Yiddish language:

> Remember, my friend, that this is the language our fathers and fathers' fathers have spoken in this land of Poland throughout the past four hundred years. *Ge'onim* have spoken, thought, and preached in it. In this tongue we even heard the speech of the Vilno *Gaon* of blessed memory. Philologically—Byk went on to explain with a striking comprehension of the issue—Yiddish is not inferior to any language in the world, for all languages have developed into literary mediums only with the passage of many generations . . . Observe that the languages of France and England, also a conglomerate of the tongues of Germany, Gaul, Rome and Greece effected through the toil of scholars from generation to generation, underwent a marked evolution over a period of three hundred years, so that now, although they contain all these mixtures, they have become fit for the noblest poetry, for the most exalted and endearing turns of phrase. German was in such a humble position but one hundred years ago. Until eighty years ago, Russian was a peasant dialect. The ancient tongues of Greece and Rome were lowly languages at the beginning of their history, until their scholars sifted and compiled grammatical inflections, achieving perfection so great that we must contemplate it with amazement. It is the mass of the people everywhere that has founded a national language; and when they originate there is no difference in prestige between one language and another: they all stammer at the beginning, and it is only the philosophers who fashion the raw material into a treasured instrument so marvellously pleasing in form.

In this eloquent defence of Yiddish, Byk also suggested that it was the duty of the scholar to attempt to advance the education of the toiling people, whose labour supported them.

On the whole, however, most of the *Maskilim* did not agree with Lefin on the translation of the Bible into Yiddish, despite the respect they showed by rising to his defence. Because of this opposition, Lefin failed to publish his remaining translation from the Writings (Hagiographa) after publishing his Yiddish version of Proverbs. These differences of opinion notwithstanding, Lefin had the satisfaction of producing several pupils who carried on his lifework in all fields. His declining years saw an impressive growth of *Haskalah* in Galicia, led by his pupils, and his pupils' pupils: Joseph Perl, Jacob Samuel Byk, Nachman Krochmal, Solomon Judah Rappoport, Judah Leib Mieses, Isaac Erter, Samson Halevi Bloch and Meir Halevi Letteris.

The Viennese group of *Haskalah* writers also played a significant role in stimulating the spread of *Haskalah* in Galicia during that period. The outstanding grammarian, Judah Leib Ben-Ze'ev, a member of this group who lived in Galicia as a youth, played a particularly important part in the dissemination of *Haskalah* not only in Galicia but throughout all of eastern Europe.

Judah Leib Ben-Ze'ev (1764-1811) was born at Lelow, near Czestochowa, and settled in Krakow, following his marriage at the age of fifteen. His life was typical of most of the *Maskilim* of his generation and country. In 1787, after innumerable wanderings through Poland, Hungary, Moravia and Prussia, he reached Berlin, where he learned German, made the acquaintance of the editors of the *Me'assef* and began to publish articles and poems in the periodical. He stayed for three years in Berlin and then returned to Krakow. However, Hassidic persecution forced him to leave his wife and city once again and settle in Breslau. He spent ten years there, working in a Hebrew printing establishment, and also publishing some of his own books. His travels round the cities of Galicia in an attempt to sell these books brought him to Brody, where he made friendships amongst the local *Maskilim*. In 1799, he moved to Vienna, where he was engaged as a proof-reader and editor in the large, German-owned Hebrew printing houses.

Despite his early death at the age of forty-seven, Ben-Ze'ev bequeathed a literary legacy of considerable proportions to his generation. He was possessed with a passionate love for the Hebrew language, inseparably linked to his love for Jewishness, which he regarded, in the spirit of the times, as identical with religious tradition, albeit refined by the process of *Haskalah*. His activities for strengthening the religious ties of the younger generation were also marked by the reactionary trend current during the age of Napoleon. But his great concern for the preservation of Jewishness was always predominant and was reinforced by his deliberate opposition to the strong movement towards assimilation in central European Jewry as a result of the intellectual trends favoured by extremist Berlin enlightenment circles. His desire to strengthen Judaism caused him to write a Hebrew textbook for young people *Me'sillat-Ha'limud* (*Pathway to Learning*), accompanied by a modern Hebrew chrestomathy *Limud-Mesharim* (*Correct Learning*), and also to publish a textbook for the study of religion, *Yesodei-Ha'dat* (*Fundamentals of Religion*), not only in the official German, but with a corresponding Hebrew text. Both the introductions to these textbooks and the texts themselves contained the conventional *Haskalah* slogans: the study of "wisdoms and sciences," and also handicrafts, loyalty to the crown and gratitude for its "favours." But his extremist monarchist loyalty did not prevent Ben-Ze'ev from incorporating the idea of the Messiah's coming, the restoration of Zion and the ingathering of the exiles into these textbooks.

By contrast with the ephemeral value of his textbooks for young people, his Hebrew translation of two Apocryphal writings, *The Scroll of Judith* and particularly *The Wisdom of Joshua Ben-Sira*, was extremely important from a linguistic point of view. Ben-Ze'ev, in his *Preface to the Holy Scriptures*, published in 1810, was the first modern Jewish scholar (specifically, the first since Spinoza) bold enough to express ideas suggestive of Biblical criticism. Following the German scholar, Eichhorn, he distinguished between First and Second *Isaiah*, and also between two authors of the book of Zechariah. However, two of his books secured him a place of honour in *Haskalah*: the Hebrew grammar entitled *Talmud Le'shon Ivri* (*Study of the Hebrew Language*), and a dictionary of Biblical Hebrew *Otzar Ha'Shorashim* (*A Thesaurus of Radicals*). In the first place, his great innovation was to establish a grammatical system for Hebrew in accordance with methods of studying modern language; secondly, regarding Hebrew as a living literary medium, his book on grammar incorporated several chapters on syntax as well as on poetic expression.

Study of the Hebrew Language had a wide circulation because of the superiority of this modern method and ran into eleven editions in the first eighty years of its publication in 1796. It was the principal text for instruction in Hebrew grammar used by east European Jews until the beginning of the twentieth century. As knowledge of the language and its grammar had become the most prominent mark of affiliation with the *Maskilim*, the appellation Ben-Ze'ev (the *Study of the Hebrew Language* was colloquially known by its author's name) was synonymous for generations with *Haskalah*, especially amongst its orthodox opponents.

CHAPTER FOURTEEN

THE LAND OF ISRAEL

A. *UNDER TURKISH RULE*

The Political and Social Régime

Palestine, the cradle of the Jewish people and the object of its passionate aspirations throughout the dispersion, was in no better a position than its exiles. At the beginning of the eighteenth century, when the condition of the Jews in Europe, and particularly in the great Jewish centre, the Kingdom of Poland, had touched the depths, *Eretz Israel*, too, was economically and politically at its lowest ebb. But the condition of the Jews in Europe had taken a sharp turn for the better by the end of the eighteenth century, with the rise of capitalism and the beginning of civil enfranchisement. Palestine, on the contrary, could resort only to temporary expedients at that period, in no way sufficient to arrest the growing process of decline and desolation. It was a victim of the feudal socio-political régime at its most decadent and corrupt phase.

Since its conquest by the Ottoman Turks in 1516, Palestine had been part of the vast Turkish Empire which stretched from the Persian frontier in the east to the borders of Morocco in the west, from the River Dniester in Bessarabia south to the Sahara desert in Africa. The tottering structure of the feudal monarchy, founded on social depredation and ruthless national oppression, was in a continuous state of collapse throughout the eighteenth century. Towards the end of the century, it reached the final stage of disintegration. Active rule was in the hands of the *pashas*, heads of the twenty-eight *pashaliks* in the Empire. The most energetic amongst them were to all intents and purposes absolute despots in their countries, mobilizing their own armies and waging individual wars against their neighbouring rivals. The office of pasha was sold to the candidate who bid the highest price and offered the largest bribe. The government of the Sublime Porte at Constantinople avoided all intervention in the administrative affairs of the *pashaliks*, but it cunningly played them off against each other, according to the principle of divide and rule. The weakness of the régime was clearly evident in the growing number of revolts by oppressed nationalities throughout the Empire.

Like all Middle East countries at the beginning of the modern period, Palestine was at a disadvantage in its economic development because of its geographical situation. The overland commercial trade route had been abandoned with the discovery of a sea route to the Indies around Africa, and Palestine and Syria lost all their importance in world commerce. However, a significant cause of Palestine's economic decline was its social and political system—a glaring example of the feudal decay that was affecting the collapsing Turkish Empire as a whole.

The agricultural workers, the *fellaheen*, bore the full burden of the prevailing régime. All land in Palestine, apart from the *waqf*, or lands owned by the Moslem religious authorities, and exceptional instances of privately owned land, or *mulk*, was in the hands of the Sultan, so that the peasants were legally in the position of tenants occupying state holdings. The collection of rentals from these tenants, like all taxes, custom and other state revenues, was farmed out annually. In most cases, the pasha himself secured the lease on village revenues together with all other state revenues collected in his province. The pashas, in their turn, handed their leases over to the district governors or to special secondary leaseholders, who collected the payments from the peasants through officials or sub-lessees, often including the village sheiks.

By the end of the eighteenth century, tenancy fees amounted to half or even two-thirds of the *fellah's* crops. The *miri* tax, which the lessees paid the government, was fixed for each village and no deductions or rebates were granted in any circumstances. If an inhabitant left a village, the total sum of the *miri* was redistributed amongst the remaining inhabitants. If an entire village was abandoned, the neighbouring villages had to make good the deficiency. Even more ruinous for the peasants was the burden of war levies, arbitrarily imposed on the villages by the pashas from time to time, especially the obligation to deliver supplies to the army. Soldiers quartered in the villages or dispatched by the pasha to collect the *miri*, mercilessly and relentlessly pillaged whatever was available. In addition, villages in certain parts of the country, especially in the frontier areas, had to make annual payments to nomadic bedouin tribes as protection fees. Not surprisingly, therefore, the peasants were deeply in debt, being forced to borrow from townsmen, from their wealthy neighbours, or from the pashas themselves. At the end of the eighteenth century, the interest rate was usually 20 per cent; at times it even rose to 30 per cent. To underwrite these loans, they mortgaged their crops, which anyhow they had to sell in advance, because of their financial distress. The exploitation of the peasants was complete when the pashas arrogated to themselves monopoly rights of trade in export commodities, particularly cotton, and required the *fellaheen* to sell to them below market price.

The *fellaheen's* standard of living continually declined under brutal oppression by state, bureaucracy, army, lessees and usurers. The French economist, François Volney, who toured the country from 1783 to 1785, described the condition of the peasants living on round, paper-thin sorghum or barley-meal bread (*pita*), eggplant and lentils. During periods of drought, they even ate wild plants and acorns. Constantly growing exploitation sapped all initiative on the part of the peasants to improve their situation by developing their land or planting new fruit groves. Whole groups of despondent peasants frequently fled into the desert or sought refuge in the cities, leaving "ghost villages" behind them.

Because of the impoverishment of the population and its total neglect by the authorities, every drought year became a year of starvation, which in turn brought plagues and epidemics. But human factors, resulting from the despotic, reckless régime, were even more responsible for the country's growing desolation and ruin. Raids by bedouin tribes, robbing and wilfully destroying fields and orchards, were particularly common during the first half of the eighteenth century, and added to the peasants' destitution. Suppression by the pashas of revolts amongst the population, and the domestic wars between the pashas themselves (the fiercest took place between 1770 and 1775), laid waste entire areas in the northern and southern parts of the country. These at least were intermittent evils compared with the incessant feuds between conflicting nomadic tribes, which also divided the *fellaheen* into rival sides. It was the custom for the *fellaheen* to make a covenant with one of the two principal tribes in the country against its rival as a means of gaining protection against bedouin assault. This sharpened the division between adjacent areas, or even between neighbouring villages within the same area. The Turkish authorities in Palestine were quite content to encourage this division of the population and even connived to provoke conflicts between the tribes and the settled communities, inciting the adversaries to open warfare.

Thus the system of oppression, exploitation and lawlessness not only reduced the agricultural population to extreme poverty but actually turned most of the countryside throughout the land into a wilderness. This oppression of the peasantry by the régime formed the chief obstacle to the development of the cities as centres of trade and handicraft. The purchasing power of the peasantry was so low that the exchange of commodities between cities and villages was confined to the barest minimum. The large number of hawkers with stalls on the streets, offering nothing but a few cakes, some dates, sweetmeats and cheap inferior-quality fancy goods were a significant indication of the poverty in the cities. Hordes of blind beggars and cripples crowding the narrow alleys completed the scene of destitution.

The turbulent political condition of the country, with incessant civil wars and uprisings, undermined all trade and industry, as it also caused the decline of agriculture. A symptom of lawlessness which directly affected commercial traffic was the disappearance of roads, destroyed by peasants in the hilly areas, in the hope of making their villages less accessible to pillage by Turkish military personnel. Transport was limited to beasts of burden, asses, mules and camels. Carts vanished because the civil and military authorities requisitioned every vehicle they could find. Furthermore, commerce throughout the country was hampered by the lack of security on the bandit-infested roads. The fear of highwaymen was so great that no one set out on a journey, however short, without joining a caravan.

For many decades, from the latter part of the eighteenth till the middle of the nineteenth centuries, the exploits of the Abu-Ghosh family were notorious throughout all Europe. The elder Abu-Ghosh, sheik of the village of Kiri el-Einab near Jerusalem,* had subjugated the neighbouring villages of Castel and Soba. Once ensconced on the high road leading from the city of Ramleh on the coastal plain to Jerusalem, he became in effect, sole ruler over the entire neighbourhood. He collected tolls at a fixed rate from all caravans, especially from Christian and Jewish pilgrims. The Jerusalem monasteries paid him an annual fee. After his death, thought to have occurred in 1817, his son inherited his office as bandit chieftain as well as his annual income of 90,000 piastres. Travellers who refused to pay the toll of seven piastres per capita plus two piastres for personal baggage were mercilessly robbed; many were seriously wounded or murdered outright. Nevertheless, travellers preferred Abu-Ghosh to the other bandit leaders and even to those authorities who could be bribed. Some travellers gave high praise to Abu-Ghosh, for he assumed the gallantry of a medieval robber-baron and was never guilty of betraying those who purchased his protection with cash.

The pashas had no qualms about raising the prices of staple foods to satisfy their insatiable avarice. A Bosnian ex-slave Ahmed, better known as El-Jezzar (The Butcher) Pasha (d. 1806), imposed the first excise duty on wine, wheat, meat and fish in the Turkish Empire, in order to increase his revenues. He also exploited tradesmen and artisans, by granting them loans at compound interest. Both El-Jezzar and his successor at Damascus, Abdallah Pasha exploited both the urban population and the peasants and bedouins with redoubled cruelty. Chateaubriand, who toured Palestine in 1806 relates how these "administrators," after raiding Transjordanian peasants and robbing them of tens of thousands of heads of cattle, goats and sheep, forced butchers to buy their plunder at twice the market price. Needless to add, it fell to the retail customers, the impoverished town dwellers, to make good this loss.

The imperial tariff system was another impediment to the development of foreign trade. The short-sighted fiscal policy of the government at Constantinople favoured foreign European traders at the expense of Ottoman subjects as trade concessions meant high payments into the Imperial Treasury. Thus, imperial subjects had to pay a 10 per cent customs duty on imports, while foreign citizens only paid 3 per cent. Furthermore, the subjects, unlike foreign citizens, had to pay customs at every port, although they had already been paid at the original port of entry. Foreign and retail trade in Palestine, as in Syria, was thus in the

* The present village of Abu-Ghosh. The original name in its Hebrew form is given to the Jewish village of Kiryat-Anavim, founded shortly after World War I.

hands of Europeans, mainly French, until the end of the eighteenth century, with Greeks and Armenians also participating.

The system of bribery, an integral part of the decadent feudal order, frustrated all efforts at reform and reorganization, in a country subject to uninhibited abuse by the authorities. In fact, the authorities acknowledged no responsibility whatsoever; sanitation in the cities was entirely in the hands of the inhabitants and depended on their cultural level and habits. The city of Acre wallowed in neglect and filth, with packs of stray dogs roaming the streets. The absence of sanitation, combined with the poor nutritive state of the urban population, increased the effects of any epidemic that broke out. Over 4,500 people died within six months in an epidemic which swept the city in 1786, according to a report by the French Consul, Renaudot. And this epidemic was primarily the result of starvation amongst the inhabitants. Renaudot reported that the starving townsfolk ate weeds growing wild in the fields in desperation, "and the authorities took measures to burn the corpses lest human beings be seen contending over them with the beasts of the field . . ."

The Economic Situation

At the end of the eighteenth century, the total population of Palestine, on both banks of the Jordan, was little more than 300,000. The situation in the middle of the nineteenth century would seem to indicate that at the beginning of the century Christians still formed a tenth of the population—three-quarters of them belonging to the Greek Orthodox Church. The number of Jews in the country had not risen to more than 5,000 or 6,000 individuals, even after the migrations of the second half of the eighteenth century.

A considerable portion of the population was concentrated in the cities—a quarter of the total by the middle of the nineteenth century—as the result of the economic policies of the authorities and the consequent flight from the villages. The largest city was Jerusalem with between 9,000 and 12,000 inhabitants, according to moderate tourist estimates. Even by 1831, the population of the harbour city of Acre had not risen above 8,000 or, at the most, 10,000 people. That period saw the beginnings of Haifa's development as a deep-water port for large ships unable to cast anchor in the shallow waters of the harbour. In 1784, François Volney had described Haifa as a village; by 1806, it was classed as a town, with several dozen shops, a few cafés and a grain market teeming with buyers. The port town of Jaffa consisted of 400-500 houses and a maximum of 3,000 inhabitants in the 1760's.

Ramleh near Jaffa numbered 400 families, according to an account in 1738, fifty years later, Volney only found 200 families there. Apparently, Ramleh, like Jaffa, was seriously affected by the war of Ali Bey in the

1770's, and part of the city was also destroyed during the Napoleonic invasion at the end of the century. Lydda (ancient and present-day Lod), which, like Ramleh, was quite important as a centre for the soap and cotton spinning industry, was described in the 1760's as a town that had declined to village status.

Among the cities of Galilee, a 1784 account depicted Safed as a village laid waste by the earthquake of 1759. By 1812, however, it was estimated to contain 600 buildings. In 1784, Volney stated that Tiberias only housed a few hundred families. Descriptions of the town in 1812, and also several years later, place the number of inhabitants at 4,000. Beisan (Bet-She'an) only contained some seventy or eighty buildings in 1812. At Nablus (Biblical She'khem), a reliable source gave 8,000 inhabitants in the 1830's. The three large cities were therefore, Jerusalem, Acre and Nablus.

Elsewhere, Jericho had never risen above village status and the population of Bethlehem was 2,500 in 1784. Hebron was estimated to have a population in 1784 of 3,000, which increased to 5,000 by 1806. Gaza contained a maximum of 2,000 individuals in 1784, according to Volney, but by the turn of the century expanded to 5,000.

The economic achievements in the country in agriculture, craft, industry, and trade were not negligible, considering the nature of the régime.

The coastal area, including most of the She'phelah and all of the Vale of Sharon, had been devastated at the end of the thirteenth century during the Mamelukes' war of conquest against the Crusaders. Until the nineteenth century, it was the most desolate area in the entire country. The most fertile district until the latter part of the eighteenth century was Galilee. It was Palestine's granary for wheat, barley, sorghum and cotton crops; tobacco, sesame and mulberry trees were also grown on a considerable scale. Vineyards spread out on hillsides in the neighbourhood of Safed and Tiberias. In market gardening, Tiberias acquired a reputation for its watermelons, which were sold as far afield as Acre and Damascus. Safed was surrounded by extensive olive groves, and olive oil was a staple product of the whole of Galilee. Large exports of wool from the port of Acre bore witness to widespread sheep raising in the north of the country and in the Samaria district. Indigo was produced in the Jordan Valley and sold to traders from Jerusalem and Hebron, as well as to dyers at Safed. The balsam plant was grown near Tiberias. East of the Jordan, the most populous and also the most fertile area was the Hauran.

The Samaria district, where grain crops, cotton, olives and mulberry trees were cultivated, came second in the fertility scale to Galilee. There were grain, cotton and tobacco fields in the south of the country, but the area was mainly noted for its vineyards, orchards, olive groves and vegetable gardens. Although most of the orchards at the approaches to Jaffa had been cut down during the wars of the 1770's and Napoleon's campaign, some still remained. Jaffa watermelons were in demand in the neighbouring lands of Syria and Egypt. Fields of cotton, tobacco and sorghum lined the road from Jaffa to Ramleh, and Ramleh was also well known for its date palms and olive groves. The region around Jerusalem abounded in olives, grapevines and fig trees, while apple, pear, mulberry and peach trees were not uncommon. The variety of first-class vegetables grown in the southern part of the country amazed tourists: kidney beans, lentils, beans, cucumbers, squash, tomatoes, cabbage, spinach, turnips, radishes and excellent sweet onions. Bethlehem produced excellent pomegranates, figs, olives and, especially, large grapes, which its Christian inhabitants used in the manufacture of white wine. Olives, grapes (dried and sold as raisins), and cotton were grown in the neighbourhood of Hebron. The regions around the cities of Askalon and Isdud (Ashdod) at the southern end of the coast stood out like oases of greenery, while the "Gardens of Gaza" were famous throughout the Middle East for their fruit: dates, lemons, oranges, figs, mulberries, pomegranates, apricots, peaches, almonds and bananas.

Craft and industry played a significant role in the country's economy, even under the prevalent socio-political and technological conditions. Volney noticed jewellers, cotton willowers, solderers, mechanics, saddlers, bakers, barbers and a few butchers along the streets in the cities he visited in the early 1780's.

Jerusalem offered a more colourful cross-section of handicrafts. It supported an industry manufacturing holy articles, ornaments and souvenirs, to cater to the needs of the Christian pilgrims and for export to Christian countries. Its products included engravings, pipestems, earthenware vessels and jewellery, which also figured as part of Palestine's exports. However, the country's most extensive industries, which also accounted for the bulk of its exports, were cotton spinning and soap manufacture. Cotton was mainly sold abroad, in a spun rather than a totally raw state. Spinning was done in villages and cities in all parts of the country—Safed, Lydda, Ramleh, Hebron and Gaza—under the domestic system. Some cities developed a cotton weaving industry for domestic consumption in conjunction with cotton growing and spinning. Nablus also manufactured woolcloth and felts. The soap industry was widespread as a result of an abundant supply of raw materials, oil and ashes. The ashes were of the best quality for the purpose. They were prepared mainly by bedouins by burning desert weeds. The production of soap gave employment to large numbers of workers in the cities of Acre, Nablus, Jaffa, Lydda, Ramleh, Jerusalem, Hebron and Gaza. Hebron was also known as a glass manufacturing centre of some importance. Sand was available on the spot: nitre was supplied by bedouins.

Domestic trade was based on transactions between cities and peasants and bedouins from the surrounding districts. The peasants offered their grains, fruit and vegetables, and the bedouins their livestock for sale on market days, once a week; in return, they bought what vessels, implements, clothing and fancy goods they needed. Every district also had a central marketing station.

Foreign trade was developed on such a large scale that the main branches of agriculture—cotton and tobacco—and all branches of industry were dependent on it. Trade with neighbouring countries as well as with Europe was conducted through the ports of Jaffa and Acre. Egypt played the most important part in Palestine's trade with the neighbouring countries. Oils, soap, ashes and indigo seeds were exported to Egypt through Jaffa and grain, cloth, sugar and, above all, rice imported. The breakdown in overland communications gave rise to a peculiar situation in the foreign trade in grain: while grain was imported from Egypt through Jaffa to supply the needs of the southern part of the country, grain from Galilee and Samaria was being exported through Acre as far afield as Constantinople, as well as to Beirut in Lebanon. Beirut traders also imported raw cotton from Acre for the textile industry.

Until the War of the Spanish Succession in 1715, Palestinian and Syrian trade with Europe had almost been a French monopoly. Even after the war, when England, Venice and Holland secured a foothold, French merchants still controlled most of the import-export trade. There were resident French vice-consuls, responsible to the Consul in the port of Sidon, at Ramleh and Acre. Raw and spun cotton formed the principal export to Europe but coarse cotton fabrics, silk, tobacco, soap, hides and nut-galls for the production of tannin in the ink industry were also sent. French traders customarily made a payment on account of the cotton harvest, and they bartered merchandise imported from France, usually cheap cotton fabrics. Imports from France included cloth, sugar, coffee, various cheap fancy goods, iron, sheet lead and tin. Volney quoted Marseilles Chamber of Commerce lists which put French imports from Sidon and Acre through Marseilles at 1,800,000 francs. Although this represented less than a tenth of all French trade with the Middle East, it was still over half France's trade with Egypt. Southern Syria and Palestine were the principal cotton exporters in the Middle East up to the beginning of the 1820's, when the large scale cultivation of cotton began in Egypt. However, following Jezzar Pasha's repressive decrees against the French traders, the French share in this trade had already begun to diminish before the Revolution. After the Marseilles Chamber of Commerce was liquidated during the Revolution, and especially following Napoleon's Palestine campaign of 1799, French preponderance in Palestine's foreign trade came to an end. England, Russia and Austria began to take an increasing share.

Religious pilgrimages provided an appreciable source of revenue for the country. At the middle of the eighteenth century, 4,000 Christian pilgrims reached Palestine annually, including about 1,000 Armenians from Armenia, Persia and Turkey. During the second half of the century, the number of Christian pilgrims noticeably declined, particularly in the case of those from western Europe, where the spread of rationalism and loss of faith in the miraculous value of visiting the holy places had made their mark. The pilgrims used to arrive in November and remain in the country until the Easter holidays. The French Revolutionary and Napoleonic Wars paralysed pilgrim traffic to a very large extent. Even when peace was restored to the country in autumn, 1806, only 700 Christian pilgrims arrived. The volume of pilgrim traffic to Palestine increased again after 1815, apparently not only because of the renewed security of sea travel but also because of the tendency towards greater religious faith current in Europe during the age of reaction.

Dhaher el-Amr and his War for the Independence of Palestine

Under the administrative division of the Turkish Empire during the eighteenth and the beginning of the nineteenth centuries, Palestine was controlled by two *pashaliks*, the *Pashalik* of Damascus and the *Pashalik* of Sidon (the latter's capital was transferred to Acre in the middle of the eighteenth century). For short periods, the southern part of the country, known as Falastin, was partitioned off as a separate *pashalik* and its governor—also with the title of Pasha—was at times in charge of the Jerusalem District, and at other odd intervals Commandant of the City of Gaza. But for the most part, administrative control was centred in the two *pashaliks* of Damascus and Sidon-Acre and this division remained in effect until the beginning of the 1830's, when Egypt took over control of the country. The *Pashalik* of Damascus included southern Syria, a part of Galilee (usually the eastern part of upper Galilee only), Samaria, Judea, the Negev, the coast and northern Transjordan. The *Pashalik* of Sidon-Acre governed southern Lebanon, the Bay of Acre, upper and lower Galilee and, at the height of its power, not only the entire coastal area of Palestine but even its southern regions.

The Pasha possessed complete jurisdiction. He commanded the army, governed, and presided at criminal trials. He himself held his office on lease and he collected all state revenues within his *Pashalik* on his own behalf—taxes, custom duties and rent from government property leases. In addition he could arbitrarily impose special levies on the population. Apart from the payment to the Sultan for their appointments, the Pashas were practically independent of Constantinople. Although their appointments were nominally for a period of one year, many eighteenth-century incumbents in Syria and Palestine governed all their lives, sometimes summarily ended by assassination by their rivals through government intrigues. The Pashas recruited private armies of their own in times of need to supplement the Imperial military forces subordinate to them, and the warships at their disposal.

District and local administration in the cities followed the pattern of feudal offices obtained on lease. The *pashaliks* were subdivided into *sanjaks*, each under a commissioner (*mutsalemin*). In Palestine, commissioners were appointed to Safed, Jerusalem, Gaza and, at first, to Nablus. The commissioner held his office on lease from the pasha and recouped this expenditure by collecting all taxes, duties and *miri* in his *sanjak* from tenant peasants. Also like the pasha in his *pashalik*, the *mutsalem* required the *sanjak* population to make payments for his own personal profit. The income of the Jerusalem Commissioner included regular tributes from Christians and Jews, permit fees for processions and licence fees for keeping the churches in repair.

The relationship between the *pashaliks* of Damascus and Sidon-Acre, which dominated all of Palestine between them, were those of two mutually hostile sovereigns. As a result, boundary demarcations between the two *pashaliks* were never stable. Entire sections of the country passed backwards and forwards between them in their incessant hostilities, throughout the eighteenth and at the beginning of the nineteenth century. The sheik of the hilly Nablus district, usually under the rule of Damascus, exploited these conflicts to secure virtual autonomy for himself. Similarly, villages in either of the *pashaliks* would revolt, capitulate to the other pasha, and form enclaves inside the territory of the surrounding *pashalik*. At the beginning of the nineteenth century ten villages between Ramleh and Hebron were under the rule of the *Pashalik* of Acre. Sheik Abu-Ghosh also acknowledged the authority of this Pasha on behalf of the villages he dominated.

Against the background of this motley feudal régime, utterly lacking in stable foundations, inter-*pashalik* wars broke out in the country and continued intermittently from the middle of the eighteenth century until the Egyptian conquest in 1831. The first of these internal wars concerned a bold attempt by a bedouin chieftain, Dhaher el-Amr, to liberate the country from Turkish rule and to unify it as an independent state.

Dhaher el-Amr, a member of the Zeidan family, was born around 1686-89 and died in 1775. His father, head of the family, was interested in his son's education and entrusted another sheik with the task of teaching him to read, write, and study the Koran and poetry. A number of years after his father's death, Dhaher became the head of the family. He gained the sympathy and aid of bedouin and Druze tribal chiefs in capturing large areas of the eastern part of upper Galilee from the district governors during his defence of the villages against oppression by the officials of the Pasha of Sidon. By a carefully planned policy, he succeeded in leasing tax collections in the conquered areas from the Pasha of Sidon and thus acquired control of the entire Tiberias District. When his tax collections had gained him sufficient wealth, he formed a large battalion and extended his domination over all of Galilee down to the Valley of Jezreel (Esdraelon). Dhaher's triumphant advance which, with the capture of Nazareth, had brought him by 1735 to the Nablus District on the border of the *Pashalik* of Damascus, filled the neighbouring Pasha with fear.

In 1742, Suleiman el-Adem, Pasha of Damascus, obtained the Sultan's consent to wage war on Dhaher and laid siege to the city of Tiberias. However, his guns and catapults failed to breach the walls of the fortress. In 1743, the Pasha set out from Damascus at the head of a large military expedition, destroyed the villages around Tiberias, and proceeded to Acre to receive a consignment of equipment that had arrived from Constantinople. On his return to Tiberias, Suleiman el-Adem, Pasha of Damascus, suddenly died.

The new Pasha of Damascus made peace with Dhaher, who even managed to take advantage of the enmity between the incumbents at Damascus and Sidon to advance his plan for further conquests. The economic consolidation of his rule in Galilee required access to the sea. He killed his cousin and as a result, inherited his lease on the Vale of Acre, held from the Pasha of Sidon. He then captured the city of Acre and its port without opposition, and the Pasha confirmed him in his post as leaseholder of the city. Shortly afterwards in about 1750, Dhaher established his domination over the entire Acre Bay area by capturing the fortress of old Haifa, near which ships of heavier tonnage could already cast anchor. Dhaher was helped by his influential connections at the Sublime Porte in Constantinople, and also by the fact that the Pasha of Damascus (in whose jurisdiction lay Haifa and the surrounding area) overlooked the sheik's violation of his borders. Dhaher also contrived to make an agreement with the bedouins in Transjordan and several other tribes. He repulsed attempts to recapture Haifa in 1761 by Othman, the new Pasha at Damascus.

Dhaher's rule marked a period of unprecedented economic advance in Galilee. The tendency in his policy towards progressive absolutism was in sharp contrast to the decadent Turkish régime. For the first time, roads were safe from brigandage and murder. The *fellaheen* were now free from bedouin raids and extortions and, furthermore, their tax burden was greatly reduced. Dhaher removed the Turkish officials and forbade the governors to accept bribes from the peasants or to collect more than the legally established sums in taxes. He reduced the tax on all crop yields from a quarter to a fifth, and occasionally granted loans for the purchase of seeds. He also encouraged the inhabitants to pave roads and to cultivate untilled soil. His desire to settle the country led him to establish Jews and Christians in Tiberias and also to permit Jews to settle at Kefar-Yassif. He granted swamp lands in the neighbourhood of Acre to Christian colonists after removing the encamped bedouins. He also encouraged the development of trade, especially in the port city of Acre. As a result of the absolute security against brigands, now ensured, many Christian pilgrims sailed to Acre instead of Jaffa. Towards the end of Dhaher's reign a decline in Acre's coastal trade set in because of the policies of his avaricious Christian vizier.

Like most absolutist rulers, Dhaher had no qualms about offending the extreme adherents of the dominant religion. He showed religious toleration towards Jews and Christians (though it cost them something in various taxes), and even allowed them to repair or erect houses of prayer (for example, the Christian churches in Tiberias and Acre). When a severe earthquake was followed by epidemics in 1759-60, Dhaher made a number of sanitary improvements in Acre, despite protests from the local Mufti on religious grounds. In fact, on this occasion, the Mufti was heavily fined.

Dhaher also embarked on large scale constructional activities as a means of strengthening his own position as well as securing the frontiers of his state. He fortified Tiberias with a wall that surrounded it completely on land, and also built a fort on a height overlooking the city from the north. He erected strongholds along the southern border of Galilee as a protection against raiding parties from Nablus. He repaired the walls of Acre, made them higher and installed two strong gates. After the attack on old Haifa by the Pasha of Damascus, he founded the new town $1\frac{1}{4}$ miles from the ancient site and fortified it with a wall and watchtowers. Similarly, Dhaher and his sons built fortresses and towers in various parts of Galilee, such as Safed, Sephoris (Zippori), Shafa-Amr (Shefar'am), Nazareth and also in the Valley of Jezreel. Some of the palaces that Dhaher and other members of his family built for their personal pleasure were fortified and equipped with cannons. Dhaher erected a mosque in Acre, while his brothers built others in their Galilean strongholds. To promote trade, Dhaher constructed a great bazaar in Acre with over a hundred shops, as well as a dock and warehouses in the port area of the city.

When war broke out between Turkey and Russia at the end of 1768, Dhaher considered the time ripe to execute his plan and wage war to establish an independent Arab state in all of Palestine. In fact, he was forced into actual hostilities by attempts by the Constantinople government to dislodge him from his control of Galilee. The state of war with Russia was encouraging uprisings in various parts of the Empire, including the Egyptian revolt, and Dhaher's powerful position as Sheik of Galilee now appeared to be extremely dangerous to Constantinople. Mameluke Ali Bey, one of the twenty-four beys who ruled Egypt in the name of the Sultan's Pasha, had stopped sending the country's taxes to the Sultan. He now declared himself ruler of Egypt and in the summer of 1770 conquered Hedjaz with the Holy City of Mecca. To prevent a similar rebellion by Dhaher, the Turkish government granted Othman Pasha of Damascus permission to open hostilities against him. Dhaher, now over eighty years old, but still full of energy and initiative, found a powerful ally in the rebellious ruler of Egypt, Ali Bey. His defensive war to maintain his supremacy in Galilee became a general Palestinian uprising against Turkish domination and joined forces with Egypt's war for independence.

In response to Dhaher's call for assistance, in November, 1770, Ali Bey dispatched advance units of his army, under the command of Ismail Bey, to Palestine. The inhabitants of the southern part of the country had revolted against the Pasha of Damascus because of his oppressive taxation on several occasions in the past. Now they joyfully welcomed Ali Bey's proclamation summoning the inhabitants of Syria and Egypt to a *Jehad*, or Holy War, against the tyrants and oppressors and citing passages from the Koran to support this case.

In March, 1771, a powerful Mameluke army, over 40,000 strong, reached Palestine from Egypt. It quickly subdued all of Palestine, with the exception of Nablus, which had never submitted to Dhaher, and even Nablus fell to the rebels after a victorious battle near Damascus at the beginning of June, 1771. Suddenly, however, the leader of the Mameluke forces, Abu Daheb, changed his tactics, apparently because he wanted control over Egypt to be in his own hands and not in those of Ali Bey. At the beginning of July he hastily returned to his own country with his army. Othman Pasha moved back to Damascus and set out for Galilee with his army to fight Dhaher. The old Sheik now demonstrated his outstanding military ability: in a surprise attack before daybreak on September 1, he dealt a mortal blow to the Pasha's army, encamped near Lake Huleh, capturing the entire force, together with its arms and cannons. By the end of October, he took Sidon, after his son had gained a victory over the Druze, who were allied with the Pasha. The sympathy of the Lebanese was of considerable help.

Following these events, the government at Constantinople removed Othman Pasha and his sons from office and attempted to come to terms with Dhaher. Dhaher, however, was hoping for the arrival of a large military force from his Egyptian ally, Ali Bey, and rejected the peace overtures. His expectations were quickly dissipated. Ali Bey, defeated by his rival Abu Daheb, had fled from Egypt and arrived in southern Palestine with only a few hundred Mamelukes. Dhaher successfully rescued his Egyptian ally from the people of Jaffa and Nablus, who had risen against him, and brought him safely to Acre, but the Turks and Druze laid siege to Sidon. Dhaher then received help from abroad. The Russian navy had hastened to help Ali Bey and was anchored off Acre. Now it sailed for Sidon to join in the battle of the Mamelukes and Dhaher's men, who fought to break the Turkish siege. Dhaher triumphed, incurring hardly any losses in the process. The Druze were the first to flee—in any case they were more inclined to side with Dhaher than with the Turks—and after that the Pasha's entire army melted away within two hours. Dhaher and Ali Bey could now proceed to the conquest of southern Palestine. By the beginning of spring, 1773, all Palestine, with the exception of Jerusalem, was in the hands of the rebels. Confident of his rear in Palestine and in Mameluke loyalty in Egypt, Ali Bey set out with a small force to reconquer his own country from Abu Daheb. His army was defeated in a battle near Cairo, and he himself taken prisoner. He died from wounds several days later. Dhaher was left to defy Turkish power alone.

His luck held out only a little longer. The Emir of Lebanon went over to his side when he became convinced that the Commissioner of Beirut, Mohammed el-Jezzar, was undermining his régime. Dhaher scored another great victory when his son, Ali, put the Turkish forces to flight in an engagement near Zahleh, in the valley between the Lebanon and Anti-Lebanon. But, as *Pride goeth before destruction* (Proverbs, 16:18), Dhaher's fortunes changed at the height of his supremacy. Prolonged warfare had laid waste the land: trade had dwindled and Dhaher's revenues were not sufficient to recruit new troops. To make matters even worse, his sons revolted against him; one of them, Ali, continued his rebellion until his father's death. The sons could not forgive their father for not abdicating in their favour in his advanced old age—he even took a new wife when nearly ninety. However, the main weakness of the independent state that Dhaher had set up in Palestine lay in the particularism of the inhabitants of the country, whose awareness of national unity against Turkey had not yet developed. It was actually impeded by the administrative methods of Dhaher's vizier and the rule of his sons, who subjected the population to heavy taxes. The signing of a peace treaty between Russia and Turkey in July, 1774, marked the end of Dhaher's rule. By command of the Sultan, a large military force came up out of Egypt led by Abu Daheb, his enemy since Ali Bey's war.

The invasion of Palestine by Egyptian forces in March, 1775, was the occasion for the violation of the alliances that united Dhaher's state. The Druze and Methuel tribesmen refused to come to his assistance and even his sons failed to rally to his side in his time of need. Ali actually supported the enemy. Abu Daheb reduced Gaza, Ramleh, and—at the end of a seven-week siege—Jaffa. In Jaffa, he dealt barbarically with the inhabitants: some 2,000 people were slaughtered in a massacre "in which there was no discrimination between Moslems, Christians and Jews." The skulls of the slain were gathered into a huge mound at the city's gates as a warning to all the inhabitants of the country. The Mamelukes captured deserted Acre without resistance and thus gained control of the entire country. Even then, Dhaher did not give up hope and was able to achieve some success for several more days. When Abu Daheb died and his forces returned to Egypt, Dhaher again seized control of the government at Acre. However, Turkish warships reached Acre Bay only a few weeks later. Dhaher's commanders defected and refused to fight the enemy and he was not even able to flee. He was shot down by Moroccan soldiers. His body was decapitated and his head, like those of the other rebels, was displayed in front of the Sultan's palace at Constantinople. This was the end of his incredible attempt to establish a Palestinian state independent of Turkey. Turkish rule was restored to the country in the person of Ahmed Pasha, known as *El-Jezzar*, "The Butcher."

Tyranny and Oppression; Napoleon's Campaign and the Restoration of Government by Pashas

In 1775, after the Dhaher el-Amr revolt had been crushed, Ahmed el-Jezzar was appointed Pasha of Sidon and Acre. His rise to power indicated the type of officers who ruled the provinces of the Turkish Empire, in the same way as his tyrannical government of Palestine exemplified the uninhibited oppression to which the Sultan's subjects were abandoned.

Ahmed was a native of Bosnia. At the age of sixteen, he had already been convicted of a felony and had to flee to Constantinople. He sold himself into slavery and was brought to Egypt, where he served in the home of a bey. He avenged his master's murder by bedouins, by ruthlessly killing every bedouin he chanced to meet, until he earned the name of "The Butcher" among the Mamelukes. These "fine qualities" gained him employment as Keeper of the Gate at the court of Ali Bey, chief of the Mameluke beys in Egypt. After he had proved his loyalty by assassinating his new master's enemies, he himself was elevated to the rank of bey. Eventually, however, he incurred Ali Bey's displeasure and fled to Constantinople and then to Damascus. Recommendations from the Pasha of Damascus secured him a reputation at the Sublime Porte in the Imperial capital: he was appointed Pasha of Sidon and Acre, and thus acquired control of all the territory that had been under the rule of Dhaher el-Amr, including Lebanon.

El-Jezzar ruled the *Pashalik* of Acre for thirty years (1775-1804), also serving as Pasha of Damascus at various periods in 1785, 1790 and 1803, which gave him domination over all Palestine. Pasha by Turkish appointment, with his residence at Acre, he recruited the men for his palace garrison (some 1,000 horsemen) from a conglomeration of Bosnians, Albanians, Berbers and brigands from all corners of the Empire. In 1785, his infantry numbered between 12,000 and 15,000 mercenaries. (Before Napoleon's campaign, this force had been reduced to 4,000 or 5,000 men.) They enabled him to crush all the uprisings against his oppressive régime, which broke out amongst the inhabitants of Palestine, Lebanon and Syria right up to the end of his rule. The people of Nablus and its dependencies were alone in refusing to submit and, despite frequent reprisals, their resistance persisted until his death.

El-Jezzar developed the exploitation of the population through taxes, war levies and monopolies into a brutal system, unprecedented even under the tyrannical Pashas. The *mutsalemin* appointed over the *sanjaks* were required to pay him the full rental on their leaseholds in advance, even before they had the opportunity to exact it from their subjects. Even the punitive levies, imposed on the cities annually or semi-annually on various pretexts, were farmed out as a regular source of revenue. The appointment of municipal councillors provided the Pasha with a similar source of income; he simply permitted the collection leaseholders to place the highest bidders on the city councils. El-Jezzar monopolized trade in cotton and other export commodities—and this was in addition to the high duty he imposed on exports of cotton through the port of Acre. To secure this monopoly, Jezzar Pasha went so far as to expel the French consuls and their vice-consuls from his lands in 1790. Most of the French merchants left Palestine at the same time as the French consuls, and French hegemony over the country's foreign trade thus ceased. All of El-Jezzar's financial affairs were handled by a Jewish banker, Haim Farhi, a native of Damascus. As Lord of the Exchequer, he virtually discharged the functions of a vizier and even influenced the Pasha's policies towards his neighbours and the emirs and sheiks under his rule. Volney estimated Jezzar Pasha's annual income at between 9,000,000 and 10,000,000 livres, while the sum he remitted in taxes to the central government never exceeded 1,500 "burses" or 1,875,000 livres.* His lessees and sub-lessees, who collected the taxes from the population, emulated their Pasha in amassing personal fortunes. This pitiless exploitation added to the destruction already wrought in the country by the fighting during the final years of Dhaher's rule.

Apart from his unlimited insatiable rapacity, Jezzar Pasha manifested all the sadistic characteristics of an oriental despot. He would cut off the heads of innocent men with his own hands and regarded removal of a victim's limb or limbs as a minor punishment. An English tourist, Lord Forbin, was shocked at the sight of the maimed victims of El-Jezzar's crimes, frequently encountered in Acre as late as 1817: people with noses, ears or even eyes missing. Once, he carried a "joke" to the lengths of hideously mutilating his Minister of the Exchequer, Haim Farhi. In fact, the Jewish vizier continued in his service after El-Jezzar had cut off his nose and one ear and gouged out one eye. El-Jezzar continued with the building of his capital, Acre, that Dhaher had begun, motivated by hope of profit, the entrenchment of his government and his own greater glory. Employing forced labour by *fellaheen* from the outskirts of the city, he built a large bazaar with the magnificent mosque in the middle that still bears his name. He equipped Acre with a water supply in the form of a Roman aqueduct (damaged during Napoleon's siege of the city), and fortified the city walls, thus converting it into an impregnable stronghold.

The Turkish government did not view Jezzar Pasha's domination of

---

* By the prevailing rate of exchange, one "burse" (500 piastres) was valued at 1,250 livres. One livre equalled £1.

Lebanon and the strengthening of his position as absolute ruler of Palestine with any favour. Although he was prompt in remitting his tax payments, they correctly suspected that he hoped eventually to establish a state independent of Constantinople. However, he was able to maintain his position by bribing ministers at the Imperial capital with gifts, while the current political situation was also propitious: the Turkish Empire had again become involved in difficult foreign and domestic wars.

At the beginning of February, 1799, Napoleon Bonaparte set out from Egypt at the head of a force of 10,000, to conquer Palestine. The immediate and principal objective of this expedition was to establish his position in Egypt on a firm basis and to guarantee French naval supplies on the Syrian coast. He also hoped to develop French trade in Palestine and Syria, which had declined in the preceding years. Apart from this, however, Napoleon had devised one of the most daring plans of his life: he hoped, after the conquest of Palestine, to invade Syria, march on Constantinople, and deliver the *coup de grace* to the tottering Turkish Empire. Bonaparte was well aware—from Volney's accounts, if from no other source—of Jezzar Pasha's brutal régime, the social subjection of the *fellaheen,* and the ruthless oppression of national and religious minorities in both Palestine and Lebanon. On February 15, 1799, immediately after the capture of El Arish, he issued a proclamation to the inhabitants of the southern area, announcing that his only purpose in coming to the country was to liberate it from Jezzar Pasha and his Egyptian Mameluke allies. He would neither harm the peaceful inhabitants nor offend their religion.

However, Napoleon made the same great political mistake in Palestine he had already committed in Egypt. This same error was more responsible for his future defeat on the battlefields of Russia than any strategical miscalculation: he had not learned from his experience of the situation in Egypt. While prosecuting his Palestine campaign, he failed to enact any reform whatsoever to improve the condition of the peasants, oppressed by the Pasha's tax farmers.

Not surprisingly, in view of this omission, the entry of Napoleon's army into Palestine failed to arouse its population to revolt against their oppressors. However, they were equally impervious to the Sultan's proclamation of a *Jehad* against the French violators of Islam, presumably because their hatred of the rule of the Turkish pashas was so strong. Instead, they adopted an attitude of watchful waiting—so that the advance of Napoleon's invading forces up the whole length of the country to the gates of Acre was in fact made easier, in that they did not encounter civil resistance.

Napoleon followed up the capture of El Arish by taking Gaza, without battle, after the forces of Jezzar Pasha and the Mamelukes had fled. By March 3, he had captured Ramleh and Lydda and was at the gates of Jaffa, fortified by El Jezzar. On March 7, he took Jaffa by storm after a three-day siege. The Turkish garrison, 2,000 strong, was annihilated, while the civilian inhabitants were pillaged and murdered by the conquerors. Napoleon committed an atrocity after the capture of Jaffa that might easily have brought the entire population of the country up in arms against him. He was saved by their hatred of the Turkish oppressors. Four thousand Turkish prisoners of war had surrendered on the promise by French officers that they would not be killed. Now, on Napoleon's orders, they were led to the seashore and shot dead to the last man. Napoleon had arrived at this callous decision after three day's reflection on the shortage of provisions, insufficient to feed thousands of prisoners. The capture of Jerusalem did not form part of Napoleon's plan. He therefore continued his advance northward from Jaffa and arrived with his army before the walls of Acre on March 19. While Acre was under siege, units of Napoleon's army advanced east through the Valley of Jezreel—where they clashed with attacking bedouin tribes and men from Nablus—to Safed and Tiberias; French army patrols even reached the Bridge of the Daughters of Jacob. On April 11, Napoleon won a great victory over the Turkish army in the battle of Mount Tabor, despite the diversionary Turkish force that had come down from Damascus to attack his army at Acre.

Disappointed in his hope of a Palestinian uprising against the Turks, Napoleon focused his ambitions exclusively on the capture of the fortress of Acre. The investment of Acre, however, proved the most outstanding failure in what he expected to be a triumphal procession. In the first place, units of the British Navy, anchored in the port under the command of Admiral Sir William Sidney Smith, supplied the Turkish military forces in the besieged city with food and ammunition. Secondly, British naval guns unceasingly pounded the besieging French army. Finally, French artillery was not in any case adequate to reduce such a powerful stronghold. On May 20, after two months of siege, Napoleon withdrew his forces from Acre, abandoning his guns in the process. His army returned to Egypt in the middle of June after many vicissitudes and much suffering, leaving thousands of dead in Palestine, killed in action before Acre or victims of the epidemic that ravaged its lines.

Jezzar Pasha reaped the benefits of the British victory over Napoleon. His prestige now soared, not only with the inhabitants of the country, but also with government circles at Constantinople. Despite his undisguised ambition to gain control over all Palestine and Syria, the Imperial government did not dare remove him from office. A year before his death, he was again appointed Pasha of Damascus and thus ruled over all Palestine. When he died in 1804, the central government inherited most of the wealth he had accumulated by his oppression, robbery, brigandage and murder. Nearly 2,500 "burses" or 3,125,000 livres in cash were transferred to the capital, and this sum excluded the money stolen from his estate by the Pasha who succeeded him, by military personnel and by the officials sent from Constantinople to administer his legacy.

Ismail Pasha, one of El Jezzar's assistants, seized the office of Pasha of Acre with the help of army troops. However, he met opposition from Suleiman Pasha, who had the support of the Sublime Porte. Suleiman also obtained considerable assistance from Haim Farhi. After Ismail had been defeated and later decapitated, Farhi personally paid off his rebellious army. Suleiman's administration (1804-19) gave the people of Palestine some relief from the abuses of his predecessor, Jezzar Pasha. The authorities treated "infidel" Christians and Jews with more tolerance and the robbery that had accompanied tax collections became less frequent. This was even more the case when the revenue system was based primarily on monopoly rights.

Haim Farhi, who had very great influence with the old Pasha was responsible for the introduction of the new financial policy. Farhi possessed such extensive power in domestic policy that his command could send a powerful sheik, who had infringed the Pasha's discipline, to jail. Several foreign tourists were loud in their praise of this Jewish finance minister as a judicious statesman possessed of remarkable talents and gracious in his intercourse with people. Lord Forbin was alone in denouncing the economic policies of the Pasha of St. Jean d'Acre and his minister, Haim Farhi, after describing the scandalous poverty of the ragged beggars who swarmed the city's streets:

> . . . Suleiman Pasha, who inhabits this palace . . . deaf to the cries of an unfortunate population. The conduct of affairs is entirely abandoned by him to a Jew named Haim Farhi . . . Haim, who is supple and adroit, has hoarded together incalculable treasures . . . Suleiman and Haim Farhi are engaged in an exclusive and despotic commerce: they are the sole proprietors of the immense grounds which surround Saint Joan d'Acre and Nazareth. The extortions, the oppressions, and the tyranny of the details of this odious government inspire the most profound contempt for those who submit to it.

Evidently Lord Forbin was mainly concerned about the Pasha's monopoly of foreign trade, which struck at the interests of British merchants, and for this reason, attributed an exaggerated share in the Pasha's revenues to the finance minister. In any event, he strongly praised the co-operation amongst the consuls of England, Russia and France in Acre for the position they adopted towards the Pasha's authorities. Another tourist, Seetzen reported in 1806 that Haim Farhi only held a few villages on lease from the Pasha. Farhi had appointed a Christian member of his household staff as overseer in two of them. During Suleiman Pasha's last years, the southern part of the country, from Gaza to Jaffa, was seized by the Mameluke Mahmed Bey Abu Nabuth. Nabuth adopted Jaffa, the capital of the rulers of Acre, as his official residence: he fortified its walls, broadened its harbour and built a wharf there. He erected luxurious water fountains in the city itself. He realized his ambition of expanding the territory under his control by moving into the Nablus area, and also held Jerusalem, until the Pasha of Acre drove him from the country.

The Sublime Porte replaced the Pashas of Damascus (though not the Pashas of Acre) at frequent intervals at that period. As before, Jerusalem was under the jurisdiction of Damascus. The French poet, Chateaubriand, saw Abdallah Pasha of Damascus during a visit to the country in 1806 and described him as a cruel miser, "the greatest of the plagues that have ever struck the inhabitants of Jerusalem." In about 1815, Suleiman Pasha of Acre captured Damascus and henceforth was Pasha of both Damascus and Acre. Thus, Palestine once again came under the control of one man. However, the first signs of invasion by the overlord of neighbouring Egypt could already be seen on the horizon amidst the incessant disturbances in Palestine and Syria, which accompanied the unsettled state of the administrative institutions in the Turkish Empire. It was not actually consummated till 1831.

B. *IMMIGRATION DURING THE EIGHTEENTH AND EARLY NINETEENTH CENTURIES*

Jewish Attachment to Palestine and the Precept of Settlement

The general population of Palestine during the turbulent period at the beginning of the nineteenth century included very few Jews. Such as there were, were worn and harassed, degraded by extreme poverty and exposed to abuse from their enemies and chastisement by their oppressors. Nonetheless, they clung desperately to the land of their heritage and looked forward to the ingathering of their people's exiles in Zion. Chateaubriand understood the mood of this wretched community and appreciated its national role. Overtones of Catholic romanticism mingled with his historical intuition in the account of his impressions of the Jewish community in Jerusalem during his travels in 1806:

> Turn to the area between Mount Zion and the Temple site, and behold another people, a small people, living in isolation, not amidst the city's other inhabitants. Singled out for every kind of contumely, it lowers its head without complaint; suffers every manner of oppression without demanding justice; without a murmur endures blows. They demand its head, and it delivers it to the curved scimitar ... It has seen Jerusalem destroyed seventeen times, yet there exists nothing in this world that can discourage it or prevent it from raising its eyes to Zion. He who beholds the Jews dispersed over the face of the earth, in keeping with the Word of God, lingers and marvels. But he will be struck with amazement, as at a miracle, who finds them still in Jerusalem and perceives them, who in law and

justice are the masters of Judea, to exist as slaves and strangers in their own land; how despite all abuses they await the King who, according to their belief, is destined to deliver them. Crushed by the Cross suspended over their heads, that reviles them, hidden away near the Temple, not a stone of whose walls remain, they persist in their deplorable blindness, which merits our compassion. The Persians, the Greeks, the Romans, have vanished from the face of the earth; and one small nation, whose nativity preceded the birth of those great ones, still exists, unsullied in race, on the ruins of its ancestral soil. If there is anything amongst the nations of the world marked with the stamp of the miraculous, this, in our opinion, is that miracle. . . .

The appeal in the Book of Psalms *For Thy servants take pleasure in her stones, and love her dust* (Psalms, 102:15) expressed the people's longing for Zion for many generations. It was woven into Talmudic legend, into the codified precepts of Maimonides and the moving verse of Judah Halevi. The pilgrimages made by hundreds of Jews annually, even in the latter part of the eighteenth century, marked the indissoluble bond between the exiled dispersed people and the land of its birth. The corresponding figure for all Christian pilgrims never reached 2,000. Pilgrimage for the purpose of "prostrating oneself on the Graves of the Fathers" was a common practice amongst Sephardi communities, geographically nearer the land than the Ashkenasim, especially in Turkey, both Asian and European.

In those days, it required considerable courage for travellers to journey to Palestine by sea, even for just a visit. The special pilgrims' ship that sailed from Constantinople once a year in the month of Elul (August or early September) before the High Holy Days (another pilgrimage season began after Shavuot—Pentecost) took ten days to reach Jaffa. "With constant wind," they might reach Sidon or Acre within a week. The journey from Alexandria in Egypt to Acre lasted five days by sea. Needless to say, the travellers had to provide their own food for the duration of the journey. The distance from Jaffa to Jerusalem was covered on donkey or camel and took a day and a night, or even thirty-six hours; the same time was required to go from Acre to Safed or Tiberias. The difficulties of the journey were increased by the danger of brigands on the roads: the stretch between Ramleh and Jerusalem was particularly vulnerable.

The purpose behind the Jewish pilgrimages to Palestine was not, as in the case of ordinary pilgrims, to seek help in personal difficulties through prayer on holy soil. They came as sons returning to the land of their birth to mourn its destruction and to pray for its rebuilding and the deliverance of the people into its bosom. An ancient tradition originating in Tannaitic legend recorded that it was customary for pilgrims who reached the land of

Israel from abroad to tear their clothes as a token of sorrow. Detailed rules decreed the order in which clothing should be torn and passages were selected for recitation to commemorate the destruction of the cities of Judah and Jerusalem, and the Temple, according to which the pilgrim saw first.

However, pilgrimages were not the only way in which the people discharged its duties and expressed its attachment to the Land. True, distinctly religious motives were interwoven in the conceptual pattern that stimulated chosen individuals amongst the pious in every generation to settle in the land of heritage and deliverance. The concept of the sanctity of the land, with its origin in tradition dating back to the Judges and the Kings, had been the subject of particularly warm contemplation by the *Tannaim* and *Amoraim*. "The Land of Israel alone," they taught, "is the land wherein the *She'khinah* resides . . . Whosoever dwells in the land of Israel is like one who possesses God, and whosoever dwells outside the land, is like one who possesses not God . . ." and "it is as though he were performing alien office." Nobody who studied Torah outside the land was equal to anyone who engaged in Torah in the Land of Israel, for the Land of Israel was the home of the Torah, "and there is no Torah like unto the Torah of the Land of Israel . . . The air of the land of Israel makes one wise." A Jew living in the Land even enjoyed great privilege in the duty of observing all the precepts of the Torah, for precepts directly connected and dependent on the land were not in force outside it. During this period too, it was the practice in Palestine to observe a number of the precepts directly dependent on the land, particularly those obligations applying to agricultural workers: the tithe (Numbers, 18:21; 26), gleanings (Leviticus, 19:9; 23:22), forgotten sheaves (Deuteronomy, 24:19), field corners (Leviticus, 19:9; 23:22), fruits forbidden for three years after the planting (Leviticus 19:23), or releases (Deuteronomy, 15:1), to name a few examples. One of the most powerful motives behind orthodox settlement in Palestine had always been desire for the privilege of burial in the holy soil. This was not only because dying in the Land of Israel spared them the need to undergo the *Gilgul Me'hilot* in the future—the rolling of the dead underground to the Holy Land—required of all dead *Tzaddikim* in the Diaspora when the day of resurrection arrived. The Jew who was privileged to die in the Land of Israel, and to be buried there, departed from this world in holiness and was assured of belonging to the next world, likewise "whomsoever did walk within the limits of the land of Israel."

These, the holy attributes of the Land and the piety attached to residing within it, had become an integral element in the people's historical consciousness, and practically all of them had been ordained as religious law in Maimonides' *Mishneh-Torah*. However, apart from the religious motive which, in fact, also embodied the factor of national consciousness in their attachment to Palestine, all generations were deeply conscious of their national obligation not to break the links with the land of their inheritance and of the mortal danger to its future which its neglect and abandonment to strangers would constitute. It was the realization of their national aspect that prompted the *Tannaim* to resolve that "residence in the Land of Israel is balanced against all the precepts in the Torah" and to formulate detailed prohibitions against permanent departure from the country. Concomitant with the ever-growing longing for deliverance in the modern period, the people's recognition of their duty to preserve their historic claim to Palestine—a claim which could not be supported unless a Jewish community remained in the country and promoted its growth—also grew stronger. This awareness penetrated all schools, whatever their trend, uniting Kabbalists, conservatives, and, at a later date, Hassidim and *Mitnagdim,* in a common, wholehearted aspiration. The two great adversaries of the mid-eighteenth century, Rabbi Jonathan Eybeschuetz, the mystic, and Rabbi Jacob Emden, the anti-visionary, incessantly urged the people not to forget the Land of Israel. Rabbi Emden's sermons on the duty of immigration and the settlement of Palestine sounded a pronounced note of realism. Commemoration of Jerusalem or good intentions and contemplation were not sufficient in his eyes:

> Every person in Israel must abidingly and firmly resolve in his heart to ascend to the Land of Israel to live in it, at all events, when he shall have acquired the expenses and some position to afford him a living . . . so that he may settle the land, which is desolate without its sons.

Rabbi Emden's strong advocacy of immigration to the country and of its colonization was consistent with his own doctrine of deliverance, whereby "Jerusalem rebuilt will precede complete deliverance." He too, regarded immigration and settlement of the country, with all the difficulties they entailed, as a practical means of strengthening the people's position in view of the collapse of the foundations of their life in the Diaspora.

> And even—he wrote—though it be a stupendous thing for one to depart from the land in which he was born, to terminate his residence and set out on a long journey, many leagues distant from his present habitat, to traverse foreign countries and states with which we are unfamiliar and whose language we know not, nevertheless let us note well how insecure is our residence in the sites of our dispersal throughout the Diaspora, and then it will be easier for us to place our path under God's guidance and seek our heritage.

At the same time as the Hassidim were spreading their doctrine of deliverance, with its cardinal tenet the sanctity of the Land of Israel, their great antagonist, the Gaon Rabbi Elijah of Vilno, was teaching:

> The meaning of Deuteronomy, 11:31, *Ye shall possess it, and dwell therein,* is that by virtue of possessing it shall you dwell

therein. And how will you possess it? Through occupation. From this you are to learn that dwelling therein means obtaining through occupying.

The Palestinian emissaries (*She'lihim*) who maintained a living link between the Land and the Diaspora, also played a large part in stimulating the people's love for the Land. Some of them were not satisfied only with appealing for support on behalf of the small, poverty-stricken community which already existed, but urged the Jews to go to Palestine and settle there. The well-known scholar Rabbi Moses Hagiz, who wrote a book at the end of the seventeenth century entitled *The Language of Truth,* specifically on the people's duties towards the Land of Israel, was one of these emissaries. His ideas became the pattern for all the appeals the *Yishuv* (i.e., the Palestine Jewish Community) and its emissaries sent out for expediting help to those holding the fort in Palestine. "The sons of the land of Israel," he had written, "are the ones who stand watch over the Tabernacle of the Lord and establish there a right of residence . . . They establish a right of residence in the Land of Israel and they stand watch over its ruins, and they are the ones who endure tribulations for the rest of their brethren in the Diaspora." Moses Hagiz had hoped that the diaspora Jews would respond to his call. "Maybe they will awaken . . . Maybe they will say, 'This is the Land which the Lord swore to our forefathers to give us.' Let each say unto his fellow, 'Let us gather strength of the cities of our Lord, which are our cities, the cities of Israel and Judah.' Perhaps they will say, "Ours is the right of deliverance, and of the first-born.' "

The appeals for help sent out to the Diaspora during the eighteenth and the beginning of the nineteenth centuries contained repeated warnings, all permeated with this overwhelming sense of the people's responsibility for maintaining the community in its Land: "Lest the country lie waste (from the refugees in Pe'ki'in, 1761); "That it remain not desolate of inhabitants" (from Safed, 1795); "Lest the soil remain devastated and deprived of its Jews" (from the Palestine Fund Administrators at Constantinople, 1763, 1800).

Revival of the Community at Tiberias, and Immigration in the 1740's

The economic decay of the country was coupled with a despotic régime which heavily oppressed the Jewish community. In these circumstances, the ground for a mass immigration to Palestine was still absolutely unprepared. Rabbi Elijah of Vilno took a realistic view of this situation and defined it in unerring terms. "Two obstacles," he stated, "exist in the Holy Land: one is the villainy of the non-believers there and the other one the poor and scanty means of livelihood." It was in general a rare occurrence for Jews of that period to pull up their roots and emigrate to distant lands, the more so overseas. However, the state of neglect and poverty in the land, the havoc and destruction extant over most of the countryside as well as the formidable trials and expense of a long journey, were mainly responsible for the fact that even the limited number of Jews who did leave the Jewish population centres of eastern and central Europe at that time, moved towards Holland and England, and not to Palestine. As in the eighteenth century and the beginning of the nineteenth, individuals and single families continued to emigrate to Palestine. The prime factor behind their re-settlement was the sanctity of the land and the consciousness of the duty to settle there. Thus, scholars were most prominent amongst the new arrivals, many of them outstanding students of the Law and accomplished Kabbalists. Some elements were assured of a more stable income in the country than other immigrants: *Yeshivot* in Palestine received special support from the Diaspora and, in addition, special bequests were often set aside for them in the legacies of the wealthy. This category of immigrants also included some well-to-do individuals who had enough funds to subsist on for a greater length of time and who, like the scholars, were motivated by the love they bore the country. At the other extreme, totally impoverished people placed their trust in the generosity of Diaspora Kehillot, or support from relatives, and went to Palestine. Only a few of these arrivals actually settled in the country with the intention of earning their livelihood by manual labour or trade. It was only when they had settled down and their support from abroad failed to arrive on time, or in sufficient quantity, that many were compelled to find a way of earning a living.

However, within the limits of the slow rate of immigration—mainly impeded by the feudalism of the Diaspora countries with large Jewish centres—a change for the better occurred during the second half of the eighteenth century and the beginning of the nineteenth. A typical manifestation of this improvement was the immigration of entire groups, which continued throughout the period. The driving force of this movement was the desire to hasten Messianic deliverance, which grew ever stronger as the foundations of their Diaspora existence were progressively eroded by the decline of the feudal system. However, the nature and extent of immigration propaganda had changed as much as the concept of deliverance had changed in the direction of evolutionism, after the débâcle of the Sabbetai Zvi movement and its offshoots, with greater emphasis on the individual's duty to repent and lead a life of sanctity. In 1700, Rabbi Judah Hassid and his faction had assembled over 1,000 immigrants, only to disintegrate in despair and frustration. Movements of this kind no longer occurred in the modern period. Instead, Kabbalists, Hassidim and Mitnagdim preached immigration and settlement in the land, in order to prepare the way for deliverance and to hasten its advent. And this immigration was mainly organized in advance, in groups of selected individuals, often with specific warnings against the emigration of any person lacking adequate spiritual or financial preparation. Some groups, from the outset, conceived immigration in principle as the duty of *Tzaddikim* and the leaders of the generation, whose settlement in Palestine would pave the way for the deliverance of the people as a whole. Frequently however, this awakening to the ideal affected broader popular circles and caused a general increase in the flow of immigration. As a result, the Jewish community in Palestine grew throughout the period, strengthened its position in the Kehillot that already existed and spread out to establish new settlements.

The first wave of organized immigrants arrived in the country as a consequence of Sheik Dhaher el-Amr's policy, which was altering the appearance of Galilee. In order to repopulate Tiberias, which was mostly in ruins, the Sheik, noted for his good sense and outstanding religious tolerance, invited Jews to settle there equally as he had made settlement widely accessible to Christians. In 1740, he approached Rabbi Haim Aboulafia, a native of Palestine, and at that time Rabbi at Smyrna (Izmir), with a request to come to Tiberias and re-establish the Kehillah, destroyed in the middle of the seventeenth century. "Arise and come up, inherit the land of Tiberias, which is the land of thy fathers!" were the Sheik's words as recorded by the chronicler, Rabbi Jacob Berav. Rabbi Berav went on to explain that Aboulafia's grandfather, the elder Rabbi Haim Aboulafia, had been Rabbi at Tiberias before its destruction. The younger Aboulafia combined the qualities of a visionary anticipating deliverance and a man of action endowed with great political ability. He was thoroughly familiar with all the Jewish settlements in the country—he himself stated that he had "been born in Hebron, grown up in Jerusalem, and given instruction in the Torah at Safed." He promptly accepted the historic opportunity that the government offered. Aboulafia regarded the revival of the Jewish community in Tiberias as the opening both of a new era in Jewish settlement in the country and of a new train of events heralding the *Athalta de'Ge'ulah*—the beginning of deliverance. He substantiated this by a quotation from the Talmud (*Rosh-Ha'shannah*, 31:b): *Israel is destined to be Delivered from Tiberias*. His letters to the Diaspora urging immigration and settlement in Tiberias also suggested that "the time was the time of love" (cf. Ezekiel, 16:8). In spring, 1742, the Rabbi and a congregation of Jews reached Tiberias, and before many years had passed they built up the city's Jewish quarter, with the Sheik's help:

> And whatever the Rabbi requested of him—the chronicler continued in praise of the Sheik—he did not withhold, and in the course of the years he built houses and courtyards for the Jews, erected a pleasing and splendid synagogue unlike any in all the land of Israel, and he constructed an appropriate bathhouse, and shops for the market day, an oil press for sesame seeds, and began to construct

roads through the land, and he also ordered the planting of fields and vineyards. And from day to day, the affection of the Princes for the Rabbi grew, and all the people of Tiberias were robust, fresh, and joyful, because the land had recovered from its fears and there was none to terrify.

The name the Rabbi gave to the *Bet-Midrash* at Tiberias symbolized his hopes for deliverance: *Mashmi'a Ye'shu'ah, He Who Announceth Salvation.*

The enlightened policy of the Galilean ruler and the initiative of the leader of the Jewish community also combined to revive the vestiges of Jewish agricultural settlement in Galilee in the middle of the eighteenth century. As a result, the agricultural community at Kefar-Yassif, near Acre, last mentioned at the end of the sixteenth century, was restored. This Jewish community was still actually in existence even in the eighteenth century. In 1741, a member of Rabbi Haim ibn 'Atr's group of immigrants had praised the community at Kefar-Yassif, which was based on the Torah and agricultural activity:

> And we found there some ten householders well situated and very free; their work is sowing and harvesting, and they deliver up their tithes and burn their heave-offering.

The community had partly or entirely disintegrated during the ensuing years because of drought and locusts. The founder of the revived settlement was Rabbi Solomon Abadi, a Kabbalist and by all indications a native of Salonica. He lived in poverty in Safed for several years, moved to Jerusalem whence he also "came forth naked," and eventually reached Kefar-Yassif, which "he chose for the beauty of the place."

Abadi, the Kabbalist, was also a man of action, and he obtained an official letter from Sheik Dhaher promising reasonable tax rates for the settlers. Soon a Jewish congregation was organized from amongst the inhabitants of the country. Several factors determined this project and the choice of site: the village provided a refuge from the epidemics that frequently ravaged the country, but was still conveniently close to Acre, where the protection of the European consuls was available. Furthermore, Kefar-Yassif was considered a holy site, both by tradition (according to popular legends, several *Tannaim* and *Amoraim* were buried there), and current practice. Jews who died at Acre were still brought there to be buried, even during the modern period: the Talmud had considered the city of Acre to be outside the boundaries of the land of Israel.

Rabbi Solomon Abadi planned to build a *Bet-Midrash* and synagogue at Kefar-Yassif, but lacked sufficient funds to complete the one or construct the other. Moreover, it never occurred to the settlers to base the economic existence of the village exclusively on the cultivation of the soil. They wanted the scholars particularly to make the study of the Law their profession and to be fully supported by the Diaspora Kehillot, like students of the Torah in the cities. In summer, 1747, the Kefar-Yassif settlers sent Rabbi Solomon Abadi to the Diaspora to collect funds for the community he had re-established. Their appeal reflected their hope for the expansion of the Jewish community in Palestine, as a result of the new political situation in Galilee under Sheik Dhaher, and for this reason they did not ask solely for monetary support but concluded their appeal with a call for immigration and settlement in their village. Support from abroad did actually help to maintain the settlement at Kefar-Yassif and even to expand it somewhat. In 1764, Rabbi Simha of Zalosce reported that there were "about twenty Jews" (i.e., households) living there, "and they till the soil." Local tradition recorded that the Jewish community at Shafa-amr (She'faram) was revived in Sheik Dhaher's time and a synagogue built there by Rabbi Haim Aboulafia, with the Sheik's help. There are grounds for supposing that the agricultural community at Pe'ki'in was also reinforced at the same period, again as a result of Rabbi Aboulafia's activity.

In those very early 1740's a considerable awakening of sentiment in favour of immigration became manifest throughout the Diaspora. It was particularly strong amongst scholars and Kabbalists who hoped to hasten deliverance by studying the Law and praying on the holy soil. The famous Kabbalist and scholar, Rabbi Haim Ben Moses ibn 'Atr (1696-1743), author of the well-known *Or-Ha'Hayim* commentary to the Pentateuch, drew attention to these ideas current amongst the "chosen scholars." He himself was so greatly impressed by Rabbi Haim Aboulafia's appeal and the resulting immigration, that he was persuaded to assemble his own group of pupils and go to Palestine.

Rabbi Haim ibn 'Atr was a native of Morocco. In 1739 he left Africa for northern Italy to embark for Palestine with his students. The propaganda he conducted in the course of his travels through Italy succeeded in setting up a foundation and maintenance fund for a new *Yeshivah* in Jerusalem. It also gained new Italian adherents to the idea of immigration, whom he accepted into his group as new pupils. In 1741, he sailed for Palestine from Leghorn at the head of a party of thirty men, women and children. An epidemic in Jerusalem when they landed forced the group to stay in Acre until 1742. After two members of his party had died, he was afraid to continue in Acre and transferred his *Yeshivah* (which he had temporarily established in Acre) to Pe'ki'in. This group proceeded to Jerusalem by way of Acre when the epidemic had died down. Rabbi Haim ibn 'Atr was able to rent a house in Jerusalem for his *Yeshivah* and distinguished students from amongst the inhabitants of Jerusalem, including Rabbi Haim Joseph David Azulai, were attracted thither. The famous Kabbalist died less than a year later, but his Torah scholarship and his solitary personal habits became the subjects of legends that circulated in Palestine and the Diaspora for generations. His own decision to go to the land had been influenced by Rabbi Haim Aboulafia's ideal. In its turn, the immigration of his group made a great impression in the Diaspora and stimulated the leaders of the rising Hassidic movement in eastern Europe to follow his example and settle in Palestine.

The Aliyah Movement in Eastern Europe: Hassidim and Pe'rushim

The development of Hassidism marked a new stage in the Aliyah movement. Thenceforth, it grew steadily, particularly in eastern European countries, where the new religious movement had spread. The yearning for deliverance, which filled the oppressed people during the Hassidic period and found expression in the new doctrine, necessarily intensified the desire to go to the Land as a means of bringing deliverance nearer. Furthermore, the mode of life, entirely enveloped in sanctity, that the Hassidim prescribed, demanded exodus from the "profane" lands of the Diaspora and settlement in the Land, which was the source and goal of holiness. The emigration of Hassidim was also prompted by their aim to establish a centre for their doctrine in Palestine. However, the same fundamental theses of Hassidism which encouraged Aliyah also set its narrow limits as a function that only a select few could fulfil. The social passiveness which marked Hassidic doctrine, basing the life of the individual on faith, precluded consideration of any practical programme for settlement or economic undertakings for the absorption of immigrants. Even projects such as Rabbi Haim Aboulafia's revival of Jewish settlement at Tiberias, or that of the Kabbalist Rabbi Solomon Abadi for Kefar-Yassif, did not evoke any response from the Hassidic settlers. Moreover, the scope of Hassidic immigration was circumscribed from the outset by the doctrine of *Tzaddikism*. It was the *Tzaddik* who effected communion at the higher levels, brought down an abundance of goodness for the people of Israel, revoked evil decrees, and accelerated the advent of salvation. Consequently it was believed that the *Tzaddik* who lived in the Holy Land and prayed "next to the portals of God" would fulfil these tasks all the more effectively. However, Hassidism, as a mass movement, was able to send more groups of immigrants at more frequent intervals than had the Kabbalists in the past. What is more, the settlement of Hassidim, by the nature of the movement itself, introduced a new element: the immigrant who was not an accomplished scholar either of the revealed Torah or of Kabbalah but whose only asset was the strength of his prayer and devotion. The Hassidic immigration also benefited from the solidarity that characterized the movement and which procured it more consistent and more efficiently organized Diaspora support for the settlement of its adherents than that received by the other organized communities (*Kole'lim*) in the country.

The Hassidim first began to go to Palestine within the lifetime of Ba'al

Shem Tov, and members of his circle were among the first to leave. Rabbi Gershon of Kuty, with his wife and small children, arrived in Palestine to settle in 1747, when he was already an ardent friend and admirer of his brother-in-law, Ba'al Shem Tov, and maintained a steady correspondence with him.

Although Ba'al Shem Tov was never able to go himself and his brilliant disciple, Rabbi Jacob Joseph, also never realized this ambition, his close associates continued to arrive during his lifetime and after his death. At first, this was a movement of individuals, but in 1764 a group of five or eight whole families of Hassidim, led by Rabbi Nachman of Horodenka and Rabbi Mendel of Przemyslany, settled in Tiberias or Safed.

No information is available on the emigration of individuals after this group movement of 1764, but it may be surmised that it continued as before. However, in 1777 a large party of Hassidim and their families—the largest group movement since Rabbi Judah Hassid and his faction in 1700—reached the country. This emigration had originally been conceived by Hassidic leaders in White Russia as a result of the peculiar circumstances of the Hassidic movement there. The grim persecutions to which the Hassidim were subjected at the instigation of the Vilno Kehillah in 1772, decided the leaders of the "Sect" to take refuge in Palestine. In their distress, Palestine appeared as an asylum from their position of double exile: their subjugation to gentile domination and the exile of "legitimate" scholars amongst the immodest. The White Russian Hassidim hoped that their immigrants would enhance the prestige of Hassidism in general, and its honour in particular, which had been hurt in their own country, and also fulfil the immediate objective of all Hassidic immigration: the hastening of deliverance through Torah and prayer in the Land of Israel.

Late in the winter of 1777, a group of Hassidim left White Russia for Palestine headed by the outstanding Hassidic leaders of the country: Rabbi Mendel of Vitebsk, Rabbi Abraham of Kolyski and Rabbi Israel of Polotzk, one of the organizers of the movement in the Mezhirich *Maggid's* time. Their journey through Volhynia and Podolia to the Moldavian border lasted five months. Apparently they stayed a while in Kehillot they passed on their travels, both to collect money for fares and the initial expenses of settling, and also to establish connections with Hassidic congregations in these Kehillot to ensure regular support once they had settled. The journey was accompanied by a good deal of publicity and a crowd of Hassidim escorted the travellers on the successive stages of their journey. This made a stirring impression on Jewish Kehillot in all the countries through which they passed, proving that although the idea of Aliyah had originated with the Hassidim of White Russia, it expressed the sentiments of all the Jewish population of eastern Europe. This was a time of great economic crisis for the Jews in the Polish Kingdom. The news of the Hassidic caravan en route to the Land of Israel, coming as it did when dejection and the sense of helplessness had reached their greatest depth, inspired them with hope for salvation and with the energy to take action. They were also encouraged by a rumour circulating amongst the masses, that the Turkish government had promised the new arrivals special privileges. In addition to the Hassidim, ordinary "poor men and paupers," who also felt a burning love for the Land, were equally encouraged to re-settle, particularly as the prospect that they might be able to exist there, either on manual labour or on support, or on both, appealed to their imagination. Efforts by Rabbi Mendel of Vitebsk and his friend, Rabbi Israel of Polotzk, to halt this emigration of the poor, lest they become a burden to the organized Hassidic group, were of no avail. The poor they met refused to heed their advice and most of the pauper immigrants did not even feel the need to join the party but preceded it "like a vanguard." This ferment of immigration among the east European Jews grew to such an extent that it attracted the attention and aroused the concern of the Polish government.

By various routes, the parties, consisting mainly of poor men, their wives and children, arrived at Constantinople. The Hassidim reached the port of Galatz on the Black Sea and from there embarked for Constantinople in a number of small vessels. One of these was wrecked at sea near the Crimean peninsula and only thirty of the eighty immigrants on board were rescued. Many lost hope on the way and returned, but over 300 people reached Palestine at the end of the summer of 1777 and travelled by donkey from Acre to their final destination at Safed.

The Hassidic leaders expressed in their letters to the Diaspora the happiness that overwhelmed them when they laid eyes on "our cherished land, the loved one of our hearts, the joy of our thoughts," after all the discomforts and vicissitudes of the long journey. They were excited not only by the "holiness of the land," but also by its fertility and abundant yield—though the country had only quietened down after the devastating wars of Sheik Dhaher and his enemies some two years previously. The new arrivals experienced no problems regarding housing: Safed had not been fully repopulated after the earthquake of 1760 and they found "many large and good houses without occupants." However, they suffered from lack of means of support, especially the poor who had reached the country with no funds at all. The Hassidic leaders therefore sent letters and special couriers appealing to the Diaspora for help. News of the adverse conditions spread rapidly and delayed the arrival of new immigrants, while many who had already come, returned.

The majority who had arrived with the Hassidic immigrants settled in the country and within a few years, after much suffering and hardship, achieved some measure of financial stability. The Hassidic leaders received special support from their adherents abroad. Most of the settlers existed either on philanthropic contributions or on their earnings from pursuing an occupation, or both. There were also some well-to-do people who required no support at all. As a result of the Hassidic re-settlement, the Jewish community in Galilee grew larger and stronger. Most of them remained in Safed with Rabbi Abraham of Kolyski. Some moved to Tiberias under the leadership of Rabbi Mendel of Vitebsk following an anti-Hassidic altercation at Safed in 1781. A few also settled at Pe'ki'in.

The movement of 1777 was not followed by a new wave of Hassidic immigrants. Its tragedy, and that of the entire Jewish people, was the glaring contrast between the deep stirrings for re-settlement amongst the Jewish masses of eastern Europe and the social and cultural feudalism which chained them. "Were they all to come, they would cover the entire land," Rabbi Mendel of Vitebsk acknowledged. After their arrival, Rabbi Mendel and his companions issued numerous warnings against further immigration of persons without means of their own or steady support from their relatives. In these circumstances, further immigration was confined to individual Hassidim, though the number of these was still higher than before 1777. These late arrivals included both Hassidic leaders, such as Rabbi Jacob Samson of Szepetovka, and laymen.

Despite its feeble consequences, the immigration of the Hassidim in 1777 marked a turning point in tightening the link between east European Jewry and Palestine. The sizeable community of Polish, Lithuanian, White Russian, and Ukrainian Jews in Palestine owed its establishment to them. Its connections with the Diaspora were not solely based on its dependence but constituted a reciprocal cultural relationship between the two. It marked the preparatory stage in the historic role the largest population centre in the Diaspora was to play in the building of the homeland during the nineteenth and twentieth centuries.

When the political situation in the country had become more stable and settlement conditions in Galilee, and particularly in Safed, had been improved, an increase in immigration also occurred amongst the Sephardi communities. At Purim, 1777, when the White Russian party of Hassidim set out on its journey to Palestine, interest in group re-settlement was also aroused at the other end of the dispersion, in North Africa. Some thirty people in Tunis "came together and formed one covenant—to go to the Holy Land." They reached the country that summer, together with the group of Hassidim. Even at the height of the Napoleonic Wars, the Sephardi immigrants—like the Ashkenasi—continued to flow to the city of Safed, because of its favourable political situation and consequent security and peace.

A new era opened in the history of the movement during the tumultuous Napoleonic period at the beginning of the nineteenth century. Here again, as at the beginning of the last quarter of the eighteenth century, it originated in the populous Diaspora centre of eastern Europe. However, whereas the earlier immigrants had been led by the Hassidim, it now issued from amongst their *Mitnaged* rivals. "To forget the holy land, Heaven forbid, prolongs the exile, [causes] the forgetting of the end of all our days!" disciples of the Vilno Gaon who had settled in Safed appealed to the Diaspora in 1810.

The Hassidim had placed the utmost emphasis on the virtue of living on the holy soil. The Mitnagdim's object in settling in Palestine before the coming of the deliverer was, primarily, to establish a Torah centre in the Land which was the source of Torah and "its abode." There are, of course, ample grounds for supposing that the additional motive of glorifying their own doctrine and approach to the Torah and the precepts through the establishment of their own community in the holy land had roused the Mitnagdim, like the Hassidim, to immigrate. The group re-settlement of the Hassidim and their eventual success in settling in the country, undoubtedly stimulated the Mitnagdim of Lithuania and White Russia to greater action in implementing their ideas for founding a Palestinian centre of their own and thus preventing their rivals from gaining predominance. However, the impelling force, as in the case of the Hassidic group in 1777, was mass enthusiasm for the idea of settling in Palestine. The scholars' initiative struck a responsive chord in the common people, who yearned for redemption. This is not surprising in view of the fact that 1808-09, when the first parties of the Gaon's disciples proceeded to Palestine, also saw the primary stages of the implementation of the Russian government's decree of 1804 expelling Jewish lessees and liquor purveyors from the villages. Many White Russian Jews were ruthlessly evicted and made homeless.

The immigration of Mitnagdim, unlike the Hassidic Aliyah that had preceded it, continued intermittently until their settlers far outnumbered their former rivals. In 1807-08, Rabbi Menahem Mendel, son of Barukh Bendit of Shklov, a well-known Kabbalist and disciple of the Vilno Gaon, emigrated to Palestine. He found Lithuanian congregations of non-Hassidim already in existence in the two cities of Safed and Tiberias and though they were numerically still small, they included distinguished scholars. In autumn 1809, Rabbi Israel of Shklov took his entire household to the country. When they arrived in Safed towards the end of the year, they found some forty families, or a total of 150 people, adhering to their outlook.

The new arrivals experienced a serious shortage of funds as none of them could engage in trade without knowledge of Arabic. An assembly of "all the great men and elders" held at the beginning of 1810, therefore decided to send Rabbi Israel of Shklov abroad to organize regular support for the community. He discharged his mission very efficiently. He founded aid institutions on behalf of the community in Safed in every city in White Russia. He was helped by Rabbi Haim of Volozhin, who also travelled to Vilno with him to arrange matters with the Palestine fund officials there. Meanwhile, an influx of new arrivals increased the community of Mitnagdim in Safed, who called themselves *Pe'rushim* (i.e., the secluded) to 461.

Unfortunately, an epidemic swept the city immediately after Rabbi

Israel's return. Together with many of the *Pe'rushim*, he fled to Jerusalem. However, the epidemic followed them there, and broke out again in 1814 after the survivors had returned to Safed. Only one daughter of Rabbi Israel's entire family survived. To add to their plight, help from abroad failed to arrive in time, and the leaders of the congregation were compelled "to tend and support the living, that they might live and not die of hunger ... to raise the orphans and to provide wet-nurses for sucklings whose mothers had died ..." Despite all these ordeals and hardships the *Pe'rushim* congregation persevered and even succeeded in gaining a foothold in Jerusalem. In October, 1815, Rabbi Mendel of Shklov, with his family and a few other members, left Safed and settled in Jerusalem. Leadership of the Safed congregation was left entirely in the hands of Rabbi Israel of Shklov.

The *Pe'rushim* immigration represented an advance on the Hassidic for all its shortcomings, which, after all, only reflected the ideology inherent in the decadent social system. Within the general framework of support from abroad, the immigrant scholars were also accompanied by working-class elements. The congregational regulations for the 1820's specified privileges for craftsmen in the distribution of charitable funds. The administrative ability of their leaders, particularly Rabbi Israel of Shklov, successfully introduced regularity and order into the financial system of the whole Ashkenazi community in the country and thus facilitated its expansion and growth. Similarly, their moderation and absence of narrow sectarianism enabled the *Pe'rushim* to maintain good relations both with the Palestine Hassidic congregation and with its Sephardim. Furthermore, they took a more realistic attitude towards the country than the Hassidim, who were inordinately and absolutely absorbed in an atmosphere of mysticism. The *Pe'rushim* were therefore much more capable of establishing firmer and more practical links between the people in the Diaspora and its Land as the immigration increased. The letter the Vilno Gaon's disciples in Safed sent to the Diaspora as early as 1810 was—both in content and in style—a fiery appeal in the name of the Land for its sons to return. The immigration of the *Pe'rushim* continued for many decades and lasted into the nineteenth century. Despite all the contrast between the old and the new worlds, the immigration of the *Hibat Zion** period of the 1880's, which inaugurated modern colonization in Palestine, was but carrying into practice the Love of Zion which had inspired the preceding Aliyoth, including that of the *Pe'rushim*.

An ill-fated project deliberately organized during that period with a view to viable agricultural colonization should also be mentioned. The oppression of the Jews in Bohemia by the régime of Francis I, the burden of special taxes, the limited number of permitted occupations, and the limitation of marriages by law had imbued at least some Jews with sufficient courage to set out for Palestine. The Austrian police files for

---

* *Hibat Zion* (i.e., Love of Zion) was the immediate precursor of the Zionist movement.

1812 recorded that a Jew, whose name was not specified, was travelling through all of southern Bohemia urging the Jews to leave for Palestine.* Some seventy or eighty families sold all their belongings and set out on carts loaded with agricultural implements. The Kehillot they passed on the way, especially those at Nikolsburg and Pressburg, welcomed them with great enthusiasm, and their rabbis, too, gave them letters of recommendation. The immigrants crossed the Danube and reached the Hungarian plain; but there they were constantly harassed on the road by bandits. After their leader had fallen in one of these clashes, a certain Jacob Meisel assumed leadership and led them southward, fighting all the way. In one of these encounters, they fought for their lives for two whole days, and only after they had lost fifty of their people did Count Esterhazy with his *Hajduks* rescue them from the attackers. As the journey continued, a severe drought, shortage of supplies, and hardships brought on illnesses.

In this plague Jacob Meisel also died. This desperate immigration was stopped on the Croatian frontier when the border estate's proprietor imprisoned the leaders for ransom and refused them passage. All but five of the immigrants returned to Bohemia. The five continued on their journey and reached Palestine.

The oppressive, absolutist régime also frustrated the movement amongst the Jews of Galicia. During 1811-12, the secret service of the Imperial Court at Vienna received information on the movement of Galician Jews, which was classed as illegal emigration. The Austrian ambassador at Constantinople reported the presence of thirty-eight Galician Jews, thirty-two with families, on their way to Palestine. At the beginning of 1812, the police was informed that fourteen other Galician Jews had gone to Palestine via Odessa and Constantinople. The government, afraid that money was being taken out of the country, forbade, by a special edict of the Emperor, all emigration by Galician Jews and warned the Kehillah *Parnassim* and rabbis that they would be held personally responsible if the emigration did not cease.

C. THE JEWISH COMMUNITY IN PALESTINE

Economic Condition; Organization of the Halukkah

The innate character of the eighteenth century Palestine Jewish community, even more than considerations of physical security, caused it to be almost entirely concentrated in "The Holy Cities." At first, these consti-

---

* The official Austrian document added that the Jew was preaching the re-establishment of the Jewish state; but this does not seem to accord with the character of this movement as depicted by the other details cited in the report. The Austrian police imputed political aims even to a peaceful movement of emigration.

tuted the three cities of Jerusalem, Hebron and Safed, but after 1740 they included the revived Kehillah in the fourth "Holy City," Tiberias. The Jewish community was far less stable numerically than the rest of the population. The Jewish population was devastated by the frequent natural disasters, common to all races—earthquakes, droughts and locusts—as well as by the incessant internal wars and their inevitable consequences—plagues, high cost of living and famine. But in addition the Jewish community was subjected to harsh decrees and discrimination at the hands of ruthless rulers and officials and to "regular" legal extortion of taxes and war levies which were so debilitating that the poor and impoverished came near to starvation on more than one occasion. The growing volume of immigration during the 1740's was mainly directed towards the cities of Galilee, Safed and Tiberias. However, because of the family and age structure of the immigrants, the increase in the size of the Jewish population was inconsiderable. Those in their prime, who arrived with their wives and children, were offset by a large proportion of aged men and women, including widows and widowers, who came "to join themselves to the land of the living" by dying there.

The largest Palestine Kehillah was still at Jerusalem, holiest of all holy cities, "the King's Sanctuary" and "City of Kingdom," which housed the remnant of the western wall surrounding the Temple. It symbolized all the majesty of the distant past and all the hopes for deliverance and the re-building of the Land. Nevertheless, its Jewish population did not increase from the middle of the eighteenth century to the beginning of the nineteenth; by all indications it actually declined. Reliable contemporary sources estimated that a maximum of 2,000 Jews lived in Jerusalem at the beginning of the nineteenth century. As late as 1834 no more than 3,000 Jews were reported in Jerusalem.

Whereas Jerusalem was the largest of the four "Holy Cities," the Hebron Kehillah, which gloried in the sanctity of the adjacent Cave of Machpelah never expanded beyond the narrow alley in which it was confined. Rabbi Gedaliah of Siemiatycze found there "approximately forty Jewish households" in 1700. A hundred years later the number was unchanged.

The two cities of Safed and Tiberias benefited most from the increased immigration of the period, as favourable settlement conditions, security and peace were more continuous in Galilee than elsewhere in the country. Of the two, Safed held a stronger attraction for new settlers, not only because of its superior tradition of holiness (associated with the graves of prophets, *tannaim*, and *amoraim* in the vicinity and also with the Kabbalist group established by Rabbi Isaac Luria in the sixteenth century) but also because of its salubrious mountain climate. The growth of the Safed community was disturbed by earthquakes in autumn, 1759, which destroyed most of the city's buildings and buried under their ruins hundreds of its inhabitants, including over a hundred Jews. Only two of the city's six synagogues survived the earthquake, and even these were severely damaged. Rabbi Simha of Zalosce, who visited Safed in 1764, estimated the number of Jews in the city after the earthquake at "about forty or fifty householders." Safed made very little progress towards rebuilding its ruins until the Hassidim came in 1777. In 1812, a learned tourist, J. L. Burckhardt, estimated that there were about 600 buildings in Safed, 150 of them occupied by Jews. However, the epidemic that swept the city in 1813-14 again wrought havoc amongst its Jewish inhabitants, forcing many to seek refuge elsewhere in the country. The Kehillah once more proceeded to reconstitute itself, but was interrupted by the calamities of the 1830's, the greatest of which was the earthquake of 1837.

The Jewish community in Tiberias grew slowly after its revival in 1740, but unlike Safed, without disturbance. It even benefited from the misfortunes of the Safed Kehillah by absorbing its refugees. All tourists, Jewish and Christian, who visited Tiberias, emphasized the fact that a high wall, with access to the city through a gate, separated the Jewish quarter, which covered the lower city down to the shore of Lake Galilee (the Sea of Kinneret), from the Arab quarter. Volney estimated the number of families in all Tiberias at a maximum of a hundred. However, in the course of time and with the various waves of immigration, the Kehillah grew so that by the end of the Napoleonic era, its population almost equalled that of Safed. Burckhardt reported in 1812 that the Jewish quarter had recently expanded by the addition of several additional streets. He calculated the number of the city's inhabitants at 4,000, including 1,000 Jews. Elsewhere in his report, he estimated that there were between 160 and 200 Jewish families in the city, forty to fifty of them from Poland and the remainder from "Spain" (i.e. Sephardim), Turkey, North Africa and Syria.

Apart from the two Kehillot, there were three Jewish village communities in Galilee at the period: in Pe'ki'in, Shafa-Amr and Kefar-Yassif, which had actually grown as a result of immigration. Pe'ki'in was particularly hallowed by a tradition which identified the carob tree, the cave, and the spring inside the cave with those of the legendary account of Rabbi Simeon Bar-Yohai and his son Eleazar.

Small Jewish communities also existed in Acre, Haifa, Nablus and Gaza. The Jewish congregation in Gaza began to decline in 1799, when many of its members fled during the crisis precipitated by Napoleon's conquering forces. According to tradition, the remaining Jews left Gaza in 1811 and moved to Hebron and Jerusalem. Individual Jews only lived in the port city of Jaffa for a few decades.

Altogether, excluding the four main Kehillot, the Jewish communities in other cities and the three villages in Galilee numbered between 500 and 750 people at the beginning of the nineteenth century. At that period, the Kehillot of the four "Holy Cities" had a population of between 5,000 and 6,000. Thus, at the end of the Napoleonic period, the Jewish population of Palestine totalled slightly over 5,000, and in any event not more than

7,000 individuals. This did not represent any significant increase over the 1,000 Jewish families reported by the Hebron emissary in 1773. However, in the intervening forty years, the Palestine Jewish community had firmly entrenched itself in the four main Kehillot, especially in the two Galilean Kehillot; it had strengthened its links with the Diaspora; and the foundations had been laid for an increased volume of immigration during the nineteenth century.

Every communication made by the emissaries who toured the Diaspora from time to time, to accelerate help to their Kehillot, told of the poverty of the Palestine Jewish community. This precarious condition was confirmed by most of the European tourists who travelled about the country at that time, especially in their descriptions of the Jewish quarter of Jerusalem. The Swedish physician and botanist, Frederick Hasselquist, had already mentioned two reasons for this situation after his visit in the middle of the eighteenth century: the Jews in Palestine had no possibility of engaging in trade; their source of income was limited to charity from pilgrims and monetary support from their co-religionists throughout the world—the greater part of which was appropriated by the Turks. Hasselquist undoubtedly arrived at the true explanation, even if he failed to analyse the wretched situation in depth.

As the impoverishment, lawlessness and chaos in the country caused by its rulers increased, it became ever more difficult for the Jewish settlers to follow the occupations they had pursued in their countries of origin. Foreign and wholesale trade at that time was almost wholly in the hands of foreign merchants, especially the French and their Armenian and Greek assistants. Peddling was almost entirely out of the question because of the danger of highwaymen on the roads. The Polish Jew, Rabbi Gedalia, who immigrated with Rabbi Judah the Hassid's party had already noted the real cause of the settlers' inability to make a living from liquor sales and innkeeping, so widespread amongst the Jews of Poland and Lithuania: "There is also this reason for their having no business affairs, and that is that no brews or honey are produced here. And even though liquors are distilled, and in the Land of Israel much wine is manufactured, nevertheless the Jews derive no income therefrom, because the Ishmaelites (i.e., the Turks) and the Arabs drink neither wine nor spirits. And if a Jew does sell an Arab or a Turk some wine or spirits and it becomes known, either through their getting drunk or in some other way, then that Jew is arrested and lashed, besides having to pay cash fines."

Nor was the third category of Jewish activity, handicraft, a feasible means of support for many settlers: apart from the low purchasing power of the population as a whole, there was very little demand for the traditional east European Jewish crafts, tailoring, hat-making, furriery, glaziery and similar professions. The system of arbitrary taxation and extortion practised by the authorities presented a further obstacle to Jewish initiative in the economic field. The Ashkenazi immigrants, in particular, encountered immense difficulties in the process of economic absorption because of their total ignorance of Arabic, not to mention Turkish, the language of the authorities.

However, despite these manifold difficulties, a fair number of Jews were economically active and self-supporting in various spheres, though for the most part, life was difficult for them and they suffered various degrees of privation. As already stated, the Jewish inhabitants of the three villages of Pe'ki'in, Shafa-Amr and Kefar-Yassif lived by manual labour, cultivating the land, though it must be assumed that there were a few scholars amongst them, aided by the city *Kole'lim*. The Jewish urban communities in Acre, Haifa and Gaza, and also the individual Jews living in Jaffa, maintained themselves unaided. The Gaza Jews were considered wealthy; by contrast the Jews of Nablus were known as "the country's poor." The Jewish inhabitants of Acre, all Sephardim, were, according to the travel account of Rabbi Simha of Zalosce, poor people but "very merciful and learned in the Torah." Only their Kehillah leader was distinguished for his wealth. They earned their living in haberdashery and silk lace manufacture. The poorest even worked as porters.

Even in the four "Holy Cities," where the bulk of the Jews lived, not all the Jews depended exclusively on support from the Diaspora—which would anyway have been impossible by sheer number. On the contrary, Jews supporting themselves by manual labour or petty trade formed the economic basis of the Sephardi community. Rabbi Simha of Zalosce compared the sources of income of the Jews of Safed with those of the Jews of Acre and his conclusions revealed a wide range of productive occupations:

> Only the *Yeshivah* scholars keep themselves completely aloof from handicrafts and support themselves penuriously on what is sent them from abroad. By contrast, the city folk support themselves as threaders of ordinary and silken clothing adornments; and so too in Acre. There are those who build houses, there are stone porters, water-carriers from wells outside the city, and a few who are employed as silver and coppersmiths.

From Rabbi Simha's description of the Safed market-place, it appears that already by the time of his visit in the middle 1760's there was a number of Jewish stores in that town. He specifically mentioned peddling as a common occupation amongst the Jews of Safed: "There are numerous Arab villages around Safed and Jewish peddlers bring their wares from Acre and canvass the Gentile villages around Safed, bartering and selling."

Jewish travel accounts give no information on the economy of the Jews of Tiberias. However, the favourable circumstances attending the revival of the Jewish community in Tiberias in 1740, its size and security and peace, which the chroniclers unanimously praised, all indicate that the

Kehillah of Tiberias was certainly not inferior to that at Safed in the number of its self-supporting Jewish merchants and craftsmen. However, mention should be made of accounts by two early nineteenth century Christian tourists—the Swiss scholar, Burckhardt, and the Bonn theologian, Professor Schultz—who both describe the Jewish community of Tiberias as depending almost entirely on support from abroad or charity. Their conclusions were apparently based on encounters (because of the affinity of their respective languages—German and Yiddish) with the Polish and Lithuanian Jews in the city (Burckhardt also visited their homes). These immigrants, like their compatriots in Safed, were not able to engage in any self-supporting trade or craft because of the language barrier. But it would appear that some of them had already succeeded in finding some kind of occupation, because the Jews who as Burckhardt reports, "openly sold wine and liquor to soldiers in the city" must have been immigrants from Poland and Lithuania.

The poverty in the largest Kehillah, Jerusalem, was more obvious than in the Jewish quarters in the other cities. The Jews of Jerusalem had not attained the legal position nor the security of the settlements in Galilee. Furthermore, the Arab inhabitants of the city did not display a consistently neighbourly attitude. Nonetheless, Jerusalem was no exception to the rule of Jewish economic activity, except that the proportion of economically active people was lower than in the Galilean cities. It may be assumed that in a normal year the proportion of totally self-supporting people in the Jerusalem Kehillah was slightly over a third of the Kehillah population.

Rabbi Gedalia of Siemiatycze described the shop and pedlar trade in Jerusalem at the beginning of the eighteenth century in the following terms:

> The Jews have some shops in the Gentile market-place, as for instance vendors of spices and such things, but they are few ... Some Jews have grocery stores, and many are in partnership with Turks . . . so that they should protect them from the robbery committed against storekeepers ... Jews from *Maghreb* (North Africa) speak Arabic and dress almost like Arabs, own donkeys, and they travel from village to village with spices and other wares and in the villages they obtain wheat and barley and other foodstuffs and bring them to Jerusalem to sell . . . but most of them are poor people.

Letters written from Palestine in those years mention the sale of soap and souvenirs to Jews from abroad. In the second half of the eighteenth century wholesale trade is mentioned in the *responsa* literature and is also referred to in the Jerusalem Kehillah regulations. This trade encompassed merchandise such as flaxen clothing, sugar—brought by caravan from Egypt, wheat, flour, glassware, cheese, wine, sesame, raisins and olive oil. The records of a law-suit brought before the authorities in 1764 against the collection of an arbitrary tariff from the Jews of Jerusalem reveal that the latter were shipping merchandise to and from Jaffa. *Responsa* of the period mention Jewish artisans in Jerusalem, including jewellers, bakers, a sausage manufacturer and an embroiderer.

The tourist, Seetzen, drew up a detailed list of Jewish trades and professions in Jerusalem in 1806:

Professionals and Tradesmen:		*Artisans and Craftsmen:*	
Physicians	3	Coppersmiths and solderers	5
Storekeepers (spices)	10	Tinsmiths	2 or 3
Storekeepers (sugar, tobacco, etc.)	10	Coffee processors	2
		Butchers	10
Dealers in sweets, vegetables, etc.	20	Painters	2
		Tailors	10
Cloth merchants	10	Flax and cotton cordmakers	2
Second-hand dealers	5		
Sulphur, thread and needle dealers	3		
Thread and silk dealers	2		
Teachers	5		
Ritual slaughterers	10		

This list accounted for 112 family heads, including sixty engaged in trade, thirty-four in crafts and another eighteen in the "free professions" (ten slaughterers, three doctors, five teachers). The family heads in the list therefore represented 22–28 per cent, or slightly over a quarter of the total number of 400–500 Jewish families in Jerusalem, Seetzen reported.* There were, however, some omissions: Seetzen mentions elsewhere, in a different context, a Jewish bookbinder and a wax candle industry supplying synagogues (as well as monasteries and mosques). The crafts the *responsa* recorded in Jerusalem are also absent from the list—jewellers, for example, or bakers (who were absolutely essential to the Kehillah). Furthermore, the list did not include people selling groceries and beverages, whose presence was required by the laws of *kashrut*: milkmen, vendors of dairy supplies, and wine dealers (also, incidentally, mentioned in the *responsa*). In particular, it should have included the pedlars, who appear in Hebrew eighteenth century sources as residents of Jerusalem. The scroll writers, cantors and beadles were omitted from the categories of "free professionals" and public service employees. These additions would raise the proportion of families supported by gainfully employed wage-earners to between 30 and 35 per cent of all the Jewish families in Jerusalem early in the nineteenth century.

Members of the self supporting group who lived on their capital were in a class by themselves in Jerusalem, or for that matter, in all four Kehillot, because of the unique character of the immigration. The difficulty of

* Seetzen actually mentioned 2,000 people without estimating the number of families.

earning a living in Palestine on the one hand, and the advanced age of many immigrants who had only come there to die on the other, meant that most of the well-to-do had immigrated with the initial intention of living on their capital. The leaders and the rabbis of the *Yishuv* who were calling for settlement in the country considered this the most desirable type of immigration. Moreover, travel accounts and letters to the Diaspora by leaders of the immigrants repeatedly warned against immigration of those who lacked sufficient capital to ensure for themselves a steady income. Those who brought their money with them loaned it out on interest, sometimes to individual gentiles, but in Jerusalem particularly to Christian monasteries, such as the French, Armenian and Greek. The monasteries especially needed these loans when the funds for their upkeep failed to arrive from abroad in time. These owners of capital also occasionally loaned money at interest both to individual Jews and to *Kole'lim* on the legal basis of "business permits."*

However, loans between Jews only represented a small percentage of the sums which Jews, as individuals or as *Kole'lim*, borrowed from Arab usurers, or from the rulers themselves, at compound interest. Some Jews with capital deposited it entirely with the *Kole'lim* on condition that they might draw a weekly rental for the rest of their lives. Other immigrants left their money abroad in the cities they had come from and received the interest on it at regular intervals to enable them to exist in Palestine. Thus, if every Jew who lived, in some way or another, on his capital were added to the list of self-supporting Jews in Jerusalem, the number of families there who did not require support (discounting drought and other disasters) would constitute two-fifths, if not half, of the total Kehillah membership.

Contemporary sources give no information on the economic life of the Hebron Jews. It would appear that this tiny community was composed principally of *Yeshivah* scholars and their pupils, and that the remaining few families earned a living either in Kehillah service or by the production of kosher foods and their sale to Kehillah members.

However appreciable their proportions, the economically active elements who supported themselves by manual labour or trade were not sufficiently numerous to shape the social and economic pattern of the Palestine Jewish community. The character of the Jewish settlements as a whole was determined by the Jews who were maintained by charity and aid funds from the Diaspora Kehillot. They included scholars who devoted themselves to "Torah and worship" in the service of the creator, as well as ordinary, respectable, poor people and beggars. This was the character of the *Yishuv*, not only in Jerusalem and in Hebron, but also, to a large extent, in the two "Holy Cities" of Galilee. Even many men who were

---

* In Aramaic: *Heter Isqa*, a formula invented in Poland in the seventeenth century to circumvent the Biblical prohibition on the taking of interest by declaring the lender of the loan a partner in the particular business for which the money was borrowed.

gainfully employed required philanthropy to supplement their meagre incomes.

Funds to support the *Yishuv* were derived from various sources. Pilgrims considered it a great act of piety to give alms to their poor brethren in Palestine. In addition, the pilgrims also made donations to charitable funds and for Kehillah requirements (it was a custom to honour them with an ascent to the reading of the Law in the synagogue on the first Sabbath after their arrival in the country). Owners of capital who settled in the country were also required to contribute to the support of the Kehillah poor. However, the principal sources of help were the donations and permanent fund organizations in the Diaspora Kehillot. The scholars and pupils of the *Yeshivot* were mostly maintained by special foundations and legacies made by donors outside Palestine. Individual scholars of exceptional prestige outside the *Yeshivot* also received regular "supplies" (allowances) from their native Kehillot or from admirers elsewhere. But aid to the Jews in general arrived through the broad channels of the *Halukkah* (allotment) funds collected throughout the Diaspora.

The *Halukkah* system developed by stages throughout the modern period until it became the mainstay of Palestine Jewry's existence. During the sixteenth century, aid funds from abroad were customarily only paid out to scholars and the helpless poor. As poverty amongst the Jews increased during the seventeenth century, the *Halukkah* began to encompass broader and broader circles, especially in times of trouble. Growing exploitation and oppression by the rulers, chiefly in the two Judean cities of Jerusalem and Hebron, made the Jewish population increasingly dependent on *Halukkah* during the eighteenth century. The economic structure of the Jews again deteriorated with the increase in the Ashkenazi congregations following the Hassidic and *Pe'rushim* immigration from eastern Europe at the end of the eighteenth and beginning of the nineteenth centuries. Because of the language barrier, the new Ashkenazi settlers lived mostly on Diaspora support, from the *Halukkah* and the "supplies." Only people with ready cash or professional training were self-sufficient.

The organization of Diaspora support also changed during this period, largely reflecting the situation that had developed within the country. When the situation deteriorated at the beginning of the sixteenth century, the Kehillah of Venice imposed an obligatory donation of a "half-shekel" (approximately a quarter ducat) on everyone who paid a minimal Kehillah tax. This practice spread to all the Kehillot of Europe. Apart from Kehillah contributions and donations, emissaries of the "Holy Cities" from time to time collected regular support from individuals, introduced by the Kehillot. "Land of Israel Collectors" were appointed and Land of Israel Chests established in large and many medium-sized communities (in Poland and Lithuania, council regulations made this compulsory for all Kehillot).

Furthermore, "Land of Israel Societies" were founded in Constantinople, Rome, Hamburg and the cities of Moravia, for example, which required their members to make regular contributions. In western Europe, contributions and donations were sent to treasurers, or "Land of Israel Presidents," in the large Kehillot of Venice, Leghorn and Amsterdam. Leghorn also served as the clearing centre for Palestine funds transmitted by the Kehillot of North Africa. In central Europe national "Presidents" (chief collectors) existed in centres such as Vienna, Prague, Hamburg and Frankfurt-on-Main during the seventeenth century. The Frankfurt-on-Main centre remained important up to the end of the eighteenth century.

Money from Kehillot in the Kingdom of Poland was sent to the Council of the Four Lands and from there to the Land of Israel collector at Lwow. During the 1750's and 1760's the "Land of Israel President" for Poland had his office in the city of Brody. The centres at Venice, Leghorn and Amsterdam sent their collections directly to the Palestinian Kehillot, according to a "donations list," while the Jews of Poland used the offices of the "Land of Israel Officials," or Palestine Fund Treasurers, at Constantinople for this purpose. At the end of the eighteenth century, following the partitions of Poland, the Palestine Collectors at Brody are mentioned as intermediaries in the transmission of support funds to the Hassidim in Galilee in the form of drafts. The Jews of European and Asian Turkey used Constantinople as the transmission centre for their Palestine funds. In fact, the Kehillah in the Turkish capital became the official and actual guardian of the Palestine Jewish community, as the result of its proximity to the country and its direct contact with the Imperial authorities.

The Diaspora did not support Palestine Jewry merely out of charity, even though the desperate appeals made during the frequent emergencies named the mortal dangers which threatened it, and help was mobilized virtually as a "ransoming of captives." The Diaspora Kehillot were fully aware of the fact that the Jews engaged in "Torah and Prayer" on the holy soil were standing guard over the people's claim to their land. They believed that the Jews living in the land were the vanguard for the rest of the people, who would ascend and join them when the Messiah came. Whenever the Jews faced an emergency, the Diaspora Kehillot made extraordinary efforts to expedite help. The Turkish Kehillot were particularly prominent in this respect, followed by the Italian; both assumed a greater share of responsibility for the situation of the Jews than any other part of the Diaspora. A letter that the Palestine collectors at Constantinople sent to the Kehillot of Rumelia in European Turkey in about 1800 urged them to emulate the Constantinople Kehillah and make a collection for Jerusalem at the rate of one piastre per capita and one half-piastre for every building. "If, Heaven forbid, we ignore this," they warned, "then the land will be waste and void of Jews."

However, despite the generosity the people in the Diaspora demonstrated towards Palestine Jewry, the *Halukkah* project was marred from its inception by a lack of unity and centralized organization which impaired the efficiency of its support. The rift between Sephardim and Ashkenazim in the Diaspora also appeared in Palestine and adversely affected fund-raising drives. Throughout the eighteenth century and into the beginning of the nineteenth, the Ashkenazim repeatedly complained that the Sephardim were not including them in the distribution of *Halukkah* income from Ashkenazi Kehillot in the Diaspora or else were allocating it unfairly. As mutual suspicion and conflict between the two communities increased, Sephardi Kehillot in western Europe accordingly refrained from supporting Ashkenazi emissaries. In the latter half of the eighteenth century, a new *Halukkah* apportionment scale was drawn up and approved both by the Palestine fund administrators in Constantinople and by Rabbi Ezekiel Landau of Prague. This agreement, divided all income from the "General Land of Israel Treasury" into twenty-eight parts, of which Jerusalem received eleven, Hebron—six, Safed—seven, and Tiberias —four. This arrangement was, in fact, instrumental in putting an end to the altercations between the small Ashkenazi community in Jerusalem and its large Sephardi community. It also prompted Ashkenazim in the Diaspora to extend more generous support to Palestine Jewry as a whole. It did not prevent the progressive disintegration of the *Halukkah* organization.

The Diaspora had been divided into three areas for the purpose of Palestine missions: Turkey in Asia and Europe, the *Maghreb*—or North Africa, and *Francia,* which covered Europe as a whole but especially western Europe. However, for the most part, each of the four "Holy Cities" sent its own emissaries abroad, and Hebron and Tiberias even established their own special campaign chests in the cities of the Diaspora. Hassidim in eastern Europe organized special support for the Hassidic community in Galilee over and above the assistance sent to Palestine Jewry as a whole (the Rabbi Meir Ba'al Ha'ness Fund). The Mitnaged *Pe'rushim* followed suit at the beginning of the nineteenth century by setting up a centre at Vilno for contributions to their *Kolel* in Palestine. Individual *Yeshivot* occasionally dispatched their own emissaries to the Diaspora to raise funds.

As a result of the absence of co-ordination and the lack of centralization Palestine donation funds frequently accumulated in Diaspora Kehillot over a period of years. In these instances, Kehillah leaders often used them for local charity purposes. An attitude of indifference towards Palestine was already appearing amongst the wealthy Jews of western Europe at the beginning of the eighteenth century, resulting from their tendency to assimilationism, a greater callousness towards the misery of their poverty-stricken fellow-Jews, and from an opposition to all philanthropy generally. Another factor, in no small measure responsible for discrediting Palestine Jewry in the eyes of the European Kehillot, even outside enlightened circles, was the large number of emissaries, which included mercenary and unscrupulous "emissaries on their own behalf."

The very *Halukkah* system eventually became an encumbrance to the Jews of Palestine, though its birth and development had stemmed from necessity. Its support largely caused the rulers of the country to intensify their system of pressure and extortion. As persecution and oppression became more powerful, the Kehillot would appeal to the Diaspora for help. And every response that the emergencies elicited led to renewed persecutions and larger demands, in the certain knowledge that they would be gratified. *Halukkah* had an even more injurious effect on the economic existence and self-respect of the Jews. The more comprehensive the *Halukkah* system became, the more Palestine Jewry came to rely on help from abroad. Its initiative and energy declined and helplessness and debility spread. The Jewish community in the birthplace of the Jewish people came to acquiesce in its status as the object of the charity of the entire Jewish people on the strength of its devotion to "Torah and Prayer on the Holy Soil."

Poverty and Oppression

The history of the Kehillot in the four "Holy Cities," and especially the Jerusalem and Hebron Kehillot at that time, offered a sordid picture of suffering and distress engendered by the many years of disaster which overshadowed the "normal" years. The decadent feudal system that afflicted the country as a whole weighed doubly on the Jewish congregations because of their disadvantage as an oppressed national and religious minority. The numerous misfortunes that ravaged the entire population— years of locust and drought, plague and illness, foreign and internal wars—affected the Jewish community with added force because of its chronic destitution, unrelieved except by assistance from abroad. The Christians in Palestine were also subjected to humiliation and contempt by the dominant religion, and also carried a heavy burden of taxes and arbitrary war levies imposed on the "infidels." But their position was infinitely better than the Jewish minority: in the first place they had the security of political protection by the European powers—France in particular carried great influence with the Sublime Porte until the end of the eighteenth century; secondly, the Christian monasteries owned innumerable assets; and finally monetary support from pilgrims and their home countries flowed steadily and copiously, even if its arrival was at times delayed.

A bitter letter of complaint from the Jerusalem Kehillah leaders in 1741 listed details of the taxes the Jews had to pay. The main levy imposed on the "infidels" (non-Moslems) was the Poll Tax collected from all males, from boys to the very aged. This tax was graded for three classes, the wealthy, intermediate, and poor, in the ratio of four, two and one piastres (in Jerusalem), or three, two, and one piastre (according to

Sheik Dhaher's apportionment for the revived Jewish settlement in Kefar-Yassif). During the 1780's, the tax ratio, according to the French tourist Volney, was from three and four to eleven piastres. The congregational heads were responsible for the payment of the Poll Tax even by impecunious indigents. The poor, according to Rabbi Gedalia, would hide in their homes when the collector came, but they were almost invariably unsuccessful in evading them, "and whosoever has not the wherewithal to pay the tax is seized, and they force the *Kahal* to pay ransom from its funds."

The letter also stated that the Jerusalem Kehillah annually sent the "compromise" sum of 1,500 piastres in Poll Tax payments for the poor.

The monthly *Mushahera* Tax was collected from merchants, artisans and landowners, without distinction as to religion. As far as obligatory gifts were concerned, reference was made in 1741 to the *Imdath*, paid for the confirmation of high officials in office or on the occasion of their visit to a city (amounting to 300 or more piastres annually in Jerusalem), and the *Ideias* Tax, a gift in honour of the Moslem holidays "to all the mighty ones in the country ... for gold, delicacies, and the sending of gifts." Other sources stated that the Jews sent money gifts and sweetmeats to the authorities during the month of *Ramadan*. High burial fees were collected, mainly by the *Qaadi* (Moslem religious judge). It was fixed at five piastres per burial during the eighteenth century, but was increased by additional fees: the *Qaadi*'s secretary collected an auxiliary fee for himself. The Jerusalem Kehillah obtained only in 1762 a *Firman* from Constantinople abolishing all burial payments, apart from the permit fee payable to the *Qaadi*. The rental for the burial ground on the slopes of the Mount of Olives alone cost one gold piece, or 0.75 piastre daily, payable to the owner of the land at daybreak.*

Apart from the taxes and obligatory gifts mentioned in the 1741 letter, seventeenth and early eighteeenth century sources recorded that the Jews of Jerusalem were required to make payments to high officials, "the dignitary and his entourage," in other words, the district commissioner and his officials. These payments altogether amounted to 500 piastres annually.

Unlike Jerusalem, the Kehillot of Tiberias and Safed occasionally experienced some relief from excessive taxation as the rulers were anxious to attract settlers there: to Tiberias when it was rebuilt from the ruins in 1740; to Safed after the earthquake of 1759. For many years, therefore, the authorities were content merely to collect the Poll Tax from the Jews, or the Poll Tax with the *miri*, or land tax, added on. But the Jews there too were not spared from arbitrary extortions by the rulers, especially during the frequent wars.

Even the regular taxes and obligatory gifts—described as the "chronic

* This coin was the *zolota*, equal to thirty paras; the piastre or *asadi*, was equal to forty paras.

ones," in the emissaries' letter—were too numerous to endure and forced the Kehillot to borrow money at interest and become involved in debt. In fact, levies for exceptional expenditure were so common that they too became routine. Thus frequent extortions by the rulers on one pretext or another were added to the hardships of the years of famine and disorders. The Kehillot could not escape from this vicious circle. The higher the taxes, the less the Kehillot were able to sustain them, and this in turn evoked further victimization by the rulers, so that the Kehillot had to borrow additional sums at continually rising rates of interest. The despots and the ruling class in the country drained the resources of the Jews in two related fashions: through taxation and through interest. Often during the eighteenth century, the Constantinople government, as a result of intercession by the Kehillah leaders of the city, intervened on behalf of the intolerably taxed Kehillot in Palestine and ordered tax apportionment by instalments, or even cancelled interest payments. This did not, however, tackle the evil at its source. Neither did the help the Kehillah emissaries brought back from the Diaspora solve the problem of indebtedness. After short periods of relief, the Kehillot were invariably again in trouble.

The false accusations and persecution that besieged the four Kehillot at the end of the eighteenth century, following the conquest of Egypt by Napoleon's forces and their invasion of Palestine, put the final mark on their suffering. A letter from Jerusalem in 1799 reported that persecutions broke out there in the summer of 1798 immediately after the French conquest of Egypt. The charge levelled against the Jews was that "the army had an advance guard of 12,000 men who are our brothers, the children of Israel." This spurious charge was, apparently, based on the presence of a number of Jewish inhabitants of North Africa in Napoleon's army in Egypt. Neither the Jerusalem Jews' loyalty to the Pasha and the Turkish government, nor their "hard work in repairing the city's fortifications," helped them on this occasion. The disorders also affected "the other nations"—in other words, the Christian minority in the city—and the Jews lived in an atmosphere of mortal danger, "hourly expecting death from within and without." At the time the letter was written, in the summer of 1799, Acre was still under siege by the French forces, and "there (were) new tribulations every day and they punish us for disobedience." We may assume that Napoleon's manifesto to the Jews on the establishment of a Jewish state in Palestine was also responsible for intensified persecution.

To add to their troubles, the cost of living rose "because of the army forces" that were stationed in Jerusalem; and there was also an outbreak of plague. Rabbi Moses Mordecai Joseph Meyuhas reported that "everybody sold all his possessions, gold and silver and even garments." He himself borrowed over 1,000 piastres at usurious rates of compound interest after having sold his possessions. The Kehillah sold all the silver ornaments from its Torah scrolls and borrowed "a vast and enormous sum" to prevent murder and, especially, the rape of its women, "as has happened to the other nations." "From the day Jerusalem was founded, we have not dwelt here in such great affliction," lamented the Kehillah elders who signed the appeal for help.

The Safed Kehillah was even more severely affected by Napoleon's campaign than the Kehillah of Jerusalem. The memory of the rioting in the Jewish quarter of Safed was still fresh in the minds of the inhabitants of the city, and Burckhardt could still record, thirteen years later, that "in 1799, after the French withdrawal from Acre, the Jewish quarter was ransacked by the Turks with not a remnant left." The Kehillah's letter of 1800 described these disorders in detail: "We were surrounded by many troubles and the evils swelled in number . . . because of quarrelling kingdoms, a band of brigands drew nigh and arrived with swords and spears and slew several living souls of Israel, may the Lord avenge them. They came with axes and began to break in the doors and windows, robbed and pillaged everything, money, outer garments, clothing, not leaving even shirts or trousers, and the women were naked in the streets of the city . . . without bread or raiments . . . Never has such a thing befallen Israel anywhere . . . May God repay the doers of evil with the measure of their evil!"

As if all this were not enough, the Kehillah incurred the displeasure of "the master of the land," Jezzar Pasha, who imposed a 50,000 piastre fine on it "on a villainous charge." As the Kehillah leaders were unable to pay, "every day the tyrants hurry to beat and to punish, and our persons are laid in iron" (*cf.* Psalms, 105: 18).

Oppression and lawlessness continued to afflict the two Galilean Kehillot also during the first years of the nineteenth century, throughout El-Jezzar's reign.

The "butcher" Pasha died in 1804. His maltreated subjects regarded his death as divine retribution "for all that he had done." But it did not mark the end of suffering for the two Kehillot in Galilee. The Jews of Safed experienced "many evils from the Gentiles and from the bandits" during the interregnum that ensued until the new pasha's administration was set up. In Tiberias, the Kehillah was only able to purchase a reprieve from a pogrom at the hands of a "heavy force" stationed there by handing over 10,000 piastres.

Under the government of Suleiman, the new Pasha of Acre, the Kehillot in Galilee gained some respite from repression and false charges. A letter from Safed dated 1810 described the Pasha as a "pure, honest ruler, undesirous of fraudulent things." Similarly, Burckhardt, describing the life of the Jews in Tiberias in 1812, remarks that, in contrast with Jezzar Pasha, who often extorted vast sums from them, Suleiman Pasha was content with collecting the Poll Tax. According to a letter from Tiberias in 1809, the main tax was the *miri* (land tax). In Tiberias, too, the boundaries of the Jewish quarter were expanded. However, the

Kehillot were still struggling with the numerous debts they had incurred under El Jezzar—they each owed 50,000 piastres. The debt of the Tiberias Kehillah was still fully outstanding in 1816, although both Kehillot (at Safed as well as at Tiberias) had obtained *Firmans* from Constantinople apportioning payment of the debt in yearly instalments, following El Jezzar's death. In 1816, the *Pe'rushim Kolel* in Safed had debts amounting to 42,000 piastres.

The two Kehillot in Judea were particularly troubled by the burden of debts at the beginning of the nineteenth century. The Jews of Hebron were unable to sustain the 1798 debt arrangement and their situation deteriorated as the years passed. A letter from the Hebron emissary in 1814 revealed that the congregation was once again threatened with expulsion and some of its rabbis had been imprisoned. The Kehillah of Jerusalem reached the depths of hardship and depression. Its indebtedness rose to 200,000 piastres as a result of the war and the "villainous charges" of 1799. Seven years later, in 1806, this sum increased to 250,000 piastres, with the usual qualification, "apart from debts due to our co-religionists." A letter to the Diaspora Kehillot in 1806 explained the political reasons for this situation: during the last years of domination by the "abusive persecutor" El Jezzar, chaos had reigned over Jerusalem and the lands around. "Every Gentile in the land wears his sword on his thigh and thinks himself a king . . . and our flock is a flock of martyrs, one lamb amongst many wolves who consume and affright us from all sides, with violence and robbery multiplying . . ."

Under the circumstances, it was impossible to demand justice, "for instead of justice there, there is iniquity." The only alternative for the Kehillah was to "stop up the mouths of the wicked men and to borrow at usurious rates of interest." A letter that the Kehillah sent to its benefactors bitterly protested against their fate as victims of the cruelty of the ruling class and their own wretched existence: "Bloodthirsty, deceitful people, . . . old and young, lap up our flowing blood, and our eyes grow dim beholding the sorrow in our lives and our years of anguish . . ."

The people endured their suffering heroically and patiently. They stubbornly and devotedly persevered, while "delivered up to harsh masters" and remained a stalwart rampart in their guardianship over "the legacy of our forefathers."

The Kole'lim and their Tax Burden

The Kehillah—during that period known as *Kolel* or *Kole'lut*, to distinguish it from the local synagogue, *Bet-Midrash* and *Yeshivah* organizations—controlled all the members of the Jewish community in its respective city. However, as a result of the split between the Ashkenazi and Sephardi communities, the Ashkenazim were organized into congregations, or *Kole'lim*, of their own, for the purpose of receiving special or additional support from abroad. When the Hassidim emigrated to Galilee, a *Kolel* uniting their congregations in Safed, Tiberias and Pe'ki'in was founded and actually sent emissaries abroad representing all the Ashkenazim in the three Galilean Kehillot. The disciples of the Vilno Gaon, who had come to Safed at the beginning of the nineteenth century and called themselves *Pe'rushim*, also formed an independent *Kolel*. However, all these Ashkenazi *Kole'lim* were subject to the authority of the Kehillot (the general *Kole'lim*) in their cities, for taxation matters, deputations to the authorities and internal Kehillah affairs.

The Kehillah was governed by an executive composed of various bodies. Contemporary references mentioned "appointees," "elected ones," "seven city optimates," "officials," a *Parnass*, and supervisors and rabbis amongst the managers of the Jerusalem Kehillah. The Kehillah leader was the *Parnass*, who represented the Kehillah before the authorities. "Appointees," "elected ones," "officials," would all seem to allude to the same office. They all served on the Kehillah's executive management, while the seven city optimates constituted its council. The rabbis and supervisors were empowered to make regulations and demand their enforcement by the "officials." An assembly of "The Chosen of the Holy City" was convened when the adoption of decisive resolutions affecting Kehillah affairs was proposed. In Safed and Tiberias, only "officials" were mentioned as Kehillah leaders; at times even the Chief Rabbi served in the capacity of an "official." The office of *Parnass* in Jerusalem was also occasionally entrusted to the Chief Rabbi. The Chief Rabbi, incidentally, was honoured with the title of *Rishon le'Zion* (the First in Zion) at the end of the eighteenth century.

However, with the progressive improvement in the *Halukkah* system, the benefactors took a more active interest in Kehillah self-administration. The "Officials of the Holy City," guardians of the remittances from Constantinople, played a decisive part in the management of the Palestine Kehillot. The appointment of the Chief Rabbi was subject to the confirmation of "the rabbis, the wealthy men, the appointed officials, and the treasurers" in Constantinople. Furthermore, the regulations and resolutions of the Jerusalem Kehillah had no validity unless they had the approval of the custodians in the imperial capital. Emissaries to Diaspora countries had first to proceed to Constantinople to have their missions confirmed and to receive letters of recommendation from the rabbis and officials in charge of the Holy City's affairs there. This was not only the case as far as the Jerusalem Kehillah was concerned. The "Hebron officials," "Safed officials" and "Tiberias officials" at Constantinople also gained virtual control of their respective Kehillot.

When Suleiman Pasha held the governorship at Acre at the beginning of the nineteenth century, his financial secretary, Haim Farhi, was the administrator and director of the Galilean Kehillot.

The *Kolel* resembled the institutionally autonomous Kehillot in all feudal countries in its diversified activities and broad jurisdiction. The *Kolel* collected government revenue and levied taxes for Kehillah requirements. The Kehillah court had the power to judge financial lawsuits, to impose fines or punishments, and to pronounce excommunications for offences against other persons or for religious transgressions. In some instances of "immodest" behaviour or of rebellion towards the Kehillah leaders, Kehillah regulations empowered the official to hand the culprit over to the "Masters of the Land" or to the "Lord of the City," to "punish him on his person and in his money . . ." The *Kolel* supervised the economic life of the Kehillah by fixing maximum prices for foodstuffs (meat, cheese), confirming rights of tenure (*Hazaqqah*) and by prohibiting inflated rents—to name but a few examples. Early in 1781, the leaders of the Jerusalem Kehillah, with the authority of "the princes and their deputies, the officials at Constantinople," passed detailed regulations governing tenants' rights with regard to the landlords: the renting of quarters from Arab landlords was monopolized by those owning rights of tenure, some of whom rented "courtyards" and then sublet the quarters, while others collected payments from the lessees for the right of *Hazaqqah*.

Kehillah regulations governing modesty in behaviour were far more stringent than in the Diaspora, quite in accordance with the character of the Palestine Jewish community. Severe and detailed regulations on such matters were particularly frequent in times of trouble and oppression, which were regarded as divine punishment for transgressions. Thus, in 1754 the "scholars, rabbis and overseers of the Holy City of Jerusalem" were urged to strengthen chastity regulations in view of "the frequent troubles and the burning wind . . . for certainly it is not for nought that God has dealt thus with this country." In the first place, it was decreed that "no daughter of Israel, not even the aged, may go to market without a covering to her garments, not even from one courtyard to the next . . . if a public thoroughfare pass between them . . . Nor may she sit in the gateway of her courtyard to converse with her friend, nor even from window to window, if a thoroughfare intervene." A woman who committed any one of these "offences" would be "an example and a lesson and shall be disgraced in the market-place and in the streets, and besides this will be fined according to the law." Men were forbidden to sell wine and beer "to any Gentile and uncircumcised person" because of the Moslem ban on the drinking of intoxicating beverages. Women, on the other hand, were forbidden to sell beverages to "any person," to safeguard their chastity. For the same reason, women under sixty were not allowed to enter non-Jewish homes to peddle wares "or in any service." To forestall a chance meeting between the two sexes in a bakery, it was decreed that bakers "shall not be able to take as servants young men, neither Jews nor Gentiles, unless married and in any event bearded"; while any woman under fifty was forbidden in general "to approach the oven, to insert or withdraw the loaf and such like." Limitations as to age and the nature of the service even surrounded the entry of a young woman into a synagogue.

The *Kolel's* rabbis and supervisors, who kept a scrupulous watch over chastity regarded all activity which involved non-preceptual merriment as licentious, and this applied particularly to games of chance. Another 1754 regulation concerning propriety decreed that "no son of Israel shall be able to patronize a purveyor of wine and drink there." The prohibition on cards and dice was renewed with redoubled severity at the same time.

The poverty, such that the bulk of the population of the *Yishuv* was dependent on financial assistance, made charity a principal Kehillah function to an extent unusual in other Jewish communities. The *Kolel* in every city was, as it were, one huge charity organization. There were, of course, as in the Diaspora, special charitable societies and charity funds in each Kehillah, all soliciting donations from Kehillah members. But in view of the unprecedented extent of poverty, the funds collected provided only a fraction of the needs, so that the greater part of the responsibility for charitable duties devolved on the *Kolel* as an institution. Their duties included the Poor Fund (*Kupat-Aniyim*), Sick Fund (*Bikkur-Holim*), Burial Fund (*Hessed va-Emet*), Teachers' Wage or Tuition Fund (*Talmud-Torah*), and, in addition, a Clothing for the Poor Fund (*Halbashat-Arumim*) and Brides' Marriage Fund (*Mohar-Ha'Be'tulot*).

However, the Kehillah's expenditure on tax payments (which also included the poll tax paid for the poor), bribes and gifts for the authorities, and payments of interest on loans exceeded all its philanthropic outlays. These expenses were the main cause of the individual's dependence on the *Kolel* within the framework of a tax system which deprived him of practically all freedom to make use of his own property.

A small portion of Kehillah revenue was derived from the sale of *Mitzvot* (i.e., the privilege of performing synagogue ceremonies), offerings and charitable contributions. Direct and indirect taxes also provided a steady source of revenue. They included an indirect tax, known in the Sephardi Kehillot as the *gabella*, imposed on meat and wine. At first, this *gabella* was leased out as a monopoly and later auctioned off annually. The tax collected on the volume of merchandise handled by the import and export merchants was also known as *gabella*.

An income tax introduced by an old regulation was levied at a rate of 10 per cent on all annual incomes of fifty piastres or more, whether it came from abroad or "from within the city." The same regulation imposed an 8 per cent income tax on "rabbis' widows arriving from abroad" and receiving an allowance from abroad. Apparently, these widows were later granted income tax deductions in view of the fact that the *Kolel* was the beneficiary on their decease.

The marriage fee for widows was also based on the *Kolel's* inheritance law. Widows, and divorcees who remarried, had to pay a marriage tax at the rate of 10 per cent of the dowry. The regulation was amended at a later date so that a widow who had an heir "here in the Holy City," only paid a 5 per cent marriage tax when she remarried. The marriage tax for widows without heirs remained at 10 per cent and was in fact raised to 20 per cent at the beginning of 1803, "the reason in principle being that since she had no heir here in the Holy City of Jerusalem, may it be rebuilt and re-established, her legacy would have passed to the *Kolel* of the Holy City." Similarly, the *Kolel* collected an indemnity for loss of revenue when a member left the city. The Jerusalem *Kolel* passed detailed and precise regulations governing the inheritance tax, "transfer fees," and "burial fees." An inheritance that a deceased bequeathed to heirs living in the city was subject to a tax deduction of 10 per cent "of all his assets—whether in the country or abroad—in silver, gold, gems, pearls, and all manner of merchandise and landholdings," only books were excepted but the debts owed to him in the city were included. The calculations were made after the deceased's own indebtedness had been discounted. In 1772, the deceased's *Hazaqqah* was added to his taxable assets. The 10 per cent tax was increased by a 3.33 per cent assessment on the legacy "to help cover the debts of the Holy City's *Kolelut*." If a man died without issue, so that his brothers or relatives inherited, the tax was levied at a rate of 20 per cent of the legacy. In 1800, the regulation was again amended to rule that "a widow must show the *Kolelut* of the Holy City of Jerusalem everything in her possession, from thread to shoelace." An "arbitration" certificate dated 1810 proved that regulations at that time already claimed for the *kolel* half the legacy inherited by a husband from his wife.

However, the unique demographic composition of the Jewish population, with its large concentration of single people, widows and widowers, who had come to "dwell in honour in the Holy City," gave the *Kolel* a greater interest in inheritance laws regarding deceased people without heirs than in the inheritance tax imposed on heirs. An old regulation, enacted at the beginning of the fifteenth century, entitled the Jerusalem *Kolel* to become the heir of anyone who died "with no legal heir known at the time of his death." This regulation had its exact counterpart in the *Lex Manus Mortuae* (Law of the Dead Hand) of the feudal monarchies, whereby the estate of a deceased with no heirs was confiscated by the royal exchequer. However, in the course of time, the *Kolel* assumed far broader inheritance rights than decreed by the *Lex Manus Mortuae*. To ensure that considerable revenue continued to accrue from that source, the inheritance regulations were constantly amended throughout the eighteenth century by various extremely severe provisions.

Regulations postponing repayment of the *Kolel's* debts to Jews pending reimbursement of "those villains," the Moslem moneylenders, were added to the Jerusalem Kehillah's economic legislation as from 1729. These regulations not only affected the well-to-do but also the immigrants of limited means who had entrusted their remaining funds to the *Kolel* "for profit." The well-to-do, whether old residents or newcomers, were able to gain exemption from most of the taxes and heavy levies as well as to retain any legacies they had inherited, intact: the *Kolel*, in its frequent instances of monetary distress, was prepared to receive lump sums in advance as exemption fees from the various taxes. Often prospective immigrants did not wait to make a compromise with the *Kolel* but obtained a written attestation from *Kolel* officials in Constantinople. Sometimes, *Kolel* representatives abroad considered themselves authorized to come to terms with prospective immigrants in questions of taxes. Only one stipulation was made: that the "compromisers" be subject to the same levies and compulsory emergency loans as the rabbis. The well-known Kabbalist, Rabbi Solomon Molcho, came to terms with the Jerusalem officials at Constantinople in 1778, when he was still in Salonica, and two years before he went to Palestine. He was exempted from any taxation on payment of 700 piastres.

The severity of the taxes and burial fees was generally justified by the argument "that there should be a *Yishuv* in the land," for the Gentile debtors were "seeking to destroy the capital . . . And Heaven forbid that the name of Israel should not be remembered in our gracious land . . ." In fact, it was poverty, indebtedness and victimization by the despots which lay heavily on the Jews and forced the *Kole'lim* to burden the Jewish population with a load of taxes and payments rarely encountered in Diaspora Kehillot. The trouble was that the prevailing system within the *Kole'lim* caused this burden to fall most heavily upon the economically active elements, the toiling and the poor. Instead of achieving its declared object—the "welfare of the Jews"—the internal régime of the *Kole'lim* actually became an impediment to the development of the *Yishuv* and, together with the country's feudal régime, was a hindrance to immigration and settlement.

Social Relations and Conflicts within the Kehillot

A book by Rabbi Gedalia of Siemiatycze, who came to the country with Rabbi Judah the Hassid's party, contained several graphic descriptions of the contrasts between the life of the rich and the poor in the Jerusalem Kehillah at the beginning of the eighteenth century. Even their methods of heating their homes in winter revealed the social distinction: "There are no winter stoves in any of Jerusalem's houses—and even bread ovens are to be found only amongst a few of the wealthy . . . For cold weather, they have large bowls, copper vessels amongst the rich, earthenware for the poor, which are filled with burning coals and thus the fire is kept."

The poor had to pay more for fuel than the rich: "Kindling wood and charcoal are brought from the villages on camels and donkeys for sale in Jerusalem. Whoever wants to, buys. But the shopkeeper who deals in wood and charcoal sells them at fixed weights and they are very expensive. The rich man profits, for he buys one or two camel-loads of wood or charcoal at a time."

The poor people drank water from whitewashed cisterns, while the rich brought "sweet and scented water" delivered by water drawers from Joab's Well, "even though they have water in their courtyard cisterns." When they travelled to the outskirts of the city, "the rich ride on donkeys, but the poor man does not ride on a donkey and goes only on foot." The social differences in the celebration of the Sabbath were apparent even in the pots in which the *Tcholent* a hot stew of kidney beans, meat, and potatoes) was prepared: "It was their manner (of the rich) to do all their cooking in copper pots. But we, most of Rabbi Judah the Hassid's party, were poor people and we put the stew into the stove in an earthenware vessel."

The principal difference, however, lay in the contents of the vessel. "The meat," Rabbi Gedalia wrote, "is expensive," and there was a special butcher "who obtained from the Turk the head and the legs, or the head and liver, and other items, and resold them." Not all the poor were in a position to buy even these scant portions of meat for the Sabbath. Rabbi Gedalia describes an event that occurred to him: "Once I went to fetch the meal from the stove, and the meal was leg of lamb and beans, and I was happy with this, for on other Sabbaths I had not even leg. But my pot had got changed with the pot of another poor man, so that when I got home, I did not even find the leg in it."

He consoled himself for his disappointment with a popular saying from Talmudical times: *Poverty follows in the poor man's wake (Baba Kama,* 92:a). But there was more to a poor man's poverty than a meatless Sabbath. "The poor people," he wrote, "stay hidden away in their homes to the best of their ability for fear of the Poll Tax collectors, and only on Sabbaths and Holidays do they venture forth ... into the city streets without any fear at all." "It is said, *And thy life shall hang in doubt before thee* (Deuteronomy, 28:66), for they do not even have enough to buy a loaf from the baker." Even those who conquered their sense of shame and begged alms were unable to support themselves on charity, because most of the people of means only had meagre incomes themselves. "And should we propose," Rabbi Gedalia reasoned, "to solicit charity, the contumely will be ours, the more so since for the most part all that is given is a small measure of wood or of charcoal, or a bit of onion, for even the *baalei-battim* (the householders) are not prosperous and the less able, therefore, to maintain others ..."

In sharp contrast with the destitution of most of the Jewish population, a perceptible section of the community enjoyed a fairly high standard of living except in years of drought, plague and the havoc of wars. The well-to-do class was quite numerous compared with the handful of fabulously wealthy men. This class included wholesale merchants, money-lenders, rabbis, heads of *Yeshivot* and also ordinary scholars, who received support from abroad in addition to *Halukkah* allotment.

An allusion in a letter that Rabbi Abraham of Kolyski sent to his confreres in White Russia in 1778 reveals just how well-off the leaders of the Hassidic congregation of Galilee and the Sephardi rabbis (*hakhamim*) were:

> The great and renowned rabbi, the godly man, our teacher, Rabbi Menahem Mendel, may his light shine forth, has concluded a match for his brilliant son, Master Moses, with (the daughter of) a great *Hakham*, renowned for his Torah, piety, and wealth. And the dowry paid was 800 piastres. And he (the bride's father) is one of the most valued and important men amongst the Sephardim in Jerusalem, and this *Hakham* is related by marriage to the *Hakham* of the *Kolel* of Tiberias.

The *responsa* literature of the period indicates that a marriage endowment on this scale was quite common amongst the well-to-do. If the principal were profitably invested, the recipient could live very well on the interest. Rabbi Menahem Mendel of Vitebsk's last will and testament offered his widow the opportunity of selling all "the important movables" he bequeathed up to the sum of 1,000 piastres, and of loaning the money thus obtained to the Ashkenazi *Kolel* "that they may earn a profit and pay her three piastres a week." This profit was enough to enable an individual to enjoy a moderate standard of living. Rabbi Haim, the son of Rabbi Tobias, a leader of the *Pe'rushim*, assured his followers in Lithuania, "that whoever can support himself on the profit derived from his capital funds abroad, will be able to live here in peace and tranquillity and secure unto himself both worlds." He made one qualification: "that one bring a maidservant, for it is impossible to obtain a maidservant here..." As compared with people of Rabbi Mendel of Vitebsk's position, the Chief Rabbi of Safed belonged to the upper level of the well-to-do class. The Safed court register contained three entries for loan transactions he concluded, each to the value of 1,000 piastres.

Scholars derived their income from two sources, the *Halukkah* and *Yeshivah* subsidies. Money donations arriving at the Sephardic *Kole'lim* from abroad, in drafts or with emissaries, were customarily distributed on the basis of a third for *Kolel* expenditure, a third for widows, orphans and the destitute poor, and a third for scholars. Thus the *Halukkah* allotments balanced the scholars against all of the Kehillah's innumerable poor. But there were even sub-classifications within the scholar class. *Halukkah* funds were distributed to the scholars twice a year, at Passover and on the Feast of Tabernacles (*Sukkot*), "to each according to his rank." Rabbis and leaders received an additional allocation between the two festivals. The second income that the scholars received, from the *Yeshivah* subsidies, was also paid according to a scale of rates varying with the rank of the individual *Yeshivah* scholar. Jerusalem's dozen or more *Yeshivot*, each usually contained ten staff scholars in addition to instructors and pupils.

Each large *Yeshivot* received an annual income of 1,000 to 1,200 piastres. An example of how this income was distributed is supplied by the classification of annual salaries at the *Haim va'Hessed Yeshivah*, founded in 1803 by a wealthy Florentine benefactor. The *Yeshivah* head received 200 piastres; his assistant, 100 piastres; the eight remaining members of the *Yeshivah* staff were divided into pairs receiving salaries of 80 piastres, 70 piastres, 60 piastres, and 50 piastres (the ninth in rank received a salary of 56 piastres). There was a fixed salary for the members of each pair. Three *Yeshivah* students who received an average of 30 piastres each, also differed in classification (34, 30 and 28 piastres per annum). The salary of the *Yeshivah* beadle was 40 piastres a year. Even *Yeshivot* whose annual income did not exceed 600 or even 400 piastres maintained a scrupulous scaling of salaries.

The *Halukkah* system also gave rise to social differences in the Ashkenazi *Kole'lim*. In the *Kolel* of Galilee, under Hassidic leaderships, a grant was made to all families in the *Kolel*, except for those "not receiving" (that is to say, of independent means); but the recipients of *Halukkah* support also customarily received private "offerings and donations" as well as pledges from their supporters in the Diaspora. Furthermore, the regulations of the *Pe'rushim Kolel* at the beginning of the 1820's would appear to indicate that from its foundation, "the family head's standing" in terms of lineage and scholarship was taken into account when support funds were apportioned.

Social differentiation within the *Kole'lim* and within the scholar class itself was much accentuated by the institutionalization of the missions to the Diaspora. A contract with the *Kolel* gave each emissary a commission of a third of the clear profits (that is to say, over and above all travel expenses) from his mission. Including travelling expenses, an emissary's share often amounted to half the funds collected for a mission even to countries as near as Turkey. Occasionally, he also received a share of the "offerings and donations" obtained as a result of letters he had written to cities that he had never actually visited. The economic position of many emmissaries also improved on their return from their missions, since their contact with benefactors in the Diaspora brought them appointments as heads of *Yeshivot* or special provisions from their supporters. The *Kole'lim* did not discourage journeys by "independent emissaries" and even helped them with letters of recommendation. They were usually scholars in reduced circumstances or in distress for a variety of other reasons—the ending of subsidies to their *Yeshivot*, or the death of a benefactor.

During the eighteenth century, the position of emissary became the monopoly of certain select families. It was passed on from generation to generation like an inheritance, as was already the case with rabbinical posts, religious judgeships, or *Yeshivah* membership. It became customary, when it came to appointing an emissary for a mission abroad, to give preference to a member of a family who had traditionally filled this office. As the emissaries themselves were usually drawn from the cream of the scholar class—rabbis, judges, heads of *Yeshivot*, and *Yeshivah* scholars—a kind of aristocracy developed within this class, which as a whole anyway enjoyed special privileges over the rest of the Jews, householders and poor alike. This aristocracy shared domination of the Kehillot with its officers: the optimates and officials, appointees and supervisors, who also transmitted their privileges to their sons and heirs.

The extra privileges the scholars enjoyed did not end with the discrimination in their favour in the allocation of *Halukkah* funds. By the end of the Middle Ages, the scholars and rabbis of Jerusalem had adopted a regulation exempting "scholars and students of the Torah from various taxes and levies, with the exception of the Poll Tax." The *Kolel* was responsible for the payment of the poll tax. Scholars also received an increasing number of concessions concerning payment of "burial fees." However, their exemption from the payment of taxes did not release them from assessments and compulsory loans in times of trouble, when even tax exemptions of individuals holding compromise agreements with the *Kolel* were suspended. In 1819, for example, the foreign trade *gabella* was imposed both on scholars engaged in trade and on traders who were generally exempt from "taxes and levies" on the basis of "compromise" contracts.

Both the householders who carried the burden of direct taxation, and the mass of the population, weighed down with indirect taxes, protested from time to time against the tax system in force. But no revolt against the exemption of scholars from payment of taxes is recorded during the latter half of the eighteenth century in contrast with the earlier period. In the middle of the century, however, there were still attempts in the Jerusalem Kehillah to abolish special taxes by public opposition. The merchants "raised a hue and cry voicing their refusal" to pay the taxation on their foreign trade returns; to no avail. At approximately the same time, many Jerusalem Jews, and especially the new immigrants, protested against the *gabella* on meat. They proposed that a new system of meat marketing be adopted in place of the established practice whereby Jewish ritual slaughtering was performed in Arab slaughterhouses, and the meat sold to the Jewish butchers who, in turn, resold it in their own shops. Instead, they suggested a system employed in many places abroad: Jewish customers would buy meat, which the ritual slaughterers marked kosher, directly from the Arab meat dealers and thus save the brokerage fee the Jewish butchers collected and which constituted the main substance of the *gabella*. The reformers collected signatures supporting their decision, but the rabbis confirmed the old practice to ensure *kashrut*.

The rabbis also won a dispute with under-privileged scholars who wanted to arrogate some of their powers. In 1760, an assembly of Jerusalem rabbis adopted a resolution designed to prevent intrigue by rebellious scholars who were trying to set up a religious court of their own. The rabbis decided to empower "the illustrious officials" on the evidence of one witness, or even of a woman, to "castigate any person who wishes to be a *dayyan*, whoever he may be, small or great," and also "anybody who shall help them." The culprits could even be handed over to "the masters of the land" for trial. All expenses would be paid by the accused, and donated to "the community in the land of Israel."

However great the success of this scholar élite in acquiring domination over the other classes of Kehillah society and crushing insubordination in its own ranks, it was compelled to yield to the authority of the "officials of the Holy City" in Constantinople, and their representatives in the country. All attempts to defy the power of the "supreme official" broke down in face of the firm stand taken by the Constantinople "officials," who did not shrink from applying sanctions by halting the transmission of aid funds or from resorting to the intervention of the authorities when the need arose.

Quarrels also broke out from time to time between the scholars and the *Parnass* of the *Kolel*. At Hebron, the *Parnassim* dealt firmly with its scholars, but in Jerusalem, the *Parnass* was often forced to defer to their demands. In 1770, the Jerusalem Kehillah succeeded in removing the *Parnass* from office by a government directive from Damascus. The rabbis wanted to secure the abolition of the life tenure of office by *Parnassim* and *Kahal* appointees in order to strengthen their power over the Kehillah. These offices had acquired the nature of *Hazaqqah* (concessions) and were even customarily bequeathed as such to the heirs of the incumbents. In 1797, the rabbis of Jerusalem revived an "old regulation" which ordained that "there shall be no *Hazaqqah* or privilege in any appointment to the public service in the Holy City of Jerusalem, may it be rebuilt and re-established." At the same time, an old resolution providing for the appointment and supervision of Kehillah officials by the rabbis and religious judges was renewed. But controversies even erupted amongst the rabbis, weakening their position in relation to the Kehillah leaders.

The communal conflict between the Sephardim and the small Ashkenazi minority in Palestine was an additional discordant element. The quarrel between the congregations in the Galilean Kehillot continued during the 1770's, even after the controversy between the Sephardic *Kolel* and the small Ashkenazi congregation over the *Halukkah* allocations had abated. A controversy broke out between the Hassidic group and the Sephardim not long after the Hassidim had settled at Safed. It was deliberately provoked by the Lithuanian Mitnagdim, who sent letters to Palestine maligning their Hassidic adversaries, but also resulted from mutual lack of tolerance for differences in communal custom. This dispute died down after some of the Hassidim moved to Tiberias, while a compromise was also reached on the apportionment of income collected by the emissaries. Even then, the disputes did not entirely disappear, as the root of the trouble, the conflict of interests between the congregations, had not been eradicated. In particular, the Hassidim, and later the *Pe'rushim*, complained about the unfair taxes which the officials of the Sephardic *Kole'lim* in Safed and Tiberias imposed on them. In 1784, an event occurred which forced both sides to request the Pasha at Acre to decide who was in the right. The *Kolel* official at Tiberias was unable to extract his dues from the Hassidim even "by force, with armed men and intimidation." He therefore seized a large sum of money, the equivalent of approximately 1,000 piastres, which had arrived for them from abroad, after lying in wait for their emissaries "at all approaches and exits by land and by sea."

Disputes even broke out within the Ashkenazi community in Galilee itself because of poverty and the *Halukkah*. When the controversy erupted between the Mitnagdim and the Hassidim in Safed, both "the Ashkenazim who had resided there from before," as well as the new arrivals from Volhynia, Podolia and the Ukraine (who had joined the Hassidic group of 1777), sided with the Sephardim and the Kehillah official. The Mitnagdim's opposition to the religious innovations of the "sect" was also permeated with social bitterness. Practically all the Mitnagdim were poor people, dependent on charity, whereas the Hassidim had brought their money with them and were anyway receiving regular subsidies from their supporters in the Diaspora. Differences of opinion within the Ashkenazi community on taxation methods also appeared in the course of time. When, in 1784, the Hassidic *Kolel* had to pay the vast sum of 1,000 piastres to the Pasha for expanding the Jewish quarter of Tiberias, "the clamour raised by the poor was: why should all of the 1,000 piastres be taken from the *Halukkah* money? Why should not the householders who receive no stipends, contribute to this just as they pay other taxes?" The "non-receivers"—the owners of cash assets—and those successfully engaged in gainful occupations, countered this with another complaint: if it were not enough that they received no share of the *Halukkah* money, now they were approached with demands that they pay extra taxes! The dispute ended in a compromise when the Hassidic *Kolel* undertook to pay half the sum from its own treasury. In 1802 dissent split the ranks of the Hassidic community in Galilee when a controversy broke out between Rabbi Abraham of Kolyski and Rabbi Shneur Zalman of Lady, who was abroad. It had originated in differences of outlook on Hassidic doctrine but soon deteriorated into a quarrel over the organization of *Halukkah* funds which lasted until Rabbi Abraham of Kolyski's death in 1810.

These interminable quarrels within the Jewish population, inseparable from its peculiar class régime, diverted its energies from opposition to the tyrants and also constituted a considerable factor in restricting its absorptive capacity. In particular, they affected its power to attract new immigrants. More than that, the social composition of the *Yishuv* as well as its weak economic foundations, caused even its spokesmen—its leaders and emissaries—not only to refrain from encouraging mass immigration from the Diaspora, but actually to warn against immigration of the poor and of people without capital. In any case, the rabbis and leaders of the *Kole'lim* were not happy about the immigration of poor people, even though, in the event, they ruled that indigent immigrants had the same right to receive aid from charity funds as the local poor in a city.

The scholars also indulged in lively rivalry within their own ranks over the financial allocations to the *Yeshivot* and therefore did not regard with any favour the immigration of members of their own class who did not possess personal sources of support.

The immigration programme of the leaders of the Jewish population envisaged a select group of wealthy immigrants who would arrive with their own capital and would even make donations to the scholars from their resources. On the other hand, some distinguished rabbis voiced opinions contrary to this "practical" attitude and advocated settlement of the country by "many of Israel" before the coming of the Messiah and the ingathering of the exiles. The contradiction between the ideal and the attitude *de facto* was only matched by the contrast between the dispersed people's longing for deliverance in its own country and the very limited possibilities of emigration. Both contradictions reflected the inner and outward conflict between the historic aspirations of the Jewish people and the bonds of the political, social, and economic feudal régime, with its antiquated cultural fabric, which fettered those aspirations.

Not surprisingly, some of the encouragement for Jewish immigration still came from people who only wanted the immigration of the aged for the privilege of burial in holy soil. However, during this period, appeals for immigration showed the first indications of attempts, however slight, to initiate activity for the constructive settlement of the country. Rabbi Jacob Emden called for the immigration of every Jew, but particularly urged it on the part of those who would be able to support themselves— that is to say, people of means generally, but particularly members of his own, wealthy class. In total contrast to the current practice of emigration of the aged, Rabbi Joseph Sopher concluded his book, *The Testimony of Joseph* (1763) with an appeal for the immigration of economically active and productive elements: "And it is but this, that whoever comes here should bring funds with him and not come empty-handed, or he should be a good artisan, capable of supporting himself. In this he will resemble the rest of the world, for nothing is given anybody *gratis*."

The immigrants from eastern Europe—the Hassidim and the disciples of the Vilno Gaon, who came after them—also conceived the idea of settlement based on economic activity. The spokesmen of the new immigrants apologized for their inability to undertake any business or employment because of their ignorance of the language (Arabic) and expressed the hope that in the course of time they would overcome these difficulties of adjustment.

Meanwhile, despite this hope for the future, the Hassidic leaders did not conceal their regret at the poor immigrants who had accompanied them against their wishes. They were therefore particularly careful to warn against the future emigration of any Jew without a steady income from capital of his own. The Hassidim and *Pe'rushim* had started out with hopes of transforming the character of Palestine Jewry. They ended with the same "practical" attitude as the scholars and leaders of the Jerusalem *Kolel*; emigration was to be restricted to scholars and "people of substance," or those receiving income from abroad.

Torah and Prayer; Culture and Popular Customs

Torah and prayer were the special functions of Palestine Jewry, both as seen by itself and by the Diaspora that maintained it. The leaders of the *Kole'lim* were not appealing for aid from their fellow-Jews in the Diaspora merely to preserve the "right of settlement" in the country. Their specific purpose was "to maintain the four cubits of *Halakhah*" in the land of the fathers, "to strengthen the hands of the Holy People in its preoccupation with the Torah on the Holy Soil" and to provide sustenance for them who *"Pray towards their Land* (Second Chronicles, 6:38) in the name of all Israel."

That generation regarded the study of the Torah on the holy soil as uniquely virtuous. Not only was Palestine the source of the Torah and the land where it might be studied "in purity," but deliverance would also be accelerated the more *Yeshivot* were established and maintained there. In fact, no community in the Diaspora equalled Palestine in numbers of *Yeshivot* and *Batei-Midrash* in relation to its Jewish population. In addition to those in the four Kehillot, others were founded in Kefar-Yassif and Pe'ki'in during the eighteenth century. At Acre, a *Yeshivah* was conducted on a temporary basis for scholars who had fled there from oppression in Safed or were preparing to move to Jerusalem like Rabbi Haim ibn 'Atr's group. In Jerusalem a special *Yeshivah* was maintained for the tiny Ashkenazi congregation. The Hassidic immigrants founded their own *Yeshivot* in the cities of Galilee, and the disciples of the Vilno Gaon who had settled in Safed also established a *Yeshivah* for themselves. However, most of the Palestine *Yeshivot* were centred in Jerusalem, both because it contained most of the Jewish population (over a half) and because of its undisputed sacred character. A record for 1758 listed twelve *Yeshivot* in Jerusalem, nine for scholars and three for householders. In 1802, a letter from the Jerusalem emissary mentioned fifteen *Yeshivot*, including one at Hebron.

The largest *Yeshivah* in Jerusalem and financially the most stable was the *Bet-Ya'akov Yeshivah*, named after its founder in 1691), the philanthropist, Jacob Pereira of Amsterdam. The *Ke'nesset Israel Yeshivah*, founded by Rabbi Haim ibn 'Atr with funds from Italian donors declined in prestige after his death in 1743, but was still in existence in the 1860's. The Palestinian *Yeshivot*, like the *Esger* of the Sephardi Kehillot, were mainly academies for adult scholars. The number of scholars attending any one institution generally never exceeded ten. The Jerusalem *Yeshivah* directory for 1758 gave the ages of nine out of ten people at the *Bet-Ya'akov Yeshivah*: two were 60 years old, one—53, three—50, one—42, one—40, and the youngest 30 years old. The scholars at these *Yeshivot* were divided by status. In addition to the head of the *Yeshivah* the Pereira *Bet-Ya'akov Yeshivah* had five people with the title of *Hakham* (Sage), and four or five *Ba'alei-Torah* (Masters of the Torah). At this *Yeshivah*, and at others too, the head of the *Yeshivah* and two of the *Hakhamim* constituted a *Bet-Din* (Court). At the *Haim va'Hessed Yeshivah*, founded in Jerusalem in 1803 by a Florentine benefactor, each of the ten students held a different scholastic rank. The usual number of students was four, although the larger ones had as many as ten, twenty and even thirty (e.g., the *Bet-Ya'akov Yeshivah*).

The articles of the *Yeshivot*, drawn up with the approval of their benefactors, outlined the details of their schedules of studies. As a rule, the members studied privately for half of the day and assembled in the *Bet-Midrash* for collective study in the afternoon. Some *Yeshivot* did not require the sages to study on their premises for more than two hours—or only one and a half hours—daily, and expressly permitted them to participate in lessons in other *Yeshivot* so "that they might support themselves appropriately." Others, however, imposed a compulsory six or even seven hours of study daily throughout the week.

The curriculum of the *Yeshivah* sages was usually divided equally between Gemara (with Rashi and the *Tosaphot*), on the one hand, and Mishnah (with the commentary of Rabbi Obadiah of Bertinoro and the *Tosaphot Yom Tov*) and the Codifiers (The *Turim* [or Columns] of Rabbi Jacob, son of Rabbi Asher Ben Yehiel, with the *Bet-Yosef*, Joseph Caro's Commentary on the *Turim*, and Maimonides' *Mishneh Torah*), on the other. At the *Neveh-Shalom Yeshivah*, the book on ethics, *Reshit Hokhmah (Fundamentals of Wisdom)* was also required reading. On the eve of the Sabbath, they customarily studied the Bible with the Commentary of Rashi. The Sabbath was devoted exclusively to the *Zohar* and to homiletics on the weekly portion of the Law. Homiletics were compulsory for sages in all the *Yeshivot*, and in some *Yeshivot* also for students who drew an allowance (all married men), in order to accustom them to appearing before the public. Every Sabbath the Chief Rabbi preached a sermon on a subject connected with the weekly portion, and it was the duty of the *Yeshivah* scribe to record "all the exegeses on the Torah originating in the *Yeshivah*." The students studied Gemara and were examined by the head of the *Yeshivah* at regular intervals.

The large *Yeshivot* also maintained auxiliary *Talmud-Torah* institutions where boys studied the Bible with the Commentary of Rashi. These *Talmud-Torahs* were usually under the direction of one to three instructors—often *Yeshivah* sages. In addition to the Yeshivot for professional scholars, there were *Yeshivot* for men of substance, who studied the Bible, Mishnah and ethical literature.

The "Pillar of Torah" was supplemented by the "Pillar of Prayer," the other part of Palestine Jewry's dual function. Palestine, "The Gateway to Heaven", was particularly suited to prayer. The people of the Diaspora respected "those who dwell on Torah and divine worship" as their apostles, who secured them divine grace through the prayers they offered on holy soil. A service was conducted after the morning prayer every Sabbath in the courtyard overlooking the Wailing Wall, and "they blessed the donors abroad and all those engaged in sending money, and they also each blessed their relatives abroad." Vigil was kept through the night (a *vilada*, in Sephardi vernacular) every Sabbath Eve and at the beginning of each new Jewish calendar month to study and recite Psalms. The *Yeshivah* articles of association made this practice compulsory. Other sections of the *Yeshivah* articles required the scholars to pray for the welfare of their donors and at times also of the Kehillah treasurers abroad who conducted the appeals for their respective *Yeshivot*.

The curriculum also included *ziara*, or visits to the graves of the *Tzaddikim* where prayer services were conducted, and the Torah studied at the traditional holy site. Such sites were numerous in Palestine. Apart from the "graves of the Patriarchs" at Hebron, the "tomb of Rachel" at Bethlehem, the "tomb of David" on Mount Zion, the "tomb of Joseph" at Nablus (Biblical Shekhem) and the "graves of the Prophets" distributed throughout the country, Galilee abounded in the graves of *Tannaim* and *Amoraim*. Guides were essential to prevent the visitor losing his way amongst the scores of graves. This function belonged by hereditary right to a Safed family of beadles, descendants of Rabbi Isaac Luria's beadle. The current incumbent would guide visitors with the help of a traditional book in his possession containing a list of every *Tannaite* and *Amoraite* grave and its location, the special prayer and invocation to be recited over the grave, and the appropriate chapter of study in commemoration of the holy man buried there. Frequent visits were also made to the graves of single *Tzaddikim*, such as Joseph's tomb at Nablus.

The tomb of Rabbi Simeon Bar Yohai at Meron was the object of particular devotion. Pilgrims from the Diaspora came to pray and make donations throughout the year while the Jewish inhabitants of the country flocked to Meron in their masses on "the days of Rabbi Simeon Bar Yohai's festival," *Lag ba'Omer*. Scholars spent two weeks twice yearly at Meron, studying the *Zohar* from beginning to end on each occasion. They also went to Pe'ki'in to study. On the eve of the anniversary of the death of the Prophet Samuel, the scholars of Jerusalem, led by the President of the Kehillah (*Nasi*), travelled to his grave (the traditional site is located a few miles north of Jerusalem) and studied there until midnight. They even studied the Bible at the traditional site of the grave of Hushai the Archite (Samuel II, 15:32, 37 etc), especially the chapters in Samuel II which told of his generous behaviour to king David. They also recited prayers and lit candles. During these visits, the Sages also prayed for the well-being of their benefactors.

The Sephardi Sages discharged their duty to their benefactors only by praying for their well-being. The Hassidic immigrants, unlike them, transplanted a custom of their sect in its entirety in Palestine. They prayed for the fulfilment of the specific wishes of any person who made a vow or gave a donation in return for his redemption payment (*pidyon*).

The Vilno Gaon's disciples in the country enrolled their supporters in the Diaspora as partners in the observance of the precepts involving physical presence in the holy land, such as gleanings, forgotten sheaves, field corners, the heave offering, the tithe and the release. As soon as they arrived in the country, they followed the advice of Rabbi Haim of Volozhin and purchased parcels of land "with grains rooted in the ground." They registered these in their own name and in the names of Diaspora Jews who had made special contributions for the purpose, "in such wise that the seller sold to the buyer and to his partners." They also urged their fellow-Jews in the Diaspora to increase their contributions for additional land purchases. Even when they did not actually possess any land, they observed the precepts of making the offering to the priests and the tithe to the Levites while they were in the country. According to Rabbi Gedalia of Siemiatycze, they made the offering and the tithe of wine and spirits respectively. Rabbi Gedalia recounts how, despite his poverty "with God's help he succeeded in purchasing a sheep in order to observe the precept of presenting a gift to the priesthood of 'the shoulder, and the two cheeks and the maw'."

Extensive literary activity in the field of *Halakhah*, unparalleled in the greatest Kehillot of the Diaspora, developed in Jerusalem, the great Torah centre where scores of brilliant scholars had gathered. At some Jerusalem *Yeshivot*, half the staff consisted of scholars who had simultaneously achieved fame as the authors of *Halakhic* books. It went without saying that all the men who filled the post of Chief Rabbi, the *Rishon le'Zion* at Jerusalem, were the authors of *Halakhic* exegeses, *responsa* compilations, glosses, commentaries and homiletic dissertations. The same was true of members of their religious tribunal, most of them scions of old Jerusalem families (for example, the Meyuhas, Algazi, Azoulai or Navon families), or had settled there in the eighteenth century. Sometimes the glosses on the four *Turim* or on the *Shulhan Arukh*, as well as queries and *responsa* (in the order of the codices) filled two or even four of the commentator's volumes. Even then, authors managed to write ten or more books and even to see most of them published in their lifetime. The emissaries discharged an important function by greatly facilitating the printing (in Constantinople,

Salonica and the cities of Italy) and distribution of these books. Some of them were authors in their own right and others were advancing the publication of manuscripts written by their fathers, relatives or associates. Their learning and the sanctity of Palestine gave these rabbinical emissaries a great deal of influence in the Diaspora Kehillot which they visited. Scholars turned to them for advice on *Halakhic* issues. They introduced reforms in the Kehillot, especially with a view to strengthening religion; they gave their approval to the publication of books; and they often ordained religious teachers. The emissaries thus united the Diaspora with Palestine in a reciprocal relationship. The Kehillot made their monetary contributions to Palestine Jewry; in return they received guidance in Torah and religion. The influence of Palestine as a spiritual and religious centre, as transmitted by its emissaries was especially important in the remote Kehillot of the Diaspora, on the fringes of the desert in North Africa, in Mesopotamia, Kurdistan, Persia, Afghanistan, India and overseas in North America and the West Indies.

However, the decline of rabbinical Judaism throughout the Diaspora at that time affected the cultural and literary creativity of Palestine Jewry even more sharply. This is not surprising in view of the cultural decline amongst the neighbouring Arab population of Palestine and also the fact that the larger part of Palestine Jewry had originated in the Sephardi communities of Turkey and the Maghreb (of North Africa)— which had also become backward and culturally stagnant by then. All the weighty tomes written during that period in Palestine barely contained one stimulating or constructive idea. Their "innovations" on the Talmud and the Codifiers produced nothing essentially new; their *responsa* rehashed old verdicts in civil law or dealt with the trivialities of observing the precepts and the laws of prayer, the reading of the Torah, blessing the palm branch and similar details, and invariably employed a tiresome *pilpulistic* method. Rabbi Moses Joseph Mordecai Meyuhas, Chief Rabbi in Jerusalem during Napoleon's Palestine campaign and revered by the people for his piety, devoted nine long pages of his book *B'rekhot Mayim* (*Water Wells*) to a discussion of whether or not it was obligatory to pronounce an additional benediction over wine suddenly brought in during a meal when those present had already blessed and drunk wine at the beginning of the meal. The rabbis of Jerusalem were still seriously engaged in solving such problems, demonstrating the utmost subtlety and learning, decades after Ba'al Shem Tov, the village teacher, had boldly ridiculed the haughty sages of Brody for spending their days discussing the problem of a man who forgot to recite the prayer *Let rise and come.**

Homiletical books were fewer in number than the books on *Halakhah*, but they too were full of *pilpul* and sterile subtlety. Although they had originally been delivered as sermons before the congregations in the synagogues, their ponderous language and involved exposition did not

---

* cf. *supra*, Chapter Twelve, pp. 459 *et seq.*, on Ba'al Shem Tov's doctrine.

distinguish them from *Halakhic* exegeses and glosses. The only homiletical author who enlivened his sermons with parables—though these too
were allegories and followed the uniform and recurring pattern of a king
and his ministers—was Rabbi Azoulai, a rabbinic emissary. He may have
been influenced in this respect by the place where he preached, the
Bet-Midrash at Leghorn. Not even the letters the *Kole'lim* or the
emissaries sent out were free from the inane, baroque style.

The ethical doctrine preached by the spokesmen for Palestine Jewry
was strongly orientated towards a rejection of this world and revulsion for
its pleasures. Disorders, plagues and droughts evoked compulsory communal fasting, and the failure of the rains was an occasion for self-
mortification on the Mondays and Thursdays of several consecutive weeks.
Rabbi Haim Joseph David Azoulai (1724–1806), mentioned earlier,
visited every magnificent building, public garden, art collection, library
and factory during a mission to Italy and described them ecstatically in
his travel journal. But he delivered solemn sermons against the pursuit of
pleasure and "the vanities of this world." He forbade not only card
playing but even chess! He regarded attendance at the theatre or circus,
going for walks or to parties, and eating delicacies on weekdays as
abhorrent and classified them as "vain and worthless things," part of "the
domain of the unholy one ... for which retribution will be made."
Instead of indulgence in pleasure there should be repentance and lamentation "over the destruction of the Temple and the exile of the *She'khinah*
and the suspension of the Law and the Temple Service these many
hundreds of years ... and then, perhaps, God will have mercy." He not
only condemned dancing as a "failing" but declared that it was a "breach
of chastity so much as to gaze upon women; and to draw near to them is a
criminal offence." And these views were held by a rabbinical emissary, a
man of stature, towering above all other contemporary Palestine emissaries, who enhanced the dignity of the Palestine Jewish community in the
eyes of world Jewry and the gentile nations more than any of his
predecessors or successors. Rabbi Azoulai was well mannered, tactful and
a natural diplomat—Louis XVI of France, noticing him from a distance at
Versailles, was said to have asked what country *l'ambassadeur* represented. He was at ease in the presence of nobles and royal ministers and
did not deny his blessings to marchionesses, who sought his company
(though with the qualification, "I chose not to rest my hand on their
heads ..."). However, his severity in matters of chastity is not surprising
in view of the fact that his father, also a member of the Jerusalem
rabbinical tribunal, had been amongst the signatories of the 1754 decree
forbidding women under the age of fifty to be seen at a bakery.*

All his contact with European culture and familiarity with the ways of
the world did not prevent Rabbi Azoulai from adhering, like all his
contemporaries in Palestine, to medieval superstition. But he also accepted

* *cf. supra*, pp. 653–4.

the austere social ethics of Rabbi Judah the Hassid and condemned fraudulence, including the defrauding of gentiles, as "a grave, sacrilegious offence." He also denounced "any *Parnass* who unduly intimidates the public not for the sake of Heaven" as a criminal on a par with unbelievers and heretics.

A unique manifestation of the belief in charms common in that generation in Palestine was the use of double and triple names. Sick children and even adults were given additional names such as Raphael, Haim or Hazekiah as a spell for effecting a cure and ensuring a long life. The frequent epidemics provided a favourable background for the spread of such customs.

The range of Rabbi Haim Joseph David Azoulai's literary interests and activities set him apart from his generation in Palestine. They extended beyond the narrow confines of *Halakhah*, Kabbalah, homiletics and ethics, although he wrote nearly a hundred works on these subjects alone. His travel book, *Maagal Tov (A Good Circle)*, contains the vast amount of information he had amassed on Jewish life during his visits to the Kehillot of Europe and Africa as an emissary. He had also objectively observed the cities and countries through which he passed and faithfully recorded all he saw. He possessed an acute historical sense and critical faculty and he examined and collected ancient manuscripts wherever possible. The fruits of this activity appeared in his book, *Shem Ha-Gedolim (Names of the Great)*, a biographical-bibliographical lexicon of Hebrew literature from the time of the *Tannaim* and *Amoraim* to his own day. These works were a marked departure from the practice of the Palestinian rabbis who not only abstained from "outer wisdom," but even failed to display any significant knowledge of Jewish history.

The prevalent atmosphere in Palestine of holiness and anticipation of deliverance was most conducive to preoccupation with occult doctrine. Small wonder, therefore, that it continued to be the centre of Kabbalist study as in former generations, except that Jerusalem replaced Safed as the meeting place of the Kabbalists in the eighteenth century. Not only was there no conflict between scholars and Kabbalists here, but the great *Halakhists*, including the Chief Rabbis, were amongst the distinguished Kabbalists. In 1737 the Kabbalist, Rabbi Gedalia Hayyon, founded a *Yeshivah* in Jerusalem, specifically devoted to the study of "the wisdom of the Truth." First known as *Midrash Hassidim*, its name was later changed to *Bet-El*, but its personnel continued to be described as "Hassidim." This *Yeshivah* hardly possessed over twelve members during the middle of the eighteenth century; by the beginning of the nineteenth, they had increased to forty. This membership was divided up and studied in three shifts round the clock, with breaks only for prayer, so that the voice of the Torah would never be absent from the *Bet-Midrash*.

The Kabbalist, Rabbi Shalom Mizrahi, known as "Shar'abi," after the town in Yemen from which he came, assumed the leadership of this

Yeshivah on the death of its founder. Many legends were woven around this central figure in Jerusalem Kabbalist society, and he was already regarded as a saint in his own lifetime. The traditional account of his youth and the manner of his revelation as "Prince Shalom Mizrahi" was similar in many biographical details to that of the founder of the Hassidic movement, his east European contemporary. After his arrival in Palestine, he earned his livelihood as a hawker of needles, forks and other fancy goods, and before his revelation was a servant in the home of Rabbi Gedalia Hayyon. Like Ba'al Shem Tov, he indulged in solitary communion, not, however, in the solitude of the outdoors, but in a sealed-off "courtyard" amongst the narrow lanes of the Old City. He recited his *Tikkun Hatzot* (midnight prayers for Israel's restoration) every night at the Wailing Wall.

However, the Jerusalem "Hassidim" and the Hassidim of Poland had nothing whatsoever in common, apart from their preoccupation with Kabbalah. In total contrast with the popular Hassidic movement conquering the Jewish masses in eastern Europe, the associates and pupils of Shalom Mizrahi the Shar'abite formed a circle of select individuals "conversant in the occult" (*yode'ei hen*) and detached from their environment by their withdrawn ways and by their practices in the study of the Torah and in prayer. These "Hassidim" in Jerusalem were pervaded by a heavy atmosphere of sadness and preparation for the next world, the antithesis of the *joie de vivre* and affirmation of this world propounded by Ba'al Shem Tov and his disciples, who "worshipped God in rejoicing." Whereas Hassidism in eastern Europe was opening up broad horizons in Kabbalist doctrine and revealing new pathways in life, the Jerusalem Kabbalists did not deviate from Rabbi Isaac Luria's interpretation of Kabbalah. The personnel of the *Bet-El Bet-Midrash* were absorbed unremittingly in the books of Rabbi Haim Vital, which they studied from the actual manuscripts. Even the works of their master, the Shar'abite, were formulated as commentaries to Luria's doctrine and meditations on *The Tree of Life* by his disciple, Haim Vital.

The Kabbalists were united by stronger bonds of companionship than existed amongst members of other *Yeshivot* in Jerusalem. The Kabbalists were not content merely with the ties of scholarship at the *Yeshivah*. The preoccupation with Kabbalah was in fact only an escape from the loneliness, insecurity and meaninglessness of drab, secular life, to the sphere of the sublime and pure spirituality. The Kabbalists used to form restricted circles in order to satisfy their need for a group life and to strengthen and encourage one another in their efforts for "the correction of the commonwealth of Israel" and the correction of the world. Groups of this sort were founded at various times and places, from the societies of Rabbi Isaac Luria, Rabbi Moses Cordovero and Rabbi Eliezer Azikri in Safed at the beginning of the sixteenth century, down to the "Covenant of Friends," founded by Rabbi Moses Haim Luzzato in Padua at the beginning of the eighteenth century. In the middle of the eighteenth century, a group of twelve Jerusalem Kabbalists ("as the number of God's tribes") made a "Contract of Affiliation" to form a spiritual community. It was renewed on a number of subsequent occasions. Its first members included Rabbi Israel Jacob Algazi, his son Rabbi Yom-Tov Algazi, the heir to the office of Chief Rabbi of Jerusalem, Rabbi Shalom Shar'abi, and Rabbi Haim Di Rosa, also an outstanding Kabbalist and already the hero of legends. The Society was already described as *Ahavat Shalom* (Love of Peace) in its 1757 and 1758 "Contracts of Affiliation," which bore the signature of "the youth, Haim Joseph David Azoulai." Its programme announced that all its members were "companions in spirit in this world and in the world to come . . . love one another greatly, in body and soul . . . are distinct only in their material existence." Together they constituted "one aboundingly glorious soul." In one of the first contracts, the members pledged that in addition to offering prayer in time of illness, they would also give charity to the poor on behalf of the deceased when one of them died without leaving any material assets. They would "endeavour to work as a group on behalf of its members as would an individual for his own son." The most prominent characteristic of this Kabbalist society for spiritual partnership was its pledge to maintain the bond of love and the duty of mutual spiritual aid even after death, in the world to come. The demarcation between this world and the next had become so blurred in the consciousness of the Kabbalists, that the document of association for 1757 bore the signature, in the first person, of Rabbi Jacob Algazi, who had died the previous year.

The continual yearning for deliverance, so clearly expressed in Kabbalist doctrine and practice, was common to all Palestine Jewry as it held on to the land of the fathers with every atom of its strength. The peculiar position of the Jewish community, subjected to cruel and alien rulers on its ancestral soil, lent the concept of deliverance in the homiletical literature of the country a character of its own. Deliverance, as preached in Palestine, more palpably took the form of the liberation of the Jewish people and the country from foreign enslavement than in the sermons preached by Diaspora Jews. Rabbi Mansour Marzuk's sermons on the exile in Egypt and the Temple's destruction provided a vehicle for a bitter outcry against his people's servitude in their own country at the hands of Ishmael, "son of the maidservant": "Woe, for what has befallen us—he lamented—Israel, sons of kings, are captives in their own land . . . Our tormentors afflict us, give us to drink of the waters of humiliation . . . We are fallen low unto dirt, we have been sold into the hands of severe masters, and Israel is for the pillagers and the wreckers." But even this lamentation was relieved by hopes of approaching Messianic redemption.

A letter to Italy in autumn, 1742, by Rabbi Haim ibn 'Atr gave the following description of the *Kol Nidre* service at the synagogue in Jerusalem: "The entire congregation was supplicating, everyone was weeping bitterly before God, that he should rebuild the Temple." However, Rabbi Abraham Meyuhas consoled his audience with the prediction that the Messiah, "that Master you wish would come quickly to his Temple, will certainly come; he will not be tardy, and if he delay, await him, for God will deliver His people." Another illustration of the reality that the coming of the Messiah possessed for that generation in Palestine is contained in a question quoted by Rabbi Azoulai in the name of his daughter's father-in-law, Rabbi Haim David Pardo, head of a Jerusalem *Yeshivah*: "When guardians of the Torah entered the *Bet-Midrash* after the Passover, they voiced one query, which was, 'If God in His Mercy will deign to send us our Messiah during these days and at this time, between first and second Passover, will we have to sacrifice on the second Passover? And if the decision is that we will, will there be any differentiation between men and women? And shall we differentiate between those residing in the land and those who will come, after the arrival of the deliverer, from the four corners of the earth?' "

It was even believed that the resurrection of the dead would not be delayed once the Messiah had come. In fact, all this mysticism concerning the revision of nature's laws only veiled the image of Messianic times in phantasy. It could not obscure the principal concept of deliverance: the redemption of the country, the Jewish people's liberation from alien bondage, the ingathering of the exiles and the restoration of the kingdom of David. In the course of his European travels, Rabbi Azoulai was impressed by the glory of the national cultures of Europe and the splendour of royal courts. As a member of a persecuted, humiliated people, these experiences evoked his intense envy. He consoled himself with the promised renewal of Israel's statehood through approaching deliverance. A description of the Tower of London, with its collection of arms, the Royal Crown and jewels, in his journal, is followed by this entry: "All these things mine eyes beheld through the wickets, and I was concerned, yet happy: for if it be thus with the transgressors of God's will, how much the more so with them who do God's will? For lo, days of glory and of honour draw nigh for the remnant of the House of Israel, and our eyes will behold the soul of our life, the Lord's Anointed One, shining forth sevenfold, ablaze with the light of the sun, crowned with the Crown of all crowns, Holiest of the holy, so be it."

His description of the coronation of Sultan Mustafa III at Constantinople in 1757 is concluded in a similar vein.

There was a wide gap between the vision of the state's future regeneration when the Messiah came, and the reality of the Palestine Jewry's submission to the reigning power. It is not surprising that the Jews of Galilee were grateful to Sheik Dhaher el-Amr for the privileges he had granted them, and they praised him incessantly and volubly for purging the land of brigands and keeping the roads safe. But even the Jews of

Jerusalem were loyal, not only to the Turkish monarchy but to the arrogant Pashas of Damascus in times of trial.

The policy the Jewish leaders followed during Napoleon's war of conquest in Palestine in 1799 was limited by the same narrow political perspective. Though a letter written by the leaders of the Jerusalem Kehillah and its rabbis, at the time of the campaign, cried out against the robbery and violence committed by the city's rulers, they found no fault with the feudal Turkish state. On the contrary, another letter in 1806 praised the Lord for the failure of Napoleon's campaign.

In normal years, the Jews also enjoyed a peaceful and mutually tolerant relationship with their Arab neighbours. Rabbi Gedalia of Siemiatycze, complaining about Arab lads assaulting Jews on the streets of Jerusalem, praised the Ishmaelites for the fact that their notables did not pass over such matters in silence. "If some important Ishmaelite," he wrote, "is apprised of this, he scolds the Arab and drives him away from the Jew or stands by until the Jew proceeds on his way." "An Ishmaelite or Arab notable" adopted the same procedure with Arab youths if they offended Jews who came to pray at the Wailing Wall. The peace and quiet which reigned in Galilee is amply and enthusiastically confirmed by travel books by pilgrims as well as by the Hassidic and *Pe'rushim* immigrants.

Pilgrimages to the holy places passed without impediment or hardship. This tolerance issued more from the reverence the Moslem Arabs themselves felt for the memory of the saints than from the monetary advantage accruing from the collection of the *jeffar* (road security tax) and the entrance fees to the sepulchres. The Hebron *Kolel*'s letters to the Diaspora constituted a lengthy chronicle of ordeals and hardships. But when it was not faced with the critical necessity of paying its debts, it enjoyed good neighbourly relations with the Arab inhabitants of the city. Rabbi Gershon of Kuty heaped abundant praise on the Hebron Arabs in a letter to his brother-in-law, Ba'al Shem Tov, in 1748. "The most distinguished of the Gentiles here," he wrote, "like the Jews very much, and when circumcision rites take place, or other festivities, they come ... in the evening and entertain the Jews, beating out rhythms and dancing amongst them, really—spare the mark!—like Jews." The notables also came to dance and to sing "praises in their tongue, Arabic" at a reception that the Hebron sages gave in honour of the guest. In contrast with the Jerusalem law discriminating against Jews (and Christians), "here (at Hebron) they walk about in garments of various hues and no one protests at this."

Normal tolerant relations were also established between the Jerusalem Kehillah and the minute Karaite congregation. This tiny community had been revived in Jerusalem in 1744 by Samuel Halevi Ben Abraham of Damascus, who had come to the country with a household of twenty-four people. It was centred around its ancient synagogue (built, according to Karaite tradition, by Anan) and depended for its existence on the Karaites of Cairo, Lithuania and, especially, the Crimea. An additional source of income was supplied by the rent it collected from fifteen or sixteen houses with rabbanite (i.e., Talmudist-Jewish) tenants. The *responsa* of the period proved that the rabbis of Jerusalem permitted the circumcision of Karaite boys (as the congregation had no *mohel* of its own) even on Sabbaths. It also honoured their oaths in matters of *kashrut*. Rabbi Raphael Me'yuhas Bar Samuel, with the consent of other rabbis, allowed rabbanite teachers to instruct the sons of Karaites in the Bible. Benjamin Ben Elijah of Tshufut-Cale, who came to Palestine in 1785 at the head of a group of Karaite pilgrims from Crimea, recorded that the Hebron Jews welcomed them with great honour and accorded them the traditional hospitality. The Karaites, in their turn, felt duty-bound to make a contribution to the synagogue of their hosts.

Normal *joie de vivre*, repressed in the *Yishuv* by ascetic practices and stringent *Kole'lim* regulations, broke out on every occasion of religiously sanctioned festivity. Weddings were celebrated by "seven days of feasting" amidst "the music of drums and cymbals." Burckhardt was amazed at the magnificent processions at weddings in Tiberias, when huge bowls, coffee urns and other silver vessels, borrowed from all the Kehillah members, were carried before the bride. In Jerusalem, it was the custom for the groom to lead his bride by the hand a distance of over four cubits to the nuptial home; a prayer shawl was wrapped around the bride and groom. A birth was the occasion for "seven celebrations by night, with song, drum and dance." The mother herself customarily brought her newborn son to the circumcision ceremony in the synagogue, "as one offers a sacrifice on the altar," and the infant was dressed in silk, with shirt and trousers.

A custom peculiar to Palestine was the celebration of *Simhat Bet Ha' shoevah* (Rejoicing of the Water Libation of Tabernacles) every night during Tabernacles week. "He who has not seen the rejoicing during *Simhat Bet Ha'shoevah* at Safed has never seen happiness in his life," Rabbi Simha of Zalosce reported, paraphrasing a Talmudical saying. The men came dancing out of the synagogue ("and the women looked on at the merrymaking outside the synagogue") with torches in their hands, and they sang to the accompaniment of drums and cymbals. The pilgrimages to the tombs of the *Tzaddikim* were also turned into joyous celebrations. The wealthy pilgrims were generally accompanied by an escort of poor men. One of these "brewed coffee, another cooked, and still another cared for the tobacco and the smoking vessels." The Hebronites showed great hospitality towards the pilgrims in order to observe "the custom of our father Abraham." They held feasts for their guests lasting three consecutive days "with royal munificence, flesh, fowl and wine, and an abundance of fruits." Besides "the repast of our father Abraham" in honour of the guests, the custom of distributing "bread and a pot of lentil porridge" to the poor, Arabs and Jews, "in honour of our father Abraham," had prevailed in Hebron as far back as the Middle Ages.

The Hassidim had brought their own customs with them to the country, especially their night-long dancing and copious consumption of spirits to stimulate "joyous worship." Needless to say, they surpassed all the Jewish communities of Palestine in their capacity for merriment.

Letters from immigrants and travel books by pilgrims expressed the Jews' rejoicing and their continually growing love for the country. They marvelled at the atmosphere of holiness in the land, with its historic memories at every turn, and also at its natural beauty, pleasant climate— especially at Safed—and abundance of fruit and vegetables. Rabbi Simha of Zalosce made some characteristic comments on the appearance and physical condition of the Jews in Galilee. "The people of Palestine," he wrote, "are naturally stronger and healthier than we are, and they carry amazingly great burdens on their heads or shoulders." Rabbi Joseph Sopher, who emigrated to Palestine from the Volhynian town of Beresteczko in 1762, concluded his Palestine letter, *The Testimony of Joseph*, with an indignant rejection of the idea that Palestine at that time was only fit to be buried in. "Whoever says that it is not good to be in the Land of Israel alive, is maligning the Land like (Joshua's) spies."

Adjustment to the country was difficult in all cases, but doubly so for arrivals from eastern Europe because of the difference in climate, language, customs, and, above all, because of the limited means of earning a living. Considerable perseverance, engendered by love for the Land, was needed to surmount these handicaps and settle down. Rabbi Abraham of Kolyski explained the problem of adjustment "to all who inquire and seek to dwell honourably in the Holy Land." The profundity of his thought and his poetic spirit permeates his words with the religious fervour of the Hassidic movement:

> Many changes, transformations and events lasting an infinity of time pass for everyone who arrives in the land until it grows upon him and he *takes pleasure in her stones and loves her dust*,* cherishes the ruins of the land of Israel more than a palace in foreign lands, prefers its dry crust of bread. And *The race is not to the swift*,† not for one day and not for two, not in a month and not in a year, but while the years multiply, until the days of adjustment pass, as it is written, *Of Zion it shall be said: this man and that was born in her.*‡ Which is to say, whosoever shall come to this sacred shrine must be conceived anew, suckled anew, and raised anew from infancy till face to face he beholds the countenance of the land and lo, his soul is bound to its soul!

These sublime words were an appropriate trumpet call to subsequent generations of immigrants to the Land. Only the overwhelming love of the

---

* The italicized passage is a paraphrase of Psalms, 102:15.
† Ecclesiastes, 9:11.
‡ Psalms, 87:5.

land in the hearts of Rabbi Abraham of Kolyski and similarly inspired men enabled the Jewish community in Palestine to survive during those distressing times, to grow, and to preserve the Jewish people's claim to its ancestral homeland.

D. PLANS TO RESTORE THE JEWISH STATE

Forerunners of Zionism during the French Revolution and under Napoleon

During the same transition period to modern times, when "the Kole'lim of the Holy Cities" were labouring under the burden of taxes and debts and appealing to the Diaspora to expedite help so that the people's hold on the land of its heritage and its future deliverance might be retained, realistic political schemes for the re-establishment of the Jewish state were conceived in Europe. True, the idea of the restoration of Zion and Israel's deliverance in its own land were still recurrent themes in Protestant theological literature, especially in England and America. Theological speculations on the renaissance of Israel had appeared in this literature as from the seventeenth century, with its most practical proposals swamped by subtle sermons on Biblical and Evangelical passages and occult premonitions of the millennium. All these theories were based on the same thesis; that the restoration of Zion and the revival of the Davidic monarchy was a precondition for the redemption of the world under the reign of Jesus of Nazareth. The promises of the Prophets concerning the salvation of Israel and the restoration of Zion had to be fulfilled in order that Jesus' gospel of "One Shepherd, one Flock" and the kingdom of heaven that would surely come, be consummated. However, side by side with this purely theological literature of "restoration," schemes for the re-establishment of a Jewish state, marked by sober political planning for definite political and economic ends, made their first appearance at the end of the eighteenth century. They became increasingly frequent at the beginning of the nineteenth.

In the past, during the eighteenth century, even the non-theologians who had planned the establishment of a Jewish state had been either mystics and religious visionaries or adventurers and dreamers (for example, the Marquis de Langallerie). By the end of the century, however, serious statesmen and economists were advocating a Jewish state. Political considerations now often even outweighed religious motives in the theologians' plans for "the restoration of Israel." The appearance of these new schemes followed the changes that were taking place in the socio-economic and political situation in Europe with the start of the modern capitalist period. Some of the proposals to restore Palestine to the Jewish people were offered as a solution to the Jewish problem for the Jews themselves and for the neighbouring peoples. Others were only intended as a means of attaining a political ambition in the competition for the domination of the Middle East.

The political and economic policy of enlightened absolutism had already given active attention to plans for "the reform of the Jews" involving the transfer of large numbers of them to useful occupations and the granting of rights in trade, industry and banking to their financial leaders. It is true that the problem of Jewish enfranchisement had been solved with the triumph of the revolution in France and the neighbouring countries. But the question of Jewish economic rehabilitation and integration with the cultural and political life of the countries in which they lived still remained unsolved. Various reform programmes advanced ideas for concentrated Jewish settlement in separate cities and villages, or even in entire countries. Some also suggested the foundation of a Jewish state in Palestine. These schemes for establishing a state of Israel originated solely with western statesmen, especially the French and English. As early as the 1780's, the European powers had conceived the idea of carving up the Turkish Empire, encouraged by its progressive deterioration and collapse following economic impoverishment, its tottering feudal régime and the revolts amongst its subject peoples. The plan was not carried out either then, or throughout the nineteenth century, only because of rivalry between the great powers over the dismemberment. The Anglo-French was during the Revolutionary and the Napoleonic eras exacerbated the Middle Eastern problem and brought the question of Palestine's future sharply to the fore. As a result, schemes were devised in every one of the rival powers of the revival of a Jewish state in Palestine which would enable the power concerned to obtain custodianship of the country.

None of these plans for a Zionist solution to the Jewish problem had any practical results. The material political conditions for the regeneration of the Jewish state were obviously absent so long as Palestine remained a province of the decaying Turkish Empire. Furthermore, the condition of the Jews in the east European population centres was such that the basic prerequisites of these schemes could not mature. A long period of capitalist development was required in this backward area of Europe before its Jewish population could attain the economic, social and cultural level commensurate with auto-emancipation and could act on its own behalf to obtain the liberation and renaissance of its own country. The first step in the dialectics of historical development was therefore the civil emancipation of the Jews in the Diaspora before they could progress to self-liberation and the consummation of their vision of deliverance in Zion. Nevertheless, the schemes for a Jewish state which appeared at the beginning of the new age, during the early period of enfranchisement, have great historic value.

The arguments in support of these plans, not only exposed the defective foundations of Jewish economic existence and status amongst the Gentiles. It also presented the indivisible national bond uniting the dispersed Jewish people, and its historic aspiration to return to the land of its national origin, as a political fact. Thenceforth, the acknowledgement of the Jewish people's historical right to its country, first expressed at that period, never disappeared from political literature, and was eventually ratified by international law.

An anonymous letter to Moses Mendelssohn in 1770 opened the series of projects for the revival of a Jewish state, worked out in the second half of the eighteenth century. At the beginning of that year (when Berlin Enlightenment circles were thrown into an uproar by the open letter from Pastor Lavater to Mendelssohn),* the latter received an unsigned letter from a highly-placed statesman, including a memorandum on the Jewish problem. The memorandum has not been preserved, but the essentials of the plan can be surmised from the draft of Mendelssohn's reply to this "man of station,"† as he addressed the author of the letter. The anonymous writer would seem to have stated that he was only concerned with "the good of the human race" and proposed that the Jewish problem be solved by the establishment of a Jewish state in Palestine. In reply, Mendelssohn cited all the difficulties which, in his opinion, precluded the implementation of this "colossal idea." The undertaking would require huge sums of money, whereas Jewish wealth was contained in credits and not in real assets. However, he thought that the greatest impediment to the execution of this programme was "the character of my nation." He sadly admitted that "it has not been adequately trained to take upon itself anything great" and offered an explanation of the historical reasons for this failure: "The pressure to which we have been subjected these many centuries has taken the vigour from our spirits. For this we are not guilty; but we may not deny that the natural urge for liberty has become completely inactive amongst us: it has changed into monk's virtue and manifests itself in prayer and suffering, but not in deeds."

Furthermore, the people in its dispersion lacked the cohesive spirit necessary for the execution of such a plan. Nor could Mendelssohn ignore the international political difficulties inherent in the competition between the great powers for the country the Jews were theoretically supposed to colonize: "It would appear to me that such a plan might be feasible only when the European Great Powers are engaged in a general war . . . In the prevailing calm, a single jealous power could frustrate the plan. It seems that the unhappy Crusades justify these misgivings only too well."

Even before Mendelssohn, Spinoza had already considered the psychological characteristics of the Jewish people as the greatest obstacle to the revival of a Jewish state in Palestine. In his *Theologico-Political*

---

* *cf.* Chapter Seven, p. 157.
† In German, *Ein Mann vom Stande*. Some sources have identified this personage with the Danish Minister at St. Petersburg, Count Friedrich von Lynar.

Treatise—which influenced Mendelssohn when he wrote his *Jerusalem*—Spinoza, discussing the question of Jewish segregationism as a principal factor in their national existence in the Diaspora, had stated:

> Nay, more, unless the fundamentals of their religion have made them effeminate in mind, I would absolutely believe that at some time they (the Jews), given the opportunity—inasmuch as human affairs are mutable—may once again establish their state, that God may choose them anew.

> (*Tractataus Theologico-Politicus*,
> Opera, I, The Hague, 1890, p. 396).

What Spinoza had conceived as a possible hindrance, Mendelssohn pronounced a certainty. This is not surprising. A vast difference had already separated the Sephardi Jews of Amsterdam, proud and intrepid descendants of the Marannos, from the abject, degraded Jews of Germany in Mendelssohn's day. The passage of time had wrought changes for the worse. In the century following the publication of Spinoza's work (in which a faint echo of the Sabbetai Zvi Messianic movement was discernible) the Jewish people had declined even further into helplessness and mere endurance, to a point where "its might was only in its mouth" and nothing could be done till Heaven took pity.

But, precisely at the time when Mendelssohn was writing these depressing words, the first signs of practical activity towards building up Palestine could be detected amongst the Jewish people. At the beginning of the 1770's, after Ali Bey and his ally, Dhaher el-Amr, had almost conquered the whole country and were at the peak of their successful attack on the Turkish armies, a Russian fleet, with several German officers on board, anchored in the Port of Leghorn.* The local Jews made contact with the Germans and asked them to mediate in forwarding a proposal for the sale of Jerusalem at a cash price to the Jewish people via Ali Bey. Ali Bey accepted their offer, and, though the price he mentioned was enormous, the Leghorn Jews accepted it and communicated with the Jews in England and Holland about raising funds. According to highly improbable accounts, they were fascinated by the idea of rebuilding the temple in the redeemed city. The negotiations collapsed with Ali Bey's defeat and death in 1773.

A substantial scheme for solving the Jewish problem by founding a Jewish state in Palestine was propounded by Prince Charles Joseph de Ligne in a memorandum drawn up in 1797 and published in 1801. De Ligne (1735-1814), a native of Belgium, was a noted diplomat, an exemplary soldier and a writer with a subtle style, whose *bons mots* circulated amongst all the aristocratic salons in Europe. His military career had been spent in the service of Austria and Russia and he had risen to the rank of Field-Marshal under both crowns. Travelling about

* *cf. supra*, pp. 614–5; also Chapter Five, pp. 113–4.

Europe, he had come into contact with the Jews of many countries and classes, from France to Bohemia, Poland and Russia, from wealthy bankers to ragged pedlars. Though de Ligne's memorandum on the Jewish question was actually written during the French revolution, the latter left no imprint whatsoever on his views. Throughout his lifetime, which lasted until the Congress of Vienna (he was the author of the *bon mot* "Congress dances but does not advance"), he held steadily to his views—those of an educated, cosmopolitan aristocrat of the era of enlightened despotism. He combined the theories of Voltaire and Rousseau with a belief in evangelical prophecies and the Pope's holiness, without being aware of any contradiction. His proposals for the solution of the Jewish problem constituted a twofold scheme: a broad series of reforms for the Jews in the lands of their domicile, and, alternatively, the reconstitution of the Jewish state in Palestine. His detailed reform programme contained no innovations as compared with the concepts held by enlightened circles during the period preceding the Revolution and civil emancipation. However, he heavily stressed the movement into productive activities and suggested, amongst other things, that the Jews should be directed into agriculture through colonization on the steppes of the southern Ukraine. He had, after all, personally observed the poverty of the Jewish masses in central and eastern Europe. De Ligne was not unconscious of the obstacles to any reform for the Jews. He was not sure that the governments would agree to his proposals and he also anticipated opposition to Jewish enfranchisement from the Christian population. The merchants would be confronted with new competitors and the working classes (artisans) would also regard them as rivals for employment. Hence, although he made no explicit decision in favour of the alternative, territorial solution of the Jewish problem, it was quite obvious that he thought it more likely to succeed.

De Ligne founded this opinion on the belief that the restoration of the Jewish centre in Palestine would infuse new blood into the Ottoman Empire. The Jews could make good the deficiencies in the declining Empire. They would revive its stagnant economy, reorganize provincial administration and also teach the Turkish army European military tactics. Above all, the Jews would restore prosperity to Palestine—to be returned to them as a kingdom under the Sultan or placed under the administration of one of his Pashas. Once they were settled in their own country, they would develop crafts, industry, agriculture and European trade. Jerusalem, a remote village, would be revived as a glorious capital. Solomon's temple would be rebuilt from its ruins. The flow of the Kedron would be regulated and directed into its proper channels. The Garden of Eden would be discovered and its four head-rivers make it into an English garden. The desert wastes and the holy places, now infested with brigands, would become settled and cultivated. The author of this chaotic mixture of a Christian-Messianic Utopia tempered by the idealism of

Rousseau and a modicum of political and economic realism, did not envisage the restoration of Zion for all classes of Jews. The restored homeland would attract the poor, the destitute and members of the Jewish middle class. Jewish *haute finance,* the wealthy bankers and merchants, as well as the enlightened Jews with their European culture, would remain in the capitals of Europe and rise to eminence "for otherwise they, the Christians, will be the losers, and rightly so."

De Ligne did nothing to implement his original plan for the re-establishment of the Jewish state. It failed to arouse the slightest response at that time, like other memoranda he had prepared—on Poland, for example. De Ligne's Zionist idea was resurrected by entirely different forces; by the leaders of that revolution which he had only regarded as a revolt by disorderly rebels. Barely a year after de Ligne had completed his document, Jewish people throughout the dispersion were fired with enthusiasm for the restoration of Zion and the re-establishment of the Jewish state at the instigation of French government circles, prompted by hard political calculations. The historically opportune hour postulated in Mendelssohn's letter of 1770 as an imperative condition for the consummation of a Jewish state, "when the great European powers are engaged in a general war," had arrived.

At the beginning of 1798, when Bonaparte was making hasty preparations for the conquest of Egypt, *A Jew's Letter to his Brethren* appeared anonymously in France, urging the Jews of the world to establish an independent Jewish state in Palestine. The manifesto began with a description of "the state of degrading humiliation" to which the Jews had been subjected for centuries wherever they lived because of "the intolerant, barbarous religions." The Jews' steadfast loyalty to their ancestral faith had not only failed to gain them the appropriate respect amongst the gentiles, but had actually strengthened the hatred felt towards them. "The time has therefore come," it declared, "to throw off this unbearable yoke—it is time to resume our rank amongst the other nations of the world." Palestine was in the hands of "despicable robbers" who were desecrating the Holy City, which the forefathers of the people had valiantly defended against the Romans. "This dauntless spirit has only slumbered. The time has come to arouse it . . . let us rebuild the temple of Jerusalem." An unconquerable nation, in whose glory the world abounds, had shown the Jews by its own example what might be achieved by love of country and it would not refuse them its assistance in view of "the philosophy that guides the leaders of that nation." The Jews as a nation numbered over 6,000,000 people dispersed over the face of the earth, "and we have in our possession untold wealth." These means had to be employed to effect a return to the homeland, for the time was ripe and the moment must not be missed.

The practical scheme that the manifesto suggested was that fifteen "tribes of Israel" should elect fifteen delegates through their deputies in the capitals of their countries. The tribes were to be divided according to country of residence: for example, Jews from Italy, Poland, Russia, Britain, Holland, Prussia, the German states and also from Turkey, Asia and Africa. These delegates would constitute a council with its seat in Paris. The council's decisions would be legally binding on all the Jews of the world. The council's agent would hold conversations with the Directory of France on the possibility of opening negotiations with the Sublime Porte at Constantinople on all matters pertinent to the restoration of Palestine to the Jewish people. The area proposed was to include lower Egypt and Palestine, from Acre to the Dead Sea and thence to the Red Sea. The territory within these boundaries lay at the centre of the world. It would be an international trading centre and, especially through the Red Sea, would control trade with India, Arabia, Ethiopia and East Africa, "the rich lands which supplied Solomon with so much gold, ivory, and precious stones." The inhabitants of these lands would be most willing to trade with the Jews of Palestine, as they themselves still retained the Law of Moses.* In return for its aid to the Jews "in returning to and occupying the country" the French government would receive financial compensation and its merchants would have sole rights in trade with the Indies and elsewhere. The important thing was that honest and intelligent men be elected as delegates to the Paris council and they would make all the detailed arrangements in consultation with the French people. The author of the manifesto concluded: "Oh, my brethren! Is there a sacrifice we shall not make to achieve this aim? Let us return to our land, live under our own laws, behold with our own eyes the Holy Places which our forefathers covered with glory in their courage and virtues! I already behold all of your awakening in holy zeal! Sons of Israel, the end to your afflictions is nigh! The hour is ripe! Beware, lest ye allow it to pass!"

This manifesto was undoubtedly written at the initiative of the French government or its army staff and with their inspiration. Its substance was fully in accordance with the objectives of the Middle Eastern campaign that the Republic was preparing. It was necessary for France to win the sympathy of Jews throughout the world to pursue this war of conquest and, above all, in areas near to the forthcoming battle-ground—in Turkey, Asia and Africa. The appeal to the Jews to revive the heroic spirit of their ancestors who fought against Rome was intended to predispose the oriental Jews to volunteer for service in Bonaparte's army. However, the vision of Zion restored and the establishment of a Jewish state in Palestine under a French protectorate was more than merely a bait to hire men and mobilize funds in wartime. It also reflected France's economic interest in the states it was preparing to conquer. France hoped to derive a good deal of benefit for its trade with the Middle East through the settlement of a Jewish population in Palestine and the adjacent areas. An article that

* The allusion is to Ethiopia where Judaism still exercised a discernible influence on religious life in the eighteenth century.

appeared on April 19, 1798 in the semi-official periodical *La Décade* in response to *A Jew's Letter to his Brethren* discussed this benefit in detail.

It began by stating the need to raise Syria and Egypt out of their economic depression and to rebuild their ruins. This could be achieved by calling upon the Jews to return to Palestine:

> We know how devoted they have been to their homeland and to the city of Jerusalem from ancient times. Dispersed throughout the world as the result of persecutions that have continued for the last 1,800 years, they still direct their gaze at Palestine in the hope that their progeny, more fortunate than they, will be brought there by some incredible miracle. They will stream back there from the four corners of the earth if but once given the sign. Their property is easy to transport. People and gold will flow. The gold they supply will suffice not only to launch the economic action but also to defray the costs of revolution in Syria and Egypt.

The article went on to explain that the negotiations of the Jews of Leghorn with Ali Bey allowed an inference from the simple to the complex: if the Jews were enthusiastic about the idea of purchasing the city of Jerusalem and rebuilding its Temple, it was all the more likely that they would react favourably to a programme for colonizing the entire country under secure conditions and with prospects for the development of trade. Miraculously, Jews were already present at all the ports that traded with the East, from the Batavian Republic (Holland) to India, and from Italy to Basra. Vast and wealthy Jewish populations existed in the North African countries and monetary administration, the minting of currency and customs collections were in their hands there. Apart from the benefits that Jewish inhabitants and Jewish capital would bring to Egypt and Syria, the Jews would also discharge a valuable function in opening up the African interior; they would enable France to eliminate England from a field of exploration where it now held the upper hand.

After a lengthy historical dissertation on Jewish misery during the Middle Ages caused by the religious fanaticism of the Christian nations, the author expressed his amazement that "this small nation" had summoned up the strength to survive in the face of its enemies. The Jews, he wrote, had been exiled from their country after heroic military struggles against their Roman oppressors. But even when they were in exile their persecutors had not been able to crush their spirit. Ancient rulers, such as Alexander the Great and Ptolemy, had been wise enough to utilize the Jews for colonizing their domains and organizing their armies. Syria and Egypt could realize even greater advantages from Jewish settlement now. Jewish acumen, Jewish capital and Jewish mercantile contacts had not yet been turned to good account even by the enlightened governments. The Jews would return to the Middle East equipped with European learning (in which they had participated), but without the defects of their old organization. "They are capable," he wrote, "of reconstruction as a body politic, or of fitting in as devoted citizens to the programme of a government founded in wisdom and daring." In conclusion, the article emphasized the advantages France could expect from this programme: "there can be no doubt whatsoever that they will become passionately attached to the nation that uplifts them." Thus, the founding of the Jewish state, enthusiastically urged by the author of *A Jew's Letter to his Brethren* was integrated into a sober and practical programme by the writer in *La Décade*, as a subsidiary matter and as only one of the possibilities. To him, the important thing was the settlement of Jews in Palestine, Syria, and Egypt for the purpose of Middle Eastern development.

Another plan was submitted to the government of France at the beginning of 1799, similar in outline and even in its reasoning to *A Jew's Letter to his Brethren*. On February 17, 1799, about a week after Napoleon had left Egypt at the head of an army to launch his campaign for the conquest of Palestine (news of this could not possibly have reached France by then), a memorandum by one Thomas Corbet* was sent from the town of Lorient, in the Brittany peninsula, to Paul Barras, a highly influential member of the Directory. The memorandum began by deploring the fate of the Jews, "a proud and noble-hearted people" plundered and ruined, who could only earn an inadequate living because of their degraded position. "Impatiently they await their regeneration as a nation" and place their confidence in the prophecies of their forthcoming deliverance. Even after the war, they would not find satisfaction in residence in France unless they were able to reconstitute themselves as a nation. The responsibility of granting the Jews a territory where they could again set up a Jewish republic rested with France. The next step would be for a member of the Directory to designate two or three Jewish notables to undertake to organize the project. The Jews in all countries would send delegates to secret conclaves, like the organization of *The United Irishmen* (the Jews had shown their sympathy for the Irish struggle for liberation as well as for the Polish), the Freemasons, or the German *Illuminati*. The Jews would conduct a fund-raising campaign to purchase the part of Egypt near the Suez isthmus and the Red Sea. The settlers in Egypt, in co-operation with France, would encourage trade with Europe. Egypt, however, would only serve as a springboard for the reconquest of their own country, Palestine. Jews would learn the trade of shipbuilding and the art of navigation in French and Italian ports. The warships that the Jews would build for Napoleon during the war would later be used to transport the immigrants to Egypt and also for trade.

---

* This surname could be English or Irish. As Thomas Corbet twice alludes sympathetically to the Irish struggle for liberation, there are grounds for assuming that he himself was Irish and a political refugee in France. It would seem, then, that this is an early evidence of Irish sympathy for the Zionist idea, which was later to be expressed even more strongly.

They would learn military tactics in Napoleon's army in Egypt and would be trained as soldiers—a role they had filled so heroically in antiquity. From Egypt they would proceed to the conquest of Palestine and would attain their heritage and resting place. They would bring with them to Asia, European scholarship, industry and skills, and would represent "a powerful instrument for the uplifting of the people of Asia." In fact, the effects of their return to Zion would extend as far as distant China.

In the event, Barras, described by Corbet as "Bonaparte's friend," did not manage to inform the Commander-in-Chief of the French armed forces in Palestine of the memorandum and its scheme. However, the memorandum constitutes important evidence of the fact that the members of the Paris government were aware of plans for the establishment of the Jewish state, although the propaganda in that direction originally issued from Napoleon's army staff.

Napoleon succeeded in rallying a considerable number of African Jews to his side during the Egyptian campaign and they fought valiantly. Rumours that spread through Palestine exaggerated this figure to record a total of 12,000 Jews in Napoleon's service. After conquering the major portion of Palestine in the spring of 1799, Napoleon considered the time ripe for a proclamation to world Jewry. He hoped that his conquest of Palestine would rouse all the peoples of Syria to revolt against Turkey. He attempted to instigate a Druze war for independence, won the sympathy of the Christians, and also attempted to gain the sympathy of the Jews. However, as far as the Jews were concerned, Napoleon was not solely interested in the tiny Jewish community in the country. He felt that the moment had come to inspire world Jewry with the idea of establishing a state for all Israel, to fire their imagination with the vision presented the year before in *A Jew's Letter to his Brethren*. On April 20, 1799, four days after the French forces had won the battle of Mount Tabor, a proclamation was issued from French Army Headquarters, Jerusalem, in the name of "Bonaparte, Commander-in-Chief of the Armies of the French Republic in Africa and Asia, to the rightful heirs of Palestine." The proclamation was composed in a solemn and restrained style befitting a historic pronouncement. It began:

> Israelites, unique nation, whom thousands of years, lust of conquest, and tyranny have been able to deprive only of their ancestral land, but not of name and national existence!
>
> Attentive and impartial observers of destinies of nations, even though not endowed with the gifts of seers like Isaiah and Joel, have long since also felt what these, with beautiful and uplifting faith, have foretold when they saw the approaching destruction of their kingdom and fatherland: *And the ransomed of the Lord shall return and come unto Zion with song and everlasting joy upon their heads; they*

shall obtain gladness and joy, and sorrow and sighing shall flee away (Isaiah, 35 : 10).

Arise, then, with gladness, ye exiled! (The French nation) avenges its own shame and the shame of the remotest nations ... and also the almost two-thousand-year-old ignominy put upon you. (France) offers to you at this very time ... Israel's patrimony ... The great nation ... herewith calls on you not indeed to conquer your patrimony, nay, only to take over that which has been conquered and, with that nation's warranty and support, to remain master of it, to maintain it against all comers.*

The proclamation urged the Jewish people to show that the courage of the Maccabees had not been stifled by "two thousand years of treatment as slaves," and ended with the appeal:

Hasten! Now is the moment, which may not return for thousands of years, to claim the restoration of civic rights amongst the population of the universe which had been shamefully withheld from you for thousands of years, your political existence as a nation amongst the nations, and the unlimited natural right to worship Jehovah in accordance with your faith publicly and most probably forever (*cf.* Joel, 4 : 20).

A letter from Jerusalem, dated the month of Nissan, 5559 (April, 1799), and signed by one Aaron Ben Levi, "Rabbi in Jerusalem," was attached to the proclamation. Rabbi Ben Levi described himself as one "of the tribe of Levi ... after the passing of numberless generations again First Rabbi and Priest in this Holy City." He informed the Jews of the Diaspora that "the glorious prophecies" contained in Joel, 4, Zephania, 2, and Malachi, 2 : 3, "have been as to their large part fulfilled by the victorious army of the great nation, and it now depends only on us to be not as the children of harlots and adulteresses, but true descendants of Israel," and to demand "the inheritance of the people of the Lord, to behold the beauty of the Lord, and to inquire in his Temple (*cf.* Psalms, 27 : 4). Take then unto yourselves the wings of the eagle and the strength of the lioness, like unto our fathers in the days of Nehemia ... and Ezra, to rebuild the walls of the orphaned city and a temple to the Lord." He called upon all the Jews of the Diaspora to "sanctify a combat," that is to say, to join battle and he exhorted "all men of Israel capable of bearing arms (to) gather and come up to us." "Aaron Ben Levi" ended with a cry to the Lord to "remember for good all that the great nation has done unto us" and raised the slogan, "A sword for the Lord and for Bonaparte!"

The proclamation and the letter did, of course, contain a number of

---

* Quoted from the translation of the Proclamation in F. Kobler, *Napoleon and the Restoration of the Jews to Palestine, New Judea*, September, 1940.

obvious distortions deliberately inserted to intensify their propaganda value amongst the Jews. For example, the proclamation was said to have been issued from Jerusalem because of its sanctity in the eyes of the people, although Napoleon never took Jerusalem. Napoleon's military staff may conceivably have thought this falsification justified after the victory near Mount Tabor, when a rapid conclusion to the siege of Acre and an easy conquest of Jerusalem and the surrounding area could be expected. But all considerations would seem to show that the signature affixed to the accompanying letter, "Aaron Ben Levi of the Tribe of Levi, First Rabbi and Priest in this Holy City" was a fraud. In the first place, the Chief Rabbi at Jerusalem at that time was Rabbi Yom Tov Algazi. Secondly, no Chief Rabbi would have jeopardized his own position or that of Palestine Jewry vis-à-vis the Turks in control of the city. Finally, he would not have proclaimed himself "Priest in this Holy City" at a time when the Temple was not standing. However, these fabrications, designed to render the propaganda more effective, can not detract from the historic importance of the proclamation.

Contemporary official publications of the French Republic also considered it politically expedient to disseminate rumours about Napoleon's projected restoration of Palestine to the Jews. At the end of May, the Paris newspapers published the following news item from Constantinople:

> Bonaparte has ordered the publication of an announcement in which he calls upon all the Jews of Asia and Africa to gather under his banner for the purpose of rebuilding ancient Jerusalem. He has already armed a great many of them and their battalions are threatening Aleppo . . .*

A month later, the official gazette published exaggerated rumours about Napoleon's alleged conquest of the Turkish Empire and added:

> It is not only in order to restore Jerusalem to the Jews that Bonaparte has conquered Syria. His original plans were much farther reaching: the capture of Constantinople.

The proclamation to the Jews of the world issued in Napoleon's name from "General Headquarters, Jerusalem," was therefore a new move in the French military and governmental policy, which had begun with the publication of *A Jew's Letter to his Brethren*. Still, in the new circumstances created by the occupation of most of Palestine by French forces, the proclamation contained no suggestion for enlisting Jewish funds. It only proposed rousing Jewish consciousness of the historical turning point

---

* There are grounds for F. Kobler's conjecture that the reference here is, as actually stated, to a proclamation solely to the Jews of Asia and Africa, and that Napoleon had issued such a proclamation some time before his Proclamation to world Jewry was published.

that had been reached; it only demanded that the Jews conclude a fraternal alliance with France and "receive into their custody" the country it had conquered. However, the French armies still needed Jewish manpower for their war effort, and the proclamation therefore urged them to revive the Maccabean spirit of heroism. In the same vein, the accompanying letter explicitly summoned "all men of Israel capable of bearing arms" to assemble under Bonaparte's flag. The proclamation's concluding exhortation to the Jews to demand the return of their civil rights, a guarantee of their religious freedom throughout the world, and political independence "as a nation amongst the nations" immediately recalls the Zionist programme of *Gegenwartsarbeit* in the twentieth century.*

However, the political interests of the war took precedence in the minds of the French even when they added these more general demands. Their aim of creating domestic unrest in the countries of their actual enemies (England and Turkey) and of their potential enemies (Austria, Prussia and Russia), and of arousing sympathy for France, not only required the Jews to aspire to the re-establishment of their state in Palestine under the tutelage of the conquering power. It also needed Jewish demands for equal rights modelled on their enfranchisement in the revolutionary countries—France, Holland and Northern Italy.

When this proclamation was written, Napoleon was still engrossed in his world-embracing plans: he hoped, after he had captured Acre, or at a later period when he could recruit the necessary troops, to march on Damascus. Then, a campaign of conquest, assisted by nations in a state of revolt, would carry him to Constantinople, where he would establish a Middle Eastern empire of his own on the ruins of the Turkish Empire.

It is therefore not unlikely that the promise to restore Palestine to "its rightful heirs" contained in the proclamation did not originally occur to him merely as a calculated manoeuvre solely for propaganda purposes. Napoleon's plan for a Middle Eastern empire may very well have made provision for a Jewish state in Palestine under French patronage. Such a step might have procured France all the political and economic advantages outlined in *A Jew's Letter to his Brethren* and in *Le Décade* on the eve of the Egyptian expedition. Napoleon's failure to reduce Acre and his retreat to Egypt thwarted his extensive aims for the Middle East and annulled plans for restoring Palestine to the Jewish people. It can be surmised that Napoleon's staff did not even manage to distribute more than a few copies of its proclamation. Meanwhile, changes in the political and military situation made it obsolete.†

* Literally, "work for the present"—all activity designed to ameliorate and maintain Jewish life in the Diaspora.

† The first, and only, copy of this proclamation came to light during the Second World War in 1940. An elderly refugee from Vienna, Herr Ernst Foges, a great-grandnephew of Rabbi Eleazar Fleckeles, brought this copy of the Proclamation, together with the accompanying letter, to London. It had been in the possession of his family, in German translation, from the time of Napoleon's Palestine campaign.

Napoleon's failure in the Palestine campaign presumably accounted for the fact that the memoirs he wrote towards the end of his life described the project for establishing a Jewish state in 1799 as a "rumour" that had circulated amongst the Jews. They made no mention whatsoever of his own share in giving it currency.

Not long after he returned from his unsuccessful expedition to the Middle East, Napoleon assumed autocratic powers in France. His Jewish policy swung to the opposite extreme. Far from desiring to restore the Jews to their country as "a nation amongst the nations," he now aimed at eradicating all memory of Jerusalem amongst the Jews and at securing their assimilation within the ruling people, to the point of national submergence. Many amongst the oppressed Jewish masses in the feudal countries still pinned their faith for national deliverance to the powerful Emperor, the creator of national boundaries, as to a new Cyrus. Furthermore, the governments of the states hostile to Napoleon still suspected that he had not given up his plans to establish a Jewish state in Palestine and would revive them in the course of a new invasion of the Middle East. Both were wrong: the Zionist propaganda in Napoleon's policy was only a passing phase; but the idea of a Jewish state, which he had temporarily supported, took root and continued to grow through all the generations until it finally came to fruition.

The idea of regenerating the Jewish state was also enthusiastically propounded outside France during the Napoleonic era. French propaganda supporting this policy had aroused particular envy in England, which was sensitive to every move Napoleon made in the Middle East. British theological literature on the "restoration" (that is to say, of the Jews to their country) had by then acquired a distinctly political tone. Already in 1790, a theologian of the "restoration" school, Pastor Richard Beere, had approached the Prime Minister, William Pitt, with a memorandum on the restoration of the Jews to Palestine "with the strength of the British fleet." A booklet by the Reverend James Bicheno on *The Restoration of the Jews and the Crisis of all Nations* was an example of the trend towards practical politics in this literature. Although it was first published in 1800, it had been written in 1799, before any news of Napoleon's Egyptian-based Palestine campaign reached England. The wars and revolutions shaking the world heralded the approach of the kingdom of heaven, which should begin—in Bicheno's opinion—with the overthrow of the Catholic and Protestant hierarchies and the destruction of the Turkish Empire. The divine prophecies indicated that the Jews would return to their country even before they returned to the Christian religion, and that they would do so through the assistance of one of the great powers, which would thus be fulfilling a divine mission. It devolved upon England to prove by its actions that it was "the instrument in the hand of Providence of recovering the unhappy Jews from the miseries of their wandering condition and of restoring them to their own land." In so doing, it would simultaneously be obeying a holy precept and thwarting its enemies. There were grounds for fear that the French might undertake this task, not to fulfil the prophecies but for their own political ends. They would enlist the millions of Jews in Europe, Asia and Africa, and awaken the love of freedom that had stirred their hearts in ancient times, for the purpose of conquering their land and again setting up a Jewish state. England must do all within its power "to prevent those possible consequences, which, were they to take place, would prove most fatal to our government and commerce. Let the rulers of this country use their influence with the Porte to give up that part of their territory from which the Jews have been expelled to its rightful owners." Even if this project cost England millions of pounds, it would yield higher returns than other expenditure, half of which was, in any case, employed unprofitably every year. However, this expenditure should logically not even be needed. England's influence with the Sublime Porte would be sufficient to persuade Turkey to give up this area, from which, in any case, it only derived a slight benefit. Bicheno concluded his undisguised political proposal on a warning note: "Wild project! It may be so, but I very much suspect that if we do not pursue some such measure as this, we shall repent it when it will be too late."

The assembly of Jewish Notables in Paris in 1806, its manifesto inviting the Jews of Europe to send delegates to the *Grand Sanhedrin* sponsored by Napoleon, and the solemn sessions of this *Sanhedrin* at the beginning of 1807, aroused new suspicions in England that Napoleon was preparing to revive his plan for restoring the Jews to Palestine. The English theologians were once again moved to verbal action to warn against French scheming. A booklet dated 1806 by L. Mayer, a "restorationist" preacher, informed the Jews that their deliverance was imminent, in fact, according to calculations based on the prophecy of Daniel, the sign would be given in 1815. However, he advised them not to hasten the end, not to revolt against reigning monarchs and particularly not "to hearken to any call from those who may come forward, influenced by motives of ambition and aggrandizement, with a view to induce you to engage in war, to accomplish your restoration."

Meanwhile, Bicheno, in a second edition of his 1807 "restorationist" pamphlet, continued to express his concern for British interests, when he inquired "if the *Sanhedrin* were to consult only what was domestic, why invite the co-operation of all Jews in Europe?" He expressed the fear that Napoleon, by restoring the Jews to their country, was attempting to increase the volume of French trade and to destroy England's status in the Middle East.

F. D. Kirwan,* who wrote the introduction to the English edition of the proceedings of the Assembly of Notables, positively stated that

---

* *cf.* Chapter Three, p. 66.

Napoleon's Jewish policy was entirely directed towards the establishment of a Jewish state in Egypt and on the banks of the Jordan. He was certain that Napoleon's demand that the Jews should acquire professions was ample proof of this. Alternative employment would be necessary if they were to prepare for their rehabilitation as a self-contained people in their own country. A nation consisting exclusively of merchants could not endure.

The English theologians feared that Napoleon's real and purported plans would harm Britain's interests in the East, but they continued as before to support the actual idea of the restoration to Zion and the establishment of the Jewish state for both political and religious reasons. On the other hand, the rulers and statesmen of Austria, Prussia and Russia were alarmed at the rumours of Napoleon's intentions in convening the *Sanhedrin*, once again because of the Jewish problem. They disliked the plan to revive the Jewish state in Palestine on its own account, even without taking French entrenchment in the Middle East into consideration. Austria, then the most reactionary state in Europe, imposed police measures to counteract Jewish sympathy for the idea of a revived Jewish state in Palestine to be procured with French help. Only Russia conceived the idea of undermining Napoleon's Jewish policy with a counter-move: the offer of an autonomous territory for the Jews. In 1806, a senior official submitted a proposal to Alexander I for setting aside for Jews a tract of land between the Don and the Dnieper, as part of a scheme for the colonization of under-populated districts. This idea might also have stimulated the Russian government to accelerate its agricultural settlement programme for the Jews in the southern Ukraine, which it launched in the same year, although not as an autonomous territory but in single colonies.

The rumours of Napoleon's purported plans in convening the *Sanhedrin* also evoked a sympathetic response across the ocean, in the United States of America. American theologians were also concerned with the religious concept of Israel's salvation as a prerequisite for the coming of the kingdom of heaven, current in England at that time. However, they were not activated by the motives of political and economic rivalry that had prompted the English theologians to come out so militantly against Napoleon's plans. The American Democratic Republican (Jeffersonian) party supported friendship with France because of its progressive régime. A lively debate on Napoleon and the plan for a Jewish state was conducted in the Virginian press during 1806–1808. A spokesman for reactionary circles exploited the rumours concerning the Paris Assembly of Notables to disparage Napoleon for presuming to be a Messiah for the Jews, and the Jews as usurers preying upon the best in all nations. On the other side, a Democratic writer, using the pseudonym of *Pacificator*, wrote a series of articles analyzing the project of a Jewish state from an economic and political point of view. In view of Turkey's decline and decay, he asserted, France had the right to undertake the liberation of the oppressed peoples of the Middle East. The Jews who settled in Syria (i.e., Palestine) under Napoleon's protectorate would transplant European science and art to the East. The Jews were "a great and rich people, endowed with initiative and intelligence." Of course, it was not reasonable to expect that all the ten million Jews, scattered over the world, would desire to return to Zion, if they were not actuated by religious fervour. But, many Jews would certainly leave the lands of the Turkish Empire for Palestine. Even if only a quarter of the world's Jews were to return, they would be able to establish an important independent state that would quickly attain greatness and disseminate a stimulating influence from the Atlantic to the Indian Ocean. Under the influence of *Pacificator's* articles, several Virginian newspapers published editorials in support of a Jewish state in Palestine, both for the "unfortunate people" and for the economic development of the East, which depended on the return of the Jews to their country.

Scarcely more than legends and even less direct historical information records the impression these plans for the establishment of a Jewish state in Palestine made on the Jewish people themselves. It may be conjectured that not even the vaguest intimation of these plans reached the Jewish townlets of eastern Europe, and whatever remote rumours did penetrate, became more remote and more distorted as they were handed on. The inhabitants of the large Kehillot apparently received more coherent political information. For example, a Hungarian paper reported in 1799:

> The proposal which has been distributed in writing throughout the world encouraging the Jews to return to Jerusalem has already exerted a powerful influence on the Jews of Lwow. They visit restaurants regularly to read the press, and one can see them agitatedly whispering amongst themselves and taking counsel on the journey to Jerusalem.

The rumours of Napoleon's attitude towards the Jews excited the imagination of the broad masses of the people and intensified their anticipation of approaching deliverance. Opinion was divided amongst the leaders of the Hassidim; some were loyal to the reigning house, while a few were inspired by faith in Napoleon as the harbinger of the Messiah.* Several legends, still current amongst the Jews of Poland and Lithuania in the twentieth century, proved that Napoleon's image as an exponent of the establishment of a Jewish state was deeply embedded in the people's memory:

> In the district of Sanok in Eastern Galicia, they used to tell the story that when Napoleon came to Palestine, the Jews welcomed him to the synagogue with great honours. They seated him on a great

---

* *cf.* Chapter Ten, pp. 364–5.

throne, from which he promised the Jews that he would restore Palestine to them and rebuild the Temple. In another town in Eastern Galicia, legend added that Napoleon rode a white charger, just like the Messiah. In one Volhynian town, the following legend was recorded: on the Ninth of Av, Napoleon happened to arrive at the Wailing Wall in Jerusalem and saw the Jews weeping at the wall. He said, "A nation that continues thus to bewail for so long a time, 1,800 years, will surely be delivered." According to a legend current in the district of Vilno, Napoleon symbolized the transition from the passive anticipation of the Messiah to a War of Liberation: when he came to Vilno, it was the Ninth of Av. He visited the synagogues and saw the Jews sitting on the floor and weeping. He asked the meaning of it. Naturally, they explained to him, they were weeping over the destruction and praying for the rebuilding of The Land. Napoleon burst out laughing, "Is that how you would regain Palestine? *This* is how to do it! " And he drew his sword . . .

The hopes that the Jews of Bohemia and Moravia placed in Napoleon were based on greater political understanding. According to Austrian police investigations in 1806, the Jews of Moravia, at Nikolsburg, for example, gave a favourable reception to the rumour of French plans to restore Palestine to the Jews and to establish an Afro-Asian commercial centre. A Prague document dated 1799 proved that Bonaparte's proclamation was actually circulated in the Kehillah, especially in Frankist circles. On the other hand, the "enlightened" Jews of Germany and western Europe rejected on principle any idea of rebuilding Palestine and sympathized with Napoleon precisely because of his assimilationist policies. Only the spokesmen of the tiny Jewish community in North America did not allow their emancipated status to inhibit their loyalty to the vision of deliverance in Zion. The news of the Paris meeting of the Assembly of Notables filled them with hope for the renewal of a state in Palestine with Napoleon's help.* In western Europe, also, inspired individuals realized the magnitude of the concept. Ludwig Börne, at the age of twenty-one, made the following entry in his journal in 1807: "At lunch we discoursed a great deal about the aims of the Jewish *Sanhedrin* in Paris . . . In reply to some of the ideas I expressed on the means for the reconstruction of the Jewish state, my Anacharsis votary† answered me in a truly shopkeeper fashion, 'I lose my breath thinking of such matters.' Breath . . . to think—what a physiological paradox! "

Not many years after the Napoleonic wars, Jews themselves took the lead in devising plans for the re-establishment of the Jewish state.

* *cf.* Chapter One, p. 14.

† A young Jew whom Börne had described in an earlier entry as a devoted reader of *The Travels of Anacharsis.*

ABBREVIATIONS

B.J.G.L.—Blätter für jüdische Geschichte und Literatur.

Festschrift Philippson—Festschrift zum 70ten Geburtstage Martin Philippsons, Leipzig, 1916.

H.J.—Historia Judaica.

HUCA—Hebrew Union College Annual, Cincinnati, Ohio.

J.G.J.C.—Jahrbuch für Geschichte der Juden in der Cechoslovakischen Republik.

J.J.G.L.—Jahrbuch für jüdische Geschichte und Literatur, Berlin.

J.J.L.G.—Jahrbuch der jüdisch-literarischen Gesellschaft, Frankfurt am Main.

J.Q.R.—Jewish Quarterly Review (New Series).

J.S.S.—Jewish Social Studies, A Quarterly Journal.

Kwartalnik Zyd—Kwartalnik poswiecony badaniu przeszlosci Zydow w Polsce. Rocznik I, zeszyt 1–3, Warsaw, 1912–13.

Maandblat—Maandblat voor de Geschiedenis der Joden in Nederland.

M.G.J.V.—Mitteilungen der Gesellschaft für jüdische Volksbunde.

M.G.W.J.—Monatsschrift für die Geschichte und Wissenschaft des Judentums.

Mies. Zyd.—Miesiecznik Zydowski, Warsaw, Tom I–IV, 1930–1935.

P.A.A.J.R.—Proceedings of the American Academy for Jewish Research.

Perezhitoye—Sbornik Tom I–IV, St. Petersburg, 1909–1913.

R.E.J.—Revue des Etudes Juives.

Voskhod—yezhemiesiatchnik, St. Petersburg, 1881–1906.

Yevr. Entziklop—Yevreyskaya Entziklopedia, Tom I–XVI, St. Petersburg.

Yevr. Starina—triekhmiesiatchnik, St. Petersburg (Leningrad), Tom I–XIII, 1909–1930.

Z.D.St.J.—Zeitschrift für Demographie und Statistik der Juden, ed. A. Ruppin, Bd. I–XVI, 1905–1920.

Z.G.J.D.—Zeitschrift für die Geschichte der Juden in Deutschland, hsg. Ludwig Geiger, Bd. I–V (1887–1892).

Z.G.J.D.(N)—Zeitschrift für die Geschichte der Juden in Deutschland, Bd. I–VII (1929–1937).

Z.G.J.T.—Zeitschrift für die Geschichte der Juden in der Tschechoslovakei.

SELECT BIBLIOGRAPHY

*(For works in Hebrew and Yiddish,
see the original Hebrew edition)*

AUSTRIA

Studies

Baron, S. W., Die Judenfrage auf dem Wiener Kongress, Vienna, 1920.

Gelber, N. M., La Police Autrichienne et le Sanhedrin de Napoleon, R.E.J., LXXXIII (1927), 1–15, 131–145.

Grunwald, M., Oesterreichs Juden in den Befreiungskriegen, Leipzig, 1908.

——, Vienna, Philadelphia, 1936.

Mayer, S., Die Wiener Juden. Kommerz, Kultur, Politik 1700–1900, 2te Aufl., Vienna, 1918.

Mitrofanow, P., Josef II, Seine Politische und Kulturelle Tätigkeit, Vienna, 1916.

Moses, L., Die Juden in Niederösterreich, Vienna, 1935.

Pollak, M., Die Juden in Wiener Neustadt, Vienna, 1927.

Pribram, A. F., Urkunden und Akten zur Geschichte der Juden in Wien, Bd. I–II, Vienna, 1918.

Spiel, H., Fanny von Arnstein oder die Emanzipation, Frankfurt am Main, 1962.

Taglicht, J., Nachlasse der Wiener Juden im 17. und 18. Jhtd., Vienna, 1917.

Tietze, H., Die Juden Wiens. Geschichte-Wirtschaft-Kultur, Vienna, 1933.

Wachstein, B., Die Gründung der Wiener Chevra Kadischa im Jahre 1763. M.G.J.V., XII (1909), 97–102, XIII (1910), 6–28.

Wertheimer, J., Die Juden in Oesterreich vom Standpunkte der Geschichte, des Rechts und des Staatsvortheils, Leipzig, 1842.

Wolf, G., Geschichte der Juden in Wien, Vienna, 1876.

BOHEMIA-MORAVIA

Studies

Adler, S., Das Judenpatent von 1797, J.G.J.C., V (1933), 199–229.

Beer, P., Geschichte, Lehren und Meinungen der religiösen Sekte der Juden, Brünn, 1822–1823.

——, Ueber die Literatur der Israeliten in den kaiserlich österreichischen Staaten im letzten Decennio des 18ten Jhdts. Sulamith, Jhg. II, Bd. I., 342–357, 421–426.

Bretholz, B., Die Judenschaft einer mährischen Kleinstadt: Markt Pirnitz im 18ten Jhdt., J.G.J.C., II, 403–455.

Brilling, B., Mähren und Erez Israel. Z.G.J.T., II (1931–1932), 237–256.

Bronner, J., Die mährischen Juden im Goldschmiedehandwerk, Z.G.J.T., I (1930–1931), 243–246.

D'Elvert, Ch., Zur Geschichte der Juden in Mähren und österreichischem Schlesien, Brünn, 1895.

Diamant, P. J., Dr. Rafael Joel, der erste jüdische Advokat im alten Oesterreich. Z.G.J.T., IV (1934), 10–17.

Flesch, H., Das Neu-Rausnitzer Steuerbuch, J.J.L.G., XXI (1930), 89–108.

——, Urkundliches über jüdische Handwerker in Mähren. M.G.W.J., LXXIV (1930), 197–217.

——, Der Pinax von Austerlitz. Jahrbuch für jüdische Volkskunde, 1924/25, (M.G.J.V., XXVI–VII), 564–616.

Frankl-Grün, A., Die Gemeindeverfassung von Kremsier. M.G.W.J., XL (1896), 180–184, 209–219, 255–261.

——, Geschichte der Juden in Kremsier, Breslau, 1896–1901.

Freimann, A., Die hebräischen Druckereien in Prag, 1733–1828. Soncino-blätter, III (1930), 113–143.

Fried, S., Kehillah kedoscha Kallady. (Kulturskizze aus jüdischer Vergangenheit.) Jüdisches Archiv, Hsg. L. Moses, Vienna, Jahrg. II (1929), 39–43, 50–51, 61–64.

Gelber, N. M., Zur Geschichte der Frankistenpropaganda im Jahre 1800. Aus zwei Jahrhunderten. Vienna, 1924, 58–69.

——, Die böhmisch-mährischen Juden und das napoleonische Sanhedrin. Z.G.J.T., I (1930–1931), 55–64, 99–103.

Gold, H., Die Juden und Judengemeinden Böhmens in Vergangenheit und Gegenwart, Bd. I, Brünn, 1934.

——, Die Juden und Judengemeinden Mährens in Vergangenheit und Gegenwart, Brünn, 1929.

Grün, N., Eine Gemeindeverordnung der israelitischen Gemeinde in Prag vom Jahre 1767. Das Jüdische Literaturblatt, hsg. Dr. Moritz Rahmer, 1893, No. 31–33.

Grunwald, M., Histoire des impôts et des professions des Juifs de Bohême, Moravie et Silésie. R.E.J., LXXXII, 439–449.

——, Memoiren eines böhmischen Juden (Josef Kraus und seine Erlebnisse in den napoleonischen Feldzügen). M.G.J.V., XVII (1914), 67–92.

Haas, T., Die Juden in Mähren, Brünn, 1908.

Heilig, B., Die Vorläufer der mährischen Konfektionsindustrie in ihrem Kampf mit den Zünften. J.G.J.C., III (1931), 307–448.

——, Ziele und Wege einer Wirtschaftsgeschichte der Juden in der C.Sl. Republik. J.G.J.C., IV (1932), 7–62.

Herrisch, I., "Koscherweinsteuer." Z.G.J.T., IV (1934), 38–41.

Hlosek, J., Zide na Moravê, Brünn, 1925.

Hoffmann, J., Geschichte der Juden in Kaaden. Z.G.J.T., II (1931/32), 21–31, 110–117, 190–197, 302–312.

Jakobovits, T., Jüdisches Gemeindeleben in Kolin. J.G.J.C., I (1929), 332–368.

——, Die jüdischen Zünfte in Prag. J.G.J.C., VIII (1936), 57–145.

Jeitteles, I., Bemerkungen über den Kulturzustand der Juden in Böhmen. Sulamith, I. Jhrg., Bd. II (1807), 209–225.

Kisch, G., Die Prager Universität und die Juden. J.G.J.C., VI (1934), 1–144.

Lieben, S. H., Rabbi Eleazar Fleckeles. J.J.L.G., X (1912), 1–33.

Müller, W., Urkundliche Beiträge zur Geschichte der mährischen Judenschaft im 17. und 18. Jhdt, Olmütz, 1903.

Ochser, S., Der Pinkas der Gemeinde Kuttenplan. M.G.J.V., XIII (1910), 32–38, 57–89.

Popper, M., Miscellen zur Wirtschaftsgeschichte der Juden in Prag zu Beginn des 19ten Jhdts. Z.G.J.D., V (1892), 276–278.

Prokes, J., Die Prager Judenkonskription vom Jahre 1729. J.G.J.C., IV, 297–331.

——, Das Ghetto zu Neu-Bidschow und die sogenannte Sekte der Bidschower Israeliten um die Mitte des XVIII Jhdts. J.G.J.C., VIII (1936), 147–308.

Richter, E. und Schmidt, A., Die Hotzenplotzer Judengemeinde, 1334–1848. M.G.J.V., XIV (1911), 29–36.

Rokycana, J., Die militärische Dienstpflicht der böhmischen Juden. Z.G.J.T., I (1930/31), 104–108.

——, Zur Geschichte der Juden in Pardubitz. J.G.J.C., IV (1932), 485–495.

Roubik, F., Zur Geschichte der Juden in Böhmen in der ersten Hälfte des 19ten Jhdts. J.G.J.C., VI (1934), 285–322.

——, Drei Beiträge zur Entwicklung der Judenemanzipation in Böhmen. J.G.J.C., V (1933), 313–428.

——, Zur Geschichte der Juden in Böhmen im 19ten Jhdt. J.G.J.C., VII (1935), 305–385.

Scari, H. v., Systematische Darstellung der in Betreff der Juden in Mähren und im k. k. Antheil Schlesiens erlassenen Gesetze und Verordnungen, Brünn, 1835.

Schwenger, H., Die Namensbeilegung der Juden in Kostel. Z.G.J.T., I (1930/31), 116–126.

——, Die Judensteuern in Kostel im Jahre 1807. Z.G.J.T., II (1931/32), 261–264.

Singer, L., Zur Geschichte der Toleranzpatente in den Sudetenländern. J.G.J.C., V, 231–311.

——, Zur Geschichte der Juden in Böhmen in den letzten Jahren Josefs II. und unter Leopold II. J.G.J.C., VI, 193–284.

——, Die Entstehung des Judensystemalpatentes von 1797. J.G.J.C., VII, 199–263.

Stein, A., Geschichte der Juden in Böhmen, Brünn, 1904.

Teply, F., Die Juden in Schwihau. J.G.J.C., II (1930), 120–184.

Vischnitser, M., Poslannie Frankistov 1800 goda, St. Petersburg, 1914.

Zacek, W., Die jüdischen Gerbereien in Mähren zu Beginn des 18ten Jhdts. J.G.J.C., V (1933), 175–197.

——, Eine Studie zur Entwicklung der jüdischen Personennamen in neurer Zeit. J.G.J.C., VIII (1936), 309–397.

——, Zu den Anfängen der Militärpflichtigkeit der Juden in Böhmen. J.G.J.C., VII (1935), 265–303.

——, Zwei Beiträge zur Geschichte des Frankismus in den böhmischen Ländern. J.G.J.C., IX (1938), 343–410.

SELECT BIBLIOGRAPHY

FRANCE

I *ON THE EVE OF REVOLUTION*

Sources

d(e) C(loots) d(u) V(al) d(e) G(race) B(aron), Lettre sur les Juifs á un Ecclesiastique de mes Amis, Berlin, 1783.

Lettres Patentes du Roi, Partout Règlement concernant les Juifs d'Alsace du 10 Juillet 1784, Colmar, 1784.

(Abbé) Grégoire, Essai sur la régéneration physique, morale et politique des Juifs, Metz, 1789.

———, Motion en faveur des Juifs, Paris, 1789.

Zalkind Hourwitz, Juif Polonais, Apologie des Juifs, Paris, 1789.

Adresse presentée à l'Assemblée Nationale le 31 Août 1789 par les députés réunis des Juifs établis à Metz, dans les trois Évêchés, en Alsace et en Lorraine, Paris, 1789.

Requête à Nosseigneurs les États Généraux en faveur des Juifs, 1789.

Opinion de M. le Comte Stanilas de Clermont-Tonnerre, député de Paris, 23 Decembre, 1789.

Opinion de M. Rabaut de Saint-Etienne, sur la motion suivante de M. le Comte de Castellane, Versailles, 1789.

L(azarus) B(endavid), Sammlung der Schriften an die Nationalversammlung, die Juden und ihre bürgerliche Verbesserung betreffend, Berlin, 1789.

Pétition des Juifs établis en France. Adressée à l'assemblée nationale le 28 Janvier 1790 sur l'ajournement du 24 Decembre 1789, Paris, 1790.

Adresse de l'Assemblée des Representants de la Commune de Paris à l'Assemblée Nationale, sur l'admission des Juifs à l'Etat Civil, Paris, 1790.

Nouveau Mémoire par les Juifs de Luneville et de Sarguemines, Presenté à l'Assemblée Nationale le 26 Février, 1790.

Pflieger, Reflexions sur les Juifs d'Alsace, Paris.

Adresse des Juifs Alsaciens au peuple d'Alsace, Février, 1790.

De Laissac, Capitaine au Régiment de Limosin, Lettre à M. le Chapelliet, membre de l'Assemblée Nationale pour demontrer—les raisons—à admettre les Juifs—aux droits de citoyens, Paris, 1790.

Requête des Marchands et Negociants de Paris, contre l'admission des Juifs, Paris, 1790.

Lettre écrite à M. Schwendt par M.M. les Maire et Officiers Municipaux de la ville de Strassbourg, le 8 Avril, 1790.

B. A. Mirabeau et les Juifs, l'Univers Israélite, Supplement, 5 Séptembre, 1913.

Studies

Révue des Études Juives, vis. I-CXVII;

Articles by E. Ginsburger, Ad. Cremieux, H. Chobat, Ab. Cahen, R. Anchel, P. A. Hildenfinger, M. Grunwald, J. Godechot, M. Ginsburger, J. Weill, M. Schwab, E. M. Levy, J. Bloch.
See especially:
Liber, M., Les Juifs et la convocation des États Généraux (Vls. 63-66);

Reuss, R., Antisémitisme dans le Bas-Rhin pendant la Révolution 1790–1793 (V. 68); R. Reuss, Quelques documents nouveaux sur l'Antisémitisme dans le Bas-Rhin de 1794 à 1799 (V. 59).

Adler, S., Geschichte der Juden in Mülhausen. Mülhausen, 1914.

Anchel, R., Les Lettres du 10 Juillet, 1784, Dubnow-Festschrift, Berlin, 1930, pp. 187–200.

Askenazy, S., Napoleon à Polska, Warsaw, 1918, V. 1, pp. 110, 164, 165, 243, V. 3, pp. 66–67.

Aulard, F. A., La Société des Jacobins, V. 5, Paris, 1895, pp. 91–93, 473, 526, 584.

——, Les Juifs de France, Paris, 1946, ch. VIII; Renseignements bibliographiques, ibid., pp. 280–285.

Bloch, M., L'Alsace Juive, Guebwiller, 1907.

Cunow, H., Die Parteien der grossen französischen Revolution und ihre Presse, Berlin, 1912.

Foa, S., La Politica economica della Casa Savoia verso gli Ebr. sec. XVI fino alla Rivoluzione francese-Nizza, Roma, 1961.

Ginsburger, E., Le Comité de surveillance de Jean Jacques Rousseau, Paris, 1934.

Ginsburger, M., Rechte und Pflichten eines Juden-Vorstehers in der Grafschaft Rappolstein, B.f.j.G.u.L., IV (1903), pp. 67–70.

——, Zwei unveröffentliche Briefe von Abbé Gregoire, Dubnow-Festschrift, Berlin, 1930, pp. 200–206.

——, Cerf-Berr und seine Zeit, Zurich, 1906.

——, Aus der Zeit des Terrorismus in Elsass, B.f.j.G.u.L., III (1902), pp. 171–176.

Glaser, A., Geschichte der Juden in Strassburg, Strassbourg, 1894.

Halphen, A. E., Recueil des lois concernants les Israélites, Paris, 1851.

Hertzberg, A., The French Enlightenment and the Jews, New York, 1968.

Jaures, J., Historie socialiste de la révolution française, V. I, La Constituante, Paris, 1922.

Kahn, L., Les Juifs de Paris pendant la Révolution, Paris, 1898.

Kulisher, M. I., Vielikaya Frantzuskaya revolutsia i yevreyskiy vopros, Leningrad, 1924.

Lacroix, S., Ce qu'on pensait des Juifs à Paris en 1790, Revue politique et littéraire, V. 9, Paris, 1898, pp. 417–424.

Léon, H., Historie des Juifs de Bayonne, Paris, 1898.

Loeb, I., Les Juifs à Strassbourg depuis 1349 jusqu'à la Révolution, Annuaire de la Société des Études Juives, V. 2, 1883, pp. 139–202.

——, Statute des Juifs d'Avignon 1779, ibid. V. 1, 1881, pp. 165–276.

Loewenstein, L., Beitrage zur Geschichte der Juden im Elsass, B.f.j.G.u.L., II (1901), pp. 18–22, 28–29, 37–38.

Lozinskyi, S. T., Zhizn Yevreyew vo Frantsii v gody ateizma i terrora (1793–1794), Yevreyskaya Lietopis, V. 1, Petrograd, 1923, pp. 18–36.

Michaud, M., Biographie Universelle.

Mahler, R., Jewish Emancipation, New York, 1942, pp. 25–26.

Malvezin, Histoire des Juifs à Bordeaux, 1875.

Netter, N., Vingt Siècles d'Histoire d'une communauté juive (Metz et son grand passé), Paris, 1938.

——, Die Schuldennot der jüdischen Gemeinde Metz 1791–1834, M.G.W.d.J., Vol. 57, pp. 591–619, Vol. 58, pp. 63–80.

Posener, S., The Social Life of the Jewish Community in France in the 18th century, J.S.S., V. 7, pp. 195–232.

Robert, A., Bourloton, E., Dictionnaire des parlamentaires français, Paris, 1891.

Reissner, H., Mirabeaus Judenpolitik, Der Morgen, V. 8, Berlin, 1932, pp. 122–130.

Sagnac, Ph., Les Juifs et la révolution française (1789–1791), Revue d'Histoire moderne et contemporaire, V. 1, Paris, 1899, pp. 5–23, 209–234.

Stillschweig, K., Die Judenemanzipation im Licht des französischen Nationsbegriffes, M.G.W.d.J., V. 81, pp. 457–478.

Szajkowski, Z., The Emancipation of Jews during the French Revolution of 1789. A Bibliography of Books, Pamphlets and Printed Documents 1789–1800, Studies in Bibliography and Booklore IV–V (1958–9).

——, The Economic Status of the Jews in Alsace, Metz and Lorraine (1648–1789), New York, 1954.

——, Articles in: H.J. XVII, 121–142, XVIII, 107–120, XIX, 148–149, XX, 97–108; J.Q.R. XLV, 205–243, XLVI, 192–193; J.S.S. XIV, 291–316, XVI, 319–334, XVIII, 118–124, XX, 215–231; P.A.A.J.R. XXIV, 137–160, XXV, 119–135, XXVI, 139–160, XXVII, 83–105, XXVIII, 103–113.

II NAPOLEONIC PERIOD

Sources
Halphen, A. E., Récueil des lois concernants les Israélites, Paris, 1851.

Tama, D., Collection des procès verbaux et décis du grand Sanhédrin, Paris, 1808.

Studies
Anchel, R., Napoléon et les Juifs, Paris, 1928.

Carmi, J. I., All' Assemblea ed al Sinedrio di Parigi, Lettere. Reggio nell' Emilia, 1905.

Grunwald, M., Die Feldzüge Napoleons, Nach Aufzeichnungen Jüdischer Teilnehmer und Augenzeugen, Vienna, 1913.

——, Un Juif fournisseur militaire de Napoléon Ier, R.E.J., 57, pp. 79–92.

Klibansky, E., Les Juifs de Francfort et le grand Sanhédrin, R.E.J. 84, pp. 96–99.

Levi, I., Napoléon Ier et le grand Sanhédrin, R.E.J. 82, pp. 265–279.

Liber, M., Napoléon Ier et les Juifs, R.E.J. 71, pp. 127–147, ibid. 72, pp. 1–23, 135–162.

Posener, S., The immediate Economic and Social Effects of the Emancipation of the Jews in France, J.S.S., Vol. 1 (1939), pp. 271–326.

——, Les Juifs sous le premier empire, R.E.J. 93, pp. 192–214, ibid. 94, pp. 157–166.

Poujol, Quelques observations concernant les Juifs en général et—ceux d'Alsace, Paris, 1806.

Sagnac, P., Napoléon Ier et les Juifs, Révue d'Histoire moderne et contemporaine, V. 2, pp. 461–484, 595–626, V. 3, pp. 461–492.

Sulamith, Jhrg. 2, Bd. 2, Heft 4 (1809), pp. 279–292.

Szajkowski, Z., The growth of the Jewish Population of France, J.S.S., Vol. 8, pp. 179–187.

——, Judaica Napoleonica, A Bibliography, 1801–1815, Studies in Bibliography and Booklore II (1956), 107–152.

——, Agricultural Credit and Napoleon's Anti-Jewish Decrees, New York, 1953.

——, Poverty and Social Welfare among French Jews (1800–1880), New York, 1954.

GALICIA

Studies

(Anonym) Über Juden und Judentum. Nuremberg, 1795, 116-175.

Balaban, M. Dzieje Żydów w Galicyi, 1772–1868. Lwow, 1914

——, Herz Homberg i szkoly józefinskie w Galicji (1787–1806). Z historji Żydów w Polsce—Szkice i Studja, Warsaw, 1920, 190–236.

——, Herz Homberg in Galizien. J.J.G.L. XIX, Berlin 1916, 189–221.

——, Historja Żydów w Krakowie i na Kazimierzu, Tom II, Cracow 1936, 525–581.

Brawer, A. J., Galizien, wie es an Österreich kam, Vienna, 1910.

Buzek, J., Wplyw polityki żydowskiej rzadu austryackiego w latach 1772–1778 na wzrost zaludnienia Żydowskiego w Galicyi. Cracow, 1903.

Finkel, L., Memorial Antoniego hr. Pergena pierwszego gubernatora Galicyi o stanie kraju (z r. 1773). Odbitka z *Kwartalnika Histor.* T. XIV, Lwow, 1900.

Gelber, N. M., Aus 2 Jahrhunderten. Vienna, 1924.

Grossman, H., Österreichs Handelspolitik mit Bezug auf Galizien in der Reformperiode 1772–1790, Vienna, 1914.

Hoffmann von Wellenhof, V., Die Sonderbesteuerung der jüdischen Bevölkerung in Galizien und Bukowina bis zum Jahr 1848. *Viertel-Jahrsschrift für Sozial und* Wirtschaftsgeschichte, XII (1914), 404–448.

Jeiteles, J., Bemerkungen eines Reisenden über den Charakter der Einwohner in Galizien. Sulamith 1807, V. 1, 181–188.

Kutrzeba, S., Historja Ustroju Polski, Tom. IV. Lwów, 1920, 133–187.

Leszczynski, J., Rzady Rosyjskie w Kraju Tarnopolskim (1809–1815). Cracow, 1903.

Lutman, T., Studja nad dziejami handlu Brodów w latach 1773–1880, Lwow, 1937.

Pribram, A., Urkunden und Akten zur Geschichte der Juden in Wien. Bd. II, Vienna, 1918, 161–172.

Rosenfeld, M., Die jüdische Bevölkerung Galiziens von 1772–1867. Z.D.St.J., X (1914), 138–143.

Rutkowski, J., Historja Gospodarcza Polski (do 1864), Warsaw 1953.

Schipper, I., Die galizische Judenschaft in wirtschaftsstatistischer Beleuchtung, 1772–1848. *Neue Jüdische Monatshefte,* Berlin, 1917, 223–233.

Schneider, L., Das Kolonisationswerk Josefs II in Galizien, Poznan, 1939.

Schnür-Peplowski, S., Galiciana 1778–1812. Lwow, 1896.

——, Z przeszłości Galicyi 1772–1862. (wyd 2) Lwow, 1895.

Schulson, S. J., Geschichte der Juden in der Bukowina, M.G.W.J., V. 72, 274–286, 371–378.

Singer, L., Zur Geschichte der Juden in Böhmen in den letzten Jahren Josefs II und unter Leopold II. J.G.J.C. VI, 204–206, 237–241, 237–277.

Stöger, M., Darstellung der gesetzlichen Verfassung der galizischen Judenschaft, V. I, II. Lwow, 1833.

Tokarz, W., Galicya w początkach ery józefinskiej w świetle ankiety urzędowej z r. 1783, Cracow, 1909.

Wischnitzer, M., Die Stellung der Brodyer Juden im internationalen Handel in der zweiten Hälfte des 18ten Jahrhunderts, Dubnow-Festschift, Berlin, 1930, 113–123.

Wolf, G., Die Versuche zur Einrichtung einer Rabbinerschule in Österreich. Z.G.J.D., V (1892), 27–53.

——, Lehrer-Seminare in Galizien, Z.G.J.D., V (1892), 146–153.

GERMANY

Sources

Bendavid, L., Etwas zur Caracteristik der Juden, Leipzig, 1793.

Borne, L., Freymuthige Bemerkungen über die neue Stettigkeits-und Schutzverordnungen für die Judenschaft in Frankfurt a.M. Z.G.J.D., IV (1890), 222–274.

Dohm, Ch. W., Ueber die bürgerliche Verbesserung der Juden. 2te Auflage, Bd. I–II, Berlin, 1783.

Ephraim, B. V., Ueber meine Verhaftung und einige andere Vorfälle meines Lebens, Berlin, 1807.

Friedlaender, D., Aktenstücke, die Reform der jüdischen Kolonien in den preussischen Staaten betreffend, Berlin, 1793.

——, Ueber die durch die neue Organisation der Judenschaft in den preussischen Staaten nothwendig gewordene Umbildung 1) ihres Gottesdienstes und Synagogen, 2) ihrer Unterrichtsanstalten und deren Gegenstände, 3) ihres Erziehungswesens überhaupt. Ein Wort zu seiner Zeit, Berlin, 1812 (hsg. M. Stern, Berlin, 1934).

Grattenauer, E. W. F., Wider die Juden, Berlin, 1803.

——, Erklärung an das Publikum über meine Schrift: Wider die Juden, Berlin, 1803.

——, Erster Nachtrag zu seiner Erklärung über seine Schrift: Wider die Juden. Ein Anhang zur fünften Auflage, Berlin, 1803.

Henle, Elkan., Ueber die Verbesserung des Judentums, Offenbach a.M. 1803. Uebergedruckt, Sulamith, Jhg. II, Bd. I., 361–382.

Hirschel, M., Apologie der Menschenrechte oder philosophisch kritische Beleuchtung der Schrift "über die physische und moralische Verfassung der heutigen Juden", Zurich, 1793.

König, J. B., Annalen der Juden in den preussischen Staaten besonders in der Mark Trandenburg, Berlin, 1790.

Kosmann, Prof., Für die Juden. Ein Wort zur Beherzigung an die Freunde der Menschheit und die wahren Verehrer Jesu, 2te Aufl, Berlin, 1803.

Maimon, S., Lebensgeschichte (hsg. Jakob Fromer), Munchen, 1911.

Mendelssohn, M., Gesammelte Schriften, Bd. 1–7, Leipzig, 1843–1845. Jubiläumsausgabe, Bd. 1, 2, 3, 7, 11, 16. Berlin, 1929–1938.

Philipson, M., Ueber die Verbesserung des Judeneids. Ein auf Befehl der Königlichen Kurfürstlichen Justizkanzlei zu Hanover verfasstes Gutachten, Neustrelitz, 1797.

Schudt, J. J., Jüdische Merkwürdigkeiten, Frankfurt a.M., 1714–1717.

Spiker, E. W., Ueber die ehemalige und jetzige Lage der Juden in Deutschland. Halle, 1809.

Sulamith, Zeitschrift, 1806–1815.

Wolff, S., Joseph, Maimoniana oder Rhapsodien zur Charakteristik S. Maimons. Aus seinem Privatleben gesammelt. Berlin, 1813.

Würfel, A., Historische Nachricht von der Judengemeinde in dem Hofmarkt Fürth. Frankfurt, 1754.

Wurtzer, H., Ueber die Fortschritte der Hamburgischen Israeliten in der wissenschaftlichen und sittlichen Bildung, besonders in der Erziehung. Von einem Nichtisraeliten. Sulamith, Jhg. III, Bd. II (1811), 239–247.

Gesetz Bulletin des Königreichs Westphalien No. 28, No. 62 Königliches Dekret vom 31 März, 1808.

Regulatiff betreffend die, von den Israeliten, als solchen zu leistenden Beiträge, Kassel, 10 Nov., 1809.

Studies

Ackerman, A., Geschichte der Juden in Brandenburg a.H. Berlin, 1906.

Adler, S., Die Entwicklung des Schulwesens der Juden zu Frankfurt a.M. bis zur Emanzipation. J.J.L.G. XVIII (1927), 143–173, XIX (1928) 237–278.

Altmann, A., ed., Studies in Nineteenth-Century Jewish Intellectual History, Cambridge, Mass., 1964.

Altmann, B., The Autonomous Federation of Jewish Communities in Paderborn. J.S.S., III, 159–188.

——, Jews and the Rise of Capitalism, Economic History and Practice in a Westphalian Community, J.S.S., V, 163–186.

Anfänger, L., Die Juden in Memmelsdorf, B.J.G.L., V, I–4.

Arendt-Stern, H., Aufklärung und Judenfrage, Z.G.J.D.(N), IV, 65–77.

Atlas, S., Solomon Maimon: The Man and his Thought. Historia Judaica, XIII, 109–120.

Auerbach, B. H., Geschichte der israelitischen Gemeinde Halberstadt. Halberstadt, 1866.

Babinger, F., Elkan Henle. M.G.W.J., LXII, 223–230.

Baer, F., Das Protokollbuch der Landjudenschaft des Herzogtums Kleve, Berlin, 1922.

Bamberger, S., Historische Berichte über die Juden der Stadt Aschaffenburg. Strassburg, 1900.

Baneth, L., Anhalt. Encyclopaedia Judaica Bd. II.

Barbeck, H., Geschichte der Juden in Nürnberg und Fürth, Nuremberg, 1878.

Baron, S. W., The Jewish Community, vol. II. Philadelphia 1942, 351–366.

——, Die Judenfrage auf dem Wiener Kongress, Vienna, 1920.

Bodenheimer, R., Beitrag zur Geschichte der Juden in Oberhessen, Giessen, 1931.

Brann, M., Etwas von der schlesischen Landgemeinde. Festschrift Jacob Guttman. Leipzig, 1915, 225–255.

——, Geschichte des Landrabbinats in Schlesien. Graetz-Jubelschrift, Breslau, 1887, 84–106, 109.

——, Geschichte und Annalen der Dyhernfurther Druckerei. M.G.W.J. XL, 474–480, 515–526, 560–574.

Buchholz, C. A., Acktenstücke, die Verbesserung des bürgerlichen Zustandes der Israeliten betreffend, Stuttgart, 1815.

Cahnmann, W., Die Münchener Judenbeschreibung von 1804. Z.G.J.D.(N), VII (1937), 180–188.

Cohen-München, A., Die Münchener Judenschaft 1750–1861. Z.G.J.D.(N), II (1930), 262–283.

Cohn, A., Beiträge zur Geschichte der Juden in Hessen-Kassel im 17. und 18. Jahrhundert, Marburg, 1933.

Cohn, W., Christian Wilhelm v. Dohm. Z.G.J.D.(N), I (1929), 255–261.

Davidsohn, L., Beiträge zur Sozial- und Wirtschaftsgeschichte der Berliner Juden vor der Emanzipation, Berlin, 1920.

Deutsch, I., Chronik der Synagogen-Gemeinde Sohrau O.S., Magdeburg, 1900.

Donath, L., Geschichte der Juden in Mecklenburg, Leipzig, 1874.

Dreifuss, E. M., Die Familiennamen der Juden, Frankfurt, 1927.

Eckstein, A., Geschichte der Juden im ehemaligen Fürstentum Bamberg. Bamberg, 1898.

——, Geschichte der Juden im Markgrafentum Bayreuth. Bayreuth, 1907.

——, Der Kampf der Juden um ihre Emanzipation in Bayern. Fürth, 1905.

Eschelbacher, J., Die Anfänge allgemeiner Bildung unter den deutschen Juden vor Mendelssohn. Festschrift Philippson, 168–177.

Fischer, H., Judentum, Staat und Heer in Preussen-Geschichte der staatlichen Judenpolitik, Tübingen, 1968.

Fraenkel, E., D. Friedländer und seine Zeit. Z.G.J.D.(N), VI (1935), 65–77.

Frank, H., Geschichte und Schicksal der Juden in Heilbronn. Heilbronn, 1963.

Freudenthal, M., Leipziger Messgäste, 1675–1764. Frankfurt a.M., 1928.

——, M., Die ersten Emanzipationsbestrebungen der Juden in Breslau. M.G.W.J., XXXVII, 41–48, 92–100, 188–197, 238–247, 331–341, 409–429, 467–483, 522–536, 565–579.

——, R. Wolf Dessau. Festschrift Philippson, 184–212.

——, Die judenfeindliche Bewegung in Preussen am Anfang dieses Jahrhunderts. Brann's Jahrbuch zur Belehrung und Unterhaltung, 1893, 15–54.

Freund, I., Die deutsche Judenfrage vor 100 Jahren. Z.G.J.D.(N), V (1935), 34–42.

——, Die Freiheitskriege und die Juden. Gemeindeblatt Berlin, 7. III. 1913.

——, Die Emanzipation der Juden in Preussen, Berlin, 1912.

Freund, S., Ein Vierteljahrtausend Hannoversches Landrabbinat 1687–1937. Hanover, 1937.

Geiger, L., Geschichte der Juden in Berlin. Berlin, 1871.

Geiger, L., Schriftenkampf für und gegen die Juden 1803–1804. Z.G.J.D., II, 301–319, III, 94–95.

——, Vor hundert Jahren, ibid, III, 185–233.

——, Mitteilungen aus Berliner Zeitungen 1741–1830. ibid, IV, 289–300.

——, Kleine Beiträge zur Geschichte der Juden in Berlin 1700–1817. ibid. IV, 29–65.

——, Die Erteilung des Bürgerrechts an die Juden in Frankfurt 1811. ibid, V, 54–74.

——, Die jüdische Gesellschaft Berlins im 18ten Jahrhundert. J.J.G.L., 1898, 190–215.

——, Aus den Akten der Gemeinde. Gemeindeblatt Berlin, Nr. 3–8, 1912.

——, Aus den Gemeindeakten der jüdischen Gemeinde zu Berlin. ibid, 8. III. 1912.

——, Aus den Akten des Königlichen Hausarchivs. ibid, 13. III. 1914.

——, Nach dem Edikt vom 11. Marz 1812. ibid, 9. VIII. 1912.

Gonsiorowski, H., Die Berufe der Juden Hamburgs von der Einwanderung bis zur Emanzipation, Hamburg, 1927.

Graetz, H., Geschichte der Juden. Bd. XI, Leipzig, 1870, 1–318.

Grotenfeld, U., Geschichte der Juden in Pommern. Baltische Studien, Neue Folge. Bd. 32, Stettin, 1930, 83–188.

Grunwald, M., Portugiesengräber auf deutscher Erde, Hamburg, 1902.

——, Juden als Reeder und Seefahrer, Berlin, 1902.

——, Hamburgs deutsche Juden, bis zur Auflösung der Dreigemeinden, 1811. Hamburg, 1904.

——, Die Statuten der Hamburg-Altonaer Gemeinde von 1726. M.G.J.V., VI (1903), Heft 11, 1–64.

——, Kleine Beiträge zur jüdischen Kulturgeschichte. ibid, VIII (1905), 144–175, IX (1906), 14–38, 96–120, XIV (1911), 63–74.

——, Gemeindeproklamationen der Dreigemeinden 1724–1734. ibid. XIV (1911), 121–127.

——, Altjüdisches Gemeindeleben. ibid, XV (1912) 1–4, 73–88. XVI (1913) Teil II, 27–31.

——, August v. Hennings, der Freund Moses Mendelssohns. J.J.G.L., 1908, 127–150.

Guggenheim, Dr., Aus der Vergangenheit der jüdischen Gemeinde zu Offenbach a.M., Offenbach, 1915.

Haenle, S., Geschichte der Juden im ehemaligen Fürstenthum Ansbach, Ansbach, 1867.

Heidenheimer, H., Zur Geschichte der Beurteilung der Juden vom 15. bis 19. Jahrhundert. M.G.W.J., LIII, 1–27, 129–158, 251–268.

Hirschfeld, H., An English Voice on the Emancipation of the Jews. Transactions of the Jewish Historical Society in England, VI, 128–137.

Horowitz, M., Frankfurter Rabbinen, Frankfurt a.M., 1882–1885.

Horwitz, L., Die Israeliten unter dem Königreich Westfalen, Berlin, 1900.

——, Die Entwicklung der jüdischen Bevölkerung in Kurhessen. Z.D.St.J., IX (1913), Heft 6, 7–8.

——, Neue Beiträge zur Geschichte und Tätigkeit des Konsistoriums der Israeliten zu Kassel 1807–1815. M.G.W.J., LIII, 513–524, 723–735.

——, Landrabbiner und Landschreiber in Kurhessen. M.G.W.J., LIV (1910) 513–534.

Jacobson, J., Jüdische Trauungen in Berlin 1723–1759, Berlin, 1938.

——, ed., Die Judenbürgerbücher der Stadt Berlin 1809–1851, Berlin, 1962.

——, ed., Jüdische Trauungen in Berlin 1759–1813, Berlin, 1968.

——, Zur Geschichte der Juden in Rogasen (MS), Berlin, 1935.

Jaraczewski, A., Die Geschichte der Juden in Erfurt, Erfurt, 1868.

Jolowicz, H., Geschichte der Juden in Königsberg, Posen, 1867.

Joseph, L. M., Mitteilung über den Verfasser der Gutachten "B'sainim Rosh", Literatur-Blatt des Orients, 1844, 711–714.

Kayserling, M., Moses Mendelssohn, 2 Aufl., Leipzig, 1888.

Kessler, G., Die Familiennamen der Juden in Deutschland, Leipzig, 1935.

Keyser, E., Bevölkerungsgeschichte Deutschlands, Leipzig, 1938.

Kober, A., Zur Vorgeschichte der Judenemanzipation in Nassau. Festschrift Philippson, 275–301.

——, Zur Geschichte der Juden Wiesbadens, Wiesbaden, 1913.

——, Die Geschichte der deutschen Juden in der historischen Forschung der letzten 35 Jahre. Z.G.J.D. (N), I (1929), 13–23.

——, Jüdische Studenten und Doktoranden der Universität Duisburg im 18. Jahrhundert. M.G.W.J. XXV (1931), 118–127.

——, The French Revolution and the Jews in Germany. J.S.S. VII (1945), 291–322.

——, und Moses, E., Aus der Geschichte der Juden in Rheinland. Jüdische Kult-und Kunstdenkmäler, Düsseldorf, 1931.

Kobler, F., Juden und Judentum in deutschen Briefen aus drei Jahrhunderten, Vienna, 1935.

——, Jüdische Geschichte in Briefen aus Ost und West, Vienna, 1938.

Kohler, M., Beiträge zur neueren jüdischen Wirtschaftsgeschichte. Die Juden in Halberstadt und Umgebung bis zur Emanzipation, Berlin, 1927.

Kopp, A., Die Dorfjuden in der Nordpfalz, Meisenheim, 1968.

Kracauer, I., Geschichte der Juden in Frankfurt a.M., 1150–1824. Frankfurt, 1925–1927.

Kroner, T., Die Juden in Württemberg. Frankfurt a.M., 1899.

Krueger, H. J., Die Judenschaft von Königsberg in Preussen 1700–1812, Marburg, 1966.

Kulisher, J. M., Yevrei v prusskoi shelkovoi promishliennosti XVIII vieka. Evr. Starina XI (1924), 129–161.

Lamm, L., Nehemias Jehuda Leib ein Martyrer für den Judenleibzoll, Berlin, 1910.

——, Ein kurzes Kapitel über Berliner Taufjuden, Berlin, 1918.

Landsberg, H., Henriette Herz, ihr Leben und ihre Zeit, Weimar, 1913.

Lazarus, F., Das Königlich Westphalische Konsistorium der Israeliten. M.G.W.J., LVIII (1914), 81–96, 178–208, 326–358, 454–482, 542–551.

——, Judenbefehlshaber, Obervorgänger und Landrabbiner im Münsterland. M.G.W.J., LXXX (1936), 106–117.

——, Die Judenbefehlshaber im Münsterland, Z.G.J.D.(N), VII (1937), 240–243.

Lebermann, J., Aus der Geschichte der Juden in Hessen. J.J.L.G., VI (1909), 105–152.

Lebermann, J., Das Darmstädter Landrabbinat. J.J.L.G., XX (1929), 181–252.

——, Jüdische Schul-und Lehrverhältnisse in Hessen, J.J.L.G., XVIII (1927), 65–142.

Levy, A., Geschichte der Juden in Sachsen, Berlin, 1900.

Levy, H., Die Entwicklung der Rechtsstellung der Hamburger Juden, Hamburg, 1933.

Lewin, A., Geschichte der badischen Juden (1738–1909), Karlsruhe, 1909.

Lewin, L., Aus dem jüdischen Kulturkampfe, J.J.L.G., XII (1918), 169–197.

——, Geschichte der israelitschen Krankenverpflegungs-Anstalt und Beerdigungs-Gesellschaft zu Breslau, 1726–1926, Breslau, 1926.

Lewinsky, Dr., Zwei Dokumente aus der älteren Geschichte der Synagogen-Gemeinde zu Hannover. B.J.G.L., I (1900), 37–39, 46–47.

Lewinsky, A., Zur Statistik der jüdischen Bevölkerung in Stadt und Hochstift Hildesheim im 18. Jahrhundert. B.J.G.L., III (1902), 113–119, 150–153, 169–171.

——, Zur Geschichte der Juden in Deutschland im 18. Jahrhundert. Festschrift Jacob Guttmann, Leipzig, 1915, 256–272.

Liebe, G., Das Judentum in der deutschen Vergangenheit, Leipzig, 1903.

Littmann, E., D. Friedlanders Sendschreiben an Probst Teller und sein Echo. Z.G.J.D.(N), VI (1935), 92–112.

Lob, A., Die Rechtsverhältnisse der Juden im ehemaligen Königreiche und der jetzigen Provinz Hannover, Frankfurt a.M., 1908.

Lowenstein, L., Zur Geschichte der Juden in Franken (1772–1775). Z.G.J.D., III (1889), 275–289.

——, Geschichte der Juden in der Kurpfalz, Frankfurt a.M., 1895.

——, Nathanel Weil, Oberlandrabbiner in Karlsruhe, Frankfurt, 1898.

——, Verzeichnis der israelitischen Einwohner von Karlsruhe im Jahre 1733, B.J.G.L., III (1902), 131–137, 154–157.

——, Zur Geschichte der Juden in Furth. J.J.L.G., VI (1909), 153–234, VIII (1911), 65–213, X (1912), 49–192.

Mahler, R., Jewish Emancipation, New York, 1942, 30–37.

Marcus, J. R., Communal Sick-care in the German-Ghetto, Cincinnati, 1947.

May, J., Die Steuern und Abgaben der Juden im Erzstift Trier. Z.G.J.D.(N), VII (1937), 156–179.

Mehring, F., Die Lessing Legende, Stuttgart, 1893.

——, Deutsche Geschichte vom Ausgang des Mittelalters, Berlin, 1923.

Meisel, W. A., Leben und Wirken Naphtali Hartwig Wesselys, Breslau, 1841.

Meisl, J., ed., Protokollbuch der jüdischen Gemeinde Berlin 1723–1854, Jerusalem, 1962.

Mendelssohn, M., Zur 200 Jährigen Wiederkehr seines Geburtstages. (Strauss, B., Cassirer, E., Bernfeld, S., Meyer, H.), Berlin, 1929.

Meyer, M. A., The origins of the Modern Jew, Detroit, 1967.

Munk, L., Die Konstituten der sämtlichen hessischen Judenschaft im Jahre 1690. Jubelschrift Dr. Israel Hildesheimer. Berlin, 1890, 69–82, 77–85 (hebr.).

——, Die Judenlandtage in Hessen-Kassel. M.G.W.J., XLI (1897), 505–522.

——, Aus dem Constitutenbuch der sämtlichen hessischen Judenschaft. Festschrift Salomon Carlebach. Berlin, 1910, 339–350.

——, Die Judenverordnungen in Hessen-Cassel. Hermann Cohen Festschrift, Berlin, 1912, 377–388.

Neubürger, F., Verfassungsrecht der gemeinen Judenschaft zu Fürth im 18. Jahrhundert. M.G.W.J., XLV (1901), 404–422, 510–539.

Offenburg, B., Das Erwachen des deutschen Nationalbewusstseins in der preussischen Judenheit, Hamburg, 1933.

Pincus, F., Saul Ascher, ein Theoretiker der Judenemanzipation. Z.G.J.D.(N), VI (1935), 28–32.

Pohle, L., Die Entwicklung des deutschen Wirtschaftslebens im letzten Jahrhundert, Leipzig, 1913.

Posener, S., Les Juifs sous le premier empire. R.E.J., XCIII, 192–214, XCIV, 157–166.

Priebatsch, F., Die Judenpolitik des fürstlichen Absolutismus im 17. und 18. Jahrhundert. Festschrift Dietrich Schäfer, Jena, 1915, 564–657.

Rabin, I., Beiträge zur Rechts- und Wirtschaftsgeschichte der Juden in Schlesien im 18. Jahrhundert, Breslau, 1932.

——, Die Juden in Zülz, Zülz, 1926.

——, Aus Dyhernfurths jüdischer Vergangenheit. (Sonderabdruck aus dem Breslauer Jüdischen Gemeindeblatt, No. 2, 1929.)

Rachel, H., Berliner Grosskaufleute und Kapitalisten, v. II: 1648–1806, Berlin, 1938.

Rexhausen, A., Die rechtliche und wirtschaftliche Lage der Juden im Hochstift Hildesheim, Hildesheim, 1914.

Rippner, B., David Friedländer und Probst Teller. Graetz-Jubelschrift, Breslau, 1887, 162–171.

Rixen, C., Geschichte und Organisation der Juden im ehemaligen Stift Münster, Münster, 1906.

Rönne, L. und Simon, H., Die früheren und gegenwärtigen Verhältnisse der Juden in den sämtlichen Landesteilen des preussischen Staates, Breslau, 1843.

Rosenthal, B., Heimatsgeschichte der badischen Juden, Baden, 1927.

——, Oberrabbiner M. Scheuer als Kritiker seiner Zeit. Z.G.J.D.(N), III (1931), 72–75.

Rosenthal, L., Zur Geschichte der Juden im Gebiet der ehemaligen Grafschaft Hanau, Hanau, 1963.

Rosenthal, S., Korrespondenz zwischen dem berühmten Talmudisten R. Mordechai Benet in Nikolsburg und R. Hirsch in Berlin. Literaturblatt des Orients, 1844, 53–55, 140–141.

Rotschild, S., Ein Rabbiner von Worms vor 100 Jahren. B.J.G.L., I (1900), 70–71.

——, Die Abgaben und die Schuldenlast der Wormser jüdischen Gemeinde, 1563–1854, Worms, 1925.

Salfeld, S., Vorboten der Judenemanzipation in Kurmainz. Hermann Cohen Festschrift, Berlin, 1912, 347–370.

Schäfer, D., Deutsche Geschichte, 2ter Band, Neuzeit, Jena, 1919.

Schiff, A., Die Namen der Frankfurter Juden zu Anfang des 19ten Jahrhunderts, Freiburg i. B., 1917.

Schnapper, A. G., Jugendarbeiten Ludwig Börnes über jüdische Dinge. Z.G.J.D., II (1888), 375–380, IV, 201–274, V, 194–222.

Schnee, H., Die Hochfinanz und der moderne Staat; Geschichte und System der Hoffaktoren im Zeitalter des Absolutismus, 6 vls., Berlin, 1953–1967.

Schwarz, St., Die Juden in Bayern im Wandel der Zeiten, Munich, 1963.

Silbergleit, H., Die Bevölkerungs- und Berufsverhältnisse der Juden im deutschen Reich. Bd. I, Freistaat Preussen, Berlin, 1930.

Silberstein, M., Wolf Breidenbach und die Aufhebung des Leibzolls in Deutschland. Z.G.J.D., V (1892), 126–145, 335–347.

Sombart, W., Die deutsche Volkswirtschaft im 19. Jahrhundert und im Anfang des 20. Jahrhunderts. 6 Aufl. Berlin, 1923.

Stern, M., Der Oberlandesälteste Jacob Moses. (Sonderabdruck aus den Mitteilungen des Gesamtarchivs der deutschen Juden, Jahrgang VI.) Berlin, 1926.

——, Zur Geschichte der Fleischgebühren in der Berliner jüdischen Gemeinde. Soncino-Blätter, II (1927), 97–108.

——, Jugendunterricht in der Berliner jüdischen Gemeinde während des 18. Jahrhunderts, J.J.L.G., XIX (1928), 39–68, XX (1929), 379–380.

——, Die Anfänge von Hirschel Löbels Berliner Rabbinat. (Sonderabdruck aus "Jeschurun", Jahrgang XVII.) Berlin, 1931.

——, Das Vereinsbuch des Berliner Bet-Hamidrasch 1743–1783. J.J.L.G., XXII (1931–1932), 401–420, I–XVIII (hebr.).

——, David Friedlaenders Schrift über die Umbildung. Berlin, 1934.

Stern, W., Die Juden in Unterfranken während der ersten Hälfte des 19ten Jahrhunderts. Z.G.J.D.(N), VI (1935), 229–238.

Stern-Täubler, S., Der preussische Staat und die Juden. Berlin, 1925.

——, Die Emanzipation der Juden in Baden. Gedenkbuch zum 125 jährigen Bestehen des Oberrats der Israeliten Badens. Frankfurt a.M., 1934, 7–104.

——, The Court Jew, Philadelphia, 1950.

Strauss, R., The Jews in the economic evolution of Central Europe. J.S.S., III (1941), 15–40.

Tänzer, A., Die Geschichte der Juden in Württemberg, Frankfurt, 1937.

Tänzer, P., Die Rechtsgeschichte der Juden in Württemberg 1806–1828, Berlin, 1922.

Treitschke, H. v., Deutsche Geschichte im 19ten Jahrhundert, I.T., Leipzig, 1927.

Unna, I., Oberrabbiner Michael Scheuer als Kritiker seiner Zeit, Z.G.J.D.(N), I (1929), 322–328.

Unna, J., Statistik der Frankfurter Juden bis zum Jahre 1866, Frankfurt, 1931.

Victor, W., Die Emanzipation der Juden in Schleswig-Holstein, Wandsbeck, 1913.

Vogelstein (red.), Festschrift zum 200 jährigen Bestehen des israelitischen Vereins für Krankenpflege und Beerdigung, Chevra Kadischa zu Königsberg i. Pr. 1704–1904, Königsberg, 1904.

Wachstein, B., Das Statut der jüdischen Bevölkerung der Grafschaft Wied-Runkel (Pinkas Runkel). Z.G.J.D.(N), IV (1932), 129–149.

Weinberg, M., Eine Statistik der Judengemeinde Schnaittach aus dem Jahre 1761. B.J.G.L., V (1904), 60–64, 69–71.

——, Geschichte der Juden in der Oberpfalz, Sulzburg, 1909.

Wiener, M., Jüdische Religion im Zeitalter der Emanzipation, Berlin, 1933.

Zunz, L., Die Ritus des synagogalen Gottesdienstes geschichtlich entwickelt. (1859), Berlin, 1919. Beilage VII, 226–228.

GREAT BRITAIN

Studies

Barnett, R. D., Anglo-Jewry in the Eighteenth Century, in: V. D. Lipman, Three Centuries of Anglo-Jewish History, London, 1961, 45–68.

Duschinsky, C., The Rabbinate of the Great Synagogue, London, 1756–1842, London, 1921.

Gaster, M., History of the Ancient Synagogue of the Spanish and Portuguese Jews in England, London, 1901.

Henriques, H. S. Q., Jews and the English Law, Oxford, 1908.

Hyamson, A. M., A History of the Jews in England, 2nd ed., London, 1928.

——, The Sephardim of England, London, 1951.

The Jewish Historical Society of England, Transactions, Vol. 6, pp. 111–127 (J. S. Meisels), Vol. 13, pp. 323–340 (J. Rumney); Vol. 17, pp. 79–90 (L. S. Sutherland), pp. 251–268 (E. Newman); Vol. 18, pp. 231–242 (J. J. Neusner). Miscellanies, Vol. 3 (1937), pp. 1–6.

Laski, N., The Laws and Charities of the Spanish and Portuguese Jews' Congregation of London, London, 1952.

Lipman, V. D., ed., Three centuries of Anglo-Jewish History, Cambridge, 1961, pp. 69–106.

Peskin, A., England's Jewish Naturalization Bill of 1753. H.J., XIX (1957), pp. 3–32.

Picciotto, J., Sketches of Anglo-Jewish History, London, 1875.

Roth, C., Anglo-Jewish Letters, London, 1938, pp. 85–243.

——, A History of the Jews in England, Oxford, 1941.

——, The Great Synagogue London (1690–1940), London, 1950.

——, The Rise of Provincial Jewry, London, 1950.

——, Essays and Portraits in Anglo-Jewish History, Philadelphia, 1963.

Rumney, J., The Anglo-Jewish Community, *The Jewish Chronicle*, December 1935, Supplement.

Wulf, J., Essays in Jewish History, London, 1934, pp. 185–201.

HOLLAND

Studies

Baasch, E., Holländische Wirtschaftsgeschichte, Jena, 1927.

de Beneditty, N., Leven en Werken van Mr. Jonas Daniel Meyer, Haarlem, 1925.

Bloom, H. I., The economic activities of the Jews of Amsterdam in the 17th and 18th centuries, Williamsport, Pa. 1937.

Boekman, E., Demographie van de Joden in Nederland, Amsterdam, 1936.

Bolle, M. E., De opheffing van de autonomio der Kehilloth in Nederland 1796, Amsterdam, 1960.

Brugmans, H., en A. Frank, ed., Geschiedenis der Joden in Nederland, Vol. 1, Amsterdam, 1940.

Carmi, J. I., op. cit., pp. 100–101, 146.

Colenbrander, H. I., De Bataafsche Republiek, Amsterdam, 1908.

De Castro, D. H., De Synagoge der Portugees-Israelietische Gemente te Amsterdam, Amsterdam, 1950.

Fuks, L., De Jiddische Kroniek van Abraham Chaim Braatbard (1740–1752), Acht en Veertigste Jaarboek Genootschap Amstelodamum, pp. 113–171.

——, Van Poerimspelen tot Poerimkranten, Maandblat 1 (5708), No. 6–7, pp. 162–176.

Hartog, J., Uit de Dagen der Patrioten, C.4 De Joden in het eerste Jaar der Bataafsche Vrijheid, pp. 195–238, Amsterdam, s.d.

Italie, H., De Emancipatie der Joden in 1796, Amsterdamsche Jaarboekje 1897, pp. 86–101.

——, Over de Societeit Felix Libertate, Oud Holland, V. 16 (1898), pp. 51–62, 79–92, 147–167.

Koenen, J., Geschiedenis der Joden in Nederland, Utrecht, 1843.

Kulischer, J., Allgemeine Wirtschaftsgeschichte, Vol. 2, Neuzeit, Munich, 1929.

Maarsen, I., De Responsa als Bron voor de Geschiedenis der Joden in Nederland, Bijdragen en Mededeelingen van het Genootschap voor de Joodsche Wetenschap in Nederland, V. 5 (1933), pp. 118–146.

Mahler, R., Jewish Emancipation, New York, 1942, pp. 27–28.

Meijer, J., Erfenis der emancipatie: het Nederlandse Jodendom in de eerste helft van de 19e eeuw, Haarlem, 1963.

——, Het Jonas Daniel Meijerplein; bezinning op drie eeuwen Amsterdams Jodendom, Amsterdam, 1961.

——, Zij lieten hun sporen achter; Joodse bijdragen tot de Nederlandse beschaving, Utrecht, 1964.

——, Problematiek per Post (Brieven van en oyer Joden in Nederland) Maandblat 1, No. 10–12.

Mendes, I., De Joodsche Gemeente te Groningen, Groningen, 1910.

Nieuw Nederlandsch Biografisch Woordenboek.

Peyster, H., Les troubles de Hollande à la veille de la révolution française 1780–1795, Paris, 1905.

Poppers, H., De Joden in Overijsel, Amsterdam, 1926.

Pozner, S., Otcherki po istorii zapadno-jevropeyskikh yevreyev v natchalie 19v. Voskhod November 1904, pp. 37–54, October 1905, pp. 76–104.

Schmidt, E., Geschiedenis van de Joden in Antwerpen, Antwerp, 1963.

Seeligman, S., Die Juden in Holland, Simonsen-Festschrift, 1923, 255 ff.

——, De Emancipatie der Joden in Nederland, Amsterdam, 1913.

——, Over de verhouding tusschen Joden en niet-Joden in de republik der Vereenigde Nederlanden, 17-18 eeuw, Amsterdam, 1922.

——, Het Nederlandsche zeewezen en de Amsterdamsche Joden in het einde der 18e eeuw. Centralblad voor Israelieten in Nederland, Vol. 16, No. 36.

——, Het geestelijk leven in de Hoogdeutsche J. G. te s' Gravenhage, The Hague, 1914.

da Silva Rosa, J. S., De bezeken van Gacham Azulay aan Nederland in de tweede Helft der 18e eeuw. Overdruk uit het Vrijdagavond en 8 April, 1927.

——, Geschiedenis der Portugeesche Joden te Amsterdam, Amsterdam, 1925.

Sluys, D. M., Bijdragen tot de geschiedenis van de Poolsch Joodsche Gemeente te Amsterdam, Bijdragen etc., V. 3, Amsterdam, 1925, pp. 138–158.

——, Het Reglement van de Adath Jeschurun, ibid. V. 5, 1933, pp. 89–90.

Wolff, M., De Houding der Joden in Holland in den Strijd tusschen Oranjegezinden en Patrioten, Bijdragen v. vad. Geschiedenis, 1907, pp. 430–470.

——, De Beteekenis der Regeering van Lodewijk Napoleon voor de Joden van Nederland, ibid. 1920, pp. 51–110.

——, De Geschiedenis der Joden te Haarlem, Haarlem, 1917.

Zuiden, D. S., De Hoogduitsche Joden in s' Gravenhage, The Hague, 1913.

Zwarts, J., De Joodsche Gemeente van Amersfoort, Amersfoort, 1927.

——, Hoofdstukken uit de Geschiedenis der Joden in Nederland, Zutphen, 1929.

HUNGARY

Studies

Bergl, J., Geschichte der ungarischen Juden. Leipzig, 1879.

Bernstein, B., Die Toleranztaxe der Juden in Ungarn. D. Kaufmann Gedenkbuch, Breslau, 1900, 599–628.

Braham, R. (ed.), Hungarian-Jewish Studies, New York, 1966.

Forbat, E., Die Geschichte des Handels und des Pressburger Handelsstandes im XVIII Jhdt, Bratislava, 1930.

Gold, H., Die Juden und die Judengemeinde Bratislava in Vergangenheit und Gegenwart. Ein Sammelwerk. Brünn, 1932.

Grunwald, M., Mattersdorf. Jahrbuch für jüdische Volkskunde, 1924–1925 (M.G.J.V., XXVI–XXVII), 402–563.

Herzog, D., Ein- und Auswanderung von Juden nach Ungarn 1806–1808. Judaica (Bratislava), Jhrg. II, No. 17–18, Juli-August 1936, 12–14.

Jeitteles, I., Ereignisse die Israeliten in Ungarn betreffend. Sulamith, Jhg. III, Bd. III (1811), 289–299.

Làszló, N., Die geistige und soziale Entwicklung der Juden in Ungarn in der ersten Hälfte des 19. Jhdts, Berlin, 1934.

Löw, L., Zur neueren Geschichte der Juden in Ungarn, Pest, 1874.

——, Gesammelte Schriften, Bd. IV, Szegedin, 1898, 371–435.

Mandl, B., Das jüdische Schulwesen in Ungarn unter Kaiser Josef II, Frankfurt a.M., 1903.

——, Zur Geschichte der jüdischen Gemeinde in Holitsch. Z.G.J.T., I (1930/1931), 180–195.

——, Zur Geschichte der jüdischen Gemeinde in Szobotiszt. Z.G.J.T., II (1931/1932), 205–214.

——, (ed.), Monumenta Hungariae Judaica. V. III, 1711–1740. Budapest, 1937.

Sas, A., Die wirtschaftlichen und sozialen Verhältnisse der Juden auf dem Dominium Munkacs-Szentmiklos im XVIII Jhdt. Jüdisches Archiv., Vienna, Jhg. II, Oktober-Dez. 1928—April 1929. No. 1–2, 1–6, No. 3–4, 33–38, No. 5–7, 38–44.

Schay, M., Die Protokolle der "Chevra Kadischa" der jüdischen Gemeinde in Palota. J.J.L.G., XVIII (1927), 195–202.

Scheiber, A. (ed.), Monumenta Hungariae Judaica, Vls. VII–XII, Budapest, 1963–1969.

Wachstein, B., Urkunden und Akten zur Geschichte der Juden in Eisenstadt und den Siebengemeinden. Vienna, 1926.

——, Die Grabschriften des alten Judenfriedhofes in Eisenstadt. Vienna, 1922.

Encyclopaedia Judaica. L. S(inger): Arad, Bazin, Györ, Gran, Kecskemet
  B. Farkas: Komorn, Levoca.
  L. Bato: Burgenland.
  Mat. Eisler: Grosswardein.

ITALY

Studies

La Rassegna Mensile di Israel, vis. 1–25 (1925–1959):
  articles by E. Artom, Ricardo Bachi, Roberto Bachi, G. Bolaffio, C. Castelbolognesi, V. Colorni, R. Curiel, E. Debenedetti, N. Diena, S. Foa, N. M. Gelber, Giorgina Levi, E. Loevinson, F. Luzzatto, S. Magrini, A. Milano, A. Ottolenghi, Cecil Roth, S. Schaerf, G. Sonnino, E. Sereni, S. Sierra, B. Terracini, A. Toaff, Gemma Volli.

Anchel, R., Napoléon et les Juifs, Paris, 1928, pp. 221–223, 267 ff.

Bachi, R. and Milano, A., Universita Israelitica di Roma, Storia e riordinamento dell' Archivio, Rome, 1929.

Balletti, A., Le istituzioni finanziarie nelle Università Israelitiche dell Emilia. Gironale delli Economisti, Serie 2, Vol. 28, Rome, 1904, pp. 359–369.

——, Gli Ebrei e gli Estensi, 2 edizione, Modena, 1930.

Berliner, A., Geschichte der Juden in Rom, Frankfurt, 1893.

Blustein, J., Storia degli Ebrei in Roma, Rome, 1921.

Castelli, E., I banchi feneratizi ebraici nel Mantovano 1386–1808, Mantua, 1959.

Castiglioni, V., L'istituto scolastico della communità israelitica di Trieste 1786–1886, Trieste, 1886.

Ciscato, A., Gli Ebrei in Padova, Padua, 1901.

Colorni, V., Gli ebrei nel sistema del diritto comune fino alla prima emancipazione, Milan, 1956.

——, Le magistrature maggiori della Communita ebraica di Mantova, Bologna, 1938.

Dezi, G., Genesi e natura del diritto di gazaga, Rome, 1872.

Formenti, G., Tributo alla verità etc., Venice, 1807.

Gabrieli, G., Italia Judaica, Rome, 1924.

Gelber, N. M., Vorgeschichte des Zionismus, ch. 3, Ein Judenstaatsprojekt in Italien, Vienna, 1927.

Glissenti, F., Gli Ebrei nel Bresciano, Brescia, 1888.

Guarnieri, G. G., Il porto di Livorno, Pisa, 1931.

Halpern, B., A Note on Ali-Bey's "Jewish State" Project, J.S.S., XVIII (1956), pp. 284–286.

Kretschmayr, H., Geschichte von Venedig, Vol. 3, Stuttgart, 1934.

Livi, L., Gli Ebrei alla luce della Statistica, 2 vols., Florence, 1918–1920.

Loevinson, E., Le basi giuridiche della communità israelitica di Livorno (1593–1787), Bulletino storico livornese, 1, Pt. 2 (1937).

——, Roma Israelitica, Frankfurt, 1927.

Luzzatto, G., Sulla condizione economica degli Ebrei veneziani nel secolo XVIII. Scriti in onore di Ricardo Bachi, 1950, pp. 161–162.

Mazzetti, R., L'antiebraismo nella cultura italiana dal 1700 al 1900. Antologia storica, Modena, 1939.

Milano, A., Storia degli Ebrei in Italia, Turin, 1963.

——, Il ghetto di Roma; illustrazioni storiche, Rome, 1964.

Modena, A., Medici e chirurghi ebrei dottorati e licenziati nell' Università di Padova del 1617 al 1816, Bologna, 1967.

Pozner, S., Ocherki etc., Voskhod, November 1904, pp. 37–54, November–December 1905, pp. 215–237.

Reumonth, A., Geschichte der Stadt Rom, Vol. 3, 2te Abt., Berlin, 1870.

Rieger, P., Geschichte der Juden in Rom, Vol. 2, Berlin, 1893.

Rodocanachi, La Saint Siège et les Juifs, Paris, 1891.

Roth, C., The History of the Jews of Italy, Philadelphia, 1946.

——, Venice, Philadelphia, 1930.

Singer, L., Zur Geschichte der Toleranzpatente in den Sudetenlandern, Widerhall des Edikts Josephs I in Italien, Jahrbuch für die Geschichte der Juden in der Cechoslovakischen Republik, Vol. 7, pp. 262–264.

Stern, M., Urkundliche Beiträge über die Stellung der Papste zu den Juden, Kiel, 1893.

Tivaroni, C., L'Italia prima della rivoluzione francese, Turin, 1888.

Zoller, I., Per la storia del 28 giugno 1799 a Siena, Rivista Israelit., Vol. 7 (1910), pp. 191–193, 240–244, Vol. 8 (1911), pp. 30–32, 65–67.

——, Theater und Tanz in den italienischen Ghettos, Mitteilungen zur Jüdischen Volkskunde, Jhrg. 29, Vienna, 1926, pp. 596–598.

PALESTINE

Sources

Badia y Leblich, Don Domingo, Viajes de Ali Bey el Abbassi por Africa y Asia durante los anos 1803–1807. Traducidos del Frances por P.P.T. III, Valencia, 1836.

Bicheno, J., The Restoration of the Jews, London, 1800.

Borsum, I. F. J., Reise nach Constantinopel, Palästina und Egypten. Berlin, 1825.

Breton, M., L'Egypte et la Syrie. T. VI, Paris, 1814.

Browne, W. S., Travels in Africa, Egypt and Syria (1792–1798). London, 1806.

Burckhardt, J. L., Reisen in Syrien, Palästina. Aus dem Englischen- W. Gesenius. Bd. 1–2, Weimar, 1823–1824.

Chateaubriand, F. A. de, Itinéraire de Paris à Jerusalem et de Jerusalem à Paris, 3 vols. Paris, 1811.

——, Journal de Jerusalem (notes inédites) Paris, 1950.

Clarke, E. D., Travels in various countries of Europe, Asia and Africa, Vol. V, 4th ed., London, 1817.
Forbin, Count, Travels in Greece, Turkey and the Holy Land, London, 1817.
Hasselquist, F., Voyages and Travels in the Levant (1749–1752), London, 1766.
J(oliffe), T. R., Letters from Palestine, London, 1820.
Korte, J., Reise nach dem Weiland gelobten Lande, 1741.
L. B., Considérations sur l'Egypte et la Syrie. La Decade Philosophique et Littéraire, An VI, 30 Germinal, 148–154.
Mariti, G., Reise von Jerusalem durch Syrien. (Aus dem Italienisichem übersetzt.) Strassburg, 1789.
Mayer, L., Restoration of the Jews, London, 1806.
Niebuhr, C., Reisebeschreibung nach Arabien und umliegenden Ländern, Vol. III, Hamburg, 1837.
Pococke, R., Beschreibung des Morgenlande, Erlangen, 1754.
Richter, O. Fr. v., Wallfahrten im Morgenlande, Berlin, 1822.
Scholz, Dr. J., Reise in der Gegend zwischen Alexandrien—Egypten, Palästina und Syrien, Leipzig, 1822.
Seetzen, U. J., Reisen nach Syrien, Palästina etc., Berlin, 1854.
Volney, C. F., Voyage en Syrie et en Egypte, 1783–1785, Paris, 1787.
Wittman, W., Travels in Turkey, Asia Minor, Syria etc., London, 1803.

Studies

Barthold, W., Die geographische und historische Erforschung des Orients, Leipzig, 1913.
Bazili, K., Siria pod turetzkim pravitielstvom, St. Petersburg, 1875.
La Custodia Francescana di Terra Santa, Jerusalem, 1933.
Gelber, N. M., Vorgeschichte des Zionismus, Vienna, 1927.
Hammer, J. v., Geschichte des Osmanischen Reiches. 2te Auflage, Pest, 1834–1836.
Hyamson, A. M., British Projects for the Restoration of Jews to Palestine. Publications of the American Jewish Historical Society, XXVI, 127–164.
Kircheisen, F. M., Napoleon im Lande der Pyramiden. Munich, 1918.
Kobler, F., Napoleon and the Restoration of the Jews to Palestine. New Judea, September 1940–February 1941.
Poliak, A. N., The demographic Evolution of the Middle East. Palestine and the Middle East, 1938, No. 5.
——, Feudalism in Egypt, Syria, Palestine and the Lebanon (1250–1900), London, 1939.
Reinach, Th., Un memoire oublié sur les Juifs. Annuaire de la Societé des études juives. Paris 1883, V. II, 93–108.
Roloff, G., Die Orientpolitik Napoleons I, Weimar, 1916.
Roux, F. Ch., Les échelles de Syrie et de Palestine au 18 siècle, Paris, 1928.
Russel, M., Palestine from the Early Period to the Present Time, Edinburgh, 1832.
Sax, C. v., Geschichte des Machtverfalles der Türkei, Vienna, 1908.
Schnapper-Arndt, G., Jugendarbeiten L. Börnes über jüdische Dinge. Z.G.J.D., II (1888), 375–378.

Shulim, J. J., Napoleon I as the Jewish Messiah: Some Contemporary Conceptions in Virginia, J.S.S., VII (1945), 275–280.
Sokolow, N., History of Zionism, 2 vols., London, 1919.
Strauss, B. u. B., Wer ist der Mann vom Stande? Occident und Orient, Gaster-Anniversary Volume. London, 1936, 518–525.
Yahuda, A. S., Napoleon and a Jewish State. Zion (incorporating New Judea), No. 7, March 1950, 29–34.

POLAND UNDER PRUSSIAN RULE; THE GRAND DUCHY
OF WARSAW

Historical Documents
Askenazy, Sz., W. dobie Księstwa Warszawskiego. Kwartalnik Żyd. I, zesz. 1, 1–14.
——, Ze spraw żydowskich w dobie kongresowej. Kwartalnik Żyd. I, zesz. 3, 1–36.
Balaban, M., red. Album Pamiątkowy ku czci Berka Joselewicza w 125 letnią rocznice. Warsaw, 1934.
——, Historja Żydów w Krakowie i na Kazimierzu. Tom II, Cracow, 1936, 582–596.
Berliner, A., Aus meiner Knabenzeit. J.J.G.L., 1913, 165–190.
Bloch, Ph., Die ersten Kulturbestrebungen der jüdischen Gemeinde Posen unter preussischer Herrschaft. Jubelschrift H. Grätz, Breslau 1871, 194–217.
C. D., Prusskiy Schutzbriew v Bielostokie. Yevr. Starina IV (1911), 587–588.
Cohn, J., Geschichte der jüdischen Gemeinde Ravitsch, Berlin, 1915.
Eisenbach, A., Struktura ludności żydowskiej w Warszawie w świetle spisu 1810 r. Biuletyn Żyd. Inst. Histor. Nr. 12–14, Warsaw, 1955, 73–121.
Feinkind, M., Dzieje Żydów w Piotrkowie i okolicy, Piotrków, 1930.
Gelber, N. M., Materialien zur Statistik der Westpreussischen Juden zu Ende des XVIIIten Jahrhunderts, Z.D.St.J., IX (1913), 56–98.
Goldshtein, M., Proyekt K. F., Voydy 1815 ob organizatzii yevreyev v Polshe. Yevr. Starina, XII (1928), 301–314.
Goldshtein, S., Iz siedleckich drevnostiey. Yevr. Starina, IV (1911), 125–129.
Grossman, H., Struktura spoleczna i gospodarcza Księswa Warszawskiego 1808–1810, Warsaw, 1925.
Grunwald, M., Jüdische Handwerker aus älterer Zeit. M.G.W.J., vol. 74, 413–421.
Handelsman, M., Prośba Żydów do Fryderyka Augusta. Kwartalnik Żyd. I, zesz. 3, 174–176.
Heppner, A., Herzberg, J., Aus Vergangenheit und Gegenwart der Juden und der jüdischen Gemeinde in den Posener Landen, Kosmin-Bydgoszcz, 1909–1929.
Herzberg, J., Geschichte der Juden in Bromberg, Frankfurt, 1903.
Hessen, J., Istoria Yevreyev v Rossii, Petrograd, 1916, 427–437.
——, V efemiernom gosudarstwie. Yevr. Starina, III (1910), 1–38.
——, Plock, Yev. Entziklop, vol. XII, 587.
Jacobsohn, J., Die Stellung der Juden in den 1793 und 1785 von Preussen

erworbenen polnischen Provinzen zur Zeit der Besitznahme. M.G.W.J., vol. 64, 209–226, 282–304; vol. 65, 42–70, 151–163, 221–245.

——, Eine Denkschrift über die Errichtung eines Lehrer Seminars für die Juden Süd- und Neuostpreussens. Allgemeine Zeitung des Judentums, Berlin 1913, Nr. 11, 17.

——, Zur Geschichte der Juden in Rogasen. (Stencil, Schocken Library, Jerusalem.)

Jaffé, M., Die Stadt Posen unter preussischer Herrschaft. Leipzig 1909.

Kandel, D., Żydzi w dobie utworzenia Królestwa Kongresowego. Kwartalnik Żyd., I, zesz. 2, 95–113.

Kempner, R., Agonia Kahalu. Kwartalnik Żyd., I, zesz. 1, 67–71.

Kirszrot, J., Prawa Żydów w Królestwie Polskiem. Warsaw 1917.

Lambert, M., Geleitzoll und Koscherfleischabgabe zwei Sondersteuern der Posener Juden. M.G.W.J., vol. 67, 273–278.

Lewin, L., Aus der Vergangenheit der jüdischen Gemeinde zu Pinne. Pinne, 1903.

——, Beiträge zur Geschichte der Juden in Kalisch, Sonderabdruck aus der Festschrift zum 70ten Geburtstage A. Harkavy's, Kempen, 1909.

——, Ein Judentag aus Süd- und Neuostpreussen. M.G.W.J., vol. 59 (1915), 180–192, 278–300.

——, Geschichte der Juden in Inowrazlaw. Poznan, 1900.

——, Geschichte der Juden in Lissa, Pinne, 1904.

Lewin, R., Die Judengesetzgebung Friedrich Wilhelms II, M.G.W.J., vol. 57 (1913), 74–98, 211–234, 363–372, 461–481, 567–590.

Loewe, H., Memoiren eines polnischen Juden. J.J.L.G., vol. 8 (1911), 87–114, 440–446.

Luninski, E., Berek Joselewicz i jego syn. Warsaw, 1909.

Nathan, N. M., Aus den "Jugenderinnerungen" Karl Friedrichs von Klöden, Festschrift Philippson, Leipzig, 1916, 249–256.

Nussbaum, H., Szkice Historyczne z Życia Żydów w Warszawie. Warsaw, 1881.

Orlowski, M., Żelazny Przemysl Hutniczy na Ziemiach Polskich. Warsaw, 1931, 34–38.

[Ostrowski, A. J.], Pomysly o potrzebie Reformy Towarzyskiej przez założyciela miasta Tomaszowa Mazowieckiego. Paris, 1834.

Prümers, R. (ed), Das Jahr 1793. (Urkunden und Aktenstücke zur Geschichte der Organisation Südpreussens.) Poznan, 1895.

Rutkowski, J., Historja Gospodarcza Polski (do 1864), Warsaw, 1953.

Schipper, I., Dzieje Handlu Żydowskiego no Ziemiach Polskich, Warsaw, 1937.

——, Samorząd żydowski w Polsce no przelomie wieku 18go 119go. Miesięcznik Zydowski, Tom 1 (1931), 513–529.

Simon, St., Żydzi inworoclawscy za czasów Księstwa Warszawkiego (1807–1815). Inowroclaw, 1939.

Skarbek hr, F., Dzieje Księstwa Warszawskiego, 3tomy, Warsaw, 1897.

Surowiecki, W., O upadku przemyslu y miast w Polsce, Warsaw, 1810.

Tokarz, W., Z dziejów sprawy żydowskiej za Księstwa Warszawskiego. Kwartalnik Historyczny, T. 16 (1902), 262–276.

Warschauer, A., Die Erziehung der Juden in der Provinz Posen durch das Elementarschulwesen. Z.G.J.D., III (1889), 29–43.

Weinryb, S. B., Neueste Wirtschaftsgeschichte der Juden in Russland und Polen. Breslau, 1934, pp. 32–36, 65–66, 234–235.

Wischnitzer, M. L., Proyekty reformy yevreyskago byta v Gertsovstvie Varshavskom i Tsarstvie Polskom. Perezhitoye, I (1909), 166–172.

Wójcicki ks., A., Dzieje Robotnikow Przemysłowych w Polsce. Warsaw, 1929, 72–78.

Wspomnienia żyda Kempinskiego. Kwartalnik Żyd. I, zesz. 3, 176–180.

RUSSIA

Sources

Akty izdavayemie Vilenskoyu kommisieyu dla razbora drevnich aktov. Tom XXXVII, Vilna, 1912.

Levanda, V. O., Polnyi khronologichesskiy sbornik zakonov, i polozhenii kasayushtchikhsia Yevreyev 1649–1873. St. Petersburg, 1874.

Regesty i nadpisi, II, III, St. Petersburg, 1899–1913.

Studies

Arndt, E. M., Erinnerungen, Leipzig, 1892, 118–163.

Averbukh, Z., Gorod Volkovysk v voynie 1812 goda. Yevr. Starina VI (1913), 536–539.

Beilin, S. Ch., Perepiska mezhdu bukharskimi i shklovskimi yevreyami 1802 g. Perezhitoye, II (1910), 274–280.

Bershadskiy, S. A., Litovskie yevrey. St. Petersburg, 1883, 54–60.

——, Polozhenie o yevreyach 1804 g. Voskhod, 1895, kn. I, 82–103, kn. III, 69–96, kn. IV, 86–109, kn. VI, 33–63.

Borovoy, S. Ia., Yevreyskaia ziemliedieltcheskaia kolonizatzia v starey Rossii. Moscow, 1928, 1–78.

Brafman, Ia. Kniga Kagala. (Vsemyrniy yevreskiy vopros), izd. tretye, Chast II. St. Petersburg, 1888.

Gessen, Iu., Deputaty yevreyskago naroda pri Aleksandrie 1, Yevr. Starina, II (1909), 17–29, 196–206.

——, Yevrey v Movskovskom gosudarstvie XV–XVIII. v. Yevr. Starina, VIII (1916), 153–172.

——, K istorii korobotchnovo sbora v Rossii. Yevr. Starina, IV (1911), 305–347.

——, "Geleitzoll", Yevr. Starina III (1910), 81–83.

——, Odessa. Yevr. Entziklopedia, XII, 50–52.

——, Stremlenie Ekateriny II vodvorit yevreyev v Rossii (1764 g.) Yevr. Starina, VIII (1916), 338–346.

——, Yevrey v Rossii. St. Petersburg, 1906.

——, Istoria Yevreyskago naroda v Rossii. Tom I., Petrograd, 1916.

Gidalevich, A., Dielo o bogokhulstvie Yevr. Starina, VIII (1916), 188–121.

Ginzburg, S. M., Iz epochi otetchestvennoy voyny. Perezhitoye IV (1913), 99–118.

Ginzburg, S., Otetchestvennaya voyna 1812 g. i russkiye yevrey, St. Petersburg, 1912.

Golitzyn, Graf N., Istoria russkago zakonodatielstva o Yevreyakh, vol. I (1649–1825), St. Petersburg, 1886.

Gordon, L., K istorii poselenía Yevreyev v Peterburgie. Voskhod, 1881, kn. II, 29–47.

Gradowsky, N. D., Torgoviya i drugiya prava Yevreyev v Rossii. St. Petersburg, 1886.

Dubnov, S. M., Sudby evreyev v epokhu zapadnoy "pervoy emantzipatzii" 1784–1815. Yevr. Starina, V (1912), 3–25, 113–143.

——, Kagal Petrovitchi. Voskhod, 1894, kn. II, 99–104.

——, Yevrey v voynie 1812 goda. Yevr. Starina, V (1912), 85–90.

Ilish, P., Ocherk istorii rizhskikh Yevreyev. Voskhod 1885, kn. VII, 61–80, kn. VIII, 10–35.

Istoria S.S.S.R. do kontza 18 v. Bolshaya Sovietskaya Entziklopedia, Tom: S.S.S.R., Moscow, 1948, 413–470.

Iwaszkiewicz, J., Litwa w roku 1812. Warsaw, 1912.

Kaganova, A., Frantsuskaia burzhuaznaia revolutzia kontza XVIII, v. i sovremiennaya russkaya pressa. Voprosy Istorii 1947, Nr. 7, 87–94.

Korobkov, Ch., Perepis yevreyskago naselenia Vitebskoy gubernii v 1772 g. Yevr. Starina, V (1912), 169–177.

——, Statistika yevreyskago naselenia Polshi i Litvi vo vtoroy polovinie XVIII vieka. Yevr. Starina, IV (1911), 541–562.

——, Utchastie yevreyev vo vnieshniey torgovlie Polshi. Yevr. Starina, IV (1911), 19–39, 197–220.

Krashinsky, I., Kaziennaya fabrika dla yevreyev pri Aleksandrie I. Yevr. Starina, VIII (1916), 345–351.

Kulisher, M., Yevrey v Kievie. Yevr. Starina, VI (1913), 417–438.

——, Ekaterina II. Voskhod, 1896, kn. XI, 134–145.

——, Istoria russkago zakonodatielstva o Yevreyach v sviazi s sistemoy nalogov vzimania i otbyvania povinnostey. Yevr. Starina, III (1910), 466–503.

Levitats, I., The Jewish Community in Russia 1772–1844. N. York, 1943.

Maggid, D. I., K istorii yevreyskich deputatov v tzarstvie Alexandra I. Perezhitoye, IV (1913), 181–191.

Moscicki, H., Żydzi polscy pod berlem Katarzyny II. Kwartalnik Żyd. I. zesz. 1, 54–66.

Nietchkin, M. V. (ed), Istoria S.S.S.R., vol. II. Moscow, 1949.

Nikitin, B., Yevreyskaia zemledielcheskaia kolonizatzia. Voskhod, 1881, kn. II, 93–119; kn. III, 87–115; kn. V, 37–70.

——, Yevrey Zemledielstsi 1807–1887. St. Petersburg, 1887.

Orshansky, N., Russkoye zakonodatielstvo o yevreyach. St. Petersburg, 1877.

Ribinskiy, V., Do istorii zhidiv na Livoberezhniy Ukraini v polov. XVIII st. Zbirnik prac Zhidowskoy istoritchno-archeografitchnoi komisii, kn. 1, Kiev, 1928, 1–97.

Schipper, I., Dzieje Handlu zydowskiego na ziemiach polskich. Warsaw, 1937, 410–435.

Stanislavskiy, Kolonizatzia Yevreyev v Novorossii. Voskhod 1887. kn. 9, 116–126.

Studnicki, W., Pożyczka wojenna wilenska 1812. Kwartalnik żyd. I, zesz. 1, 115–120.

Toporovski, B., Dva ukaza imperatora Alexandra I. Yevr. Starina, VI (1913), 407–408.

Trotzkiy, L., Yevrey v kievskoy gubernii v 1812g. Yevr. Starina, XIII (1930), 131–134.

Weinryb, B., Neueste Wirtschaftsgeschichte der Juden in Russland und Polen. Breslau, 1934.

Wischnitzer, M., Jüdische Geschichtsschreibung in russischer Sprache. M.G.W.J., vol. 71, 306–308.

Yushkov, S. V., Istoria gosudarstva i prava S.S.S.R. Chast. 1. Moscow, 1950, 325–349, 371–375.

SWITZERLAND

Sources

Bulletin Helvétique 1798–1800.

Journal du Corps Législatif et Bulletin Officiel.

(Bulletin Officiel du Directoire Helvétique) Vols. 1–16.

Studies

Alte Endinger Volkslieder, Jüdisches Jahrbuch für die Schweiz, v. 5 (1920–1921), pp. 198–199.

Ambrunnen, A. (Alfred Zander), 1. Dokumente zur Judenfrage in der Schweiz, 2. Dokumente zur Judenfrage in der Schweiz seit 1798, Zurich, 1935.

Brisac, J., Ce que les Israélites doivent à la France, Lausanne, 1916.

Erlanger, I., Beiträge zur Geschichte der Schweizer Juden, Jud. Jhrb. für die Schweiz, v. 4 (1919–1920), pp. 178–185.

Frohlich, J., Kleine Urkunden aus dem schweizerisch-jüdischen Gemeindeleben, ibid. v. 1 (1916–1917), pp. 112–117.

Guggenheim, P., Zur Geschichte der Schweizer Juden, Zurich, 1934.

Guggenheim-Gruenberg, F., Aus einem alten Endingen Gemeindebuch, Zurich, 1952.

——, Die ältesten jüdischen Familien in Lengnau und Endingen, Zurich, 1954.

Nordemann, Th., Zur Geschichte der Juden in Basel, Basel, 1955.

Weldler, A. and Guggenheim-Gruenberg, F., Geschichte der Juden in der Schweiz, Bd. Goldach, 1966.

UNITED STATES

Sources

The Constitution of the Commonwealth of Pennsylvania, Philadelphia, 1776.

The Constitution of the Commonwealth of Pennsylvania, to which is added a report of the Committee as adopted by the Council of the Censor, Philadelphia, 1784.

The Constitution of the Commonwealth of Pennsylvania, Philadelphia, 1790.

The Constitution of the State of New York together with the New York State—Constitutions of 1777, 1821, 1846, Albany, 1894.

The New York Gazette & Weekly Post Boy, July 23, 30, 1770. (New York Historical Society.)

Karigal, H. I., The Salvation of Israel, a Sermon, Newport, 1773.

Seixas, Rev. G., A Religious Discourse, New York, 1789 (Historical Society of Pennsylvania).

——, Discourse, New York, 1798 (The American Jewish Historical Society).

Carvalho, E. N., A Sermon, preached on occasion of the death of the Rev. Mr. Gershom Mendes Seixas, Philadelphia, 1816.

de la Motta, J., M.D., Funeral Address, pronounced in the Synagogue previous to the interment of the relics of the Rev. Gershom M. Seixas, New York, 1816.

Phillips, N., Eulogy, 1816.

Publications of the American Jewish Historical Society, American Jewish Historical Society Quarterly, vols. 1–59 (1893–1970).

Studies

Beard, C. A., A History of the American Civilization, New York, 1940.

Benjamin, J. J., Drei Jahre in America, Hanover, 1862.

Blau, J. L. and Baron, S. W., The Jews of the United States 1790–1840; A Documentary History, 3 vols., New York, 1963.

Blum, I., The Jews of Baltimore, Baltimore, 1910.

Bridenbaugh, C. and Harrison, P., Chapel Hill, 1949.

Cobb, S. H., The Rise of Religious Liberty in America, New York, 1902.

Ehrenfried, A., A Chronicle of Boston Jewry, from the Colonial Settlement to 1900, Boston, 1963.

Elzas, B. A., The Jews in South Carolina, Philadelphia, 1905.

Ezekiel, Lichtenstein, H. T. and G., The History of the Jews in Richmond, Richmond, 1917.

Fish, M., Aaron Levy, Founder of Aaronsburg, New York, 1951.

Franklin, L. M., Jews in Michigan, Michigan History Magazine, XXIII, pp. 77–92.

Freund, M. K., Jewish Merchants in Colonial America, New York, 1939.

Friedman, L. M., Rabbi Haim Isaac Carigal, Boston, 1940.

——, Jewish Pioneers and Patriots, Philadelphia, 1945.

——, Pilgrims in a New Land, New York, 1948.

——, Some further Sidelights on Aaron Lopez, J.Q.R., XLV, pp. 562–567.

Glanz, R., Jews in early German-American Literature, J.S.S., 4, pp. 99–120.

——, Notes on early Jewish peddling in America, J.S.S., 7, pp. 119–136.

Goodman, A. V., The American Overture, Jewish Rights in Colonial Times, Philadelphia, 1947.

Grinstein, H. B., The Rise of the Jewish Community of New York, 1654–1860, Philadelphia, 1945.

Gutstein, M. A., The Story of the Jews of Newport, New York, 1936.

Hershkowitz, L., Wills of early New York Jews (1704–1799), New York, 1967.

Hershkowitz, L. and Meyer, I. S., ed. Letters of the Franks Family (1733–1748), Waltham, Mass., 1968.

Humphrey, E. F., Nationalism and Religion in America, 1774–1789, Boston, 1924.

Lebeson, A. L., Jewish Pioneers in America, 1492–1848, New York, 1931.

Mahler, R., Jewish Emancipation, A Selection of Documents, New York, 1942, pp. 13–15, 22–24.

Marcus, J. R., Early American Jewry, vol. I (1649–1794), vol. II (1655–1790), Philadelphia (1951–1953).

——, Light on Early Connecticut Jewry, The American Jewish Archives, vol. I, pp. 3–52.

——, American Jewry. Documents—Eighteenth Century, Cincinnati, 1959.

——, Memoirs of American Jews 1775–1865, vol. I, Philadelphia. 1955.

Morais, H. S., The Jews of Philadelphia, Philadelphia, 1894.

Pool, de Sola D., Portraits etched in stone — early Jewish settlers 1682–1831, New York, 1952.

——, An old faith in the new world; portrait of Shearith Israel, 1654–1954, New York, 1955.

——, Early Relations Between Palestine and American Jewry, The Brandeis Avukah Annual, Boston, 1932, pp. 536–548.

Reznikoff, C., Engelman, U. Z., The Jews of Charleston, Philadelphia, 1950.

Roth, C., Anglo-Jewish Letters (Nrs. 69, 70, 71, 76, 82), London, 1938.

Schappes, M. U., A Documentary History of the Jews in the United States (1654–1875), New York, 1950 (new ed.).

Simonhoff, H., Jewish Notables in America, 1776–1865, New York, 1956.

Stiles, E., The Literary Diary, vol. 1, New York, 1901.

Thorning, J. F., Religious Liberty in Transition, first series: New England, Washington, D.C., 1931.

Wiernik, P., History of the Jews in America, New York, 1912.

Wolf, E. and Whiteman, M., The History of the Jews of Philadelphia from Colonial times to the age of Jackson, Philadelphia, 1957.

Wolf, S., The American Jew as Patriot, Soldier and Citizen, Philadelphia, 1895.

BEGINNINGS OF HASKALA IN EASTERN EUROPE

Studies

Auerbach, B. H., Geschichte der israelitischen Gemeinde in Halberstadt, Halberstadt, 1866, Beilage III.

Bettan, I., The Dubno Maggid. HUCA XXIII part 2 (1950–1951), pp. 267–293.

Delitzsch, F., Zur Geschichte der jüdischen Poesie, Leipzig, 1836, 99–110.

Kogan, D., Rodoslovnaya Gurvitshey. Perezhitoye II (1910), 268–273.

Regesty i Nadpisi. Tom III, St. Petersburg, 1913, Nr. 2299.

Rozenfeld, S., R. Menashe Ilier. Perezhitoye IV (1913), 65–98.

Schechter, S., Rabbi Elijah Vilna, Gaon. Studies in Judaism, First Series, Philadelphia, 1911, 73–98.

Stanislavskiy, S., Tuvia Feder. Yevr. Starina, V (1912), 460–466.

Weissberg, M., Język literacki Żydów w Galicji. Kwartalnik Żyd. zesz. 2, 1–16.

Weissberg, M., Literatura nowohebrajska w Galicji. Kwartalnik Żyd. zesz. I, 35–53.

——, Die neuhebräische Aufklärungsliteratur in Galizien, M.G.W.J., vol. 71 (1927), 54–62, 100–109.

Zinberg, S. L., Predietchi yevreyskoy zhurnalistiki v Rossii, Perezhitoye, IV (1913), 119–148.

——, Shklov i yego "prosvietitieli" kontza XVIII vieka, Yevr. Starina, XII (1928), 17–44.

HASSIDISM

Studies

Aesucoli—Weintraub, A. Z., le Hassidisme, essai Critique, Paris, 1928.

Bloch, Ch., Die Gemeinde der Chassidim. Berlin, 1920.

Buber, M., For the Sake of Heaven (2nd ed.), New York, 1953.

——, Jewish Mysticism and the Legend of Baal Shem, London, 1931.

Chajes, Ch., Baal Szem Tow u chrzescijan. Mies, Żyd, IV (1934), 440–459, 550–565.

Dubnow, S. M., Vmieshatielstvo russkago pravitielstva v antihasidskuyu borbu (1800–1801), Yevr. Starina, III (1910), 84–109, 253–282.

Graetz, H., Geschichte der Juden, Bd. XI, Leipzig, 1870.

Gulkowitsch, L., Das kulturhistorische Bild des Chassidismus. Tartu, 1938.

Loehr, M., Beiträge zur Geschichte des Chassidismus. Leipzig, 1925.

Maggid, D. G., Klistorii borby s hasidizmom. Perezhitoye II (1910), 116–129.

Marek, P. S., Krizis yevreyskago samoupravlenia y hasidizm. Yevr. Starina, XII (1928), 45–101.

——, Vnutrennaya borba v yevrestvie v 18 viekie. Yevr. Starina, XII (1928), 102–178.

Newman, L., The Hassidic Anthology, New York, 1934.

Schapiro-Memel, H., Ein jüdischer Pater Loyola, Das jüdische Literaturblatt XXII (1893), Nr. 26–30.

Scholem, G., Devekuth, or Communion with God. The Review of Religion, Jan. 1950, 115–139.

——, Major Trends in Jewish Mysticism, Jerusalem, 1941 (new ed.).

Ysander, T., Studien zum bestischen Hassidismus in seiner religions-geschicht-lichen Sonderart, Upsala, 1933.

INDEX